KT-215-391

RAF Squadrons

RAF Squadrons

A Comprehensive Record of the Movement and Equipment of all RAF Squadrons and their Antecedents since 1912.

Wing Commander C G Jefford MBE RAF

Airlife
England

For my father, Sqn Ldr C W 'Jeff' Jefford, and my father-in-law, Sqn Ldr D L 'Slim' Rowell, who between them gave 75 years of service to the Royal Air Force.

First published 1988
by Airlife Publishing Ltd
Reprinted 1994

Jefford, C G
RAF squadrons
1. Great Britain. Royal Air Force.
Squadrons to 1987
I. Title
358.4'131'0941

ISBN 1 85310 053 6

Printed in England by Livesey Ltd., Shrewsbury

Airlife Publishing Ltd.

101 Longden Road, Shrewsbury, England

CONTENTS

Foreword

By Air Commodore Henry Probert,
Head of the Air Historical Branch (RAF)

At first sight this volume may appear to be just another 'squadron reference book', so many of which have appeared over the years, all in their own way serving useful purposes though sometimes adding little to the overall fund of knowledge. Occasionally, however, a new work appears which represents an invaluable addition to the existing works of reference in this particular field, and it is for this reason that I welcome Wing Commander Jefford's book.

A serving Royal Air Force officer with wide operational experience, 'Jeff' has devoted a great deal of his spare time over many years to the necessary research. Much of this has had to be done in the Public Records Office, where the earlier squadron records now reside, but he has also been a regular visitor to the Air Historical Branch, where I have discussed his work with him from time to time. He has carried out his research meticulously, pursuing every missing detail and cross-checking between different types of record in the attempt to ensure absolute accuracy. While the Operations Record Books have obviously been prime sources, he recognises that they are only as good as the men who compiled them at the time. Consequently, in order to ensure that the dates he quotes are accurate, he has also consulted the Air Ministry Organisation Memoranda (SD155) and their precursors; since these actually authorised the formation, moves, re-equipment and disbandment of units, the dates quoted in them are rightly preferred in cases of doubt.

This book will, I believe, be quickly recognised by the experts and enthusiasts in this field as probably the most detailed work of reference on the squadrons of the RAF and its World War I predecessors, with the various appendices providing rapid means of checking specific points. Of these the airfield location maps strike me as particularly useful, and certainly the book as a whole will be a standard work of reference for us in AHB. It represents a great achievement on the part of its author and I wish it well.

Air Commodore H. A. Probert, MBE MA RAF (Retd)
1988

Preface

In compiling this book (the format and content would make a claim to have 'written' it something of an overstatement) my aim was to produce, as accurately and comprehensively as possible, a record of the movements of, and the aircraft types flown by, all the squadrons of the Royal Air Force and their immediate predecessors in the Royal Flying Corps and Royal Naval Air Service. This is already fairly well trodden ground and, in order to keep the size of the book within reasonable bounds, I have not included any form of narrative account of each unit's exploits. This omission is also, at least partly, justified by the availability of a number of excellent books by other authors which do provide adequate brief histories of each unit's activities. The only reasonable criticism of these accounts is their inherent brevity and an improvement could only be made by providing longer and more detailed versions. Unfortunately this would result in an extremely large, and prohibitively expensive, book. The end product is presented therefore as a mass of easily interpreted, cross-referenced data and is intended to provide, as definitively as possible, a source book containing the essential facts about all RAF squadron histories. It is a book for reference, not for reading.

The information contained in this book has taken me over twenty years to assemble, cross-check and collate. My primary source material has been the original documentation held by the Public Record Office and the Air Historical Branch of the Ministry of Defence. The study of these records has enabled me to make many corrections and additions to previously published accounts. I have also been able to extend and update these since I have had access to official material of a more recent date.

I would like to think that I have made two significant contributions to the recording of the history of the Royal Air Force. The first concerns the refinement of previously accepted accounts of squadron movements, particularly in the period 1916-19. Most of the readily available information concerning this era has been based on the digests of each squadron's service prepared by the Air Historical Branch of the Air Ministry in the early 1920s. However, research at that time seems to have concentrated on the operational phase of each unit's career. Consequently the work up and/or run down periods were often recorded inaccurately or omitted altogether. Indeed the very existence of many of the squadrons which actually formed during World War One, but which subsequently failed to reach a combat zone, has been only sketchily acknowledged. I have been able both to amend, where necessary, previously published accounts, and to unearth the essential facts, which until now have remained obscure, about the non-operational units. Even so some gaps remain to be filled.

The second innovation is the provision of a series of maps showing the locations, world-wide, at which Royal Air Force units of squadron status have been based. This is the first time that this information has been presented in an easily assimilated form between one set of covers. In the course of identifying these locations it became apparent that there were a number of long-standing misconceptions over the whereabouts, and even the existence, of some airfields. Many of these, I believe, have now been clarified.

Having already observed that a number of books are available which record various aspects of Royal Air Force unit histories I wish to express my admiration for and to acknowledge my debt to their authors. In particular the published work of the following writers has been of great value to me: J M Bruce, E F Cheesman, Christopher Coles, J J Halley, Tim Mason, P J Moyes, J D R Rawlings, Bruce Robertson, O G Thetford and R C C Sturtivant. I also wish to register publicly my thanks to the many correspondents who have helped me by providing elusive pieces of information or photographs and in this context I would mention especially: Rick Barker of the Royal Air Force Museum, Chaz Bowyer, Maj John Cross of the Museum of Army Flying, Peter Green, Jim Halley of Air Britain, Sqn Ldr Ray Leach, Stuart Leslie, Bill Morgan of Cross and Cockade, Ian O'Neill of the International Auster Pilots Club, Jock Ross of the RAAF Historical Section, Chris Shores, Ray Sturtivant, Flt Lt Andy Thomas, Geoff Thomas and Sqn Ldr Joe Warne. In addition I wish to thank the staff of the Public Record Office, numerous serving officers who have been approached over the years during their stewardship of their squadron's archives and, especially, the staff of the Air Historical Branch of the Ministry of Defence.

In selecting the illustrations for this book I was often obliged to choose between quality and originality. I have tried to include a proportion of 'new' pictures. Where a poor quality photograph has been used it is because I decided that the interest value of the subject matter made it a better choice than, a more familiar, posed photograph. The majority of the photographs used have been generously contributed by those named above. The most appropriate source has been acknowledged in the caption to each picture, however, the widespread practice of copying photographs has obscured the true origins of some. This may have led to some of the credits given in this book being incorrect, if this has indeed occurred then it was unintentional and I do apologise.

My final, and most important, acknowledgement must be to my family. I wish to express to them my heartfelt gratitude for their forebearance in putting up with my preoccupation with this project for so long with such fortitude and good humour.

August 1988

C G Jefford
High Wycombe
Bucks

Introduction

Having set out to produce a book which records the movements and equipment of all Royal Air Force squadrons, it would be as well to define some terms. These notes are intended to enlarge on the concept of a 'squadron' and to establish the ground rules which were used in the compilation of these records. Having said that, it will become apparent that, in the course of the last 75 years or so, sufficient anomalies have occurred to make 'rules' something of a misnomer. Perhaps 'guidelines', being less precise, would be a more appropriate term.

The Squadron as an Entity

The term 'squadron' is not an exclusively Air Force one. It has a long tradition of usage in both the Royal Navy and the British Army and was thus a convenient designation to apply to the air units sponsored by these services when they first began to appear. Perhaps surprisingly, 'squadron' does not have a particularly well-defined meaning within the Royal Air Force. It is used as a convenient administrative label to identify a variety of formations or units. Squadrons are, generally, smaller than (and may be constituent parts of) Wings; and larger than (and may be sub-divided into) Flights. All three of these terms are in widespread use and are not only applied to flying units. They are used, for instance: to designate units of the Royal Air Force Regiment; to identify the administrative, technical and support elements which constitute the organisation of any Station; and, in a ceremonial context, to describe the various formations in a formal parade. What distinguishes most flying squadrons, however, is that they have a discrete status. Their existence is not conditional upon that of a parent Station or Wing organisation. A squadron's independence is signified by its individual number. This is allocated to it from a centrally controlled series administered at Ministry level.

Squadrons on parade. Nos 6, 208 and 216 Sqns with their Gordons, Audaxes and Valentias at Heliopolis in Apr 38. (RAF Museum P11057)

Further refinement of this description of a squadron is not practical, since an example can be found which will confound any attempt to provide a more precise definition. It would be convenient to consider a squadron as the smallest self-contained combat formation — which is probably how most people think of it. However, for a variety of reasons, this simply will not do. To start with, there have been many operational units having only 'Flight' status which have been larger than most squadrons. Then again, not all squadrons have been 'self-contained'. Many have operated under various systems of centralised-servicing, as a result of which their aeroplanes and groundcrews have been withdrawn and pooled within a common-user supporting formation. Finally, not all squadrons have been intended to function as combat units. Many have been formed specifically to carry out second-line or support tasks and even the most famous of units have spent periods of their histories on supporting, non-combat, sometimes even non-flying, duties. These characteristics may be summarised as size, status and role, and are examined in greater depth below.

The size of a squadron can vary greatly. For example, towards the end of World War Two, No 101 Sqn had an establishment of 30 Lancasters; however, at times it had as many as 45 aircraft on charge. By contrast, when No 21 Sqn was operating Twin Pioneers in East Africa in the early 1960s, it had only three aeroplanes. The spectrum is equally broad in terms of manpower. When a squadron is operating under a centralised-servicing system it may number only its aircrews and one or two supporting staff, perhaps an Adjutant or an Intelligence Officer. In the case of a World War Two single-seat fighter-bomber unit this might total fewer than 20 men. On the other hand, a completely autonomous unit flying large aeroplanes, like Liberators, could well have had 300 men. Further, contrasting, examples are provided by: an indepen-

By 1945 a squadron flying large aeroplanes could have a considerable strength of personnel; there are 196 men in this picture of No 626 Sqn with one of their Lancasters. (RAF Museum P7885)

Under a centralised servicing system a squadron's strength in men is reduced to the minimum. This picture shows all but one of the fifty-five aircrew (eleven five-man crews) plus the Adjutant of No 83 Sqn with XL443, one of the Scampton Wing's Blue Steel-armed Vulcan B.2s. The photograph was taken in Jun 69, shortly before the unit's final disbandment. The CO, Wg Cdr (later Air Cdre) J M Pack, is 9th from the left in the front row; the author is 3rd from the left in the middle row. (Author's collection)

dent bomber squadron mobilising in the UK in 1918, which was intended to have 264 men to operate its ten Handley Page 0/400s; and a Vulcan bomber unit in 1965, which had only its eleven crews of five men each.

The lower extreme is approached when a squadron is reduced to a cadre, in which case it will have a minimal establishment of both manpower and equipment, indeed often no aircraft at all, being intended to provide a nucleus on which to build a full-scale unit if and when required. The majority of squadrons went through a period of cadre status in 1919, prior to demobilisation after the First World War. The official establishment of such units at the time was 15: 2 officers, 1 Senior NCO, and 12 men of various trades. There were no aeroplanes allotted. Other examples of cadre units were the Special Reserve Squadrons (Nos 500-504) of the late 1920s and most UK-based squadrons immediately after the Second World War when, for example, No 138 Sqn, along with most other Lincoln units, had an establishment of just six aeroplanes.

Ultimately a unit may be reduced to a 'Numberplate Only' basis, in which case it will have only a notional existence. For instance when No 1 Fighter Wing was disbanded in Australia on 31 Oct 45, two of its units, Nos 548 and 549 Sqns, disbanded with it. The third unit however, No 54 Sqn, was reduced to a Numberplate Only. This Numberplate was transferred to the UK and brought back into use on 15 Nov 45 by renumbering No 183 Sqn. A more recent example is provided by No 20 Sqn, which was reduced to a Numberplate in Germany on 30 Dec 60. The Numberplate was transferred to the Far East Air Force on 1 May 61 and the unit was re-established at Tengah on 1 Sep 61.

Within this book some latitude has been allowed in the use of some of these terms. 'Cadre' has been used loosely to denote a unit which has been reduced to a completely non-effective status but which still retains some physical presence. 'Numberplate Only' status has not been acknowledged at all, since such units have no tangible existence.

Squadron functions are usually perceived as being the classic combat roles of bomber, fighter, reconnaissance and so on. However, radar calibration, the provision of gunnery targets and electronic warfare training facilities, along with meteorological reconnaissance and light communications are just some of the less obvious, and less glamorous tasks which have occupied units of squadron strength. Such mundane tasks have often involved dedicated units; however, the vast majority of squadrons, including most of the now famous Numbers, spent the first few months after their formation in 1915-18 engaged in flying training duties. Some random examples of well known squadrons which have been obliged to spend some time on second-line tasks include: Nos 1 and 41 Sqns which were Instrument Rating Squadrons in 1947-48;

Illustrating two of the more unusual and specialised roles in which units of squadron status have been engaged are: (above) a Hastings Met 1, TG622, of No 202 Sqn which was used for meteorological reconnaissance (Air Britain M1107); *and (below) a modified Canberra B.6, WJ775, which was used by No 51 Sqn for signals duties.* (RAF Museum P19778)

This Canberra TT 18, WJ721, of No 7 Sqn was photographed during that unit's period of service as a target facilities squadron and illustrates the fact that a long and distinguished history does not secure any unit a permanent place in the front line. (Andrew Thomas)

Nos 5, 17, 20 and 34 Sqns which were gunnery co-operation squadrons in 1949-51; No 7 Sqn which was a target facilities unit in 1970-82; Nos 15 and 22 Sqns which were trials units within the Aeroplane and Armament Experimental Establishment at Martlesham Heath in 1923-34; and Nos 46 and 52 Sqns which served as Maintenance Units in the Middle East in 1941-42. This list is far from comprehensive but it serves to illustrate the range of non-combat roles in which squadrons may be called upon to serve, and to show that a long and proud history is no guarantee that a unit will avoid being assigned to such tasks.

To summarise the above, it will be seen that a squadron: may have many men, or few; may have large numbers of aircraft on charge, or none at all; may be established as a self-contained unit, or otherwise; may have operational, cadre, or Numberplate Only status; and may be a combat, or a support unit. In view of the breadth of this spectrum, only a fairly loose definition will embrace all of its aspects. A squadron is a unit which has been allocated a number from within the series of numbers which has been reserved for the designation of units having squadron status. That, for all practical purposes, is all that may be said — a squadron is a squadron because the Ministry (through the office of the Air Member for Supply and Organisation) says it is one.

An example of the early training machines used to provide ab initio pilot instruction was the Farman Shorthorn. This one was with No 5 Reserve Squadron at Castle Bromwich. No 5 RS provided the nucleus for No 54 Sqn; its predecessor, No 5 RAS, had provided the basis for No 19 Sqn. (K M Molson)

An Armstrong Whitworth FK8, B297, of No 50 Training Squadron at Narborough. This unit had no connection whatsoever with No 50 Sqn, which was an operational Home Defence squadron.
(J M Bruce/G S Leslie collection)

The Evolution of Squadron Numbers 1912-1918

The Royal Flying Corps (RFC) was created on 13 Apr 12 and on 13 May it absorbed the Air Battalion of the Royal Engineers, which had itself only been formed on 1 Apr 11. The initial RFC flying units were Nos 1, 2 and 3 Sqns of the Military Wing, the Naval Wing's flying unit at Eastchurch, and the Central Flying School. The Royal Navy was never very deeply committed to this organisation, which placed its air assets under Army control, and after the publication of Admiralty Circular Letter CW 13964/14 dated 1 Jul 14, (which introduced the term Royal Naval Air Service [RNAS] and promulgated details of the service's internal organisation and its distinctive rank titles), naval aviation effectively went its own way. The independent status of the RNAS was finally formalised a year later on the authority of Admiralty Order 1204/15 of 29 Jul 15. Until they were amalgamated again on the formation of the Royal Air Force (RAF) on 1 Apr 18 the two air services formed and designated their units independently.

Typical of the early types with which the RFC was established in 1912 was this Breguet G3, No 211. Seen here at Upper Heyford, this aeroplane served with Nos 2 and 4 Sqns before WW I.
(RAF Museum P12185)

Within the RFC (and later the RAF) the process leading to the formation of new operational squadrons was subject to progressive changes throughout World War One as the Service itself evolved and grew. Although a handful of squadrons was formed from scratch, after 1915 the normal practice was to provide the nucleus of each new squadron from the resources of a unit which already existed. Initially the parent unit would often be another operational squadron. This led to some quite complex genealogies; for instance – No 8 Sqn begat No 13 Sqn, which begat No 22 Sqn, which begat No 45 Sqn, which begat No 64 Sqn. Parent units were not always operational squadrons however, and as the war proceeded it became more common for a new squadron's nucleus to be drawn from a training unit. Since this process was an integral part of the wartime flying training system, it is worthwhile digressing a little to examine this system briefly in order to appreciate its influence on the creation of new units.

From shortly after the beginning of the war and concurrent with the formation of Service Squadrons, i.e. those intended for operations, a separate series of numbered training units began to appear. These were designated initially as Reserve Aeroplane Squadrons (RAS), then, from 13 Jan 16, as Reserve Squadrons (RS), and finally, from 31 May 17, as Training Squadrons (TS). The numbers allocated to these units duplicated those given to the Service Squadrons although they were in fact quite unrelated. There was, for example, both a No 11 Service Squadron and a No 11 Reserve (later Training) Squadron. Before these training units began to be superseded by a new type of organisation, starting in mid-1917, the designations of Training Squadrons extended from No 1 to No 75, (higher numbers in this series, reaching to No 93, were allocated to further training units initially formed in the UK but deployed for service in Canada). Since Service Squadrons usually spent the first few months of their existence in a training role, they were sometimes loosely referred to as 'training squadrons' and this has given rise to some confusion in later years. To complicate matters further, yet another series of second-line units began to form from late 1917 onwards. These, Depot Squadrons and Night Training Squadrons, were allocated numbers broadly in reverse, working backwards from No 200, and eventually reaching to No 186. The histories of none of these training units have been dealt with in this book, but where they acted as the parent unit of a new Service Squadron this contribution has been noted.

When the nucleus of a new Service Squadron was authorised to form, its personnel were initially posted onto the

This Pup, B1750, was at Waddington in late 1917 and is representative of the obsolescent operational types flown by students to consolidate experience gained on Farmans, Avros or DH 6s. (P I C Payne)

strength of its appointed parent unit for training. Eventually the new unit would be issued with training machines of its own and it would assume an independent existence acting as a training unit itself. In the beginning these embryo squadrons provided basic flying training on types like Farmans and Avro 504s, but as the training system developed this became the province of the RS/TS. The Service Squadron began to be equipped with a 'service type' and function broadly in the role of a modern Operational Conversion Unit (OCU). Ultimately the squadron would be ordered to 'mobilise'. It would be issued with its operational aircraft type and, after a work-up period of perhaps four weeks, be deployed overseas. An element would often be left behind to form the basis of another new unit, either another Service Squadron or a Reserve/Training Squadron. This system prevailed from mid-1915 until early-1918. Thereafter the initial 'parented' stage was effectively omitted. Although a parent unit was nominated its responsibilities were not significant and personnel drafted to the new unit were taken on strength directly.

As the war progressed, discrete operational roles for aeroplanes became more and more clearly defined. This led to distinctly different aircraft types and dedicated role equipment. To meet the consequent need for increased specialisation the training system was extensively revised. From mid-1917 a new series of basic flying training units, Training Depot Stations (TDS), began to form, initially on a trial basis. A TDS was organised internally into three squadrons, lacking any formal designation (rather like the squadrons within a modern Flying Training School). These new establishments were able to capitalise on the systematic approach to flying training devised by Major Smith-Barry and developed at the School of Special Flying at Gosport. Each TDS taught basic flying skills and provided role related training, specialising in the production of, for instance, Day Bomber, Corps Reconnaissance or Single-Seat Fighter pilots. Accompanying this rationalisation of basic pilot training was a parallel revision of observer training and the creation of a series of advanced and specialised instructional facilities. These included Schools of Aerial Fighting, Schools of Navigation and Bomb Dropping, Wireless Schools, Schools of Aerial Gunnery, a Photography School, and so on. The graduates of this system were posted to the embryo Service Squadrons as these began their work-up for deployment to France.

By mid-1918 the new training system was a demonstrable success and Air Ministry letter C.4519 of 4 Jul 18 authorised the wholesale transfer of pilot training to the TDS concept and simultaneously removed the Service Squadrons from the training organisation altogether. Beginning on 15 Jul 18 many additional TDSs began to form from the resources made available by the progressive disbandment of the previous generation of Training Squadrons, this process continuing into early Sep 18. Another consequence of the change in policy was the disbandment, in Jul and Aug, of many of the prospective Service Squadrons which were then engaged in training duties under the old system. Their resources too were absorbed into the expanding TDS organisation. Contemporary plans for the formation of additional new squadrons were cancelled. By this time squadron numbers, with associated locations and formation dates, had (with only a few exceptions) been formally allocated up to No 165. Although some of these squadrons were eventually formed under revised plans some of the higher numbers did not actually come into use until the Second World War. This is discussed more fully at Appendix 1.

Under the new system, squadrons were to form from four elements, a HQ, and A, B and C Flts, drawn from four separate TDSs. These elements were to move independently to a common location which would be one of the newly designated Mobilisation Stations, e.g. Upper Heyford, Kenley, Wyton — these having no connection at all with the training system. Here over a period of eight weeks, they would be issued with their operational equipment and moulded into a fighting unit prior to their deployment to France.

Of course, the new organisation for creating squadrons was not introduced overnight, since any such major change needs time to work its way through the system. The flow of new units to France was sustained from a number of existing nucleus Service Squadrons which had been retained from the old system. There was, however, a discernible decline in the rate of deployment in mid-1918. During the first six months of the year, nineteen new squadrons were despatched to France. The Programme of Development for the RAF published by the Air Ministry on 13 Jul 18 (Air Organisation Memorandum AO 939)

The early equipment of the specialised training units which began to proliferate from 1917 onwards tended to be obscure or superseded operational types. A typical example is provided by this Armstrong Whitworth FK 3 'Little Ack' of the School of Aerial Fighting at Loch Doon, Ayr. (via Chaz Bowyer)

forecast another forty one squadrons crossing the Channel in the period Aug-Nov 1918, although a revised Programme (AO 999, dated 17 Aug 18) reduced this target to seventeen. What was actually achieved over this period was the deployment of just six squadrons. It is not suggested that the revision of the pattern of training was the sole cause of this under-achievement. Other factors, like shortages of manpower, delays in the development of new types of aeroplanes and engines, and bottlenecks in the production of existing designs, allied to the over-optimism which seemed to be inherent in each successive Programme of Development, would all have been contributory causes. The new system was just beginning to produce results as the war ended. The Programme current at that time (AO 1147, dated 5 Nov 18) envisaged the last twelve of the 'old-type' squadrons being deployed to France in Nov-Dec 1918, to be followed by the first thirteen of the units raised from the TDS organisation in Jan-Feb 1919. These new units were just beginning to form as the war came to an end but the indications were that slippage in planned deployment dates would occur again.

Despite the changes in policy outlined above, which had affected their formation, the designation of RFC Service Squadrons had progressed steadily and logically and by the time that the RAF was formed the allocation of numbers to units formed or planned had extended to about No 150. The

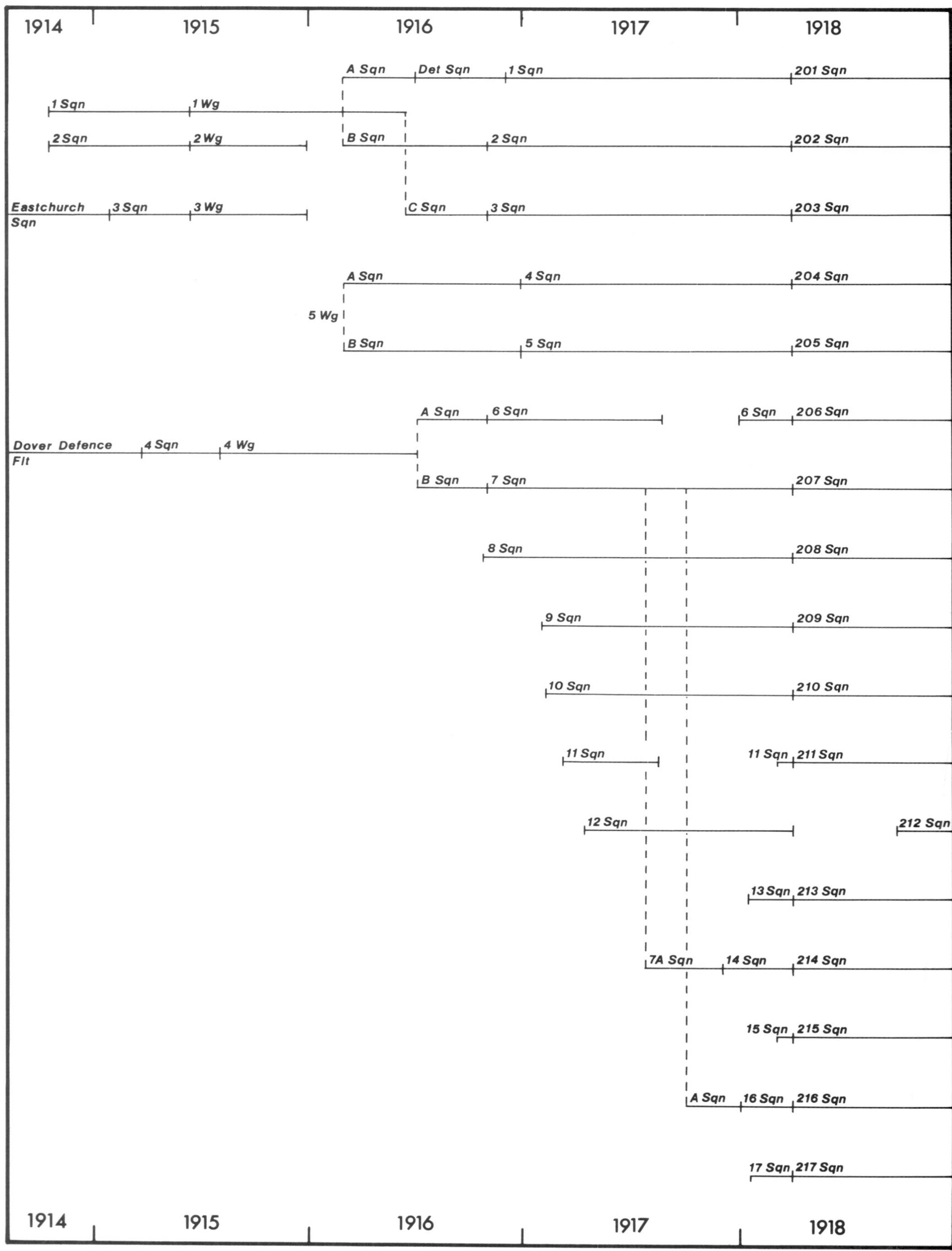
1914
1915
1916
1917
1918
A Sqn
Det Sqn
1 Sqn
201 Sqn
1 Sqn
1 Wg
2 Sqn
2 Wg
B Sqn
2 Sqn
202 Sqn
Eastchurch Sqn
3 Sqn
3 Wg
C Sqn
3 Sqn
203 Sqn
A Sqn
4 Sqn
204 Sqn
5 Wg
B Sqn
5 Sqn
205 Sqn
A Sqn
6 Sqn
6 Sqn
206 Sqn
Dover Defence Flt
4 Sqn
4 Wg
B Sqn
7 Sqn
207 Sqn
8 Sqn
208 Sqn
9 Sqn
209 Sqn
10 Sqn
210 Sqn
11 Sqn
11 Sqn
211 Sqn
12 Sqn
212 Sqn
13 Sqn
213 Sqn
7A Sqn
14 Sqn
214 Sqn
15 Sqn
215 Sqn
A Sqn
16 Sqn
216 Sqn
17 Sqn
217 Sqn
1914
1915
1916
1917
1918

Fig 1

No 12 Sqn RNAS represented a deviation from the norm in that it disbanded on 1 Apr 18 instead of becoming No 212 Sqn, RAF as might have been expected. When No 212 Sqn did form later in the year it took part in trials of a parasite fighter concept using the rigid airship R.23 as host. Several aeroplanes were involved but Lt Keys made the first live drop on 6 Nov 18, probably in Sopwith 2F1 Camel, N6814, seen here suspended beneath the R.23 at Pulham. (MOD H315)

No 81 Sqn was one of the units whose development was heavily influenced by the changes in organisational planning which took place in the latter half of 1918. After a series of false starts (see Appendix 1) it was finally reformed, with Canadian personnel, a few days after the Armistice. This Dolphin, E4764, graphically displays No 81 Sqn's alias as No 1 Sqn, Canadian Air Force. (via G S Leslie)

Following the creation of the RAF a formal system of nomenclature was imposed upon the ex-RNAS flying organisation. Naval seaplanes had, for example, been operating from Hornsea Mere since 1917. On 27 May 18 the Sopwith Baby-equipped unit was designated as No 453 Flt while that operating Short seaplanes became No. 405 Flt on 15 Jun 18. They were joined on 15 Aug 18 by No 404 (Short) Flt from Killingholme and thereafter were jointly known as No 248 Sqn. This Short 184, N1274, was photographed (minus its port wingtip float) at Hornsea. (J M Bruce/G S Leslie collection)

development of the RNAS, by contrast, had been punctuated by a series of reorganisations and rationalisations which had led to its comparatively few operational units being designated successively as numbered squadrons, numbered wings, lettered squadrons, and, finally numbered squadrons again. An impression of this complex evolutionary process can be gained from Fig 1.

When the RAF was created the RFC units retained their original numbers and those squadrons of the RNAS which were retained were distinguished by having 200 added to their existing designations, e.g. No 3 (Naval) Sqn, RNAS became No 203 Sqn, RAF. In this book the movements and equipment of the ex-RNAS units have only been recorded in detail from the formation of the numbered squadrons which immediately preceded their absorption into the RAF. The RNAS had also included a large number of additional flying units stationed in the UK, in Italy and around the Mediterranean and Aegean Seas. These, although operational, lacked any coherent system of identification. After being taken over by the RAF some of these units were allocated squadron numbers while others were identified as numbered flights. These flights, while retaining their independent designations, were subsequently, grouped into yet more new squadrons numbered in the 200-series. This system underwent continual development and expansion until the Armistice. Since the squadrons involved were often equipped with both landplanes and seaplanes, and frequently had elements detached away from the HQ location, this semi-autonomous sub-organisation within the unit was well suited to maritime operations. Within the main text the numbered flights of those squadrons which were constituted in this way have been listed. It should be noted, however, that flights were sometimes transferred between squadrons, and occasionally operated independently. It should not, therefore, be inferred that the dates given for a squadron's existence also applied to the flights concerned.

The highest squadron number allotted before demobilisation brought an end to further expansion in Nov 18 was No 274. Some of the intervening numbers had not been used however, nor had all of the squadrons which had been formed become operational. A significant number of units had existed for only a few weeks, being disbanded during the reorganisation of training in the summer of 1918. Others planned to form at this time were cancelled, and yet another group had their formations suspended or pre-empted by the Armistice. On 11 Nov 18 the RAF had some 204 squadron numbers in use. Of these perhaps 180 could be regarded as having had operational status.

Between the Wars

Demobilisation began almost as soon as the First World War ended. Most squadrons in the process of forming were abandoned within a matter of days, and the units in France

No 274 was the highest number allocated to a squadron during WW 1. Plans to form the unit with Vimys in Nov 18 in the anti-submarine role did not reach fruition and the squadron did not come into being until eight months after the Armistice. This picture shows one of the squadron's Handley Page V/1500s, E8293, at Bircham Newton in 1919. (RAF Museum P15272)

The last squadron to reach France intact before the Armistice was No 94 Sqn which moved to Senlis-le-Sec on 31 Oct 18. It had been briefed for its first patrol when hostilities ended; the sortie was cancelled and No 94 Sqn missed becoming operational during WW I by a matter of hours. The next unit due to arrive in France, No 39 Sqn, had just begun to move when its deployment was cancelled on 16 Nov 18. This picture shows No 94 Sqn's SE 5As at Upper Heyford shortly before they left for France. The aeroplanes include: F871 'A', E6032 'B', F896 'C', H680 'D' and H678 'E'. (RAF Museum P1884)

were rapidly reduced to a cadre basis and withdrawn to the UK where they languished for up to a year before formally disbanding. The RAF reached its lowest strength on 1 Mar 20 when it numbered just twenty nine squadrons. These were distributed as follows: Nos 1, 3, 20, 31, 48, 97, 99 and 114 Sqns in India (note that Nos 1 and 3 Sqns were temporarily identified as "B" and "A" Sqns respectively on this date); Nos 2 and 100 Sqns in Ireland; Nos 4, 24, 39, 203, 207, 210, 230 and 238 Sqns in the UK; Nos 6 and 30 Sqns in Iraq; No 12 Sqn in Germany; No 14 Sqn in Palestine; Nos 47, 55, 56, 70, 208 and 216 Sqns in Egypt; and No 267 Sqn in Malta. Of these, seven existed only as cadres and few of the others were at full strength. Thereafter a slow resurgence took place and by the beginning of 1924 there were thirty four permanent squadrons with a further seven joining them during the year. The size of the service continued to increase slowly, until there were over sixty squadrons when the Expansion Programmes of the late 1930s began.

Representative of the RAF at its lowest ebb in the early 1920s is this DH 10, E7845, of No 216 Sqn at Heliopolis. (RAF Museum P11024)

During this period two innovations were introduced which both affected squadron numbering and led to the creation of new units. The first was the establishment of the Special Reserve and the Auxiliary Air Force. The difference between them was that the Special Reserve squadrons were commanded by regular officers and had a significant nucleus of regular officers and men, the balance being made up by reservists. The Auxiliary squadrons, by contrast, were almost wholly manned by volunteer, part-time personnel. The first of these units was formed in 1925. The Special Reserve squadrons were numbered as Nos 500-504, while the Auxiliaries were numbered from No 600, eventually reaching No 616, although No 606 never materialised. During 1936-37 the Special Reserves were transferred to the Auxiliary Air Force, but retained their original numbers. The second change was the redesignation of seaplane units as squadrons. For the greater part of the 1920s maritime units had operated as Flights, but from Jan 29 they were restored to squadron status. They were allocated disused numbers from the ex-RNAS 200-series to acknowledge their maritime connection.

The Special Reserve began to form from 1925. They are represented here by this Fairey Fawn, J7981, of No 503 Sqn at Waddington. (D Allison)

The realisation that another war in Europe was becoming increasingly likely led to a series of RAF Expansion Programmes being authorised and from 1935 new squadrons began to proliferate. By the time that hostilities broke out there were 158 squadron numbers in use. Most of the new units had been formed by detaching a Flight from an established squadron and expanding it to squadron size — a similar practice to that commonly used during the First World War.

When maritime Flights were upgraded to Squadron status in 1929 No 482 Flt became No 203 Sqn. Shortly afterwards the squadron moved to the head of the Persian Gulf where this Southampton II, S1298, is seen cruising over the Shatt el Arab circa 1930. (RAF Museum P12862)

The Second World War

With the collapse of Continental Europe in 1940, refugee airmen began to arrive in the UK in such numbers that it

New squadrons raised in response to the demands of the RAF Expansion Schemes were often created from a nucleus drawn from an existing unit. This Harrow II, K6962, is of No 115 Sqn which was reformed at Marham on 15 Jun 37 by expanding B Flt of No 38 Sqn. (MOD H201)

became possible to form squadrons manned largely by these Allied personnel. These squadrons were allocated numbers in blocks dedicated to each nationality from the 300 series. In addition, volunteers from the USA began to join the RAF and three fighter squadrons, Nos 71, 121 and 133, were formed from this contingent. These American-manned units were eventually transferred to the USAAF in 1942.

Under the terms of the British Commonwealth Air Training Plan (BCATP) agreement which was signed on 13 Dec 39, Australia, Canada and New Zealand undertook to train aircrew, both for their own Air Forces and for service in the RAF. Article XV of the BCATP also committed these Dominions to forming additional squadrons and under subsequent agreements some of these were assigned to serve under RAF control. In Feb 41 these agreements were given substance. The rate of formation of Dominion squadrons planned at that time envisaged that by 30 Jun 42 there would be an additional 25 RCAF, 18 RAAF and 6 RNZAF squadrons serving with the RAF. To cater for these units the following number blocks were allocated: from No 400 — Canada; from No 450 — Australia; and from No 485 — New Zealand. To avoid confusion with existing RAF units Nos 110, 1 and 2 Sqns, RCAF, which were already serving in the UK, were renumbered on 1 Mar 41 as Nos 400, 401 and 402 Sqns, respectively. For the same reason, and at the same time, independent RAF Flights numbered in the then current 400-series had 1000 added to their designations; thus, for example, No 430 Flt became No 1430 Flt. By contrast those RAAF squadrons already serving under RAF operational control all retained their original numbers. These units were: No 3 Sqn in the Middle East, No 10 Sqn in the UK and Nos 1, 8 and 21 Sqns in the Far East. No 75 (New Zealand) Sqn and No 242 (Canadian) Sqn were other possible candidates for renumbering but since these were actually RAF, rather than Dominion, squadrons and there was no risk of their numbers being duplicated it was decided not to alter their status but to continue to man them with New Zealand and Canadian personnel whenever possible. After the war, on 1 Apr 46, the No 75 numberplate was transferred to the RNZAF in perpetuity, in recognition of the unit's wartime exploits. The number remains in use with the RNZAF today (1988).

No 10 Sqn, RAAF, was one of the Commonwealth squadrons already in being which retained its identity rather than being redesignated, as might have been expected, following the introduction of dedicated number blocks in 1941. The wartime censor has retouched this picture of No 10 Sqn's Sunderland II, W3984/RB·S, to remove the, then classified, ASV radar aerials. (F G Swanborough via Andrew Thomas)

No 306 Sqn was one of the Allied units formed from the influx of refugee Polish airmen which began to arrive in the UK in 1940. This picture shows one of the squadron's Spitfire IIBs, P8342/UZ·N. Photographed on 31 Aug 41 the aeroplane sports the flying duck badge of the Polish 4th (Torun) Air Regt on the cowling below the exhaust stubs, a cartoon character just ahead of the windscreen and the Polish national emblem on the fuselage aft of the roundel. The tail section exhibits substantial battle damage. (RAF Museum P15047)

A group of New Zealanders converting to Wellingtons in the UK when the war broke out eventually became No 75 (NZ) Sqn of the RAF and flew with Bomber Command throughout the war operating in turn the Wellington, Stirling and Lancaster. In recognition of the contribution which the unit's New Zealand personnel had made the numberplate was transferred to the RNZAF in perpetuity on 1 Apr 46 on the authority of SD155/1946 No 731. This picture shows one of No 75 Sqn's Stirling IIIs, EF466/AA·K, in 1943. (RAF Museum P15451)

This Warwick I, BV531/AQ·P, of No 276 Sqn is representative of a ten-squadron batch of numbers, 275-284, which were dedicated to Air-Sea Rescue units. This aircraft flew with No 276 Sqn's Portreath detachment and is pictured in its full operational rig, complete with ASV aerials, an airborne lifeboat and 'Invasion Stripes'. (RAF Museum P21387)

Squadron numbers between 651 and 673 were allocated to Army-associated units. The first of these to operate in direct support of troops in combat was No 651 Sqn. This photograph shows one of the squadron's Auster Is hidden beneath camouflage netting in Tunisia in 1942 during this initial deployment. (Billingham via the Museum of Army Flying)

This Spitfire IV, BP880, named 'Flying Scotsman', is seen at Chandina in Jan 44. It belonged to No 681 Sqn, one of the units numbered in a block allocated to overseas based photo-reconnaissance squadrons. (F D Proctor)

While these allocations were being made to Allied units, the indigenous RAF continued to expand, using numbers outside these special blocks. There were, needless to say, some anomalies. For instance, Nos 67, 68, 69 and 71, numbers which had been used by Australian-manned units within the RFC in 1917-18, were bypassed in the expansion of the 1930s and were not re-used until after the Australians had been allocated their own block of numbers in the 400-series.

Within the RAF number allocation, squadrons were formed on a fairly random basis; however, some sub-blocks are apparent as a result of batches of units being formed in response to a tactical or administrative requirement. For instance: Nos 275-284 Sqns were Air-Sea Rescue units; Nos 285-291 Sqns were for Anti-Aircraft Co-operation training; Nos 295-299 Sqns were transport units; Nos 530-539 were the short-lived Turbinlite squadrons; Nos 540-544 and 680-684 Sqns were photo-reconnaissance units for service at home and abroad respectively. In this connection it should be noted that a contingency plan was conceived, when an invasion of the UK was considered to be a strong possibility, which envisaged the use of fighter OTUs as operational squadrons. These were to have had the numbers 551-566 which would have been created by adding 500 to the existing OTU designation. In the event, the plan was never put into effect, although there was desultory use of some of the numbers by the OTUs for a short period. Despite their lack of formal activation, this block of numbers has never been reallocated for use by other units. The final significant sub-block was 651-673. These numbers were used by Army-oriented units formed within the RAF. The first sixteen of these were operational AOP squadrons, while the last six, although formed as glider squadrons in India, never saw action.

The RAF allocation of squadron numbers, including Commonwealth and Allied units, extended to 699. Of this allocation, 538 numbers have been used at some time, the highest actual number used being No 695. Although strictly beyond the scope of this book, it is worth recording that the allocation of numbers did, and still does, run on in a logical sequence up to 1999. These numbers are summarised at Appendix 2. As ever, there is an anomaly. No 1435 Flt, in Malta, was a fighter unit which, being both a large and an operational unit, assumed the title of No 1435 Sqn. This was subsequently recognised by officialdom and, by default, the RAF acquired a squadron number which it should never have had.

Post War

With the end of World War Two the RAF again underwent a sharp reduction in size. Having peaked at a strength of 504 numbers in use on 1 Jan 45, it had shrunk to 479 squadrons by VE-Day (8 May 45) and to 397 by VJ-Day (14 Aug 45). By

Norway is one of several countries which have sustained the identities of their national squadrons which served within the RAF during WW II. This F-104 of No 331 Sqn RNoAF, was photographed off Northern Norway in Sep 78 after intercepting a Vulcan of No 50 Sqn. (Author)

Among the numberplates especially selected to remain in use after WW II was that of No 511 Sqn in recognition of its work as the pioneer long-range transport squadron. The squadron had this Lancastrian, VW701, on charge in 1945/46 and used it to conduct a 34,000 mile round-the-world flight and a return trip to Java. It is seen here at Kallang during the second route-proving exercise. (Sqn Ldr N J Haine)

early Apr 47 progressive demobilisation had reduced the RAF's size to just over 140 squadrons. All the 300 and 400 series numbers disappeared from the RAF's Order of Battle as these units either disbanded or flew back to their various homelands. In many cases these squadrons were absorbed into their existing national air service organisations and in others they formed the nuclei of new services being re-established after Liberation. Some of the original RAF squadron numbers have been perpetuated by these Air Forces, and in Canada, Greece, Norway and the Netherlands, for example, they are still in use.

The Auxiliary Air Force squadrons had been mobilised into the RAFVR in 1939 and had lost their special status in the process. The old Auxiliary squadron numbers disappeared along with the others in the wholesale post-war demobilisation programme. However, on 10 May 46 the Auxiliary Air Force was reconstituted although, since local recruiting had first to take place, it was some months before the new squadrons actually began to materialise. On 16 Dec 47 the prefix 'Royal' was granted to the 'week-end flyers' who then became the RAuxAF. The RAuxAF, as a flying organisation, survived for not quite ten years for, on 10 Mar 57, all the squadrons were disbanded at a stroke. By that time the Auxiliaries comprised all the pre-war numbers, less No 503 Sqn, plus Nos 661-664 and 666 (AOP) Sqns and had briefly also included No 622 Sqn as a transport unit. Later in 1957, on 1 Sep, the four remaining regular AOP squadrons were transferred to Army control and their subsequent histories fall outside the scope of this volume. Suffice to say that the original numbers have been retained by the Army and they are still in use.

Once the RAF had settled down to its peacetime existence a squadron numbering policy became discernible. In general, those squadrons which already had the longest histories would be those which would continue to serve. Thus if a unit had served through the 1920s and 1930s its future was fairly well assured. However, there were some over-riding considerations. Several additional numbers belonging to squadrons with particularly significant or distinguished war records were also selected and retained in use, notwithstanding their relatively brief service. Examples of these are: No 120 Sqn, which had been the most successful land-based anti-submarine unit; No 230 Sqn as an example of a flying-boat unit; No 511 Sqn, the original long-range transport squadron; No 617 Sqn, the famous 'Dambusters'; and No 543 Sqn which was representative of the wartime photo-reconnaissance squadrons. Another factor to be acknowledge in the selection of unit numbers was historical association with a specific role. Thus, when helicopters began to be introduced for rescue duties, Nos 275 and 284 Sqns were reformed to operate them at home and in the Mediterranean area respectively, these squadrons having been wartime rescue units in those theatres. In line with this policy it was decided, when two joint RAF/RN electronic

The 'Auxiliaries' were recreated from 10 May 46. This Spitfire F.22, PK497, RAD·V, of No 504 Sqn was photographed at Hucknall on 13 Jun 48, by which time most of the squadrons of the new volunteer force had become fairly well established. (R C Sturtivant)

Auster AOP 9, WZ717, was issued to No 656 Sqn on 22 May 56 when it was still an RAF unit. It was still on charge on 1 Sep 57 when the four remaining operational AOP squadrons were absorbed into the Army Air Corps. The aeroplane did not survive for long in the hands of its new owners since it was Struck Off Charge on 20 Dec 57. (M Fearne via the Museum of Army Flying)

In 1975/76, following the withdrawal of British forces from most of their permanent overseas bases it was concluded that the six squadron force of Hercules transports was larger than its commitments warranted. Two units were accordingly disbanded; these were Nos 36 and 48 Sqns, those with the least cumulative service. Since the Hercules force operated on a pool basis no unit markings were carried; the loss of the two units was not, therefore, readily apparent. This photograph, taken at Gatow in Jun 75, shows one of Lyneham's Hercules C.1s, XV206, in the desert-style camouflage which was in vogue for RAF transport aircraft in the 1970s. (Author)

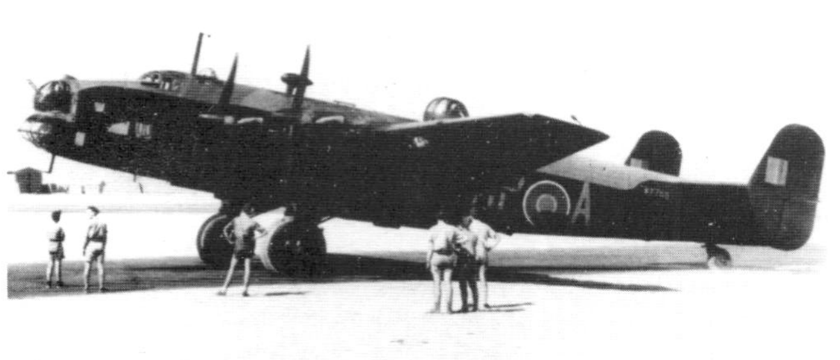

One of the earliest examples of a linked squadron was No 76/454 which served in Palestine and Egypt in 1942. The Servicing Echelon was later replaced, making the link No 76/462 Sqn. This Halifax II Srs I, W7755/MP-A, was one of the original sixteen aircraft detachment of No 76 Sqn which flew out to the Middle East in Jul 42. (RAF Museum P20070)

countermeasures training squadrons were to be formed, to break new ground. The new units were formed as Nos 360 and 361 Sqns. Neither of these numbers had been used before, which avoided the units' having predominantly Air Force or Naval backgrounds so that both services could contribute to building a history from scratch.

In recent years, with the number of squadrons steadily decreasing, the dominant, though not exclusive, consideration in the selection of squadron numbers has become length of service, with historical role having only secondary importance. This principle could be seen in action when it became necessary to disband two, of the existing six, Hercules squadrons in 1976. Nos 36 and 48 Sqns were, despite their distinguished records, the ones to go, since the others had all accumulated more actual service. Another manifestation of the desire to sustain suitable squadron numbers could be seen earlier when, in 1969, the Communications Squadrons were allocated formal unit numbers. Previously such units had usually, although not exclusively, had names relating to formations or regions, e.g. RAF Germany Communications Squadron and Northern Communications Squadron.

The progressive expansions and contractions of the RAF and its predecessors, which have been summarised in the above paragraphs, are further reviewed and illustrated diagrammatically at Appendix 3.

Linked Numbers

During the Second World War linked unit numbers were used intermittently in the Middle East. This usually occurred when the air echelon of a squadron detached from the UK, eg No 10 Sqn, was combined with the ground echelon of another unit which had as yet received no aircraft of its own, eg No 227 Sqn. The combined unit, in this case, operated as No 10/227 Sqn until it was incorporated, with No 76/462 Sqn, into an independently established No 462 Sqn. A particularly unusual example of this practice was the merging of an RAF unit with one from the FAA to form No 33/806 Sqn. This link was formally constituted from 8 Jun 41 until 28 Jul 41.

A second series of linked numbers manifested itself in 1949 and persisted for some 10 years in an effort to extend the histories of units which had in effect been disbanded. This is discussed in more detail at Appendix 4.

Shadow Squadrons

Since the mid-1950s it has been the practice to allocate the numbers of defunct operational squadrons to certain second-line or training units for use in the event of general mobilisation. This is dealt with in more detail at Appendix 5.

Squadron Titles

From time to time various schemes have been devised under which some squadrons have had a name incorporated into their titles. This is discussed at Appendix 6.

Squadron Roles

From 27 Mar 24, on the authority of AMWO 218, a squadron's role was included in its title (and badge frame after these were

Hunter F.6, XF526, of No 229 OCU at Chivenor wearing the markings of its 'shadow' identity – No 234 Sqn. (via R C Sturtivant)

introduced in Jan 36 by AMO A.14) so that squadrons were designated: No 1 (Fighter) Sqn; No 2 (Army Co-operation) Sqn; No 9 (Bombing) Sqn; and so on. The term 'Bombing' was replaced by 'Bomber' after the publication of AMWO 221 on 4 Apr 29. Further descriptive terms, eg General Reconnaissance and Bomber-Transport, were introduced as required.

This practice was officially terminated in May 39 by AMO A.185 which stated that titles were no longer to appear in badge frames or be part of the unit's title. Notwithstanding this regulation, over forty years later some squadrons still incorporate their role, particularly where this has never changed, in their title, albeit unofficially. The reasons for the deletion of roles were twofold. Firstly security considerations made it unwise to advertise a unit's function within its designation; and secondly, the system was becoming subject to too many changes as units switched roles. For instance No 6 Sqn changed from Army Co-operation to Bomber in Apr 31, No 45 Sqn changed from Bomber Transport to Bombing in Apr 27 while No 216 Sqn switched in the reverse sense some four years later, and No 30 Sqn changed from Bomber to Fighter in Mar 41. Changes such as these became ever more frequent as the Second World War dictated changes in tactics and these in turn required units to be re-equipped and carry out different tasks. No 27 Sqn is a good example of the way in which a unit number may be used to designate a series of formations operating in a wide variety of roles. No 27 Sqn originally deployed to France in 1916 as a fighter squadron but rapidly evolved into a bomber unit, in which role it continued to function until 1939. During World War Two it operated in turn as a flying training school, a fighter squadron, a Beaufighter strike unit, and as an Air-Jungle Rescue squadron. After the war it flew on the Berlin Air Lift as a Dakota squadron then reverted to bomber operations with Canberras and Vulcans. A second period of service with Vulcans, this time in the Maritime Surveillance role, was followed by its current reincarnation as a Tornado strike-attack unit.

Within this book no attempt has been made to reflect a squadron's role although this can usually be deduced from the types of aircraft which it flew.

Aircraft Types and Variants

Where feasible, all the aircraft types that a squadron has

In 1936, while it was still the practice to include a squadron's function in its title, the format of RAF unit badges was regularised. At the same time three standard, role related badge frames were introduced for display on a squadron's aeroplanes. These were: an arrowhead for fighter squadrons; a star for reconnaissance units; and a grenade for bomber squadrons. An example of the star form can be seen on the fin of this Hector, K9703, of No 53 Sqn. (RAF Museum P17216)

Having exchanged roles between bomber and bomber-transport Nos 45 and 216 Sqns continued to serve together in Egypt. This incident took place at Heliopolis and involved Wellesley, K7761, and Valentia, JR9765. The Valentia carries its No 216 Sqn badge on its nose in the appropriate grenade-shaped frame. (RAF Museum P11060)

During the 1920s and 1930s most squadrons adopted some form of pseudo-heraldic device with which to identify their aeroplanes. This Hart, K4468, of No 6 Sqn exhibits that unit's pre-1936 emblem on its fin. When this was submitted to Chester Herald, the newly appointed Inspector of RAF Badges, for official sanction in 1936 it was disallowed since it featured the squadron's actual number – which was against the rules. The design was resubmitted with the figure '6' restyled in the form of a writhing serpent – it was duly approved. (RAF Museum P10740)

Military budgets in the 1920s were subject to extreme stringency. It was contemporary RAF policy to invest most of its limited resources into the training of its personnel and a capital works programme. As a result most service aeroplanes in the early post-war era were either wartime types or adaptations of them. This Walrus, N9534, of No 3 Sqn, seen visiting Cranwell in 1923, was the DH 9A of 1918 re-engined with a Napier Lion and optimised for the Fleet Spotter role. (RAF Museum P22408)

operated as its primary equipment have been recorded in each unit's listing in the main text. This has not always been possible for the earliest days of some of the original RFC squadrons. As observed previously, it was common practice in the First World War for a newly formed squadron to spend its first few months of service on training duties. During this period the earliest squadrons generally flew a varied collection of obsolete or training aircraft, typically Avro 504s, assorted BE models and a variety of Farmans. Units formed later tended to fly more up-to-date Service machines. Records are not often comprehensive for this early phase of many squadrons' service and so it has not always been possible to be specific about which types were used or for how long. However, after a few months a unit would be mobilised for overseas service and equipped with its operational aircraft. From this stage onwards it has been possible to note all the types flown, broken down into variants where these were significantly different.

Broadly speaking the progressive re-equipment of squadrons was, at first, a straightforward process of replacing the current type with a completely new and improved one. As aeroplanes became more sophisticated (and expensive), however, this practice was gradually superseded and new equipment tended to take the form of progressive developments of a basic design. These variants were distinguished by 'mark numbers', expressed in Roman numerals, e.g. Halifax I, II, III, etc. Further sub-variants were indicated by a suffix letter, thus: Hurricane IIA, IIB, IIC, etc. In late 1942 a further refinement, role prefixes, was introduced, for instance B for bombers, GR for general reconnaissance types, RP for aircraft modified for the firing of rocket projectiles, and so on. However, despite official sanction the use of these prefixes was somewhat sporadic and they did not become universally accepted until later.

The intensive development of basic designs during World War Two led to many variants being evolved. However, large numbers expressed in Roman numerals, e.g. XIV, XVI, XVIII

When role prefixes were introduced for mark numbers in 1943 the letters GR stood for General Reconnaissance and were appropriate to types such as this Wellington GR XIV of No 14 Sqn at Chivenor. (Chaz Bowyer)

Today GR stands for Ground Attack/Reconnaissance and is applied to high performance types like the Jaguar and Tornado. These are Harrier GR 3s of No 3 Sqn, XZ132 nearest. (British Aerospace, Kingston)

As variants of basic designs proliferated it was found that large mark numbers expressed in Roman numerals became increasingly cumbersome and in 1948 Arabic numerals were introduced and role prefixes became commonplace. This is a Spitfire XVIII (later FR 18), TP448/GZ·?, of No 32 Sqn photographed over Palestine on 21 July 47 from a Lancaster. (RAF Museum P10503)

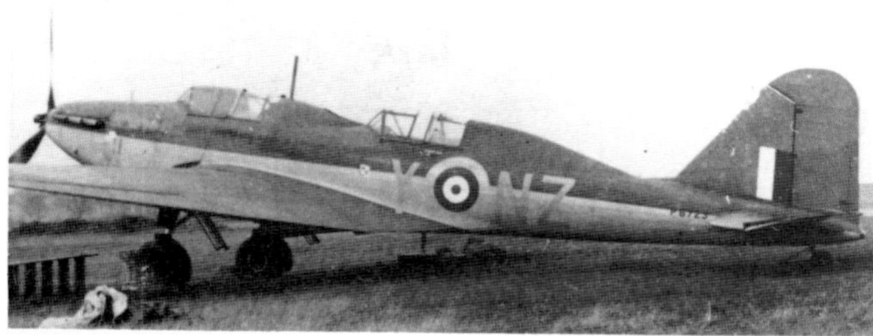

Before becoming operational many newly-formed squadrons flew interim second-line types. This Battle Trainer, P6723/NZ·Y, was flown by No 304 Sqn in 1940. Note the Polish chequerboard insignia just below the rear cockpit sill. (RAF Museum P17883)

Although not generally listed in the histories in this book squadrons often carry second-line or training aircraft on their inventories. This Meteor T.7, VW442, is wearing the red chevrons of No 65 Sqn. (R C Sturtivant)

and XXXIV, were clumsy, inconvenient and potentially confusing. AMO N.1000 dated 28 Aug 41 ruled that engine mark numbers, which had proliferated more rapidly than those of airframes, above 20/XX would thenceforth be expressed in Arabic numerals. From Jan 45 the same practice was applied to aircraft, and, on the authority of AMO N.438, the use of Roman numerals was abandoned altogether from 3 Jun 48. From this time on, the use of role prefixes became widespread.

In this book an attempt has been made to reflect these changes without going to the lengths of the extensive duplication of recording which would be necessary to register each change in style of designation as it affected each squadron. Roman numerals without role prefixes have generally been used until the end of 1945 (or until disbandment, where this took place shortly afterwards) and Arabic numerals with prefixes thereafter.

Two dates have been noted against each aircraft type/mark. These are the dates of introduction into, and withdrawal from, service. These dates have been drawn, in general, from the squadrons' Operations Record Books (RAF Form 540). It should be appreciated that isolated examples of phased-out types were sometimes retained on charge for a while after a squadron had re-equipped. The withdrawal date recorded is that after which the type/mark's use by the squadron ceased to be significant.

Many squadrons have, from time to time, employed examples of second-line types or training variants of operational aircraft for a variety of reasons. Examples include: the use of Ansons, Oxfords, Tiger Moths, Magisters, etc. as squadron 'hacks', either officially or otherwise; the use of types like Harvards, Battles or Masters, while a squadron converted to retractable undercarriage monoplanes in the period immediately prior to the Second World War, or as interim equipment pending the receipt of the intended first-line type; and the use of dual-controlled variants like the Vampire T.11 or Harrier T.4 for pilot checks and Instrument Ratings. In these histories, the listing of squadron equipment has been confined to the primary operational types and these ancillary types/marks have not usually been recorded. However, in units where these aeroplanes formed the primary equipment, Communications or Calibration Squadrons for instance, they have been noted.

Appendix 7 provides a cross-reference by aircraft type to the main unit history Section of the book. Aircraft manufacturers have been omitted in both the main listings and in the cross-reference, but they are recorded at Appendix 8.

Formations and Disbandments

As a general rule the formation and disbandment of units is always authorised at Ministry level. Over the years various documents have served as the channel through which this executive authority has been communicated. The earliest of these included: Directives issued by the Director of Military Aeronautics; Programmes of Development published by the Director of Air Organisation; and Air Organisation Memoranda (the 'AO' series). The latter first appeared in 1916 and were originally published under the auspices of the War Office. The Air Ministry inherited this responsibility in 1918 and continued their publication until 1933. From 1927 onwards the term 'Air Order' became increasingly prevalent in references to these documents. In 1933 a new series, 'Confidential Organisation Memoranda', was started. These continued until 15 Sep 39 when the last in the series, No 427, announced that all such matters would subsequently be classified as Secret. The first Secret Organisation Memorandum had already been

The formal announcement of the original formation of No 141 Sqn was contained in Air Organisation Memorandum AO 714, dated 31 Dec 17. This picture was taken shortly after the unit had won an inter-squadron competition involving all the squadrons of the VIth (Home Defence) Brigade in 1918. As the winners No 141 Sqn became the 'Cock Squadron', hence the device on the fin of this Bristol Fighter, E2604. The officer is Maj B E Baker, the CO. As a footnote it should be recorded that as the champions took off from Suttons Farm, the venue for the competition's final events, to return to Biggin Hill one of the victorious crew fired a celebratory Verey light which set fire to the VIP tent . . . (Author's collection)

Confidential Organisation Memoranda were the contemporary authoritative documents governing unit formations during the RAF's expansion in the 1930s. No 46 Sqn, one of whose Gauntlet IIs, K5315, is seen here after a landing accident at Kenley on 17 Jun 37, was reformed on the authority of OM No 41, dated 8 Jul 36. (RAF Museum P4386)

Since 1939 the Secret Document (SD) 155 has been the authority for unit formations. No 25 Sqn, for example, was reformed at Waterbeach on 2 Jul 58 by renumbering No 153 Sqn on the authority of SD155/1958 No 320. This is a 1960 photograph of one of No 25 Sqn's Javelin FAW 9s, XH772. (Air Britain M2579)

published, on 5 Apr 39, in the first issue of the 'Secret Document (SD) 155'. The SD 155 continues to represent the formal authority on which the formation and disbandment of squadrons is based today.

Exceptions to this formal process can occur, of course, especially in wartime, when planned actions may be supplanted by reactions to unforeseen events. A classic example of this occurred in the Far East in 1942, when several squadrons were effectively disbanded by the Japanese, rather than by an executive decision of the Air Council. In such cases a notional disbandment date has been established from an examination of the surviving records.

Another adaptation of the system which is sometimes used involves official sanction being given to the formation or disbandment of a unit, but implementation of the decision being delegated to the discretion of the local Commander concerned. An example of this is provided by SD 155/1940 No 549, which ordered the disbandment of No 81 Sqn "by 19 Jun 40". The F 540 for RAF Hendon records that the squadron actually ceased to exist on 15 Jun 40.

Having established that there is usually an appointed date on which squadrons are to form or disband, it must also be conceded that this, although recognised, cannot always be rigidly adhered to by subordinate organisations. For instance the formation date of a unit may have to be postponed because of a lack of personnel or other resources. However, in general, the formation does take place, although occasionally it may be some time before a unit takes on more than a notional existence. For instance, Nos 181 and 182 Sqns were both authorised to form on 25 Aug 42 (on the authority of SD 155/1942 No 799) although the squadrons' F 540s did not open until the following month.

Air Ministry Weekly Orders were not, in the context of unit formations and disbandments, authoritative documents in themselves, but they were used in the 1920s and 1930s to publicise changes in organisation. For instance, an announcement of the reformation of No 32 Sqn (to consist at first of only a HQ and one Flight) on 1 Apr 23 was contained in AMWO No 201 of 1923. Expansion of the squadron to full three Flight strength was the subject of AMWO No 445 of 1924. This picture shows one of No 32 Sqn's Snipes, E6268, during this period wearing the original verison of the unit's distinctive blue-bar-with-white-diagonals markings. (RAF Museum P19363)

Although personnel had already been drafted to Gosport for No 60 Sqn and equipment, including aeroplanes, had been provided, indeed the CO was appointed on 1 May 16, the squadron was not officially formed until 15 May. Before the end of the month No 60 Sqn had moved to France equipped with a variety of Moranes including this model BB, possibly 5176. (Capt D S Glover)

An example of a unit which ran on beyond its promulgated disbandment date is provided by No 298 Sqn which was officially disbanded on 21 Dec 46 by SD155/1947 No 26. However, it continued to operate under local authorisation until 27 Dec 46. This is one of No 298 Sqn's Halifax A7s, NA356, seen visiting Santa Cruz in Feb 46. (RAF Museum P7083)

The converse is also true, in that some squadrons begin to assemble before their formation is officially recognised. Two examples of this practice, from the First World War, are provided by No 55 Sqn, which was officially formed on 8 Jun 16 (notified by HQ VIth Brigade letter 6B/791, dated 21 Jun 16); and No 60 Sqn, which, together with Nos 50, 51, 53 and 54 Sqns, was authorised from 15 May 16 (by Director of Air Organisation letter 87/6649, dated 22 May 16). While it is true that correspondence concerning these squadrons took place earlier, and even that personnel were posted onto their strengths before these dates, the fact remains that these events predated their **officially** recognised formation.

Disbandment dates may also, on occasion, be implemented rather flexibly. For instance, a squadron may begin to run down some weeks in advance of the prescribed date as its personnel are posted away to other units and its equipment is withdrawn for reallocation. Little of substance may remain when the appointed day finally arrives.

On the other hand the arrival of an official disbandment date

This Mosquito VI, HR609, of No 618 Sqn crashed on 12 Jun 45 as a result of engine failure. The squadron was authorised to disband in the following month but it continued to exist until the turn of the year. (D Vincent)

sometimes has little or no apparent effect. During the large-scale demobilisation of 1945-46 the administrative system was not always able to react promptly to a peremptory notification of a unit's disbandment. Since it might take days, even weeks, formally to dispose of a squadron's effects, units sometimes continued to function under their own momentum although, technically, they were existing in a kind of 'legal limbo'. No 126 Sqn, for instance, was officially disbanded on 10 Mar 46 (by SD 155/1946 No 512) but it took several weeks for all of the squadron's Spitfires to be flown away and the Squadron Orderly Room did not finally close until 26 Apr. Perhaps the most extreme case is provided by No 618 Sqn, which was disbanded in Australia with effect from 21 Jul 45 (on the authority of SD 155/1945 No 1601). The squadron, however, continued to function, and to maintain its F 540, until 31 Dec 45.

One other cause of alternative dates appearing in squadron records should be mentioned. When a squadron is reduced to a Numberplate Only this implies an intention to reform it in the not too distant future, however, these plans may not come to fruition. The situation should then be regularised by formal disbandment of the nominal unit. Sometimes this is done retroactively, but sometimes a new date is promulgated. An example of the first practice is provided by No 132 Sqn which was reduced to a Numberplate on 15 Apr 46 (by SD 155/1946 No 780). More than two years later this date was redesignated as the disbandment date on the authority of SD 155/1948 No 39. On the other hand No 658 Sqn was reduced to a Numberplate on 15 Oct 46 (by SD 155/1946 No 2159), but when it was formally disbanded, (by SD 155/1947 No 402), this event was deemed to have occurred on 1 Apr 47. Other examples of a second date being applied are provided by Nos 70 and 104 Sqns which were reduced to Numberplate Only and 'unmanned' status respectively on 1 Apr 47 (by SD 155/1947 No 383), but not disbanded until 9 Feb 48 (by SD 155/1948 No 188). As stated earlier in the Introduction, within this book Numberplate Only status has not been acknowledged and, where applicable, the date of reduction has been quoted as the effective disbandment date, even when this technically occurred later.

Throughout this book the dates of formation and disbandment given have, whenever possible, been drawn from the appropriate authoritative contemporary official documents. Where these are missing, or never existed, the records of the controlling Command and/or Group Headquarters have been consulted. As a result the dates quoted sometimes differ from those which have appeared in previously published accounts, and even from those in squadrons' F 540s. At times of stress, when the "fog of war" was at its thickest, it was quite possible for a squadron, which is at a relatively low level within the organisational structure, not to be fully aware of what decisions were being implemented. Consequently, while it is acknowledged that a squadron's F 540 reflects the unit's perception of events, it is not always the best source from which to extract the 'facts'. The following examples, drawn

Hurricane IIB, BM995, of No 258 Sqn at Colombo after its reformation following the loss of the original No 258 Sqn in the fall of Singapore and the East Indies. (S Searle)

Thunderbolt II, KJ194/GQ·N, of No 134 Sqn. This aeroplane was later reported to be with No 131 Sqn following the renumbering exercise of Jun/Jul 45. (W Wright)

from units serving in South East Asia Command, illustrate this point:

a. An examination of No 258 Sqn's Operations Record Book for the spring of 1942, when the squadron was reforming in Ceylon, indicates that some confusion existed at unit level as to the squadron's precise status. This was a case, as described above, of a unit being formed under the aegis of a local commander, rather than on the specific direction of the Air Council. The details of No 258 Sqn's reformation given in the accompanying account were drawn from the records of HQ No 222 Group, which are quite specific on the subject.

b. HQ ACSEA Administrative Instruction 128/45 dated 9 Jun 45 ordered the disbandment of Nos 123, 134 and 135 (Thunderbolt) Sqns and the transfer of their aircraft, equipment and personnel to Nos 81, 131 and 615 (Spitfire) Sqns. Although not actually specified this implied the effective disbandment of the existing Nos 81, 131 and 615 Sqns (since their personnel were to be posted away and their Spitfires withdrawn, to re-equip Indian squadrons) and their immediate reformation by the renumbering of the Thunderbolt units. All this was to be effective on 10 Jun 45. (These changes were subsequently ratified by SD 155/1945 No 1754). The way in which each of the units concerned implemented the directive is discussed below. The Spitfire squadrons were all in comparatively stable situations and were able to react promptly, once they learned of the reorganisation.

(1) No 81 Sqn, at No 22 APC, Amarda Road, received the instructions on 14 Jun 45 and within two days its pilots had left and its aircraft, their Ace of Spades markings erased, awaited disposal. The last date recorded in the 'old' No 81 Sqn's F 540 is 19 Jun 45, i.e. nine days after the unit had technically ceased to exist.

(2) No 131 Sqn, at Dalbhumgarh, had not long been in India and had yet to become operational in the theatre. It disbanded almost immediately, the unit's F 540 for the month of Jun 45 being a single page summary.

(3) No 615 Sqn, at Chakulia, learned of their disbandment on 17 Jun and had implemented the instructions by 28 Jun. The last entry in the F 540 is dated 29 Jun.

By contrast the Thunderbolt squadrons were all in the throes of redeployment when the decision was announced and, being somewhat scattered, took some weeks to reassemble their assets and assume their new identities.

(4) No 123 Sqn moved from Kyaukpyu to Bobbili during Jun 45. The aircraft, flying via Cox's Bazaar, Baigachi and Vizagapatam, arrived on 25 Jun. The groundcrew preceded them by ten days having travelled to Madras by sea, completing their journey by train. No mention is made of the reorganisation in the F 540 which continues to 30 Jun, however, the next month's records were kept as No 81 Sqn.

Camouflaged Thunderbolt Is of No 135 Sqn at Chittagong in Dec 44. Six months later this unit was disbanded and its assets were transferred to No 615 Sqn; in the process the new squadron was re-equipped with unpainted Thunderbolt IIs. (via G J Thomas)

(5) No 134 Sqn's F 540 for Jun 45 is a one page summary covering the unit's move from Kyaukpyu to Ulunderpet and acknowledging that the squadron was disbanded on 10 Jun and that its personnel were to be posted to No 131 Sqn. The new No 131 Sqn's F 540 begins on 1 Jul.

(6) No 135 Sqn's F 540 ends on 30 Apr 45 with the unit at Akyab. No records have survived for May and Jun, but the No 615 Numberplate was taken into use at some time during Jun as the 'old' No 615 (Spitfire) Sqn's diary contains complaints that their mail was not arriving since it was being redirected to the 'new' unit. The unit's records are resumed in Jul 45 as No 615 Sqn.

c. No 67 Sqn's official disbandment date was 31 Jul 45 but the squadron was not notified of this until 8 Aug. As a result the unit's F 540 runs on until 31 Aug covering the events of the squadron's run down.

Although No 136 Sqn ceased to exist on 8 May 46 when it was renumbered as No 152 Sqn this Spitfire FR 14E, RN193, still sported No 136 Sqn's HM codes when it was photographed at Bangalore in 1947. (R C Sturtivant)

Although confusion surrounded some of the unit renumberings which followed WW II this was not always the case. No 605 Sqn was renumbered as No 4 Sqn on 31 Aug 45 on the authority of SD155/1945 No 2098. This transformation duly took place as scheduled. This photograph was taken in the late 1940s and shows one of No 4 Sqn's Mosquito FB 6s, RS679. (RAF Museum P19014)

d. SD 155/1946 No 1298 renumbered No 136 Sqn as No 152 Sqn with effect from 8 May 46. However No 136 Sqn was on board the SS *Pachaug Victory* in the Bay of Bengal en route from Malaya to India on that date and did not arrive in Bombay until four days later. As a result 12 May is sometimes quoted as the date of this renumbering.

Confusion at squadron level over the date of a renumbering was not confined to the Far East. Other instances occurred in Europe. For instance, among the changes authorised by SD 155/1945 No 2098 (dated 3 Sep 45) were the following, which were to be effective from 19 Sep 45:

a. No 487 Sqn to be reduced to a Numberplate Only.

b. No 16 Sqn to disband and reform immediately from No 487 Sqn.

On 3 Oct 45 these changes were amended (by SD 155/1945 No 2383), still with an effective date of 19 Sep 45, to be:

c No 487 Sqn to be reduced to a Numberplate Only.

d. No 268 Sqn to disband and reform immediately from No 487 Sqn.

e. No 16 Sqn to disband and reform immediately from No 268 Sqn.

Since there was a time delay in these dates being notified to the units concerned it will be appreciated that for a matter of weeks there would have been some uncertainty at squadron level as to exactly which Numberplate applied to which unit, and from when.

A similar revision of dates led to confusion over the renumbering of No 107 Sqn as No 11 Sqn. SD 155/1948 No 630 authorised this change with effect from 15 Sep 48. The effective date was subsequently changed to 4 Nov 48 (by an amendment), however, SD 155/1948 No 746 ordered that the original date was to stand.

As can be seen from the foregoing examples, so many factors have influenced the formation and disbandment of squadrons that it is difficult to devise universally applicable rules to decide what the effective dates of these events should be. One solution might be to recognise a unit only after it has become 'operational', or (in modern, international terms) been 'assigned' (to NATO). Since the 1970s a step has been taken in this direction to cover the periods during which combat squadrons undergo re-equipment. In practice today "re-equipment" frequently means the creation of a completely new, replacement formation and, until it has worked-up, there may be two squadrons using the same number; the new unit often has the term "Designate" incorporated into its title, to distinguish it from the 'real' squadron, until it finally takes over as the effective unit.

Although superficially attractive such a pragmatic approach, of recognising a unit only after it has become operational, would fail to acknowledge the time and effort spent by those

Since the 1970s it has become a frequent practice for re-equipment programmes to result in two units using the same numberplate at the same time. When No 29 Sqn converted to Phantoms the nominal change occurred on New Year's Day 1975. In fact a new and independent unit, No 29 Sqn (Designate) had formed on 1 Oct 74 to work-up on Phantoms so that it could assume the sole right to the numberplate on 1 Jan 75 without any loss of operational capability, the Lightning unit remaining fully available until 31 Dec 74. This photograph shows one of No 29 Sqn's Phantom FGR 2s, XV400. (Air Britain M751)

units which never 'made it', or which took a long time to do so. Thus the many squadrons which existed, but which never saw combat, during the First World War would go unacknowledged, as would for example, the months spent by No 84 Sqn at Habbaniyah in 1949 while it struggled to introduce the first Brigands into service.

In a book devoted to the history of any particular squadron it is possible to: discourse at length on the effective status of the unit at any particular time; to record its perception of the events surrounding each formation and disbandment; and to reflect on the parochial implications of periods spent at less than full strength or while considered to be non-operational. Within the confines of this book, however, the aim has had to be more fundamental. It has been to record the actual, the formal, the official periods of existence of each squadron. To this end the primary (but not exclusive) sources used to establish the formation and disbandment dates in this book have been the enabling executive documents, and not unit records.

Movement Dates

Under wartime conditions the tactical movement of squadrons within a theatre is usually at the discretion of the Operational Commander concerned. Such movements will be influenced strongly by events and the notice given may vary from weeks to minutes. Depending upon the circumstances the relevant orders may be passed in writing, by signal or, in extremis, by telephone.

On the other hand redeployments between theatres in wartime, and almost all permanent changes of base in peacetime, are directed from Ministry level, using the same executive documents as those specified previously in the context of unit formation and disbandment. The creation of a squadron, however, is an absolute event which can be considered to have occurred administratively, whether or not it had any immediate tangible effect. The same is not true of movements, which must involve positive action and which take a finite time to implement. Although executive orders to move usually specify a timescale these are, in practical terms, really notional dates — targets to be aimed at. The achievement of the aim on schedule, however, is subject to a variety of unpredictable factors such as: the weather; the availability of transport resources, air, land or sea; en route diversions; and enemy action.

In view of the above it will be appreciated that, unlike formations and disbandments, it is not the executive documents that provide the critical information but the individual unit records. These should have recorded the actual events which occurred and they have been used, whenever possible, as the primary reference source for movement details. Where squadron F 540s are missing, or have been inadequately compiled, the records of the concerned Stations, Wings, Groups, Commands, or other associated formations have been consulted as necessary to establish the dates of events.

Although each squadron's movements have, where possible been noted in the main text as if they had occurred on a specific day, these dates should be treated with some circumspection. Few squadron moves actually take place in one day. Typically an advance party precedes the main element and a rear party follows on behind. This practice can lead to a variety of dates for a given unit movement being recorded in different contemporary records. For instance, in its own Operations Record Book a hypothetical squadron might record itself as having moved on (say) the 10th of a month, probably because that was the date of arrival at the new location of the air echelon, or because it was the date on which the CO or the Squadron's Adjutant or Recording Officer moved. However, the receiving Station may note the allocation of accommodation to the advance party on the 8th as the effective movement date. By contrast, from its point of view, the losing Station might perceive the 13th, when the squadron's old offices were finally vacated by the rear party, to be the significant date. For good measure the relevant Group

Unit movements are often supported by air transport. The earliest type operated in this role was the Vernon. This is a Vernon I of No 45 Sqn. (RAF Museum P20445)

The ultimate development of the bomber-transport theme begun with the Vernon was the Bombay which operated in both roles in the Middle East during WW II. In Mar/Apr 42 four Bombays of No 216 Sqn (L5820, L5825, L5831 and L5843) were engaged in a shuttle service up and down the Persian Gulf. This is believed to be one of these aircraft at Karachi (note the Valentia – of No 31 Sqn? – in the hangar), a southern extension of the normal route which was visited on five occasions by these aircraft. (via D W Warne)

Mainstay of the RAF's transport force in the immediate post-war years was the York. This one, wearing the TB codes of No 51 Sqn, was photographed at Mauripur in Oct 47. (R C Sturtivant)

Squadron redeployments, especially those involving aircraft with relatively short ranges, could often be quite complex exercises in logistics. This picture shows a Spitfire F.24 of No 80 Sqn being moved ashore by lighter after having been ferried from the UK to Hong Kong by HMS Ocean. (RAF Museum P15536)

Headquarters' records may reflect the 11th as the movement date, because that was the first day on which the unit was available for operations from its new location.

To take a simple example to illustrate this point, consider the redeployment of No 30 Sqn from Egypt to Ceylon in 1942. This transfer was carried out via HMS *Indomitable*. The Hurricanes were flown off the carrier on 6 Mar and landed at Ratmalana. The ship docked at Trincomalee the following day and the squadron groundcrew disembarked, being reunited with their pilots and aircraft on 8 Mar. Did the unit arrive on 6 Mar or 8 Mar ? Within the confines of this book only one date has been given for each move and sometimes a degree of judgement has had to be exercised over its selection. The aim has been to try to reflect where the 'core' of the squadron was.

The duration of a unit move will be influenced by a number of factors, the dominant one of course being the distance to be covered. Others of major significance are the size of the unit and, in wartime especially, tactical considerations such as the speed of an advance or the proximity of the enemy during a retreat. As the reliability and capability of aeroplanes have improved over the years, so the time taken to move a unit has correspondingly decreased and distance has become less significant. Three examples will serve to illustrate this (distances quoted are Great Circle 'straight lines', not route miles flown, which would have been considerably greater in each case):

No 216 Sqn, France to Egypt, 1919. The first three HP 0/400s of No 216 Sqn left Marquise on 10 Jul, an Advance Party having previously departed on 22 Jun. None of these aircraft reached Egypt: one was wrecked in a gale at Istres on 12 Jul; one fell in the sea off Spezia; the last, having already been subject to delays, finally crashed at Pisa on 3 Sep. The second element, this time for four aircraft, was more successful. These departed on 17 Jul and arrived at Qantara on 12 and 23 Aug, 14 Sep and 16 Oct. The final three aircraft left on 21 Jul. Two made it, arriving on 12 and 24 Aug, while the third was lost at Taranto. The 1,810 nms move had taken some three months and four of the ten aircraft involved had been lost in the process.

No 203 Sqn, Ceylon to UK, 1946. Twelve Liberator VIIIs of No 203 Sqn left Kankesanterai, in three elements of four aircraft each, on 15, 19 and 23 May. Routeing via Karachi, Shaibah, Lydda, Castel Benito and St Mawgan, all the aircraft had arrived at Leuchars by 2 Jun — a move of 4,680 nms in 19 days.

No 74 Sqn, UK to Singapore, 1967. On 4 Jun the first six Lightning F.6s of No 74 Sqn left Leuchars followed by five more on 5 Jun and a final pair a day later. Refuelled en route by Victor tankers of Nos 55, 57 and 214 Sqns, the aircraft made intermediate stops only at Akrotiri, Masirah and Gan. By 12 Jun the whole squadron was operational at Tengah — 5,890 nms in 8 days.

With a view to reducing the constraints imposed by time and distance the RAF introduced air-to-air refuelling (AAR), using the probe and drogue method, from the late 1950s. This picture shows a Valiant tanker of No 90 Sqn 'towing' a Vulcan B.1A. In the course of trials testing the concept of an airborne alert posture in Jul 62 No 50 Sqn kept one (of its eight) Vulcans airborne at all times for 14 consecutive days and nights; average sortie length was extended to over 8 hours by the use of AAR.
(RAF Waddington archives)

The Second World War created the most concentrated and wide-ranging period of movement in the RAF's history, and it is worthwhile examining how some of the moves were carried out. For a squadron to be capable of rapid redeployment, it is generally true to say that it must be organised as a mobile tactical unit, which tends to confine the capability to squadrons operating relatively small and simple aircraft which can fly from comparatively primitive airstrips without much sophisticated support equipment. The wartime RAF devised several concepts to meet the need for tactical mobility, each tailored to meet the demands imposed by a particular situation.

The fighter squadrons of the Western Desert Air Force were probably the finest exponents of the art of tactical mobility, initially in North Africa and later in Italy. In Africa the (mainly Hurricane and Kittyhawk equipped) fighter squadrons were engaged in a two year campaign which involved a series of advances and retreats during land battles, to which were added, during more static phases of the fighting, forward deployments for operations and withdrawals for re-equipment and rest periods. The theatre stretched some 700 nms from the Nile Delta to Benghazi, and the distances to be covered in each move, or series of moves, could be relatively large. This scenario led to a system under which squadrons were organised into A and B echelons which moved independently, sometimes leapfrogging each other in the process. The single representative date noted for a change of base in the

The perfection of practical AAR techniques has enhanced the RAF's ability to move individual aircraft or whole squadrons about the globe. This Lightning F.6, XR725, of No 23 Sqn was photographed in Canada having flown non-stop from Leuchars to Toronto in company with XS936 on 28 Aug 68 to take part in several North American air shows.
(Air Britain M7740)

No 73 Sqn was one of the fighter squadrons involved in the highly mobile campaign which ebbed and flowed across the North African desert in 1940-42. Despite being highly unofficial No 73 Sqn persisted in painting their distinctive peacetime arrowhead insignia on their aircraft for most of their service with Desert Air Force. This is an early (1941) example of this practice with the blue and yellow marking applied to a Hurricane I.
(via Chris Shores)

"Proximity to the front line was a force multiplier." These Spitfire XVIs of No 443 Sqn are seen parked at B 114/Diepholz in Apr 45 on a dispersal laid with Square Meshed Track. Although all these aircraft have clipped wings, making them LF XVIs, some display the early rounded rudder while others have the later pointed version. (RAF Museum P21635)

accompanying accounts is usually the date on which the aircraft arrived. However, elements of the squadron, particularly the groundcrew, travelling via the single coastal road in their motor convoys, may well have arrived both before and after the quoted date.

For the invasion of France and the subsequent advance through North West Europe the need for mobility was again to be vital if the tactical Typhoon, Spitfire and Mustang squadrons were to stay sufficiently close to the front-line to realise their full potential (proximity to the front was a 'force multiplier' if the security of the forward operating base could be assured). European movements involved much shorter distances than those which had had to be contended with in North Africa and a different approach to mobility was adopted. The fighter and fighter-bomber squadrons of the Second Tactical Air Force employed a system of 'centralised servicing'. Each squadron comprised only its pilots and their aircraft. Three or four such squadrons would be grouped together and supported by a Wing Operations organisation. Engineering and maintenance needs were met by Servicing Echelons. These too were mobile and in the event tended to become associated with a particular Wing. This went some way towards re-establishing the sense of unit identity which had been lost in the withdrawal of the groundcrews from their squadrons, and also provided an element of continuity in aircraft maintenance. This 'stripped down' squadron organisation made a move-in-a-day a realistic proposition. For example, when No 3 Sqn moved to Warmwell on 3 Apr 45, the transfer was just as straightforward as it sounds. The pilots would have boarded their Tempests and, despatched by the Servicing Echelon working with No 122 Wing, flown the single stage to the UK. At Warmwell the squadron's aircraft would have been looked after by the groundcrew of No 17 Armament Practice Camp, whose facilities the squadron had flown home to use. On their return to Volkel the pilots and aircraft would have rejoined No 122 Wing and resumed routine operations.

Following its prolonged transit to the Far East No 22 Sqn operated its Beauforts from Ceylon for two years. This ASV radar-equipped example, JM509, suffered a mishap at Katukurunda. (via G J Thomas)

Moving small slow aeroplanes over long distances, as was sometimes necessary in India, was an uneconomic proposition as it absorbed a disproportionate number of the airframe's available flying hours. One solution to the problem was to move aeroplanes by road. This picture shows an Auster III, NX509, of No 1587 AOP Refresher Flt at Deolali rigged on a vehicle portee. (R D Henshaw via Museum of Army Flying)

South East Asia Command probably imposed the greatest difficulties on movement, both on reaching the theatre because of its remoteness (from the UK), and subsequently, on intra-theatre movement owing to the vast size of the Indian sub-continent and the limited capabilities of the railway-based surface communications and logistic facilities. A closer look at some examples will illustrate the complexities involved and the time required to move a unit to and through this region.

No 22 Sqn. The transfer of Beaufort squadrons from the UK to the Far East in 1942 provides a suitable case to examine in more detail. No 22 Sqn's air echelon moved to Thorney Island on 1 Feb, where it was attached to No 86 Sqn prior to setting off for the Middle East. After positioning at Portreath, thirteen aircraft left for Gibraltar in two waves on 18 and 19 Mar. By 5 Apr they had reached LG 86 in Egypt after staging through Luqa and Sidi Barrani en route. Meanwhile the squadron's groundcrews had assembled at No 1 Personnel Despatch Centre at West Kirby, boarding the SS *Ormonde* at Liverpool on 12 Feb. The convoy sailed on 16 Feb, reaching Freetown on 1 Mar and Durban on 21 Mar. Here the squadron disembarked and lived under canvas at Blairwood for a fortnight before sailing again, this time in the SS *Nieuw Amsterdam*, on 6 Apr. Reaching Suez ten days later, they disembarked once more and were billeted at Kasfareet. Here an element was detached to become the advance party and flew out to Ceylon from Amiriya and Almaza. The air echelon, now only a few miles away across the Nile Delta, also began to move again. Having transferred some of its aeroplanes to local units as reinforcements, the remaining eight aircraft set off on 21 Apr for Habbaniyah and proceeded, via Shaibah on 23 Apr and Sharjah on 24 Apr, to Karachi, which was reached the following day. After 24 hours rest, the unit moved to Hyderabad on 27 Apr and flew to Ratmalana, their destination, on 28 Apr. One aeroplane was lost en route and others experienced delays but the seventh

No 47 Sqn was one of the torpedo-bomber units resident in Egypt which preyed on the assets of the Beaufort squadrons passing through the Mediterranean theatre in 1942 en route to the Far East. This is Beaufort I, DW380, of No 47 Sqn pictured at Misurata in Apr 43. (F F Smith via Chris Shores)

and last finally arrived in Ceylon on 31 May. In the meantime the ground echelon had re-embarked on HMT *Talma* at Suez on 22 Apr, arriving at Bombay on 7 May. Twelve days were spent at Colaba Camp before boarding HMT *City of Canterbury* for the final stage of the journey, although the ship did not sail until 25 May, reaching Colombo on the 28th. The groundcrews completed their journey to Ratmalana on 29 May, just two days before the last of the Beauforts arrived.

No 42 Sqn. Although No 22 Sqn's three-and-a-half month transit may seem to have been a major saga, it was about par for that particular course. By contrast No 42 Sqn, which undertook a similar redeployment beginning in Jun 42, took nearly six months. In their case the ground echelon spent two months ashore at Durban while the air echelon was subject to a corresponding delay in the Mediterranean theatre, being retained for operations from Malta and Egypt with Nos 39 and 47 Sqns. The squadron was not re-united until it reached Yelahanka in early Dec 42.

No 217 Sqn. No 217 Sqn attempted the same journey but fared even worse. The ground echelon made reasonable progress, departing Liverpool on 7 May and arriving at Minneriya on 11 Aug. Like No 42 Sqn before it, however, No 217 Sqn's air echelon failed to negotiate the Mediterranean chicane and was effectively absorbed by No 39 Sqn whilst operating from Luqa. None of No 217 Sqn's Beauforts reached Ceylon and the squadron was eventually reconstituted with Hudsons.

Once established in India, movement was still difficult and protracted. In the accompanying account of No 110 Sqn's movements there appears '5 Jun 44 to Kalyan'. What did this actually involve, for the groundcrew in particular? Having seen off their aircraft, the squadron paraded at Silchar at 0845hrs on 6 Jun. Entraining at 1030hrs, they set off for Chandpur, arriving at 0200hrs the next morning. Transferring to a river steamer, they sailed at 1130hrs to travel the 70 or so miles upstream to Gaolundo Ghat, arriving there at 0130hrs on 8 Jun. A further train journey, lasting from 0145hrs to 1130hrs, took them to Calcutta. After a meal in a transit camp and a few hours in the city, the squadron was back at Howrah Station for a 2015hrs departure. The train was late and, after sleeping in the station, they finally moved off again at 1100hrs on 9 Jun. For four days the squadron traversed India from East to West in a series of fits and starts, periods of progress being interspersed with pauses to take on water. The squadron's Operations Record Book observes that over the first 600 miles they averaged just 9 mph! After thirteen intermediate stops the groundcrew finally reached Kalyan at 1815hrs on 13 Jun.

It is hoped that these notes will have sounded an appropriate note of caution over the unquestioning acceptance of specific single dates of movements. Nevertheless, if the reservations and considerations discussed above are taken into account, the movement information recorded in this book may be regarded as good 'working dates'.

When No 110 Sqn's groundcrews undertook their epic journey from Silchar to Kalyan in Jun 44 the squadron was flying the unusually camera-shy Vengeance. This one, coded OB·V, belonged to No 45 Sqn and bore a 'Saint' emblem on the forward fuselage. (RAF Museum PC/73/4/763)

This photograph illustrates the fact that there are exceptions to any rules where squadron formations and movements are concerned. No 74 Sqn was notionally formed at Hornchurch with effect from 1 Sep 35, as an additional fighter unit for deployment to the Middle East/Mediterranean area in response to Italian aggression in Abyssinia. In reality the squadron assembled on board HMT Neuralia *at Southampton on 3 Sep 35 and sailed for Malta, its equipment following on the SS* Mainar *from Ellesmere Port. Arriving in Hal Far on 11 Sep, the unit was initially referred to as 'the Demon Flights'; it was not permitted to assume its true identity until 14 Nov 35. This picture of one of No 74 Sqn's Demons, K3769, at Hal Far illustrates an early pre-war use of camouflage. Using locally available dopes, No 74 Sqn began to apply a colour scheme 'based on a 1918 pattern' (presumably that developed for the Sopwith Salamander) to its aircraft on 3 Oct 35 and by the time the squadron's presence in Malta was revealed all of its aircraft had been painted.* (RAF Museum P1566)

The Squadrons

1 Sqn

3 May 12 F @ Farnborough — from No 1 (Airship) Coy, Air Btn, RE
May 12 **Beta** (Jan 14)
May 12 **Gamma** (Jan 14)
May 12 **Delta** (Jan 14)
May 12 **Zeta** (Jan 14)
Sep 13 **Eta** (Jan 14)
1 Jan 14 all airships transferred to the control of RN
1 May 14 unit restyled 'Airship Detachment, RFC'
1 May 14 re-established at Brooklands as a cadre
4 Aug 14 embodied
Aug 14 **Longhorn** (Feb 15)
Aug 14 **Vickers Boxkite** (Oct 14)
Sep 14 **Bristol Boxkite** (Nov 14)
Oct 14 **Martinsyde S.1** (Nov 14)
3 Nov 14 to Netheravon
Feb 15 **Avro 504** (Oct 15)
Mar 15 **BE 8** (Jun 15)
Mar 15 **Caudron G.III** (Oct 15)
7 Mar 15 to St-Omer
9 Mar 15 to Bailleul (Asylum Ground)
Apr 15 **Bristol Scout** (Oct 15)
Apr 15 **Morane L** (Dec 15)
Apr 15 **Martinsyde S.1** (Aug 15)
Oct 15 **Morane N** (Mar 16)
Nov 15 **Morane LA** (Jan 17)
Jan 16 **Morane BB** (Jan 17)
Mar 16 **Nieuport 16** (Aug 16)
Jun 16 **Nieuport 20** (Jan 17)
Jul 16 **Morane P** (Jan 17)
Jul 16 **Nieuport 17** (Dec 17)
May 17 **Nieuport 23** (Dec 17)
Aug 17 **Nieuport 24** (Dec 17)
Sep 17 **Nieuport 27** (Dec 17)
Jan 18 **SE 5A** (Feb 19)
9 Mar 18 to Ste-Marie-Cappel
3 Apr 18 to Clairmarais South
5 Aug 18 to Fienvillers
6 Oct 18 to Senlis-le-Sec
6 Oct 18 to Bouvincourt
8 Nov 18 to Le Hameau
3 Mar 19 to London Colney as a cadre
9 Sep 19 to Uxbridge
1 Jan 20 re-established at Risalpur, initially identified as 'B' Sqn
Feb 20 **Snipe** (Nov 26)
1 Apr 20 'B' Sqn redesignated as No 1 Sqn
1 May 20 to Bangalore
Apr 21 to Hinaidi
det Sulaimania
Apr 23 **Nighthawk** (Sep 23)
1 Nov 26 DB
—
1 Feb 27 RF @ Tangmere
Feb 27 **Siskin IIIA** (Feb 32)
Feb 32 **Fury I** (Nov 38)
Feb 37 **Gladiator I** (Mar 37)
Oct 38 **Hurricane I** (Apr 41)
Sep 39 to Octeville
Sep 39 to Norrent-Fontes
Oct 39 to Vassincourt
det Rouvres
1 Apr 40 to Berry-au-Bac
Apr 40 to Vassincourt
May 40 to Berry-au-Bac
7 May 40 to Condé/Vraux
3 May 40 to Anglure
3 Jun 40 to Châteaudun
1 Jun 40 to Boos
5 Jun 40 to Angers
7 Jun 40 to Nantes
3 Jun 40 to Northolt
det Hawkinge
3 Jul 40 to Tangmere
1 Aug 40 to Northolt
dets Tangmere, Manston, North Weald, Heathrow
Sep 40 to Wittering
15 Dec 40 to Northolt
5 Jan 41 to Kenley
Feb 41 **Hurricane IIA** (Jun 41)
7 Apr 41 to Croydon
Apr 41 **Hurricane IIB** (Jan 42)
1 May 41 to Redhill
1 Jun 41 to Kenley
14 Jun 41 to Redhill
1 Jul 41 to Tangmere
Jul 41 **Hurricane IIC** (Sep 42)
Apr 42 **Hurricane I** (Jul 42)
Jun 42 **Hurricane IIB** (Sep 42)
8 Jul 42 to Acklington
Jul 42 **Typhoon IB** (Apr 44)
9 Feb 43 to Biggin Hill
15 Mar 43 to Lympne
15 Feb 44 to Martlesham Heath
3 Apr 44 to North Weald
Apr 44 **Spitfire IXB** (May 45)
22 Apr 44 to Ayr
29 Apr 44 to Predannack
20 Jun 44 to Harrowbeer
22 Jun 44 to Detling
11 Jul 44 to Lympne
10 Aug 44 to Detling
18 Dec 44 to Manston
8 Apr 45 to Coltishall
14 May 45 to Ludham
May 45 **Spitfire F.21** (Oct 46)
23 Jul 45 to Hutton Cranswick
24 Sep 45 to Hawkinge
22 Oct 45 to Hutton Cranswick
30 Apr 46 to Tangmere
17 Jun 46 to Acklington
22 Jul 46 to Tangmere
Oct 46 **Meteor F.3** (Aug 47)
24 Feb 47 to Acklington
1 Apr 47 to Tangmere
29 Apr 47 to Lübeck
26 Jun 47 to Tangmere
Aug 47 **Harvard T.2B** (Jun 48)
Aug 47 **Oxford T.2** (Jun 48)
Jun 48 **Meteor F.4** (Aug 50)
Aug 50 **Meteor F.8** (Oct 55)
Sep 55 **Hunter F.5** (Jun 58)
1 Jul 58 DB
—
2 Jul 58 RF @ Stradishall — No 263 Sqn renumbered
Jul 58 **Hunter F.6** (Mar 60)
Jan 60 **Hunter FGA 9** (Jul 69)
7 Nov 61 to Waterbeach
13 Aug 63 to West Raynham
18 Jul 69 to Wittering
Jul 69 **Harrier GR 1** ( )
Nov 73 **Harrier GR 3** ( )
det Port Stanley

2 Sqn

13 May 12 F @ Farnborough — from No 2 (Aeroplane) Coy, Air Btn, RE
May 12 **Bristol Boxkite** (Dec 12)
May 12 **Breguet Biplane** (Dec 12)
May 12 **BE 1** ( )
May 12 **Longhorn** (Aug 14)
Jul 12 **BE 2** (Aug 12)
Jul 12 **Henry Farman Biplane** (Dec 12)
Feb 13 **BE 2A** (Aug 15)
26 Feb 13 to Montrose
det Limerick
Apr 13 **BE 2** (Sep 14)
Apr 14 **Shorthorn** (Mar 15)
30 Jun 14 to Netheravon
5 Aug 14 to Farnborough
Aug 14 **RE 1** (Aug 14)
12 Aug 14 to Swingate Down
13 Aug 14 to Amiens
16 Aug 14 to Maubeuge
24 Aug 14 to Berlaimont
25 Aug 14 to Le Cateau
25 Aug 14 to St-Quentin
26 Aug 14 to La Fère
28 Aug 14 to Compiègne
30 Aug 14 to Senlis
31 Aug 14 to Juilly
2 Sep 14 to Serris
Sep 14 **BE 2C** (Dec 14)
3 Sep 14 to Touquin
4 Sep 14 to Melun
7 Sep 14 to Touquin
9 Sep 14 to Coulommiers
12 Sep 14 to Fère-en Tardenois
Sep 14 **RE 5** (Feb 15)
17 Oct 14 to St-Omer
27 Nov 14 to Merville
det St-Omer
Feb 15 **Vickers FB 5** (Feb 15)
Feb 15 **BE 2B** (Aug 15)
Feb 15 **BE 2C** (Jun 17)
30 Jun 15 to Hesdigneul
Jul 15 **Bristol Scout** (Dec 15)
Jul 16 **BE 2D** (Jun 17)
Jan 17 **BE 2E** (Jun 17)
Apr 17 **AW FK 8** (Feb 19)
9 Jun 18 to Floringham
20 Oct 18 to Mazingarbe
26 Oct 18 to Genech
14 Feb 19 to Bicester as a cadre
Sep 19 to Weston-on-the-Green
20 Jan 20 DB
—
1 Feb 20 RF @ Oranmore – No No 105 Sqn renumbered
Feb 20 **Bristol F2b Fighter** (Jan 30)
dets Castlebar, Fermoy
Jul 20 to Fermoy
det Oranmore
13 Feb 22 to Digby
2 Jun 22 to Aldergrove
27 Sep 22 to Farnborough
det Aldergrove
17 Sep 23 to Andover
31 Mar 24 to Manston
20 Apr 27 en route China via HMS *Hermes*
31 May 27 to Shanghai Racecourse
13 Sep 27 en route UK via HMS *Hermes*
27 Oct 27 to Manston
Dec 29 **Atlas** (Jun 33)
May 33 **Audax** (Nov 37)
30 Nov 35 to Hawkinge
Nov 37 **Hector** (Sep 38)
Jul 38 **Lysander I** (Feb 40)
29 Sep 39 to Abbeville/Drucat
Feb 40 **Lysander II** (Sep 40)
dets Senon, Ronchin, Lubuissière
17 May 40 to Labuissière
det Wevelghem
19 May 40 to Boulogne
20 May 40 to Lympne
20 May 40 to Bekesbourne
8 Jun 40 to Hatfield
1 Aug 40 to Cambridge
det Sawbridgeworth
Sep 40 **Lysander III** (Jul 42)
24 Oct 40 to Sawbridgeworth
19 Jul 41 to Firbeck
23 Jul 41 to Sawbridgeworth
4 Aug 41 to Weston Zoyland
10 Aug 41 to Sawbridgeworth
Aug 41 **Tomahawk I & II** (Apr 42)
5 Dec 41 to Martlesham Heath
7 Dec 41 to Sawbridgeworth
det Gatwick
Apr 42 **Mustang I** (Feb 44)
31 Jan 43 to Bottisham
dets Westcott, Newmarket, Cranfield, Duxford
19 Mar 43 to Fowlmere
27 Apr 43 to Sawbridgeworth
16 Jul 43 to Gravesend
7 Aug 43 to Odiham
22 Sep 43 to Hutton Cranswick
6 Oct 43 to Odiham
14 Nov 43 to North Weald
30 Nov 43 to Sawbridgeworth
22 Jan 44 to North Weald
det Benson
Feb 44 **Mustang IA** (Jun 44)
29 Feb 44 to Sawbridgeworth
11 Mar 44 to Dundonald
24 Mar 44 to Sawbridgeworth
4 Apr 44 to Gatwick
Jun 44 **Mustang II** (Jan 45)
27 Jun 44 to Odiham
29 Jul 44 to B 10/Plumetot
14 Aug 44 to B 4/Bény-sur-Mer
1 Sep 44 to B 27/Boisney
6 Sep 44 to B 31/Fresnoy-Folny
11 Sep 44 to B 43/Fort Rouge
27 Sep 44 to B 61/St Denis-Westrem
10 Oct 44 to B 70/Deurne
23 Nov 44 to B 77/Gilze-Rijen
Nov 44 **Spitfire XIV** (Jan 51)
9 Mar 45 to B 89/Mill
18 Apr 45 to B 106/Twente
30 May 45 to B 118/Celle
17 Jun 45 to B 150/Hustedt
6 Jul 45 to Warmwell
20 Jul 45 to B 150/Hustedt
19 Sep 45 to B 118/Celle
Sep 45 **Spitfire XI** (Mar 46)
Jan 46 **Spitfire PR 19** (Jun 51)
10 Feb 46 to Sylt
5 Mar 46 to Celle
19 Aug 46 to Sylt
16 Sep 46 to Celle
15 Apr 47 to Wunstorf
22 Nov 47 to Lübeck
11 Dec 47 to Wunstorf
28 Jun 48 to Wahn
15 Sep 49 to Wunstorf
29 Jun 50 to Bückeburg
Dec 50 **Meteor FR 9** (Jun 56)
Mar 51 **Meteor PR 10** (Jun 51)
15 May 52 to Gütersloh
1 Jul 53 to Wahn
28 Oct 55 to Geilenkirchen
Feb 56 **Swift FR 5** (Mar 61)
10 Oct 57 to Jever
Mar 61 **Hunter FR 10** (Mar 71)
9 Sep 61 to Gütersloh
1 Dec 70 redesignated as No 2 (Hunter) Sqn
31 Mar 71 DB
—
1 Dec 70 RF @ Brüggen as No 2 (Phantom) Sqn
Dec 70 **Phantom FGR 2** (Sep 76)
3 May 71 to Laarbruch
30 Sep 76 DB
—
1 Jun 76 Training at Laarbruch as No 2 Sqn (Designate)
—
1 Oct 76 RF @ Laarbruch
Oct 76 **Jaguar GR 1** ( )

3 Sqn

13 May 12 F @ Larkhill — from det of No 2 (Aeroplane) Coy, Air Btn, RE
May 12 **Henry Farman III** (Jun 12)
May 12 **Avro Type E** (Aug 12)
May 12 **Bristol Boxkite** (Aug 12)
May 12 **Deperdussin Monoplane** (Sep 12)
May 12 **Nieuport Monoplane** (Sep 12)
May 12 **Bristol Prier Monoplane** (Sep 12)
May 12 **BE 3** (Oct 13)
Aug 12 **BE 4** (Mar 14)
Sep 12 **Bristol Coanda Monoplane** (Sep 12)
Sep 12 **Longhorn** (Aug 13)
Oct 12 **Bleriot XXI** (Apr 13)
Mar 13 **BE 2A** (Apr 13)
Mar 13 **Henry Farman F.20** (Dec 14)
Apr 13 **Bleriot XI** (Jun 15)
May 13 **Avro Type Es** (Aug 13)
16 Jun 13 to Netheravon
Mar 14 **SE 2** (May 14)
Aug 14 **BE 2C** (Aug 14)

Aug 14 **Bleriot Parasol** (Mar 15)
12 Aug 14 to Swingate Down
13 Aug 14 to Amiens
Aug 14 **BE 8** (Aug 14)
16 Aug 14 to Maubeuge
24 Aug 14 to Le Cateau
Aug 14 **Tabloid** (Sep 14)
25 Aug 14 to St-Quentin
26 Aug 14 to La Fère
28 Aug 14 to Compiègne
30 Aug 14 to Senlis
31 Aug 14 to Juilly
Sep 14 **BE 8** (Sep 14)
2 Sep 14 to Serris
3 Sep 14 to Touquin
4 Sep 14 to Melun
7 Sep 14 to Touquin
9 Sep 14 to Coulommiers
12 Sep 14 to Fère-en Tardenois
Sep 14 **Bristol Scout** ( )
5 Oct 14 to Amiens
8 Oct 14 to Abbeville
9 Oct 14 to Moyenneville
12 Oct 14 to St-Omer
det Hinges
Oct 14 **SE 2** (Mar 15)
24 Nov 14 to Gonneham
Dec 14 **Morane L** (Sep 15)
1 Jun 15 to Lozinghem
Sep 15 **Morane LA** (Jan 17)
Oct 15 **Morane N** (Jul 16)
Dec 15 **Morane BB** (Dec 16)
16 Mar 16 to Bruay
1 Apr 16 to Bertangles
10 Apr 16 to Lahoussoye
May 16 **Nieuport 16** (16)
Aug 16 **Morane P** (Oct 17)
23 Jan 17 to Laviéville
15 Jul 17 to Longavesnes
26 Aug 17 to Lechelle
10 Oct 17 to Warloy
Oct 17 **Camel** (Feb 19)
25 Mar 18 to Vert Galand
26 Mar 18 to Valheureux
15 Oct 18 to Léchelle
4 Nov 18 to Inchy
15 Feb 19 to Wye as a cadre
2 May 19 to Swingate Down
15 Oct 19 to Croydon
27 Oct 19 to Uxbridge
21 Jan 20 re-established at Ambala, initially identified as 'A' Sqn
22 Mar 20 to Bangalore
1 Apr 20 'A' Sqn redesignated as No 3 Sqn
Jun 20 **Snipe** (Mar 21)
1 Apr 21 to Ambala
30 Sep 21 DB
—
1 Oct 21 RF @ Leuchars — from a Flt of No 205 Sqn
Oct 21 **DH 9A (3-seater)** (Oct 22)
Jan 22 **Walrus** (Apr 23)
8 Nov 22 to Gosport
1 Apr 23 DB — split into Nos 420, 421 & 422 Flts
—
1 Apr 24 RF @ Manston
Apr 24 **Snipe** (Aug 25)
30 Apr 24 to Upavon
May 25 **Woodcock II** (Aug 28)
Aug 28 **Gamecock I** (Jun 29)
Jun 29 **Bulldog II/IIA** (Jul 37)
10 May 34 to Kenley
18 Oct 35 to Port Sudan
22 Oct 35 to Khartoum
22 Jan 36 to Port Sudan
28 Aug 36 to Kenley
Mar 37 **Gladiator I** (Mar 38)
Mar 38 **Hurricane I** (Jul 38)
Jul 38 **Gladiator I** (Jul 39)
1 May 39 to Biggin Hill
May 39 **Hurricane I** (Apr 41)
2 Sep 39 to Croydon
10 Sep 39 to Manston
17 Sep 39 to Croydon
12 Oct 39 to Manston
13 Nov 39 to Croydon
det Hawkinge
28 Jan 40 to Kenley
10 May 40 to Merville
20 May 40 to Kenley
30 May 40 to Wick
3 Sep 40 to Castletown
14 Sep 40 to Turnhouse
dets Montrose, Dyce
13 Oct 40 to Castletown
7 Jan 41 to Skaebrae
det Sumburgh
10 Feb 41 to Castletown
det Sumburgh
3 Apr 41 to Martlesham Heath
Apr 41 **Hurricane IIB** (Oct 41)
Apr 41 **Hurricane IIC** (Feb 43)
23 Jun 41 to Stapleford Tawney
9 Aug 41 to Hunsdon
dets Manston, Shoreham
Feb 43 **Typhoon IB** (Apr 44)
14 May 43 to West Malling
11 Jun 43 to Manston
28 Dec 43 to Swanton Morley
14 Feb 44 to Manston
Feb 44 **Tempest V** (Apr 48)
6 Mar 44 to Bradwell Bay
6 Apr 44 to Ayr
14 Apr 44 to Bradwell Bay
28 Apr 44 to Newchurch
21 Sep 44 to Matlask
28 Sep 44 to B 60/Grimbergen
1 Oct 44 to B 80/Volkel
1 Apr 45 to Warmwell
17 Apr 45 to B 112/Hopsten
26 Apr 45 to B 152/Fassberg
21 Jun 45 to B 160/Kastrup
18 Jul 45 to B 156/Lüneburg
8 Aug 45 to B 158/Lübeck
5 Sep 45 to B 155/Dedelsdorf
14 Sep 45 to B 106/Twente
16 Sep 45 to B 155/Dedelsdorf
6 Oct 45 to B 170/Sylt
23 Oct 45 to B 152/Fassberg
24 Jan 46 to Wunstorf
27 Mar 46 to Gatow
6 May 46 to Dedelsdorf
2 Jun 46 to Manston
12 Jun 46 to Dedelsdorf
5 Sep 46 to Manston
19 Sep 46 to Wunstorf
22 Oct 46 to Sylt
25 Nov 46 to Wunstorf
4 Jan 47 to Gatow
3 Feb 47 to Wunstorf
2 Sep 47 to Duxford
16 Sep 47 to Wunstorf
1 Oct 47 to Gatow
3 Nov 47 to Wunstorf
5 Jan 48 to Lübeck
11 Feb 48 to Wunstorf
Apr 48 **Vampire F.1** (May 49)
25 Jun 48 to Gütersloh
9 Aug 48 to Lübeck
4 Sep 48 to Gütersloh
May 49 **Vampire FB 5** (May 53)
1 Apr 52 to Wildenrath
May 53 **Sabre F.4** (Jun 56)
21 Jul 53 to Geilenkirchen
May 56 **Hunter F.4** (Jun 57)
15 Jun 57 DB
—
21 Jan 59 RF @ Geilenkirchen — No 96 Sqn renumbered
Jan 59 **Javelin FAW 4** (Jan 61)
4 Jan 61 DB
—
4 Jan 61 RF @ Geilenkirchen — No 59 Sqn renumbered
Jan 61 **Canberra B(I) 8** (Dec 71)
15 Jan 68 to Laarburch
31 Dec 71 DB
—
1 Jan 72 RF @ Wildenrath
Jan 72 **Harrier GR 1** (Dec 74)
Dec 73 **Harrier GR 3** ( )
1 Apr 77 to Gütersloh

4 Sqn

16 Sep 12 F @ Farnborough — nucleus from No 2 Sqn
Dec 12 **Cody V** (Mar 13)
Dec 12 **Breguet Biplane** (Jan 14)
Jan 13 **BE 4** (Feb 13)
Jan 13 **Longhorn** (Aug 14)
Apr 13 **BE 1** ( )
Apr 13 **Caudron G II** (Apr 14)
May 13 **Shorthorn** (Jul 14)
14 Jun 13 to Netheravon
Nov 13 **BE 2** (Sep 14)
Jan 14 **BE 2A** (Oct 15)
Jul 14 **BE 2C** (Aug 14)
21 Jul 14 to Eastchurch (A & B Flts)
det Netheravon (C Flt)
Aug 14 **Shorthorn** (Aug 14)
13 Aug 14 to Amiens
det Swingate Down (C Flt) until 20 Sep 14
16 Aug 14 to Maubeuge
24 Aug 14 to Le Cateau
25 Aug 14 to St-Quentin
26 Aug 14 to La Fère
28 Aug 14 to Compiègne
30 Aug 14 to Senlis
31 Aug 14 to Juilly
2 Sep 14 to Serris
3 Sep 14 to Touquin
4 Sep 14 to Melun
7 Sep 14 to Touquin
9 Sep 14 to Coulommiers
12 Sep 14 to Fére-en Tardenois
Sep 14 **Shorthorn** (15)
6 Oct 14 to Amiens
8 Oct 14 to Abbeville
9 Oct 14 to Moyenneville
12 Oct 14 to St-Omer
dets Poperinghe, Dunkirk, Bailleul (Town Ground)
Dec 14 **Tabloid** (Jan 15)
Jan 15 **BE 2B** (Oct 15)
Feb 15 **Martinsyde S.1** (Apr 15)
Feb 15 **Voisin LA** (Jul 15)
Mar 15 **Bristol Scout** (Mar 16)
21 Apr 15 to Bailleul (Town Ground)
Apr 15 **BE 2C** (May 17)
May 15 **Caudron G III** (Jun 15)
Jun 15 **Morane H** (Sep 15)
20 Jul 15 to Vert Galand
5 Aug 15 to Baizieux
7 Nov 15 to Allonville
Feb 16 to Baizieux
Feb 16 to Marieux
27 Mar 16 to Baizieux
Jul 16 **BE 2D** (May 17)
Jul 16 **BE 2E** (May 17)
Jan 17 **BE 2G** (May 17)
28 Feb 17 to Warloy
30 May 17 to Abeele
Jun 17 **RE 8** (Feb 19)
18 Nov 17 to Chocques
8 Apr 18 to Treizennes
16 Apr 18 to St-Omer
18 Sep 18 to Ste-Marie-Cappel
21 Oct 18 to Linselles
16 Nov 18 to Ascq
3 Dec 18 to Linselles
13 Feb 19 to Northolt as a cadre
20 Sep 19 to Uxbridge
30 Apr 20 to Farnborough, re-established
Apr 20 **Bristol F2b Fighter** (Oct 29)
dets Stonehenge, Aldergrove, Baldonnel
26 Sep 22 en route Turkey via HMS *Ark Royal* & HMS *Argus*
11 Oct 22 to Kilya Bay
11 Dec 22 to Kilid el Bahr
5 Sep 23 en route UK
18 Sep 23 to Farnborough
Oct 29 **Atlas** (Feb 32)
Dec 31 **Audax** (Jul 37)
16 Feb 37 to Odiham
May 37 **Hector** (Jan 39)
Dec 38 **Lysander II** (Sep 40)
24 Sep 39 to Mons-en-Chaussée
3 Oct 39 to Monchy-Lagache
det Ronchin
16 May 40 to Ronchin
dets Aspelaere, Clairmarais
21 May 40 to Clairmarais
det Ronchin
22 May 40 to Dunkirk
det Detling
24 May 40 to Ringway
9 Jun 40 to Linton-on-Ouse
27 Aug 40 to Clifton
Sep 40 **Lysander III** (Jul 41)
May 41 **Lysander IIIA** (Jun 42)
Apr 42 **Tomahawk IIA** (Apr 43
May 42 **Mustang I** (Mar 44)
1 Mar 43 to Barford St John
5 Mar 43 to Cranfield
8 Mar 43 to Duxford
12 Mar 43 to Clifton
20 Mar 43 to Bottisham
16 Jul 43 to Gravesend
7 Aug 43 to Odiham
15 Sep 43 to Funtington
6 Oct 43 to Odiham
14 Nov 43 to North Weald
30 Nov 43 to Sawbridgeworth
Dec 43 **Mosquito XVI** (May 44)
3 Jan 44 to Aston Down
Jan 44 **Spitfire XI** (Aug 45)
3 Mar 44 to Sawbridgeworth
4 Apr 44 to Gatwick
27 Jun 44 to Odiham
det B 10/Plumetot
16 Aug 44 to B 4/Bény-sur-Mer
1 Sep 44 to B 27/Boisney
6 Sep 44 to B 31/Fresnoy-Folny
11 Sep 44 to B 43/Fort Rouge
27 Sep 44 to B 61/St Denis-Westrem
Oct 44 **Typhoon FR IB** (Jan 45
16 Oct 44 to B 70/Deurne
23 Nov 44 to B 77/Gilze-Rijen
8 Mar 45 to B 89/Mill
17 Apr 45 to B 106/Twente
30 May 45 to B 118/Celle
31 Aug 45 DB — became High Level PR Flt of No 2 S
—
1 Sep 45 RF @ Volkel — No 60 Sqn renumbered
Sep 45 **Mosquito FB 6** (Jul 50)
13 Sep 45 to Gilze-Rijen
8 Nov 45 to Gütersloh
4 Feb 46 to Sylt
17 Feb 46 to Gütersloh
2 Jun 46 to Manston
12 Jun 46 to Gütersloh
27 Jun 46 to Handorf
12 Aug 46 to Gütersloh
6 Sep 46 to Sylt
9 Oct 46 to Gütersloh
5 Aug 47 to Sylt
22 Aug 47 to Gütersloh
13 Nov 47 to Wahn
1 Mar 48 to Gatow
31 Mar 48 to Wahn
1 May 48 to Lübeck
5 Jun 48 to Wahn
4 Aug 48 to Lübeck
28 Aug 48 to Wahn
19 Sep 49 to Celle
10 Jul 50 to Wunstorf
Jul 50 **Vampire FB 5** (May 54
1 Mar 52 to Jever
Nov 53 **Vampire FB 9** (May 54
Mar 54 **Sabre F.4** (Aug 55)
Jul 55 **Hunter F.4** (Feb 57)
Feb 57 **Hunter F.6** (Dec 60)
30 Dec 60 DB
—
30 Dec 60 RF @ Gütersloh — No 79 Sqn renumberec
Dec 60 **Swift FR 5** (Mar 61)
Dec 60 **Hunter FR 10** (May 70
16 Mar 61 to Jever
6 Sep 61 to Gütersloh
30 May 70 DB

—
1 Sep 69 'UK Echelon' formed at West Raynham — from No 54 Sqn
Sep 69 **Hunter FGA 9** (May 70)
13 Mar 70 to Wittering
Apr 70 **Harrier GR 1** (Sep 70) det Wildenrath
30 Sep 70 DB — joined main squadron in Germany
—
1 Jun 70 RF @ Wildenrath
Jun 70 **Harrier GR 1** (Nov 74)
Nov 73 **Harrier GR 3** ( )
4 Jan 77 to Gütersloh

5 Sqn

26 Jul 13 F @ South Farnborough — nucleus from No 3 Sqn
Jul 13 **Avro Type Es** (Jul 14)
Jul 13 **Longhorn** (Aug 14)
Jul 13 **Henry Farman F.20** (Mar 15)
Jan 14 **SE 2A** (Mar 14)
Feb 14 **Sopwith Three-Seater** (Aug 14)
14 **BE 1** (Aug 14)
Jun 14 **Tabloid** (Aug 14)
28 May 14 to Netheravon
6 Jul 14 to Gosport (Fort Grange)
Jul 14 **Avro 504** (Oct 15)
14 Aug 14 to Swingate Down
15 Aug 14 to Amiens
Aug 14 **BE 8** (Sep 14)
18 Aug 14 to Maubeuge
24 Aug 14 to Le Cateau
25 Aug 14 to St-Quentin
26 Aug 14 to La Fère
28 Aug 14 to Compiègne
30 Aug 14 to Senlis
31 Aug 14 to Juilly
Sep 14 **Henry Farman F.27** (Sep 14)
2 Sep 14 to Serris
3 Sep 14 to Pezarche
4 Sep 14 to Melun
6 Sep 14 to La Boiserotte
7 Sep 14 to Touquin
8 Sep 14 to Rebais
9 Sep 14 to Coulommiers
2 Sep 14 to Fére-en Tardenois
Sep 14 **Bristol Scout** (Oct 14)
30 Sep 14 to Amiens
8 Oct 14 to Abbeville
9 Oct 14 to Moyenneville
2 Oct 14 to St-Omer dets Ebblinghem, Wallon-Cappel, Meteren, Bailleul (Town Ground)
3 Oct 14 to Bailleul (Town Ground) det St-Omer
1 Jan 15 to Bailleul (Asylum Ground) dets St-Omer, Poperinghe, Morbecque
Jan 15 **Martinsyde S.1** (Aug 15)
Feb 15 **Voisin LA** (Mar 15)
Mar 15 **Bleriot Parasol** (May 15)
Mar 15 **Vickers FB 5** (Jan 16)
15 **Bristol Scout** (Mar 15)
Apr 15 **Caudron G III** (May 15)
7 Apr 15 to Abeele
Jul 15 **DH 2** (Aug 15)
Aug 15 **BE 2C** (Apr 17)
Dec 15 **FE 8** (May 16)
Jan 16 **DH 2** (May 16)
1 Mar 16 to Droglandt
Jun 16 **BE 2D** (17)
2 Oct 16 to Marieux
Jan 17 **BE 2E** (Jun 17)
Jan 17 **BE 2F** (Jun 17)
Jan 17 **BE 2G** (Jun 17)
4 Mar 17 to La Gorgue
7 Apr 17 to Savy
Jun 17 **RE 8** (Sep 19)
2 Jun 17 to Acq dets Les Moëres
25 May 18 to Le Hameau
4 Aug 18 to Bovelles
24 Aug 18 to Le Hameau
14 Oct 18 to Pronville
24 Oct 18 to Emerchicourt
8 Nov 18 to Aulnoy
16 Nov 18 to Pecq
27 Nov 18 to Cognelée
7 Dec 18 to Elsenborn
21 Dec 18 to Hangelar
Mar 19 **Bristol F2b Fighter** (Oct 19)
19 Sep 19 to Bicester
9 Oct 19 reduced to a cadre
20 Jan 20 DB
—
1 Apr 20 RF @ Quetta — No 48 Sqn renumbered
Apr 20 **Bristol F2b Fighter** (May 31) det Loralai
26 Oct 22 to Ambala det Saugor
10 Mar 24 to Dardoni
22 Jan 25 to Kohat dets Tank, Miranshah, Jhelum
15 Oct 25 to Risalpur dets Quetta, Miranshah, Hassani Abdel, Jhelum
15 Dec 28 to Quetta dets Risalpur, Drigh Road
16 May 30 to Kohat det Miranshah
15 Mar 31 to Quetta
May 31 **Wapiti** (Jun 40) dets Secunderabad, Poona, Jubbulpore, Ford Sandeman
9 Jun 35 to Drigh Road as a cadre
31 Jul 35 re-established
1 Aug 35 to Risalpur
15 Oct 35 to Chaklala dets Julalpur, Lahore, Risalpur, Kohat, Miranshah
6 Mar 37 to Miranshah
20 Apr 37 to Risalpur dets Miranshah, Chaklala
8 Nov 37 to Chaklala dets Miranshah
23 Apr 38 to Risalpur dets Arawali, Kohat, Miranshah, Fort Sandeman, Hakimpet, Sialkot
10 Oct 39 to Ford Sandeman dets Quetta, Kohat, Miranshah
10 Jun 40 to Lahore
Jun 40 **Hart** (Feb 41) det Miranshah
26 Feb 41 to Risalpur
Feb 41 **Audax** (May 42) det Dum Dum
15 Dec 41 to Dum Dum
Dec 41 **Mohawk IV** (Jun 43) det Dinjan
5 May 42 to Dinjan — (No 5 Sqn det at Dinjan absorbed No 146 Sqn to become No 5 Sqn, while No 146 Sqn det at Dum Dum absorbed the remainder of No 5 Sqn to become No 146 Sqn) det Tezpur
2 Oct 42 to Agartala dets Chittagong, 'Reindeer'
1 Jun 43 to Kharagpur
Jul 43 **Hurricane IID** (Dec 43)
Aug 43 **Hurricane IIC** (Oct 44)
22 Nov 43 to Amarda Road
7 Dec 43 to Sapam
24 Mar 44 to Wangjing det Patharkandi
30 Mar 44 to Lanka
6 Jun 44 to Dergaon
25 Jun 44 to Vizagapatam
16 Sep 44 to Yelahanka
Oct 44 **Thunderbolt I** (Feb 46)
Oct 44 **Thunderbolt II** (Jan 45)
24 Oct 44 to Cholavaram
29 Oct 44 to Trichinopoly det St Thomas Mount
14 Dec 44 to Nazir dets Cox's Bazaar, Sadaung, Sinthe
19 Apr 45 to Cox's Bazaar
28 Apr 45 to Kyaukpyu
6 Jun 45 to Cox's Bazaar
10 Jun 45 to Vizagapatam
24 Jun 45 to Bobbili
30 Aug 45 to Vizagapatam
12 Sep 45 to Baigachi
25 Sep 45 to Zayatkwin
30 Sep 45 to Baigachi
2 Oct 45 to Bobbili
2 Nov 45 to Vizagapatam
5 Dec 45 to Baigachi
17 Feb 46 to Bhopal
Mar 46 **Tempest F.2** (Aug 47)
1 Jun 46 to Poona
3 Nov 46 to Yelahanka
10 Nov 46 to Poona det Risalpur
22 Jan 47 to Peshawar dets Poona, Risalpur, Yelahanka, Miranshah
3 Jul 47 to Mauripur
1 Aug 47 DB
—
11 Feb 49 RF @ Pembrey — No 595 Sqn renumbered
Feb 49 **Martinet TT 1** (Jan 50)
Feb 49 **Harvard T.2B** (Mar 51)
Feb 49 **Spitfire LF 16E** (Aug 51)
Feb 49 **Oxford T.2** (Aug 51)
26 Oct 49 to Chivenor
Jan 50 **Beaufighter TT 10** (Aug 51)
Dec 50 **Vampire F.3** (Aug 51)
13 Mar 51 to Llandow
1 Aug 51 DB
—
1 Mar 52 RF @ Wunstorf
Mar 52 **Vampire FB 5** (Jun 53)
Nov 52 **Venom FB 1** (Aug 55)
Jul 55 **Venom FB 4** (Oct 57)
10 Oct 55 to Fassberg
9 Oct 56 to Wunstorf
11 Oct 57 DB
—
21 Jan 59 RF @ Laarbruch — No 68 Sqn renumbered
Jan 59 **Meteor NF 11** (Jun 60)
Jan 60 **Javelin FAW 5** (Nov 62)
Nov 62 **Javelin FAW 9** (Oct 65) — ex No 33 Sqn
11 Dec 62 to Geilenkirchen
7 Oct 65 to Binbrook
Dec 65 **Lightning F.6** (Dec 87)
Jun 70 **Lightning F.1A** (Sep 72)
Oct 72 **Lightning F.3** (Sep 87)
31 Dec 87 DB
—
1 Jan 88 RF @ Coningsby
Jan 88 **Tornado F.3** ( )

6 Sqn

31 Jan 14 F @ South Farnborough
Jan 14 **Longhorn** (Sep 14)
Feb 14 **BE 2** (Aug 14)
Mar 14 **Shorthorn** (Aug 14)
May 14 **RE 1** (Aug 14)
Jun 14 **RE 5** (Sep 14)
Aug 14 **BE 8** (Jan 15)
Sep 14 **Vickers FB 'Gun Carrier'** (Sep 14)
Sep 14 **Henry Farman F.20** (Dec 14)
Sep 14 **BE 2A** (Sep 15)
21 Sep 14 to Netheravon
4 Oct 14 to Farnborough
7 Oct 14 to Bruges
8 Oct 14 to Ostende
13 Oct 14 to St-Pol dets Ypres, Boulogne
20 Oct 14 to Poperinghe
21 Oct 14 to St-Omer
18 Nov 14 to Bailleul det St-Omer
Nov 14 **Bleriot XI** (Jan 15)
Jan 15 **Martinsyde S.1** (Aug 15)
Jan 15 **BE 2C** (Feb 17)
8 Mar 15 to Poperinghe
24 Apr 15 to Abeele det Droglandt
May 15 **FE 2A** (Mar 16)
Jun 15 **Bristol Scout** (Jun 16)
Nov 15 **Martinsyde G.100** (Feb 16)
Dec 15 **FE 2B** (Feb 16)
Jun 16 **BE 2D** (May 17)
Oct 16 **BE 2E** (Nov 16)
Dec 16 **BE 2F** (Feb 17)
Dec 16 **BE 2G** (May 17)
Apr 17 **RE 8** (Jul 20)
16 Nov 17 to Bertangles
23 Mar 18 to St-André-aux Bois
26 Mar 18 to Le Crotoy dets Treizennnes, Rely, Auxi-le-Chateau
18 Jul 18 to Fienvillers
5 Aug 18 to Bovelles
17 Aug 18 to Auxi-le-Chateau
27 Aug 18 to Acq
27 Sep 18 to Moislains
6 Oct 18 to Longavesnes
19 Oct 18 to Bertry West
20 Oct 18 to Maretz
9 Nov 18 to Gondecourt
16 Nov 18 to Pecq
6 Dec 18 to Gerpinnes
Feb 19 **Bristol F2b Fighter** (Apr 19)
19 Mar 19 to Sart
14 Apr 19 en route ME via Marseiles
16 Jul 19 to Basrah
6 Sep 19 to Baghdad West dets Bushire, Abu Kemal, Annah
Jul 20 **Bristol F2b Fighter** (Jun 32) dets Samawah, Hillah, Kirkuk, Mosul, Sulaimania
9 Oct 22 to Hinaidi
19 May 24 to Mosul
20 Oct 26 to Hinaidi
28 Oct 29 to Ismailia dets Semakh, Ramleh, Haifa, Qasaba
Jun 31 **Gordon** (Oct 35)
Sep 35 **Hart** (Jan 38)
Oct 35 **Demon** (Nov 36)
29 May 36 to Ramleh det Semakh
19 Nov 36 to Ismailia
22 Nov 37 to Ramleh
Jan 38 **Hardy** (Apr 40) dets Haifa, Ismailia
Aug 39 **Gauntlet I & II** (Apr 40)
Sep 39 **Lysander I** (Dec 39)
Feb 40 **Lysander II** (Jun 41) dets Qasaba, Siwa, Tobruk
17 Feb 41 to Aqir
24 Feb 41 to Barce
Feb 41 **Hurricane I** (Jul 41) dets Heliopolis, Agedabia, Antelat, Msus
4 Apr 41 to Marawa
5 Apr 41 to Derna
8 Apr 41 to El Gubbi East
9 Apr 41 to El Gubbi West
19 Apr 41 to Maaten Bagush
23 Apr 41 to Qasaba
1 Jul 41 to Tel Aviv
26 Aug 41 to Wadi Halfa
Aug 41 **Gladiator I & II** (Jan 42) det Kufra

Aug 41 **Lysander I & II** (Jan 42)
Sep 41 **Hurricane I** (Feb 42)
Nov 41 **Blenheim IV** (Jan 42)
13 Jan 42 to Helwan
22 Jan 42 to Kilo 26
Apr 42 **Hurricane IID** (Dec 42)
28 Apr 42 to Shandur
4 Jun 42 to Gambut dets LG 102, LG 108, Shandur
17 Jun 42 to LG 75 det Shandur
18 Jun 42 to LG 102 det Shandur
27 Jun 42 to LG 106 det Shandur
29 Jun 42 to LG 91 det Shandur
29 Jul 42 to LG 89 dets Shandur, LG 37, LG 172
6 Nov 42 to LG 172 det Shandur
10 Dec 42 to Idku dets Shandur, LG 106
Dec 42 **Hurricane IIC** (Feb 43)
31 Jan 43 to Bu Amud
Feb 43 **Hurricane IID** (Jul 43)
2 Mar 43 to Castel Benito
8 Mar 43 to Sorman
17 Mar 43 to Senem
3 Apr 43 to Gabes
13 Apr 43 to Sfax
16 Apr 43 to Goubrine
2 Jun 43 to Ben Gardane
Jul 43 **Hurricane IV** (Jan 47)
22 Sep 43 to Fayid dets El Bassa, LG 91
24 Feb 44 to Grottaglie dets Borgo, Vis
4 Jul 44 to Foggia dets Pescara, Vis, Falconara
16 Aug 44 to Canne dets Vis, Brindisi, Araxos, Falconara, Niksic, Prkos
4 Apr 45 to Prkos
14 May 45 to Campomarino
18 May 45 to Canne
13 Jul 45 to Megiddo
3 Sep 45 to Petah Tiqva
28 Sep 45 to Ramat David
Feb 46 **Sptifire LF 9** (Jan 47)
2 Jun 46 to Ein Shemar
3 Oct 46 to Nicosia
Dec 46 **Tempest F.6** (Dec 49)
5 Sep 47 to Shallufa
26 Nov 47 to Khartoum det Mogadishu
5 May 48 to Fayid
1 Sep 48 to Deversoir
Oct 49 **Vampire FB 5** (Apr 52)
7 Jan 50 to Habbaniyah
9 Feb 50 to Deversoir
1 Jun 50 to Mafraq
29 Jun 50 to Deversoir
22 Nov 50 to Habbaniyah
21 Dec 50 to Deversoir
5 Apr 51 to Nicosia
22 May 51 to Deversoir
18 Jun 51 to Shaibah
19 Sep 51 to Habbaniyah
13 Nov 51 to Abu Sueir
27 Nov 51 to Habbaniyah
28 Jan 52 to Abu Sueir
Feb 52 **Vampire FB 9** (May 54)
31 May 52 to Nicosia
11 Jul 52 to Habbaniyah
28 Jul 52 to Abu Sueir
18 Aug 52 to Habbaniyah dets Sharjah, Mafraq
20 Jan 53 to Sharjah
18 Feb 53 to Habbaniyah dets Shaibah, Mafraq, Shallufa, Nicosia
10 Jan 54 to Amman
Feb 54 **Venom FB 1** (Aug 55)
7 Jun 54 to Habbaniyah
28 Aug 54 to Nicosia
5 Oct 54 to Habbaniyah dets Mafraq, Shaibah
Jun 55 **Venom FB 4** (Jun 57)
26 Sep 55 to Amman
10 Oct 55 to Habbaniyah
7 Nov 55 to Nicosia
12 Dec 55 to Habbaniyah
6 Apr 56 to Akrotiri det Coningsby for Canberra
Jul 57 **Canberra B.2** (Jan 60)
Dec 59 **Canberra B.6** (May 63)
Jan 62 **Canberra B.16** (Jan 69)
13 Jan 69 to Coningsby as a cadre
7 May 69 re-established
May 69 **Phantom FGR 2** (Sep 74)
30 Sep 74 DB

—

1 Jul 74 training at Lossiemouth as No 6 Sqn (Designate)

—

1 Oct 74 RF @ Lossiemouth
Oct 74 **Jaguar GR 1** ( )
15 Nov 74 to Coltishall

7 Sqn

1 May 14 F @ Farnborough
May 14 **Longhorn** (Aug 14)
May 14 **BE 8** (Aug 14)
May 14 **Tabloid** (Aug 14)
8 Aug 14 DB — personnel transferred to other units

—

29 Sep 14 RF @ Farnborough
Sep 14 **Henry Farman F.20** (Oct 14)
Sep 14 **Morane H** (Oct 14)
Sep 14 **Bleriot XI** (Oct 14)
Sep 14 **Avro Type E** (Apr 15)
Sep 14 **Vickers FB 'Gun Carrier'** (Apr 15) dets Swingate Down, Netheravon
24 Oct 14 to Netheravon
Oct 14 **RE 5** (Sep 15)
8 Apr 15 to St-Omer det Boulogne
Apr 15 **Voisin LA** (Sep 15)
Jun 15 **Bristol Scout** (Jun 16)
Jul 15 **BE 2C** (Feb 17)
11 Sep 15 to Droglandt
12 Dec 15 to Bailleul
Dec 15 **Morane LA** (Dec 15)
May 16 **BE 2D** (Oct 16)
30 Jul 16 to Warloy
Oct 16 **BE 2E** (Jun 17)
Dec 16 **BE 2F** (May 17)
Dec 16 **BE 2G** (Jun 17)
6 Feb 17 to Moreuil
15 Apr 17 to Matigny det Nesle
23 May 17 to Proven
May 17 **RE 8** (Oct 19)
13 Apr 18 to Droglandt
3 Sep 18 to Proven
22 Oct 18 to Bisseghem
1 Nov 18 to Stacegham
5 Nov 18 to Menin
15 Nov 18 to Stacegham
25 Nov 18 to Peronnes
26 Nov 18 to Fort Cognelée
6 Dec 18 to Elsenborn
15 Dec 18 to Bickendorf
20 Dec 18 to Spich
11 May 19 to Buchheim
7 Aug 19 to Heumar
21 Sep 19 to Old Sarum
9 Oct 19 reduced to a cadre
27 Oct 19 to Eastleigh
19 Nov 19 to Farnborough
31 Dec 19 DB

—

1 Jun 23 RF @ Bircham Newton — from 'D' Flt, No 100 Sqn
Jun 23 **Vimy** (Apr 27)
May 24 **Virginia III** (May 25)
Sep 24 **Virginia II** (Feb 27)
Sep 24 **Virginia IV** (Jun 25)
Jan 25 **Virginia V** (May 26)
Jun 25 **Virginia VI** (Aug 26)
Mar 27 **Virginia VII** (Jan 33)
7 Apr 27 to Worthy Down
Sep 27 **Virginia IX** (Aug 33)
Nov 28 **Virginia X** (Mar 36)
Apr 35 **Heyford II** (Apr 38)
Apr 36 **Heyford III** (Apr 38)
3 Sep 36 to Finningley
Apr 37 **Wellesley** (Apr 38)
Mar 38 **Whitley II** (Dec 38)
Nov 38 **Whitley III** (May 39)
Mar 39 **Anson I** (Apr 40)
Apr 39 **Hampden** (Apr 40)
1 Sep 39 to Doncaster
15 Sep 39 to Finningley
23 Sep 39 to Upper Heyford
8 Apr 40 DB — merged into No 16 OTU

—

30 Apr 40 RF @ Finningley (for Hampden)
20 May 40 DB

—

1 Aug 40 RF @ Leeming
Aug 40 **Stirling I** (Aug 43)
29 Oct 40 to Oakington
Mar 43 **Stirling III** (Aug 43)
May 43 **Lancaster I & III** (Aug 45)
25 Jul 45 to Mepal
Aug 45 **Lancaster B.1 (FE)** (Jan 50)
29 Jul 46 to Upwood
Sep 49 **Lincoln B.2** (Jan 56)
1 Jan 56 DB

—

1 Nov 56 RF @ Honington
Nov 56 **Valiant B(PR) 1** (Sep 62)
Jan 57 **Valiant B.1** (Sep 62)
Jan 57 **Valiant B(K) 1** (Sep 62)
26 Jul 60 to Wittering
Aug 61 **Valiant B(PR)K 1** (May 62)
30 Sep 62 DB

—

1 May 70 RF @ St Mawgan
May 70 **Canberra TT 18** (Jan 82)
Dec 70 **Canberra B.2** (Oct 75)
5 Jan 82 DB

1 Sep 82 RF @ Odiham
Sep 82 **Chinook HC 1** ( ) det Port Stanley

8 Sqn

1 Jan 15 F @ Brooklands
Jan 15 **BE 2C** (Aug 17)
6 Jan 15 to Gosport (Fort Grange)
Feb 15 **BE 2A** (Oct 15)
Feb 15 **BE 2B** (Oct 15)
15 Apr 15 to St-Omer
1 May 15 to Abeele
May 15 to Oxelaere
Jun 15 **Bristol Scout** (May 16)
Jun 15 **BE 8** (Jul 15)
24 Jul 15 to Vert Galand
Aug 15 to Marieux
20 Feb 16 to La Bellevue
Jun 16 **BE 2D** (17)
3 Feb 17 to Soncamp
Feb 17 **BE 2E** (Aug 17)
9 May 17 to Boiry-St-Martin
Aug 17 **AW FK 8** (Dec 18)
18 Oct 17 to Longavesnes
29 Oct 17 to Mons-en-Chaussée
11 Mar 18 to Nurlu
22 Mar 18 to Chipilly
24 Mar 18 to Poulainville
28 Mar 18 to Vert Galand
12 Apr 18 to Auxi-le-Chateau dets Bruay, Poulainville, Avesnes-le-Comte, Vignacourt
5 Aug 18 to Vignacourt
18 Aug 18 to La Bellevue det Foucaucourt
22 Sep 18 to Estrées-en-Chaussée
8 Oct 18 to Hervilly
18 Oct 18 to Malincourt
16 Nov 18 to La Bellevue
Dec 18 **Bristol F2b Fighter** (Jul 19)
11 May 19 to Sart
28 Jul 19 to Duxford as a cadre
20 Jan 20 DB

—

18 Oct 20 RF @ Helwan
Oct 20 **DH 9A** (Jun 28)
11 Dec 20 to Suez
23 Feb 21 to Basrah
4 Mar 21 to Baghdad West
29 Dec 21 to Hinaidi
27 Feb 27 to Khormaksar
Jan 28 **Fairey IIIF** (Mar 35)
Feb 35 **Vincent** (Nov 40)
Oct 35 **Demon** (Oct 35 — one F only) det Burao
Apr 39 **Blenheim I** (Oct 41) dets Riyan, Berbera, Sheikh Othman
Jul 40 **Maryland I** (Dec 40)
Aug 40 **Swordfish** (Dec 40) — floatplanes
Jan 41 **Blenheim IV** (Aug 42)
May 41 **Vincent** (Apr 42) dets Perim Island, Assab Aischa, Riyan
Sep 42 **Blenheim V** (Jan 44) dets Bandar Kassim, Riyan, Salalah, Scuscuiban
Feb 43 **Hudson VI** (Dec 43)
Dec 43 **Wellington XIII** (May 45
1 May 45 DB

—

15 May 45 RF @ Jessore — No 20 Sqn renumbered
May 45 **Liberator VI** (Nov 45)
21 May 45 to Minneriya det Sigiriya
15 Nov 45 DB

—

1 Sep 46 RF @ Khormaksar — No 114 Sqn renumbered
Sep 46 **Mosquito FB 6** (May 47)
Mar 47 **Tempest F.6** (Dec 49) det Eastleigh
Jun 49 **Brigand B.1** (Jan 53) dets Mogadishu, Asmara
Jul 50 **Anson C.19** (Feb 52)
Jul 50 **Auster AOP 6** (Feb 52)
14 Aug 50 to Nicosia
25 Sep 50 to Khormaksar det Habbaniyah
31 May 51 to Shaibah
8 Sep 51 to Khormaksar
23 Feb 52 to Nicosia
9 Apr 52 to Khormaksar
Dec 52 **Vampire FB 9** (Jul 55) det Sheikh Othman
7 Jul 53 to Nicosia
14 Aug 53 to Deversoir
23 Sep 53 to Habbaniyah
1 Oct 53 to Deversoir
23 Nov 53 to Khormaksar dets Eastleigh, Khartou
Mar 55 **Venom FB 1** (Nov 55)
Oct 55 **Venom FB 4** (Jan 60)
24 Jul 56 to Habbaniyah
5 Sep 56 to Akrotiri
20 Dec 56 to Khormaksar
Dec 56 **Venom FB 1** (Apr 57)
Jan 58 **Meteor FR 9** (Aug 59)
Jan 60 **Hunter FGA 9** (Dec 71)
Apr 61 **Hunter FR 10** (May 63)
30 Jun 61 to Bahrain
1 Jul 61 to Farwania
10 Jul 61 to Bahrain
8 Aug 61 to Farwania
8 Sep 61 to Bahrain
14 Oct 61 to Khormaksar dets Masirah, Sharjah, Muharraq

8 Aug 67 to Masirah
8 Sep 67 to Muharraq
Sep 67 **Hunter FR 10** (Dec 71)
dets Sharjah, Masirah
21 Dec 67 DB
—
1 Jan 72 RF @ Kinloss
Jan 72 **Shackleton AEW 2** ( )
14 Aug 73 to Lossiemouth

9 Sqn

8 Dec 14 F @ St-Omer — Wireless Flt redesignated
Dec 14 **BE 2A** (Feb 15)
Dec 14 **Longhorn** (Feb 15)
Dec 14 **Bleriot XI** (Mar 15)
Dec 14 **Shorthorn** (Mar 15)
Jan 15 **BE 2B** (Feb 15)
Jan 15 **BE 2C** (Feb 15)
Jan 15 **Bleriot Parasol** (Mar 15)
dets Bailleul, Chocques
2 Mar 15 DB — elements incorporated into Nos 2, 5, 6 & 15 Sqns
—
1 Apr 15 RF @ Brooklands
Apr 15 **BE 2** (Jul 15)
Apr 15 **Bleriot XI** (Aug 15)
Apr 15 **Longhorn** (Nov 15)
3 Jul 15 to Swingate Down
Jul 15 **BE 8A** (Nov 15)
Jul 15 **Avro 504** (Nov 15)
Jul 15 **Martinsyde S.1** (Nov 15)
Aug 15 **BE 2C** (Oct 16)
Nov 15 **RE 7** (Nov 15)
2 Dec 15 to St-Omer
Dec 15 **Bristol Scout** (Jun 16)
4 Dec 15 to Bertangles
6 Mar 16 to Allonville
Jun 16 **BE 2D** (Sep 16)
5 Jul 16 to Chipilly
Aug 16 **BE 2E** (Jun 17)
3 Sep 16 to Morlancourt
dets Mons-en-Chaussée
7 Apr 17 to Nurlu
May 17 **RE 8** (May 19)
6 May 17 to Estrées-en-Chaussée
0 Jun 17 to Proven
1 Apr 18 to Calais
6 Jun 18 to Agenvillers
Jul 18 **Bristol F2b Fighter** (Oct 18)
7 Jul 18 to Quevauvillers
5 Aug 18 to Amiens
7 Sep 18 to Proyart
5 Sep 18 to Athies
5 Oct 18 to Montigny Farm
3 Oct 18 to Prémont Farm
9 Oct 18 to Tarcienne
Dec 18 to Fort Cognelée
9 Dec 18 to Clavier
3 Jan 19 to Ludendorf
Feb 19 **Bristol F2b Fighter** (Jul 19)
0 Jul 19 to Castle Bromwich as a cadre
Dec 19 DB
—
Apr 24 RF @ Upavon
Apr 24 **Vimy** (Oct 25)
Apr 24 to Manston
Sep 24 **Virginia IV** (Mar 27)
Jan 25 **Virginia V** (May 26)
Jun 25 **Virginia VI** (Apr 27)
Jul 26 **Virginia VII** (Jun 30)
Jan 27 **Virginia VIII** (Mar 27)
Jul 27 **Virginia IX** (Feb 32)
Jan 29 **Virginia X** (Apr 36)
Nov 30 to Boscombe Down
Oct 35 to Andover
Jan 36 to Aldergrove
Mar 36 **Heyford III** (May 39)
Oct 36 to Scampton
Mar 38 to Stradishall
Jan 39 **Wellington I** (Dec 39)
Jul 39 to Honington
Sep 39 **Wellington IA** (Sep 40)
det Lossiemouth
Feb 40 **Wellington IC** (Oct 41)
Mar 41 **Wellington II** (Aug 41)
Jul 41 **Wellington III** (Aug 42)
May 42 **Wellington IC** (Jun 42)
7 Aug 42 to Waddington
Sep 42 **Lancaster I & III** (Dec 45)
14 Apr 43 to Bardney
dets Lossiemouth, Yagodnik
6 Jul 45 to Waddington
Nov 45 **Lancaster B.7** (Apr 46)
19 Jan 46 to Salbani
19 Apr 46 to Binbrook
May 46 **Lancaster B.1 & 3** (Jul 46)
Jul 46 **Lincoln B.2** (May 52)
May 52 **Canberra B.2** (Jun 56)
Sep 55 **Canberra B.6** (Jul 61)
2 Jun 59 to Coningsby
13 Jul 61 DB
—
1 Mar 62 RF @ Coningsby
Apr 62 **Vulcan B.2** (Apr 82)
10 Nov 64 to Cottesmore
26 Feb 69 to Akrotiri
15 Jan 75 to Waddington
1 May 82 DB
—
1 Jun 82 RF @ Honington
Jun 82 **Tornado GR 1** ( )
1 Oct 86 to Brüggen

10 Sqn

1 Jan 15 F @ Farnborough — nucleus from No 1 RAS
Jan 15 **Longhorn** (Apr 15)
Jan 15 **Shorthorn** (Apr 15)
Jan 15 **Bleriot XI** (Apr 15)
Jan 15 **Martinsyde S.1** (Apr 15)
Jan 15 **BE 2C** (Apr 17)
8 Jan 15 to Brooklands
1 Apr 15 to Hounslow
7 Apr 15 to Netheravon
27 Jul 15 to St-Omer
30 Jul 15 to Aire
7 Aug 15 to Chocques
Jun 16 **BE 12** (Jul 16)
Jul 16 **BE 2D** (Feb 17)
Dec 16 **BE 2E** (Jul 17)
Jan 17 **BE 2F** (Jul 17)
Jan 17 **BE 2G** (Jul 17)
Jul 17 **AW FK 8** (Feb 19)
18 Nov 17 to Abeele
12 Apr 18 to Droglandt
Jun 18 **Bristol F2b Fighter** (Oct 18)
22 Sep 18 to Abeele
21 Oct 18 to Menin
5 Nov 18 to Staceghem
15 Nov 18 to Menin
1 Dec 18 to Reckem
17 Feb 19 to Ford Junction as a cadre
15 Oct 19 to Croydon
31 Dec 19 DB
—
3 Jan 28 RF @ Upper Heyford
Jan 28 **Hyderabad** (Nov 31)
Dec 30 **Hinaidi** (Sep 32)
1 Apr 31 to Boscombe Down
Sep 32 **Virginia X** (Jan 35)
Aug 34 **Heyford IA** (Jan 36)
Nov 35 **Heyford III** (Jun 37)
25 Jan 37 to Dishforth
Mar 37 **Whitley I** (Jun 39)
May 39 **Whitley IV** (May 40)
dets Villeneuve, Kinloss
May 40 **Whitley V** (Dec 41)
8 Jul 40 to Leeming
Dec 41 **Halifax I** (Aug 42)
Dec 41 **Halifax II** (Mar 44)
det Lossiemouth
5 Jul 42 det Aqir (as No 10/227 Sqn — became No 462 Sqn wef 7 Sep 42
19 Aug 42 to Melbourne
Mar 44 **Halifax III** (May 45)
May 45 **Dakota** (Dec 47)
6 Aug 45 to Broadwell
28 Aug 45 en route FE
10 Sep 45 to Bilaspur
5 Oct 45 to Poona
dets Chaklala, Meiktila
5 Jun 46 to Mauripur
15 Dec 47 DB
—
4 Oct 48 RF @ Oakington — No 238 Sqn renumbered
Oct 48 **Dakota** (Feb 50)
dets Lübeck for BAL
20 Feb 50 DB
—
15 Jan 53 RF @ Scampton
Jan 53 **Canberra B.2** (Dec 56)
16 May 55 to Honington
15 Jan 57 DB
—
15 Apr 58 RF @ Cottesmore
Apr 58 **Victor B.1** (Mar 64)
1 Mar 64 DB
—
1 Jul 66 RF @ Fairford
Jul 66 **VC 10 C.1** ( )
23 May 67 to Brize Norton

11 Sqn

14 Feb 15 F @ Netheravon — nucleus from No 7 Sqn
Feb 15 **Henry Farman F.20** (Jun 15)
Feb 15 **Vickers FB 'Gun Carrier'** (Jun 15)
Jun 15 **Vickers FB 5** (Jul 16)
25 Jul 15 to St-Omer
29 Jul 15 to Vert Galand
20 Sep 15 to Villers-Bretonneux
det Vert Galand
27 Oct 15 to Bertangles
Dec 15 **Bristol Scout** (Feb 16)
Jan 16 to Savy
Feb 16 **DH 2** (Mar 16)
Apr 16 **Nieuport 16** (Aug 16)
May 16 **Vickers ES 1** (Jun 16)
May 16 **Bristol Scout** (Aug 16)
May 16 **Vickers FB 9** (Jul 16)
Jun 16 **FE 2B** (Jun 17)
Jul 16 **Nieuport 17** (Aug 16)
31 Aug 16 to Izel-le-Hameau
May 17 **Bristol F2b Fighter** (Oct 19)
1 Jun 17 to La Bellevue
27 Mar 18 to Fienvillers
16 Apr 18 to Remaisnil
7 Jul 18 to Le Quesnoy
19 Sep 18 to Vert Galand
15 Oct 18 to Mory
1 Nov 18 to Béthencourt
18 Nov 18 to Aulnoye
19 Dec 18 to Nivelles
20 May 19 to Spich
3 Sep 19 to Scopwick
9 Oct 19 reduced to a cadre
31 Dec 19 DB
—
15 Jan 23 RF @ Andover — from cadre of the Air Pilotage School
Jan 23 **DH 9A** (Apr 24)
16 Sep 23 to Bircham Newton
Apr 24 **Fawn** (May 27)
31 May 24 to Netheravon
Nov 26 **Horsley** (Nov 28)
Oct 28 **Wapiti** (Aug 32)
29 Dec 28 en route India
22 Jan 29 to Risalpur
det Miranshah
Feb 32 **Hart** (Jul 39)
dets Gilgit, Arawali, Miranshah
Jul 39 **Blenheim I** (Jan 41)
7 Aug 39 to Tengah
9 Sep 39 to Kallang
20 Apr 40 to Lahore
5 May 40 to Karachi
9 May 40 to Ismailia
det Heliopolis
16 Jun 40 to Sheikh Othman
1 Dec 40 to Helwan
det Fuka
Jan 41 **Blenheim IV** (Sep 43)
28 Jan 41 to Larissa
det Paramythia
16 Mar 41 to Almyros
17 Apr 41 to Menidi
23 Apr 41 to Argos
16 May 41 to Ramleh
25 May 41 to Aqir
9 Aug 41 to Habbaniyah
27 Sep 41 to LG 09
9 Oct 41 to LG 104
25 Oct 41 to LG 116
dets LG 76, Bu Amud
26 Dec 41 to Bu Amud
27 Jan 42 to LG 116
dets Bu Amud, Gambut
22 Feb 42 to Helwan
17 Mar 42 to Colombo
12 Jan 43 to Baigachi
13 Feb 43 to Feni
det Ranchi
15 Aug 43 to Yelahanka
det Ranchi
15 Sep 43 to St Thomas Mount
Sep 43 **Hurricane IIC** (Jun 45)
15 Oct 43 to Cholavaram
det Lalmai
2 Dec 43 to Lalmai
25 Jan 44 to 'Lyons'
2 Mar 44 to Sapam
5 Mar 44 to Tulihal
14 Apr 44 to Lanka
dets Imphal, Kangla
1 Jul 44 to Dimapur
det Imphal
1 Oct 44 to Imphal
9 Nov 44 to Tamu
26 Jan 45 to Kan
11 Feb 45 to Sinthe
1 May 45 to Magwe
19 May 45 to Feni
29 May 45 to Chettinad
31 May 45 to Tanjore
7 Jun 45 to Chettinad
Jun 45 **Spitfire XIV** (Feb 48)
17 Aug 45 to Madura
18 Sep 45 to Kelanang via HMS *Trumpeter*
21 Sep 45 to Kuala Lumpur
23 Sep 45 to Tengah
25 Sep 45 to Seletar
7 Jan 46 to Kuala Lumpur
12 Apr 46 to Seletar
23 Apr 46 to Iwakuni via HMS *Vengeance*
6 May 46 to Miho
23 Feb 48 DB (date retrospectively amended to 31 Mar 48)
—
15 Sep 48 RF @ Wahn — No 107 Sqn renumbered
Sep 48 **Mosquito FB 6** (Aug 50)
17 Sep 49 to Celle
14 Aug 50 to Wunstorf
Aug 50 **Vampire FB 5** (Dec 52)
Aug 52 **Venom FB 1** (Aug 55)
Aug 55 **Venom FB 4** (Nov 57)
26 Sep 55 to Fassberg
15 Oct 56 to Wunstorf
16 Nov 57 DB
—
21 Jan 59 RF @ Geilenkirchen — No 256 Sqn renumbered
Jan 59 **Meteor NF 11** (Feb 60)
Oct 59 **Javelin FAW 4** (Mar 62)
Aug 61 **Javelin FAW 5** (Dec 62)
Dec 62 **Javelin FAW 9** (Jan 66) — ex No 25 Sqn
11 Jan 66 DB
—
3 Apr 67 RF @ Leuchars
Apr 67 **Lightning F.6** ( )
28 Mar 72 to Binbrook
Oct 72 **Lightning F.3** (May 86)

12 Sqn

14 Feb 15 F @ Netheravon — nucleus from No 1 Sqn
May 15 **Avro 504** (Sep 15)
Jun 15 **BE 2C** (Feb 17)
6 Sep 15 to St-Omer
Sep 15 **Martinsyde S.1** (Oct 15)
Sep 15 **BE 2B** (Nov 15)
Sep 15 **Voisin LA** (Nov 15)
Sep 15 **RE 7** (Jan 16)
Sep 15 **RE 5** (Feb 16)
Oct 15 **Morane H** (Nov 15)
Nov 15 **Bristol Scout** (May 16)
Nov 15 **Morane LA** (Feb 16)
28 Feb 16 to Vert Galand
Feb 16 **FE 2B** (Feb 16)
3 Mar 16 to Avesnes-le-Comte
Feb 16 **Morane BB** (Feb 16)
Jul 16 **BE 2D** (Aug 17)
Dec 16 **BE 2E** (Aug 17)
9 May 17 to Wagnonlieu
7 Jul 17 to Ablainzevelle
Aug 17 **RE 8** (Jul 19)
Aug 17 to Courcelles-le-Comte
16 Dec 17 to Boiry-St-Martin
22 Mar 18 to Soncamp
Mar 18 **Bristol F2b Fighter** (Jul 22)
17 Sep 18 to Mory
14 Oct 18 to Estourmel
29 Nov 18 to Gerpinnes
6 Dec 18 to Clavier
19 Dec 18 to Düren
5 May 19 to Heumar
17 Nov 20 to Bickendorf
27 Jul 22 DB
—
1 Apr 23 RF @ Northolt
Apr 23 **DH 9A** (Mar 24)
24 Mar 24 to Andover
Mar 24 **Fawn** (Dec 26)
Jun 26 **Fox** (Jan 31)
Jan 31 **Hart** (Oct 36)
4 Oct 35 en route Aden
20 Oct 35 to Khormaksar
25 Nov 35 to Robat
23 Mar 36 to Khormaksar
18 May 36 to Robat
28 Jul 36 to Khormaksar
11 Aug 36 en route UK
29 Aug 36 to Andover
Oct 36 **Hind** (Feb 38)
Feb 38 **Battle** (Nov 40)
9 May 39 to Bicester
2 Sep 39 to Berry-au-Bac
8 Dec 39 to Amifontaine det Perpignan/La Salanque
16 May 40 to Echemines
8 Jun 40 to Sougé
16 Jun 40 to Finningley
3 Jul 40 to Binbrook
Nov 40 **Wellington II** (Nov 42) det Thruxton
Aug 42 **Wellington III** (Nov 42)
25 Sep 42 to Wickenby
Nov 42 **Lancaster I & III** (Jul 46)
24 Sep 45 to Binbrook
26 Jul 46 to Waddington
Aug 46 **Lincoln B.2** (Apr 52)
18 Sep 46 to Binbrook
12 Jan 48 to Hemswell
14 Mar 48 to Binbrook
Mar 52 **Canberra B.2** (Jun 55)
May 55 **Canberra B.6** (Jul 61)
Aug 57 **Canberra B.2** (Mar 59)
2 Jul 59 to Coningsby
13 Jul 61 DB
—
1 Jul 62 RF @ Coningsby
Jul 62 **Vulcan B.2** (Dec 67)
17 Nov 64 to Cottesmore
31 Dec 67 DB
—
1 Oct 69 RF @ Honington
Oct 69 **Buccaneer S.2** ( )
4 Aug 80 to Lossiemouth — (No 216 Sqn redesignated — original unit remained as 'No 12 Sqn (South)' until 1 Nov 80)

13 Sqn

10 Jan 15 F @ Gosport (Fort Grange) — nucleus from No 8 Sqn
Jan 15 **BE 2C** (Apr 17)
15 **Bristol Scout** (May 16)
19 Oct 15 to St-Omer
21 Oct 15 to Vert Galand
12 Mar 16 to Le Hameau
18 Mar 16 to Savy
Jul 16 **BE 2D** (Jul 17)
Sep 16 **BE 2E** (Jan 17)
Apr 17 **BE 2E** (Jul 17)
9 May 17 to Etrun
Jun 17 **RE 8** (Mar 19)
22 Mar 18 to Le Hameau
22 Sep 18 to Mory
19 Oct 18 to Carnières
1 Dec 18 to Vert Galand
19 Jan 19 to St-Omer
27 Mar 19 to Sedgeford as a cadre
31 Dec 19 DB
—
1 Apr 24 RF @ Kenley — from the Signals Co-operation Flt
Apr 24 **Bristol F2b Fighter** (Jan 28)
30 May 24 to Andover
Aug 27 **Atlas** (Jul 32)
23 Sep 29 to Netheravon
May 32 **Audax** (May 37)
3 May 35 to Old Sarum
16 Feb 37 to Odiham
May 37 **Hector** (Feb 39)
Jan 39 **Lysander II** (Jan 41)
24 Sep 39 to Mons-en-Chaussée
Apr 40 to Flamicourt
11 May 40 to Douai
22 May 40 to Abbeville det Clairmarais
26 May 40 to Châteaubriant
29 May 40 to Bekesbourne
30 May 40 to Hooton Park
17 Jun 40 to Speke
14 Jul 40 to Hooton Park
Nov 40 **Lysander III** (Jul 41)
17 Jul 41 to Odiham
Jul 41 **Blenheim IV** (Sep 42) dets Detling, Wattisham, Thruxton
1 Aug 42 to Macmerry
10 Aug 42 to Odiham
Sep 42 **Blenheim V** (Dec 43)
15 Nov 42 en route N Africa, via Gibraltar
18 Nov 42 to Blida dets Canrobert, Setif
5 Dec 42 to Canrobert
8 Feb 43 to Oulmene
22 May 43 to Blida dets Monastir, La Sebala
4 Sep 43 to Protville II
12 Oct 43 to Sidi Ahmed
26 Oct 43 to Sidi Amor
Oct 43 **Ventura V** (Dec 43) det Bo Rizzo
19 Dec 43 to Kabrit
Jan 44 **Baltimore IV** (Jun 44)
Jan 44 **Baltimore V** (Oct 44)
22 Mar 44 to Biferno
2 May 44 to Regina
22 Jun 44 to Tarquinia
18 Jul 44 to Cecina det Perugia
27 Oct 44 to Iesi
Oct 44 **Boston IV** (Feb 46)
Nov 44 **Boston V** (Apr 46) dets Perugia, Marcianese
30 Dec 44 to Falconara
7 Mar 45 to Forli
13 May 45 to Aviano
14 Sep 45 to Hassani
19 Apr 46 DB
—
1 Sep 46 RF @ Ein Shemar — No 680 Sqn renumbered
Sep 46 **Mosquito PR 34** (Mar 52)
14 Dec 46 to Kabrit
5 Feb 47 to Fayid
Apr 47 **Spitfire PR 11** (Dec 47)
28 Feb 51 to Kabrit
Dec 51 **Meteor PR 10** (Aug 56) det Eastleigh
1 Jan 55 to Abu Sueir
10 Feb 56 to Akrotiri
Feb 56 **Canberra PR 7** (Dec 61)
Jul 61 **Canberra PR 9** (Oct 76)
1 Sep 65 to Luqa
6 Jan 72 to Akrotiri
Apr 72 **Canberra PR 7** (Jan 82)
10 Oct 72 to Luqa
22 Oct 78 to Wyton
5 Jan 82 DB

14 Sqn

3 Feb 15 F @ Shoreham — nucleus from No 3 RAS
Feb 15 **Longhorn** (Aug 15)
11 May 15 to Hounslow
May 15 **BE 2C** (Nov 17)
May 15 **Caudron G.III** (Aug 15)
5 Aug 15 to Gosport (Fort Grange)
7 Nov 15 en route Egypt
19 Nov 15 to Alexandria
23 Nov 15 to Ismailia
Nov 15 **Shorthorn** (16)
Nov 15 **BE 2E** (Sep 18)
Nov 15 **Martinsyde S.1** ( ) dets Mersah Matruh, Fayoum, Heliopolis
6 Dec 15 to Heliopolis dets Ismailia, Abu Gandir, Qantara
29 Jan 16 to Ismailia dets El Hammam, Sidi Barrani, Sollum, Mersah Matruh, Suez, Heliopolis, Port Said, Salmana, Rabigh, Mustabig
16 **Martinsyde G.100** (17)
Jun 16 **DH 1A** (Mar 17)
20 Jan 17 to Kilo 143/Ujret el Zol dets Yenbo, El Weigh
25 Mar 17 to Rafah dets Deir el Ballah, El Weigh
27 Apr 17 to Deir el Ballah dets Suez, Kilo 143, El Weigh, Aqaba
Jul 17 **Vickers FB 19 Mk II** (Aug 17)
Oct 17 **RE 8** (Nov 18)
20 Nov 17 to Julis
30 Nov 17 to Junction Station dets Jericho, Jerusalem
Feb 18 **Nieuport 17** (Oct 18)
24 Oct 18 to Qantara
6 Nov 18 to Mikra Bay
9 Dec 18 en route UK
1 Jan 19 to Tangmere as a cadre
4 Feb 19 DB
—
1 Feb 20 RF @ Ramleh — No 111 Sqn renumbered
Feb 20 **Bristol F2b Fighter** (Feb 26) dets Amman, Damascus, Aleppo, Mafraq, Beersheba
Jun 24 **DH 9A** (Mar 30)
15 Feb 26 to Amman dets Ramleh
Nov 29 **Fairey IIIF** (Sep 32)
Jul 32 **Gordon** (Apr 38)
Mar 38 **Wellesley** (Dec 40)
24 Aug 39 to Ismailia dets Qasaba
19 Dec 39 to Amman det Port Sudan
24 May 40 to Port Sudan
Jun 40 **Gladiator I** (Mar 41)
Sep 40 **Blenheim IV** (Aug 42)
12 Apr 41 to Heliopolis
1 May 41 to LG 21
7 Jul 41 to Petah Tiqva
10 Aug 41 to Habbaniyah
24 Aug 41 to Qaiyarh
8 Oct 41 to Habbaniyah
26 Oct 41 to Lydda
4 Nov 41 to LG 15
18 Nov 41 to LG 75
18 Dec 41 to Gambut
27 Jan 42 to Bu Amud
6 Feb 42 to LG 76
8 Feb 42 to LG 116 dets Gambut, Bir el Baheira
1 May 42 to El Firdan det Kabrit
4 Jun 42 to LG 116
28 Jun 42 to Qassassin dets LG 97, LG 98, LG 88
Jul 42 **Baltimore II** (Aug 42)
10 Aug 42 to LG 224
Aug 42 **Marauder I** (Sep 44)
25 Aug 42 to Fayid dets Berka III, Gambut No 3
23 Feb 43 to Gambut No 3 dets Berka, Shallufa
1 Mar 43 to Telergma dets Berka III, Gambut No 3, Shallufa
10 Mar 43 to Blida dets Gambut No 3, Shallufa, Bone, Kasfareet
May 43 **Mustang I** (Jun 43)
2 Jun 43 to Protville I dets Bone, Grottaglie
27 Oct 43 to Sidi Amor dets Bone, Ghisonaccia, Grottaglie
5 Dec 43 to Ghisonaccia dets Blida, Grottaglie
13 Jan 44 to Blida dets Grottaglie, Ghisonaccia, Telergma
11 Apr 44 to Alghero dets Grottaglie, Ghisonaccia, Telergma, Foggia
Jun 44 **Marauder II** (Aug 44)
Jun 44 **Marauder III** (Sep 44)
23 Sep 44 to Grottaglie
3 Oct 44 to Gragnano (No 56 PTC
24 Oct 44 to Chivenor
Nov 44 **Wellington XIV** (May 45
25 May 45 DB
—
25 May 45 RF @ Banff — No 143 Sqn renumbered
May 45 **Mosquito VI** (Mar 46)
29 Aug 45 to Gatwick
1 Oct 45 to B 72/Cambrai/Epinoy
4 Dec 45 to Sylt
19 Dec 45 to B 72/Cambrai/Epinoy
31 Mar 46 DB
—
1 Apr 46 RF @ Wahn — No 128 Sqn renumbered
Apr 46 **Mosquito B.16** (Aug 48)
16 Aug 47 to Gatow
11 Sep 47 to Wahn
29 Sep 47 to West Malling
17 Oct 47 to Wahn
Dec 47 **Mosquito B.35** (Feb 51)
13 May 48 to West Malling
4 Jun 48 to Wahn
16 Sep 49 to Celle
1 Nov 50 to Fassberg
Feb 51 **Vampire FB 5** (Jul 54)
May 53 **Venom FB 1** (Jun 55)
23 Jun 55 to Oldenburg
Jun 55 **Hunter F.4** (May 57)
Apr 57 **Hunter F.6** (Dec 62)
26 Sep 57 to Ahlhorn
15 Sep 58 to Gütersloh
16 Mar 61 to Jever

6 Sep 61 to Gütersloh
17 Dec 62 DB
—
17 Dec 62 RF @ Wildenrath — No 88 Sqn renumbered
Dec 62 **Canberra B(I) 8** (Jun 70)
30 Jun 70 DB
—
1 Jul 70 RF @ Brüggen
Jul 70 **Phantom FGR 2** (Nov 75)
30 Nov 75 DB
—
1 May 75 training at Brüggen as No 14 Sqn (Designate)
—
1 Dec 75 RF @ Brüggen
Dec 75 **Jaguar GR 1** (Nov 85)
1 Nov 85 DB
—
1 Jul 85 training at Brüggen as No 14 Sqn (Designate)
—
1 Nov 85 RF @ Brüggen
Nov 85 **Tornado GR 1** ( )

15 Sqn

1 Mar 15 F @ South Farnborough — nucleus from No 1 RAS
3 Apr 15 to Hounslow
Apr 15 **Henry Farman F.20** (Oct 15)
Apr 15 **Longhorn** (Oct 15)
Apr 15 **Shorthorn** (Oct 15)
Apr 15 **Avro 504** (Oct 15)
Apr 15 **Bleriot XI** (Sep 15)
Apr 15 **BE 2C** (Jul 17)
1 May 15 to Swingate Down
Oct 15 **Morane H** (Dec 15)
Nov 15 **Morane L** (Dec 15)
3 Dec 15 to St-Omer
5 Jan 16 to Droglandt
8 Mar 16 to Vert Galand
7 Mar 16 to Marieux
Aug 16 **BE 2D** (Aug 17)
2 Oct 16 to Léalvillers (Clairfaye Farm)
Oct 16 **BE 2E** (May 17)
Jan 17 **BE 2F** (May 17)
Jan 17 **BE 2G** (May 17)
May 17 **RE 8** (Feb 19)
6 Jun 17 to Courcelles-le-Comte
7 Jul 17 to La Gorgue det Clairmarais
8 Aug 17 to Savy
0 Aug 17 to Longavesnes
8 Oct 17 to Léchelle
0 Nov 17 to Bapaume
5 Dec 17 to Léchelle
2 Mar 18 to Laviéville
5 Mar 18 to Lahoussoye
5 Mar 18 to Fienvillers
0 Apr 18 to Vert Galand
4 Sep 18 to Senlis-le-Sec
2 Oct 18 to Léchelle (Quatre Vents Farm)
5 Oct 18 to Selvigny (Ferme Guillemin)
3 Dec 18 to Vignacourt
6 Feb 19 to Fowlmere as a cadre
1 Dec 19 DB
—
) Mar 24 RF @ Martlesham Heath as A & AEE trials unit
Mar 24 **DH 9A** (Oct 26)
Oct 26 **Horsley** (May 34)
May 34 DB — note that equipment was largely notional and would have been that operated in the event of mobilisation
—
Jun 34 RF @ Abingdon
Jun 34 **Hart** (Jun 36)
Mar 36 **Hind** (Jul 38)
Jun 38 **Battle** (Dec 39)
2 Sep 39 to Bétheniville
11 Sep 39 to Condé/Vraux
10 Dec 39 to Wyton
Dec 39 **Blenheim IV** (Oct 40)
14 Apr 40 to Alconbury
15 May 40 to Wyton det Lossiemouth
Nov 40 **Wellington IC** (May 41)
Apr 41 **Stirling I** (Apr 43)
13 Aug 42 to Bourn
Jan 43 **Stirling III** (Dec 43)
14 Apr 43 to Mildenhall
Dec 43 **Lancaster I & III** (Mar 47)
19 Aug 46 to Wyton
Feb 47 **Lincoln B.2** (Nov 50)
29 Nov 50 to Marham
4 Feb 51 to Coningsby
Feb 51 **Washington B.1** (Apr 53)
May 53 **Canberra B.2** (Apr 57)
19 May 54 to Cottesmore
18 Feb 55 to Honington
15 Apr 57 DB
—
1 Sep 58 RF @ Cottesmore
Sep 58 **Victor B.1** (Oct 64)
1 Oct 64 DB
—
1 Oct 70 RF @ Honington
Oct 70 **Buccaneer S.2** (Jul 83)
11 Jan 71 to Laarbruch
1 Jul 83 absorbed by No 16 Sqn
—
1 Jul 83 training at Laarbruch as No 15 Sqn (Designate)
—
1 Sep 83 re-established at Laarbruch
Sep 83 **Tornado GR 1** ( )

16 Sqn

10 Feb 15 F @ St Omer — from Flts of Nos 2 & 6 Sqns
Feb 15 **RE 5** (Feb 15)
Feb 15 **Vickers FB 5** (Mar 15)
Feb 15 **Bleriot XI** (Mar 15)
26 Feb 15 Flt added from No 5 Sqn
Feb 15 **Martinsyde S.1** (May 15)
6 Mar 15 to La Gorgue det Aire
Mar 15 **Voisin LA** (May 15)
Mar 15 **BE 2C** (Apr 17)
May 15 **BE 2A** (Jul 15)
May 15 **Shorthorn** (Nov 15)
1 Jun 15 to Chocques
Jun 15 **BE 2B** (Jun 15)
18 Jul 15 to Merville
Aug 15 **Bristol Scout** (Jun 16)
Oct 15 **FE 2A** (Jan 16)
Oct 15 **FE 2B** (Feb 16)
12 Dec 15 to La Gorgue
Jun 16 **BE 2D** (Nov 16)
Jul 16 **BE 2E** (May 17)
31 Aug 16 to Bruay
Apr 17 **BE 2F** (May 17)
Apr 17 **BE 2G** (Aug 17)
25 May 17 to Camblain-l'Abbé
May 17 **RE 8** (Feb 19)
21 Oct 18 to La Brayelle
25 Oct 18 to Auchy
14 Feb 19 to Fowlmere as a cadre
31 Dec 19 DB
—
1 Apr 24 RF @ Old Sarum — Co-op Sqn of School of Army Co-operation redesignated
Apr 24 **Bristol F2b Fighter** (Mar 31)
Jan 31 **Atlas** (Jan 34)
Dec 33 **Audax** (Oct 38)
May 38 **Lysander I** (Apr 39)
Apr 39 **Lysander II** (Nov 40)
17 Feb 40 to Hawkinge
13 Apr 40 to Amiens
14 Apr 40 to Bertangles
19 May 40 to Lympne
May 40 **Lysander I** (Sep 40)
3 Jun 40 to Redhill
29 Jun 40 to Cambridge
3 Aug 40 to Okehampton det Cambridge
15 Aug 40 to Weston Zoyland
Oct 40 **Lysander III** (Jul 41) dets Okehampton, Roborough, Tilshead, St Just, Bolt Head
May 41 **Lysander IIIA** (Jul 42)
4 Jun 41 to Okehampton
6 Jun 41 Weston Zoyland dets Lee-on-Solent, Tilshead
9 Sep 41 to Okehampton
11 Sep 41 to Weston Zoyland
25 Sep 41 to Thruxton
3 Oct 41 to Weston Zoyland det Farnborough
23 Nov 41 to Lympne
27 Nov 41 to Weston Zoyland det Okehampton
Apr 42 **Mustang I** (Oct 43) dets Middle Wallop, Exeter
1 Jan 43 to Andover
Feb 43 **Tomahawk II** (Jun 43)
Feb 43 **Spitfire V** (Feb 43)
26 Feb 43 to Ford
13 Mar 43 to Andover
6 Apr 43 to Weston Zoyland
9 Apr 43 to Andover
16 May 43 to Weston Zoyland
22 May 43 to Andover
1 Jun 43 to Middle Wallop
29 Jun 43 to Hartford Bridge
Aug 43 **Spitfire XI** (Sep 45)
16 Apr 44 to Northolt
Jul 44 **Spitfire IX** (Nov 44)
4 Sep 44 to A 12/Balleroy
9 Sep 44 to B 48/Amiens/Glisy
27 Sep 44 to B 58/Melsbroek
Mar 45 **Spitfire XIX** (Sep 45)
10 Apr 45 to B 78/Eindhoven
17 Sep 45 Flts to Nos 2, 26 & 268 Sqns
19 Sep 45 DB
—
19 Sep 45 RF @ Celle — No 268 Sqn renumbered
Sep 45 **Spitfire XIX** (Apr 46)
Sep 45 **Spitfire XIV** (Apr 46)
Sep 45 **Spitfire XVI** (Apr 46)
1 Apr 46 DB
—
1 Apr 46 RF @ Fassberg — No 56 Sqn renumbered
Apr 46 **Tempest F.5** (Aug 46)
1 Jun 46 to Manston
12 Jun 46 to Fassberg
21 Jun 46 to Sylt
14 Jul 46 to Fassberg
Aug 46 **Tempest F.2** (Dec 48)
5 Sep 46 to Manston
16 Sep 46 to Fassberg
4 Feb 47 to Gatow
21 Mar 47 to Fassberg
8 May 47 to Ahlhorn
20 May 47 to Fassberg
13 Jul 47 to Zeltweg
12 Aug 47 to Fassberg
6 Oct 47 to Middle Wallop
17 Oct 47 to Fassberg
3 Nov 47 to Lübeck
24 Nov 47 to Fassberg
1 Dec 47 to Gütersloh
6 Jan 48 to Gatow
2 Feb 48 to Gütersloh
14 Jul 48 to Lübeck
7 Aug 48 to Gütersloh
Dec 48 **Vampire FB 5** (Jun 54)
2 Nov 50 to Celle
Jan 54 **Venom FB 1** (Jun 57)
1 Jun 57 DB
—
1 Mar 58 RF @ Laarbruch
Mar 58 **Canberra B(I) 8** (Jun 72)
6 Jun 72 DB
—
1 Oct 72 training at Laarbruch as No 16 Sqn (Designate)
—
8 Jan 73 RF @ Laarbruch
Jan 73 **Buccaneer S.2** (Feb 84)
29 Feb 84 DB
—
1 Jan 84 training at Laarbruch as No 16 Sqn (Designate)
—
1 Mar 84 RF @ Laarbruch
Mar 84 **Tornado GR 1** ( )

17 Sqn

1 Feb 15 F @ Gosport (Fort Grange)
Feb 15 **BE 2C** (Nov 15)
5 Aug 15 to Hounslow
15 Nov 15 en route Egypt
11 Dec 15 to Alexandria
18 Dec 15 to Heliopolis
Dec 15 **BE 2C** (Jun 18) Flts @ El Hammam, Suez, Kharga, Port Sudan, dets Fayoum, Minya, Assiyut, Rahad, Nahud, Jebel el Hillah
2 Jul 16 en route Salonika
21 Jul 16 to Mikra Bay
Jul 16 **Bristol Scout** (Sep 16)
Jul 16 **DH 2** ( ) Flts @ Lahana, Avret Hisar, Orlyak, Marian, Amberkoj
Nov 16 **BE 12A** (Sep 18)
Jul 17 **SPAD S.VII** (Dec 17)
Aug 17 det Florina (used loaned French Nieuport 17 (Dec 17))
Dec 17 **SE 5A** (Apr 18)
8 Dec 17 to Lahana Flt @ Amberkoj det Mudros
Mar 18 **AW FK 8** (Dec 18)
Aug 18 **DH 9** (Nov 19)
22 Sep 18 to Amberkoj
26 Sep 18 to Stojakovo Flt @ Amberkoj
2 Oct 18 to Radovo Flt @ Amberkoj
13 Oct 18 to Amberkoj Flts @ Phillipopolis, Mustapha Pasha, Mikra Bay, Batum
Dec 18 **Camel** (Nov 19)
28 Jan 19 to San Stephano dets Kars, Tiflis
14 Nov 19 DB
—
1 Apr 24 RF @ Hawkinge
Apr 24 **Snipe** (Mar 26)
Mar 26 **Woodcock II** (Jan 28)
14 Oct 26 to Upavon
Jan 28 **Gamecock I** (Sep 28)
Sep 28 **Siskin IIIA** (Oct 29)
Oct 29 **Bulldog II/IIA** (Aug 36)
10 May 34 to Kenley
Aug 36 **Gauntlet II** (Jun 39)
23 May 39 to North Weald
Jun 39 **Hurricane I** (Feb 41)
2 Sep 39 to Croydon
9 Sep 39 to Debden det Wattisham
16 Dec 39 to Martlesham Heath
24 Dec 39 to Debden
30 Dec 39 to Martlesham Heath
8 Jan 40 to Debden
13 Jan 40 to Martlesham Heath
20 Jan 40 to Debden
30 Jan 40 to Martlesham Heath
11 Feb 40 to Debden
22 Feb 40 to Martlesham Heath
27 Feb 40 to Debden
5 Mar 40 to Martlesham Heath
12 Mar 40 to Debden
19 Mar 40 to Martlesham Heath
20 Mar 40 to Debden
23 Mar 40 to Martlesham Heath

27 Mar 40 to Debden
5 Apr 40 to Martlesham Heath
13 Apr 40 to Debden
23 Apr 40 to Martlesham Heath
30 Apr 40 to Debden
7 May 40 to Hawkinge
22 May 40 to Debden
25 May 40 to Kenley
8 Jun 40 to Le Mans
15 Jun 40 to Dinard
18 Jun 40 to Jersey
det Guernsey
19 Jun 40 to Debden
19 Aug 40 to Tangmere
2 Sep 40 to Debden
9 Oct 40 to Martlesham Heath
26 Feb 41 to Croydon
Feb 41 **Hurricane IIA** (Apr 41)
1 Apr 41 to Martlesham Heath
5 Apr 41 to Castletown
Apr 41 **Hurricane I** (Aug 41)
dets Elgin, Sumburgh
16 Jun 41 to Elgin
dets Sumburgh, Dyce, Montrose
Jul 41 **Hurricane IIB** (Nov 41)
17 Sep 41 to Tain
31 Oct 41 to Catterick
10 Nov 41 en route ME, diverted to FE
16 Jan 42 to Mingaladon
Jan 42 **Hurricane IIA** (Jun 42)
dets, Akyab, 'Highland Queen', Zayatkwin, Magwe
2 Mar 42 to 'Highland Queen'
6 Mar 42 to Mingaladon
7 Mar 42 to Zigon
9 Mar 42 to 'Park Lane'
11 Mar 42 to Magwe
29 Mar 42 to Loiwing
dets Lashio, Pankham Fort
14 Apr 42 to Alipore
May 42 to Jessore
Jun 42 **Hurricane IIB** (Aug 42)
23 Aug 42 to Red Road
Aug 42 **Hurricane IIC** (Jun 44)
6 Mar 43 to Kalyanpur
17 Apr 43 to Alipore
30 May 43 to Agartala
28 Aug 43 to China Bay
14 Jan 44 to Minneriya
Mar 44 **Spitfire VIII** (Jun 45)
29 Jun 44 to Vavuniya
det China Bay
20 Nov 44 to Sapam
30 Nov 44 to Palel
18 Dec 44 to Taukkyan
20 Jan 45 to Tabingaung
3 Feb 45 to Ywadon
11 Apr 45 to Meiktila
18 Apr 45 to Thedaw
28 Apr 45 to 'Tennant'
11 May 45 to Thedaw
18 Jun 45 to Madura
Jun 45 **Spitfire XIVE** (Feb 48)
18 Sep 45 to Kelanang via HMS *Trumpeter*
21 Sep 45 to Kuala Lumpur
23 Sep 45 to Tengah
25 Sep 45 to Seletar
8 Jan 46 to Kuala Lumpur
12 Apr 46 to Seletar
23 Apr 46 to Iwakuni via HMS *Vengeance*
6 May 46 to Miho
23 Feb 48 DB (date retrospectively amended to 31 Mar 48)
—
11 Feb 49 RF @ Chivenor — No 691 Sqn renumbered
Feb 49 **Martinet TT 1** (Jan 50)
Feb 49 **Spitfire LF 16E** (Mar 51)
Feb 49 **Harvard T.2B** (Mar 51)
Feb 49 **Oxford T.2** (Mar 51)
Jun 49 **Beaufighter TT 10** (Mar 51)
13 Mar 51 DB
—
1 Jun 56 RF @ Wahn
Jun 56 **Canberra PR 7** (Dec 69)
3 Apr 57 to Wildenrath
31 Dec 69 DB
—
1 Sep 70 RF @ Brüggen
Sep 70 **Phantom FGR 2** (Jan 76)
30 Jan 76 DB
—
1 Sep 75 training at Brüggen as No 17 Sqn (Designate)
—
1 Feb 76 RF @ Brüggen
Feb 76 **Jaguar GR 1** (Mar 85)
1 Mar 85 DB
—
6 Jan 85 training at Brüggen as No 17 Sqn (Designate)
—
1 Mar 85 RF @ Brüggen
Mar 85 **Tornado GR 1** ( )

18 Sqn

11 May 15 F @ Northolt — nucleus from No 4 RAS
May 15 **Martinsyde S.1** (Oct 15)
May 15 **Shorthorn** (Nov 15)
15 **Bristol Scout** (15)
16 Aug 15 to Mousehold Heath
Sep 15 **Vickers FB 5** (Apr 16)
18 Nov 15 to St-Omer
25 Nov 15 to Treizennes
12 Feb 16 to Auchel
Jan 16 **DH 2** (Apr 16)
Mar 16 **Martinsyde G.100** (Jun 16)
1 Apr 16 to Bruay
Apr 16 **FE 2B** (Jun 17)
22 Jul 16 to Treizennes
2 Aug 16 to Bruay
6 Sep 16 to Laviéville
10 Dec 16 to St-Leger-les-Authie
27 Jan 17 to Bertangles
25 May 17 to Baizieux
Jun 17 **DH 4** (Oct 18)
10 Jul 17 to La Bellevue
11 Oct 17 to Auchel
2 Feb 18 to Treizennes
9 Apr 18 to Serny
17 Aug 18 to Maisoncelle
Sep 18 **DH 9A** (Aug 19)
13 Oct 18 to Le Hameau
27 Oct 18 to La Brayelle
28 Nov 18 to Maubeuge
24 Jan 19 to Bickendorf
1 May 19 to Merheim
9 Sep 19 to Weston-on-the-Green as a cadre
31 Dec 19 DB
—
20 Oct 31 RF @ Upper Heyford
Oct 31 **Hart** (May 36)
7 Jan 36 to Bircham Newton
Apr 36 **Hind** (May 39)
7 Sep 36 to Upper Heyford
May 39 **Blenheim I** (May 40)
24 Sep 39 to Roye/Amy
18 Oct 39 to Rosières-en-Santerre
Mar 40 **Blenheim IV** (Sep 42)
17 May 40 to Guyencourt
18 May 40 to Crécy
19 May 40 to Lympne
21 May 40 to Watton
26 May 40 to Gatwick
12 Jun 40 to West Raynham
9 Sep 40 to Great Massingham
3 Apr 41 to Oulton
13 Jul 41 to Horsham St Faith
det Manston
13 Oct 41 air echelon det Luqa, to Egypt (Helwan, LG 05, Fuka) in Jan 42. 21 Mar 42 absorbed by local units
5 Nov 41 to Oulton
5 Dec 41 to Horsham St Faith
9 Dec 41 to Wattisham
4 Mar 42 re-established @ Wattisham
dets Dundonald, Heathfield
24 Aug 42 to West Raynham
Sep 42 **Blenheim V** (Apr 43)
11 Nov 42 to Blida
30 Nov 42 to Canrobert
det Setif
Feb 43 **Boston III** (Oct 44)
7 Mar 43 to Oulmene
17 Apr 43 to Souk el Khemis ('Kings Cross')
1 Jun 43 to Grombalia
1 Aug 43 to Monte Lungo
det Ponte Olivo
9 Aug 43 to Comiso
24 Aug 43 to Gerbini
8 Oct 43 to Brindisi
31 Oct 43 to Celone
16 Feb 44 to Marcianese
15 Jun 44 to La Banca
27 Jun 44 to Tarquinia
18 Jul 44 to Cecina
Jul 44 **Boston IV** (Mar 46)
15 Oct 44 to Falconara
Jan 45 **Boston V** (Mar 46)
8 Mar 45 to Forli
10 May 45 to Aviano
14 Sep 45 to Hassani
31 Mar 46 DB
—
1 Sep 46 RF @ Ein Shemar — No 621 Sqn renumbered
Sep 46 **Lancaster GR 3** (Oct 46)
15 Sep 46 DB — absorbed as 'B' Flt, No 38 Sqn
—
15 Mar 47 RF @ Butterworth — No 1300 Flt renumbered
Mar 47 **Mosquito FB 6** (Nov 47)
16 Apr 47 to Mingaladon
1 Oct 47 to Butterworth
15 Nov 47 DB
—
8 Dec 47 RF @ Netheravon
Dec 47 **Dakota** (Feb 50)
11 Dec 47 to Waterbeach
dets Wunstorf, Fassberg, Lübeck for BAL
5 Sep 48 to Oakington
det Lübeck for BAL
6 Oct 49 to Waterbeach
20 Feb 50 DB
—
1 Aug 53 RF @ Scampton
Aug 53 **Canberra B.2** (Jan 57)
22 May 55 to Upwood
1 Feb 57 DB
—
17 Dec 58 RF @ Finningley — from 'C' Flt, No 199 Sqn
Dec 58 **Valiant B.1** (Mar 63)
31 Mar 63 DB
—
27 Jan 64 RF @ Odiham — from the Wessex Trials Unit
Jan 64 **Wessex HC 2** (Nov 80)
1 Jan 65 to Gütersloh
5 Jan 68 to Acklington
8 Aug 69 to Odiham
1 Sep 70 to Gütersloh
30 Nov 80 DB
—
4 Aug 81 RF @ Odiham
Aug 81 **Chinook HC 1** ( )
det Port Stanley
6 Aug 83 to Gütersloh

19 Sqn

1 Sep 15 F @ Castle Bromwich — nucleus from No 5 RAS
Sep 15 **Shorthorn** (Oct 15)
Sep 15 **Avro 504** (Oct 15)
Sep 15 **Caudron G.III** (Oct 15)
Oct 15 **BE 2C** (Dec 15)
Dec 15 **RE 7** (Dec 15)
31 Jan 16 to Netheravon
Feb 16 **Avro 504** (Jun 16)
Feb 16 **Caudron G.III** (Jul 16)
Feb 16 **Bristol Scout** (Jul 16)
Feb 16 **Martinsyde S.1** (Jul 16)
Feb 16 **BE 2C** (Jul 16)
Feb 16 **FE 2B** (Jul 16)
Feb 16 **RE 5** (Jul 16)
Feb 16 **RE 7** (Jul 16)
Feb 16 **BE 12** (Feb 17)
29 Mar 16 to Filton
30 Jul 16 to St-Omer
1 Aug 16 to Fienvillers
Oct 16 **SPAD S. VII** (Jan 18)
2 Apr 17 to Vert Galand
31 May 17 to Liettres
14 Aug 17 to Poperinghe
5 Sep 17 to Bailleul (Asylum Ground)
Nov 17 **Dolphin** (Feb 19)
25 Dec 17 to Ste-Marie-Cappel
13 Feb 18 to Bailleul
23 Mar 18 to Ste-Marie-Cappel
31 Mar 18 to Savy
17 Aug 18 to Cappelle
23 Sep 18 to Savy
24 Oct 18 to Abscon
9 Feb 19 to Genech
18 Feb 19 to Ternhill as a cadre
31 Dec 19 DB
—
1 Apr 23 RF @ Duxford — one flt only, attached to No 2 FTS
Apr 23 **Snipe** (Dec 24)
1 Jun 24 brought up to squadron strength
Dec 24 **Grebe II** (Apr 28)
Mar 28 **Siskin IIIA** (Sep 31)
Sep 31 **Bulldog IIA** (Jan 35)
Jan 35 **Gauntlet I** (Mar 39)
Sep 36 **Gauntlet II** (Feb 39)
Aug 38 **Spitfire I** (Dec 40)
17 Apr 40 to Horsham St Faith
16 May 40 to Duxford
25 May 40 to Hornchurch
5 Jun 40 to Duxford
Jun 40 **Spitfire IB** (Sep 40)
25 Jun 40 to Fowlmere
3 Jul 40 to Duxford
24 Jul 40 to Fowlmere
det Eastchurch
Sep 40 **Spitfire IIA** (Nov 41)
1 Nov 40 to Duxford
6 Feb 41 to Fowlmere
dets West Malling
16 Aug 41 to Matlask
Oct 41 **Spitfire VB** (Aug 43)
1 Dec 41 to Ludham
4 Apr 42 to Hutton Cranswick
6 May 42 to Perranporth
1 Jun 42 to Warmwell
14 Jun 42 to Perranporth
1 Jul 42 to Biggin Hill
7 Jul 42 to Perranporth
23 Jul 42 to Colerne
31 Jul 42 to Perranporth
16 Aug 42 to Southend
20 Aug 42 to Perranporth
Sep 42 **Spitfire VC** (Mar 43)
dets Exeter, Fairwood Common, Harrowbeer
1 Mar 43 to Middle Wallop
10 Mar 43 to Membury
13 Mar 43 to Middle Wallop
5 Apr 43 to Fairlop
17 May 43 to Digby
4 Jun 43 to Matlask
20 Jun 43 to Gravesend
6 Jun 43 to Bognor
2 Jul 43 to Newchurch
18 Aug 43 to Kingsnorth
Aug 43 **Spitfire IX** (Jan 44)
29 Sep 43 to Weston Zoyland
15 Oct 43 to Gatwick
24 Oct 43 to Gravesend
Jan 44 **Mustang III** (Apr 45)
15 Apr 44 to Ford
12 May 44 to Southend
20 May 44 to Funtington

15 Jun 44 to Ford
25 Jun 44 to B 7/Martragny
15 Jul 44 to B 12/Ellon
2 Sep 44 to B 24/St-André-de-l'Eure
3 Sep 44 to B 40/Beauvais/Nivillers
9 Sep 44 to B 60/Grimbergen
28 Sep 44 to Matlask
14 Oct 44 to Andrews Field
13 Feb 45 to Peterhead
Apr 45 **Mustang IV** (Mar 46)
23 May 45 to Acklington
13 Aug 45 to Bradwell Bay
7 Sep 45 to Molesworth
Mar 46 **Spitfire LF 16E** (Nov 46)
2 May 46 to Lübeck
29 Jun 46 to Wittering
10 Sep 46 to Biggin Hill
16 Sep 46 to Wittering
Oct 46 **Hornet F.1** (May 48)
23 Apr 47 to Church Fenton
Mar 48 **Hornet F.3** (Jan 51)
Jan 51 **Meteor F.4** (Jun 51)
Apr 51 **Meteor F.8** (Jan 57)
Oct 56 **Hunter F.6** (Feb 63)
29 Jun 59 to Leconfield
Dec 62 **Lightning F.2** (Oct 69)
23 Sep 65 to Gütersloh
Jan 68 **Lightning F.2A** (Dec 76)
31 Dec 76 DB
—
1 Oct 76 training at Wildenrath as No 19 Sqn (Designate)
—
1 Jan 77 RF @ Wildenrath
Jan 77 **Phantom FGR 2** ( )

20 Sqn

1 Sep 15 F @ Netheravon — nucleus from No 7 RAS
Sep 15 **Curtiss JN 3**(Jan 16)
Sep 15 **BE 2C** (Jan 16)
Oct 15 **Martinsyde S.1** (Nov 15)
5 Dec 15 to Filton
Dec 15 **FE 2B** (Jun 16)
6 Jan 16 to St-Omer
3 Jan 16 to Clairmarais
Feb 16 **FE 2A** (Mar 16)
Feb 16 **Martinsyde G.100** (Jun 16)
Jun 16 **FE 2D** (Sep 17)
Sep 16 **RE 7** (Jan 17)
9 Jan 17 to Boisdinghem
5 Apr 17 to Ste-Marie-Cappel
Aug 17 **Bristol F2b Fighter** (May 19)
3 Apr 18 to Boisdinghem
6 Aug 18 to Vignacourt
6 Sep 18 to Suzanne
4 Sep 18 to Proyart
7 Oct 18 to Moislains
5 Oct 18 to Iris Farm
3 Dec 18 to Ossogne
0 Apr 19 en route India
6 Jun 19 to Risalpur
Jul 19 **Bristol F2b Fighter** (Mar 32) dets Tank, Sorarogha
1 Jul 19 to Parachinar dets Risalpur, Bannu
2 Sep 19 to Bannu det Tank
8 Jul 20 to Parachinar det Tank
5 Nov 20 to Tank
0 Apr 21 to Parachinar
7 Oct 21 to Ambala
4 Oct 22 to Quetta det Loralai
5 Jan 25 to Peshawar det Miranshah
2 May 25 to Kohat dets Miranshah
2 Oct 25 to Peshawar dets Miranshah, Quetta, Manzai
Jan 32 **Wapiti** (Dec 35) dets Miranshah, Hassani Abdel, Jhelum, Quetta
Dec 35 **Audax** (Dec 41)
2 Dec 36 to Miranshah
24 Dec 36 to Peshawar dets Risalpur, Hassani Abdel, Arawali
7 Jan 37 to Miranshah
16 Jan 37 to Peshawar
20 Apr 37 to Miranshah
14 Aug 37 to Peshawar det Miranshah
13 May 38 to Miranshah
20 May 39 to Peshawar dets Miranshah, Kohat, Parachinar
29 Aug 39 to Miranshah dets Manzai, Peshawar
29 Oct 39 to Peshawar det Miranshah
8 Apr 40 to Kohat dets Miranshah, Peshawar, Risalpur, Quetta, Juhu, St Thomas Mount
10 Jun 41 to Begumpet dets Poona, Peshawar, Saugor, Deolali, Delhi, Bangalore, Juhu, Miranshah
Dec 41 **Lysander II** (Apr 43)
2 Mar 42 to Peshawar
1 May 42 to Chakulia
5 May 42 to Jamshedpur dets Tezpur, Dinjan, Feni, Imphal, Chittagong
11 Dec 42 to Charra dets Imphal, Chittagong, Maungdaw
Jan 43 **Hurricane IIB** (May 43)
Mar 43 **Hurricane IID** (Sep 45)
16 May 43 to Kalyan det Poona
5 Dec 43 to Nidania
25 Feb 44 to Mardhaibunia dets Lanka, Ramu
25 May 44 to Chiringa dets Imphal
31 Jul 44 to Trichinopoly dets Cuttack
21 Sep 44 to St Thomas Mount dets Cuttack, Imphal, Ranchi, Sambre
Dec 44 **Hurricane IV** (Sep 45)
23 Dec 44 to Sapam
17 Jan 45 to Thazi
12 Feb 45 to Monywa
11 Apr 45 to Thedaw
28 Apr 45 to 'Tennant'
8 May 45 to Thedaw
5 Jun 45 to Chettinad
7 Jun 45 to St Thomas Mount
27 Aug 45 to Amarda Road
Sep 45 **Spitfire VIII** (Apr 46)
28 Sep 45 to Don Muang
Nov 45 **Spitfire XIV** (Dec 46)
27 Jan 46 to Mingaladon
12 Apr 46 to Agra
May 46 **Tempest F.2** (Jul 47)
25 Jul 47 to Mauripur
1 Aug 47 DB
—
11 Feb 49 RF @ Llanbedr — No 631 Sqn renumbered
Feb 49 **Martinet TT 1** (Jun 50)
Feb 49 **Vampire F.1** (Mar 51)
Feb 49 **Spitfire LF 16E** (Sep 51)
Feb 49 **Harvard T.2B** (Sep 51)
19 Jul 49 to Valley
Oct 49 **Oxford T.2** (Sep 51)
Nov 49 **Vampire F.3** (Sep 51)
Feb 50 **Beaufighter TT 10** (Sep 51)
16 Sep 51 DB
—
14 Jun 52 RF @ Jever
Jun 52 **Vampire FB 9** (Dec 53)
28 Jul 52 to Oldenburg
Nov 52 **Vampire FB 5** (Jan 54)
Oct 53 **Sabre F.4** (Nov 55)
Nov 55 **Hunter F.4** (Jun 57)
May 57 **Hunter F.6** (Dec 60)
23 Sep 57 to Ahlhorn
30 Aug 58 to Gütersloh
30 Dec 60 DB
—
1 Sep 61 RF @ Tengah
Sep 61 **Hunter FGA 9** (Feb 70) dets Chieng Mai, Kuching, Labuan
Jan 69 **Pioneer CC 1** (Dec 69)
18 Feb 70 DB
—
1 Dec 70 RF @ Wildenrath
Dec 70 **Harrier GR 1** (Mar 73)
Oct 72 **Harrier GR 3** (Feb 77)
1 Mar 77 DB
—
1 Mar 77 RF @ Brüggen
Mar 77 **Jaguar GR 1** (Jun 84)
30 Jun 84 DB
—
1 Apr 84 training at Laarbruch as No 20 Sqn (Designate)
—
30 Jun 84 RF @ Laarbruch
Jun 84 **Tornado GR 1** ( )

21 Sqn

23 Jul 15 F @ Netheravon — nucleus from No 8 RAS
Jul 15 **RE 7** (Aug 16)
23 Jan 16 to Boisdinghem
Feb 16 **Bristol Scout** (Mar 16)
Apr 16 **BE 2C** (Aug 16)
2 Apr 16 to Ste-André-aux-Bois
Apr 16 **BE 2E** (Aug 16)
Jun 16 **Martinsyde G.100** (Jun 16)
19 Jun 16 to Fienvillers
28 Jul 16 to Boisdinghem
Aug 16 **BE 12** (Feb 17)
25 Aug 16 to Bertangles
Feb 17 **RE 8** (Feb 19)
16 Feb 17 to Boisdinghem
24 Mar 17 to Droglandt
19 May 17 to La Lovie
13 Apr 18 to St-Inglevert
22 Apr 18 to Floringhem
19 Oct 18 to Hesdigneul
25 Oct 18 to Seclin
11 Nov 18 to Froidmont
16 Nov 18 to Sweveghem
18 Dec 18 to Coucou
14 Feb 19 to Fowlmere as a cadre
1 Oct 19 DB
—
3 Dec 35 RF @ Bircham Newton — nucleus from No 82 Sqn
Dec 35 **Hind** (Aug 38)
25 Jul 36 to Abbotsinch
3 Nov 36 to Lympne
15 Aug 38 to Eastchurch
Aug 38 **Blenheim I** (Sep 39)
2 Mar 39 to Watton
Sep 39 **Blenheim IV** (Mar 42) dets Bassingbourn, Horsham St Faith, Bodney
24 Jun 40 to Lossiemouth
30 Oct 40 to Watton dets Bodney, Manston, Lossiemouth, Luqa
25 Dec 41 to Luqa
14 Mar 42 DB
—
14 Mar 42 RF @ Bodney
Mar 42 **Blenheim IV** (Jul 42) det Abbotsinch
May 42 **Ventura I & II** (Sep 43)
31 Oct 42 to Methwold det Exeter
1 Apr 43 to Oulton
19 Aug 43 to Hartford Bridge
27 Sep 43 to Sculthorpe
Sep 43 **Mosquito VI** (Nov 47)
31 Dec 43 to Hunsdon
17 Apr 44 to Gravesend det Dunsfold
18 Jun 44 to Thorney Island
6 Feb 45 to B 87/Rosières-en-Santerre
17 Apr 45 to B 58/Melsbroek
9 Nov 45 to Sylt
30 Nov 45 to Gütersloh
30 Mar 46 to Sylt
27 Apr 46 to Gütersloh
27 Jun 46 to Handorf det Nuremburg/Furth
9 Aug 46 to Gütersloh
3 Sep 46 to Wahn
6 Sep 46 to Manston
18 Sep 46 to Wahn
26 Sep 46 to Gütersloh
6 Nov 46 to Sylt
12 Dec 46 to Gütersloh
7 Nov 47 DB
—
21 Sep 53 RF @ Scampton
Sep 53 **Canberra B.2** (Jun 57)
1 Jun 55 to Waddington
30 Jun 57 DB
—
1 Oct 58 RF @ Upwood — No 542 Sqn renumbered
Oct 58 **Canberra B.2** (Jan 59)
Oct 58 **Canberra B.6** (Jan 59) det Laverton
15 Jan 59 DB
—
1 May 59 RF @ Benson
May 59 **Twin Pioneer CC 1** (Sep 67)
15 Sep 59 to Eastleigh
1 Jun 65 to Khormaksar
Aug 65 **Dakota** (Sep 67)
Feb 67 **Andover CC 2** (Sep 67)
9 Sep 67 DB
—
3 Feb 69 RF @ Andover — Western Communications Sqn redesignated
Feb 69 **Devon C.2** (Jan 76)
Feb 69 **Pembroke C.1** (Jan 76)
31 Jan 76 DB

22 Sqn

1 Sep 15 F @ Gosport (Fort Grange) — nucleus from No 13 Sqn
Sep 15 **Longhorn** (Oct 15)
Sep 15 **BE 2C** (Mar 16)
Sep 15 **Bleriot XI** (Mar 16)
24 Sep 15 to Gosport (Fort Rowner)
Oct 15 **Caudron G.III** (Oct 15)
Oct 15 **BE 8A** (Nov 15)
Oct 15 **Curtiss JN 3** (Jan 16)
Oct 15 **Martinsyde S.1A** (Jun 16)
Dec 15 **Bristol Scout** (Mar 16)
Jan 16 **Avro 504** (Mar 16)
Mar 16 **FE 2B** (Aug 17)
1 Apr 16 to St-Omer
1 Apr 16 to Vert Galand
16 Apr 16 to Bertangles
27 Apr 17 to Chipilly
1 May 17 to Flez
3 Jul 17 to Warloy
5 Jul 17 to Izel-le-Hameau
Jul 17 **Bristol F2b Fighter** (Aug 19)
14 Aug 17 to Boisdinghem
10 Sep 17 to Estrée-Blanche
22 Jan 18 to Auchel
2 Feb 18 to Treizennes
21 Mar 18 to Serny
23 Mar 18 to Vert Galand
9 Apr 18 to Serny
30 Jul 18 to Maisoncelle
22 Oct 18 to Izel-le-Hameau
26 Oct 18 to Aniche
17 Nov 18 to Aulnoye

22 Nov 18 to Wiheries
20 Dec 18 to Nivelles
21 May 19 to Spich
31 Aug 19 to Ford Junction as a cadre
20 Nov 19 to Croydon
31 Dec 19 DB
—
24 Jul 23 RF @ Martlesham Heath as A & AEE trials unit
Jul 23 **DH 9A** (Oct 26)
Oct 26 **Horsley** (May 34)
1 May 34 DB — note that equipment was largely notional and would have been that operated in the event of mobilisation
—
1 May 34 RF @ Donibristle
May 34 **Vildebeeste I** (Oct 35)
May 35 **Vildebeeste III** (Feb 40)
10 Oct 35 to Hal Far
29 Aug 36 to Donibristle
10 Mar 38 to Thorney Island
Mar 38 **Vildebeeste IV** (Feb 40)
Sep 39 **Vildebeeste I** (Nov 39)
Nov 39 **Beaufort I** (Jul 44)
8 Apr 40 to North Coates dets Manston, St Eval, Wick
25 Jun 41 to Thorney Island
28 Oct 41 to St Eval
1 Feb 42 to Thorney Island
16 Feb 42 en route FE by sea. Air echelon flew via ME and was retained for operations from Luqa, Sidi Barrani & LG 86.
28 Apr 42 to Ratmalana
30 Sep 42 to Minneriya
15 Feb 43 to Vavuniya
21 Apr 44 to Ratmalana
May 44 **Beaufighter X** (Sep 45)
7 Jul 44 to Vavuniya
23 Dec 44 to Kumbhirgram
26 Jan 45 to Jorri
18 Apr 45 to Chiringa
21 Jun 45 to Gannavaram
30 Sep 45 DB
—
1 May 46 RF @ Seletar — No 89 Sqn renumbered
May 46 **Mosquito FB 6** (Aug 46)
15 Aug 46 DB
—
15 Feb 55 RF @ Thorney Island
Mar 55 **Sycamore HC 12** (Jan 56)
Jun 55 **Whirlwind HAR 2** (Aug 62) dets Valley, Felixstowe, Martlesham Heath
4 Jun 56 to St Mawgan dets Chivenor, Felixstowe, Tangmere, Thorney Island, Valley, Manston, Coltishall
Aug 62 **Whirlwind HAR 10** (Nov 81)
1 Apr 74 to Thorney Island dets Valley, Chivenor, Coltishall, Brawdy
26 Jan 76 to Finningley dets Valley, Chivenor, Brawdy, Leuchars, Manston, Leconfield
Jun 76 **Wessex HC 2** ( )

23 Sqn

1 Sep 15 F @ Gosport (Fort Grange) — nucleus from No 14 Sqn
Sep 15 **Bleriot XI** (Oct 15)
Sep 15 **Caudron G.III** (Dec 15)
Sep 15 **Shorthorn** (Jan 16)
Sep 15 **Avro 504A** (Mar 16)
Oct 15 **Martinsyde S.1** (Mar 16)
Oct 15 **BE 2C** (Mar 16) det Suttons Farm
Jan 16 **FE 2B** (Apr 17)
15 Mar 16 to St-Omer
16 Mar 16 to Fienvillers
18 Mar 16 to Le Hameau
Mar 16 **Martinsyde G.100** (May 16)
1 Sep 16 to Fienvillers
5 Sep 16 to Vert Galand
Feb 17 **SPAD S.VII** (Apr 18)
5 Mar 17 to Baizieux
23 May 17 to Auchel
29 May 17 to Bruay dets Erquinghem
13 Jun 17 to La Lovie
Dec 17 **SPAD S.XIII** (May 18)
16 Feb 18 to Matigny
22 Mar 18 to Moreuil
28 Mar 18 to Bertangles
29 Apr 18 to St-Omer
Apr 18 **Dolphin** (Mar 19)
16 May 18 to Bertangles
13 Sep 18 to Cappy
11 Oct 18 to Hancourt
25 Oct 18 to Bertry East
3 Dec 18 to Clermont
15 Mar 19 to Waddington as a cadre
31 Dec 19 DB
—
1 Jul 25 RF @ Henlow
Jul 25 **Snipe** (Apr 26)
Apr 26 **Gamecock I** (Sep 31)
6 Feb 27 to Kenley
Jul 31 **Bulldog IIA** (Apr 33)
Jul 31 **Hart Fighter** (Jul 32)
Jul 32 **Demon** (Dec 38)
17 Sep 32 to Biggin Hill
21 Dec 36 to Northolt
16 May 38 to Wittering
Dec 38 **Blenheim IF** (Apr 41)
31 May 40 to Collyweston
16 Aug 40 to Wittering
12 Sep 40 to Ford
Mar 41 **Havoc I** (Aug 42) dets Manston, Tangmere, Bradwell Bay, Middle Wallop
Feb 42 **Boston III** (Aug 42)
Jun 42 **Mosquito II** (Aug 43)
6 Aug 42 to Manston
14 Aug 42 to Bradwell Bay
21 Aug 42 to Manston det Bradwell Bay
13 Oct 42 to Bradwell Bay
27 Dec 42 to Luqa
May 43 **Mosquito VI** (Sep 45) dets Sigonella, Gerbini, Pomigliano
7 Dec 43 to Alghero det Blida
2 Jun 44 to Little Snoring
Aug 45 **Mosquito XXX** (Sep 45)
25 Sep 45 DB
—
1 Sep 46 RF @ Wittering — No 219 Sqn renumbered
Sep 46 **Mosquito NF 30** (Nov 46)
22 Sep 46 to Lübeck
Oct 40 **Mosquito NF 36** (Jun 52)
4 Oct 46 to Wittering
23 Jan 47 to Coltishall
28 Apr 47 to Acklington
6 Jun 47 to Coltishall
29 Aug 47 to Lübeck
11 Sep 47 to Coltishall
11 Mar 48 to Lübeck
25 Mar 48 to Coltishall
4 Oct 48 to Acklington
16 Nov 48 to Coltishall
19 Nov 49 to Church Fenton
22 Sep 50 to Coltishall
Sep 51 **Vampire NF 10** (Jan 54)
15 Jan 52 to Horsham St Faith
4 Jul 52 to Coltishall
Nov 53 **Venom NF 2** (Mar 56)
Sep 55 **Venom NF 3** (May 57)
12 Oct 56 to Horsham St Faith
Mar 57 **Javelin FAW 4** (Jul 59)
28 May 57 to Coltishall
7 Sep 58 to Horsham St Faith
Apr 59 **Javelin FAW 7** (Jul 60)
5 Jun 59 to Coltishall
31 Mar 60 to Horsham St Faith
Apr 60 **Javelin FAW 9R** (Oct 64)
11 Jul 60 to Coltishall
Apr 62 **Javelin FAW 7** (Sep 62)
9 Mar 63 to Leuchars
Aug 64 **Lightning F.3** (Nov 67)
May 67 **Lightning F.6** (Oct 75)
May 72 **Lightning F.3** (Oct 75)
31 Oct 75 DB
—
6 Oct 75 training at Coningsby as No 23 Sqn (Designate)
—
1 Nov 75 RF @ Coningsby
Nov 75 **Phantom FGR 2** (Mar 83)
25 Feb 76 to Wattisham
30 Mar 83 DB
—
30 Mar 83 RF @ Port Stanley — from det of No 29 Sqn
Mar 83 **Phantom FGR 2** ( )
21 Apr 86 to Mount Pleasant

24 Sqn

1 Sep 15 F @ Hounslow — nucleus from No 17 Sqn
Oct 15 **Curtiss JN 4** (Nov 15)
Oct 15 **Caudron G.III** (Nov 15)
Oct 15 **Avro 504** (Nov 15)
Oct 15 **BE 2C** (Nov 15)
Oct 15 **Bleriot XI** (Nov 15)
Oct 15 **Bristol Scout** (Nov 15)
Oct 15 **Longhorn** (Nov 15)
Oct 15 **Shorthorn** (Nov 15)
Nov 15 **Vickers FB 5** (Feb 16)
Jan 16 **DH 2** (Jun 17)
7 Feb 16 to St-Omer
10 Feb 16 to Bertangles
17 Dec 16 to Chipilly
17 Apr 17 to Flez
May 17 **DH 5** (Jan 18)
10 Jul 17 to Baizieux
23 Sep 17 to Teteghem
24 Nov 17 to Marieux
Dec 17 **SE 5A** (Jan 19)
30 Dec 17 to Villers-Bretonneux
26 Jan 18 to Matigny
22 Mar 18 to Moreuil
26 Mar 18 to Bertangles
28 Mar 18 to Conteville
14 Aug 18 to Bertangles
8 Sep 18 to Cappy
6 Oct 18 to Athies
27 Oct 18 to Busigny
11 Nov 18 to Bisseghem
16 Nov 18 to Ennetières
11 Dec 18 to Bisseghem
12 Feb 19 to London Colney as a cadre
19 Sep 19 to Uxbridge
1 Feb 20 re-established at Kenley from the Air Council Inspection Sqn
Feb 20 **Bristol F2b Fighter** (Jul 30)
Jul 20 **DH 9A** (Jun 27)
15 Jan 27 to Northolt
Jan 27 **Avro 504N** (33)
Jan 27 **Moth** (Jul 33)
Jun 28 **Wapiti** (30)
Jul 28 **Fairey IIIF** (33)
Jul 30 **Tomtit** (33)
Nov 31 **Tutor** (Oct 32)
Jan 33 **Hart C** (Jul 41)
Jun 33 **Tiger Moth** (Jun 38)
10 Jul 33 to Hendon
Jul 33 **Audax** (Feb 38)
Mar 35 **Dragon Rapide/Dominie** (Oct 44)
Jul 37 **Nighthawk** (Sep 38)
Oct 37 **DH 86 Express** (Mar 43)
Jun 38 **Magister I** (40)
Jun 38 **Anson I** (Jun 38)
Oct 38 **Mentor** (Aug 44)
Nov 38 **Vega Gull** (Oct 42)
Sep 39 **Leopard Moth** (Apr 40)
Sep 39 **Fox Moth** (Jul 40)
Sep 39 **Dragon** (Jul 41)
Sep 39 **Electra** (May 42)
Sep 39 **Percival Q.6** (Oct 42)
Oct 39 **Puss Moth** (Apr 40)
Dec 39 **Flamingo** (Nov 44)
Mar 40 **Envoy** (Oct 40)
Mar 40 **Whitney Straight** (Apr 42
Apr 40 **Phoenix** (Dec 40)
May 40 dets Reims, Echemines
May 40 **SM 73P** (May 40)
May 40 **DC 3** (Jun 40)
May 40 **Anson I** (Jul 40)
May 40 **Ensign** (Nov 40)
Jun 40 **Hornet Moth** (Oct 42)
Jul 40 **Oxford** (Oct 44)
Feb 41 **Reliant** (Sep 43)
May 41 **Cygnet** (Jan 42)
May 41 **Botha** (Oct 42)
May 41 **Beech 17 Traveller** (45)
Jun 41 **Heck III** (Aug 41)
Jun 41 **Leopard Moth** (Apr 42)
Aug 41 **Hudson I** (Apr 43)
Sep 41 **Hudson II** (Feb 42)
Sep 42 **Messerschmitt Bf 108** (Aug 42)
Sep 41 **Hudson V** (Nov 43)
Jan 42 **Fokker XXII** (Apr 43)
Feb 42 **Hudson IV** (Jun 42)
Feb 42 **Hudson III** (Sep 45)
Jun 42 **Wicko** (Dec 42)
Jul 42 **Phoenix** (Aug 42)
Jul 42 **Hudson VI** (Jun 43)
Jul 42 **Lockheed 12** (Aug 44)
Aug 42 **Proctor** (43)
Jan 43 **Goose** (Jan 44)
Feb 43 **Wellington XVI** (Jan 44
Mar 43 **York I** (Oct 44)
Apr 43 **Dakota** (Nov 52)
Aug 44 **Anson X** ( )
Nov 44 **Skymaster I** (Feb 45)
25 Feb 46 to Bassingbourn
Jul 46 **Lancastrian C.2** (Oct 4
Jul 46 **York C.1** (Dec 51)
11 Jun 49 to Waterbeach
25 Feb 50 to Oakington
Feb 50 **Valetta C.1** (Nov 50)
27 Nov 50 to Lyneham
Nov 50 **Hastings C.1** (Jan 68)
9 Feb 51 to Topcliffe
Jun 51 **Hastings C.2** (Jan 68)
Oct 51 **Hastings C.4** ( )
6 May 53 to Abingdon
1 Jan 57 to Colerne
5 Jan 68 to Lyneham
Feb 68 **Hercules C.1** ( )
Mar 80 **Hercules C.3** ( )

25 Sqn

25 Sep 15 F @ Montrose — nucle from No 6 RAS
Sep 15 **Shorthorn** (Nov 15)
Sep 15 **Caudron G.III** (Nov 15
Sep 15 **Curtiss JN 4** (Dec 15)
Sep 15 **Martinsyde S.1** (Dec 1
Sep 15 **Avro 504** (Dec 15)
Nov 15 **BE 2C** (Dec 15)
31 Dec 15 to Thetford
Jan 16 **Vickers FB 5** (Feb 16)
Feb 16 **FE 2B** (May 17)
Feb 16 **Morane L** (Feb 16)
19 Feb 16 to Folkestone
20 Feb 16 to St-Omer
1 Apr 16 to Lozinghem
Jul 16 **FE 2C** (Jul 16)
Mar 17 **FE 2D** (Aug 17)
Jun 17 **DH 4** (Aug 19)
11 Oct 17 to Boisdinghem
3 Feb 18 to Serny
6 Mar 18 to Villers-Bretonneux
24 Mar 18 to Beauvois
29 Mar 18 to Ruisseauville
27 Oct 18 to La Brayelle
Oct 18 **DH 9A** (Oct 19)
29 Nov 18 to Maubeuge
26 May 19 to Bickendorf
7 Jul 19 to Merheim

6 Sep 19 to South Carlton
9 Oct 19 reduced to a cadre
3 Dec 19 to Scopwick
31 Jan 20 DB
—
26 Apr 20 RF @ Hawkinge
Apr 20 **Snipe** (Oct 24)
28 Sep 22 en route Turkey
1 Oct 22 to San Stephano
22 Sep 23 en route UK
3 Oct 23 to Hawkinge
Oct 24 **Grebe II** (Jul 29)
May 29 **Siskin IIIA** (Mar 32)
Feb 32 **Fury I** (37)
Nov 36 **Fury II** (Oct 37)
Oct 37 **Demon** (Jun 38)
Jun 38 **Gladiator I** (Feb 39)
6 Sep 38 to Northolt
2 Oct 38 to Hawkinge
Dec 38 **Blenheim IF** (Jan 41)
2 Aug 39 to Northolt
5 Sep 39 to Filton
4 Oct 39 to Northolt
det Martlesham Heath
6 Jan 40 to North Weald
det Martlesham Heath
0 May 40 to Hawkinge
2 May 40 to North Weald
9 Jun 40 to Martlesham Heath
2 Sep 40 to North Weald
Sep 40 **Beaufighter IF** (Jan 43)
8 Oct 40 to Debden
7 Dec 40 to Wittering
Jul 41 **Havoc I** (Aug 41)
6 Jan 42 to Ballyhalbert
7 May 42 to Church Fenton
det Predannack
Oct 42 **Mosquito II** (Jan 44)
Aug 43 **Mosquito VI** (Sep 43)
9 Dec 43 to Acklington
Dec 43 **Mosquito XVII** (Oct 44)
5 Feb 44 to Coltishall
Sep 44 **Mosquito XXX** (Sep 46)
7 Oct 44 to Castle Camps
Jan 45 **Mosquito VI** (Feb 45)
4 Jul 45 to Bradwell Bay
Aug 45 to Castle Camps
5 Oct 45 to Lübeck
Oct 45 to Castle Camps
Jan 46 to Boxted
7 Jan 46 to Lübeck
Feb 46 to Boxted
7 Apr 46 to Lübeck
May 46 to Boxted
3 Jul 46 to Lübeck
Aug 46 to Boxted
5 Sep 46 to West Malling
Sep 46 **Mosquito NF 36** (Oct 51)
Apr 47 to Lübeck
May 47 to West Malling
5 Jun 47 to Acklington
7 Jul 47 to West Malling
5 Jan 48 to Acklington
7 Feb 48 to West Malling
Apr 48 to Lübeck
May 48 to West Malling
Jul 51 **Vampire NF 10** (Feb 54)
Mar 54 **Meteor NF 12** (Jun 58)
Mar 54 **Meteor NF 14** (Jun 58)
Sep 57 to Tangmere
Jul 58 DB
—
Jul 58 RF @ Waterbeach — No 153 Sqn renumbered
Jul 58 **Meteor NF 12** (Apr 59)
Jul 58 **Meteor NF 14** (Apr 59)
Dec 58 **Javelin FAW 7** (Jan 61)
Dec 59 **Javelin FAW 9** (Dec 62)
Oct 61 to Leuchars
Apr 62 **Javelin FAW 7** (Sep 62)
Dec 62 DB
—
Oct 73 **Bloodhound II** @ North Coates
Jan 71 to Brüggen, Flts at Laarbruch & Wildenrath
Mar 83 to Wyton, Flts at Barkston Heath & Wattisham

26 Sqn

8 Oct 15 F @ Netheravon — from personnel of the South African Flying Unit
23 Dec 15 en route East Africa
31 Jan 16 to Mombasa
Jan 16 **BE 2C** (Jan 18)
1 Feb 16 to Mbuyuni
23 Mar 16 to Taveta
28 Mar 16 to Mbuyuni
May 16 **Henry Farman F.27** (Jan 18)
Flts @ Kahe, Marago-Opuni, Lassiti, Kwa-Lokua, Palms Mbagui, Dakawa, Morogoro, Dar-es-Salaam, Tulo, Kilwa, Dodoma, Iringa, Ubena, Itigi, Shinyanga, Songea, Narungombe, Missindyi, Nahunga, Mtua.
dets @ Fort Johnson, Mtonia, Mwembe, Songea, Likuju, Itigi, Tabora, Maranda, Mbarangandu, Tunduru.
Jan 18 to Dar-es-Salaam
8 Feb 18 en route South Africa
4 Mar 18 to Capetown
6 Jun 18 en route UK
8 Jul 18 to Blandford
8 Jul 18 DB
—
11 Oct 27 RF @ Catterick
Oct 27 **Atlas** (Sep 33)
Jul 33 **Audax** (Sep 37)
Aug 37 **Hector** (May 39)
Feb 39 **Lysander III** (Nov 40)
3 Oct 39 to Abbeville/Drucat
det Ronchin
Apr 40 to Dieppe
det Arras
15 May 40 to Laon/Athies
22 May 40 to Lympne
8 Jun 40 to West Malling
dets Cambridge, Odiham
3 Sep 40 to Gatwick
Nov 40 **Lysander III** (Jun 42)
Feb 41 **Tomahawk II** (Mar 42)
14 Jul 41 to Weston Zoyland
18 Jul 41 to Leconfield
22 Jul 41 to Gatwick
4 Aug 41 to Detling
8 Aug 41 to Gatwick
29 Aug 41 to Warmwell
1 Sep 41 to Gatwick
27 Sep 41 to Barton Bendish
30 Sep 41 to Twinwood Farm
1 Oct 41 to Upwood
2 Oct 41 to Snailwell
2 Oct 41 to Honington
3 Oct 41 to Gatwick
12 Oct 41 to Manston
15 Oct 41 to Gatwick
det Manston
22 Nov 41 to Manston
30 Nov 41 to Gatwick
Jan 42 **Mustang I** (Mar 44)
8 Feb 42 to Weston Zoyland
23 Feb 42 to Gatwick
det Madley
19 May 42 to West Malling
31 May 42 to Gatwick
26 Jul 42 to West Malling
31 Jul 42 to Gatwick
13 Jan 43 to Detling
1 Mar 43 to Stoney Cross
10 Mar 43 to Eastmanton Down
11 Mar 43 to Red Barn
13 Mar 43 to Stoney Cross
det Weston Zoyland
7 Apr 43 to Gatwick
22 Jun 43 to Detling
11 Jul 43 to Martlesham Heath
16 Jul 43 to Detling
19 Jul 43 to Ballyhalbert
21 Jul 43 to Church Fenton
det Ballyhalbert
28 Dec 43 to Hutton Cranswick
det Ballyhalbert
12 Feb 44 to Scorton
28 Feb 44 to Hutton Cranswick
Mar 44 **Spitfire VA** (Nov 44)
31 Mar 44 to Peterhead
10 Apr 44 to Dundonald
21 Apr 44 to Ayr
26 Apr 44 to Hutton Cranswick
29 Apr 44 to Lee-on-Solent
Aug 44 **Hurricane IIC** (Dec 44)
6 Oct 44 to Hawkinge
11 Oct 44 to Tangmere
1 Nov 44 to Manston
4 Nov 44 to Tangmere
Nov 44 **Mustang I** (Jun 45)
8 Dec 44 to Exeter
14 Jan 45 to Harrowbeer
21 Jan 45 to North Weald
det Coltishall
3 Apr 45 to Harrowbeer
13 Apr 45 to Cognac/Château Bernard
1 May 45 to Harrowbeer
23 May 45 to Chilbolton
Jun 45 **Spitfire XIV** (Apr 46)
20 Aug 45 to B 164/Schleswig
Sep 45 **Spitfire XI** (Apr 46)
7 Sep 45 to B 158/Lübeck
8 Dec 45 to B 170/Sylt
24 Dec 45 to B 158/Lübeck
1 Apr 46 DB
—
1 Apr 46 RF @ Wunstorf — No 41 Sqn renumbered
Apr 46 **Tempest F.5** (Jul 46)
13 Apr 46 to Fassberg
7 May 46 to Gatow
17 Jun 46 to Fassberg
Jun 46 **Tempest F.2** (Apr 49)
24 Sep 46 to Chivenor
23 Oct 46 to Fassberg
6 Jan 47 to Sylt
14 Feb 47 to Fassberg
8 May 47 to Ahlhorn
20 May 47 to Fassberg
13 Jul 47 to Zeltweg
11 Aug 47 to Fassberg
19 Nov 47 to Gütersloh
5 Dec 47 to Gatow
5 Jan 48 to Gütersloh
11 Feb 48 to Lübeck
6 Mar 48 to Gütersloh
7 Jun 48 to Lübeck
5 Jul 48 to Gütersloh
Apr 49 **Vampire FB 5** (Dec 53)
7 Jan 50 to Wunstorf
Jun 52 **Vampire FB 9** (Dec 53)
12 Aug 52 to Oldenburg
Nov 53 **Sabre F.4** (Jul 55)
Jun 55 **Hunter F.4** (Sep 57)
10 Sep 57 DB
—
7 Jun 58 RF @ Ahlhorn
Jun 58 **Hunter F. 6** (Dec 60)
8 Sep 58 to Gütersloh
30 Dec 60 DB
—
1 Jun 62 RF @ Odiham
Jun 62 **Belvedere HC 1** (Nov 65)
1 Mar 63 to Khormaksar
30 Nov 65 DB — aircraft to Singapore via HMS *Albion* for No 66 Sqn
—
3 Feb 69 RF @ Wyton — Training Command Communciations Sqn (ex-NCS) renumbered
Feb 69 **Basset CC 1** (May 74)
Feb 69 **Devon C.2** (Mar 76)
31 Mar 76 DB

27 Sqn

5 Nov 15 F @ Hounslow — nucleus from No 24 Sqn, used various aircraft
10 Dec 15 to Swingate Down
Feb 16 **Martinsyde G.100/102** (Nov 17)
1 Mar 16 to St-Omer
2 Mar 16 to Treizennes
7 Jun 16 to St-André-aux Bois
19 Jun 16 to Fienvillers
31 May 17 to Clairmarais North
12 Oct 17 to Serny
Oct 17 **DH 4** (Oct 18)
7 Mar 18 to Villers-Bretonneux
24 Mar 18 to Beauvois
29 Mar 18 to Ruisseauville
3 Jun 18 to Fourneuil
21 Jun 18 to Ruisseauville
15 Jul 18 to Chailly
7 Aug 18 to Beauvois
Sep 18 **DH 9** (Mar 19)
29 Oct 18 to Villers-lès-Cagnicourt
28 Nov 18 to Bavay
18 Mar 19 to Shotwick as a cadre
22 Jan 20 DB
—
1 Apr 20 RF @ Mianwali — No 99 Sqn renumbered
Apr 20 **DH 9A** (May 30)
14 Apr 20 to Risalpur
dets Tank, Dardoni
14 Dec 22 to Dardoni
20 Apr 23 to Risalpur
dets Dardoni, Miranshah, Arawali
26 May 25 to Peshawar
12 Oct 25 to Risalpur
det Miranshah
17 Dec 28 to Kohat
Apr 30 **Wapiti** (Nov 40)
dets Manzai, Miranshah, Juhu, Arawali, Gilgit, St Thomas Mount
25 Sep 39 to Risalpur
1 Oct 39 unit tasked as an FTS until 21 Oct 40
Oct 39 **Tiger Moth** (Oct 40)
Oct 39 **Hart** (Oct 40)
dets Kohat, Miranshah
Nov 40 **Blenheim IF** (Feb 42)
10 Feb 41 unit reverted to operational status
13 Feb 41 to Kallang
14 May 41 to Butterworth
21 Aug 41 to Sungei Patani
9 Dec 41 to Butterworth
12 Dec 41 to Kallang
24 Jan 42 to P II
18 Feb 42 DB — sqn dispersed
—
19 Sep 42 RF @ Amarda Road
Nov 42 **Beaufighter VIF** (Jul 44)
8 Jan 43 to Kanchrapara
8 Feb 43 to Agartala
Apr 43 **Mosquito II** (Jun 43)
Oct 43 **Beaufighter X** (Feb 46)
Dec 43 **Mosquito VI** (May 44)
8 Feb 44 to Parashuram
7 Mar 44 to Cholavaram
14 Sep 44 to Ranchi
18 Oct 44 to Agartala
29 Oct 44 to Dohazari
19 Nov 44 to Chiringa
dets Akyab, Monywa, Meiktila, Mingaladon
Apr 45 **Sentinel** (Jan 46)
19 Jun 45 to Akyab
dets Mingaladon
12 Oct 45 to Mingaladon
dets Kemajoran, Bayan Lepas
1 Feb 46 DB
—
1 Nov 47 RF @ Abingdon — nucleus from No 46 Sqn
24 Nov 47 to Oakington
Nov 47 **Dakota** (Nov 50)
dets Wunstorf, Fassberg for BAL
det Ikeja
1 Mar 50 to Abingdon
10 Jun 50 to Netheravon
10 Nov 50 DB

—
15 Jun 53 RF @ Scampton
Jun 53 **Canberra B.2** (Dec 57)
26 May 55 to Waddington
31 Dec 57 DB
—
1 Apr 61 RF @ Scampton
Apr 61 **Vulcan B.2** (Mar 72)
29 Mar 72 DB
—
1 Nov 73 RF @ Scampton
Nov 73 **Vulcan B.2 (MRR)** (Mar 82)
31 Mar 82 DB
—
1 May 83 RF @ Marham
May 83 **Tornado GR 1** ( )

28 Sqn

7 Nov 15 F @ Gosport (Fort Grange) — nucleus from No 22 Sqn
Nov 15 **BE 2A** ( )
Nov 15 **Avro 504** (Apr 17)
Nov 15 to Gosport (Fort Rowner)
Dec 15 **BE 2C** (Apr 17)
Apr 17 **Henry Farman F.20** (Jul 17)
Apr 17 **FE 2B** (Jul 17)
Apr 17 **DH 2** (Jul 17)
12 May 17 to Gosport (Fort Grange)
23 Jul 17 to Yatesbury
Jul 17 **Pup** (Sep 17)
Jul 17 **DH 5** (Sep 17)
Jul 17 **Avro 504** (Sep 17)
Jul 17 **Bristol Scout** (Sep 17)
Aug 17 **Camel** (Feb 19)
8 Oct 17 to St-Omer
10 Oct 17 to Droglandt
29 Oct 17 to Candas
12 Nov 17 to Milan
17 Nov 17 to Ghedi
22 Nov 17 to Verona
28 Nov 17 to Grossa
20 Aug 18 to Sarcedo
22 Oct 18 to Treviso
6 Nov 18 to Sarcedo
10 Mar 19 to Yatesbury as a cadre
29 Mar 19 to Leighterton
20 Oct 19 to Eastleigh
20 Jan 20 DB
—
1 Apr 20 RF @ Ambala — No 114 Sqn renumbered
Apr 20 **Bristol F2b Fighter** (Sep 31)
15 Oct 21 to Kohat
dets Dardoni, Tank
15 Apr 22 to Parachinar
10 Oct 22 to Kohat
12 Dec 22 to Dardoni
17 Mar 23 to Tank
19 Apr 23 to Peshawar
dets Dardoni, Hassani Abdel, Tank
5 Jan 25 to Quetta
det Poona
15 Dec 26 to Ambala
dets Poona, Bangalore, Deolali, Secunderabad, Jubbulpore, Saugor, Miranshah
13 Aug 30 to Risalpur
1 Dec 30 to Ambala
Sep 31 **Wapiti** (Jul 36)
dets Jhelum, Delhi, Peshawar, Mhow, Jullundur
Jun 36 **Audax** (Dec 41)
det Delhi
23 Apr 37 to Manzai
det Miranshah
6 Jul 37 to Ambala
dets Delhi, Juhu, Miranshah
3 Mar 39 to Kohat
dets Miranshah, Peshawar, Arawali, Manzai, Risalpur, Quetta, Drigh Road, Dum Dum, Fort Sandeman, Sialkot, Jullundur, Jhelum
Sep 41 **Lysander II** (Dec 42)
31 Jan 42 to Lashio
dets Zayatkwin, Port Blair
8 Feb 42 to Magwe
det Mingaladon
6 Mar 42 to Asansol
7 Mar 42 to Lahore
7 Apr 42 to Ranchi
dets Dum Dum, Jamshedpur
18 Jul 42 to Kohat
31 Aug 42 to Ranchi
Dec 42 **Hurricane IIB** (Apr 44)
dets Maungdaw, Imphal, Cox's Bazaar, Ramu
4 Jun 43 to Alipore
dets Agartala, Imphal, Cox's Bazaar
1 Nov 43 to Imphal
dets Ratnap, Cox's Bazaar
Mar 44 **Hurricane IIC** (Oct 45)
5 Apr 44 to Jorhat
dets Imphal, Dalbumgarh
6 Jul 44 to Dalbumgarh
2 Aug 44 to Ranchi
2 Oct 44 to Dalbumgarh
10 Dec 44 to Tamu
11 Jan 45 to Kalemyo
30 Jan 45 to Ye-U
13 Feb 45 to Sadaung
5 Apr 45 to Meiktila
22 May 45 to Mingaladon
May 45 **Hurricane IV** (Jun 45)
det Meiktila
Jul 45 **Spitfire XI** (Sep 45)
Oct 45 **Spitfire VIII** (Nov 45)
Oct 45 **Spitfire XIV** (May 47)
7 Oct 45 to Zayatkwin
3 Nov 45 to Bayan Lepas
10 Apr 46 to Kuala Lumpur
1 Feb 47 to Tengah
Apr 47 **Spitfire FR 18** (Feb 51)
26 Jan 48 to Sembawang
11 May 49 to Kai Tak
1 May 50 to Sek Kong
7 Oct 50 to Kai Tak
Jan 51 **Vampire FB 5** (Feb 52)
28 Mar 51 to Sek Kong
Feb 52 **Vampire FB 9** (Aug 56)
15 Aug 55 to Kai Tak
5 Dec 55 to Sek Kong
Feb 56 **Venom FB 1** (Nov 59)
14 Jun 57 to Kai Tak
Nov 59 **Venom FB 4** (Jul 62)
May 62 **Hunter FGA 9** (Jan 67)
2 Jan 67 DB
—
1 Mar 68 RF @ Kai Tak — from det of No 103 Sqn
Mar 68 **Whirlwind HC 10** (Aug 72)
Jan 72 **Wessex HC 2** ( )
17 May 78 to Sek Kong

29 Sqn

7 Nov 15 F @ Gosport (Fort Grange) — nucleus from No 23 Sqn
Nov 15 **Longhorn** (Mar 16)
Nov 15 **Avro 504A** (Mar 16)
Nov 15 **Caudron G.III** (Mar 16)
Dec 15 **BE 2C** (Mar 16)
Feb 16 **BE 2B** (Mar 16)
Mar 16 **DH 2** (Mar 17)
25 Mar 16 to St-Omer
15 Apr 16 to Abeele
Jun 16 **FE 8** (Aug 16)
23 Oct 16 to Le Hameau
Mar 17 **Nieuport 16** (Apr 17)
Apr 17 **Nieuport 17** (Nov 17)
May 17 **Nieuport 23** (Nov 17)
5 Jul 17 to Poperinghe
Aug 17 **Nieuport 24** (Dec 17)
Oct 17 **Nieuport 27** (Apr 18)
16 Feb 18 to La Lovie
11 Apr 18 to Tetegham
Apr 18 **SE 5A** (Aug 19)
22 Apr 18 to St-Omer
11 Jun 18 to Vignacourt
22 Jul 18 to St-Omer
1 Aug 18 to Hoog Huis
25 Sep 18 to La Lovie
5 Oct 18 to Hoog Huis
23 Oct 18 to Marcke
26 Nov 18 to Nivelles
19 Dec 18 to Bickendorf
11 Aug 19 to Spittlegate as a cadre
31 Dec 19 DB
—
1 Apr 23 RF @ Duxford
Apr 23 **Snipe** (Jan 25)
Jan 25 **Grebe II** (Mar 28)
Mar 28 **Siskin IIIA** (Jun 32)
1 Apr 28 to North Weald
Jun 32 **Bulldog IIA** (Apr 35)
Mar 35 **Demon** (Mar 36)
31 Oct 35 to Amiriya
Mar 36 **Gordon** (Aug 36)
20 Jul 36 to Helwan
6 Aug 36 to Amiriya
12 Sep 36 to North Weald
Oct 36 **Demon (Turret)** (Dec 38)
22 Nov 37 to Debden
Dec 38 **Blenheim IF** (Feb 41)
det Martlesham Heath
4 Apr 40 to Drem
10 May 40 to Debden
det Martlesham Heath
27 Jun 40 to Digby
27 Jul 40 to Wellingore
Sep 40 **Beaufighter IF** (May 43)
27 Apr 41 to West Malling
det Coltishall
Mar 43 **Beaufighter VIF** (May 43)
13 May 43 to Bradwell Bay
May 43 **Mosquito XII** (Apr 44)
Jul 43 **Mosquito VI** (Aug 43)
3 Sep 43 to Ford
Oct 43 **Mosquito XIII** (Feb 45)
1 Mar 44 to Drem
1 May 44 to West Malling
19 Jun 44 to Hunsdon
22 Feb 45 to Colerne
Feb 45 **Mosquito XXX** (Aug 46)
11 May 45 to Manston
21 Sep 45 to Lübeck
6 Oct 45 to Manston
29 Oct 45 to West Malling
12 Jan 46 to Lübeck
27 Jan 46 to West Malling
11 Feb 46 to Spilsby
21 Mar 46 to West Malling
6 Apr 46 to Lübeck
17 Apr 46 to West Malling
Jul 46 **Mosquito NF 36** (Oct 50)
5 Oct 46 to Lübeck
18 Oct 46 to West Malling
26 Feb 47 to Acklington
31 Mar 47 to West Malling
3 May 47 to Lübeck
16 May 47 to West Malling
16 Jun 47 to Acklington
24 Jul 47 to West Malling
5 Jan 48 to Acklington
26 Feb 48 to West Malling
14 May 48 to Lübeck
27 May 48 to West Malling
Oct 50 **Mosquito NF 30** (Aug 51)
25 Nov 50 to Tangmere
Jul 51 **Meteor NF 11** (Dec 57)
14 Jan 57 to Acklington
Nov 57 **Javelin FAW 6** (Aug 61)
Feb 58 **Meteor NF 12** (Jul 58)
22 Jul 58 to Leuchars
Apr 61 **Javelin FAW 9** (May 67)
1 Mar 63 to Nicosia
16 Mar 64 to Akrotiri
3 Dec 65 to Ndola
det Lusaka
3 Sep 66 to Akrotiri
10 May 67 to Wattisham
May 67 **Lightning F.3** (Dec 74)
31 Dec 74 DB
—
1 Oct 74 training at Coningsby as No 29 Sqn (Designate
—
1 Jan 75 RF @ Coningsby
Jan 75 **Phantom FGR 2** (Mar 87
det Port Stanley (became No 23 Sqn)
30 Mar 87 DB
—
1 Apr 87 RF @ Coningsby
Apr 87 **Tornado F.3** ( )

30 Sqn

24 Mar 15 RFC Detached Flt at Moascar redesignated as No 30 Sqn, although this date was not notified to the unit until 31 Jul 15
Mar 15 **Longhorn** (Nov 15)
Mar 15 **Shorthorn** (Oct 16)
Mar 15 **BE 2C** (Feb 18)
5 Aug 15 "Air unit personnel" in Mesopotamia gazetted to the RFC. This unit was using the types above, plus:
Aug 15 **Caudron G.III** (Sep 15)
Aug 15 **Martinsyde S.1** (Nov 15)
7 Nov 15 No 30 Sqn organised wit HQ and B Flt (a reinforcement draft which had arrived 4 Nov at Basra, and A Flt (the original air unit personnel) deployed forward at Aziziya wher it was joined by B Flt on 9 Nov and detached a section to Lajj
26 Nov 15 Flt in Egypt relieved by A Flt, No 14 Sqn and began to move to Basra
28 Nov 15 to Kut al Imara
7 Dec 15 to Ali Gharbi
27 Dec 15 Element from Egypt arrived to become C Flt remaining at Basra until 30 Apr 16.
6 Jan 16 to Musandeg
10 Jan 16 to Sheikh Saad
16 Jan 16 to Ora
28 Feb 16 RNAS unit joined No 3 Sqn and remained until 29 Jun 16 flying **BE 2C, Short 827, Voisin LA.S** and **Henry Farman F.27**
1 Apr 16 to Camp Wadi
6 May 16 to Sheikh Saad
Flts @ Basra, Arab Village
dets Zobeir, Barjisayah
Jun 16 **Voisin LA.S** (Nov 16)
Jul 16 **Henri Farman F.27** (May 17)
Sep 16 **Martinsyde G.100** (Nov 17)
9 Oct 16 to Arab village
Flt @ Sinn Abtar, det Nasiriyah
26 Feb 17 to Shumran
Flt @ Sinn Abtar, det Nasiriyah
2 Mar 17 to Sheikh Jaad
Flt @ Sinn Abtar, det Nasiriyah
3 Mar 17 to Aziziya
Flt @ Sinn Abtar, det Nasiriyah
5 Mar 17 to Zeur
Flt @ Sinn Abtar, det Nasiriyah
8 Mar 17 to Bustan

Flt @ Bawi, det Nasiriyah
1 Mar 17 to Baghdad
Flts @ Bawi, Kasirin, Baquba, Fort Kermea, det Nasiriyah
7 Apr 17 to Fort Kermea
Flts @ Sindiya, Barura, Baghdad
0 Apr 17 to Barura
Flt @ Baghdad
Apr 17 **Bristol Scout** (Oct 17)
4 May 17 to Baghdad
dets Sindiya, Jadida, Baquba
May 17 **BE 2E** (Apr 19)
Sep 17 **SPAD S.VII** (May 18)
3 Sep 17 to Baquba
Flts @ Falluja, Madhij
8 Oct 17 to Shahraban
Flts @ Baquba, Falluja
5 Oct 17 to Baquba
Flt @ Falluja
Oct 17 **RE 8** (Apr 19)
Nov 17 **Vickers FB 19 Mk II** (Nov 17)
2 Dec 17 to Qalat Mufti
Flt @ Falluja
8 Dec 17 to Baquba
Flts @ Falluja, Ramadi
Dec 17 **DH 4** (Jan 18)
Jan 18 **Martinsyde G.100** (Apr 18)
1 Mar 18 to Qubba
Flts @ Ramadi, Hit
5 Apr 18 to Baquba
Flts @ Ramadi, Kifri, Hit, dets Hamadan, Tuz Khurmatli
8 Sep 18 to Kifri
Flt @ Baquba, dets Hamadan, Zinjan
3 Nov 18 to Baquba
Flts @ Kifri, Kazvin, Baghdad, Bushire
Dec 18 **Martinsyde G.100** (Feb 19)
Jan 19 **SE 5A** (Feb 19)
2 Apr 19 to Baghdad
9 Apr 19 reduced to a cadre
1 Feb 20 re-established at Baghdad West from No 63 Sqn
Feb 20 **RE 8** (Jan 21)
dets Mosul, Kazvin, Bushire, Ramadi, Samawah
Jan 21 **DH 9A** (Sep 29)
3 Dec 22 to Hinaidi
det Kirkuk
1 Apr 27 to Kirkuk
dets Hinaidi, Sulaimania
7 Oct 27 to Hinaidi
Apr 29 **Wapiti** (Aug 35)
3 Oct 29 to Mosul
Apr 35 **Hardy** (Apr 38)
9 Oct 36 to Dhibban
Jan 38 **Blenheim I** (Mar 41)
5 Aug 39 to Ismailia
det El Daba
Jun 40 **Blenheim IF** (May 41)
dets Amiriya, Helwan, Maaten Bagush, Qasaba, Gerawala
9 Jul 40 to Ikingi
dets Amiriya, Helwan, Maaten Bagush, Fuka, Haifa
3 Nov 40 to Elevsis
dets Paramythia, Heraklion, Maleme
8 Apr 41 to Maleme
8 May 41 to Amiriya
Jun 41 **Hurricane I** (Aug 42)
2 Jun 41 to Idku
det Ikingi
2 Oct 41 to LG 102
8 Nov 41 to LG 05
4 Jan 42 to LG 121
9 Feb 42 to Heliopolis
25 Feb 42 en route Ceylon via HMS *Indomitable*
8 Mar 42 to Ratmalana
31 Aug 42 to Dambulla
Aug 42 **Hurricane IIC** (Sep 44)
dets Minneriya, St Thomas Mount, Colombo
15 Feb 43 to Colombo
31 Aug 43 to Dambulla
dets Kalametiya, Feni
12 Jan 44 to Fazilpur
det Feni
10 Apr 44 to Comilla
25 May 44 to Yelahanka
Jul 44 **Thunderbolt I** (Jan 45)
13 Sep 44 to Arkonam
5 Oct 44 to Chittagong
Oct 44 **Thunderbolt II** (Mar 46)
det Cox's Bazaar
10 Dec 44 to Jumchar
det Cox's Bazaar
24 Apr 45 to Akyab
18 May 45 to Chakulia
3 Jul 45 to Vizagapatam
12 Sep 45 to Baigachi
24 Sep 45 to Zayatkwin
30 Sep 45 to Baigachi
2 Oct 45 to Vizagapatam
4 Dec 45 to Baigachi
21 Feb 46 to Bhopal
Mar 46 **Tempest F.2** (Dec 46)
27 May 46 to Agra
1 Dec 46 DB
—
1 Nov 47 RF @ Abingdon — nucleus from No 238 Sqn
24 Nov 47 to Oakington
Nov 47 **Dakota** (Jan 51)
dets Wunstorf, Fassberg, Lübeck for BAL
27 Nov 50 to Abingdon
Nov 50 **Valetta C.1** (May 57)
2 May 52 to Benson
15 Apr 53 to Dishforth
Apr 57 **Beverley C.1** (Sep 67)
15 Nov 59 to Eastleigh
1 Sep 64 to Muharraq
7 Sep 67 DB
—
1 May 68 RF @ Fairford
Jun 68 **Hercules C.1** ( )
1 Feb 71 to Lyneham
Mar 80 **Hercules C.3** ( )

31 Sqn

11 Oct 15 'A' Flt F @ South Farnborough — from No 1 RAS
Nov 15 **BE 2C** (Feb 20)
27 Nov 15 en route India
29 Dec 15 to Nowshera
18 Jan 16 'B' Flt F @ Gosport — from No 22 Sqn
1 Mar 16 'A' & 'B' Flts to Risalpur
Apr 16 'A' Flt to Murree
10 May 16 'C' Flt F @ Gosport — from HD Brigade
4 Jul 16 'C' Flt to Murree
29 Jul 16 'B' Flt to Murree
5 Oct 16 to Risalpur
Mar 17 **Henry Farman F.27** (18)
Oct 17 **BE 2E** (Feb 20)
dets Bannu, Tank, Khanpur, Dera Ismail Khan, Dera Ghazi Khan, Lahore
Jun 19 **Bristol F2b Fighter** (Apr 31)
dets Bannu, Tank, Kohat
15 Apr 20 to Mhow
26 Nov 20 to Cawnpore
31 Oct 21 to Peshawar
dets Tank, Dardoni
17 Apr 23 to Dardoni
13 Mar 24 to Ambala
dets Quetta
15 Dec 26 to Quetta
dets Jubbulpore, Mhow, Ford Sandeman, Loralai
Feb 31 **Wapiti** (Aug 39)
dets Fort Sandeman, Secunderabad, Hakimpet, Mhow
8 Jun 35 to Drigh Road as a cadre
1 Aug 35 re-established
dets Quetta, Hakimpet, Jubbulpore, Fort Sandeman, Poona, Risalpur
27 Oct 38 to Lahore
dets Ford Sandeman, Jubbulpore, Ambala, Risalpur
Apr 39 **Valentia** (Aug 41)
Dec 39 to Peshawar
Feb 41 to Lahore
26 Mar 41 to Drigh Road
Apr 41 **DC 2** (Apr 43)
dets Shaibah, Basrah
Sep 41 to Lahore
dets Bilbeis, Maaten Bagush
Feb 42 to Akyab
Mar 42 to Dum Dum
det Dinjan
Apr 42 to Lahore
Apr 42 **DC 3** (Apr 43)
dets Dinjan, Tezpur
21 Feb 43 to Palam
dets Agartala, Tezpur
19 Mar 43 to Dhubalia
det Agartala
Apr 43 **Dakota** (Sep 46)
23 May 43 to Kharagpur
dets Agartala, Tezpur
21 Jun 43 to Agartala
dets Dinjan, Kharagpur, Tezpur
11 Jul 44 to Basal
31 Oct 44 to Agartala
1 Jan 45 to Comilla
6 Feb 45 to Hathazari
15 May 45 to Ramree/Kyaukpyu
dets Toungoo, Tilda, Akyab, Mingaladon
Aug 45 to Akyab
dets Toungoo, Tilda, Mingaladon, Kyaukpyu
30 Sep 45 to Kallang
det Kemajoran
20 Jan 46 to Kemajoran
30 Sep 46 DB
—
1 Nov 46 RF @ Mauripur — No 77 Sqn renumbered
Nov 46 **Dakota** (Dec 47)
2 Sep 47 to Palam
6 Nov 47 to Mauripur
15 Dec 47 DB
—
19 Jul 48 RF @ Hendon — Metropolitan Communications Sqn renamed
Jul 48 **Anson C.12** (Mar 55)
Jul 48 **Anson C.19** (Mar 55)
Jul 48 **Proctor** (Jul 53)
Jul 48 **Spitfire PR 19** (Apr 49)
Jan 49 **Devon C.1** (Mar 55)
Mar 49 **Spitfire LF 16** (May 54)
Jul 50 **Tiger Moth** (Mar 54)
Jun 52 **Prentice T.1** (May 54)
Apr 53 **Chipmunk T.10** (Mar 55)
1 Mar 55 DB — reverted to Metropolitan Communications Sqn
—
1 Mar 55 RF @ Laarbruch
Mar 55 **Canberra PR 7** (Mar 71)
31 Mar 71 DB
—
20 Jul 71 RF @ Brüggen
Jul 71 **Phantom FGR 2** (Jun 76)
30 Jun 76 DB
—
1 Jan 76 training at Brüggen as No 31 Sqn (Designate)
—
30 Jun 76 RF @ Brüggen
Jun 76 **Jaguar GR 1** (Nov 84)
1 Nov 84 DB
—
1 Sep 84 training at Brüggen as No 31 Sqn (Designate)
—
1 Nov 84 RF @ Brüggen
Nov 84 **Tornado GR 1** ( )

32 Sqn

12 Jan 16 F @ Netheravon — nucleus from No 21 Sqn
Jan 16 **Henry Farman F.20** (May 16)
Jan 16 **Vickers FB 5** (May 16)
May 16 **Vickers ES 1** (Jul 16)
Feb 16 **DH 2** (Jul 17)
28 May 16 to St-Omer
4 Jun 16 to Auchel
7 Jun 16 to Treizennes
21 Jul 16 to Vert Galand
25 Oct 16 to Léalvillers
May 17 **DH 5** (Mar 18)
3 Jul 17 to Abeele
8 Jul 17 to Droglandt
Dec 17 **SE 5A** (Mar 19)
5 Mar 18 to Bailleul
27 Mar 18 to Belleville Farm
29 Mar 18 to Beauvois
3 Jun 18 to Fouquerolles
21 Jun 18 to Ruisseauville
18 Jul 18 to Touquin
3 Aug 18 to La Bellevue
27 Oct 18 to Pronville
1 Nov 18 to La Brayelle
16 Nov 18 to Le Hameau
18 Jan 19 to Serny
5 Mar 19 to Tangmere as a cadre
8 Oct 19 to Croydon
31 Dec 19 DB
—
1 Apr 23 RF @ Kenley
Apr 23 **Snipe** (Dec 24)
Nov 24 **Grebe II** (Jan 27)
Sep 26 **Gamecock I** (Apr 28)
Apr 28 **Siskin IIIA** (Jan 31)
Jan 31 **Bulldog IIA** (Jul 36)
21 Sep 32 to Biggin Hill
Jul 36 **Gauntlet II** (Oct 38)
Oct 38 **Hurricane I** (Jul 41)
3 Jan 40 to Gravesend
8 Mar 40 to Manston
22 Mar 40 to Gravesend
27 Mar 40 to Biggin Hill
26 May 40 to Wittering
4 Jun 40 to Biggin Hill
27 Aug 40 to Acklington
15 Dec 40 to Middle Wallop
16 Feb 41 to Ibsley
17 Apr 41 to Pembrey
det Carew Cheriton
1 Jun 41 to Angle
Jul 41 **Hurricane IIB** (Nov 42)
27 Nov 41 to Manston
Nov 41 **Hurricane IIC** (Aug 43)
Apr 42 **Hurricane I** (Jun 42)
5 May 42 to West Malling
14 Jun 42 to Friston
7 Jul 42 to West Malling
14 Aug 42 to Friston
20 Aug 42 to West Malling
10 Sep 42 to Honiley
19 Oct 42 to Baginton
25 Nov 42 en route N Africa
7 Dec 42 to Phillipeville
det Maison Blanche
10 Jan 43 to Maison Blanche
det Souk el Khemis ('Paddington')
Apr 43 **Spitfire VC** (Nov 43)
21 May 43 to Tingley
Jun 43 **Spitfire IX** (Jul 44)
19 Aug 43 to La Sebala

18 Oct 43 to Montecorvino
17 Nov 43 to Reghaia
dets Tafaraoui, La Senia, Merrakesh, Foggia
Dec 43 **Spitfire VIII** (Jul 44)
28 Feb 44 to Foggia Main
May 44 **Spitfire VC** (Sep 45)
16 Jul 44 to Canne
dets Leverano, Metokhi
26 Sep 44 to Brindisi
dets Metokhi, Araxos
17 Oct 44 to Kalamaki
13 Nov 44 to Sedes
25 Feb 45 to Ramat David
Aug 45 **Spitfire IX** (May 47)
27 Sep 45 to Petah Tiqva
15 Mar 46 to Aqir
6 Jun 46 to Ramat David
3 Oct 46 to Ein Shemar
Apr 47 **Spitfire FR 18** (Mar 49)
det Ramat David
25 Mar 48 to Nicosia
det Ramat David
Jul 48 **Vampire F.3** (Jul 50)
Jun 50 **Vampire FB 5** (Sep 54)
4 Jan 51 to Shallufa
27 Jan 52 to Deversoir
Apr 52 **Vampire FB 9** (Sep 54)
15 Sep 54 to Kabrit
Sep 54 **Venom FB 1** (Jan 57)
14 Jan 55 to Shaibah
16 Oct 55 to Ta Kali
28 Aug 56 to Amman
29 Oct 56 to Ma'fraq
11 Jan 57 to Nicosia
det Weston Zoyland for Canberra
Jan 57 **Canberra B.2** (Mar 62)
18 Mar 57 to Akrotiri
Jul 61 **Canberra B.15** (Feb 69)
dets Tengah, Kuantan
3 Feb 69 DB
—
3 Feb 69 RF @ Northolt — Metropolitan Communications Sqn redesignated
Feb 69 **Pembroke C.1** (Sep 69)
Feb 69 **Sycamore HC 14** (Aug 72)
Feb 69 **Basset CC 1** (May 74)
Feb 69 **Andover CC 2** ( )
Jan 70 **Whirlwind HCC 12** (Oct 81)
Mar 71 **HS 125 CC 1** ( )
Apr 73 **HS 125 CC 2** ( )
Sep 75 **Andover C.1** ( )
May 76 **Gazelle HCC 4** ( )
Aug 83 **HS 125 CC 3** ( )

33 Sqn

12 Jan 16 F @ Filton — nucleus from No 20 Sqn
Jan 16 **BE 2C** (Jun 17)
29 Mar 16 to Tadcaster
dets York (the Knavesmire), Bramham Moor, Coal Aston, Beverley
Jun 16 **BE 12** (Jun 17)
Jul 16 **Bristol Scout** (Nov 16)
3 Oct 16 to Gainsborough
dets Scampton, Kirton-in-Lindsey, Elsham
Jan 17 **BE 2E** (Sep 17)
Jun 17 **BE 12A** (Sep 17)
Jun 17 **FE 2B** (Aug 18)
Jun 17 **FE 2D** (Aug 18)
12 Jun 18 to Kirton-in-Lindsey
dets Scampton, Elsham
Jun 18 **Bristol F2b Fighter** (Aug 18)
Aug 18 **Avro 504K (NF)** (Jun 19)
2 Jun 19 to Harpswell
13 Jun 19 DB
—
1 Mar 29 RF @ Netheravon
Mar 29 **Horsley** (Mar 30)
14 Sep 29 to Eastchurch
Feb 30 **Hart** (Feb 38)
5 Nov 30 to Bicester
27 Nov 34 to Upper Heyford
4 Oct 35 en route Egypt
25 Oct 35 to Mersah Matruh
det Ramleh
13 Jul 36 to Amman
det Ramleh
10 Aug 36 to Gaza
14 Nov 36 to Ismailia
Feb 38 **Gladiator I** (Jun 40)
det Ramleh
29 Sep 38 to Heliopolis
det Ramleh
3 Oct 38 to Ismailia
21 Oct 38 to Ramleh
dets Lydda, Amman
24 Apr 39 to Helwan
25 May 39 to Ismailia
dets El Daba, Qasaba
5 Aug 39 to Qasaba
1 Sep 39 to Mersah Matruh
23 Oct 39 to Qasaba
28 Oct 39 to Mersah Matruh
det Sidi Barrani
Feb 40 **Gauntlet II** (Jun 40)
Mar 40 **Gladiator II** (Oct 40)
17 Jun 40 to Qasaba
dets Gerawala, Sidi Barrani
25 Jun 40 to Helwan
Sep 40 **Hurricane I** (Feb 42)
22 Sep 40 to Fuka
15 Jan 41 to Amiriya
1 Feb 41 to Elevsis
det Paramythia
4 Mar 41 to Larissa
18 Apr 41 to Elevsis
22 Apr 41 to Argos
24 Apr 41 to Maleme
1 Jun 41 to Amiriya
dets Heliopolis, Gerawala, El Gamil, Fuka
1 Sep 41 to Sidi Haneish
10 Sep 41 to Gerawala
8 Nov 41 to Giarabub
20 Nov 41 to LG 125
1 Jan 42 to Msus
15 Jan 42 to Antelat
22 Jan 42 to Msus
24 Jan 42 to Mechili
28 Jan 42 to Gazala No 1
3 Feb 42 to Gambut
10 Feb 42 to LG 101
30 Mar 42 to Gambut
Mar 42 **Hurricane IIB** (Jun 42)
17 Jun 42 to Sidi Azeiz
18 Jun 42 to LG 75
20 Jun 42 to LG 76
23 Jun 42 to LG 12
Jun 42 **Hurricane IIC** (Dec 43)
26 Jun 42 to El Daba
27 Jun 42 to LG 154
24 Jul 42 to LG 172
27 Jul 42 to LG 85
5 Aug 42 to Idku
31 Aug 42 to LG 85
3 Oct 42 to LG 154
23 Oct 42 to LG 172
12 Nov 42 to LG 101
18 Nov 42 to El Adem
28 Nov 42 Benina
Feb 43 **Spitfire VB** (Jun 43)
11 Feb 43 to Bersis
24 Jun 43 to Misurata West
9 Sep 43 to Bersis
det Benina
Nov 43 **Spitfire VB** (Feb 44)
Dec 43 **Spitfire VC** (Apr 44)
17 Jan 44 to Mersah Matruh
1 Apr 44 en route UK
23 Apr 44 to North Weald
Apr 44 **Spitfire LF IXE** (Dec 44)
17 May 44 to Lympne
3 Jul 44 to Tangmere
17 Jul 44 to Funtington
6 Aug 44 to Selsey
10 Aug 44 to Fairwood Common
18 Aug 44 to Selsey
19 Aug 44 to B 10/Plumetot
20 Aug 44 to Tangmere
31 Aug 44 to B 17/Carpiquet
7 Sep 44 to Lympne
10 Sep 44 to B 35/Godelmesnil
12 Sep 44 to B 53/Merville
2 Nov 44 to B 65/Maldeghem
15 Dec 44 to Lasham
15 Dec 44 to Predannack
Dec 44 **Tempest V** (Nov 46)
21 Feb 45 to B 77/Gilze-Rijen
7 Apr 45 to B 91/Kluis
20 Apr 45 to B 109/Quackenbrück
19 Aug 45 to B 155/Dedelsdorf
14 Sep 45 to B 106/Twente
16 Sep 45 to B 155/Dedelsdorf
17 Sep 45 to B 170/Sylt
6 Oct 45 to B 155/Dedelsdorf
23 Oct 45 to B 152/Fassberg
2 Jan 46 to Gatow
17 Feb 46 to Fassberg
31 Mar 46 to Sylt
8 May 46 to Fassberg
1 Jun 46 to Manston
12 Jun 46 to Fassberg
18 Jun 46 to Gatow
18 Jul 46 to Fassberg
27 Aug 46 to Gatow
24 Sep 46 to Fassbeg
Oct 46 **Tempest F.2** (Jun 51)
8 May 47 to Ahlhorn
20 May 47 to Fassberg
13 Jul 47 to Zeltweg
11 Aug 47 to Fassberg
12 Sep 47 to Gatow
29 Sep 47 to Fassberg
31 Nov 47 to Gütersloh
5 Jan 48 to Lübeck
11 Feb 48 to Gütersloh
30 Apr 48 to Gatow
5 Jun 48 to Gütersloh
2 Jul 49 to Renfrew
14 Jul 49 en route FE via HMS *Ocean*
9 Aug 49 to Changi
10 Sep 49 to Butterworth
13 Oct 49 to Changi
18 Mar 50 to Tengah
dets Kuala Lumpur
30 May 50 to Butterworth
det Tengah
May 51 **Hornet F.3** (Mar 55)
7 Aug 51 to Tengah
5 Jan 52 to Butterworth
31 Mar 55 DB
—
15 Oct 55 RF @ Driffield
Dec 55 **Venom NF 2A** (Jul 57)
31 Jul 57 DB
—
30 Sep 57 RF @ Leeming — No 264 Sqn renumbered
Sep 57 **Meteor NF 14** (Aug 58)
Jul 58 **Javelin FAW 7** (Jan 62)
30 Sep 58 to Middleton St George
Oct 60 **Javelin FAW 9** (Nov 62)
31 Dec 62 DB
—
1 Mar 65 **Bloodhound II** at Butterworth
31 Jan 70 DB
—
14 Jun 71 RF @ Odiham
Jun 71 **Puma HC 1** ( )

34 Sqn

12 Jan 16 F @ Castle Bromwich — nucleus from No 19 Sqn
Feb 16 **Caudron G. III** (16)
Feb 16 **BE 2C** (Jan 17)
May 16 **BE 2E** (Jan 17)
15 Jun 16 to Lilbourne
10 Jul 16 to Allonville
Dec 16 **BE 2F** (Feb 17)
Dec 16 **BE 2G** (Feb 17)
Jan 17 **RE 8** (May 19)
1 Feb 17 to Villers-Bretonneux
18 Apr 17 to Estrées-en-Chaussée
16 May 17 to Nurlu
26 May 17 to Villers-Bretonneux
10 Jun 17 to Estrées-en-Chaussée
29 Jun 17 to Bray-Dunes
1 Nov 17 to Candas
13 Nov 17 to Milan
18 Nov 17 to Ghedi
22 Nov 17 to Verona
28 Nov 17 to Grossa
3 Dec 17 to Istrana
det Marcon
30 Mar 18 to Villaverla
Apr 18 **Bristol F2b Fighter** (Jul 18)
23 Oct 18 to San Luca
16 Nov 18 to Villaverla
28 Feb 19 to Caldiero
3 May 19 to Old Sarum as a cadre
25 Oct 19 DB
—
3 Dec 35 RF @ Bircham Newton — nucleus from No 18 Sqn
Jan 36 **Hind** (Jul 38)
30 Jul 36 to Abbotsinch
3 Nov 36 to Lympne
12 Jul 38 to Upper Heyford
Jul 38 **Blenheim I** (Nov 41)
2 Mar 39 to Watton
12 Aug 39 en route FE
10 Sep 39 to Tengah
Jun 41 **Blenheim IV** (Feb 42)
det Butterworth
18 Jan 42 to P I
dets Tengah, Kemajoran, Lahat
24 Jan 42 to P II
15 Feb 42 to Lahat
18 Feb 42 to Kalidjati
20 Feb 42 DB — absorbed by No 8 Sqn
—
1 Apr 42 RF from elements at Chakrata and Karachi
15 Apr 42 to Allahabad
Apr 42 **Blenheim IV** (Jan 43)
det Ondal
13 Jun 42 to Ondal
det Peshawar
8 Dec 42 to Baigachi
Dec 42 **Blenheim V** (Jul 43)
30 Jan 43 to Jessore
det Silchar West
7 Mar 43 to Silchar West
18 Mar 43 to Kumbhirgram
3 May 43 to St Thomas Mount
det Kumbhirgram
Aug 43 **Hurricane IIC** (Apr 45)
15 Sep 43 to Cholavaram
16 Oct 43 to Alipore
30 Oct 43 to Palel
Dec 43 **Hurricane IIB** (Jan 44)
11 Apr 44 to Dergaon
15 Jul 44 to Palel
20 Dec 44 to Yazagyo
23 Jan 45 to Onbauk
det Wangjing
Mar 45 **Thunderbolt II** (Oct 45)
15 Mar 45 to Ondaw
20 Apr 45 to Kwetnge
11 May 45 to Myingyan
det Kinmagon
1 Jun 45 to Kinmagon
1 Jul 45 to Meiktila
18 Aug 45 to Zayatkwin
15 Oct 45 DB
—
1 Aug 46 RF @ Palam — No 681 Sqn renumbered
Aug 46 **Spitfire PR 19** (Jul 47)
det Kohat
1 Aug 47 DB
—
11 Feb 49 RF @ Horsham St Fait — No 695 Sqn renumbered
Feb 49 **Martinet TT 1** (Jun 49)

Feb 49 **Spitfire LF 16E** (Mar 51)
Feb 49 **Harvard T.2B** (Jul 51)
Feb 49 **Oxford T.2** (Jul 51)
Feb 49 **Beaufighter TT 10** (Jul 51)
Jul 51 DB
—
Aug 54 RF @ Tangmere
Aug 54 **Meteor F.8** (Dec 55)
Oct 55 **Hunter F.5** (Jan 58)
Jan 58 DB — aircraft to No 208 Sqn
—
Oct 60 RF @ Seletar — from Beverley Flight of No 48 Sqn
Oct 60 **Beverley C.1** (Dec 67)
Dec 67 DB

5 Sqn

Feb 16 F @ Thetford — nucleus from No 9 RS
Feb 16 **BE 2C** (Apr 16)
Feb 16 **FE 2B** (Dec 16)
Feb 16 **Vickers FB 5** (Dec 16)
Apr 16 **DH 2** (Jun 16)
Apr 16 **Henry Farman F.20** (Jun 16)
Jun 16 to Narborough
Oct 16 **AW FK 8** (Jan 19)
Jan 17 to St-Omer
Feb 17 to St-André-aux Bois
Apr 17 to Savy
May 17 to Villers-Bretonneux
May 17 to Mons-en-Chaussée
Jul 17 to Savy
Aug 17 to La Gorgue
Oct 17 to La Lovie
Oct 17 to Bruay
Nov 17 to Estrées-en-Chaussée
Feb 18 **Bristol F2b Fighter** (Jul 18)
Mar 18 to Chipilly
Mar 18 to Poulainville
Mar 18 to Abbeville
Apr 18 to Poulainville
May 18 to Flesselles
Sep 18 to Suzanne
Sep 18 to Moislains
Sep 18 **Bristol F2b Fighter** (Jan 19)
Oct 18 to Longavesnes
Oct 18 to Elincourt
Nov 18 to Flaumont
Nov 18 to Grand Fayt
Nov 18 to Elincourt
Nov 18 to La Bellevue
Jan 19 to Ste-Marie-Cappel as a cadre
Mar 19 to Netheravon
Jun 19 DB
—
Mar 29 RF @ Bircham Newton
Mar 29 **DH 9A** (Jan 30)
Nov 29 **Fairey IIIF** (Sep 32)
Jul 32 **Gordon** (Aug 36)
Oct 35 en route ME
Oct 35 to Ed Damer
Apr 36 to Gebeit
Aug 36 en route UK
Aug 36 to Worthy Down
Nov 36 **Gordon** (Sep 37)
Jul 37 **Wellesley** (May 38)
Apr 38 **Battle** (Feb 40)
Apr 38 to Cottesmore
Jul 39 **Anson I** (Apr 40)
Aug 39 to Cranfield
Nov 39 **Blenheim IV** (Apr 40)
Dec 39 to Bassingbourn
Feb 40 to Upwood
Apr 40 DB — merged into No 17 OTU
—
Nov 40 RF @ Boscombe Down
Nov 40 **Halifax I** (Feb 42)
Nov 40 to Leeming
Dec 40 to Linton-on-Ouse
Oct 41 **Halifax II** (Jan 44)
15 Aug 42 to Graveley
Oct 43 **Halifax III** (Mar 44)
Mar 44 **Lancaster I & III** (Sep 49)
18 Sep 46 to Stradishall
10 Feb 49 to Mildenhall
Aug 49 **Lincoln B.2** (Feb 50)
23 Feb 50 DB — became the basis of the B-29 Conversion Unit
—
1 Sep 51 RF @ Marham — Washington Conversion Unit redesignated
Sep 51 **Washington B.1** (Feb 54)
Apr 54 **Canberra B.2** (Sep 61)
16 Jul 56 to Upwood
11 Sep 61 DB
—
1 Dec 62 RF @ Coningsby
Dec 62 **Vulcan B.2** (Feb 82)
2 Nov 64 to Cottesmore
1 Jan 69 to Akrotiri
16 Jan 75 to Scampton
1 Mar 82 DB

36 Sqn

1 Feb 16 F @ Cramlington — from HD Flt
Feb 16 **BE 2C** (Jun 17)
Feb 16 **Bristol Scout** (Jul 16)
May 16 **BE 12** (Aug 17)
dets Seaton Carew, Ashington, Hylton
12 Oct 16 to Newcastle
dets Seaton Carew, Ashington, Hylton
Dec 16 **BE 2E** (Aug 17)
Jun 17 **FE 2B** (Aug 18)
Sep 17 **FE 2D** (Aug 18)
Apr 18 **Pup** (Nov 18)
Apr 18 **Bristol F2b Fighter** (Jun 19)
1 Jul 18 to Hylton/Usworth
dets Seaton Carew, Ashington
13 Jun 19 DB
—
9 Oct 28 RF @ Donibristle — Coastal Defence Torpedo Flt redesignated
Oct 28 **Horsley** (Jul 35)
14 Oct 30 to FE by sea via Leuchars
14 Nov 30 to Seletar
Jul 35 **Vildebeeste III** (Mar 42)
dets Kota Bahru, Gong Kedak, Kuantan
Dec 41 **Albacore** (Feb 42)
1 Feb 42 to Kalidjati
15 Feb 42 to Tjikampek
27 Feb 42 to Madioen
28 Feb 42 to Andir
1 Mar 42 to Tjikembar
4 Mar 42 to Tasikmalaja
9 Mar 42 DB — captured
—
22 Oct 42 RF @ Tanjore
Dec 42 **Wellington IC** (Jul 43)
Feb 43 **Wellington VIII** (Sep 43)
8 Apr 43 to Dhubalia
24 Jun 43 to Blida
Jun 43 **Wellington X** (Nov 43)
Jul 43 **Wellington XI** (Sep 43)
Jul 43 **Wellington XII** (Dec 43)
Jul 43 **Wellington XIII** (Dec 43)
dets Bone, Montecorvino, La Senia, Gibraltar, Tafaraoui, Grottaglie, Bo Rizzo, Ghisonaccia
Sep 43 **Wellington XIV** (Jun 45)
30 Apr 44 to Reghaia
dets La Senia, Grottaglie, Bone, Alghero
18 Sep 44 to Tarquinia
26 Sep 44 to Chivenor
9 Mar 45 to Benbecula
4 Jun 45 DB
—
1 Oct 46 RF @ Thorney Island — No 248 Sqn renumbered
Oct 46 **Mosquito FB 6** (Oct 47)
15 Oct 47 DB
—
1 Jul 53 RF @ Topcliffe
Jul 53 **Neptune MR 1** (Feb 57)
28 Feb 57 DB
—
1 Sep 58 RF @ Colerne — No 511 Sqn renumbered
Sep 58 **Hastings C.1** (Jul 67)
Sep 58 **Hastings C.2** (Jul 67)
1 Jul 67 to Lyneham
Jul 67 **Hercules C.1** (Nov 75)
3 Nov 75 DB

37 Sqn

15 Apr 16 F @ Norwich — nucleus from No 9 RS
16 Apr 16 to Orfordness
20 May 16 DB — absorbed by Experimental Establishment
—
15 Sep 16 RF @ Woodford Green — nucleus from No 39 Sqn
29 Sep 16 to Woodham Mortimer
dets Goldhanger, Stow Maries, Rochford
Sep 16 **BE 2D** (Feb 18)
Sep 16 **BE 12** (May 18)
Dec 16 **BE 2E** (Apr 18)
Dec 16 **BE 12A** (May 18)
May 17 **1½ Strutter** (Aug 17)
Jun 17 **Pup** (Jul 17)
Jun 17 **RE 7** (Oct 17)
Dec 17 **BE 12B** (May 18)
May 18 **SE 5A** (Jul 18)
22 Jun 18 to Stow Maries
det Goldhanger
Jul 18 **Camel** (Jul 19)
Dec 18 **Snipe** (Jul 19)
17 Mar 19 to Biggin Hill
1 Jul 19 DB — renumbered as No 39 Sqn
—
26 Apr 37 RF @ Feltwell — from 'B' Flt, No 214 Sqn
Apr 37 **Harrow** (Jun 39)
May 39 **Wellington I** (Nov 39)
Oct 39 **Wellington IA** (Aug 40)
det Salon
Jun 40 **Wellington IC** (Apr 43)
13 Nov 40 to Luqa
1 Dec 40 to Fayid
17 Dec 40 to Shallufa
dets Menidi, Paramythia, Shaibah, LG 76, LG 09, Luqa
27 Apr 42 to LG 09
26 Jun 42 to LG 224
29 Jun 42 to Abu Sueir
6 Nov 42 to LG 224
13 Nov 42 to LG 106
29 Nov 42 to LG 140
det Benina
20 Jan 43 to Benina
28 Jan 43 to El Magrun
14 Feb 43 to Gardabia East
25 Feb 43 to Gardabia West
Mar 43 **Wellington III** (Apr 43)
Mar 43 **Wellington X** (Oct 44)
30 May 43 to Kairouan
16 Nov 43 to Djedeida
16 Dec 43 to Cerignola
det Tortorella
13 Jan 44 to Tortorella
Oct 44 **Liberator VI** (Mar 46)
16 Oct 45 to Aqir
12 Dec 45 to Shallufa
31 Mar 46 DB
—
15 Apr 46 RF @ Fayid — No 214 Sqn renumbered
Apr 46 **Lancaster B.3** (Jun 46)
Jun 46 **Lancaster B.7** (Mar 47)
26 Aug 46 to Kabrit
16 Sep 46 to Shallufa
1 Apr 47 DB
—
14 Sep 47 RF @ Ein Shemar — nucleus from No 38 Sqn
Sep 47 **Lancaster MR 3** (Sep 53)
dets Ramat David, Shallufa
31 Mar 48 to Luqa
Jul 53 **Shackleton MR 2** (Sep 67)
21 Aug 57 to Khormaksar
7 Sep 67 DB

38 Sqn

1 Apr 16 F @ Thetford — nucleus from No 12 RS
22 May 16 DB — redesignated as No 25 RS
—
14 Jul 16 RF @ Castle Bromwich — nucleus from No 54 Sqn
Jul 16 **BE 12** (Jul 17)
1 Oct 16 to Melton Mowbray
dets Stamford, Leadenham, Buckminster
Nov 16 **BE 2E** (Sep 17)
Nov 16 **FE 2B** (Jan 19)
Jul 17 **FE 2D** (Apr 18)
25 May 18 to Buckminster
dets Leadenham, Stamford
31 May 18 to Cappelle — depot remained at Buckminster until 14 Aug 18; became No 90 Sqn
24 Aug 18 to Beauregard
29 Sep 18 to St-Pol
26 Oct 18 to Harlebeke
16 Dec 18 to Serny
14 Feb 19 to Hawkinge as a cadre
4 Jul 19 DB
—
16 Sep 35 RF @ Mildenhall — nucleus from 'B' Flt, No 99 Sqn
Sep 35 **Heyford III** (Jun 37)
Nov 36 **Hendon II** (Jan 39)
5 May 37 to Marham
Nov 38 **Wellington I** (Apr 40)
Sep 39 **Wellington IA** (Jun 40)
Apr 40 **Wellington IC** (Aug 42)
12 Nov 40 en route Egypt
24 Nov 40 to Ismailia
7 Dec 40 to Fayid
det LG 60
18 Dec 40 to Shallufa
dets Gambut, Sidi Azeiz, Fuka, Elevsis, El Adem, Luqa, LG 117, LG 09, LG 226, Berka III, Gianaclis
Aug 41 **Wellington II** (Oct 41)
May 42 **Wellington VIII** (Sep 43)
28 Feb 43 to Berka III
dets Misurata, LG 91, St Jean
Jun 43 **Wellington XI** (May 44)
Jun 43 **Wellington XII** (Sep 43)
Sep 43 **Wellington XIII** (Jan 45)
14 Nov 44 to Kalamaki
13 Dec 44 to Grottaglie
Jan 45 **Wellington XIV** (Dec 46)
31 Jan 45 to Foggia Main
dets Rosignano, Hal Far
21 Apr 45 to Falconara
13 Jul 45 to Luqa
Jul 45 **Warwick ASR 1** (Nov 46)
dets Elmas, Benina, Hassani
Jul 46 **Lancaster GR 3** (Feb 54)
det Ein Shemar

12 Dec 46 to Ein Shemar
31 Mar 48 to Luqa
Sep 53 **Shackleton MR 2** (Mar 67)
30 Oct 65 to Hal Far
31 Mar 67 DB

39 Sqn

15 Apr 16 F @ Hounslow — from elements of No 19 RS
Apr 16 **BE 2C** (Nov 17)
dets Suttons Farm, Hainault Farm
Apr 16 **Bristol Scout** (Jun 16)
30 Jun 16 to Woodford Green
dets Suttons Farm, Hainault Farm, North Weald Basset, Gosport, Biggin Hill
Jun 16 **BE 12** (Dec 17)
Dec 16 **BE 12A** (Dec 17)
Dec 16 **BE 2E** (Jan 18)
Apr 17 **Nieuport 20** (Jun 17)
May 17 **AW FK 8** (Jul 17)
Jun 17 **SE 5** (Aug 17)
Jul 17 **Camel** (Aug 17)
Dec 17 **Bristol F2b Fighter** (Nov 18)
9 Dec 17 to North Weald
16 Nov 18 DB — deployment to Bavichove abandoned before completion
—
1 Jul 19 RF @ Biggin Hill — No 37 Sqn renumbered
Jul 19 **Snipe** (Oct 19)
14 Oct 19 reduced to a cadre
20 Dec 19 to Uxbridge
12 Apr 20 to Kenley
12 Mar 21 to Spittlegate — re-established
Apr 21 **DH 9A** (Nov 28)
12 Jan 28 to Bircham Newton
29 Dec 28 en route India
22 Jan 29 to Risalpur
Mar 29 **Wapiti** (Dec 31)
dets Miranshah, Gilgit, Peshawar
Nov 31 **Hart** (Jul 39)
dets Jhelum, Delhi, Gilgit, Miranshah
Jun 39 **Blenheim I** (Jan 41)
12 Aug 39 to Tengah
9 Sep 39 to Kallang
19 Apr 40 to Lahore
7 May 40 to Heliopolis
13 May 40 to Sheikh Othman
1 Dec 40 to Helwan
det Qotafiyah
Dec 40 **Blenheim IV** (Jan 41)
23 Jan 41 to Heliopolis
Jan 41 **Maryland I** (Jan 42)
21 Mar 41 to Shandur
dets LG 15, LG 16
8 May 41 to Wadi Natrun
dets Burgh el Arab, Idku, LG 16
Aug 41 **Beaufort I** (Nov 42)
15 Oct 41 to Maryut
dets LG 15, LG 17, LG 05, El Gubbi, Bu Amud, LG 16
27 Dec 41 to LG 86
dets Sidi Barrani, Bu Amud, Luqa, Shallufa, Shandur, El Gubbi
Apr 42 **Beaufort II** (Jun 43)
1 Jul 42 to Shandur
dets Gianaclis, Luqa
20 Aug 42 to Luqa — absorbed elements of Nos 86 & 217 Sqns
dets Gianaclis, Helwan, Shandur
2 Oct 42 to Shallufa
det Gianaclis
6 Nov 42 to Luqa
det Shallufa
9 Dec 42 to Shallufa
det Luqa
21 Jan 43 to Luqa
dets Shallufa, Gianaclis
1 Jun 43 to Protville II
3 Jun 43 to LG 224
11 Jun 43 to Protville II
Jun 43 **Beaufighter X** (Feb 45)
det Shallufa
17 Oct 43 to Protville I
19 Oct 43 to Sidi Amor
det Grottaglie
20 Nov 43 to Reghaia
dets Grottaglie, Merrakesh
21 Feb 44 to Alghero
det Grottaglie
15 Jul 44 to Biferno
dets Reghaia, Hassani
Dec 44 **Marauder III** (Sep 46)
6 Jun 45 to Rivolto
16 Oct 45 to Khartoum
Feb 46 **Mosquito VI** (Sep 46)
Feb 46 **Mosquito FB 26** (Sep 46)
det Eastleigh
8 Sep 46 DB
—
1 Apr 48 RF @ Khartoum
det Manston
Jun 48 **Tempest F.6** (Feb 49)
det Asmara
28 Feb 49 DB
—
1 Mar 49 RF @ Fayid
Jun 49 **Mosquito NF 36** (Mar 53)
26 Feb 51 to Kabrit
Mar 53 **Meteor NF 13** (Jun 58)
10 Jan 55 to Luqa
9 Aug 56 to Nicosia
23 Mar 57 to Luqa
det Nicosia
19 May 58 to Nicosia
18 Jun 58 to Luqa
30 Jun 58 DB
—
1 Jul 58 RF @ Luqa — No 69 Sqn renumbered
Jul 58 **Canberra PR 3** (Apr 63)
Nov 62 **Canberra PR 9** (May 82)
1 Oct 70 to Wyton
Oct 70 **Canberra PR 7** (Feb 72)
1 Jun 82 DB

40 Sqn

26 Feb 16 F @ Gosport (Fort Grange) — nucleus from No 23 Sqn
Feb 16 **BE 2C** (Aug 16)
Feb 16 **Avro 504** (Aug 16)
Aug 16 **FE 8** (Mar 17)
19 Aug 16 to St-Omer
25 Aug 16 to Treizennes
Mar 17 **Nieuport 17** (Oct 17)
25 Apr 17 to Auchel
29 Apr 17 to Bruay
May 17 **Nieuport 23** (Oct 17)
Aug 17 **Nieuport 24** (Oct 17)
Oct 17 **SE 5** (18)
Oct 17 **SE 5A** (Feb 19)
4 Jun 18 to Bryas
24 Oct 18 to Aniche
29 Dec 18 to Orcq
13 Feb 19 to Tangmere as a cadre
4 Jul 19 DB
—
1 Apr 31 RF @ Upper Heyford
Apr 31 **Gordon** (Nov 35)
8 Oct 32 to Abingdon
Nov 35 **Hart (Special)** (Mar 36)
Mar 36 **Hind** (Aug 38)
Jul 38 **Battle** (Dec 39)
2 Sep 39 to Bétheniville
3 Dec 39 to Wyton
Dec 39 **Blenheim IV** (Nov 40)
Nov 40 **Wellington IC** (Feb 42)
2 Feb 41 to Alconbury
31 Oct 41 to Luqa
14 Feb 42 DB — UK echelon renumbered as No 156 Sqn
—
1 May 42 RF @ Abu Sueir — from remains of ME detachment
May 42 **Wellington IC** (Jun 43)
23 Jun 42 to Shallufa
20 Aug 42 to Kabrit
8 Nov 42 to LG 222A
13 Nov 42 to LG 104
det Luqa
26 Nov 42 to LG 237
det Luqa
13 Jan 43 to Heliopolis
det Luqa
20 Jan 43 to LG 237
det El Magrun
14 Feb 43 to Gardabia East
13 Mar 43 to Gardabia South
Mar 43 **Wellington III** (Apr 44)
28 May 43 to El Alem East
May 43 **Wellington X** (Mar 45)
25 Jun 43 to Hani West
18 Nov 43 to Oudna No 1
16 Dec 43 to Cerignola No 2
30 Dec 43 to Foggia Main
Feb 45 **Liberator VI** (Jan 46)
31 Oct 45 to Abu Sueir
Jan 46 **Lancaster B.7** (Mar 47)
17 Sep 46 to Shallufa
1 Apr 47 DB
—
1 Dec 47 RF @ Abingdon
Dec 47 **York C.1** (Mar 50)
det Wunstorf for BAL
25 Jun 49 to Bassingbourn
15 Mar 50 DB
—
28 Oct 53 RF @ Coningsby
Oct 53 **Canberra B.2** (Feb 57)
24 Feb 54 to Wittering
31 Oct 56 to Upwood
1 Feb 57 DB

41 Sqn

15 Apr 16 F @ Gosport (Fort Rowner) — nucleus from No 28 Sqn
22 May 16 DB — renumbered as No 27 RS
—
14 Jul 16 RF @ Gosport (Fort Rowner) — nucleus from No 27 RS
Jul 16 **Vickers FB 5** (Oct 16)
Jul 16 **DH 2** (Oct 16)
Sep 16 **FE 8** (Jul 17)
15 Oct 16 to St-Omer
21 Oct 16 to Abeele
24 May 17 to Hondschoote
15 Jun 17 to Abeele
3 Jul 17 to Léalvillers
Jul 17 **DH 5** (Nov 17)
Nov 17 **SE 5A** (Feb 19)
22 Mar 18 to Marieux
27 Mar 18 to Fienvillers
29 Mar 18 to Alquines
9 Apr 18 to Savy
11 Apr 18 to Serny
19 May 18 to Estrée-Blanche
1 Jun 18 to Conteville
14 Aug 18 to St-Omer
20 Sep 18 to Droglandt
23 Oct 18 to Halluin
10 Feb 19 to Tangmere as a cadre
8 Oct 19 to Croydon
31 Dec 19 DB
—
1 Apr 23 RF @ Northolt
Apr 23 **Snipe** (May 24)
May 24 **Siskin III** (Mar 27)
Mar 27 **Siskin IIIA** (Nov 31)
Oct 31 **Bulldog IIA** (Aug 34)
Jul 34 **Demon** (Oct 37)
4 Oct 35 en route Aden
20 Oct 35 to Khormaksar
18 Mar 36 to Sheikh Othman
11 Aug 36 en route UK
25 Sep 36 to Catterick
Oct 37 **Fury II** (Jan 39)
Jan 39 **Spitfire I** (Nov 40)
19 Oct 39 to Wick
25 Oct 39 to Catterick
28 May 40 to Hornchurch
17 Jun 40 to Catterick
26 Jul 40 to Hornchurch
8 Aug 40 to Catterick
3 Sep 40 to Hornchurch
Nov 40 **Spitfire IIA** (Aug 41)
23 Feb 41 to Catterick
Mar 41 **Spitfire I** (Apr 41)
28 Jul 41 to Merston
Aug 41 **Spitfire VB** (Mar 43)
16 Dec 41 to Westhampnett
1 Apr 42 to Merston
15 Jun 42 to Martlesham Heath
30 Jun 42 to Hawkinge
8 Jul 42 to Debden
1 Aug 42 to Longtown
11 Aug 42 to Llanbedr
17 Aug 42 to Tangmere
20 Aug 42 to Llanbedr
22 Sep 42 to Eglinton
30 Sep 42 to Llanbedr
5 Oct 42 to Tangmere
11 Oct 42 to Llanbedr
25 Feb 43 to High Ercall
Feb 43 **Spitfire XII** (Sep 44)
12 Apr 43 to Hawkinge
21 May 43 to Biggin Hill
28 May 43 to Friston
21 Jun 43 to Westhampnett
4 Oct 43 to Tangmere
6 Feb 44 to Southend
20 Feb 44 to Tangmere
11 Mar 44 to Friston
29 Apr 44 to Bolt Head
16 May 44 to Fairwood Common
24 May 44 to Bolt Head
19 Jun 44 to West Malling
28 Jun 44 to Westhampnett
3 Jul 44 to Friston
11 Jul 44 to Lympne
Sep 44 **Spitfire XIV** (Sep 45)
5 Dec 44 to B 64/Diest
31 Dec 44 to Y 32/Ophoven
27 Jan 45 to B 80/Volkel
7 Mar 45 to Warmwell
18 Mar 45 to B 78/Eindhoven
8 Apr 45 to B 106/Twente
16 Apr 45 to B 118/Celle
9 May 45 to B 160/Kastrup
21 Jun 45 to B 172/Husum
11 Jul 45 to B 158/Lübeck
20 Aug 45 to Warmwell
6 Sep 45 to B 158/Lübeck
Sep 45 **Tempest V** (Apr 46)
31 Jan 46 to B 116/Wunstorf
28 Feb 46 to B 170/Sylt
29 Mar 46 to B 116/Wunstorf
1 Apr 46 DB — renumbered as No 26 Sqn
—
1 Apr 46 RF @ Dalcross — No 12 Sqn renumbered
Apr 46 **Spitfire F.21** (Aug 47)
15 Apr 46 to Wittering
29 Jun 46 to Lübeck
30 Aug 46 to Wittering
11 Nov 46 to Acklington
20 Dec 46 to Wittering
17 Apr 47 to Church Fenton
Aug 47 **Oxford T.2** (Sep 48)
Aug 47 **Harvard T.2B** (Sep 48)
Jun 48 **Hornet F.1** (Aug 48)
Jul 48 **Hornet F.3** (Mar 51)
Jan 51 **Meteor F.4** (Apr 51)
29 Mar 51 to Biggin Hill
Apr 51 **Meteor F.8** (Jul 55)
Jun 55 **Hunter F.5** (Jan 58)
31 Jan 58 DB

—
1 Feb 58 RF @ Coltishall — No 141 Sqn renumbered
Feb 58 **Javelin FAW 4** (Feb 60)
5 Jul 58 to Wattisham
Aug 58 **Javelin FAW 5** (Feb 60)
Nov 59 **Javelin FAW 8** (Dec 63)
Dec 63 DB
—
Sep 65 **Bloodhound II** at West Raynham
Jul 70 DB
—
Apr 72 RF @ Coningsby
Apr 72 **Phantom FGR 2** (Mar 77)
Mar 77 DB
—
Oct 76 training at Coltishall as No 41 Sqn (Designate)
—
Apr 77 RF @ Coltishall
Apr 77 **Jaguar GR 1** ( )

2 Sqn

Feb 16 F @ Netheravon — nucleus from No 19 Sqn
Apr 16 to Filton
Apr 16 **BE 2D** (Aug 16)
Apr 16 **BE 2E** (Apr 17)
Aug 16 to St-Omer
Aug 16 to Bailleul (Town Ground)
Sep 16 to La Gorgue
Nov 16 to Bailleul (Town Ground)
Apr 17 **RE 8** (Feb 19) det Abeele
Nov 17 to Fienvillers
Nov 17 to Candas
Dec 17 to Padua
Dec 17 to San Pelagio
Dec 17 to Istrana
Dec 17 to Grossa dets Limbraga, San Luca
Feb 18 to San Luca
Mar 18 to Poggio Renatico
Mar 18 to Fienvillers
Mar 18 to Chocques
Apr 18 to Treizennes
Apr 18 to Rely
Oct 18 to Chocques
Oct 18 to Ascq
Nov 18 to Marquain
Nov 18 to Aulnoy
Dec 18 to Saultain
Dec 18 to Abscon
Feb 19 to Netheravon as a cadre
Jun 19 DB
—
Dec 36 RF @ Donibristle — from 'B' Flt, No 22 Sqn
Dec 36 **Vildebeeste III** (Dec 37)
Jan 37 **Vildebeeste I** (Mar 37)
Mar 37 **Vildebeeste IV** (Apr 40)
Mar 38 to Thorney Island dets Eastleigh, Lee-on-Solent, Tangmere, Gosport
ep 38 to Thornaby
ct 38 to Thorney Island
ug 39 to Bircham Newton
ep 39 **Vildebeeste III** (Apr 40)
pr 40 **Beaufort I** (Apr 42)
pr 40 to Thorney Island
un 40 to Wick det Thorney Island
lar 41 to Leuchars dets North Coates, Sumburgh, Coltishall, St Eval, Wick
lar 42 **Beaufort II** (Oct 42)
un 42 to FE by sea. Air echelon flew via ME; retained to operate from Luqa & Shandur. Moved on to India in Nov 42.
17 Oct 42 to Ratmalana
7 Dec 42 to Yelahanka
Dec 42 **Beaufort I** (Feb 43) det Vizagapatam
Feb 43 **Blenheim V** (Oct 43) det Rajyeswarpur
12 Mar 43 to Rajyeswarpur det Kumbhirgram
1 May 43 to Kumbhirgram det Yelahanka
Oct 43 **Hurricane IV** (Jun 45)
10 Nov 43 to St Thomas Mount
18 Dec 43 to Palel
2 May 44 to Kangla
6 Jul 44 to Tulihal
Sep 44 **Hurricane IIC** (Dec 44)
16 Nov 44 to Kangla
19 Jan 45 to Onbauk
14 Mar 45 to Ondaw
23 Apr 45 to Sinthe
Apr 45 **Hurricane IIC** (Jun 45)
30 Apr 45 to 'Maida Vale'
18 May 45 to Chakulia
22 May 45 to Dalbumgarh
30 Jun 45 DB
—
1 Jul 45 RF @ Meiktila — No 146 Sqn renumbered
Jul 45 **Thunderbolt II** (Dec 45)
30 Dec 45 DB
—
1 Oct 46 RF @ Thorney Island — No 254 Sqn renumbered
Oct 46 **Beaufighter TF 10** (Oct 47)
15 Oct 47 DB
—
28 Jun 52 RF @ St Eval
Jun 52 **Shackleton MR 1A** (Jul 54)
Jan 53 **Shackleton MR 2** (Jun 66)
8 Oct 58 to St Mawgan
Nov 65 **Shackleton MR 3** (Sep 71)
Apr 71 **Nimrod MR 1** (Jun 84)
Jun 83 **Nimrod MR 2** ( )

43 Sqn

15 Apr 46 F @ Montrose — nucleus from No 18 RS
19 Apr 16 to Stirling
May 16 **AW FK 3** (Aug 16)
Jun 16 **BE 2C** (Aug 16)
Jun 16 **Avro 504** (Aug 16)
30 Aug 16 to Netheravon
Aug 16 **Bristol Scout** (Dec 16)
Nov 16 **BE 2C** (Nov 16)
Dec 16 **1½ Strutter** (Sep 17)
9 Dec 16 to Northolt
17 Jan 17 to St-Omer
25 Jan 17 to Treizennes
30 May 17 to Lozinghem
Sep 17 **Camel** (Oct 18)
15 Jan 18 to La Gorgue
22 Mar 18 to Avesnes-le-Comte
3 Jun 18 to Fouquerolles
21 Jun 18 to Estrée-Blanche
14 Jul 18 to Touquin
2 Aug 18 to Fienvillers
Aug 18 **Snipe** (Sep 19)
6 Oct 18 to Senlis-le-Sec
31 Oct 18 to Bouvincourt
15 Nov 18 to Bisseghem
26 Nov 18 to Fort Cognelée
19 Dec 18 to Bickendorf
12 Aug 19 to Eil
25 Aug 19 to Spittlegate
28 Sep 19 reduced to a cadre
31 Dec 19 DB
—
1 Jul 25 RF @ Henlow
Jul 25 **Snipe** (May 26)
Apr 26 **Gamecock I** (Jun 28)
12 Dec 26 to Tangmere
Jun 28 **Siskin IIIA** (May 31)
May 31 **Fury I** (Jan 39)
Dec 38 **Hurricane I** (Apr 41)
18 Nov 39 to Acklington
26 Feb 40 to Wick
31 May 40 to Tangmere det Northolt
8 Sep 40 to Usworth
12 Dec 40 to Drem
22 Feb 41 to Crail
1 Mar 41 to Drem
Apr 41 **Hurricane IIA** (Aug 42)
Apr 41 **Hurricane IIB** (Aug 42)
4 Oct 41 to Acklington det Ford
Dec 41 **Hurricane IIC** (Aug 42)
16 Jun 42 to Tangmere
1 Sep 42 to Kirton-in-Lindsey
Sep 42 **Hurricane I** (Nov 42)
28 Oct 42 en route N Africa via Gibraltar
8 Nov 42 to Maison Blanche
Nov 42 **Hurricane IIC** (Mar 43)
17 Mar 43 to Jemappes
Mar 43 **Spitfire VC** (Jan 44)
19 Apr 43 to Tingley
2 May 43 to Nefza
26 May 43 to Mateur I
5 Jun 43 to Sfax
9 Jun 43 to Hal Far
14 Jul 43 to Comiso
1 Aug 43 to Pachino
Aug 43 **Spitfire IX** (May 47)
29 Aug 43 to Panebianco
30 Aug 43 to Catania
2 Sep 43 to Cassala
6 Sep 43 to Falcone
16 Sep 43 to Tusciano
11 Oct 43 to Capodichino
16 Jan 44 to Lago
21 May 44 to Nettuno
5 Jun 44 to Tre Cancelli
14 Jun 44 to Tarquinia
25 Jun 44 to Grosseto
5 Jul 44 to Piombino
20 Jul 44 to Calvi
Aug 44 **Spitfire VIII** (Nov 44)
20 Aug 44 to Ramatuelle
25 Aug 44 to Sisteron
7 Sep 44 to Lyons/Bron
27 Sep 44 to La Jasse
13 Oct 44 to Peretola
16 Nov 44 to Rimini
17 Feb 45 to Ravenna
5 May 45 to Rivolto
11 May 45 to Klagenfurt
10 Sep 45 to Zeltweg
24 Sep 46 to Tissano
18 Jan 47 to Treviso
16 May 47 DB
—
11 Feb 49 RF @ Tangmere — No 266 Sqn renumbered
Feb 49 **Meteor F.4** (Sep 50)
Sep 50 **Meteor F.8** (Sep 54)
11 Nov 50 to Leuchars
Jul 54 **Hunter F.1** (Nov 56)
Feb 56 **Hunter F.4** (Jul 58)
Nov 56 **Hunter F.6** (Dec 56)
Jan 58 **Hunter F.6** (Jul 60)
May 60 **Hunter FGA 9** (Oct 67)
21 Jun 61 to Nicosia
1 Mar 63 to Khormaksar
7 Nov 67 DB
—
1 Sep 69 RF @ Leuchars
Sep 69 **Phantom FG 1** ( )

44 Sqn

15 Apr 16 F @ Catterick — nucleus from No 6 RS
18 Apr 16 to Turnhouse
22 May 16 DB — redesignated as No 26 RS
—
24 Jul 17 RF @ Hainault Farm — nucleus from No 39 Sqn
Jul 17 **1½ Strutter** (Sep 17)
Aug 17 **Camel** (Jun 19)
1 Jul 19 to North Weald Basset as a cadre
31 Dec 19 DB
—
8 Mar 37 RF @ Wyton
Mar 37 **Hind** (Dec 37)
18 Mar 37 to Andover
16 Jun 37 to Waddington
Dec 37 **Blenheim I** (Feb 39)
Feb 39 **Anson I** (Jun 39)
Feb 39 **Hampden** (Dec 41) det Lossiemouth
Dec 41 **Lancaster I & III** (Sep 47) dets Lossiemouth, Nutts Corner
31 May 43 to Dunholme Lodge
30 Sep 44 to Spilsby
21 Jul 45 to Mepal
25 Aug 45 to Mildenhall
Oct 45 **Lincoln B.2** (May 46)
29 Aug 46 to Wyton
Dec 46 **Lincoln B.2** (Mar 47)
May 47 **Lincoln B.2** (Jan 51)
7 Feb 51 to Marham
Feb 51 **Washington B.1** (Jan 53)
9 Apr 51 to Coningsby
Apr 53 **Canberra B.2** (Jul 57)
20 May 54 to Cottesmore
20 Feb 55 to Honington
15 Jul 57 DB
—
10 Aug 60 RF @ Waddington — nucleus from No 83 Sqn
Aug 60 **Vulcan B.1** (Sep 67)
Sep 66 **Vulcan B.2** (Dec 82)
21 Dec 82 DB

45 Sqn

1 Mar 16 F @ Gosport (Fort Grange) — nucleus from No 22 Sqn
Mar 16 **Avro 504** (Apr 16)
Mar 16 **Martinsyde S.1** (Sep 16)
Mar 16 **BE 2C** (Sep 16)
Mar 16 **Bristol Scout** (Sep 16)
Apr 16 **FE 2B** (Sep 16)
3 May 16 to Thetford
21 May 16 to Sedgeford
May 16 **Henry Farman F.20** (Sep 16)
Sep 16 **1½ Strutter** (Aug 17)
12 Oct 16 to St-Omer
15 Oct 16 to Fienvillers det Boisdinghem
4 Dec 16 to Ste-Marie-Cappel
Apr 17 **Nieuport 12** (May 17)
Apr 17 **Nieuport 10** (May 17)
Jul 17 **Camel** (Jan 19)
16 Nov 17 to Fienvillers
16 Dec 17 to Candas
18 Dec 17 to Padua
18 Dec 17 to San Pelagio
26 Dec 17 to Istrana
17 Mar 18 to Grossa
22 Sep 18 to Bettoncourt
Oct 18 **Snipe** (Jan 19)
21 Nov 18 to Izel-le-Hameau
19 Jan 19 to Liettres
17 Feb 19 to Rendcomb as a cadre
15 Oct 19 to Eastleigh
31 Dec 19 DB
—
1 Apr 21 RF @ Helwan
Apr 21 **DH 9A** (Jul 21)
11 Jul 21 to Almaza
Jul 21 **Vimy** (Feb 22)
Feb 22 **Vernon** (Jan 27)
14 Mar 22 to Basrah
14 Apr 22 to Baghdad West
16 May 22 to Hinaidi
17 Jan 27 to Helwan as a cadre
25 Apr 27 re-established at Heliopolis
Apr 27 **DH 9A** (Sep 29)
21 Oct 27 to Helwan det Ramleh
Aug 29 **Fairey IIIF** (Dec 35) dets Amman, Gaza, Ismailia, Hinaidi, Mosul, Shaibah, Eastleigh

Sep 35 **Hart** (Jan 36)
Nov 35 **Vincent** (Dec 37)
Jan 36 **Gordon** (Dec 36) — Eastleigh det only; became No 223 Sqn
Nov 37 **Wellesley** (Jun 39)
3 Jan 39 to Ismailia
Jun 39 **Blenheim I** (Feb 41)
4 Aug 39 to Fuka
18 Jun 40 to Helwan dets El Daba, Carthago, Summit
26 Sep 40 to Wadi Gazouza
28 Nov 40 to Helwan
8 Dec 40 to Qotafiyah
30 Dec 40 to LG 81
31 Dec 40 to Menastir
6 Feb 41 to Helwan
Feb 41 **Blenheim IV** (Aug 42)
4 Apr 41 to Derna
6 Apr 41 to Gazala
7 Apr 41 to Gambut Main
10 Apr 41 to Qasaba
12 Apr 41 to El Gubsi
13 Apr 41 to Fuka
May 41 **Blenheim IVF** (Jan 42)
1 Jun 41 to Wadi Natrun
23 Jun 41 to Aqir det Muqueibila
21 Aug 41 to Habbaniyah
24 Sep 41 to LG 16
14 Nov 41 to LG 75
18 Dec 41 to Gambut det Wadi Natrun
6 Jan 42 to Helwan det Bu Amud
13 Feb 42 en route FE
Feb 42 to Mingaladon dets Zayatkwin, 'Highland Queen', 'John Haig', 'Johnny Walker'
21 Feb 42 to Magwe dets 'Highland Queen', 'John Haig', 'Johnny Walker', Akyab, Asansol
29 Mar 42 to Loiwing dets Fyzabad, Kanchrapara, Dum Dum, Lashio
14 Apr 42 to Lashio
30 Apr 42 to Dum Dum (where HQ had been since 26 Mar)
16 Aug 42 to Asansol
9 Nov 42 to Cholavaram
Dec 42 **Vengeance IA & II** (Feb 44) det Asansol
8 Mar 43 to Asansol
18 May 43 to Digri dets Chittagong, Ranchi, Kumbhirgram
14 Oct 43 to Kumbhirgram
12 Feb 44 to Yelahanka
Feb 44 **Mosquito VI** (Dec 46)
1 May 44 to Amarda Road
29 May 44 to Dalbhumgarh
27 Aug 44 to Ranchi
22 Sep 44 to Kumbhirgram
26 Apr 45 to Joari det Chiringa
17 May 45 to Cholavaram
14 Oct 45 to St Thomas Mount
29 May 46 to Negombo
Dec 46 **Beaufighter TF 10** (Feb 50)
Apr 47 **Mosquito FB 6** (Jun 47) det Kuala Lumpur
May 49 **Brigand Met 3** (Jun 49) — to No 1301 Flt wef 14 Jun 49
16 May 49 to Kuala Lumpur dets Negombo, Butterworth, Tengah
Oct 49 **Brigand B.1** (Feb 52)
5 Dec 49 to Tengah
Jan 52 **Hornet F.3** (May 55) dets Butterworth, Kuala Lumpur
31 Mar 55 to Butterworth
May 55 **Vampire FB 9** (Jan 56)
Oct 55 **Venom FB 1** (Nov 57) det Coningsby for Canberra
15 Nov 57 to Tengah
Nov 57 **Canberra B.2** (Dec 62)
Sep 62 **Canberra B.15** (Feb 70) dets Labuan, Kuching, Kuantan, Kai Tak
18 Feb 70 DB
—
1 Aug 72 RF @ West Raynham
Aug 72 **Hunter FGA 9** (Jul 76)
29 Sep 72 to Wittering
26 Jul 76 DB

46 Sqn

19 Apr 16 F @ Brooklands — nucleus from No 2 RS
20 Apr 16 to Wyton
Apr 16 **BE 2C** (Sep 16)
16 **BE 2E** (Sep 16)
Sep 16 **Nieuport 12** (Apr 17)
20 Oct 16 to St-Omer
26 Oct 16 to Droglandt
Jan 17 **Nieuport 20** (Apr 17)
25 Apr 17 to Boisdinghem
Apr 17 **Pup** (Nov 17)
12 May 17 to La Gorgue
6 Jul 17 to Bruay
10 Jul 17 to Suttons Farm
30 Aug 17 to Ste-Marie-Cappel
7 Sep 17 to Filescamp Farm
Nov 17 **Camel** (Feb 19)
16 May 18 to Liettres
17 Jun 18 to Serny
14 Aug 18 to Poulainville
8 Sep 18 to Cappy
6 Oct 18 to Athies
27 Oct 18 to Busigny
16 Nov 18 to Baizieux
10 Feb 19 to Rendcomb as a cadre
31 Dec 19 DB
—
3 Sep 36 RF @ Kenley — from 'B' Flt, No 17 Sqn
Sep 36 **Gauntlet II** (Mar 39)
15 Nov 37 to Digby
Mar 39 **Hurricane I** (May 41)
10 Dec 39 to Acklington
17 Jan 40 to Digby
9 May 40 to Scapa Flow for HMS *Glorious*
26 May 40 to Skaanland
27 May 40 to Bardufoss
8 Jun 40 to HMS *Glorious* — sunk 8 Jun 40
13 Jun 40 re-established at Digby det Ternhill
1 Sep 40 to Stapleford
8 Nov 40 to North Weald
14 Dec 40 to Digby
28 Feb 41 to Church Fenton
1 Mar 41 to Sherburn-in-Elmet
20 May 41 to ME, aircrew left in Malta for No 126 Sqn
16 Jul 41 to Abu Sueir as an MU
10 Sep 41 to Kilo 17
2 May 42 to Idku — re-established from an element of No 89 Sqn
May 42 **Beaufighter IF** (Sep 43) dets Abu Sueir, El Gubbi, Ramat David, Bersis, St Jean, Nicosia, Lakatamia, Tocra, Gambut, Luqa, LG 224, Berka, Bu Amud, El Adem
Jan 43 **Beaufighter VIF** (Dec 44)
Sep 43 **Beaufighter XI** (Nov 43)
Nov 43 **Beaufighter VIC** (Dec 43)
Feb 44 **Beaufighter X** (Apr 44)
Aug 44 **Mosquito XII** (Dec 44)
13 Dec 44 to Shallufa (No 39 PTC)
21 Dec 44 en route UK
9 Jan 45 to Stoney Cross
Feb 45 **Stirling V** (May 46)
Nov 45 **Stirling IV** (Jan 46)
Feb 46 **Dakota** (Feb 50)
11 Oct 46 to Manston
16 Dec 46 to Abingdon
24 Nov 47 to Oakington dets Wunstorf, Fassberg, Lübeck for BAL
20 Feb 50 DB
—
15 Aug 54 RF @ Odiham
Aug 54 **Meteor NF 12** (Feb 56)
Aug 54 **Meteor NF 14** (Feb 56)
Feb 56 **Javelin FAW 1** (Oct 57)
Aug 57 **Javelin FAW 2** (Jun 61)
May 58 **Javelin FAW 6** (Oct 58)
17 Jul 59 to Waterbeach
30 Jun 61 DB — nucleus remained to ferry Javelins to FE for No 60 Sqn
—
1 Sep 66 RF @ Abingdon
Sep 66 **Andover C.1** (Aug 75)
9 Sep 70 to Thorney Island
29 Aug 75 DB

47 Sqn

1 Mar 16 F @ Beverley
Mar 16 **BE 2C** (Aug 16)
Mar 16 **AW FK 3** (Sep 16)
Jun 16 **Bristol Scout** (Jul 16)
5 Sep 16 en route Salonika
20 Sep 16 to Mikra Bay
Oct 16 **BE 12** (Apr 18) Flt @ Yanesh
Feb 17 **DH 2** (Jan 18)
Feb 17 **AW FK 3** (Jul 18)
Jun 17 **Vickers FB 19 Mk II** (Apr 18)
Sep 17 **BE 12A** (Feb 18)
Oct 17 **BE 2E** (Apr 18)
27 Oct 17 to Yanesh Flts @ Mikra Bay, Kukush, Snevche, Hadzi Junas, Kirec, Kalabac, Hajdarli, Amberkoj dets Thasos, Florina, Mudros, Gmuldjina, Dedeagatch
Nov 17 **SE 5A** (Apr 18)
Feb 18 **Bristol M.1C** (May 18)
Mar 18 **AW FK 8** (Jan 19)
Aug 18 **DH 9** (Oct 19)
14 Feb 19 to Amberkoj
24 Apr 19 to Novorossisk
4 Jun 19 to Ekaterinodar Flts @ Velikoknya-jaskaya, Zimovniki, Kotelnikovo, Gniloaksaiskaya, Beketovka
Aug 19 **DH 9A** (Oct 19)
Sep 19 **Camel** (Oct 19)
7 Oct 19 to Beketovka
20 Oct 19 DB — redesignated as Nos 11, 12 and 13 Sqns, Russian 7th Division
—
1 Feb 20 RF @ Helwan — No 206 Sqn renumbered
Feb 20 **DH 9** (Sep 20) det Khartoum
Jun 20 **DH 9A** (Jun 28)
21 Oct 27 to Khartoum
Dec 27 **Fairey IIIF** (Jan 33)
Jan 33 **Gordon** (Dec 39)
Jul 36 **Vincent** (Aug 40)
Jun 39 **Wellesley** (Mar 43) det Kapoeta
28 May 40 to Erkowit/Carthago dets Gordon's Tree, Gedaref, Sennar
27 Nov 40 to Gordon's Tree dets Sennar, Kassala, Agordat, Asmara, Blackdown
24 Apr 41 to Asmara
9 Dec 41 to Massawa
22 Dec 41 to Kasfareet
25 Jan 42 to Burgh el Arab
10 Feb 42 to LG 87
18 Mar 42 to Kasfareet
—
16 Apr 42 Operational **(Wellesley)** echelon established at LG 89
1 Jul 42 to Shandur
16 Jul 42 to St Jean
10 Nov 42 to LG 227
30 Nov 42 to LG 08
4 Jan 43 to LG 07
3 Mar 43 DB (Operational echelon
—
8 Sep 42 to Shandur — re-established from elements of Nos 39 and 42 Sqns
Sep 42 **Beaufort I** (Jun 43) det Gianaclis
29 Jan 43 to Gianaclis det Berka
3 Mar 43 to Misurata West
Jun 43 **Beaufighter X** (Oct 44)
22 Jun 43 to Protville II
17 Oct 43 to Sidi Amor det El Adem
14 Nov 43 to El Adem
25 Nov 43 to Gambut No 3
16 Mar 44 to Amiriya
25 Mar 44 en route India
20 Apr 44 to Cholavaram
7 Oct 44 to Yelahanka
Oct 44 **Mosquito VI** (Nov 44)
6 Nov 44 to Ranchi
Dec 44 **Beaufighter X** (Apr 45)
13 Jan 45 to Kumbhirgram det Thazi
Feb 45 **Mosquito VI** (Mar 46)
28 Apr 45 to Kinmagon
15 Aug 45 to Hmawbi dets Meiktila, Kemajora
15 Jan 46 to Butterworth det Kemajoran
21 Mar 46 DB
—
1 Sep 46 RF @ Qastina — No 64 Sqn renumbered
Sep 46 **Halifax A.7** (Nov 46)
Sep 46 **Halifax A.9** (Sep 48)
30 Sep 46 to Fairford
14 Sep 48 to Dishforth
Sep 48 **Hastings C.1** (Mar 56) det Schleswig for BAL
22 Aug 49 to Topcliffe
Feb 53 **Hastings C.2** (Mar 56)
13 May 53 to Abingdon
Mar 56 **Beverley C.1** (Oct 67)
31 Oct 67 DB
—
1 Mar 68 RF @ Fairford
Mar 68 **Hercules C.1** ( )
1 Feb 71 to Lyneham
Mar 80 **Hercules C.3** ( )

48 Sqn

15 Apr 16 F @ Netheravon — nucleus from No 7 RS, used various aircraft
8 Jun 16 to Rendcomb
Mar 17 **Bristol F2a Fighter** (Jul 17)
8 Mar 17 to La Bellevue
May 17 **Bristol F2b Fighter** (May 19)
10 Jul 17 to Bray-Dunes
15 Sep 17 to Leffrinckhoucke
22 Dec 17 to Flez
22 Mar 18 to Champien
24 Mar 18 to Bertangles
28 Mar 18 to Conteville
3 Apr 18 to Bertangles
26 Aug 18 to Boisdinghem

30 Sep 18 to Ste-Marie-Cappel
29 Oct 18 to Reckem
17 Nov 18 to Nivelles
19 Dec 18 to Bickendorf
26 May 19 en route India
27 Jun 19 to Quetta
Aug 19 **Bristol F2b Fighter** (Apr 20)
det Loralai
1 Apr 20 DB — renumbered as No 5 Sqn
—
25 Nov 35 RF @ Bicester — from 'C' Flt, No 101 Sqn
6 Dec 35 to Manston
Jan 36 **Cloud** (Jun 36) — 'B' Flt, Seaplane Training Sqn attached from Calshot 17 Jan-20 Jun 36
6 Jan 36 'X' Flt, School of Air Navigation attached until 1 Sep 38
Mar 36 **Anson I** (Dec 41)
1 Sep 38 to Eastchurch
8 Sep 38 to Thorney Island
0 Oct 38 to Eastchurch
4 Aug 39 to Manston
3 Aug 39 to Eastchurch
5 Aug 39 to Thorney Island
dets Bircham Newton, Detling, Guernsey, Carew Cheriton
Jun 40 **Beaufort I** (Nov 40)
det St Eval
6 Jul 40 to Hooton Park
dets Aldergrove, Port Ellen, Carew Cheriton, Limavady, Stornoway
3 Aug 41 to Stornoway
dets Aldergrove, Limavady
Sep 41 **Hudson V** (Nov 42)
Sep 41 **Hudson III** (Dec 42)
0 Oct 41 to Skitten
5 Jan 42 to Wick
dets Sumburgh, Kaldadarnes
3 Sep 42 to Sumburgh
0 Nov 42 to Gosport
Nov 42 **Hudson VI** (Feb 44)
3 Dec 42 to Gibraltar
det Agadir
Jul 43 **Beaufighter IIF** (Aug 43)
Feb 44 to Bircham Newton
3 Feb 44 to Down Ampney
Feb 44 **Dakota** (Jan 46)
det Birch
4 Aug 45 en route FE
3 Sep 45 to Patenga
5 Jan 46 DB
—
5 Feb 46 RF @ Kallang — No 215 Sqn renumbered
Feb 46 **Dakota** (May 51)
det Kemajoran
4 Apr 46 to Changi
Jun 49 to Kuala Lumpur
2 Dec 49 to Changi
Jun 50 **Valetta C.1** (Sep 50)
May 51 **Valetta C.1** (Dec 57)
May 57 **Hastings C.1 & C.2** (Mar 67)
Jun 59 **Beverley C.1** (Oct 60) — became No 34 Sqn
Apr 67 DB
—
Oct 67 RF @ Changi
Oct 67 **Hercules C.1** (Jan 76)
Sep 71 to Lyneham
Jan 76 DB

9 Sqn

Apr 16 F @ Swingate Down — nucleus from No 13 RS
Apr 16 **BE 2C** (Nov 17)
Apr 16 **Avro 504** (Nov 17)
Dec 16 **RE 7** (Nov 17)
Apr 17 **Martinsyde G.100** (Nov 17)
Apr 17 **DH 4** (Apr 18)
12 Nov 17 to La Bellevue
26 Mar 18 to Les Eauvis
29 Mar 18 to Boisdinghem
30 Mar 18 to Petite Synthe
Apr 18 **DH 9** (Jul 19)
3 May 18 to Conteville
2 Jun 18 to Fourneuil
21 Jun 18 to Beauvois
15 Jul 18 to Rozay-en-Brie
4 Aug 18 to Beauvois
29 Oct 18 to Villers-lès-Cagnicourt
24 Nov 18 to Bavai
29 May 19 to Bickendorf
18 Jul 19 DB
—
10 Feb 36 RF @ Bircham Newton — from 'C' Flt, No 18 Sqn
Feb 36 **Hind** (Dec 38)
8 Aug 36 to Worthy Down
14 Mar 38 to Scampton
Sep 38 **Hampden** (Apr 42)
det Kinloss
Apr 42 **Manchester** (Jun 42)
Jun 42 **Lancaster I & III** (Mar 50)
2 Jan 43 to Fiskerton
16 Oct 44 to Fulbeck
22 Apr 45 to Syerston
28 Sep 45 to Mepal
29 Jul 46 to Upwood
Oct 49 **Lincoln B.2** (Jul 55)
25 Jun 52 to Waddington
1 Aug 53 to Wittering
23 Feb 54 to Upwood
1 Aug 55 DB
—
1 May 56 RF @ Wittering
May 56 **Valiant B.1** (Mar 63)
dets Christmas Island, Edinburgh Field
Jun 56 **Valiant B(PR) 1** (Nov 56)
Nov 56 **Valiant B(K) 1** (Dec 64)
26 Jun 61 to Marham
1 May 65 DB

50 Sqn

15 May 16 F @ Swingate Down — nucleus from No 20 RS
May 16 **BE 2C** (Sep 17)
May 16 **BE 12** (May 18)
Jun 16 **Vickers ES 1** (Jul 17)
23 Oct 16 to Harrietsham
dets Detling, Bekesbourne, Throwley
Dec 16 **BE 12A** (Aug 17)
Dec 16 **BE 2E** (Feb 18)
Mar 17 **Bristol M.1B** (Mar 17)
May 17 **RE 8** (Jun 17)
May 17 **AW FK 8** (Jan 18)
Jun 17 **Pup** (Jul 17)
Jan 18 **BE 12B** (Jun 18)
5 Mar 18 to Bekesbourne
May 18 **SE 5A** (Jul 18)
Jul 18 **Camel** (Jun 19)
13 Jun 19 DB
—
3 May 37 RF @ Waddington
May 37 **Hind** (Jan 39)
Dec 38 **Hampden** (Apr 42)
dets Lossiemouth, Wick, Kinloss
10 Jul 40 to Hatfield Woodhouse/Lindholme
20 Jul 41 to Swinderby
26 Nov 41 to Skellingthorpe
Apr 42 **Manchester** (Jun 42)
May 42 **Lancaster I & III** (Oct 46)
20 Jun 42 to Swinderby
16 Oct 42 to Skellingthorpe
16 Jun 45 to Sturgate
26 Jan 46 to Waddington
Jul 46 **Lincoln B.2** (Jan 51)
31 Jan 51 DB
—
15 Aug 52 RF @ Binbrook
Aug 52 **Canberra B.2** (Oct 59)
8 Jan 56 to Upwood
1 Oct 59 DB
—
1 Aug 61 RF @ Waddington — nucleus from No 617 Sqn
Aug 61 **Vulcan B.1** (Oct 66)
Jan 66 **Vulcan B.2** (Mar 84)
Jun 82 **Vulcan B.2(K)** (Mar 84)
31 Mar 84 DB

51 Sqn

15 May 16 F @ Norwich — nucleus from No 9 RS
May 16 **BE 2C** (Jan 17)
May 16 **BE 12** (Jan 17)
1 Jun 16 to Thetford
23 Sep 16 to Hingham
dets Harling Road, Mattishall, Narborough, Tydd St Mary
Oct 16 **FE 2B** (Nov 18)
Dec 16 **BE 2E** (Mar 17)
7 Aug 17 to Marham
dets Mattishall, Tydd St Mary
17 **Martinsyde G.100** (17)
Jan 18 **BE 12B** (18)
Oct 18 **Camel** (Jun 19)
14 May 19 to Suttons Farm
13 Jun 19 DB
—
15 Mar 37 RF @ Driffield — from 'B' Flt, No 58 Sqn
Mar 37 **Virginia X** (Feb 38)
24 Mar 37 to Boscombe Down
Mar 37 **Anson I** (Feb 38)
Feb 38 **Whitley II** (Dec 39)
20 Apr 38 to Linton-on-Ouse
Aug 38 **Whitley III** (Mar 40)
Nov 39 **Whitley IV** (May 40)
det Kinloss
9 Dec 39 to Dishforth
Jan 40 **Whitley V** (Oct 42)
det Andover
6 May 42 to Chivenor
27 Oct 42 to Snaith
Nov 42 **Halifax II** (Jan 44)
Jan 44 **Halifax III** (May 45)
20 Apr 45 to Leconfield
Jun 45 **Stirling V** (Apr 46)
21 Aug 45 to Stradishall
Nov 45 **Stirling IV** (Jan 46)
Jan 46 **York C.1** (Oct 50)
20 Aug 46 to Waterbeach
det Wunstorf for BAL
1 Dec 47 to Abingdon
25 Jun 49 to Bassingbourn
30 Oct 50 DB
—
21 Aug 58 RF @ Watton — No 192 Sqn renumbered
Aug 58 **Canberra B.2** (Jul 59)
Aug 58 **Canberra B.6** (Oct 76)
Aug 58 **Comet C.2(R)** (Jan 75)
Feb 63 **Hastings C.1** (Mar 67)
31 Mar 63 to Wyton
Jul 71 **Nimrod R.1** ( )

52 Sqn

15 May 16 F @ Hounslow — nucleus from No 39 Sqn
May 16 **BE 2C** (Nov 16)
May 16 **BE 12** (Nov 16)
Nov 16 **RE 8** (Feb 17)
17 Nov 16 to St-Omer
18 Nov 16 to Bertangles
15 Dec 16 to Chipilly
25 Jan 17 to Méaulte
Feb 17 **BE 2F** (May 17)
Feb 17 **BE 2G** (May 17)
29 Mar 17 to Longavesnes
May 17 **RE 8** (Feb 19)
15 Jun 17 to Bray-Dunes
6 Dec 17 to Izel-le-Hameau
4 Jan 18 to Lahoussoye
12 Jan 18 to Matigny
23 Jan 18 to Golancourt
22 Mar 18 to Catigny
24 Mar 18 to Lahoussoye
25 Mar 18 to Poulainville
28 Mar 18 to Abbeville
3 May 18 to Mont-de-Soissons
5 May 18 to Fismes
27 May 18 to Cramaille
28 May 18 to La Ferté
29 May 18 to Trécon
30 Jun 18 to Auxi-le-Chateau
4 Aug 18 to Izel-le-Hameau
24 Aug 18 to Savy
19 Oct 18 to Bourlon
21 Oct 18 to Escadoeuvres
25 Oct 18 to Avesnes-le-Sec
10 Nov 18 to Aulnoy
16 Nov 18 to Linselles
23 Nov 18 to Aulnoy
18 Feb 19 to Netheravon as a cadre
28 Jun 19 to Lopcombe Corner
23 Oct 19 DB
—
18 Jan 37 RF @ Abingdon — from 'B' Flt, No 15 Sqn
Jan 37 **Hind** (Dec 37)
1 Mar 37 to Upwood
Nov 37 **Battle** (Apr 40)
Feb 39 **Anson I** (Apr 40)
det Alconbury
9 Sep 39 to Abingdon
det Kidlington
18 Sep 39 to Benson
6 Apr 40 DB — merged into No 12 OTU
—
1 Jul 41 RF @ Habbaniyah as a servicing unit
Jul 41 **Audax** (Jan 42)
17 Aug 42 to Mosul
Oct 42 **Blenheim IV** (Feb 43)
Jan 43 **Baltimore III** (Feb 43)
22 Feb 43 to LG 91
Feb 43 **Baltimore IIIA** (Mar 44)
4 Jun 43 to Protville I
Aug 43 **Baltimore IV** (Mar 44)
1 Nov 43 to Bo Rizzo
det Gibraltar
Feb 44 **Baltimore V** (Mar 44)
20 Feb 44 to Gibraltar
31 Mar 44 DB
—
1 Jul 44 RF @ Dum Dum — from 'C' & 'D' Flts, No 353 Sqn
Jul 44 **Dakota** (Sep 51)
Dec 44 **Liberator VI** (Feb 45)
Aug 45 **Liberator VI** (Dec 45)
30 Oct 46 to Mingaladon
30 Jul 47 to Changi
21 Nov 48 to Kuala Lumpur
31 May 49 to Seletar
27 Aug 49 to Changi
12 Jul 50 to Kuala Lumpur
12 Jan 51 to Changi
Jun 51 **Valetta C.1** (Apr 66)
1 Aug 59 to Kuala Lumpur
det Bayan Lepas — Voice Flt
Nov 59 **Dakota** (Jul 60) — Voice Flt
23 Sep 60 to Butterworth
25 Apr 66 DB
—
1 Dec 66 RF @ Abingdon
Dec 66 **Andover C.1** (Dec 69)
22 Dec 66 to Seletar
17 Feb 69 to Changi
31 Dec 69 DB

53 Sqn

15 May 16 F @ Catterick — nucleus from No 14 RS
May 16 **AW FK 3** (Dec 16)

May 16 **Avro 504** (Dec 16)
May 16 **BE 12** (Dec 16)
11 Dec 16 to Farnborough
Dec 16 **BE 2E** (Apr 17)
26 Dec 16 to St-Omer
Dec 16 **BE 2G** (Apr 17)
4 Jan 17 to Baiileul (Town Ground)
Feb 17 **RE 8** (Apr 19)
1 Feb 18 to Abeele
21 Feb 18 to Villeselve
23 Mar 18 to Allonville
24 Mar 18 to Fienvillers
26 Mar 18 to Boisdinghem
6 Apr 18 to Abeele
12 Apr 18 to Ste-Marie-Cappel
12 Apr 18 to Clairmarais South
21 Sep 18 to Abeele
21 Oct 18 to Coucou
6 Nov 18 to Sweveghem
16 Nov 18 to Seclin
24 Nov 18 to Reumont
28 Nov 18 to Laneffe
15 Mar 19 to Old Sarum as a cadre
25 Oct 19 DB

—

28 Jun 37 RF @ Farnborough
Jun 37 **Hector** (Mar 39)
8 Apr 38 to Odiham
Jan 39 **Blenheim IV** (Aug 41)
20 Sep 39 to Plivot
11 Oct 39 to Poix
det Vitry-en-Artois
19 May 40 to Crécy
20 May 40 to Lympne
21 May 40 to Andover
1 Jun 40 to Eastchurch
13 Jun 40 to Gatwick
3 Jul 40 to Detling
det Bircham Newton
24 Nov 40 to Thorney Island
dets Bircham Newton, St Eval
20 Mar 41 to St Eval
3 Jul 41 to Bircham Newton
Jul 41 **Hudson V** (Feb 43)
dets St Eval, Limavady
20 Oct 41 to St Eval
17 Dec 41 to Limavady
18 Feb 42 to North Coates
16 May 42 to St Eval
3 Jul 42 en route USA
30 Jul 42 to Quonset Point, Rhode Island
12 Aug 42 to Waller Field, BWI
22 Aug 42 to Edinburgh Field, BWI
23 Nov 42 to Norfolk, Virginia
30 Nov 42 en route UK
1 Jan 43 to Davidstow Moor
18 Feb 43 to Docking
Feb 43 **Whitley VII** (Apr 43)
18 Mar 43 to Bircham Newton
29 Apr 43 to Thorney Island
May 43 **Liberator VA** (Feb 45)
25 Sep 43 to Beaulieu
3 Jan 44 to St Eval
May 44 **Liberator VI** (Apr 45)
13 Sep 44 to Reykjavik
det Ballykelly
Jan 45 **Liberator VIII** (Feb 46)
1 Jun 45 to St Davids
Aug 45 **Liberator VI** (Feb 46)
17 Sep 45 to Merryfield
1 Dec 45 to Gransden Lodge
28 Feb 46 DB

—

28 Feb 46 RF @ Upwood — No 102 Sqn renumbered
Feb 46 **Liberator VI** (Jun 46)
Feb 46 **Liberator VIII** (Jun 46)
det Tempsford
15 Jun 46 DB

—

1 Dec 46 RF @ Netheravon — No 187 Sqn renumbered
Dec 46 **Dakota** (Jul 49)
11 Dec 47 to Waterbeach
dets Wunstorf, Fassberg, Lübeck for BAL
31 Jul 49 DB

—

1 Aug 49 RF @ Topcliffe — nucleus from Nos 47 & 297 Sqns
Aug 49 **Hastings C.1** (Feb 57)
9 Feb 51 to Lyneham
Jun 52 **Hastings C.2** (Feb 57)
1 Jan 57 to Abingdon
Jan 57 **Beverley C.1** (Jun 63)
30 Jun 63 DB — absorbed by No 47 Sqn

—

1 Jan 66 RF @ Fairford
Jan 66 **Belfast C.1** (Sep 76)
23 May 67 to Brize Norton
14 Sep 76 DB

54 Sqn

15 May 16 F @ Castle Bromwich — nucleus from No 5 RS
May 16 **BE 2C** (Dec 16)
Jun 16 **BE 12** (Jun 16)
Jul 16 **Avro 504** ( )
22 Dec 16 to London Colney
Dec 16 **Pup** (Dec 17)
24 Dec 16 to St-Omer
26 Dec 16 to Bertangles
11 Jan 17 to Chipilly
18 Apr 17 to Flez
18 Jun 17 to Bray-Dunes
16 Jul 17 to Leffrinckhoucke
8 Sep 17 to Teteghem
6 Dec 17 to Bruay
Dec 17 **Camel** (Feb 19)
18 Dec 17 to Lahoussoye
1 Jan 18 to Flez
22 Mar 18 to Champien
24 Mar 18 to Bertangles
28 Mar 18 to Conteville
7 Apr 18 to Clairmarais North
29 Apr 18 to Caffiers
1 Jun 18 to St-Omer
11 Jun 18 to Vignacourt
16 Jun 18 to Boisdinghem
30 Jun 18 to Liettres
14 Jul 18 to Touquin
4 Aug 18 to Fienvillers
25 Aug 18 to Avesnes-le-Comte
17 Oct 18 to Rely
24 Oct 18 to Merchin
17 Feb 19 to Yatesbury as a cadre
25 Oct 19 DB

—

15 Jan 30 RF @ Hornchurch
Jan 30 **Siskin IIIA** (Dec 30)
Apr 30 **Bulldog IIA** (Sep 36)
Aug 36 **Gauntlet II** (May 37)
Apr 37 **Gladiator I** (Apr 39)
Mar 39 **Spitfire I** (Feb 41)
28 Oct 39 to Rochford
3 Nov 39 to Hornchurch
17 Nov 39 to Rochford
2 Dec 39 to Hornchurch
16 Dec 39 to Rochford
29 Dec 39 to Hornchurch
16 Jan 40 to Rochford
14 Feb 40 to Hornchurch
23 Mar 40 to Rochford
20 Apr 40 to Hornchurch
28 May 40 to Catterick
4 Jun 40 to Hornchurch
25 Jun 40 to Rochford
24 Jul 40 to Hornchurch
28 Jul 40 to Catterick
8 Aug 40 to Hornchurch
3 Sep 40 to Catterick
23 Feb 41 to Hornchurch
Feb 41 **Spitfire IIA** (May 41)
31 Mar 41 to Southend
20 May 41 to Hornchurch
May 41 **Spitfire VA** (Aug 41)
11 Jun 41 to Debden
13 Jun 41 to Hornchurch
Jul 41 **Spitfire VB** (Nov 41)
4 Aug 41 to Martlesham Heath
Aug 41 **Spitfire IIA** (Aug 41)
25 Aug 41 to Hornchurch
17 Nov 41 to Castletown
Nov 41 **Spitfire IIB** (Mar 42)
Mar 42 **Spitfire VB** (Jun 42)
2 Jun 42 to Wellingore
18 Jun 42 en route Australia
13 Aug 42 to Melbourne (No 1 PD)
24 Aug 42 to Richmond
det Laverton
Nov 42 **Spitfire VC** (May 44)
25 Jan 43 to Darwin/Nightcliffe
dets Millingimbi, Drysdale Mission, Learmonth, Winnellie
Apr 44 **Spitfire VIII** (Sep 45)
8 Jun 44 to Livingstone
21 Oct 44 to Darwin/Civil
23 Sep 45 to Melbourne (No 1 PD)
31 Oct 45 DB

—

15 Nov 45 RF @ Chilbolton — No 183 Sqn renumbered
Nov 45 **Tempest F.2** (Oct 46)
28 Jun 46 to Odiham
9 Aug 46 to Acklington
27 Aug 46 to Odiham
5 Sep 46 to Molesworth
1 Oct 46 to Odiham
Oct 46 **Vampire F.1** (Aug 48)
6 Oct 47 to Acklington
27 Nov 47 to Odiham
Apr 48 **Vampire F.3** (Nov 49)
Oct 49 **Vampire FB 5** (Apr 52)
Apr 52 **Meteor F.8** (Mar 55)
Feb 55 **Hunter F.1** (Sep 55)
Sep 55 **Hunter F.4** (Jan 57)
Jan 57 **Hunter F.6** (Mar 60)
17 Jul 59 to Stradishall
Mar 60 **Hunter FGA 9** (Sep 69)
23 Nov 61 to Waterbeach
14 Aug 63 to West Raynham
1 Sep 69 to Coningsby
Sep 69 **Phantom FGR 2** (Apr 74)
22 Apr 74 DB

—

28 Mar 74 training at Lossiemouth as No 54 Sqn (Designate)

—

23 Apr 74 RF @ Lossiemouth
Apr 74 **Jaguar GR 1** ( )
15 Aug 74 to Coltishall

55 Sqn

8 Jun 16 F @ Castle Bromwich — nucleus from No 34 Sqn & No 5 RS
Jun 16 **BE 2C** (Feb 17)
10 Jun 16 to Lilbourne
Jun 16 **AW FK 3** (Feb 17)
Jun 16 **Avro 504K** (Feb 17)
Jan 17 **DH 4** (Jan 19)
5 Mar 17 to Fienvillers
31 May 17 to Boisdinghem
11 Oct 17 to Ochey
7 Nov 17 to Tantonville
5 Jun 18 to Azelot
16 Nov 18 to Le Planty
2 Dec 18 to St-André-aux Bois
1 Feb 19 to Renfrew as a cadre
1 Jan 20 to Shotwick
22 Jan 20 DB

—

1 Feb 20 RF @ Suez — No 142 Sqn renumbered
Feb 20 **DH 9** (Sep 20)
det Ramleh
Jun 20 **DH 9A** (Feb 30)
8 Jul 20 en route Turkey
12 Jul 20 to Maltepe
3 Sep 20 en route Basra via HMS *Ark Royal*
23 Sep 20 to Basra
30 Sep 20 to Baghdad West
dets Bushire, Mosul
20 Mar 21 to Mosul
19 May 24 to Hinaidi
Feb 30 **Wapiti** (Mar 37)
Feb 37 **Vincent** (May 39)
14 Sep 37 to Dhibban/Habbaniyah
Mar 39 **Blenheim I** (Dec 40)
25 Aug 39 to Ismailia
11 Jun 40 to Fuka
Dec 40 **Blenheim IV** (Jun 41)
10 Jan 41 to LG 79
16 Jan 41 to Amseat
5 Feb 41 to Bu Amud
15 Feb 41 to Heliopolis
dets Benina, Barce
10 Mar 41 to Marawa
4 Apr 41 to Derna
7 Apr 41 to Gazala North
8 Apr 41 to Gambut
10 Apr 41 to LG 15
2 May 41 to LG 95
det LG 15
3 Jun 41 to Helwan
1 Jul 41 to LG 100
det LG 21
11 Aug 41 to Aqir
Aug 41 **Blenheim IV** (Mar 42)
22 Sep 41 to LG 17
dets Sidi Barrani, El Gubbi
8 Jan 42 to Bu Amud
det El Gubbi
12 Jan 42 to Benina
20 Jan 42 to Berka
25 Jan 42 to El Gubbi
31 Jan 42 to Gambut
3 Feb 42 to Fuka
22 Mar 42 to Helwan
3 Apr 42 to Luxor
May 42 **Baltimore II** (Dec 42)
11 May 42 to LG 99
30 Jun 42 to LG 207
dets LG 98, LG'Y'
29 Aug 42 to LG 86
dets Lydda, Derna, LG'Y', Kilo 61
Oct 42 **Baltimore III** (Feb 43)
Feb 43 **Baltimore IIIA** (Oct 43)
7 Mar 43 to Sirtan
14 Mar 43 to Ben Gardane
5 Apr 43 to Medanine
16 Apr 43 to La Fauconnerie South
2 Jun 43 to Enfidaville
21 Jun 43 to Reyville
Jul 43 **Baltimore IV** (May 44)
det Luqa
10 Aug 43 to Monte Lungo
21 Aug 43 to Sigonella
28 Sep 43 to Brindisi
29 Oct 43 to Celone
4 Jan 44 to Kabrit
Jan 44 **Baltimore V** (Oct 44)
24 Mar 44 to Biferno
3 May 44 to Regina
23 Jun 44 to Tarquinia
20 Jul 44 to Cecina
dets Perugia, Marcianese
25 Oct 44 to Ancona
Oct 44 **Boston IV** (Jul 46)
Oct 44 **Boston V** (Jul 46)
3 Nov 44 to Porto Potenza
det Marcianese
11 Dec 44 to Falconara
det Marcianese
9 Mar 45 to Forli
12 May 45 to Aviano
20 Sep 45 to Hassani
Jul 46 **Mosquito FB 26** (Nov 46)
1 Dec 46 DB

—

1 Sep 60 RF @ Honington
Sep 60 **Victor B.1** (May 65)
24 May 65 to Marham
May 65 **Victor B(K) 1A** (Apr 67)
Feb 67 **Victor K.1/1A** (Aug 76)
Jul 75 **Victor K.2** ( )

56 Sqn

8 Jun 16 F @ Gosport (Fort Rowner) — nucleus from No 28 Sqn, used various aircraft
14 Jul 16 to London Colney

Mar 17 **SE 5** (Aug 17)
Apr 17 to St-Omer
Apr 17 to Vert Galand
May 17 to Liettres
Jun 17 **SE 5A** (Feb 19)
Jun 17 to Bekesbourne det Rochford
Jul 17 to Estrée-Blanche
Nov 17 to Laviéville
Jan 18 to Baizieux
Mar 18 to Valheureux
Oct 18 to Léchelle
Oct 18 to Esnes
Oct 18 to La Targette
Nov 18 to Béthencourt
Feb 19 to Narborough as a cadre
Dec 19 to Bircham Newton
Jan 20 DB

—

Feb 20 RF @ Aboukir — No 80 Sqn renumbered
Feb 20 **Snipe** (Sep 22) det San Stephano (remained until Aug 23)
Sep 22 DB

—

Nov 22 RF @ Hawkinge
Nov 22 **Snipe** (Nov 24)
May 23 to Biggin Hill
Sep 24 **Grebe II** (Sep 27)
Sep 27 **Siskin IIIA** (Oct 32)
Oct 27 to North Weald
Oct 32 **Bulldog IIA** (May 36)
May 36 **Gauntlet II** (Jul 37)
Jul 37 **Gladiator I** (May 38)
Apr 38 **Hurricane I** (Feb 41)
Oct 39 to Martlesham Heath det North Weald
Feb 40 to North Weald dets Manston, Vitry-en-Artois, Norrent-Fontes, Boulogne, Biggin Hill
May 40 to Digby
Jun 40 to North Weald
Sep 40 to Boscombe Down
Nov 40 to Middle Wallop
Dec 40 to North Weald
Feb 41 **Hurricane IIB** (Mar 42)
Jun 41 to Martlesham Heath
Jun 41 to Duxford
Sep 41 **Typhoon IA** (Dec 42)
Mar 42 to Snailwell
Mar 42 **Typhoon IB** (May 44)
May 42 to Manston det Tangmere
Jun 42 to Snailwell
Aug 42 to Matlask
Jul 43 to Manston
Aug 43 to Martlesham Heath
Aug 43 to Manston
Aug 43 to Bradwell Bay
Oct 43 to Martlesham Heath
Feb 44 to Scorton
Feb 44 to Acklington
Mar 44 to Scorton
Mar 44 to Ayr
Apr 44 to Scorton
Apr 44 **Spitfire IX** (Jun 44)
Apr 44 to Newchurch
Jun 44 **Tempest V** (Apr 46)
Sep 44 to Matlask
Sep 44 to B 60/Grimbergen
Oct 44 to B 80/Volkel
Apr 45 to B 112/Hopsten
Apr 45 to B 152/Fassberg
May 45 to Warmwell
May 45 to B 152/Fassberg
Jun 45 to Manston
Jun 45 to B 160/Kastrup
Aug 45 to B 164/Schleswig
Sep 45 to B 155/Dedelsdorf
Sep 45 to B 106/Twente
Sep 45 to B 155/Dedelsdorf
Oct 45 to B 152/Fassberg
Dec 45 to B 170/Sylt
Jan 46 to B 152/Fassberg
Feb 46 to Gatow
Mar 46 to B 152/Fassberg
Apr 46 DB — renumbered as No 16 Sqn

—

1 Apr 46 RF @ Bentwaters — No 124 Sqn renumbered
Apr 46 **Meteor F.3** (Sep 48)
16 Sep 46 to Boxted
5 Nov 46 to Acklington
20 Dec 46 to Wattisham
17 Apr 47 to Duxford
2 Oct 47 to Lübeck
31 Nov 47 to Duxford
2 Feb 48 to Thorney Island
3 May 48 to Lübeck
23 Jun 48 to Thorney Island
Sep 48 **Meteor F.4** (Dec 50)
10 May 50 to Waterbeach
Dec 50 **Meteor F.8** (Jun 55)
Feb 54 **Swift F.1** (Mar 55)
Aug 54 **Swift F.2** (Mar 55)
May 55 **Hunter F.5** (Nov 58)
Nov 58 **Hunter F.6** (Jan 61)
10 Jul 59 to Wattisham
Dec 60 **Lightning F.1A** (Apr 65)
Mar 65 **Lightning F.3** (Dec 71)
11 Apr 67 to Akrotiri
Sep 71 **Lightning F.6** (Jun 76)
21 Jan 75 to Wattisham
28 Jun 76 DB

—

31 Mar 76 training at Coningsby as No 56 Sqn (Designate)

—

29 Jun 76 RF @ Coningsby
Jun 76 **Phantom FGR 2** ( )
9 Jul 76 to Wattisham

57 Sqn

8 Jun 16 F (HQ & A Flt) @ Companthorpe — nucleus from No 33 Sqn, B & C Flts @ Tadcaster
Jun 16 **BE 2C** (Oct 16)
Jun 16 **Avro 504K** (Oct 16)
20 Aug 16 to Tadcaster
Oct 16 **FE 2D** (Jun 17)
16 Dec 16 to St-André-aux Bois
22 Jan 17 to Fienvillers
May 17 **DH 4** (May 19)
11 Jun 17 to Droglandt
27 Jun 17 to Boisdinghem
23 Nov 17 to Ste-Marie-Cappel
29 Mar 18 to Le Quesnoy
19 Sep 18 to Vert Galand
22 Oct 18 to Mory
9 Nov 18 to Beauvois
22 Nov 18 to Vert Galand
24 Nov 18 to Le Casteau det Spa
12 Dec 18 to Spy dets La Louveterie, Franc Waret
7 Jan 19 to Morville
Feb 19 **DH 9A** (Jul 19) dets Sart, Maisoncelle, Nivelles, Marquise
4 Aug 19 to South Carlton as a cadre
31 Dec 19 DB

—

20 Oct 31 RF @ Netheravon
Nov 31 **Hart** (May 36)
5 Sep 32 to Upper Heyford
May 36 **Hind** (May 38)
Mar 38 **Blenheim I** (May 40)
24 Sep 39 to Roye/Amy
17 Oct 39 to Rosiéres-en-Santerre
Mar 40 **Blenheim IV** (Nov 40) det Rennes
18 May 40 to Poix
19 May 40 to Crécy
22 May 40 to Wyton
29 May 40 to Gatwick
11 Jun 40 to Wyton
23 Jun 40 to Lossiemouth
14 Aug 40 to Bogs O'Mayne
6 Nov 40 to Wyton
20 Nov 40 to Feltwell
Nov 40 **Wellington IA** (Nov 40)
Nov 40 **Wellington IC** (Jun 42)
Jul 41 **Wellington II** (Nov 41)
Jan 42 **Wellington III** (Sep 42) det Methwold
Sep 42 **Lancaster I & III** (Nov 45)
4 Sep 42 to Scampton
29 Aug 43 to East Kirkby
Aug 45 **Lincoln B.2** (Nov 45)
25 Nov 45 DB

—

25 Nov 45 RF @ Elsham Wolds — No 103 Sqn renumbered
Nov 45 **Lancaster I & III** (May 46)
Nov 45 **Lincoln B.2** (May 51) dets East Kirkby, Scampton
2 Dec 45 to Scampton
1 May 46 to Lindholme
7 Oct 46 to Waddington
4 Apr 51 to Marham
Apr 51 **Washington B.1** (Mar 53)
4 Jun 51 to Waddington
2 Apr 52 to Coningsby
May 53 **Canberra B.2** (Dec 57)
22 May 54 to Cottesmore
19 Feb 55 to Honington
15 Nov 56 to Coningsby
9 Dec 57 DB

—

1 Jan 59 RF @ Honington
Jan 59 **Victor B.1** (Jun 66)
1 Dec 65 to Marham
Feb 66 **Victor K.1** (May 77)
Jun 76 **Victor K.2** (Jun 86)
30 Jun 86 DB

58 Sqn

8 Jun 16 F @ Cramlington — nucleus from No 36 Sqn, used various aircraft
Dec 17 **FE 2B** (Oct 18)
22 Dec 17 to Dover
10 Jan 18 to St-Omer
13 Jan 18 to Treizennes
1 Feb 18 to Clairmarais
25 Mar 18 to Auchel det Le Hameau
23 Apr 18 to Fauquembergues
31 Aug 18 to Alquines
Sep 18 **HP 0/400** (Jan 20)
27 Oct 18 to Provin
12 Apr 19 en route Egypt via Marseilles
2 May 19 to Heliopolis
Jul 19 **Vimy** (Jan 20)
1 Feb 20 DB — renumbered as No 70 Sqn

—

1 Apr 24 RF @ Worthy Down
Apr 24 **Vimy** (May 25)
Dec 24 **Virginia V** (Nov 26)
Mar 25 **Virginia III** (Apr 26)
Jul 25 **Virginia VI** (May 27)
Aug 26 **Virginia VII** (Dec 30)
Apr 27 **Virginia IX** (Apr 34)
Jan 28 **Virginia X** (Jan 38)
13 Jan 36 to Upper Heyford
3 Sep 36 to Driffield
Feb 37 **Anson I** (Nov 37)
24 Mar 37 to Boscombe Down
Oct 37 **Whitley I** (Apr 38)
Oct 37 **Whitley II** (Jul 39)
20 Apr 38 to Linton-on-Ouse
Apr 39 **Heyford III** (May 39)
May 39 **Whitley III** (Apr 40) dets Reims, Boscombe Down
30 Sep 39 to Boscombe Down
14 Feb 40 to Linton-on-Ouse
Mar 40 **Whitley V** (Dec 42)
8 Apr 42 to St Eval det Wick
Jun 42 **Whitley VII** (Dec 42)
30 Aug 42 to Stornoway
2 Dec 42 to Holmsley South
Dec 42 **Halifax II** (Mar 45)
31 Mar 43 to St Eval
29 Jun 43 to Holmsley South
6 Dec 43 to St Davids
1 Sep 44 to Stornoway
Mar 45 **Halifax III** (May 45)
25 May 45 DB

—

1 Oct 46 RF @ Benson — No 540 Sqn renumbered
Oct 46 **Anson C.11** (Jul 47)
Oct 46 **Mosquito PR 34** (Dec 47)
Jul 47 **Anson C.19** (Dec 51)
Apr 49 **Mosquito PR 34** (Aug 51)
Nov 50 **Lincoln B.2** (Sep 51)
Jul 51 **Mosquito PR 34A** (Dec 53)
Nov 51 **Mosquito PR 35** (Mar 54)
31 Mar 53 to Wyton
Dec 53 **Canberra PR 3** (Oct 55)
Jan 55 **Canberra PR 7** (Sep 70)
Jan 60 **Canberra PR 9** (Nov 62)
30 Sep 70 DB

—

1 Aug 73 RF @ Wittering — nucleus from No 45 Sqn
Aug 73 **Hunter FGA 9** (Jul 76)
26 Jul 76 DB

59 Sqn

21 Jun 16 F @ Narborough — nucleus from No 35 Sqn, used various aircraft
Feb 17 **RE 8** (Aug 19)
13 Feb 17 to St-Omer
23 Feb 17 to La Bellevue
1 Jun 17 to Le Hameau
15 Jun 17 to Longavesnes
15 Jul 17 to Mons-en-Chaussée
29 Oct 17 to Longavesnes
30 Nov 17 to Estrées-en-Chaussée
16 Dec 17 to Courcelles-le-Comte
22 Mar 18 to Léalvillers
26 Mar 18 to Fienvillers
12 Apr 18 to Vert Galand
Apr 18 **Bristol F2b Fighter** (Aug 19)
17 Sep 18 to Beugnâtre
14 Oct 18 to Caudry
29 Nov 18 to Gerpinnes
14 Mar 19 to Bickendorf
3 May 19 to Düren
4 Aug 19 DB

—

28 Jun 37 RF @ Old Sarum
Jun 37 **Hector** (Sep 39)
May 39 **Blenheim IV** (Aug 41)
11 May 39 to Andover
5 Oct 39 to Poix dets Vitry-en-Artois, Rennes
19 May 40 to Crécy
20 May 40 to Lympne
21 May 40 to Andover
31 May 40 to Eastchurch dets Boos, Dreux
6 Jun 40 to Odiham
3 Jul 40 to Thorney Island dets Manston, Bircham Newton, Detling
23 Jun 41 to Detling
22 Jul 41 to Thorney Island
Jul 41 **Hudson III** (Dec 41 — ferried to FE for No 62 Sqn) dets Detling, Bircham Newton
Dec 41 **Hudson V** (Aug 42)
17 Jan 42 to North Coates
Jul 42 **Hudson VI** (Aug 42)
29 Aug 42 to Thorney Island
Aug 42 **Liberator III** (Dec 42) det St Eval
Dec 42 **Fortress IIA** (Apr 43) det Chivenor
6 Feb 43 to Chivenor det St Eval

27 Mar 43 to Thorney Island
det St Eval
Apr 43 **Liberator V** (Mar 45)
11 May 43 to Aldergrove
15 Sep 43 to Ballykelly
Mar 45 **Liberator VIII** (Jun 46)
14 Sep 45 to Waterbeach
Sep 45 **Liberator VI** (Jun 46)
15 Jun 46 DB
—
1 Dec 47 RF @ Abingdon
Dec 47 **York C.1** (Oct 50)
det Wunstorf for BAL
25 Jun 49 to Bassingbourn
30 Oct 50 DB
—
1 Sep 56 RF @ Gütersloh — from No 102 Sqn
Sep 56 **Canberra B.2** (Mar 57)
Feb 57 **Canberra B(I) 8** (Jan 61)
15 Nov 57 to Geilenkirchen
4 Jan 61 DB — renumbered as No 3 Sqn

60 Sqn

15 May 16 F @ Gosport — nucleus from No 1 RS
May 16 **Morane H** (May 16)
28 May 16 to St-Omer
31 May 16 to Boisdinghem
May 16 **Morane LA** (Jun 16)
May 16 **Morane BB** (Aug 16)
May 16 **Morane N** (Sep 16)
16 Jun 16 to Vert Galand
Jul 16 **Morane I** (Oct 16)
Jul 16 **Morane V** (Oct 16)
3 Aug 16 to St-André-aux Bois
Aug 16 **Nieuport 16** (Apr 17)
Aug 16 **Nieuport 17** (Aug 17)
23 Aug 16 to Le Hameau
1 Sep 16 to Savy
18 Jan 17 to Filescamp Farm
Mar 17 **Nieuport 23** (Aug 17)
Jul 17 **SE 5** (Oct 17)
Aug 17 **SE 5A** (Jan 19)
7 Sep 17 to Ste-Marie-Cappel
8 Mar 18 to Bailleul
23 Mar 18 to La Bellevue
27 Mar 18 to Fienvillers
12 Apr 18 to Boffles
17 Sep 18 to Baizieux
14 Oct 18 to Beugnâtre
31 Oct 18 to Quiévy
23 Nov 18 to Inchy
17 Feb 19 to Narborough as a cadre
1 Jan 20 to Bircham Newton
22 Jan 20 DB
—
1 Apr 20 RF @ Risalpur — No 97 Sqn renumbered
Apr 20 **DH 10/10A** (Apr 23)
dets Mianwali, Rajkot, Juhu, Karachi, Tank, Dardoni
Mar 23 **DH 9A** (May 30)
dets Hassani Abdel, Dardoni, Quetta, Arawali, Delhi, Miranshah
29 May 25 to Peshawar
dets Quetta, Drigh Road
15 Oct 25 to Kohat
dets Risalpur, Delhi, Miranshah, Quetta, Arawali, Drigh Road
Mar 30 **Wapiti** (Jul 39)
dets Miranshah, Delhi, Seletar, Drigh Road, Arawali, Manzai, Gilgit, Dum Dum, Kanpur
3 Mar 39 to Ambala
Mar 39 **Blenheim I** (Feb 42)
dets Dum Dum, St Thomas Mount, Juhu, Drigh Road, Sharjah, Peshawar
19 Sep 40 to Lahore
dets Peshawar, Jiwani
14 Feb 41 to Mingaladon
dets Lashio, Mergui, Victoria Point, Moulmein, Akyab, Zayatkwin, 'Johnny Walker'
Jul 41 **Buffalo I** (Oct 41)
9 Feb 42 to Magwe
Feb 42 sqn dispersed
—
1 Mar 42 re-established at Lahore
Mar 42 **Blenheim IV** (Aug 43)
dets Peshawar, St Thomas Mount
12 May 42 to Asansol
dets Cuttack, Dinjan
20 Dec 42 to Jessore
dets Feni
22 Jan 43 to Dohazari
14 May 43 to Yelahanka
det St Thomas Mount
7 Jul 43 to St Thomas Mount
31 Jul 43 to Yelahanka
Aug 43 **Hurricane IIC** (Jul 45)
det Vavuniya
1 Sep 43 to St Thomas Mount
2 Oct 43 to Cholavaram
14 Nov 43 to Agartala
20 Mar 44 to Silchar West
3 May 44 to Dergaon
dets Singerbil, Agartala, Silchar West
2 Jul 44 to Kumbhirgram
det Imphal
20 Sep 44 to Kangla
5 Jan 45 to Taukkyan
10 Feb 45 to Monywa
14 Apr 45 to Thedaw
28 Apr 45 to Kalaywa
det 'Tennant'
17 May 45 to Zayatkwin
21 May 45 to Thedaw
30 Jun 45 to Tanjore
det Yelahanka
Jul 45 **Thunderbolt II** (Nov 46)
25 Sep 45 to Baigachi
1 Oct 45 to Zayatkwin
2 Oct 45 to Port Swettenham
2 Oct 45 to Kuala Lumpur
21 Oct 45 to Kemajoran
det Soerabaya
1 Dec 45 to Soerabaya
12 May 46 to Kemajoran
det Medan
2 Dec 46 to Tengah
Jan 47 **Spitfire F.18** (Jan 51)
24 Jan 48 to Sembawang
31 Aug 49 to Tengah
15 Oct 49 to Butterworth
6 Dec 49 to Kuala Lumpur
Mar 50 **Spitfire FR 18** (Nov 50)
31 May 50 to Tengah
Dec 50 **Vampire FB 5** (Mar 52)
Mar 52 **Vampire FB 9** (Aug 55)
Apr 55 **Venom FB 1** (Apr 57)
Apr 57 **Venom FB 4** (Nov 59)
27 May 59 det Leeming for Meteor
Oct 59 **Meteor NF 14** (Aug 61)
Jul 61 **Javelin FAW 9** (Apr 68)
dets Butterworth, Kuching, Labuan, Kai Tak
1 May 68 DB
—
3 Feb 69 RF @ Wildenrath — RAF Germany Communications Sqn redesignated
Feb 69 **Pembroke C.1** ( )
Feb 69 **Heron C.4** (Jul 72)
Oct 71 **Andover CC 2** (Nov 75)
Mar 87 **Andover CC 2** ( )
Apr 87 **Andover C.1** ( )

61 Sqn

5 Jul 16 F @ Wye — nucleus from No 20 RS
24 Aug 16 DB — absorbed into No 63 Sqn
—
24 Jul 17 RF @ Rochford — nucleus from No 37 Sqn
Jul 17 **Pup** (Jan 18)
Dec 17 **SE 5A** (Jul 18)
Jun 18 **Camel** (Jun 19)
13 Jun 19 DB
—
8 Mar 37 RF @ Hemswell
Mar 37 **Audax** (Apr 37)
Mar 37 **Anson I** (Feb 38)
Jan 38 **Blenheim I** (Mar 39)
Feb 39 **Hampden** (Oct 41)
det Wick
Jun 41 **Manchester** (Jun 42)
17 Jul 41 to North Luffenham
Sep 41 to Woolfox Lodge
Apr 42 **Lancaster I & III** (Jun 46)
5 May 42 to Syerston
det St Eval
Jan 43 **Lancaster II** (Mar 43)
16 Nov 43 to Skellingthorpe
12 Jan 44 to Coningsby
15 Apr 44 to Skellingthorpe
16 Jun 45 to Sturgate
25 Jan 46 to Waddington
May 46 **Lincoln B.2** (Aug 54)
6 Aug 53 to Wittering
Aug 54 **Canberra B.2** (Mar 58)
30 Jun 55 to Upwood
31 Mar 58 DB

62 Sqn

28 Jul 16 F @ Netheravon — nucleus from No 42 Sqn & No 7 RS
8 Aug 16 to Filton — used various aircraft
May 17 **Bristol F2b Fighter** (Jul 19)
17 Jul 17 to Rendcomb
23 Jan 18 to St-Omer
30 Jan 18 to Serny
8 Mar 18 to Cachy
24 Mar 18 to Remaisnil
29 Mar 18 to Planques
7 Aug 18 to Croisette
26 Sep 18 to La Bellevue
29 Oct 18 to Villers-lès-Cagnicourt
18 Nov 18 to Aulnoye
14 Dec 18 to Bouge
20 Dec 18 to Nivelles
2 May 19 to Spich
31 Jul 19 DB
—
3 May 37 RF @ Abingdon — from 'B' Flt, No 40 Sqn
May 37 **Hind** (Mar 38)
12 Jul 37 to Cranfield
Feb 38 **Blenheim I** (Jan 42)
12 Aug 39 en route FE
22 Sep 39 to Tengah
dets Alor Star, Kallang, Kuching, Miri
8 Feb 41 to Alor Star
dets Sembawang, Kuantan
8 Dec 41 to Butterworth
10 Dec 41 to Taiping
24 Dec 41 to Tengah
27 Jan 42 to P II
Jan 42 **Hudson III** (Feb 42)
16 Feb 42 to Semplak
18 Feb 42 DB — merged into No 1 Sqn, RAAF
—
30 Apr 42 RF @ Dum Dum — No 139 Sqn renumbered
Apr 42 **Hudson III** (Dec 43)
14 Jun 42 to Cuttack
dets Vizagapatam, Asansol
24 Jan 43 to Dhubalia
21 Feb 43 to Jessore
Mar 43 **Hudson VI** (Dec 43)
24 May 43 to Chaklala
Jul 43 **Dakota** (Mar 46)
3 Jan 44 to Comilla
30 Apr 44 to Chandina
det Agartala
12 Jul 44 to Agartala
9 Aug 44 to Basal
3 Nov 44 to Agartala
29 Dec 44 to Comilla
dets Kangla, Tulihal, Akyab, Hathazari
21 Mar 45 to Akyab
18 Sep 45 to Mingaladon
dets Akyab, Don Muang, Meiktila
15 Mar 46 DB
—
1 Sep 46 RF @ Palam — No 76 Sqn renumbered
Sep 46 **Dakota** (Mar 47)
det Dum Dum
1 Mar 47 reduced to a cadre
16 Jun 47 re-established @ Mauripur
Jun 47 **Dakota** (Aug 47)
det Chaklala
10 Aug 47 DB
—
8 Dec 47 RF @ Manston
Dec 47 **Dakota** (Jun 49)
10 Dec 47 to Waterbeach
dets Fassberg, Lübeck for BAL
1 Jun 49 DB
—
1 Feb 60 **Bloodhound I** at Woolfox Lodge
30 Sep 64 DB

63 Sqn

5 Jul 16 F @ Stirling — nucleus from Nos 43 & 61 Sqns
Jul 16 **DH 4** (Jun 17)
Oct 16 **BE 12** (May 17)
Oct 16 **BE 2E** (Dec 19)
Oct 16 **Avro 504** (May 17)
Oct 16 **AW FK 3** (May 17)
31 Oct 16 to Cramlington
May 17 **RE 8** (Jun 17)
23 Jun 17 en route ME
13 Aug 17 to Basra
Aug 17 **DH 4** (Apr 19)
Aug 17 **Bristol Scout** (Feb 18)
Sep 17 **RE 8** (Feb 20)
det Baghdad
5 Sep 17 to Samarra
Oct 17 **SPAD S.VII** (Apr 18)
Oct 17 **Martinsyde G.100** (Apr 18)
dets Akab, Ramadi, Hi[t], Baquba, Tuz Khurmatli
17 Oct 18 to Tikrit
Oct 18 **Martinsyde G.102** (Aug 19)
12 Nov 18 to Samarra
dets Mosul, Ramadi
Jan 19 **Bristol M.1C** (Dec 19)
17 Feb 19 to Baghdad
dets Ramadi, Kazvin, Bushire, Kermanshah, Mosul, Kirkuk
Feb 19 **SE 5A** (Apr 19)
May 19 **Camel** (Sep 19)
29 Feb 20 DB — used to re-establish No 30 Sqn
—
15 Feb 37 RF @ Andover — fro[m] 'B' Flt, No 12 Sqn
Feb 37 **Hind** (Apr 37)
3 Mar 37 to Upwood
Mar 37 **Audax** (Aug 37)
May 37 **Battle** (Apr 40)
Mar 39 **Anson I** (Apr 40)
9 Sep 39 to Abingdon
17 Sep 39 to Benson
dets Squires Gate, Weston Zoyland, Penrhos

6 Apr 40 DB — merged into No 12 OTU
—
15 Jun 42 RF @ Gatwick — nucleus from No 239 Sqn
Jun 42 **Mustang I** (Nov 43)
16 Jul 42 to Catterick
6 Nov 42 to Weston Zoyland
13 Nov 42 to Catterick
21 Nov 42 to Macmerry dets Lossiemouth, Odiham, Dalcross, Acklington
27 Jul 43 to Turnhouse det Macmerry
8 Nov 43 to Thruxton
Nov 43 **Mustang IA** (May 44)
2 Nov 43 to Sawbridgeworth
30 Nov 43 to North Weald det Benson
2 Jan 44 to Turnhouse dets Tealing, Peterhead, Dundonald
7 Apr 44 to Woodvale
Apr 44 **Hurricane IV** (Jun 44)
May 44 **Spitfire VB** (Jan 45) det Ballyhalbert
8 May 44 to Lee-on-Solent
2 Jul 44 to Woodvale det Ballyhalbert
0 Aug 44 to Lee-on-Solent
0 Sep 44 to North Weald
1 Nov 44 to Manston
4 Nov 44 to North Weald
1 Feb 45 DB
—
1 Sep 46 RF @ Middle Wallop — No 164 Sqn renumbered
Sep 46 **Spitfire LF 16E** (May 48)
3 Sep 46 to Lübeck
0 Oct 46 to Middle Wallop
5 Jan 48 to Thorney Island
Apr 48 **Meteor F.3** (Jun 48)
4 May 48 to Lübeck
9 Jun 48 to Thorney Island
Jul 48 **Meteor F.4** (Dec 50)
0 May 50 to Waterbeach
Dec 50 **Meteor F.8** (Jan 57)
Nov 56 **Hunter F.6** (Oct 58)
0 Oct 58 DB

4 Sqn

Aug 16 F @ Sedgeford — nucleus from No 45 Sqn
Aug 16 **Henry Farman F.20** (Jun 17)
Aug 16 **BE 2C** (Dec 16)
Aug 16 **FE 2B** (Jun 17)
Jun 17 **Pup** (Oct 17)
Jun 17 **Avro 504** (Oct 17)
Jun 17 **DH 5** (Mar 18)
Oct 17 to St-Omer
Oct 17 to Le Hameau
Jan 18 **SE 5A** (Feb 19)
Oct 18 to Aniche
Nov 18 to Saultain
Dec 18 to Froidmont
Feb 19 to Narborough as a cadre
Dec 19 DB
—
Mar 36 RF @ Heliopolis — nucleus from Nos 6 & 208 Sqns, via No 29 Sqn
Mar 36 **Demon** (Dec 38)
Apr 36 to Ismailia
Aug 36 to Aboukir
Aug 36 en route UK
Sep 36 to Martlesham Heath
May 38 to Church Fenton
Dec 38 **Blenheim IF** (Apr 40)
Aug 39 to Duxford
Aug 39 to Sutton Bridge
Aug 39 to Church Fenton dets Leconfield, Evanton, Catterick
Apr 40 **Spitfire I** (Jan 41)
May 40 to Usworth
May 40 to Kenley
19 Aug 40 to Leconfield det Ringway
13 Oct 40 to Biggin Hill
15 Oct 40 to Coltishall
11 Nov 40 to Hornchurch
27 Jan 41 to Southend
Jan 41 **Spitfire IIA** (Nov 41)
31 Mar 41 to Hornchurch
9 May 41 to Martlesham Heath
15 May 41 to Hornchurch
16 May 41 to Turnhouse
17 May 41 to Drem
6 Aug 41 to Turnhouse
4 Oct 41 to Drem
16 Nov 41 to Hornchurch
Nov 41 **Spitfire VB** (Jul 42)
6 Feb 42 to Fairlop
22 Feb 42 to Hornchurch
31 Mar 42 to Southend
1 May 42 to Hornchurch
Jun 42 **Spitfire IX** (Mar 43)
19 Jul 42 to Martlesham Heath
27 Jul 42 to Hornchurch
8 Sep 42 to Fairlop
14 Nov 42 to Hornchurch
9 Dec 42 to Predannack
2 Jan 43 to Fairlop
15 Mar 43 to Hornchurch
28 Mar 43 to Ayr
Mar 43 **Spitfire VB** (Sep 43)
6 Aug 43 to Friston
19 Aug 43 to Gravesend
Sep 43 **Spitfire VC** (Jul 44)
6 Sep 43 to West Malling
25 Sep 43 to Coltishall
21 Jan 44 to Ayr
2 Feb 44 to Coltishall
29 Apr 44 to Deanland
26 Jun 44 to Harrowbeer
Jun 44 **Spitfire IX** (Nov 44)
30 Aug 44 to Bradwell Bay
Nov 44 **Mustang III** (May 46)
29 Dec 44 to Bentwaters
15 Aug 45 to Horsham St Faith
Aug 45 **Mustang IV** (May 46)
Feb 46 **Hornet F.1** (May 48)
6 Aug 46 to Linton-on-Ouse
8 Mar 48 to Acklington
Apr 48 **Hornet F.3** (Mar 51)
30 Apr 48 to Linton-on-Ouse
Dec 50 **Meteor F.4** (Apr 51)
Mar 51 **Meteor F.8** (Nov 56)
15 Aug 51 to Duxford
Sep 56 **Meteor NF 12** (Sep 58)
Sep 56 **Meteor NF 14** (Sep 58)
Aug 58 **Javelin FAW 7** (Oct 60)
Jul 60 **Javelin FAW 9** (Jun 67)
17 Jul 61 to Waterbeach
24 Aug 62 to Binbrook
1 Apr 65 to Tengah dets Kuching, Labuan
15 Jun 67 DB

65 Sqn

1 Aug 16 F @ Wyton — nucleus from No 46 Sqn, used various aircraft
29 May 17 to Wye
Jul 17 **Camel** (Feb 19)
24 Oct 17 to La Lovie
4 Nov 17 to Bailleul (Asylum Ground)
17 Feb 18 to Poperinghe
21 Mar 18 to Droglandt
24 Mar 18 to Clairmarais
28 Mar 18 to Conteville
6 Apr 18 to Bertangles
12 Aug 18 to Cappelle
16 Aug 18 to Bray-Dunes
19 Sep 18 to Petite Synthe
25 Oct 18 to Bisseghem
12 Feb 19 to Yatesbury as a cadre
25 Oct 19 DB
—
1 Aug 34 RF @ Hornchurch
Aug 34 **Demon** (Jul 36)
Jul 36 **Gauntlet II** (Jun 37)
Jun 37 **Gladiator I** (Apr 39)
Mar 39 **Spitfire I** (Apr 41)
2 Oct 39 to Northolt
28 Mar 40 to Hornchurch
28 May 40 to Kirton-in-Lindsey
5 Jun 40 to Hornchurch
27 Aug 40 to Turnhouse
29 Nov 40 to Tangmere
Jan 41 **Spitfire IIA** (Sep 41)
26 Feb 41 to Kirton-in-Lindsey
Sep 41 **Spitfire IIB** (Oct 41)
28 Sep 41 to Oulton
3 Oct 41 to Kirton-in-Lindsey
7 Oct 41 to Westhampnett
Oct 41 **Spitfire VB** (Aug 43)
22 Dec 41 to Debden
14 Apr 42 to Great Sampford
9 Jun 42 to Martlesham Heath
15 Jun 42 to Great Sampford
30 Jun 42 to Hawkinge
7 Jul 42 to Great Sampford
29 Jul 42 to Gravesend
14 Aug 42 to Eastchurch
20 Aug 42 to Gravesend
26 Sep 42 to Drem
2 Oct 42 to Lympne
11 Oct 42 to Drem
3 Jan 43 to Machrihanish (and HMS *Argus*)
10 Jan 43 to Drem
29 Mar 43 to Perranporth
18 May 43 to Fairlop
31 May 43 to Selsey
1 Jul 43 to Kingsnorth
Aug 43 **Spitfire IX** (Jan 44)
5 Oct 43 to Ashford
15 Oct 43 to Gatwick
24 Oct 43 to Gravesend
Dec 43 **Mustang III** (Mar 45)
15 Apr 44 to Ford
14 May 44 to Funtington
28 May 44 to Southend
4 Jun 44 to Funtington
15 Jun 44 to Ford
25 Jun 44 to B 7/Martragny
17 Jul 44 to B 12/Ellon
1 Sep 44 to B 24/St-André-de-l'Eure
3 Sep 44 to B 40/Beauvais/Nivillers
9 Sep 44 to B 60/Grimbergen
29 Sep 44 to Matlask
3 Oct 44 to Peterhead
4 Oct 44 to Matlask
14 Oct 44 to Andrews Field
16 Jan 45 to Peterhead
28 Jan 45 to Banff
1 Feb 45 to Peterhead
Mar 45 **Mustang IV** (May 46)
6 May 45 to Andrews Field
15 May 45 to Bentwaters
13 Aug 45 to Fairwood Common
6 Sep 45 to Hethel
Feb 46 **Spitfire LF 16E** (Oct 46)
13 Feb 46 to Spilsby
14 Mar 46 to Horsham St Faith
Jun 46 **Hornet F.1** (Jun 48)
11 Aug 46 to Linton-on-Ouse
22 Mar 48 to Acklington
Apr 48 **Hornet F.3** (Feb 51)
12 May 48 to Linton-on-Ouse
Dec 50 **Meteor F.4** (Mar 51)
Feb 51 **Meteor F.8** (Feb 57)
15 Aug 51 to Duxford
Nov 56 **Hunter F.6** (Mar 61)
31 Mar 61 DB
—
1 Jan 64 **Bloodhound II** at Seletar
30 Mar 70 DB

66 Sqn

24 Jun 16 F @ Filton nucleus from No 19 Sqn
2 Jul 16 to Netheravon
Jul 16 **BE 2B, 2C & 2D** (Feb 17)
Jul 16 **BE 12** (Feb 17)
Jul 16 **Avro 504K** (Feb 17)
27 Jul 16 to Filton
Feb 17 **Pup** (Oct 17)
3 Mar 17 to St-Omer
18 Mar 17 to Vert Galand
31 May 17 to Liettres
20 Jun 17 to Calais
6 Jul 17 to Estrée-Blanche
Oct 17 **Camel** (Mar 19)
11 Nov 17 to Candas
22 Nov 17 to Milan
29 Nov 17 to Verona
4 Dec 17 to Grossa
18 Feb 18 to Treviso
10 Mar 18 to San Pietro-in-Gu
1 Nov 18 to Arcade
6 Nov 18 to San Pietro-in-Gu
10 Mar 19 to Yatesbury as a cadre
29 Mar 19 to Leighterton
25 Oct 19 DB
—
20 Jul 36 RF @ Duxford — from 'C' Flt, No 19 Sqn
Jul 36 **Gauntlet II** (Dec 38)
Oct 38 **Spitfire I** (Nov 40)
16 May 40 to Horsham St Faith
29 May 40 to Coltishall
3 Sep 40 to Kenley
10 Sep 40 to Gravesend
30 Oct 40 to West Malling
Oct 40 **Spitfire IIA** (Apr 42)
7 Nov 40 to Biggin Hill
24 Feb 41 to Exeter
Feb 41 **Spitfire I** (Mar 41)
27 Apr 41 to Perranporth
14 Dec 41 to Portreath
8 Feb 42 to Warmwell
22 Feb 42 to Portreath
Feb 42 **Spitfire VA** (Mar 42)
Mar 42 **Spitfire VB & VC** (Nov 43)
27 Apr 42 to Ibsley
3 Jul 42 to Tangmere
7 Jul 42 to Ibsley
16 Aug 42 to Tangmere
20 Aug 42 to Ibsley
24 Aug 42 to Zeals
26 Sep 42 to Predannack
29 Sep 42 to Zeals
8 Oct 42 to Hawkinge
9 Oct 42 to Zeals
1 Nov 42 to Warmwell
14 Nov 42 to Zeals
23 Dec 42 to Ibsley
9 Feb 43 to Skaebrae det Sumburgh
May 43 **Spitfire VI** (Jun 43)
28 Jun 43 to Church Stanton
10 Aug 43 to Redhill
13 Aug 43 to Kenley
17 Sep 43 to Perranporth
8 Nov 43 to Hornchurch
Nov 43 **Spitfire LF IXB** (Sep 44)
16 Nov 43 to Southend
1 Dec 43 to Hornchurch
22 Feb 44 to Llanbedr
1 Mar 44 to North Weald
31 Mar 44 to Bognor
22 Apr 44 to Southend
25 Apr 44 to Bognor
8 May 44 to Castletown
14 May 44 to Bognor
22 Jun 44 to Tangmere
6 Aug 44 to Funtington
12 Aug 44 to Ford
20 Aug 44 to B 16/Villons-les-Buissons
6 Sep 44 to B 33/Campneuseville
11 Sep 44 to B 57/Lille/Nord
Sep 44 **Spitfire IXE** (Nov 44)
6 Oct 44 to B 60/Grimbergen
Nov 44 **Spitfire LF XVIE** (Apr 45)
22 Dec 44 to B 79/Woensdrecht
20 Feb 45 to Fairwood Common
16 Mar 45 to B 85/Schjndel
18 Apr 45 to B 106/Twente
30 Apr 45 DB
—

1 Sep 46 RF @ Duxford — No 165 Sqn renumbered
Sep 46 **Spitfire LF 16E** (Mar 47)
2 Sep 46 to Lübeck
2 Nov 46 to Duxford
Mar 47 **Meteor F.3** (May 48)
5 Sep 47 to Lübeck
31 Oct 47 to Duxford
10 Mar 48 to Lübeck
29 Apr 48 to Duxford
May 48 **Meteor F.4** (Jan 51)
7 Oct 49 to Linton-on-Ouse
Jan 51 **Meteor F.8** (Apr 54)
Jan 54 **Sabre F.4** (Mar 56)
Mar 56 **Hunter F.4** (Jan 57)
Oct 56 **Hunter F.6** (Sep 60)
14 Feb 57 to Acklington
30 Sep 60 DB
—
15 Sep 61 RF @ Odiham — from the Belvedere Trials Unit
Sep 61 **Belvedere HC 1** (Mar 69)
26 May 62 to Seletar
dets Kuching, Brunei, Labuan, Butterworth
17 Mar 69 DB

67 Sqn

12 Sep 16 F @ Heliopolis — No 1 Sqn AFC renumbered
Sep 16 **BE 2C** (Nov 17)
Sep 16 **Avro 504K** (Dec 16)
Sep 16 **BE 2E** (Feb 18)
Sep 16 **Martinsyde G.100/102** (Feb 18)
dets Suez, Sherika, Qantara
17 Dec 16 to Mustabig
Dec 16 **Bristol Scout** (17)
12 Jan 17 to Kilo 143/Ujret el Zol
26 Mar 17 to Rafah
15 Jun 17 to Deir el Ballah
Jul 17 **BE 12A** (Feb 18)
17 Sep 17 to Weli Sheikh Nuran
Oct 17 **RE 8** (Feb 18)
13 Dec 17 to Julis
Jan 18 **Bristol F2b Fighter** (Feb 18)
6 Feb 18 DB — renumbered as No 1 Sqn AFC
—
12 Mar 41 RF @ Kallang
Mar 41 **Buffalo I** (Mar 42)
13 Oct 41 to Mingaladon
det Mergui
Feb 42 **Hurricane IIB** (Mar 42)
Feb 42 to Toungoo
Feb 42 to Magwe
Mar 42 to Akyab
27 Mar 42 Sqn dispersed

Jun 42 Sqn re-established @ Alipore
Jun 42 **Hurricane IIC** (Feb 44)
1 Apr 43 to Chittagong
det Ramu
30 Nov 43 to Alipore
Feb 44 **Spitfire VIII** (Jul 45)
7 Mar 44 to Amarda Road
28 Mar 44 to Alipore
12 Apr 44 to Baigachi
8 Jul 44 to Comilla
dets Chittagong, Cox's Bazaar
30 Nov 44 to Double Moorings
1 Jan 45 to Maunghnama
8 Jan 45 to Akyab Main
6 Feb 45 to Dabaing 4
14 May 45 to Akyab Main
31 Jul 45 DB
—
1 Sep 50 RF @ Gütersloh
Sep 50 **Vampire FB 5** (Jun 53)
5 May 52 to Wildenrath
May 53 **Sabre F.4** (Mar 56)
5 Jul 55 to Brüggen
Jan 56 **Hunter F.4** (May 57)
31 May 57 DB

68 Sqn

30 Jan 17 F @ Harlaxton
Jan 17 **DH 5** (Jan 18)
21 Sep 17 to Baizieux
Jan 18 **SE 5A** (Jan 18)
19 Jan 18 DB — renumbered as No 2 Sqn, AFC
—
7 Jan 41 RF @ Catterick
Jan 41 **Blenheim IF** (May 41)
23 Apr 41 to High Ercall
May 41 **Beaufighter IF** (Feb 43)
8 Mar 42 to Coltishall
det Peterhead
Feb 43 **Beaufighter VIF** (Jul 44)
5 Feb 44 to Coleby Grange
1 Mar 44 to Fairwood Common
23 Jun 44 to Castle Camps
Jul 44 **Mosquito XVII** (Feb 45)
Jul 44 **Mosquito XIX** (Feb 45)
28 Oct 44 to Coltishall
8 Feb 45 to Wittering
Feb 45 **Mosquito XXX** (Apr 45)
27 Feb 45 to Coltishall
16 Mar 45 to Church Fenton
20 Apr 45 DB
—
1 Jan 52 RF @ Wahn
Feb 52 **Meteor NF 11** (Jan 59)
22 Jul 57 to Laarbruch
21 Jan 59 DB — renumbered as No 5 Sqn

69 Sqn

28 Dec 16 F @ South Carlton — No 2 Sqn, AFC renumbered, used various aircraft
Aug 17 **RE 8** (Jan 18)
24 Aug 17 to Lympne
9 Sep 17 to St-Omer
10 Sep 17 to Savy
9 Nov 17 to Bailleul (Town Ground)
19 Jan 18 DB — renumbered as No 3 Sqn, AFC
—
10 Jan 41 RF @ Luqa — No 431 Flt renumbered
Jan 41 **Maryland I** (Apr 42)
May 41 **Hurricane I** (Jul 41)
May 41 **Hurricane IIC** (Jan 42)
Aug 41 **Beaufort I** (Sep 41)
31 Oct 41 to Ta Kali
29 Nov 41 to Luqa
Jan 42 **Mosquito I** (Mar 42)
Jan 42 **Beaufighter I** (Apr 42)
Jan 42 **Spitfire IV** (Feb 43) — to No 683 Sqn
Jun 42 **Baltimore I** (Dec 42)
Jun 42 **Baltimore II** (Apr 43)
Aug 42 **Wellington VIII** (Feb 43) — to No 458 Sqn
Apr 43 **Baltimore III** (Sep 43)
Sep 43 **Baltimore IV** (Apr 44)
Jan 44 **Baltimore V** (Apr 44)
9 Feb 44 to Montecorvino
10 Apr 44 en route UK
22 Apr 44 to Glasgow (No 10 PTC)
28 Apr 44 sqn dispersed
5 May 44 sqn re-established @ Northolt
May 44 **Wellington XIII** (Aug 45)
4 Sep 44 to A 12/Balleroy
11 Sep 44 to B 48/Amiens/Glisy
26 Sep 44 to B 58/Melsbroek
15 Apr 45 to B 78/Eindhoven
det Aalborg
7 Aug 45 DB
—
7 Aug 45 RF @ Cambrai/Epinoy — No 613 Sqn renumbered
Aug 45 **Mosquito VI** (Mar 46)
9 Oct 45 to Sylt
27 Oct 45 to Cambrai/Epinoy
31 Mar 46 DB
—
31 Mar 46 RF @ Wahn — No 180 Sqn renumbered
Mar 46 **Mosquito B.16** (Nov 47)
det Manston
13 Nov 46 to Gatow
13 Dec 46 to Wahn
19 Apr 47 to Tangmere
16 May 47 to Wahn
7 Nov 47 DB
—
1 Oct 54 RF @ Gütersloh
Oct 54 **Canberra PR 3** (Jul 58)
13 Dec 54 to Laarbruch
1 Apr 58 to Luqa
1 Jul 58 DB — renumbered as No 39 Sqn

70 Sqn

22 Apr 16 F @ South Farnborough
Apr 16 **1½ Strutter** (Jul 17)
31 May 16 'A' Flt to Fienvillers
3 Jul 16 'B' Flt to Fienvillers
1 Aug 16 'C' Flt to Fienvillers
16 Dec 16 to Auchel
2 Mar 17 to Vert Galand
2 Apr 17 to Fienvillers
14 May 17 to Boisdinghem
Jun 17 **Camel** (Mar 19)
27 Jun 17 to Liettres
8 Sep 17 to Poperinghe
15 Mar 18 to Marieux
28 Mar 18 to Fienvillers
16 Apr 18 to Remaisnil
8 Jul 18 to Boisdinghem
1 Aug 18 to Esquerdes
22 Sep 18 to Droglandt
23 Oct 18 to Menin
25 Nov 18 to Fort Cognelée
7 Dec 18 to Elsenborn
18 Dec 18 to Bickendorf
Jan 19 **Snipe** (Sep 19)
27 Aug 19 to Spittlegate
28 Sep 19 reduced to a cadre
22 Jan 20 DB
—
1 Feb 20 RF @ Heliopolis — No 58 Sqn renumbered
Feb 20 **HP 0/400** (Apr 20)
Feb 20 **Vimy** (Nov 22)
16 Jan 22 to Baghdad West
Nov 22 **Vernon** (Dec 26)
31 May 22 to Hinaidi
Jan 24 **Victoria I** (Mar 26)
Feb 26 **Victoria III** (Jun 34)
Nov 28 **Victoria IV** (May 34)
Apr 30 **Victoria V** (Aug 35)
Jul 31 **Victoria VI** (Nov 35)
Nov 35 **Valentia** (Oct 40)
16 Oct 37 to Dhibban/Habbaniyah
30 Aug 39 to Helwan
det Habbaniyah
11 Jun 40 to Heliopolis
9 Sep 40 to Kabrit
Sep 40 **Wellington IC** (Jan 43)
dets Tatoi, El Adem, Shaibah
17 Jan 42 to LG 75
5 Feb 42 to LG 104
26 Jun 42 to LG 224
29 Jun 42 to Abu Sueir
6 Nov 42 to LG 224
11 Nov 42 to LG 106
30 Nov 42 to LG 140
det Benina
Jan 43 **Wellington III** (Nov 43)
19 Jan 43 to Benina
23 Jan 43 to El Magrun
10 Feb 43 to Gardabia East
25 Feb 43 to Gardabia West
Apr 43 **Wellington X** (Jan 45)
25 May 43 to Temmar
15 Nov 43 to Djedeida
20 Dec 43 to Cerignola
det Tortorella
29 Dec 43 to Tortorella
Jan 45 **Liberator VI** (Mar 46)
12 Oct 45 to Aqir
12 Dec 45 to Shallufa
31 Mar 46 DB
—
15 Apr 46 RF @ Fayid — No 178 Sqn renumbered
Apr 46 **Lancaster B 1(FE)** (Apr 47)
21 Aug 46 to Kabrit
17 Sep 46 to Shallufa
1 Apr 47 DB
—
1 May 48 RF @ Kabrit — No 215 Sqn renumbered
May 48 **Dakota** (Jan 50)
Jan 50 **Valetta C.1** (Jan 56)
26 Feb 51 to Fayid
12 Dec 55 to Nicosia
Jan 56 **Hastings C.1** (Jan 68)
Jan 56 **Hastings C.2** (Jan 68)
12 Jul 66 to Akrotiri
Oct 67 **Argosy C.1** (Feb 75)
Dec 70 **Hercules C.1** ( )
15 Jan 75 to Lyneham
Mar 80 **Hercules C.3** ( )

71 Sqn

27 Mar 17 F @ Castle Bromwich, used various aircraft
Dec 17 **Camel** (Jan 18)
18 Dec 17 to St-Omer
22 Dec 17 to Bruay
19 Jan 18 DB — renumbered as No 4 Sqn, AFC
—
19 Sep 40 RF @ Church Fenton
Sep 40 **Buffalo I** (Nov 40)
Nov 40 **Hurricane I** (May 41)
23 Nov 40 to Kirton-in-Lindsey
5 Apr 41 to Martlesham Heath
Apr 41 **Hurricane IIA** (Aug 41)
23 Jun 41 to North Weald
Aug 41 **Spitfire IIA** (Sep 41)
Sep 41 **Spitfire VB** (Sep 42)
14 Dec 41 to Martlesham Heath
2 May 42 to Debden
14 Aug 42 to Gravesend
20 Aug 42 to Debden
29 Sep 42 DB — redesignated as 334th Sqn, 4th Pursuit Group, USAAF
—
16 Sep 50 RF @ Gütersloh
Sep 50 **Vampire FB 5** (Oct 53)
8 Apr 52 to Wildenrath
Oct 53 **Sabre F.4** (May 56)
7 Jul 55 to Brüggen
Apr 56 **Hunter F.4** (May 57)
31 May 57 DB

72 Sqn

28 Jun 17 F @ Upavon — nucleus from 'A' Flt, CFS
8 Jul 17 to Netheravon
Jul 17 **Avro 504** (Dec 17)
Jul 17 **Pup** (Dec 17)
1 Nov 17 to Sedgeford
25 Dec 17 en route Persian Gulf
2 Mar 18 to Basra
Mar 18 **DH 4** (Jun 18)
Mar 18 **Bristol M.1C** (Feb 19)
Mar 18 **SE 5A** (Feb 19)
Mar 18 to Baghdad
Mar 18 **SPAD S.VII** (Jan 19)
Apr 18 **Martinsyde G.100** (Nov 18)
Flts @ Mirjana, Samarr
dets Hamadan, Tikrit, Baku, Kazvin, Zinjan
25 Nov 18 Sqn reunited at Baghda
1 Feb 19 reduced to a cadre
22 Sep 19 DB
—

2 Feb 37 RF @ Tangmere — nucleus from No 1 Sqn
Mar 37 **Gladiator I** (May 39)
1 Jun 37 to Church Fenton
Apr 39 **Spitfire I** (Apr 41)
7 Oct 39 to Leconfield
det Drem
1 Nov 39 to Church Fenton
det Drem
1 Dec 39 to Drem
2 Jan 40 to Leconfield
3 Jan 40 to Church Fenton
2 Mar 40 to Acklington
Mar 40 **Gladiator I & II** (Mar 40)
1 Jun 40 to Gravesend
5 Jun 40 to Acklington
1 Aug 40 to Biggin Hill
1 Sep 40 to Croydon
2 Sep 40 to Biggin Hill
3 Oct 40 to Leconfield
Oct 40 to Coltishall
Oct 40 to Matlask
2 Nov 40 to Coltishall
Nov 40 to Leuchars
5 Dec 40 to Acklington
Apr 41 **Spitfire IIA** (Jul 41)
Apr 41 **Spitfire IIB** (Jul 41)
Jul 41 to Gravesend
Jul 41 **Spitfire VB** (Jul 42)
Jul 41 to Biggin Hill
Oct 41 to Gravesend
Mar 42 to Biggin Hill
Jun 42 to Lympne
Jul 42 to Biggin Hill
Jul 42 **Spitfire VC** (Feb 43)
Jul 42 **Spitfire IX** (Aug 42)
Aug 42 to Morpeth
Aug 42 **Spitfire VB** (Nov 42)
Aug 42 to Ayr
det Drem
Sep 42 to Ouston
Nov 42 en route N Africa via Gibraltar
Nov 42 to Maison Blanche
Nov 42 to Bone
Nov 42 to Souk el Arba
Jan 43 to Souk el Khemis ('Euston')
Feb 43 to Constantine
Feb 43 **Spitfire IX** (Oct 44)
Feb 43 to Souk el Khemis ('Euston')
May 43 to La Sebala I
det Utique
May 43 to Mateur
Jun 43 to Hal Far
Jun 43 **Spitfire VC** (Jan 44)
Jul 43 to Comiso
Jul 43 to Pachino
Aug 43 to Panebianco
Sep 43 to Cassala
Sep 43 to Falcone
Sep 43 to Tusciano
Oct 43 to Capodichino
Jan 44 to Lago
Jun 44 to Tre Cancelli
Jun 44 to Tarquinia
Jun 44 to Grosseto
Jul 44 to Piombino
Jul 44 to Calvi
Aug 44 to Ramatuelle
Aug 44 to Sisteron
Sep 44 to Lyons/Bron
Sep 44 to La Jasse
Oct 44 to Peretola
Oct 44 **Spitfire LF IX** (Dec 46)
Nov 44 to Rimini
Feb 45 to Ravenna
May 45 to Rivolto
May 45 to Klagenfurt
Sep 45 to Zeltweg
Oct 45 to Campoformido
Oct 45 to Zeltweg
Sep 46 to Tissano
Dec 46 DB
—
Feb 47 RF @ Odiham — No 130 Sqn renumbered
Feb 47 **Vampire F.1** (Oct 48)
Oct 47 to Acklington
28 Nov 47 to Odiham
Jun 48 **Vampire F.3** (Nov 49)
Nov 49 **Vampire FB 5** (May 53)
22 Mar 50 to North Weald
Jul 52 **Meteor F.8** (Feb 56)
9 May 53 to Church Fenton
Feb 56 **Meteor NF 12** (Jun 59)
Feb 56 **Meteor NF 14** (Jun 59)
Apr 59 **Javelin FAW 4** (Jun 61)
Jun 59 **Javelin FAW 5** (Jun 61)
28 Jun 59 to Leconfield
30 Jun 61 DB
—
15 Nov 61 RF @ Odiham
Nov 61 **Belvedere HC 1** (Aug 64)
Aug 64 **Wessex HC 2** ( )
det Manston (SAR)
16 Apr 81 to Benson
12 Nov 81 to Aldergrove

73 Sqn

2 Jul 17 F @ Upavon — nucleus from 'B' Flt, CFS, used various aircraft
10 Jul 17 to Lilbourne
Nov 17 **Camel** (Feb 19)
9 Jan 18 to St-Omer
12 Jan 18 to Liettres
5 Mar 18 to Champien
23 Mar 18 to Cachy
24 Mar 18 to Remaisnil
30 Mar 18 to Beauvois
3 Jun 18 to Fouquerolles
21 Jun 18 to Planques
14 Jul 18 to Touquin
4 Aug 18 to La Bellevue
16 Sep 18 to Foucaucourt
23 Sep 18 to Estrées-en-Chaussée
8 Oct 18 to Hervilly
17 Oct 18 to Malincourt
15 Nov 18 to Baizieux
10 Feb 19 to Yatesbury as a cadre
2 Jul 19 DB
—
15 Mar 37 RF @ Mildenhall
Mar 37 **Fury II** (Jul 37)
12 Jun 37 to Debden
Jun 37 **Gladiator I** (Jul 38)
9 Nov 37 to Digby
Jul 38 **Hurricane I** (Jan 42)
9 Sep 39 to Le Havre/Octeville
28 Sep 39 to Norrent-Fontes
9 Oct 39 to Rouvres
11 Apr 40 to Reims
19 Apr 40 to Rouvres
10 May 40 to Reims
11 May 40 to Rouvres
14 May 40 to Reims
16 May 40 to Villeneuve
18 May 40 to Gaye
3 Jun 40 to Echemines
7 Jun 40 to Ruaudin
15 Jun 40 to Saumur
15 Jun 40 to Nantes/Château Bougon
16 Jun 40 to Bagneux
18 Jun 40 to Church Fenton
det Sherburn-in-Elmet
5 Sep 40 to Castle Camps
6 Nov 40 to ME via HMS *Furious*
30 Nov 40 to Heliopolis
det Dekheila
30 Dec 40 to Sidi Haneish
11 Jan 41 to Amseat
30 Jan 41 to Gazala
det El Adem
10 Mar 41 to Bu Amud
9 Apr 41 to El Gubbi
25 Apr 41 to Sidi Haneish
det Heraklion
6 Sep 41 to El Gamil
Sep 41 **Tomahawk IIB** (Nov 41)
Oct 41 **Hurricane IIB** (Feb 42)
Oct 41 **Hurricane IIC** (Jul 43)
dets Shandur, Gazala, Kilo 8
3 Feb 42 to El Adem
18 Feb 42 to Gasr el Arid
21 Feb 42 to Gambut No 2
27 Feb 42 to Gasr el Arid
12 Mar 42 to Gambut No 1
17 Apr 42 to Gambut Main
20 May 42 to El Adem
27 May 42 to Gambut
18 Jun 42 to LG 115
19 Jun 42 to LG 76
24 Jun 42 to Qasaba
27 Jun 42 to El Daba
det LG 20
28 Jun 42 to LG 39
2 Jul 42 to LG 89
23 Jul 42 to El Ballah
31 Jul 42 to Shandur
det El Bassa
22 Aug 42 to LG 85
det Burgh el Arab
24 Oct 42 to LG 89
7 Nov 42 to LG 21
9 Nov 42 to LG 13
11 Nov 42 to LG 155
13 Nov 42 to Gambut West
17 Nov 42 to El Adem
det Bu Amud
28 Nov 42 to El Magrun
23 Dec 42 to El Merduma
2 Jan 43 to Alem el Chel
11 Jan 43 to Tamet
21 Jan 43 to Bir Dufan
4 Feb 43 to Gasr Garabulli
16 Feb 43 to El Assa
det Castel Benito
19 Mar 43 to Nefatia
8 Apr 43 to Gabes
12 Apr 43 to Sfax
20 Apr 43 to El Alem
21 Apr 43 to Monastir
29 May 43 to La Sebala II
Jun 43 **Spitfire VC** (Sep 44)
det Luqa
28 Jul 43 to La Sebala I
Oct 43 **Spitfire IX** (Apr 48)
18 Oct 43 to Montecorvino
2 Dec 43 to Foggia Main
1 Jul 44 to Canne
16 Jul 44 to Foggia Main
det Vis
Jul 44 **Spitfire VIII** (Sep 44)
12 Sep 44 to Canne
det Kalamaki
2 Apr 45 to Prkos
15 May 45 to Brindisi
3 Jul 45 to Hal Far
15 Jul 46 to Ta Kali
Jul 47 **Spitfire F.22** (Oct 48)
Jul 48 **Vampire F.3** (Oct 50)
21 Apr 49 to Nicosia
27 May 49 to Ta Kali
20 Feb 50 to Nicosia
27 Mar 50 to Ta Kali
May 50 **Vampire FB 5** (Feb 52)
14 Feb 51 to Nicosia
21 Mar 51 to Ta Kali
21 Jun 51 to Castel Benito
20 Jul 51 to Ta Kali
18 Sep 51 to Shaibah
10 Oct 51 to Ta Kali
Nov 51 **Vampire FB 9** (Sep 54)
1 Feb 52 to Kabrit
29 Feb 52 to Ta Kali
5 Mar 52 to Kabrit
6 Jun 52 to Ta Kali
20 Sep 52 to Idris
30 Sep 52 to Ta Kali
24 Oct 52 to Nicosia
25 Nov 52 to Ta Kali
23 Mar 53 to El Adem
29 Mar 53 to Ta Kali
4 May 53 to Habbaniyah
17 Jul 53 to Deversoir
20 Jul 53 to Habbaniyah
19 Sep 53 to Nicosia
25 Oct 53 to Habbaniyah
5 Jan 54 to Shaibah
dets Sharjah, Muharraq
25 Mar 54 to Nicosia
21 Apr 54 to Habbaniyah
Jul 54 **Venom FB 1** (Dec 56)
dets Sharjah
2 May 55 to Nicosia
12 Oct 55 to Amman
5 Nov 55 to Nicosia
30 Jul 56 to Khormaksar
21 Dec 56 to Akrotiri
Dec 56 **Venom FB 4** (Mar 57)
det Weston Zoyland for Canberra
Mar 57 **Canberra B.2** (Aug 62)
Jun 62 **Canberra B.15** (Feb 69)
17 Mar 69 DB

74 Sqn

1 Jul 17 F @ Northolt — nucleus from No 2 TS, used various aircraft
10 Jul 17 to London Colney
25 Mar 18 to Goldhanger
Mar 18 **SE 5A** (Feb 19)
30 Mar 18 to St-Omer
2 Apr 18 to Teteghem
9 Apr 18 to La Lovie
11 Apr 18 to Clairmarais North
7 Aug 18 to Clairmarais South
28 Sep 18 to La Lovie
3 Oct 18 to Clairmarais South
23 Oct 18 to Marcke
1 Nov 18 to Cuerne
17 Nov 18 to Froidmont
30 Nov 18 to Halluin
10 Feb 19 to Lopcombe Corner as a cadre
3 Jul 19 DB
—
1 Sep 35 RF @ Hornchurch — initially referred to as "the Demon Flights"
3 Sep 35 established on board HMT *Neuralia* en route Malta
Sep 35 **Demon** (Apr 37)
11 Sep 35 to Hal Far
21 Sep 36 to Hornchurch
Mar 37 **Gauntlet II** (Feb 39)
Feb 39 **Spitfire I** (Sep 40)
22 Oct 39 to Rochford
29 Oct 39 to Hornchurch
3 Nov 39 to Rochford
14 Nov 39 to Hornchurch
2 Dec 39 to Rochford
16 Dec 39 to Hornchurch
29 Dec 39 to Rochford
16 Jan 40 to Hornchurch
14 Feb 40 to Rochford
23 Mar 40 to Hornchurch
20 Apr 40 to Rochford
27 May 40 to Leconfield
6 Jun 40 to Rochford
Jun 40 **Spitfire IIA** (May 41)
26 Jun 40 to Hornchurch
14 Aug 40 to Wittering
21 Aug 40 to Kirton-in-Lindsey
9 Sep 40 to Coltishall
15 Oct 40 to Biggin Hill
20 Feb 41 to Manston
30 Apr 41 to Gravesend
May 41 **Spitfire VB** (Mar 42)
9 Jul 41 to Acklington
Jul 41 **Spitfire IIA** (Dec 41)
3 Oct 41 to Llanbedr
24 Jan 42 to Long Kesh
25 Mar 42 to Atcham
10 Apr 42 en route ME
21 Jun 42 to Helwan
8 Jul 42 to Ramat David
4 Sep 42 to Hadera
18 Oct 42 to Doshen Tapeh
1 Dec 42 to Meherabad
Dec 42 **Hurricane IIB** (Aug 43)
dets Abadan, Shaibah
11 Apr 43 to Shaibah
dets Meherabad, Abadan
Apr 43 **Hurricane I** (May 43)
17 May 43 to Habbaniyah
23 May 43 to LG 106
dets LG 08, LG 101,

LG 105, Idku, St Jean
26 Aug 43 to Idku
Aug 43 **Spitfire VB** (Apr 44)
Aug 43 **Spitfire VC** (Apr 44)
dets Nicosia, LG 106
22 Sep 43 to Nicosia
dets Cos, Idku
11 Oct 43 to Peristerona
Oct 43 **Spitfire IX** (Apr 44)
22 Oct 43 to Nicosia
23 Oct 43 to Idku
dets Nicosia, Cairo West
22 Nov 43 to Dekheila
det Idku
12 Dec 43 to Idku
dets Maryut, LG 106, Dekheila
21 Jan 44 to Dekheila
dets Idku, St Jean
4 Mar 44 to Idku
det St Jean
7 Apr 44 en route UK
24 Apr 44 to North Weald
Apr 44 **Spitfire LF IXE** (Mar 45)
15 May 44 to Lympne
3 Jul 44 to Tangmere
17 Jul 44 to Selsey
26 Jul 44 to Southend
6 Aug 44 to Tangmere
20 Aug 44 to B 8/Sommervieu
2 Sep 44 to B 29/Bernay
10 Sep 44 to B 37/Corroy
12 Sep 44 to B 51/Lille/Vendeville
17 Sep 44 to B 55/Wevelghem
25 Nov 44 to B 70/Deurne
3 Feb 45 to B 85/Schjindel
Mar 45 **Spitfire LF XVIE** (May 45)
16 Apr 45 to B 105/Drope
16 May 45 to Colerne
May 45 **Meteor F.3** (Mar 48)
7 Jan 46 to Fairwood Common
15 Feb 46 to Colerne
2 Jun 46 to Bentwaters
9 Jun 46 to Colerne
14 Aug 46 to Horsham St Faith
23 Sep 46 to Acklington
30 Oct 46 to Horsham St Faith
1 Jul 47 to Lübeck
28 Aug 47 to Horsham St Faith
Dec 47 **Meteor F.4** (Oct 50)
1 Jul 50 to Tangmere
8 Jul 50 to Acklington
4 Aug 50 to Horsham St Faith
Oct 50 **Meteor F.8** (Mar 57)
Mar 57 **Hunter F.4** (Jan 58)
Nov 57 **Hunter F.6** (Nov 60)
8 Jun 59 to Coltishall
Jun 60 **Lightning F.1** (Apr 64)
2 Mar 64 to Leuchars
Apr 64 **Lightning F.3** (Sep 67)
Sep 66 **Lightning F.6** (Aug 71)
12 Jun 67 to Tengah
1 Sep 71 DB
—
19 Oct 84 RF @ Wattisham
Oct 84 **Phantom (F-4J (UK))** ( )

75 Sqn

1 Oct 16 F @ Tadcaster — nucleus from No 33 Sqn
Oct 16 **BE 2C** (Sep 17)
12 Oct 16 to Goldhanger
dets Yelling, Old Weston, Therfield
Oct 16 **BE 12** (Jul 18)
Jan 17 **BE 2E** (Jul 18)
8 Sep 17 to Elmswell
dets Harling Road, Hadleigh
Sep 17 **FE 2B** (Oct 17)
Jan 18 **BE 12B** (Jul 18)
Jul 18 **Avro 504K(NF)** (Jun 19)
22 May 19 to North Weald Basset
13 Jun 19 DB
—
15 Mar 37 RF @ Driffield — from 'B' Flt, No 215 Sqn
Mar 37 **Virginia X** (Sep 37)
Mar 37 **Anson I** (Nov 37)
Sep 37 **Harrow** (Jul 39)
11 Jul 38 to Honington
Mar 39 **Anson I** (Oct 39)
Jul 39 **Wellington I** (Apr 40)
13 Jul 39 to Stradishall
14 Sep 39 to Harwell
dets Squires Gate, Carew Cheriton, Honington
8 Apr 40 DB — merged into No 15 OTU
—
8 Apr 40 RF @ Feltwell — New Zealand Sqn redesignated
Apr 40 **Wellington I** (Aug 40)
Apr 40 **Wellington IA** (Aug 40)
May 40 **Wellington IC** (Jan 42)
det Salon
Jan 42 **Wellington III** (Nov 42)
15 Aug 42 to Mildenhall
det Oakington
1 Nov 42 to Newmarket
Nov 42 **Stirling I** (Jul 43)
Mar 43 **Stirling III** (Apr 44)
28 Jun 43 to Mepal
Mar 44 **Lancaster I & III** (Oct 45)
21 Jul 45 to Spilsby
Sep 45 **Lincoln B.2** (Oct 45)
15 Oct 45 DB — number transferred to RNZAF

76 Sqn

15 Sep 16 F @ Cramlington — nucleus from No 36 sqn
Sep 16 **BE 2C** (17)
Sep 16 **BE 12** (Aug 18)
Sep 16 **DH 6** (17)
10 Oct 16 to Ripon
dets Copmanthorpe, Helperby, Catterick
Dec 16 **BE 2E** (Aug 18)
Dec 16 **BE 12A** (Aug 18)
May 17 **RE 8** (Jul 18)
Mar 18 **BE 12B** (Aug 18)
Jul 18 **Bristol F2b Fighter** (Aug 18)
Aug 18 **Avro 504K(NF)** (May 19)
18 Mar 19 to Helperby
dets Copmanthorpe, Catterick
30 May 19 to Tadcaster as a cadre
13 Jun 19 DB
—
12 Apr 37 RF @ Finningley — from 'B' Flt, No 7 Sqn
Apr 37 **Wellesley** (Apr 39)
Mar 39 **Hampden** (Apr 40)
May 39 **Anson I** (Apr 40)
23 Sep 39 to Upper Heyford
8 Apr 40 DB — merged into No 16 OTU
—
30 Apr 40 RF @ West Raynham (for Hampden)
20 May 40 DB
—
1 May 41 RF @ Linton-on-Ouse — from 'C' Flt, No 35 Sqn
May 41 **Halifax I** (Mar 42)
4 Jun 41 to Middleton St George
Oct 41 **Halifax II** (Apr 43)
dets Lossiemouth, Tain, Aqir, Shallufa, LG 224, Fayid (ME det, initially as No 76/454 and later as No 76/462 Sqn, was absorbed into No 462 Sqn on 7 Sep 42)
16 Sep 42 to Linton-on-Ouse
Feb 43 **Halifax V** (Feb 44)
16 Jun 43 to Holme-on-Spalding Moor
Jan 44 **Halifax III** (Apr 45)
Mar 45 **Halifax VI** (May 45)
May 45 **Dakota** (Sep 46)
8 Aug 45 to Broadwell
28 Aug 45 en route FE
10 Sep 45 to Tilda
18 Oct 45 to Poona
25 May 46 to Palam
1 Sep 46 DB — renumbered as No 62 Sqn
—
9 Dec 53 RF @ Wittering
Dec 53 **Canberra B.2** (Dec 55)
15 Nov 55 to Weston Zoyland
Dec 55 **Canberra B.6** (Dec 60)
dets Pearce, Edinburgh Field, Christmas Island
1 Apr 57 to Hemswell
17 Jul 58 to Upwood
30 Dec 60 DB

77 Sqn

1 Oct 16 F @ Thetford — nucleus from No 51 Sqn
16 Oct 16 to Edinburgh
dets Turnhouse, New Haggerston, Whiteburn, Penston
Oct 16 **BE 2C** (Nov 18)
Oct 16 **BE 12** (Nov 18)
Oct 16 **DH 6** (Dec 16)
Oct 16 **BE 2D** (Dec 16)
Jan 17 **BE 2E** (Nov 18)
May 17 **RE 8** (Jul 18)
Dec 17 **BE 12B** (Sep 18)
May 18 to Penston
det Whiteburn
Sep 18 **Avro 504K(NF)** (Jun 19)
13 Jun 19 DB
—
14 Jun 37 RF @ Finningley — from 'B' Flt, No 102 Sqn
Jun 37 **Audax** (Nov 37)
7 Jul 37 to Honington
Nov 37 **Wellesley** (Nov 38)
25 Jul 38 to Driffield
Nov 38 **Whitley III** (Oct 39)
Sep 39 **Whitley V** (Oct 42)
dets Villeneuve, Kinloss
28 Aug 40 to Linton-on-Ouse
5 Oct 40 to Topcliffe
5 Sep 41 to Leeming
6 May 42 to Chivenor
5 Oct 42 to Elvington
Oct 42 **Halifax II** (Jun 44)
Apr 44 **Halifax V** (May 44)
15 May 44 to Full Sutton
May 44 **Halifax III** (Mar 45)
Mar 45 **Halifax VI** (Aug 45)
Jul 45 **Dakota** (Nov 46)
31 Aug 45 to Broadwell
20 Sep 45 en route FE
30 Sep 45 to Kargi Road
22 Oct 45 to Mauripur
1 Nov 46 DB — renumbered as No 31 Sqn
—
1 Dec 46 RF @ Broadwell — No 271 Sqn renumbered
Dec 46 **Dakota** (Jun 49)
17 Dec 46 to Manston
10 Dec 47 to Waterbeach
dets Wunstorf, Fassberg, Lübeck for BAL
1 Jun 49 DB
—
1 Sep 58 **Thor** at Feltwell
10 Jul 63 DB

78 Sqn

1 Nov 16 F @ Newhaven
det Telscombe Cliffs
Nov 16 **BE 2C** (Sep 17)
Nov 16 **BE 12** (Jan 18)
25 Dec 16 to Hove
dets Telscombe Cliffs, Gosport, Chiddingstone Causeway
Dec 16 **BE 2E** (Dec 17)
Dec 16 **BE 12A** (Jan 18)
Jul 17 **SE 5** (Jul 17)
Aug 17 **1½ Strutter** (Feb 18)
20 Sep 17 to Suttons Farm
det Biggin Hill
Sep 17 **FE 2D** (Oct 17)
Dec 17 **BE 12B** (Jan 18)
Jan 18 **Camel** (Jul 19)
Oct 18 **Snipe** (Jul 19)
1 Jul 19 reduced to a cadre
31 Dec 19 DB
—
1 Nov 36 RF @ Boscombe Down — from 'B' Flt, No 10 Sqn
Nov 36 **Heyford III** (Oct 37)
1 Feb 37 to Dishforth
Jul 37 **Whitley I** (Dec 39)
Jun 39 **Whitley IVA** (Jun 40)
det Ternhill
Aug 39 **Whitley V** (Mar 42)
det Linton-on-Ouse
13 Dec 39 to Linton-on-Ouse
det Brackley
16 Jul 40 to Dishforth
dets Ringway, Luqa
7 Apr 41 to Middleton St George
20 Oct 41 to Croft
Mar 42 **Halifax II** (Jan 44)
10 Jun 42 to Middleton St George
16 Sep 42 to Linton-on-Ouse
16 Jun 43 to Breighton
Jan 44 **Halifax III** (Apr 45)
Apr 45 **Halifax VI** (Jul 45)
Jun 45 **Dakota** (May 50)
20 Sep 45 to Almaza
19 Sep 46 to Kabrit
2 Mar 50 to Mogadishu
6 Mar 50 to Eastleigh
13 Apr 50 to Kabrit
Apr 50 **Valetta C.1** (Sep 54)
21 Feb 51 to Fayid
30 Sep 54 DB
—
15 Apr 56 RF @ Khormaksar
Apr 56 **Pioneer CC 1** (Aug 59)
Jun 58 **Pembroke C.1** (Jun 59)
Oct 58 **Twin Pioneer CC 1** (Jun 65)
Jun 65 **Wessex HC 2** (Dec 71)
13 Oct 67 to Sharjah
21 Dec 71 DB
—
1 May 86 RF @ Mount Pleasant from Nos 1310 & 1564 Flts
May 86 **Sea King HAR 3** ( )
May 86 **Chinook HC 1** ( )

79 Sqn

1 Aug 17 F @ Gosport — nucleu from No 27 TS, used various aircraft
8 Aug 17 to Beaulieu
Dec 17 **Dolphin** (Jul 19)
20 Feb 18 to St-Omer
22 Feb 18 to Estrée-Blanche
5 Mar 18 to Champien
22 Mar 18 to Cachy
24 Mar 18 to Beauvois
16 May 18 to Ste-Marie-Cappel
22 Oct 18 to Reckem
26 Nov 18 to Nivelles
20 Dec 18 to Bickendorf
15 Jul 19 DB
—
22 Mar 37 RF @ Biggin Hill — fr 'B' Flt, No 32 Sqn
Mar 37 **Gauntlet II** (Nov 38)
Nov 38 **Hurricane I** (Jul 41)
12 Nov 39 to Manston
8 Mar 40 to Biggin Hill
det Manston
10 May 40 to Merville

2 May 40 to Norrent-Fontes
5 May 40 to Merville
1 May 40 to Biggin Hill
7 May 40 to Digby
5 Jun 40 to Biggin Hill
1 Jul 40 to Hawkinge
1 Jul 40 to Sealand
3 Jul 40 to Acklington
7 Aug 40 to Biggin Hill
8 Sep 40 to Pembrey
Jun 41 **Hurricane IIB** (Dec 41)
4 Jun 41 to Fairwood Common
4 Dec 41 to Baginton
4 Mar 42 en route India
7 Jun 42 to Kanchrapara
Jun 42 **Hurricane IIC** (Jul 44)
det Chittagong
Jan 43 to Dohazari
2 Jan 43 to Ramu
dets 'Hay', 'Lyons', 'Ritz'
May 43 to Comilla
Jul 43 to Ranchi
Oct 43 to Alipore
5 Dec 43 to Chittagong
3 Jan 44 to Dohazari
5 May 44 to Yelahanka
Jun 44 **Thunderbolt I** (Dec 44)
Jun 44 **Thunderbolt II** (Dec 45)
7 Sep 44 to Arkonam
Oct 44 to Manipur Road
Nov 44 to Wangjing
3 Mar 45 to Palel
3 Mar 45 to Wangjing
Apr 45 to Myingyan North
Apr 45 to 'Tennant'
May 45 to Myingyan North
7 Jun 45 to Meiktila
Dec 45 DB
—
5 Nov 51 RF @ Gütersloh
Nov 51 **Meteor FR 9** (Aug 56)
3 Nov 54 to Laarbruch
Nov 55 to Wunstorf
Jun 56 **Swift FR 5** (Dec 60)
5 Sep 56 to Gütersloh
Dec 60 **Hunter FR 10** (Dec 60)
Dec 60 DB — renumbered as No 4 Sqn

80 Sqn

Aug 17 F @ Thetford — nucleus from No 36 TS, used various aircraft
Aug 17 to Montrose
Nov 17 to Beverley
Dec 17 **Camel** (Dec 18)
Jan 18 to Boisdinghem
Feb 18 to Serny
Mar 18 to Champien
Mar 18 to Cachy
Mar 18 to Remaisnil
Mar 18 to Wamin
Mar 18 to Belleville Farm
Apr 18 to La Bellevue
Jun 18 to Fouquerolles
Jun 18 to Liettres
Jul 18 to Touquin
Aug 18 to Vignacourt
Aug 18 to Allonville
Sep 18 to Assevillers
Oct 18 to Bouvincourt
Oct 18 to Bertry West
Nov 18 to Flaumont
Nov 18 to Grand Fayt
Dec 18 to Strée A
Dec 18 **Snipe** (Feb 20)
Mar 19 to Clermont
May 19 en route Egypt via Marseilles
Jun 19 to Aboukir
Feb 20 DB — renumbered as No 56 Sqn
—
Mar 37 RF @ Kenley — from 'B' Flt, No 17 Sqn
Mar 37 **Gauntlet II** (May 37)
15 Mar 37 to Henlow
May 37 **Gladiator I** (Nov 40)
9 Jun 37 to Debden
30 Apr 38 en route Egypt
10 May 38 to Ismailia
det Ramleh
24 Sep 38 to Amiriya
9 Oct 38 to Ismailia
16 Jan 39 to Helwan
21 Apr 39 to Amiriya
19 May 39 to Helwan
det Amiriya
15 Jul 39 to Amiriya
Jun 40 **Hurricane I** (Aug 40)
det Sidi Barrani
22 Aug 40 to Sidi Barrani
31 Aug 40 to Sidi Haneish South
det Bir Kenayis
8 Nov 40 to Abu Sueir
Nov 40 **Gladiator II** (Mar 41)
19 Nov 40 to Elevsis
23 Nov 40 to Trikkala
det Yanina
4 Dec 40 to Larissa
det Yanina
16 Jan 41 to Yanina
dets Elevsis, Paramythia
Jan 41 **Hurricane I** (Jan 42)
27 Feb 41 to Paramythia
5 Mar 41 to Elevsis
22 Apr 41 to Argos
24 Apr 41 to Maleme
29 Apr 41 en route Palestine
1 May 41 to Aqir
dets Maleme, Nicosia, Haifa
23 Jun 41 to Haifa
dets Nicosia, Aqir
20 Jul 41 to Nicosia
det Famagusta
16 Aug 41 to Aqir
9 Sep 41 to Rayak
det Beirut
19 Oct 41 to LG 103
6 Nov 41 to LG 111
19 Nov 41 to LG 128
2 Dec 41 to LG 123
5 Dec 41 to LG 133
11 Dec 41 to El Gubbi
18 Dec 41 to Gazala No 2
28 Dec 41 to El Adem
Jan 42 **Hurricane IIC** (Apr 43)
3 Feb 42 to LG 109
10 Feb 42 to LG 102
4 Mar 42 to Gambut
1 Jun 42 to LG 121
22 Jun 42 to LG 18
27 Jun 42 to LG 92
22 Sep 42 to El Bassa
13 Oct 42 to LG 85
20 Oct 42 to LG 37
11 Nov 42 to LG 13
18 Nov 42 to Bu Amud
Apr 43 **Spitfire VC** (Apr 44)
15 May 43 to Idku
det El Gamil
5 Jul 43 to Savoia
17 Aug 43 to St Jean
7 Sep 43 to Derna
Sep 43 **Spitfire IX** (Jan 44)
dets Bu Amud, Savoia
19 Oct 43 to Savoia
9 Nov 43 to Kabrit
dets Heliopolis, Dekheila
20 Jan 44 to Madna
Jan 44 **Spitfire VB** (Apr 44)
23 Feb 44 to Canne
13 Mar 44 to Trigno
2 Apr 44 to Portici (No 3 BPD)
10 Apr 44 en route UK
24 Apr 44 to Sawbridgeworth
5 May 44 to Hornchurch
May 44 **Spitfire IX** (Aug 44)
19 May 44 to Detling
22 Jun 44 to Merston
27 Jun 44 to Gatwick
5 Jul 44 to West Malling
Aug 44 **Tempest V** (Feb 48)
29 Aug 44 to Manston
20 Sep 44 to Coltishall
29 Sep 44 to B 70/Deurne
1 Oct 44 to B 82/Grave
7 Oct 44 to B 80/Volkel
12 Apr 45 to B 112/Hopsten
19 Apr 45 to Warmwell
7 May 45 to B 152/Fassberg
24 Jun 45 to B 160/Kastrup
6 Sep 45 to B 158/Lübeck
28 Oct 45 to B 170/Sylt
18 Nov 45 to B 158/Lübeck
31 Jan 46 to Wunstorf
17 Apr 46 to Dedelsdorf
4 May 46 to Sylt
12 Jun 46 to Dedelsdorf
19 Jul 46 to Gatow
26 Aug 46 to Dedelsdorf
5 Sep 46 to Manston
19 Sep 46 to Wunstorf
14 Feb 47 to Sylt
22 Mar 47 to Wunstorf
5 May 47 to Middle Wallop
16 May 47 to Wunstorf
3 Jun 47 to Gatow
30 Jun 47 to Wunstorf
2 Sep 47 to Duxford
17 Sep 47 to Wunstorf
Jan 48 **Spitfire F.24** (Dec 51)
4 Feb 48 to Thorney Island
11 Feb 48 to Wunstorf
2 Apr 48 to Lübeck
29 Apr 48 to Wunstorf
10 May 48 to Thorney Island
5 Jun 48 to Wunstorf
22 Jun 48 to Gatow
14 Jul 48 to Gütersloh
22 Jul 48 to Lübeck
24 Aug 48 to Gütersloh
2 Jul 49 to Renfrew
14 Jul 49 en route Hong Kong via HMS *Ocean*
20 Aug 49 to Kai Tak
3 Jan 50 to Sek Kong
1 Feb 50 to Kai Tak
7 Mar 50 to Sek Kong
28 Apr 50 to Kai Tak
Dec 51 **Hornet F.3** (Apr 55)
1 May 55 DB
—
1 Aug 55 RF @ Laarbruch — No 214 Sqn renumbered
Aug 55 **Canberra PR 7** (Sep 69)
11 Jun 57 to Brüggen
30 Sep 69 DB

81 Sqn

7 Jan 17 F @ Gosport — nucleus from No 1 RS, used various aircraft
15 Jan 17 to Scampton
4 Jul 18 DB — merged into No 34 TDS
—
25 Nov 18 RF @ Upper Heyford — also designated No 1 Sqn, CAF
Nov 18 **Dolphin** (Apr 19)
2 May 19 to Shoreham
May 19 **SE 5A** (Jan 20)
28 Jan 20 DB
—
21 Nov 39 RF @ Mont Jois — from the Air Component Communications Sqn
Dec 39 **Tiger Moth** (Jun 40)
Dec 39 **Cierva C.40** (Dec 39)
5 May 40 to Hendon
15 Jun 40 DB
—
28 Jul 41 RF @ Leconfield — from 'A' Flt, No 504 Sqn
Jul 41 **Hurricane IIB** (Nov 41)
12 Aug 41 en route USSR via HMS *Argus*
7 Sep 41 to Vaenga
28 Nov 41 en route UK
6 Dec 41 to Turnhouse
Dec 41 **Spitfire VA** (Apr 42)
6 Jan 42 to Ouston
14 Feb 42 to Turnhouse
15 Mar 42 to Ouston
29 Mar 42 to Turnhouse
dets Drem, Ouston, Ayr
Apr 42 **Spitfire VB** (Oct 42)
13 Apr 42 to Ouston
det Ayr
14 May 42 to Hornchurch
17 Jul 42 to Fairlop
1 Sep 42 to Wellingore
30 Oct 42 en route N Africa via Gibraltar
Oct 42 **Spitfire VC** (Nov 43)
8 Nov 42 to Maison Blanche
13 Nov 42 to Bone
5 Jan 43 to Constantine
Jan 43 **Spitfire IX** (Nov 43)
26 Jan 43 to Tingley
17 Mar 43 to Souk el Khemis ('Paddington')
12 May 43 to La Sebala I
20 May 43 to Utique
3 Jun 43 to Ta Kali
18 Jul 43 to Lentini
6 Sep 43 to Milazzo
23 Sep 43 to Serretelle
10 Oct 43 to Gioia del Colle
3 Nov 43 en route FE
Nov 43 **Spitfire VIII** (Jun 45)
8 Dec 43 to Alipore
7 Jan 44 to Tulihal
9 Feb 44 to Ramu/'Reindeer I'
19 Feb 44 to Tulihal
29 Feb 44 to Kangla
det 'Broadway'
2 Mar 44 to Tulihal
dets Kangla, Palel, Kumbhirgram
28 Apr 44 to Kumbhirgram
dets Kangla, Imphal
10 Aug 44 to Minneriya
15 Dec 44 to Ratmalana
27 Apr 45 to Amarda Road
10 Jun 45 DB
—
10 Jun 45 RF @ Bobbili — No 123 Sqn (at Baigachi) renumbered
Jun 45 **Thunderbolt II** (Jun 46)
30 Aug 45 to Vizagapatam
25 Sep 45 to Baigachi
30 Sep 45 to Zayatkwin
6 Oct 45 to Port Swettenham
6 Oct 45 to Kuala Lumpur
21 Oct 45 to Kemajoran
30 Jun 46 DB
—
1 Sep 46 RF @ Seletar — No 684 Sqn renumbered
Sep 46 **Spitfire PR 19** (Jan 50)
Sep 46 **Mosquito PR 34** (Dec 55)
dets Kemajoran, Mingaladon, Labuan
1 Oct 47 to Changi
dets Butterworth, Kai Tak, Mingaladon
1 Feb 48 to Tengah
dets Kai Tak, Kuala Lumpur, Tan Son Nhut, Labuan
Jul 48 **Spitfire FR 18** (Mar 50)
Oct 49 **Anson C.19** (Jun 51)
16 Mar 50 to Seletar
dets Butterworth, Kai Tak, Labuan
Nov 50 **Spitfire FR 18** (Jan 51)
Jan 51 **Spitfire PR 19** (Jun 54)
Jan 54 **Meteor PR 10** (Jul 61)
Dec 55 **Pembroke C(PR) 1** (Aug 60)
1 Apr 58 to Tengah
det Labuan
Feb 60 **Canberra PR 7** (Jan 70)
16 Jan 70 DB

82 Sqn

7 Jan	17	F @ Doncaster — nucleus from No 15 RS, used various aircraft
6 Feb	17	to Beverley
30 Mar	17	to Waddington
Jul	17	**AW FK 8** (Feb 19)
17 Nov	17	to St-Omer
20 Nov	17	to Savy
22 Jan	18	to Golancourt
22 Mar	18	to Catigny
24 Mar	18	to Allonville
27 Mar	18	to Bertangles
28 Mar	18	to Agenvillers
7 Jun	18	to Quevauvillers
15 Jul	18	to Haussimont
2 Aug	18	to Quelmes
3 Sep	18	to Droglandt
20 Sep	18	to Proven
22 Oct	18	to Bisseghem
6 Nov	18	to Menin
19 Nov	18	to Bertangles
15 Feb	19	to Shoreham as a cadre
May	19	to Tangmere
4 Jul	19	DB
		—
14 Jun	37	RF @ Andover — from 'B' Flt, No 142 Sqn
Jun	37	**Hind** (Mar 38)
8 Jul	37	to Cranfield
Mar	38	**Blenheim I** (Sep 39)
22 Aug	39	to Watton
Aug	39	**Blenheim IV** (Mar 42) dets Odiham, Lossiemouth, Tangmere, Luqa
21 Mar	42	en route FE
24 May	42	to Karachi
11 Jun	42	to Quetta
6 Jul	42	to Cholavaram
Aug	42	**Vengeance I & IA** (Jul 44) dets Drigh Road, Madhaiganj
5 Mar	43	to Madhaiganj
11 Apr	43	to Asansol
Apr	43	**Vengeance II** (Jul 44) det Salbani
25 May	43	to Salbani det Chittagong
9 Aug	43	to Feni
21 Nov	43	to Dohazari
23 Jan	44	to Jumchar
Mar	44	**Vengeance III** (Jul 44)
20 Mar	44	to Kumbhirgram
9 Apr	44	to Jumchar
28 May	44	to Kolar
Jul	44	**Mosquito VI** (Mar 46) det Ranchi
30 Sep	44	to Ranchi
8 Dec	44	to Charra
15 Dec	44	to Kumbhirgram det Charra
26 Apr	45	to Joari
27 May	45	to Cholavaram
12 Oct	45	to St Thomas Mount
15 Mar	46	DB
		—
1 Oct	46	RF @ Benson — from elements of No 541 Sqn
Oct	46	**Spitfire PR 19** (Oct 47)
Oct	46	**Lancaster PR 1** (Dec 53) dets Accra, Kano, Yundum, Eastleigh, Leuchars
18 Jun	47	to Leuchars dets Eastleigh, Dar-es-Salaam, Lusaka
6 Oct	47	to Benson
31 Oct	47	Benson (Spitfire) element to No 541 Sqn. HQ now Eastleigh dets Swartkop, Tabora, Shallufa
6 Nov	48	to Takoradi dets Ikeja, Lungi, Eastleigh
21 Mar	49	to Eastleigh dets Dar-es-Salaam, Tabora
5 Aug	49	to Takoradi dets Eastleigh, Ikeja, Kano
26 Mar	51	to Eastleigh dets Takoradi, Tabora, Livingstone, Habbaniyah
30 Oct	52	to Benson
31 Mar	53	to Wyton
Nov	53	**Canberra PR 3** (Feb 55)
Oct	54	**Canberra PR 7** (Sep 56)
1 Sep	56	DB
		—
22 Jul	59	**Thor** at Shepherds Grove
10 Jul	63	DB

83 Sqn

7 Jan	17	F @ Montrose — nucleus from No 18 RS, used various aircraft
15 Jan	17	to Spittlegate
15 Sep	17	to Wyton
12 Dec	17	to Narborough
Dec	17	**FE 2B** (Feb 19)
6 Mar	18	to St-Omer
7 Mar	18	to Auchel
2 May	18	to Franqueville
9 Oct	18	to Lahoussoye
26 Oct	18	to Estrées-en-Chaussée
13 Dec	18	to Serny
14 Feb	19	to Hawkinge as a cadre
Sep	19	to Lympne
15 Oct	19	to Croydon
31 Dec	19	DB
		—
4 Aug	36	RF @ Turnhouse
Aug	36	**Hind** (Dec 38)
14 Mar	38	to Scampton
Nov	38	**Hampden** (Jan 42) det Lossiemouth
Dec	41	**Manchester** (Jun 42)
May	42	**Lancaster I & III** (Jul 46)
15 Aug	42	to Wyton
18 Apr	44	to Coningsby
Jul	46	**Lincoln B.2** (Dec 55)
5 Nov	46	to Hemswell
1 Jan	56	DB
		—
21 May	57	RF @ Waddington
Jul	57	**Vulcan B.1** (Aug 60)
10 Aug	60	reduced to a cadre
10 Oct	60	re-established at Scampton
Dec	60	**Vulcan B.2** (Aug 69)
31 Aug	69	DB

84 Sqn

7 Jan	17	F @ Beaulieu — nucleus from No 16 RS
Jan	17	**BE 12A** (Mar 17)
Jan	17	**BE 12** (Mar 17)
Jan	17	**BE 2C** (Mar 17)
22 Mar	17	to Lilbourne
Mar	17	**Nieuport 12** (Aug 17)
Mar	17	**Curtiss JN 4** (Aug 17)
Mar	17	**Avro 504** (Aug 17)
Mar	17	**1½ Strutter** (Aug 17)
Aug	17	**SE 5A** (Aug 19)
23 Sep	17	to Liettres
12 Nov	17	to Le Hameau
29 Dec	17	to Flez
22 Mar	18	to Champien
23 Mar	18	to Vert Galand
28 Mar	18	to Conteville
4 Apr	18	to Bertangles
8 Sep	18	to Assevillers
8 Oct	18	to Bouvincourt
25 Oct	18	to Bertry West
3 Dec	18	to Thuilles
13 May	19	to Bickendorf
6 Jul	19	to Eil
12 Aug	19	to Tangmere as a cadre
8 Oct	19	to Croydon
Jan	20	to Kenley
30 Jan		DB
		—
13 Aug	20	RF @ Baghdad West
Aug	20	**DH 9A** (Jan 29)
20 Sep	20	to Shaibah dets Baghdad West, Nasiriyah, Bushire
Jun	28	**Wapiti** (Jan 35)
Dec	34	**Vincent** (Jun 39)
Feb	39	**Blenheim I** (Apr 41) det Sharjah
24 Sep	40	to Heliopolis dets Fuka, Qotafiyah, Tatoi
16 Nov	40	to Menidi det Paramythia
Mar	41	**Blenheim IV** (Mar 42)
Apr	41	to Heraklion
Apr	41	to Heliopolis
26 Apr	41	to Aqir dets Habbaniyah, H.4
24 May	41	to Habbaniyah
7 Jun	41	to Mosul det Shaibah
27 Sep	41	to Habbaniyah dets Aqir, Amiriya
9 Nov	41	to Amiriya
25 Nov	41	to LG 116
26 Nov	41	to LG 75
18 Dec	41	to Gambut
2 Jan	42	to Heliopolis
14 Jan	42	en route FE
23 Jan	42	to P I
26 Jan	42	to P II
16 Feb	42	to Kalidjati
1 Mar	42	Sqn dispersed
		—
18 Mar	42	re-established at Drigh Road
3 Jun	42	to Quetta
17 Nov	42	to Vizagapatam
Dec	42	**Vengeance I, IA, II** (Jun 44)
13 Jan	43	to Cholavaram
8 Apr	43	to Ratmalana det Yelahanka
28 Aug	43	to Ranchi det Drigh Road
7 Dec	43	to Maharajpur
10 Feb	44	to Kumbhirgram
Mar	44	**Vengeance III** (Oct 44)
22 Jul	44	to Samungli
31 Oct	44	to Yelahanka
Dec	44	**Vengeance II** (Feb 45)
Dec	44	**Vengeance III** (Mar 45)
Feb	45	**Mosquito VI** (Dec 46)
23 Apr	45	to Charra det St Thomas Mount
26 Jun	45	to St Thomas Mount det Guindy
2 Sep	45	to Baigachi
10 Sep	45	to Hmawbi
12 Sep	45	to Kallang
22 Sep	45	to Seletar dets Kemajoran, Soerabaya
16 Jan	46	to Kemajoran
21 May	46	to Kuala Lumpur
11 Sep	46	to Seletar
Dec	46	**Beaufighter X** (Oct 48)
26 Sep	47	to Changi
1 Feb	48	to Tengah det Kuala Lumpur
11 Oct	48	en route ME
28 Nov	48	to Habbaniyah
Feb	49	**Brigand B.1** (Feb 53) det Mogadishu
8 Apr	50	to Tengah
20 Feb	53	DB
		—
20 Feb	53	RF @ Fayid — No 204 Sqn renumbered
Feb	53	**Valetta C.1** (Dec 56)
3 Dec	55	to Abu Sueir
11 Mar	56	to Nicosia
31 Dec	56	DB
		—
31 Dec	56	RF @ Khormaksar — Aden Protectorate Communications and Support Sqn renumbered
Dec	56	**Valetta C.1** (Aug 60)
Dec	56	**Sycamore HR 14** (May 57)
Dec	56	**Pembroke C.1** (Jun 57)
May	58	**Beverley C.1** (Aug 67)
Aug	67	**Andover C.1** (Sep 71)
3 Sep	67	to Sharjah
30 Dec	70	to Muharraq
1 Oct	71	DB
		—
17 Jan	72	RF @ Akrotiri — from No 1536 Flt & No 230 Sqn det
Jan	72	**Whirlwind HC 10** (Mar 82) det Nicosia
Mar	82	**Wessex HC 2** ( )

85 Sqn

1 Aug	17	F @ Upavon — nucleus from 'C' Flt, CFS, used various aircraft
10 Aug	17	to Norwich
27 Nov	17	to Hounslow
May	18	**SE 5A** (Feb 19)
22 May	18	to Marquise
25 May	18	to Petite Synthe
11 Jun	18	to St-Omer
13 Aug	18	to Bertangles
5 Sep	18	to Savy
23 Sep	18	to Foucaucourt
9 Oct	18	to Estrées-en-Chaussée
27 Oct	18	to Escaufourt
9 Nov	18	to Phalempin
7 Dec	18	to Ascq
19 Feb	19	to Lopcombe Corner as a cadre
3 Jul	19	DB
		—
1 Jun	38	RF @ Debden — from 'A' Flt, No 87 Sqn
Jun	38	**Gladiator I** (Sep 38)
Sep	38	**Hurricane I** (Apr 41)
18 Oct	38	to Aldergrove
4 Nov	38	to Debden
9 Sep	39	to Rouen/Boos
29 Sep	39	to Merville
5 Nov	39	to Lille/Seclin dets Le Touquet, St-Inglevert
10 Apr	40	to Mons-en-Chaussée
26 Apr	40	to Lille/Seclin
19 May	40	to Merville
20 May	40	to Boulogne
23 May	40	to Debden dets Martlesham Heath, Castle Camps
19 Aug	40	to Croydon
3 Sep	40	to Castle Camps
5 Sep	40	to Church Fenton
23 Oct	40	to Kirton-in-Lindsey dets Caistor, Debden, Gravesend
23 Nov	40	to Gravesend
1 Jan	41	to Debden
Jan	41	**Defiant I** (Feb 41)
Feb	41	**Havoc I** (Nov 41)
3 May	41	to Hunsdon
Jul	41	**Havoc II** (Sep 42)
Aug	42	**Mosquito II** (Jun 43)
Mar	43	**Mosquito XV** (Aug 43)
Mar	43	**Mosquito XII** (Feb 44)
13 May	43	to West Malling det Predannack
Oct	43	**Mosquito XIII** (May 44
Nov	43	**Mosquito XVII** (Nov 4
1 May	44	to Swannington
21 Jul	44	to West Malling
29 Aug	44	to Swannington
Nov	44	**Mosquito XXX** (Jan 46
27 Jun	45	to Castle Camps
13 Aug	45	to Bradwell Bay
7 Sep	45	to Castle Camps
11 Oct	45	to Tangmere
20 Oct	45	to Lübeck
3 Nov	45	to Tangmere

Jan 46 **Mosquito NF 36** (Oct 51)
Aug 46 to Acklington
Sep 46 to Tangmere
Oct 46 to Lübeck
Nov 46 to Tangmere
Apr 47 to West Malling
Jun 47 to Acklington
Jun 47 to West Malling
Jan 48 to Acklington
Feb 48 to West Malling
May 48 to Lübeck
Jun 48 to West Malling
Sep 51 **Meteor NF 11** (Apr 54)
Apr 54 **Meteor NF 12** (Nov 58)
Apr 54 **Meteor NF 14** (Nov 58)
Sep 57 to Church Fenton
Nov 58 DB
—
Nov 58 RF @ Stradishall — No 89 Sqn renumbered
Nov 58 **Javelin FAW 2** (Mar 60)
Nov 58 **Javelin FAW 6** (Jun 60)
Jun 59 to West Malling
Mar 60 **Javelin FAW 8** (Mar 63)
Sep 60 to West Raynham
Mar 63 DB
—
Apr 63 RF @ West Raynham — from the Target Facilities Sqn
Apr 63 **Canberra T.11** (Apr 69)
Apr 63 to Binbrook
Sep 64 **Meteor F (TT) 8** (Aug 70)
Nov 64 **Canberra B.2** (Dec 75)
Aug 65 **Canberra T.19** (Dec 75)
Aug 68 **Canberra PR 3** (Apr 69)
Jan 72 to West Raynham
Dec 75 DB — absorbed by No 100 Sqn
—
Dec 75 **Bloodhound II** @ West Raynham, dets North Coates, Bawdsey

6 Sqn

Sep 17 F @ Shoreham — nucleus from No 3 TS, used various aircraft
Sep 17 to Wye
Dec 17 to Northolt
Jul 18 DB — absorbed by No 30 TDS
—
Dec 40 RF @ Gosport
Dec 40 **Blenheim IV** (Jun 41)
Feb 41 to Leuchars
Mar 41 to Wattisham
det Ipswich
May 41 to North Coates
Jun 41 **Beaufort I** (Feb 42)
det St Eval
Dec 41 **Beaufort II** (Aug 42)
Jan 42 to St Eval
det Thorney Island, Wick
Mar 42 to Skitten
det Sumburgh
Jul 42 to Luqa (air echelon only — absorbed by No 39 Sqn, 26 Aug 42)
Aug 42 to Thorney Island
Oct 42 **Liberator IIIA** (Oct 44)
Mar 43 to Aldergrove
Apr 43 **Liberator V** (Sep 43)
Sep 43 to Ballykelly
Mar 44 to Reykjavik
det Tain
Jul 44 to Tain
Jul 44 **Liberator V** (Mar 45)
Jan 45 **Liberator VIII** (Apr 46)
Aug 45 to Oakington
Aug 45 **Liberator VI** (Apr 46)
Apr 46 DB

87 Sqn

1 Sep 17 F @ Upavon — nucleus from 'D' Flt, CFS, used various aircraft
15 Sep 17 to Sedgeford
19 Dec 17 to Hounslow
Dec 17 **Dolphin** (Feb 19)
24 Apr 18 to St-Omer
27 Apr 18 to Petite Synthe
27 May 18 to Estrées-lès-Crécy
29 Jun 18 to Rougefay
19 Sep 18 to Soncamp
4 Nov 18 to Boussières
9 Feb 19 to Ternhill as a cadre
24 Jun 19 DB
—
15 Mar 37 RF @ Tangmere — nucleus from No 54 Sqn
Mar 37 **Fury II** (Jun 37)
7 Jun 37 to Debden
Jun 37 **Gladiator I** (Aug 38)
Jul 38 **Hurricane I** (Sep 42)
4 Sep 39 to Rouen/Boos
29 Sep 39 to Merville
5 Nov 39 to Lille/Seclin
det Le Touquet
22 Feb 40 to Le Touquet
8 Mar 40 to Lille/Seclin
15 Apr 40 to Amiens
3 May 40 to Senon
10 May 40 to Lille/Seclin
20 May 40 to Merville
22 May 40 to Debden
24 May 40 to Church Fenton
5 Jul 40 to Exeter
dets Hullavington, Bibury
28 Nov 40 to Colerne
det Charmy Down
18 Dec 40 to Charmy Down
det St Mary's
Jun 41 **Hurricane IIC** (Jan 44)
7 Aug 41 to Colerne
det St Mary's
27 Jan 42 to Charmy Down
det St Mary's
2 Nov 42 en route N Africa
7 Dec 42 to Phillipeville
dets Gibraltar, Setif
22 Dec 42 to Djedjelli
dets Setif, Taher
Feb 43 to Taher
det Setif
Apr 43 **Spitfire VB & VC** (Aug 44)
22 May 43 to Tingley
Jun 43 **Spitfire IX** (Jun 44)
1 Jul 43 to Monastir
21 Jul 43 to Tingley
13 Aug 43 to La Sebala I
1 Oct 43 to Bo Rizzo
det Palermo
6 Dec 43 to Palermo
Dec 43 **Spitfire VIII** (May 44)
3 Apr 44 to Catania
21 Jun 44 to Foggia
23 Jul 44 to Perugia
23 Aug 44 to Loreto
Aug 44 **Spitfire IX** (Dec 46)
4 Sep 44 to Fano
16 Sep 44 to Borghetto
2 Oct 44 to Fano
det Rimini
17 Nov 44 to Peretola
31 Dec 44 to Pontedera
24 Apr 45 to Bologna
1 May 45 to Villafranca
12 May 45 to Campoformido
22 Aug 45 to Treviso
23 Sep 46 to Zeltweg
2 Dec 46 to Tissano
15 Dec 46 to Zeltweg
30 Dec 46 DB
—
1 Jan 52 RF @ Wahn
Mar 52 **Meteor NF 11** (Dec 57)
2 Jul 57 to Brüggen
Aug 57 **Javelin FAW 1** (Jan 61)
Sep 58 **Javelin FAW 5** (Oct 60)
Nov 59 **Javelin FAW 4** (Jan 61)
3 Jan 61 DB

88 Sqn

24 Jul 17 F @ Gosport — nucleus from No 1 TS, used various aircraft
2 Aug 17 to Harling Road
Mar 18 **Bristol F2b Fighter** (Aug 19)
2 Apr 18 to Kenley
16 Apr 18 to Cappelle
19 Jul 18 to Drionville
2 Aug 18 to Serny
21 Oct 18 to Floringhem
23 Oct 18 to Ascq
26 Oct 18 to Gondecourt
28 Oct 18 to Bersée
18 Nov 18 to Aulnoy
13 Dec 18 to Dour
14 Dec 18 to Franc Waret
18 Dec 18 to Nivelles
10 Aug 19 DB
—
7 Jun 37 RF @ Waddington — nucleus from No 110 Sqn
Jun 37 **Hind** (Dec 37)
17 Jul 37 to Boscombe Down
Dec 37 **Battle** (Aug 41)
11 Sep 39 to Auberives-sur-Suippes
13 Sep 39 to Mourmelon-le-Grande
dets Perpignan/La Salanque
16 May 40 to Les Grandes-Chappelles
4 Jun 40 to Moisy
dets Echemines, Faux-Villecerf
14 Jun 40 to Driffield
23 Jun 40 to Sydenham
Feb 41 **Boston I & II** (Aug 41)
Feb 41 **Blenheim I** (Jul 41)
8 Jul 41 to Swanton Morley
Jul 41 **Blenheim IV** (Feb 42)
Jul 41 **Boston III** (Jun 43)
1 Aug 41 to Attlebridge
dets Manston, Long Kesh, Abbotsinch, Ford, Winfield, Charmy Down
29 Sep 42 to Oulton
dets Ford, Hurn
30 Mar 43 to Swanton Morley
Mar 43 **Boston IIIA** (Apr 45)
dets Charmy Down, Lossiemouth, Dalcross Shobdon
19 Aug 43 to Hartford Bridge
dets Swanton Morley, Beaulieu
Jun 44 **Boston IV** (Apr 45)
16 Oct 44 to B 50/Vitry-en-Artois
6 Apr 45 DB
—
1 Sep 46 RF @ Kai Tak — No 1430 Flt renumbered
Sep 46 **Sunderland GR 5** (Oct 54)
dets Iwakuni, Seletar
24 Jun 51 to Seletar
dets Iwakuni, Kai Tak
1 Oct 54 DB
—
15 Jan 56 RF @ Wildenrath
Jan 56 **Canberra B(I) 8** (Dec 62)
17 Dec 62 DB — renumbered as No 14 Sqn

89 Sqn

24 Jul 17 F @ Catterick — nucleus from No 6 TS, used various aircraft
7 Aug 17 to Harling Road
17 Jul 18 to Upper Heyford
Jul 18 **SE 5A** (Jul 18)
29 Jul 18 DB
—
25 Sep 41 RF @ Colerne
Oct 41 **Beaufighter IF** (Apr 43)
19 Nov 41 en route Egypt
10 Dec 41 to Abu Sueir
dets Idku, Ta Kali, Luqa, El Gamil, Dekheila, Fuka, Hurghada, Cairo West, Shandur, Bu Amud, Benina, Bersis, Maison Blanche
Aug 42 **Beaufighter VIF** (Jun 45)
28 Jan 43 to Bersis
8 Mar 43 to Castel Benito
dets Bersis, Misurata West
18 Aug 43 to Bu Amud
dets Idku, Bersis, St Jean
19 Sep 43 to Idku
15 Oct 43 en route FE
26 Oct 43 to Vavuniya
dets St Thomas Mount, Ratmalana, Vizagapatam
29 Mar 44 to Minneriya
25 Jun 44 to Vavuniya
dets St Thomas Mount, Minneriya, Ratmalana
18 Aug 44 to Baigachi
dets Chittagong, Tulihal, Cox's Bazaar, Tabingaung, Sadaung, Dwelha, Kwetnge, Chiringa, Akyab, Meiktila, Mingaladon
Feb 45 **Mosquito VI** (Apr 45)
Mar 45 **Mosquito XIX** (Mar 46)
6 Sep 45 to Hmawbi
25 Sep 45 to Kuala Lumpur
26 Sep 45 to Seletar
Mar 46 **Walrus** (Apr 46)
1 May 46 DB — renumbered as No 22 Sqn
—
15 Dec 55 RF @ Stradishall
Jan 56 **Venom NF 3** (Nov 57)
Sep 57 **Javelin FAW 6** (Nov 58)
Oct 57 **Javelin FAW 2** (Nov 58)
30 Nov 58 DB — renumbered as No 85 Sqn

90 Sqn

8 Oct 17 F @ Shawbury — nucleus from No 10 TS, used various aircraft
18 Oct 17 to Shotwick
15 Jul 18 to Brockworth
Jul 18 **Dolphin** (Jul 18)
29 Jul 18 DB
—
14 Aug 18 RF @ Buckminster — from No 38 Sqn Depot
Aug 18 **FE 2B** (Sep 18)
dets Stamford, Leadenham
Sep 18 **Avro 504K(NF)** (Jun 19)
13 Jun 19 DB
—
15 Mar 37 RF @ Bicester — from 'A' Flt, No 101 Sqn
Mar 37 **Hind** (Jun 37)
May 37 **Blenheim I** (Apr 39)
Mar 39 **Blenheim IV** (Apr 40)
10 May 39 to West Raynham
13 Aug 39 to Penrhos
27 Aug 39 to West Raynham
3 Sep 39 to Bircham Newton
7 Sep 39 to Weston-on-the-Green
11 Sep 39 to West Raynham
14 Sep 39 to Weston-on-the-Green
16 Sep 39 to Upwood
Sep 39 **Blenheim I** (Apr 40)
6 Apr 40 DB — merged into No 17 OTU
—
3 May 41 RF @ Watton
May 41 **Fortress I** (Feb 42)
det Great Massingham

15 May 41	to West Raynham
30 Aug 41	to Polebrook dets Kinloss, Shallufa — absorbed by No 220 Sqn det
Oct 41	**Blenheim IV** (Feb 42)
10 Feb 42	DB — absorbed by No 1653 HCU
	—
7 Nov 42	RF @ Bottesford
Nov 42	**Stirling I** (May 43)
29 Dec 42	to Ridgewell
Mar 43	**Stirling III** (Jun 44)
31 May 43	to West Wickham/ Wratting Common
13 Oct 43	to Tuddenham
May 44	**Lancaster I & III** (Sep 47)
11 Nov 46	to Wyton
Apr 47	**Lincoln B.2** (Aug 50)
1 Sep 50	DB
	—
4 Oct 50	RF @ Marham
Jan 51	**Washington B.1** (Mar 54)
Nov 53	**Canberra B.2** (May 56)
1 May 56	DB
	—
1 Jan 57	RF @ Honington
Mar 57	**Valiant B(K) 1** (Dec 64)
May 57	**Valiant B(PR) 1** (Dec 60)
May 57	**Valiant B(PR)K 1** (Mar 61)
1 Mar 65	DB

91 Sqn

1 Sep 17	F @ Spittlegate — nucleus from No 11 TS, used various aircraft
14 Sep 17	to Chattis Hill
15 Mar 18	to Tangmere
27 Aug 18	to Kenley
Oct 18	**Dolphin** (Jul 19)
7 Mar 19	to Lopcombe Corner
3 Jul 19	DB
	—
9 Jan 41	RF @ Hawkinge — No 421 Flt renumbered
Jan 41	**Spitfire IIA** (Jun 41)
Mar 41	**Spitfire VB** (May 43) det Lympne
2 Oct 42	to Lympne
9 Oct 42	to Hawkinge det Lympne
23 Nov 42	to Lympne det Hawkinge
11 Jan 43	to Hawkinge
20 Apr 43	to Honiley
Apr 43	**Spitfire XII** (Mar 44)
9 May 43	to Wittering det Kingscliffe
21 May 43	to Hawkinge
28 Jun 43	to Westhampnett
4 Oct 43	to Tangmere
8 Feb 44	to Hutton Cranswick
20 Feb 44	to Tangmere
29 Feb 44	to Castle Camps
Mar 44	**Spitfire XIV** (Aug 44)
17 Mar 44	to Drem
23 Apr 44	to West Malling
21 Jul 44	to Deanland
Aug 44	**Spitfire IXB** (Apr 45)
7 Oct 44	to Biggin Hill
29 Oct 44	to Manston
Jan 45	**Spitfire XXI** (Oct 46)
8 Apr 45	to Ludham
14 Jul 45	to Fairwood Common
18 Aug 45	to Dyce
21 Mar 46	to Duxford
3 Jun 46	to West Malling
10 Jun 46	to Duxford
29 Jun 46	to Lübeck
29 Aug 46	to Duxford
Oct 46	**Meteor F.3** (Jan 47)
6 Jan 47	to Acklington
31 Jan 47	DB — renumbered as No 92 Sqn

92 Sqn

1 Sep 17	F @ London Colney — nucleus from No 56 TS
Sep 17	**Pup** (Apr 18)
14 Sep 17	to Chattis Hill
17 Mar 18	to Tangmere
May 18	**SE 5A** (Aug 19)
2 Jul 18	to Bray-Dunes
19 Jul 18	to Drionville
2 Aug 18	to Serny
27 Sep 18	to Proyart
9 Oct 18	to Estrées-en-Chaussée
25 Oct 18	to Bertry East
3 Dec 18	to Thuilles
14 Jun 19	to Eil
7 Aug 19	DB
	—
10 Oct 39	RF @ Tangmere — nucleus from No 601 Sqn
Oct 39	**Blenheim IF** (Mar 40)
30 Dec 39	to Croydon det Gatwick
Mar 40	**Spitfire I** (Feb 41)
9 May 40	to Northolt
9 Jun 40	to Hornchurch
18 Jun 40	to Pembrey
8 Sep 40	to Biggin Hill
9 Jan 41	to Manston
20 Feb 41	to Biggin Hill
Feb 41	**Spitfire VB** (Feb 42)
24 Sep 41	to Gravesend
20 Oct 41	to Digby
12 Feb 42	en route ME
16 Apr 42	to Fayid
30 Apr 42	to Heliopolis
4 Aug 42	to LG 173
Aug 42	**Spitfire VB & VC** (Sep 43)
6 Nov 42	to LG 21
12 Nov 42	to LG 13
14 Nov 42	to Gambut West
25 Nov 42	to Msus
4 Dec 42	to El Hassiet
9 Dec 42	to El Nogra
21 Dec 42	to El Merduma
1 Jan 43	to El Chel
3 Jan 43	to Tamet
9 Jan 43	to Hamraiet
19 Jan 43	to Darragh/Wadi Surri
6 Feb 43	to Castel Benito
26 Feb 43	to Hazbub
2 Mar 43	to Ben Gardane
10 Mar 43	to Bu Grara
Apr 43	**Spitfire IX** (Aug 43)
12 Apr 43	to La Fauconnerie
15 Apr 43	to Goubrine
6 May 43	to Hergla
21 May 43	to Ben Gardane
14 Jun 43	to Luqa
13 Jul 43	to Pachino
17 Jul 43	to Cassibile
25 Jul 43	to Lentini West
Jul 43	**Spitfire VIII** (Dec 46)
14 Sep 43	to Grottaglie
24 Sep 43	to Gioia del Colle
5 Oct 43	to Tortorella
18 Oct 43	to Triolo
22 Nov 43	to Canne
17 Jan 44	to Marcianese
23 Apr 44	to Venafro
12 Jun 44	to Littorio
17 Jun 44	to Fabrica
3 Jul 44	to Perugia det Rosignano
24 Aug 44	to Loreto det Rosignano
4 Sep 44	to Fano
4 Dec 44	to Bellaria
3 May 45	to Treviso
Jun 46	**Spitfire IX** (Dec 46)
23 Sep 46	to Zeltweg
30 Dec 46	DB
	—
31 Jan 47	RF @ Acklington — No 91 Sqn renumbered
Jan 47	**Meteor F.3** (May 48)
15 Feb 47	to Duxford
31 Aug 47	to Lübeck
30 Oct 47	to Duxford
10 Mar 48	to Lübeck
29 Apr 48	to Duxford
May 48	**Meteor F.4** (Oct 50)
7 Oct 49	to Linton-on-Ouse
Oct 50	**Meteor F.8** (Feb 54)
Feb 54	**Sabre F.4** (Apr 56)
Apr 56	**Hunter F.4** (Mar 57)
1 Mar 57	to Middleton St George
Mar 57	**Hunter F.6** (Apr 63)
30 Sep 57	to Thornaby
1 Oct 58	to Middleton St George
22 May 61	to Leconfield
Apr 63	**Lightning F.2** (Jul 71)
29 Dec 65	to Geilenkirchen
24 Jan 68	to Gütersloh
Aug 68	**Lightning F.2A** (Mar 77)
31 Mar 77	DB
	—
1 Jan 77	training at Wildenrath as No 92 Sqn (Designate)
	—
1 Apr 77	RF @ Wildenrath
Apr 77	**Phantom FGR 2** ( )

93 Sqn

23 Sep 17	F @ Croydon — nucleus from No 40 TS, used various aircraft
3 Oct 17	to Chattis Hill
19 Mar 18	to Tangmere
17 Aug 18	DB
	—
14 Oct 18	RF @ Port Meadow
Nov 18	**Dolphin** (Nov 18)
21 Nov 18	DB
	—
7 Dec 40	RF @ Middle Wallop — No 420 Flt renumbered
Dec 40	**Harrow II (LAM)** (Apr 41)
Dec 40	**Havoc I** (Nov 41) dets Coltishall, Hibaldstow, Exeter
Mar 41	**Wellington IC** (Jul 41)
Mar 41	**Boston I** (Jun 41)
Oct 41	**Havoc I (Turbinlite)** (Nov 41)
18 Nov 41	DB — redesignated as No 1458 Flt
	—
1 Jun 42	RF @ Andreas
Jun 42	**Spitfire VB** (Oct 42)
8 Sep 42	to Kingscliffe
20 Oct 42	en route North Africa via Gibraltar
Nov 42	**Spitfire VC** (Feb 44)
13 Nov 42	to Maison Blanche
16 Nov 42	to Souk el Arba
23 Dec 42	to Souk el Khemis ('Euston')
13 May 43	to La Sebala I
26 May 43	to Mateur
12 Jun 43	to Hal Far
14 Jul 43	to Comiso
Jul 43	**Spitfire IX** (Sep 45)
30 Jul 43	to Pachino
28 Aug 43	to Panebianco
2 Sep 43	to Cassala
6 Sep 43	to Falcone
28 Sep 43	to Battipaglia
11 Oct 43	to Capodichino
15 Jan 44	to Lago det Nettuno
5 Jun 44	to Tre Cancelli
14 Jun 44	to Tarquinia
25 Jun 44	to Grosseto
5 Jul 44	to Piombino
20 Jul 44	to Calvi
20 Aug 44	to Ramatuelle
25 Aug 44	to Sisteron
9 Sep 44	to Lyons/Bron
27 Sep 44	to La Jasse
10 Oct 44	to Peretola
16 Nov 44	to Rimini
17 Feb 45	to Ravenna
5 May 45	to Campoformido
16 May 45	to Klagenfurt
5 Sep 45	DB
	—
1 Jan 46	RF @ Lavariano — No 237 Sqn renumbere
Jan 46	**Mustang IV** (Dec 46)
24 Jan 46	to Tissano
30 Apr 46	to Lavariano
16 Sep 46	to Treviso
29 Nov 46	to Lavariano
4 Dec 46	to Treviso
30 Dec 46	DB
	—
15 Nov 50	RF @ Celle
Nov 50	**Vampire FB 5** (Apr 54)
3 Mar 52	to Jever
Mar 54	**Sabre F.4** (Jan 56)
Jan 56	**Hunter F.4** (Mar 57)
Mar 57	**Hunter F.6** (Dec 60)
30 Dec 60	DB

94 Sqn

30 Jul 17	F @ Gosport — nucleu from No 55 TS, used various aircraft
2 Aug 17	to Harling Road
27 Jul 18	to Shoreham
19 Aug 18	to Upper Heyford
Sep 18	**SE 5A** (Jan 19)
31 Oct 18	to Senlis-le-Sec
19 Nov 18	to Izel-le-Hameau
17 Jan 19	reduced to a cadre
3 Feb 19	to Tadcaster
30 Jun 19	DB
	—
26 Mar 39	RF to Khormaksar
Mar 39	**Gladiator I** (Apr 40)
Mar 39	**Gladiator II** (Jun 41)
2 May 39	to Sheikh Othman dets Berbera, Laferug, Little Aden
19 Apr 41	to Amiriya
22 Apr 41	to Ismailia det Habbaniyah
May 41	**Hurricane I** (Dec 41)
29 Aug 41	to El Ballah
27 Oct 41	to LG 103
14 Nov 41	to LG 109
18 Nov 41	to LG 124
Dec 41	**Hurricane IIB** (Jan 42
12 Dec 41	to Sidi Rezegh
19 Dec 41	to Gazala No 2
22 Dec 41	to Mechili
24 Dec 41	to Msus
12 Jan 42	to Antelat
23 Jan 42	to Msus
25 Jan 42	to Mechili
26 Jan 42	to Gazala
28 Jan 42	to LG 110
Feb 42	**Kittyhawk I** (May 42)
15 Feb 42	to El Adem
17 Feb 42	to Gasr-el-Arid
26 Feb 42	to LG 115
17 Mar 42	to Gasr-el-Arid det LG 115
16 May 42	to Maryut
1 Jun 42	to El Gamil
Jun 42	**Hurricane I** (Aug 42)
Jun 42	**Hurricane IIC** (Apr 4
Dec 42	**Spitfire VC** (Jan 43)
14 Jan 43	to Martuba
1 Apr 43	to Cyrene det Apollonia
1 May 43	to Savoia
25 May 43	to Apollonia det Savoia
19 Jun 43	to Savoia
Aug 43	**Spitfire VB** (Sep 43)
29 Oct 43	to Bu Amud
2 Nov 43	to El Adem
Feb 44	**Spitfire IX** (Aug 44)
Mar 44	**Spitfire VC** (Feb 45)
6 Apr 44	to Bu Amud
15 Jul 44	to Savoia
Aug 44	**Spitfire VB** (Feb 45) dets Almaza (No 22 PT & Aboukir (No 24 PT
17 Oct 44	to Kalamaki

4 Feb 45 to Sedes
Feb 45 **Spitfire VIII** (Apr 45)
Feb 45 **Spitfire IX** (Apr 45)
0 Apr 45 DB
—
1 Dec 50 RF @ Celle
Dec 50 **Vampire FB 5** (Jun 54)
Jan 54 **Venom FB 1** (Sep 57)
4 Sep 57 DB
—
1 Oct 60 **Bloodhound I** at Misson
0 Jun 63 DB

95 Sqn

8 Oct 17 F @ Ternhill — nucleus from No 43 TS, used various aircarft
0 Oct 17 to Shotwick
4 Jul 18 DB
—
Oct 18 RF @ Kenley (for Buzzard) — nucleus from Nos 21, 28, 30 and 51 TDSs
) Nov 18 DB
—
5 Jan 41 RF @ Pembroke Dock — nucleus from No 210 Sqn
Jan 41 **Sunderland I** (Dec 42)
Mar 41 to Freetown (Fourah Bay)
dets Apapa, Bathurst, Libreville, Pointe Noire, Gibraltar
Jul 41 **Hurricane I** (Oct 41) — at Hastings
Apr 42 to Jui
dets Bathurst, Fishermans Lake
Jul 42 **Sunderland III** (Jun 45)
Mar 43 to Bathurst/Half Die
Mar 43 **Sunderland I** (Nov 43)
dets Jui, Dakar, Port Etienne
Jun 45 DB

96 Sqn

Oct 17 F @ South Carlton — nucleus from No 45 TS, used various aircraft
Oct 17 to Shotwick
Jul 18 DB — absorbed by No 51 TDS
—
Sep 18 RF @ Wyton — nucleus from Nos 2, 32, 38 and 46 TDSs
Nov 18 **Salamander** (Dec 18)
Dec 18 DB
—
Dec 40 RF @ Cranage — No 422 Flt renumbered
Dec 40 **Hurricane I** (May 41)
Mar 41 **Defiant I** (Feb 42)
det Squires Gate
Sep 41 **Hurricane IIC** (Jan 42)
Oct 41 to Wrexham
Feb 42 **Defiant IA** (May 42)
det Honiley
Apr 42 **Defiant II** (Jul 42)
May 42 **Beaufighter IIF** (Feb 43)
Sep 42 **Beaufighter VIF** (Nov 43)
Oct 42 to Honiley
dets Tangmere, Ford
Aug 43 to Church Fenton
Sep 43 to Drem
Oct 43 **Mosquito XIII** (Dec 44)
Nov 43 to West Malling
Jun 44 to Ford
Sep 44 to Odiham
Dec 44 DB
—
Dec 44 RF @ Leconfield
Dec 44 **Halifax III** (Apr 45)

30 Mar 45 to Cairo West
Apr 45 **Dakota** (Jun 46)
1 May 45 to Bilaspur
det Comilla
4 Sep 45 to Hmawbi
16 Apr 46 to Kai Tak
1 Jun 46 DB — renumbered as No 110 Sqn
—
17 Nov 52 RF @ Ahlhorn
Nov 52 **Meteor NF 11** (Jan 59)
12 Feb 58 to Geilenkirchen
Sep 58 **Javelin FAW 4** (Jan 59)
21 Jan 59 DB — renumbered as No 3 Sqn

97 Sqn

1 Dec 17 F @ Waddington — nucleus from No 51 TS, used various aircraft
21 Jan 18 to Stonehenge
31 Mar 18 to Netheravon
Jun 18 **HP 0/400** (Mar 19)
3 Aug 18 to Xaffévillers
17 Nov 18 to St-Inglevert
4 Mar 19 to Ford Junction
Apr 19 **DH 10** (Mar 20)
19 Jul 19 en route India
23 Aug 19 to Allahabad
dets Lahore, Risalpur, Mianwali
15 Nov 19 to Lahore
dets Mianwali, Karachi, Juhu, Rajkot
28 Mar 20 to Risalpur
1 Apr 20 DB — renumbered as No 60 Sqn
—
16 Sep 35 RF @ Catfoss — from 'B' Flt, No 10 Sqn
Sep 35 **Heyford IA** (Jan 36)
26 Sep 35 to Boscombe Down
Nov 35 **Heyford III** (Feb 39)
7 Jan 37 to Leconfield
Feb 39 **Anson I** (Apr 40)
Feb 39 **Whitley II** (Apr 40)
Feb 39 **Whitley III** (Apr 40)
17 Sep 39 to Abingdon
8 Apr 40 DB — merged into No 10 OTU
—
30 Apr 40 RF @ Driffield (for Whitley)
20 May 40 DB
—
25 Feb 41 RF @ Waddington — nucleus from No 207 Sqn
Feb 41 **Manchester** (Feb 42)
10 Mar 41 to Coningsby
Jul 41 **Hampden** (Aug 41)
Jan 42 **Lancaster I & III** (Jul 46)
2 Mar 42 to Woodhall Spa
18 Apr 43 to Bourn
dets Graveley, Gransden Lodge, Oakington
18 Apr 44 to Coningsby
Jul 46 **Lincoln B.2** (Dec 55)
7 Nov 46 to Hemswell
1 Jan 56 DB
—
1 Dec 58 **Thor** at Hemswell
24 May 63 DB
—
25 May 63 RF @ Watton — No 151 Sqn renumbered
May 63 **Varsity T.1** (Jan 67)
May 63 **Canberra B.2** (Jan 67)
May 63 **Hastings C.2** (Jan 67)
2 Jan 67 DB

98 Sqn

15 Aug 17 F @ Harlaxton — nucleus from No 44 TS, used various aircraft
30 Aug 17 to Old Sarum
Feb 18 **DH 9** (Mar 19)
1 Mar 18 to Lympne
1 Apr 18 to St-Omer
3 Apr 18 to Clairmarais
12 Apr 18 to Alquines
25 May 18 to Coudekerque
6 Jun 18 to Ruisseauville
21 Jun 18 to Drionville
13 Jul 18 to Chailly
3 Aug 18 to Blangermont
27 Oct 18 to Abscon
27 Dec 18 to Marquain
19 Jan 19 to Alquines
28 Mar 19 to Shotwick as a cadre
24 Jun 19 DB
—
17 Feb 36 RF @ Abingdon — from 'C' Flt, No 15 Sqn
Feb 36 **Hind** (Jun 38)
21 Aug 36 to Hucknall
Jun 38 **Battle** (Jul 41)
dets Weston Zoyland, Upwood, Bassingbourn
2 Mar 40 to Scampton
dets Bassingbourn, Old Sarum
19 Mar 40 to Finningley
16 Apr 40 to Château Bougon
15 Jun 40 to Gatwick
31 Jul 40 to Kaldadarnes
Jun 41 **Hurricane I** (Jul 41)
15 Jul 41 DB — Hurricane element became No 1423 Flt
—
12 Sep 42 RF @ West Raynham
Sep 42 **Mitchell II** (Sep 45)
15 Oct 42 to Foulsham
det Honiley
18 Aug 43 to Dunsfold
det Swanton Morley
18 Oct 44 to B 58/Melsbroek
Nov 44 **Mitchell III** (Sep 45)
28 Apr 45 to B 110/Achmer
det Fersfield
18 Sep 45 to B 58/Melsbroek
Sep 42 **Mosquito XVI** (Aug 48)
15 Mar 46 to Wahn
1 Jul 47 to Gatow
9 Aug 47 to Wahn
4 Nov 47 to Gatow
4 Dec 47 to Wahn
Dec 47 **Mosquito B.35** (Feb 51)
19 Sep 49 to Celle
1 Nov 50 to Fassberg
Feb 51 **Vampire FB 5** (Aug 53)
Aug 53 **Venom FB 1** (Apr 55)
19 Apr 55 to Jever
Apr 55 **Hunter F.4** (Jul 57)
25 Jul 57 DB
—
1 Aug 59 **Thor** at Driffield
18 Apr 63 DB
—
19 Apr 63 RF @ Tangmere — No 245 Sqn renumbered
Apr 63 **Canberra B.2** (Feb 76)
1 Oct 63 to Watton
17 Apr 69 to Cottesmore
Aug 70 **Canberra E.15** (Feb 76)
27 Feb 76 DB

99 Sqn

15 Aug 17 F @ Yatesbury — nucleus from No 13 TS, used various aircraft
30 Aug 17 to Ford Farm
Mar 18 **DH 9** (Nov 18)
25 Apr 18 to St-Omer
4 May 18 to Tantonville
5 Jun 18 to Azelot
Sep 18 **DH 9A** (Mar 20)
16 Nov 18 to Auxi-le-Chateau
29 Nov 18 to St-André-aux Bois
12 Dec 18 to Aulnoy
14 May 19 en route India, via Marseilles
15 Jun 19 to Ambala
26 Sep 19 to Mianwali
det Ambala
1 Apr 20 DB — renumbered as No 27 Sqn
—
1 Apr 24 RF @ Netheravon
Apr 24 **Vimy** (Dec 24)
31 May 24 to Bircham Newton
Aug 24 **Aldershot III** (Dec 25)
Dec 25 **Hyderabad** (Jan 31)
5 Jan 28 to Upper Heyford
Oct 29 **Hinaidi** (Dec 33)
Dec 33 **Heyford** (Nov 38)
15 Nov 34 to Mildenhall
Oct 38 **Wellington I** (Dec 39)
1 Sep 39 to Newmarket
Sep 39 **Wellington IA** (Apr 40)
dets Lossiemouth, Salon
Mar 40 **Wellington IC** (Feb 42)
8 Mar 41 to Waterbeach
Jul 41 **Wellington II** (Oct 41)
12 Feb 42 en route India, sqn split up
1 Jun 42 re-established @ Ambala
dets Solan (No 2 Hill Depot), Pandeveswar
12 Sep 42 to Pandeveswar
Oct 42 **Wellington IC** (May 43)
24 Oct 42 to Digri
3 Apr 43 to Chaklala
Apr 43 **Wellington III** (Aug 44)
Apr 43 **Wellington X** (Aug 44)
14 Jun 43 to Jessore
dets Agartala, Kumbhirgram
27 Aug 44 to Dhubalia
Sep 44 **Liberator VI** (Nov 45)
1 Aug 45 to Cocos Island
15 Nov 45 DB
—
17 Nov 47 RF @ Lyneham
Nov 47 **York C.1** (Sep 49)
det Wunstorf for BAL
Aug 49 **Hastings C.1 & C.2** (Jun 59)
Jun 59 **Britannia C.1 & C.2** (Jan 76)
16 Jun 70 to Brize Norton
7 Jan 76 DB

100 Sqn

11 Feb 17 F @ Hingham — nucleus from No 51 Sqn
23 Feb 17 to Farnborough
Feb 17 **BE 2C** (Jan 18)
21 Mar 17 to St-André-aux Bois
Mar 17 **FE 2B** (Aug 18)
1 Apr 17 to Izel-le-Hameau
Apr 17 **BE 2E** (Aug 17)
16 May 17 to Treizennes
5 Oct 17 to Ochey
Jan 18 **FE 2C** (Aug 18)
3 Apr 18 to Villesneux
9 May 18 to Ochey
10 Aug 18 to Xaffévillers
Aug 18 **HP 0/400** (Sep 19)
25 Nov 18 to Ligescourt
dets St-Inglevert, Quilen
16 Jun 19 to St-Inglevert
12 Sep 19 to Baldonnel as a cadre
1 Feb 20 re-established (absorbed cadre of No 141 Sqn)
Feb 20 **DH 9A** (Jun 21)
Feb 20 **Bristol F2b Fighter** (Mar 22)
dets Castlebar, Oranmore
4 Feb 22 to Spittlegate
Feb 22 **DH 9A** (May 24)
Feb 22 **Avro 504K** (May 24)
Feb 22 **Vimy** (May 24)
May 24 to Eastchurch
May 24 **Fawn** (Dec 26)
Jul 24 to Spittlegate
Aug 26 **Horsley** (Apr 33)

10 Jan 28 to Bicester
3 Nov 30 to Donibristle
Nov 32 **Vildebeeste I** (Sep 33)
Aug 33 **Vildebeeste II** (Jan 41)
7 Dec 33 en route FE
6 Jan 34 to Seletar
Dec 37 **Vildebeeste III** (Feb 42)
Dec 41 **Beaufort I** (Jan 42) det Kuantan
31 Jan 42 to Kemajoran
8 Feb 42 DB — merged into No 36 Sqn
—
14 Dec 42 RF @ Waltham
Dec 42 **Lancaster I & III** (May 46)
1 Apr 45 to Elsham Wolds
15 Dec 45 to Scampton
8 May 46 to Lindholme
May 46 **Lincoln B.2** (Apr 54)
28 Oct 46 to Hemswell
23 Mar 50 to Waddington
2 Aug 53 to Wittering
Apr 54 **Canberra B.2** (Sep 59)
Aug 56 **Canberra B.6** (Sep 59)
Aug 56 **Canberra PR 7** (Jun 57) dets Wyton, Christmas Island
Aug 56 **Canberra B(I) 8** (Sep 59)
1 Sep 59 DB
—
1 May 62 RF @ Wittering
May 62 **Victor B.2** (Sep 68)
30 Sep 68 DB
—
1 Feb 72 RF @ West Raynham
Feb 72 **Canberra B.2** ( )
Feb 72 **Canberra T.19** (Jul 80)
5 Jan 76 to Marham
Feb 76 **Canberra E.15** ( )
5 Jan 82 to Wyton
Jan 82 **Canberra PR 7** ( )
Jan 82 **Canberra TT 18** ( )

101 Sqn

12 Jul 17 F @ Farnborough
25 Jul 17 to St-André-aux Bois
Jul 17 **FE 2B** (Mar 19)
Jul 17 **BE 12** (Mar 18)
Jul 17 **BE 12A** (Mar 18)
7 Aug 17 to Le Hameau
31 Aug 17 to Clairmarais South
2 Feb 18 to Auchel
16 Feb 18 to Catigny
24 Mar 18 to Fienvillers
25 Mar 18 to Haute Vissée
7 Apr 18 to Famechon
8 Sep 18 to Lahoussoye
8 Oct 18 to Proyart East
25 Oct 18 to Hancourt
12 Nov 18 to Catillon
29 Nov 18 to Strée
13 Dec 18 to Morville
12 Mar 19 to Laneffe as a cadre
18 Mar 19 to Filton
11 Oct 19 to Eastleigh
31 Dec 19 DB
—
21 Mar 28 RF @ Bircham Newton
Apr 28 **Sidestrand** (Jul 36)
12 Oct 29 to Andover
1 Dec 34 to Bicester
Jan 35 **Overstrand** (Aug 38)
Jun 38 **Blenheim I** (Apr 39)
Apr 39 **Blenheim IV** (Jul 41)
9 May 39 to West Raynham dets Manston, Brize Norton
Apr 41 **Wellington IC** (Feb 42)
6 Jul 41 to Oakington
11 Feb 42 to Bourn
Feb 42 **Wellington III** (Oct 42)
11 Aug 42 to Stradishall
29 Sep 42 to Holme-on-Spalding Moor
Oct 42 **Lancaster I & III** (Aug 46)
15 Jun 43 to Ludford Magna
1 Oct 45 to Binbrook
Aug 46 **Lincoln B.2** (Jun 51)
Jun 51 **Canberra B.2** (Aug 54)
Jun 54 **Canberra B.6** (Jan 57)
1 Feb 57 DB
—
15 Oct 57 RF @ Finningley
Oct 57 **Vulcan B.1** (Dec 67)
26 Jun 61 to Waddington
Dec 67 **Vulcan B.2** (Aug 82)
4 Aug 82 DB
—
1 May 84 RF @ Brize Norton
May 84 **VC 10 K.2** ( )
Feb 85 **VC 10 K.3** ( )

102 Sqn

9 Aug 17 F @ Hingham
24 Sep 17 to St-André-aux Bois
Sep 17 **FE 2B** (Mar 19)
28 Sep 17 to Le Hameau
3 Oct 17 to Treizennes
5 Mar 18 to Le Hameau
10 Apr 18 to Surcamps
19 Sep 18 to Famechon
19 Oct 18 to Hurtebise Farm
23 Oct 18 to La Targette
27 Oct 18 to Bévillers
14 Dec 18 to Serny
26 Mar 19 to Lympne as a cadre
3 Jul 19 DB
—
1 Oct 35 RF @ Worthy Down — from 'B' Flt, No 7 Sqn
Oct 35 **Heyford II & III** (Nov 38)
3 Sep 36 to Finningley
7 Jul 37 to Honington
11 Jul 38 to Driffield
Oct 38 **Whitley III** (Jan 40) det Villeneuve
Nov 39 **Whitley V** (Feb 42) det Kinloss
25 Aug 40 to Leeming
1 Sep 40 to Prestwick det Aldergrove
10 Oct 40 to Linton-on-Ouse
15 Nov 40 to Topcliffe
15 Nov 41 to Dalton
Dec 41 **Halifax II** (May 44)
7 Jun 42 to Topcliffe
7 Aug 42 to Pocklington
May 44 **Halifax III** (Feb 45)
Feb 45 **Halifax VI** (Sep 45)
8 Sep 45 to Bassingbourn
Sep 45 **Liberator VI** (Feb 46)
Sep 45 **Liberator VIII** (Feb 46)
15 Feb 46 to Upwood
28 Feb 46 DB — renumbered as No 53 Sqn
—
20 Oct 54 RF @ Gütersloh
Oct 54 **Canberra B.2** (Aug 56)
20 Aug 56 DB
—
1 Aug 59 **Thor** at Full Sutton
27 Apr 63 DB

103 Sqn

1 Sep 17 F @ Beaulieu — nucleus from No 16 TS, used various aircraft
8 Sep 17 to Old Sarum
Mar 18 **DH 9** (Mar 19)
12 May 18 to Serny
3 Jun 18 to Fourneuil
21 Jun 18 to Serny
21 Oct 18 to Floringhem
26 Oct 18 to Ronchin
26 Jan 19 to Maisoncelle
28 Mar 19 to Shotwick as a cadre
1 Oct 19 DB
—
10 Aug 36 RF @ Andover
Aug 36 **Hind** (Aug 38)
26 Feb 37 to Usworth
Jul 38 **Battle** (Oct 40)
2 Sep 38 to Abingdon
1 Apr 39 to Benson
2 Sep 39 to Challerange
28 Nov 39 to Plivot
15 Feb 40 to Bétheniville
16 May 40 to St-Lucien Ferme
4 Jun 40 to Ozouer-le-Doyen dets Echemines, Faux-Villecerf
14 Jun 40 to Sougé
15 Jun 40 to Abingdon
18 Jun 40 to Honington
3 Jul 40 to Newton
Oct 40 **Wellington IC** (Jul 42)
11 Jul 41 to Elsham Wolds
Jul 42 **Halifax II** (Oct 42)
Oct 42 **Lancaster I & III** (Nov 45)
25 Nov 45 DB — renumbered as No 57 Sqn
—
30 Nov 54 RF @ Gütersloh
Nov 54 **Canberra B.2** (Jul 56)
1 Aug 56 DB
—
1 Aug 59 RF @ Nicosia — No 284 Sqn renumbered
Aug 59 **Sycamore HR 14** (Jul 63) det El Adem
31 Jul 63 DB — renumbered as No 1563 Flt (Nicosia) and No 1564 Flt (El Adem)
—
1 Aug 63 RF @ Seletar — from 'B' Flt, No 110 Sqn
Aug 63 **Whirlwind HC 10** (Dec 72) dets Kuching, Labuan, Kai Tak
28 Mar 69 to Changi
15 Sep 71 to Tengah
Nov 72 **Wessex HC 2** (Jul 75)
1 Aug 75 DB

104 Sqn

1 Sep 17 F @ Wyton — nucleus from No 20 TS, used various aircraft
16 Sep 17 to Andover
Apr 18 **DH 9** (Feb 19)
19 May 18 to St-Omer
20 May 18 to Azelot
20 Nov 18 to Maisoncelle
Nov 18 **DH 10** (Feb 19)
1 Feb 19 to Turnhouse
3 Mar 19 to Crail as a cadre
30 Jun 19 DB
—
7 Jan 36 RF @ Abingdon — from 'C' Flt, No 40 Sqn
Jul 36 **Hind** (May 38)
21 Aug 36 to Hucknall
2 May 38 to Bassingbourn
May 38 **Blenheim I** (Apr 40)
May 39 **Anson I** (Apr 40)
17 Sep 39 to Bicester
Nov 39 **Blenheim IV** (Apr 40)
6 Apr 40 DB — merged into No 13 OTU
—
7 Mar 41 RF @ Driffield
Apr 41 **Wellington II** (Aug 43)
14 Oct 41 15 aircraft det Luqa
14 Feb 42 UK echelon renumbered as No 158 Sqn
14 Jan 42 to Kabrit
13 May 42 to LG 106 det Luqa
26 Jun 42 to Kabrit
7 Nov 42 to LG 224 det Luqa
12 Nov 42 to LG 104 det Luqa
27 Nov 42 to LG 237 det Luqa
6 Feb 43 to Soluch
14 Feb 43 to Gardabia Main
26 May 43 to Cheria
24 Jun 43 to Hani West
Jul 43 **Wellington X** (Feb 45)
18 Nov 43 to Oudna
13 Dec 43 to Cerignola No 3
30 Dec 43 to Foggia Main
Feb 45 **Liberator VI** (Jan 46)
31 Oct 45 to Abu Sueir
Nov 45 **Lancaster B.7(FE)** (Mar 47)
1 Jul 46 to Shallufa
1 Apr 47 DB
—
15 Mar 55 RF @ Gütersloh
Mar 55 **Canberra B.2** (Aug 56)
1 Aug 56 DB
—
22 Jul 59 **Thor** at Ludford Magna
24 May 63 DB

105 Sqn

23 Sep 17 F @ Waddington — nucleus from No 51 TS, used various aircraft
3 Oct 17 to Andover
Apr 18 **RE 8** (Dec 18)
16 May 18 to Ayr
19 May 18 to Omagh dets Oranmore, Castlebar
Dec 18 **Bristol F2b Fighter** (Feb 20)
28 Jan 19 to Oranmore dets Castlebar, the Curragh, Tallaght, Fermoy
1 Feb 20 DB — renumbered as No 2 Sqn
—
12 Apr 37 RF @ Upper Heyford — from 'B' Flt, No 18 Sqn
26 Apr 37 to Harwell
Apr 37 **Audax** (Oct 37)
Aug 37 **Battle** (May 40)
2 Sep 39 to Reims
12 Sep 39 to Villeneuve (Vertus) dets Perpignan/La Salanque, Echemines
18 May 40 to Echemines det Villeneuve (Vertus)
22 May 40 to Nantes/Château Bougon
14 Jun 40 to Honington
Jun 40 **Blenheim IV** (Dec 41)
10 Jul 40 to Watton
31 Oct 40 to Swanton Morley dets Lossiemouth, Luqa
Nov 41 **Mosquito IV** (Mar 44)
9 Dec 41 to Horsham St Faith det Leuchars
22 Sep 42 to Marham
Jun 43 **Mosquito IX** (Aug 45)
23 Mar 44 to Bourn
Mar 44 **Mosquito XVI** (Feb 46)
29 Jun 45 to Upwood
1 Feb 46 DB
—
21 Feb 62 RF @ Benson
May 62 **Argosy C.1** (Jan 68)
15 Jun 62 to Khormaksar
6 Aug 67 to Muharraq
1 Feb 68 DB

106 Sqn

23 Sep 17 F @ Spittlegate — nucleus from No 49 TS used various aircraft
3 Oct 17 to Andover
May 18 **RE 8** (Jan 19)
21 May 18 to Ayr
30 May 18 to Fermoy

Jan 19 **Bristol F2b Fighter** (Oct 19)
dets Birr, Oranmore
Oct 19 DB
—
Jun 38 RF @ Abingdon — from 'A' Flt, No 15 Sqn
Jun 38 **Hind** (Jul 38)
Jul 38 **Battle** (May 39)
Sep 38 to Thornaby
Sep 38 to Grantham
Oct 38 to Thornaby
May 39 **Anson I** (Sep 39)
May 39 **Hampden** (Mar 42)
det Evanton
Sep 39 to Cottesmore
Oct 39 to Finningley
Feb 41 to Coningsby
Feb 42 **Manchester** (Jun 42)
May 42 **Lancaster I & III** (Feb 46)
Sep 42 to Syerston
Nov 43 to Metheringham
Feb 46 DB
—
Jul 59 **Thor** at Bardney
May 63 DB

7 Sqn

Oct 17 F @ Catterick — nucleus from No 46 TS, used various aircraft
Oct 17 to Stonehenge
Dec 17 to Lake Down
May 18 **DH 9** (Mar 19)
Jun 18 to Le Quesnoy
Jun 18 to Drionville
Jul 18 to Chailly
Aug 18 to Ecoivres
Oct 18 to Moislains
Nov 18 to Bavay
Dec 18 to Franc Waret
Dec 18 to Nivelles
Jan 19 to Maubeuge
Mar 19 to Hounslow as a cadre
Aug 19 DB
—
Aug 36 RF @ Andover
Sep 36 **Hind** (Sep 38)
Feb 37 to Old Sarum
Jun 37 to Harwell
Aug 38 **Blenheim I** (Jun 39)
May 39 to Wattisham
May 39 **Blenheim IV** (Feb 42)
dets Lossiemouth, Newmarket, Swanton Morley, Hunsdon, Horsham St Faith, Ipswich
Mar 41 to Leuchars
May 41 to Great Massingham
dets Luqa, Ford, Manston
Jan 42 **Boston III** (Mar 43)
Aug 42 to Annan
Aug 42 to Great Massingham
det Charmy Down
Feb 43 **Boston IIIA** (Mar 44)
Aug 43 to Hartford Bridge
Feb 44 to Lasham
Feb 44 **Mosquito VI** (Sep 48)
det Swanton Morley
Oct 44 to Hartford Bridge
Nov 44 to A 75/Cambrai/Epinoy
Jul 45 to Fersfield
Jul 45 to A 75/Cambrai/Epinoy
Jul 45 to B 58/Melsbroek
Nov 45 to Y 99/Gütersloh
Jan 46 to Sylt
Feb 46 to Gütersloh
Jun 46 to Handorf
Jul 46 to Sylt
Aug 46 to Gütersloh
Sep 46 to Wahn
Sep 46 to Manston
Sep 46 to Wahn
Sep 46 to Gütersloh
Feb 47 to Sylt
24 Feb 47 to Gütersloh
26 Feb 47 to Sylt
22 Mar 47 to Gütersloh
26 Sep 47 to Sylt
18 Oct 47 to Gütersloh
13 Nov 47 to Wahn
8 Mar 48 to Lübeck
30 Mar 48 to Wahn
5 Jun 48 to Gatow
5 Jul 48 to Wahn
31 Jul 48 to Lübeck
16 Aug 48 to Wahn
15 Sep 48 DB — renumbered as No 11 Sqn
—
22 Jul 59 **Thor** at Tuddenham
10 Jul 63 DB

108 Sqn

1 Nov 17 F @ Montrose — nucleus from No 52 TS, used various aircraft
12 Nov 17 to Stonehenge
2 Dec 17 to Lake Down
14 Jun 18 to Kenley
Jun 18 **DH 9** (Feb 19)
22 Jul 18 to Cappelle
27 Oct 18 to Bisseghem
16 Nov 18 to Gondecourt
16 Feb 19 to Lympne as a cadre
3 Jul 19 DB
—
4 Jan 37 RF @ Upper Heyford — from 'B' Flt, No 57 Sqn
Jan 37 **Hind** (Jun 38)
18 Feb 37 to Farnborough
7 Jul 37 to Cranfield
2 May 38 to Bassingbourn
Jun 38 **Blenheim I** (Apr 40)
May 39 **Anson I** (Apr 40)
18 Sep 39 to Bicester
Oct 39 **Blenheim IV** (Apr 40)
6 Apr 40 DB — merged into No 13 OTU
—
1 Aug 41 RF @ Kabrit
Aug 41 **Wellington IC** (Nov 42)
12 Sep 41 to Fayid
dets LG 09, LG 105
Nov 41 **Liberator II** (Jun 42) — to No 159 Sqn
20 May 42 to LG 105
det Fayid
26 Jun 42 to Kabrit
19 Aug 42 to LG 237
13 Nov 42 to LG 09
det LG 106
26 Nov 42 to LG 237
Nov 42 **Liberator II** (Dec 42) — Special Operations Flt
25 Dec 42 DB
—
10 Mar 43 RF @ Shandur
Mar 43 **Beaufighter VIF** (Mar 45)
dets Luqa, Bersis, Bu Amud
3 Jun 43 to Luqa
dets Bersis, Bu Amud, Castel Benito, Idku, Alghero, Catania
Feb 44 **Mosquito XII** (May 44)
Mar 44 **Mosquito XIII** (Jul 44)
1 Jul 44 to Hal Far
det Alghero
26 Jul 44 to Idku
det Gambut
18 Oct 44 to Araxos
25 Oct 44 to Kalamaki
2 Mar 45 to Lecce (No 54 PTC)
28 Mar 45 DB

109 Sqn

1 Nov 17 F @ South Carlton — nucleus from No 61 TS, used various aircraft
12 Nov 17 to Stonehenge
2 Dec 17 to Lake Down
Jul 18 **DH 9** (Aug 18)
19 Aug 18 DB
—
10 Dec 40 RF @ Boscombe Down — Wireless Intelligence Development Unit redesignated
Dec 40 **Whitley V** (Jan 41)
Dec 40 **Anson I** (Jun 42)
Dec 40 **Wellington IC** (Dec 42)
Jul 41 **Wellington I** (Sep 41)
19 Jan 42 to Tempsford
dets Wyton, Upper Heyford, Boscombe Down, Stradishall
Mar 42 **Wellington VI** (Jul 42)
6 Apr 42 to Stradishall
det Upper Heyford
Jul 42 **Lancaster I** (Oct 42)
7 Aug 42 to Wyton
Dec 42 **Mosquito IV** (May 44)
Jun 43 **Mosquito IX** (Sep 45)
5 Jul 43 to Marham
Mar 44 **Mosquito XVI** (Sep 45)
2 Apr 44 to Little Staughton
30 Apr 45 DB
—
1 Oct 45 RF @ Woodhall Spa — No 627 Sqn renumbered
Oct 45 **Mosquito XVI** (Dec 48)
19 Oct 45 to Wickenby
27 Nov 45 to Hemswell
4 Nov 46 to Coningsby
Apr 48 **Mosquito B.35** (Jul 52)
31 Mar 50 to Hemswell
Aug 52 **Canberra B.2** (Dec 54)
Dec 54 **Canberra B.6** (Jan 57)
1 Jan 56 to Binbrook
1 Feb 57 DB

110 Sqn

1 Nov 17 F @ Rendcomb — nucleus from No 38 TS, used various aircraft
12 Nov 17 to Dover (Swingate Down)
26 Nov 17 to Sedgeford
15 Jun 18 to Kenley
Aug 18 **DH 9A** (Aug 19)
1 Sep 18 to Bettoncourt
20 Nov 18 to Auxi-le-Chateau
30 Nov 18 to Maisoncelle
3 Jul 19 to Marquise
27 Aug 19 DB
—
18 May 37 RF @ Waddington
May 37 **Hind** (Jan 38)
Jan 38 **Blenheim I** (Sep 39)
11 May 39 to Wattisham
Jun 39 **Blenheim IV** (Jun 42)
dets Lossiemouth, Horsham St Faith, Manston, Lindholme, Ipswich, Martlesham Heath, Brize Norton, Luqa, Swanton Morley
17 Mar 42 en route FE
19 May 42 to Karachi
10 Jun 42 to Quetta
det Karachi
11 Oct 42 to Ondal
Oct 42 **Vengeance I, IA, II** (Dec 44)
1 Nov 42 to Pandeveswar
6 Dec 42 to Madhaiganj
dets Dohazari, Chittagong
13 Jun 43 to Digri
dets Ranchi, Amarda Road
15 Oct 43 to Kumbhirgram
det Allahabad
Jun 44 **Vengeance III** (Jan 45)
5 Jun 44 to Kalyan
Jun 44 **Vengeance IV** (Dec 44)
det Takoradi
6 Oct 44 to Kolar
26 Oct 44 to Yelahanka
Nov 44 **Mosquito VI** (Apr 46)
11 Mar 45 to Joari
22 May 45 to Kinmagon
16 Aug 45 to Hmawbi
11 Sep 45 to Bayan Lepas
11 Sep 45 to Kallang
22 Sep 45 to Seletar
dets Kemajoran, Labuan
27 Feb 46 to Labuan
det Seletar
7 Apr 46 DB
—
1 Jun 46 RF @ Kai Tak — No 96 Sqn renumbered
Jun 46 **Dakota** (Jul 47)
21 Jul 47 reduced to a cadre
15 Sep 47 re-established at Changi
Sep 47 **Dakota** (May 52)
2 Jul 48 to Kuala Lumpur
20 Nov 48 to Changi
27 May 49 to Seletar
27 Aug 49 to Changi
11 Dec 49 to Kuala Lumpur
det Changi
12 Jul 50 to Changi
19 Jul 51 to Kuala Lumpur
26 Oct 51 to Changi
det Kuala Lumpur
Oct 51 **Valetta C.1** (Dec 57)
31 Dec 57 DB
—
3 Jun 59 RF @ Kuala Lumpur — from Nos 155 & 194 Sqns
Jun 59 **Whirlwind HAR 4** (Jul 60)
1 Sep 59 to Butterworth
Apr 60 **Sycamore HR 14** (Oct 64)
dets Brunei, Labuan, Sibu
Jul 63 **Whirlwind HAR 10** (Feb 71)
17 Jan 64 to Seletar
dets Butterworth, Labuan, Kuching
6 Mar 69 to Changi
15 Feb 71 DB

111 Sqn

1 Aug 17 F @ Deir-el-Ballah — nucleus from No 14 Sqn
Aug 17 **Bristol Scout** (Oct 17)
Aug 17 **Bristol M.1B** (Jan 18)
Aug 17 **DH 2** (Dec 17)
Aug 17 **Vickers FB 19 Mk II** (Jan 18)
Sep 17 **Bristol F2b Fighter** (Feb 18)
Oct 17 **SE 5A** (Jan 19)
det Julis
1 Dec 17 to Julis
Jan 18 **Nieuport 17, 23 & 24** (Jul 18)
det Sarona
30 Mar 18 to Ramleh
det Sarona
18 Oct 18 to Qantara
Jan 19 **Bristol F2b Fighter** (Feb 20)
6 Feb 19 to Ramleh
dets Damascus, Aleppo
1 Feb 20 DB — renumbered as No 14 Sqn
—
1 Oct 23 RF @ Duxford
Oct 23 **Grebe II** (Jan 25)
Apr 24 **Snipe** (Jan 25)
Jun 24 **Siskin II** (Nov 26)
Sep 26 **Siskin IIIA** (Feb 31)
1 Apr 28 to Hornchurch

Jan 31 **Bulldog IIA** (Jun 36)
12 Jul 34 to Northolt
Jun 36 **Gauntlet I & II** (Jan 38)
Dec 37 **Hurricane I** (Apr 41)
27 Oct 39 to Acklington
7 Dec 39 to Drem
27 Feb 40 to Wick
13 May 40 to Northolt
21 May 40 to Digby
30 May 40 to North Weald
4 Jun 40 to Croydon
19 Aug 40 to Debden
3 Sep 40 to Croydon
8 Sep 40 to Drem
12 Oct 40 to Dyce det Montrose
Apr 41 **Spitfire I** (May 41)
May 41 **Spitfire IIA** (Aug 41)
20 Jul 41 to North Weald
Aug 41 **Spitfire VB** (Oct 42)
1 Nov 41 to Debden
15 Dec 41 to North Weald
22 Dec 41 to Debden
30 Jun 42 to Gravesend
7 Jul 42 to Debden
28 Jul 42 to Kenley
21 Sep 42 to Martlesham Heath
27 Sep 42 to Fowlmere
20 Oct 42 en route N Africa via Gibraltar
Oct 42 **Spitfire VC** (Jan 44)
11 Nov 42 to Maison Blanche
14 Nov 42 to Bone
3 Dec 42 to Souk el Arba
22 Dec 42 to Souk el Khemis ('Waterloo')
13 May 43 to Protville I
25 May 43 to Mateur
10 Jun 43 to Safi
Jun 43 **Spitfire IXE** (May 47)
15 Jul 43 to Comiso
30 Jul 43 to Pachino
29 Aug 43 to Panebianco
2 Sep 43 to Cassala
6 Sep 43 to Falcone
23 Sep 43 to Montecorvino
28 Sep 43 to Battipaglia
11 Oct 43 to Capodichino
15 Jan 44 to Lago
5 Jun 44 to Tre Cancelli
14 Jun 44 to Tarquinia
25 Jun 44 to Grosseto
5 Jul 44 to Piombino
20 Jul 44 to Calvi
20 Aug 44 to Ramatuelle
25 Aug 44 to Sisteron
7 Sep 44 to Lyons/Bron
26 Sep 44 to La Jasse
2 Oct 44 to Peretola
13 Nov 44 to Rimini
17 Feb 45 to Ravenna
4 May 45 to Rivolto
16 May 45 to Klagenfurt
12 Sep 45 to Zeltweg
23 Sep 46 to Tissano
16 Jan 47 to Treviso
16 May 47 DB

—

2 Dec 53 RF @ North Weald
Dec 53 **Meteor F.8** (Jun 55)
Jun 55 **Hunter F.4** (Nov 56)
Nov 56 **Hunter F.6** (Aug 61)
19 Feb 58 to North Luffenham
18 Jun 58 to Wattisham
Apr 61 **Lightning F.1A** (Feb 65)
Dec 64 **Lightning F.3** (Sep 74)
May 74 **Lightning F.6** (Sep 74)
30 Sep 74 DB

—

1 Jul 74 training at Coningsby as No 111 Sqn (Designate)

—

1 Oct 74 RF @ Coningsby
Oct 74 **Phantom FGR 2** (Jul 79)
3 Nov 75 to Leuchars
Jan 78 **Phantom FG 1** ( )

112 Sqn

25 Jul 17 F @ Detling — from 'B' Flt, No 50 Sqn
30 Jul 17 to Throwley
Jul 17 **Pup** (Mar 18)
Mar 18 **Camel** (Jun 19)
19 **Snipe** (Jun 19)
13 Jun 19 DB

—

16 May 39 RF on board HMS *Argus*
26 May 39 to Helwan
Jun 39 **Gladiator I & II** (Jun 41) dets Port Sudan, Summit, Erkowit
Mar 40 **Gauntlet II** (Jul 40)
19 Jul 40 to Gerawala det Summit, Sidi Barrani, 'Y' LG, 'Z' LG
7 Sep 40 to Sidi Haneish dets LG 79, 'Z' LG
1 Jan 41 to Amiriya
23 Jan 41 to Elevsis
18 Feb 41 to Yanina det Paramythia
Feb 41 **Hurricane I** (Mar 41)
15 Apr 41 to Agrinion
16 Apr 41 to Kalamaki
22 Apr 41 to Heraklion det Aboukir
31 May 41 to Fayid
Jun 41 **Tomahawk I** (Sep 41) dets Haifa, Maryut
12 Sep 41 to LG 102
Sep 41 **Tomahawk IIA & IIB** (Dec 41)
14 Nov 41 to LG 110
19 Nov 41 to LG 122
19 Dec 41 to El Adem
21 Dec 41 to Msus
Dec 41 **Kittyhawk IA** (Oct 42)
13 Jan 42 to Antelat
21 Jan 42 to Msus
24 Jan 42 to Mechili
28 Jan 42 to Gazala
2 Feb 42 to El Adem
3 Feb 42 to Gambut
15 Feb 42 to El Adem
17 Feb 42 to Gambut
16 Mar 42 to Sidi Haneish
15 Apr 42 to Gambut No 1
17 Jun 42 to Sidi Azeiz
18 Jun 42 to LG 75
24 Jun 42 to LG 102
26 Jun 42 to LG 106
28 Jun 42 to LG 91 det LG 175
Oct 42 **Kittyhawk III** (Apr 44)
6 Nov 42 to LG 106
8 Nov 42 to LG 115
9 Nov 42 to LG 76
15 Nov 42 to Gazala No 2
19 Nov 42 to Martuba
29 Nov 42 to Antelat
6 Dec 42 to Belandah
9 Jan 43 to Hamraiet
19 Jan 43 to Bir Dufan
25 Jan 43 to Castel Benito
15 Feb 43 to El Assa
8 Mar 43 to Nefatia
21 Mar 43 to Medanine
3 Apr 43 to El Hamma
14 Apr 43 to El Djem
18 Apr 43 to Kairouan
21 May 43 to Zuara
9 Jul 43 to Safi
18 Jul 43 to Pachino
2 Aug 43 to Agnone
15 Sep 43 to Grottaglie
20 Sep 43 to Brindisi
23 Sep 43 to Bari
3 Oct 43 to Foggia
26 Oct 43 to Mileni
30 Jan 44 to Cutella
Apr 44 **Kittyhawk IV** (Jun 44)
23 May 44 to San Angelo
13 Jun 44 to Guidonia
24 Jun 44 to Falerium
Jun 44 **Mustang III** (Jun 45)
10 Jul 44 to Creti det Rosignano
25 Aug 44 to Iesi
18 Nov 44 to Fano
25 Feb 45 to Cervia
Feb 45 **Mustang IV** (Dec 46)
19 May 45 to Lavariano
1 Mar 46 to Tissano
23 Sep 46 to Treviso det Lavariano
30 Dec 46 DB

—

12 May 51 RF @ Fassberg
May 51 **Vampire FB 5** (Feb 54)
7 Mar 52 to Jever
6 Jul 53 to Brüggen
Jan 54 **Sabre F.4** (Apr 56)
Apr 56 **Hunter F.4** (May 57)
31 May 57 DB

—

1 Aug 60 **Bloodhound I** at Church Fenton
7 Nov 60 to Breighton
31 Mar 64 DB

—

2 Nov 64 **Bloodhound II** at Woodhall Spa
1 Oct 67 to Episkopi
20 Jun 69 to Paramali
1 Jul 75 DB

113 Sqn

1 Aug 17 F @ Ismailia
Aug 17 **BE 2E** (Apr 18)
Sep 17 **RE 8** (Feb 20) det Sheikh Nuran
10 Oct 17 to Sheikh Nuran
23 Nov 17 to Julis det Khirbet Deiran
5 Dec 17 to Khirbet Deiran
17 Jan 18 to Sarona
Feb 18 **Nieuport 17, 23 & 24** (Oct 18) dets El Affule, Haifa
18 Nov 18 to Qantara
16 Feb 19 to Ismailia
Feb 19 **BE 2E** (Dec 19)
1 Feb 20 DB — renumbered as No 208 Sqn

—

18 May 37 RF @ Upper Heyford
May 37 **Hind** (Jun 39)
31 Aug 37 to Grantham
30 Apr 38 en route Egypt
11 May 38 to Heliopolis
29 Sep 38 to Mersah Matruh
11 Oct 38 to Heliopolis
21 Apr 39 to El Daba
21 May 39 to Heliopolis
Jun 39 **Blenheim I** (Apr 40)
Mar 40 **Blenheim IV** (Apr 41)
10 Jun 40 to Maaten Bagush
28 Sep 40 to 'Waterloo'
15 Jan 41 to Sidi Barrani
4 Feb 41 to Gambut det Barce
22 Feb 41 to Kabrit
14 Mar 41 to Alexandria
23 Mar 41 to Menidi
29 Mar 41 to Larissa
4 Apr 41 to Niamata
16 Apr 41 to Menidi
22 Apr 41 to Maleme
24 Apr 41 to Suda Bay
15 May 41 to Ramleh
May 41 **Blenheim IV** (Dec 42)
31 May 41 to Maaten Bagush det Luqa
14 Nov 41 to Giarabub dets LG 75, LG 125
30 Nov 41 to LG 116
23 Dec 41 to Helwan
30 Dec 41 en route India
6 Jan 42 to Toungoo
7 Jan 42 to Mingaladon
8 Jan 42 to Lashio
19 Jan 42 to Mingaladon dets Zayatkwin, 'Johnny Walker', Toungoo
21 Feb 42 to Magwe dets Zayatkwin, Mingaladon, 'Highland Queen', 'John Haig'
12 Mar 42 sqn dispersed — absorbed by No 45 Sq
6 Apr 42 reassembled at Fyzabad
8 Apr 42 to Asansol dets Loiwing, Tezpur, Dum Dum
Oct 42 **Blenheim V** (Aug 43)
19 Dec 42 to Jessore
21 Jan 43 to Feni
28 Feb 43 to Chandina det Agartala
4 May 43 to Comilla
27 Jun 43 to Feni det Dudhkundi
31 Aug 43 to Yelahanka det Dudhkundi
Sep 43 **Hurricane IIC** (Apr 4
2 Oct 43 to St Thomas Mount det Dudhkundi
9 Nov 43 to Cholavaram
22 Dec 43 to Manipur Road/ Dimapur
15 Mar 44 to Tulihal dets Silchar, Palel, Jorhat, Patharkandi, Kangla
25 May 44 to Palel
19 Dec 44 to Yazagyo
22 Jan 45 to Onbauk
14 Mar 45 to Ondaw det Wangjing
Apr 45 **Thunderbolt I** (May 4
20 Apr 45 to Kwetnge
7 May 45 to Myingyan det Kinmagon
5 Jun 45 to Kinmagon
Jun 45 **Thunderbolt II** (Oct 4
30 Jun 45 to Meiktila
17 Aug 45 to Zayatkwin
15 Oct 45 DB

—

1 Sep 46 RF @ Aqir — No 62 Sqn renumbered
Sep 46 **Halifax A.7** (Apr 47)
Sep 46 **Halifax A.9** (Apr 47)
Sep 46 **Dakota** (Apr 47)
1 Apr 47 DB

—

1 May 47 RF @ Fairford
May 47 **Dakota** (Sep 48)
1 Sep 48 DB

—

22 Jul 59 **Thor** at Mepal
10 Jul 63 DB

114 Sqn

22 Sep 17 F @ Lahore — from two Flts of No 31 Sc
Sep 17 **BE 2C** (Oct 19)
Sep 17 **Henry Farman F.27** (18)
Sep 17 **BE 2E** (Apr 20) dets Quetta, Aden
22 Jul 18 to Quetta
5 Nov 18 to Lahore det Jubbulpore
26 Mar 19 to Quetta dets Lahore, Cawnp
20 May 19 to Lahore dets Quetta, Cawnp Kohat
16 Jun 19 to Quetta dets Bannu, Loralai
2 Oct 19 to Ambala
Oct 19 **Bristol F2b Fighter** (Apr 20) det Agra
1 Apr 20 DB — renumbered

No 28 Sqn
—
1 Dec 36 RF @ Wyton
Dec 36 **Hind** (Mar 37)
Mar 37 **Audax** (Apr 37)
Mar 37 **Blenheim I** (May 39)
May 39 **Blenheim IV** (Sep 42)
9 Dec 39 to Condé/Vraux dets Perpignan/La Salanque, Crécy
1 May 40 to Nantes
1 May 40 to Wattisham
0 Jun 40 to Horsham St Faith
0 Aug 40 to Oulton det Hornchurch
2 Mar 41 to Thornaby
3 May 41 to Leuchars
9 Jul 19 to West Raynham dets Lossiemouth, Prestwick, Odiham, Wigtown
Sep 42 **Blenheim V** (Apr 43)
3 Nov 42 en route N Africa
5 Nov 42 to Blida
5 Dec 42 to Setif det Canrobert
7 Dec 42 to Canrobert
Mar 43 **Boston III** (Jul 44)
4 Apr 43 to Souk-el-Khemis ('Kings Cross')
May 43 to Grombalia
Aug 43 to Monte Lungo det Ponte Olivo
Aug 43 to Comiso
Aug 43 to Sigonella
Oct 43 to Brindisi
Oct 43 to Celone det Pomigliano
Apr 44 to Marcianese det Regina
Jun 44 to La Banca
Jun 44 to Tarquinia
Jun 44 **Boston IV** (May 46)
Jul 44 to Cecina det Perugia
Oct 44 to Falconara det Perugia
Jan 45 **Boston V** (May 46)
Mar 45 to Forli
May 45 to Aviano
Sep 45 to Khormaksar
Nov 45 **Mosquito VI** (May 46)
May 46 reduced to a cadre
Sep 46 DB — renumbered as No 8 Sqn
—
Aug 47 RF @ Kabrit
Aug 47 **Dakota** (Nov 49)
Sep 49 **Valetta C.1** (Dec 57)
Feb 51 to Fayid
Dec 55 to Abu Sueir
Mar 56 to Nicosia
Dec 57 DB
—
Nov 58 RF @ Hullavington
Nov 58 **Chipmunk T.10** (Mar 59)
Dec 58 to Nicosia
Mar 59 DB
—
Apr 59 RF @ Colerne
Apr 59 **Hastings C.1 & C.2** (Sep 61)
Sep 61 DB
—
Oct 61 RF @ Benson
Feb 62 **Argosy C.1** (Oct 71)
Oct 71 DB

15 Sqn

Dec 17 F @ Catterick — used various aircraft
Apr 18 to Netheravon
Jul 18 **HP 0/400** (Mar 19)
Jul 18 to Castle Bromwich
Aug 18 to Roville-aux-Chênes
Nov 18 to St-Inglevert
Mar 19 to Ford Junction as a cadre
18 Oct 19 DB
—
15 Jun 37 RF @ Marham — from 'B' Flt, No 38 Sqn
Jun 37 **Hendon II** (Aug 37)
Jun 37 **Harrow** (Jun 39)
Mar 39 **Wellington I** (Oct 39)
Sep 39 **Wellington IA** (Aug 40) det Kinloss
Jun 40 **Wellington IC** (Feb 42)
Feb 42 **Wellington III** (Mar 43)
24 Sep 42 to Mildenhall
8 Nov 42 to East Wretham
Mar 43 **Lancaster II** (May 44)
6 Aug 43 to Little Snoring
26 Nov 43 to Witchford
Mar 44 **Lancaster I & III** (46)
10 Sep 45 to Graveley
46 **Lancaster B.1 (FE)** (49)
9 Sep 46 to Stradishall
15 Feb 49 to Mildenhall
Sep 49 **Lincoln B.2** (Feb 50)
1 Mar 50 DB
—
13 Jun 50 RF @ Marham
Jun 50 **Washington B.1** (Mar 54)
Feb 54 **Canberra B.2** (May 57)
1 Jun 57 DB
—
21 Aug 58 RF @ Watton — No 116 Sqn renumbered
Aug 58 **Varsity T.1** (Aug 70)
25 Aug 58 to Tangmere
Aug 63 **Valetta C.1** (May 64)
1 Oct 63 to Watton
Jan 67 **Hastings C.2** (Jan 69)
Feb 68 **Argosy E.1** (Jan 78)
9 Apr 69 to Cottesmore
23 Feb 76 to Brize Norton
Nov 76 **Andover E.3** ( )
4 Jan 83 to Benson

116 Sqn

1 Dec 17 F @ Andover — used various aircraft
31 Mar 18 to Netheravon
27 Jul 18 to Kenley
Aug 18 **HP 0/400** (Nov 18)
28 Sep 18 to Feltham
20 Nov 18 DB
—
17 Feb 41 RF @ Hatfield — from No 1 AACU
Feb 41 **Lysander III** (Mar 43)
24 Apr 41 to Hendon
Nov 41 **Hurricane I** (Aug 42)
20 Apr 42 to Heston
Jun 42 **Hornet Moth** (Jan 43)
Jul 42 **Tiger Moth** (Apr 43)
Nov 42 **Oxford II** (May 45)
Nov 42 **Anson I** (May 45)
12 Dec 42 to Croydon
2 Jul 44 to North Weald
27 Aug 44 to Gatwick
7 Sep 44 to Redhill
Mar 45 **Anson XII** (May 45)
2 May 45 to Hornchurch
26 May 45 DB
—
1 Aug 52 RF @ Watton — 'N' Calibration Sqn redesignated
Aug 52 **Anson C.19** (Aug 54)
Aug 52 **Lincoln B.2** (Apr 54)
Sep 53 **Hastings C.1** (Apr 56)
Dec 53 **Varsity T.1** (Aug 58)
21 Aug 58 DB — renumbered as No 115 Sqn

117 Sqn

1 Jan 18 F @ Waddington, used various aircraft
3 Apr 18 to Hucknall
15 Jul 18 to Norwich
Oct 18 **DH 9** (Oct 19)
30 Nov 18 to Wyton
23 Mar 19 to Tallaght
24 Apr 19 to Gormanston
6 Oct 19 DB — absorbed by No 141 Sqn
—
30 Apr 41 RF @ Khartoum — from 'C' Flt, No 216 Sqn
Apr 41 **Bombay** (Nov 41)
Apr 41 **Wellesley** (Nov 41)
Apr 41 **Proctor** (Nov 41)
Apr 41 **Gladiator I** (Nov 41)
May 41 **SM 79K** (Nov 41)
Oct 41 **DC 2** (Jul 42)
3 Nov 41 to Bilbeis
Mar 42 **DH 86 Express** (May 42)
May 42 **Hudson VI** (Sep 43)
May 42 **Lodestar** (Sep 42)
May 42 **DC 3** (Aug 42)
Jul 42 **Hudson IV** (Sep 43)
3 Nov 42 operational element to Amiriya
19 Nov 42 operational element to El Adem
9 Jan 43 operational element to Marble Arch
Feb 43 **DC 2** (Jul 43)
6 Mar 43 operational element to Castel Benito
13 Apr 43 operational element to Gabes
23 Apr 43 operational element to El Djem
23 May 43 operational element to Castel Benito
Jun 43 **Dakota** (Dec 45)
5 Jul 43 to Castel Benito
3 Sep 43 to Catania
2 Oct 43 to Bari
1 Nov 43 to Mauripur
6 Nov 43 to Dhamial
19 Jan 44 to Lalmai det Tulihal
14 Mar 44 to Sylhet
25 Jun 44 to Agartala det Sylhet
1 Nov 44 to Risalpur
26 Nov 44 to Bikram
10 Dec 44 to Hathazari
Jan 45 **Sentinel** (Jun 45)
15 Apr 45 to Kyaukpyu det Hathazari
16 Jun 45 to Patenga
19 Aug 45 to Hmawbi
17 Dec 45 DB

118 Sqn

1 Jan 18 F @ Catterick (for HP 0/400), used various aircraft
15 Apr 18 to Netheravon
7 Aug 18 to Bicester
7 Sep 18 DB
—
20 Feb 41 RF @ Filton
Feb 41 **Spitfire I** (Apr 41) det Pembrey
7 Apr 41 to Colerne
Apr 41 **Spitfire IIA** (Jul 41)
9 Apr 41 to Warmwell
18 Apr 41 to Ibsley
Jul 41 **Spitfire IIB** (Sep 41)
Sep 41 **Spitfire VB** (Jan 44) dets Perranporth, Predannack
23 Feb 42 to Warmwell
7 Mar 42 to Ibsley
3 Jul 42 to Tangmere
7 Jul 42 to Ibsley
16 Aug 42 to Tangmere
24 Aug 42 to Zeals
23 Dec 42 to Ibsley
3 Jan 43 to Wittering
17 Jan 43 to Coltishall
15 Aug 43 to Westhampnett
24 Aug 43 to Merston
20 Sep 43 to Peterhead
Sep 43 **Spitfire VI** (Oct 43) det Skaebrae
19 Oct 43 to Castletown det Peterhead
20 Jan 44 to Detling
23 Jan 44 to Peterhead
Jan 44 **Spitfire IXC** (Mar 44)
5 Feb 44 to Detling
10 Mar 44 to Skaebrae
Mar 44 **Spitfire VB** (Jul 44)
Mar 44 **Spitfire VII** (Jul 44) det Sumburgh
12 Jul 44 to Detling
Jul 44 **Spitfire IXC** (Jan 45)
9 Aug 44 to Peterhead
29 Aug 44 to Westhampnett
25 Sep 44 to Manston
15 Dec 44 to Bentwaters
Jan 45 **Mustang III** (Mar 46)
11 Aug 45 to Fairwood Common
8 Sep 45 to Horsham St Faith
10 Mar 46 DB
—
10 May 51 RF @ Fassberg
May 51 **Vampire FB 5** (Jun 54)
Sep 53 **Venom FB 1** (May 55)
6 May 55 to Jever
May 55 **Hunter F.4** (Aug 57)
22 Aug 57 DB
—
1 Sep 59 RF @ Aldergrove — from Flt of No 228 Sqn
Sep 59 **Sycamore HR 14** (Apr 61)
14 Apr 61 DB
—
15 Apr 61 RF @ Aldergrove
Apr 61 **Sycamore HR 14** (Aug 62)
31 Aug 62 DB

119 Sqn

1 Jan 18 F @ Andover, used various aircraft
1 Mar 18 to Duxford
19 Aug 18 to Thetford
26 Sep 18 to Wyton
Sep 18 **DH 9** (Dec 18)
6 Dec 18 DB
—
13 Mar 41 RF @ Bowmore — 'G' Flt redesignated
Mar 41 **Short S.26M** (Oct 41)
Apr 41 **Short S.23M** (Aug 41)
Jun 41 **Catalina IB** (Jul 41)
4 Aug 41 to Pembroke Dock
Oct 41 reduced to a cadre
16 Apr 42 re-established at Lough Erne
May 42 **Catalina IIIA** (Oct 42)
6 Sep 42 to Pembroke Dock
Sep 42 **Sunderland III** (Apr 43)
17 Apr 43 DB
—
19 Jul 44 RF @ Manston — from Albacore Flt of No 415 Sqn
Jul 44 **Albacore** (Feb 45)
9 Aug 44 to Swingfield
2 Oct 44 to Bircham Newton dets B 63/St Croix, B 65/Maldeghem, B 83/Knocke le Zout
Jan 45 **Swordfish III** (May 45)
21 Feb 45 to B 83/Knocke le Zout
22 May 45 to Bircham Newton
22 May 45 DB

120 Sqn

1 Jan 18 F @ Cramlington, used various aircraft
3 Aug 18 to Bracebridge Heath
23 Nov 18 to Wyton
Nov 18 **DH 9** (Oct 19)
20 Feb 19 to Hawkinge

17 Jul 19 to Lympne
21 Oct 19 DB
—
2 Jun 41 RF @ Nutts Corner
Jun 41 **Liberator I** (Oct 43)
Nov 41 **Liberator II** (Oct 42)
21 Jul 42 to Ballykelly
Jul 42 **Liberator III** (Jan 44) dets Reykjavik, Aldergrove, Predannack
14 Feb 43 to Aldergrove det Reykjavik
15 Apr 43 to Reykjavik det Aldergrove
Dec 43 **Liberator V** (Jan 45)
24 Mar 44 to Ballykelly
Dec 44 **Liberator III** (Jun 45)
4 Jun 45 DB
—
1 Oct 46 RF @ Leuchars — No 160 Sqn renumbered
Oct 46 **Liberator VIII** (Jun 47)
Nov 46 **Lancaster GR 3** (Apr 51)
14 Dec 50 to Kinloss
Mar 51 **Shackleton MR 1** (Oct 56)
1 Apr 52 to Aldergrove
Apr 53 **Shackleton MR 2** (Aug 54)
Oct 56 **Shackleton MR 2** (Nov 58)
Sep 58 **Shackleton MR 3** (Feb 71)
1 Apr 59 to Kinloss
Oct 70 **Nimrod MR 1** (Feb 82)
Apr 81 **Nimrod MR 2** ( )

121 Sqn

1 Jan 18 F @ Narborough (for DH 9), used various aircraft
10 Aug 18 to Filton
17 Aug 18 DB
—
5 May 41 RF @ Kirton-in-Lindsey
May 41 **Hurricane I** (Jul 41)
Jul 41 **Hurricane IIB** (Nov 41)
28 Sep 41 to Digby
3 Oct 41 to Kirton-in-Lindsey
Oct 41 **Spitfire IIA** (Nov 41)
Nov 41 **Spitfire VB** (Sep 42)
16 Dec 41 to North Weald
3 Jun 42 to Southend
23 Sep 42 to Debden
29 Sep 42 DB — redesignated as 335th Sqn, 4th Fighter Group, USAAF

122 Sqn

1 Jan 18 F @ Sedgeford (for DH 9), used various aircraft
17 Aug 18 DB
—
29 Oct 18 RF @ Upper Heyford (for DH 10) — nucleus from Nos 9, 10, 11 and 15 TDSs.
20 Nov 18 DB
—
5 May 41 RF @ Turnhouse
May 41 **Spitfire I** (Oct 41)
26 Jun 41 to Ouston
31 Aug 41 to Catterick
Sep 41 **Spitfire IIA** (Oct 41)
6 Oct 41 to Scorton
Oct 41 **Spitfire IIB** (Jan 42)
Nov 41 **Spitfire VB** (Oct 42)
1 Apr 42 to Hornchurch
8 Jun 42 to Fairlop
29 Jun 42 to Martlesham Heath
6 Jul 42 to Fairlop
17 Jul 42 to Hornchurch
Sep 42 **Spitfire IX** (May 43)
29 Sep 42 to Martlesham Heath
3 Oct 42 to Hornchurch
16 Nov 42 to Fairlop
9 Dec 42 to Hornchurch
Apr 43 **Spitfire VB** (Aug 43)
18 May 43 to Eastchurch
1 Jun 43 to Bognor
1 Jul 43 to Kingsnorth
Aug 43 **Spitfire IX** (Feb 44) det Brenzett
5 Oct 43 to Ashford
15 Oct 43 to Weston Zoyland
3 Nov 43 to Gravesend
Jan 44 **Mustang III** (May 45)
15 Apr 44 to Ford
14 May 44 to Funtington
21 May 44 to Southend
28 May 44 to Funtington
15 Jun 44 to Ford
26 Jun 44 to B 7/Martragny
16 Jul 44 to B 12/Ellon
2 Sep 44 to B 24/St-André-de-l'Eure
3 Sep 44 to B 40/Beauvais/Nivilllers
9 Sep 44 to B 60/Grimbergen
28 Sep 44 to Matlask
14 Oct 44 to Andrews Field
1 May 45 to Peterhead
May 45 **Mustang IV** (Aug 45)
3 Jul 45 to Dyce
Aug 45 **Spitfire IX** (Feb 46)
29 Aug 45 to Wick
24 Sep 45 to Hawkinge
19 Oct 45 to Wick
3 Jan 46 to Dalcross
Feb 46 **Spitfire F.21** (Apr 46)
1 Apr 46 DB — renumbered as No 41 Sqn

123 Sqn

1 Feb 18 F @ Waddington (for DH 9), used various aircraft
1 Mar 18 to Duxford
17 Aug 18 DB
—
20 Nov 18 RF @ Upper Heyford — also designated No 2 Sqn, CAF
Nov 18 **DH 9A** (Feb 20)
31 Mar 19 to Shoreham
5 Feb 20 DB
—
10 May 41 RF @ Turnhouse
May 41 **Spitfire I** (Sep 41)
6 Aug 41 to Drem
Sep 41 **Spitfire IIA** (Apr 42)
22 Sep 41 to Castletown det Tain
Jan 42 **Spitfire VB** (Apr 42)
11 Apr 42 en route Egypt
19 Jun 42 to Aboukir
19 Jul 42 to Muqueibila
5 Sep 42 to Hadera
9 Oct 42 to Habbaniyah
Oct 42 **Gladiator II** (Nov 42) det Abadan
22 Oct 42 to Doshen Tapeh
24 Nov 42 to Meherabad
Nov 42 **Hurricane IIC** (Sep 44)
12 Jan 43 to Abadan
3 May 43 to Bu Amud
May 43 **Spitfire VC** (Sep 43)
Jul 43 **Spitfire IX** (Aug 43)
1 Nov 43 to Qassassin
16 Nov 43 en route India
11 Dec 43 to Feni
7 Jan 44 to Patharkandi
1 Jun 44 to St Thomas Mount
20 Sep 44 to Yelahanka
Sep 44 **Thunderbolt I** (Dec 44)
24 Oct 44 to Cholavaram
29 Oct 44 to Kajamalai
3 Dec 44 to Baigachi
Dec 44 **Thunderbolt II** (Jun 45)
18 Dec 44 to Nazir det Cox's Bazaar
28 Apr 45 to Kyaukpyu
6 Jun 45 to Cox's Bazaar
10 Jun 45 to Baigachi
10 Jun 45 DB — renumbered as No 81 Sqn, aircraft ferried to Bobbili

124 Sqn

1 Feb 18 F @ Old Sarum (for DH 9), used various aircraft
1 Mar 18 to Fowlmere
17 Aug 18 DB
—
10 May 41 RF @ Castletown
May 41 **Spitfire I** (Nov 41)
Oct 41 **Spitfire IIB** (Nov 41)
Nov 41 **Spitfire VA** (Feb 42)
Nov 41 **Spitfire VB** (Jul 42)
17 Nov 41 to Biggin Hill
3 May 42 to Gravesend
30 Jun 42 to Eastchurch
5 Jul 42 to Martlesham Heath
13 Jul 42 to Gravesend
Jul 42 **Spitfire VI** (Jul 43)
29 Jul 42 to Debden
25 Sep 42 to Tangmere
29 Oct 42 to Westhampnett
7 Nov 42 to North Weald
7 Dec 42 to Martlesham Heath
21 Dec 42 to North Weald
29 Dec 42 to Drem
21 Jan 43 to North Weald
Jan 43 **Spitfire IX** (May 43)
1 Mar 43 to Croughton
5 Mar 43 to Duxford
12 Mar 43 to North Weald
Mar 43 **Spitfire VB** (Jun 43)
Mar 43 **Spitfire VII** (Jul 44) dets Colerne, Exeter, Ibsley, Fairwood Common
26 Jul 43 to Northolt
20 Sep 43 to West Malling
5 Jan 44 to Southend
18 Jan 44 to West Malling
18 Mar 44 to Church Fenton
23 Apr 44 to Bradwell Bay
26 Jul 44 to Detling
Jul 44 **Spitfire HF IXE** (Aug 45)
9 Aug 44 to Westhampnett
25 Sep 44 to Manston
10 Feb 45 to Coltishall
7 Apr 45 to Hawkinge
10 Apr 45 to Hutton Cranswick
15 Jul 45 to Bradwell Bay
10 Aug 45 to Hutton Cranswick
20 Aug 45 to Molesworth
Aug 45 **Meteor F.3** (Apr 46)
5 Oct 45 to Bentwaters
18 Feb 46 to Fairwood Common
20 Mar 46 to Bentwaters
1 Apr 46 DB — renumbered as No 56 Sqn

125 Sqn

1 Feb 18 F @ Old Sarum (for DH 9), used various aircraft
1 Mar 18 to Fowlmere
17 Aug 18 DB
—
16 Jun 41 RF @ Colerne
Jun 41 **Defiant I** (May 42)
7 Aug 41 to Charmy Down
24 Sep 41 to Fairwood Common
Oct 41 **Defiant II** (May 42)
25 Jan 42 to Colerne det Fairwood Common
Feb 42 **Beaufighter IIF** (Sep 42) dets Charmy Down, Fairwood Common
14 May 42 to Fairwood Common
Sep 42 **Beaufighter VIF** (Mar 44) dets Sumburgh, Peterhead
15 Apr 43 to Exeter
14 Nov 43 to Valley det Ballyhalbert
Feb 44 **Mosquito XVII** (Mar 45)
25 Mar 44 to Hurn
31 Jul 44 to Middle Wallop det Bradwell Bay
18 Oct 44 to Coltishall
Feb 45 **Mosquito XXX** (Nov 45)
24 Apr 45 to Church Fenton
20 Nov 45 DB — renumbered as No 264 Sqn
—
31 Mar 55 RF @ Stradishall
Mar 55 **Meteor NF 11** (Jan 56)
Dec 55 **Venom NF 3** (May 57)
10 May 57 DB

126 Sqn

1 Feb 18 F @ Old Sarum (for DH 9), used various aircraft
1 Mar 18 to Fowlmere
17 Aug 18 DB
—
28 Jun 41 RF @ Ta Kali — nucleus from No 46 Sqn
Jun 41 **Hurricane IIA** (Mar 42)
Jun 41 **Hurricane IIB** (Mar 42)
Mar 42 **Spitfire VB** (Mar 44)
Mar 42 **Spitfire VC** (Mar 44)
6 Apr 42 to Luqa
Mar 43 **Spitfire IX** (Nov 43)
10 Jun 43 to Safi
23 Sep 43 to Gerbini
16 Oct 43 to Grottaglie
1 Apr 44 en route UK
30 Apr 44 to Sawbridgeworth
Apr 44 **Spitfire IXB** (Dec 44)
22 May 44 to Culmhead
3 Jul 44 to Harrowbeer
30 Aug 44 to Bradwell Bay
Dec 44 **Mustang III** (Apr 46)
30 Dec 44 to Bentwaters
Aug 45 **Mustang IV** (Mar 46)
5 Sep 45 to Hethel
15 Sep 45 to Bradwell Bay
5 Oct 45 to Hethel
Feb 46 **Spitfire LF XVIE** (Mar 46)
10 Mar 46 DB

127 Sqn

1 Feb 18 F @ Catterick (for DH 9), used various aircraft
4 Jul 18 DB — absorbed by No 4 TDS
—
29 Jun 41 RF @ Habbaniyah — from 'F' Flt, No 4 SFTS
Jun 41 **Gladiator I & II** (Jul 41)
Jun 41 **Hurricane I** (Jul 41)
29 Jun 41 to Haditha (K.3)
30 Jun 41 to T.1
6 Jul 41 to Tahoune Guemac
12 Jul 41 DB — absorbed by No 261 Sqn
—
26 Aug 41 RF @ Kasfareet — from No 249 Sqn groundcrews ex-UK
29 Sep 41 to Hurghada
22 Feb 42 to St Jean
Feb 42 **Hurricane I** (Jun 42) det Nicosia
14 Jun 42 to Shandur
Jun 42 **Hurricane IIB** (Oct 43) dets Sidi Barrani, Gerawala, LG 15
27 Jun 42 to LG 92
14 Jul 42 to LG 172

0 Aug 42 to LG 88
9 Sep 42 to Kilo 8
0 Oct 42 to LG 89
3 Oct 42 to LG 37
9 Nov 42 to LG 20
8 Nov 42 to LG 08
6 Jan 43 to St Jean det Nicosia
6 Jan 43 to Ramat David
Jan 43 **Spitfire VC** (Oct 43) det Nicosia
3 Mar 43 to St Jean dets Nicosia, Beirut, Paphos, Meherabad, Gaza, Lakatamia
Jul 43 **Hurricane IIC** (Apr 44)
Mar 44 **Spitfire VB** (Mar 44)
Mar 44 **Spitfire VC** (Mar 44)
Mar 44 **Spitfire IX** (Mar 44)
1 Apr 44 en route UK
3 Apr 44 to North Weald
May 44 **Spitfire HF IX** (Jul 44)
5 May 44 to Lympne
4 Jul 44 to Tangmere
Jul 44 **Spitfire LF IXE** (Nov 44)
2 Jul 44 to Southend
3 Jul 44 to Tangmere
5 Aug 44 to Funtington
2 Aug 44 to Ford
Aug 44 to B 16/Villons-les-Buissons
Sep 44 to B 33/Campneuseville
Sep 44 to B 57/Lille/Nord
Oct 44 to B 60/Grimbergen
Nov 44 **Spitfire XVI** (Apr 45)
Dec 44 to B 79/Woensdrecht
Feb 45 to Fairwood Common
Mar 45 to B 85/Schjindel
Apr 45 to B 106/Twente
Apr 45 DB

28 Sqn

Feb 18 F @ Thetford (for DH 9), used various aircraft
Jul 18 DB
—
Oct 41 RF @ Hastings, Sierra Leone — from Fighter Flt, No 95 Sqn
Oct 41 **Hurricane I** (Jan 43) dets Jeswang, Port Loko, Yundum
Nov 42 **Hurricane IIB** (Mar 43)
Mar 43 DB
—
Sep 44 RF @ Wyton
Sep 44 **Mosquito XX** (Nov 44)
Oct 44 **Mosquito XXV** (Nov 44)
Oct 44 **Mosquito XVI** (Mar 46)
Jun 45 to Warboys
Oct 45 to B 58/Melsbroek dets Blackbushe, Wahn
Mar 46 to Wahn
Mar 46 DB — renumbered as No 14 Sqn

29 Sqn

Mar 18 F @ Duxford (for DH 9), used various aircraft
Jul 18 DB
—
Jun 41 RF @ Leconfield
Jun 41 **Spitfire I** (Aug 41)
Aug 41 to Westhampnett
Aug 41 **Spitfire IIA** (Aug 41)
Aug 41 **Spitfire VB** (Jun 43)
Nov 41 to Debden
Dec 41 to Westhampnett
Jul 42 to Ipswich
Jul 42 to Westhampnett
Jul 42 to Thorney Island
Sep 42 to Grimsetter dets Sumburgh, Skaebrae
Dec 42 **Spitfire VC** (Jan 43)
Dec 42 **Spitfire VI** (Jan 43)
19 Jan 43 to Skaebrae
13 Feb 43 to Ibsley
28 Feb 43 to Tangmere
13 Mar 43 to Ibsley
28 Jun 43 to Hornchurch
Jun 43 **Spitfire IX** (Apr 44)
17 Jan 44 to Peterhead
16 Mar 44 to Heston
Mar 44 **Mustang III** (May 45)
30 Mar 44 to Llanbedr
3 Apr 44 to Coolham
22 Jun 44 to Holmsley South
24 Jun 44 to Ford
8 Jul 44 to Brenzett
11 Oct 44 to Andrews Field
11 Dec 44 to Bentwaters
May 45 **Spitfire IXE** (Sep 46)
26 May 45 to Dyce
10 Jun 45 to Vaernes
16 Jul 45 to Gardermoen
9 Nov 45 to Molesworth
3 Dec 45 to Hutton Cranswick
7 Jan 46 to Spilsby
9 Feb 46 to Hutton Cranswick
2 May 46 to Lübeck
28 Jun 46 to Church Fenton
1 Sep 46 DB — renumbered as No 257 Sqn

130 Sqn

1 Mar 18 F @ Wyton (for DH 9), used various aircraft
1 Apr 18 to Hucknall
4 Jul 18 DB
—
16 Jun 41 RF @ Portreath
Jun 41 **Spitfire IIA** (Dec 41)
25 Oct 41 to Harrowbeer
Oct 41 **Spitfire VA** (Dec 41)
Oct 41 **Spitfire VB** (Nov 42)
30 Nov 41 to Warmwell
5 Dec 41 to Perranporth
Apr 42 **Spitfire VC** (Mar 43)
12 Jul 42 to Warmwell
17 Jul 42 to Perranporth
4 Aug 42 to West Freugh
12 Aug 42 to Perranporth
16 Aug 42 to Thorney Island
20 Aug 42 to Perranporth
21 Oct 42 to Warmwell
31 Oct 42 to Perranporth
30 Mar 43 to Drem
Mar 43 **Spitfire VB** (Feb 44)
30 Apr 43 to Ballyhalbert
5 Jul 43 to Honiley
5 Aug 43 to West Malling
18 Sep 43 to Catterick
10 Nov 43 to Scorton
16 Nov 43 to Ayr
30 Nov 43 to Scorton
21 Dec 43 to Acklington
4 Jan 44 to Scorton
Jan 44 **Spitfire VC** (Feb 44)
13 Feb 44 DB
—
5 Apr 44 RF @ Lympne — No 186 Sqn renumbered
Apr 44 **Spitfire VB** (Aug 44)
30 Apr 44 to Horne
19 Jun 44 to Westhampnett
27 Jun 44 to Merston
3 Aug 44 to Tangmere
Aug 44 **Spitfire XIV** (May 45)
11 Aug 44 to Lympne
30 Sep 44 to B 70/Deurne
1 Oct 44 to B 82/Grave
1 Nov 44 to B 64/Diest
31 Dec 44 to Y 32/Ophoven
27 Jan 45 to B 78/Eindhoven
3 Feb 45 to Warmwell
21 Feb 45 to B 78/Eindhoven
7 Apr 45 to B 106/Twente
17 Apr 45 to B 118/Celle
7 May 45 to B 152/Fassberg
May 45 **Spitfire IXB** (Oct 46)
10 May 45 to North Weald
24 May 45 to Dyce
20 Jun 45 to Kristiansand/Kjevik
29 Jul 45 to Stavangar/Sola
31 Jul 45 to Kristiansand/Kjevik
13 Oct 45 to Gardermoen
4 Nov 45 to Manston
1 Dec 45 to Charterhall
24 Jan 46 to Acklington
27 Jan 46 to Manston
17 Jun 46 to Acklington
23 Jul 46 to Odiham
Oct 46 **Vampire F.1** (Jan 47)
31 Jan 47 DB — renumbered as No 72 Sqn
—
1 Aug 53 RF @ Brüggen
Aug 53 **Sabre F.4** (May 56)
Apr 56 **Hunter F.4** (May 57)
31 May 57 DB
—
1 Dec 59 **Thor** at Polebrook
23 Aug 63 DB

131 Sqn

15 Mar 18 F @ Shawbury (for DH 9), used various aircraft
17 Aug 18 DB
—
30 Jun 41 RF @ Ouston
Jun 41 **Spitfire IA** (Nov 41)
10 Jul 41 to Catterick
6 Aug 41 to Ternhill
Sep 41 **Spitfire IIA** (Jan 42)
27 Sep 41 to Atcham
Dec 41 **Spitfire VB** (Sep 43)
9 Feb 42 to Llanbedr
4 Mar 42 to Valley
16 Apr 42 to Llanbedr
14 May 42 to Merston
22 Aug 42 to Tangmere
24 Aug 42 to Ipswich
31 Aug 42 to Tangmere
24 Sep 42 to Thorney Island
7 Nov 42 to Westhampnett
Dec 42 **Spitfire VC** (Jan 43)
22 Jan 43 to Castletown
26 Jun 43 to Exeter
Jun 43 **Spitfire VC** (Sep 43)
16 Aug 43 to Redhill
17 Sep 43 to Church Stanton/Culmhead
Sep 43 **Spitfire IX** (Mar 44)
10 Feb 44 to Colerne
22 Feb 44 to Fairwood Common
29 Feb 44 to Colerne
Mar 44 **Spitfire VII** (Oct 44)
24 Mar 44 to Harrowbeer
24 May 44 to Culmhead
28 Aug 44 to Friston
Nov 44 en route FE
5 Feb 45 to Amarda Road
Feb 45 **Spitfire VIII** (Jun 45)
3 Apr 45 to Dalbhumgarh
10 Jun 45 DB
—
10 Jun 45 RF @ Ulunderpet — No 134 Sqn (at Kyaukpyu) renumbered
Jun 45 **Thunderbolt II** (Dec 45)
29 Aug 45 to Bobbili
31 Aug 45 to Baigachi
11 Sep 45 to Zayatkwin
20 Sep 45 to Kuala Lumpur
31 Dec 45 DB

132 Sqn

1 Mar 18 F @ Ternhill (for HP 0/400), used various aircraft
19 Aug 18 to Castle Bromwich
23 Dec 18 DB
—
7 Jul 41 RF @ Peterhead
Jul 41 **Spitfire I** (Nov 41)
Sep 41 **Spitfire IIB** (Apr 42) dets Montrose, Tain
16 Feb 42 to Skaebrae det Sumburgh
Mar 42 **Spitfire VB** (Jun 43)
11 Jun 42 to Grimsetter det Sumburgh
23 Sep 42 to Martlesham Heath
2 Oct 42 to Hornchurch
9 Oct 42 to Martlesham Heath
28 Feb 43 to Zeals
5 Apr 43 to Eastchurch
18 May 43 to Perranporth
May 43 **Spitfire VC** (Jun 43)
20 Jun 43 to Gravesend
Jun 43 **Spitfire VB** (Oct 43)
3 Jul 43 to Newchurch
Sep 43 **Spitfire IXB** (Jan 44)
12 Oct 43 to Detling
17 Jan 44 to Castletown
Jan 44 **Spitfire VB** (Mar 44)
Jan 44 **Spitfire VI** (Mar 44)
10 Mar 44 to Detling
13 Mar 44 to Fairwood Common
19 Mar 44 to Detling
Mar 44 **Spitfire IXB** (Jul 44)
18 Apr 44 to Ford
Jun 44 **Spitfire IXE** (Sep 44)
25 Jun 44 to B 11/Longues
13 Aug 44 to B 19/Lingèvres
4 Sep 44 to B 40/Beauvais/Nivillers
6 Sep 44 to B 52/Douai
17 Sep 44 to B 70/Deurne
Sep 44 **Spitfire IXB** (Nov 44)
29 Sep 44 to Hawkinge
14 Dec 44 en route FE
20 Jan 45 to Vavuniya
Jan 45 **Spitfire VIII** (May 45)
May 45 **Spitfire XIV** (Apr 46)
25 Jun 45 to Madura
2 Sep 45 en route Hong Kong via HMS *Smiter*
15 Sep 45 to Kai Tak
15 Apr 46 DB

133 Sqn

1 Mar 18 F @ Ternhill (for HP 0/400), used various aircraft
4 Jul 18 DB
—
31 Jul 41 RF @ Coltishall
Aug 41 **Hurricane IIB** (Dec 41)
15 Aug 41 to Duxford
28 Sep 41 to Collyweston
3 Oct 41 to Fowlmere
8 Oct 41 to Eglinton
Oct 41 **Spitfire IIA** (Jan 42)
2 Jan 42 to Kirton-in-Lindsey
Jan 42 **Spitfire VA** (Mar 42)
Feb 42 **Spitfire VB** (Sep 42) det West Malling
3 May 42 to Biggin Hill
30 Jun 42 to Lympne
12 Jul 42 to Biggin Hill
31 Jul 42 to Gravesend
17 Aug 42 to Lympne
22 Aug 42 to Martlesham Heath
31 Aug 42 to Biggin Hill
23 Sep 42 to Great Sampford
Sep 42 **Spitfire IX** (Sep 42)
29 Sep 42 DB — redesignated as 336th Sqn, 4th Fighter Group, USAAF

134 Sqn

1 Mar 18 F @ Ternhill (for HP 0/400), used various aircraft
4 Jul 18 DB
—

28 Jul 41 RF @ Leconfield — nucleus from No 17 Sqn
Jul 41 **Hurricane IIB** (Oct 41)
12 Aug 41 en route USSR via HMS *Argus*
7 Sep 41 to Vaenga
16 Nov 41 en route UK
7 Dec 41 to Catterick
Dec 41 **Spitfire VA** (Feb 42)
30 Dec 41 to Eglinton
Dec 41 **Spitfire IIA** (Feb 42)
Jan 42 **Hurricane IIB** (Feb 42)
Jan 42 **Spitfire VB** (Mar 42)
26 Mar 42 to Baginton
10 Apr 42 en route Egypt
9 Jun 42 to Helwan
6 Jul 42 to Lydda
16 Nov 42 to LG 222
22 Jan 43 to Shandur
Jan 43 **Hurricane IIB** (Oct 43)
6 Feb 43 to LG 121
Mar 43 **Hurricane IIC** (Apr 43) det LG 219
13 Apr 43 to LG 219 det Sousse
14 May 43 to Bu Amud det Sousse
23 Jun 43 to Bersis
Jun 43 **Spitfire VB & VC** (Aug 43)
31 Oct 43 to Qassassin
Nov 43 **Hurricane IIC** (Aug 44)
14 Nov 43 en route India
30 Nov 43 to Comilla
15 Dec 43 to Parashuram
20 Jan 44 to Fazilpur
3 Feb 44 to 'Hay'
23 May 44 to Arkonam dets Salbani, Cuttack
15 Aug 44 to Yelahanka
Sep 44 **Thunderbolt I** (Jan 45)
Sep 44 **Thunderbolt II** (Jun 45)
6 Oct 44 to Arkonam
19 Nov 44 to Baigachi
26 Nov 44 to Ratnap det Cox's Bazaar
28 Apr 45 to Kyaukpyu
10 Jun 45 DB — renumbered as No 131 Sqn, aircraft ferried to Ulunderpet

135 Sqn

1 Apr 18 F @ Hucknall (for DH 9), used various aircraft
4 Jul 18 DB
—
15 Aug 41 RF @ Baginton
Aug 41 **Hurricane IIA** (Nov 41)
4 Sep 41 to Honiley
Nov 41 **Hurricane IIC** (Nov 41)
10 Nov 41 en route FE
16 Jan 42 to Zayatkwin
28 Jan 42 to Mingaladon
Feb 42 **Hurricane IIB** (Oct 43) dets Zayatkwin, 'Highland Queen', Akyab, Magwe
2 Mar 42 to 'Highland Queen'
6 Mar 42 to Mingaladon
7 Mar 42 to Zigon
9 Mar 42 to 'Park Lane'
11 Mar 42 to Magwe
27 Mar 42 to Dum Dum dets Akyab, Cuttack, Vizagapatam
23 Jan 43 to 'George' det 'Hove'
13 May 43 to 'Reindeer'
16 May 43 to Dohazari
30 May 43 to St Thomas Mount
6 Jul 43 to Yelahanka
Oct 43 **Hurricane IIC** (Sep 44)
22 Nov 43 to St Thomas Mount
16 Jan 44 to Minneriya
May 44 **Thunderbolt I** (Jun 45) det Amarda Road
9 Oct 44 to Chittagong det Cox's Bazaar
9 Dec 44 to Jumchar det Cox's Bazaar
15 Apr 45 to Cox's Bazaar
24 Apr 45 to Akyab
17 May 45 to Chakulia (air echelon)
10 Jun 45 DB — renumbered as No 615 Sqn (groundcrew at Akyab)

136 Sqn

1 Apr 18 F @ Lake Down (for DH 9), used various aircraft
4 Jul 18 DB
—
20 Aug 41 RF @ Kirton-in-Lindsey
Aug 41 **Hurricane IIB** (Nov 41)
Oct 41 **Hurricane IIA** (Nov 41)
9 Nov 41 en route FE
3 Feb 42 to Rangoon
26 Feb 42 to Dum Dum dets Mingaladon, Akyab
27 Feb 42 to Asansol dets Mingaladon, Akyab
31 Mar 42 to Alipore
Apr 42 **Hurricane IIB** (Mar 43) det Maidan
26 Jun 42 to Red Road det Vizagapatam
17 Aug 42 to Alipore det Vizagapatam
6 Sep 42 to Dum Dum
26 Dec 42 to Chittagong
Mar 43 **Hurricane IIC** (Oct 43)
21 Jun 43 to Baigachi
Oct 43 **Spitfire VC** (Feb 44)
5 Nov 43 to Amarda Road
21 Nov 43 to Baigachi
1 Dec 43 to 'Lyons'
7 Dec 43 to Alipore
20 Dec 43 to 'Lyons'
27 Dec 43 to 'Hay'
Jan 44 **Spitfire VIII** (May 46)
25 Jan 44 to Rumkha
5 Mar 44 to Sapam
11 Mar 44 to Wangjing
23 Apr 44 to Chittagong
7 Jul 44 to Ratmalana
15 Dec 44 to Minneriya
7 Apr 45 to Cocos Island
22 Oct 45 to Tengah via HMS *Smiter*
26 Nov 45 to Kuala Lumpur
Feb 46 **Spitfire XIV** (May 46)
5 May 46 en route Bombay
8 May 46 DB — renumbered as No 152 Sqn

137 Sqn

1 Apr 18 F @ Shawbury (for DH 9), used various aircraft
4 Jul 18 DB
—
20 Feb 41 RF @ Charmy Down
Feb 41 **Whirlwind I** (Jun 43)
8 Nov 41 to Coltishall
31 Nov 41 to Matlask det Snailwell
2 Aug 42 to Drem
11 Aug 42 to Matlask
24 Aug 42 to Snailwell
17 Sep 42 to Manston
12 Jun 43 to Southend
Jun 43 **Hurricane IV** (Jan 44)
8 Aug 43 to Manston
14 Dec 43 to Lympne
2 Jan 44 to Colerne
Jan 44 **Typhoon IB** (Aug 45)
4 Feb 44 to Lympne
1 Apr 44 to Manston
14 Aug 44 to B 6/Coulombs
28 Aug 44 to B 30/Créton
3 Sep 44 to B 48/Amiens/Glisy
6 Sep 44 to B 58/Melsbroek
23 Sep 44 to B 78/Eindhoven
13 Jan 45 to B 86/Helmond
7 Mar 45 to Warmwell
19 Mar 45 to B 86/Helmond
11 Apr 45 to B 106/Twente
14 Apr 45 to B 112/Hopsten
17 Apr 45 to B 120/Langenhagen
1 May 45 to B 156/Lüneburg
7 May 45 to B 118/Celle
9 May 45 to B 160/Kastrup
21 Jun 45 to B 172/Husum
11 Jul 45 to B 158/Lübeck
20 Aug 45 to Warmwell
26 Aug 45 DB — renumbered as No 174 Sqn

138 Sqn

30 Sep 18 F @ Chingford — nucleus from Nos 1, 5 36 & 45 TDSs
Oct 18 **Bristol F2b Fighter** (Feb 19)
1 Feb 19 DB
—
25 Aug 41 RF @ Newmarket — No 1419 Flt renumbered
Aug 41 **Lysander IIIA** (Mar 42)
Aug 41 **Whitley V** (Nov 42) det Luqa (**Whitley**)
Aug 41 **Halifax II** (Aug 44)
16 Dec 41 to Stradishall
11 Mar 42 to Tempsford
Jan 43 **Halifax V** (Aug 44)
Jun 44 **Stirling IV** (Mar 45)
9 Mar 45 to Tuddenham
Mar 45 **Lancaster I & III** (Sep 47)
12 Nov 46 to Wyton
Sep 47 **Lincoln B.2** (Aug 50)
1 Sep 50 DB
—
1 Jan 55 RF @ Gaydon
Feb 55 **Valiant B.1** (Mar 62)
6 Jul 55 to Wittering
Mar 56 **Valiant B(PR) 1** (May 61)
Mar 56 **Valiant B(PR)K 1** (Aug 61)
Jun 56 **Valiant B(K) 1** (Apr 62)
1 Apr 62 DB

139 Sqn

3 Jul 18 F @ Villaverla — from 'Z' Flt of No 34 Sqn
Jul 18 **Bristol F2b Fighter** (Feb 19)
10 Oct 18 to Grossa
2 Nov 18 to Arcade
14 Nov 18 to Grossa
30 Jan 19 to Caldiero
25 Feb 19 to Blandford as a cadre
7 Mar 19 DB
—
3 Sep 36 RF @ Wyton
Sep 36 **Hind** (Jul 37)
Jul 37 **Blenheim I** (Sep 39)
Jul 39 **Blenheim IV** (Dec 41)
1 Dec 39 to Bétheniville
15 Feb 40 to Plivot
30 May 40 to West Raynham
10 Jun 40 to Horsham St Faith det Luqa
13 Jul 41 to Oulton dets Manston, Luqa
23 Oct 41 to Horsham St Faith
9 Dec 41 to Oulton
Dec 41 **Hudson III** (Apr 42)
Jan 42 en route FE
Jan 42 to Port Blair
Mar 42 to Akyab
Mar 42 to Dum Dum
30 Apr 42 DB — renumbered as No 62 Sqn
—
8 Jun 42 RF @ Horsham St Faith
Jun 42 **Blenheim V** (Nov 42)
Jun 42 **Mosquito IV** (Jul 44)
15 Jun 42 to Oulton
26 Jun 42 to Horsham St Faith
29 Sep 42 to Marham
4 Jul 43 to Wyton
Sep 43 **Mosquito IX** (Aug 44)
Dec 43 **Mosquito XX** (Aug 45)
1 Feb 44 to Upwood
Feb 44 **Mosquito XVI** (Jul 48)
Oct 44 **Mosquito XXV** (May 45)
4 Feb 46 to Hemswell
4 Nov 46 to Coningsby
Feb 48 **Mosquito B.35** (Jan 53)
1 Apr 50 to Hemswell
Nov 52 **Canberra B.2** (Jul 55)
Feb 55 **Canberra B.6** (Dec 59)
1 Jan 56 to Binbrook
31 Dec 59 DB
—
1 Feb 62 RF @ Wittering
Feb 62 **Victor B.2** (Dec 68)
31 Dec 68 DB

140 Sqn

17 Sep 41 F @ Benson — from No 1416 Flt
Sep 41 **Spitfire C** (Aug 42)
Sep 41 **Spitfire I** (Apr 43)
Sep 41 **Spitfire IV** (Nov 43)
Sep 41 **Blenheim IV** (Aug 43)
29 Oct 41 to Weston Zoyland
4 Nov 41 to Benson det Mount Farm
20 May 42 to Mount Farm dets Benson, St Eval
16 Mar 43 to Hartford Bridge
Apr 43 **Ventura I** (Jan 44)
Jun 43 **Spitfire PR VII** (Jul 43)
Sep 43 **Spitfire XI** (Apr 44)
Nov 43 **Mosquito IX** (Jul 44)
Dec 43 **Mosquito XVI** (Jul 45)
7 Apr 44 to Northolt
3 Sep 44 to A 12/Balleroy
9 Sep 44 to B 48/Amiens/Glisy
26 Sep 44 to B 58/Melsbroek
15 Apr 45 to B 78/Eindhoven
9 Jul 45 to Fersfield
12 Jul 45 to Acklington
19 Sep 45 to Fersfield
20 Sep 45 DB

141 Sqn

1 Jan 18 F @ Rochford — from 'A' Flt, No 61 Sqn
Jan 18 **Dolphin** (Apr 18)
Jan 18 **BE 12** (Mar 18)
9 Feb 18 to Biggin Hill
Feb 18 **BE 12B** (Mar 18)
Feb 18 **Pup** (Mar 18)
Feb 18 **BE 2E** (Mar 18)
Mar 18 **Bristol F2b Fighter** (Feb 20)
1 Mar 19 to Tallaght dets the Curragh, Birr
14 Dec 19 to Baldonnel dets Gormanston, Birr
1 Feb 20 DB — absorbed into No 100 Sqn
—
4 Oct 39 RF @ Turnhouse
Oct 39 **Gladiator I** (Apr 40)
19 Oct 39 to Grangemouth
Nov 39 **Blenheim IF** (May 40)
13 Feb 40 to Prestwick
22 Feb 40 to Grangemouth
Apr 40 **Defiant I** (Sep 41)
28 Jun 40 to Turnhouse
11 Jul 40 to West Malling det Biggin Hill

25 Jul 40 to Prestwick det Grangemouth
22 Aug 40 to Dyce det Montrose
30 Aug 40 to Turnhouse dets Biggin Hill, Gatwick
15 Oct 40 to Drem det Gatwick
22 Oct 40 to Gatwick
3 Nov 40 to Gravesend
29 Apr 41 to Ayr dets Acklington Drem
Jun 41 **Beaufighter IF** (Jun 43)
29 Jan 42 to Acklington det Drem
23 Jun 42 to Tangmere
10 Aug 42 to Ford
18 Feb 43 to Predannack
30 Apr 43 to Wittering det Drem
May 43 **Beaufighter VIF** (Jan 44)
Nov 43 **Mosquito II** (Aug 44)
4 Dec 43 to West Raynham
Aug 44 **Mosquito VI** (Apr 45) det Fiskerton
Apr 45 **Mosquito XXX** (Sep 45)
3 Jul 45 to Little Snoring
7 Sep 45 DB
—
17 Jun 46 RF @ Wittering
Jun 46 **Mosquito NF 36** (Dec 51)
21 Sep 46 to Lübeck
5 Oct 46 to Wittering
9 Jan 47 to Acklington
15 Feb 47 to Coltishall
28 Apr 47 to Acklington
5 Jun 47 to Coltishall
12 Sep 47 to Lübeck
26 Sep 47 to Coltishall
2 Apr 48 to Lübeck
16 Apr 48 to Coltishall
21 Nov 49 to Church Fenton
23 Sep 50 to Coltishall
Aug 51 **Meteor NF 11** (Sep 55)
Jun 55 **Venom NF 3** (Mar 57)
14 Oct 56 to Horsham St Faith
Feb 57 **Javelin FAW 4** (Jan 58)
28 May 57 to Coltishall
1 Feb 58 DB — renumbered as No 41 Sqn
—
1 Apr 59 **Bloodhound I** at Dunholme Lodge
31 Mar 64 DB

142 Sqn

2 Feb 18 F @ Ismailia
Feb 18 **BE 12A** (Jun 18)
3 Feb 18 to Julis
Mar 18 **Martinsyde G.102** (Jun 18)
Apr 18 **RE 8** (Apr 19)
8 Apr 18 to Ramleh det Jerusalem
May 18 **AW FK 8** (Apr 19)
Jun 18 **BE 2E** (Mar 19)
8 Sep 18 to Sarona dets Jerusalem, El Affule
4 Oct 18 to Ramleh dets Damascus, Haifa
5 Nov 18 to Qantara
Jan 19 **DH 9** (Feb 20)
6 Feb 19 to Suez
1 Feb 20 DB — renumbered as No 55 Sqn
—
1 Jun 34 RF @ Netheravon
Jun 34 **Hart** (Nov 36)
3 Jan 35 to Andover
3 Oct 35 en route ME
3 Oct 35 to Aboukir
5 Oct 35 to Mersah Matruh det Helwan
3 Aug 36 to Ismailia
5 Nov 36 to Aboukir
0 Nov 36 en route UK
3 Dec 36 to Andover
Jan 37 **Hind** (Apr 38)
Mar 38 **Battle** (Nov 40)
9 May 39 to Bicester
2 Sep 39 to Berry-au-Bac
12 Sep 39 to Plivot
16 Sep 39 to Berry-au-Bac det Perpignan/La Salanque
16 May 40 to Faux-Villecerf
6 Jun 40 to Villiersfaux
15 Jun 40 to Waddington
3 Jul 40 to Binbrook
12 Aug 40 to Eastchurch
6 Sep 40 to Binbrook
Nov 40 **Wellington II** (Oct 41)
26 Nov 41 to Waltham
Oct 41 **Wellington IV** (Sep 42)
Sep 42 **Wellington III** (Aug 43)
19 Dec 42 to Blida
19 Dec 42 to Kirmington — UK echelon only, merged with No 150 Sqn to form No 166 Sqn wef 27 Jan 43
Jun 43 **Wellington X** (Oct 44)
5 May 43 to Fontaine Chaude
26 May 43 to Kairouan
15 Nov 43 to Oudna
21 Dec 43 to Cerignola No 3
15 Feb 44 to Amendola
4 Jul 44 to Regina
5 Oct 44 DB
—
25 Oct 44 RF @ Gransden Lodge
Oct 44 **Mosquito XXV** (Sep 45)
28 Sep 45 DB
—
1 Feb 59 RF @ Eastleigh
Feb 59 **Venom FB 4** (Apr 59)
1 Apr 59 DB — renumbered as No 208 Sqn
—
22 Jul 59 **Thor** at Coleby Grange
24 May 63 DB

143 Sqn

1 Feb 18 F @ Throwley — nucleus from No 112 Sqn
Feb 18 **AW FK 8** (Mar 18)
14 Feb 18 to Detling
Mar 18 **SE 5A** (Aug 18)
Aug 18 **Camel** (Oct 19)
Jun 19 **Snipe** (Oct 19)
31 Oct 19 DB
—
15 Jun 41 RF @ Aldergrove — nucleus from No 252 Sqn
Jun 41 **Beaufighter IC** (Nov 41)
5 Jul 41 to Thornaby
20 Jul 41 to Dyce
27 Sep 41 to Sumburgh
5 Dec 41 to Dyce
Dec 41 **Blenheim IV** (Sep 42)
16 Dec 41 to Aldergrove
23 Apr 42 to Limavady
11 Jun 42 to Thorney Island
27 Jul 42 to Docking
Aug 42 **Beaufighter IC** (Sep 42)
27 Aug 42 to North Coates
Sep 42 **Beaufighter IIF** (Mar 43)
Mar 43 **Beaufighter XI** (May 44)
28 Aug 43 to St Eval
16 Sep 43 to Portreath
Sep 43 **Beaufighter X** (Oct 44)
12 Feb 44 to North Coates det Manston
23 May 44 to Manston
9 Sep 44 to North Coates
Sep 44 **Mosquito II** (Oct 44)
23 Oct 44 to Banff
Oct 44 **Mosquito VI** (May 45)
25 May 45 DB — renumbered as No 14 Sqn

144 Sqn

20 Mar 18 F @ Port Said
Apr 18 **BE 2E** (Jul 18)
May 18 **BE 12A** (Aug 18)
Jun 18 **Martinsyde S.1** (Aug 18)
Jul 18 **RE 8** (Jul 18)
14 Aug 18 to Junction Station
Aug 18 **DH 9** (Dec 18) dets Haifa, Mudros
6 Nov 18 to Mikra Bay dets Mudros, Amberkoj
4 Dec 18 en route UK
16 Dec 18 to Ford Junction as a cadre
4 Feb 19 DB
—
11 Jan 37 RF @ Bicester — from 'B' Flt, No 101 Sqn
Jan 37 **Overstrand** (Feb 37)
Jan 37 **Anson I** (Sep 37)
9 Feb 37 to Hemswell
Mar 37 **Audax** (Sep 37)
Aug 37 **Blenheim I** (Apr 39)
Mar 39 **Hampden** (Mar 43)
17 Jul 41 to North Luffenham
22 Apr 42 to Leuchars dets Skitten, Sumburgh, Wick, Afrikanda, Vaenga
Jan 43 **Beaufighter VIC** (May 43)
8 Apr 43 to Tain
May 43 **Beaufighter X** (Jul 43) dets Wick, Blida, Protville II
9 Jul 43 to Benson det Protville II
5 Aug 43 to Tain
Aug 43 **Beaufighter X** (May 45)
20 Oct 43 to Wick
10 May 44 to Davidstow Moor
1 Jul 44 to Strubby
3 Sep 44 to Banff
23 Oct 44 to Dallachy
25 May 45 DB
—
1 Dec 59 **Thor** at North Luffenham
23 Aug 63 DB

145 Sqn

15 May 18 F @ Aboukir
1 Jun 18 to Abu Sueir
Aug 18 **SE 5A** (Feb 19) det Junction Station
25 Aug 18 to Qantara
13 Sep 18 to Ramleh
20 Oct 18 to Qantara
8 Feb 19 reduced to a cadre
16 Feb 19 to Suez
6 Sep 19 DB
—
10 Oct 39 RF @ Croydon
Oct 39 **Blenheim IF** (May 40)
Mar 40 **Hurricane I** (Feb 41)
9 May 40 to Filton
10 May 40 to Tangmere
23 Jul 40 to Westhampnett
14 Aug 40 to Drem dets Dyce, Montrose
31 Aug 40 to Dyce det Montrose
9 Oct 40 to Tangmere
Jan 41 **Spitfire I** (Mar 41)
Feb 41 **Spitfire IIA** (Feb 42)
May 41 **Spitfire IIB** (Jul 41)
28 May 41 to Merston
28 Jul 41 to Catterick
Sep 41 **Spitfire IIB** (Feb 42)
Nov 41 **Spitfire VB** (Feb 42)
11 Feb 42 en route ME
30 Apr 42 to Helwan
Apr 42 **Spitfire VB** (Sep 43)
25 May 42 to Gambut
18 Jun 42 to LG 155
20 Jun 42 to LG 76
24 Jun 42 to LG 13
26 Jun 42 to LG 15
29 Jun 42 to LG 154 dets LG 39, LG 172
5 Aug 42 to Idku det Dekheila
21 Aug 42 to LG 154 dets Dekheila, Idku
26 Sep 42 to LG 92
7 Oct 42 to LG 173
7 Nov 42 to LG 21
12 Nov 42 to LG 155
14 Nov 42 to Gambut
25 Nov 42 to Msus
4 Dec 42 to El Hassiet
9 Dec 42 to Agedabia
21 Dec 42 to El Merduma
30 Dec 42 to Sidi Azzab
4 Jan 43 to Hamraiet
24 Jan 43 to Wadi Surri det Castel Benito
17 Feb 43 to Castel Benito
23 Feb 43 to Medanine
2 Mar 43 to Ben Gardane
10 Mar 43 to Bu Grara
Mar 43 **Spitfire IX** (Sep 43)
12 Apr 43 to La Fauconnerie
15 Apr 43 to Goubrine
7 May 43 to Hergla det Goubrine
21 May 43 to Ben Gardane
14 Jun 43 to Luqa
Jun 43 **Spitfire VIII** (Aug 45)
13 Jul 43 to Pachino
17 Jul 43 to Cassibile
25 Jul 43 to Lentini West
24 Sep 43 to Gioia del Colle
5 Oct 43 to Tortorella
18 Oct 43 to Triolo
20 Nov 43 to Canne
17 Jan 44 to Marcianese
23 Apr 44 to Venafro
21 May 44 to Lago
4 Jun 44 to Venafro
12 Jun 44 to Littorio
17 Jun 44 to Fabrica
3 Jul 44 to Perugia det Rosignano
25 Aug 44 to Loreto
5 Sep 44 to Fano
4 Dec 44 to Bellaria
3 May 45 to Treviso
May 45 **Spitfire IX** (Aug 45)
19 Aug 45 DB
—
1 Mar 52 RF @ Celle
Mar 52 **Vampire FB 5** (Aug 54)
Mar 54 **Venom FB 1** (Oct 57)
15 Oct 57 DB

146 Sqn

15 Oct 41 F @ Risalpur — from 'B' Flt, No 5 Sqn
Oct 41 **Audax** (Sep 42)
26 Nov 41 to Dum Dum det Dinjan
2 Dec 41 to Dinjan
Mar 42 **Mohawk IV** (May 42)
Mar 42 **Buffalo I** (May 42)
5 May 42 to Dum Dum (No 5 Sqn det @ Dum Dum renumbered as No 146 Sqn)
May 42 **Hurricane IIB** (Jan 44)
6 Sep 42 to Alipore dets Chittagong, 'Reindeer'
3 May 43 to Feni dets Chittagong
26 Jun 43 to Comilla dets Chittagong
3 Dec 43 to Baigachi
Dec 43 **Hurricane IIC** (May 44)
1 Mar 44 to St Thomas Mount
5 Jun 44 to Yelahanka
Jun 44 **Thunderbolt I** (Mar 45)
13 Aug 44 to Arkonam

5 Sep 44 to Kumbhirgram
Sep 44 **Thunderbolt II** (Oct 44) dets Cox's Bazaar
21 Nov 44 to Wangjing det Sinthe
Mar 45 **Thunderbolt II** (Jul 45)
18 Mar 45 to Palel
23 Mar 45 to Wangjing
20 Apr 45 to Myingyan North
30 Apr 45 to 'Tennant'
6 May 45 to Myingyan North
7 Jun 45 to Meiktila
1 Jul 45 DB — renumbered as No 42 Sqn

147 Sqn

17 Oct 41 Formation authorised. Initially intended to take over No 216 Sqn's Bombays. By Jun 42 planned role had changed to bomber and groundcrew were employed to support the operations of Nos 159 and 160 Sqns pending receipt of their own Liberators.
Jun 42 @ Fayid
2 Jul 42 to St Jean
12 Aug 42 to Aqir
18 Nov 42 to Shandur
15 Feb 43 DB — absorbed into No 178 Sqn
—
1 Sep 44 RF @ Croydon
Sep 44 **Dakota** (Sep 46)
Sep 44 **Anson XII** (Sep 45)
Apr 46 **Anson C.19** (Sep 46)
15 Sep 46 DB
—
1 Feb 53 RF @ Abingdon — from Overseas Ferry Unit
16 Apr 53 to Benson
15 Sep 58 DB — merged with No 167 Sqn to form the Ferry Sqn

148 Sqn

10 Feb 18 F @ Andover
1 Mar 18 to Ford Junction
Mar 18 **FE 2B** (Feb 19)
25 Apr 18 to Auchel
3 May 18 to Sains-lès-Pernes
22 Oct 18 to Camblain-l'Abbé
31 Oct 18 to Erre
9 Dec 18 to Serny
17 Feb 19 to Tangmere as a cadre
4 Jul 19 DB
—
7 Jun 37 RF @ Scampton — nucleus from No 9 Sqn
Jun 37 **Audax** (Jul 37)
Jun 37 **Wellesley** (Nov 38)
10 Mar 38 to Stradishall
Nov 38 **Heyford III** (Mar 39)
Mar 39 **Wellington I** (Apr 40)
Apr 39 **Anson I** (Apr 40)
6 Sep 39 to Harwell
8 Apr 40 DB — merged into No 15 OTU
—
30 Apr 40 RF @ Stradishall
Apr 40 **Wellington IC** (May 40)
20 May 40 DB
—
1 Dec 40 RF @ Luqa
Dec 40 **Wellington IC** (Oct 41)
26 Mar 41 to Kabrit dets Luqa, LG 60, LG 104
Oct 41 **Wellington II** (Apr 42)
Apr 42 **Wellington IC** (Dec 42)
15 May 42 to LG 106
26 Jun 42 to Kabrit
19 Aug 42 to LG 237
12 Nov 42 to LG 106
13 Nov 42 to LG 09
1 Dec 42 to LG 167 dets Luqa, Kilo 40
31 Dec 42 DB
—
14 Mar 43 RF @ Gambut — Special Liberator Flight redesignated
Mar 43 **Liberator II** (Feb 44)
Mar 43 **Halifax II** (May 45)
5 Apr 43 to Derna
1 Sep 43 to Tocra
31 Jan 44 to Brindisi
Feb 44 **Lysander IIIA** (Jun 45) det Calvi (Lysander)
Jul 44 **Halifax V** (May 45)
Nov 44 **Stirling IV** (Dec 44)
28 Jun 45 to Foggia
Jun 45 **Liberator VI** (Jan 46)
8 Nov 45 to Gianaclis
15 Jan 46 DB
—
4 Nov 46 RF @ Upwood
Nov 46 **Lancaster B.1(FE)** (Feb 50)
Jan 50 **Lincoln B.2** (Jun 55)
1 Jul 55 DB
—
1 Jul 56 RF @ Marham
Jul 56 **Valiant B(K) 1** (Dec 64)
Dec 56 **Valiant B.1** (Dec 64)
Dec 57 **Valiant B(PR) 1** (Dec 64)
Feb 58 **Valiant B(PR)K 1** (Dec 64)
1 May 65 DB

149 Sqn

1 Mar 18 F @ Ford Junction
Mar 18 **FE 2B** (Aug 19)
2 Jun 18 to Marquise
4 Jun 18 to Quilen
16 Jun 18 to Alquines dets Abeele, Clairmarais North
16 Sep 18 to Clairmarais North
25 Oct 18 to Ste-Marguerite
26 Nov 18 to Fort Cognelée
24 Dec 18 to Bickendorf
26 Mar 19 to Tallaght as a cadre
1 Aug 19 DB
—
12 Apr 37 RF @ Mildenhall — from 'B' Flt, No 99 Sqn
Apr 37 **Heyford III** (May 37)
May 37 **Heyford IA** (Mar 39)
Jan 39 **Wellington I** (Dec 39)
Sep 39 **Wellington IA** (Jun 40)
Mar 40 **Wellington IC** (Dec 41) det Salon
Nov 41 **Stirling I** (Jul 43) det Lakenheath
6 Apr 42 to Lakenheath
Feb 43 **Stirling III** (Sep 44) det Tempsford
15 May 44 to Methwold
Aug 44 **Lancaster I & III** (Nov 49) det Woodbridge
29 Apr 46 to Tuddenham
4 Nov 46 to Stradishall
28 Feb 49 to Mildenhall
Oct 49 **Lincoln B.2** (Mar 50)
1 Mar 50 DB
—
9 Aug 50 RF @ Marham
17 Oct 50 to Coningsby
Nov 50 **Washington B.1** (Feb 53)
Mar 53 **Canberra B.2** (Aug 56)
22 May 54 to Cottesmore
24 Aug 54 to Ahlhorn
17 Sep 54 to Gütersloh
31 Aug 56 DB

150 Sqn

1 Apr 18 F @ Kirec — from elements of Nos 17 and 47 Sqns
Apr 18 **Bristol M.1C** (Jan 19)
Apr 18 **SE 5A** (Feb 19) det Marian
May 18 **Camel** (Feb 19)
Jul 18 **BE 12A** (Dec 18)
Aug 18 **BE 2E** (Jan 19) det Amberkoj
20 Oct 18 to Mikra Bay dets Kirec, Gumuljina, Dedeagatch
Dec 18 **AW FK 8** (Jan 19)
15 Mar 19 reduced to a cadre
11 Jun 19 to San Stephano
18 Sep 19 DB
—
8 Aug 38 RF @ Boscombe Down
Aug 38 **Battle** (Sep 40)
3 Apr 39 to Benson
2 Sep 39 to Challerange
11 Sep 39 to Écury-sur-Coole dets Perpignan/La Salanque
15 May 40 to Pouan
3 Jun 40 to Houssay
18 Jun 40 to Stradishall
3 Jul 40 to Newton
Oct 40 **Wellington IA** (Dec 40)
Oct 40 **Wellington IC** (Dec 42)
10 Jul 41 to Snaith
Sep 42 **Wellington III** (Aug 43)
Oct 42 to Kirmington
19 Dec 42 to Blida — UK element became No 166 Sqn wef 27 Jan 43
Apr 43 **Wellington X** (Oct 44)
5 May 43 to Fontaine Chaude
26 May 43 to Kairouan West
15 Nov 43 to Oudna No 2
21 Dec 43 to Cerignola No 3
15 Feb 44 to Amendola
4 Jul 44 to Regina
5 Oct 44 DB
—
1 Nov 44 RF @ Fiskerton — from 'C' Flt, No 550 Sqn
Nov 44 **Lancaster I & III** (Nov 45)
22 Nov 44 to Hemswell
7 Nov 45 DB
—
1 Aug 59 **Thor** at Carnaby
9 Apr 63 DB

151 Sqn

12 Jun 18 F @ Hainault Farm — from Flts of Nos 44, 78 & 112 Sqns
Jun 18 **Camel** (Feb 19)
19 Jun 18 to Marquise
23 Jun 18 to Fontaine-sur-Maye det Famechon
8 Sep 18 to Vignacourt
8 Oct 18 to Bancourt
5 Dec 18 to Liettres
21 Feb 19 to Gullane as a cadre
10 Sep 19 DB
—
4 Aug 36 RF @ North Weald — from 'B' Flt, No 56 Sqn
Aug 36 **Gauntlet II** (Mar 39)
Dec 38 **Hurricane I** (Jun 41) dets Martlesham Heath
13 May 40 to Martlesham Heath
17 May 40 to Abbeville
18 May 40 to Vitry-en-Artois
18 May 40 to Manston
20 May 40 to North Weald dets Manston, Rochford
29 Aug 40 to Stapleford
1 Sep 40 to Digby det Wittering
28 Nov 40 to Bramcote det Wittering
Dec 40 **Defiant I** (Oct 41)
22 Dec 40 to Wittering det Coltishall
Jun 41 **Hurricane IIC** (Jan 42)
Sep 41 **Defiant II** (Jul 42)
Apr 42 **Mosquito II** (Jul 43)
30 Apr 43 to Colerne
Jul 43 **Mosquito XII** (Mar 44)
16 Aug 43 to Middle Wallop
Aug 43 **Mosquito VI** (Aug 43) dets Coltishall
17 Nov 43 to Colerne dets Coltishall
Dec 43 **Mosquito XIII** (Sep 44)
25 Mar 44 to Predannack
Jul 44 **Mosquito VI** (Sep 44)
Aug 44 **Mosquito XXX** (Oct 46)
8 Oct 44 to Castle Camps
19 Nov 44 to Hunsdon
1 Mar 45 to Bradwell Bay
17 May 45 to Predannack
3 Jan 46 to Lübeck
12 Jan 46 to Predannack
27 Mar 46 to Lübeck
6 Apr 46 to Predannack
19 Apr 46 to Exeter
11 Jul 46 to Weston Zoyland
23 Aug 46 to Lübeck
6 Sep 46 to Weston Zoyland
10 Oct 46 DB
—
15 Sep 51 RF @ Leuchars
Feb 52 **Vampire NF 10** (May 5
Mar 53 **Meteor NF 11** (Oct 55)
Sep 55 **Venom NF 3** (Jun 57)
17 Jun 57 to Turnhouse
Jun 57 **Javelin FAW 5** (Sep 61)
15 Nov 57 to Leuchars
19 Sep 61 DB
—
1 Jan 62 RF @ Watton — Signa Development Sqn redesignated
Jan 62 **Lincoln B.2** (Mar 63)
Jan 62 **Hastings C.1 & C.2** (May 63)
Jan 62 **Varsity T.1** (May 63)
Jan 62 **Canberra B.2** (May 63)
25 May 63 DB — renumbered as No 97 Sqn

152 Sqn

1 Oct 18 F @ Rochford
Oct 18 **Camel** (Feb 19)
18 Oct 18 to Carvin
29 Nov 18 to Liettres
21 Feb 19 to Gullane as a cadre
30 Jun 19 DB
—
2 Oct 39 RF @ Acklington
Oct 39 **Gladiator I & II** (Jan 4(dets Leconfield, Sumburgh
Dec 39 **Spitfire I** (Mar 41)
12 Jul 40 to Warmwell
Mar 41 **Spitfire IIA** (Jun 42)
9 Apr 41 to Portreath
25 Aug 41 to Snailwell
31 Aug 41 to Swanton Morley
17 Dec 41 to Coltishall
17 Jan 42 to Eglinton
Apr 42 **Spitfire VB** (Oct 42)
16 Aug 42 to Angle
27 Sep 42 to Collyweston
30 Sep 42 to Wittering
10 Nov 42 en route N Africa
14 Nov 42 to Maison Blanche
Nov 42 **Spitfire VB** (Mar 43)
24 Nov 42 to Bone
25 Nov 42 to Souk el Arba
31 Dec 42 to Constantine
15 Jan 43 to Setif
3 Feb 43 to Souk el Khemis ('Paddington')
Mar 43 **Spitfire VC** (Nov 43)
16 May 43 to Protville
30 May 43 to Sousse

4 Jun 43 to Ta Kali
22 Jul 43 to Lentini
Aug 43 **Spitfire IX** (Nov 43)
6 Sep 43 to Milazzo
16 Sep 43 to Asa
25 Sep 43 to Serretelle
13 Oct 43 to Gioia del Colle
3 Nov 43 en route India
4 Dec 43 to Baigachi
Dec 43 **Spitfire VIII** (Mar 46)
21 Feb 44 to Double Moorings det Ramu
31 Mar 44 to Chittagong
17 Apr 44 to Rumkha
1 May 44 to Comilla
31 May 44 to Palel
6 Jul 44 to Imphal
5 Sep 44 to Tulihal
29 Oct 44 to Tamu
15 Jan 45 to Kan
7 Feb 45 to Sinthe
30 Apr 45 to 'Maida Vale'
25 May 45 to Thedaw
19 Jul 45 to Toungoo
29 Jul 45 to Thedaw
20 Aug 45 to Zayatkwin
11 Sep 45 to Bayan Lepas
12 Sep 45 to Kallang
26 Sep 45 to Tengah
Jan 46 **Spitfire XIV** (Mar 46)
0 Mar 46 DB
—
8 May 46 RF en route Malaya-India — No 136 Sqn renumbered
2 May 46 to Worli
3 May 46 to Yelahanka
May 46 **Spitfire VIII** (Jul 46)
8 Jun 46 to Risalpur
Jul 46 **Tempest F.2** (Jan 47)
5 Jan 47 DB
—
0 Jun 54 RF @ Wattisham
Jun 54 **Meteor NF 12** (Jul 58)
Jun 54 **Meteor NF 14** (Jul 58)
8 Jun 56 to Stradishall
6 Jan 57 to Wattisham
8 Aug 57 to Stradishall
1 Jul 58 DB
—
1 Oct 58 RF @ Muharraq — No 1417 Flt renumbered
Oct 58 **Pembroke C.1** (Nov 67)
Dec 58 **Twin Pioneer CC 1** (Nov 67)
Aug 63 **Twin Pioneer CC 2** (Nov 67) det Sharjah
5 Nov 67 DB

53 Sqn

Nov 18 F @ Hainault Farm — nucleus from 6th Bde units
Nov 18 **Camel** (Jun 19)
Jun 19 DB
—
Oct 41 RF @ Ballyhalbert — from 'A' Flt, No 256 Sqn
Oct 41 **Defiant I** (Apr 42) dets Limavady, Ballykelly, Eglinton, St Angelo
Jan 42 **Beaufighter IF** (Jan 43)
Nov 42 **Beaufighter VIF** (Sep 44)
Dec 42 to Portreath det Ballyhalbert
Dec 42 to Maison Blanche dets Ballyhalbert, Youks les Bains, Bone, Taher, La Sebala
Jul 43 to Reghaia dets Taher, La Sebala, La Senia, Alghero
Aug 44 **Hurricane IIC** (Sep 44)
Aug 44 **Spitfire VIII** (Sep 44)
Aug 44 **Spitfire IX** (Sep 44)
5 Sep 44 DB
—
7 Oct 44 RF @ Kirmington — nucleus from No 166 Sqn
Oct 44 **Lancaster I & III** (Sep 45)
15 Oct 44 to Scampton
28 Sep 45 DB
—
28 Feb 55 RF @ West Malling
Feb 55 **Meteor NF 12** (Jun 58)
Feb 55 **Meteor NF 14** (Jun 58)
17 Sep 57 to Waterbeach
2 Jul 58 DB — renumbered as No 25 Sqn

154 Sqn

7 Aug 18 F @ Chingford (for Bristol F2b Fighter) — nucleus from Nos 33, 37, 39 and 44 TDSs
11 Sep 18 DB
—
17 Nov 41 RF @ Fowlmere
Nov 41 **Spitfire IIA** (Apr 42)
Jan 42 **Spitfire IIB** (Apr 42)
Feb 42 **Spitfire VA** (Apr 42)
Feb 42 **Spitfire VB** (Aug 43)
12 Mar 42 to Coltishall det Fowlmere
5 Apr 42 to Fowlmere
7 May 42 to Church Stanton
7 Jun 42 to Hornchurch
27 Jul 42 to Fairlop
10 Aug 42 to Ipswich
15 Aug 42 to Fairlop
1 Sep 42 to Wellingore
1 Nov 42 en route N Africa
Nov 42 **Spitfire VC** (Feb 44)
12 Nov 42 to Djedjelli
5 Jan 43 to Bone
17 Jan 43 to Tingley
16 Mar 43 to Souk el Khemis ('Victoria')
13 May 43 to Protville
29 May 43 to Sousse
4 Jun 43 to Ta Kali
20 Jul 43 to Lentini
Jul 43 **Spitfire IX** (Oct 44)
6 Sep 43 to Milazzo
23 Sep 43 to Serretelle
13 Oct 43 to Gioia del Colle det Foggia
23 Dec 43 to Minnigh dets Lakatamia, Ramat David
18 Feb 43 to Almaza (No 22 PTC) dets Ramat David, Muqueibila
30 Mar 44 to Ajaccio
11 Apr 44 to Alto
19 Apr 44 to Poretta
11 Jul 44 to Calenzana
Aug 44 **Spitfire VIII** (Oct 44)
23 Aug 44 to Frejus
5 Sep 44 to Montelimar
19 Sep 44 to Le Vallon
11 Oct 44 to Gragnano (No 56 PTC)
29 Oct 44 DB
—
5 Nov 44 RF @ Biggin Hill
Nov 44 **Spitfire VII** (Feb 45)
Feb 45 **Mustang IV** (Mar 45)
1 Mar 45 to Hunsdon
19 Mar 45 DB

155 Sqn

14 Sep 18 F @ Chingford — nucleus from Nos 1, 26, 55 and 57 TDSs
Sep 18 **DH 9A** (Dec 18)
7 Dec 18 DB
—
1 Apr 42 RF @ Peshawar
2 Jun 42 to Lower Topa (No 1 Hill Depot)
27 Jun 42 to Peshawar
9 Jul 42 to St Thomas Mount
Aug 42 **Mohawk IV** (Jan 44) det Vizagapatam
18 Oct 42 to Alipore
24 Nov 42 to Agartala
1 Feb 43 to Rajyeswarpur det Imphal
4 Mar 43 to Imphal
1 Jul 43 to Agartala
10 Sep 43 to Imphal
8 Jan 44 to Alipore
Jan 44 **Spitfire VIII** (Dec 45)
22 Feb 44 to Baigachi
20 Mar 44 to Kalyanpur
23 Apr 44 to Baigachi
14 Aug 44 to Palel
30 Nov 44 to Sapam det Tamu
8 Jan 45 to Tulihal det Tabingaung
11 Feb 45 to Sadaung
6 Apr 45 to Dwelha
19 Apr 45 to Kwetnge
28 Apr 45 to 'Tennant' det Thedaw
23 May 45 to Toungoo
15 Aug 45 to Zayatkwin
11 Sep 45 to Bayan Lepas
12 Sep 45 to Kallang
24 Sep 45 to Tengah
Dec 45 **Spitfire XIV** (Aug 46)
4 Feb 46 to Medan
31 Aug 46 DB
—
1 Sep 54 RF @ Kuala Lumpur
Sep 54 **Whirlwind HAR 4** (Jun 59) dets Seletar, Kluang
3 Jun 59 DB — merged with No 194 Sqn to form No 110 Sqn

156 Sqn

12 Oct 18 F @ Wyton — nucleus Nos 27, 35, 52 and 53 TDSs
Nov 18 **DH 9A** (Nov 18)
9 Dec 18 DB
—
14 Feb 42 RF @ Alconbury — from UK echelon of No 40 Sqn
Feb 42 **Wellington IC** (Jun 42)
Feb 42 **Wellington III** (Jan 43)
8 Aug 42 to Warboys
Jan 43 **Lancaster I & III** (Sep 45)
5 Mar 44 to Upwood
27 Jun 45 to Wyton
25 Sep 45 DB

157 Sqn

14 Jul 18 F @ Upper Heyford — nucleus from CFS and Nos 3, 43 and 56 TDSs, used various aircraft
Nov 18 **Salamander** (Feb 19)
1 Feb 19 DB
—
15 Dec 41 RF @ Debden
18 Dec 41 to Castle Camps
Jan 42 **Mosquito II** (Jun 44)
15 Mar 43 to Bradwell Bay
13 May 43 to Hunsdon
Jul 43 **Mosquito VI** (Apr 44)
9 Nov 43 to Predannack
26 Mar 44 to Valley
7 May 44 to Swannington
May 44 **Mosquito XIX** (May 45)
21 Jul 44 to West Malling
29 Aug 44 to Swannington
Feb 45 **Mosquito XXX** (Aug 45)
16 Aug 45 DB

158 Sqn

4 Sep 18 F @ Upper Heyford (for Salamander) — nucleus from CFS and Nos 42, 50 and 53 TDSs
20 Nov 18 DB
—
14 Feb 42 RF @ Driffield — from UK echelon of No 104 Sqn
Feb 42 **Wellington II** (Jun 42)
6 Jun 42 to East Moor
Jun 42 **Halifax II** (Dec 43) dets Beaulieu, Manston
6 Nov 42 to Rufforth
28 Feb 43 to Lisset
Dec 43 **Halifax III** (May 45)
Apr 45 **Halifax VI** (May 45)
May 45 **Stirling V** (Dec 45)
17 Aug 45 to Stradishall
Nov 45 **Stirling IV** (Dec 45)
28 Dec 45 DB

159 Sqn

2 Jan 42 F @ Molesworth (ground echelon)
12 Feb 42 en route ME
15 Apr 42 to Fayid
10 May 42 en route FE (element remained Fayid)
24 May 42 to Deolali
1 Jun 42 to Chakrata
27 Sep 42 to Salbani
—
Jan 42 air echelon training at Polebrook (No 1653 HCU)
26 Apr 42 to Lyneham
May 42 **Liberator II** (Aug 43)
7 Jun 42 to Fayid (personnel from Nos 147, 159, 160, 454 & 458 Sqns)
2 Jul 42 to St Jean
12 Aug 42 to Aqir
16 Sep 42 joint sqn restyled as No 160 Sqn. No 159 Sqn aircraft to FE
27 Sep 42 to Salbani
—
Jul 43 **Liberator V** (Aug 43)
Aug 43 **Liberator III** (Jun 44) det Dudhkundi
24 Oct 43 to Digri det Dhubalia
9 Mar 44 to Dhubalia
Mar 44 **Liberator VI** (Jul 45) det Madhaiganj
15 Apr 44 to Digri
Jul 44 **Liberator V** (Feb 45) dets Jessore, Akyab, China Bay, Drigh Road, Pegu
Jun 45 **Liberator VIII** (Jun 46)
2 Oct 45 to Salbani dets Pegu, Santa Cruz, Sookerating
1 Jun 46 DB

160 Sqn

16 Jan 42 F @ Thurleigh (ground echelon)
12 Feb 42 en route FE
4 Jun 42 to Drigh Road
17 Jun 42 to Quetta
—
Jan 42 air echelon training at Polebrook (No 1653 HCU)
26 Apr 42 to Lyneham
May 42 **Liberator II** (Jan 43)
7 May 42 to Nutts Corner
30 May 42 to Lyneham
11 Jun 42 to Fayid (effectively absorbed into No 159 Sqn)

16 Sep 42 to Aqir — No 159 Sqn (jointly manned by personnel from Nos 147, 159, 160 and 454 Sqns) restyled as No 160 Sqn
8 Nov 42 to Shandur
15 Jan 43 absorbed by No 178 Sqn
—
22 Nov 42 to Salbani
19 Feb 43 to Ratmalana
Mar 43 **Liberator III** (Oct 45)
Jun 43 **Liberator V** (Nov 45)
2 Aug 43 to Sigiriya
dets Cuttack, Addu Atoll
Jan 44 **Liberator VI** (Feb 45)
31 Jul 44 to Kankesanterai
dets Addu Atoll, Kandy
7 Feb 45 to Minneriya
Sep 45 **Liberator VIII** (Oct 46)
17 Oct 45 to Kankesanterai
23 Jun 46 to Leuchars
Aug 46 **Lancaster GR 3** (Oct 46)
1 Oct 46 DB — renumbered as No 120 Sqn

161 Sqn

15 Feb 42 F @ Newmarket — nucleus from No 138 Sqn & the King's Flt
Feb 42 **Lysander IIIA** (Jun 45)
Feb 42 **Hudson I** (Aug 44)
Feb 42 **Whitley V** (Dec 42)
1 Mar 42 to Graveley
8 Apr 42 to Tempsford
Sep 42 **Halifax II** (Dec 42)
Oct 42 **Halifax V** (Oct 44)
Oct 42 **Albemarle I** (Apr 43)
Oct 42 **Havoc I** (Dec 43)
det St Eval (Albemarle, Havoc, Hudson)
det Tangmere (Lysander)
det Kinloss (Halifax)
Sep 43 **Hudson IIIA** (Jun 45)
Sep 43 **Hudson V** (Jun 45)
det Winkleigh (Lysander)
Sep 44 **Stirling IV** (Jun 45)
2 Jun 45 DB

162 Sqn

4 Jan 42 F @ Kabrit — from a detachment of No 109 Sqn. At first referred to as 'the Signals Squadron' but by 1 Mar 42 the No 162 Sqn numberplate was in use.
Jan 42 **Wellington IC** (Feb 44)
6 Jan 42 to Shallufa
dets LG 09, Idku, LG 104, Aqir, Nicosia, Bilbeis
Feb 42 **Blenheim IV** (Jul 42)
12 Apr 42 to Bilbeis
dets Maaten Bagush, Habbaniyah, Shaibah, Nicosia, Luqa, Rayak, LG 86, Mersah Matruh, Aqir, Lydda, Gambut, Misurata, Mellaha
Jul 42 **Blenheim V** (Jan 44)
4 Apr 43 to Benina
dets Gambut, Luqa, Lydda, Mellaha
27 Aug 43 to LG 91
dets Gambut, Nicosia
Sep 43 **Wellington III** (Nov 43)
Sep 43 **Baltimore II** (Jan 44)
Oct 43 **Baltimore I** (Nov 43)
Oct 43 **Mosquito VI** (Jan 44)
Jan 44 **Wellington III** (Jul 44)
Jan 44 **Baltimore III** (Sep 44)
Mar 44 **Wellington DW I** (Jul 44)
20 Apr 44 to Idku
dets Lakatamia, St Jean, Benina
Apr 44 **Wellington X** (Sep 44)
Apr 44 **Mosquito VI** (Jul 44)
25 Sep 44 DB
—
16 Dec 44 RF @ Bourn
Dec 44 **Mosquito XXV** (Jul 46)
Feb 45 **Mosquito XX** (Jul 46)
10 Jul 45 to Blackbushe
14 Jul 46 DB

163 Sqn

10 Jul 42 F @ Suez
15 Jul 42 to Asmara
Jul 42 **Hudson IIIA** (Aug 42)
Jul 42 **Hudson VI** (Dec 42)
18 Dec 42 reduced to a cadre
16 Jun 43 DB
—
25 Jan 45 RF @ Wyton
Jan 45 **Mosquito XXV** (May 45)
May 45 **Mosquito XVI** (Aug 45)
10 Aug 45 DB

164 Sqn

6 Apr 42 F @ Peterhead
Apr 42 **Spitfire VA** (Sep 42)
5 May 42 to Skaebrae
det Sumburgh
10 Sep 42 to Peterhead
Sep 42 **Spitfire VB** (Feb 43)
det Tangmere
29 Jan 43 to Fairwood Common
det Peterhead
Feb 43 **Hurricane IID** (May 43)
Feb 43 **Hurricane IV** (Feb 44)
8 Feb 43 to Middle Wallop
20 Jun 43 to Warmwell
6 Aug 43 to Manston
22 Sep 43 to Fairlop
4 Jan 44 to Twinwood Farm
13 Jan 44 to Fairlop
Jan 44 **Typhoon IB** (May 45)
11 Feb 44 to Twinwood Farm
8 Mar 44 to Acklington
16 Mar 44 to Thorney Island
12 Apr 44 to Llanbedr
21 Apr 44 to Thorney Island
18 Jun 44 to Funtington
22 Jun 44 to Hurn
17 Jul 44 to B 8/Sommervieu
20 Jul 44 to B 7/Martragny
3 Sep 44 to B 23/Morainville
6 Sep 44 to B 35/Godelmesnil
13 Sep 44 to B 53/Merville
30 Oct 44 to B 67/Ursel
26 Nov 44 to B 77/Gilze-Rijen
12 Dec 44 to Fairwood Common
26 Dec 44 to B 77/Gilze-Rijen
1 Jan 45 to A 84/Chiévres
19 Jan 45 to B 77/Gilze-Rijen
21 Mar 45 to B 91/Kluis
17 Apr 45 to B 103/Plantlunne
27 May 45 to B 116/Wunstorf
17 Jun 45 to Milfield
17 Jun 45 to Turnhouse
Jun 45 **Spitfire IX** (Jul 46)
20 Nov 45 to Fairwood Common
6 Jan 46 to Turnhouse
25 Mar 46 to Tangmere
26 Apr 46 to Middle Wallop
Jul 46 **Spitfire LF XVIE** (Aug 46)
31 Aug 46 DB — renumbered as No 63 Sqn

165 Sqn

6 Apr 42 F @ Ayr
Apr 42 **Spitfire VA** (Jun 42)
dets Drem, Turnhouse
May 42 **Spitfire VB** (Oct 43)
15 Aug 42 to Eastchurch
20 Aug 42 to Gravesend
dets Martlesham Heath, Tangmere, Predannack
2 Nov 42 to Tangmere
9 Mar 43 to Martlesham Heath
23 Mar 43 to Tangmere
29 Mar 43 to Peterhead
det Dyce
30 Jun 43 to Ibsley
Jul 43 **Spitfire VC** (Oct 43)
30 Jul 43 to Exeter
8 Aug 43 to Kenley
17 Sep 43 to Church Stanton/ Culmhead
Sep 43 **Spitfire IXB** (Jan 45)
10 Feb 44 to Colerne
1 Mar 44 to Fairwood Common
7 Mar 44 to Colerne
10 Mar 44 to Culmhead
2 Apr 44 to Predannack
20 Jun 44 to Harrowbeer
22 Jun 44 to Detling
12 Jul 44 to Lympne
10 Aug 44 to Detling
15 Dec 44 to Bentwaters
Jan 45 **Mustang III** (May 45)
May 45 **Spitfire IXE** (Sep 46)
29 May 45 to Dyce
15 Jun 45 to Vaernes
30 Dec 45 to Charterhall
24 Jan 46 to Duxford
3 Jul 46 to Middle Wallop
8 Jul 46 to Duxford
1 Sep 46 DB — renumbered as No 66 Sqn

166 Sqn

13 Jun 18 F @ Bircham Newton
Jun 18 **FE 2B** (Oct 18)
Oct 18 **HP V/1500** (May 19)
31 May 19 DB
—
1 Nov 36 RF @ Boscombe Down — from 'B' Flt, No 97 Sqn
Nov 36 **Heyford III** (Sep 39)
20 Jan 37 to Leconfield
Jun 39 **Whitley I** (Feb 40)
dets Benson, Boscombe Down
17 Sep 39 to Abingdon
Dec 39 **Whitley III** (Apr 40)
det Jurby
6 Apr 40 DB — merged into 10 OTU
—
27 Jan 43 RF @ Kirmington — from the UK echelons of Nos 142 & 150 Sqns
Jan 43 **Wellington III** (Apr 43)
Feb 43 **Wellington X** (Sep 43)
Sep 43 **Lancaster I & III** (Nov 45)
18 Nov 45 DB

167 Sqn

18 Nov 18 F @ Bircham Newton
Nov 18 **HP V/1500** (May 19)
21 May 19 DB
—
6 Apr 42 RF @ Scorton
Apr 42 **Spitfire VB** (Jun 43)
det Acklington
1 Jun 42 to Castletown
det Peterhead
14 Oct 42 to Ludham
Oct 42 **Spitfire VC** (Jun 43)
1 Mar 43 to Kidlington
5 Mar 43 to Fowlmere
13 Mar 43 to Ludham
13 May 43 to Digby
18 May 43 to Hornchurch
21 May 43 to Westhampnett
12 Jun 43 to Woodvale
12 Jun 43 DB — renumbered as No 322 Sqn
—
1 Oct 44 RF @ Holmsley South
Nov 44 **Warwick I** (May 45)
Nov 44 **Warwick III** (Feb 46)
30 Mar 45 to Blackbushe
Apr 45 **Anson XII** (Feb 46)
det Croydon
Jun 45 **Dakota** (Jan 46) — @ Croydon, No 147 Sqn aircraft
1 Feb 46 DB
—
1 Feb 53 RF @ Abingdon — from the Overseas Ferry Unit
16 Apr 53 to Benson
15 Sep 58 DB — merged with No 147 Sqn to form the Ferry Sqn

168 Sqn

15 Jun 42 F @ Snailwell — nucleus from No 268 Sqn
Jun 42 **Tomahawk II** (Nov 42)
13 Jul 42 to Bottisham
det Tangmere
18 Nov 42 to Odiham
Nov 42 **Mustang I** (Aug 43)
1 Mar 43 to Weston Zoyland
17 Mar 43 to Odiham
Aug 43 **Mustang IA** (Feb 44)
20 Sep 43 to Hutton Cranswick
10 Oct 43 to Huggate
15 Oct 43 to Thruxton
12 Nov 43 to Sawbridgeworth
30 Nov 43 to North Weald
21 Jan 44 to Llanbedr
4 Feb 44 to North Weald
det Benson
21 Feb 44 to Odiham
Feb 44 **Mustang I** (Oct 44)
det Benson
6 Mar 44 to Gatwick
31 Mar 44 to Odiham
29 Jun 44 to B 8/Sommervieu
14 Aug 44 to B 21/Ste-Honorine-de Ducy
2 Sep 44 to B 34/Avrilly
21 Sep 44 to B 66/Blankenberg
Sep 44 **Typhoon IB** (Feb 45)
4 Oct 44 to B 78/Eindhoven
26 Feb 45 DB

169 Sqn

15 Jun 42 F @ Twinwood Farm — nucleus from No 613 Sq
Jun 42 **Mustang I** (Sep 43)
27 Jun 42 to Doncaster
dets Twinwood Farm, Kirton-in-Lindsey, Clifton
12 Oct 42 to Weston Zoyland
18 Oct 42 to Doncaster
det Kirton-in-Lindsey
15 Nov 42 to Clifton
18 Dec 42 to Duxford
1 Mar 43 to Barford St John
5 Mar 43 to Gransden Lodge
10 Mar 43 to Bottisham
12 Mar 43 to Duxford
26 Mar 43 to Andover
21 Jun 43 to Middle Wallop
30 Sep 43 DB
—
1 Oct 43 RF @ Ayr
8 Dec 43 to Little Snoring
Jan 44 **Mosquito II** (Jul 44)
4 Jun 44 to Great Massingham
Jun 44 **Mosquito VI** (Aug 45)
Jan 45 **Mosquito XIX** (Aug 45)
10 Aug 45 DB

170 Sqn

Jun 42 F @ Weston Zoyland
Jun 42 **Mustang I** (Aug 43)
Jun 42 to Hurn
Oct 42 to Thruxton
Oct 42 to Andover
dets Weston Zoyland, Ibsley, Snailwell, Barford St John
Feb 43 to Ford
Mar 43 to Andover
Mar 43 to Snailwell
det Weston Zoyland
Jun 43 to Odiham
det Tangmere
Aug 43 **Mustang IA** (Jan 44)
Sep 43 to Hutton Cranswick
Oct 43 to Huggate
Oct 43 to Thruxton
det Benson
Nov 43 to Sawbridgeworth
Jan 44 DB
—
Oct 44 RF @ Kelstern — from 'C' Flt, No 625 Sqn
Oct 44 **Lancaster I & III** (Nov 45)
Oct 44 to Dunholme Lodge
Nov 44 to Hemswell
Nov 45 DB

171 Sqn

Jun 42 F @ Gatwick
Jun 42 **Tomahawk I** (Dec 42)
Jul 42 to Odiham
Aug 42 to Gatwick
Sep 42 **Mustang IA** (Dec 42)
Sep 42 to Weston Zoyland
Sep 42 to Gatwick
Dec 42 to Hartford Bridge
Feb 43 DB — provided nucleus for No 430 Sqn
—
Sep 44 RF @ North Creake — from 'C' Flt, No 199 Sqn
Sep 44 **Stirling III** (Jan 45)
Oct 44 **Halifax III** (Jul 45)
Jul 45 DB

172 Sqn

Apr 42 F @ Chivenor — from No 1417 (Leigh Light) Flt
Apr 42 **Wellington VIII** (Mar 43)
det Skitten
Dec 42 **Wellington XII** (Oct 43)
Aug 43 **Wellington XIV** (Jun 45)
dets Lagens, Gibraltar
Sep 44 to Limavady
Jun 45 DB

173 Sqn

Jul 42 F @ Heliopolis
Jun 42 **Audax** (Feb 43)
Jul 42 **Lysander II** (Jul 43)
Jul 42 **Hart** (Aug 43)
Jul 42 **Hurricane I** (Sep 43)
Jul 42 **Blenheim IV** (Sep 43)
Jul 42 **Oxford** (Sep 43)
Jul 42 **Moth Major** (Oct 43)
Jul 42 **Gull Six** (Oct 43)
Jul 42 **Magister I** (Oct 43)
Jul 42 **Boston III** (Jan 44)
Jul 42 **Electra** (Jan 44)
Jul 42 **Proctor I** (Feb 44)
Jul 42 **Lodestar** (Feb 44)
Jul 42 **Argus** (Feb 44)
Aug 42 **Dragon Rapide** (Oct 42)
Dec 42 **SM 79** (Jan 43)
Feb 43 **Reliant** (Feb 43)
Feb 43 **Junkers Ju 52/3m** (Feb 43)
Feb 43 **Scion Senior** (Sep 43)
Mar 43 **Hardy** (Apr 43)
Apr 43 **Beaufighter IF** (Sep 43)
Sep 43 **Anson I** (Feb 44)
29 Feb 44 DB — renamed ME Communications Sqn
—
1 Feb 53 RF @ Hawarden — No 4 (Home) Ferry Unit renamed
Feb 53 **Anson C.19** (Sep 57)
Feb 55 **Varsity T.1** (Sep 57)
2 Sep 57 DB

174 Sqn

3 Mar 42 F @ Manston — nucleus from No 607 Sqn
Mar 42 **Hurricane IIB** (Apr 43)
det Ford
9 Jul 42 to Fowlmere
12 Jul 42 to Manston
1 Sep 42 to Warmwell
21 Sep 42 to Manston
6 Dec 42 to Odiham
1 Mar 43 to Chilbolton
11 Mar 43 to Grove
12 Mar 43 to Zeals
det Odiham
5 Apr 43 to Gravesend
Apr 43 **Typhoon IB** (Apr 45)
12 Jun 43 to Merston
1 Jul 43 to Lydd
det Wigtown
10 Oct 43 to Westhampnett
21 Jan 44 to Eastchurch
4 Feb 44 to Westhampnett
1 Apr 44 to Holmsley South
17 Jun 44 to B 5/Camilly
19 Jun 44 to B 2/Bazenville
24 Jun 44 to B 5/Camilly
28 Aug 44 to B 24/St-André-de-l'Eure
2 Sep 44 to B 40/Beauvais
4 Sep 44 to B 50/Vitry-en-Artois
17 Sep 44 to B 70/Deurne
1 Oct 44 to B 80/Volkel
10 Nov 44 to Warmwell
21 Nov 44 to B 80/Volkel
21 Mar 45 to B 100/Goch
10 Apr 45 DB
—
26 Aug 45 RF @ B 158/Lübeck — No 137 Sqn renumbered
Aug 45 **Typhoon IB** (Sep 45)
7 Sep 45 DB
—
7 Sep 45 RF @ Warmwell — No 274 Sqn renumbered
Sep 45 **Tempest V** (Apr 46)
19 Sep 45 to B 155/Dedelsdorf
19 Oct 45 to Gatow
26 Nov 45 to B 152/Fassberg
20 Apr 46 DB

175 Sqn

3 Mar 42 F @ Warmwell
Mar 42 **Hurricane IIB** (Apr 43)
det Ibsley
10 Oct 42 to Harrowbeer
9 Dec 42 to Gatwick
14 Jan 43 to Odiham
1 Mar 43 to Stoney Cross
11 Mar 43 to Lasham
13 Mar 43 to Odiham
19 Mar 43 to Stoney Cross
8 Apr 43 to Colerne
Apr 43 **Typhoon IB** (Sep 45)
29 May 43 to Lasham
2 Jun 43 to Appledram
1 Jul 43 to Lydd
det Wigtown
9 Oct 43 to Westhampnett
24 Feb 44 to Eastchurch
8 Mar 44 to Westhampnett
1 Apr 44 to Holmsley South
20 Jun 44 to B 3/Ste-Croix-sur-Mer
24 Jun 44 to B 5/Camilly
28 Aug 44 to B 24/St-André-de-l'Eure
2 Sep 44 to B 42/Tillé
4 Sep 44 to B 50/Vitry-en-Artois
17 Sep 44 to B 70/Deurne
30 Sep 44 to B 80/Volkel
21 Nov 44 to Warmwell
4 Dec 44 to B 80/Volkel
21 Mar 45 to B 100/Goch
11 Apr 45 to B 110/Achmer
19 Apr 45 to B 150/Hustedt
27 May 45 to Warmwell
11 Jun 45 to Manston
16 Jun 45 to B 164/Schleswig
22 Aug 45 to B 160/Kastrup
5 Sep 45 to B 164/Schleswig
30 Sep 45 DB

176 Sqn

15 Jan 43 F @ Dum Dum — from det of No 89 Sqn
Jan 43 **Beaufighter IF** (Aug 43)
Jan 43 **Beaufighter VIF** (Aug 45)
6 Feb 43 to Baigachi
May 43 **Hurricane IIC** (Jan 44)
dets Feni, Kangla, Chittagong, Tulihal, Ratmalana, Vavuniya
18 Aug 44 to Vavuniya
dets Ratmalana, St Thomas Mount
21 Aug 44 to Minneriya
dets Ratmalana, St Thomas Mount, Chittagong, Cox's Bazaar
31 Mar 45 to Baigachi
dets Cox's Bazaar, Akyab, Mingaladon
Jun 45 **Mosquito XVI** (Jul 45)
Jul 45 **Mosquito XIX** (Jun 46)
1 Jun 46 DB

177 Sqn

11 Jan 43 F @ Amarda Road
16 Mar 43 to Allahabad
May 43 **Beaufighter VIC** (May 44)
6 May 43 to Phaphamau
13 Aug 43 to Chittagong
25 Aug 43 to Feni
Nov 43 **Beaufighter X** (Jul 45)
Nov 43 **Beaufighter XI** (May 44)
31 May 44 to Ranchi
det Tulihal
14 Aug 44 to Chiringa
det Tulihal
1 Feb 45 to Ranchi
10 Feb 45 to Chiringa
24 Jun 45 to Hathazari
1 Jul 45 DB

178 Sqn

15 Jan 43 F @ Shandur — aircrews from No 160 Sqn, ME Det. Groundcrews from Nos 147 Sqn, and Nos 159 & 160 Sqns, ME Dets
Jan 43 **Liberator II** (Dec 43)
4 Mar 43 to Hosc Raui (Ghemines)
det Shandur
May 43 **Halifax II** (Sep 43)
Sep 43 **Liberator III** (Jul 44)
1 Oct 43 to Terria
det El Adem
1 Jan 44 to El Adem
Jan 44 **Liberator VI** (Jan 46)
1 Mar 44 to Celone
4 Jul 44 to Amendola
det Ein Shemar
25 Aug 45 to Ein Shemar
5 Nov 45 to Fayid
Nov 45 **Lancaster III** (Apr 46)
15 Apr 46 DB — renumbered as No 70 Sqn

179 Sqn

1 Sep 42 F @ Skitten — from Flt of No 172 Sqn
Sep 42 **Wellington VIII** (Sep 43)
18 Nov 42 to Gibraltar
dets Agadir, Blida
Aug 43 **Wellington XIV** (Nov 44)
det Lagens
28 Apr 44 to Predannack
6 Sep 44 to Chivenor
21 Sep 44 to Benbecula
23 Oct 44 to Chivenor
1 Nov 44 to St Eval
Nov 44 **Warwick V** (May 46)
Feb 46 **Lancaster ASR 3** (Sep 46)
30 Sep 46 DB — absorbed into No 210 Sqn

180 Sqn

11 Sep 42 F @ West Raynham
Sep 42 **Mitchell II** (Apr 45)
19 Oct 42 to Foulsham
18 Aug 43 to Dunsfold
det Aston Down
12 Apr 44 to Swanton Morley
26 Apr 44 to Dunsfold
18 Oct 44 to B 58/Melsbroek
Dec 44 **Mitchell III** (Sep 45)
30 Apr 45 to B 110/Achmer
7 Jun 45 to Fersfield
14 Jun 45 to B 110/Achmer
det A 75/Epinoy
17 Sep 45 to B 58/Melsbroek
Sep 45 **Mosquito XVI** (Mar 46)
8 Mar 46 to Wahn
31 Mar 46 DB — renumbered as No 69 Sqn

181 Sqn

25 Aug 42 F @ Duxford
Sep 42 **Hurricane I** (Dec 42)
Sep 42 **Typhoon IA** (Dec 42)
Sep 42 **Typhoon IB** (Sep 45)
10 Dec 42 to Snailwell
1 Mar 43 to Cranfield
8 Mar 43 to Snailwell
24 Mar 43 to Gravesend
5 Apr 43 to Lasham
2 Jun 43 to Appledram
3 Jul 43 to New Romney
8 Oct 43 to Merston
31 Dec 43 to Odiham
13 Jan 44 to Merston
6 Feb 44 to Eastchurch
21 Feb 44 to Merston
1 Apr 44 to Hurn
20 Jun 44 to B 6/Coulombs
31 Aug 44 to B 30/Créton
3 Sep 44 to B 48/Amiens/Glisy
6 Sep 44 to B 58/Melsbroek
22 Sep 44 to B 78/Eindhoven
12 Jan 45 to Warmwell
3 Feb 45 to B 86/Helmond
11 Apr 45 to B 106/Twente
13 Apr 45 to B 112/Hopsten
18 Apr 45 to B 120/Langenhagen
1 May 45 to B 156/Lüneburg
7 May 45 to B 158/Lübeck
7 Jul 45 to B 160/Kastrup
21 Jul 45 to Warmwell
4 Aug 45 to B 160/Kastrup
6 Sep 45 to B 166/Flensburg
9 Sep 45 to B 164/Schleswig
30 Sep 45 DB

182 Sqn

25 Aug 42 F @ Martlesham Heath
Sep 42 **Hurricane I** (Oct 42)
Sep 42 **Typhoon IA** (Jan 43)
Sep 42 **Typhoon IB** (Sep 45)
7 Dec 42 to Sawbridgeworth
17 Jan 43 to Snailwell
20 Jan 43 to Sawbridgeworth
30 Jan 43 to Martlesham Heath
1 Mar 43 to Middle Wallop
5 Apr 43 to Fairlop
29 Apr 43 to Lasham
2 Jun 43 to Appledram
2 Jul 43 to New Romney det Wigtown
12 Oct 43 to Merston
31 Dec 43 to Odiham
5 Jan 44 to Eastchurch
23 Jan 44 to Merston
1 Apr 44 to Hurn
20 Jun 44 to B 6/Coulombs
22 Jun 44 to Holmsley South
3 Jul 44 to B 6/Coulombs
28 Aug 44 to B 30/Créton
3 Sep 44 to B 48/Amiens/Glisy
6 Sep 44 to B 58/Melsbroek
22 Sep 44 to B 78/Eindoven
13 Jan 45 to B 86/Helmond
3 Feb 45 to Warmwell
21 Feb 45 to B 86/Helmond
11 Apr 45 to B 106/Twente
13 Apr 45 to B 112/Hopsten
17 Apr 45 to B 120/Langenhagen
1 May 45 to B 156/Lüneburg
7 May 45 to B 158/Lübeck
11 Jul 45 to B 160/Kastrup
5 Aug 45 to Warmwell
19 Aug 45 to B 160/Kastrup
5 Sep 45 to B 166/Flensburg
8 Sep 45 to B 164/Schleswig
30 Sep 45 DB

183 Sqn

1 Nov 42 F @ Church Fenton
Nov 42 **Hurricane I** (Feb 43)
Nov 42 **Typhoon IA** (Dec 42)
Nov 42 **Typhoon IB** (Jun 45)
1 Mar 43 to Cranfield
8 Mar 43 to Snailwell
12 Mar 43 to Church Fenton
24 Mar 43 to Colerne
8 Apr 43 to Gatwick
3 May 43 to Lasham
30 May 43 to Colerne
5 Jun 43 to Harrowbeer
4 Aug 43 to Tangmere
18 Sep 43 to Perranporth
14 Oct 43 to Predannack
1 Feb 44 to Tangmere
15 Mar 44 to Manston
1 Apr 44 to Thorney Island
11 Apr 44 to Llanbedr
22 Apr 44 to Thorney Island
18 Jun 44 to Funtington
1 Jul 44 to Hurn
14 Jul 44 to Eastchurch
25 Jul 44 to B 7/Martragny
3 Sep 44 to B 23/Morainville
6 Sep 44 to B 35/Godelmesnil
11 Sep 44 to B 53/Merville
29 Oct 44 to B 67/Ursel
26 Nov 44 to B 77/Gilze-Rijen
1 Jan 45 to A 84/Chièvres
19 Jan 45 to B 77/Gilze-Rijen
21 Mar 45 to B 91/Kluis
17 Apr 45 to B 103/Plantlunne
27 May 45 to B 116/Wunstorf
16 Jun 45 to Milfield
17 Jun 45 to Chilbolton
Jun 45 **Spitfire IX** (Nov 45)
8 Oct 45 to Fairwood Common
Oct 45 **Tempest II** (Nov 45)
15 Nov 45 to Chilbolton
15 Nov 45 DB — renumbered as No 54 Sqn

184 Sqn

1 Dec 42 F @ Colerne
Dec 42 **Hurricane IID** (May 43) det Milfield
1 Mar 43 to Chilbolton
11 Mar 43 to Grove
12 Mar 43 to Zeals
5 Apr 43 to Eastchurch det Milfield
May 43 **Hurricane IV** (Mar 44)
31 May 43 to Merston
12 Jun 43 to Manston
14 Aug 43 to Kingsnorth
18 Aug 43 to Newchurch
15 Sep 43 to Snailwell
17 Sep 43 to Newchurch
Oct 43 **Spitfire VB** (Oct 43)
12 Oct 43 to Detling
6 Mar 44 to Odiham
Mar 44 **Typhoon IB** (Sep 45)
11 Mar 44 to Eastchurch
3 Apr 44 to Odiham
23 Apr 44 to Westhampnett
14 May 44 to Holmsley South
20 May 44 to Westhampnett
17 Jun 44 to Holmsley South
27 Jun 44 to B 10/Plumetot
16 Jul 44 to B 5/Camilly
28 Aug 44 to B 24/St-André-de-l'Eure
2 Sep 44 to B 42/Tillé
4 Sep 44 to B 50/Vitry-en-Artois
17 Sep 44 to B 70/Deurne
30 Sep 44 to B 80/Volkel
4 Dec 44 to Warmwell
18 Dec 44 to B 80/Volkel
21 Mar 45 to B 100/Goch
11 Apr 45 to B 110/Achmer
18 Apr 45 to B 150/Hustedt
7 May 45 to Warmwell
28 May 45 to B 164/Schleswig
2 Aug 45 to B 160/Kastrup
29 Aug 45 DB

185 Sqn

21 Oct 18 F @ East Fortune — nucleus from Nos 31, 33, 39 & 49 TDS
Nov 18 **Cuckoo** (Apr 19)
9 Apr 19 reduced to a cadre
14 Apr 19 DB — (listed as a cadre until 6 Nov 19 when it was DB retrospectively)
—
1 Mar 38 RF @ Abingdon — from 'B' Flt, No 40 Sqn
Mar 38 **Hind** (Jul 38)
Jun 38 **Battle** (Jun 39) det Thornaby
1 Sep 38 to Thornaby
27 Sep 38 to Grantham
15 Oct 38 to Thornaby
Jun 39 **Hampden** (Apr 40)
Aug 39 **Hereford** (Apr 40)
Aug 39 **Anson I** (Apr 40)
24 Aug 39 to Cottesmore
8 Apr 40 DB — merged into No 14 OTU
—
8 Apr 40 RF @ Cottesmore
Apr 40 **Hampden** (May 40)
17 May 40 DB
—
12 May 41 RF @ Hal Far — from elements of No 261 Sqn & No 1430 Flt
May 41 **Hurricane I** (Jun 42)
May 41 **Hurricane IIA & IIC** (Jun 42) dets Ta Kali, Luqa
May 42 **Spitfire VC** (Sep 44)
5 Jun 43 to Krendi
Jun 43 **Spitfire IX** (Jul 44)
23 Sep 43 to Hal Far dets Grottaglie, Brindisi, Catania
29 Jul 44 to Grottaglie
2 Aug 44 to Perugia
Aug 44 **Spitfire VIII** (Sep 44)
23 Aug 44 to Loreto
4 Sep 44 to Fano
17 Sep 44 to Borghetto
Sep 44 **Spitfire IX** (Aug 45)
2 Oct 44 to Fano
17 Nov 44 to Peretola
31 Dec 44 to Pontedera
Mar 45 **Spitfire VIII** (Apr 45)
25 Apr 45 to Bologna
1 May 45 to Villafranca
16 May 45 to Campoformido
14 Aug 45 DB
—
15 Sep 51 RF @ Hal Far
Sep 51 **Vampire FB 5** (May 53)
23 Jul 52 to Luqa
14 Aug 52 to Idris
8 Sep 52 to Nicosia
13 Oct 52 to Habbaniyah
1 May 53 DB

186 Sqn

Formed from volunteers from No 185 Sqn on board HMS *Argus*, No 186 Sqn was intended for anti-shipping operations in the Caspian Sea from Baku. Deployment was cancelled 17 Feb 19 and the sqn was put ashore at Gosport (via Devonport) where it was re-established as a torpedo development unit. The planned aircraft were replaced by DH 9As and delivered to Russia by HMS *Ark Royal* where they were used by Nos 47 and 221 Sqns.

31 Dec 18 F on board HMS *Argus*
17 Feb 19 to Gosport
Jun 19 **Cuckoo** (Feb 20)
1 Feb 20 DB — renumbered as No 210 Sqn
—
27 Apr 43 RF @ Drem
3 Aug 43 to Ayr
Aug 43 **Hurricane IV** (Jan 44)
Nov 43 **Typhoon IB** (Feb 44)
7 Jan 44 to Tain
Feb 44 **Spitfire VB** (Apr 44)
1 Mar 44 to Lympne
5 Apr 44 DB — renumbered as No 130 Sqn
—
1 Oct 44 RF @ Tuddenham
Oct 44 **Lancaster I & III** (Jul 45)
17 Dec 44 to Stradishall
17 Jul 45 DB

187 Sqn

1 Feb 45 F @ Merryfield — nucleus from Halifax Development Flt of No 246 Sqn
Feb 45 **Halifax III** (Mar 45)
Mar 45 **Dakota** (Oct 46)
17 Sep 45 to Membury det Bari
11 Oct 46 to Netheravon dets Bari, Schwecat
1 Dec 46 DB — renumbered as No 53 Sqn
—
1 Feb 53 RF @ Aston Down — No 2 Home Ferry Unit renumbered
Feb 53 **Anson C.19** (Sep 57)
Mar 55 **Varsity T.1** (Sep 57)
Apr 55 **Anson C.12** (Sep 57)
2 Sep 57 DB

189 Sqn

15 Oct 44 F @ Bardney
Oct 44 **Lancaster I & III** (Nov 45)
2 Nov 44 to Fulbeck
8 Apr 45 to Bardney
15 Oct 45 to Metheringham
20 Nov 45 DB

190 Sqn

17 Feb 43 F @ Sullom Voe — nucleus from No 210 S
Feb 43 **Catalina IB** (Dec 43) det Reykjavik
Oct 43 **Catalina IV** (Dec 43)
1 Jan 44 DB — renumbered as No 210 Sqn
—
5 Jan 44 RF @ Leicester East
Jan 44 **Stirling IV** (Jun 45)
25 Mar 44 to Fairford
14 Oct 44 to Great Dunmow
May 45 **Halifax III** (Jan 46)
May 45 **Halifax VII** (Jan 46)
21 Jan 46 DB — renumbered as No 295 Sqn (at Tarran Rushton)

191 Sqn

17 May 43 F @ Korangi Creek
May 43 **Catalina IB** (Nov 44) dets Red Hills Lake, Jiwani, Trombay, Coc
Aug 44 **Catalina IVB** (Jun 45)
18 Nov 44 to Red Hills Lake dets Coconada, Trombay, Korangi Creek, Koggala
27 Apr 45 to Koggala
Apr 45 **Catalina IB** (Jun 45) det Korangi Creek
15 Jun 45 DB

192 Sqn

4 Jan 43 F @ Gransden Lodge from No 1474 Flt
Jan 43 **Wellington IC** (Mar 4
Jan 43 **Wellington III** (Mar 4
Jan 43 **Wellington X** (Jan 45)
Jan 43 **Mosquito IV** (Mar 45)
Mar 43 **Halifax II** (Jul 43)
5 Apr 43 to Feltwell
Jul 43 **Halifax V** (Mar 44)
25 Nov 43 to Foulsham
Mar 44 **Halifax III** (Aug 45)
Feb 45 **Mosquito XVI** (Aug 4
Aug 45 **Anson I** (Aug 45)
Aug 45 **Oxford** (Aug 45)
22 Aug 45 DB — became Centra Signals Establishment
—
15 Jul 51 RF @ Watton
Jul 51 **Mosquito PR 34** (Sep
Jul 51 **Lincoln B.2** (Feb 53)
Apr 52 **Washington B.1** (Feb
Jan 53 **Canberra B.2** (Aug 58
Jul 54 **Canberra B.6** (Aug 58
Dec 54 **Varsity T.1** (Mar 56)
Jul 57 **Comet C.2(R)** (Aug 58
21 Aug 58 DB — renumbered as No 51 Sqn

93 Sqn

Dec 42 F @ Harrowbeer
Jan 43 **Hurricane II** (Feb 43)
Jan 43 **Typhoon IB** (Aug 45)
Aug 43 to Gravesend
Sep 43 to Harrowbeer
Feb 44 to Fairlop
Mar 44 to Thorney Island
Apr 44 to Llanbedr
Apr 44 to Needs Oar Point
Jul 44 to Hurn
Jul 14 to B 15/Ryes
Jul 44 to B 3/Ste-Croix-sur-Mer
Sep 44 to B 23/Morainville
Sep 44 to Manston
Sep 44 to B 51/Lille/Vendeville
Sep 44 to Fairwood Common
Oct 44 to B 70/Deurne
Feb 45 to B 89/Mill
Apr 45 to B 105/Drope
Apr 45 to B 111/Ahlhorn
Jan 45 to Hildesheim
Aug 45 DB

94 Sqn

Oct 42 F @ Lahore
Oct 42 **Hudson VI** (Aug 43) dets Tezpur, Dum Dum
Feb 43 to Palam
May 43 **Dakota** (Feb 46)
Sep 43 to Basal det Chaklala
Feb 44 to Comilla
Feb 44 to Agartala det Imphal
Sep 44 to Imphal
Nov 44 to Basal
Dec 44 to Agartala det Imphal
Jan 45 **Sentinel** (Sep 45) dets Kangla, Monywa
Mar 45 to Akyab dets Monywa, Wangjing, Meiktila
Aug 45 to Mingaladon
Feb 46 DB
—
Feb 53 RF @ Sembawang — from FE Casevac Flt
Feb 53 **Dragonfly HC 2** (Jun 56) det Kuala Lumpur
May 53 to Kuala Lumpur
Apr 54 **Sycamore HR 14** (Jun 59)
Jun 59 DB — merged with No 155 Sqn to form No 110 Sqn

5 Sqn

Nov 42 F @ Duxford
Nov 42 to Hutton Cranswick
Nov 42 **Typhoon IB** (Feb 44)
Feb 43 to Woodvale
May 43 to Ludham
Jul 43 to Matlask
Aug 43 to Coltishall
Sep 43 to Fairlop
Feb 44 DB
—
Oct 44 RF @ Witchford — from 'C' Flt, No 115 Sqn
Oct 44 **Lancaster I & III** (Aug 45)
Nov 44 to Wratting Common
Aug 45 DB

6 Sqn

Nov 42 F @ Driffield
Dec 42 to Leconfield
Dec 42 **Wellington III** (Dec 42)
Dec 42 **Wellington X** (Jul 43)

19 Jul 43 to Witchford
Jul 43 **Stirling III** (Jan 44)
18 Nov 43 to Leicester East
7 Jan 44 to Tarrant Rushton
Jan 44 **Stirling IV** (Mar 46)
14 Mar 44 to Keevil
9 Oct 44 to Wethersfield
26 Jan 45 to Shepherds Grove
Jan 46 **Stirling V** (Mar 46)
16 Mar 46 DB

197 Sqn

21 Nov 42 F @ Turnhouse
25 Nov 42 to Drem
Nov 42 **Typhoon IA** (Jan 43)
Nov 42 **Typhoon IB** (Aug 45)
28 Mar 43 to Tangmere
15 Mar 44 to Manston
1 Apr 44 to Tangmere
10 Apr 44 to Needs Oar Point
3 Jul 44 to Hurn
20 Jul 44 to B 3/Ste-Croix-sur-Mer
3 Sep 44 to Manston
11 Sep 44 to B 51/Lille/Vendeville
2 Oct 44 to B 70/Deurne
25 Nov 44 to Fairwood Common
12 Dec 44 to B 70/Deurne
8 Feb 45 to B 89/Mill
16 Apr 45 to B 105/Drope
30 Apr 45 to B 111/Ahlhorn
8 Jun 45 to Hildesheim
31 Aug 45 DB

198 Sqn

7 Dec 42 F @ Digby
Dec 42 **Typhoon IA** (May 43)
Dec 42 **Typhoon IB** (Sep 45)
23 Jan 43 to Ouston
9 Feb 43 to Acklington
24 Mar 43 to Manston
15 May 43 to Woodvale
5 Jun 43 to Martlesham Heath
19 Aug 43 to Bradwell Bay
22 Aug 43 to Manston
16 Mar 44 to Tangmere
30 Mar 44 to Llanbedr
6 Apr 44 to Thorney Island
22 Apr 44 to Llanbedr
30 Apr 44 to Thorney Island
18 Jun 44 to Funtington
22 Jun 44 to Hurn
1 Jul 44 to B 10/Plumetot det Hurn
8 Jul 44 to B 5/Camilly
11 Jul 44 to B 10/Plumetot
19 Jul 44 to B 7/Martragny
3 Sep 44 to B 23/Morainville
6 Sep 44 to B 35/Godelmesnil
11 Sep 44 to B 53/Merville
30 Oct 44 to B 67/Ursel
6 Nov 44 to Fairwood Common
21 Nov 44 to B 67/Ursel
26 Nov 44 to B 77/Gilze-Rijen
31 Dec 44 to A 84/Chièvres
19 Jan 45 to B 77/Gilze-Rijen
21 Mar 45 to B 91/Kluis
17 Apr 45 to B 103/Plantlunne
27 May 45 to B 116/Wunstorf
15 Sep 45 DB

199 Sqn

7 Nov 42 F @ Blyton
Nov 42 **Wellington III** (Apr 43)
3 Feb 43 to Ingham
Mar 43 **Wellington X** (Jun 43)
21 Jun 43 to Lakenheath
Jul 43 **Stirling III** (Mar 45)
1 May 44 to North Creake
Feb 45 **Halifax III** (Jul 45)
29 Jul 45 DB
—

15 Jul 51 RF @ Watton
Jul 51 **Lincoln B.2** (Sep 57)
Jan 52 **Mosquito NF 36** (Oct 53)
17 Apr 52 to Hemswell
Jul 54 **Canberra B.2** (Dec 58)
May 57 **Valiant B.1** (Dec 58) — det Honington
1 Oct 57 to Honington — Lincoln element remained at Hemswell as No 1321 Flt
17 Dec 58 DB — renumbered as No 18 Sqn at Finningley

200 Sqn

25 May 41 F @ Bircham Newton — nucleus from No 206 Sqn
Jun 41 **Hudson IV** (Nov 42)
18 Jun 41 to Jeswang dets Takoradi, Accra, Apapa, Hastings, Robertsfield, Port Etienne, Pointe Noire, Waterloo
Feb 42 **Hudson III** (Sep 43)
Jun 42 **Hudson IIIA** (Oct 43)
Nov 42 **Hudson VI** (Sep 43)
13 Mar 43 to Yundum dets Jeswang, Port Etienne, Hastings, Robertsfield, Rufisque, Waterloo
Jul 43 **Liberator V** (Sep 44) dets Port Etienne, Robertsfield, Rufisque
Feb 44 **Liberator VI** (May 45)
4 May 44 to St Thomas Mount dets Cuttack, Sigiriya
1 Apr 45 to Jessore
15 May 45 DB — renumbered as No 8 Sqn

201 Sqn

The original No 1 Sqn, RNAS formed at Fort Grange, Gosport on 17 Oct 14. It moved to France on 28 Feb 15 and in Jun 15 was restyled as No 1 Wg, RNAS. On 1 Mar 16 'A' Sqn of No 1 Wg was detached and from 3 Jul 16 it was referred to as the 'Detached Squadron, RNAS'. The unit was again redesignated, as No 1 (Naval) Sqn, on 3 Dec 16.

3 Dec 16 F @ Furnes as No 1 (Naval) Sqn — 'Detached Sqn, RNAS' renamed
Dec 16 **Nieuport 17** (Feb 17)
Dec 16 **Sopwith Triplane** (Dec 17)
15 Feb 17 to Chipilly
11 Apr 17 to La Bellevue
1 Jun 17 to Bailleul (Asylum Ground)
2 Nov 17 to Middle Aerodrome
10 Dec 17 to Dover (Guston Road)
Dec 17 **Camel** (Jan 19)
16 Feb 18 to Teteghem
27 Mar 18 to Ste-Marie-Cappel
28 Mar 18 to Fienvillers
1 Apr 18 redesignated as No 201 Sqn, RAF
12 Apr 18 to Nouex-les-Auxi
20 Jul 18 to Ste-Marie-Cappel
6 Aug 18 to Poulainville
14 Aug 18 to Nouex-les-Auxi
19 Sep 18 to Baizieux
14 Oct 18 to Beugnâtre
27 Oct 18 to La Targette
Oct 18 **Snipe** (Oct 18)

22 Nov 18 to Béthencourt
5 Feb 19 reduced to a cadre
17 Feb 19 to Lake Down
2 Sep 19 to Eastleigh
31 Dec 19 DB
—
1 Jan 29 RF @ Calshot — No 480 Flt renumbered
Jan 29 **Southampton II** (Dec 36)
Apr 36 **London I** (Jun 38)
Jan 38 **London II** (Apr 40)
29 Sep 38 to Invergordon
7 Oct 38 to Calshot
9 Aug 39 to Sullom Voe
6 Nov 39 to Invergordon
Apr 40 **Sunderland I** (Jan 42)
26 May 40 to Sullom Voe
May 41 **Sunderland II** (Mar 44)
9 Oct 41 to Lough Erne
Jan 42 **Sunderland III** (Jun 45)
8 Apr 44 to Pembroke Dock
3 Nov 44 to Castle Archdale
Feb 45 **Sunderland V** (Feb 57)
2 Aug 45 to Pembroke Dock
Mar 46 **Seaford I** (Apr 46)
1 Apr 46 to Calshot det Finkenwerder for BAL
18 Jan 49 to Pembroke Dock
28 Feb 57 DB
—
1 Oct 58 RF @ St Mawgan — No 220 Sqn renumbered
Oct 58 **Shackleton MR 3** (Dec 70)
1 Jul 65 to Kinloss
Jul 70 **Nimrod MR 1** (Feb 83)
Jan 82 **Nimrod MR 2** ( )

202 Sqn

No 2 Sqn, RNAS was formed at Eastchurch on 17 Oct 14. In Jun 15 it was redesignated as No 2 Wg and on 2 Aug 15 it moved to France. On 12 Aug 15 the unit was withdrawn to Dover for redeployment to Imbros for operations in the Aegean. A new No 2 Sqn was formed from 'B' Sqn of No 1 Wg, RNAS on 5 Nov 16.

5 Nov 16 F @ St-Pol as No 2 (Naval) Sqn — ex 'B' Sqn, No 1 Wg, RNAS
Nov 16 **Pup** (17)
Nov 16 **Farman F.40** (17)
Nov 16 **1½ Strutter** (Nov 17)
Mar 17 **DH 4** (Mar 19)
26 Jan 18 to Bergues
1 Apr 18 redesignated as No 202 Sqn, RAF
May 18 **DH 9** (Sep 18)
25 Nov 18 to Varssenaere
27 Mar 19 to Driffield as a cadre
Dec 19 to Spittlegate
22 Jan 20 DB
—
9 Apr 20 RF @ Alexandria — from a Flt of No 267 Sqn
Apr 20 **Short 184** (May 21)
16 May 21 DB
—
1 Jan 29 RF @ Kalafrana — No 481 Flt renumbered
Jan 29 **Fairey IIID** (Sep 30)
Jul 30 **Fairey IIIF** (Aug 35)
May 35 **Scapa** (Nov 37)
Sep 37 **London II** (Jun 41)
10 Sep 39 to Gibraltar
Oct 40 **Swordfish** (Jun 41) — floatplanes
Apr 41 **Catalina IB** (Jan 45)
Dec 41 **Sunderland I** (Sep 42)
Dec 41 **Sunderland II** (Sep 42)
Mar 42 **Sunderland III** (Sep 42)
3 Sep 44 to Castle Archdale
Oct 44 **Catalina IV** (Jun 45)

4 Jun 45 DB
—
1 Oct 46 RF @ Aldergrove — No 518 Sqn renumbered
Oct 46 **Halifax GR 6** (May 51)
Aug 49 **Halifax A.9** (Dec 50)
dets Gibraltar
Oct 50 **Hastings Met 1** (Aug 64)
28 Aug 64 DB
—
29 Aug 64 RF @ Leconfield — No 228 Sqn renumbered
Aug 64 **Whirlwind HAR 10** (Nov 79)
dets Acklington, Ouston, Coltishall, Leuchars
1 Sep 76 to Finningley
dets Boulmer, Leconfield, Coltishall, Lossiemouth, Brawdy
Jul 78 **Sea King HAR 3** ( )
det Port Stanley
Nov 82 **Wessex HAR 2** ( )

203 Sqn

The 'Eastchurch Squadron' of the RNAS formed in May 14. This unit deployed to Ostend on 27 Aug 14, moving to St-Pol on 1 Sep 14. The squadron withdrew to Dover on 26 Feb 15, where it was redesignated No 3 Sqn, RNAS before moving to the Aegean in the following month. In Jun 15 it was restyled No 3 Wg and disbanded at the end of the year. A new No 3 Sqn, RNAS was formed by redesignating an element of No 1 Wg, RNAS on 5 Nov 16.

5 Nov 16 F @ St-Pol as No 3 (Naval) Sqn, RNAS — ex 'C' Sqn, No 1 Wg, RNAS
Nov 16 **Nieuport 11** (Feb 17)
Nov 16 **Bristol Scout** (Feb 17)
Feb 17 **Pup** (Jul 17)
1 Feb 17 to Vert Galand
28 Feb 17 to Bertangles
26 Mar 17 to Marieux
15 Jun 17 to Furnes
Jul 17 **Camel** (Mar 19)
6 Sep 17 to Bray-Dunes
1 Nov 17 to Walmer
2 Jan 18 to Bray-Dunes
11 Mar 18 to St-Eloi
28 Mar 18 to Treizennes
1 Apr 18 redesignated as No 203 Sqn, RAF
9 Apr 18 to Liettres
16 May 18 to Filescamp Farm
14 Aug 18 to Allonville
6 Sep 18 to Filescamp Farm
23 Sep 18 to Le Hameau
24 Oct 18 to Bruille
24 Nov 18 to Auberchicourt
22 Dec 18 to Orcq
18 Jan 19 to Boisdinghem
27 Mar 19 to Waddington as a cadre
Dec 19 to Scopwick
21 Jan 20 DB
—
1 Mar 20 RF @ Leuchars
Mar 20 **Camel** (Aug 22)
Aug 22 **Nightjar** (Apr 23)
18 Sep 22 en route Turkey via HMS *Argus*
27 Sep 22 to Kilya Bay
19 Dec 22 en route UK via HMS *Argus*
4 Jan 23 to Leuchars
1 Apr 23 DB — split into Nos 401 & 402 Flts
—
1 Jan 29 RF @ Mount Batten — No 482 Flt renumbered
Jan 29 **Southampton II** (Apr 31)
28 Feb 29 en route Persian Gulf
14 Mar 29 to Basrah
Mar 29 **Fairey IIIF** (Apr 29)
Mar 31 det Felixstowe for **Rangoon** (Sep 35)
Aug 35 det Pembroke Dock for **Singapore III** (Mar 40)
26 Sep 35 to Isthmus
24 Aug 36 to Basrah
2 Sep 39 to Isthmus
15 Feb 40 to Sheikh Othman
Mar 40 **Blenheim I** (May 40)
May 40 **Blenheim IV** (Nov 42)
18 May 40 to Khormaksar
det Berbera
16 Apr 41 to Kabrit
24 Apr 41 to Heraklion
30 Apr 41 to Kabrit
dets Lydda, Habbaniyah, H.4
20 Jun 41 to LG 101
dets Fuka, Sidi Barrani, El Gubbi, Burgh el Arab, Berka, Nicosia, Lakatamia
16 Jan 42 to Berka III
24 Jan 42 to El Gubbi
1 Feb 42 to Gambut
3 Feb 42 to LG 05
6 Feb 42 to LG 39
Feb 42 **Hudson III** (Feb 42)
Feb 42 **Maryland I** (Dec 42)
dets LG 05, Bu Amud, Gambut
30 Jun 42 to LG 'Y'
dets LG 226, LG 'X'
9 Jul 42 to LG 'X'
det LG 226
Aug 42 **Baltimore I** (Nov 43)
Aug 42 **Baltimore II** (Nov 43)
17 Oct 42 to LG 227
Oct 42 **Blenheim V** (Nov 42)
dets Berka, Gambut
Dec 42 **Baltimore III** (Nov 43)
4 Mar 43 to Berka III
Jun 43 **Baltimore IIIA** (Nov 43)
Jul 43 **Baltimore IV** (Nov 43)
4 Nov 43 to LG 91
15 Nov 43 to Santa Cruz
Nov 43 **Wellington XIII** (Oct 44)
9 Oct 44 to Madura
Oct 44 **Liberator VI** (Apr 46)
dets Cochin, St Thomas Mount, Ratmalana, Sigiriya, Vizagapatam
28 Feb 45 to Kankesanterai
dets Akyab, Cocos Islands
Jan 46 **Liberator VIII** (Oct 46)
19 May 46 to Leuchars
Jul 46 **Lancaster GR 3** (Mar 53)
16 Jan 47 to St Eval
15 Aug 52 to Topcliffe
Mar 53 **Neptune MR 1** (Aug 56)
1 Sep 56 DB
—
1 Nov 58 RF @ Ballykelly — No 240 Sqn renumbered
Nov 58 **Shackleton MR 1A** (Feb 59)
Dec 58 **Shackleton MR 3** (Jul 62)
Apr 62 **Shackleton MR 2** (Dec 66)
Jun 66 **Shackleton MR 3** (Dec 71)
1 Feb 69 to Luqa
Oct 71 **Nimrod MR 1** (Dec 77)
12 Jan 72 to Sigonella
23 Apr 72 to Luqa
31 Dec 77 DB

204 Sqn

The RNAS Defence Flight at Dover became No 4 Sqn, RNAS on 29 Mar 15. On 3 Aug 15 the unit moved to Eastchurch and was redesignated as No 4 Wg. A new No 4 Sqn was formed from an element of No 5 Wg on 31 Dec 16.

31 Dec 16 F @ Coudekerque as No 4 (Naval) Sqn — ex 'A' Sqn, No 5 Wg, RNAS
Dec 16 **1½ Strutter** (Mar 17)
Mar 17 **Pup** (Jun 17)
1 Apr 17 to Bray-Dunes
Jun 17 **Camel** (Feb 19)
2 Jan 18 to Walmer
6 Mar 18 to Bray-Dunes
1 Apr 18 redesignated as No 204 Sqn, RAF
13 Apr 18 to Teteghem
30 Apr 18 to Cappelle
9 May 18 to Teteghem
24 Oct 18 to Heule
11 Feb 19 to Waddington as a cadre
31 Dec 19 DB
—
1 Feb 29 RF @ Mount Batten
Feb 29 **Southampton II** (Oct 35)
Aug 35 **Scapa** (Jan 37)
27 Sep 35 to Aboukir
22 Oct 35 to Alexandria
5 Aug 36 to Mount Batten
Oct 36 **London I & II** (Jul 39)
Jun 39 **Sunderland I** (Sep 43)
2 Apr 40 to Sullom Voe
5 Apr 41 to Reykjavik
Jun 41 **Sunderland II** (Mar 43)
det Pembroke Dock
15 Jul 41 to Gibraltar
28 Aug 41 to Bathurst/Half Die
dets Gibraltar, Jui, Port Etienne
Oct 42 **Sunderland III** (Jun 45)
28 Jan 44 to Jui
dets Half Die, Port Etienne
1 Apr 44 to Half Die
8 Apr 44 to Jui
dets Half Die, Port Etienne, Fishermans Lake, Abidjan
Apr 45 **Sunderland V** (Jun 45)
30 Jun 45 DB
—
1 Aug 47 RF @ Kabrit
Aug 47 **Dakota** (Jul 49)
May 49 **Valetta C.1** (Feb 53)
22 Feb 51 to Fayid
20 Feb 53 DB — renumbered as No 84 Sqn
—
1 Jan 54 RF @ Ballykelly
Jan 54 **Shackleton MR 2** (May 58)
May 58 **Shackleton MR 1A** (Feb 60)
May 59 **Shackleton MR 2C** (Mar 71)
1 Apr 71 DB
—
1 Apr 71 RF @ Honington — from the Majunga Detachment Support Unit
Apr 71 **Shackleton MR 2C** (Apr 72)
dets Majunga, Tengah, Masirah
1 May 72 DB

205 Sqn

31 Dec 16 F @ Coudekerque as No 5 (Naval) Sqn — ex 'B' Sqn, No 5 Wg, RNAS
Dec 16 **1½ Strutter** (Jul 17)
1 Apr 17 to Petite Synthe
Apr 17 **DH 4** (Sep 18)
6 Mar 18 to Villers-Brettoneux
11 Mar 18 to Mons-en-Chaussée
22 Mar 18 to Champien
24 Mar 18 to Bertangles
28 Mar 18 to Bois-de-Roche
1 Apr 18 redesignated as No 205 Sqn, RAF
25 Aug 18 to Bovelles
16 Sep 18 to Proyart East
Sep 18 **DH 9A** (Mar 19)
7 Oct 18 to Moislains
27 Nov 18 to Maubeuge
12 Jan 19 to La Louveterie
21 Mar 19 to Hucknall as a cadre
Dec 19 to Scopwick
22 Jan 20 DB
—
15 Apr 20 RF @ Leuchars
Apr 20 **Panther** (Apr 23)
1 Apr 23 DB — became Nos 44 441 & 442 Flts
—
8 Jan 29 RF @ Seletar — from Far East Flight
Jan 29 **Southampton II** (Feb 3
Apr 35 **Singapore III** (Oct 41)
Apr 41 **Catalina I** (Mar 42)
dets Port Victoria, Koggala, China Bay, Batavia
31 Jan 42 to Batavia
det Seletar
1 Feb 42 to Oesthaven
16 Feb 42 to Tjilitjap
1 Mar 42 to Fremantle
31 Mar 42 DB
—
23 Jul 42 RF @ Koggala
Jul 42 **Catalina I** (Feb 45)
dets Red Hills Lake, Addu Atoll, Diego Garcia, Cocona China Bay, Kelai, Cocos Islands
May 44 **Catalina IVB** (Sep 45)
Jun 45 **Sunderland GR 5** (May 59)
det Iwakuni
15 Sep 49 to Seletar
dets Iwakuni, China B Kai Tak, Changi
1 Mar 58 to Changi
det Seletar
May 58 **Shackleton MR 1A** (Sep 62)
Feb 62 **Shackleton MR 2C** (Oct 71)
31 Oct 71 DB

206 Sqn

The first No 6 Sqn, R was formed on 1 Nov by redesignating 'A' S of No 4 Wg. This unit disbanded in Aug 17. new No 6 (Naval) Sqn formed on 1 Nov 17.

1 Nov 17 F @ Dover (Guston Road) as No 6 (Naval) Sqn — from the Waln Defence Flight
Nov 17 **DH 4** (Mar 18)
14 Jan 18 to Petite Synthe
Feb 18 **DH 9** (Jan 20)
31 Mar 18 to Ste-Marie-Cappel
1 Apr 18 redesignated as No 20 Sqn, RAF

Apr 18 to Boisdinghem
Apr 18 to Alquines
May 18 to Boisdinghem
Jun 18 to Alquines
Oct 18 to Ste-Marie-Cappel
Oct 18 to Linselles
Nov 18 to Nivelles
Dec 18 to Bickendorf
May 19 to Maubeuge
Jun 19 en route Egypt via Marseilles
Jun 19 to Heliopolis
Jun 19 to Helwan
Feb 20 DB — renumbered as No 47 Sqn
—
Jun 36 RF @ Manston — from 'C' Flt, No 48 Sqn
Jun 36 **Anson I** (Jun 40)
Aug 36 to Bircham Newton
Mar 40 **Hudson I** (Aug 42) det St Eval
Apr 41 **Hudson II, III, IV** (Aug 42)
May 41 to St Eval
Aug 41 to Aldergrove
Oct 41 **Hudson V** (Aug 42)
Jul 42 to Benbecula
Jul 42 **Fortress II** (Mar 44)
Oct 43 to Lagens
Mar 44 to Davidstow Moor
Mar 44 **Liberator VI** (Apr 45)
Apr 44 to St Eval
Jul 44 to Leuchars
Mar 45 **Liberator VIII** (Apr 46)
Jul 45 to Oakington
Apr 46 DB
—
Nov 47 RF @ Lyneham
Nov 47 **York C.1** (Aug 49) dets Wunstorf for BAL
Aug 49 DB
—
Dec 49 RF @ Waterbeach
Dec 49 **Dakota** (Feb 50)
Feb 50 DB
—
Sep 52 RF @ St Eval
Sep 52 **Shackleton MR 1A** (May 58)
Feb 53 **Shackleton MR 2** (Jun 54)
Jan 58 to St Mawgan
Jan 58 **Shackleton MR 3** (Oct 70)
Jul 65 to Kinloss
Aug 70 **Nimrod MR 1** (Feb 81)
Feb 80 **Nimrod MR 2** ( )

7 Sqn

Nov 16 F @ Petite Synthe as No 7 (Naval) Sqn — ex 'B' Sqn, No 4 Wg, RNAS
Nov 16 **Caudron G.IV** (Dec 16)
Nov 16 **1½ Strutter** (Apr 17)
Nov 16 **Short Bomber** (Jun 17)
Apr 17 to Coudekerque
Apr 17 **HP 0/100** (Apr 18)
Jul 17 split into Nos 7 & 7A Sqns, RNAS det Redcar, later Manston — det became 'A' Sqn, RNAS
Apr 18 redesignated as No 207 Sqn, RAF
Apr 18 to Netheravon
Apr 18 **HP 0/400** (Aug 19)
May 18 to Andover
Jun 18 to Ligescourt
Oct 18 to Estrées-en-Chaussée
Dec 18 to Carvin
Jan 19 to Merheim
May 19 to Hangelar
Aug 19 to Tangmere as a cadre
Oct 19 to Croydon
Jan 20 to Kenley
Jan 20 to Uxbridge

20 Jan 20 DB
—
1 Feb 20 RF @ Bircham Newton as a cadre — nucleus from No 274 Sqn
Apr 21 **DH 9A** (Jan 28)
29 Sep 22 en route Turkey
11 Oct 22 to San Stephano
22 Sep 23 en route UK
3 Oct 23 to Eastchurch
Dec 27 **Fairey IIIF** (Sep 32)
9 Nov 29 to Bircham Newton
Aug 32 **Gordon** (Apr 36)
28 Oct 36 to Ed Damer
6 Apr 36 to Gebeit
Apr 36 **Vincent** (Jul 36)
29 Aug 36 to Worthy Down
Aug 36 **Gordon** (Nov 37)
Sep 37 **Wellesley** (Apr 38)
20 Apr 38 to Cottesmore
Apr 38 **Battle** (Apr 40)
Jul 39 **Anson I** (Apr 40)
24 Aug 39 to Cranfield
9 Dec 39 to Cottesmore
5 Apr 40 to Cranfield
19 Apr 40 DB — merged into Nto 12 OTU
—
1 Nov 40 RF @ Waddington
Nov 40 **Manchester** (Mar 42)
Jul 41 **Hampden** (Aug 41)
17 Nov 41 to Bottesford
Mar 42 **Lancaster I & III** (Aug 49)
20 Sep 42 to Langar
12 Oct 43 to Spilsby
30 Oct 45 to Methwold
29 Apr 46 to Tuddenham
8 Nov 46 to Stradishall
28 Feb 49 to Mildenhall
Jul 49 **Lincoln B.2** (Feb 50)
1 Mar 50 DB
—
4 Jun 51 RF @ Marham
Jun 51 **Washington B.1** (Mar 54)
Mar 54 **Canberra B.2** (Feb 56)
27 Mar 56 DB
—
1 Apr 56 RF @ Marham
Jun 56 **Valiant B(PR) 1** (Dec 64)
Jun 56 **Valiant B(K) 1** (Dec 64)
Mar 62 **Valiant B.1** (Dec 64)
1 May 65 DB
—
3 Feb 69 RF @ Northolt — Strike Command Communications Sqn redesignated
Feb 69 **Basset CC1** (May 74)
Feb 69 **Pembroke C.1** (Nov 75)
Feb 69 **Devon C.2** (Jun 84) dets Wyton, Turnhouse
30 Jun 84 DB

208 Sqn

25 Oct 16 F @ St-Pol as No 8 (Naval) Sqn — one Flt from each of Nos 1, 4 and 5 Wgs.
26 Oct 16 to Vert Galand
Oct 16 **1½ Strutter** (Nov 16)
Oct 16 **Nieuport 17** (Dec 16)
Oct 16 **Pup** (Feb 17)
Feb 17 **Sopwith Triplane** (Sep 17)
7 Feb 17 to Furnes
28 Mar 17 to Auchel
16 May 17 to St-Eloi
Sep 17 **Camel** (Nov 18)
28 Feb 18 to Bray-Dunes
1 Mar 18 to Walmer
29 Mar 18 to Teteghem
1 Apr 18 redesignated as No 208 Sqn, RAF
2 Apr 18 to La Gorgue
9 Apr 18 to Serny
30 Jul 18 to Tramecourt
22 Sep 18 to Foucaucourt
9 Oct 18 to Estrées-en-Chaussée

26 Oct 18 to Maretz
Nov 18 **Snipe** (Nov 19)
3 Dec 18 to Strée B
23 May 19 to Heumar
7 Aug 19 to Eil
9 Sep 19 to Netheravon
7 Nov 19 DB
—
1 Feb 20 RF @ Ismailia — No 113 Sqn renumbered
Feb 20 **RE 8** (Nov 20) det Ramleh
Oct 20 **Bristol F2b Fighter** (May 30)
28 Sep 22 to San Stephano
26 Sep 23 to Ismailia
27 Oct 27 to Heliopolis det Ramleh
May 30 **Atlas** (Aug 35)
Apr 34 **Audax** (Jan 39)
Sep 35 **Demon** (Mar 36) — 'D' Flt only dets Mersah Matruh, Amiriya
24 Jan 36 to Mersah Matruh
18 Apr 36 to Heliopolis dets Ramleh, Fayid, Helwan, Burrumbul, Mersah Matruh, Aboukir
28 Sep 38 to Mersah Matruh
13 Oct 38 to Heliopolis
Jan 39 **Lysander I & II** (May 42)
26 Feb 39 to Mersah Matruh
16 Mar 39 to Heliopolis
7 Aug 39 to Mersah Matruh
1 Sep 39 to Qasaba
23 Oct 39 to Maaten Bagush
28 Oct 39 to Qasaba
15 Nov 39 to Heliopolis dets Mersah Matruh, Qasaba
9 Jun 40 to Qasaba dets Sidi Barrani, Bir Kanayis, Siwa
Nov 40 **Hurricane I** (Sep 42) det Halfaya, Bir Mella
10 Jan 41 to Gambut
22 Jan 41 to Tmimi dets Mechili, Agedabia
4 Feb 41 to Marawa
6 Feb 41 to Barce
3 Mar 41 to Heliopolis
5 Apr 41 to Mersah Matruh
6 Apr 41 to Kazaklar dets Larissa, Pharsala
17 Apr 41 to Amphiklia
18 Apr 41 to Kalamaki
19 Apr 41 to Elevsis dets Amphiklia, Kalamaki
22 Apr 41 to Argos
24 Apr 41 to Maleme
28 Apr 41 to Aboukir
1 May 41 to Gaza
May 41 **Audax** (Jun 41) dets Habbaniyah, Amman, H.4, Haifa
21 Jun 41 to Ramleh dets Haifa, Muqueibila, Rosh Pinna, H.4, Rayak, Deir-es-Zor
29 Sep 41 to Aqir
19 Oct 41 to LG 10 dets Gabr Saleh, LG 75
14 Nov 41 to LG 112 det LG 134
21 Nov 41 to LG 134
24 Nov 41 to LG 123
28 Nov 41 to LG 128 det LG 134
30 Nov 41 to LG 134
10 Dec 41 to El Gubbi dets LG 134, LG 131
19 Dec 41 to Tmimi dets Mechili, Antelat, Msus, Benina, Martuba
3 Feb 42 to Acroma
8 Feb 42 to Sidi Azeiz dets Acroma, Bir el Regal, El Adem

27 Mar 42 to Moascar
Apr 42 **Tomahawk IIB** (Sep 42)
May 42 **Hurricane IIA & IIB** (Jan 44)
15 May 42 to Sidi Azeiz dets El Adem, Bir el Gubi, Sidi Rezegh, Gasr el Arid, LG 79
15 Jun 42 to LG 103 det LG 79
27 Jun 42 to LG 100 dets LG 103, LG 79
30 Jun 42 to Heliopolis det LG 39
12 Jul 42 to LG 100 det LG 39
17 Sep 42 to LG 202 dets LG 39, LG 104
18 Nov 42 to LG 28
15 Jan 43 to Aqsu
12 Feb 43 to K.1 (Kirkuk) dets Hinaidi, Beirut
1 Jul 43 to Rayak
16 Nov 43 to El Bassa
Dec 43 **Spitfire VC** (Aug 44) dets Muqueibila, Megiddo
7 Jan 44 to Megiddo dets Heliopolis, Bersis
Mar 44 **Spitfire IX** (May 47)
17 Mar 44 to Trigno
1 May 44 to San Angelo
1 Jun 44 to Venafro
4 Jun 44 to Aquino
11 Jun 44 to Osa
17 Jun 44 to Falerium
23 Jun 44 to Orvieto
5 Jul 44 to Castiglione
Jul 44 **Spitfire VIII** (Sep 44)
1 Aug 44 to Malignano
20 Sep 44 to Peretola
26 Apr 45 to Bologna
28 Apr 45 to Villafranca
15 May 45 to Tissano
30 Jun 45 to Bari
5 Jul 45 to Ramat David
13 Aug 45 to Petah Tiqva
12 Mar 46 to Aqir
6 Jun 46 to Ein Shemar
Aug 46 **Spitfire FR 18** (Apr 51)
26 Mar 48 to Nicosia det Ramat David
17 Nov 48 to Fayid
25 May 50 to Khartoum
10 Aug 50 to Fayid
Jan 51 **Meteor FR 9** (Mar 58)
19 Feb 51 to Kabrit dets Castel Benito, Habbaniyah
16 Sep 51 to Nicosia
19 Oct 51 to Abu Sueir dets Nicosia, El Adem, Habbaniyah, Sharjah
17 Jan 56 to Hal Far
26 Mar 56 to Akrotiri det Khormaksar
7 Aug 56 to Ta Kali det Bahrain
Jan 58 det Tangmere for Hunter — ex No 34 Sqn
1 Mar 58 to Nicosia
Mar 58 **Hunter F.6** (Mar 59) det Amman
31 Mar 59 DB
—
1 Apr 59 RF @ Eastleigh — No 142 Sqn renumbered
Apr 59 **Venom FB 4** (Mar 60)
29 Mar 60 to Stradishall
Mar 60 **Hunter FGA 9** (Sep 71)
3 Jun 60 to Eastleigh
30 Jun 61 to Bahrain
1 Jul 61 to Farwania
8 Aug 61 to Bahrain
8 Sep 61 to Farwania
10 Oct 61 to Bahrain
15 Nov 61 to Khormaksar
30 Nov 61 to Eastleigh det Khormaksar
9 Dec 61 to Khormaksar

dets Muharraq
8 Jun 64 to Muharraq dets Sharjah
10 Sep 71 DB
—
1 Jul 74 RF @ Honington
Oct 74 **Buccaneer S.2** ( )
1 Jul 83 to Lossiemouth

209 Sqn

1 Feb 17 F @ St Pol as No 9 (Naval) Sqn — nucleus from No 8 (Naval) Sqn
Feb 17 **Nieuport 17** (Jun 17)
Feb 17 **Pup** (Jul 17)
Feb 17 **Sopwith Triplane** (Jul 17)
15 May 17 to Furnes
15 Jun 17 to Flez
Jul 17 **Camel** (Feb 19)
5 Jul 17 to Le Hameau
10 Jul 17 to Frontier Aerodrome
25 Jul 17 to Leffrinckhoucke
1 Oct 17 to Frontier Aerodrome
10 Oct 17 to Middle Aerodrome
16 Feb 18 to Dover (Guston Road)
20 Mar 18 to Middle Aerodrome
21 Mar 18 to Teteghem
21 Mar 18 to Bray-Dunes
23 Mar 18 to Cappelle
27 Mar 18 to Bailleul
29 Mar 18 to Clairmarais
1 Apr 18 redesignated as No 209 Sqn, RAF
7 Apr 18 to Bertangles
20 Jul 18 to Quelmes
6 Aug 18 to Bertangles
14 Aug 18 to Le Hameau
24 Oct 18 to Bruille
22 Nov 18 to Saultain
11 Dec 18 to Froidmont
14 Feb 19 to Scopwick as a cadre
24 Jun 19 DB
—
15 Jan 30 RF @ Mount Batten
Feb 30 **Iris III** (Dec 32)
Feb 32 **Saro A.7** (Jul 32)
Jun 32 **Iris V** (Jun 34)
Aug 32 **Singapore II** (Nov 32)
Feb 33 **Southampton II** (Jun 34)
Jan 34 **Perth** (Dec 34)
Oct 34 **Southampton II** (Nov 34)
Oct 34 **London I** (Nov 34)
Jan 35 **Southampton II** (Feb 35)
Jan 35 **London I** (Feb 36)
Feb 35 **Stranraer** (Sep 35)
Apr 35 **Short R.24/31** (Sep 35)
1 May 35 to Felixstowe
Jul 35 **Perth** (May 36)
Jan 36 **Southampton II** (Jul 36)
Feb 36 **Singapore III** (Mar 39)
22 Sep 37 to Kalafrana
31 Sep 37 to Arzeu
17 Dec 37 to Felixstowe
27 Sep 38 to Invergordon
8 Oct 38 to Felixstowe
Dec 38 **Stranraer** (Apr 40)
22 May 39 to Stranraer
17 Jun 39 to Felixstowe
12 Aug 39 to Invergordon
22 Aug 39 to Felixstowe
30 Aug 39 to Invergordon det Falmouth
7 Oct 39 to Oban det Falmouth
Dec 39 **Lerwick I** (May 41)
12 Jul 40 to Pembroke Dock
3 Jan 41 to Stranraer
23 Mar 41 to Lough Erne
Apr 41 **Catalina I** (Jun 45)
26 Jul 41 to Reykjavik
10 Oct 41 to Pembroke Dock
30 Mar 42 en route East Africa
15 Jun 42 to Kipevu
Jul 42 **Catalina IIA** (Jun 45) dets Kisumu, Pamanzi, Diego Suarez, Congella, Tulear, Port Victoria, Aden, Masirah
Feb 45 **Sunderland V** (Jan 55)
21 Jul 45 to Koggala
17 Sep 45 to Kai Tak
28 Apr 46 to Seletar dets Iwakuni, Kai Tak
1 Jan 55 DB
—
1 Nov 58 RF @ Kuala Lumpur — No 267 Sqn renumbered
Nov 58 **Auster AOP 6** (Mar 59)
Nov 58 **Dakota** (Nov 59)
Nov 58 **Pembroke C.1** (Feb 60)
Nov 58 **Pioneer CC 1** (Dec 68)
Mar 59 **Twin Pioneer CC 1** (Dec 68)
1 Oct 59 to Seletar
Oct 60 **Twin Pioneer CC 2** (Dec 68) dets Labuan, Kuching, Bayan Lepas
31 Dec 68 DB

210 Sqn

12 Feb 17 F @ St-Pol as No 10 (Naval) Sqn, RNAS
Feb 17 **Nieuport 12** (May 17)
Feb 17 **Nieuport 17** (May 17)
Feb 17 **Sopwith Triplane** (Jul 17)
27 Mar 17 to Furnes
15 May 17 to Droglandt
Jul 17 **Camel** (Feb 19)
4 Oct 17 to Leffrinckhoucke
27 Nov 17 to Tetegham
1 Apr 18 redesignated as No 210 Sqn, RAF
1 Apr 18 to Treizennes
9 Apr 18 to Liettres
27 Apr 18 to St-Omer
30 May 18 to Ste-Marie-Cappel
9 Jul 18 to Teteghem
22 Jul 18 to Eringhem
23 Oct 18 to Boussières
17 Feb 19 to Scopwick as a cadre
24 Jun 19 DB
—
1 Feb 20 RF @ Gosport — No 186 Sqn renumbered
Feb 20 **Cuckoo** (Apr 23)
1 Apr 23 DB — renumbered as Nos 460 & 461 Flts
—
1 Mar 31 RF @ Felixstowe
May 31 **Southampton II** (Aug 35)
15 Jun 31 to Pembroke Dock
Nov 34 **Singapore III** (Apr 35) — ferried to No 205 Sqn
Jul 35 **Singapore III** (Aug 35) — ferried to No 203 Sqn
Aug 35 **Rangoon** (Sep 36) — from No 203 Sqn
28 Sep 35 to Gibraltar
Oct 35 **London II** (Nov 35)
Oct 35 **Stranraer** (Nov 35)
7 Aug 36 to Pembroke Dock
Aug 36 **Singapore III** (Nov 38)
22 Sep 37 to Arzeu
18 Dec 37 to Pembroke Dock
Jun 38 **Sunderland I** (Apr 41)
29 Sep 38 to Tayport
8 Oct 38 to Pembroke Dock
23 Oct 39 to Invergordon
6 Nov 39 to Pembroke Dock
24 Nov 39 to Invergordon det Sullum Voe
21 May 40 to Pembroke Dock
13 Jul 40 to Oban dets Reykjavik, Sullom Voe, Stranraer
Apr 41 **Catalina I** (Aug 43)
28 Feb 42 to Sullom Voe det Grasnaya
Jul 42 **Catalina II** (Mar 43)
Aug 42 **Catalina IB** (Dec 43)
4 Oct 42 to Pembroke Dock det Gibraltar
21 Apr 43 to Hamworthy det Gibraltar
31 Dec 43 DB
—
1 Jan 44 RF @ Sullom Voe — No 190 Sqn renumbered
Jan 44 **Catalina IB** (Mar 44)
Jan 44 **Catalina IV** (Jun 45) det Pembroke Dock
4 Jun 45 DB
—
1 Jun 46 RF @ St Eval — No 179Y Sqn renumbered
Jun 46 **Lancaster ASR 3** (Dec 52)
10 Sep 52 to Ballykelly
26 Sep 52 to Topcliffe
Feb 53 **Neptune MR 1** (Jan 57)
31 Jan 57 DB
—
1 Dec 58 RF @ Ballykelly — No 269 Sqn renumbered
Dec 58 **Shackleton MR 2** (Oct 70)
31 Oct 70 DB
—
1 Nov 70 RF @ Sharjah
Nov 70 **Shackleton MR 2** (Nov 71)
15 Nov 71 DB

211 Sqn

The first No 11 Sqn, RNAS, formed at Dunkerque on 8 Mar 17 but, after moving to Hondschoote on 11 Jul 17, it disbanded on 27 Aug 17.

10 Mar 18 RF @ Petite Synthe as No 11 (Naval) Sqn, RNAS
Mar 18 **DH 4** (Apr 18)
Mar 18 **DH 9** (Mar 19)
1 Apr 18 redesignated as No 211 Sqn, RAF
24 Oct 18 to Iris Farm
3 Dec 18 to Thuilles
15 Mar 19 to Wyton as a cadre
24 Jun 19 DB
—
24 Jun 37 RF @ Mildenhall
Jul 37 **Audax** (Oct 37)
Aug 37 **Hind** (May 39)
2 Sep 37 to Grantham
12 May 38 to Helwan
18 Jul 38 to Ramleh det Semakh
29 Sep 38 to Helwan
31 Jan 39 to Ismailia
Apr 39 **Blenheim I** (Nov 41) det El Daba
10 Aug 39 to El Daba det Qotafiyah
17 Jul 40 to Qotafiyah
8 Nov 40 to Ismailia
17 Nov 40 to Tatoi/Menidi det Paramythia
9 Feb 41 to Paramythia det Menidi
17 Apr 41 to Arginion
19 Apr 41 to Menidi
22 Apr 41 to Heraklion
23 Apr 41 to Heliopolis (air echelon only)
27 Apr 41 to Ramleh
30 Apr 41 to Lydda
10 May 41 to Aqir
May 41 **Blenheim IV** (Feb 42)
5 Jun 41 to Heliopolis
10 Jun 41 to Wadi Gazouza
18 Nov 41 absorbed into No 72 OTU
20 Dec 41 re-established
25 Jan 42 en route FE
4 Feb 42 to P II
16 Feb 42 to Kalidjati
19 Feb 42 DB — abosrbed by No 84 Sqn
—
14 Aug 43 RF @ Phaphamau
Oct 43 **Beaufighter X** (May 45)
10 Nov 43 to Ranchi
23 Dec 43 to Silchar West
26 Jan 44 to Bhatpara dets Nazir, Ramu
26 May 44 to Feni
10 Jul 44 to Chiringa det Ranchi
31 May 45 to Yelahanka
Jun 45 **Mosquito VI** (Feb 46)
11 Jul 45 to St Thomas Mount
2 Nov 45 to Akyab
27 Nov 45 to Don Muang
15 Mar 46 DB

212 Sqn

No 12 (Naval) Sqn was training unit formed at Pol in Apr 17, moving Petite Synthe on 1 Jul Unlike other RNA squadrons it disband on 1 Apr 18 rather th being absorbed into t RAF as No 212 Sqn.

20 Aug 18 F @ Great Yarmouth (Nos 490, 557 & 558 Fl
Aug 18 **DH 4** (Jan 19)
Aug 18 **DH 9A** (Feb 20)
Aug 18 **DH 9** (19)
Oct 18 **Camel** (Jan 19)
7 Mar 19 to Swingate Down
9 Feb 20 DB
—
10 Feb 40 RF @ Meaux — overse element of PDU
Feb 40 **Spitfire C** (Jun 40)
Feb 40 **Blenheim IV** (Jun 40)
Feb 40 **Hudson I** (Jun 40) dets Lille/Seclin, Nancy
9 Jun 40 to Orléans/Bricy
14 Jun 40 to Heston dets Poitiers, La Rochelle
18 Jun 40 DB
—
22 Oct 42 RF @ Korangi Creek
30 Nov 42 sqn established
Dec 42 **Catalina IB** (Oct 44) dets Masirah, Jiwani, Bahrain, Red Hills Lak Trombay, Cochin, Koggala, Bally
Sep 44 **Catalina IV** (Jun 45)
Feb 45 **Catalina IB** (Jun 45)
1 May 45 to Red Hills Lake dets Akyab, Bally
1 Jul 45 DB — renumbered as No 240 Sqn

213 Sqn

15 Jan 18 F @ St-Pol as No 13 (Naval) Sqn — ex St-P Defence Sqn
Jan 18 **Camel** (Mar 19)
25 Jan 18 to Bergues
1 Apr 18 redesignated as No 213 Sqn, RAF
27 Nov 18 to Stalhille
19 Mar 19 to Scopwick as a cadre
31 Dec 19 DB
—
8 Mar 37 RF @ Northolt — from 'A' Flt, No 111 Sqn
Mar 37 **Gauntlet II** (Mar 39)
1 Jul 37 to Church Fenton
18 May 38 to Wittering
Jan 39 **Hurricane I** (Mar 42)
May 40 dets Manston, Merville Biggin Hill
9 Jun 40 to Biggin Hill
18 Jun 40 to Exeter
7 Sep 40 to Tangmere

Nov 40 to Leconfield
Jan 41 to Driffield
Feb 41 to Castletown
May 41 en route Egypt via HMS *Furious*
May 41 to Abu Sueir det Maaten Bagush
Jul 41 to Lydda
Jul 41 to Haifa det Nicosia
Jul 41 to Nicosia dets Famagusta, Ismailia, Idku, Abu Zenima, Shandur, El Khanka
Dec 41 to LG 90 dets El Khanka, Dekheila
Jan 42 to Idku
Jan 42 **Hurricane IIC** (May 44) det El Khanka
May 42 to LG 12
Jun 42 to Gambut West
Jun 42 to LG 155
Jun 42 to LG 75
Jun 42 to LG 76
Jun 42 to LG 07
Jun 42 to LG 12
Jun 42 to LG 05
Jun 42 to LG 154
Jul 42 to LG 172
Jul 42 to LG 154
Aug 42 to Kilo 8
Aug 42 to LG 85
Oct 42 to LG 172
Nov 42 to LG 20
Nov 42 to LG 101
Nov 42 to LG 125
Nov 42 to El Adem
Nov 42 to Martuba
Jan 43 to Misurata West
Jul 43 to Idku dets Paphos, St Jean, Lakatamia
Feb 44 **Spitfire VC** (May 44)
Feb 44 **Spitfire IX** (Jun 44)
Feb 44 to El Gamil dets St Jean, Lakatamia, Idku
May 44 to Idku
May 44 **Mustang III** (Feb 47)
Jul 44 to Leverano
Jul 44 to Biferno
Feb 45 **Mustang IV** (Feb 57)
May 45 to Prkos
May 45 to Biferno
Jun 45 to Brindisi
Sep 45 to Ramat David
Sep 46 to Nicosia
Jan 47 **Tempest F.6** (Jan 50)
Sep 47 to Shallufa
Oct 47 to Khartoum
Aug 48 to Mogadishu
Oct 48 to Deversoir
Dec 49 **Vampire FB 5** (May 52)
Apr 52 **Vampire FB 9** (Sep 54)
Aug 53 to Shallufa
Oct 53 to Deversoir
Sep 54 DB
—
Sep 55 RF @ Ahlhorn
Mar 56 **Canberra B(I) 6** (Dec 69)
Aug 57 to Brüggen
Dec 69 DB

4 Sqn

Dec 17 F @ Coudekerque as No 14 (Naval) Sqn — from No 7A Sqn, RNAS
Dec 17 **HP 0/100** (18)
Mar 18 to Alquines
Mar 18 to Coudekerque
Apr 18 redesignated as No 214 Sqn, RAF
Jun 18 to St-Inglevert
Jun 18 **HP 0/400** (Feb 20)
Oct 18 to Quilen
Oct 18 to Chemy
4 Jul 19 to Abu Sueir
1 Feb 20 DB — absorbed into No 216 Sqn
—
16 Sep 35 RF @ Boscombe Down — from 'B' Flt, No 9 Sqn
Sep 35 **Virginia X** (Apr 37)
15 Oct 35 to Andover det Aldergrove
1 Oct 36 to Scampton
Jan 37 **Harrow** (Jun 39)
19 Apr 37 to Feltwell
May 39 **Wellington I** (May 40)
3 Sep 39 to Methwold
Sep 39 **Wellington IA** (Sep 40)
14 Feb 40 to Stradishall
Jul 40 **Wellington IC** (Apr 42)
Nov 41 **Wellington II** (Dec 41)
5 Jan 42 to Honington
12 Jan 42 to Stradishall
Apr 42 **Stirling I** (Feb 44)
1 Oct 42 to Chedburgh
Feb 43 **Stirling III** (Jan 44)
10 Dec 43 to Downham Market
6 Jan 44 to Sculthorpe
Jan 44 **Fortress II** (Jul 45)
16 May 44 to Oulton
Nov 44 **Fortress III** (Jul 45)
27 Jul 45 DB
—
27 Jul 45 RF @ Amendola — No 614 Sqn renumbered
Jul 45 **Liberator VIII** (Nov 45)
24 Aug 45 to Ein Shemar
7 Nov 45 to Fayid
Nov 45 **Lancaster B.1** (Apr 46)
15 Apr 46 DB — renumbered as No 37 Sqn
—
5 Nov 46 RF @ Upwood
Nov 46 **Lancaster B.1(FE)** (Mar 50)
Feb 50 **Lincoln B.2** (Dec 54)
30 Dec 54 DB
—
15 Jun 55 RF @ Laarbruch
Jun 55 **Canberra PR 7** (Aug 55)
1 Aug 55 DB — renumbered as No 80 Sqn
—
21 Jan 56 RF @ Marham
Jan 56 **Valiant B(PR) 1** (Dec 57)
Mar 56 **Valiant B.1** (Nov 57)
Apr 56 **Valiant B(PR)K 1** (Dec 64)
Jan 57 **Valiant B(K) 1** (Dec 64)
1 Mar 65 DB
—
1 Jul 66 RF @ Marham
Jul 66 **Victor K.1** (Jan 77)
28 Jan 77 DB

215 Sqn

10 Mar 18 F @ Coudekerque as No 15 (Naval) Sqn — nucleus from Nos 7 and 14 Sqns, RNAS.
Mar 18 **HP 0/100** (May 18)
1 Apr 18 redesignated as No 215 Sqn, RAF
23 Apr 18 to Netheravon
May 18 **HP 0/400** (Feb 19)
13 May 19 to Andover
4 Jul 18 to Alquines
19 Aug 18 to Xaffévillers
21 Nov 18 to Alquines
2 Feb 19 to Ford Junction as a cadre
18 Oct 19 DB
—
1 Oct 35 RF @ Worthy Down — from 'C' Flt, No 58 Sqn
Oct 35 **Virginia X** (Sep 37)
14 Jan 36 to Upper Heyford
3 Sep 36 to Driffield
Feb 37 **Anson I** (Nov 37)
Aug 37 **Harrow** (Dec 39)
25 Jul 38 to Honington
Jul 39 **Wellington I** (Apr 40)
10 Sep 39 to Bramcote
24 Sep 39 to Bassingbourn dets Silloth, Jurby, Squires Gate, Harwell
Jan 40 **Anson I** (Apr 40)
8 Apr 40 DB — merged into No 11 OTU
—
8 Apr 40 RF @ Honington
Apr 40 **Wellington IA** (May 40)
18 May 40 to Bassingbourn
22 May 40 DB — merged into No 11 OTU
—
9 Dec 41 RF @ Newmarket
5 Jan 42 to Stradishall
12 Feb 42 ground echelon en route India
21 Feb 42 air echelon formed at Waterbeach
Feb 42 **Wellington IC** (Sep 43)
19 Mar 42 air echelon en route India
14 Apr 42 to Asansol
17 Apr 42 to Pandeveswar dets Dum Dum, Alipore
13 Aug 42 to St Thomas Mount dets Vizagapatam
13 Oct 42 to Chaklala det St Thomas Mount
12 Mar 43 to Jessore dets Digri, Chittagong, Cuttack
Sep 43 **Wellington X** (Aug 44) dets Kolar, Amarda Road
Jul 44 **Liberator VI** (Apr 45)
17 Sep 44 to Digri det Amarda Road
28 Dec 44 to Dhubalia
Apr 45 **Dakota** (Feb 46)
5 May 45 to Tulihal
3 Jun 45 to Basal
9 Jul 45 to Chittagong
19 Aug 45 to Hmawbi
23 Oct 45 to Kallang det Kai Tak
15 Feb 46 DB — renumbered as No 48 Sqn
—
1 Aug 47 RF @ Kabrit
Aug 47 **Dakota** (May 48)
31 Oct 47 to Aqir
23 Nov 47 to Kabrit
1 May 48 DB — renumbered as No 70 Sqn
—
30 Apr 56 RF @ Dishforth
May 56 **Pioneer CC 1** (Sep 58)
1 Sep 58 DB — renumbered as No 230 Sqn
—
1 May 63 RF @ Benson
May 63 **Argosy C.1** (Dec 67)
31 Jul 63 to Changi
31 Dec 67 DB

216 Sqn

8 Jan 18 F @ Ochey as No 16 (Naval) Sqn — ex 'A' Sqn, RNAS
Jan 18 **HP 0/100** (18)
Mar 18 **HP 0/400** (Oct 21)
30 Mar 18 to Villesneux
1 Apr 18 redesignated as No 216 Sqn, RAF det Cramaille
9 May 18 to Ochey
26 Aug 18 to Autreville
28 Sep 18 to Roville-aux-Chênes
17 Nov 18 to Quilen
14 Dec 18 to Marquise
3 Jul 19 to Qantara
Jul 20 to Abu Sueir
Aug 20 **DH 10** (Jun 22)
15 Apr 21 to Heliopolis
Jun 22 **Vimy** (Jan 26)
Dec 25 **Victoria II** (Oct 26)
Jul 26 **Victoria III** (Apr 35)
Feb 29 **Victoria V** (Aug 34)
Apr 29 **Victoria IV** (Apr 31)
Apr 33 **Victoria VI** (Nov 35)
Feb 35 **Valentia** (Sep 41) det Eastleigh
Oct 39 **Bombay** (May 43)
7 Oct 41 to El Khanka
Nov 41 **DH 86 Express** (Apr 42) dets Maaten Bagush, Gazala, Amiriya, El Adem
Jul 42 **Hudson VI** (Apr 43)
27 Nov 42 to Cairo West dets Ramat David, Habbaniyah, Khartoum, Eastleigh, Karachi, Agartala, Bari, Khormaksar
Apr 43 **Dakota** (Dec 49)
15 Jul 45 to Almaza
5 Sep 46 to Fayid
14 Feb 47 to Kabrit
Nov 49 **Valetta C.1** (Nov 55)
26 Feb 51 to Fayid
8 Nov 55 to Lyneham
Jun 56 **Comet C.2** (May 67)
Feb 62 **Comet C.4** (Jun 75)
30 Jun 75 DB
—
1 Jul 79 RF @ Honington
Jul 79 **Buccaneer S.2** (Aug 80)
4 Jul 80 to Lossiemouth
4 Aug 80 'DB' — personnel and equipment absorbed by No 12 Sqn but unit was never formally disbanded
—
1 Nov 84 'RF' (reactivated) at Brize Norton
Nov 84 **Tristar C.1** ( )
Mar 86 **Tristar K.1** ( )

217 Sqn

23 Jan 18 F @ Bierne as No 17 (Naval) Sqn — ex-RN Seaplane Base
Jan 18 **DH 4** (Mar 19)
1 Feb 18 to Bergues
1 Apr 18 redesignated as No 217 Sqn, RAF
10 Jul 18 to Crochte
25 Nov 18 to Varssenaere
29 Mar 19 to Driffield as a cadre
19 Oct 19 DB
—
15 Mar 37 RF @ Boscombe Down
Mar 37 **Anson I** (Dec 40)
7 Jun 37 to Tangmere
16 Aug 37 to Bicester
13 Sep 37 to Tangmere
28 Sep 38 to Warmwell
10 Oct 38 to Tangmere
25 Aug 39 to Warmwell
2 Oct 39 to St Eval det Carew Cheriton
Sep 40 **Beaufort I** (Nov 41)
29 Oct 41 to Thorney Island
Nov 41 **Beaufort II** (Aug 42) dets St Eval, Manston, North Coates, Skitten
6 Mar 42 to Leuchars dets Sumburgh, Skitten
7 Mar 42 en route FE, air echelon via Luqa — absorbed by No 39 Sqn
11 Aug 42 to Minneriya
Oct 42 **Hudson IIIA** (Jun 43)
Jan 43 **Hudson VI** (May 43)
10 Feb 43 to Vavuniya
Apr 43 **Beaufort I** (Aug 44) dets Addu Atoll, Santa Cruz, Cochin, Ratmalana
29 Apr 44 to Ratmalana
Jul 44 **Beaufighter X** (Sep 45)

7 Sep 44 to Vavuniya
29 Jun 45 to Gannavaram
30 Sep 45 DB
—
14 Jan 52 RF @ St Eval
Jan 52 **Neptune MR 1** (Mar 57)
7 Apr 52 to Kinloss
31 Mar 57 DB
—
1 Feb 58 RF @ St Mawgan — No 1360 Flt renumbered
Feb 58 **Whirlwind HAR 4** (Nov 59)
det Christmas Island
13 Nov 59 DB

218 Sqn

24 Apr 18 F @ Dover (Guston Road)
Apr 18 **DH 9** (Feb 19)
23 May 18 to Petite Synthe
7 Jul 18 to Fréthun
25 Oct 18 to Reumont
16 Nov 18 to Vert Galand
11 Feb 19 to Hucknall as a cadre
24 Jun 19 DB
—
16 Mar 36 RF @ Upper Heyford — from 'C' Flt, No 57 Sqn
Mar 36 **Hart** (Mar 38)
Jan 38 **Battle** (May 40)
22 Apr 38 to Boscombe Down
2 Sep 39 to Auberives-sur-Suippes
det Perpignan/La Salanque
16 May 40 to St-Lucien Ferme
21 May 40 to Nantes
13 Jun 40 to Mildenhall
Jul 40 **Blenheim IV** (Nov 40)
18 Jul 40 to Oakington
Nov 40 **Wellington IC** (Feb 42)
25 Nov 40 to Marham
May 41 **Wellington II** (Dec 41)
Jan 42 **Stirling I** (Jun 43)
8 Jul 42 to Downham Market
Feb 43 **Stirling III** (Aug 44)
7 Mar 44 to Woolfox Lodge
det Methwold
4 Aug 44 to Methwold
Aug 44 **Lancaster I & III** (Aug 45)
5 Dec 44 to Chedburgh
10 Aug 45 DB
—
1 Dec 59 **Thor** at Harrington
23 Aug 63 DB

219 Sqn

22 Jul 18 F @ Westgate (seaplanes — Nos 406 & 442 Flts) and Manston (landplanes — Nos 470, 555 & 556 Flts)
dets Bacton, Burgh Castle
Jul 18 **Hamble Baby** (Oct 18)
Jul 18 **Sopwith Baby** (Nov 18)
Jul 18 **DH 9** (Jun 19)
Jul 18 **Camel** (Jun 19)
Jul 18 **Short 184** (Feb 20)
Oct 18 **Fairey IIIB** (Feb 20)
7 Feb 20 DB
—
4 Oct 39 RF @ Catterick
Oct 39 **Blenheim IF** (Feb 41)
dets Scorton, Leeming, Redhill
Sep 40 **Beaufighter IF** (May 43)
12 Oct 40 to Redhill
dets Tangmere, Debden
10 Dec 40 to Tangmere
det Valley
23 Jun 42 to Acklington
det Drem
21 Oct 42 to Scorton
det Ayr
25 Apr 43 to Catterick
May 43 **Beaufighter VIF** (Jan 44)
14 May 43 en route N Africa
15 Jun 43 to Bone
dets La Sebala, Maison Blanche, Taher, Monastir, Luqa
21 Aug 43 to La Sebala
dets Bo Rizzo, Bone, Sidi Ahmed
19 Oct 43 to Sidi Amor
det Bone
29 Jan 44 en route UK
27 Feb 44 to Woodvale
Feb 44 **Mosquito XVII** (Nov 44)
15 Mar 44 to Honiley
26 Mar 44 to Colerne
1 Apr 44 to Bradwell Bay
Jun 44 **Mosquito XXX** (Sep 46)
29 Aug 44 to Hunsdon
10 Oct 44 to B 48/Amiens/Glisy
dets B 77/Gilze-Rijen
4 Apr 45 to B 77/Gilze-Rijen
det B 51/Lille/Vendeville
8 Jun 45 to B 106/Twente
14 Aug 45 to Acklington
17 Nov 45 to Lübeck
2 Dec 45 to Acklington
26 Feb 46 to Lübeck
9 Mar 46 to Acklington
25 Mar 46 to Spilsby
17 Apr 46 to Acklington
1 May 46 to Wittering
10 May 46 to Lübeck
25 May 46 to Wittering
1 Sep 46 DB — renumbered as No 23 Sqn
—
1 Mar 51 RF @ Kabrit
Mar 51 **Mosquito NF 36** (Mar 53)
Mar 53 **Meteor NF 13** (Sep 54)
1 Sep 54 DB
—
5 Sep 55 RF @ Driffield
Sep 55 **Venom NF 2A** (Jul 57)
31 Jul 57 DB

220 Sqn

1 Apr 18 F @ Imbros* — from 'C' Sqn (later Nos 475, 476 & 477 Flts)
Apr 18 **DH 4** (Jan 19)
Jun 18 **DH 9** (Jan 19)
Jul 18 **Camel** (Jan 19)
Sep 18 adopted No 220 Sqn numberplate
det San Stephano
Feb 19 to Mudros as a cadre
21 May 19 DB
—
17 Aug 36 RF @ Bircham Newton — nucleus from No 206 Sqn
Aug 36 **Anson I** (Dec 39)
21 Aug 39 to Thornaby
Sep 39 **Hudson I, III & VI** (Jun 42)
dets St Eval, Wick
28 Apr 41 to Wick
1 Dec 41 No 90 Sqn det, Shallufa, renumbered as No 220 Sqn det
Dec 41 **Fortress I** (Aug 42)
9 Jan 42 to Nutts Corner
det Polebrook
2 May 42 Shallufa det transferred to FE (and leaves No 220 Sqn)
20 Jun 42 to Ballykelly
Jul 42 **Fortress II** (Dec 44)
dets Benbecula, Reykjavik
14 Feb 43 to Aldergrove
20 Mar 43 to Benbecula
18 Oct 43 to Lagens
dets Gibraltar, Thorney Island
Jul 44 **Fortress III** (Apr 45)
Dec 44 **Liberator VI** (Jul 45)
1 Jun 45 to St Davids
Jul 45 **Liberator VIII** (May 46)
22 Sep 45 to Waterbeach
Sep 45 **Liberator VI** (May 46)
25 May 46 DB
—
24 Sep 51 RF @ Kinloss
Sep 51 **Shackleton MR 1** (Feb 58)
14 Nov 51 to St Eval
Mar 53 **Shackleton MR 2** (Jul 54)
4 Dec 56 to St Mawgan
Mar 57 **Shackleton MR 2** (Oct 57)
Aug 57 **Shackleton MR 3** (Oct 58)
1 Oct 58 DB — renumbered as No 201 Sqn
—
22 Jul 59 **Thor** at North Pickenham
10 Jul 63 DB

*see Appendix 12

221 Sqn

1 Apr 18 F @ Stavros* — from 'D' Sqn (later Nos 552, 553 & 554 Flts)
Apr 18 **DH 4** (Oct 18)
Apr 18 **Camel** (Sep 18)
Jul 18 **DH 9** (Oct 18)
Sep 18 adopted No 221 Sqn numberplate
15 Oct 18 to Mudros — assets absorbed by No 222 Sqn
Dec 18 re-established
Dec 18 **DH 9** (Sep 19)
29 Dec 18 en route South Russia via HMS *Riviera* & HMS *Empress*
5 Jan 19 to Batum
10 Jan 19 to Baku
15 Jan 19 to Petrovsk Kaskar
dets Chechen, Lagan
Apr 19 **DH 9A** (Sep 19)
18 Aug 19 began evacuation
1 Sep 19 DB
—
21 Nov 40 RF @ Bircham Newton
Nov 40 **Wellington IC** (Dec 41)
dets Limavady, St Eval
2 May 41 to Limavady
dets Bircham Newton, St Eval, Reykjavik
29 Sep 41 to Reykjavik
det Limavady
25 Dec 41 to Docking
Jan 42 **Wellington VIII** (Sep 43)
8 Jan 42 to LG 39
det Luqa
24 Feb 42 to LG 87 (attached to No 47 Sqn)
dets LG 05, Luqa, St Jean
14 Mar 42 re-established at LG 89
dets LG 05, Luqa, LG 99
30 Jun 42 to Shandur
dets Gianaclis, St Jean, Luqa
11 Aug 42 to Shallufa Satellite
22 Aug 42 to Shallufa
dets Idku, St Jean, Gianaclis, LG 143, Berka II
1 Feb 43 to Luqa
Jun 43 **Wellington XI** (Dec 43)
det Grottaglie
Sep 43 **Wellington XII** (Oct 43)
Oct 43 **Wellington XIII** (Aug 45)
31 Mar 44 to Grottaglie
det Foggia
23 Oct 44 to Kalamaki/Hassani
8 Apr 45 to Idku
dets Aqir, El Adem, Benina
21 Aug 45 DB

*see Appendix 12

222 Sqn

1 Apr 18 F @ Thasos* — from 'A' Sqn (later Nos 478, 479 & 480 Flts)
Apr 18 **DH 4** (Feb 19)
Apr 18 **Camel** (Feb 19)
det Stavros
6 May 18 to Stavros (combined with 'B' Sqn to form 'F' Sqn)
6 May 18 to Thasos
13 May 18 to Marian
14 May 18 to Thasos
22 May 18 to Mudros
Jun 18 **DH 9** (Feb 19)
6 Jul 18 to Imbros
7 Jul 18 to Mudros
Sep 18 adopted No 222 Sqn numberplate
dets Amberkoj, Dedeagatch
15 Nov 18 to San Stephano
23 Nov 18 to Mudros
27 Feb 19 DB
—
4 Oct 39 RF @ Duxford
Oct 39 **Blenheim IF** (Mar 40)
Mar 40 **Spitfire I** (Mar 41)
10 May 40 to Digby
23 May 40 to Kirton-in-Lindsey
28 May 40 to Hornchurch
4 Jun 40 to Kirton-in-Lindsey
29 Aug 40 to Hornchurch
11 Nov 40 to Coltishall
Mar 41 **Spitfire IIA** (Jun 41)
Mar 41 **Spitfire IIB** (Aug 41)
6 Jun 41 to Matlask
1 Jul 41 to Manston
19 Jul 41 to Southend
18 Aug 41 to North Weald
Aug 41 **Spitfire VB** (Jun 43)
30 Jun 42 to Manston
7 Jul 42 to North Weald
4 Aug 42 to Winfield
10 Aug 42 to Drem
15 Aug 42 to Biggin Hill
21 Aug 42 to Drem
22 Oct 42 to Ayr
27 Mar 43 to Southend
1 Apr 43 to Martlesham Heath
29 Apr 43 to Hornchurch
May 43 **Spitfire IX** (Aug 43)
Aug 43 **Spitfire LF IXB** (Dec
20 Dec 43 to Southend
27 Dec 43 to Hornchurch
30 Dec 43 to Woodvale
14 Feb 44 to Catterick
25 Feb 44 to Acklington
10 Mar 44 to Hornchurch
4 Apr 44 to Southend
9 Apr 44 to Selsey
30 Jun 44 to Coolham
4 Jul 44 to Funtington
6 Aug 44 to Selsey
19 Aug 44 to Tangmere
26 Aug 44 to B 17/Carpiquet
10 Sep 44 to B 35/Godelmesnil
12 Sep 44 to B 53/Merville
2 Nov 44 to B 65/Maldeghem
15 Dec 44 to Predannack
Jan 45 **Tempest V** (Oct 45)
21 Feb 45 to B 77/Gilze-Rijen
7 Apr 45 to B 91/Kluis
20 Apr 45 to B 109/Quackenbrü
4 Jun 45 to Fairwood Commo
25 Jun 45 to B 155/Dedelsdorf
3 Sep 45 to Manston
5 Sep 45 to Weston Zoyland
10 Sep 45 to Chilbolton
15 Sep 45 to Weston Zoyland
23 Oct 45 to Molesworth

Oct 45 **Meteor F.3** (Jul 48)
Dec 45 to Exeter
Mar 46 to Spilsby
Apr 46 to Exeter
Jun 46 to Boxted
Jun 46 to Exeter
Jul 46 to Weston Zoyland
Oct 46 to Tangmere
Apr 47 to Lübeck
Jun 47 to Tangmere
Dec 47 **Meteor F.4** (Oct 50)
May 48 to Lübeck
Jun 48 to Thorney Island
May 50 to Leuchars
Sep 50 **Meteor F.8** (Dec 54)
Dec 54 **Hunter F.1** (Aug 56)
Aug 56 **Hunter F.4** (Nov 57)
Nov 57 DB
—
May 60 **Bloodhound I** at Woodhall Spa
Jun 64 DB

e Appendix 12

3 Sqn

Apr 18 F @ Mitylene* — ex 'B' Sqn (later Nos 559, 560 & 561 Flts)
Apr 18 **Camel** (May 19)
Apr 18 to Stavros
May 18 **DH 4** (May 19)
Jul 18 **DH 9** (May 19)
Sep 18 adopted No 223 Sqn numberplate
Nov 18 to Mudros
May 19 DB
—
Dec 36 RF @ Nairobi — from Flt of No 45 Sqn
Dec 36 **Gordon** (Feb 37)
Feb 37 **Vincent** (Jul 38)
Jun 38 **Wellesley** (Apr 41) dets Summit
Sep 39 to Summit
Jan 40 to Gordon's Tree
May 40 to Summit dets Perim Island, Gordon's Tree
Dec 40 to Wadi Gazouza
Apr 41 to Shandur
May 41 **Maryland** (Apr 42)
May 41 Sqn acting as OTU until Jan 42
Jun 41 **Blenheim I** (Jan 42)
Nov 41 **Boston III** (Jan 42) operational (Maryland) recce flt det Fuka, El Gubbi, Timimi, Sidi Azeiz, LG 121 (Oct 41-Mar 42)
Jan 42 **Baltimore I** (Jul 42)
Mar 42 **Baltimore II** (Jul 42)
Apr 42 to LG 116 det Baheira
Jun 42 to LG 99
Jun 42 to LG 'Y'
Jul 42 **Baltimore III** (Feb 43) dets LG 86, LG 98
Sep 42 to LG 86 dets LG 'Y', LG 209, Habbaniyah, Derna, Abu Sueir
Jan 43 **Baltimore IIIA** (Sep 43)
Mar 43 to Sirtan West
Mar 43 to Sirtan North
Mar 43 to Ben Gardane
Apr 43 to Medanine
Apr 43 to La Fauconnerie
Jun 43 to Enfidaville
Jun 43 to Reyville dets Luqa
Jul 43 **Baltimore IV** (Aug 44)
Aug 43 to Monte Lungo
Aug 43 to Sigonella
Sep 43 to Brindisi
Oct 43 to Celone
Mar 44 **Baltimore V** (Aug 44)
14 Mar 44 to Biferno
26 Jun 44 to Pescara
12 Aug 44 DB — renumbered as No 30 Sqn, SAAF
—
23 Aug 44 RF @ Oulton
Aug 44 **Liberator IV** (Jun 45)
Apr 45 **Fortress II** (Jul 45)
Apr 45 **Fortress III** (Jul 45)
29 Jul 45 DB
—
1 Dec 59 **Thor** at Folkingham
23 Aug 63 DB

*see Appendix 12

224 Sqn

1 Apr 18 F @ Alimini — (Nos 496, 497 & 498 Flts)
Apr 18 **DH 4** (Apr 19)
Jun 18 **DH 9** (Apr 19)
14 Jun 18 to Andrano
9 Nov 18 to Pizzone
15 Apr 19 DB
—
1 Feb 37 RF @ Manston — from 'C' Flt, No 48 Sqn
Feb 37 **Anson I** (Jul 39)
15 Feb 37 to Boscombe Down
9 Jul 37 to Thornaby
17 Jan 38 to Eastleigh dets Montrose, Gosport
26 Mar 38 to Thornaby
1 Sep 38 to Leuchars
May 39 **Hudson I** (May 41) det Aldergrove
Mar 41 **Hudson III** (Feb 42)
15 Apr 41 to Limavady
May 41 **Hudson V** (Sep 42)
20 Dec 41 to St Eval
19 Feb 42 to Limavady det Stornoway
16 Apr 42 to Tiree
Jul 42 **Liberator III** (Apr 43)
10 Sep 42 to Beaulieu
Nov 42 **Liberator II** (Apr 43)
Jan 43 **Liberator V** (Dec 44)
23 Apr 43 to St Eval
11 Sep 44 to Milltown
Dec 44 **Liberator VI** (Mar 45)
Feb 45 **Liberator VIII** (Nov 46)
20 Jul 45 to St Eval
Oct 46 **Lancaster GR 3** (Nov 47)
10 Nov 47 DB
—
1 Mar 48 RF @ Aldergrove
Mar 48 **Halifax GR 6** (Mar 52) det Gibraltar
18 Oct 48 to Gibraltar det Aldergrove
Jul 51 **Shackleton MR 1** (Aug 54)
May 53 **Shackleton MR 2** (Oct 66)
31 Oct 66 DB

225 Sqn

1 Apr 18 F @ Alimini — (Nos 481, 482 & 483 Flts)
Apr 18 **1½ Strutter** (Jun 18)
Apr 18 **Hamble Baby Convert** (Jun 18)
Apr 18 **Camel** (Dec 18) det Pizzone
14 Jun 18 to Andrano
9 Nov 18 to Pizzone
18 Dec 18 DB
—
9 Oct 39 RF @ Odiham — from 'B' Flt, No 614 Sqn ('No 614A Sqn')
Oct 39 **Lysander II** (Sep 40)
9 Jun 40 to Old Sarum
1 Jul 40 to Tilshead dets Okehampton, Shoreham, Pembrey, Exeter, Staverton
Sep 40 **Lysander III** (Jun 42)
29 Jul 41 to Thruxton dets Weston Zoyland, Dumfries
Jan 42 **Hurricane I** (Jun 42)
Jan 42 **Hurricane IIC** (May 42)
13 May 42 to Abbotsinch
19 May 42 to Thruxton
May 42 **Mustang I** (Oct 42) det Macmerry
31 Aug 42 to Macmerry
30 Oct 42 en route N Africa via Gibraltar
13 Nov 42 to Maison Blanche
Nov 42 **Hurricane IIB** (Apr 43) det Bone
19 Nov 42 to Bone det Souk el Arba
23 Dec 42 to Souk el Arba det Souk el Khemis ('Waterloo'), Constantine
Jan 43 **Spitfire VB** (Dec 43)
Apr 43 **Mustang II** (Jul 43)
22 May 43 to Ariana det Korba
10 Jun 43 to Bou Ficha
Jul 43 **Spitfire VC** (Jan 45)
22 Aug 43 to San Francesco
7 Sep 43 to Milazzo — sqn split into two echelons:

15 Sep 43 'A' echelon to Asa
28 Sep 43 'A' echelon to Serretelle
6 Oct 43 'A' echelon to Capodichino
17 Jan 44 'A' echelon to Lago

17 Sep 43 'B' echelon to Crotone
24 Sep 43 'B' echelon to Scanzano
27 Sep 43 'B' echelon to Gioia del Colle
29 Sep 43 'B' echelon to Palazzo
5 Oct 43 'B' echelon to Celone
15 Jan 44 'B' echelon to Lago

17 Jan 44 Sqn reunited at Lago det Tre Cancelli
12 Jun 44 to Galeria
19 Jun 44 to Voltone
Jun 44 **Spitfire IX** (Dec 46)
2 Jul 44 to Follonica
20 Jul 44 to Calvi dets Rosignano, Malignano
20 Aug 44 to Ramatuelle
28 Aug 44 to Sisteron
8 Sep 44 to Lyons/Satolas
24 Sep 44 to La Jasse
28 Sep 44 to Peretola
25 Apr 45 to Bologna det Villafranca
30 Apr 45 to Villafranca
15 May 45 to Tissano
13 Aug 45 to Lavariano
19 Oct 45 to Klagenfurt
11 Jun 46 to Tissano
9 Jul 46 to Campoformido
30 Dec 46 DB
—
1 Jan 60 RF @ Andover — JEHU redesignated
Jan 60 **Sycamore HC 14** (Feb 62)
Jan 60 **Whirlwind HC 2** (Feb 62)
17 May 60 to Odiham
Nov 61 **Whirlwind HC 10** (Nov 65)
15 Nov 63 to Seletar
8 Dec 63 to Kuching
1 Nov 65 DB

226 Sqn

1 Apr 18 F @ Pizzone — (Nos 472, 473 & 474 Flts)
Apr 18 **DH 4** (Nov 18)
Jun 18 **DH 9** (Nov 18)
Jun 18 **Camel** (Nov 18)
1 Oct 18 to Andrano
3 Oct 18 to Pizzone
8 Oct 18 to Mudros
11 Nov 18 to Taranto
18 Dec 18 DB
—
15 Mar 37 RF @ Upper Heyford — from 'B' Flt, No 57 Sqn
Mar 37 **Audax** (Nov 37)
16 Apr 37 to Harwell
Oct 37 **Battle** (May 41)
2 Sep 39 to Reims dets Perpignan/La Salanque
16 May 40 to Faux-Villecerf
15 Jun 40 to Artins
18 Jun 40 to Thirsk
27 Jun 40 to Sydenham
27 May 41 to Wattisham
May 41 **Blenheim IV** (Dec 41) dets Manston, Long Kesh
Nov 41 **Boston III** (Apr 43)
9 Dec 41 to Swanton Morley dets Ouston, Thruxton, Drem
Jan 43 **Boston IIIA** (Jun 43)
May 43 **Mitchell II** (Sep 45)
13 Feb 44 to Hartford Bridge
17 Oct 44 to B 50/Vitry-en-Artois
Dec 44 **Mitchell III** (Sep 45)
22 Apr 45 to B 77/Gilze-Rijen det Fersfield
20 Sep 45 DB
—
1 Aug 59 **Thor** at Catfoss
9 Mar 63 DB

227 Sqn

1 Apr 18 F @ Pizzone — (Nos 499, 550 & 551 Flts)
Apr 18 **Caproni Ca 42** (Apr 18)
Apr 18 **DH 4** (Dec 18)
Jun 18 **DH 9** (Dec 18)
9 Dec 18 DB (without every having become fully established)
—
1 Jul 42 established at Aqir as No 10/227 Sqn operating Halifaxes pending arrival of Beaufighters
7 Sep 42 merged with No 76/462 Sqn to become No 462 Sqn
—
20 Aug 42 RF @ Luqa — from det of No 248 Sqn
Aug 42 **Beaufighter IC** (Feb 43)
Aug 42 **Beaufighter VIC** (Aug 44)
26 Nov 42 to Ta Kali
1 Mar 43 to Idku det Gambut
5 May 43 to Derna
24 Jun 43 to El Magrun
8 Jul 43 to Gardabia West
19 Jul 43 to Derna
16 Aug 43 to Limassol
23 Sep 43 to Lakatamia
Sep 43 **Beaufighter XI** (Aug 44)
Oct 43 **Beaufighter X** (Dec 43)
31 Nov 43 to Berka III det Reghaia
11 Aug 44 to Biferno
12 Aug 44 DB — renumbered as No 19 Sqn SAAF
—
7 Oct 44 RF @ Bardney — ex 'A' Flt, No 9 Sqn & 'B' Flt, No 619 Sqn (at Strubby)

Oct 44 **Lancaster I & III** (Sep 45)
12 Oct 44 to Balderton
5 Apr 45 to Strubby
8 Jun 45 to Graveley
5 Sep 45 DB

228 Sqn

20 Aug 18 F @ Great Yarmouth — (Nos 324, 325 & 326 Flts)
Aug 18 **Felixstowe F.2A** (Mar 19)
Aug 18 **Curtiss H.12/16** ( )
30 Apr 19 to Brough as a cadre
5 Jun 19 to Killingholme
30 Jun 19 DB
—
15 Dec 36 RF @ Pembroke Dock
Feb 37 **Scapa** (Aug 38)
Feb 37 **London I** (Sep 38)
Apr 37 **Singapore III** (Sep 37)
Apr 37 **Stranraer** (Apr 39)
29 Sep 38 to Invergordon
9 Oct 38 to Pembroke Dock
Nov 38 **Sunderland I** (Aug 41)
5 Jun 39 to Alexandria
10 Sep 39 to Pembroke Dock
10 Jun 40 to Alexandria det Kalafrana
19 Jul 40 to Aboukir det Kalafrana
13 Sep 40 to Kalafrana det Alexandria
25 Mar 41 to Alexandria
16 Jun 41 en route West Africa by sea
28 Aug 41 to Bathurst (aircraft arrived 1 Aug) det Calshot (aircraft returned to UK)
26 Sep 41 en route UK
9 Oct 41 re-established at Stranraer
Nov 41 **Sunderland I** (Mar 43)
Nov 41 **Sunderland II** (Mar 43)
10 Mar 42 to Oban
Mar 42 **Sunderland III** (Apr 45)
11 Dec 42 to Lough Erne/Castle Archdale
4 May 43 to Pembroke Dock
Feb 45 **Sunderland V** (Jun 45)
4 Jun 45 DB
—
1 Jun 46 RF @ St Eval — No 224Y Sqn renumbered
Jun 46 **Liberator VIII** (Sep 46)
30 Sep 46 DB
—
1 Jul 54 RF @ St Eval — nucleus from No 206 Sqn
Jul 54 **Shackleton MR 2** (Mar 59)
29 Nov 56 to St Mawgan
14 Jan 58 to St Eval
6 Mar 59 DB
—
1 Sep 59 RF @ Leconfield — No 275 Sqn renumbered
Sep 59 **Whirlwind HAR 2** (Dec 62)
Sep 59 **Whirlwind HAR 4** (Dec 62)
Sep 59 **Anson T.21** (Mar 60)
Sep 59 **Sycamore HR 14** (Jun 60) dets Acklington, Leuchars, Horsham St Faith
Sep 62 **Whirlwind HAR 10** (Aug 64)
28 Aug 64 DB — renumbered as No 202 Sqn

229 Sqn

20 Aug 18 F @ Great Yarmouth — (Nos 428, 429, 454 & 455 Flts)
Aug 18 **Sopwith Baby** (Oct 18)
Aug 18 **Hamble Baby** (Oct 18)
Aug 18 **Short 184** (Mar 19)
Aug 18 **Short 320** (Mar 19)
Nov 18 **Fairy IIIC** (Mar 19)
3 Mar 19 to Killingholme as a cadre
31 Dec 19 DB
—
4 Oct 39 RF @ Digby
Oct 39 **Blenheim IF** (Mar 40) dets Biggin Hill, Kenley
Mar 40 **Hurricane I** (Sep 41)
26 Jun 40 to Wittering det Bircham Newton
9 Sep 40 to Northolt
15 Dec 40 to Wittering
22 Dec 40 to Speke
20 May 41 en route Egypt. Air echelon via HMS *Furious* & Malta, attached to Nos 6, 73, 208, 213 & 274 Sqns pending arrival of ground echelon.
1 Sep 41 Sqn re-established @ LG 93
Sep 41 **Hurricane IIC** (Apr 42)
14 Sep 41 to LG 12 dets LG 111, LG 123
20 Nov 41 to LG 123
12 Dec 41 to Bu Amud
16 Dec 41 to Gazala
21 Dec 41 to Msus
23 Dec 41 to Mechili
9 Jan 42 to Antelat
23 Jan 42 to Mechili
25 Jan 42 to Gazala
2 Feb 42 to LG 111
7 Feb 42 to LG 102
15 Feb 42 to El Firdan
26 Mar 42 to Gambut
28 Mar 42 to Hal Far
29 Apr 42 DB
—
3 Aug 42 RF @ Ta Kali — air echelon of No 603 Sqn renumbered
Aug 42 **Spitfire VC** (Apr 44)
10 Dec 42 to Krendi
25 Sep 43 to Hal Far
Oct 43 **Spitfire IX** (Apr 44) det Catania
30 Jan 44 to Catania
5 Apr 44 to Portici (No 3 BPD)
24 Apr 44 to Hornchurch
May 44 **Spitfire IX** (Dec 44)
19 May 44 to Detling
22 Jun 44 to Tangmere
24 Jun 44 to Merston
28 Jun 44 to Gatwick
1 Jul 44 to Coltishall
25 Sep 44 to Manston
22 Oct 44 to Matlask
20 Nov 44 to Swannington
Dec 44 **Spitfire LF XVIE** (Jan 45)
2 Dec 44 to Coltishall
10 Jan 45 DB — renumbered as No 603 Sqn

230 Sqn

20 Aug 18 F @ Felixstowe — (Nos 327, 328 & 487 Flts)
Aug 18 **Curtiss H.16** (Mar 19)
Aug 18 **Felixstowe F.2A** (Mar 19)
Sep 18 **Camel** (Dec 18) det Butley
18 **Felixstowe F.3** (Mar 19)
18 **Short 184** (Mar 19)
Oct 18 **Fairey IIIB/C** (Mar 19)
13 Mar 19 reduced to a cadre
31 Dec 19 re-established from No 4 (Communications) Sqn
Jan 20 **Felixstowe F.3** (Sep 21)
Jan 20 **Fairey IIIC** (Jun 21)
Jan 20 **Felixstowe F.2A** (Apr 23)
Jan 20 **Felixstowe F.5** (Apr 23)
7 May 22 to Calshot
1 Apr 23 DB — renumbered as No 480 Flt
—
1 Dec 34 RF @ Pembroke Dock
Apr 35 **Singapore III** (Dec 38))
23 Sep 35 en route Egypt
24 Oct 35 to Alexandria
24 Nov 35 to Lake Timsah
1 Dec 35 to Alexandria
30 Jul 36 en route UK
3 Aug 36 to Pembroke Dock
14 Oct 36 en route FE
8 Jan 37 to Seletar
Jun 38 **Sunderland I** (Jan 43) dets Trincomalee, Colombo, Penang, Koggala
13 Feb 40 to Koggala
6 May 40 to Alexandria dets Kalafrana, Aboukir, Scaramanga
19 Jun 41 to Aboukir
Jun 41 **Dornier Do 22** (Feb 42) — No 2 Yugoslav Sqn attached
Oct 41 **Sunderland II** (Sep 42)
Mar 42 **Sunderland III** (Apr 45)
3 Jul 42 to Fanara
28 Jul 42 to Aboukir
9 Jan 43 to Dar-es-Salaam dets Aboukir, Bizerta, Jui, Tulear, Pamanzi
7 Feb 44 to Koggala dets Diego Garcia, Addu Atoll, Kelai, Lake Indawgyi
Feb 45 **Sunderland V** (Feb 57)
17 Apr 45 to Akyab (SS *Manela*) dets Red Hills Lake, Koggala
23 May 45 to Rangoon
26 Jul 45 to Red Hills Lake det Seletar
1 Dec 45 to Seletar
15 Apr 46 to Pembroke Dock
10 Aug 46 to Castle Archdale
16 Sep 46 to Calshot det Finkenwerder (BAL)
25 Feb 49 to Pembroke Dock
28 Feb 57 DB
—
1 Sep 58 RF @ Dishforth — No 215 Sqn renumbered
Sep 58 **Pioneer CC 1** (Dec 62)
27 Nov 58 to Nicosia
7 Apr 59 to Dishforth
30 Apr 59 to Upavon
Feb 60 **Twin Pioneer CC 1** (Jan 63)
30 May 60 to Odiham det Mamfe
Feb 62 **Twin Pioneer CC 2** (Jan 63)
Jul 62 **Whirlwind HC 10** (Dec 71)
15 Jan 63 to Gütersloh det Nicosia
31 Dec 64 to Odiham
10 Mar 65 to Labuan dets Kuching, Tawau, Sepulot
25 Nov 66 to Odiham det Nicosia
10 Mar 69 to Wittering det Nicosia
3 Dec 71 DB
—
1 Oct 71 Training at Odiham as No 230 Sqn (Puma Echelon)
—
1 Jan 72 RF @ Odiham
Jan 72 **Puma HC 1** ( )
14 Oct 80 to Gütersloh

231 Sqn

20 Aug 18 F @ Felixstowe — (Nos 329 & 330 Flts)
Aug 18 **Felixstowe F.2A** (Mar 19)
Aug 18 **Felixstowe F.3** (Mar 19)
Nov 18 **Felixstowe F.5** (Mar 19)
13 Mar 19 reduced to a cadre
7 Jul 19 DB
—
1 Jul 40 RF @ Aldergrove — from No 416 Flt
Jul 40 **Lysander II** (Aug 41)
15 Jul 40 to Newtownards
Nov 40 **Lysander III** (May 43)
Oct 41 **Tomahawk I & IIB** (Jul 43)
11 Dec 41 to Long Kesh
6 Jan 42 to Maghaberry
20 Nov 42 to Long Kesh
2 Jan 43 to Nutts Corner dets Ballyhalbert
21 Mar 43 to Clifton
Mar 43 **Mustang I** (Jan 44) dets Ballyhalbert
6 Jul 43 to Dunsfold
11 Jul 43 to Weston Zoyland
21 Jul 43 to Dunsfold
28 Jul 43 to Woodchurch
15 Oct 43 to Redhill
15 Jan 44 DB
—
7 Sep 44 RF @ Dorval
Sep 44 **Dakota** (Jan 46)
Sep 44 **Hudson IIIA** (Jan 46)
Sep 44 **Hudson VI** (Dec 45)
Sep 44 **Liberator I** (Jan 46)
Sep 44 **Liberator II** (Jan 46)
Sep 44 **Liberator III** (Jan 46)
Sep 44 **Coronado** (Jan 46)
Sep 44 **Spartan Executive** (Sep 45)
44 **Marauder (B-26A)** (Jul 45)
Feb 45 **Liberator IX** (Jan 46)
Sep 45 det Bermuda for Coronado operations
1 Dec 45 Flt formed at Full Sutton for Lancastrian
Dec 45 **Lancastrian C.2** (Jan 46
15 Jan 46 DB — UK Flt became Lancastrian Training Unit/No 1699 HCU

232 Sqn

20 Aug 18 F @ Felixstowe — (Nos 333, 334 & 335 Flts)
Aug 18 **Felixstowe F.2A** (Jan 19
Aug 18 **Felixstowe F.3** (Jan 19)
5 Jan 19 DB — redesignated as No 4 (Communications Sqn
—
17 Jul 40 RF @ Sumburgh — fro 'B' Flt, No 3 Sqn
Jul 40 **Hurricane I** (Apr 41)
18 Sep 40 to Castletown
13 Oct 40 to Skitten
24 Oct 40 to Drem
11 Nov 40 to Skitten
4 Dec 40 to Elgin
29 Apr 41 to Montrose
19 Jul 41 to Abbotsinch
Jul 41 **Hurricane I** (Nov 41)
21 Jul 41 to Ouston
Aug 41 **Hurricane IIB** (Feb 42)
11 Nov 41 en route ME, diverted FE
13 Jan 42 to Seletar (personnel from Nos 17, 135, 136 232 Sqns — sometimes referred to as '232(I)' S — see No 242 Sqn) det Kallang
5 Feb 42 to P I dets Kallang
14 Feb 42 to P II

Feb 42 to Tjilitjan
Feb 42 DB — absorbed by No 242/'232(II)' Sqn
—
Apr 42 RF @ Atcham
Apr 42 **Spitfire VB** (Nov 42)
May 42 to Llanbedr
dets Ayr, Merston
Aug 42 to Turnhouse
Aug 42 to Gravesend
Aug 42 to Debden
Sep 42 to Turnhouse
Nov 42 en route N Africa
Dec 42 to Phillipeville
Dec 42 to Constantine
Jan 43 to Bone
Jan 43 **Spitfire VB** (Feb 44)
Jan 43 to Tingley
Mar 43 to Souk el Khemis ('Victoria')
May 43 to Protville
May 43 to Sousse
Jun 43 to Ta Kali
Jun 43 **Spitfire IX** (Oct 44)
Jul 43 to Lentini East
Jul 43 **Spitfire VC** (Feb 44)
Sep 43 to Milazzo East
Sep 43 to Asa
Sep 43 to Serretelle
Oct 43 to Gioia del Colle
Dec 43 to Bab-el-Haoua
dets Lakatamia, Ramat David
Feb 44 to Almaza (No 22 PTC)
dets Ramat David, Muqueibila
Mar 44 to Ajaccio
Apr 44 to Alto
Apr 44 to Poretta
Jul 44 to Calenzana
Aug 44 to Frejus
Oct 44 to Gragnano (No 56 PTC)
Oct 44 DB
—
Nov 44 RF @ Stoney Cross
Dec 44 **Wellington XVI** (Feb 45)
Jan 45 reduced to a cadre — dispersed between No 243 Sqn and No 1315 Flt
Feb 45 re-established at Stoney Cross
Feb 45 **Liberator VII** (Aug 46)
Feb 45 to Palam
det Holmsley South
May 45 **Skymaster I** (Apr 46)
Jul 45 **Liberator III** (Dec 45)
dets Ratmalana, Negombo
Sep 45 **Liberator VI** (Aug 46)
Jan 46 **Liberator VIII** (Aug 46)
Mar 46 **Lancastrian C.2** (Aug 46)
Jun 46 to Poona
Aug 46 DB

3 Sqn

Aug 18 F @ Dover (Harbour and Guston Road) — (Nos 407, 471 & 491 Flts)
Aug 18 **Camel** (Nov 18)
det Walmer
Aug 18 **DH 9** (Mar 19)
Aug 18 **Short 184** (May 19)
Jan 19 **DH 4** (May 19)
May 19 DB
—
May 37 RF @ Upper Heyford
May 37 **Anson I** (Dec 39)
Jul 37 to Thornaby
Sep 38 to Leuchars
Sep 38 to Montrose
Oct 38 to Leuchars
Aug 39 **Hudson I** (Jun 41)
Oct 39 **Blenheim IV** (Jan 40)
det Bircham Newton
Aug 40 to Aldergrove
Sep 40 to Leuchars
Dec 40 to Aldergrove
Jan 41 **Hudson III** (Mar 44)
Jun 41 **Hudson V** (Aug 42)
16 Aug 41 to St Eval
dets Thorney Island, Gibraltar
2 Jan 42 to Thorney Island
dets St Eval, Gibraltar
12 Jul 42 to Gibraltar
Jul 42 **Hudson IIIA** (Mar 44)
det Lagens
5 Mar 44 to Blakehill Farm
Mar 44 **Dakota** (Dec 45)
8 Jun 45 to Odiham
15 Aug 45 en route FE
1 Sep 45 to Tulihal
det Toungoo
15 Dec 45 DB — absorbed by No 215 Sqn
—
1 Sep 60 RF @ Khormaksar — from Valetta Flight of No 84 Sqn
Sep 60 **Valetta C.1** (Jan 64)
31 Jan 64 DB

234 Sqn

Aug 18 F @ Trescoe — (Nos 350, 351, 352 & 353 Flts)
Aug 18 **Curtiss H.12** ( )
Aug 18 **Short 184** (May 19)
Aug 18 **Felixstowe F.3** (May 19)
15 May 19 DB
—
30 Oct 39 RF @ Leconfield
Nov 39 **Battle** (Mar 40)
Nov 39 **Blenheim IF** (Mar 40)
Nov 39 **Gauntlet II** (Dec 39)
Mar 40 **Spitfire I** (Apr 41)
22 May 40 to Church Fenton
18 Jun 40 to St Eval
14 Aug 40 to Middle Wallop
11 Sep 40 to St Eval
24 Feb 41 to Warmwell
Mar 41 **Spitfire IIA** (Sep 41)
Sep 41 **Spitfire VB** (Oct 44)
5 Nov 41 to Ibsley
24 Dec 41 to Predannack
31 Dec 41 to Ibsley
23 Mar 42 to Warmwell
4 Apr 42 to Ibsley
27 Apr 42 to Portreath
23 Aug 42 to Charmy Down
30 Aug 42 to Portreath
dets Predannack, Perranporth
28 Oct 42 to Perranporth
Oct 42 **Spitfire IV** (Apr 43)
26 Nov 42 to Portreath
26 Dec 42 to Perranporth
19 Jan 43 to Grimsetter
Jan 43 **Spitfire VI** (May 43)
det Sumburgh
24 Apr 43 to Skaebrae
26 Jun 43 to Church Stanton
8 Jul 43 to Honiley
5 Aug 43 to West Malling
16 Sep 43 to Southend
15 Oct 43 to Hutton Cranswick
31 Dec 43 to Church Fenton
28 Jan 44 to Coltishall
18 Mar 44 to Bolt Head
29 Apr 44 to Deanland
19 Jun 44 to Predannack
28 Aug 44 to North Weald
Sep 44 **Mustang III** (Apr 45)
17 Dec 44 to Bentwaters
Mar 45 **Mustang IV** (Aug 45)
1 May 45 to Peterhead
3 Jul 45 to Dyce
27 Jul 45 to Bentwaters
27 Aug 45 to Hawkinge
21 Sep 45 to Bentwaters
Aug 45 **Spitfire IX** (Feb 46)
12 Feb 46 to Molesworth
Feb 46 **Meteor F.3** (Sep 46)
28 Mar 46 to Boxted
1 Sep 46 DB — renumbered as No 266 Sqn
—
1 Aug 52 RF @ Oldenburg
Aug 52 **Vampire FB 5** (Jan 54)
Aug 52 **Vampire FB 9** (Jan 54)
Nov 53 **Sabre F.4** (May 56)
8 Jan 54 to Geilenkirchen
May 56 **Hunter F.4** (Jul 57)
15 Jul 57 DB

235 Sqn

Aug 18 F @ Newlyn — (Nos 424 & 425 Flts)
Aug 18 **Short 184** (Feb 19)
22 Feb 19 DB
—
30 Oct 39 RF @ Manston
Dec 39 **Battle** (Feb 40)
Feb 40 **Blenheim IVF** (Dec 41)
27 Feb 40 to North Coates
Feb 40 **Blenheim IF** (May 40)
25 Apr 40 to Bircham Newton
26 May 40 to Detling
10 Jun 40 to Thorney Island
24 Jun 40 to Bircham Newton
dets Thorney Island, Aldergrove
4 Jun 41 to Dyce
det Sumburgh
Dec 41 **Beaufighter IC** (Sep 42)
25 Mar 42 to Sumburgh
31 May 42 to Docking
16 Jul 42 to Chivenor
Jul 42 **Beaufighter VIC** (Oct 43)
21 Jan 43 to Leuchars
dets Sumburgh, Tain, St Eval
29 Aug 43 to Portreath
Oct 43 **Beaufighter X** (May 44)
det St Angelo
21 Feb 44 to St Angelo
27 Mar 44 to Portreath
Apr 44 **Beaufighter XI** (Jun 44)
Jun 44 **Mosquito VI** (Jul 45)
6 Sep 44 to Banff
10 Jul 45 DB

236 Sqn

Aug 18 F @ Mullion — (Nos 493, 515 & 516 Flts)
Aug 18 **DH 6** (Mar 19)
Aug 18 **DH 9** (May 19)
31 May 19 DB
—
30 Oct 39 RF @ Stradishall
Nov 39 **Blenheim IF** (Jul 40)
9 Dec 39 to Martlesham Heath
29 Feb 40 to North Coates
29 Apr 40 to Speke
25 May 40 to Filton
14 Jun 40 to Middle Wallop
4 Jul 40 to Thorney Island
Jul 40 **Blenheim IVF** (Feb 42)
det St Eval
8 Aug 40 to St Eval
21 Mar 41 to Carew Cheriton
det St Eval
Oct 41 **Beaufighter IC** (Feb 42)
9 Feb 42 to Wattisham and reduced to a cadre (crews to ME)
14 Mar 42 re-established
Mar 42 **Beaufighter IC** (Feb 43)
3 Jul 42 to Oulton
18 Sep 42 to North Coates
Sep 42 **Beaufighter VIC** (Jul 43)
dets Wick, Sumburgh, Predannack
Jul 43 **Beaufighter X** (May 45)
25 May 45 DB

237 Sqn

Aug 18 F @ Cattewater — (Nos 420, 421, 422 & 423 Flts)
Aug 18 **Short 184** (May 19)
15 May 19 DB
—
22 Apr 40 RF @ Nairobi — No 1 Sqn, SRAF redesignated
Apr 40 **Audax** (Sep 40)
Apr 40 **Hardy** (Apr 41)
dets Wajir, Malindini, Buna, Garissa
Jun 40 **Hart** (Sep 40)
30 Sep 40 to Gordons Tree
Nov 40 **Lysander I & II** (Nov 41)
dets Blackdown
30 Jan 41 to Umtali
dets Blackdown, Agordat
9 Mar 41 to Barentu
det Agordat
Mar 41 **Gladiator II** (Aug 41)
27 Mar 41 to Umritsar
7 Apr 41 to Asmara
30 May 41 to Wadi Halfa
det Kufra
24 Aug 41 to Kasfareet
Sep 41 **Hurricane I** (Dec 42)
21 Sep 41 to 'Y' LG
30 Oct 41 to LG 10
14 Nov 41 to LG 75
dets LG 112, LG 132
22 Nov 41 to LG 128
12 Dec 41 to Gambut
det Bu Amud
21 Dec 41 to Tmimi
31 Dec 41 to Berka
7 Jan 42 to Tmimi
28 Jan 42 to El Firdan
6 Feb 42 to Ismailia
1 Mar 42 to Mosul
9 Jul 42 to Qaiyarh
13 Sep 42 to Kermanshah
det Abadan
1 Dec 42 to Kirkuk
Jan 43 en route Egypt
6 Feb 43 to Shandur
Feb 43 **Hurricane IIC** (Dec 43)
17 Feb 43 to LG 106
10 Jun 43 to Bersis
12 Sep 43 to Idku
det Paphos
Dec 43 **Spitfire VB** (Feb 44)
Dec 43 **Spitfire VC** (Mar 44)
9 Dec 43 to Savoia
31 Jan 44 to Sidi Barrani
25 Feb 44 to Idku
det Aboukir
Mar 44 **Spitfire IX** (Sep 45)
19 Apr 44 to Poretta
23 May 44 to Serragia
9 Jul 44 to Calvi
27 Aug 44 to Cuers
4 Oct 44 to Falconara
dets Pisa, Rosignano
24 Feb 45 to Rosignano
8 Oct 45 to Lavariano as a cadre
1 Jan 46 DB — renumbered as No 93 Sqn

238 Sqn

20 Aug 18 F @ Cattewater — (Nos 347, 348 & 349 Flts)
Aug 18 **Curtiss H.16** ( )
Aug 18 **Short 184** (May 19)
Aug 18 **Felixstowe F.2A** (May 19)
Aug 18 **Felixstowe F.3** (May 19)
dets Holy Island, Killingholme, Calshot
15 May 19 reduced to a cadre
20 Mar 22 DB
—
16 May 40 RF @ Tangmere
May 40 **Spitfire I** (Jun 40)
20 Jun 40 to Middle Wallop
Jun 40 **Hurricane I** (Mar 41)
det Warmwell

14 Aug 40 to St Eval
10 Sep 40 to Middle Wallop
30 Sep 40 to Chilbolton
Jan 41 to Middle Wallop
1 Feb 41 to Chilbolton
Mar 41 **Hurricane IIA** (May 41)
1 Apr 41 to Pembrey det Carew Cheriton
16 Apr 41 to Chilbolton
May 41 **Hurricane I** (Sep 41)
20 May 41 en route Egypt. Air echelon via HMS *Victorious*, Ta Kali, LG 07 & Gerawala (attached to No 274 Sqn until 20 Aug 41)
17 Jul 41 to El Firdan (ground echelon)
24 Jul 41 to LG 92 (ground echelon)
Sep 41 **Hurricane IIC** (Jan 42)
15 Sep 41 to LG 12
13 Nov 41 to LG 123 dets Sidi Haneish, Gazala, Mechili
26 Dec 41 to Msus
1 Jan 42 to Antelat
19 Jan 42 to El Gubbi
Jan 42 **Hurricane I** (May 42)
3 Feb 42 to Gambut
14 May 42 to LG 121
May 42 **Hurricane IIB** (Oct 42)
1 Jun 42 to Gambut West
16 Jun 42 to LG 155
20 Jun 42 to LG 76
24 Jun 42 to LG 13 det LG 15
26 Jun 42 to LG 105
28 Jun 42 to LG 92
Sep 42 **Hurricane IIC** (Sep 43)
26 Sep 42 to LG 154
23 Oct 42 to LG 172
7 Nov 42 to LG 20
9 Nov 42 to LG 12
11 Nov 42 to LG 101
13 Nov 42 to LG 125
20 Nov 42 to El Adem
25 Nov 42 to Benina
28 Nov 42 to Martuba
13 Jan 43 to El Gamil
Feb 43 **Spitfire VB** (Apr 43)
Feb 43 **Spitfire VC** (Apr 43)
Aug 43 **Spitfire VC** (Mar 44)
Aug 43 **Spitfire IX** (Oct 44)
29 Jan 44 to LG 106
28 Apr 44 to Poretta
1 May 44 to Serragia
Jun 44 **Spitfire VIII** (Oct 44)
8 Jul 44 to Calvi
30 Aug 44 to Cuers
22 Sep 44 to Le Vallon
9 Oct 44 to Gragnano (No 56 PTC)
26 Oct 44 DB
—
1 Dec 44 RF @ Merryfield
Jan 45 **Dakota** (Dec 45)
22 Feb 45 to Raipur
13 Mar 45 to Comilla
26 Jun 45 en route Australia
2 Jul 45 to Parafield
27 Dec 45 DB
—
1 Dec 46 RF @ Abingdon — No 525 Sqn renumbered
Dec 46 **Dakota** (Oct 48) det Schwecat
24 Nov 47 to Oakington
4 Oct 48 DB — renumbered as No 10 Sqn

239 Sqn

Aug 18 F @ Torquay — (No 418 Flt)
Aug 18 **Short 184** (May 19)
31 May 19 DB
—
18 Sep 40 RF @ Hatfield — nucleus from Nos 16 and 225 Sqns
Sep 40 **Lysander II** (May 41) dets Gatwick, Cambridge
22 Jan 41 to Gatwick
Apr 41 **Lysander III** (Jan 42)
Jun 41 **Tomahawk I & II** (Sep 42)
6 Jul 41 to Weston Zoyland
13 Jul 41 to Gatwick
26 Sep 41 to Netheravon
30 Sep 41 to Kidlington
3 Oct 41 to Gatwick
Jan 42 **Hurricane I** (May 42)
Jan 42 **Hurricane IIC** (May 42)
3 May 42 to Abbotsinch
May 42 **Mustang I** (Sep 43)
14 May 42 to Gatwick
19 May 42 to Detling
31 May 42 to Gatwick
31 Aug 42 to Twinwood Farm dets Snailwell, Gatwick
22 Oct 42 to Cranfield det Sawbridgeworth
18 Nov 42 to Odiham
6 Dec 42 to Hurn
25 Jan 43 to Stoney Cross
10 Mar 43 to Eastmanton Down
11 Mar 43 to Lasham
12 Mar 43 to Stoney Cross
7 Apr 43 to Gatwick
21 Jun 43 to Fairlop
27 Jun 43 to Martlesham Heath
9 Jul 43 to Fairlop
15 Aug 43 to Hornchurch
30 Sep 43 to Ayr
Oct 43 **Beaufighter IF** (Jan 44)
10 Dec 43 to West Raynham
Jan 44 **Mosquito II** (Aug 44)
Aug 44 **Mosquito VI** (Jan 45)
Jan 45 **Mosquito XXX** (Jul 45)
1 Jul 45 DB

240 Sqn

20 Aug 18 F @ Calshot — (Nos 345, 346, 410 & 411 Flts)
Aug 18 **Curtiss H.12** ( )
Aug 18 **Short 184** (May 19)
Aug 18 **Short 320** (May 19)
Aug 18 **Campania** (May 19)
Aug 18 **Felixstowe F.2A** (May 19)
15 May 19 DB
—
30 Mar 37 RF @ Calshot — ex 'C' Flt, Seaplane Training Sqn
Mar 37 **Scapa** (Jan 39)
Nov 38 **Singapore III** (Jul 39)
Jul 39 **Lerwick I** (Sep 39)
Jul 39 **London II** (Jul 40)
12 Aug 39 to Invergordon det Falmouth
4 Nov 39 to Sullom Voe
12 Feb 40 to Invergordon
27 Mar 40 to Sullom Voe
27 May 40 to Pembroke Dock
Jun 40 **Stranraer** (Apr 41)
30 Jul 40 to Stranraer det Lough Erne
Mar 41 **Catalina I** (Jun 45)
28 Mar 41 to Kiladeas
23 Aug 41 to Lough Erne
Mar 42 **Catalina IIA** (Nov 44)
29 May 42 en route FE
4 Jul 42 to Red Hills Lake dets Coconada, Cochin, Koggala, Addu Atoll, Kelai, Diego Garcia, China Bay
Jul 44 **Catalina IV** (Jun 45)
1 Jul 45 DB
—
1 Jul 45 RF @ Red Hills Lake — from elements of Nos 212 & 240 Sqns
Jul 45 **Catalina I** (Oct 45)
Jul 45 **Catalina IV** (Aug 45)
Jul 45 **Sunderland V** (Mar 46) dets Bally, China Bay, Penang, Rangoon
10 Jan 46 to Koggala
21 Mar 46 DB
—
1 May 52 RF @ Aldergrove — nucleus from No 120 Sqn
May 52 **Shackleton MR 1** (Nov 58)
27 May 52 to St Eval
5 Jun 52 to Ballykelly
Mar 53 **Shackleton MR 2** (Aug 54)
1 Nov 58 DB — renumbered as No 203 Sqn
—
1 Aug 59 **Thor** at Breighton
8 Jan 63 DB

241 Sqn

Aug 18 F @ Portland — (Nos 416, 417 & 513 Flts) det Chickerall
Aug 18 **DH 6** (Jan 19)
Aug 18 **Short 184** (Jun 19)
Aug 18 **Campania** (Jun 19)
Aug 18 **Wight Converted** (Jun 19)
18 Jun 19 DB
—
25 Sep 40 RF @ Longman — ex 'A' Flts of Nos 4 & 614 Sqns
Sep 40 **Lysander II** (Dec 40)
Nov 40 **Roc** (Nov 40)
Dec 40 **Lysander III** (May 42)
11 Apr 41 to Bury St Edmunds
1 Jul 41 to Bottisham
Aug 41 **Tomahawk IIA** (May 42) dets Snailwell, Macmerry, Henlow, Docking
Mar 42 **Mustang I** (Nov 42)
2 May 42 to Ayr det Turnhouse
12 Nov 42 en route N Africa
30 Nov 42 to Maison Blanche
Dec 42 **Hurricane IIB** (Dec 43)
15 Dec 42 to Constantine
21 Dec 42 to Souk el Arba
16 Jan 43 to Souk el Khemis ('Euston')
Feb 43 **Spitfire VC** (Mar 43) dets Constantine, Thelepte
15 May 43 to Ariana
15 Jun 43 to Bou Ficha
25 Oct 43 to Phillipeville
Dec 43 **Spitfire IX** (Aug 45)
23 Dec 43 to El Aouina
31 Dec 43 to Palata
Jan 44 **Spitfire VIII** (Oct 44) det Canne
20 Jan 44 to Madna
22 Feb 44 to Canne det Pomigliano
7 Apr 44 to Trigno det San Angelo
1 Jun 44 to Sinello
18 Jun 44 to San Vito
27 Jun 44 to Tortoreto
1 Jul 44 to Fermo
29 Jul 44 to Falconara
24 Aug 44 to Chiaravalle
1 Sep 44 to Piagiolino
17 Sep 44 to Cassandro
28 Sep 44 to Rimini
6 Nov 44 to Fano
4 Dec 44 to Bellaria
3 May 45 to Treviso
14 Aug 45 DB

242 Sqn

Aug 18 F @ Newhaven — (Nos 408, 409 & 514 Flts)
Aug 18 **Short 184** (May 19)
Aug 18 **DH 6** (Jan 19)
Oct 18 **Campania** (Nov 18) det Telscombe Cliffs
15 May 19 DB
—
30 Oct 39 RF @ Church Fenton
Dec 39 **Blenheim I** (Dec 39)
Dec 39 **Battle** (Feb 40)
Feb 40 **Hurricane I** (Mar 41)
21 May 40 to Biggin Hill
8 Jun 40 to Châteaudun
14 Jun 40 to Ancenis
16 Jun 40 to Nantes
18 Jun 40 to Coltishall
26 Oct 40 to Duxford
30 Nov 40 to Coltishall
16 Dec 40 to Martlesham Heath
Mar 41 **Hurricane IIB** (Mar 4
9 Apr 41 to Stapleford Tawney
22 May 41 to North Weald
19 Jul 41 to Manston
16 Sep 41 to Valley
1 Nov 41 en route FE via HMS *Argus*
12 Nov 41 pilots diverted to Mal via HMS *Argus* & HM *Ark Royal*
7 Jan 42 established at Ta Kali dets Hal Far, Luqa
17 Mar 42 DB — absorbed by N 126 Sqn
30 Jan 42 to P I (personnel from Nos 232, 242 and 605 Sqns — sometimes referred to as '232(II) Sqn)
5 Feb 42 to Tengah
5 Feb 42 to Kallang
10 Feb 42 to P I
14 Feb 42 to P II
18 Feb 42 to Tjilitjan
2 Mar 42 to Andir
7 Mar 42 to Tasikmalaja
10 Mar 42 DB — dispersed
—
10 Apr 42 RF @ Turnhouse
Apr 42 **Spitfire VB** (Dec 43)
15 May 42 to Ouston
1 Jun 42 to Drem
11 Aug 42 to North Weald
14 Aug 42 to Manston
20 Aug 42 to North Weald
1 Sep 42 to Digby
30 Oct 42 en route N Africa
8 Nov 42 to Maison Blanche
14 Nov 42 to Djedjelli
23 Nov 42 to Bone
5 Jan 43 to Constantine det Setif
24 Jan 43 to Tingley
29 Jan 43 to Setif det Constantine
23 Feb 43 to Souk el Khemis ('Paddington')
13 Mar 43 to Tingley
19 Apr 43 to Souk el Khemis ('Marylebone')
13 May 43 to Sidi Athman
30 May 43 to Sousse
5 Jun 43 to Ta Kali
Jul 43 **Spitfire VC** (Feb 44)
Jul 43 **Spitfire IX** (Nov 44)
22 Jul 43 to Lentini East
6 Sep 43 to Milazzo East
16 Sep 43 to Asa
24 Sep 43 to Serretelle
13 Oct 43 to Gioia del Colle
23 Dec 43 to Afisse North det Ramat David
18 Feb 44 to Almaza (No 22 PT det Ramat David
30 Mar 44 to Ajaccio
5 Apr 44 to Alto
19 Apr 44 to Poretta
11 Jul 44 to Calenzana
23 Aug 44 to Frejus
4 Sep 44 to Montelimar

1 Sep 44 to Le Vallon
6 Oct 44 to Gragnano (No 56 PTC)
4 Nov 44 DB
—
5 Nov 44 RF @ Stoney Cross
Jan 45 **Wellington XVI** (Feb 45)
Feb 45 **Stirling V** (Dec 45)
Apr 45 **York I** (Jul 45)
Sep 45 **Stirling IV** (Dec 45)
9 Dec 45 to Merryfield
Dec 45 **York C.1** (Sep 49)
7 May 46 to Oakington
7 Nov 47 to Waterbeach
1 Dec 47 to Abingdon det Wunstorf for BAL
5 Jun 49 to Lyneham
Aug 49 **Hastings C.1** (Apr 50)
1 May 50 DB
—
1 Oct 59 **Bloodhound I** at Marham
0 Sep 64 DB

43 Sqn

Aug 18 F @ Cherbourg — (Nos 414 & 415 Flts)
Aug 18 **Short 184** (Mar 19)
Aug 18 **Wight Converted** (Mar 19)
5 Mar 19 DB
—
Mar 41 RF @ Kallang
Apr 41 **Buffalo I** (Jan 42) det Kota Bahru
) Jan 42 DB — evacuated
—
Jun 42 RF @ Ouston
Jun 42 **Spitfire VB** (Oct 42) det Greatham
Sep 42 to Turnhouse
Nov 42 en route North Africa
Dec 42 to Phillipeville
Jan 43 **Spitfire VB** (Feb 44)
Jan 43 **Spitfire VC** (Feb 44)
Jan 43 to Constantine
Jan 43 to Bone
Jan 43 to Tingley
Jan 43 to Souk el Khemis ('Euston')
May 43 to La Sebala II
May 43 to Mateur
Jun 43 to Hal Far
Jun 43 **Spitfire IX** (Sep 44)
Jul 43 to Comiso
Jul 43 to Pachino
Aug 43 to Panebianco
Aug 43 to Catania
Sep 43 to Cassala
Sep 43 to Falcone
Sep 43 to Tusciano
Oct 43 to Capodichino
Nov 43 to Gioia del Colle
Dec 43 to Aleppo dets Nicosia, Ramat David
Feb 44 to Almaza (No 22 PTC) dets Ramat David, Muqueibila
Mar 44 to Ajaccio
Apr 44 to Alto
Apr 44 to Poretta
Jul 44 to Calenzana
Aug 44 to Frejus
Sep 44 to Montelimar
Sep 44 to Le Vallon
Oct 44 to Gragnano (No 56 PTC)
Oct 44 DB
—
Dec 44 RF @ Morecambe (No 2 PDC) — advanced air echelon
Dec 44 en route Canada
Dec 44 to Dorval
Dec 44 **Dakota** (Apr 46)
Jan 45 en route Australia
Feb 45 to Camden

Dec 44 ground echelon assembled West Kirby (No 1 PDC)
22 Dec 44 en route Australia
27 Jan 45 to Camden

4 Jan 45 rear air echelon F @ Stoney Cross — from No 232 Sqn
6 Jan 45 to Merryfield
Jan 45 **Dakota** (Mar 45)
9 Mar 45 to Morecambe (No 2 PDC)
13 Mar 45 en route Canada
21 Mar 45 to Dorval
Mar 45 **Dakota** (Apr 46)
4 Apr 45 en route Australia
15 Apr 45 to Camden

15 Apr 46 DB

244 Sqn

25 Jul 18 F @ Bangor — (Nos 521, 522 & 530 Flts)
Jul 18 **DH 6** (Jan 19) dets Tallaght, Llangefni, Luce Bay
22 Jan 19 DB
—
1 Nov 40 RF @ Shaibah — from 'S' Sqn
Nov 40 **Vincent** (Jan 43) dets Mosul, Sharjah
Apr 42 **Blenheim IV** (Dec 42)
May 42 to Sharjah
Oct 42 **Blenheim V** (Apr 44) dets Ras al Hadd, Jask, Masirah
Feb 44 **Wellington XIII** (May 45)
17 Mar 44 to Masirah dets Khormaksar, Mogadishu, Santa Cruz
1 May 45 DB

245 Sqn

Aug 18 F @ Fishguard — (Nos 426 & 427 Flts)
Aug 18 **Short 184** (May 19)
10 May 19 DB
—
30 Oct 39 RF @ Leconfield
Nov 39 **Blenheim IF** (Mar 40)
Feb 40 **Battle** (Mar 40) dets Church Fenton, Acklington
Mar 40 **Hurricane I** (Aug 41)
12 May 40 to Drem det Hawkinge
5 Jun 40 to Turnhouse det Hawkinge
20 Jul 40 to Aldergrove dets Limavady, Ballyhalbert
14 Jul 41 to Ballyhalbert det Limavady
Aug 41 **Hurricane IIB** (Sep 42)
1 Sep 41 to Chilbolton
17 Nov 41 to Warmwell
23 Nov 41 to Chilbolton
19 Dec 41 to Middle Wallop det Shoreham
May 42 **Hurricane IIC** (Jan 43)
26 Oct 42 to Charmy Down
Dec 42 **Typhoon IB** (Aug 45)
29 Jan 43 to Peterhead
30 Mar 43 to Gravesend dets Matlask, Ludham, Lympne
28 May 43 to Fairlop
2 Jun 43 to Selsey
1 Jul 43 to Lydd
10 Oct 43 to Westhampnett
1 Apr 44 to Holmsley South
25 Apr 44 to Eastchurch
30 Apr 44 to Holmsley South
12 May 44 to Eastchurch
22 May 44 to Holmsley South
27 Jun 44 to B 5/Camilly
28 Aug 44 to B 24/St-André-de-l'Eure
2 Sep 44 to B 42/Tillé
4 Sep 44 to B 50/Vitry-en-Artois
17 Sep 44 to B 70/Deurne
30 Sep 44 to B 80/Volkel
19 Dec 44 to Warmwell
6 Jan 45 to B 80/Volkel
20 Mar 45 to B 100/Goch
11 Apr 45 to B 110/Achmer
16 Apr 45 to B 150/Hustedt
28 May 45 to B 164/Schleswig
16 Jun 45 to Warmwell
4 Jul 45 to B 164/Schleswig
10 Aug 45 DB
—
10 Aug 45 RF @ Colerne — No 504 Sqn renumbered
Aug 45 **Meteor F.3** (Apr 48)
18 Feb 46 to Fairwood Common
20 Mar 46 to Colerne
2 Jun 46 to Bentwaters
9 Jun 46 to Colerne
16 Aug 46 to Horsham St Faith
29 Oct 46 to Lübeck
15 Dec 46 to Horsham St Faith
30 Jun 47 to Lübeck
30 Aug 47 to Horsham St Faith
Dec 47 **Meteor F.4** (Jul 50)
Jun 50 **Meteor F.8** (Apr 57)
27 Jun 55 to Stradishall
Apr 57 **Hunter F.4** (Jun 57)
30 Jun 57 DB
—
21 Aug 58 RF @ Watton — No 527 Sqn renumbered
Aug 58 **Canberra B.2** (Apr 63)
25 Aug 58 to Tangmere
19 Apr 63 DB — renumbered as No 98 Sqn

246 Sqn

Aug 18 F @ Seaton Carew — (Nos 402, 403, 451, 452 & 495 Flts)
Aug 18 **FE 2B** (Oct 18)
Aug 18 **Kangaroo** (Nov 18)
Aug 18 **Short 184** (Mar 19)
Aug 18 **Sopwith Baby** (Oct 18)
15 Mar 19 DB
—
5 Aug 42 RF @ Bowmore
Oct 42 **Sunderland III** (Apr 43)
30 Apr 43 DB
—
11 Oct 44 RF @ Lyneham — nucleus from No 511 Sqn
Oct 44 **Liberator VII** (Jul 45)
Nov 44 **Halifax III** (Mar 45)
1 Dec 44 to Holmsley South
Dec 44 **York I** (Oct 46) det Northolt
Feb 45 **Liberator III** (Dec 45)
Feb 45 **Liberator VI** (Nov 45)
Apr 45 **Skymaster I** (Nov 45)
16 Oct 46 DB — renumbered as No 511 Sqn

247 Sqn

20 Aug 18 F @ Felixstowe — (Nos 336, 337 & 338 Flts)
Aug 18 **Felixstowe F.2A** (Jan 19)
Aug 18 **Felixstowe F.3** (Jan 19)
22 Jan 19 DB
—
1 Aug 40 RF @ Roborough — Sumburgh Fighter Flt redesignated
Aug 40 **Gladiator II** (Feb 41) det St Eval
Jan 41 **Hurricane I** (Jun 41)
10 Feb 41 to St Eval
17 Feb 41 to Roborough det St Eval
10 May 41 to Portreath
Jun 41 **Hurricane IIA** (Dec 41)
18 Jun 41 to Predannack
Aug 41 **Hurricane IIB** (Dec 41)
Aug 41 **Hurricane IIC** (Mar 43) det Exeter
Apr 42 **Hurricane I** (Sep 42)
17 May 42 to Exeter dets Predannack, Middle Wallop, Charmy Down
Aug 42 **Hurricane IIB** (Mar 43)
21 Sep 42 to High Ercall det Valley
Jan 43 **Typhoon IB** (Aug 45)
28 Feb 43 to Middle Wallop
5 Apr 43 to Fairlop
29 May 43 to Gravesend
4 Jun 43 to Bradwell Bay
10 Jul 43 to New Romney
7 Aug 43 to Attlebridge
13 Aug 43 to New Romney
11 Oct 43 to Merston
31 Oct 43 to Snailwell
5 Nov 43 to Merston
31 Dec 43 to Odiham
13 Jan 44 to Merston
1 Apr 44 to Eastchurch
24 Apr 44 to Hurn
20 Jun 44 to B 6/Coulombs det Hurn
28 Aug 44 to B 30/Créton
3 Sep 44 to B 48/Amiens/Glisy
6 Sep 44 to B 58/Melsbroek
22 Sep 44 to B 78/Eindhoven
13 Jan 45 to B 86/Helmond
21 Feb 45 to Warmwell
7 Mar 45 to B 86/Helmond
12 Apr 45 to B 106/Twente
13 Apr 45 to B 112/Hopsten
17 Apr 45 to B 120/Langenhagen
1 May 45 to B 156/Lüneburg
6 May 45 to B 158/Lübeck
20 Aug 45 to Chilbolton
Sep 45 **Tempest F.2** (May 46)
7 Jan 46 to Fairwood Common
16 Feb 46 to Chilbolton
Mar 46 **Vampire F.1** (May 49)
1 Jun 46 to West Malling
12 Jun 46 to Chilbolton
27 Jun 46 to Odiham
7 Sep 46 to West Malling
16 Sep 46 to Odiham
7 Oct 47 to Acklington
27 Nov 47 to Odiham
Jul 48 **Vampire F.3** (Dec 49)
Nov 49 **Vampire FB 5** (May 52)
Apr 52 **Meteor F.8** (Jun 55)
May 55 **Hunter F.4** (Mar 57)
Mar 57 **Hunter F.6** (Dec 57)
31 Dec 57 DB
—
1 Jul 60 **Bloodhound I** at Carnaby
31 Dec 63 DB

248 Sqn

Aug 18 F @ Hornsea — (Nos 404, 405 & 453 Flts)
Aug 18 **Sopwith Baby** (Nov 18)
Aug 18 **Short 184** (Mar 19)
Aug 18 **Short 320** (Mar 19) det North Coates
10 Mar 19 DB
—
30 Oct 39 RF @ Hendon
Dec 39 **Blenheim IF** (May 40)
24 Feb 40 to North Coates
Mar 40 **Blenheim IVF** (Jul 41)
8 Apr 40 to Thorney Island
16 Apr 40 to Gosport
22 May 40 to Dyce det Montrose
14 Jul 40 to Sumburgh
6 Jan 41 to Dyce det Wick

15 Jun 41 to Bircham Newton
dets St Eval, Portreath
Jul 41 **Beaufighter IC** (Jun 42)
17 Feb 42 to Dyce
May 42 **Beaufighter VIC** (Sep 42)
30 May 42 to Sumburgh
air echelon det Ta Kali
Jul-Sep 42 — aircraft
left for No 227 Sqn
5 Aug 42 to Dyce
13 Sep 42 to Talbenny
Sep 42 **Beaufighter VIC** (Jun 43)
3 Nov 42 to Pembrey
5 Dec 42 to Talbenny
18 Jan 43 to Predannack
det Gibraltar
Jun 43 **Beaufighter X** (Dec 43)
Dec 43 **Mosquito VI** (Oct 46)
Jan 44 **Mosquito XVIII** (Jan 45)
— ex No 618 Sqn det
17 Feb 44 to Portreath
12 Sep 44 to Banff
19 Jul 45 to Chivenor
8 Dec 45 to Ballykelly
17 Dec 45 to Chivenor
30 May 46 to Thorney Island
1 Oct 46 DB — renumbered as
No 36 Sqn

249 Sqn

18 Aug 18 F @ Dundee — (Nos 400, 401, 419 & 450 Flts)
Aug 18 **Sopwith Baby** (Nov 18)
Aug 18 **Hamble Baby** (Nov 18)
Aug 18 **Short 184** (Mar 19)
3 Mar 19 to Killingholme as
a cadre
8 Oct 19 DB
—
16 May 40 RF @ Church Fenton
May 40 **Hurricane II** (May 40)
17 May 40 to Leconfield
May 40 **Spitfire I** (Jun 40)
Jun 40 **Hurricane I** (Feb 41)
8 Jul 40 to Church Fenton
14 Aug 40 to Boscombe Down
1 Sep 40 to North Weald
Feb 41 **Hurricane IIA** (Apr 41)
May 41 en route Malta via HMS *Furious* & HMS *Ark Royal*
21 May 41 to Ta Kali
May 41 **Hurricane I** (Aug 41)
Jun 41 **Hurricane IIB** (Mar 42)
Jun 41 **Hurricane IIC** (Mar 42)
Mar 42 **Spitfire VB** (Jan 44)
May 42 **Spitfire VC** (Sep 44)
23 Nov 42 to Krendi
Jun 43 **Spitfire IX** (Nov 43)
24 Sep 43 to Hal Far
23 Oct 43 to Grottaglie
10 Nov 43 to Brindisi
10 Dec 43 to Grottaglie
15 Jul 44 to Canne
dets Leverano, Vis,
Brindisi
Sep 44 **Mustang III** (Apr 45)
dets Brindisi
Apr 45 **Spitfire IX** (May 45)
17 Apr 45 to Prkos
15 May 45 to Campomarino
May 45 **Mustang III** (Jun 45)
27 Jun 45 to Brindisi
Jun 45 **Mustang IV** (Aug 45)
16 Aug 45 DB
—
23 Oct 45 RF @ Eastleigh — No 500 Sqn renumbered
Oct 45 **Baltimore V** (Apr 46)
Mar 46 **Mosquito FB 26** (Aug 46)
27 Jun 46 to Habbaniyah
Dec 46 **Tempest F.6** (Mar 50)
13 Apr 48 to Ramat David
17 May 48 to Habbaniyah
29 Mar 49 to Deversoir
28 Jun 49 to Nicosia
8 Aug 49 to Deversoir
Jan 50 **Vampire FB 5** (May 52)
24 Jun 50 to Nicosia
10 Aug 50 to Deversoir
det Negombo
16 Apr 51 to Mafraq
27 Apr 51 to Deversoir
14 Jul 51 to Shaibah
24 Oct 51 to Deversoir
16 Apr 52 to Nicosia
9 May 52 to Deversoir
May 52 **Vampire FB 9** (Nov 54)
8 Jun 54 to Amman
Oct 54 **Venom FB 1** (Nov 55)
Jul 55 **Venom FB 4** (Oct 57)
26 Sep 55 to Nicosia
4 Nov 55 to Amman
27 Aug 56 to Akrotiri
11 Mar 57 to El Adem
3 May 57 to Ta Kali
4 Jun 57 to El Adem
13 Jul 57 to Eastleigh
det Sharjah
15 Oct 57 DB
—
6 Aug 57 training at Coningsby as No 249 Sqn (Designate)
—
15 Oct 57 RF @ Akrotiri
Oct 57 **Canberra B.2** (Jan 60)
Nov 59 **Canberra B.6** (Apr 62)
Nov 61 **Canberra B.16** (Feb 69)
24 Feb 69 DB

250 Sqn

10 May 18 F @ Padstow — (Nos 494, 500, 501, 502 & 503 Flts)
May 18 **DH 6** (May 19)
May 18 **DH 9** (May 19)
det Westward Ho!
31 May 19 DB
—
1 Apr 41 RF @ Aqir — from 'K' Flt
Apr 41 **Tomahawk IIB** (Apr 42)
dets Amiriya, Nicosia
25 May 41 to Maryut
13 Jun 41 to LG 13
31 Aug 41 to LG 07
8 Sep 41 to LG 13
det LG 110
14 Nov 41 to LG 109
19 Nov 41 to LG 123
2 Dec 41 to LG 122
5 Dec 41 to LG 123
11 Dec 41 to El Gubbi
19 Dec 41 to Gazala No 3
21 Dec 41 to Mechili
27 Dec 41 to Msus
12 Jan 42 to Antelat
21 Jan 42 to Msus
24 Jan 42 to Mechili
28 Jan 42 to Gazala No 1
3 Feb 42 to El Gamil
Feb 42 **Hurricane I** (Apr 42)
Feb 42 **Hurricane IIC** (Apr 42)
Apr 42 **Kittyhawk I** (Oct 42)
16 Apr 42 to LG 12
21 Apr 42 to Gambut No 1
12 Jun 42 to Gambut No 2
18 Jun 42 to LG 75
23 Jun 42 to LG 102
27 Jun 42 to LG 106
29 Jun 42 to LG 91
Oct 42 **Kittyhawk III** (Jan 44)
6 Nov 42 to LG 106
9 Nov 42 to LG 101
11 Nov 42 to LG 76
13 Nov 42 to Gambut No 1
15 Nov 42 to Gazala No 3
19 Nov 42 to Martuba No 4
8 Dec 42 to Belandah
18 Dec 42 to Marble Arch
31 Dec 42 to Alem el Chel
11 Jan 43 to Hamraiet
17 Jan 43 to Sedadah
19 Jan 43 to Bir Dufan
24 Jan 43 to Castel Benito
15 Feb 43 to El Assa
8 Mar 43 to Nefatia
21 Mar 43 to Medanine
3 Apr 43 to El Hamma
14 Apr 43 to El Djem
18 Apr 43 to Kairouan
21 May 43 to Zuara
9 Jul 43 to Hal Far
13 Jul 43 to Luqa
19 Jul 43 to Pachino
4 Aug 43 to Agnone
16 Sep 43 to Grottaglie
23 Sep 43 to Bari/Palese
3 Oct 43 to Foggia
26 Oct 43 to Mileni
28 Dec 43 to Cutella
Jan 44 **Kittyhawk IV** (Aug 45)
24 May 44 to San Angelo
13 Jun 44 to Guidonia
23 Jun 44 to Falerium
9 Jul 44 to Creti
26 Aug 44 to Iesi
18 Nov 44 to Fano
25 Feb 45 to Cervia
19 May 45 to Lavariano
Aug 45 **Mustang III** (Dec 46)
Aug 45 **Mustang IV** (Dec 46)
22 Jan 46 to Tissano
23 Sep 46 to Treviso
19 Nov 46 to Lavariano
25 Nov 46 to Treviso
30 Dec 46 DB

251 Sqn

May 18 F @ Hornsea — (Nos 504, 505, 506 & 510 Flts)
May 18 **DH 6** (Jan 19)
dets Atwick, Greenland Top, West Ayton, Owthorne, Seaton Carew, Redcar
Nov 18 **DH 9** (Jan 19)
31 Jan 19 to Killingholme as
a cadre
30 Jun 19 DB
—
1 Aug 44 RF @ Reykjavik — No 1407 Flt redesignated
Aug 44 **Ventura I** (Oct 44)
Aug 44 **Hudson III** (Aug 45)
Aug 44 **Anson I** (Oct 45)
Mar 45 **Fortress II** (Oct 45)
Aug 45 **Warwick I** (Oct 45)
30 Oct 45 DB

252 Sqn

May 18 F @ Tynemouth — (Nos 495, 507, 508, 509 & 510 Flts)
May 18 **DH 6** (Jan 19)
May 18 **Kangaroo** (Aug 18)
dets Cramlington, Seaton Carew, Redcar
31 Jan 19 to Killingholme as a cadre
30 Jun 19 DB
—
21 Nov 40 RF @ Bircham Newton
1 Dec 40 to Chivenor
Dec 40 **Blenheim IF** (Apr 41)
Dec 40 **Blenheim IVF** (Apr 41)
Dec 40 **Beaufighter IC** (Jun 41)
6 Apr 41 to Aldergrove
air echelon det Luqa, Heraklion, Abu Sueir
15 Jun 41 DB — UK echelon renumbered as
No 143 Sqn
—
ME det continued to operate with No 272 Sqn at Idku. No 252 Sqn nameplate in use from
3 Sep 41
—
14 Nov 41 re-established @ Idku
Nov 41 **Beaufighter IC** (Jan 44
Sep 42 **Beaufighter VIC** (Jan
dets El Gubbi, Berka, Fuka, Luqa, Paphos, St Jean, LG 05
18 Jan 43 to Berka III
21 Feb 43 to El Magrun
dets Berka III, Misura Gambut, Bersis
Jun 43 **Beaufighter XI** (Jan 44
3 Aug 43 to Berka III
dets El Magrun, Gamb LG 91
11 Sep 43 to Limassol
23 Sep 43 to Lakatamia
16 Dec 43 to LG 91
det Shallufa
Jan 44 **Beaufighter X** (Dec 46
21 Jan 44 to Mersah Matruh
20 Jun 44 to Gambut
30 Nov 44 to Mersah Matruh
6 Feb 45 to Aboukir
10 Feb 45 to Gianaclis
18 Feb 45 to Hassani
28 Aug 45 to Araxos
1 Dec 46 DB

253 Sqn

7 Jun 18 F @ Bembridge — (N 412, 413, 511, 512 & Flts)
Jun 18 **Hamble Baby** (18)
Jun 18 **Short 184** (May 19)
Jun 18 **Campania** (May 19)
Aug 18 **DH 6** (Jan 19)
dets Brading, Chicker
31 May 19 DB
—
30 Oct 39 RF @ Manston
Dec 39 **Battle** (Apr 40)
Feb 40 **Hurricane I** (Sep 41)
14 Feb 40 to Northolt
8 May 40 to Kenley
det Poix
24 May 40 to Kirton-in-Lindsey
dets Coleby Grange, Ringway
21 Jul 40 to Turnhouse
23 Aug 40 to Prestwick
29 Aug 40 to Kenley
3 Jan 41 to Leconfield
10 Feb 41 to Skaebrae
Jul 41 **Hurricane IIB** (Sep 4
21 Sep 41 to Hibaldstow
Oct 41 **Hurricane IIA** (Feb 4
Jan 42 **Hurricane IIC** (Sep 4
Apr 42 **Hurricane I** (Sep 42)
May 42 **Hurricane IIA** (Sep 4
24 May 42 to Shoreham
30 May 42 to Hibaldstow
14 Jun 42 to Friston
7 Jul 42 to Hibaldstow
16 Aug 42 to Friston
20 Aug 42 to Hibaldstow
Nov 42 en route N Africa
13 Nov 42 to Maison Blanche
Nov 42 **Hurricane IIC** (Sep 4
22 Nov 42 to Phillipeville
5 Jan 43 to Setif
13 Feb 43 to Jemappes
13 Mar 43 to Maison Blanche
Mar 43 **Spitfire VC** (Mar 43)
Apr 43 to Jemappes
21 May 43 to Phillipeville
7 Jun 43 to Jemappes
15 Jun 43 to Sousse
24 Jun 43 to Lampedusa
8 Aug 43 to La Sebala I
Aug 43 **Spitfire VC** (Nov 44)
Sep 43 **Spitfire IX** (May 44)
17 Oct 43 to Montecorvino
28 Nov 43 to Capodichino
24 Feb 44 to Borgo
Feb 44 **Spitfire VB** (Apr 44)

May 44 to Foggia
det Vis
Jul 44 to Canne
dets Leverano, Brindisi
Nov 44 **Spitfire VIII** (May 47)
Nov 44 **Spitfire IX** (May 47)
Apr 45 to Prkos
May 45 to Brindisi
Aug 45 to Treviso
Sep 46 to Zeltweg
Jan 47 to Treviso
Mar 47 **Spitfire XI** (May 47)
May 47 DB
—
Apr 55 RF @ Waterbeach
Apr 55 **Venom NF 2A** (Aug 57)
Sep 57 DB

54 Sqn

May 18 F @ Prawle Point — (Nos 492, 515, 516, 517 & 518 Flts)
May 18 **DH 6** (Feb 19)
May 18 **DH 9** (Feb 19)
det Mullion
Feb 19 DB
—
Oct 39 RF @ Stradishall
Nov 39 **Blenheim IF** (Apr 40)
Dec 39 to Sutton Bridge
Jan 40 to Bircham Newton
Jan 40 **Blenheim IVF** (Aug 42)
det Lossiemouth
Apr 40 to Hatston
May 40 to Sumburgh
Aug 40 to Dyce
dets Aldergrove, St Eval
Jan 41 to Sumburgh
May 41 to Aldergrove
Dec 41 to Dyce
Feb 42 to Carew Cheriton
Jun 42 to Dyce
Jul 42 **Beaufighter VIF** (Sep 43)
dets Wick, Abbotsinch
Oct 42 to Docking
Nov 42 to North Coates
Aug 43 **Beaufighter X** (Oct 46)
Mar 45 **Mosquito XVIII** (May 45)
Jun 45 to Chivenor
Nov 45 to Langham
May 46 to Thorney Island
Oct 46 DB — renumbered as No 42 Sqn
—
Dec 59 **Thor** @ Melton Mowbray
Aug 63 DB

55 Sqn

Jul 18 F @ Pembroke — (Nos 519, 520, 521, 522, 523 & 524 Flts)
Jul 18 **DH 6** (Jan 19)
dets Llangefni, Luce Bay
Jan 19 DB
—
Nov 40 RF @ Kirton-in-Lindsey
Nov 40 **Defiant I** (Sep 41)
Mar 41 **Hurricane I** (Jul 41)
May 41 to Hibaldstow
Jul 41 **Beaufighter IIF** (May 42)
det Coltishall
Sep 41 to Coltishall
det West Malling
Mar 42 to High Ercall
Mar 42 **Beaufighter VIF** (Feb 45)
Jun 42 to Honiley
Nov 42 to Maison Blanche
det Souk el Arba
Dec 42 to Bone
det Souk el Arba
Dec 42 to Setif
dets Souk el Arba, Tingley, Bone, Maison Blanche, Souk el Khemis

('Paddington'), La Sebala II
21 May 43 to La Sebala II
det Monastir
17 Aug 43 to Bo Rizzo
14 Nov 43 to Grottaglie
det Pomigliano
24 Jan 44 to Foggia Main
dets Grottaglie, Pomigliano, Falconara, Hal Far, Catania, Rosignano
Feb 45 **Mosquito XIX** (Apr 46)
9 Feb 45 to Rosignano
dets Falconara, Le Vallon, Istres, Hal Far
4 Sep 45 to Hal Far
31 Jan 46 to Gianaclis
Jan 46 **Mosquito XXX** (Apr 46)
30 Apr 46 DB

256 Sqn

Jun 18 F @ Seahouses — (Nos 495, 525, 526, 527 & 528 Flts)
Jun 18 **DH 6** (Jan 19)
dets New Haggerston, Rennington, Cairncross, Ashington
Nov 18 **Kangaroo** (Jan 19)
31 Jan 19 to Killingholme as a cadre
30 Jun 19 DB
—
23 Nov 40 RF @ Catterick
Nov 40 **Defiant I** (May 42)
4 Jan 41 to Pembrey
6 Feb 41 to Colerne
det Middle Wallop
26 Mar 41 to Squires Gate
det Ballyhalbert
May 41 **Hurricane I** (Jul 41)
Jul 41 **Hurricane IIB** (Oct 41)
May 42 **Defiant II** (Jun 42)
May 42 **Beaufighter IF** (Nov 42)
1 Jun 42 to Woodvale
det Ballyhalbert
Oct 42 **Beaufighter VIF** (May 43)
24 Apr 43 to Ford
May 43 **Mosquito XII** (Jul 44)
det Luqa
25 Aug 43 to Woodvale
det Luqa
25 Sep 43 to Luqa
dets Catania, Alghero, Pomigliano
Jan 44 **Mosquito XIII** (Sep 45)
7 Apr 44 to La Senia
May 44 **Spitfire VIII** (Aug 44
May 44 **Spitfire IX** (Aug 44)
dets Reghaia, Alghero, Gibraltar
Jun 44 **Hurricane IIC** (Aug 44)
15 Aug 44 to Alghero
4 Sep 44 to Foggia
dets Le Vallon, Falconara
26 Feb 45 to Forli
Feb 45 **Mosquito XII** (Sep 45)
Apr 45 **Mosquito VI** (Oct 45)
4 Jun 45 to Aviano
24 Aug 45 to Lecce (No 54 PTC)
13 Sep 45 to El Ballah
Oct 45 **Mosquito XIX** (Sep 46)
16 Dec 45 to Deversoir
May 46 **Mosquito XVI** (Sep 46)
13 Jul 46 to Nicosia
12 Sep 46 DB
—
17 Nov 52 RF @ Ahlhorn
Nov 52 **Meteor NF 11** (Jan 59)
12 Feb 58 to Geilenkirchen
21 Jan 59 DB — renumbered as No 11 Sqn

257 Sqn

18 Aug 18 F @ Dundee — (Nos 318 & 319 Flts)
Aug 18 **Curtiss H.16** (18)
Aug 18 **Felixstowe F.2A** (Apr 19)
Apr 19 reduced to a cadre
30 Jun 19 DB
—
16 May 40 RF @ Hendon
May 40 **Spitfire I** (Jun 40)
Jun 40 **Hurricane I** (Jun 41)
4 Jul 40 to Northolt
15 Aug 40 to Debden
5 Sep 40 to Martlesham Heath
8 Oct 40 to North Weald
7 Nov 40 to Martlesham Heath
16 Dec 40 to Coltishall
Apr 41 **Hurricane IIC** (Aug 41)
May 41 **Hurricane IIB** (Sep 42)
7 Nov 41 to Honiley
Nov 41 **Hurricane IIA** (Aug 42)
Jan 42 **Hurricane IIC** (Sep 42)
Jan 42 **Hurricane I** (Jul 42)
Apr 42 **Spitfire VB** (May 42)
6 Jun 42 to High Ercall
Jul 42 **Typhoon IA** (May 43)
Jul 42 **Typhoon IB** (May 45)
21 Sep 42 to Exeter
det Bolt Head
8 Jan 43 to Warmwell
det Ibsley
12 Aug 43 to Gravesend
17 Sep 43 to Warmwell
20 Jan 44 to Beaulieu
3 Feb 44 to Tangmere
10 Apr 44 to Needs Oar Point
11 Apr 44 to Fairwood Common
12 Apr 44 to Needs Oar Point
2 Jul 44 to Hurn
8 Jul 44 to B 15/Ryes
15 Jul 44 to B 3/Ste-Croix-sur-Mer
11 Aug 44 to Fairwood Common
30 Aug 44 to B 3/Ste-Croix-sur-Mer
1 Sep 44 to Manston
2 Sep 44 to B 3/Ste-Croix-sur-Mer
4 Sep 44 to Manston
6 Sep 44 to B 23/Morainville
11 Sep 44 to B 51/Lille/Vendeville
2 Oct 44 to B 70/Deurne
8 Feb 45 to B 89/Mill
5 Mar 45 DB
—
1 Sep 46 RF @ Church Fenton — No 129 Sqn renumbered
Sep 46 **Meteor F.3** (Mar 48)
12 Jan 47 to Acklington
16 Feb 47 to Church Fenton
15 Apr 47 to Horsham St Faith
31 Jun 47 to Lübeck
28 Aug 47 to Horsham St Faith
Feb 48 **Meteor F.4** (Oct 50)
Sep 50 **Meteor F.8** (Mar 55)
27 Oct 50 to Wattisham
Sep 54 **Hunter F.2** (Mar 57)
10 Jun 56 to Wymeswold
15 Jan 57 to Wattisham
31 Mar 57 DB
—
1 Jul 60 **Bloodhound I** at Warboys
31 Dec 63 DB

258 Sqn

25 Jul 18 F @ Luce Bay — (Nos 523, 524 & 529 Flts)
Jul 18 **DH 6** (Mar 19)
Nov 18 **Fairey IIIA** (Mar 19)
5 Mar 19 DB
—
22 Nov 40 RF @ Leconfield
1 Dec 40 to Duxford
4 Dec 40 to Drem
Dec 40 **Hurricane I** (Apr 41)
17 Dec 40 to Acklington
1 Feb 41 to Jurby
17 Apr 41 to Valley
det Penrhos

22 Apr 41 to Kenley
Apr 41 **Hurricane IIA** (Feb 42)
1 Jun 41 to Redhill
14 Jun 41 to Kenley
10 Jul 41 to Martlesham Heath
3 Oct 41 to Debden
1 Nov 41 en route FE, arrived via HMS *Indomitable*
28 Jan 42 to Seletar
30 Jan 42 to Tengah
1 Feb 42 to P I
3 Feb 42 to Tengah
4 Feb 42 to P I
14 Feb 42 to P II
18 Feb 42 to Tjilitjan
23 Feb 42 DB — absorbed by Nos 242/'232(II)' and 605 Sqns
—
1 Mar 42 RF @ Ratmalana
Mar 42 **Hurricane I** (Jan 43)
Mar 42 **Hurricane IIB** (Dec 43)
23 Mar 42 to Colombo (Racecourse)
dets Dum Dum, China Bay
20 Feb 43 to Dambulla
dets Kalemetiya, Kolar
31 Jul 43 to Comilla
5 Nov 43 to Dohazari
Nov 43 **Hurricane IIC** (Aug 44)
13 Dec 43 to Chittagong
25 Jan 44 to 'Hay'
30 Jan 44 to 'Hove'
25 Feb 44 to 'Reindeer I'
3 Jun 44 to Arkonam
14 Aug 44 to Yelahanka
Sep 44 **Thunderbolt I** (Jan 45)
Oct 44 **Thunderbolt II** (Dec 45)
8 Oct 44 to Arkonam
26 Nov 44 to Ratnap
dets Cox's Bazaar, Sadaung
1 May 45 to Kyaukpyu
8 Jun 45 to Ulunderpet
21 Aug 45 to Bobbili
7 Sep 45 to Baigachi
11 Sep 45 to Zayatkwin
25 Sep 45 to Kuala Lumpur
31 Dec 45 DB

259 Sqn

No 259 Sqn was officially authorised to form at Felixstowe on 20 Aug 18 and was to have comprised Nos 342, 343 and 344 Flts operating Felixstowe F.2As. Although usually annotated as having been formally disbanded on 13 Sep 19 it is unlikely that the squadron ever had more than a notional existence.

—
16 Feb 43 RF @ Kipevu
Feb 43 **Catalina IB** (Apr 45)
dets Congella, Langebaan, Tulear
14 Sep 43 to Dar-es-Salaam
dets Diego Suarez, Khormaksar, Masirah, Port Victoria, Tulear, Mauritius
Mar 45 **Sunderland V** (Apr 45)
1 May 45 DB

260 Sqn

Aug 18 F @ Westward Ho! — (Nos 502 & 503 Flts)
Aug 18 **DH 6** (Feb 19)
Aug 18 **DH 9** (Feb 19)
22 Feb 19 DB
—

22 Nov 40 RF @ Castletown
5 Dec 40 to Skitten
Dec 40 **Hurricane I** (Feb 42)
7 Jan 41 to Castletown
10 Feb 41 to Skitten
16 Apr 41 to Drem
19 May 41 en route ME
10 Aug 41 to Haifa dets Beirut, El Bassa
17 Aug 41 to El Bassa det Beirut
20 Sep 41 to Haifa dets Beirut, El Bassa
25 Oct 41 to LG 115 dets LG 124, LG 109, LG 101
12 Dec 41 to Sidi Rezegh
19 Dec 41 to Gazala No 2
24 Dec 41 to Msus
12 Jan 42 to Antelat
16 Jan 42 to Benina
22 Jan 42 to Martuba
23 Jan 42 to LG 109
1 Feb 42 to LG 101
Feb 42 **Tomahawk II** (Mar 42)
15 Feb 42 to LG 115
Feb 42 **Kittyhawk I** (Sep 42)
10 Mar 42 to Gasr-el-Arid
23 May 42 to Gambut No 2
6 Jun 42 to Bir el Baheira
18 Jun 42 to LG 76
19 Jun 42 to LG 115
19 Jun 42 to LG 85
Jun 42 **Kittyhawk IIA** (May 43)
11 Jul 42 to LG 97
6 Nov 42 to LG 75
10 Nov 42 to Sidi Azeiz
15 Nov 42 to Gazala No 2
19 Nov 42 to Martuba No 4
10 Dec 42 to Belandah
18 Dec 42 to Marble Arch
Dec 42 **Kittyhawk III** (Mar 44)
31 Dec 42 to Gzina
1 Jan 43 to Hamraiet I
4 Jan 43 to Hamraiet 3
12 Jan 43 to Bir Dufan
18 Jan 43 to Sedadah
24 Jan 43 to Castel Benito
7 Feb 43 to Sorman
14 Feb 43 to El Assa
2 Mar 43 to Ben Gardane
8 Mar 43 to Nefatia
20 Mar 43 to Medanine
4 Apr 43 to El Hamma
18 Apr 43 to Kairouan
21 May 43 to Zuara
17 Jul 43 to Luqa
19 Jul 43 to Pachino
4 Aug 43 to Agnone
27 Sep 43 to Bari
3 Oct 43 to Foggia
26 Oct 43 to Mileni
3 Jan 44 to Cutella
Apr 44 **Mustang III** (Aug 45)
21 May 44 to San Angelo
10 Jun 44 to Guidonia
23 Jun 44 to Falerium
7 Jul 44 to Creti
23 Aug 44 to Iesi
17 Nov 44 to Fano
23 Feb 45 to Cervia
18 May 45 to Lavariano
Jun 45 **Mustang IV** (Aug 45)
19 Aug 45 DB

261 Sqn

No 261 Sqn was officially authorised to form at Felixstowe on 20 Aug 18 and was to have comprised Nos 339, 340, 341 Flts operating Felixstowe F.2As. Although usually annotated as having been formally disbanded on 13 Sep 19 it is unlikely that the squadron ever had more than a notional existence.

—

2 Aug 40 RF @ Luqa — No 418 & Malta Fighter Flts redesignated
Aug 40 **Sea Gladiator I** (Jan 41)
Aug 40 **Hurricane I** (May 41)
20 Nov 40 to Ta Kali
12 May 41 DB — absorbed by No 185 Sqn

—

12 Jul 41 RF @ Habbaniyah — No 127 Sqn renumbered
Jul 41 **Gladiator I** (Sep 41)
Jul 41 **Hurricane I** (May 42) det Deir es Zor
10 Aug 41 to Shaibah
27 Sep 41 to Mosul dets Haifa, Nicosia
1 Jan 42 to Haifa dets Nicosia, St Jean
14 Jan 42 to St Jean dets Nicosia, Beirut
26 Feb 42 en route FE via HMS *Indomitable*
6 Mar 42 to China Bay
Mar 42 **Hurricane IIB** (Nov 43) dets Ratmalana, St Thomas Mount
14 Jan 43 to Dum Dum
7 Feb 43 to Baigachi det 'Reindeer'
25 Jun 43 to Chittagong
22 Oct 43 to Chiringa
Oct 43 **Hurricane IIC** (Jun 44)
29 Feb 44 to Baigachi
8 Mar 44 to Alipore
27 Apr 44 to Yelahanka
Jun 44 **Thunderbolt I** (Oct 44)
15 Aug 44 to Arkonam
Aug 44 **Thunderbolt II** (Sep 45)
2 Sep 44 to Kumbhirgram det Cox's Bazaar
22 Nov 44 to Wangjing
18 Mar 45 to Palel
23 Mar 45 to Wangjing det Sinthe
22 Apr 45 to Myingyan North
30 Apr 45 to 'Tennant'
7 May 45 to Myingyan North
1 Jul 45 to Tanjore
25 Sep 45 DB

262 Sqn

29 Sep 42 F @ Hednesford (No 104 PRDU)
29 Sep 42 en route South Africa
12 Nov 42 to Congella
Feb 43 **Catalina IB** (Feb 45)
Sep 44 **Catalina IVB** (Feb 45) dets St Lucia, Tulear, Langebaan
15 Feb 45 DB — renumbered as No 35 Sqn, SAAF

263 Sqn

27 Sep 18 F @ Otranto — (Nos 359, 435, 436 & 441 Flts)
Sep 18 **Sopwith Baby** (May 19)
Sep 18 **Hamble Baby** ( )
Sep 18 **Short 184** (May 19)
Sep 18 **Short 320** (May 19)
Sep 18 **Felixstowe F.3** (May 19) det Santa Maria di Leucca
Nov 18 to Taranto
16 May 19 DB

—

2 Oct 39 RF @ Filton
Oct 39 **Gladiator I & II** (Apr 40)
24 Apr 40 to Lake Lesjeskog via HMS *Glorious*
25 Apr 40 to Aandalsnes
28 Apr 40 to UK by sea
1 May 40 to Scapa Flow
2 May 40 to Turnhouse
May 40 **Gladiator II** (Jun 40)
21 May 40 to Bardufoss via HMS *Furious* det Bodö
7 Jun 40 to HMS *Glorious*
8 Jun 40 HMS *Glorious* sunk
10 Jun 40 re-established at Drem
Jun 40 **Hurricane I** (Nov 40)
28 Jun 40 to Grangemouth
Jul 40 **Whirlwind I** (Dec 43) det Montrose
2 Sep 40 to Drem dets Macmerry, Prestwick
28 Nov 40 to Exeter det St Eval
24 Feb 41 to St Eval
18 Mar 41 to Portreath
10 Apr 41 to Filton
7 Aug 41 to Charmy Down
19 Dec 41 to Warmwell
23 Dec 41 to Charmy Down
28 Jan 42 to Colerne
10 Feb 42 to Fairwood Common
18 Apr 42 to Angle det Portreath
15 Aug 42 to Colerne det Warmwell
13 Sep 42 to Warmwell dets Predannack, Fairwood Common
20 Feb 43 to Harrowbeer
15 Mar 43 to Warmwell dets Bolt Head, Predannack
19 Jun 43 to Zeals
12 Jul 43 to Warmwell
7 Sep 43 to Manston
10 Sep 43 to Warmwell
Dec 43 **Typhoon IB** (Aug 45)
5 Dec 43 to Ibsley
5 Jan 44 to Fairwood Common
23 Jan 44 to Beaulieu
6 Mar 44 to Warmwell
19 Mar 44 to Harrowbeer
19 Jun 44 to Bolt Head
10 Jul 44 to Hurn
23 Jul 44 to Eastchurch
6 Aug 44 to B 3/Ste-Croix-sur-Mer
6 Sep 44 to Manston
11 Sep 44 to B 51/Lille/Vendeville
2 Oct 44 to B 70/Deurne
13 Jan 45 to Fairwood Common
10 Feb 45 to B 89/Mill
16 Apr 45 to B 105/Drope
30 Apr 45 to B 111/Ahlhorn
8 Jun 45 to R 16/Hildesheim
30 Aug 45 DB

—

30 Aug 45 RF @ Lübeck — No 616 Sqn renumbered
Aug 45 **Meteor F.3** (Mar 48)
1 Sep 45 to Manston
21 Sep 45 to Acklington
24 Jan 46 to Charterhall
1 Mar 46 to Acklington
2 Apr 46 to Church Fenton
1 Jun 46 to Boxted
9 Jun 46 to Church Fenton
31 Oct 46 to Lübeck
17 Dec 46 to Church Fenton
15 Apr 47 to Horsham St Faith
1 Jul 47 to Lübeck
28 Aug 47 to Horsham St Faith
Dec 47 **Meteor F.4** (Dec 50)
8 Aug 49 to Acklington
1 Sep 49 to Horsham St Faith
Oct 50 **Meteor F.8** (Apr 55)
23 Oct 50 to Acklington
22 Nov 50 to Wattisham
Feb 55 **Hunter F.2** (Aug 56)
May 55 **Hunter F.5** (Aug 56)
10 Jun 56 to Wymeswold
Aug 56 **Hunter F.6** (Jul 58)
15 Jan 57 to Wattisham
30 Aug 57 to Stradishall
2 Jul 58 DB

—

1 Jun 59 **Bloodhound I** at Watto
30 Jun 63 DB

264 Sqn

27 Sep 18 F @ Suda Bay — (Nos 439 & 440 Flts)
Sep 18 **Short 184** (Dec 18) det Siros
Dec 18 reduced to a cadre, personnel withdrawn to Malta
1 Mar 19 DB

—

30 Oct 39 RF @ Sutton Bridge
7 Dec 39 to Martlesham Heath
Dec 39 **Defiant I** (Sep 41) det Wittering
10 May 40 to Duxford
3 Jul 40 to Fowlmere
23 Jul 40 to Kirton-in-Lindsey dets Coleby Grange, Ringway
22 Aug 40 to Hornchurch
29 Aug 40 to Kirton-in-Lindsey dets Northolt, Luton, Martlesham Heath
29 Oct 40 to Southend
27 Nov 40 to Debden
31 Dec 40 to Gravesend
11 Jan 41 to Biggin Hill
14 Apr 41 to West Malling
Sep 41 **Defiant II** (Jul 42)
1 May 42 to Colerne
May 42 **Mosquito II** (Jan 44) dets Bradwell Bay, Treblezue, Portreath
30 Apr 43 to Predannack
7 Aug 43 to Fairwood Common
12 Aug 43 to Predannack
Aug 43 **Mosquito VI** (Oct 43)
7 Nov 43 to Coleby Grange
18 Dec 43 to Church Fenton
Dec 43 **Mosquito XIII** (Aug 45
7 May 44 to Hartford Bridge
26 Jul 44 to Hunsdon
11 Aug 44 to A 8/Picauville
4 Sep 44 to B 6/Coulombs
5 Sep 44 to B 17/Carpiquet
25 Sep 44 to Predannack
30 Nov 44 to Colerne
1 Dec 44 to Odiham
9 Jan 45 to B 51/Lille/Vendevill
26 Apr 45 to B 77/Gilze-Rijen
7 May 45 to B 108/Rheine
16 May 45 to B 77/Gilze-Rijen
6 Jun 45 to B 106/Twente
25 Aug 45 DB

—

20 Nov 45 RF @ Church Fenton — No 125 Sqn renumbere
Nov 45 **Mosquito NF 30** (May 4
2 Dec 45 to Lübeck
14 Dec 45 to Church Fenton
7 Jan 46 to Spilsby
7 Feb 46 to Church Fenton
Mar 46 **Mosquito NF 36** (Jan 5
22 Jul 46 to Linton-on-Ouse
12 Aug 46 to Lübeck
23 Aug 46 to Linton-on-Ouse
20 Apr 47 to Wittering
28 Apr 47 to Acklington
5 Jun 47 to Wittering
20 Jun 47 to Lübeck
4 Jul 47 to Wittering
13 Jan 48 to Coltishall
16 Apr 48 to Lübeck
30 Apr 48 to Coltishall
19 Nov 49 to Church Fenton
2 Oct 50 to Coltishall
24 Aug 51 to Linton-on-Ouse
Nov 51 **Meteor NF 11** (Oct 54)
14 Feb 52 to Leuchars
7 Aug 52 to Acklington
25 Aug 52 to Linton-on-Ouse
Oct 54 **Meteor NF 14** (Oct 57)

Feb 57 to Middleton St George
Sep 57 to Leeming
Sep 57 DB — renumbered as No 33 Sqn
—
Dec 58 **Bloodhound I** at North Coates
Nov 62 DB

65 Sqn

Intended to form at Gibraltar with Nos 364, 365 & 366 Flts to operate Short 184s and Felixstowe F.3s. However the squadron does not appear to have ever been formally embodied.

Mar 43 F @ Kipevu
Apr 43 **Catalina IB** (Apr 45)
Apr 43 to Diego Suarez dets Jui, Pamanzi, Kipevu, Mauritius, Tulear, Masirah, Port Victoria, Khormaksar, St Lucia, Congella
May 45 DB

66 Sqn

Sep 18 F @ Mudros — (Nos 437 & 438 Flts)
Sep 18 **Short 184** (Mar 19)
Sep 18 **Short 320** (Mar 19) det Skyros
Mar 19 to Petrovsk Port det Chechen
Sep 19 DB
—
Oct 39 RF @ Sutton Bridge
Dec 39 **Battle** (May 40)
Jan 40 **Spitfire I** (Sep 40)
Mar 40 to Martlesham Heath det Wittering
May 40 to Wittering det Collyweston
Aug 40 to Eastchurch
Aug 40 to Hornchurch
Aug 40 to Wittering
Sep 40 **Spitfire IIA** (Oct 40)
Oct 40 **Spitfire I** (Apr 41)
Mar 41 **Spitfire IIA** (Sep 41)
Sep 41 to Martlesham Heath
Sep 41 **Spitfire IIB** (Sep 41)
Sep 41 **Spitfire VB** (Jun 42)
Oct 41 to Collyweston
Oct 41 to Kingscliffe
Jan 42 to Duxford
Jan 42 **Typhoon IA** (Sep 42)
Mar 42 **Typhoon IB** (Jul 45) det Ccltishall
Aug 42 to Matlask
Aug 42 to Duxford
Sep 42 to Warmwell det Predannack
Jan 43 to Exeter det Warmwell
Sep 43 to Gravesend
Sep 43 to Exeter
Sep 43 to Harrowbeer
Mar 44 to Bolt Head
Mar 44 to Harrowbeer
Mar 44 to Acklington
Mar 44 to Tangmere
Apr 44 to Needs Oar Point
Apr 44 to Snaith
May 44 to Needs Oar Point
Jun 44 to Eastchurch
Jul 44 to Hurn
Jul 44 to B 3/Ste-Croix-sur-Mer
Jul 44 to B 8/Sommervieu
Sep 44 to B 23/Morainville
Sep 44 to Manston
Sep 44 to Tangmere
10 Sep 44 to Manston
11 Sep 44 to B 51/Lille/Vendeville
2 Oct 44 to B 70/Deurne
14 Feb 45 to B 89/Mill
16 Apr 45 to B 105/Drope
25 Apr 45 to Fairwood Common
4 Jun 45 to B 111/Ahlhorn
8 Jun 45 to Hildesheim
6 Aug 45 DB
—
1 Sep 46 RF @ Boxted — Nos 234 Sqn renumbered
Sep 46 **Meteor F.3** (Apr 48)
24 Sep 46 to Acklington
31 Oct 46 to Boxted
4 Nov 46 to Wattisham
5 Dec 46 to Boxted
4 Jan 47 to Wattisham
16 Apr 47 to Tangmere
28 Apr 47 to Lübeck
26 Jun 47 to Tangmere
Feb 48 **Meteor F.4** (Feb 49)
5 Jul 48 to Acklington
24 Aug 48 to Tangmere
11 Feb 49 DB — renumbered as No 43 Sqn
—
14 Jul 52 RF @ Wunstorf
Aug 52 **Vampire FB 5** (May 53)
Apr 53 **Venom FB 1** (Aug 55)
Jul 55 **Venom FB 4** (Nov 57)
15 Oct 55 to Fassberg
15 Oct 56 to Wunstorf
16 Nov 57 DB
—
1 Dec 59 **Bloodhound I** at Rattlesden
30 Jun 64 DB

267 Sqn

27 Sep 18 F @ Kalafrana — (Nos 360, 361, 362 & 363 Flts)
Sep 18 **Short 184** (21)
Sep 18 **Felixstowe F.2A** (Feb 23)
Sep 18 **Felixstowe F.3** (Jun 21) det Alexandria
Dec 20 **Fairey IIID** (Aug 23) dets HMS *Ark Royal*, Kilya Bay
1 Aug 23 DB — redesignated as No 481 Flt
—
20 Aug 40 RF @ Heliopolis — Heliopolis Communications Flt redesignated
Aug 40 **Proctor I** (Jun 42)
Aug 40 **Anson I** (Jun 42)
Aug 40 **Magister I** (Jun 42)
Aug 40 **Hudson I** (Sep 41)
Aug 40 **Hind** (Nov 41)
Aug 40 **Percival Q.6** (May 42)
Aug 40 **Vega Gull** (Jun 42)
Dec 40 **Lockheed 14** (Nov 41)
Jan 41 **Lysander I & II** (Jun 42)
Jan 41 **Lodestar** (Oct 42)
Feb 41 **Simoun** (Aug 41)
Mar 41 **Gladiator I & II** (Jun 42)
May 41 **Electra** (Dec 41)
Aug 41 **Wellesley** (Mar 42)
Aug 41 **Blenheim I** (Apr 42)
Sep 41 **DC 2** (Oct 41)
Nov 41 **Audax** (Jun 42)
Dec 41 **Messerschmitt Bf 110C** (Mar 42)
Dec 41 **Moth** (Jun 42)
Feb 42 **Hurricane I** (Jun 42)
Feb 42 **Messerschmitt Bf 109F** (Oct 42)
Mar 42 **Hudson IV** (Jun 43)
Apr 42 **Hudson III** (Jul 42)
Jun 42 **Boston III** (Jun 42)
Jul 42 **Hudson VI** (Jun 43)
Aug 42 **DC 3** (Dec 42)
18 Aug 42 to Bilbeis dets Amiriya, El Adem
9 Jan 43 to Marble Arch
19 Jan 43 to LG 224
May 43 **Dakota** (Jul 46) det Catania
18 Nov 43 to Bari
10 Feb 45 to Bilaspur
24 Mar 45 to Tulihal
31 Mar 45 to Akyab det Mauripur
30 Aug 45 to Mingaladon det Mauripur
21 Jul 46 DB
—
15 Feb 54 RF @ Kuala Lumpur
Feb 54 **Dakota** (Nov 58)
Feb 54 **Auster AOP 6** (Nov 58)
Feb 54 **Pioneer CC 1** (Nov 58)
Sep 54 **Pembroke C.1** (Nov 58)
Nov 54 **Harvard T.2B** (Dec 56)
1 Nov 58 DB — renumbered as No 209 Sqn
—
1 Nov 62 RF @ Benson
Nov 62 **Argosy C.1** (Jun 70)
30 Jun 70 DB

268 Sqn

Aug 18 F @ Kalafrana — (Nos 433 & 434 Flts)
Aug 18 **Short 184** (Oct 19)
Aug 18 **Short 320** (Oct 19)
11 Oct 19 DB
—
30 Sep 40 RF @ Bury St Edmunds — crews from Nos 2 & 26 Sqns
Sep 40 **Lysander II** (Apr 41) dets Cambridge
Feb 41 **Lysander III** (Mar 42)
1 Apr 41 to Snailwell
26 Apr 41 to Ipswich
28 Apr 41 to Snailwell
May 41 **Tomahawk IIA** (Aug 42)
20 Jun 41 to West Raynham
21 Jun 41 to Barton Bendish
25 Jun 41 to Snailwell
21 Jul 41 to Weston Zoyland
27 Jul 41 to Snailwell
4 Aug 41 to Penshurst
8 Aug 41 to Snailwell
28 Sep 41 to Barton Bendish
30 Sep 41 to Twinwood Farm
1 Oct 41 to Snailwell
25 Oct 41 to Barton Bendish
26 Oct 41 to Snailwell
24 Nov 41 to Weston Zoyland
8 Dec 41 to Snailwell dets Docking, Ibsley
Apr 42 **Mustang I** (Jul 43)
20 May 42 to Weston Zoyland
2 Jun 42 to Snailwell
9 Aug 42 to Weston Zoyland
16 Aug 42 to Snailwell det Duxford
2 Mar 43 to Wing
6 Mar 43 to Bottisham
10 Mar 43 to Snailwell
31 May 43 to Odiham
Jul 43 **Mustang IA** (Nov 44) det Tangmere
15 Sep 43 to Funtington
9 Oct 43 to Odiham
15 Oct 43 to Thruxton
8 Nov 43 to Turnhouse
17 Jan 44 to North Weald
7 Feb 44 to Llanbedr
20 Feb 44 to North Weald
1 Mar 44 to Sawbridgeworth
26 Mar 44 to Dundonald
8 Apr 44 to Gatwick
27 Jun 44 to Odiham det B 10/Plumetot
Jul 44 **Typhoon FR 1B** (Oct 44)
10 Aug 44 to B 10/Plumetot
13 Aug 44 to B 4/Bény-sur-Mer
1 Sep 44 to B 27/Boisney
6 Sep 44 to B 31/Fresnoy-Folny
11 Sep 44 to B 43/Fort Rouge
27 Sep 44 to B 61/St Denis-Westrem
10 Oct 44 to B 70/Deurne
Nov 44 **Mustang II** (Aug 45)
23 Nov 44 to B 77/Gilze-Rijen
13 Jan 45 to Fairwood Common
9 Feb 45 to B 77/Gilze-Rijen
9 Mar 45 to B 89/Mill
18 Apr 45 to B 106/Twente
Apr 45 **Spitfire XIVE** (Sep 45)
30 May 45 to B 118/Celle
18 Jun 45 to B 150/Hustedt
17 Sep 45 to B 118/Celle
Sep 45 **Spitfire XIX** (Sep 45)
19 Sep 45 DB — renumbered as No 16 Sqn
—
19 Sep 45 RF @ Cambrai/Epinoy — No 487 Sqn renumbered
Sep 45 **Mosquito VI** (Mar 46) det Melsbroek
31 Mar 46 DB

269 Sqn

6 Oct 18 F @ Port Said — (Nos 431 & 432 Flts)
Oct 18 **BE 2E** (Mar 19)
Oct 18 **Short 184** (Nov 19)
Dec 18 **DH 9** (Mar 19)
15 Sep 19 to Alexandria
15 Nov 19 DB — absorbed by No 267 Sqn
—
7 Dec 36 RF @ Bircham Newton — from 'C' Flt, No 220 Sqn
Dec 36 **Anson I** (Jun 40)
30 Dec 36 to Abbotsinch
17 Jan 38 to Eastleigh
24 Mar 38 to Abbotsinch
29 Sep 38 to Thornaby
6 Oct 38 to Abbotsinch
25 Aug 39 to Montrose
10 Oct 39 to Wick
Apr 40 **Hudson I** (May 41) det Kaldadarnes
May 41 **Hudson III** (Dec 43)
31 May 41 to Kaldadarnes
6 Mar 43 to Reykjavik
8 Jan 44 to Davidstow Moor
Feb 44 **Hudson IIIA** (Aug 45)
Feb 44 **Martinet** (Jul 44)
Feb 44 **Walrus** (Mar 46)
Feb 44 **Spitfire VB** (Mar 46)
8 Mar 44 to Lagens
Sep 44 **Warwick I** (Mar 46)
10 Mar 46 DB
—
1 Jan 52 RF @ Gibraltar — nucleus from No 224 Sqn
Jan 52 **Shackleton MR 1** (Nov 58)
24 Mar 52 to Ballykelly
Mar 53 **Shackleton MR 2** (Aug 54)
Oct 58 **Shackleton MR 2** (Nov 58)
1 Dec 58 DB — renumbered as No 210 Sqn
—
22 Jul 59 **Thor** at Caistor
24 May 63 DB

270 Sqn

Apr 19 F @ Alexandria — (Nos 354, 355 & 356 Flts)
Apr 19 **Felixstowe F.3** (Sep 19)
Apr 19 **Sopwith Baby** (Apr 19)
Apr 19 **DH 9** ( )
Apr 19 **Short 184** (Sep 19)
15 Sep 19 DB — merged into No 269 Sqn
—

12 Nov 42 RF @ Jui
Nov 42 **Catalina IB** (Apr 44)
dets Bathurst, Fisherman's Lake
23 Jul 43 to Apapa
dets Jui, Abidjan, Libreville
Dec 43 **Sunderland III** (Jun 45)
30 Jun 45 DB

271 Sqn

27 Sep 18 F @ Taranto — (Nos 357, 358, 359 & 367 Flts)
det Otranto
Sep 18 **Short 184** (Dec 18)
Sep 18 **Felixstowe F.3** (Dec 18)
9 Dec 18 DB
—
1 May 40 RF @ Doncaster — from No 1680 Flt
May 40 **SM 73P** (May 40)
May 40 **Ford 5AT-D** (Sep 40)
May 40 **HP 42** (Dec 40)
May 40 **Magister I** (Jan 41)
May 40 **Bombay** (Feb 41)
May 40 **Harrow** (May 45)
Sep 40 **Whitney Straight** (Mar 43)
Oct 40 **Albatross** (Apr 42)
dets Hendon, Donibristle
Dec 41 **Hudson V** (May 42)
Apr 42 **Dominie** (Feb 44)
Aug 43 **Dakota** (Dec 46)
29 Feb 44 to Down Ampney
dets Doncaster, Blakehill Farm, Northolt, Croydon
10 Aug 45 to Odiham
5 Oct 45 to Broadwell
1 Dec 46 DB — renumbered as No 77 Sqn

272 Sqn

25 Jul 18 F @ Machrihanish — (Nos 531, 532 & 533 Flts)
Jul 18 **DH 6** (Mar 19)
Nov 18 **Fairey IIIA** (Mar 19)
5 Mar 19 DB
—
18 Nov 40 RF @ Aldergrove — from Flts of Nos 235 & 236 Sqns
Nov 40 **Blenheim IVF** (Apr 41)
3 Apr 41 to Chivenor
Apr 41 **Beaufighter IC** (Jul 43)
det Sumburgh
28 May 41 to Abu Sueir
14 Jun 41 to Idku
dets Luqa, LG 10
12 Jan 42 to LG 10
14 Mar 42 to Idku
dets LG 10, LG 05, LG 07, LG 143, LG 104, El Khanka, Heliopolis, Paphos, Nicosia, St Jean, Gianaclis
6 Nov 42 to Ta Kali
det Luqa
Nov 42 **Beaufighter VIC** (Feb 44)
4 Jun 43 to Luqa
5 Jul 43 to Gardabia
17 Jul 43 to Luqa
Sep 43 **Beaufighter XI** (May 44)
3 Sep 43 to Bo Rizzo
21 Oct 43 to Catania
Dec 43 **Beaufighter X** (Apr 45)
3 Feb 44 to Alghero
dets Bo Rizzo, Borgo, Reghaia
15 Sep 44 to Foggia
det Falconara
20 Mar 45 to Falconara
24 Apr 45 to Gragnano (No 56 PTC)
30 Apr 45 DB

273 Sqn

Aug 18 F @ Burgh Castle — (Nos 470, 485, 486 & 534 Flts)
Aug 18 **DH 4** (Mar 19)
Aug 18 **DH 9** (Mar 19)
Aug 18 **Camel** (Mar 19)
dets Covehithe, Westgate, Manston
14 Mar 19 reduced to a cadre
Jun 19 to Great Yarmouth
5 Jul 19 DB
—
1 Aug 39 RF @ China Bay
Aug 39 **Seal** (Mar 42)
Aug 39 **Vildebeeste III** (Mar 42)
det Ratmalana
Mar 42 **Fulmar II** (Sep 42)
18 Jun 42 to Katukurunda
Aug 42 **Hurricane I** (Nov 42)
Aug 42 **Hurricane IIB** (Dec 43)
1 Sep 42 to Ratmalana
15 Feb 43 to China Bay
1 Aug 43 to Ratmalana
Dec 43 **Hurricane IIC** (May 44)
Mar 44 **Spitfire VIII** (Dec 45)
9 Jul 44 to Chittagong
26 Aug 44 to Cox's Bazaar
31 Dec 44 to Maunghnama
det Cox's Bazaar
27 Jan 45 to Kyaukpyu
5 May 45 to Mingaladon
11 Sep 45 to Don Muang
19 Sep 45 to Tan Son Nhut
Nov 45 **Spitfire XIV** (Jan 46)
31 Jan 46 DB

274 Sqn

No 274 Sqn was first authorised to form at Seaton Carew in Nov 18 and was to have flown Vimys in the anti-submarine role. This plan was never fulfilled.

—
15 Jun 19 F @ Bircham Newton — nucleus from No 5 (Communications) Sqn
Jun 19 **HP V/1500** (Jan 20)
20 Jan 20 DB — to become the nucleus of No 207 Sqn
—
19 Aug 40 RF @ Amiriya — from elements of Nos 33, 80 & 112 Sqns
Aug 40 **Gladiator II** (Nov 40)
Aug 40 **Hurricane I** (Oct 41)
det Sidi Haneish
6 Dec 40 to LG 13
10 Jan 41 to Sidi Azeiz
dets Mechili, Marawa
12 Feb 41 to Amiriya
det Ismailia
17 Apr 41 to Gerawala
det Sidi Barrani
10 Sep 41 to Maryut
det El Khanka
Oct 41 **Hurricane IIB** (May 42)
26 Oct 41 to LG 103
det LG 110
6 Nov 41 to LG 130
20 Nov 41 to LG 124
25 Nov 41 to LG 103
19 Dec 41 to Gazala No 1
27 Dec 41 to Gazala No 2
dets Msus, LG 165
24 Jan 42 to Mechili
det Gazala
26 Jan 42 to LG 111
dets El Adem, Gambut
17 Feb 42 to Gasr el Arid
det Gambut 2
9 Mar 42 to Gambut Main
8 Apr 42 to Sidi Haneish
6 May 42 to Gambut
May 42 **Hurricane IIC** (Nov 43)
18 Jun 42 to El Dwabis
23 Jun 42 to LG 07
24 Jun 42 to Sidi Haneish
27 Jun 42 to LG 105
29 Jun 42 to LG 92
14 Jul 42 to LG 173
19 Aug 42 to LG 88
9 Sep 42 to LG 229
10 Oct 42 to LG 89
23 Oct 42 to LG 37
27 Nov 42 to Martuba 1
21 Dec 42 to Benina
20 Jan 43 to Misurata
26 Jan 43 to Mellaha
Apr 43 **Spitfire VB** (Aug 43)
Apr 43 **Spitfire VC** (Aug 43)
9 Aug 43 to Derna
det Paphos
7 Oct 43 to Idku
det Paphos
Oct 43 **Spitfire VC** (Apr 44)
Nov 43 **Spitfire VB** (Feb 44)
det Madna
22 Feb 44 to Canne
3 Apr 44 to Portici (No 3 BPD)
24 Apr 44 to Hornchurch
May 44 **Spitfire IX** (Aug 44)
19 May 44 to Detling
22 Jun 44 to Merston
28 Jun 44 to Gatwick
5 Jul 44 to West Malling
17 Aug 44 to Manston
Aug 44 **Tempest V** (Sep 45)
20 Sep 44 to Coltishall
29 Sep 44 to B 70/Deurne
2 Oct 44 to B 82/Grave
7 Oct 44 to B 80/Volkel
17 Mar 45 to B 77/Gilze-Rijen
7 Apr 45 to B 91/Kluis
20 Apr 45 to B 109/Quackenbrück
20 Jun 45 to B 155/Dedelsdorf
3 Sep 45 to Warmwell
7 Sep 45 DB — renumbered as No 174 Sqn

275 Sqn

15 Oct 41 F @ Valley
dets Andreas, Eglinton
Oct 41 **Lysander III** (Sep 43)
Oct 41 **Walrus** (Feb 45)
May 42 **Defiant I** (Jun 43)
Mar 43 **Anson I** (Oct 44)
20 Apr 44 to Warmwell
Apr 44 **Spitfire VC** (Feb 45)
7 Aug 44 to Bolt Head
det Portreath
22 Oct 44 to Exeter
dets Bolt Head, Portreath
12 Jan 45 to Harrowbeer
dets Bolt Head, Portreath
15 Feb 45 DB
—
1 Mar 53 RF @ Linton-on-Ouse
Apr 53 **Sycamore HR 13** (Nov 55)
det North Weald
Jan 54 **Auster AOP 5** (Aug 54)
Feb 54 **Hiller HTE-2** (May 55)
Jul 54 **Anson T.21** (Sep 59)
Jul 54 **Chipmunk T.10** (Mar 56)
Jul 54 **Sycamore HR 14** (Sep 59)
18 Nov 54 to Thornaby
dets Leuchars, Leconfield, North Coates, Chivenor, Aldergrove, Horsham St Faith
9 Oct 57 to Leconfield
dets Acklington, Leuchars, Horsham St Faith, Chivenor, Aldergrove
Mar 59 **Whirlwind HAR 4** (Sep 59)
Aug 59 **Whirlwind HAR 2** (Sep 59)
1 Sep 59 DB — renumbered as No 228 Sqn

276 Sqn

21 Oct 41 F @ Harrowbeer
Oct 41 **Lysander IIIA** (May 43)
Nov 41 **Hurricane I** (Jan 42)
Jan 42 **Walrus** (Nov 45)
dets Roborough, Portreath, Warmwell, Perranporth, Fairwood Common
Mar 42 **Spitfire IIA** (Apr 42)
May 42 **Defiant I** (Jun 43)
Feb 43 **Spitfire IIA** (May 44)
Mar 43 **Anson I** (Mar 44)
Feb 44 **Sea Otter** (May 44)
4 Apr 44 to Portreath
Apr 44 **Warwick I** (Nov 44)
May 44 **Spitfire VB** (Jun 45)
dets Bolt Head, A 23/Querqueville
18 Sep 44 to A 23/Querqueville
30 Sep 44 to B 48/Amiens/Glisy
dets Portreath, B 61/St Denis-Westrem
25 Oct 44 to B 63/St Croix
dets B 67/Ursel, B 61/St Denis-Westrem
14 Dec 44 to B 83/Knocke le Zout
det B 61/St Denis-Westrem
6 Jun 45 to Andrews Field
23 Aug 45 to Kjevik
dets Vaernes, Sola
22 Oct 45 to Gardemoen
10 Nov 45 to Dunsfold
14 Nov 45 DB

277 Sqn

22 Dec 41 F @ Stapleford Tawney
dets Martlesham Heath, Hawkinge, Shoreham
Dec 41 **Lysander III** (Jun 44)
Dec 41 **Walrus** (Feb 45)
May 42 **Defiant I** (May 43)
7 Dec 42 to Gravesend
dets Hawkinge, Martlesham Heath, Shoreham
Feb 43 **Spitfire IIC** (May 44)
Nov 43 **Sea Otter** (Feb 45)
15 Apr 44 to Shoreham
dets Martlesham Heath, Warmwell, Hurn, Hawkinge
Apr 44 **Spitfire VB** (Feb 45)
5 Oct 44 to Hawkinge
det Warmwell
Nov 44 **Warwick I** (Feb 45)
det Portreath
15 Feb 45 DB

278 Sqn

1 Oct 41 F @ Matlask — from 3 ASR Flt
Oct 41 **Lysander IIIA** (Feb 43
Oct 41 **Walrus** (Oct 45)
det North Coates
21 Apr 42 to Coltishall
dets North Coates, Woolsington, Acklington, Hutton Cranswick, Ayr, Drem, Castletown, Peterhead, Sumburgh
Feb 43 **Anson I** (May 44)
21 Apr 44 to Bradwell Bay
Apr 44 **Spitfire IIA** (May 44)
Apr 44 **Warwick I** (Jan 45)

May 44 **Spitfire VB** (Feb 45)
det Martlesham Heath
27 Sep 44 to Martlesham Heath
det Hornchurch
15 Feb 45 to Thorney Island
dets Hawkinge, Beccles, Exeter
May 45 **Sea Otter** (Oct 45)
15 Oct 45 DB

279 Sqn

16 Nov 41 F @ Bircham Newton
Nov 41 **Hudson III, V, VI** (Dec 44)
31 Oct 44 to Thornaby
Nov 44 **Warwick I** (Sep 45)
Feb 45 **Hurricane IIC** (Sep 45)
dets Banff, Wick, Fraserburgh, Tain, Reykjavik
Jul 45 **Sea Otter** (Sep 45)
3 Sep 45 to Beccles
Sep 45 **Lancaster ASR III** (Mar 46)
det Pegu
10 Mar 46 DB — Lancaster element at Pegu absorbed by No 1348 Flt

280 Sqn

12 Dec 41 F @ Thorney Island
Jan 42 **Anson I** (Oct 43)
10 Feb 42 to Detling
det Bircham Newton
30 Jul 42 to Langham
det Bircham Newton
5 Nov 42 to Bircham Newton
25 Sep 43 to Thorney Island
Oct 43 **Warwick I** (Jun 46)
21 Oct 43 to Thornaby
1 May 44 to Strubby
det Thornaby
6 Sep 44 to Langham
det Thornaby
30 Oct 44 to Beccles
dets Langham, Thorney Island, St Eval
3 Nov 45 to Langham
dets Thorney Island, St Eval, Aldergrove, Lagens
23 Nov 45 to Thornaby
dets Thorney Island, Aldergrove, Tain, Reykjavik, Lossiemouth
21 Jun 46 DB

281 Sqn

29 Mar 42 F @ Ouston
det Drem
Mar 42 **Defiant I** (Jun 43)
Jan 43 **Walrus** (Nov 43)
Mar 43 **Anson I** (Nov 43)
14 Jun 43 to Woolsington
det Drem
9 Oct 43 to Drem
det Ayr
22 Nov 43 DB — absorbed by No 282 Sqn
—
22 Nov 43 RF @ Thornaby
Dec 43 **Warwick I** (Oct 45)
det Davidstow Moor
27 Feb 44 to Tiree
dets Wick, Davidstow Moor, Great Orton, Leuchars, Dallachy, Banff, Mullaghmore
7 Feb 45 to Mullaghmore
det Tireee
Mar 45 **Sea Otter** (Oct 45)
31 Mar 45 to Limavady
dets Tiree, Valley
Apr 45 **Warwick VI** (May 45)
13 Aug 45 to Ballykelly
Aug 45 **Wellington XIII** (Sep 45)
dets Tiree, Tain
24 Oct 45 DB

282 Sqn

1 Jan 43 F @ Castletown
dets Peterhead, Drem, Ayr
Jan 43 **Walrus** (Jan 44)
Mar 43 **Anson I** (Jan 44)
12 Jan 44 DB — absorbed by No 278 Sqn
—
1 Feb 44 RF @ Davidstow Moor — nucleus from No 269 Sqn
Feb 44 **Warwick I** (Jul 45)
19 Sep 44 to St Eval
dets St Mawgan, Great Orton, Exeter
Mar 45 **Walrus** (Jul 45)
Mar 45 **Sea Otter** (Jul 45)
9 Jul 45 DB

283 Sqn

11 Feb 43 F @ Algiers (Hussein Day)
Apr 43 **Walrus** (Apr 44)
6 May 43 to Maison Blanche
13 May 43 to Tingley
30 May 43 to La Sebala
28 Aug 43 to Palermo
25 Dec 43 to Ajaccio
29 Dec 43 to Borgo
6 Apr 44 to Hal Far
Apr 44 **Warwick I** (Mar 46)
dets Castel Benito, Blida, Kalamaki/Hassani, Saki
31 Mar 46 DB

284 Sqn

7 May 43 F @ Gravesend
17 May 43 to Martlesham Heath
13 Jun 43 en route N Africa
17 Jul 43 established at Hal Far
Jul 43 **Walrus** (Sep 44)
27 Jul 43 to Cassibile
22 Aug 43 to Lentini East
det Milazzo
25 Sep 43 to Scanzano
2 Oct 43 to Gioia del Colle
15 Nov 43 to Brindisi
14 Mar 44 to Alghero
Mar 44 **Warwick I** (Sep 45)
dets Ghisonaccia, Ramatuelle, Calvi, Bone
17 Sep 44 to Elmas
Sep 44 **Hurricane IIC** (Mar 45)
dets Calvi, Bone, El Aouina
14 Nov 44 to Bone
dets Elmas, Istres, Pomigliano
13 Apr 45 to Pomigliano
21 Sep 45 DB
—
15 Oct 56 RF @ Nicosia
Oct 56 **Sycamore HR 14** (Aug 59)
1 Aug 59 DB — renumbered as No 103 Sqn

285 Sqn

1 Dec 41 F @ Wrexham — from No 9 Gp AAC Flt
dets Honiley, Woodvale
Dec 41 **Blenheim I** (Feb 42)
Dec 41 **Hudson III** (Feb 42)
Dec 41 **Lysander III** (Jun 42)
Mar 42 **Oxford** (Jun 45)
Mar 42 **Defiant I** (Jul 43)
29 Oct 42 to Honiley
dets Woodvale, High Ercall, Valley
Dec 42 **Defiant III** (Dec 43)
Jul 43 **Martinet** (Nov 43)
25 Aug 43 to Woodvale
dets High Ercall, Honiley, Croydon, Colerne, Fairwood Common
Sep 43 **Beaufighter IF** (Nov 44)
Jan 44 **Hurricane IIC** (Jun 45)
Mar 44 **Hurricane IV** (Apr 44)
19 Nov 44 to Andover
dets Farnborough, Middle Wallop
4 Jan 45 to North Weald
dets Farnborough, Hunsdon
Feb 45 **Mustang I** (Jun 45)
20 Jun 45 to Weston Zoyland
26 Jun 45 DB

286 Sqn

17 Nov 41 F @ Filton — from No 10 Gp AAC Flt
Nov 41 **Master III** (Jul 43)
Nov 41 **Defiant III** (Nov 43)
Nov 41 **Defiant I** (Jul 44)
Nov 41 **Hurricane I** (Jun 43)
Nov 41 **Oxford** (May 45)
30 Dec 41 to Colerne
24 Jan 42 to Lulsgate Bottom
2 Mar 42 to Colerne
30 Apr 42 to Lulsgate Bottom
Apr 42 **Hurricane IIC** (May 45)
dets (at various times over the next two years) at: Colerne, Middle Wallop, Exeter, Harrowbeer, Carew Cheriton, Fairwood Common, Pengam Moors, Kemble, Perranporth, Warmwell, Portreath, Charmy Down, Winkleigh
26 May 42 to Zeals
31 Aug 42 to Colerne
10 Oct 42 to Weston-super-Mare
Jul 43 **Martinet** (Nov 44)
29 Nov 43 to Weston Zoyland
10 Apr 44 to Culmhead
20 May 44 to Colerne
28 Jul 44 to Zeals
28 Sep 44 to Weston Zoyland
Nov 44 **Master III** (Feb 45)
16 May 45 DB

287 Sqn

19 Nov 41 F @ Croydon — from No 11 Gp AAC Flt
dets Debden, Hornchurch, Merston, Martlesham Heath, Fairlop, Biggin Hill, Northolt, Ipswich, Ford, Honiley, Hunsdon, Southend, Farnborough
Nov 41 **Blenheim IV** (Jan 42)
Nov 41 **Hudson III** (Mar 42)
Nov 41 **Lysander III** (Apr 42)
Nov 41 **Hurricane I, IIB, IV** (Mar 45)
Feb 42 **Master III** (Aug 42)
Mar 42 **Defiant I** (Oct 43)
Mar 42 **Oxford** (Jun 46)
Jan 43 **Defiant III** (Oct 43)
Jul 43 **Martinet** (Jun 46)
Nov 43 **Spitfire VB** (Mar 44)
3 Jul 44 to North Weald
dets Farnborough, Gatwick
27 Aug 44 to Gatwick
dets North Weald
Sep 44 **Beaufighter VI** (Jul 45)
Nov 44 **Spitfire IX** (Sep 45)
Nov 44 **Tempest V** (Jun 46)
20 Jan 45 to Redhill
det North Weald
3 May 45 to Hornchurch
dets Hunsdon, North Weald
15 Jun 45 to Bradwell Bay
Aug 45 **Spitfire XVI** (Jun 46)
10 Sep 45 to West Malling
15 Jun 46 DB

288 Sqn

18 Nov 41 F @ Digby — from No 12 Gp AAC Flt
dets Church Fenton, Duxford
Nov 41 **Blenheim IV** (Feb 42)
Nov 41 **Lysander II & III** (Mar 42)
Nov 41 **Hudson III** (Mar 42)
Nov 41 **Hurricane I** (44)
Mar 42 **Defiant I** (Apr 43)
6 Dec 42 to Wellingore
dets Church Fenton, Duxford
Dec 42 **Spitfire VB & IX** (Jun 46)
18 Jan 43 to Digby
dets Church Fenton, Duxford, Wittering, Coltishall, Bottisham, Collyweston
Mar 43 **Oxford** (May 45)
Jul 43 **Martinet** ( )
9 Nov 43 to Coleby Grange
dets Church Fenton, Coltishall, Collyweston
25 Nov 43 to Digby
dets Church Fenton, Coltishall, Collyweston
12 Jan 44 to Collyweston
dets Church Fenton, Coltishall, Docking, Fairwood Common, Ford, North Weald
Mar 44 **Beaufighter VI** (Nov 44)
20 Nov 44 to Church Fenton
dets Collyweston, Ouston, Acklington
May 45 **Vengeance IV** (Jun 46)
13 Aug 45 to Hutton Cranswick
det Acklington
24 May 46 to East Moor
det Acklington
15 Jun 46 DB
—
16 Mar 53 RF @ Middle Wallop
Mar 53 **Spitfire LF 16E** (May 53)
Apr 53 **Balliol T.2** (Sep 57)
30 Sep 57 DB

289 Sqn

17 Nov 41 F @ Kirknewton — from No 13 Gp AAC Flt
Nov 41 **Blenheim IV** (Jan 42)
Nov 41 **Lysander III** (Mar 42)
Nov 41 **Hudson III** (Mar 42)
Nov 41 **Hurricane I, IIC, IV** (Jun 45)
Mar 42 **Oxford** (Jun 45)
Mar 42 **Defiant I & III** (Jul 43)
dets Ayr, Longman
18 May 42 to Turnhouse
dets West Freugh, Dyce, Ouston, Drem, Catterick
Jun 43 **Martinet** (Mar 45)

Mar 45 **Vengeance IV** (Jun 45)
7 May 45 to Acklington det West Freugh
18 May 45 to Eshott
5 Jun 45 to Andover
26 Jun 45 DB

290 Sqn

1 Dec 43 F @ Newtownards — from Nos 1617 & 1480 Flts det West Freugh
Dec 43 **Hurricane IIC** (Jan 45)
Dec 43 **Oxford** (Oct 45)
Dec 43 **Martinet** (Oct 45)
25 Mar 44 to Long Kesh det West Freugh
25 Aug 44 to Turnhouse dets West Freugh, Farnborough, Long Kesh
Dec 44 **Spitfire VB** (Oct 45)
1 Feb 45 to B 83/Knocke le Zout
27 Oct 45 DB

291 Sqn

1 Dec 43 F @ Hutton Cranswick — from Nos 1613, 1629 & 1634 Flts dets Southend, Eastchurch, Ouston, Acklington, Eshott
Dec 43 **Henley III** (Mar 44)
Dec 43 **Martinet** (Jun 45)
Mar 44 **Hurricane IIC** (Nov 44)
Apr 44 **Hurricane IV** (Jun 45)
Nov 44 **Vengeance IV** (Jun 45)
26 Jun 45 DB

292 Sqn

1 Feb 44 F @ Jessore
Feb 44 **Walrus** (Jun 45)
Apr 44 **Warwick I** (Jun 45) dets Ratmalana
Nov 44 **Sea Otter** (Jun 45)
Dec 44 **Liberator VI** (Jun 45)
5 Feb 45 to Agartala dets Kankesanterai, Chittagong
15 Jun 45 DB — split into Nos 1347, 1348 & 1349 Flts

293 Sqn

28 Nov 43 F @ Blida
Nov 43 **Warwick I** (Apr 46)
1 Dec 43 to Bone det Pomigliano
28 Mar 44 to Pomigliano
Apr 44 **Walrus** (Apr 46) dets Pisa, Rosignano, Foggia, Rivolto, Cesenatico, Udine
21 Mar 45 to Foggia dets Cesenatico, Udine
27 Jun 45 to Pomigliano
5 Apr 46 DB

294 Sqn

24 Sep 43 F @ Berka — ASR Flt redesignated
Sep 43 **Walrus** (Apr 46)
Sep 43 **Wellington IC** (Mar 44) dets LG 07, Lakatamia, Mellaha, Limassol, Derna, Gambut
5 Oct 43 to LG 91 dets Derna, Lakatamia, Berka III, LG 07, Mellaha, St Jean, Gambut, Castel Benito
29 Mar 44 to Idku dets Berka III, Gambut No 3, LG 07, St Jean, Ramat David, Lakatamia, Luxor, Benina, El Adem, Aboukir, Nicosia, Aqir, Hassani, Lydda
Mar 44 **Wellington XI** (Jun 45)
Jun 44 **Wellington XIII** (Apr 46)
Oct 44 **Warwick I** (Apr 46)
6 Jun 45 to Basrah dets Sharjah, Masirah, Muharraq
8 Apr 46 DB

295 Sqn

3 Aug 42 F @ Netheravon — nucleus from No 296 Sqn
Aug 42 **Whitley V** (Nov 43)
Feb 43 **Halifax V** (Nov 43)
1 May 43 to Holmsley South det Goubrine II
30 Jun 43 to Hurn
Oct 43 **Albemarle II** (Jul 44)
Nov 43 **Albemarle I** (Jul 44)
15 Mar 44 to Harwell
Apr 44 **Albemarle V** (Jul 44)
Jun 44 **Stirling IV** (Jan 46)
11 Oct 44 to Rivenhall
21 Jan 46 DB
—
21 Jan 46 RF @ Tarrant Rushton — No 190 Sqn renumbered
Jan 46 **Halifax A.7** (Apr 46)
1 Apr 46 DB — renumbered as No 297 Sqn
—
10 Sep 47 RF @ Fairford
Sep 47 **Halifax A.9** (Oct 48)
1 Nov 48 DB

296 Sqn

25 Jan 42 F @ Ringway — the Glider Exercise Unit redesignated
Jan 42 **Hector** (Aug 42)
Jan 42 **Hart** (Aug 42)
1 Feb 42 to Netheravon
May 42 **Whitley V** (Mar 43)
25 Jul 42 to Hurn
25 Oct 42 to Andover
19 Dec 42 to Hurn
Jan 43 **Albemarle I** (Oct 44)
3 Jun 43 air echelon to Froha
3 Jun 43 to Stoney Cross (ground echelon)
24 Jun 43 air echelon to Goubrine II det Cassibile
15 Oct 43 to Hurn
Nov 43 **Albemarle II** (Oct 44)
14 Mar 44 to Brize Norton
Apr 44 **Albemarle V** (Oct 44)
Aug 44 **Albemarle VI** (Oct 44)
Sep 44 **Halifax V** (Feb 45)
29 Sep 44 to Earles Colne
Feb 45 **Halifax III** (Jan 46)
Dec 45 **Halifax A.7** (Jan 46)
23 Jan 46 DB

297 Sqn

22 Jan 42 F @ Netheravon — the Parachute Exercise Sqn redesignated
Feb 42 **Whitley V** (Feb 44)
5 Jun 42 to Hurn
24 Oct 42 to Thruxton
Jul 43 **Albemarle I** (Dec 44)
25 Aug 43 to Stoney Cross
Feb 44 **Albemarle II** (Dec 44)
14 Mar 44 to Brize Norton
Apr 44 **Albemarle V** (Dec 44)
Jul 44 **Albemarle VI** (Dec 44)
30 Sep 44 to Earls Colne
Oct 44 **Halifax V** (Feb 45)
Feb 45 **Halifax III** (Apr 46)
Dec 45 **Halifax A.7** (Apr 46)
1 Apr 46 DB
—
1 Apr 46 RF @ Tarrant Rushton — No 295 Sqn renumbered
Apr 46 **Halifax A.7** (Mar 47)
5 Sep 46 to Brize Norton
Jan 47 **Halifax A.9** (Oct 48)
21 Aug 47 to Fairford
1 Nov 48 to Dishforth
Nov 48 **Hastings C.1** (Nov 50) det Schleswig for BAL
22 Aug 49 to Topcliffe
15 Nov 50 DB

298 Sqn

24 Aug 42 F @ Thruxton — nucleus from No 297 Sqn
Aug 42 **Whitley V** (Oct 42)
19 Oct 42 DB — formation suspended
—
4 Nov 43 RF @ Tarrant Rushton — from a Flt of No 295 Sqn
Nov 43 **Halifax V** (Nov 44)
Sep 44 **Halifax III** (Jul 45)
Mar 45 **Halifax A.7** (Dec 46)
5 Jul 45 en route India
15 Jul 45 to Raipur dets Akyab, Alipore
9 Dec 45 to Digri dets Alipore, Meiktila, Chaklala
20 May 46 to Baroda
24 Jul 46 to Mauripur det Risalpur
21 Dec 46 DB

299 Sqn

4 Nov 43 F @ Stoney Cross — from 'C' Flt, No 297 Sqn
Nov 43 **Ventura I & II** (Jan 44)
Jan 44 **Stirling IV** (Feb 46)
15 Mar 44 to Keevil
9 Oct 44 to Wethersfield
25 Jan 45 to Shepherds Grove
Jan 45 **Stirling V** (Feb 46)
15 Feb 46 DB

300 Sqn

1 Jul 40 F @ Bramcote
Jul 40 **Battle** (Nov 40)
22 Aug 40 to Swinderby
Dec 40 **Wellington IC** (Sep 41)
18 Jul 41 to Hemswell
Aug 41 **Wellington IV** (Jan 43)
18 May 42 to Ingham
31 Jan 43 to Hemswell
Jan 43 **Wellington III** (Apr 43)
Mar 43 **Wellington X** (Mar 44)
22 Jun 43 to Ingham
1 Mar 44 to Faldingworth
Apr 44 **Lancaster I & III** (Oct 46)
2 Jan 47 DB

301 Sqn

22 Jul 40 F @ Bramcote
Jul 40 **Battle** (Nov 40)
29 Aug 40 to Swinderby
Oct 40 **Wellington IC** (Aug 41
18 Jul 41 to Hemswell
Aug 41 **Wellington IV** (Apr 43)
7 Apr 43 DB
—
7 Nov 44 RF @ Brindisi — No 1586 Flt redesignated
Nov 44 **Halifax II** (Mar 45)
Nov 44 **Halifax V** (Mar 45)
Nov 44 **Liberator VI** (Mar 45)
4 Apr 45 to Blackbushe
May 45 **Warwick I** (Jul 45)
May 45 **Warwick III** (Feb 46)
2 Jul 45 to North Weald
4 Sep 45 to Chedburgh
Jan 46 **Halifax VIII** (Dec 46)
18 Dec 46 DB

302 Sqn

13 Jul 40 F @ Leconfield
Jul 40 **Hurricane I** (Mar 41) dets Duxford
11 Oct 40 to Northolt
23 Nov 40 to Westhampnett
Mar 41 **Hurricane IIA** (May 41
7 Apr 41 to Kenley
29 May 41 to Jurby
May 41 **Hurricane I** (Jul 41)
Jul 41 **Hurricane IIB** (Oct 41)
7 Aug 41 to Church Stanton
5 Sep 41 to Warmwell
11 Oct 41 to Ibsley
Oct 41 **Spitfire IIA** (Nov 41)
Oct 41 **Spitfire VB** (Sep 43)
1 Nov 41 to Harrowbeer
27 Apr 42 to Warmwell
1 May 42 to Harrowbeer
5 May 42 to Heston
30 Jun 42 to Croydon
7 Jul 42 to Heston
21 Sep 42 to Ipswich
29 Sep 42 to Heston
1 Feb 43 to Kirton-in-Lindsey det Digby
17 Apr 43 to Hutton Cranswick
1 Jun 43 to Heston
20 Jun 43 to Perranporth
Jul 43 **Spitfire VC** (Sep 43)
19 Aug 43 to Fairlop
18 Sep 43 to Tangmere
Sep 43 **Spitfire IX** (May 44)
21 Sep 43 to Northolt
2 Dec 43 to Fairwood Common
19 Dec 43 to Northolt
1 Mar 44 to Llanbedr
7 Mar 44 to Northolt
1 Apr 44 to Deanland
12 Apr 44 to Southend
14 Apr 44 to Deanland
26 Apr 44 to Chailey
May 44 **Spitfire IXE** (Feb 45)
28 Jun 44 to Appledram
16 Jul 44 to Ford
4 Aug 44 to B 10/Plumetot
30 Aug 44 to Fairwood Common
16 Sep 44 to B 51/Lille/Vendeville
3 Oct 44 to B 70/Deurne
11 Oct 44 to B 61/St Denis-Westrem
Jan 45 **Spitfire XVIE** (Dec 46)
23 Jan 45 to B 60/Grimbergen
9 Mar 45 to B 77/Gilze-Rijen
13 Apr 45 to B 101/Nordhorn
30 Apr 45 to B 113/Varrelbusch
27 Aug 45 to B 170/Sylt
14 Sep 45 to B 113/Varrelbusch
16 Sep 45 to B 111/Ahlhorn
27 Aug 46 to Sylt
31 Aug 46 to Ahlhorn
7 Oct 46 to Hethel
18 Dec 46 DB

303 Sqn

22 Jul 40 F @ Northolt
Aug 40 **Hurricane I** (Jan 41)
11 Oct 40 to Leconfield
3 Jan 41 to Northolt
Jan 41 **Spitfire I** (Mar 41)
Mar 41 **Spitfire IIA** (Jun 41)
May 41 **Spitfire IIB** (Aug 41)
15 Jul 41 to Speke
Aug 41 **Spitfire I** (Oct 41)
Aug 41 **Hurricane I** (Oct 41)
7 Oct 41 to Northolt
Oct 41 **Spitfire VB** (Jul 43)
16 Jun 42 to Kirton-in-Lindsey
15 Aug 42 to Redhill
20 Aug 42 to Kirton-in-Lindsey
2 Feb 43 to Northolt
5 Feb 43 to Heston
5 Mar 43 to Debden
12 Mar 43 to Heston
26 Mar 43 to Martlesham Heath
8 Apr 43 to Heston
1 Jun 43 to Northolt
Jun 43 **Spitfire IXC** (Nov 43)
12 Nov 43 to Ballyhalbert
Nov 43 **Spitfire LF VB** (Feb 45)
30 Apr 44 to Horne
19 Jun 44 to Westhampnett
27 Jun 44 to Merston
Jul 44 **Spitfire IXC** (Apr 45)
9 Aug 44 to Westhampnett
25 Sep 44 to Coltishall
Feb 45 **Spitfire XVI** (Apr 45)
4 Apr 45 to Andrews Field
Apr 45 **Mustang I** (May 45)
Apr 45 **Mustang IV** (Nov 46)
6 May 45 to Coltishall
0 Aug 45 to Andrews Field
1 Dec 45 to Turnhouse
5 Jan 46 to Wick
6 Mar 46 to Charterhall
3 Mar 46 to Hethel
1 Dec 46 DB

304 Sqn

2 Aug 40 F @ Bramcote
Aug 40 **Battle** (Nov 40)
Nov 40 **Wellington IC** (Apr 43)
2 Dec 40 to Syerston
9 Jul 41 to Lindholme
0 May 42 to Tiree
5 Jun 42 to Dale
3 Nov 42 to Talbenny
0 Dec 42 to Dale
2 Apr 43 to Docking
Apr 43 **Wellington X** (Jun 43)
7 Jun 43 to Davidstow Moor
Jun 43 **Wellington XIII** (Sep 43)
Sep 43 **Wellington XIV** (Dec 45)
3 Dec 43 to Predannack
9 Feb 44 to Chivenor
1 Sep 44 to Benbecula
det Limavady
6 Mar 45 to St Eval
9 Jul 45 to North Weald
Jul 45 **Warwick I** (Nov 45)
Jul 45 **Warwick III** (May 46)
5 Sep 45 to Chedburgh
May 46 **Halifax VIII** (Dec 46)
8 Dec 46 DB

305 Sqn

9 Aug 40 F @ Bramcote
Aug 40 **Battle** (Nov 40)
Nov 40 **Wellington IC** (Jul 41)
2 Dec 40 to Syerston
Jul 41 to Lindholme
Jul 41 **Wellington II** (Aug 42)
2 Jul 42 to Hemswell
Aug 42 **Wellington IV** (May 43)
May 43 **Wellington X** (Aug 43)
2 Jun 43 to Ingham
Sep 43 to Swanton Morley
Sep 43 **Mitchell II** (Dec 43)
18 Nov 43 to Lasham
Dec 43 **Mosquito VI** (Nov 46)
23 Oct 44 to Hartford Bridge
25 Oct 44 to Lasham
30 Oct 44 to Hartford Bridge
19 Nov 44 to A 75/Cambrai/Epinoy
30 Jul 45 to B 80/Volkel
7 Sep 45 to B 77/Gilze-Rijen
24 Nov 45 to B 58/Melsbroek
2 Jan 46 to Sylt
19 Jan 46 to Melsbroek
11 Mar 46 to Wahn
18 Jun 46 to Sylt
11 Jul 46 to Wahn
25 Jul 46 to Handorf
16 Aug 46 to Wahn
7 Sep 46 to Manston
16 Sep 46 to Wahn
15 Oct 46 to Faldingworth
6 Jan 47 DB

306 Sqn

29 Aug 40 F @ Church Fenton
Aug 40 **Hurricane I** (Apr 41)
7 Nov 40 to Ternhill
3 Apr 41 to Northolt
Apr 41 **Hurricane IIA** (Jul 41)
Jun 41 **Spitfire IIB** (Sep 41)
Sep 41 **Spitfire VB** (Oct 41)
7 Oct 41 to Speke
Oct 41 **Spitfire IIA** (Dec 41)
12 Dec 41 to Church Stanton
Dec 41 **Spitfire VB** (Oct 42)
3 May 42 to Kirton-in-Lindsey
16 Jun 42 to Northolt
Oct 42 **Spitfire IX** (Mar 43)
12 Mar 43 to Hutton Cranswick
Mar 43 **Spitfire VB** (Apr 44)
30 May 43 to Catterick
det Thornaby
11 Aug 43 to Gravesend
19 Aug 43 to Friston
22 Sep 43 to Heston
19 Dec 43 to Llanbedr
1 Jan 44 to Heston
15 Mar 44 to Llanbedr
20 Mar 44 to Heston
1 Apr 44 to Coolham
Apr 44 **Mustang III** (Jan 47)
22 Jun 44 to Holmsley South
27 Jun 44 to Ford
8 Jul 44 to Brenzett
10 Oct 44 to Andrews Field
10 Aug 45 to Coltishall
8 Oct 45 to Fairwood Common
18 Nov 45 to Coltishall
6 Jan 47 DB

307 Sqn

5 Sep 40 F @ Kirton-in-Lindsey
Sep 40 **Defiant I** (Aug 41)
7 Nov 40 to Jurby
dets Cranage, Squires Gate
23 Jan 41 to Squires Gate
26 Mar 41 to Colerne
26 Apr 41 to Exeter
det Pembrey
Aug 41 **Beaufighter IIF** (May 42)
May 42 **Beaufighter VIF** (Jan 43)
Dec 42 **Mosquito II** (Mar 44)
15 Apr 43 to Fairwood Common
det Predannack
7 Aug 43 to Predannack
Aug 43 **Mosquito VI** (Oct 43)
9 Nov 43 to Drem
det Sumburgh
Jan 44 **Mosquito XII** (Jan 45)
2 Mar 44 to Coleby Grange
6 May 44 to Church Fenton
det Coltishall
Oct 44 **Mosquito XXX** (Nov 46)
27 Jan 45 to Castle Camps
31 May 45 to Coltishall
24 Aug 45 to Horsham St Faith
4 Nov 45 to Lübeck
15 Nov 45 to Horsham St Faith
9 Feb 46 to Lübeck
24 Feb 46 to Horsham St Faith
29 Nov 46 reduced to a cadre
2 Jan 47 DB

308 Sqn

5 Sep 40 F @ Squires Gate
12 Sep 40 to Speke
25 Sep 40 to Baginton
Oct 40 **Hurricane I** (Apr 41)
Mar 41 **Spitfire I** (May 41)
31 May 41 to Chilbolton
May 41 **Spitfire IIA** (Aug 41)
24 Jun 41 to Northolt
Aug 41 **Spitfire VB** (Nov 43)
12 Dec 41 to Woodvale
Jan 42 **Spitfire IIA** (Feb 42)
1 Apr 42 to Exeter
7 May 42 to Hutton Cranswick
1 Jul 42 to Redhill
7 Jul 42 to Hutton Cranswick
30 Jul 42 to Heston
15 Sep 42 to Ipswich
21 Sep 42 to Heston
29 Oct 42 to Northolt
29 Apr 43 to Church Fenton
5 Jul 43 to Hutton Cranswick
7 Sep 43 to Friston
13 Sep 43 to Hutton Cranswick
21 Sep 43 to Heston
11 Nov 43 to Northolt
Nov 43 **Spitfire IX** (Mar 45)
2 Dec 43 to Hutton Cranswick
18 Dec 43 to Northolt
8 Mar 44 to Llanbedr
15 Mar 44 to Northolt
1 Apr 44 to Deanland
28 Apr 44 to Chailey
28 Jun 44 to Appledram
16 Jul 44 to Ford
4 Aug 44 to B 10/Plumetot
6 Sep 44 to B 31/Fresnoy-Folny
10 Sep 44 to B 51/Lille/Vendeville
3 Oct 44 to B 70/Deurne
11 Oct 44 to B 61/St Denis-Westrem
13 Jan 45 to B 60/Grimbergen
9 Mar 45 to B 77/Gilze-Rijen
Mar 45 **Spitfire XVI** (Dec 46)
13 Apr 45 to B 101/Nordhorn
26 Apr 45 to Fairwood Common
2 Jun 45 to B 113/Varrelbusch
16 Sep 45 to B 111/Ahlhorn
22 Jan 46 to Sylt
9 Feb 46 to Ahlhorn
7 Oct 46 to Hethel
18 Dec 46 DB

309 Sqn

7 Oct 40 F @ Abbotsinch
Nov 40 **Lysander III** (May 41)
6 Nov 40 to Renfrew
det Perth/Scone
8 May 41 to Dunino
May 41 **Lysander IIIA** (Jul 42)
dets Gatwick, Longman, Findo Gask
Aug 42 **Mustang I** (Feb 44)
26 Nov 42 to Findo Gask
dets Peterhead, Gatwick
10 Mar 43 to Kirknewton
3 Jun 43 to Snailwell
6 Nov 43 to Wellingore
24 Nov 43 to Snailwell
Feb 44 **Hurricane IV** (Apr 44)
dets Drem, Hutton Cranswick
23 Apr 44 to Drem
dets Hutton Cranswick, Acklington, Peterhead
Apr 44 **Hurricane IIC** (Sep 44)
Sep 44 **Mustang I** (Oct 44)
Oct 44 **Mustang III** (Nov 46)
14 Nov 44 to Peterhead
14 Dec 44 to Andrews Field
10 Aug 45 to Coltishall
9 Oct 45 to Bradwell Bay
det Coltishall
17 Nov 45 to Coltishall
6 Jan 47 DB

310 Sqn

10 Jul 40 F @ Duxford
Jul 40 **Hurricane I** (Mar 41)
Mar 41 **Hurricane IIA** (Dec 41)
26 Jun 41 to Martlesham Heath
Jun 41 **Hurricane IIB** (Dec 41)
20 Jul 41 to Dyce
det Montrose
Oct 41 **Spitfire IIA** (Dec 41)
Nov 41 **Spitfire VB** (Feb 44)
24 Dec 41 to Perranporth
9 Feb 42 to Predannack
11 Feb 42 to Perranporth
8 Mar 42 to Warmwell
21 Mar 42 to Perranporth
7 May 42 to Exeter
1 Jul 42 to Redhill
7 Jul 42 to Exeter
det Bolt Head
Jul 42 **Spitfire VC** (Jun 43)
16 Aug 42 to Redhill
21 Aug 42 to Exeter
det Bolt Head
26 Jun 43 to Castletown
Jul 43 **Spitfire VI** (Sep 43)
det Sumburgh
19 Sep 43 to Ibsley
Sep 43 **Spitfire VC** (Feb 44)
2 Dec 43 to Llanbedr
15 Dec 43 to Ibsley
Jan 44 **Spitfire LF IX** (Jul 44)
19 Feb 44 to Mendlesham
21 Feb 44 to Hutton Cranswick
25 Feb 44 to Mendlesham
28 Mar 44 to Southend
3 Apr 44 to Appledram
22 Jun 44 to Tangmere
28 Jun 44 to B 10/Plumetot
29 Jun 44 to Tangmere
1 Jul 44 to Lympne
11 Jul 44 to Digby
Jul 44 **Spitfire VB** (Sep 44)
det Hutton Cranswick
28 Aug 44 to North Weald
Aug 44 **Spitfire LF IX** (Feb 46)
29 Dec 44 to Bradwell Bay
27 Feb 45 to Manston
7 Aug 45 to Hildesheim
13 Aug 45 to Prague
15 Feb 46 DB — transferred to Czech control

311 Sqn

29 Jul 40 F @ Honington
Aug 40 **Wellington IC** (Jun 43)
16 Sep 40 to East Wretham
det Stradishall
28 Apr 42 to Aldergrove
12 Jun 42 to Talbenny
26 May 43 to Beaulieu
Jun 43 **Liberator IIIA** (43)
Jun 43 **Liberator V** (Mar 45)
23 Feb 44 to Predannack
7 Aug 44 to Tain
Mar 45 **Liberator VI** (Feb 46)
6 Aug 45 to Manston
13 Aug 45 to Prague
15 Feb 46 DB — transferred to Czech control

312 Sqn

29 Aug 40 F @ Duxford
Aug 40 **Hurricane I** (May 41)
26 Sep 40 to Speke dets Penrhos
3 Mar 41 to Valley dets Penrhos
25 Apr 41 to Jurby
29 May 41 to Kenley
May 41 **Hurricane IIB** (Dec 41)
20 Jul 41 to Martlesham Heath
19 Aug 41 to Ayr det Turnhouse
Oct 41 **Spitfire IIA** (Dec 41)
Nov 41 **Spitfire IIB** (Jan 42)
Dec 41 **Spitfire VB** (Feb 44)
1 Jan 42 to Fairwood Common
24 Jan 42 to Angle det Fairwood Common
18 Apr 42 to Fairwood Common
20 Apr 42 to Warmwell
24 Apr 42 to Fairwood Common
2 May 42 to Harrowbeer
19 May 42 to Warmwell
31 May 42 to Harrowbeer
1 Jul 42 to Redhill
8 Jul 42 to Harrowbeer
16 Aug 42 to Redhill
20 Aug 42 to Harrowbeer
Aug 42 **Spitfire VC** (Jun 43)
10 Oct 42 to Church Stanton
20 Feb 43 to Warmwell
14 Mar 43 to Church Stanton
24 Jun 43 to Skaebrae det Peterhead
21 Sep 43 to Ibsley
Sep 43 **Spitfire VC** (Feb 44)
2 Dec 43 to Llanbedr
18 Dec 43 to Ibsley
Jan 44 **Spitfire LF IXB** (Jun 44)
19 Feb 44 to Mendlesham
23 Feb 44 to Southend
3 Mar 44 to Mendlesham
4 Apr 44 to Appledram
22 Jun 44 to Tangmere
Jun 44 **Spitfire HF IX** (Feb 46)
28 Jun 44 to B 10/Plumetot
29 Jun 44 to Tangmere
4 Jul 44 to Lympne
11 Jul 44 to Coltishall
27 Aug 44 to North Weald
3 Oct 44 to Bradwell Bay
27 Feb 45 to Manston
7 Aug 45 to Hildesheim
13 Aug 45 to Prague
15 Feb 46 DB — transferred to Czech control

313 Sqn

10 May 41 F @ Catterick
May 41 **Spitfire I** (Aug 41)
1 Jul 41 to Leconfield
Aug 41 **Spitfire IIA** (Nov 41)
26 Aug 41 to Portreath
Oct 41 **Spitfire VB** (Feb 44)
23 Nov 41 to Warmwell
29 Nov 41 to Portreath
15 Dec 41 to Hornchurch
6 Feb 42 to Southend
7 Mar 42 to Hornchurch
29 Apr 42 to Fairlop
8 Jun 42 to Church Stanton
Jul 42 **Spitfire VC** (Jul 43)
28 Jun 43 to Peterhead det Sumburgh
Jun 43 **Spitfire VI** (Jul 43)
21 Aug 43 to Hawkinge
18 Sep 43 to Ibsley
Nov 43 **Spitfire VC** (Feb 44)
6 Jan 44 to Woodvale
10 Jan 44 to Ayr
20 Jan 44 to Ibsley
Feb 44 **Spitfire IX** (Jul 44)
20 Feb 44 to Mendlesham
14 Mar 44 to Southend
20 Mar 44 to Mendlesham
4 Apr 44 to Appledram
22 Jun 44 to Tangmere
28 Jun 44 to B 10/Plumetot
29 Jun 44 to Tangmere
4 Jul 44 to Lympne
11 Jul 44 to Skaebrae
Jul 44 **Spitfire VB** (Oct 44)
Jul 44 **Spitfire VII** (Aug 44) det Sumburgh
4 Oct 44 to North Weald
Oct 44 **Spitfire IX** (Feb 46)
29 Dec 44 to Bradwell Bay
27 Feb 45 to Manston
7 Aug 45 to Hildesheim
13 Aug 45 to Prague
15 Feb 46 DB — transferred to Czech control

315 Sqn

8 Jan 41 F @ Acklington
Feb 41 **Hurricane I** (Jul 41)
13 Mar 41 to Speke
14 Jul 41 to Northolt
Jul 41 **Spitfire IIA** (Aug 41)
Aug 41 **Spitfire IIB** (Sep 41)
Aug 41 **Spitfire VB** (Nov 42)
1 Apr 42 to Woodvale det Valley
5 Sep 42 to Northolt
Nov 42 **Spitfire IX** (May 43)
Feb 43 **Spitfire VB** (Apr 44)
2 Jun 43 to Hutton Cranswick
6 Jul 43 to Ballyhalbert
13 Nov 43 to Heston
19 Dec 43 to Llanbedr
1 Jan 44 to Heston
Mar 44 **Mustang III** (Dec 46)
24 Mar 44 to Llanbedr
28 Mar 44 to Heston
1 Apr 44 to Coolham
22 Jun 44 to Holmsley South
25 Jun 44 to Ford
10 Jul 44 to Brenzett
10 Oct 44 to Andrews Field
24 Oct 44 to Coltishall
1 Nov 44 to Peterhead
16 Jan 45 to Andrews Field
8 Aug 45 to Coltishall
19 Nov 45 to Fairwood Common
20 Dec 45 to Coltishall
14 Jan 47 DB

316 Sqn

12 Feb 41 F @ Pembrey
Feb 41 **Hurricane I** (Aug 41)
18 Jun 41 to Colerne
Jun 41 **Hurricane IIA** (Nov 41)
Jun 41 **Hurricane IIB** (Oct 41)
2 Aug 41 to Church Stanton
Oct 41 **Spitfire IIA** (Nov 41)
Oct 41 **Spitfire VB** (Jul 43)
13 Dec 41 to Northolt
23 Apr 42 to Heston
30 Jul 42 to Hutton Cranswick
12 Mar 43 to Northolt
Mar 43 **Spitfire IX** (Sep 43)
22 Sep 43 to Acklington
Sep 43 **Spitfire LF VB** (Apr 44)
15 Feb 44 to Woodvale
Apr 44 **Mustang III** (Nov 46)
28 Apr 44 to Coltishall
4 Jul 44 to West Malling
11 Jul 44 to Friston
27 Aug 44 to Coltishall
24 Oct 44 to Andrews Field
16 May 45 to Coltishall
10 Aug 45 to Andrews Field
17 Sep 45 to Fairwood Common
5 Oct 45 to Andrews Field
28 Nov 45 to Wick
15 Mar 46 to Hethel
11 Dec 46 DB

317 Sqn

19 Feb 41 F @ Acklington
Feb 41 **Hurricane I** (Jul 41)
29 Apr 41 to Ouston
26 Jun 41 to Colerne
27 Jun 41 to Fairwood Common
Jul 41 **Hurricane IIB** (Nov 41)
21 Jul 41 to Exeter
Oct 41 **Spitfire VB** (Sep 43)
1 Apr 42 to Northolt
30 Jun 42 to Croydon
7 Jul 42 to Northolt
5 Sep 42 to Woodvale
13 Feb 43 to Kirton-in-Lindsey
29 Apr 43 to Martlesham Heath
1 Jun 43 to Heston
21 Jun 43 to Perranporth
21 Aug 43 to Fairlop
21 Sep 43 to Northolt
Sep 43 **Spitfire IX** (May 45)
2 Dec 43 to Southend
18 Dec 43 to Northolt
1 Apr 44 to Deanland
26 Apr 44 to Chailey
28 Jun 44 to Appledram
16 Jul 44 to Ford
4 Aug 44 to B 10/Plumetot
6 Sep 44 to B 31/Fresnoy-Folny
10 Sep 44 to B 51/Lille/Vendeville
3 Oct 44 to B 70/Deurne
11 Oct 44 to B 61/St Denis-Westrem
22 Nov 44 to Fairwood Common
11 Dec 44 to B 61/St Denis-Westrem
13 Jan 45 to B 60/Grimbergen
9 Mar 45 to B 77/Gilze-Rijen
2 Apr 45 to B 82/Grave
4 Apr 45 to B 77/Gilze-Rijen
13 Apr 45 to B 101/Nordhorn
30 Apr 45 to B 113/Varrelbusch
May 45 **Spitfire XVI** (Dec 46)
15 Sep 45 to B 111/Ahlhorn
Jul 46 to Sylt
16 Aug 46 to Ahlhorn
7 Oct 46 to Hethel
18 Dec 46 DB

318 Sqn

20 Mar 43 F @ Detling
Apr 43 **Hurricane I** (Aug 43) det Weston Zoyland
5 Aug 43 en route Egypt
31 Aug 43 to Almaza
10 Sep 43 to Muqueibila
Sep 43 **Hurricane IIB** (Mar 44)
14 Oct 43 to Gaza
21 Nov 43 to LG 207
Mar 44 **Spitfire VB** (Mar 45)
Mar 44 **Spitfire VC** (Mar 45)
23 Apr 44 to Helwan
24 Apr 44 to Marble Arch
25 Apr 44 to Castel Benito
28 Apr 44 to Madna
1 May 44 to Trigno
17 Jun 44 to San Vito
26 Jun 44 to Tortoreto
2 Jul 44 to Fermo det Castiglione
30 Jul 44 to Falconara
24 Aug 44 to Chiaravalle
31 Aug 44 to Piagiolino
16 Sep 44 to Cassandro
27 Sep 44 to Rimini det Iesi
Sep 44 **Spitfire IX** (Jul 46)
6 Nov 44 to Bellaria
4 Dec 44 to Forli
3 May 45 to La Russia
6 May 45 to Treviso
14 May 45 to Tissano
21 Aug 45 to Lavariano
24 Jan 46 to Tissano
9 Mar 46 to Treviso
15 Aug 46 en route UK
19 Aug 46 to Coltishall
12 Dec 46 DB

320 Sqn

1 Jun 40 F @ Pembroke Dock
Jun 40 **Fokker T VIIIw/G** (Nov 40)
Jun 40 **Anson I** (Oct 41) det Carew Cheriton
1 Oct 40 to Leuchars det Silloth
Oct 40 **Hudson I** (Sep 42)
18 Jan 41 to Carew Cheriton — absorbed No 321 Sqn
21 Mar 41 to Leuchars
Mar 41 **Hudson II** (Sep 41)
Jul 41 **Hudson III** (Sep 42)
Jan 42 **Hudson V** (May 42)
21 Apr 42 to Bircham Newton
Aug 42 **Hudson VI** (Mar 43)
15 Mar 43 to Methwold
Mar 43 **Mitchell II** (Aug 45)
30 Mar 43 to Attlebridge
30 Aug 43 to Lasham
18 Feb 44 to Dunsfold
6 May 44 to Swanton Morley
18 May 44 to Dunsfold
18 Oct 44 to B 58/Melsbroek
Feb 45 **Mitchell III** (Aug 45)
30 Apr 45 to B 110/Achmer
2 Aug 45 DB — transferred to Netherlands Navy control

321 Sqn

1 Jun 40 F @ Pembroke Dock
24 Jun 40 to Carew Cheriton
Jun 40 **Anson I** (Jan 41)
18 Jan 41 DB — absorbed by No 320 Sqn
—
15 Aug 42 RF @ China Bay — from Dutch elements assembling since Mar 42. '321' numberplate in use from May 42.
Aug 42 **Catalina II** (Feb 45)
Oct 42 **Catalina III** (Dec 45) dets Addu Atoll, Red Hills Lake, Cochin, Socotra, Langebaan, Congella, Masirah
May 44 **Catalina IVB** (Feb 45) – loaned from No 205 Sqn
Dec 44 **Liberator VI** (Dec 45)
Apr 45 **Catalina IVB** (Dec 45) dets Cocos, Kemajoran, Soerabaya
Oct 45 to Kemajoran
8 Dec 45 DB — transferred to Dutch control

322 Sqn

12 Jun 43 F @ Woodvale — No 167 Sqn renumbered
Jun 43 **Spitfire VB** (Apr 44)
15 Nov 43 to Llanbedr
30 Nov 43 to Woodvale
31 Dec 43 to Hawkinge
Feb 44 **Spitfire VC** (Apr 44)
25 Feb 44 to Ayr
1 Mar 44 to Hawkinge
10 Mar 44 to Acklington
Mar 44 **Spitfire XIV** (Aug 44)
24 Apr 44 to Hartford Bridge
20 Jun 44 to West Malling
21 Jul 44 to Deanland
Aug 44 **Spitfire LF IXE** (Nov 4
10 Oct 44 to Fairwood Common
31 Oct 44 to Biggin Hill
Nov 44 **Spitfire LF XVIE** (Oct 45)
3 Jan 45 to B 79/Woensdrecht
21 Feb 45 to B 85/Schjindel
18 Apr 45 to B 106/Twente
30 Apr 45 to B 113/Varrelbusch

Jul 45 to B 116/Wunstorf
Oct 45 DB

326 Sqn

Dec 43 F @ Ajaccio — GCII/7 'Nice'
Dec 43 **Spitfire VC** (Oct 44)
Apr 44 **Spitfire VIII** (Apr 44)
Apr 44 **Spitfire IX** (Nov 45)
Aug 44 to Calvi
Sep 44 to Le Vallon
Sep 44 to Bron
Sep 44 to Longevic
Sep 44 to Luxeuil
Mar 45 to Colmar
Apr 45 to Entzheim
Apr 45 to Grossachsenheim
Nov 45 DB — transferred to French control

327 Sqn

Dec 43 F @ Ajaccio — GC I/3 'Corse'
Dec 43 **Spitfire VC** (Nov 45)
Apr 44 to Borgo
Apr 44 **Spitfire IX** (Nov 45) det Ajaccio
Jun 44 **Spitfire VIII** (Nov 45)
Aug 44 to Ajaccio
Sep 44 to Calvi
Sep 44 to Le Vallon
Sep 44 to Bron
Sep 44 to Longevic
Sep 44 to Luxeuil det Nancy
Mar 45 to Colmar
Apr 45 to Entzheim
May 45 to Sersheim
Nov 45 DB — transferred to French control

328 Sqn

Dec 43 F @ Reghaia — GC I/7 'Provence'
Dec 43 **Spitfire VC** (Sep 44)
Jan 44 to Taher
Apr 44 **Spitfire IX** (Nov 45)
May 44 to Borgo
Jul 44 **Spitfire VIII** (Nov 45)
Jul 44 to Ajaccio
Aug 44 to Calvi
Sep 44 to Istres
Sep 44 to Bron
Sep 44 to Longevic
Sep 44 to Luxeuil det Nancy
Mar 45 to Colmar
Apr 45 to Entzheim
Apr 45 to Grossachsenheim
Nov 45 DB — transferred to French control

329 Sqn

Jan 44 F @ Ayr — GC I/2 'Cicognes'
Jan 44 to Perranporth
Feb 44 **Spitfire VB** (Mar 44)
Feb 44 **Spitfire VC** (Mar 44)
Feb 44 **Spitfire IX** (Mar 45)
Mar 44 to Ayr
Mar 44 to Perranporth
Apr 44 to Merston
May 44 to Llanbedr
May 44 to Merston
Jun 44 to Funtington
Jul 44 to Selsey
Aug 44 to Tangmere
Aug 44 to B 8/Sommervieu
2 Sep 44 to B 29/Bernay
10 Sep 44 to B 37/Corroy
12 Sep 44 to B 51/Lille/Vendeville
17 Sep 44 to B 55/Wevelghem
25 Nov 44 to B 70/Deurne
6 Feb 45 to B 85/Schjindel
Feb 45 **Spitfire XVI** (Apr 45)
9 Mar 45 to Turnhouse
3 Apr 45 to Skaebrae
Apr 45 **Spitfire IX** (Nov 45)
25 May 45 to Harrowbeer
16 Jun 45 to A 41/Dreux
19 Jun 45 to Harrowbeer
16 Jul 45 to Fairwood Common
10 Aug 45 to Exeter
17 Nov 45 DB — transferred to French control

330 Sqn

25 Apr 41 F @ Reykjavik
May 41 **Northrop N3P-B** (Jun 43) dets Akureyri, Budareyri
Jul 42 **Catalina III** (Jan 43)
28 Jan 43 to Oban dets Reykjavik, Budayeri
Feb 43 **Sunderland III** (Apr 45)
Mar 43 **Sunderland II** (Mar 44)
12 Jul 43 to Sullom Voe
Apr 45 **Sunderland V** (Nov 45)
14 Jun 45 to Stavanger/Sola
21 Nov 45 DB — transferred to Norwegian control

331 Sqn

21 Jul 41 F @ Catterick
Jul 41 **Hurricane I** (Aug 41)
Aug 41 **Hurricane IIB** (Nov 41)
21 Aug 41 to Castletown
21 Sep 41 to Skaebrae dets Sumburgh, Dyce
Nov 41 **Spitfire IIA** (Apr 42)
Apr 42 **Spitfire VB** (Oct 42)
4 May 42 to North Weald
30 Jun 42 to Manston
7 Jul 42 to North Weald
14 Aug 42 to Manston
20 Aug 42 to North Weald
7 Sep 42 to Ipswich
14 Sep 42 to North Weald
2 Oct 42 to Manston
9 Oct 42 to North Weald
Oct 42 **Spitfire IXB** (Apr 45)
5 Jan 44 to Llanbedr
21 Jan 44 to North Weald
5 Mar 44 to Southend
13 Mar 44 to North Weald
31 Mar 44 to Bognor
22 Jun 44 to Tangmere
6 Aug 44 to Funtington
13 Aug 44 to Ford
30 Aug 44 to B 16/Villons-les-Buissons
1 Sep 44 to B 33/Campneuseville det Manston
11 Sep 44 to B 57/Lille/Nord
19 Sep 44 to Fairwood Common
6 Oct 44 to B 60/Grimbergen
22 Dec 44 to B 79/Woensdrecht
21 Feb 45 to B 85/Schjindel
14 Mar 45 to Fairwood Common
2 Apr 45 to B 85/Schjindel
18 Apr 45 to B 106/Twente
22 Apr 45 to Dyce
Apr 45 **Spitfire IXE** (Nov 45)
22 May 45 to Gardermoen
21 Nov 45 DB — transferred to Norwegian control

332 Sqn

15 Jan 42 F @ Catterick
Jan 42 **Spitfire VA** (Apr 42)
Apr 42 **Spitfire VB** (Nov 42) det Thornaby
19 Jun 42 to North Weald
14 Aug 42 to Manston
20 Aug 42 to North Weald
1 Sep 42 to Martlesham Heath
6 Sep 42 to North Weald
2 Oct 42 to Manston
9 Oct 42 to North Weald
Nov 42 **Spitfire IXB** (Apr 45)
May 43 **Spitfire VB** (Jun 43)
5 Jan 44 to Llanbedr
21 Jan 44 to North Weald
21 Mar 44 to Southend
27 Mar 44 to North Weald
31 Mar 44 to Bognor
21 Jun 44 to Tangmere
6 Aug 44 to Funtington
12 Aug 44 to Ford
20 Aug 44 to B 16/Villons-les-Buissons
6 Sep 44 to B 33/Campneuseville
11 Sep 44 to B 57/Lille/Nord
6 Oct 44 to B 60/Grimbergen
11 Dec 44 to Fairwood Common
31 Dec 44 to B 79/Woensdrecht
21 Feb 45 to B 85/Schjindel
18 Apr 45 to B 106/Twente
22 Apr 45 to Dyce
Apr 45 **Spitfire IXE** (Nov 45)
22 May 45 to Gardermoen
16 Jul 45 to Vaernes
21 Nov 45 DB — transferred to Norwegian control

333 Sqn

5 May 43 F @ Woodhaven ('A' Flt) & Leuchars ('B' Flt) — No 1477 Flt renumbered
May 43 **Catalina IB** (Jan 45)
May 43 **Mosquito II** (Oct 43) dets Sullom Voe
Sep 43 **Mosquito VI** (May 45)
May 44 **Catalina IV** (Nov 45)
1 Sep 44 to Banff ('B' Flt)
Jun 45 to Fornebu
21 Nov 45 DB — transferred to Norwegian control

334 Sqn

26 May 45 F @ Banff — 'B' Flt, No 333 Sqn renumbered
May 45 **Mosquito VI** (Nov 45)
8 Jun 45 to Gardermoen
21 Nov 45 DB — transferred to Norwegian control

335 Sqn

10 Oct 41 F @ Aqir
Oct 41 **Hurricane I** (Sep 42)
6 Dec 41 to St Jean
27 Jan 42 to LG 20 det LG 121
28 May 42 to LG 10
24 Jun 42 to LG 20
29 Jun 42 to Idku
Aug 42 **Hurricane IIC** (Oct 42)
8 Aug 42 to Dekheila
19 Sep 42 to LG 173
Sep 42 **Hurricane IIB** (Oct 43)
3 Oct 42 to LG 85
24 Oct 42 to LG 37 det LG 104
11 Nov 42 to LG 13
18 Nov 42 to LG 121
8 Feb 43 to LG 08
Sep 43 **Hurricane IIC** (Jan 44)
Jan 44 **Spitfire VB** (Sep 44)
Jan 44 **Spitfire VC** (Jul 46)
12 Jan 44 to Tocra
28 Jan 44 to Benina
2 Feb 44 to Tocra
1 Mar 44 to Bersis
17 Sep 44 to Nuova
4 Oct 44 to Biferno
12 Nov 44 to Kalamaki/Hassani
10 Sep 45 to Sedes
31 Jul 46 DB — transferred to Greek control

336 Sqn

25 Feb 43 F @ LG 219
Feb 43 **Hurricane IIC** (Jul 44)
7 Apr 43 to LG 121
Oct 43 **Spitfire VC** (Jun 46)
31 Jan 44 to El Adem
5 Mar 44 to Bu Amud
3 Apr 44 to LG 08 det Idku
May 44 **Spitfire IX** (Jun 44)
13 Jul 44 to El Adem
16 Sep 44 to Canne
18 Sep 44 to Nuova det Araxos
4 Nov 44 to Grottaglie
14 Nov 44 to Kalamaki/Hassani
16 May 45 to Sedes
31 Jul 46 DB — transferred to Greek control

340 Sqn

7 Nov 41 F @ Turnhouse — GC IV/2 'Ile de France'
Nov 41 **Spitfire IIA** (Mar 42) det Drem
20 Dec 41 to Drem
1 Jan 42 to Ayr
Mar 42 **Spitfire VB** (Oct 42)
1 Apr 42 to Redhill
7 Apr 42 to Westhampnett
20 Jul 42 to Ipswich
26 Jul 42 to Westhampnett
28 Jul 42 to Hornchurch
23 Sep 42 to Biggin Hill
Oct 42 **Spitfire IXB** (Mar 43)
21 Mar 43 to Turnhouse
Mar 43 **Spitfire VB** (Feb 44) det Drem
30 Apr 43 to Drem det Ayr
9 Nov 43 to Perranporth
Feb 44 **Spitfire IXB** (Feb 45)
17 Apr 44 to Merston
15 May 44 to Llanbedr
19 May 44 to Merston
22 Jun 44 to Funtington
1 Jul 44 to Selsey
14 Aug 44 to Tangmere
19 Aug 44 to B 8/Sommervieu
2 Sep 44 to B 29/Bernay
10 Sep 44 to B 37/Corroy
12 Sep 44 to B 51/Lille/Vendeville
17 Sep 44 to B 55/Wevelghem
2 Nov 44 to Biggin Hill
17 Dec 44 to Drem
30 Jan 45 to Turnhouse
8 Feb 45 to B 85/Schjindel
Feb 45 **Spitfire LF XVI** (Nov 45)
16 Apr 45 to B 105/Drope
16 Jun 45 to A 41/Dreux
19 Jun 45 to B 105/Drope
5 Jul 45 to B 58/Melsbroek
8 Jul 45 to B 152/Fassberg
3 Sep 45 to Tangmere
6 Sep 45 to Warmwell
17 Sep 45 to B 152/Fassberg
25 Nov 45 to Friedrichshaven
27 Nov 45 DB — transferred to French control

341 Sqn

18 Jan 43 F @ Turnhouse — GC III/2 'Alsace'
Jan 43 **Spitfire VB** (Mar 43)
21 Mar 43 to Biggin Hill
Mar 43 **Spitfire IXB** (Oct 43)
11 Oct 43 to Perranporth
Oct 43 **Spitfire VB** (Feb 44)
Feb 44 **Spitfire IXB** (Feb 45)
14 Apr 44 to Merston
11 May 44 to Llanbedr
16 May 44 to Merston
22 Jun 44 to Funtington
1 Jul 44 to Selsey
6 Aug 44 to Tangmere
19 Aug 44 to B 8/Sommervieu
2 Sep 44 to B 29/Bernay
10 Sep 44 to B 37/Corroy
12 Sep 44 to B 51/Lille/Vendeville
17 Sep 44 to B 55/Wevelghem
25 Nov 44 to B 70/Deurne
1 Feb 45 to Turnhouse
Feb 45 **Spitfire XVI** (Nov 45)
9 Feb 45 to B 85/Schjindel
16 Apr 45 to B 105/Drope
16 Jun 45 to A 41/Dreux
19 Jun 45 to B 105/Drope
6 Jul 45 to B 152/Fassberg
8 Nov 45 to Entzheim
9 Nov 45 to Friedrichshaven
27 Nov 45 DB — transferred to French control

342 Sqn

1 Apr 43 F @ West Raynham — GB I/20 'Lorraine'
Apr 43 **Boston IIIA** (Apr 45)
15 May 43 to Sculthorpe
19 Jul 43 to Great Massingham
6 Sep 43 to Hartford Bridge
Aug 44 **Boston IV** (Apr 45)
17 Oct 44 to B 50/Vitry-en-Artois
Mar 45 **Mitchell II** (May 45)
Mar 45 **Mitchell III** (Dec 45)
22 Apr 45 to B 77/Gilze-Rijen
2 Dec 45 DB — transferred to French control

343 Sqn

29 Nov 43 F @ Dakar — from Flotille 7E
Nov 43 **Sunderland III** (Nov 45) dets Port Etienne
27 Nov 45 DB — transferred to French control

344 Sqn

29 Nov 43 F @ Dakar — from Flotille 1E
Nov 43 **Wellington XI** (Nov 45)
Nov 43 **Wellington XIII** (Nov 45) dets Port Etienne
27 Nov 45 DB — transferred to French control

345 Sqn

30 Jan 44 F @ Ayr — GC II/2 'Berry'
Mar 44 **Spitfire VB** (Sep 44)
26 Apr 44 to Shoreham
16 Aug 44 to Deanland
Sep 44 **Spitfire HF IX** (Apr 45)
10 Oct 44 to Fairwood Common
28 Oct 44 to Biggin Hill
1 Nov 44 to B 55/Wevelghem
25 Nov 44 to B 70/Deurne
6 Feb 45 to B 85/Schjindel
16 Mar 45 to Fairwood Common
2 Apr 45 to B 85/Schjindel
Apr 45 **Spitfire XVI** (Nov 45)
16 Apr 45 to B 105/Drope
16 Jun 45 to A 41/Dreux
19 Jun 45 to B 105/Drope
7 Jul 45 to B 152/Fassberg det B 77/Gilze-Rijen
21 Nov 45 to Friedrichshaven
27 Nov 45 DB — transferred to French control

346 Sqn

15 May 44 F @ Elvington — GB II/23 'Guyenne'
May 44 **Halifax V** (Jun 44)
Jun 44 **Halifax III** (Apr 45)
Mar 45 **Halifax VI** (Nov 45)
20 Oct 45 to Bordeaux/Merignac
15 Nov 45 DB — transferred to French control

347 Sqn

20 Jun 44 F @ Elvington — GB I/25 'Tunisie'
Jun 44 **Halifax V** (Jul 44)
Jul 44 **Halifax III** (Apr 45)
Mar 45 **Halifax VI** (Nov 45)
20 Oct 45 to Bordeaux/Merignac
15 Nov 45 DB — transferred to French control

349 Sqn

9 Jan 43 F @ Ikeja
Jan 43 **Tomahawk I** (Apr 43)
3 May 43 DB

5 Jun 43 RF @ Wittering
Jun 43 **Spitfire VA** (Sep 43)
8 Jun 43 to Collyweston det Kingscliffe
29 Jun 43 to Kingscliffe
5 Aug 43 to Wellingore
16 Aug 43 to Digby
25 Aug 43 to Acklington det Digby
Sep 43 **Spitfire LF VB** (Feb 44)
22 Oct 43 to Friston
Oct 43 **Spitfire VC** (Feb 44)
26 Oct 43 to Southend
10 Nov 43 to Friston
Feb 44 **Spitfire LF IXE** (Feb 45)
11 Mar 44 to Hornchurch
6 Apr 44 to Llanbedr
11 Apr 44 to Selsey
30 Jun 44 to Coolham
4 Jul 44 to Funtington
6 Aug 44 to Selsey
19 Aug 44 to Tangmere
26 Aug 44 to B 17/Carpiquet
8 Sep 44 to B 35/Godelmesnil
12 Sep 44 to B 53/Merville
2 Nov 44 to B 65/Maldeghem
13 Jan 45 to B 77/Gilze-Rijen
16 Feb 45 to Predannack
Feb 45 **Tempest V** (Apr 45)
19 Apr 45 to B 106/Twente
Apr 45 **Spitfire IXB** (May 45)
30 Apr 45 to B 113/Varrelbusch
May 45 **Spitfire LF XVIE** (Oct 46)
29 Jun 45 to B 116/Wunstorf
1 Sep 45 to B 56/Evere
4 Sep 45 to B 116/Wunstorf
30 Nov 45 to B 152/Fassberg
2 May 46 to Brustem
6 May 46 to Fassberg
8 May 46 to Sylt
14 Jun 46 to Fassberg
15 Oct 46 to Beauvechain
24 Oct 46 DB — transferred to Belgian control

350 Sqn

12 Nov 41 F @ Valley — nucleus from Belgian Flt of No 131 Sqn
Nov 41 **Spitfire IIA** (Apr 42)
19 Feb 42 to Atcham
Mar 42 **Spitfire VB** (Dec 43)
5 Apr 42 to Warmwell
15 Apr 42 to Debden
30 Jun 42 to Gravesend
7 Jul 42 to Martlesham Heath
16 Jul 42 to Kenley
31 Jul 42 to Redhill
7 Sep 42 to Martlesham Heath
15 Sep 42 to Redhill
23 Sep 42 to Southend
7 Dec 42 to Hornchurch
Dec 42 **Spitfire VC** (Mar 43)
1 Mar 43 to Heston
5 Mar 43 to Debden
13 Mar 43 to Hornchurch
15 Mar 43 to Fairlop
23 Mar 43 to Acklington
8 Jun 43 to Ouston
20 Jul 43 to Acklington
25 Aug 43 to Digby
7 Sep 43 to West Malling
19 Sep 43 to Digby
1 Oct 43 to Hawkinge
12 Oct 43 to Southend
31 Oct 43 to Hawkinge
Dec 43 **Spitfire VC** (Dec 43)
30 Dec 43 to Hornchurch
Dec 43 **Spitfire IXB** (Mar 44)
8 Feb 44 to Llanbedr
19 Feb 44 to Hornchurch
10 Mar 44 to Hawkinge
14 Mar 44 to Peterhead
Mar 44 **Spitfire VB** (Jul 44)
Mar 44 **Spitfire VC** (Jul 44)
25 Apr 44 to Friston
3 Jul 44 to Westhampnett
Jul 44 **Spitfire IX** (Aug 44)
8 Aug 44 to Hawkinge
Aug 44 **Spitfire XIV** (Oct 46)
29 Sep 44 to Lympne
3 Dec 44 to B 56/Evere
31 Dec 44 to Y 32/Ophoven
27 Jan 45 to B 78/Eindhoven
18 Mar 45 to Warmwell
2 Apr 45 to B 78/Eindhoven
7 Apr 45 to B 106/Twente
16 Apr 45 to B 118/Celle
6 May 45 to B 152/Fassberg
21 Jun 45 to B 172/Husum
13 Jul 45 to B 116/Wunstorf
1 Sep 45 to B 56/Evere
4 Sep 45 to B 116/Wunstorf
29 Nov 45 to B 152/Fassberg
Aug 46 **Spitfire XVI** (Oct 46)
7 Mar 46 to Sylt
29 Mar 46 to Fassberg
2 May 46 to Brustem
6 May 46 to Fassberg
15 Oct 46 to Beauvechain
24 Oct 46 DB — transferred to Belgian control

351 Sqn

1 Jul 44 F @ Benina
Jul 44 **Hurricane IIC** (Sep 44) det Shallufa
Sep 44 **Hurricane IV** (Jun 45)
29 Sep 44 to Canne dets Vis, Prkos
12 Mar 45 to Prkos det Vis
15 Jun 45 DB — transferred to Yugoslav control

352 Sqn

22 Apr 44 F @ Benina
Apr 44 **Hurricane IIC** (Jun 44)
6 May 44 to Lete
Jun 44 **Spitfire VB** (Aug 44)
Jun 44 **Spitfire VC** (Jun 45)
9 Aug 44 to Canne det Vis
25 Jan 45 to Vis
4 Apr 45 to Prkos
15 Jun 45 DB — transferred to Yugoslav control

353 Sqn

1 Jun 42 F @ Dum Dum — from crews of No 62 Sqn and No 103 CD Flt
Jun 42 **Hudson III** (Oct 44)
1 Aug 42 to Cuttack det Dum Dum
24 Feb 43 to Dhubalia
2 Apr 43 to Tanjore
24 Aug 43 to Palam
Oct 43 **Hudson VI** (Jul 44)
Apr 44 **Dakota** (Oct 46) det Dum Dum
Aug 44 **Anson X** (Jan 45)
Nov 44 **Warwick III** (Apr 45)
Jan 45 **Expediter I** (Jul 45)
1 Oct 46 DB

354 Sqn

10 May 43 F @ Drigh Road
17 Aug 43 to Cuttack
Aug 43 **Liberator V** (Aug 44)
Dec 43 **Liberator IIIA** (Apr 44
Feb 44 **Liberator VI** (May 45) dets St Thomas Mount, Sigiriya
12 Oct 44 to Minneriya dets Cuttack, Kankesanterai
18 Jan 45 to Cuttack det Kankesanterai
18 May 45 DB

355 Sqn

18 Aug 43 F @ Salbani
Nov 43 **Liberator III** (Jul 44)
Feb 44 **Liberator VI** (Dec 45) det Dhubalia
Aug 45 **Liberator VIII** (May 46 dets Digri, Pegu
3 Jan 46 to Digri det Pegu
3 Apr 46 to Salbani det Pegu
1 Jun 46 DB

356 Sqn

15 Jan 44 F @ Salbani
Jan 44 **Liberator VI** (Nov 45)
22 Jul 45 to Cocos Island
15 Nov 45 DB

357 Sqn

1 Feb 44 F @ Digri — from No 1576 Flt
Feb 44 **Hudson III** (Jan 45)
Feb 44 **Liberator III** (Jan 45) dets Dum Dum, China Bay
Feb 44 **Catalina IV** (Mar 44) det Red Hills Lake
15 Sep 44 to Jessore
Sep 44 **Liberator VI** (Nov 45) dets Minneriya, China Bay

Oct 44 **Dakota** (Nov 45) dets Dum Dum, Toungoo, Mingaladon
Jan 45 **Sentinel** (Mar 45) dets Cox's Bazaar, Akyab, Kyaukpyu
Mar 45 **Lysander IIIA** (Nov 45) — ex Flt of No 161 Sqn dets Meiktila, Mingaladon, Don Muang
Nov 45 DB

58 Sqn

Nov 44 F @ Kolar — from No 1673 HCU
Nov 44 **Liberator VI** (Nov 45)
Jan 45 to Digri
Feb 45 to Jessore
Nov 45 to Bishnapur
Nov 45 DB

60 Sqn

Sep 66 F @ Watton — from 'B' Flt, No 97 Sqn. Numberplate in use from 1 Apr 66
Sep 66 **Canberra B.2** (Aug 67)
Sep 66 **Canberra B.6** (Mar 67)
Dec 66 **Canberra T.17** ( )
Apr 69 to Cottesmore
Sep 75 to Wyton

61 Sqn

Jan 67 F @ Watton
May 67 **Canberra T.17** (Jul 67)
Jul 67 DB

'Article XV' Squadrons

der Article XV of the British mmonwealth Air Training Plan was agreed, by their respective vernments, that trained Canadian, stralian and New Zealand air and und crews would be provided to ve with the RAF; this contribution to be in addition to the, previously eed, training of British personnel in se countries. In return the UK vernment undertook to pay the men to provide their equipment. The lisation of these commitments, ch were subsequently amended in ail, led to the formation of 70 adrons, of which 67 were num- ed in the 400-series. Although tly units of the RCAF, RAAF and ZAF (as indicated by the slightly ering forms of their badge frames) e squadrons served under British rational control and are con- ionally regarded as having been an gral part of the RAF's organisation ng the War Years.

0 Sqn

Mar 41 F @ Odiham — No 110 Sqn, RCAF renumbered
Mar 41 **Lysander III** (Dec 41) dets Redhill, Gatwick
Apr 41 **Tomahawk I, IIA & IIB** (Jul 42)
un 41 to Bottisham
un 41 to Odiham dets Gatwick, Weston Zoyland
un 42 **Mustang I** (Feb 44) dets Weston Zoyland, Middle Wallop
4 Dec 42 to Dunsfold dets Middle Wallop, Portreath, Treblezue
27 Dec 42 to Middle Wallop det Treblezue
1 Feb 43 to Dunsfold
8 Feb 43 to Weston Zoyland
22 Feb 43 to Dunsfold
28 Jul 43 to Woodchurch
15 Oct 43 to Redhill
2 Dec 43 to Kenley
Dec 43 **Mosquito XVI** (Apr 44)
Dec 43 **Spitfire XI** (Aug 45)
30 Dec 43 to Redhill
18 Feb 44 to Odiham
1 Jul 44 to B 8/Sommervieu det Odiham
15 Aug 44 to B 21/Ste-Honorine -de-Ducy
1 Sep 44 to B 34/Avrilly
20 Sep 44 to B 66/Blankenberg
3 Oct 44 to B 78/Eindhoven
7 Mar 45 to B 90/Petit Brogel
10 Apr 45 to B 108/Rheine
16 Apr 45 to B 116/Wunstorf
28 Apr 45 to B 154/Reinsehlen
7 May 45 to B 156/Lüneburg
18 Jul 45 to B 160/Kastrup
2 Aug 45 to B 156/Lüneburg
7 Aug 45 DB

401 Sqn

1 Mar 41 F @ Digby — No 1 Sqn, RCAF renumbered
Mar 41 **Hurricane I** (May 41)
May 41 **Hurricane IIA** (Sep 41)
Sep 41 **Spitfire IIA** (Oct 41)
20 Oct 41 to Biggin Hill
Oct 41 **Spitfire VB** (Aug 42)
19 Mar 42 to Gravesend
3 Jul 42 to Eastchurch
Jul 42 **Spitfire IX** (Dec 42)
28 Jul 42 to Martlesham Heath
3 Aug 42 to Biggin Hill
14 Aug 42 to Lympne
21 Aug 42 to Biggin Hill
24 Sep 42 to Kenley
23 Jan 43 to Catterick
Jan 43 **Spitfire VB** (Oct 43) det Thornaby
29 May 43 to Redhill
21 Jul 43 to Martlesham Heath
31 Jul 43 to Redhill
7 Aug 43 to Staplehurst
13 Oct 43 to Biggin Hill
Oct 43 **Spitfire IXB** (Apr 45)
8 Apr 44 to Fairwood Common
18 Apr 44 to Tangmere
18 Jun 44 to B 4/Bény-sur-Mer
8 Aug 44 to B 18/Cristot
1 Sep 44 to B 28/Evreux
2 Sep 44 to B 24/St-André-de-l'Eure
3 Sep 44 to B 44/Poix
7 Sep 44 to B 56/Evere
21 Sep 44 to B 68/Le Culot
3 Oct 44 to B 84/Rips
14 Oct 44 to B 80/Volkel
24 Oct 44 to Warmwell
4 Nov 44 to B 80/Volkel
6 Dec 44 to B 88/Heesch
12 Apr 45 to B 108/Rheine
15 Apr 45 to B 116/Wunstorf
13 May 45 to B 152/Fassberg
May 45 **Spitfire XIVE** (Jun 45)
Jun 45 **Spitfire XVI** (Jun 45)
23 Jun 45 DB

402 Sqn

1 Mar 41 F @ Digby — No 2 Sqn, RCAF renumbered
Mar 41 **Hurricane I** (May 41)
May 41 **Hurricane IIA** (Jul 41)
Jun 41 **Hurricane IIB** (Mar 42)
23 Jun 41 to Martlesham Heath
10 Jul 41 to Ayr
19 Aug 41 to Southend
6 Nov 41 to Warmwell
4 Mar 42 to Colerne
Mar 42 **Spitfire VB** (May 42)
17 Mar 42 to Fairwood Common
14 May 42 to Kenley
31 May 42 to Redhill
29 Jun 42 to Ipswich
1 Jul 42 to Redhill
Aug 42 **Spitfire IX** (Mar 43)
3 Aug 42 to Martlesham Heath
9 Aug 42 to Redhill
13 Aug 42 to Kenley
21 Mar 43 to Digby
Mar 43 **Spitfire VB** (Jun 44)
Apr 43 **Spitfire VC** (Jun 44)
7 Aug 43 to Merston
19 Sep 43 to Digby
19 Dec 43 to Ayr
2 Jan 44 to Digby
12 Feb 44 to Wellingore
12 Apr 44 to Peterhead
22 Apr 44 to Wellingore
30 Apr 44 to Horne
19 Jun 44 to Westhampnett
27 Jun 44 to Merston
Jul 44 **Spitfire IX** (Aug 44)
8 Aug 44 to Hawkinge
Aug 44 **Spitfire XIVE** (Jun 45)
30 Sep 44 to B 70/Deurne
1 Oct 44 to B 82/Grave
1 Nov 44 to B 64/Diest
27 Dec 44 to B 88/Heesch
14 Jan 45 to Warmwell
2 Feb 45 to B 88/Heesch
12 Apr 45 to B 108/Rheine
15 Apr 45 to B 116/Wunstorf
12 May 45 to B 152/Fassberg
Jun 45 **Spitfire XVI** (Jul 45)
1 Jul 45 DB

403 Sqn

19 Feb 41 F @ Baginton
Mar 41 **Tomahawk I & IIA** (Jun 41)
May 41 **Spitfire I** (Jul 41)
30 May 41 to Ternhill
Jul 41 **Spitfire IIA** (Sep 41)
Aug 41 **Spitfire VB** (Jan 43)
4 Aug 41 to Hornchurch
25 Aug 41 to Debden
3 Oct 41 to Martlesham Heath
22 Dec 41 to North Weald
2 May 42 to Southend
3 Jun 42 to Martlesham Heath
19 Jun 42 to Catterick det West Hartlepool
1 Jul 42 to Manston
8 Jul 42 to Catterick
23 Jan 43 to Kenley
Jan 43 **Spitfire IXB** (Dec 44)
7 Aug 43 to Lashenden
20 Aug 43 to Headcorn
14 Oct 43 to Kenley
24 Feb 44 to Hutton Cranswick
29 Feb 44 to Kenley
18 Apr 44 to Tangmere
16 Jun 44 to B 2/Bazenville
26 Aug 44 to B 26/Illiers-l'Evêque
22 Sep 44 to B 68/Le Culot
23 Sep 44 to Fairwood Common
3 Oct 44 to B 82/Grave
28 Oct 44 to B 58/Melsbroek
3 Nov 44 to B 56/Evere
Dec 44 **Spitfire XVI** (Jul 45)
4 Jan 45 to Warmwell
14 Jan 45 to B 56/Evere
2 Mar 45 to B 90/Petit Brogel
31 Mar 45 to B 78/Eindhoven
11 Apr 45 to B 100/Goch
28 Apr 45 to B 154/Reinsehlen
1 Jul 45 DB

404 Sqn

15 Apr 41 F @ Thorney Island
Apr 41 **Blenheim IVF** (Jan 43)
20 Jun 41 to Castletown
27 Jul 41 to Skitten
9 Oct 41 to Dyce det Sumburgh
3 Dec 41 to Sumburgh
26 Mar 42 to Dyce
5 Aug 42 to Sumburgh
Sep 42 **Beaufighter IIF** (Apr 43)
24 Sep 42 to Dyce
22 Jan 43 to Chivenor
Mar 43 **Beaufighter XI** (Nov 43)
2 Apr 43 to Tain
20 Apr 43 to Wick
Sep 43 **Beaufighter X** (Mar 45)
8 May 44 to Davidstow Moor
1 Jul 44 to Strubby dets Davidstow Moor
3 Sep 44 to Banff
22 Oct 44 to Dallachy
Mar 45 **Mosquito VI** (May 45)
3 Apr 45 to Banff
25 May 45 DB

405 Sqn

23 Apr 41 F @ Driffield
May 41 **Wellington II** (Apr 42)
20 Jun 41 to Pocklington
Apr 42 **Halifax II** (Sep 43)
7 Aug 42 to Topcliffe
25 Oct 42 to Beaulieu
1 Mar 43 to Topcliffe
6 Mar 43 to Leeming
19 Apr 43 to Gransden Lodge
Aug 43 **Lancaster I & III** (May 45)
26 May 45 to Linton-on-Ouse
May 45 **Lancaster X** (Sep 45)
16 Jun 45 en route Canada
21 Jun 45 to Greenwood, NS
5 Sep 45 DB

406 Sqn

5 May 41 F @ Acklington
May 41 **Blenheim IF** (Jun 41)
May 41 **Blenheim IVF** (Jun 41)
Jun 41 **Beaufighter IIF** (Jul 42)
1 Feb 42 to Ayr det Scorton
16 Jun 42 to Scorton
Jun 42 **Beaufighter VIF** (Aug 44)
4 Sep 42 to Predannack
8 Dec 42 to Middle Wallop
31 Mar 43 to Valley
15 Nov 43 to Exeter
Apr 44 **Mosquito XII** (Jul 44)
14 Apr 44 to Winkleigh
Jul 44 **Mosquito XXX** (Aug 45)
17 Sep 44 to Colerne
27 Nov 44 to Manston
14 Jun 45 to Predannack
1 Sep 45 DB

407 Sqn

8 May 41 F @ Thorney Island
May 41 **Blenheim IV** (Jul 41)
Jun 41 **Hudson III** (May 42)
Jun 41 **Hudson V** (Apr 43)
8 Jul 41 to North Coates
18 Feb 42 to Thorney Island
31 Mar 42 to Bircham Newton
1 Oct 42 to St Eval
10 Nov 42 to Docking det Thorney Island
Jan 43 **Wellington XI** (Apr 43)
16 Feb 43 to Skitten
Mar 43 **Wellington XII** (Feb 44)
1 Apr 43 to Chivenor

Jun 43 **Wellington XIV** (Jun 45)
3 Nov 43 to St Eval
2 Dec 43 to Chivenor
29 Jan 44 to Limavady
28 Apr 44 to Chivenor
24 Aug 44 to Wick
11 Nov 44 to Chivenor
4 Jun 45 DB

408 Sqn

15 Jun 41 F @ Lindholme
Jun 41 **Hampden** (Sep 42)
20 Jul 41 to Syerston
9 Dec 41 to Balderton det North Luffenhem
14 Sep 42 to Leeming
Sep 42 **Halifax V** (Dec 42)
Dec 42 **Halifax II** (Oct 43)
27 Aug 43 to Linton-on-Ouse
Oct 43 **Lancaster II** (Sep 44)
Sep 44 **Halifax III** (Feb 45)
Sep 44 **Halifax VII** (May 45)
May 45 **Lancaster X** (Sep 45)
14 Jun 45 en route Canada
18 Jun 45 to Greenwood, NS
5 Sep 45 DB

409 Sqn

16 Jun 41 F @ Digby
Jul 41 **Defiant I** (Sep 41)
26 Jul 41 to Coleby Grange
Aug 41 **Beaufighter IIF** (Jun 42) dets Kirton-in-Lindsey, Hibaldstow
Jun 42 **Beaufighter VIF** (Apr 44)
23 Feb 43 to Acklington dets Drem, Coleby Grange, Peterhead, Coltishall
19 Dec 43 to Coleby Grange dets Peterhead, Coltishall
5 Feb 44 to Acklington
Mar 44 **Mosquito XIII** (Jun 45)
1 Mar 44 to Hunsdon
14 May 44 to West Malling det Church Fenton
19 Jun 44 to Hunsdon
25 Aug 44 to B 17/Carpiquet
10 Sep 44 to B 24/St-André-de-l'Eure
27 Sep 44 to B 48/Amiens/Glisy
4 Oct 44 to B 68/Le Culot
12 Oct 44 to B 51/Lille/Vendeville
19 Apr 45 to B 108/Rheine
15 May 45 to B 77/Gilze-Rijen
11 Jun 45 to B 106/Twente
1 Jul 45 DB

410 Sqn

30 Jun 41 F @ Ayr
Jun 41 **Defiant I** (May 42)
6 Aug 41 to Drem dets Acklington, Ouston, Dyce
Apr 42 **Beaufighter IIF** (Jan 43)
15 Jun 42 to Ayr det Drem
1 Sep 42 to Scorton
20 Oct 42 to Acklington
Oct 42 **Mosquito II** (Dec 43)
21 Feb 43 to Coleby Grange det Predannack
Jul 43 **Mosquito VI** (Sep 43)
20 Oct 43 to West Malling
8 Nov 43 to Hunsdon
Dec 43 **Mosquito XIII** (Aug 44)
30 Dec 43 to Castle Camps
29 Apr 44 to Hunsdon
18 Jun 44 to Zeals
28 Jul 44 to Colerne
Aug 44 **Mosquito XXX** (Jun 45)
9 Sep 44 to Hunsdon
22 Sep 44 to B 48/Amiens/Glisy
3 Nov 44 to B 51/Lille/Vendeville
7 Jan 45 to B 48/Amiens/Glisy
6 Apr 45 to B 77/Gilze-Rijen
9 Jun 45 DB

411 Sqn

16 Jun 41 F @ Digby
Jun 41 **Spitfire I** (Sep 41)
Jun 41 **Spitfire IIA** (Oct 41)
Oct 41 **Spitfire VB** (Oct 43)
19 Nov 41 to Hornchurch
7 Mar 42 to Southend
30 Mar 42 to Digby
5 Jun 42 to Shawbury
7 Jun 42 to Digby
5 Aug 42 to Shawbury
8 Aug 42 to Digby
1 Mar 43 to Kidlington
5 Mar 43 to Fowlmere
12 Mar 43 to Digby
22 Mar 43 to Kenley
8 Apr 43 to Redhill
7 Aug 43 to Staplehurst
13 Oct 43 to Biggin Hill
Oct 43 **Spitfire IXB** (Sep 44)
24 Feb 44 to Peterhead
29 Feb 44 to Biggin Hill
16 Apr 44 to Tangmere
17 Apr 44 to Fairwood Common
22 Apr 44 to Tangmere
19 Jun 44 to B 4/Bény-sur-Mer
8 Aug 44 to B 18/Cristot
1 Sep 44 to B 24/St-André-de-l'Eure
2 Sep 44 to B 26/Illiers-l'Evêque
3 Sep 44 to B 44/Poix
7 Sep 44 to B 56/Evere
Sep 44 **Spitfire IXE** (May 45)
21 Sep 44 to B 68/Le Culot
4 Oct 44 to B 84/Rips
15 Oct 44 to Warmwell
23 Oct 44 to B 84/Rips
24 Oct 44 to B 80/Volkel
6 Dec 44 to B 88/Heesch
12 Apr 45 to B 108/Rheine
15 Apr 45 to B 116/Wunstorf
14 May 45 to B 152/Fassberg
May 45 **Spitfire XVIE** (May 45)
24 May 45 to Warmwell
7 Jun 45 to B 152/Fassberg
Jun 45 **Spitfire XIV** (Mar 46)
5 Jul 45 to B 174/Utersen
16 Nov 45 to B 170/Sylt
4 Dec 45 to B 174/Utersen
15 Mar 46 DB

412 Sqn

30 Jun 41 F @ Digby
Jul 41 **Spitfire IIA** (Oct 41)
20 Oct 41 to Wellingore
Oct 41 **Spitfire VB** (Nov 43)
1 May 42 to Martlesham Heath
4 Jun 42 to North Weald
19 Jun 42 to Merston
24 Aug 42 to Tangmere
23 Sep 42 to Redhill
2 Nov 42 to Kenley
29 Jan 43 to Angle
8 Feb 43 to Fairwood Common
1 Mar 43 to Hurn
6 Mar 43 to Odiham
7 Mar 43 to Lasham
8 Apr 43 to Fairwood Common
13 Apr 43 to Perranporth
21 Jun 43 to Friston
14 Jul 43 to Redhill
8 Aug 43 to Staplehurst
14 Oct 43 to Biggin Hill
Nov 43 **Spitfire IXB** (Sep 44)
5 Jan 44 to Hutton Cranswick
20 Jan 44 to Biggin Hill
30 Mar 44 to Fairwood Common
7 Apr 44 to Biggin Hill
15 Apr 44 to Tangmere
18 Jun 44 to B 4/Bény-sur-Mer
8 Aug 44 to B 18/Cristot
29 Aug 44 to B 28/Evreux
1 Sep 44 to B 24/St-André-de-l'Eure
2 Sep 44 to B 26/Illiers-l'Evêque
3 Sep 44 to B 44/Poix
6 Sep 44 to B 56/Evere
Sep 44 **Spitfire IXE** (May 45)
21 Sep 44 to B 68/Le Culot
4 Oct 44 to B 84/Rips
15 Oct 44 to B 80/Volkel
6 Dec 44 to B 88/Heesch
13 Apr 45 to B 108/Rheine
16 Apr 45 to B 116/Wunstorf
13 May 45 to B 152/Fassberg
May 45 **Spitfire XVIE** (Jun 45)
6 Jun 45 to Warmwell
20 Jun 45 to B 152/Fassberg
Jun 45 **Spitfire XIV** (Mar 46)
6 Jul 45 to B 174/Utersen
7 Dec 45 to B 170/Sylt
21 Dec 45 to B 174/Utersen
15 Mar 46 DB

413 Sqn

30 Jun 41 F @ Stranraer
Jul 41 **Catalina I** (Dec 44)
Jul 41 **Catalina IV** (Dec 44)
1 Oct 41 to Sullom Voe
4 Mar 42 en route Ceylon
2 Apr 42 to Koggala dets Addu Atoll, Port Victoria, Kipevu, Bahrain, Langebaan, Aden
21 Jan 45 en route UK
21 Feb 45 to Bournemouth (No 3 PRC)
23 Feb 45 DB

414 Sqn

12 Aug 41 F @ Croydon
Aug 41 **Lysander III** (Jun 42)
Aug 41 **Tomahawk I & II** (Jun 42)
Jun 42 **Mustang I** (Aug 44)
5 Dec 42 to Dunsfold
1 Feb 43 to Middle Wallop det Predannack
20 Feb 43 to Dunsfold det Predannack
9 Apr 43 to Middle Wallop
26 May 43 to Harrowbeer
4 Jun 43 to Portreath
20 Jun 43 to Dunsfold
5 Jul 43 to Gatwick
31 Jul 43 to Weston Zoyland
10 Aug 43 to Gatwick
13 Aug 43 to Ashford
5 Oct 43 to Woodchurch
15 Oct 43 to Redhill
3 Nov 43 to Gatwick
5 Feb 44 to Peterhead
20 Feb 44 to Odiham
29 Feb 44 to Dundonald
11 Mar 44 to Gatwick
1 Apr 44 to Odiham
Aug 44 **Spitfire IX** (Apr 45)
15 Aug 44 to B 21/Ste-Honorine-de-Ducy
29 Aug 44 to B 26/Illiers-l'Evêque
3 Sep 44 to B 44/Poix
7 Sep 44 to B 56/Evere
20 Sep 44 to B 66/Blankenberg
3 Oct 44 to B 78/Eindhoven
7 Mar 45 to B 90/Petit Brogel
Apr 45 **Spitfire XIV** (Aug 45)
11 Apr 45 to B 108/Rheine
17 Apr 45 to B 116/Wunstorf
28 Apr 45 to B 154/Reinsehlen
7 May 45 to B 118/Celle
8 May 45 to B 156/Lüneburg
23 Jun 45 to Warmwell
6 Jul 45 to B 156/Lüneburg
7 Aug 45 DB

415 Sqn

20 Aug 41 F @ Thorney Island
Sep 41 **Beaufort I** (Feb 42)
Jan 42 **Hampden** (Sep 43)
11 Apr 42 to St Eval
16 May 42 to Thorney Island
5 Jun 42 to North Coates
5 Aug 42 to Wick dets Tain, Leuchars
1 Sep 42 to Tain
6 Sep 42 to Leuchars dets St Eval, Thorney Island
11 Nov 42 to Thorney Island
Sep 43 **Wellington XIII** (Jul 4
Oct 43 **Albacore** (Jul 44)
15 Nov 43 to Bircham Newton dets (Wellington) Nor Coates, Docking dets (Albacore) Manst Thorney Island, Winkleigh
26 Jul 44 to East Moor
Jul 44 **Halifax III** (May 45)
Mar 45 **Halifax VII** (May 45)
15 May 45 DB

416 Sqn

22 Nov 41 F @ Peterhead
Nov 41 **Spitfire IIA** (Mar 42)
Mar 42 **Spitfire VB** (Mar 43)
14 Mar 42 to Dyce dets Montrose, Peterhead
3 Apr 42 to Peterhead det Dyce
25 Jun 42 to Westhampnett
7 Jul 42 to Peterhead det Dyce
16 Jul 42 to Martlesham Heath
14 Aug 42 to Hawkinge
20 Aug 42 to Martlesham Heath
23 Sep 42 to Redhill
8 Nov 42 to Martlesham Heath
24 Nov 42 to Redhill
1 Feb 43 to Kenley
Mar 43 **Spitfire IX** (Jun 43)
29 May 43 to Wellingore
7 Jun 43 to Digby
Jun 43 **Spitfire VB** (Feb 44)
Jun 43 **Spitfire VC** (Jun 43)
9 Aug 43 to Merston
19 Sep 43 to Wellingore
2 Oct 43 to Digby
Jan 44 **Spitfire IXB** (Dec 44)
12 Feb 44 to Kenley
17 Apr 44 to Tangmere
16 Jun 44 to B 2/Bazenville
28 Aug 44 to B 26/Illiers-l'Evêqu
22 Sep 44 to B 68/Le Culot
30 Sep 44 to B 82/Grave
22 Oct 44 to B 58/Melsbroek
4 Nov 44 to B 56/Evere
Dec 44 **Spitfire XVI** (Sep 45)
3 Mar 45 to B 90/Petit Brogel
31 Mar 45 to B 78/Eindhoven
12 Apr 45 to B 100/Goch
14 Apr 45 to B 114/Diepholz
26 Apr 45 to B 154/Reinsehlen
2 Jul 45 to B 152/Fassberg
5 Jul 45 to B 174/Utersen
Sep 45 **Spitfire XIVE** (Mar 4
15 Mar 46 DB

417 Sqn

27 Nov 41 F @ Charmy Down
Dec 41 **Spitfire IIA** (Feb 42)
26 Jan 42 to Colerne
Feb 42 **Spitfire VB** (Mar 42)
24 Feb 42 to Tain
13 Apr 42 en route ME
4 Jun 42 to Kasfareet
18 Jul 42 to Deversoir
5 Sep 42 to Shandur
Sep 42 **Hurricane IIB** (Oct 42)
Sep 42 **Hurricane IIC** (Jan 43)
det Heliopolis
0 Oct 42 to Idku
Oct 42 **Spitfire VB** (Sep 43)
Oct 42 **Spitfire VC** (Sep 43)
dets Heliopolis, Kufra
5 Jan 43 to LG 175
9 Feb 43 to Castel Benito
8 Feb 43 to Mellaha
det Ben Gardane
2 Apr 43 to La Fauconnerie
5 Apr 43 to Goubrine
6 May 43 to Hergla
1 May 43 to Ben Gardane
9 Jun 43 to Luqa
6 Jul 43 to Cassibile
6 Jul 43 to Lentini West
Aug 43 **Spitfire VIII** (Apr 45)
9 Sep 43 to Grottaglie
5 Sep 43 to Gioia del Colle
5 Oct 43 to Tortorella
8 Oct 43 to Triolo
6 Nov 43 to Canne
7 Jan 44 to Marcianese
Mar 44 **Spitfire IX** (May 44)
dets Canne, Nettuno
4 Apr 44 to Venafro
3 Jun 44 to Littorio
7 Jun 44 to Fabrica
Jul 44 to Perugia
Aug 44 to Loreto
5 Sep 44 to Fano
5 Dec 44 to Bellaria
Apr 45 **Spitfire IX** (Jul 45)
May 45 to Treviso
Jul 45 DB

18 Sqn

Nov 41 F @ Debden
Nov 41 **Boston III** (Jul 43)
Apr 42 to Bradwell Bay
Mar 43 to Ford
Mar 43 **Mosquito II** (Nov 44)
Apr 44 to Holmsley South
Jul 44 to Hurn
Jul 44 to Middle Wallop
Aug 44 to Hunsdon
Nov 44 **Mosquito VI** (Sep 45)
Nov 44 to Blackbushe
Mar 45 to B 71/Coxyde
Apr 45 to B 80/Volkel
Sep 45 DB

19 Sqn

Dec 41 F @ Mildenhall
Jan 42 **Wellington IC** (Nov 42)
Feb 42 **Wellington III** (Nov 42)
Aug 42 to Leeming
Aug 42 to Topcliffe
Oct 42 to Croft
Nov 42 **Halifax II** (Apr 44)
Nov 42 to Middleton St George
Mar 44 **Lancaster X** (Sep 45)
Jun 45 en route Canada
Jun 45 to Yarmouth, NS
Sep 45 DB

0 Sqn

Dec 41 F @ Waddington
Jan 42 **Hampden** (Aug 42)
7 Aug 42 to Skipton-on-Swale
Aug 42 **Wellington III** (Apr 43)
16 Oct 42 to Middleton St George
Feb 43 **Wellington X** (Oct 43)
16 May 43 en route N Africa
19 Jun 43 to Kairouan
29 Sep 43 to Hani East
17 Oct 43 en route UK
6 Nov 43 to Dalton
12 Dec 43 to Tholthorpe
Dec 43 **Halifax III** (May 45)
Apr 45 **Lancaster X** (Sep 45)
12 Jun 45 en route Canada
16 Jun 45 to Debert, NS
5 Sep 45 DB

421 Sqn

6 Apr 42 F @ Digby
Apr 42 **Spitfire VA** (May 42)
3 May 42 to Fairwood Common
May 42 **Spitfire VB** (May 43)
14 Jun 42 to Warmwell
28 Jun 42 to Fairwood Common
29 Jun 42 to Exeter
det Bolt Head
8 Jul 42 to Fairwood Common
16 Aug 42 to Ibsley
22 Aug 42 to Fairwood Common
6 Oct 42 to Kenley
11 Oct 42 to Fairwood Common
det Zeals
26 Oct 42 to Angle
1 Nov 42 to Zeals
14 Nov 42 to Angle
30 Nov 42 to Charmy Down
4 Dec 42 to Angle
29 Jan 43 to Kenley
1 Mar 43 to Croughton
5 Mar 43 to Gransden Lodge
10 Mar 43 to Fowlmere
13 Mar 43 to Kenley
det Manston
23 Mar 43 to Redhill
10 Apr 43 to Martlesham Heath
22 Apr 43 to Redhill
17 May 43 to Kenley
May 43 **Spitfire IX** (Feb 44)
6 Aug 43 to Lashenden
20 Aug 43 to Headcorn
14 Oct 43 to Kenley
Feb 44 **Spitfire IXB** (Dec 44)
2 Mar 44 to Hutton Cranswick
8 Mar 44 to Kenley
18 Apr 44 to Tangmere
16 Jun 44 to B 2/Bazenville
29 Aug 44 to B 26/Illiers-l'Evêque
22 Sep 44 to B 68/Le Culot
1 Oct 44 to B 82/Grave
23 Oct 44 to B 58/Melsbroek
3 Nov 44 to B 56/Evere
6 Dec 44 to Warmwell
18 Dec 44 to B 56/Evere
Dec 44 **Spitfire XVIE** (Jul 45)
2 Mar 45 to B 90/Petit Brogel
31 Mar 45 to B 78/Eindhoven
11 Apr 45 to B 100/Goch
13 Apr 45 to B 114/Diepholz
28 Apr 45 to B 154/Reinsehlen
2 Jul 45 to B 152/Fassberg
8 Jul 45 to B 174/Utersen
23 Jul 45 DB

422 Sqn

2 Apr 42 F @ Lough Erne
Jul 42 **Lerwick I** (Sep 42)
Aug 42 **Catalina IB** (Nov 42)
30 Oct 42 to Long Kesh
5 Nov 42 to Oban
Nov 42 **Sunderland III** (Jun 45)
det Jui
8 May 43 to Bowmore
3 Nov 43 to St Angelo
13 Apr 44 to Castle Archdale
4 Nov 44 to Pembroke Dock
25 Jul 45 to Bassingbourn
Aug 45 **Liberator VI** (Sep 45)
Aug 45 **Liberator VIII** (Sep 45)
4 Sep 45 DB

423 Sqn

18 May 42 F @ Oban
Jul 42 **Sunderland II** (Apr 43)
Sep 42 **Sunderland III** (May 45)
2 Nov 42 to Lough Erne/Castle Archdale
8 Aug 45 to Bassingbourn
Aug 45 **Liberator VI** (Sep 45)
Aug 45 **Liberator VIII** (Sep 45)
4 Sep 45 DB

424 Sqn

15 Oct 42 F @ Topcliffe
Oct 42 **Wellington III** (Apr 43)
Feb 43 **Wellington X** (Oct 43)
8 Apr 43 to Leeming
3 May 43 to Dalton
16 May 43 en route N Africa
23 Jun 43 to Kairouan
30 Sep 43 to Hani East
26 Oct 43 en route UK
6 Nov 43 to Skipton-on-Swale
Dec 43 **Halifax III** (Jan 45)
Jan 45 **Lancaster I & III** (Oct 45)
15 Oct 45 DB

425 Sqn

25 Jun 42 F @ Dishforth
Aug 42 **Wellington III** (Apr 43)
Apr 43 **Wellington X** (Oct 43)
16 May 43 en route N Africa
23 Jun 43 to Kairouan
30 Sep 43 to Hani East
26 Oct 43 en route UK
6 Nov 43 to Dishforth
10 Dec 43 to Tholthorpe
Dec 43 **Halifax III** (May 45)
May 45 **Lancaster X** (Sep 45)
13 Jun 45 en route Canada
15 Jun 45 to Debert, NS
5 Sep 45 DB

426 Sqn

15 Oct 42 F @ Dishforth
Oct 42 **Wellington III** (Apr 43)
Mar 43 **Wellington X** (Jun 43)
18 Jun 43 to Linton-on-Ouse
Jul 43 **Lancaster II** (May 44)
Apr 44 **Halifax III** (Jun 44)
Jun 44 **Halifax VII** (May 45)
Dec 44 **Halifax III** (Mar 45)
25 May 45 to Driffield
Jun 45 **Liberator VI** (Dec 45)
Jun 45 **Liberator VIII** (Dec 45)
25 Jun 45 to Tempsford
31 Dec 45 DB

427 Sqn

7 Nov 42 F @ Croft
Nov 42 **Wellington III** (Mar 43)
Feb 43 **Wellington X** (May 43)
5 May 43 to Leeming
May 43 **Halifax V** (Feb 44)
Jan 44 **Halifax III** (Mar 45)
Mar 45 **Lancaster I & III** (May 46)
31 May 46 DB

428 Sqn

7 Nov 42 F @ Dalton
Nov 42 **Wellington III** (Apr 43)
Apr 43 **Wellington X** (Jun 43)
4 Jun 43 to Middleton St George
Jun 43 **Halifax V** (Jan 44)
Nov 43 **Halifax II** (Jun 44)
Jun 44 **Lancaster X** (Sep 45)
31 May 45 en route Canada
25 Jul 45 to Yarmouth, NS
5 Sep 45 DB

429 Sqn

7 Nov 42 F @ East Moor
Nov 42 **Wellington III** (Aug 43)
Jan 43 **Wellington X** (Aug 43)
13 Aug 43 to Leeming
Aug 43 **Halifax II** (Jan 44)
Nov 43 **Halifax V** (Mar 44)
Mar 44 **Halifax III** (Mar 45)
Mar 45 **Lancaster I & III** (May 46)
31 May 46 DB

430 Sqn

1 Jan 43 F @ Hartford Bridge — nucleus from No 171 Sqn
Jan 43 **Tomahawk I & II** (Feb 43)
8 Jan 43 to Dunsfold
Jan 43 **Mustang I** (Dec 44)
25 Apr 43 to Weston Zoyland
5 May 43 to Dunsfold
5 Jul 43 to Gatwick
13 Aug 43 to Ashford
15 Oct 43 to Gatwick
4 Jan 44 to Peterhead
31 Jan 44 to Gatwick
10 Feb 44 to Clifton
27 Feb 44 to Gatwick
1 Apr 44 to Odiham
29 Jun 44 to B 8/Sommervieu
14 Aug 44 to B 21/Ste-Honorine-de-Ducy
1 Sep 44 to B 34/Avrilly
20 Sep 44 to B 66/Blankenberg
4 Oct 44 to B 78/Eindhoven
Nov 44 **Spitfire XIV** (Aug 45)
det Y 32/Ophoven
7 Mar 45 to B 90/Petit Brogel
10 Apr 45 to B 108/Rheine
16 Apr 45 to B 116/Wunstorf
28 Apr 45 to B 154/Reinsehlen
8 May 45 to B 156/Lüneburg
23 Jul 45 to Warmwell
2 Aug 45 to B 156/Lüneburg
7 Aug 45 DB

431 Sqn

13 Nov 42 F @ Burn
Dec 42 **Wellington X** (Jul 43)
15 Jul 43 to Tholthorpe
Jul 43 **Halifax V** (Apr 44)
10 Dec 43 to Croft
Mar 44 **Halifax III** (Oct 44)
Oct 44 **Lancaster X** (Sep 45)
7 Jun 45 en route Canada
12 Jun 45 to Dartmouth, NS
5 Sep 45 DB

432 Sqn

1 May 43 F @ Skipton-on-Swale
May 43 **Wellington X** (Nov 43)
19 Sep 43 to East Moor
Oct 43 **Lancaster II** (Feb 44)
Feb 44 **Halifax III** (Jul 44)
Jul 44 **Halifax VII** (May 45)
15 May 45 DB

433 Sqn

25 Sep 43 F @ Skipton-on-Swale
Nov 43 **Halifax III** (Jan 45)
Jan 45 **Lancaster I & III** (Oct 45)
15 Oct 45 DB

434 Sqn

15 Jun 43 F @ Tholthorpe
Jun 43 **Halifax V** (May 44)
11 Dec 43 to Croft
May 44 **Halifax III** (Dec 44)
Dec 44 **Lancaster X** (Sep 45)
Feb 45 **Lancaster I & III** (Mar 45)
10 Jun 45 en route Canada
15 Jun 45 to Dartmouth, NS
5 Sep 45 DB

435 Sqn

1 Nov 44 F @ Gujrat
Nov 44 **Dakota** (Mar 46)
18 Dec 44 to Tulihal
27 Aug 45 en route UK
29 Aug 45 to Down Ampney det Croydon
31 Mar 46 DB

436 Sqn

20 Aug 44 F @ Gujrat
Oct 44 **Dakota** (Jun 46)
14 Jan 45 to Kangla
17 Mar 45 to Akyab
12 May 45 to Kyaukpyu det Kinmagon
24 Aug 45 en route UK
29 Aug 45 to Down Ampney det Biggin Hill
4 Apr 46 to Odiham
22 Jun 46 DB

437 Sqn

1 Sep 44 F @ Blakehill Farm
Sep 44 **Dakota** (Jun 46)
7 May 45 to B 75/Nivelles
7 Jun 45 to B 58/Melsbroek dets Gardemoen, Odiham
15 Sep 45 to B 56/Evere
15 Nov 45 to Odiham dets B 56/Evere, Croydon
15 Jun 46 DB

438 Sqn

10 Nov 43 F @ Digby — No 118 Sqn, RCAF renumbered
Nov 43 **Hurricane IV** (May 44)
19 Dec 43 to Wittering
10 Jan 44 to Ayr
Jan 44 **Typhoon IB** (Aug 45)
18 Mar 44 to Hurn
3 Apr 44 to Funtington
19 Apr 44 to Hurn
27 Jun 44 to B 9/Lantheuil
31 Aug 44 to B 24/St-André-de-l'Eure
3 Sep 44 to B 48/Amiens/Glisy
6 Sep 44 to B 58/Melsbroek
26 Sep 44 to B 78/Eindhoven
19 Mar 45 to Warmwell
3 Apr 45 to B 100/Goch
12 Apr 45 to B 110/Achmer
21 Apr 45 to B 150/Hustedt
29 May 45 to B 166/Flensburg
26 Aug 45 DB

439 Sqn

1 Jan 44 F @ Wellingore — No 123 Sqn, RCAF renumbered
Jan 44 **Hurricane IV** (Apr 44)
8 Jan 44 to Ayr
Feb 44 **Typhoon IB** (Aug 45)
18 Mar 44 to Hurn
2 Apr 44 to Funtington
19 Apr 44 to Hurn
11 May 44 to Hutton Cranswick
20 May 44 to Hurn
27 Jun 44 to B 9/Lantheuil
31 Aug 44 to B 24/St-André-de-l'Eure
3 Sep 44 to B 48/Amiens/Glisy
7 Sep 44 to B 58/Melsbroek
25 Sep 44 to B 78/Eindhoven
30 Mar 45 to B 100/Goch
3 Apr 45 to Warmwell
22 Apr 45 to B 150/Hustedt
29 May 45 to B 166/Flensburg
26 Aug 45 DB

440 Sqn

8 Feb 44 F @ Ayr — No 111 Sqn, RCAF renumbered
Feb 44 **Hurricane IV** (Mar 44)
Mar 44 **Typhoon IB** (Aug 45)
18 Mar 44 to Hurn
3 Apr 44 to Funtington
20 Apr 44 to Hurn
28 Jun 44 to B 9/Lantheuil
31 Aug 44 to B 24/St-André-de-l'Eure
3 Sep 44 to B 48/Amiens/Glisy
6 Sep 44 to B 58/Melsbroek
26 Sep 44 to B 78/Eindhoven
30 Mar 45 to B 100/Goch
11 Apr 45 to B 110/Achmer
20 Apr 45 to B 150/Hustedt
23 Apr 45 to Warmwell
8 May 45 to B 150/Hustedt
29 May 45 to B 166/Flensburg
26 Aug 45 DB

441 Sqn

8 Feb 44 F @ Digby — No 125 Sqn, RCAF renumbered
Feb 44 **Spitfire VB** (Mar 44)
Mar 44 **Spitfire IXB** (Jan 45)
18 Mar 44 to Holmsley South
1 Apr 44 to Westhampnett
12 Apr 44 to Hutton Cranswick
23 Apr 44 to Funtington
13 May 44 to Ford
15 Jun 44 to B 3/Ste-Croix-sur-Mer
15 Jul 44 to B 11/Longues
13 Aug 44 to B 19/Lingèvres
2 Sep 44 to B 40/Beauvais/Nivillers
5 Sep 44 to B 52/Douai
17 Sep 44 to B 70/Deurne
1 Oct 44 to Hawkinge
30 Dec 44 to Skaebrae
Jan 45 **Spitfire IX** (May 45)
3 Apr 45 to Hawkinge
29 Apr 45 to Hunsdon
17 May 45 to Digby
May 45 **Mustang III** (Aug 45)
16 Jul 45 to Molesworth
7 Aug 45 DB

442 Sqn

8 Feb 44 F @ Digby — No 14 Sqn, RCAF renumbered
Feb 44 **Spitfire VB** (Mar 44)
Mar 44 **Spitfire IXB** (Sep 44)
18 Mar 44 to Holmsley South
1 Apr 44 to Westhampnett
23 Apr 44 to Funtington
25 Apr 44 to Hutton Cranswick
1 May 44 to Funtington
15 May 44 to Ford
15 Jun 44 to B 3/Ste-Croix-sur-Mer
15 Jul 44 to B 4/Bény-sur-Mer
8 Aug 44 to B 18/Cristot
1 Sep 44 to B 24/St-André-de-l'Eure
2 Sep 44 to B 26/Illiers-l'Evêque
3 Sep 44 to B 44/Poix
7 Sep 44 to B 56/Evere
Sep 44 **Spitfire IXE** (Mar 45)
21 Sep 44 to B 68/Le Culot
3 Oct 44 to B 84/Rips
14 Oct 44 to B 80/Volkel
14 Nov 44 to Warmwell
25 Nov 44 to B 80/Volkel
6 Dec 44 to B 88/Heesch
23 Mar 45 to Hunsdon
Mar 45 **Mustang III** (Aug 45)
17 May 45 to Digby
17 Jul 45 to Molesworth
7 Aug 45 DB

443 Sqn

8 Feb 44 F @ Digby — No 127 Sqn, RCAF renumbered
Feb 44 **Spitfire VB** (Mar 44)
Mar 44 **Spitfire IXB** (Feb 45)
18 Mar 44 to Holmsley South
27 Mar 44 to Hutton Cranswick
8 Apr 44 to Westhampnett
22 Apr 44 to Funtington
15 May 44 to Ford
15 Jun 44 to B 3/Ste-Croix-sur-Mer
15 Jul 44 to B 2/Bazenville
28 Aug 44 to B 26/Illiers-l'Evêque
21 Sep 44 to B 68/Le Culot
30 Sep 44 to B 82/Grave
22 Oct 44 to B 58/Melsbroek
4 Nov 44 to B 56/Evere
18 Dec 44 to Warmwell
3 Jan 45 to B 56/Evere
Jan 45 **Spitfire XVI** (Jan 46)
3 Mar 45 to B 90/Petit Brogel
31 Mar 45 to B 78/Eindhoven
12 Apr 45 to B 100/Goch
13 Apr 45 to B 114/Diepholz
28 Apr 45 to B 154/Reinsehlen
2 Jul 45 to B 152/Fassberg
7 Jul 45 to B 174/Utersen
Jan 46 **Spitfire XIV** (Mar 46)
15 Mar 46 DB

450 Sqn

16 Feb 41 F @ Williamstown
9 Apr 41 en route ME
12 May 41 to Abu Sueir
23 Jun 41 to Aqir
Jun 41 **Hurricane I** (Oct 41)
29 Jun 41 to Amman
11 Jul 41 to Damascus
18 Jul 41 to Haifa
4 Aug 41 to El Bassa
19 Aug 41 to Rayak
25 Oct 41 to Burgh el Arab (as an aircraft RDU)
12 Dec 41 to LG 'Y'
Dec 41 **Kittyhawk I** (Sep 42)
30 Jan 42 to LG 12
16 Feb 42 to Gambut Main det El Adem
22 Feb 42 to Gambut No 1
9 Mar 42 to Gambut Main
16 Apr 42 to Gambut No 1
17 Jun 42 to Sidi Azeiz
18 Jun 42 to LG 75
24 Jun 42 to LG 102
27 Jun 42 to LG 106
30 Jun 42 to LG 91
Sep 42 **Kittyhawk III** (Oct 4
2 Oct 42 to LG 224
14 Oct 42 to LG 175
6 Nov 42 to LG 106
9 Nov 42 to LG 101
11 Nov 42 to LG 76
14 Nov 42 to Gambut No 1
15 Nov 42 to Gazala
19 Nov 42 to Martuba 4 det Antelat
8 Dec 42 to Belandah
18 Dec 42 to Marble Arch
1 Jan 43 to Alem el Chel
9 Jan 43 to Hamraiet 3
18 Jan 43 to Sedadah
24 Jan 43 to Castel Benito
14 Feb 43 to El Assa det Ben Gardane
8 Mar 43 to Nefatia
21 Mar 43 to Medanine
6 Apr 43 to El Hamma
14 Apr 43 to El Djem
18 Apr 43 to Kairouan
18 May 43 to Zuara
13 Jul 43 to Luqa
18 Jul 43 to Pachino
2 Aug 43 to Agnone
16 Sep 43 to Grottaglie
23 Sep 43 to Bari
3 Oct 43 to Foggia
27 Oct 43 to Mileni
Oct 43 **Kittyhawk IV** (Aug
28 Dec 43 to Cutella
22 May 44 to San Angelo
12 Jun 44 to Guidonia
23 Jun 44 to Falerium
9 Jul 44 to Creti
28 Aug 44 to Iesi
11 Sep 44 to Foiano
20 Sep 44 to Iesi
17 Nov 44 to Fano
Nov 44 **Mustang III** (Dec 44
25 Feb 45 to Cervia
19 May 45 to Lavariano
May 45 **Mustang III** (Aug 45
20 Aug 45 DB

451 Sqn

25 Feb 41 F @ Bankstown
8 Apr 41 en route ME
12 May 41 to Aboukir
May 41 **Hurricane I** (Jan 43)
1 Jul 41 to Qasaba dets LG 90, LG 75
10 Oct 41 to LG 75 dets LG 131, LG 13 Sidi Azeiz
24 Nov 41 to LG 132
25 Nov 41 to LG 75 det LG 128
29 Nov 41 to LG 128
9 Dec 41 to El Gubbi
18 Dec 41 to LG 131
24 Dec 41 to Sidi Azeiz
27 Jan 42 to Heliopolis
16 Feb 42 to Rayak dets El Bassa, Nicos Lakatamia, Gaza
15 Aug 42 to Estabel dets El Bassa, Gaza, Lakatamia
18 Sep 42 to El Bassa dets Lakatamia, Gaz
14 Oct 42 to Estabel dets Lakatamia, Gaz
14 Nov 42 to St Jean det Lakatamia
1 Jan 43 to LG 08
Jan 43 **Hurricane IIC** (Oct
8 Feb 43 to Idku
Mar 43 **Spitfire VC** (Mar 44)
27 Aug 43 to LG 106 dets Almaza, Mersa Matruh
Dec 43 **Spitfire IX** (Oct 44)
4 Feb 44 to El Gamil det Almaza

Apr 44 to Poretta
May 44 to Serragia
Jul 44 to St Catherine (Calvi)
Aug 44 to Cuers
Aug 44 **Spitfire VIII** (Oct 44)
Oct 44 to Gragnano (No 56 PTC)
Nov 44 en route UK
Dec 44 to Hawkinge
Dec 44 **Spitfire IXB** (Jan 45)
Jan 45 **Spitfire XVI** (Jun 45)
Feb 45 to Manston
Feb 45 to Matlask
Feb 45 to Swannington
Mar 45 to Matlask
Apr 45 to Lympne
May 45 to Hawkinge
May 45 to Skaebrae
Jun 45 to Lasham
Aug 45 **Spitfire XIV** (Jan 46)
Sep 45 to B 152/Fassberg
Sep 45 to B 116/Wunstorf
Nov 45 to Gatow
Dec 45 to B 116/Wunstorf
Jan 46 DB

2 Sqn

Apr 41 F @ Kirton-in-Lindsey
Apr 41 **Spitfire I** (May 41)
May 41 **Spitfire IIA** (Aug 41)
Jul 41 to Kenley
Aug 41 **Spitfire VB** (May 42)
Oct 41 to Redhill
Jan 42 to Kenley
Mar 42 to Andreas
Jun 42 en route Australia
Aug 42 to Melbourne
Sep 42 to Mascot
Sep 42 **Spitfire VC** (Jan 45)
Jan 43 to Batchelor
Feb 43 to Strauss
dets Wyndham, Millingimbi
Jan 44 **Spitfire VIII** (Oct 45)
Mar 44 to Guildford
Mar 44 to Strauss
May 44 to Sattler
un 44 transferred to No 80 Wg, RAAF and ceased to have any further direct association with the RAF. Eventually disbanded at Tarakan on 17 Nov 45

3 Sqn

May 41 F @ Bankstown
Jul 41 en route Singapore
Aug 41 to Sembawang
Aug 41 **Buffalo I** (Feb 42)
Dec 41 to Ipoh
Dec 41 to Kuala Lumpur
Dec 41 to Sembawang
Feb 42 to P II
Feb 42 to Kemajoran
Feb 42 en route Australia
Mar 42 to Adelaide
Mar 42 DB
—
Jun 42 RF @ Drem
Jun 42 **Spitfire VB** (Apr 43)
Sep 42 to Hornchurch
Oct 42 to Southend
Nov 42 to Martlesham Heath
Dec 42 to Southend
Mar 43 to Westcott
Mar 43 to Newmarket
Mar 43 to Southend
Mar 43 to Hornchurch
Mar 43 **Spitfire IXB** (Jun 43)
Jun 43 to Ibsley
Jun 43 **Spitfire VB** (Jan 44)
Jun 43 **Spitfire VC** (Oct 43)
Aug 43 to Perranporth
Oct 43 to Skaebrae
det Sumburgh

19 Jan 44 to Detling
Jan 44 **Spitfire IXB** (Jul 44)
21 Jan 44 to Hutton Cranswick
4 Feb 44 to Detling
13 Mar 44 to Peterhead
19 Mar 44 to Detling
18 Apr 44 to Ford
25 Jun 44 to B 11/Longues
Jul 44 **Spitfire IXE** (Sep 44)
13 Aug 44 to B 19/Lingèvres
2 Sep 44 to B 40/Beauvais/Nivillers
5 Sep 44 to B 52/Douai
17 Sep 44 to B 70/Deurne
Sep 44 **Spitfire IXB** (Nov 44)
30 Sep 44 to Coltishall
18 Oct 44 to Matlask
Nov 44 **Spitfire LF XVI** (Jun 45)
20 Nov 44 to Swannington
15 Mar 45 to Matlask
6 Apr 45 to Lympne
2 May 45 to Hawkinge
14 Jun 45 to Lasham
Aug 45 **Spitfire XIV** (Jan 46)
14 Sep 45 to B 152/Fassberg
16 Sep 45 to Gatow
18 Oct 45 to B 116/Wunstorf
21 Jan 46 DB

454 Sqn

23 May 41 F @ Williamstown (ground echelon only)
11 Jul 41 DB — absorbed by No 458 Sqn
—
2 Apr 42 RF @ Blackpool as a nucleus of groundcrew only. Moved to ME and became servicing echelon of No 76/454 Sqn at Aqir and assisted in the maintenance of Nos 159 and 160 Sqn's Liberators.
dets Shallufa, LG 224, Fayid
—
30 Sep 42 established at Aqir
19 Oct 42 to Qaiyarh
Nov 42 **Blenheim V** (Jan 43)
24 Jan 43 to LG 227
Feb 43 **Baltimore III** (Oct 43)
16 Feb 43 to LG 91
13 Apr 43 to Gambut 3
Jul 43 **Baltimore IV** (Nov 44)
7 Aug 43 to LG 91
dets Lakatamia, St Jean
21 Oct 43 to St Jean
Oct 43 **Baltimore V** (Aug 45)
dets LG 91, Lakatamia
4 Nov 43 to Berka III
det Gambut
27 Jul 44 to Pescara
18 Aug 44 to Falconara
8 Dec 44 to Cesenatico
det Forli
16 May 45 to Villa Orba
20 Aug 45 DB

455 Sqn

6 Jun 41 F @ Swinderby
30 Jun 41 Australian echelon formed at Williamstown
15 Jul 41 en route UK
Jul 41 **Hampden** (Dec 43)
1 Sep 41 Australian echelon arrives UK
8 Feb 42 to Wigsley
28 Apr 42 to Leuchars
dets Sumburgh, Vaenga, Benbecula, Tain, Wick
Dec 43 **Beaufighter X** (May 45)
14 Apr 44 to Langham
dets Thorney Island, Manston

20 Oct 44 to Dallachy
25 May 45 DB

456 Sqn

30 Jun 41 F @ Valley
Jun 41 **Defiant I** (Nov 41)
Sep 41 **Beaufighter IIF** (Mar 43)
Jul 42 **Beaufighter VIF** (Jan 43)
Dec 42 **Mosquito II** (Apr 44)
det Colerne
29 Mar 43 to Middle Wallop
dets Castle Camps, Predannack
Jun 43 **Mosquito VI** (Oct 43)
17 Aug 43 to Colerne
17 Nov 43 to Fairwood Common
Jan 44 **Mosquito XVII** (Feb 45)
29 Feb 44 to Ford
31 Dec 44 to Church Fenton
Dec 44 **Mosquito XXX** (Jun 45)
16 Mar 45 to Bradwell Bay
15 Jun 45 DB

457 Sqn

16 Jun 41 F @ Baginton
Jun 41 **Spitfire I** (Oct 41)
7 Aug 41 to Jurby
Sep 41 **Spitfire IIA** (Mar 42)
3 Oct 41 to Andreas
Dec 41 **Spitfire VB** (May 42)
23 Mar 42 to Redhill
31 May 42 to Kirton-in-Lindsey
18 Jun 42 en route Australia
13 Aug 42 to Melbourne
6 Sep 42 to Richmond
Sep 42 **Spitfire VC** (Jul 44)
7 Nov 42 to Camden
18 Jan 43 to Batchelor
31 Jan 43 to Livingstone
dets Drysdale Mission, Millingimbi
10 Jan 44 to Sattler
19 Jan 44 to Livingstone
11 Mar 44 to Guildford
25 Mar 44 to Livingstone
10 May 44 to Sattler
dets Learmonth, Drysdale Mission
Jul 44 **Spitfire VIII** (Oct 45)
Jul 44 transferred to No 80 Wg, RAAF and ceased to have any further direct association with the RAF. Eventually disbanded at Labuan on 7 Nov 45

458 Sqn

10 Jul 41 F @ Williamstown
7 Aug 41 en route UK
25 Aug 41 established at Holme-on-Spalding Moor
Aug 41 **Wellington IV** (Jan 42)
Feb 42 **Wellington IC** (Apr 42)
23 Mar 42 en route ME
Mar 42 aircrews attached Nos 104, 108 & 148 Sqns at Kabrit, and Nos 37 & 70 Sqns at Abu Sueir. Groundcrews to No 159 Sqn at Fayid, St Jean and Aqir, and to USAAF Halverson Detachment at Lydda
1 Sep 42 re-established at Shallufa
Sep 42 **Wellington IC** (Nov 42)
Sep 42 **Wellington VIII** (Sep 43)
dets Gambut, Berka, Luqa
30 Mar 43 to LG 91
dets Luqa, Blida

18 Jun 43 to Protville
Jun 43 **Wellington XIII** (May 44)
9 Oct 43 to Bone
dets Blida, Luqa, Grottaglie, Ghisonaccia, Bo Rizzo, Reghaia
Jan 44 **Wellington XIV** (Jun 45)
25 May 44 to Alghero
3 Sep 44 to Foggia
dets Falconara, Le Vallon, Rosignano
29 Jan 45 to Gibraltar
8 Jun 45 DB

459 Sqn

10 Feb 42 F @ LG 39
Feb 42 **Blenheim IV** (May 42)
Mar 42 **Hudson III** (Jan 44)
dets LG 05, Gambut
13 May 42 to LG 40
1 Jul 42 to LG 'Z'
dets LG 226, St Jean, Khormaksar, Gambut
18 Nov 42 to LG 227
dets Khormaksar, LG 208, Gambut 3
28 Nov 42 to Gianaclis
dets Khormaksar, Gambut 3, Berka III, LG 227
18 Dec 42 to LG 143
dets Khormaksar, Berka III, LG 227, LG 91, LG 07, Lydda
Aug 43 **Hudson VI** (Mar 44)
Dec 43 **Ventura V** (Jul 44)
dets Berka III, LG 07, Gianaclis, Nicosia, El Adem, St Jean, Lydda, Ramat David
5 Apr 44 to Ramat David
15 May 44 to St Jean
Jul 44 **Baltimore IV** (Feb 45)
Jul 44 **Baltimore V** (Feb 45)
9 Aug 44 to Berka III
17 Feb 45 to Almaza (No 22 PTC)
25 Feb 45 en route UK
14 Mar 45 to Chivenor
10 Apr 45 DB

460 Sqn

15 Nov 41 F @ Molesworth — from 'C' Flt, No 458 Sqn
Nov 41 **Wellington IV** (Sep 42)
4 Jan 42 to Breighton
Aug 42 **Halifax II** (Oct 42)
Oct 42 **Lancaster I & III** (Oct 45)
14 May 43 to Binbrook
27 Jul 45 to East Kirkby
10 Oct 45 DB

461 Sqn

26 Apr 42 F @ Mount Batten
Apr 42 **Sunderland II** (May 43)
Aug 42 **Sunderland III** (Jun 45)
5 Sep 42 to Hamworthy Junction (Poole Harbour)
20 Apr 43 to Pembroke Dock
Feb 45 **Sunderland V** (Jun 45)
4 Jun 45 DB

462 Sqn

7 Sep 42 F @ Fayid — from a merger of Nos 10/227 & 76/462 Sqns
Sep 42 **Halifax II** (Feb 44)
13 Nov 42 to LG 237
det LG 09
29 Nov 42 to LG 167

14 Dec 42 to LG 237
18 Jan 43 to LG 167
24 Jan 43 to Soluch
14 Feb 43 to Gardabia Main
22 May 43 to Hosc Raui
1 Oct 43 to Terria det El Adem
1 Jan 44 to El Adem
15 Feb 44 DB en route Celone — renumbered as No 614 Sqn
—
12 Aug 44 RF @ Driffield
Aug 44 **Halifax III** (Sep 45)
22 Dec 44 to Foulsham
24 Sep 45 DB

463 Sqn

25 Nov 43 F @ Waddington — from 'C' Flt, No 467 Sqn
Nov 43 **Lancaster I & III** (Sep 45)
3 Jul 45 to Skellingthorpe
25 Sep 45 DB

464 Sqn

15 Aug 42 F @ Feltwell
Sep 42 **Ventura I & II** (Nov 43)
3 Apr 43 to Methwold
21 Jul 43 to Sculthorpe
Aug 43 **Mosquito VI** (Sep 45)
31 Dec 43 to Hunsdon
25 Mar 44 to Swanton Morley
9 Apr 44 to Hunsdon
17 Apr 44 to Gravesend
18 Jun 44 to Thorney Island det B 87/Rosières-en-Santerre
7 Feb 45 to B 87/Rosières-en-Santerre
18 Apr 45 to B 58/Melsbroek
25 Sep 45 DB

466 Sqn

15 Oct 42 F @ Driffield
Oct 42 **Wellington II** (Nov 42)
Nov 42 **Wellington X** (Sep 43)
22 Dec 42 to Leconfield
Sep 43 **Halifax II** (Nov 43)
Nov 43 **Halifax III** (May 45)
3 Jun 44 to Driffield
May 45 **Halifax VI** (Aug 45)
6 Sep 45 to Bassingbourn
Oct 45 **Liberator VIII** (Oct 45)
26 Oct 45 DB

467 Sqn

7 Nov 42 F @ Scampton
Nov 42 **Lancaster I & III** (Sep 45)
24 Nov 42 to Bottesford
13 Nov 43 to Waddington
15 Jun 45 to Metheringham
30 Sep 45 DB

485 Sqn

1 Mar 41 F @ Driffield
Mar 41 **Spitfire I** (Jun 41)
21 Apr 41 to Leconfield
Jun 41 **Spitfire IIA** (Aug 41)
1 Jul 41 to Redhill
Aug 41 **Spitfire VB** (Jul 43)
21 Oct 41 to Kenley
8 Jul 42 to Kingscliffe
16 Aug 42 to West Malling
22 Aug 42 to Kingscliffe
24 Oct 42 to Kirkistown
5 Nov 42 to Eglinton
13 Nov 42 to Kingscliffe
2 Jan 43 to Westhampnett
21 May 43 to Merston
1 Jul 43 to Biggin Hill
Jul 43 **Spitfire IXB** (Nov 43)
18 Oct 43 to Hornchurch
21 Nov 43 to Drem
Nov 43 **Spitfire VB** (Feb 44)
Feb 44 **Spitfire IXB** (Jul 44)
28 Feb 44 to Hornchurch
21 Mar 44 to Llanbedr
7 Mar 44 to Hornchurch
7 Apr 44 to Selsey
30 Jun 44 to Coolham
Jul 44 **Spitfire IXE** (Feb 45)
3 Jul 44 to Funtington
7 Aug 44 to Selsey
19 Aug 44 to Tangmere
31 Aug 44 to B 17/Carpiquet
7 Sep 44 to B 35/Godelmesnil
12 Sep 44 to B 53/Merville
2 Nov 44 to B 65/Maldeghem
5 Nov 44 to Fairwood Common
24 Nov 44 to B 65/Maldeghem
13 Jan 45 to B 77/Gilze-Rijen
25 Feb 45 to Predannack
Feb 45 **Tempest V** (Mar 45)
Mar 45 **Typhoon IB** (Apr 45)
19 Apr 45 to B 106/Twente
Apr 45 **Spitfire IXB** (Aug 45)
29 Apr 45 to B 105/Drope
26 Aug 45 DB

486 Sqn

3 Mar 42 F @ Kirton-in-Lindsey
Mar 42 **Hurricane IIB** (Jul 42)
9 Apr 42 to Wittering
Jul 42 **Typhoon IB** (Apr 44)
27 Sep 42 to North Weald
10 Oct 42 to West Malling
29 Oct 42 to Tangmere
Jan 44 **Tempest V** (Feb 44)
31 Jan 44 to Beaulieu
28 Feb 44 to Drem
6 Mar 44 to Castle Camps
21 Mar 44 to Ayr
29 Mar 44 to Castle Camps
Apr 44 **Tempest V** (Sep 45)
29 Apr 44 to Newchurch
19 Sep 44 to Matlask
28 Sep 44 to B 60/Grimbergen
1 Oct 44 to B 80/Volkel
10 Apr 45 to B 112/Hopsten
26 Apr 45 to B 150/Hustedt
6 May 45 to B 118/Celle
8 May 45 to B 160/Kastrup
6 Jul 45 to B 158/Lübeck
7 Sep 45 DB

487 Sqn

15 Aug 42 F @ Feltwell
Sep 42 **Ventura II** (Sep 43)
3 Apr 43 to Methwold
20 Jul 43 to Sculthorpe
Aug 43 **Mosquito VI** (Sep 45)
31 Dec 43 to Hunsdon
18 Apr 44 to Gravesend
26 Apr 44 to Swanton Morley
30 Apr 44 to Gravesend
18 Jun 44 to Thorney Island det B 87/Rosières-en-Santerre
5 Feb 45 to B 87/Rosières-en-Santerre
18 Apr 45 to B 58/Melsbroek
20 Jul 45 to A 75/Cambrai/Epinoy
19 Sep 45 DB — renumbered as No 268 Sqn

488 Sqn

Sep 41 F @ Rongotai
Oct 41 en route Singapore
10 Oct 41 to Kallang det Kluang
Oct 41 **Buffalo I** (Jan 42)
Jan 42 **Hurricane IIB** (Feb 42)
8 Feb 42 to Batavia
15 Feb 42 to Tjilitjan
23 Feb 42 survivors evacuated
2 Mar 42 to Fremantle
2 Mar 42 DB — formed nucleus of No 14 Sqn, RNZAF
—
25 Jun 42 RF @ Church Fenton
Jun 42 **Beaufighter IIF** (May 43)
1 Sep 42 to Ayr dets Drem, Coltishall
Mar 43 **Beaufighter VIF** (Sep 43)
3 Aug 43 to Drem
Aug 43 **Mosquito XII** (Mar 44)
3 Sep 43 to Bradwell Bay
Oct 43 **Mosquito XIII** (Oct 44)
3 May 44 to Colerne
12 May 44 to Zeals
29 Jul 44 to Colerne
9 Oct 44 to Hunsdon
Oct 44 **Mosquito XXX** (Apr 45)
15 Nov 44 to B 48/Amiens/Glisy
4 Apr 45 to B 77/Gilze-Rijen
26 Apr 45 DB

489 Sqn

12 Aug 41 F @ Leuchars
Aug 41 **Beaufort I** (Jan 42)
Jan 42 **Blenheim IV** (Mar 42)
8 Mar 42 to Thorney Island
Mar 42 **Hampden I** (Oct 43) det St Eval
5 Aug 42 to Skitten
24 Sep 42 to Wick det Leuchars
6 Oct 43 to Leuchars
Oct 43 **Beaufighter X** (May 45)
8 Apr 44 to Langham
24 Oct 44 to Dallachy
16 Jun 45 to Banff
Jun 45 **Mosquito VI** (Aug 45)
1 Aug 45 DB

490 Sqn

28 Mar 43 F @ Jui det Stranraer
Jun 43 **Catalina IB** (Jul 44) dets Fisherman's Lake, Apapa, Half Die, Abidjan
May 44 **Sunderland III** (Jun 45)
30 Jun 45 DB

500 Sqn

16 Mar 31 F @ Manston as a Special Reserve Sqn
Mar 31 **Virginia X** (Jan 36)
Jan 36 **Hart** (May 37)
25 May 36 transferred to AAF
Feb 37 **Hind** (Mar 39)
28 Sep 38 to Detling
Mar 39 **Anson I** (Apr 41)
30 Jul 39 to Warmwell
13 Aug 39 to Detling
Apr 41 **Blenheim IV** (Nov 41)
30 May 41 to Bircham Newton dets Carew Cheriton, Limavady
Nov 41 **Hudson V** (Apr 44)
22 Mar 42 to Stornoway
30 Aug 42 to St Eval
5 Nov 42 to Gibraltar det Tafaraoui
19 Nov 42 to Blida det Tafaraoui
4 May 43 to Tafaraoui dets Blida, Bone, Ghisonaccia, Montecorvino, Grottaglie
Dec 43 **Ventura V** (Jul 44)
6 Jan 44 to La Senia dets Blida, Bone, Ghisonaccia, Bo Rizzo
Jun 44 **Hudson VI** (Jul 44)
11 Jul 44 DB — aircraft to No 27 Sqn, SAAF
—
13 Jul 44 RF @ La Senia
21 Aug 44 to Maison Carrée (No 1 BPD)
28 Aug 44 to Portici (No 3 BPD)
14 Sep 44 to Pescara
Sep 44 **Baltimore IV** (Feb 45)
Sep 44 **Baltimore V** (Oct 45)
15 Oct 44 to Perugia
9 Dec 44 to Cesenatico
11 May 45 to Villa Orba
27 Aug 45 to Lecce (No 54 PTC) det Villa Orba
12 Sep 45 to Almaza (No 22 PTC) dets Villa Orba, Eastleig
19 Oct 45 to Eastleigh
23 Oct 45 DB — renumbered as N 249 Sqn
—
10 May 46 RF @ West Malling
13 Jun 46 embodied
Feb 47 **Mosquito NF 19** (Aug 47
Apr 47 **Mosquito NF 30** (Oct 48
May 48 **Spitfire F.22** (Oct 48)
Jul 48 **Meteor F.3** (Oct 51)
Jul 51 **Meteor F.4** (Feb 52)
Nov 51 **Meteor F.8** (Mar 57)
10 Mar 57 DB

501 Sqn

14 Jun 29 F @ Filton as a Special Reserve Sqn
Mar 30 **DH 9A** (Nov 30)
Sep 30 **Wapiti** (Mar 33)
Jan 33 **Wallace** (Jul 36)
1 May 36 transferred to AAF
Jul 36 **Hart** (Mar 38)
Mar 38 **Hind** (Mar 39)
Mar 39 **Hurricane I** (May 41)
27 Nov 39 to Tangmere
10 May 40 to Bétheniville
16 May 40 to Anglure
2 Jun 40 to Le Mans
16 Jun 40 to Dinard
19 Jun 40 to St Helier
21 Jun 40 to Croydon
4 Jul 40 to Middle Wallop
25 Jul 40 to Gravesend
10 Sep 40 to Kenley
17 Dec 40 to Filton
9 Apr 41 to Colerne
Apr 41 **Spitfire I** (Jun 41)
Jun 41 **Spitfire IIA** (Oct 41)
25 Jun 41 to Chilbolton
5 Aug 41 to Ibsley
Sep 41 **Spitfire VB** (Jul 44)
25 Jan 42 to Warmwell
7 Feb 42 to Ibsley
May 42 **Spitfire VC** (Oct 42)
3 Jul 42 to Tangmere
7 Jul 42 to Ibsley
24 Aug 42 to Middle Wallop
8 Oct 42 to Hawkinge
10 Oct 42 to Middle Wallop
19 Oct 42 to Ballyhalbert det Eglinton
30 Apr 43 to Westhampnett
17 May 43 to Martlesham Heath
5 Jun 43 to Woodvale
12 Jun 43 to Westhampnett
21 Jun 43 to Hawkinge
Jun 43 **Spitfire IX** (Apr 44)
21 Jan 44 to Southend
4 Feb 44 to Hawkinge

Apr 44 to Friston
Jul 44 to Westhampnett
Jul 44 **Tempest V** (Apr 45)
Aug 44 to Manston
Sep 44 to Bradwell Bay
Mar 45 to Hunsdon
Apr 45 DB

—

May 46 RF @ Filton
Jun 46 embodied
Oct 46 **Spitfire LF 16E** (May 49)
Nov 48 **Vampire F.1** (Jun 51)
Apr 51 **Vampire FB 5** (Mar 57)
Feb 55 **Vampire FB 9** (Feb 57)
Mar 57 DB

2 Sqn

May 25 F @ Aldergrove as a Special Reserve Sqn
Jun 25 **Vimy** (Jul 28)
Jul 28 **Hyderabad** (Feb 32)
Dec 31 **Virginia X** (Oct 35)
Oct 35 **Wallace** (Apr 37)
Apr 37 **Hind** (Apr 39)
Jul 37 transferred to AAF
Jan 39 **Anson I** (Oct 40) det Hooton Park
Aug 40 **Botha I** (Nov 40)
Sep 40 **Whitley V** (Feb 42)
Jan 41 to Limavady det St Eval
Jan 42 to Bircham Newton dets Docking, St Eval
Feb 42 **Whitley VII** (Feb 43)
Feb 42 to St Eval det Holmsley South
Feb 43 **Halifax II** (Mar 45)
Mar 43 to Holmsley South
Mar 43 to St Eval
Jun 43 to Holmsley South
Dec 43 to St Davids
Sep 44 to Stornoway
Feb 45 **Halifax III** (May 45)
May 45 DB

—

May 46 RF @ Aldergrove
Jul 46 embodied
Mar 47 **Mosquito B.25** (Jan 48)
Dec 47 **Mosquito NF 30** (Oct 48)
Sep 48 **Spitfire F.22** (Mar 51)
Jan 51 **Vampire F.3** (Mar 51)
Feb 51 **Vampire FB 5** (Mar 57)
Jul 54 **Vampire FB 9** (Mar 57)
Mar 57 DB

3 Sqn

Oct 26 F @ Waddington as a Special Reserve Sqn
Oct 26 **Fawn** (Jun 29)
Feb 29 **Hyderabad** (Jan 34)
Oct 33 **Hinaidi** (Nov 35)
Oct 35 **Wallace** (Jul 36)
May 36 transferred to AAF
Jun 36 **Hart** (Nov 38)
Jun 38 **Hind** (Nov 38)
Nov 38 DB — moved to Doncaster and renumbered as No 616 Sqn

4 Sqn

Mar 28 F @ Hucknall as a Special Reserve Sqn
Oct 29 **Horsley** (Mar 34)
Mar 34 **Wallace I** (May 37)
Mar 36 **Wallace II** (May 37)
May 36 transferred to AAF
May 37 **Hind** (Nov 38)
Nov 38 **Gauntlet II** (Aug 39)
May 39 **Hurricane I** (Jul 41)
Aug 39 to Digby

9 Oct 39 to Debden det Wattisham
24 Dec 39 to Martlesham Heath
30 Dec 39 to Debden
8 Jan 40 to Martlesham Heath
13 Jan 40 to Debden
20 Jan 40 to Martlesham Heath
30 Jan 30 to Debden
11 Feb 40 to Martlesham Heath
22 Feb 40 to Debden
27 Feb 40 to Martlesham Heath
5 Mar 40 to Debden
12 Mar 40 to Martlesham Heath
18 Mar 40 to Debden
27 Mar 40 to Martlesham Heath
4 Apr 40 to Debden
13 Apr 40 to Martlesham Heath
23 Apr 40 to Debden
30 Apr 40 to Martlesham Heath
7 May 40 to Debden
12 May 40 to Lille/Marcq
19 May 40 to Norrent-Fontes
20 May 40 to Manston
21 May 40 to Debden
22 May 40 to Wick
21 Jun 40 to Castletown
2 Sep 40 to Catterick
6 Sep 40 to Hendon
26 Sep 40 to Filton
18 Dec 40 to Exeter
21 Jul 41 to Fairwood Common
Jul 41 **Hurricane IIB** (Nov 41)
11 Aug 41 to Chilbolton
26 Aug 41 to Ballyhalbert
Oct 41 **Spitfire IIA** (Feb 42)
Dec 41 **Spitfire IIB** (Feb 42)
Jan 42 **Spitfire VB** (Jan 44)
12 Jan 42 to Kirkistown
19 Jun 42 to Ballyhalbert dets Kirkistown, Eglinton
19 Oct 42 to Middle Wallop
Oct 42 **Spitfire VC** (Sep 43)
30 Dec 42 to Ibsley
30 Jun 43 to Church Stanton
14 Aug 43 to Redhill
19 Sep 43 to Castletown
Sep 43 **Spitfire VI** (Jan 44) det Sumburgh
18 Oct 43 to Peterhead
19 Jan 44 to Hornchurch
Jan 44 **Spitfire IXB** (Mar 44)
28 Jan 44 to Llanbedr
4 Feb 44 to Hornchurch
10 Mar 44 to Castletown
Mar 44 **Spitfire VB** (Jul 44)
30 Apr 44 to Digby det Acklington
11 Jul 44 to Lympne
Jul 44 **Spitfire IXE** (Mar 45)
12 Jul 44 to Detling
13 Aug 44 to Manston
25 Feb 45 to Hawkinge
26 Feb 45 to B 65/Maldeghem
28 Feb 45 to Hawkinge
28 Mar 45 to Colerne
Apr 45 **Meteor III** (Aug 45) dets Andrews Field, Lübeck
10 Aug 45 DB — renumbered as No 245 Sqn

—

10 May 46 RF @ Syerston
11 Jun 46 embodied
8 Nov 46 to Hucknall
May 47 **Mosquito NF 30** (May 48)
May 48 **Spitfire F.22** (Mar 50)
2 Apr 49 to Wymeswold
Oct 49 **Meteor F.4** (Mar 52)
Mar 52 **Meteor F.8** (Feb 57)
10 Mar 57 DB

510 Sqn

15 Oct 42 F @ Hendon — nucleus from No 24 Sqn
Oct 42 **Lysander I** (Jan 43)
Oct 42 **Reliant** (Oct 43)
Oct 42 **Hornet Moth** (Dec 43)
Oct 42 **Puss Moth** (Dec 43)
Oct 42 **Oxford** (Apr 44)
Oct 42 **Spitfire I** (Apr 44)
Oct 42 **Tiger Moth** (Apr 44)
Oct 42 **Proctor I & III** (Apr 44)
Oct 42 **Vega Gull** (Apr 44)
Oct 42 **Mohawk III** (Apr 44)
Oct 42 **Percival Q.6** (Apr 44)
Oct 42 **Gipsy Moth** (Apr 44)
Oct 42 **Hart** (Jan 44)
Oct 42 **Stampe SV 4B** (Apr 44)
Dec 42 **Anson I** (Apr 44)
May 43 **Koolhoven FK 43** (Dec 43)
Aug 43 **Cygnet** (Dec 43)
Mar 44 **Proctor IV** (Apr 44)
8 Apr 44 DB — became Metropolitan Communications Sqn

511 Sqn

10 Oct 42 F @ Lyneham — from No 1425 Flt
Oct 42 **Liberator I** (Mar 44)
Oct 42 **Liberator II** (May 44)
Nov 42 **Albemarle I** (Mar 44) det Gibraltar
Dec 42 **Halifax II** (Dec 42)
Sep 43 **Dakota** (Jul 44)
Nov 43 **York** (Oct 46)
Jul 44 **Liberator VII** (Dec 44)
Oct 45 **Lancastrian C.2** (Apr 46)
7 Oct 46 DB

—

16 Oct 46 RF @ Lyneham — No 246 Sqn renumbered
Oct 46 **York C.1** (Aug 49) det Wunstorf for BAL
Sep 49 **Hastings C.1** (Sep 58)
51 **Hastings C.2** (Sep 58)
1 May 57 to Colerne
1 Sep 58 DB — renumbered as No 36 Sqn

—

15 Dec 59 RF @ Lyneham
Dec 59 **Britannia C.1** (Dec 75)
Dec 59 **Britannia C.2** (Dec 75)
16 Jun 70 to Brize Norton
7 Jan 76 DB

512 Sqn

18 Jun 43 F @ Hendon
Aug 43 **Dakota** (Mar 46)
14 Feb 44 to Broadwell det B 56/Evere
6 Aug 45 to Holme-on-Spalding Moor
8 Oct 45 to Qastina
24 Oct 45 to Gianaclis
2 Dec 45 to Bari
14 Mar 46 DB

513 Sqn

15 Sep 43 F @ Witchford
Oct 43 **Stirling III** (Nov 43)
21 Nov 43 DB

514 Sqn

1 Sep 43 F @ Foulsham
Sep 43 **Lancaster II** (Jul 44)
23 Nov 43 to Waterbeach
Jun 44 **Lancaster I & III** (Aug 45)
22 Aug 45 DB

515 Sqn

1 Oct 42 F @ Northolt — from the 'Defiant Flt'
Oct 42 **Defiant II** (Dec 43)
29 Oct 42 to Heston
1 Jun 43 to Hunsdon
Jun 43 **Beaufighter IIF** (Apr 44)
15 Dec 43 to Little Snoring
Feb 44 **Mosquito II** (Apr 44)
Mar 44 **Mosquito VI** (Jun 45)
10 Jun 45 DB

516 Sqn

28 Apr 43 F @ Dundonald — No 1441 Flt renumbered
Apr 43 **Hurricane IIB** (Jun 43)
Apr 43 **Lysander II** (Dec 43)
Apr 43 **Mustang I** (Mar 44)
Apr 43 **Anson I** (Dec 44)
Apr 43 **Blenheim IV** (Dec 44)
Dec 43 **Hurricane IIB** (Dec 44)
Dec 43 **Hurricane IIC** (Dec 44) dets Ayr, Havorfordwest
2 Dec 44 DB

517 Sqn

7 Aug 43 F @ St Eval — No 1404 Flt renumbered
Aug 43 **Hudson III** (Sep 43)
Aug 43 **Hampden** (Dec 43)
Sep 43 **B-17F Fortress** (Nov 43) — USAAF aircraft attached
25 Nov 43 to St Davids
Nov 43 **Halifax V** (Jun 45)
1 Feb 44 to Brawdy
Mar 45 **Halifax III** (Jun 46)
30 Nov 45 to Chivenor
21 Jun 46 DB

518 Sqn

6 Jul 43 F @ Stornoway
Jul 43 **Halifax V** (Jun 45)
25 Sep 43 to Tiree
Mar 45 **Halifax III** (46) dets Wick, Tain
18 Sep 45 to Aldergrove — (absorbed No 1402 Flt)
Sep 45 **Hurricane IIC** (Oct 46)
Sep 45 **Spitfire VII** (Oct 46) det Tain
Mar 46 **Halifax VI** (Oct 46)
1 Oct 46 DB — renumbered as No 202 Sqn

519 Sqn

7 Aug 43 F @ Wick — from Nos 1406 & 1408 Flts
Aug 43 **Hampden** (Oct 43)
Aug 43 **Spitfire VI** (Nov 44)
Sep 43 **Hudson IIIA** (Oct 43)
Sep 43 **Ventura V** (Oct 44)
10 Dec 43 to Skitten
Aug 44 **Hudson III** (Mar 45)
28 Nov 44 to Wick
Oct 44 **Fortress II** (Sep 45)
Nov 44 **Spitfire VII** (Dec 45)
17 Aug 45 to Tain
Aug 45 **Halifax III** (May 46)
8 Nov 45 to Leuchars
31 May 46 DB

520 Sqn

20 Sep 43 F @ Gibraltar — from No 1403 Flt
Sep 43 **Hudson III** (Mar 44)
Sep 43 **Gladiator II** (Aug 44)
Feb 44 **Halifax V** (May 45)
Feb 44 **Spitfire V** (Apr 44)
Jun 44 **Hurricane IIC** (Apr 46)
Sep 44 **Martinet** (Jan 46)
Jan 45 **Hudson III** (Jan 46)
May 45 **Halifax III** (Apr 46)
Jul 45 **Warwick I** (Apr 46)
Oct 45 **Hudson VI** (Jan 46)
25 Apr 46 DB

521 Sqn

22 Jul 42 F @ Bircham Newton — from No 1401 Flt
Jul 42 **Blenheim IV** (Mar 43)
Jul 42 **Gladiator II** (Mar 43)
Jul 42 **Spitfire V** (Mar 43)
Jul 42 **Mosquito IV** (Mar 43)
Jul 42 **Hudson IIIA** (Mar 43)
22 Mar 43 DB — split into Nos 1401 & 1409 Flts
—
1 Sep 43 RF @ Docking
Sep 43 **Hudson III** (Dec 43)
Sep 43 **Hampden** (Dec 43)
Sep 43 **Gladiator II** (Mar 45)
Sep 43 **Spitfire IX** (Nov 45)
Oct 43 **Ventura V** (Dec 44)
Aug 44 **Hurricane IIC** (Nov 45)
Sep 44 **Hudson VI** (Mar 45)
1 Nov 44 to Langham
Dec 44 **Fortress II** (Feb 46)
det Brawdy
May 45 **Fortress III** (Feb 46)
3 Nov 45 to Chivenor
Dec 45 **Halifax III** (Mar 46)
31 Mar 46 DB

524 Sqn

20 Oct 43 F @ Oban
Oct 43 **Mariner I** (Dec 43)
7 Dec 43 DB
—
7 Apr 44 RF @ Davidstow Moor
Apr 44 **Wellington XIII** (Jan 45)
1 Jul 44 to Docking
23 Jul 44 to Bircham Newton
17 Oct 44 to Langham
Dec 44 **Wellington XIV** (May 45)
25 May 45 DB

525 Sqn

1 Sep 43 F @ Weston Zoyland
Sep 43 **Warwick I** (Sep 44)
6 Feb 44 to Lyneham
Jun 44 **Dakota** (Dec 46)
Jul 44 **Stirling III** (Nov 44)
Aug 44 **Warwick III** (Sep 44)
15 Jul 45 to Membury
det Schwecat
31 Oct 46 to Abingdon
det Schwecat
1 Dec 46 DB — renumbered as No 238 Sqn

526 Sqn

15 Jun 43 F @ Longman
Jun 43 **Blenheim IV** (May 45)
Jun 43 **Hornet Moth** (May 45)
Jun 43 **Oxford** (May 45)
Aug 43 **Dominie** (May 45)
1 May 45 DB — absorbed by No 527 Sqn

527 Sqn

15 Jun 43 F @ Castle Camps
Jun 43 **Hurricane I** (Sep 44)
Jun 43 **Hornet Moth** (Sep 44)
Jun 43 **Blenheim IV** (May 45)
Jun 43 **Hurricane IIB** (Jul 45)
28 Feb 44 to Snailwell
28 Apr 44 to Digby
dets Longman, Tealing
Jul 44 **Spitfire VB** (Apr 46)
Sep 44 **Oxford** (Apr 46)
Apr 45 **Wellington X** (Apr 46)
Apr 45 **Dominie** (Apr 46)
12 Nov 45 to Watton
15 Apr 46 DB
—
1 Aug 52 RF @ Watton — 'R' Calibration Sqn redesignated
Aug 52 **Mosquito B.35** (Jan 54)
Aug 52 **Anson C.19** (Mar 54)
Aug 52 **Lincoln B.2** (Sep 54)
Jun 53 **Meteor NF 11** (Jul 55)
Jan 54 **Varsity T.1** (Mar 56)
Aug 54 **Meteor NF 14** (Oct 55)
Dec 54 **Canberra B.2** (Aug 58)
Apr 56 **Canberra PR 7** (Jun 56)
Sep 57 **Meteor NF 11** (Nov 57)
21 Aug 58 DB — renumbered as No 245 Sqn

528 Sqn

15 Jun 43 F @ Filton
Jun 43 **Blenheim IV** (Sep 44)
Jun 43 **Hornet Moth** (Sep 44)
15 May 44 to Digby
1 Sep 44 DB — absorbed by No 527 Sqn

529 Sqn

15 Jun 43 F @ Halton — from No 1448 Flt
Jun 43 **Rota I** (Oct 45)
Jun 43 **Hornet Moth** (Oct 45)
18 Aug 44 to Henley (Crazies Hill)
Aug 44 **Oxford** (Oct 45)
Apr 45 **Hoverfly I** (Oct 45)
20 Oct 45 DB

Nos 530-539, the Turbinlite Sqns
All ten Turbinlite Flights were raised to squadron status on 2 Sep 42. However, for administrative reasons it was not possible to implement this change simultaneously for all the units and the formal creation of five of the squadrons was postponed until 8 Sep 42 by HQ Fighter Command.

530 Sqn

8 Sep 42 F @ Hunsdon — No 1451 Flt redesignated
Sep 42 **Havoc II (Turbinlite)** (Jan 43)
Sep 42 **Boston III (Turbinlite)** (Jan 43)
Sep 42 **Hurricane IIC** (Jan 43)
25 Jan 43 DB

531 Sqn

8 Sep 42 F @ West Malling — No 1452 Flt redesignated
Sep 42 **Havoc I (Turbinlite)** (Jan 43)
Sep 42 **Boston III (Turbinlite)** (Jan 43)
Sep 42 **Hurricane IIC** (Jan 43)
Sep 42 **Havoc I** (Jan 43)
2 Oct 42 to Debden
9 Oct 42 to West Malling
25 Jan 43 DB

532 Sqn

2 Sep 42 F @ Wittering — No 1453 Flt redesignated
Sep 42 **Havoc I (Turbinlite)** (Jan 43)
Sep 42 **Boston III (Turbinlite)** (Jan 43)
Sep 42 **Hurricane IIB** (Jan 43)
Sep 42 **Hurricane IIC** (Jan 43)
Sep 42 **Boston III** (Jan 43)
det Hibaldstow
9 Nov 42 to Hibaldstow
25 Jan 43 DB

533 Sqn

8 Sep 42 F @ Charmy Down — No 1454 Flt redesignated
Sep 42 **Havoc I (Turbinlite)** (Sep 42)
Sep 42 **Havoc II (Turbinlite)** (Jan 43)
Sep 42 **Boston III (Turbinlite)** (Jan 43)
Sep 42 **Hurricane IIB** (Jan 43)
Sep 42 **Hurricane IIC** (Jan 43)
Sep 42 **Havoc I** (Jan 43)
25 Jan 43 DB

534 Sqn

2 Sep 42 F @ Tangmere — No 1455 Flt redesignated
Sep 42 **Havoc I (Turbinlite)** (Jan 43)
Sep 42 **Havoc II (Turbinlite)** (Jan 43)
Sep 42 **Boston III (Turbinlite)** (Jan 43)
Sep 42 **Hurricane IIC** (Jan 43)
Sep 42 **Boston I** (Jan 43)
25 Jan 43 DB

535 Sqn

2 Sep 42 F @ High Ercall — No 1456 Flt redesignated
Sep 42 **Havoc I (Turbinlite)** (Sep 42)
Sep 42 **Havoc II (Turbinlite)** (Jan 43)
Sep 42 **Boston III (Turbinlite)** (Jan 43)
Sep 42 **Hurricane IIC** (Jan 43)
25 Jan 43 DB

536 Sqn

8 Sep 42 F @ Predannack — No 1457 Flt redesignated
Sep 42 **Havoc II (Turbinlite)** (Jan 43)
Sep 42 **Hurricane IIC** (Jan 43)
27 Oct 42 to Fairwood Common
det Exeter
25 Jan 43 DB

537 Sqn

8 Sep 42 F @ Middle Wallop — No 1458 Flt redesignated
Sep 42 **Havoc I (Turbinlite)** (Jan 43)
Sep 42 **Boston III (Turbinlite)** (Jan 43)
Sep 42 **Hurricane IIB** (Jan 43)
Sep 42 **Hurricane IIC** (Jan 43)
Sep 42 **Havoc I** (Jan 43)
25 Jan 43

538 Sqn

2 Sep 42 F @ Hibaldstow — No 1459 Flt redesignated
Sep 42 **Havoc I (Turbinlite)** (Jan 43)
Sep 42 **Havoc II (Turbinlite)** (Jan 43)
Sep 42 **Boston III (Turbinlite)** (Jan 43)
Sep 42 **Hurricane I** (Jan 43)
Sep 42 **Hurricane IIC** (Jan 43)
25 Jan 43 DB

539 Sqn

2 Sep 42 F @ Acklington — No 1460 Flt redesignated
Sep 42 **Havoc I (Turbinlite)** (Jan 43)
Sep 42 **Havoc II (Turbinlite)** (Jan 43)
Sep 42 **Boston III (Turbinlite)** (Jan 43)
Sep 42 **Hurricane IIC** (Jan 43)
Sep 42 **Boston I** (Jan 43)
25 Jan 43 DB

540 Sqn

19 Oct 42 F @ Leuchars — from 'H' & 'L' Flts, No 1 PF
dets Benson, Gibraltar
Oct 42 **Spitfire IV** (Dec 42)
Oct 42 **Mosquito I** (May 43)
Oct 42 **Mosquito IV** (Aug 43)
Dec 42 **Mosquito VIII** (Aug 43
Jul 43 **Mosquito IX** (Mar 45)
29 Feb 44 to Benson
dets Gibraltar, Dyce, Yagodnik
May 44 **Mosquito XVI** (Dec 45
Nov 44 **Mosquito VI** (Jun 45)
Nov 44 **Mosquito XXXII** (Aug 45)
29 Mar 45 to Coulommiers
det Trondheim
23 Sep 45 to Mount Farm
det Trondheim
Nov 45 **Mosquito XXXIV** (Oct 46)
6 Nov 45 to Benson
1 Oct 46 DB — renumbered as 58 Sqn
—
1 Dec 47 RF @ Benson — from Mosquito element of 58 Sqn
Dec 47 **Mosquito PR 34** (Oct
Apr 51 **Mosquito PR 34A** (Sep 53)
Dec 52 **Canberra PR 3** (Oct
26 Mar 53 to Wyton
Jun 53 **Canberra B.2** (Sep 54
Jun 54 **Canberra PR 7** (Mar
31 Mar 56 DB

541 Sqn

19 Oct 42 F @ Benson — from 'B' & 'F' Flts, No 1 F
Oct 42 **Spitfire D** (Jan 43)
Oct 42 **Spitfire IV** (Sep 44)

Nov 42 **Spitfire IX** (Dec 42)
Dec 42 **Spitfire XI** (Mar 46) dets St Eval, Gibraltar
May 44 **Spitfire X** (Apr 45)
Jun 44 **Spitfire XIX** (Oct 46)
Jul 44 **Mustang III** (Jun 45) det Coulommiers
Oct 45 **Meteor F.3** (Apr 46)
Feb 46 **Lancaster PR 1** (Oct 46) dets Yundum, Takoradi, Kano, Accra
Oct 46 DB — renumbered as No 82 Sqn
—
Nov 47 RF @ Benson — from Spitfire element of No 82 Sqn
Nov 47 **Spitfire PR 19** (May 51)
Dec 50 **Meteor PR 10** (Sep 57)
Jun 51 to Bückeburg
Apr 52 to Gütersloh
Jul 54 to Bückeburg
Sep 54 to Gütersloh
Nov 54 to Laarbruch
Nov 55 to Wunstorf
Sep 57 DB

542 Sqn

Oct 42 F @ Benson — from 'A' & 'E' Flts, No 1 PRU
Oct 42 **Spitfire IV** (Jul 43)
Mar 43 **Spitfire XI** (Aug 45)
May 44 **Spitfire X** (Aug 45)
Jun 44 **Spitfire XIX** (Aug 45)
Aug 45 DB
—
May 54 RF @ Wyton
May 54 **Canberra PR 7** (Oct 55)
Oct 55 DB
—
Nov 55 RF @ Wyton — No 1323 Flt renumbered
Nov 55 **Canberra B.2** (Oct 58)
Nov 55 **Canberra B.6** (Oct 58)
Dec 55 to Weston Zoyland dets Darwin, Edinburgh Field, Laverton
Mar 57 to Hemswell
Jul 58 to Upwood
Oct 58 DB — renumbered as No 21 Sqn

543 Sqn

Oct 42 F @ Benson — from elements of No 1 PRU
Oct 42 **Spitfire IV** (Oct 43) dets St Eval, Mount Farm, Vaenga
Apr 43 **Spitfire XI** (Oct 43)
Oct 43 DB
—
Apr 55 RF @ Gaydon
Jun 55 **Valiant B(PR) 1** (Dec 64)
Nov 55 to Wyton
Feb 65 **Valiant B(PR)K 1** (Dec 64)
May 65 **Victor B.2(SR)** (May 74)
May 74 DB

544 Sqn

Oct 42 F @ Benson — from elements of No 1 PRU
Oct 42 **Anson I** (Mar 43)
Oct 42 **Maryland I** (Mar 43)
Oct 42 **Wellington IV** (Mar 43)
Oct 42 **Spitfire IV** (Oct 43) dets Gibraltar, Merrakesh, Agadir, Leuchars
Mar 43 **Mosquito IV** (Oct 43)
Aug 43 **Spitfire XI** (Oct 43)
Aug 43 **Mosquito IX** (Feb 45)
Mar 44 **Mosquito XVI** (Aug 45)
Oct 44 **Mosquito XXXII** (Oct 45)
Apr 45 **Mosquito XXXIV** (Oct 45)
13 Oct 45 DB

547 Sqn

22 Oct 42 F @ Holmsley South
Oct 42 **Wellington VIII** (May 43)
10 Dec 42 to Chivenor
22 Jan 43 to Tain
2 Apr 43 to Chivenor det Tain
May 43 **Wellington XI** (Nov 43)
31 May 43 to Davidstow Moor
25 Oct 43 to Thorney Island
Oct 43 **Wellington XIII** (Nov 43) det Aldergrove
Nov 43 **Liberator V** (Oct 44)
14 Jan 44 to St Eval
Aug 44 **Liberator VI** (May 45)
1 Oct 44 to Leuchars
Mar 45 **Liberator VIII** (Jun 45)
4 Jun 45 DB

548 Sqn

15 Dec 43 F @ Lawntown
19 Jan 44 to Strathpine
Apr 44 **Spitfire VIII** (Sep 45)
28 May 44 to Amberley
15 Jun 44 to Livingstone det Truscott
22 Oct 44 to Darwin/Civil det Truscott
23 Sep 45 to Melbourne (No 1 PD)
31 Oct 45 DB

549 Sqn

15 Dec 43 F @ Lawntown
1 Jan 44 to Strathpine
Apr 44 **Spitfire VIII** (Sep 45)
24 May 44 to Amberley
16 Jun 44 to Strauss det Truscott
23 Oct 44 to Darwin/Civil det Truscott
23 Sep 45 to Melbourne (No 1 PD)
31 Oct 45 DB

550 Sqn

25 Nov 43 F @ Waltham — from 'C' Flt, No 100 Sqn
Nov 43 **Lancaster I & III** (Oct 45)
3 Jan 44 to North Killingholme
1 Nov 45 DB

567 Sqn

1 Dec 43 F @ Detling — from No 1624 Flt det Eastchurch
Dec 43 **Barracuda II** (Jul 44)
Dec 43 **Martinet** (Apr 45)
Dec 43 **Hurricane IV** (Aug 45)
Dec 43 **Oxford** (Jun 46)
14 Nov 44 to Hornchurch dets Hawkinge, Lympne, Eastchurch
Jan 45 **Vengeance IV** (Jun 46)
Jun 45 **Spitfire VB** (Sep 45)
13 Jun 45 to Hawkinge
Jul 45 **Spitfire XVI** (Jun 46)
21 Aug 45 to Manston det Eastchurch
26 Apr 46 to West Malling
15 Jun 46 DB

569 Sqn

No 46 Gp, which was formed on 17 Jan 44, was created as a Transport Support Force and was initially intended to have five squadrons at three new bases (Down Ampney, Blakehill Farm and Broadwell). The squadrons were to be Nos 271 and 512, redeployed from 'airline' operations, and three new units to be designated Nos 569, 575 and 597 Sqns. It was planned to retrain and expand the two existing squadrons and split off nucleii from these to form the new units. In the event only one of the new numbers (No 575) was taken up, the other two units being provided by transferring the existing Nos 48 and 233 Sqns from Coastal Command. The Nos 567 and 597 numberplates, which had been allocated on 10 Jan 44, were withdrawn on 1 Mar 44 without ever having taken on any substantial form although some personnel under training with No 512 Sqn at Hendon had been earmarked for No 569 Sqn.

570 Sqn

15 Nov 43 F @ Hurn
Nov 43 **Albemarle I** (Aug 44)
Nov 43 **Albemarle II** (Aug 44)
14 Mar 44 to Harwell
May 44 **Albemarle V** (Aug 44)
Jul 44 **Stirling IV** (Dec 45)
8 Oct 44 to Rivenhall
28 Dec 45 DB

571 Sqn

5 Apr 44 F @ Downham Market
Apr 44 **Mosquito XVI** (Sep 45) det Graveley
24 Apr 44 to Oakington
20 Jul 45 to Warboys
20 Sep 45 DB

575 Sqn

1 Feb 44 F @ Hendon — nucleus from No 512 Sqn
Feb 44 **Dakota** (Aug 46)
14 Feb 44 to Broadwell det B 56/Evere
6 Aug 45 to Melbourne
24 Nov 45 to Blakehill Farm
31 Jan 46 to Bari
26 Jul 46 to Kabrit
15 Aug 46 DB

576 Sqn

25 Nov 43 F @ Elsham Wolds — from 'C' Flt, No 103 Sqn
Nov 43 **Lancaster I & III** (Sep 45)
31 Oct 44 to Fiskerton
19 Sep 45 DB

577 Sqn

1 Dec 43 F @ Castle Bromwich — from elements of Nos 6, 7 & 8 AACUs dets Wrexham, Sealand, Montford Bridge, Shobdon, Bodorgan, Ipswich, Mona, Fairwood Common, Woodvale, Atcham, Barrow-in-Furness, Hawarden at various times
Dec 43 **Hurricane IV** (Jul 45)
Dec 43 **Oxford** (Jun 46)
May 44 **Hurricane IIC** (Jul 45)
Nov 44 **Beaufighter I** (Jul 45)
Jun 45 **Spitfire VB** (Aug 45)
Jun 45 **Spitfire XVI** (Jun 46)
Jul 45 **Vengeance IV** (Jun 46)
15 Jun 46 DB

578 Sqn

14 Jan 44 F @ Snaith — from 'C' Flt, No 51 Sqn
Jan 44 **Halifax III** (Mar 45)
6 Feb 44 to Burn
15 Apr 45 DB

582 Sqn

1 Apr 44 F @ Little Staughton — from 'C' Flts of Nos 7 & 156 Sqns
Apr 44 **Lancaster I & III** (Sep 45)
10 Sep 45 DB

586 Sqn

No 586 Sqn was conceived as the British element of a joint USAAF/RAF electronic warfare force. Its formation, with Fortress IIs, was authorised with effect from 10 Dec 43, however, at that date no location for the unit had been nominated. In the event it was decided to employ No 214 Sqn in the role and No 586 Sqn's formation was cancelled on 30 Dec 43 without its ever having taken on any tangible form.

587 Sqn

1 Dec 43 F @ Weston Zoyland — from Nos 1600, 1601 & 1625 Flts
Dec 43 **Oxford** (Feb 44)
Dec 43 **Henley III** (May 44)
Dec 43 **Hurricane IV** (Jun 45)
Dec 43 **Martinet** (Aug 45)
Mar 44 **Hurricane IIC** (Jun 45)
10 Apr 44 to Culmhead dets Pengam Moors, Colerne, Carew Cheriton
1 Oct 44 to Weston Zoyland dets Middle Wallop, Ibsley
Oct 44 **Vengeance IV** (Jun 46)
Apr 45 **Mustang I** (May 45)
Jul 45 **Spitfire XVI** (Jun 46)
1 Jun 46 to Tangmere
15 Jun 46 DB

595 Sqn

1 Dec 43 F @ Aberporth — from Nos 1607, 1608 & 1609 Flts dets Manorbier, Fairwood Common, Poulton, Wrexham, Brawdy at various times
Dec 43 **Henley III** (Jun 44)
Dec 43 **Hurricane IIC** (Jul 44)
Dec 43 **Martinet** (Feb 49)
Apr 44 **Oxford** (Feb 49)
Jun 44 **Hurricane IV** (Mar 45)
Nov 44 **Vengeance IV** (Jul 45)
Dec 44 **Spitfire VB** (45)
Dec 44 **Spitfire XII** (Jul 45)

Jul 45 **Spitfire IX** (48)
Sep 45 **Spitfire XVI** (Feb 49)
27 Apr 46 to Fairwood Common
22 Oct 46 to Pembrey
Dec 46 **Vampire F.1** (Oct 48)
Jun 48 **Spitfire F.21** (Feb 49)
11 Feb 49 DB — renumbered as No 5 Sqn

597 Sqn

See No 569 Sqn

598 Sqn

1 Dec 43 F @ Peterhead — from Nos 1479 & 1632 Flts and No 289 Sqn det
dets Longman, Skaebrae, Sumburgh, Montrose, Turnhouse
Dec 43 **Lysander IIIA** (Jan 44)
Dec 43 **Oxford** (Apr 45)
Dec 43 **Martinet** (Apr 45)
Feb 44 **Hurricane IV** (Apr 45)
Jun 44 **Hurricane IIC** (Apr 45)
12 Mar 45 to Bircham Newton
dets Lympne, Peterhead, Hutton Cranswick
Apr 45 **Beaufighter I** (Apr 45)
30 Apr 45 DB

600 Sqn

14 Oct 25 F @ Northolt
Oct 25 **DH 9A** (Oct 29)
18 Jan 27 to Hendon
Aug 29 **Wapiti** (Jan 35)
Jan 35 **Hart** (May 37)
Feb 37 **Demon** (Apr 39)
1 Oct 38 to Kenley
4 Oct 38 to Hendon
Jan 39 **Blenheim IF** (Oct 41)
25 Aug 39 to Northolt
2 Oct 39 to Hornchurch
16 Oct 39 to Rochford
20 Oct 39 to Hornchurch
det Manston
Nov 39 **Blenheim IV** (Jun 40)
27 Dec 39 to Manston
14 May 40 to Northolt
20 Jun 40 to Manston
24 Aug 40 to Hornchurch
Sep 40 **Beaufighter IF** (Jun 41)
12 Sep 40 to Redhill
12 Oct 40 to Catterick
dets Drem, Acklington, Prestwick
14 Mar 41 to Drem
dets Prestwick
27 Apr 41 to Colerne
Apr 41 **Beaufighter IIF** (Apr 42)
18 Jun 41 to Fairwood Common
det Predannack
27 Jun 41 to Colerne
det Predannack
6 Oct 41 to Predannack
Mar 42 **Beaufighter VIF** (Feb 45)
2 Sep 42 to Church Fenton
18 Nov 42 to Blida
7 Dec 42 to Maison Blanche
10 Jan 43 to Setif
dets Souk el Khemis ('Paddington'), Bone, Tingley, Monastir
25 Jun 43 to Luqa
26 Jul 43 to Cassibile
30 Sep 43 to Montecorvino
dets Brindisi, Tortorella, Gaudo, Lago
2 Feb 44 to Marcianese
22 Mar 44 to Pomigliano
1 Apr 44 to Marcianese
13 Jun 44 to La Banca
19 Jun 44 to Voltone
5 Jul 44 to Follonica
29 Jul 44 to Rosignano
det Falconara
25 Aug 44 to Falconara
dets Rosignano, Iesi, Bellaria
15 Dec 44 to Cesenatico
Dec 44 **Mosquito XIX** (Aug 45)
24 May 45 to Campoformido
26 Jul 45 to Aviano
21 Aug 45 DB
—
10 May 46 RF @ Biggin Hill
6 Jun 46 embodied
Oct 46 **Spitfire F.14** (Nov 47)
Apr 47 **Spitfire F.21** (Nov 50)
Sep 48 **Spitfire F.22** (Mar 50)
Mar 50 **Meteor F.4** (Apr 52)
Nov 51 **Meteor F.8** (Mar 57)
10 Mar 57 DB

601 Sqn

14 Oct 25 F @ Northolt
Jun 26 **DH 9A** (Oct 30)
18 Jan 27 to Hendon
Nov 29 **Wapiti** (Jun 33)
Feb 33 **Hart** (Aug 37)
Aug 37 **Demon** (Dec 38)
Dec 38 **Gauntlet II** (Mar 39)
Jan 39 **Blenheim IF** (Feb 40)
2 Sep 39 to Biggin Hill
30 Dec 39 to Tangmere
Feb 40 **Hurricane I** (Mar 41)
dets Merville, St-Valéry
1 Jun 40 to Middle Wallop
17 Jun 40 to Tangmere
19 Aug 40 to Debden
2 Sep 40 to Tangmere
7 Sep 40 to Exeter
17 Dec 40 to Northolt
Mar 41 **Hurricane IIB** (Jan 42)
1 May 41 to Manston
30 Jun 41 to Matlask
Aug 41 **Airacobra I** (Mar 42)
16 Aug 41 to Duxford
6 Jan 42 to Acaster Malbis
Mar 42 **Spitfire VB** (Apr 42)
25 Mar 42 to Digby
10 Apr 42 en route Egypt
20 Apr 42 aircrew to Luqa via USS *Wasp*
May 42 **Spitfire VC** (Jan 44)
23 Jun 42 sqn re-united at Maryut
25 Jun 42 to LG 13
29 Jun 42 to LG 154
24 Jul 42 to LG 173
29 Jul 42 to LG 85
5 Aug 42 to LG 219
11 Aug 42 to Helwan
22 Aug 42 to LG 154
26 Sep 42 to LG 92
7 Nov 42 to LG 21
9 Nov 42 to LG 13
12 Nov 42 to LG 155
14 Nov 42 to Gambut West
25 Nov 42 to Msus
4 Dec 42 to El Hassiet
8 Dec 42 to El Nogra
21 Dec 42 to El Merduma
31 Dec 42 to El Chel
9 Jan 43 to Hamraiet
20 Jan 43 to Darragh North
17 Feb 43 to Castel Benito
26 Feb 43 to Hazbub Main
1 Mar 43 to Ben Gardane South
9 Mar 43 to Hazbub North
11 Mar 43 to Bu Grara
det El Hamma
4 Apr 43 to Gabes Main
12 Apr 43 to La Fauconnerie
16 Apr 43 to Goubrine
7 May 43 to Hergla North
21 May 43 to Ben Gardane
15 Jun 43 to Luqa
Jun 43 **Spitfire IX** (Aug 43)
13 Jul 43 to Pachino
17 Jul 43 to Cassibile
25 Jul 43 to Lentini West
Jul 43 **Spitfire VIII** (Jun 44)
5 Oct 43 to Tortorella
18 Oct 43 to Triolo
26 Nov 43 to Canne
18 Jan 44 to Marcianese
det Madna
23 Apr 44 to Venafro
Jun 44 **Spitfire IXB** (Aug 45)
12 Jun 44 to Littorio
17 Jun 44 to Fabrica
3 Jul 44 to Perugia
24 Aug 44 to Loreto
4 Sep 44 to Fano
4 Dec 44 to Bellaria
3 May 45 to Treviso
14 Aug 45 DB
—
10 May 46 RF @ Hendon
27 Jun 46 embodied
Oct 46 **Spitfire LF 16E** (Jan 50)
27 Mar 49 to North Weald
Nov 49 **Vampire F.3** (Sep 52)
Aug 52 **Meteor F.8** (Mar 57)
10 Mar 57 DB

602 Sqn

12 Sep 25 F @ Renfrew
Oct 25 **DH 9A** (Jan 28)
Sep 27 **Fawn** (Oct 29)
Jul 29 **Wapiti** (Apr 34)
20 Jan 33 to Abbotsinch
Feb 34 **Hart** (Jun 36)
Jun 36 **Hind** (Nov 38)
Nov 38 **Hector** (Jan 39)
Jan 39 **Gauntlet II** (May 39)
May 39 **Spitfire I** (Jun 41)
7 Oct 39 to Grangemouth
13 Oct 39 to Drem
14 Apr 40 to Dyce
det Montrose
22 May 40 to Drem
13 Aug 40 to Westhampnett
17 Dec 40 to Prestwick
15 Apr 41 to Ayr
det Montrose
May 41 **Spitfire IIA** (Aug 41)
10 Jul 41 to Kenley
Jul 41 **Spitfire VB** (Sep 42)
14 Jan 42 to Redhill
dets Kenley
4 Mar 42 to Kenley
13 May 42 to Redhill
dets Kenley
17 Jul 42 to Peterhead
16 Aug 42 to Biggin Hill
20 Aug 42 to Peterhead
10 Sep 42 to Skaebrae
det Sumburgh
Sep 42 **Spitfire VA** (Oct 42)
Sep 42 **Spitfire VI** (Nov 42)
Oct 42 **Spitfire VC** (Apr 43)
20 Jan 43 to Perranporth
Jan 43 **Spitfire VB** (Oct 43)
14 Apr 43 to Lasham
29 Apr 43 to Fairlop
1 Jun 43 to Bognor
1 Jul 43 to Kingsnorth
13 Aug 43 to Newchurch
Oct 43 **Spitfire IXB** (Jan 44)
12 Oct 43 to Detling
17 Jan 44 to Skaebrae
Jan 44 **Spitfire LF VB** (Mar 44)
12 Mar 44 to Detling
13 Mar 44 to Llanbedr
20 Mar 44 to Detling
Mar 44 **Spitfire IXB** (Aug 44)
18 Apr 44 to Ford
25 Jun 44 to B 11/Longues
Aug 44 **Spitfire IXE** (Sep 44)
13 Aug 44 to B 19/Lingèvres
2 Sep 44 to B 40/Beauvais/Nivillers
5 Sep 44 to B 52/Douai
17 Sep 44 to B 70/Deurne
30 Sep 44 to Coltishall
Sep 44 **Spitfire IXB** (Nov 44)
18 Oct 44 to Matlask
Nov 44 **Spitfire XVI** (May 45)
20 Nov 44 to Swannington
19 Feb 45 to Coltishall
23 Feb 45 to Ludham
5 Apr 45 to Coltishall
15 May 45 DB
—
10 May 46 RF @ Abbotsinch
11 Jun 46 embodied
Oct 46 **Spitfire F.14** (Oct 48)
Aug 47 **Spitfire F.21** (Jan 51)
Oct 48 **Spitfire F.22** (May 51)
Jan 51 **Vampire FB 5** (Mar 57)
15 Apr 51 to Leuchars
13 Jul 51 to Abbotsinch
15 Apr 52 to Renfrew
18 Jun 54 to Abbotsinch
10 Mar 57 DB

603 Sqn

14 Oct 25 F @ Turnhouse
Oct 25 **DH 9A** (May 30)
Mar 30 **Wapiti** (Mar 34)
Feb 34 **Hart** (Feb 38)
Feb 38 **Hind** (Mar 39)
Mar 39 **Gladiator II** (Oct 39)
Sep 39 **Spitfire I** (Nov 40)
16 Dec 39 to Prestwick
17 Jan 40 to Dyce
det Montrose
14 Apr 40 to Drem
5 May 40 to Turnhouse
dets Montrose, Dyce
28 Aug 40 to Hornchurch
Oct 40 **Spitfire IIA** (May 41)
3 Dec 40 to Southend
13 Dec 40 to Drem
27 Feb 41 to Turnhouse
16 May 41 to Hornchurch
May 41 **Spitfire VA** (Dec 41)
16 Jun 41 to Southend
9 Jul 41 to Hornchurch
Aug 41 **Spitfire VB** (Mar 42)
12 Nov 41 to Fairlop
15 Dec 41 to Dyce
14 Mar 42 to Peterhead
13 Apr 42 ground echelon en rou
Egypt
20 Apr 42 air echelon to Ta Kali
USS *Wasp*
Apr 42 **Spitfire VC** (Aug 42)
3 Aug 42 air echelon at Ta Kali renumbered as No 229 Sqn
4 Jun 42 ground echelon to Kasfareet
28 Jun 42 to Nicosia
dets Lakatamia, Paphc
21 Dec 42 to Aboukir (No 24 PT
25 Jan 43 to Idku
Feb 43 **Beaufighter IC** (Nov 4
Feb 43 **Beaufighter VIC** (Oct
dets Berka III
27 Mar 43 to Misurata West
dets Berka III, El Magrun
Aug 43 **Beaufighter XI** (Oct 43
6 Sep 43 to Bo Rizzo
4 Oct 43 to LG 91
Oct 43 **Beaufighter X** (Dec 44
18 Oct 43 to Gambut 3
det El Adem
Dec 44 en route UK via Port Said
26 Dec 44 DB
—
10 Jan 45 RF @ Coltishall — No 229 Sqn renumber
Jan 45 **Spitfire LF XVIE** (Aug 45)
24 Feb 45 to Ludham
5 Apr 45 to Coltishall
28 Apr 45 to Turnhouse
7 May 45 to Drem
14 Jun 45 to Skaebrae

8 Jul 45 to Turnhouse
5 Aug 45 DB
—
0 May 46 RF @ Turnhouse
1 Jun 46 embodied
Oct 46 **Spitfire LF 16E** (Jun 48)
Feb 48 **Spitfire F.22** (Jul 51)
May 51 **Vampire FB 5** (Feb 57)
6 Jul 51 to Leuchars
4 Oct 51 to Turnhouse
0 Mar 57 DB

604 Sqn

7 Mar 30 F @ Hendon
Apr 30 **DH 9A** (Oct 30)
Sep 30 **Wapiti** (34)
Sep 34 **Hart** (Jun 35)
Jun 35 **Demon** (Jan 39)
Jan 39 **Blenheim I** (May 41)
2 Sep 39 to North Weald
det Martlesham Heath
5 Jan 40 to Northolt
May 40 **Gladiator I** (May 40)
5 May 40 to Manston
) Jun 40 to Northolt
3 Jul 40 to Gravesend
7 Jul 40 to Middle Wallop
Sep 40 **Beaufighter IF** (Apr 43)
det Coltishall
Aug 42 to Warmwell
Aug 42 to Middle Wallop
Dec 42 to Predannack
Feb 43 to Ford
Apr 43 to Scorton
Apr 43 **Beaufighter VIF** (Apr 44)
Feb 44 **Mosquito XIII** (Apr 45)
Mar 44 **Mosquito XII** (May 44)
Apr 44 to Church Fenton
May 44 to Hurn
Jul 44 to Colerne
Jul 44 to Zeals
Jul 44 to Colerne
det A 15/Maupertus
Aug 44 to A 8/Picauville
Sep 44 to B 17/Carpiquet
Sep 44 to Predannack
Dec 44 to Odiham
Dec 44 to B 51/Lille/Vendeville
Apr 45 DB
—
May 46 RF @ Hendon
Jun 46 embodied
Oct 46 **Spitfire LF 16E** (May 50)
Mar 49 to North Weald
Nov 49 **Vampire F.3** (Aug 52)
Aug 52 **Meteor F.8** (Mar 57)
Mar 57 DB

605 Sqn

Oct 26 F @ Castle Bromwich
Oct 26 **DH 9A** (Jul 30)
Apr 30 **Wapiti** (Nov 34)
Feb 34 **Hart** (Sep 36)
Aug 36 **Hind** (Jan 39)
Apr 39 **Gladiator I** (Nov 39)
Jun 39 **Hurricane I** (Dec 40)
Aug 39 to Tangmere
Feb 40 to Leuchars
Feb 40 to Wick
May 40 to Hawkinge
May 40 to Drem
Sep 40 to Croydon
Nov 40 **Hurricane IIA** (Sep 41)
Feb 41 to Martlesham Heath
Mar 41 to Ternhill
May 41 to Baginton
Aug 41 **Hurricane IIB** (Mar 42)
Sep 41 to Honiley
Nov 41 en route FE via HMS *Argus*
—
Nov 41 majority of pilots diverted to Malta via HMS *Argus* & HMS *Ark Royal*

7 Jan 42 established at Hal Far
dets Luqa, Ta Kali
17 Mar 42 DB — absorbed by No 185 Sqn
—
27 Jan 42 to P I (groundcrew and remainder of pilots — operated with No 242/ '232(I)' Sqn)
det Seletar
14 Feb 42 to P II
18 Feb 42 to Tjilitjan
28 Feb 42 DB — absorbed by No 242 Sqn
—
7 Jun 42 RF @ Ford
Jul 42 **Havoc I** (Aug 42)
Jul 42 **Havoc II** (Aug 42)
Jul 42 **Boston III** (Feb 43)
det Hunsdon
Feb 43 **Mosquito II** (Jul 43)
15 Mar 43 to Castle Camps
Jul 43 **Mosquito VI** (Aug 45)
6 Oct 43 to Bradwell Bay
7 Apr 44 to Manston
21 Nov 44 to Blackbushe
15 Mar 45 to B 71/Coxyde
25 Apr 45 to B 80/Volkel
det Fersfield
31 Aug 45 DB — renumbered as No 4 Sqn
—
10 May 46 RF @ Honiley
11 Jun 46 embodied
May 47 **Mosquito NF 30** (Sep 48)
Jul 48 **Vampire F.1** (May 51)
Feb 50 **Vampire F.3** (Oct 52)
Apr 51 **Vampire FB 5** (Mar 57)
10 Mar 57 DB

607 Sqn

17 Mar 30 F @ Usworth
Dec 32 **Wapiti** (Jan 37)
Sep 36 **Demon** (Aug 39)
Dec 38 **Gladiator I** (May 40)
10 Oct 39 to Acklington
det Drem
14 Nov 39 to Croydon
15 Nov 39 to Merville
13 Dec 39 to Vitry-en-Artois
dets Abbeville, St-Inglevert
Mar 40 **Hurricane I** (May 40)
12 Apr 40 to Abbeville
26 Apr 40 to Vitry-en-Artois
18 May 40 to Labuissière
22 May 40 to Croydon
4 Jun 40 to Usworth
Jun 40 **Hurricane I** (Sep 41)
1 Sep 40 to Tangmere
10 Oct 40 to Turnhouse
8 Nov 40 to Drem
12 Dec 40 to Usworth
16 Jan 41 to Macmerry
2 Mar 41 to Drem
16 Apr 41 to Skitten
Jun 41 **Hurricane IIA** (Nov 41)
Jul 41 **Hurricane IIB** (Mar 42)
27 Jul 41 to Castletown
20 Aug 41 to Martlesham Heath
10 Oct 41 to Manston
20 Mar 42 en route India
25 May 42 to Alipore
Jun 42 **Hurricane IIC** (Feb 43)
23 Aug 42 to Jessore
16 Dec 42 to Feni
24 Jan 43 to Chittagong
Feb 43 **Hurricane IIB** (Sep 43)
2 Apr 43 to Alipore
Sep 43 **Spitfire VC** (Mar 44)
1 Oct 43 to Amarda Road
16 Oct 43 to Alipore
30 Nov 43 to Ramu
25 Feb 44 to Nidania
21 Mar 44 to Rumkha
Mar 44 **Spitfire VIII** (Aug 45)
17 Apr 44 to Wangjing
27 Apr 44 to Imphal

6 Jul 44 to Baigachi
24 Nov 44 to Sapam
11 Dec 44 to Tulihal
16 Jan 45 to Tabingaung
5 Apr 45 to Dwelha
19 Apr 45 to Kwetnge
28 Apr 45 to Kalaywa
8 May 45 to Thedaw
det 'Tennant'
14 May 45 to Mingaladon
19 Aug 45 DB
—
10 May 46 RF @ Ouston
11 Jun 46 embodied
Nov 46 **Spitfire FR 14** (Mar 49)
Jan 49 **Spitfire F.22** (Jun 51)
Mar 51 **Vampire FB 5** (Mar 57)
10 Mar 57 DB

608 Sqn

17 Mar 30 F @ Thornaby
Jun 30 **Wapiti** (Jan 37)
Jan 37 **Demon** (Mar 39)
Mar 39 **Anson I** (May 41)
Jun 40 **Botha I** (Nov 40)
Feb 41 **Blenheim I** (Aug 41)
Mar 41 **Blenheim IV** (Sep 41)
Jul 41 **Hudson V** (Jul 44)
Aug 41 **Hudson III** (Aug 42)
2 Jan 42 to Wick
det Skitten
29 Jul 42 to Sumburgh
Jul 42 **Hudson IIIA** (Aug 42)
27 Aug 42 to Gosport
9 Nov 42 to Gibraltar
18 Dec 42 to Blida
det Bone
Mar 43 **Hudson VI** (Jul 44)
6 Aug 43 to Protville
2 Sep 43 to Augusta
4 Sep 43 to Bo Rizzo
det Grottaglie, Montecorvino
17 Nov 43 to Montecorvino
dets Grottaglie, Gaudo
Dec 43 **Hudson IIIA** (Jul 44)
4 Jan 44 to Grottaglie
dets Gaudo, Montecorvino
17 Feb 44 to Montecorvino
det Bo Rizzo
24 Jun 44 to Pomigliano
22 Jul 44 DB
—
1 Aug 44 RF @ Downham Market
Aug 44 **Mosquito XX** (Apr 45)
Oct 44 **Mosquito XXV** (Apr 45)
Mar 45 **Mosquito XVI** (Aug 45)
24 Aug 45 DB
—
10 May 46 RF @ Thornaby
12 Jun 46 embodied
Jul 47 **Mosquito NF 30** (Jun 48)
May 48 **Spitfire F.22** (Jan 51)
May 50 **Vampire F.3** (Jul 52)
Apr 52 **Vampire FB 5** (Mar 57)
Apr 51 **Vampire F.1** (Jun 51)
Apr 56 **Vampire FB 9** (Feb 57)
10 Mar 57 DB

609 Sqn

10 Feb 36 F @ Yeadon
May 36 **Hart** (Jan 38)
Jan 38 **Hind** (Aug 39)
Aug 39 **Spitfire I** (May 41)
27 Aug 39 to Catterick
7 Oct 39 to Acklington
17 Oct 39 to Drem
5 Dec 39 to Kinloss
10 Jan 40 to Drem
20 May 40 to Northolt
6 Jul 40 to Middle Wallop
2 Oct 40 to Warmwell
24 Feb 41 to Biggin Hill
Feb 41 **Spitfire IIA** (Jun 41)

Jun 41 **Spitfire VB** (May 42)
28 Jul 41 to Gravesend
24 Sep 41 to Biggin Hill
19 Nov 41 to Digby
30 Mar 42 to Duxford
Apr 42 **Typhoon IA** (42)
42 **Typhoon IB** (Sep 45)
26 Aug 42 to Bourn
30 Aug 42 to Duxford
18 Sep 42 to Biggin Hill
2 Nov 42 to Manston
22 Jul 43 to Matlask
18 Aug 43 to Lympne
14 Dec 43 to Manston
6 Feb 44 to Fairwood Common
20 Feb 44 to Manston
16 Mar 44 to Tangmere
21 Mar 44 to Acklington
1 Apr 44 to Thorney Island
22 Apr 44 to Llanbedr
30 Apr 44 to Thorney Island
18 Jun 44 to Funtington
1 Jul 44 to B 10/Plumetot
det Hurn
9 Jul 44 to B 5/Camilly
19 Jul 44 to B 7/Martragny
3 Sep 44 to B 23/Morainville
6 Sep 44 to B 35/Godelmesnil
det Manston
11 Sep 44 to B 53/Merville
30 Oct 44 to B 67/Ursel
26 Nov 44 to B 77/Gilze-Rijen
31 Dec 44 to A 84/Chièvres
19 Jan 45 to B 77/Gilze-Rijen
21 Mar 45 to B 91/Kluis
17 Apr 45 to B 103/Plantlunne
27 May 45 to B 116/Wunstorf
2 Jun 45 to Lasham
4 Jun 45 to Fairwood Common
23 Jun 45 to B 116/Wunstorf
15 Sep 45 DB
—
10 May 46 RF @ Church Fenton
11 Jun 46 embodied
5 Nov 46 to Yeadon
Apr 47 **Mosquito NF 30** (Sep 48)
Apr 48 **Spitfire LF 16E** (Feb 51)
18 Oct 50 to Church Fenton
Nov 50 **Vampire FB 5** (Jan 51)
Jan 51 **Meteor F.4** (Jul 51)
Jun 51 **Meteor F.8** (Mar 57)
10 Mar 57 DB

610 Sqn

10 Feb 36 F @ Hendon
16 Apr 36 to Hooton Park
May 36 **Hart** (May 38)
May 38 **Hind** (Sep 39)
Sep 39 **Hurricane I** (Sep 39)
Sep 39 **Spitfire I** (Feb 41)
10 Oct 39 to Wittering
4 Apr 40 to Prestwick
10 May 40 to Biggin Hill
27 May 40 to Gravesend
8 Jul 40 to Biggin Hill
31 Aug 40 to Acklington
15 Dec 40 to Westhampnett
Feb 41 **Spitfire IIA** (Nov 41)
Jul 41 **Spitfire VB** (Aug 41)
29 Aug 41 to Leconfield
Nov 41 **Spitfire VB** (Mar 44)
14 Jan 42 to Hutton Cranswick
4 Apr 42 to Ludham
16 Aug 42 to West Malling
21 Aug 42 to Ludham
Aug 42 **Spitfire VC** (Oct 42)
15 Oct 42 to Castletown
20 Jan 43 to Westhampnett
30 Apr 43 to Perranporth
May 43 **Spitfire VC** (Feb 44)
26 Jun 43 to Bolt Head
19 Dec 43 to Fairwood Common
4 Jan 44 to Exeter
Jan 44 **Spitfire XIV** (Mar 45)
7 Apr 44 to Culmhead
23 Apr 44 to Fairwood Common
30 Apr 44 to Culmhead

16 May 44 to Bolt Head
24 May 44 to Harrowbeer
19 Jun 44 to West Malling
27 Jun 44 to Westhampnett
2 Jul 44 to Friston
12 Sep 44 to Lympne
4 Dec 44 to B 56/Evere
31 Dec 44 to Y 32/Ophoven
27 Jan 45 to B 78/Eindhoven
21 Feb 45 to Warmwell
3 Mar 45 DB
—
10 May 46 RF @ Hooton Park
16 Jun 46 embodied
Nov 46 **Spitfire F.14** (Apr 49)
Mar 49 **Spitfire F.22** (Aug 51)
Jul 51 **Meteor F.4** (May 52)
Mar 52 **Meteor F.8** (Mar 57)
10 Mar 57 DB

611 Sqn

10 Feb 36 F @ Hendon
1 Apr 36 to Liverpool
6 May 36 to Speke
Jun 36 **Hart** (Apr 38)
Apr 38 **Hind** (May 39)
May 39 **Spitfire I** (Sep 40)
13 Aug 39 to Duxford
10 Oct 39 to Digby
dets North Coates, Ternhill
Aug 40 **Spitfire IIA** (Oct 40)
Oct 40 **Spitfire I** (Mar 41)
13 Dec 40 to Southend
27 Jan 41 to Hornchurch
Feb 41 **Spitfire IIA** (May 41)
20 May 41 to Southend
May 41 **Spitfire VA** (Jul 41)
14 Jun 41 to Hornchurch
Jun 41 **Spitfire VB** (Nov 41)
12 Nov 41 to Drem
Nov 41 **Spitfire IIA** (Feb 42)
Nov 41 **Spitfire IIB** (Jan 42)
Jan 42 **Spitfire VB** (Jul 42)
3 Jun 42 to Kenley
13 Jul 42 to Martlesham Heath
20 Jul 42 to Redhill
Jul 42 **Spitfire IX** (Jul 43)
27 Jul 42 to Ipswich
1 Aug 42 to Redhill
14 Aug 42 to Kenley
20 Aug 42 to Redhill
23 Sep 42 to Biggin Hill
1 Jul 43 to Matlask
Jul 43 **Spitfire LF VB** (Jul 44)
31 Jul 43 to Ludham
4 Aug 43 to Coltishall
6 Sep 43 to Southend
13 Sep 43 to Coltishall
8 Oct 43 to Manston
13 Oct 43 to Coltishall
19 Nov 43 to Ford
22 Nov 43 to Coltishall
8 Feb 44 to Ayr
19 Feb 44 to Coltishall
30 Apr 44 to Deanland
24 Jun 44 to Harrowbeer
3 Jul 44 to Predannack
17 Jul 44 to Bolt Head
Jul 44 **Spitfire IX** (Mar 45)
30 Aug 44 to Bradwell Bay
3 Oct 44 to Skaebrae
det Sumburgh
Dec 44 **Spitfire VII** (Dec 44)
31 Dec 44 to Hawkinge
3 Mar 45 to Hunsdon
Mar 45 **Mustang IV** (Aug 45)
7 May 45 to Peterhead
15 Aug 45 DB
—
10 May 46 RF @ Speke
26 Jun 46 to Hooton Park and embodied
22 Jul 46 to Woodvale
Nov 46 **Spitfire FR 14** (Aug 49)
Feb 49 **Spitfire F.22** (Nov 51)
May 51 **Meteor F.4** (Apr 52)
9 Jul 51 to Hooton Park
Mar 52 **Meteor F.8** (Mar 57)
10 Mar 57 DB

612 Sqn

1 Jun 37 F @ Dyce
Dec 37 **Hector** (Nov 39)
Jun 39 **Anson I** (Jan 41)
dets Stornoway, Wick
Nov 40 **Whitley V** (Jan 42)
1 Apr 41 to Wick
dets Limavady, St Eval, Reykjavik
Sep 41 **Whitley VII** (Jun 43)
15 Dec 41 to Reykjavik
18 Aug 42 to Thorney Island
23 Sep 42 to Wick
det Skitten
Nov 42 **Wellington VIII** (Mar 43)
Mar 43 **Wellington XIII** (Mar 44)
18 Apr 43 to Davidstow Moor
25 May 43 to Chivenor
Jun 43 **Wellington XIV** (Jul 45)
1 Nov 43 to St Eval
3 Dec 43 to Chivenor
26 Jan 44 to Limavady
1 Mar 44 to Chivenor
9 Sep 44 to Limavady
19 Dec 44 to Langham
9 Jul 45 DB
—
10 May 46 RF @ Dyce
11 Jun 46 embodied
Nov 46 **Spitfire F.14** (Oct 49)
Nov 48 **Spitfire LF 16E** (Jun 51)
Jun 51 **Vampire FB 5** (Mar 57)
14 Jul 51 to Leuchars
14 Oct 51 to Edzell
12 Nov 52 to Dyce
10 Mar 57 DB

613 Sqn

1 Mar 39 F @ Ringway
Apr 39 **Hind** (Apr 40)
2 Oct 39 to Odiham
Nov 39 **Hector** (May 40)
dets Weston Zoyland, Hawkinge
Apr 40 **Lysander II** (Jan 41)
30 Jun 40 to Netherthorpe
7 Sep 40 to Firbeck
dets Clifton, Netherthorpe, Sutton Bridge, Doncaster, Martlesham Heath
Jan 41 **Lysander IIIA** (Sep 42)
8 Jul 41 to Doncaster
Aug 41 **Tomahawk II** (Apr 42)
26 Sep 41 to Andover
6 Oct 41 to Doncaster
dets Odiham, Weston Zoyland
15 Apr 42 to Twinwood Farm
Apr 42 **Mustang I** (Oct 43)
28 Aug 42 to Ouston
dets Odiham, Gatwick
1 Mar 43 to Wing
7 Mar 43 to Bottisham
19 Mar 43 to Ringway
30 Mar 43 to Wellingore
28 May 43 to Clifton
20 Jun 43 to Portreath
15 Jul 43 to Snailwell
12 Oct 43 to Lasham
Oct 43 **Mosquito VI** (Aug 45)
12 Apr 44 to Swanton Morley
24 Apr 44 to Lasham
23 Oct 44 to Hartford Bridge
25 Oct 44 to Lasham
30 Oct 44 to Hartford Bridge
20 Nov 44 to A 75/Cambrai/Epinoy
det Fersfield
7 Aug 45 DB — renumbered as No 69 Sqn
—
10 May 46 RF @ Ringway
12 Jun 46 embodied
Dec 46 **Spitfire F.14** (Dec 48)
Oct 48 **Spitfire F.22** (Mar 51)
Feb 51 **Vampire F.1** (Apr 51)
Feb 51 **Vampire FB 5** (Mar 57)
Jun 54 **Vampire FB 9** (Mar 57)
10 Mar 57 DB

614 Sqn

1 Jun 37 F @ Pengam Moors
Jun 37 **Hind** (39)
Apr 38 **Hector** (Feb 40)
Jul 39 **Lysander II** (Jul 41)
2 Oct 39 to Odiham
det Weston Zoyland
8 Jun 40 to Grangemouth
dets Evanton, Montrose, Longman, Dumfries, Tangmere
5 Mar 41 to Macmerry
dets Westhampnett, Dalcross, Elgin, Clifton
Apr 41 **Lysander III** (Jan 42)
Jul 41 **Blenheim IV** (Aug 42)
dets West Raynham, Odiham, Thruxton
14 Aug 42 to Thruxton
21 Aug 42 to Macmerry
26 Aug 42 to Odiham
Aug 42 **Blenheim V** (Jan 44)
dets Weston Zoyland, Snailwell
16 Nov 42 en route N Africa
18 Nov 42 to Blida
5 Dec 42 to Canrobert
8 Feb 43 to Oulmene
22 May 43 to Tafaroui
28 Aug 43 to Bo Rizzo
25 Jan 44 DB
—
15 Feb 44 RF en route El Adem-Celone — No 462 Sqn renumbered
Feb 44 **Halifax II** (Mar 45)
28 Feb 44 to Celone
10 May 44 to Stornara
15 Jul 44 to Amendola
Aug 44 **Liberator VIII** (Jul 45)
27 Jul 45 DB — renumbered as No 214 Sqn
—
10 May 46 RF @ Llandow
11 Jun 46 embodied
Jan 47 **Spitfire LF 16E** (Sep 48)
Jul 48 **Spitfire F.22** (Jul 50)
Jul 50 **Vampire F.3** (Dec 51)
Dec 51 **Vampire FB 5** (Mar 57)
Feb 55 **Vampire FB 9** (Feb 56)
10 Mar 57 DB

615 Sqn

1 Jun 37 F @ Kenley
Nov 37 **Audax** (Mar 38)
Nov 37 **Hector** (Feb 39)
Dec 38 **Gauntlet II** (Sep 39)
Jun 39 **Gladiator I** (Oct 39)
2 Sep 39 to Croydon
Oct 39 **Gladiator II** (May 40)
15 Nov 39 to Merville
13 Dec 39 to Vitry-en-Artois
det St-Inglevert
12 Apr 40 to Poix
det St-Inglevert
27 Apr 40 to Abbeville
dets St-Inglevert, Le Touquet
Apr 40 **Hurricane I** (Feb 41)
22 May 40 to Kenley
det Manston (Gladiator)
29 Aug 40 to Prestwick
10 Oct 40 to Northolt
16 Dec 40 to Kenley
Feb 41 **Hurricane IIA** (Apr 41)
21 Apr 41 to Valley
Apr 41 **Hurricane I** (Jul 41)
Jul 41 **Hurricane IIB** (Mar 42)
Jul 41 **Hurricane IIC** (Mar 42)
11 Sep 41 to Manston
27 Nov 41 to Angle
23 Jan 42 to Fairwood Common
17 Mar 42 en route FE
17 Jun 42 to Jessore
Jul 42 **Hurricane IIC** (Sep 43)
6 Dec 42 to Feni
7 May 43 to Alipore
Sep 43 **Spitfire VC** (Jul 44)
1 Nov 43 to Chittagong
13 Dec 43 to Dohazari
26 Feb 44 to Nazir
19 Mar 44 to Silchar West
10 May 44 to Dergaon
23 May 44 to Palel
Jun 44 **Spitfire VIII** (Jun 45)
10 Aug 44 to Baigachi
24 Feb 45 to Nidania
det Kyaukpyu
23 Apr 45 to Charra
22 May 45 to Chakulia
29 May 45 to Cuttack
10 Jun 45 DB
—
10 Jun 45 RF @ Akyab — No 135 Sqn renumbered
Jun 45 **Thunderbolt II** (Sep 45)
det Chakulia (air echelon)
8 Jul 45 to Vizagapatam
25 Sep 45 DB
—
10 May 46 RF @ Biggin Hill
1 Jul 46 embodied
Oct 46 **Spitfire F.14** (Jan 49)
Jan 47 **Spitfire F.21** (Jun 50)
Jul 48 **Spitfire F.22** (Oct 50)
Sep 50 **Meteor F.4** (Sep 51)
Sep 51 **Meteor F.8** (Mar 57)
10 Mar 57 DB

616 Sqn

1 Nov 38 F @ Doncaster — from No 503 Sqn
Nov 38 **Hind** (Jan 39)
Jan 39 **Gauntlet II** (Dec 39)
May 39 **Battle** (Nov 39)
23 Oct 39 to Leconfield
Oct 39 **Spitfire I** (Feb 41)
det Catfoss
27 May 40 to Rochford
6 Jun 40 to Leconfield
19 Aug 40 to Kenley
3 Sep 40 to Coltishall
9 Sep 40 to Kirton-in-Lindsey
26 Feb 41 to Tangmere
Feb 41 **Spitfire IIA** (Jul 41)
9 May 41 to Westhampnett
Jul 41 **Spitfire VB** (Jun 42)
6 Oct 41 to Kirton-in-Lindsey
Oct 41 **Spitfire IIB** (Nov 41)
30 Jan 42 to Kingscliffe
Apr 42 **Spitfire VI** (Nov 43)
3 Jul 42 to West Malling
7 Jul 42 to Kingscliffe
8 Jul 42 to Kenley
29 Jul 42 to Great Sampford
14 Aug 42 to Hawkinge
20 Aug 42 to Great Sampford
1 Sep 42 to Ipswich
7 Sep 42 to Great Sampford
23 Sep 42 to Tangmere
29 Oct 42 to Westhampnett
2 Jan 43 to Ibsley
15 Mar 43 to Harrowbeer
18 Mar 43 to Ibsley
17 Sep 43 to Exeter
Sep 43 **Spitfire VII** (Aug 44)
16 Nov 43 to Fairwood Common
1 Dec 43 to Exeter
18 Mar 44 to West Malling

24 Apr 44 to Fairwood Common
16 May 44 to Culmhead
Jul 44 **Meteor I** (Jan 45)
21 Jul 44 to Manston det Debden
17 Jan 45 to Colerne
Jan 45 **Meteor III** (Aug 45) det B 58/Melsbroek
28 Feb 45 to Andrews Field det B 58/Melsbroek
31 Mar 45 to B 77/Gilze-Rijen
13 Apr 45 to B 91/Kluis
20 Apr 45 to B 109/Quackenbrück
26 Apr 45 to B 152/Fassberg
3 May 45 to B 156/Lüneburg
7 May 45 to B 158/Lübeck
30 Aug 45 DB — renumbered as No 263 Sqn
—
10 May 46 RF @ Finningley
11 Jul 46 embodied
Sep 47 **Mosquito NF 30** (May 49)
Jan 49 **Meteor F.3** (May 51)
Apr 51 **Meteor F.4** (Dec 51)
Dec 51 **Meteor F.8** (Mar 57)
23 May 55 to Worksop
10 Mar 57 DB

617 Sqn

23 Mar 43 F @ Scampton
Mar 43 **Lancaster III (Spec)** (May 43)
Mar 43 **Lancaster I & III** (Jun 45)
30 Aug 43 to Coningsby det Tempsford
0 Jan 44 to Woodhall Spa
Apr 44 **Mosquito VI** (Mar 45) dets Yagodnik, Lossiemouth
7 Jun 45 to Waddington
Jun 45 **Lancaster VII (FE)** (Sep 46)
9 Jan 46 to Digri
1 May 46 to Binbrook
Sep 46 **Lincoln B.2** (Jan 52)
Jan 52 **Canberra B.2** (Apr 55)
Feb 55 **Canberra B.6** (Dec 55)
5 Dec 55 DB
—
1 May 58 RF @ Scampton
May 58 **Vulcan B.1** (Jul 61)
Sep 61 **Vulcan B.2** (Dec 81)
1 Dec 81 DB
—
1 Jan 83 RF @ Marham
Jan 83 **Tornado GR 1** ( )

618 Sqn

5 Mar 43 F @ Skitten
Apr 43 **Mosquito IV** (Oct 43)
Apr 43 **Beaufighter II** (Jun 43) dets Manston, Turnberry, Dyce, Benson, Wick
Oct 43 **Mosquito XVIII** (Jan 44) det Predannack
Jul 44 to Wick
Jul 44 **Mosquito VI** (Oct 44)
Aug 44 to Beccles
Sep 44 **Mosquito IV** (Jul 45) det Dallachy
Sep 44 **Mosquito XVI** (Jul 45)
Oct 44 en route Australia via HMS *Fencer* & HMS *Striker*
Dec 44 to Melbourne
Feb 45 to Narromine
Feb 45 **Mosquito VI** (Jul 45)
Jul 45 DB

619 Sqn

18 Apr 43 F @ Woodhall Spa — nucleus from No 97 Sqn
Apr 43 **Lancaster I & III** (Jul 45)
9 Jan 44 to Coningsby
17 Apr 44 to Dunholme Lodge
28 Sep 44 to Strubby
1 Jul 45 to Skellingthorpe
18 Jul 45 DB

620 Sqn

17 Jun 43 F @ Chedburgh
Jun 43 **Stirling I** (Aug 43)
Aug 43 **Stirling III** (Mar 44)
22 Nov 43 to Leicester East det Hurn
18 Mar 44 to Fairford
Feb 44 **Stirling IV** (Jul 45)
18 Oct 44 to Great Dunmow
Jul 45 **Halifax A.VII** (Sep 46)
15 Jan 46 to Aqir
6 Mar 46 to Cairo West det Shallufa
14 Jun 46 to Aqir
Jun 46 **Dakota** (Sep 46)
Aug 46 **Halifax A.IX** (Sep 46)
1 Sep 46 DB — renumbered as No 113 Sqn

621 Sqn

12 Sep 43 F @ Port Reitz det Mogadishu
Sep 43 **Wellington XIII** (Nov 45)
1 Nov 43 to Mogadishu dets Scuscuiban, Bandar Kassim, Riyan
5 Dec 43 to Khormaksar dets Scuscuiban, Bandar Kassim, Riyan, Socotra, Mogadishu
Jan 45 **Wellington XIV** (Dec 45)
12 Nov 45 to Mersah Matruh
Dec 45 **Warwick V** (Aug 46) dets Aqir, Benina
20 Apr 46 to Aqir
Apr 46 **Lancaster ASR III** (Aug 46)
6 Jun 46 to Ein Shemar
1 Sep 46 DB — renumbered as No 18 Sqn

622 Sqn

10 Aug 43 F @ Mildenhall — from 'C' Flt, No 15 Sqn
Aug 43 **Stirling III** (Jan 44)
Dec 43 **Lancaster I & III** (Aug 45)
15 Aug 45 DB
—
1 Nov 50 RF @ Blackbushe
Dec 50 **Valetta C.1** (Sep 53)
30 Sep 53 DB

623 Sqn

10 Aug 43 F @ Downham Market — from an element of No 218 Sqn
Aug 43 **Stirling III** (Dec 43)
6 Dec 43 DB

624 Sqn

22 Sep 43 F @ Blida — from No 1575 Flt
Sep 43 **Ventura II** (Oct 43)
Sep 43 **Halifax II** (Sep 44)
Sep 43 **Halifax V** (Feb 44) dets Protville, Sidi Amor, Tocra
2 Dec 43 to Tocra
23 Dec 43 to Brindisi
15 Feb 44 to Blida det Bone
Jul 44 **Stirling IV** (Sep 44)
5 Sep 44 DB
—
28 Dec 44 RF @ Grottaglie
Jan 45 **Walrus** (Nov 45) dets Foggia, Hassani
21 Feb 45 to Foggia dets Hassani, Falconara, Rosignano
30 Apr 45 to Falconara dets Hassani, Rosignano, Treviso, Hal Far, Sedes
9 Jul 45 to Rosignano dets Hal Far, Sedes
21 Aug 45 to Littorio dets Hal Far, Sedes
30 Nov 45 DB

625 Sqn

1 Oct 43 F @ Kelstern — from 'C' Flt, No 100 Sqn
Oct 43 **Lancaster I & III** (Oct 45)
5 Apr 45 to Scampton
7 Oct 45 DB

626 Sqn

7 Nov 43 F @ Wickenby — from 'C' Flt, No 12 Sqn
Nov 43 **Lancaster I & III** (Oct 45)
14 Oct 45 DB

627 Sqn

12 Nov 43 F @ Oakington — from Flt of No 139 Sqn
Nov 43 **Mosquito IV** (Sep 45)
15 Apr 44 to Woodhall Spa
Jul 44 **Mosquito XX** (Sep 45)
Oct 44 **Mosquito XXV** (Sep 45)
Mar 45 **Mosquito XVI** (Sep 45)
30 Sep 45 DB — renumbered No 109 Sqn

628 Sqn

21 Mar 44 F @ Red Hills Lake — from 'B' Flt, No 357 Sqn
Mar 44 **Catalina IB** (Oct 44)
Jul 44 **Catalina IV** (Oct 44)
1 Oct 44 DB

630 Sqn

15 Nov 43 F @ East Kirkby — from 'B' Flt, No 57 Sqn
Nov 43 **Lancaster I & III** (Jul 45)
18 Jul 45 DB

631 Sqn

1 Dec 43 F @ Towyn — from Nos 1605 & 1628 Flts det Llanbedr
Dec 43 **Henley III** (Mar 45)
Mar 44 **Hurricane IIC** (Aug 45)
Aug 44 **Oxford** (Jul 45)
Sep 44 **Martinet** (Jan 45)
Jan 45 **Vengeance IV** (May 47)
10 May 45 to Llanbedr
Jun 45 **Spitfire VB** (Sep 45)
Aug 45 **Spitfire XVI** (Feb 49)
Jan 47 **Martinet** (Feb 49)
Aug 48 **Vampire F.1** (Feb 49)
11 Feb 49 DB — renumbered as No 20 Sqn

635 Sqn

20 Mar 44 F @ Downham Market — from 'B' Flt, No 35 Sqn & 'C' Flt, No 97 Sqn
Mar 44 **Lancaster III** (Aug 45)
Jul 44 **Lancaster VI** (Nov 44)
1 Sep 45 DB

639 Sqn

1 Dec 43 F @ Cleave — from Nos 1602, 1603 & 1604 Flts
Dec 43 **Henley III** (Apr 45)
Aug 44 **Hurricane IV** (Apr 45) dets Perranporth, Portreath
30 Apr 45 DB

640 Sqn

7 Jan 44 F @ Leconfield — from 'C' Flt, No 158 Sqn
Jan 44 **Halifax III** (Mar 45)
Mar 45 **Halifax VI** (May 45)
7 May 45 DB

644 Sqn

23 Feb 44 F @ Tarrant Rushton — nucleus from No 298 Sqn
Mar 44 **Halifax V** (Nov 44)
Oct 44 **Halifax III** (Jun 45)
Mar 45 **Halifax A.VII** (Sep 46)
1 Dec 45 to Qastina
Aug 46 **Halifax A.IX** (Sep 46)
1 Sep 46 DB — renumbered as No 47 Sqn

650 Sqn

1 Dec 43 F @ Cark — from No 1614 Flt & D Flt, No 289 Sqn
Dec 43 **Martinet** (Jun 45)
Dec 43 **Hurricane IV** (Jun 45)
18 Nov 44 to Bodorgan dets Cark, Woodvale, Valley, Hutton Cranswick
26 Jun 45 DB

Nos 651-666, the AOP Squadrons
The AOP squadrons were raised from 1941 onwards and were manned jointly by both Army and RAF personnel. The former providing the pilots and the latter being responsible for much of the maintenance. Once committed to battle the AOP units led an extremely nomadic existence moving, at times, daily. Typically a squadron would be allocated to a Corps. Flights would serve Divisions within the Corps and would be located close to the Divisional HQ. On occasion Sections of one or two aircraft might be assigned to yet smaller formations. Thus it was not unusual for an AOP squadron in the field to be operating from as many

as eight locations at once, and four was quite normal. During fast moving campaigns like the break-out from the Normandy beach-head, the advance into Germany, and the capture of Rangoon, a squadron HQ could even loose touch with some of its elements for several days at a time.
The locations listed in the following histories, for the wartime period, are generally those occupied by the squadron HQ. In some cases these were recorded in the Operations Record Books as contemporary grid references. Where this was the case they have been converted into a more easily interpreted form and expressed as a latitude and longitude. No attempt has been made to record the complex movements of the Flights and Sections of each squadron. Similarly the numerous temporary landing grounds in the UK which were used during work-up exercises have also been omitted.
After the war, on 1 Jan 47, the constituent Flights of the few remaining AOP squadrons were given individual numbers in the 1900 series. These Flights usually operated as sub-units of squadrons but they could be transferred from one to another. When this occurred they retained their discrete Flight number, for instance No 1902 Flt was transferred from the control of No 657 Sqn in the UK to that of No 652 Sqn in Germany on 12 Feb 52. Alternatively a Flight could operate independently without any squadron affiliation at all. An example of this practice is provided by No 1910 Flt which left the control of No 651 Sqn on 20 Jul 52 and spent the next two years as an autonomous unit in Eritrea. This book is concerned chiefly with units of squadron status, however, the significance of the numbered AOP Flights has been recognised and where they were part of a squadron this has been acknowledged in the accompanying listings.

651 Sqn

1 Aug 41 F @ Old Sarum
Aug 41 **Taylorcraft Plus C** (Jul 42)
Sep 41 **Taylorcraft Plus D** (Oct 41)
Feb 42 **Taylorcraft Plus C.2** (Sep 42)
Jul 42 **Auster I** (Nov 43)
31 Jul 42 to Dumfries
11 Aug 42 to Kidsdale
30 Oct 42 to Gourock en route N Africa
13 Nov 42 to Algiers
17 Nov 42 to Bone
11 Dec 42 to Beja
12 Jan 43 to Souk el Arba
19 Apr 43 to Medjez el Bab
14 May 43 to La Marsa
22 May 43 to Sfax
25 May 43 to Sousse
4 Jun 43 to Castel Benito
9 Jun 43 to Sousse
19 Jul 43 to Syracuse
21 Jul 43 to Lentini
5 Aug 43 to 3727N 1500E
14 Aug 43 to Lentini
Aug 43 **Auster III** (Dec 44)
1 Sep 43 to Scordia
17 Sep 43 to Vibo Valentia
21 Sep 43 to Firmo
24 Sep 43 to Gioia del Colle
27 Sep 43 to Altamura
30 Sep 43 to Canosa
2 Oct 43 to San Severo
10 Oct 43 to Torremaggiore
1 Nov 43 to Serracapriola
8 Nov 43 to Vasto
7 Mar 44 to Bari
6 Apr 44 to Paglieta
May 44 **Auster IV** (Nov 45)
9 Jun 44 to San Vito
20 Jun 44 to Roseto degli Abruzzi
23 Jun 44 to Torre di Palme
29 Jun 44 to Fermo
3 Jul 44 to Recanati
21 Jul 44 to San Bernadino
29 Jul 44 to Monte Marciano
19 Aug 44 to Fabriano
25 Aug 44 to Pergola
29 Aug 44 to Fossombrone
5 Sep 44 to Morciano
25 Sep 44 to Serravalle
4 Oct 44 to 4402N 1230E
15 Oct 44 to Santa Arcangelo
29 Oct 44 to Cesena
16 Nov 44 to Forli (Villa Carpena)
Dec 44 **Auster V** (Jun 47)
24 Jan 45 to Porto San Elpidio
28 Feb 45 to Forli
6 Mar 45 to Villa Brocchi
31 Mar 45 to 4428N 1214E
12 Apr 45 to 4424N 1202E
15 Apr 45 to 4431N 1204E
24 Apr 45 to Montesanto
27 Apr 45 to Ferrara
1 May 45 to Padua
4 May 45 to Udine
10 May 45 to Klagenfurt
7 Oct 45 to Gorizia
9 Nov 45 to Aboukir
10 Nov 45 to Ismailia
2 Feb 46 to Ramleh
Flts det Ein Shemar, Ismailia, Qastina
10 Jul 46 to Petah Tiqva
Flts det Ein Shemar, Ramleh, Ramat David, Qastina
Mar 47 **Auster AOP 6** (Oct 55)
1 Jun 47 to Qastina (Nos 1906, 1907, 1908 & 1910 Flts)
No 1909 Flt det Ramat David
11 Feb 48 to Petah Tiqva (Nos 1908 & 1910 Flts)
No 1909 Flt det Ramat David
28 Apr 48 to Sarafand (Nos 1908 & 1910 Flts)
No 1909 Flt det Ramat David
12 May 48 to Fayid (Nos 1908 & 1910 Flts)
No 1909 Flt det Ramat David, Haifa, Amman
26 Aug 48 to Castel Benito/Idris (Nos 1908 & 1910 Flts)
No 1908 Flt det Habbaniyah, Ismailia
Nov 49 **Auster AOP 5** (Mar 52)
15 Nov 51 to Ismailia (Nos 1908 & 1910 Flts)
No 1908 Flt det Kasfareet, Idris, Barce
No 1910 Flt det Famagusta
1 Nov 55 DB
—
1 Nov 55 RF @ Middle Wallop — No 657 Sqn renumbered
Nov 55 **Sycamore HC 11** (Sep 57) (No 1906 Flt)
Nov 55 **Auster AOP 6** (Sep 57) (Nos 1903 & 1913 Flts)
No 1903 Flt at Detling, Feltwell
No 1913 Flt at Middle Wallop, Andover, Aldergrove
4 Apr 57 to Feltwell (Nos 1903 & 1913 Flts)
No 1906 Flt at Middle Wallop
1 Sep 57 transferred to Army Air Corps as 3, 6 & 13 Flts

652 Sqn

1 May 42 F @ Old Sarum
May 42 **Tiger Moth** (Nov 42)
15 Jun 42 to Bottisham
11 Aug 42 to Westley
Aug 42 **Taylorcraft Plus C.2** (Mar 43)
Oct 42 **Auster I** (Mar 43)
1 Jan 43 to Dumfries
20 Feb 43 to Sawbridgeworth
28 Mar 43 to Methven
Mar 43 **Auster III** (Apr 44)
2 Jul 43 to Ayr
7 Dec 43 to Ipswich
Feb 44 **Auster IV** (Aug 46)
25 Mar 44 to Denham
29 Apr 44 to Cobham
6 Jun 44 to Bény-sur-Mer ('A' Flt)
7 Jun 44 to Plumetot
8 Jul 44 to Reviers
1 Aug 44 to Blainville
13 Aug 44 to Grentheville
17 Aug 44 to St-Pierre-sur-Dives
23 Aug 44 to Lisieux
26 Aug 44 to 4913N 0029E
3 Sep 44 to Foucart
4 Sep 44 to Angerville-l'Orcher
14 Sep 44 to Héricourt-en-Caux
17 Sep 44 to Parfondeval
23 Sep 44 to Bueken
27 Sep 44 to Zoersal
5 Oct 44 to Het Gehaul
13 Oct 44 to Turnhout
19 Oct 44 to 5117½N 0439E
23 Oct 44 to Maria ter Heide
1 Nov 44 to Brasschaat
4 Nov 44 to Roosendaal
10 Nov 44 to Brasschaat
31 Dec 44 to Tilburg
Dec 44 **Auster V** (Dec 53)
1 Apr 45 to Kleve
3 Apr 45 to Zutphen
30 Apr 45 to Rhede
14 Jun 45 to Deilinghofen
16 Nov 45 to Hoya
29 Apr 46 to Celle (Nos 1902, 1903 & 1904 Flts)
Sep 46 **Auster AOP 6** (Sep 57)
1 Dec 47 to Lüneburg (Nos 1902, 1903, 1904 & 1905 Flts)
1 May 49 to Detmold (Nos 1901, 1904, 1905 & 1909 Flts)
Jan 56 **Auster AOP 9** (Sep 57)
1 Sep 57 transferred to Army control as 1, 4, 5 and 9 Flights

653 Sqn

20 Jun 42 F @ Old Sarum
Jun 42 **Tiger Moth** (Sep 42)
8 Jul 42 to Farnborough
Aug 42 **Taylorcraft Plus C.2** (Jul 43)
Aug 42 **Auster I** (Mar 43)
7 Sep 42 to Penshurst
Mar 43 **Auster III** (Apr 44)
17 Aug 43 to Sissinghurst
18 Aug 43 to Chart Court
17 Sep 43 to Penshurst
6 Dec 43 to Weston Zoyland
17 Dec 43 to Penshurst
Feb 44 **Auster IV** (Sep 45)
27 Jun 44 to Rucqueville
Jul 44 **Auster V** (Sep 45)
13 Jul 44 to Bretteville
6 Aug 44 to Cheux
10 Aug 44 to Landes
14 Aug 44 to Forêt de Cinglais
18 Aug 44 to St-Germain-Langot
23 Aug 44 to Trun
26 Aug 44 to La Barre-en-Ouche
28 Aug 44 to le Mesnil-Jourdain
30 Aug 44 to Saussay-la-Campagne
1 Sep 44 to Coudray-en-Vexin
3 Sep 44 to Gouy-l'Hopital
4 Sep 44 to Gouy-Servins
8 Sep 44 to Renaix
9 Sep 44 to Willebroek
15 Sep 44 to Boischot
23 Sep 44 to Eindhoven
6 Oct 44 to Hoeven
7 Oct 44 to Nijmegen
18 Oct 44 to Hoeven
24 Oct 44 to Dinther
29 Oct 44 to Helvoirt
8 Nov 44 to Peer
13 Nov 44 to Weert
8 Dec 44 to Boshoven
22 Dec 44 to Stein
25 Jan 45 to Geleen
6 Feb 45 to Diest
19 Mar 45 to 5123N 0445E
26 Mar 45 to 5140N 0505E
30 Mar 45 to 5145N 0509E
31 Mar 45 to 5150N 0515E
1 Apr 45 to Ahaus
7 Apr 45 to Westerkapellen
9 Apr 45 to Kirchdorf
4 May 45 to Harburg
7 May 45 to Hamburg/Altona
22 Jun 45 to Hoya
15 Sep 45 DB

654 Sqn

15 Jul 42 F @ Old Sarum
Jul 42 **Tiger Moth** (Sep 42)
15 Sep 42 to Firbeck
Sep 42 **Taylorcraft Plus C.2** (Nov 42)
Sep 42 **Auster I** (Dec 42)
20 Nov 42 to Bottisham
Dec 42 **Auster III** (Feb 43)
20 Feb 43 to Gourock
4 Mar 43 to Algiers (PTC Husse Dey)
18 Mar 43 to le Kroube
Mar 43 **Auster III** (Dec 44)
4 Apr 43 to Sbiba
11 Apr 43 to Kairouan
14 Apr 43 to Msaken
15 May 43 to Hergla
27 May 43 to Sfax (Sidi Mansour
23 Jun 43 to Hergla
4 Aug 43 to Syracuse
12 Aug 43 to Comiso
4 Sep 43 to Milazzo
9 Sep 43 to Tusciano
30 Sep 43 to Castellamare
3 Oct 43 to Cercola
7 Oct 43 to Capodichino
21 Oct 43 to 4105N 1413E
1 Nov 43 to Sparinese
24 Nov 43 to 4113½N 1404½E
31 Mar 44 to Santa Maria la Fos
29 Apr 44 to Presenzano
21 May 44 to San Giorgio
27 May 44 to Pontecorvo
8 Jun 44 to Alatri
9 Jun 44 to 4201N 1235E
Jun 44 **Auster IV** (Mar 47)
14 Jun 44 to Otricole
15 Jun 44 to Narni
22 Jun 44 to Perugia
8 Jul 44 to Umbertide
27 Jul 44 to Arezzo
15 Aug 44 to Senigallia
28 Aug 44 to Borgo Lucrezia
11 Sep 44 to Cassandro
16 Sep 44 to Riccione
16 Oct 44 to San Piero in Bagn
16 Nov 44 to Forli
Dec 44 **Auster V** (Jun 47)
28 Feb 45 to Rimini
1 Apr 45 to La Russia
30 Apr 45 to Rovigo
1 May 45 to Tricesimo
18 Sep 45 to Ronchi (Nos 1906 1907 Flts)
31 Mar 47 to Campoformido (N 1906 & 1907 Flts)
24 Jun 47 DB

655 Sqn

30 Nov 42 F @ Old Sarum
Dec 42 **Auster I** (Mar 43)
Feb 43 **Auster III** (Aug 43)
24 Feb 43 to Fowlmere
14 Mar 43 to Old Sarum
22 Mar 43 to Gatwick
7 Apr 43 to Detling
12 Aug 43 en route N Africa
25 Aug 43 to Algiers (No 1 BPD Fort de l'Eau)
1 Oct 43 to Bone
Oct 43 **Auster III** (Aug 44)
31 Oct 43 to Châteaudun
6 Dec 43 to Sidi Ahmed
9 Dec 43 en route Italy
25 Dec 43 to LG S of River Sangro
2 Jan 44 to Paglieta det Anzio
Jun 44 **Auster IV** (Aug 45)
9 Jun 44 to Santa Maria la Fossa
11 Jul 44 to Giovanni
23 Aug 44 to Figline
2 Sep 44 to Incisa
12 Sep 44 to Scandicci
22 Sep 44 to Vicchio
16 Oct 44 to Borgo San Lorenzo
Jan 45 **Auster V** (Aug 45)
16 Apr 45 to Lugo
19 Apr 45 to Medicina
22 Apr 45 to Budrio
23 Apr 45 to San Marco
24 Apr 45 to Coronella
27 Apr 45 to Canda
30 Apr 45 to Mestre
2 May 45 to Portogruaro
3 May 45 to Ronchi dets Udine, Venice
31 Aug 45 DB

656 Sqn

31 Dec 42 F @ Westley
Jan 43 **Tiger Moth** (Aug 43)
Jan 43 **Auster I** (Mar 43)
Feb 43 **Auster III** (Aug 43)
16 Mar 43 to Stapleford Tawney
31 Aug 43 en route FE
15 Sep 43 to Worli (Base Reception Centre)
21 Sep 43 to Juhu
1 Oct 43 to Deolali
Nov 43 **Auster III** (Jun 45)
29 Jan 44 to Maunghnama
8 Feb 44 to Bawli
12 Apr 44 to Dimapur
24 Jun 44 to Ranchi
Oct 44 **Auster IV** (Jun 45)
18 Oct 44 to Palel
4 Jan 45 to Kalemyo
14 Feb 45 to Monywa
Feb 45 **Auster V** (Jan 47)
26 Apr 45 to Meiktila
6 May 45 to Mingaladon
7 Jun 45 to Madras by sea
7 Jun 45 to Coimbatore
24 Sep 45 operational element to Kelanang via HMS *Trumpeter* Flts to Port Swettenham, Ipoh, Kuala Lumpur (Noble Field), Johore Bahru, Kuala Trengganu
4 Nov 45 to Kuala Lumpur (Noble Field) Flts to Kemajoran, Kuala Trengganu, Ipoh
5 Jan 46 to Kemajoran Flts to Soerabaya, Bandoeng, Padang, Semerang, Medan
8 Nov 46 to Kuala Lumpur (Noble Field)
5 Jan 47 DB — reduced to No 1914 Flt
—

29 Jun 48 RF @ Sembawang — from No 1914 Flt
Jun 48 **Auster AOP 5** (May 51)
15 Jul 48 Nos 1902, 1903 & 1907 Flts added dets Taiping (No 1902 Flt), Seremban (No 1903 Flt), Kai Tak (No 1903 Flt), Kuala Lumpur (No 1907 Flt), Kluang (No 1914 Flt)
17 Aug 49 to Changi dets Taiping (No 1902 Flt), Kuala Lumpur (No 1907 Flt), Kluang (No 1914 Flt), Temerloh (No 1914 Flt), Muar (No 1907 Flt)
12 Apr 50 to Kuala Lumpur dets Taiping (Nos 1902, 1907 & 1914 Flts), Changi (Nos 1902 & 1911 Flts), Benta (Nos 1902, 1907, 1911 & 1914 Flts), Sembawang (Nos 1902, 1907 & 1911 Flts), Ipoh (No 1902 Flt), Johore Bahru (No 1907 Flt), Kluang (Nos 1907 & 1911 Flts), Seremban (Nos 1907 & 1911 Flts), Temerloh (Nos 1911 & 1914 Flts), Port Dickson (No 1914 Flt)
Jul 50 **Auster AOP 6** (Apr 56)
Sep 55 **Auster AOP 9** (Sep 57)
1 Sep 57 transferred to Army Air Corps control as 2, 7, 11 and 14 Flights

657 Sqn

31 Jan 43 F @ Ouston
Feb 43 **Auster I** (May 43)
May 43 **Auster III** (Oct 44)
1 May 43 to Westley
26 Jun 43 to Clifton
15 Aug 43 en route N Africa
24 Aug 43 to Algiers (No 1 BPD, Fort de l'Eau)
22 Sep 43 to Bone
16 Oct 43 to Phillipeville
9 Jan 44 to Châteaudun
16 Jan 44 en route Italy
28 Feb 44 to Vasto
8 Apr 44 to Presenzano
11 May 44 to Campozillone
5 Jun 44 to Anagni
9 Jun 44 to Civita Castellana
Jun 44 **Auster IV** (Mar 45)
23 Jun 44 to Citta della Pieve
29 Jun 44 to Ravigliano
4 Jul 44 to Creti
18 Jul 44 to Carraia
19 Aug 44 to Iesi
1 Sep 44 to LG on S bank of River Foglia
6 Oct 44 to Rimini
21 Oct 44 to Savignano
4 Nov 44 to Cesena
29 Nov 44 to Cervia
15 Dec 44 to San Pancrazio
Dec 44 **Auster V** (Mar 45)
21 Mar 45 to Ravenna
24 Mar 45 to Leghorn
30 Mar 45 to Marseilles en route Holland
11 Apr 45 to Gilze-Rijen
Apr 45 **Auster V** (Nov 52)
16 Apr 45 to Doetchinem
21 Apr 45 to Otterloo
4 May 45 to Teuge
16 May 45 to Hilversum
20 Jun 45 to Goslar
16 Nov 45 to Rollestone Camp
26 Jan 46 to Andover (Nos 1900 and 1901 Flts)
Mar 46 **Auster AOP 4** (Dec 52)
Jun 46 **Auster AOP 6** (Nov 55)
Apr 47 **Hoverfly 2** (Mar 48) — No 1901 Flt only No 1901 Flt det Beaulieu
19 Jan 48 to Middle Wallop (at various times comprised Nos 1900, 1901, 1903, 1906, 1912 and 1913 Flts)
May 50 **Hoverfly 2** (Apr 51) — No 1906 Flt only
Sep 51 **Sycamore HC 11** (Nov 55) — No 1906 Flt only No 1903 Flt at Detling No 1913 Flt at Middle Wallop
1 Nov 55 DB — renumbered as No 651 Sqn

658 Sqn

30 Apr 43 F @ Old Sarum
Apr 43 **Auster III** (Apr 44)
6 Aug 43 to Oatland Hill
29 Aug 43 to Clifton
1 Jan 44 to Burn
7 Jan 44 to Doncaster
21 Jan 44 to Burn
14 Mar 44 to Collyweston
Mar 44 **Auster IV** (Sep 45)
19 Apr 44 to Hartfield
25 Jun 44 to Ellon
13 Jul 44 to Secqueville-en-Bessin
15 Aug 44 to Fresney-le-Vieux
Aug 44 **Auster V** (Sep 45)
26 Aug 44 to Gacé
27 Aug 44 to Autouillet
31 Aug 44 to Thilliers-les-Vexin
2 Sep 44 to Wailly
4 Sep 44 to Blairville
6 Sep 44 to Maulde
8 Sep 44 to Perk
15 Sep 44 to Diest
20 Sep 44 to Bourg Leopold
22 Sep 44 to Eindhoven/Schaft
29 Sep 44 to Gemert
2 Oct 44 to Escharen
4 Nov 44 to St Hubert
5 Mar 45 to Tienraij
29 Mar 45 to Diersfordt
8 Apr 45 to Osnabrück
20 Apr 45 to Dorfmark
22 Jun 45 to Deilinghofen
2 Jul 45 to Hawkinge
6 Jul 45 to Stapleford Tawney
10 Jul 45 to Matlask
3 Sep 45 to West Kirby (No 1 PDC)
2 Oct 45 en route India
22 Oct 45 to Worli (Base Reception Depot)
1 Nov 45 to Dhubalia
Nov 45 **Auster V** (Dec 45)
3 Jan 46 to Calcutta (No 35 PTC)
31 Mar 46 to Hakimpet
Jun 46 **Auster V** (Oct 46)
15 Oct 46 DB

659 Sqn

30 Apr 43 F @ Firbeck
May 43 **Auster III** (Apr 44)
17 Aug 43 to Clifton
31 Dec 43 to Burn
1 Jan 44 to Clifton
Mar 44 **Auster IV** (Jul 45)
23 Apr 44 to East Grinstead
14 Jun 44 to Cully
23 Jun 44 to Lantheuil
Jul 44 **Auster V** (Jul 45)
18 Jul 44 to Basly
20 Jul 44 to Bény-sur-Mer
30 Jul 44 to Noron-la-Poterie
2 Aug 44 to La Fouquerie
7 Aug 44 to La Terrière
21 Aug 44 to St-Paul
1 Sep 44 to Flers
13 Sep 44 to St-Germain
16 Sep 44 to Diest
18 Sep 44 to Linde
28 Sep 44 to Geldrop
3 Oct 44 to Mill
1 Nov 44 to Mierlo
7 Mar 45 to Horst
13 Mar 45 to Issum
28 Mar 45 to Wesel
30 Mar 45 to Erle
1 Apr 45 to Gescher
2 Apr 45 to Greven
4 Apr 45 to Tecklenburg
5 Apr 45 to Bissendorf
6 Apr 45 to Hille
12 Apr 45 to Negenborn
14 Apr 45 to Celle
15 Apr 45 to Habighorst
17 Apr 45 to Hösseringen
20 Apr 45 to Lüneburg
2 May 45 to Wangelau
5 May 45 to Lübeck
10 May 45 to Kiel/Holtenau
4 Jul 45 to Lympne
10 Jul 45 to Matlask
3 Sep 45 to West Kirby (No 1 PDC)
2 Oct 45 en route India
23 Oct 45 to Worli (Base Reception Depot)
4 Nov 45 to Dhubalia
Nov 45 **Auster V** (Aug 47)
12 Jan 46 to Peshawar dets Deolali, Miranshah, Razmak, Lahore, Ambala
1 Jan 47 to Lahore dets Razmak, Deolali, Jullundur, Peshawar
May 47 **Auster AOP 6** (Aug 47)
14 Aug 47 DB

660 Sqn

31 Jul 43 F @ Old Sarum
Jul 43 **Auster III** (Feb 44)
21 Sep 43 to Andover
20 Nov 43 to East Grinstead
Feb 44 **Auster IV** (May 46)
23 Apr 44 to Westenhanger
8 Jul 44 to Pierrepont
12 Jul 44 to Lasson
22 Jul 44 to Mondeville
15 Aug 44 to Brettville-sur-Laize
19 Aug 44 to Perrières
23 Aug 44 to Ste-Foy-de-Montgommery
25 Aug 44 to Le Planquay
27 Aug 44 to Ailly
31 Aug 44 to Boos
3 Sep 44 to Moyenneville
9 Sep 44 to Cassel
12 Sep 44 to Ardres
Sep 44 **Auster V** (May 46)
30 Sep 44 to Ghent
9 Nov 44 to Nijmegen
23 Feb 45 to Reichswalde
4 Mar 45 to Berg en Dal
Mar 45 to Kleve
Apr 45 to Vermeppen
Jun 45 to B 56/Evere
29 Jun 45 to Kiel/Holtenau
31 May 46 DB

661 Sqn

31 Aug 43 F @ Old Sarum
Aug 43 **Auster III** (May 44)
27 Nov 43 to Andover
19 Feb 44 to Fairchildes
Mar 44 **Auster IV** (Oct 45)
27 Jun 44 to Penshurst
7 Aug 44 to Amblie
17 Aug 44 to Pont-de-Fresney

19 Aug 44 to Ernes
26 Aug 44 to Le Favril
3 Sep 44 to Cailly
9 Sep 44 to Fauquembergues
28 Sep 44 to Ghent
18 Oct 44 to Breda
Nov 44 **Auster V** (Oct 45)
4 Dec 44 to Tilburg
12 Mar 45 to Schaijk
26 Mar 45 to Grave
12 Apr 45 to Doetinchem
17 Apr 45 to 5158N 0559E
18 Apr 45 to Arnhem
23 Apr 45 to Delden
28 Apr 45 to Borne
5 Jun 45 to Apeldoorn
6 Jul 45 to Rostrup
11 Sep 45 to Ghent
31 Oct 45 DB
—
1 May 49 RF @ Kenley as RAuxAF unit comprising:
No 1957 Flt —
1 May 49 F @ Kenley
No 1958 Flt —
1 Jul 49 F @ Hendon
No 1959 Flt —
1 May 49 F @ Henlow
17 Oct 55 to Hornchurch
No 1960 Flt —
1 May 49 F @ Kenley
No 1961 Flt —
1 May 49 F @ Henlow
May 49 **Auster AOP 5** (Oct 51)
May 49 **Auster AOP 6** (Feb 57)
Jul 49 **Auster AOP 4** (Feb 50)
10 Mar 57 DB

662 Sqn

30 Sep 43 F @ Old Sarum
Sep 43 **Auster III** (Apr 44)
4 Feb 44 to Westley
Mar 44 **Auster IV** (Dec 45)
8 Jun 44 to Le Hamel
13 Jun 44 to Bayeux
1 Aug 44 to St-André
6 Aug 44 to Canteloup
17 Aug 44 to Ondefontaine
18 Aug 44 to Taillebois
23 Aug 44 to St-André-d'Eschauffour
26 Aug 44 to Douains
29 Aug 44 to La Queue-d'Haye
31 Aug 44 to Hébécourt
1 Sep 44 to Bernaville
4 Sep 44 to B 58/Melsbroek
7 Sep 44 to Diest
Sep 44 **Auster V** (Dec 45)
15 Sep 44 to Bourg Leopold
19 Sep 44 to Nijmegen
9 Nov 44 to Beek
21 Dec 44 to Bourg Leopold
23 Dec 44 to Rillaar
29 Dec 44 to Temploux
2 Jan 45 to Dinant
18 Jan 45 to Diest
31 Jan 45 to Schaijk
20 Feb 45 to Reichswalde
4 Mar 45 to Goch
6 Mar 45 to Ossenpass
10 Mar 45 to Goch
26 Mar 45 to Appeldorn
1 Apr 45 to Aalten
7 Apr 45 to Nordhorn
10 Apr 45 to Freren
13 Apr 45 to Anstedt
23 Apr 45 to Wester-Wisch
29 Apr 45 to Bassen
1 May 45 to Zeven
5 May 45 to Elm
9 May 45 to Bremerhaven
22 May 45 to Hoya
10 Jun 45 to Goslar
4 Jul 45 to Neheim
10 Jul 45 to Deilinghofen
3 Nov 45 to B 58/Melsbroek
15 Dec 45 DB
—
1 Feb 49 RF @ Colerne as RAuxAF unit comprising:
No 1956 Flt —
1 Feb 49 F @ Colerne
No 1962 Flt —
1 Sep 49 F @ Middle Wallop
No 1963 Flt —
1 Feb 49 F @ Colerne
Feb 49 **Auster AOP 5** (Oct 51)
Feb 49 **Auster AOP 6** (Feb 57)
Oct 49 **Auster AOP 4** (Jan 50)
10 Mar 57 DB

663 Sqn

14 Aug 44 F @ San Basilio
Oct 44 **Auster IV** (Feb 46)
2 Nov 44 to Eboli
Nov 44 **Auster V** (Feb 46)
17 Dec 44 to Montecorvino
2 Jan 45 to Forli
7 Jan 45 to Castrocaro
10 Jan 45 to Meldola
30 Jan 45 to Villa Carpena
16 Apr 45 to Villa Arzana
12 May 45 to Porto San Giorgio
26 May 45 to Imola
10 Jul 45 to Lonato
3 Oct 45 to Monza
10 Oct 46 en route UK
29 Oct 46 DB
—
1 Jul 49 RF @ Hooton Park as RAuxAF unit comprising:
No 1951 Flt —
1 Jul 49 F @ Ringway
No 1952 Flt —
1 Jul 49 F @ Llandow
15 Oct 50 to Pengam Moors
18 Jun 53 to Llandow
No 1953 Flt —
1 Jul 49 F @ Hooton Park
No 1954 Flt —
1 Sep 49 F @ Wolverhampton
27 Mar 53 to Castle Bromwich
No 1955 Flt —
1 Jul 49 F @ Hooton Park
Jul 49 **Auster AOP 5** (Oct 51)
Jul 49 **Auster AOP 6** (Feb 57)
10 Mar 57 DB

664 Sqn

9 Dec 44 F @ Andover
Dec 44 **Auster IV** (May 46)
Dec 44 **Auster V** (May 46)
2 Feb 45 to Penshurst
23 Mar 45 to Tilburg
1 Apr 45 to Breda
22 Apr 45 to Meppen
6 May 45 to Rostrup
17 Jun 45 to Apeldoorn
1 Sep 45 to Jever
12 Sep 45 to Rostrup
31 May 46 DB
—
1 Sep 49 RF @ Hucknall as RAuxAF unit comprising:
No 1964 Flt —
1 Sep 49 F @ Yeadon
2 Feb 53 to Rufforth
1 Jun 54 to Yeadon
No 1965 Flt —
1 Sep 49 F @ Ouston
14 Feb 54 to Usworth
No 1969 Flt —
1 Sep 49 F @ Desford
17 Jan 53 to Hucknall
15 Jul 54 to Wymeswold
No 1970 Flt —
1 Sep 49 F @ Hucknall
Sep 49 **Auster AOP 5** (Oct 51)
Sep 49 **Auster AOP 6** (Mar 57)
10 Mar 57 DB

665 Sqn

22 Jan 45 F @ Andover
Jan 45 **Auster V** (Jul 45)
17 Mar 45 to Oatland Hill
21 Apr 45 to Gilze-Rijen
27 May 45 to Borne
7 Jun 45 to Apeldoorn
10 Jul 45 DB

666 Sqn

5 Mar 45 F @ Andover
Mar 45 **Auster V** (Sep 45)
18 Apr 45 to Friston
28 May 45 to Gilze-Rijen
6 Jun 45 to Hilversum
25 Jun 45 to Apeldoorn
30 Sep 45 DB
—
1 May 49 RF @ Perth/Scone as RAuxAF unit comprising:
No 1966 Flt —
1 May 49 F @ Perth/Scone
No 1967 Flt —
1 Dec 51 F @ Renfrew
5 Dec 52 to Abbotsinch
No 1968 Flt —
1 May 49 F @ Turnhouse
Jun 49 **Auster AOP 5** (Nov 51)
Jun 49 **Auster AOP 6** (Mar 57)
10 Mar 57 DB

667 Sqn

1 Dec 43 F @ Gosport — from from Nos 1622 & 1631 Flts
det Shoreham
Dec 43 **Defiant I** (Dec 44)
Dec 43 **Defiant III** (Feb 45)
Jan 44 **Hurricane IIC** (Sep 45)
Mar 44 **Barracuda II** (Jul 45)
Apr 44 **Oxford** (Dec 45)
Oct 44 **Vengeance IV** (Dec 45)
Jul 45 **Spitfire XVI** (Dec 45)
20 Dec 45 DB

Nos 668-673 Glider Sqns
Nos 668-673 Sqns were intended to operate Hadrian and, later, Horsa gliders in conjunction with Dakota and Halifax tugs in SEAC. However, their formation and work-up was a disjointed and protracted affair and none of the six units ever became operational. Various preparatory courses were undergone, eg in jungle warfare at Belgaum, and some training flying was carried out on **Hadrians** and **Tiger Moths** with which all of the squadrons were equipped for varying periods. Some operational flying was carried out by some of the pilots of Nos 671, 672 and 673 Sqns who were detached to other units to fly Dakotas and L-5 Sentinels.

668 Sqn

16 Nov 44 F @ Calcutta
4 Feb 45 to Lalaghat
30 Apr 45 to Belgaum
28 Jun 45 to Fatejhang
5 Jul 45 to Upper Topa
21 Aug 45 to Fatehjang
10 Nov 45 DB

669 Sqn

16 Nov 44 F @ Bikram
31 Dec 44 DB — renumbered as No 671 Sqn
—
1 Jan 45 RF @ Basal
19 Mar 45 to Belgaum
27 May 45 to Upper Topa
23 Jun 45 to Basal
7 Jul 45 to Fatehjang
10 Nov 45 DB

670 Sqn

30 Dec 44 F @ Fatehjang
15 Mar 45 to Belgaum
30 May 45 to Dhamial
1 Jun 45 to Basal
23 Jun 45 to Upper Topa
26 Jul 45 to Fatehjang
det Upper Topa
1 Apr 46 to Chaklala
1 Jul 46 DB

671 Sqn

1 Jan 45 F @ Bikram — No 669 Sqn renumbered
9 Feb 45 to Belgaum
3 Apr 45 to Bikram
26 Aug 45 to Kargi Road
25 Oct 45 DB

672 Sqn

21 Jan 45 F @ Bikram
26 Feb 45 to Belgaum
30 Apr 45 to Bikram
8 Aug 45 to Kargi Road
19 Nov 45 to Fatehjang
1 Apr 46 to Chaklala
1 Jul 46 DB

673 Sqn

27 Jan 45 F @ Bikram
22 Feb 45 to Belgaum
6 Apr 45 to Bikram
det Bilaspur
24 Aug 45 to Tilda
31 Aug 45 to Bilaspur
16 Sep 45 to Kargi Road
25 Oct 45 DB

679 Sqn

1 Dec 43 F @ Ipswich — from Nos 1616 & 1627 Flts
Dec 43 **Henley III** (Feb 44)
Dec 43 **Martinet** (Jun 45)
Dec 43 **Hurricane IIC** (Jun 45)
Mar 44 **Hurricane IV** (Jun 45)
Apr 44 **Barracuda II** (Jan 45)
Apr 45 **Vengeance IV** (Jun 45)
26 Jun 45 DB

680 Sqn

1 Feb 43 F @ LG 219 — No 2 PRU redesignated
Feb 43 **Spitfire IV** (Jun 44)
Feb 43 **Spitfire VI** (Aug 43)

Feb 43 **Electra** (Feb 45)
Feb 43 **Beaufighter I** (Mar 43)
Feb 43 **Spitfire IX** (Sep 43)
Feb 43 **Hurricane I** (Mar 44)
dets El Djem, Monastir, Castel Benito, Senem, Derna, Tocra, Lakatamia, Nicosia, San Severo, Hassani
Aug 43 **Spitfire XI** (Jul 46)
Aug 43 **Hurricane PR II** (Dec 44)
Feb 44 **Mosquito IX** (Mar 45)
Feb 44 **Mosquito XVI** (Jul 46)
Dec 44 **Baltimore V** (Jul 46)
Feb 45 to Deversoir
Feb 45 **Argus** (Jul 46)
dets Habbaniyah, Aqir, Meherabad, Hassani, Sharjah, Shaibah
Jul 46 **Mosquito XXXIV** (Sep 46)
Jul 46 to Ein Shemar
Sep 46 DB — renumbered as No 13 Sqn

81 Sqn

Jan 43 F @ Dum Dum — No 3 PRU redesignated
Jan 43 **Hurricane IIC** (Nov 43)
Jan 43 **Mitchell II** (Nov 43)
Jan 43 **Spitfire IV** (Nov 44)
det Agartala
Aug 43 **Mosquito II** (Nov 43)
Aug 43 **Mosquito VI** (Nov 43)
Sep 43 **Mosquito IX** (Nov 43)
Sep 43 **Spitfire XI** (Aug 46)
Dec 43 to Chandina
Jan 44 to Dum Dum
May 44 to Alipore
dets Comilla, Imphal, Mingaladon, Meiktila
May 45 to Mingaladon
det Alipore
Aug 45 **Spitfire XIX** (Aug 46)
Sep 45 to Kai Tak
Dec 45 to Kuala Lumpur
Jan 46 to Seletar
dets Don Muang, Mingaladon, Tan Son Nhut, Kemajoran
May 46 to Palam
Aug 46 DB — renumbered as No 34 Sqn

682 Sqn

1 Feb 43 F @ Maison Blanche — No 4 PRU redesignated
Feb 43 **Spitfire IV** (Jul 43)
Feb 43 **Spitfire XI** (Sep 45)
6 Jun 43 to La Marsa
det Foggia
8 Dec 43 to San Severo
dets Trigno, Pomigliano, Alghero, Nettuno, Voltone, Follonica, Borgo, Cecina, Le Luc, Valence, Lyons/Bron, Longevic, Malignano, Peretola, Nancy
Sep 44 **Spitfire XIX** (Sep 45)
14 Sep 45 DB

683 Sqn

8 Feb 43 F @ Luqa — from 'B' Flt, No 69 Sqn
Feb 43 **Spitfire IV** (Jul 43)
Feb 43 **Spitfire IX** (Mar 43)
Feb 43 **Spitfire XI** (Sep 45)
May 43 **Mosquito IV** (Jun 43)
20 Nov 43 to El Aouina
20 Dec 43 to San Severo
dets Vasto, Aquino, Osa, Falerium, Orvieto, Castiglione, Malignano, Chiaravalle, Piagiolino, Cassandro, Rimini, Bellaria, Forli, La Russia, Treviso, Udine, Hassani
Sep 44 **Spitfire XIX** (Sep 45)
21 Sep 45 DB
—
1 Aug 50 RF @ Fayid
Oct 50 **Lancaster PR 1** (Nov 53)
Nov 50 **Valetta C.1** (Nov 53)
26 Feb 51 to Kabrit
23 Apr 51 to Eastleigh
dets Livingstone, Dar-es-Salaam
24 Sep 51 to Kabrit
det Shaibah
18 Dec 51 to Khormaksar
det Habbaniyah
10 Jun 52 to Habbaniyah
det Sharjah
30 Nov 53 DB

684 Sqn

29 Sep 43 F @ Dum Dum — from elements of No 681 Sqn
Sep 43 **Mitchell II** (Sep 45)
Sep 43 **Mosquito II** (Dec 43)
Sep 43 **Mosquito VI** (Feb 44)
Oct 43 **Mosquito IX** (Feb 45)
9 Dec 43 to Comilla
31 Jan 44 to Dum Dum
Feb 44 **Mosquito XVI** (May 46)
5 May 44 to Alipore
dets Yelahanka, China Bay, Cocos
May 45 **Beaufighter VI** (Jul 45)
Jul 45 **Mosquito XXXIV** (Sep 46)
Jul 45 **Beaufighter X** (Jul 46)
11 Oct 45 to Saigon/Tan Son Nhut
dets Cocos, Seletar
20 Jan 46 to Don Muang
dets Seletar, Tan Son Nhut
Aug 46 to Seletar
1 Sep 46 DB — renumbered as No 81 Sqn

691 Sqn

1 Dec 43 F @ Roborough — from No 1623 Flt
Dec 43 **Barracuda II** (Mar 45)
Dec 43 **Defiant I & III** (Apr 45)
Dec 43 **Hurricane I** (Mar 44)
Dec 43 **Oxford** (Feb 49)
Mar 44 **Hurricane IIC** (Apr 45)
21 Feb 45 to Harrowbeer
Apr 45 **Vengeance IV** (May 47)
Jul 45 **Spitfire VB** (Aug 45)
1 Aug 45 to Exeter
Aug 45 **Martinet** (Feb 49)
Aug 45 **Spitfire XVI** (Feb 49)
Nov 45 **Harvard IIB** (Feb 49)
29 Apr 46 to Weston Zoyland
Jul 46 to Fairwood Common
4 Oct 46 to Chivenor
11 Feb 49 DB — renumbered as No 17 Sqn

692 Sqn

1 Jan 44 F @ Graveley
Jan 44 **Mosquito IV** (Jun 44)
Mar 44 **Mosquito XVI** (Sep 45)
4 Jun 45 to Gransden Lodge
20 Sep 45 DB

695 Sqn

1 Dec 43 F @ Bircham Newton — from Nos 1611 & 1612 Flts
Dec 43 **Lysander I & II** (Jan 44)
Dec 43 **Henley III** (Jun 44)
Dec 43 **Martinet** (May 45)
Dec 43 **Hurricane IIC** (Sep 45)
Sep 44 **Spitfire VB** (Aug 45)
Mar 45 **Vengeance IV** (May 47)
Jul 45 **Spitfire XVI** (Feb 49)
11 Aug 45 to Horsham St Faith
Jun 46 **Oxford** (Feb 49)
Dec 46 **Martinet** (Feb 49)
Dec 46 **Harvard IIB** (Feb 49)
Dec 48 **Beaufighter TT 10** (Feb 49)
11 Feb 49 DB — renumbered as No 34 Sqn

1435 Sqn

2 Aug 42 F @ Luqa — No 1435 Flt redesignated
Aug 42 **Spitfire VB** (Nov 43)
Aug 42 **Spitfire VC** (Nov 43)
Mar 43 **Spitfire IX** (Apr 45)
27 Oct 43 to Grottaglie
9 Nov 43 to Brindisi
det Vis
30 May 44 to Grottaglie
det Vis
May 44 **Spitfire VC** (Sep 44)
3 Jun 44 to Brindisi
det Vis
2 Jul 44 to Grottaglie
dets Hal Far, Catania, Vis, Foggia
13 Feb 45 to Falconara
dets Hal Far, Vis
29 Apr 45 to Gragnano No (56 PTC)
9 May 45 DB

Appendix 1

The Reorganisation of Training and Mobilisation in Mid-1918

Something of a mystery has surrounded the origins of over forty squadrons which were caught up in a major reorganisation of the flying services in the UK shortly after the formation of the RAF. A number of interpretations of the immediate and residual effects of this upheaval on the squadrons concerned have been published. None has been very accurate; however, sufficient original documentation has survived to permit a reasonably precise reconstruction to be made. This Appendix is intended to present these 'new' facts.

Since the details given below differ in many respects from the fragmentary accounts which have appeared previously the relevant contemporary source documents have been identified as footnotes and the significance of each of these has been indicated within the notes on each squadron. Seven of these documents are particularly important and provide three critical dates; these are:

a. **Air Organisation Memorandum 875.** A0 875, dated 25 May 18, covered the last Programme of Development for the RAF published prior to the implementation of the rationalisation process. In most cases this document provides the baseline for the accompanying notes on each squadron.

b. **Air Ministry letter C4519.** C4519, dated **4 Jul 18,** and signed by the Master General of Personnel, Godfrey Paine, introduced a major revision of policy. In the context of this book the most significant of the objectives set out in the letter was "To separate clearly Training from Mobilisation". The practical effects of this were: the immediate disbandment of thirteen Service Squadrons, then functioning as training units; the simultaneous cancellation of contemporary plans for the formation of a further twelve such squadrons; and the creation, from the resources thus made available and the amalgamation of Training Squadrons, of a number of new Training Depot Stations, beginning on 15 Jul 18. A new Programme of Development, replacing and extensively revising A0 875, accompanied this policy letter.

c. **Air Organisation Memorandum 939.** A0 939, dated 13 Jul 18, published the Programme of Development accompanying Godfrey Paine's letter of 4 Jul 18, and made the new plans more widely available.

d. **Air Organisation Memorandum 961.** It is evident that the plans detailed in A0 939 had proved over-ambitious and A0 961, dated **29 Jul 18,** placed the whole programme in abeyance, apart from a handful of units which were allowed to continue mobilising.

e. **Air Organisation Memorandum 999.** After a recasting and scaling-down of plans A0 999, dated **17 Aug 18,** was published, covering a revised Programme of Development. This involved the disbandment of a further eight squadrons, which had survived the curtailment of 4 Jul, and excluded sixteen planned units which had featured under A0 939. No further sweeping changes were introduced but the programme covered by A0 999 was subsequently subjected to extensive amendment in detail. Most squadrons had their planned locations or intended equipment altered, or their formation and/or deployment dates postponed.

f. **Air Organisation Memorandum 1147.** A0 1147, dated 5 Nov 18, provided a complete restatement of the Programme of Development to replace that issued under A0 999. It incorporated all the interim amendments that had accrued thus far and introduced further changes. A0 1147 was the last plan to be published before the Armistice, which was declared just six days later.

g. **Air Organisation Memorandum 1155.** A0 1155, dated 15 Nov 18, ordered the disbandment of the majority of units which were at an early stage of mobilisation, and cancelled plans for additional units scheduled to form against the programme published under A0 1147. Only eight squadrons from the Programme were authorised to proceed with their mobilisation but plans for their deployment overseas were abandoned.

The notes below deal with those squadrons which have not previously had their early development adequately recorded. Their periods of actual existence are included in the main text, but this Appendix enlarges on this basic information by including details of the changes in plan to which these units were subject while they were still in the conceptual stage.

No 26 Sqn. Having returned to the UK after service in East Africa, No 26 Sqn disbanded on 8 Jul 18 whilst notionally located at the Records Office, Blandford. The squadron was soon programmed to reform at Chingford, with Puma-engined Bristol Fighters, on 14 Nov 18 and move to France on 14 Jan 19[19]. Replaced in the programme by No 126 Sqn, on 17 Oct 18[33], the unit was rescheduled to form on 17 Dec 18, at Port Meadow with Salamanders, from a contingent of South African personnel training at No 50 TDS, for deployment to France on 14 Feb 19[37]. This plan was pre-empted by the Armistice[38].

No 81 Sqn, one of whose Dolphins is seen here at Scampton, was one of the Service Squadrons which disbanded in the summer of 1918. In this case the unit was absorbed into the expanding organisation of Training Depot Stations, No 34 TDS in this instance. (Author's collection)

No 81 Sqn. During a prolonged gestation No 81 Sqn was, at various times, projected to deploy to France with: Clerget-powered Sopwith Triplanes on 10 Apr 17[1]; SPADs on 31 Oct 17[2]; SE 5s on 23 Jan 18[3]; and Dolphins on 26 Apr 18[4]. Throughout this period the squadron served at Scampton in a training role. It was finally planned to begin working up on Dolphins from 14 Sep 18 in preparation for deployment to France on 21 Oct 18[10], but in the event, the squadron was disbanded on 4 Jul 18[12]. Immediately scheduled to reform at Bicester, again with Dolphins, on 21 Aug 18 and move to France on 21 Oct 18[12], No 81 Sqn's formation and deployment were both subsequently delayed by one month[13]. Reprogrammed yet again, this time to form at Fowlmere, still with Dolphins, on 13 Nov 18 and move to France on 13 Jan 19[19], the unit's planned locations was later changed, first to Wyton[20], and then to Upper Heyford[26]. Subsequently the squadron's formation date was postponed to 20 Nov 18, with deployment to follow on 24 Jan 19[33]. Shortly afterwards it was decided that the group of Canadians earmarked for No 93 Sqn would be used to form No 81 Sqn instead[34]. The final revision of plans involved a delay of just five days to the formation date, to 25 Nov 18, deployment still being envisioned on 24 Jan 19[37]. Despite the Armistice No 81 Sqn's formation was allowed to continue[38] and the unit duly came into being.

No 81 Sqn represented something of a departure from the general pattern of events following the Armistice of 11 Nov 18 in that its formation took place while other similar, planned or embryonic, units had their formation cancelled or suspended. This photograph was taken at Shoreham in 1919 after the, Canadian manned, squadron had exchanged its original Dolphins for SE 5As. The aeroplanes include F9100, F7955, F7982, F9025 and D381. (via G S Leslie)

No 86 Sqn. Initially planned to deploy to France with Dolphins on 13 Jun 18[4], No 86 Sqn's mobilisation was subject to a series of deferments and the squadron was still serving at Northolt in a training role, but was planned to begin working up on Dolphins from 21 Oct 18 in preparation for deployment to France on 28 Nov 18[10], when it was disbanded on 4 Jul 18[12]. The squadron was immediately scheduled to reform at Brockworth, with Dolphins, on 28 Sep 18 and move to France on 28 Nov 18[12]. Shortly afterwards, both formation and deployment were postponed by one month[13]. The unit was then reprogrammed to form, still at Brockworth, but with Salamanders, on 30 Oct 18 and move to France on 30 Dec 18[19]. Reprogrammed yet again, this time to form at Bircham Newton with Salamanders on 14 Nov 18 and move to France on 28 Jan 19[37]. This plan was abandoned shortly after the Armistice[38].

No 89 Sqn. No 89 Sqn was initially intended to deploy to France in Mar 18 with Camels[3], the proposed aircraft later being changed to SE 5s[4]. The squadron's mobilisation was repeatedly deferred but it was just beginning to work up on SE 5As at Upper Heyford, in preparation for deployment to France on 10 Aug 18[14], when the unit was disbanded on 29 Jul 18[15]. The squadron was reprogrammed to form at Fowlmere with Buzzards on 11 Nov 18 and move to France on 11 Jan 19[19]. The planned location was later changed, first to Wyton[20], and then to Leeds (Sherburn-in-Elmet)[26]. The unit was finally planned to form at Chingford with Dolphins on 14 Dec 18 and move to France on 13 Feb 19[37]. Implementation of this plan was pre-empted by the Armistice[38].

No 93 Sqn. No 93 Sqn was initially planned to deploy to France with SE 5s on 27 Apr 18[4]. After repeated delays in the implementation of this plan, during which the squadron served at Tangmere in a training role, it was intended to move the unit to Brockworth on 19 Aug 18 and begin its mobilisation, in preparation for deployment to France, with Dolphins, on 29 Sep 18[10]. This plan was later postponed by one month[13], but in the event the squadron was disbanded on 17 Aug 18[19]. No 93 Sqn was then scheduled to reform, with Canadian personnel[17], at Bicester, again with Dolphins, on 14 Oct 18 and move to France on 14 Dec 18[19]. The planned location was later changed to Oxford (Port Meadow)[29]. The unit's formation took place against this plan, but not with the Canadians, who had been reassigned to No 81 Sqn[34]. No 93 Sqn was disbanded shortly after the Armistice[38].

No 95 Sqn. No 95 Sqn was initially intended to deploy to France with Camels in Apr 18[3], but the intended aircraft were later changed to Dolphins[4]. Repeated delays in mobilisation were experienced and during this period the squadron served in a training role at Shotwick. It was finally planned to begin working up the unit, on Dolphins, from 21 Sep 18 in preparation for deployment to France on 28 Oct 18[10], but the squadron was disbanded on 4 Jul 18[12]. The unit was immediately scheduled to reform at Kenley, still with Dolphins, on 28 Aug 18 and move to France on 28 Oct 18[12]. Both formation and deployment were later deferred by one month[13]. No 95 Sqn was reprogrammed once again, this time to form on 1 Oct 18, still at Kenley, but with Buzzards, and move to France on 1 Dec 18[19]. After the squadron had formed lack of aircraft led to deployment being deferred to 15 Jan 19[37]. The unit disbanded shortly after the Armistice[38] without having received any aircraft, although two Buzzards were being prepared for delivery from Brooklands as the war ended.

No 96 Sqn. No 96 Sqn was initially intended to deploy to France with Camels in May 18[3] but, while repeated delays were imposed on the planned deployment date, the intended aircraft type was changed, first to Dolphins[7], and then to Snipes[8]. In the meantime No 96 Sqn served at Shotwick in a training role. It was finally scheduled to begin working up, with Salamanders, from 23 Sep 18 in preparation for deployment to France on 30 Oct 18[9], but it was disbanded on 4 Jul 18[12]. The squadron was immediately scheduled to reform at Upper Heyford, still with Salamanders, on 30 Aug 18 and move to France on 30 Oct 18[12]. Reprogrammed yet again, this time to form at Fowlmere, again with Salamanders, on 28 Sep 18 and move to France on 28 Nov 18[19], the squadron's planned location was later changed to Wyton[20]. Formation took place against this last plan, deployment later being postponed to 14 Dec 18[37] due to slow delivery of aircraft. Salamanders began to arrive on the squadron just before the Armistice but the unit was disbanded shortly after this[38] without having become fully mobilised.

No 109 Sqn. No 109 Sqn spent some time at Lake Down in a training role but was eventually planned to deploy to France with DH 9s on 20 Aug 18[12]. The planned type was later changed to DH 9As[15] and deployment was postponed, first to 20 Sep 18[15] and then to 4 Oct 18[19]. In the event No 109 Sqn disbanded on 19 Aug 18[20] and did not feature in any subsequent plans.

No 118 Sqn. Originally intended to be equipped with HP 0/400s, No 118 Sqn spent some time attempting, unsuccessfully, to mobilise, finally disbanding at Bicester on 7 Sep 18[23]. It was later programmed to reform at Feltham with Vimys on 16 Dec 18 for deployment to France on 14 Feb 19[37], but this plan was pre-empted by the Armistice[38].

This DH 6, A9738, was on the strength of No 121 Sqn at Narborough during the unit's early service in a training role. Other types used were FK 3s and RE 8s. (Capt D S Glover)

No 121 Sqn. No 121 Sqn, after service at Narborough in a training role, moved to Filton on 10 Aug 18 to begin working up on DH 9s for deployment to France on 20 Sep 18[12]. In the event the squadron was disbanded on 17 Aug 18[19]. Initially scheduled to reform at Filton with DH 9s on 14 Oct 18 and move to France on 14 Dec 18[19], No 121 Sqn's planned location was later changed, first to Thetford[22], and then to Feltham[26]. Later still formation was deferred to 1 Nov 18[32]. The unit was finally reprogrammed to form at Leeds (Sherburn-in-Elmet), this time with DH 10s, on 1 Dec 18 and move to France on 31 Jan 19[37]. This plan was abandoned shortly after the Armistice[38].

No 122 Sqn. No 122 Sqn was serving at Sedgeford in a training role and planned to move to Hamble on 18 Aug 18 to work up on DH 9s for deployment to France on 28 Sep 18[12] when it was disbanded on 17 Aug 18[19]. In the meantime the nominated mobilisation station had been changed to Upper Heyford[16], but disbandment occurred the day before the move was to have taken place. The squadron was rescheduled to form at Upper Heyford with DH9s on 29 Oct 18 and move to France on 29 Dec 18[19]. Formation took place as planned but the intended equipment was later changed to DH 10s and deployment was deferred to 11 Jan 19[37]. No operational aircraft had been received before the squadron's mobilisation was abandoned with the Armistice[38].

No 123 Sqn. Serving at Duxford in a training role and planned to work up on DH 9s from 26 Aug 18 in preparation for deployment to France on 2 Oct 18[12], No 123 Sqn was disbanded on 17 Aug 18[19]. Initially rescheduled to form, with Canadian personnel[17], at Bicester, still with DH 9s, on 3 Nov 18 and move to France on 3 Jan 19[19], the squadron's planned location was later changed to Port Meadow[29]. No 123 Sqn's formation was later postponed to 20 Nov 18, with deployment to take place on 14 Jan 19[33]. Later still the planned aircraft type was changed to DH 9As[37]. Despite the Armistice the squadron's formation was authorised to continue, but with its location changed to Upper Heyford[38], its aircraft being reallocated from No 156 Sqn as that squadron simultaneously disbanded.

No 123 Sqn had a dual identity during its second existence since it was also No 2 Sqn, Canadian Air Force. This picture shows a DH 9A, F2755, of No 123 Sqn at Shoreham in 1919 in the company of a captured Rumpler C.VII, 9949. (via G S Leslie)

No 124 Sqn. Serving at Fowlmere in a training role, and planned to begin working up on DH 9s on 2 Sep 18 in preparation for deployment to France on 9 Oct 18[12], No 124 Sqn was disbanded on 17 Aug 18[19]. The squadron did not feature in any subsequent plans.

No 125 Sqn. Serving at Fowlmere in a training role, and planned to begin working up on DH 9s from 7 Sep 18 in preparation for deployment to France on 14 Oct 18[12], No 125 Sqn was disbanded on 17 Aug 18[19]. The squadron did not feature in any subsequent plans.

No 126 Sqn. Serving at Fowlmere in a training role, and planned to begin working up on DH 9s from 16 Sep 18 in preparation for deployment to France on 23 Oct 18[12], No 126 Sqn disbanded on 17 Aug 18[19]. The squadron was later reprogrammed to form, in place of No 26 Sqn, with Puma-engined Bristol Fighters at Chingford on 14 Nov 18 and move to France on 14 Jan 19[33]. This plan was abandoned with the Armistice[38].

No 127 Sqn. Serving at Catterick in a training role, and planned to begin working up on DH 9s from 18 Aug 18 in preparation for deployment to France on 25 Sep 18[9], No 127 Sqn was disbanded on 4 Jul 18[12]. The squadron was immediately scheduled to reform at Norwich with DH 9s on 25 Aug 18 and move to France on 25 Oct 18[12]. This plan was suspended on 29 Jul 18[15] and No 127 Sqn did not appear in any subsequent programmes.

No 128 Sqn. Serving at Thetford in a training role, and planned to begin working up on DH 9s from 22 Aug 18 in preparation for deployment to France on 29 Sep 18[9], No 128 Sqn was disbanded on 4 Jul 18[12]. The squadron was immediately scheduled to reform at Feltham, again with DH 9s, on 29 Aug 18 and move to France on 29 Oct 18[12]. This plan was put into abeyance on 29 Jul 18[15] and No 128 Sqn did not feature in any subsequent plans.

No 129 Sqn. Serving at Duxford in a training role, and planned to begin working up on DH 9s from 26 Aug 18 in preparation for deployment to France on 3 Oct 18[9], No 129 Sqn was disbanded on 4 Jul 18[12]. The squadron was immediately scheduled to reform at Shoreham, again with DH 9s, on 3 Sep 18 and move to France on 3 Nov 18[12]. This plan was put into abeyance on 29 Jul 18[15] and No 129 Sqn did not appear in any subsequent plans.

No 130 Sqn. Serving at Hucknall in a training role, and planned to begin working up on DH 9s from 1 Sep 18 in preparation for deployment to France on 8 Oct 18[9], No 130 Sqn was disbanded on 4 Jul 18[12]. The squadron was immediately scheduled to reform at Bracebridge Heath, again with DH 9s, on 8 Sep 18 and move to France on 8 Nov 18[12]. This plan was suspended on 29 Jul 18[15] and No 130 Sqn did not appear in any subsequent programmes.

No 131 Sqn. Serving at Shawbury in a training role, and planned to move to Kenley on 26 Aug 18 and begin working up on DH 9s in preparation for deployment to France on 5 Oct 18[12], No 131 Sqn was disbanded on 17 Aug 18[19] before the move took place. The squadron did not appear in any further programmes.

No 132 Sqn. Serving at Ternhill in a training role, and planned to begin working up with HP 0/400s from 22 Aug 18 in preparation for deployment to France on 29 Sep 18[9], No 132 Sqn was later moved to Castle Bromwich, on 19 Aug 18[12], to mobilise. Delays in the delivery of aircraft caused postponements to the deployment, first to 13 Nov 18[19] and then to 20 Dec 18[30]. The latter change was accompanied by a change of aircraft type to DH 9As[30]. The final deployment date scheduled was 13 Jan 19[37] but No 132 Sqn's mobilisation was abandoned[38] before any operational aircraft had been received.

No 133 Sqn. Serving at Ternhill in a training role, and planned to begin working up on HP 0/400s from 31 Aug 18 in preparation for deployment to France on 7 Oct 18[9], No 133 Sqn was disbanded on 4 Jul 18[12]. The squadron was immediately scheduled to reform at Bicester, still with 0/400s, on 7 Aug 18 and move to France on 7 Oct 18[12]. Reprogrammed to form at Feltham, again with 0/400s, on 28 Oct 18 and move to France on 28 Dec 18[19], No 133 Sqn was subsequently replanned to form on 25 Nov 18, still at Feltham, but with the equipment changed to DH 9As and deployment delayed to 25 Jan 19[30]. The final plan for the unit involved its formation at Castle Bromwich on 21 Dec 18 for eventual service with the Grand Fleet[37]. All aircraft were supposed to have been delivered by 31 Jan 19, but the unit's formation was pre-empted by the Armistice[38].

No 134 Sqn. Serving at Ternhill in a training role, and planned to begin working up on DH 9As from 6 Sep 18 in preparation for deployment to France on 13 Oct 18[9], No 134 Sqn was disbanded on 4 Jul 18[12]. The squadron was immediately scheduled to reform at Upper Heyford on DH 9As on 13 Sep 18 and move to France on 13 Nov 18[12]. This plan was put in abeyance on 29 Jul 18[15] and No 134 Sqn did not feature in any subsequent programmes.

No 135 Sqn. Serving at Hucknall in a training role, and planned to begin working up on DH 9s from 14 Sep 18 in preparation for deployment to France on 21 Oct 18[9], No 135 Sqn was disbanded on 4 Jul 18[12]. The squadron was immediately scheduled to reform at Bicester with DH 9As on 21 Sep 18 and move to France on 21 Nov 18[12]. This plan was suspended on 29 Jul 18[15] and No 135 Sqn did not appear in any later programmes.

No 136 Sqn. Serving at Lake Down in a training role, and planned to begin working up on DH 9s from 22 Sep 18 in preparation for deployment to France on 29 Oct 18[9], No 136 Sqn was disbanded on 4 Jul 18[12]. The squadron was immediately scheduled to reform at Castle Bromwich with DH 9As on 29 Sep 18 and move to France on 29 Nov 18[12]. This plan was put in abeyance on 29 Jul 18[15] and No 136 Sqn did not appear in any subsequent programmes.

No 137 Sqn. Serving at Shawbury in a training role, and planned to begin working up on DH 9s from 28 Sep 18 in preparation for deployment to France on 4 Nov 18[9], No 137 Sqn was disbanded on 4 Jul 18[12]. Immediately scheduled to reform at Chingford on 4 Oct 18 and move to France on 4 Dec 18, the squadron was now planned to receive DH 9As[12]. This plan was suspended on 29 Jul 18[15] and No 137 Sqn did not appear in any later programmes.

No 138 Sqn. The earliest plans for No 138 Sqn projected its formation at Catterick with HP 0/400s for deployment to France on 7 Oct 18[5]. This plan was superseded by one which envisaged the squadron's formation at Port Meadow, with either 0/400s or DH 9s, on 1 Apr 18[6]. These plans were later postponed by one month[6] and finally cancelled, being replaced by an intention to form No 138 Sqn with Hispano-engined Bristol Fighters and move it to France on 5 Oct 18[9]. No location or formation date had been fixed before these plans were abandoned on 4 Jul 18[12]. The squadron was immediately rescheduled to form at Chingford, still with (Hispano) Bristol Fighters, on 5 Aug 18 and move to France on 5 Oct 18[12]. This plan was suspended on 29 Jul 18[15] and the unit was reprogrammed to form on 30 Sep 18, still at Chingford, but with Puma-engined Bristol Fighters, and move to France on 30 Nov 18[19]. Formation took place on the last appointed date but in the event the aircraft supplied were Falcon-powered. The unit was on the point of moving overseas[36] when the war ended and the move was cancelled[38]. No 138 Sqn was one of those units which escaped immediate disbandment after the Armistice[38].

No 139 Sqn. No 139 Sqn was initially projected as a bomber squadron to form on 1 Apr 18 and deploy to France on 17 Oct 18 with either DH 9s or HP 0/400s[6]. Formation was later postponed to 1 May 18 but a location had still not been nominated[6] before the squadron was deleted from the Programme of Development. The numberplate was subsequently allocated to 'Z' Flt in Italy where it came into use from 3 Jul 18.

No 140 Sqn. The earliest plans for No 140 Sqn envisaged its formation on 1 Apr 18 with either DH 9s or HP 0/400s[6]. The planned formation date was later postponed to 1 May 18 but no location had been decided before the squadron was deleted from the Programme of Development. No 140 Sqn did not feature in any subsequent programmes.

No 146 Sqn. No 146 Sqn was initially planned[5] as a bombing squadron which was to be equipped with DH 9s ready for deployment from the UK to Egypt by 30 Apr 18. This deployment date was later amended to 3 Jun 18[8] and 14 Jul 18[9]. However, no place of formation had been published before the unit disappeared from the Programme of Development in Jul 18[12], although there are later references which indicate that, had it formed, it had been intended to operate in the Aegean, from Mudros. No 146 Sqn did not feature in any subsequent plans.

No 147 Sqn. No 147 Sqn was initially planned[5] as a bombing squadron which was to be equipped with DH 9s ready for deployment from the UK to Egypt by 31 May 18. This deployment date was later amended to 3 Jul 18[8] and then to 14 Aug 18[9]. However, no place of formation had been nominated before the unit disappeared from the Programme of Development in Jul 18[12]. Despite this, repeated references were made to No 147 Sqn in a variety of documents dated between Jun 18 and Mar 19. In all cases the unit was described as 'mobilising in Egypt' but no location or parent formation was ever recorded. It is very doubtful that No 147 Sqn ever had more than a notional existence; it certainly does not figure in any HQ Middle East documents after its formation, along with that of No 146 Sqn, had been indefinitely postponed in May 18[39].

No 154 Sqn. No 154 Sqn was initially projected as a Falcon-powered Bristol Fighter unit to be deployed to France on 3 Oct 18[8]. No location or formation date had been fixed before these plans were abandoned on 4 Jul 18[12]. No 154 Sqn was immediately rescheduled to form at Chingford, still with (Falcon) Bristol Fighters, on 3 Aug 18 and move to France on 3 Oct 18[12]. This plan was suspended on 29 Jul 18[15] but formation was subsequently authorised on 7 Aug 18[18]. Ten days later the squadron's deployment date was fixed as 29 Oct 18[19] but on 11 Sep 18 the squadron was disbanded[24]. It did not appear in any subsequent plans.

No 155 Sqn. No 155 Sqn was initially projected as a DH 9A squadron to be deployed to France on 22 Sep 18[8]. Shortly afterwards deployment was rescheduled for 6 Oct 18 but no date or place of formation had been decided[9] before these plans were abandoned on 4 Jul 18[12]. The squadron was immediately rescheduled to form at Coventry with DH 9As on 6 Sep 18 and move to France on 6 Nov 18[12]. These plans were suspended on 29 Jul 18 and the squadron was subsequently rescheduled to form at Feltham, still with DH 9As, on 14 Sep 18 and move to France on 14 Nov 18[19]. The planned location was later changed to Chingford[25] and deployment was postponed to 21 Nov 18[37]. No 155 Sqn's formation took place as planned but the unit's deployment, which had been authorised[35], was cancelled[38] with the Armistice, although the unit was not required to disband immediately.

No 155 Sqn was scheduled to complete its mobilisation ten days after the Armistice was signed on 11 Nov 18; on 15 Nov its deployment to France was cancelled. This is one of the squadron's DH 9As, E8553. (RAF Museum P5089)

No 156 Sqn. No 156 Sqn was initially projected as a DH 9A squadron to be deployed to France on 29 Sep 18[8]. Shortly afterwards deployment was rescheduled for 12 Oct 18, but no place or date of formation had been fixed[9] before this plan was abandoned on 4 Jul 18[12]. The squadron was immediately reprogrammed to form at Duxford with DH 9As on 12 Sep 18 and to move to France on 12 Nov 18[12]. These plans were suspended on 29 Jul 18[15] and the squadron was subsequently reprogrammed with its formation and deployment dates delayed by exactly one month[19]. The planned location was later changed, first to Thetford[20], and then to Wyton[26], and deployment was further postponed to 12 Dec 18[37]. The squadron duly formed at Wyton on 12 Oct 18[27], but mobilisation was abandoned shortly after the Armistice[38] and on 20 Nov 18 its aircraft were transferred to No 123 Sqn.

No 157 Sqn. No 157 Sqn was initially projected as a Snipe squadron to be deployed to France on 26 Aug 18[8]. This plan was dropped and No 157 Sqn was next envisaged as the first Salamander unit and was to be deployed to France on 31 Aug 18[9], but no place or date of formation had been fixed before these plans were abandoned on 4 Jul 18[12]. The squadron was immediately rescheduled to form at Upper Heyford, still with Salamanders, on 14 Jul 18 and move to France on 14 Sep 18[12]. Formation took place on the appointed date but lack of aircraft led to delays in the planned deployment date, first to 14 Oct 18[19], and then to 14 Nov 18[21]. At the time of the Armistice the squadron had a full complement of Salamanders and was due to move overseas on 21 Nov 18[37]. The move was cancelled with the end of the war[38] but the squadron remained in existence for a while.

No 158 Sqn. No 158 Sqn was initially projected as a Snipe squadron to be deployed to France on 7 Sep 18[8]. Shortly afterwards the planned aircraft were changed to Salamanders and deployment was rescheduled for 30 Sep 18[9]; however, no date or place of formation had been fixed[9] before these plans were abandoned on 4 Jul 18[12]. No 158 Sqn was immediately reprogrammed to form at Upper Heyford, again with Salamanders, on 14 Aug 18 and move to France on 14 Oct 18[12]. These plans were suspended on 29 Jul 18[15]. The squadron's formation was next scheduled for 4 Sep 18, with deployment to follow on 4 Nov 18[19]. Formation took place at Upper Heyford as planned but lack of aircraft led to progressive delays to the planned deployment date, initially to 14 Dec 18[31], and, by the time of the Armistice, to 3 Jan 19[37]. The squadron was disbanded shortly after the war ended[38] without ever having received any Salamanders.

No 159 Sqn. No 159 Sqn was initially projected to be a fighter squadron, with either SE 5As or Dolphins, to be deployed to France on 30 Sep 18. No place or date of formation had been fixed however[8], before the unit was dropped from the programme. No 159 Sqn did not feature in any subsequent plans.

No 160 Sqn. No 160 Sqn was initially projected as a DH 9A unit to be deployed to France on 7 Oct 18[8]. Shortly afterwards the deployment date was rescheduled for 20 Oct 18[9] but no date or place of formation had been appointed[9] before these plans were abandoned on 4 Jul 18[12]. No 160 Sqn was immediately rescheduled to form at Bristol (Filton) with DH 9As on 20 Sep 18 and move to France on 20 Nov 18[12]. These plans were suspended on 29 Jul 18[15] and No 160 Sqn did not appear in any subsequent plans.

No 161 Sqn. No 161 Sqn was initially projected as a DH 9A squadron to be deployed to France on 13 Oct 18[8]. Shortly afterwards deployment was deferred to 27 Oct 18, but no place or date of formation had been fixed[9] before this plan was abandoned on 4 Jul 18[12]. No 161 Sqn was immediately rescheduled to form at Hamble, with DH 9As, on 27 Sep 18 and move to France on 27 Nov 18[12]. This plan was suspended on 29 Jul 18[15] and the squadron did not appear in any subsequent programmes.

No 162 Sqn. No 162 Sqn was initially projected as a DH 9A squadron to be deployed to France on 19 Oct 18[8]. Shortly afterwards deployment was deferred to 2 Nov 18, but no place or date of formation had been decided[9] before this plan was abandoned on 4 Jul 18[12]. No 162 Sqn was immediately rescheduled to form at Chingford on 4 Oct 18 and move to France on 4 Dec 18[12]. This programme was put into abeyance on 29 Jul 18[15] and the squadron did not feature in any subsequent plans.

No 163 Sqn. No 163 Sqn was initially projected as a DH 9A squadron to be deployed to France on 26 Oct 18[8]. Shortly afterwards deployment was deferred to 9 Nov 18, but no place or date of formation had been fixed[9] before this plan was abandoned on 4 Jul 18[12]. No 163 Sqn was immediately rescheduled to form at Fowlmere, with DH 9As, on 9 Oct 18 and move to France on 9 Dec 18[12]. This plan was suspended on 29 Jul 18[15] and the squadron did not appear in any subsequent programmes.

No 164 Sqn. No 164 Sqn was initially projected as a DH 9A squadron to be deployed to France on 31 Oct 18[8]. Shortly afterwards deployment was deferred to 15 Nov 18, but no place or date of formation had been published[9] before this plan was abandoned on 4 Jul 18[12]. No 164 Sqn was immediately rescheduled to form at Fowlmere, again with DH 9As, on 25 Oct 18 and move to France on 25 Dec 18[12]. This plan was put into abeyance on 29 Jul 18[15] and the squadron did not feature in any subsequent programmes.

No 165 Sqn. No 165 Sqn was initially projected as a DH 10 squadron to be deployed to France on 8 Oct 18[8]. Shortly afterwards deployment was postponed to 22 Oct 18, but no place or date of formation had been decided[9] before this plan was abandoned on 4 Jul 18[12]. No 165 Sqn was immediately rescheduled to form at Duxford, again with DH 10s, on 22 Aug 18 and move to France on 22 Oct 18[12]. This plan was suspended on 29 Jul 18[15] and No 164 Sqn did not appear in any subsequent programmes.

No 166 Sqn. No 166 Sqn was initially projected as a Snipe squadron to be deployed to France on 28 Sep 18, but no place or date of formation had been decided[8] before the squadron disappeared from the Programme of Development[9]. Rescheduled to form with HP V/1500s[12], this took place at Bircham Newton on 13 Jun 18[11], i.e. before the new Programme had been published.

No 166 Sqn was intended to fly Handley Page V/1500s like this one as part of a strategic bombing force. The Armistice prevented the initial demonstration of this concept by a matter of days. This picture was taken at Bircham Newton, No 166 Sqn's home base. The immense size of these aeroplanes can be judged from the diminutive figure leaning from the front cockpit. (RAF Museum P12552)

Footnotes

1. Air Organisation Memorandum A0 309 dated 22 Dec 16
2. Air Organisation Memorandum A0 476 dated 20 Jun 17
3. Air Organisation Memorandum A0 567 dated 15 Sep 17
4. Air Organisation Memorandum A0 657 dated 16 Nov 17
5. Air Organisation Memorandum A0 755 dated 26 Jan 18
6. HQ Training Division letter HQ/1041 dated 20 Feb 18
7. HQ Training Division letter TD/733/200 dated 14 Mar 18
8. Air Organisation Memorandum A0 860 dated 9 May 18
9. Air Organisation Memorandum A0 875 dated 27 May 18
10. Air Organisation Memorandum A0 883 dated 8 Jun 18
11. Air Organisation Memorandum A0 900 dated 13 Jun 18
12. Air Ministry letter C4519 dated 4 Jul 18
 & Air Organisation Memorandum A0 939 dated 13 Jul 18
13. Air Ministry letter C4519(N.5) dated 17 Jul 18
14. Air Organisation Memorandum A0 946 dated 18 Jul 18
15. Air Organisation Memorandum A0 961 dated 29 Jul 18
16. Air Organisation Memorandum A0 971 dated 3 Aug 18
17. Air Organisation Memorandum A0 967 dated 5 Aug 18
18. Air Organisation Memorandum A0 976 dated 7 Aug 18
19. Air Organisation Memorandum A0 999 dated 17 Aug 18
20. Air Organisation Memorandum A0 1002 dated 19 Aug 18
21. Air Organisation Memorandum A0 1015 dated 29 Aug 18
22. Air Organisation Memorandum A0 1028 dated 6 Sep 18
23. Air Organisation Memorandum A0 1030 dated 7 Sep 18
24. Air Organisation Memorandum A0 1039 dated 11 Sep 18
25. Air Organisation Memorandum A0 1045 dated 12 Sep 18
26. Air Organisation Memorandum A0 1056 dated 17 Sep 18
27. Air Organisation Memorandum A0 1074 dated 24 Sep 18
28. Air Organisation Memorandum A0 1085 dated 27 Sep 18
29. Air Organisation Memorandum A0 1086 dated 27 Sep 18
30. Air Organisation Memorandum A0 1100 dated 5 Oct 18
31. Air Organisation Memorandum A0 1102 dated 9 Oct 18
32. Air Organisation Memorandum A0 1110 dated 12 Oct 18
33. Air Organisation Memorandum A0 1113 dated 17 Oct 18
34. Air Organisation Memorandum A0 1117 dated 19 Oct 18
35. Air Organisation Memorandum A0 1127 dated 25 Oct 18
36. Air Organisation Memorandum A0 1139 dated 30 Oct 18
37. Air Organisation Memorandum A0 1147 dated 5 Nov 18
38. Air Organisation Memorandum A0 1155 dated 15 Nov 18
39. HQ Middle East letter JPP dated 31 May 18

As indicated in the foregoing, many service squadrons spent their early months serving in a training role. No 65 Sqn was slightly unusual in that it was given a Home Defence commitment during its pre-deployment work-up at Wye where this picture of one of its Camels was taken. (J D Steer)

The adoption of obligatory RAF style organisation from 1 Apr 18 did not suit some of the more remotely located elements of the RNAS, leading to subsequent uncertainty over the early days of some of these units. Those based in southern Italy, exemplified here by No 225 Sqn's Camels (above) and No 226 Sqn's DH 9s (below) made an effort to conform, although there were still differences between the designations adopted and those nominated by London. Units serving in the Aegean theatre were even more recalcitrant and it was not until Sep 18 that they finally began to use RAF squadron numbers. This is enlarged upon in Appendix 12. (J M Bruce/G S Leslie collection)

Appendix 2

Unit Number Allocations

The numbers allocated to RAF squadrons are part of a series which extends from 1 to 1999. Within this series, blocks of numbers have been allotted to a variety of air units of all three services. These blocks are listed below. It should be appreciated that not every number within each block has been taken up.

Numbers	**Allocations**
1-299	RFC/RAF allocation. Those from No 201 onwards had predominantly maritime (RNAS) origins. No 188 has never been used.
300-309	Polish squadrons.
310-313	Czechoslovak squadrons.
315-318	Polish squadrons.
320-322	Dutch squadrons.
326-329	French squadrons.
330-334	Norwegian squadrons.
335-336	Greek squadrons.
340-347	French squadrons.
349-350	Belgian squadrons.
351-352	Jugoslav squadrons.
353-399	RAF allocation. Only Nos 353-358, 360 and 361 have been used.
400-445	Canadian squadrons. Nos 444 and 445 were not used.
450-467	Australian squadrons. No 465 was not used.
485-490	New Zealand squadrons.
500-509	Special Reserve (later Auxiliary, then Royal Auxiliary, Air Force) squadrons. Only 500-504 were used.
510-599	RAF allocation. Nos 522, 523, 545, 546, 568, 569, 572-574, 579-581, 583-586, 588-594, 596, 597 and 599 were never used. Some squadrons were planned within these numbers but they failed to materialise before being overtaken by events. In addition Nos 551-566 were allocated to potentially operational fighter OTUs but the option was never taken up.

Spitfire VB, AB824/RF·S, of No 303 (Polish) Sqn being recovered by a team of Luftwaffe personnel after it had been lost over St Omer on 4 Apr 42 in the hands of Flt Lt Kustrynski. (via Chaz Bowyer)

A Czech Liberator GR VI, KG870/PP·H, of No 311 Sqn. This picture was taken after the war; RAF roundels have been deleted and the fins display the Czech Air Force emblem. No 311 Sqn flew back to its homeland in Aug 45 transporting men and equipment of Nos 310, 312 and 313 (Spitfire) Sqns all of which were returning to Prague at the same time. (via Chaz Bowyer)

Hudson I, T9316/TO·A, of No 320 Sqn. A black-edged orange triangle can just be discerned among the glazed nose panels identifying the aircraft as belonging to a Dutch-manned unit. (RAF Museum P8096)

Before No 342 Sqn was established in the UK an earlier Free French 'Lorraine' Squadron had operated with the Allies in East and North Africa. These Blenheim IVs, T1875 and Z5728, were photographed in service with the unit in the Sudan. Their French association is boldly displayed. (ECP Armées)

Clipped winged Belgian Spitfire VB, AA944/GE·U, of No 349 Sqn caught striking an undignified pose. (via Chaz Bowyer)

600-616	Auxiliary (later Royal Auxiliary) Air Force squadrons. No 606 was not used.
617-650	RAF allocation. Nos 617-620 were originally intended as Auxiliaries but not formed as such. Nos 629, 632-634, 636-638, 641-643 and 645-649 were not used. No 622 was re-used post-war as an Auxiliary squadron.
651-673	Army-associated allocation. Nos 651-666 were AOP units, of which No 663 was a Polish squadron and Nos 664-666 were Canadian. Nos 668-673 were glider units in India. Nos 661-664 were re-used post-war as Auxiliary squadrons. Since 1 Sep 57 this block of numbers has been dedicated to Army Air Corps units.
674-699	RAF allocation. Only Nos 679-684, 691, 692 and 695 have been used.
700-799	Originally allocated to Fleet Air Arm catapult units but later changed to second-line Naval squadrons.
800-899	Allocated to carrier- and land-based operational squadrons of the Fleet Air Arm.
900-999	Barrage balloon squadrons.
1000-1299	Not used.
1300-1399	Allocated to miscellaneous Flights and some Conversion Units.
1400-1499	Allocated to miscellaneous Flights. Introduced on 1 Mar 41 when Commonwealth squadrons began to form in the 400 block. Potential confusion with existing Flights numbered in the 400s under a previous system was avoided by renumbering them in the 1400s by adding 1000 to the current number; thus, for example, No 430 Flt became No 1430 Flt. Note that No 1435 Flt retained its number on becoming No 1435 Sqn.
1500-1699	Allocated to Flights and Conversion Units.
1700-1799	Second allocation for Fleet Air Arm second-line squadrons.
1800-1899	Second allocation for Fleet Air Arm operational squadrons.
1900-1999	Allocated to AOP Flights.

A Spitfire FR XIVE of the Australian No 453 Sqn after the end of the war. No 453 Sqn formed part of BAFO until Jan 46; one month of this period was spent on garrison duty in Berlin. (T Stone)

No 489 Sqn was one of six New Zealand-manned units which flew with the RAF in Europe during WW II. These three Hampden torpedo-bombers of No 489 Sqn are being led by AE261. (RAF Museum P7181)

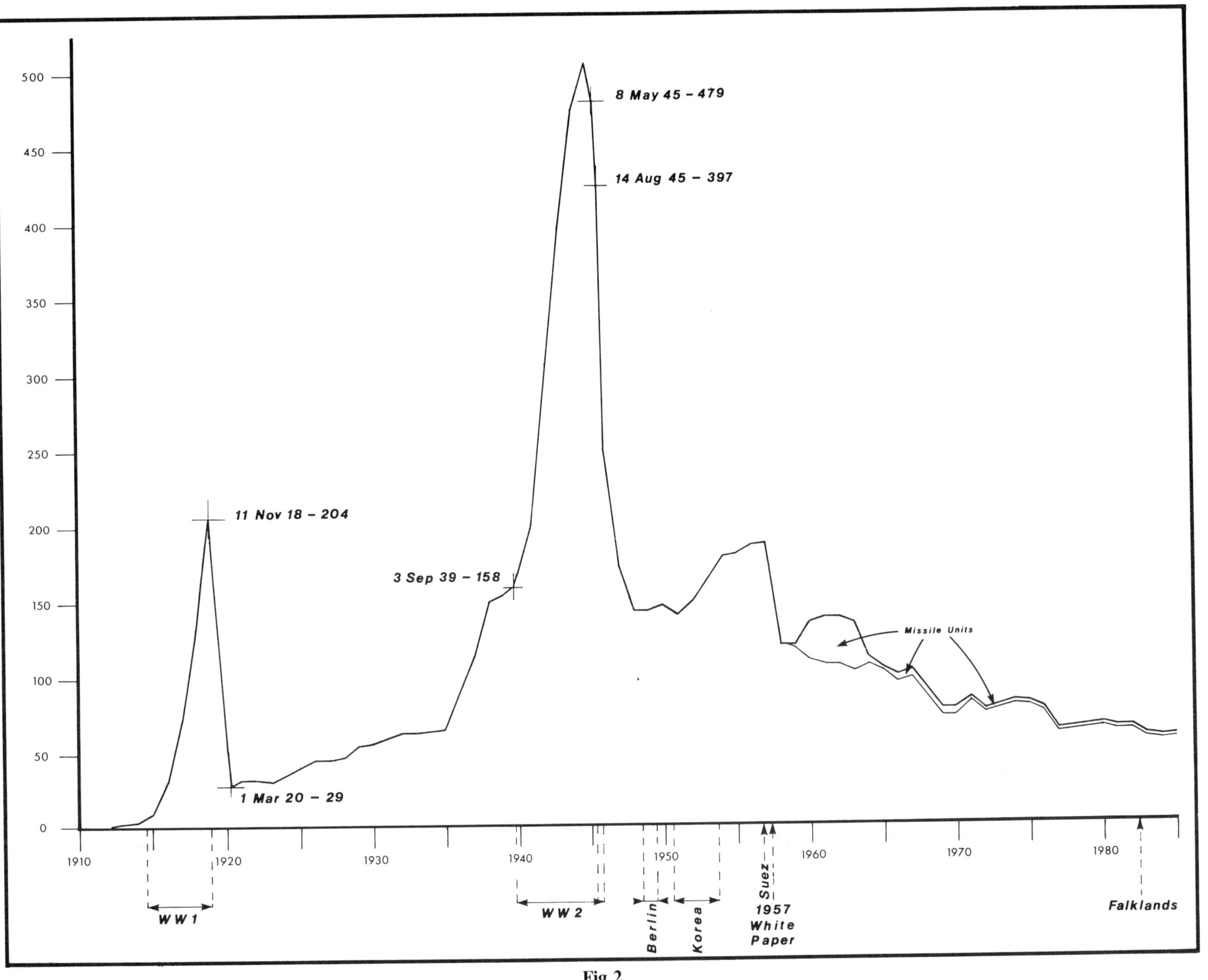

500
450
400
350
300
250
200
150
100
50
0
8 May 45 – 479
14 Aug 45 – 397
11 Nov 18 – 204
3 Sep 39 – 158
Missile Units
1 Mar 20 – 29
1910
1920
1930
1940
1950
1960
1970
1980
WW 1
WW 2
Berlin
Korea
Suez
1957 White Paper
Falklands

Fig 2

Appendix 3

Graphical Illustrations

The illustrations in this Appendix are intended to provide an easily assimilated impression of the way in which the size of the RAF has fluctuated. The accompanying notes expand on the information contained in the charts and in the text of the Introduction to the book.

Figure 2. Figure 2 plots the size of the RAF and its antecedents, measured in numbers of squadrons in service as at 1 Jan each year. Five particularly significant additional dates have also been highlighted.

If the graph is read from left to right the salient points of the RAF's history are evident. The RFC began with just three squadrons in 1912 and by the outbreak of World War One there were seven. Thereafter expansion took place at a rapid rate until a peak strength had been reached by the time of the Armistice of 11 Nov 18, when 204 squadron numbers were in use, although not all of these units were operational. Demobilisation was even more rapid and by 1 Mar 20 the RAF had reached its nadir. A nominal 29 squadrons existed — with an effective strength of perhaps half that number — and these were spread out between the UK and India.

When WW I ended the RAF had over 200 squadrons. It was still expanding and was on the point of introducing a new generation of combat types including the Vimy, DH 10, Salamander, Buzzard and V/1500. The Snipe was the first of these and was the only one to fly operationally before the Armistice. This one, E8057, belonged to No 70 Sqn and was photographed at Bickendorf in 1919. (J M Bruce/G S Leslie collection)

Over the next three years the RAF's size stabilised at just over 30 squadrons. In 1923 a committee was set up under the chairmanship of the Marquess of Salisbury to report on both national and imperial defence, with particular regard to the contribution to be made by the RAF. The committee advised, among other things, that the UK element of the service should be expanded to a strength of 52 squadrons, an increase of 34 units. This recommendation was accepted and a slow expansion was put in hand. Many of the additional squadrons were created through the formation of units of the Special Reserve and the Auxiliary Air Force from 1925 onwards and, later, by the redesignation of flying boat Flights as Squadrons. The target was reached in the early 1930s and by 1 Jan 35 there was a total of 65 squadrons. Over the next two years, however, the potential size and strength of the newly revealed Luftwaffe led to a succession of Expansion Programmes being authorised, each enlarging on its predecessor. These were acted upon with some urgency; over the next three years the RAF more than doubled in size and by 1 Jan 38 it could field 149 squadrons. When war was declared on 3 Sep 39 this total had increased slightly to 158.

The creation of new units proceeded steadily and rapidly during the years of the Second World War. The rate of expansion did not decline until 1944 and even then the change was slight. However, by the end of that year the end of the war was within sight and expansion was replaced by contraction. On 1 Jan 45 there were 504 squadron numbers in use. By VE-Day this had fallen to 479 and a further 82 units had disbanded by VJ-Day. Post-war, although many units were significantly reduced in strength compared to their wartime establishments, further reduction in numbers of squadrons was checked by the prevailing tensions in Europe which culminated in the Berlin Airlift. By this time the size of the RAF had stabilised at just under 150 squadrons and this strength was

One of the handful of unit designations selected to constitute the small post-war Air Force (and thus incidentally ensure that it was likely to remain in use more or less permanently) was that of No 27 Sqn. This picture was taken at Risalpur in 1920 and shows DH 9As of 27 Sqn, H64, H28, J587, E8461 and (possibly) E774, still wearing wartime camouflage. (Chaz Bowyer)

The creation of the Special Reserve contributed to the steady consolidation of the RAF's strength in the 1920s. This Hyderabad, J9297, which is apparently being dismantled, perhaps after a forced-landing, is of No 503 Sqn, the second of the Reserve squadrons to be formed. (RAF Waddington archives)

No 50 Sqn was one of the many units reformed under the Expansion Programmes of the mid-1930s. This Hind, K6741, is seen just to the south of Waddington in 1938; the WW I hangars can be seen in the top left hand corner of the picture – see Appendix 10, Figure 15. (No 50 Sqn archives)

maintained until a further deterioration in international relations associated with the Cold War and ultimately leading to the conflict in Korea gave rise to a re-expansion between 1951 and 1957. 1957 proved to be a particularly significant year in the fortunes of the RAF. That year's Defence White Paper postulated that, since a defence against incoming nuclear bombers or ballistic missles could not be 100% effective, it was not sensible to maintain an unnecessarily large fighter force in an effort to achieve the impossible. National security in the future therefore was to rest on deterrence, not on direct defence. It was planned to concentrate the remaining air defences on the protection of the deterrent forces and, further, it was intended to replace existing fighter aircraft with surface-to-air missiles (SAM). This was to lead to a marked decline in the strength of the service, mostly through the disbandment of fighter and light bomber squadrons in the UK and Germany. The initial reduction in strength, however, was as a result of the disbandment of the flying units of the RAuxAF, on economic grounds, which removed 25 squadrons at a stroke on 10 Mar 57. Four more squadrons were lost on 1 Sep 57, when the remaining AOP units were transferred to the control of the Army.

Further effects of the 1957 White Paper's policy became apparent from 1958 as the new missile squadrons began to form. At one time consideration was given to creating a discrete block of numbers for missile units, but in the event it was decided to allocate defunct numbers from within the already existing series of squadron numbers. The missile era proved to be short-lived, lasting effectively only from 1959 until 1964. It involved four complexes of Thor IRBM launch sites protected by Bloodhound Mk 1 SAM installations. The geographical deployment of these units is illustrated at Figure 3.

After the disbandment of the first-generation missile units, a much reduced commitment to the use of SAM (now Bloodhound Mk 2) continued and is maintained today (1988). However the number of SAM units fell to two as the RAF realigned

A Thor IRBM at lift-off. Sixty of these liquid-fuelled rockets were deployed by the RAF in Eastern England in the early 1960s under joint British/US control. Being immobile they were inherently vulnerable, however, and they were withdrawn after the successful development of the long-range Atlas missile which could reach their targets from the relative safety and security of launch sites in the USA. (RAF Museum P15254)

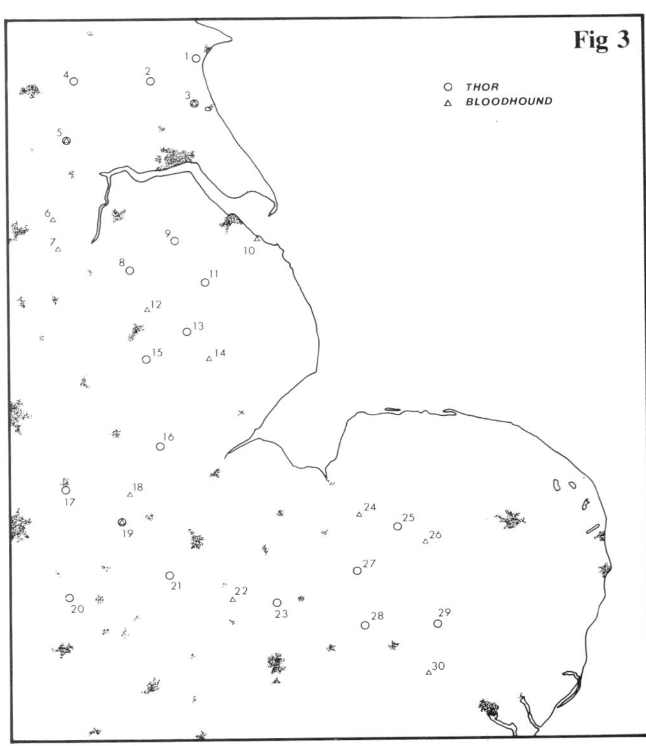

Thor

2 Driffield — Wg HQ & No 98 Sqn
1 Carnaby — No 150 Sqn
3 Catfoss — No 226 Sqn
4 Full Sutton — No 102 Sqn
5 Breighton — No 240 Sqn

8 Hemswell — Wg HQ & No 97 Sqn
9 Caistor — No 269 Sqn
11 Ludford Magna — No 104 Sqn
13 Bardney — No 106 Sqn
15 Coleby Grange — No 142 Sqn

19 North Luffenham — Wg HQ & No 144 Sqn
16 Folkingham — No 223 Sqn
17 Melton Mowbray — No 254 Sqn
20 Harrington — No 218 Sqn
21 Polebrook — No 130 Sqn

27 Feltwell — Wg HQ & No 77 Sqn
23 Mepal — No 113 Sqn
25 North Pickenham — No 220 Sqn
28 Tuddenham — No 107 Sqn
29 Shepherds Grove — No 82 Sqn

Bloodhound I

6 Lindholme — No 21 Wg HQ
3 Catfoss — No 247 Sqn
5 Breighton — No 112 Sqn
7 Misson — No 94 Sqn

19 North Luffenham — No 151 Wg HQ
18 Woolfox Lodge — No 62 Sqn
22 Warboys — No 257 Sqn

10 North Coates — No 148 Wg HQ & No 264 Sqn
12 Dunholme Lodge — No 141 Sqn
14 Woodhall Spa — No 222 Sqn

26 Watton — No 24 Wg HQ & No 263 Sqn
24 Marham — No 242 Sqn
30 Rattlesden — No 266 Sqn

itself into a NATO-orientated, European-based force. This process occupied some 13 years in the 1960s and 1970s and was a consequence of the UK's withdrawal from its colonial responsibilities. During this period the RAF left East Africa (1965), Aden (1967), Libya (1970), Singapore (1971), the Persian Gulf (1971) and Malta (1978). Although base facilities, and a permanent presence at (helicopter) squadron strength, are maintained in Hong Kong and Cyprus, the need for combat squadrons to be permanently based outside Europe has become minimal. The steady disbandment of overseas based units from 1964 onwards has led to a progressive decline in the strength of the RAF, more or less in line with its commitments. The only significant change in this trend has been the establishment of two overseas squadrons in the Falkland Islands since the South Atlantic campaign of 1982. It is interesting to note from the chart that when the RAF went to war in 1982 it had fewer squadrons from which to assemble a force than at any time since 1931 . . .

Following the withdrawal of British forces from most of their overseas commitments few squadrons have been permanently based outside Europe since 1978. One of the RAF's traditional 'colonial' units which has continued to serve abroad is No 84 Sqn which is stationed in Cyprus where this picture of a Whirlwind HAR 10, XD184, was taken. (Andrew Thomas)

On 15 Jul 53 the RAF mounted its Coronation Review at Odiham. This was the greatest ever concentration of British military aircraft. This photograph conveys some impression of the size of the event – there were 305 aircraft on the ground and a further 641 flew past, taking 27 minutes to do so. Identifiable in the picture are Canberras, Varsities, Neptunes, Valettas, Meteors of various types, Hastings, Lancasters and Lincolns. (MOD PRB6595)

Graphically portraying the UK's post-1957 deterrent posture, this photograph shows a Valiant BK 1, WZ390, of No 214 Sqn being towed past the Bloodhound Mk 1s of No 242 Sqn at RAF Marham. (RAF Museum P15122)

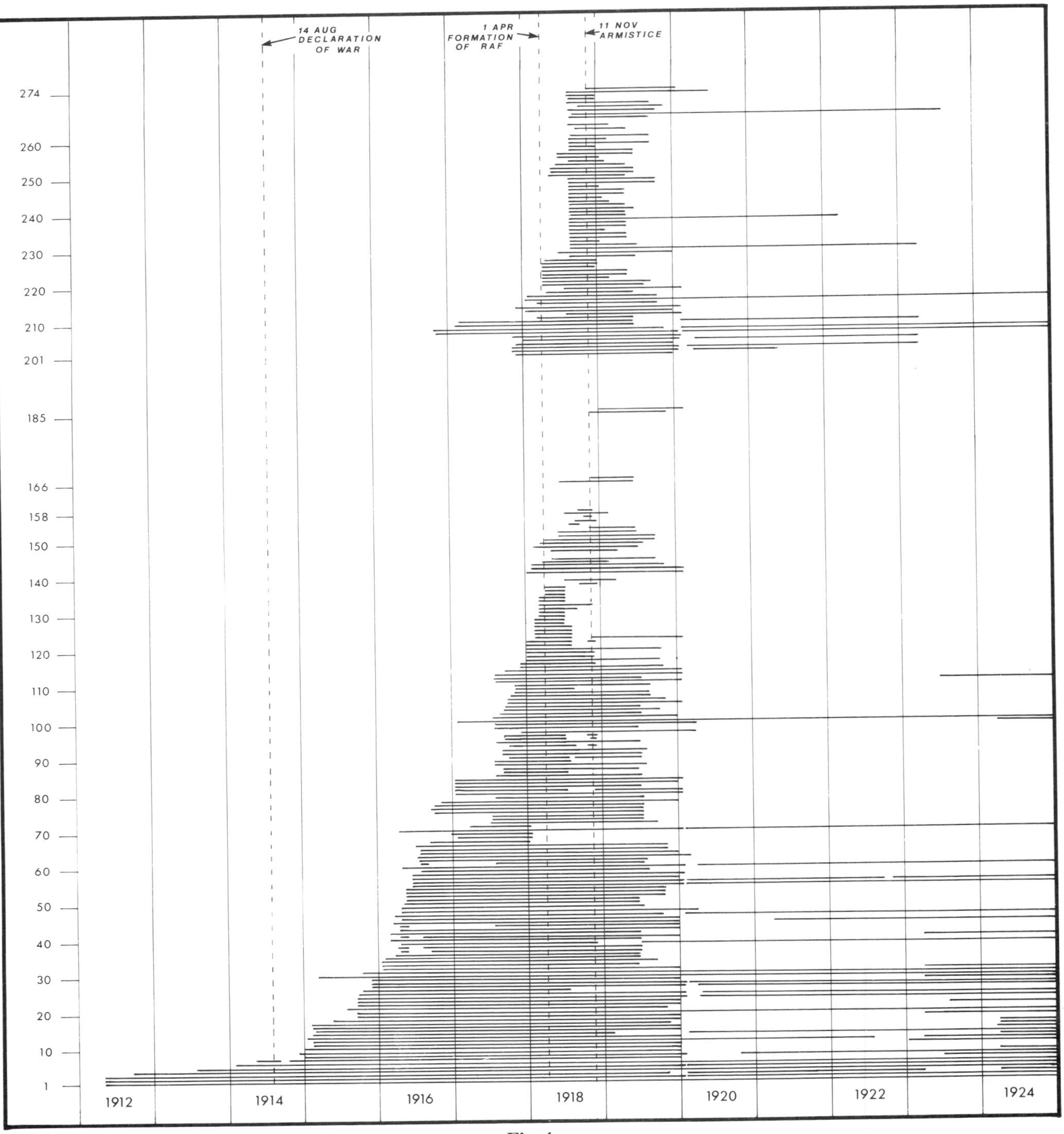

14 AUG DECLARATION OF WAR

1 APR FORMATION OF RAF

11 NOV ARMISTICE

274
260
250
240
230
220
210
201
185
166
158
150
140
130
120
110
100
90
80
70
60
50
40
30
20
10
1

1912 1914 1916 1918 1920 1922 1924

Fig 4

For much of 1919 a British occupation force remained in Germany. Most RAF units involved were based around Cologne. This is a Dolphin, C8043, of No 79 Sqn at Bickendorf in 1919. (RAF Museum P8296)

Figure 4. Figure 4 presents the first 13 years of British military aviation in the form of a chart showing the periods of existence of the various Service Squadrons of the RFC, the RNAS and the RAF. The steady extension of the RFC/RAF series of unit numbers (Nos 1-200) is apparent. The creation of RNAS/RAF squadrons (No 201 onwards) can be seen to have followed a different pattern. The senior naval units are illustrated here only as detailed in the main text of this book their earlier service under various other designations is illustrated at Figure 1. Also evident from this chart is the creation of a large extension of the maritime-oriented block of squadrons in mid-1918 by the formation and/or redesignation of various types of coastal defence Flights and naval air stations.

The effects of post-war demobilisation 1918-19 can be clearly seen, as can the subsequent reshuffling of unit designations in the early 1920s resulting, by the end of 1924, in a stable selection of 'permanent' squadron indentities.

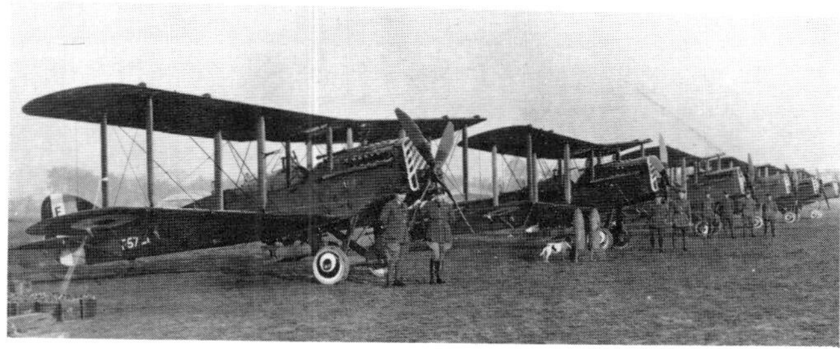

On 1 April 18 No 17 Sqn, RNAS, along with other Naval air units serving in France was renumbered, becoming No 217 Sqn, RAF. This picture shows a line-up of the squadron's DH 4s; the nearest aeroplane is F5721. (RAF Museum P14493)

Following the initial period of demobilisation plans for a peacetime Air Force were laid. The original concept envisaged a force of 84 squadrons but this was rapidly pruned to 32. The unit numbers selected for permanent service were personally approved by the Chief of the Air Staff, MRAF Sir Hugh (later Lord) Trenchard in Dec 19 and were to be: Nos 1, 2, 3, 4, 5, 6, 14, 20, 24, 25, 27, 28, 30, 31, 39, 47, 55, 56, 60, 70, 84, 100, 202, 203, 205, 207, 208, 210, 216, 230, 238 and 267 Sqns. Not all of these numbers were in use at the time and there followed a spate of disbandments, reformations and renumberings in the early months of 1920 to achieve the aim. Representing these 'permanent' units are (above) a group of Bristol Fighters, including H1530 'A' and F4403 'C', of No 5 Sqn at Quetta in 1922 (Chaz Bowyer); and (below) a pair of Snipes, E6977 and E7601, of No 25 Sqn at San Stephano in 1923. (RAF Museum P4053)

No 84 Sqn was one of the units nominated in Dec 19 to form part of the permanent Air Force. Intended to operate DH 10s in Mesopotamia, No 84 Sqn's formation was dogged by complications and when it did finally reform in Aug 20 it was with DH 9As, the DH 10s going instead to No 216 Sqn in Egypt. The squadron spent the next 20 years in Iraq, based at Shaibah. This picture shows one of its Wapitis, J9835, displaying No 84 Sqn's scorpion insignia, over the River Tigris near Basrah. (RAF Museum P9685)

Fig 6

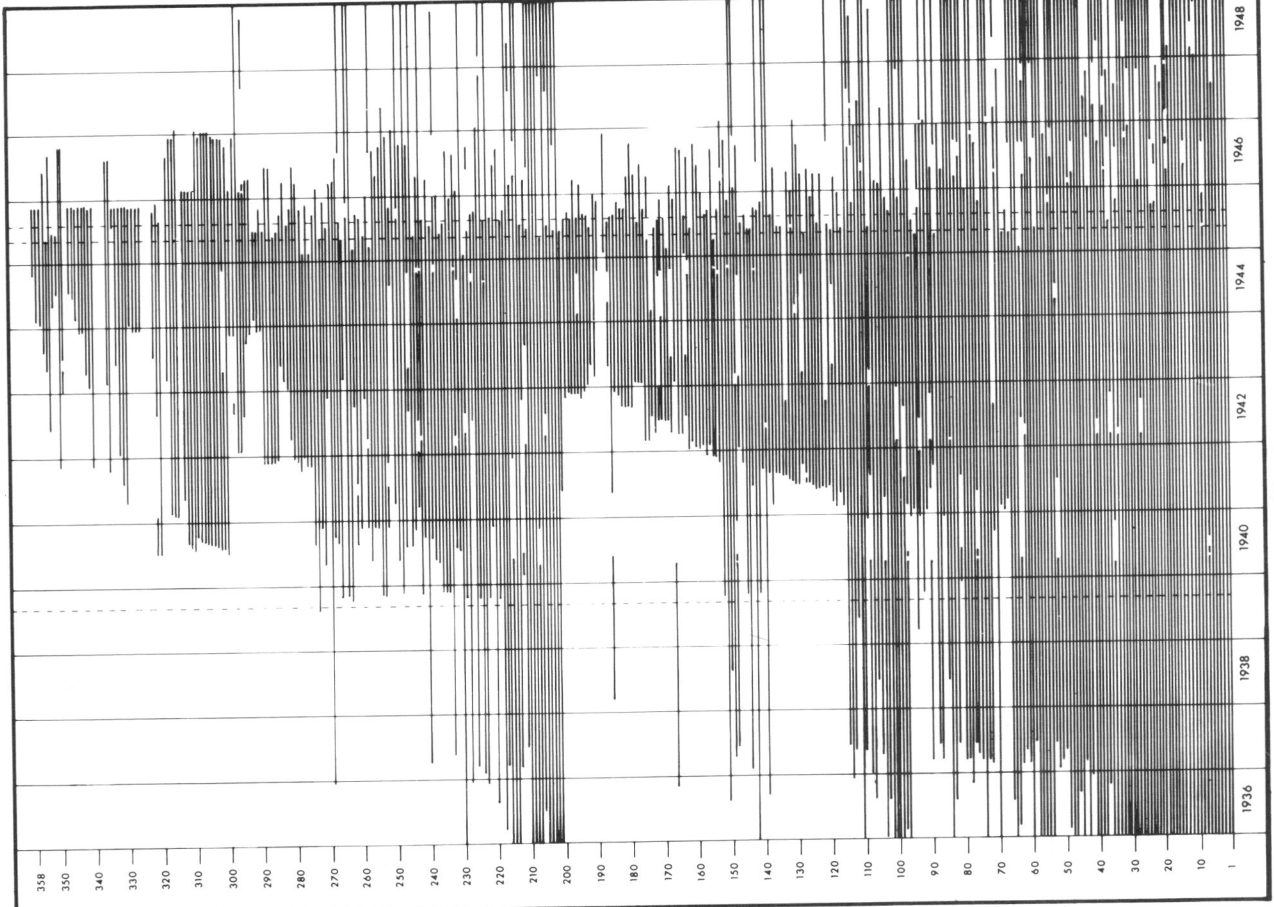

Fig 5

Figures 5 and 6. Figures 5 and 6 illustrate the use of squadron numbers in the period 1936-1948. Compared to the end of 1924 (see Fig 4), when 41 numbers were in use, there were 88 squadrons by the beginning of 1936. This increase had been made up from a steady rise in the numbers of permanent squadrons plus the redesignation of maritime Flights as new Squadrons, numbered in the 200-series, and the creation of the Special Reserve and the Auxiliary Air Force, which formed the squadrons in the 500- and 600-series, with a noticeable decline in the rate of creation of new units after mid-1944.

The establishment of Allied units in the 300-series, from 1940 onwards can be seen, as can the opening of the three blocks of Commonwealth numbers, (Canadian from 400, Australian from 450, and New Zealand from 485), from early-1941, and their subsequent development.

The end of the War brought mass disbandments and during 1945 the RAF lost more than half its strength. 267 squadrons were shed and the year ended with 249 numbers still in use. The salient features of 1946 were the re-establishment of the Auxiliary Air Force and, among the continuing disbandments, (a further net loss of 77 units during the year), the reformation of many of the senior squadrons — frequently by the renumbering of shorter-lived units. This process continued at a reduced rate in 1947 and then stabilised. Gains and losses in 1948 balanced and that year began and ended with 143 numbers in use.

Representative of the Commonwealth units numbered in the 400-series is this Boston III, W8268/TH·0, of No 418 Sqn. This aeroplane was reported missing from a sortie on 20 May 42. (RAF Museum P21641)

One of the squadrons formed during the expansion period in the 1930s was No 228 Sqn. This Scapa, K7306, was used temporarily pending delivery of the squadron's Stranraers. (via Andrew Thomas)

Although many units were disbanded in 1945-47 there was still a need for a substantial Air Force, both at home and overseas, in view of the political uncertainties of the early post-war years. One of the units retained to police the peace with No 26 Sqn, one of whose Tempest F.2s, MW418/XC·A, is seen here at Zeltweg during a deployment of No 135 Wg (Nos 16, 26 and 33 Sqns) to Austria in the summer of 1947. (Sqn Ldr D L Rowell)

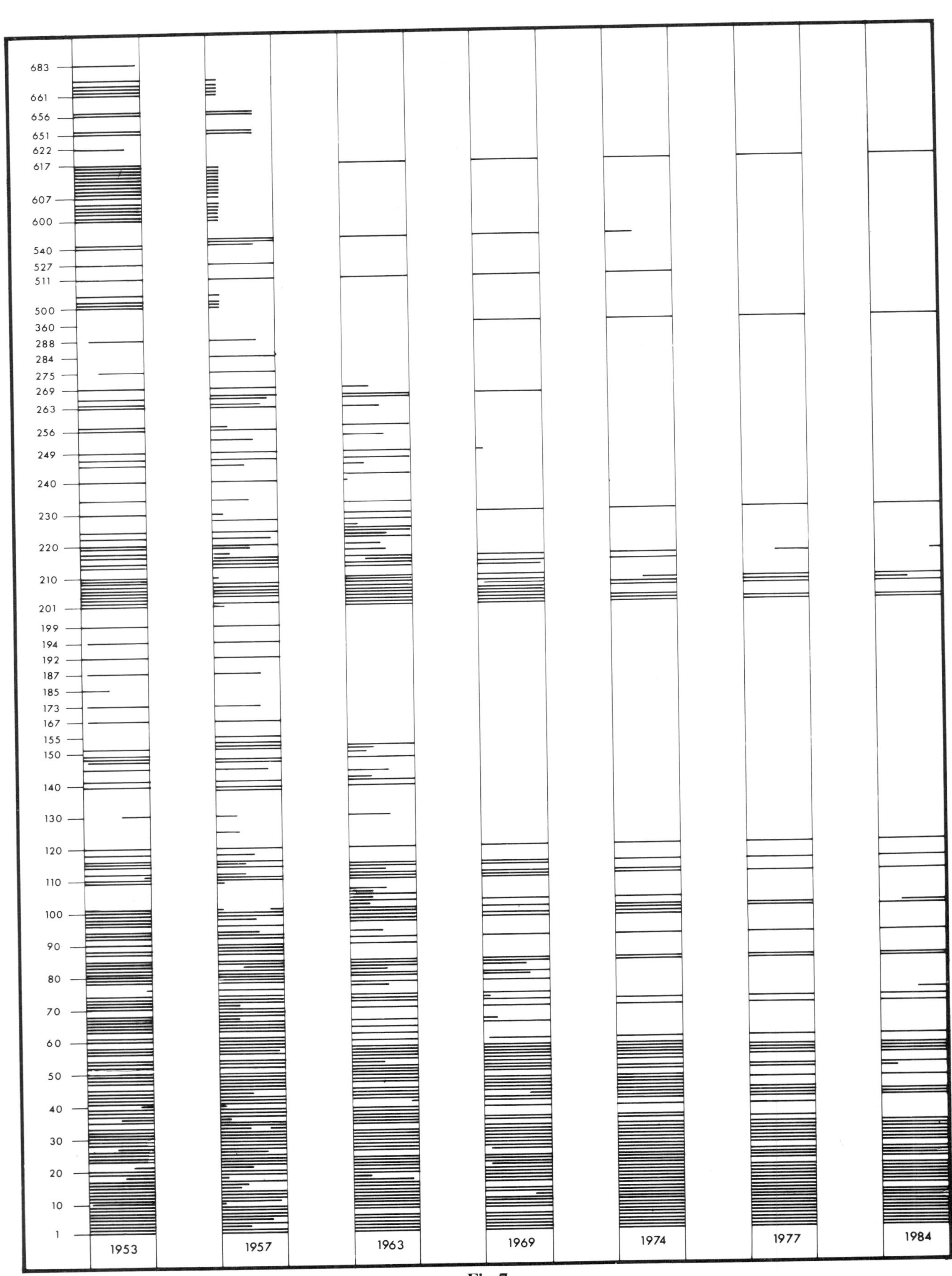
683
661
656
651
622
617
607
600
540
527
511
500
360
288
284
275
269
263
256
249
240
230
220
210
201
199
194
192
187
185
173
167
155
150
140
130
120
110
100
90
80
70
60
50
40
30
20
10
1
1953
1957
1963
1969
1974
1977
1984

Fig 7

Figure 7. Figure 7 continues the pattern established in the previous charts but examines random years rather than a continuous period. 1953 opened with 163 squadrons in the line, 20 more than had been available at the end of 1948 (see Fig 5/6). Most of the increase (14 units) had occurred during 1952 as the expansion associated with the Korean War period began. This increase in numbers continued until, by the beginning of 1957, there were 187 squadrons serving.

1957, however, was a watershed year for the RAF. It was the year in which the RAuxAF flying squadrons were withdrawn and in which the surviving AOP squadrons were transferred to the control of the Army. Other disbandments attributable to changes in Defence Policy resulted in an overall reduction of 68 squadrons, so that 1957 ended with only 119 numbers still in use.

The next year illustrated, 1963, represents the beginning of the end of the RAF's large-scale involvement with missiles. At the start of the year there were 135 squadron numbers in use, of which 30 were missile units. By year's end these figures had fallen to 112 and 8 respectively. Thus, despite the reduction in numbers of operational squadrons available, there was a net loss over the year of only one flying unit.

The next 3 years illustrated, 1969, 1974 and 1977, are representative of the period of the RAF's withdrawal from overseas commitments. Compared to 1963, the last year examined, which had closed with 112 squadrons, 1977 ended with only 64, 2 of them equipped with missiles. Significant years in this period were 1965, 1967 and 1968 which involved losses of 7, 12 and 13 units respectively. The RAF maintained a strength of 80 or so squadrons throughout the years 1969 — 1975 but in 1976 further disbandments reduced that figure to 63 by the end of the year. Thereafter, the total of numbers in use has remained at that level, with only a slight overall tendency towards a continuing decline in strength — a peak of 66 squadrons was reached at the beginning of 1980 but four years later there were only 58.

A core element of the RAF throughout most of the period covered by Fig 7 was the V-Force. This picture of a Valiant B(PR)K 1, WZ395, of No 214 Sqn was taken at Colerne on 15 Sep 56 and shows the relatively short-lived 'high speed silver' finish which was rapidly superseded by an overall anti-flash white for all V-bombers. WZ395 spent most of its service with No 214 Sqn, finally being grounded in Dec 64 when the remaining Valiants were diagnosed as being structurally unsound due to metal fatigue. (R C Sturtivant)

Another stalwart of the mid-1950-1970 period was the Hunter. This one is a Hunter FGA 9, XG205, of No 43 Sqn seen at Nicosia wearing the unit's black and white checks and a cartoon version of its fighting cock badge on the nose. No 43 Sqn fell victim to the UK's policy of colonial withdrawal, being disbanded in late 1967 as the RAF left Aden. (Air Britain X69)

A Victor B.2(SR), XL161, of No 543 Sqn, the last of the RAF's strategic reconnaissance squadrons, which finally disbanded in 1974.

No 612 Sqn was one of the RAuxAF units disbanded in 1957. One of its Vampire FB 5s, WA397/8W·L, is seen here over Aberdeen, its home town. (Sqn Ldr R Robertson)

The remaining AOP squadrons were transferred from RAF to Army control in 1957. No 656 Sqn was one of these; this is one of the squadron's Auster AOP 6s, WJ367. The aircraft was lost in a crash near Ipoh on 22 Mar 56. (M D N Fisher via the Museum of Army Flying)

Appendix 4

Linked Squadrons

As the RAF contracted from 1945 onwards many of its squadrons were disbanded completely, however, some of those with longer, or more distinguished, histories were reduced to 'Numberplate Only' status in anticipation of their re-establishment, either as additional new units, or by the relabelling of existing squadrons. For a brief period in 1946-47, in an effort to give these potential squadrons more substance, some numberplates were appended to existing units as their 'B Flights'.

An example of this is provided by the association of Nos 27 and 45 Sqns. Notice had been given, by SD 155/1946 No 1365, of an intention to reform No 27 Sqn at Seletar. This plan was cancelled shortly afterwards but, in order to sustain the No 27 numberplate SD 155/1946 No 2201 applied it, from 1 Nov 46, to No 45 Sqn in Ceylon where it was to serve as that unit's 'B(27) Flight'. This arrangement continued until 1 Oct 47 when the designation was withdrawn, on the authority of SD 155/1947 No 997, since an independent No 27 Sqn was about to be formed in the UK. Similar arrangements led to a B(18) Flight serving within No 38 Sqn from 15 Sep 46 until the end of the year, when its designation was changed to B(87) Flight in the expectation that a new No 18 Sqn was likely to form, the '87' being withdrawn in turn on 31 Aug 47.

This approach to sustaining inactive squadron numberplates was not very successful since, in practice, the 'parasite' squadrons were scarcely acknowledged by their parent units. It was not widely used. Nevertheless it was still felt that a system was needed which would prolong the effective service, and thus extend the histories, of selected squadrons from among those which had been disbanded following the Second

No 85 Sqn shed its alter ego, No 145 Sqn, at the end of Feb 52. By that time the parent unit was introducing red and black fuselage markings and applying its WW I insignia of a white hexagon to the fins of its aircraft. This Mosquito NF 36, RL148, displays both styles of marking. (RAF Museum P19019)

When this photograph of one of No 45 Sqn's Beaufighter TF 10s, RD824/OB·K, over Ceylon was taken (1947) the unit also held No 27 Sqn's numberplate in safe-keeping. The parasite unit's presence was, however, a rather low-key affair. (E W Johnson)

This photograph shows a Washington B.1, WF504, in 1951. The unit code, LS·C, identifies the aircraft as belonging to No 15 Sqn. However, since the unit was 'linked' at the time, it was, more precisely, owned by No 15/21 Sqn. In practice the active units in such arrangements rarely paid much regard to these nominal affiliations. (N J Roberson)

This Meteor NF 11, WD725, only wears the red triple-X markings of No 29 Sqn although it was actually on the strength of No 29/22 Sqn. (R C Sturtivant)

World War. A further attempt was made to provide some of these with a 'spiritual', if not a physical, existence by the creation of Linked Squadrons. AMO A.86 formalised this requirement, and the system was introduced from Feb 49. In each case the inactive squadron was the second element of the linked pair. In the event this also proved to be a rather unrealistic concept which never gained much popular support. Although the upper echelons of the RAF bureaucracy acknowledged the 'alter egos', at squadron level they received little more than tacit recognition. Despite its somewhat intangible nature time accrued as a linked unit was considered to be reckonable (by both squadrons) towards the 25 years service needed to qualify for the award of a Squadron Standard. The Linked Squadron concept was overtaken by the expansion of the RAF during the period of tension associated with the Korean War in the early 1950s, which allowed most of the dormant numbers to be re-established in their own right. Units linked together under this scheme were:

Squadrons	From		To
7/76	1 Feb 49	-	8 Dec 53
15/21	1 Feb 49	-	20 Sep 53
19/152	11 Feb 49	-	31 May 54
23/151	11 Feb 49	-	14 Sep 51
29/22	11 Feb 49	-	20 Dec 54
41/253	11 Feb 49	-	15 Apr 55
43/17	13 Mar 51	-	31 May 56
44/55	1 Feb 49	-	14 Jul 57
45/33	31 Mar 55	-	14 Oct 55
49/102	1 Feb 49	-	19 Oct 54
50/103	1 Feb 49	-	30 Nov 54
50/40	1 Feb 57	-	1 Oct 59
56/87	11 Feb 49	-	31 Dec 51
57/104	1 Feb 49	-	14 Mar 55
61/144	1 Feb 49	-	31 Mar 58
66/111	11 Feb 49	-	1 Nov 53
74/34	20 Jul 51	-	31 Jul 54
83/150	1 Feb 49	-	1 Jan 56
85/145	11 Feb 49	-	28 Feb 52
109/105	1 Feb 49	-	1 Feb 57
115/218	1 Feb 49	-	1 Mar 50
115/218	13 Jun 50	-	1 Jun 57
120/220	15 Feb 49	-	23 Sep 51
141/42	11 Feb 49	-	27 Jun 52
203/36	15 Feb 49	-	30 Jun 53
205/209	1 Jan 55	-	1 Nov 58
210/217	15 Feb 49	-	13 Jan 52
224/269	15 Feb 49	-	1 Jan 52
230/240	15 Feb 49	-	30 Apr 52
240/204	20 Feb 53	-	1 Jan 54
245/266	11 Feb 49	-	13 Jul 52
264/79	11 Feb 49	-	14 Nov 51

Meteor F.4s displaying the LZ codes of No 66 Sqn, including VT139/D, VW273/E and VT138/F, in 1949. At this time the unit was technically designated as No 66/111 Sqn. (RAF Museum P3610)

Appendix 5

Shadow Squadrons

To take advantage of the pools of experienced instructor aircrew and the operational aircraft on charge within various post-graduate training units, notably the OCUs, it has been the intention, since the mid-1950's, to realise the potential of these assets in time of crisis. This might involve either the use of crews and aircraft to reinforce existing front-line squadrons or the mobilisation of selected units as additional operational squadrons in their own right. Where the latter has been the plan, 'shadow squadron' numbers have been allocated as follows:

Shadow Number	Unit	Aircraft	Base(s)	Period
11 Sqn	228 OCU	Javelin	Leuchars	1966
38 Sqn	236 OCU	Nimrod	St Mawgan & Kinloss	1970-date
45 Sqn	TWCU	Tornado	Honington	1984-date
63 Sqn	229 OCU & TWU	Hunter & Hawk	Chivenor & Brawdy	1963-date
64 Sqn	228 OCU	Phantom	Coningsby	1970-date
65 Sqn	226 OCU	Lightning	Coltishall	1971-1974
65 Sqn	229 OCU	Tornado	Coningsby	1986-date
79 Sqn	229 OCU & TWU	Hunter & Hawk	Chivenor & Brawdy	1967-date
127 Sqn	229 OCU	Hunter	Chivenor	1957-1958
131 Sqn	229 OCU	Hunter	Chivenor	1958
137 Sqn	228 OCU	Javelin	Leeming	1956-1961
145 Sqn	229 OCU	Hunter	Chivenor	1958-1963
145 Sqn	226 OCU	Lightning	Middleton St George & Coltishall	1963-1971
151 Sqn	No 2 TWU	Hawk	Chivenor	1981-date
219 Sqn	AWF Combat School	Javelin	West Raynham	1957-1962
220 Sqn	236 OCU	Shackleton	Kinloss & St Mawgan	mid-1960s
229 Sqn	229 OCU	Hunter	Chivenor	1955-1957
234 Sqn	229 OCU & TWU	Hunter	Chivenor & Brawdy	1958-date

The Tornado Weapons Conversion Unit has the alternative identity of No 45 Sqn. This 1984 picture of Tornado GR 1, ZA397, shows the red and blue diamonds which were first used on the squadron's Hunters in 1972. Why it was considered necessary to devise this new marking is uncertain as No 45 Sqn has a traditional fighter-style marking, a white dumbell, dating back to 1917. First used on Camels, it last appeared, on a red ground, on Venoms. *(J M Webber)*

Appendix 6

Named Squadrons

From time to time various schemes have been devised under which some squadrons have had a name incorporated into their titles. These were sometimes included in the standard badge frame. Such titles fell into several official and semi-official categories, broadly, thus:

a. UK regional or city titles were used by the Auxiliary Air Force squadrons and those of the Special Reserve, e.g. No 607 (County of Durham) Squadron.

b. Allied squadrons formed within the RAF included their nationality within their title, e.g. No 320 (Netherlands) Squadron.

c. Some allied-manned squadrons adopted a regional title from their homeland, e.g. No 301 (Pomeranian) Squadron and No 342 (Lorraine) Squadron.

d. RAF squadrons which were manned by a large proportion of Commonwealth personnel, or which had a significant element of their equipment funded by a region or organisation, had this acknowledged by the incorporation of a suitable title. Examples are: No 237 (Rhodesia) Squadron which was largely manned by colonials; No 139 (Jamaica) Squadron whose aircraft were largely purchased by contributions from Jamaica; and No 193 (Fellowship of the Bellows) Squadron whose aircraft were bought by an association of expatriate Britons living in Brazil.

e. Although not formally incorporated into their titles the nicknames of the Canadian squadrons numbered in the 400 series were of particular significance to the units concerned. These names would, typically, be of an animal, either one indigenous to Canada or one noted for its aggressive nature, or of an adoptive city, e.g. No 424 (Tiger) Squadron and No 432 (Leaside) Squadron.

A close regional association was fundamental to the concept of the Auxiliary Air Force. This Wapiti, J9861, served with No 605 (County of Warwick) Sqn between 1930 and 1934. (RAF Museum P21133)

A Mitchell II, NO·K, of No 320 (Netherlands) Sqn. (Chaz Bowyer)

When the AuxAF was reformed in 1946 its regional links were re-established. This Meteor F.8, WH450, wears the markings of No 500 (County of Kent) Sqn; a blue bar with a white edged green zig-zag. The photograph was taken at Odiham on 15 Jul 53 during the Coronation Review which accounts, at least in part, for the aircraft's pristine condition. (R C Sturtivant)

Spitfire VB, BL479/SZ·X, of No 316 (Warsaw) Sqn. (RAF Museum P100603)

Some RAF squadrons had official regional affiliations. Some individual aeroplanes also had associations with regions or with organisations which had contributed funds towards its purchase. This picture shows a Typhoon IA, R8224/US·H, of No 56 (Punjab) Sqn; the aeroplane carries the donor name 'Land Girl' on the 'car-door type' cockpit entry. (RAF Museum 5962-15)

f. Prior to their transfer to the USAAF in 1942 the three fighter squadrons formed within the RAF from American pilots were referred to as 'Eagle' squadrons.

The practice of donating aeroplanes or gifts of money with which to purchase aircraft, referred to above, was not peculiar to the Second World War; indeed the custom had been widespread in World War One. As a result of this, No 110 Sqn took the name 'Hyderabad' on the strength of the fact that the Nizam of Hyderabad had funded the unit's entire complement of DH 9As in 1918 and when regional titles came into vogue in 1939 the association was recalled.

There was a less formal scheme of regional association during World War Two, under which some squadrons were affiliated to towns in the UK. This was intended both to provide the unit with a territorial link and to give the related town a more personal stake in the war. Examples of these associations are: No 61 (City of Lincoln) Squadron, No 144 (Grimsby) Squadron, and No 166 (Huddersfield) Squadron.

From Apr 39 some squadrons were affiliated to UK towns and cities, although these associations were not incorporated into the units' formal titles. No 15 Sqn was an example of such a unit, having been linked to Oxford. The squadron is represented here by two pictures of the same Lancaster. ME844 was delivered to No 15 Sqn on 16 Jun 44 and coded as LS·C; it is seen here (above) in this guise with 22 mission symbols painted beneath the cockpit. The aeroplane survived the war, as can be seen from the post-war picture (below) (white code letters were introduced from Jul 45) in which the mission tally has increased to the very respectable total of 78. (N J Roberson)

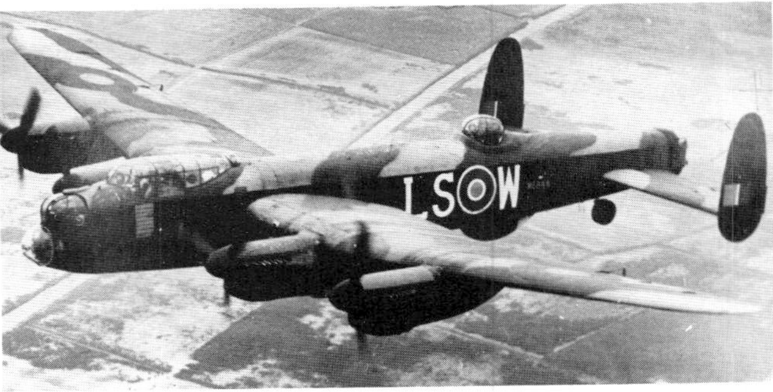

These loose affiliations, however, were not formalised into the unit's title.

The official titles, including Canadian nicknames, which have been used are:

Squadron	Title
No 18	Burma
No 24	Commonwealth
No 26	South African
No 35	Madras Presidency
No 43	China-British
No 44	Rhodesia
No 46	Uganda
No 56	Punjab
No 65	East India
No 71	Eagle
No 72	Basutoland
No 74	Trinidad
No 75	New Zealand
No 79	Madras Presidency
No 82	United Provinces
No 87	United Provinces
No 88	Hong Kong

All Canadian squadrons had an individual name. This Catalina I, W8434/QL·F, belonged to No 413 (Tusker) Sqn; the aeroplane was lost at Sullom Voe on 2 Jan 42 when it collided with an obstruction on take-off. (P H T Green)

Squadron	Title
No 91	Nigeria
No 92	East India
No 97	Straits Settlements
No 99	Madras Presidency
No 102	Ceylon
No 110	Hyderabad
No 114	Hong Kong
No 121	Eagle
No 122	Bombay
No 123	East India
No 124	Baroda
No 125	Newfoundland
No 126	Persian Gulf
No 129	Mysore
No 130	Punjab
No 131	County of Kent
No 132	City of Bombay
No 133	Eagle
No 139	Jamaica
No 149	East India
No 152	Hyderabad
No 154	Motor Industries
No 164	Argentine-British
No 165	Ceylon
No 167	Gold Coast
No 174	Mauritius
No 183	Gold Coast
No 193	Fellowship of the Bellows (Brazil)
No 209	Hong Kong
No 213	Ceylon
No 214	Federated Malay States
No 218	Gold Coast
No 219	Mysore
No 222	Natal
No 234	Madras Presidency
No 237	Rhodesia
No 242	Canadian
No 245	Northern Rhodesian
No 247	China-British

Squadron	Title
No 249	Gold Coast
No 250	Sudan
No 253	Hyderabad State
No 257	Burma
No 263	Fellowship of the Bellows (Argentina)
No 264	Madras Presidency
No 266	Rhodesia
No 300	Masovian
No 301	Pomeranian
No 302	Poznan
No 303	Kosciusko
No 304	Silesian
No 305	Wielpolska
No 306	Torun
No 307	Lwow
No 308	Krakow
No 309	Ziema Czerwienska
Nos 310-313	Czechoslovak
No 315	Deblin
No 316	Warsaw
No 317	Wilno
No 318	Danzig
Nos 320-321	Netherlands
No 322	Dutch
No 326	GC II/7 'Nice'
No 327	GC I/3 'Corse'
No 328	GC I/7 'Provence'
No 329	GC I/2 'Cicognes'
Nos 330-334	Norwegian
Nos 335-336	Greek
No 340	GC IV/2 'Ile de France'
No 341	GC III/2 'Alsace'
No 342	GB I/20 'Lorraine'
No 343	Flotille 7E
No 344	Flotille 1E
No 345	GC II/2 'Berry'
No 346	GB II/23 'Guyenne'
No 347	GB I/25 'Tunisie'
Nos 349-350	Belgian

Spitfire IX, MH448/AP·P, of No 130 (Punjab) Sqn in Norway in 1945. *(RAF Museum P9606)*

Whirlwind, P7062/HE·L, of No 263 (Fellowship of the Bellows) Sqn. *(RAF Museum P9515)*

Mustang IV, KM348/AK·V, of No 213 (Ceylon) Sqn at Nicosia in 1946. *(Andrew Thomas)*

Wellington X, HF598/BH·E, of No 300 Sqn (Masovian) Sqn. *(J B Cynk)*

Squadron	Title
Nos 351-352	Jugoslav
No 400	City of Toronto
No 401	Ram
No 402	Winnipeg Bear
No 403	Wolf
No 404	Buffalo
No 405	Vancouver
No 406	Lynx
No 407	Demon
No 408	Goose
No 409	Nighthawk
No 410	Cougar
No 411	Grizzly Bear
No 412	Falcon
No 413	Tusker
No 414	Sarnia Imperials
No 415	Swordfish
No 416	City of Oshawa
No 417	City of Windsor
No 418	City of Edmonton
No 419	Moose
No 420	Snowy Owl

Squadron	Title
No 421	Red Indian
No 422	Flying Yachtsman
No 423	Bald Eagle
No 424	Tiger
No 425	Alouette
No 426	Thunderbird
No 427	Lion
No 428	Ghost
No 429	Bison
No 430	City of Sudbury
No 431	Iroquois
No 432	Leaside
No 433	Porcupine
No 434	Bluenose
No 435	Chinthe
No 436	Elephant
No 437	Husky
No 438	Wild Cat
No 439	Westmount
No 440	City of Ottawa and Beaver
No 441	Silver Fox
No 442	Caribou

When discrete blocks of numbers were allocated to Commonwealth squadrons in 1941 No 110 Sqn, RCAF was redesignated as No 400 Sqn. This is one of the unit's Tomahawk Is, AH851/SP·F, at Odiham; this aeroplane was written off following a crash landing on 19 Oct 41. (PAC PL34966)

Lancaster II, DS689/OW·S, of No 426 (Thunderbird) Sqn. (Chas Bowyer)

No 443 Hornet
No 500 County of Kent
No 501 County of Gloucester (changed from City of Bristol on 1 May 30)
No 502 Ulster
No 503 County of Lincoln
No 504 County of Nottingham
No 600 City of London
No 601 County of London
No 602 City of Glasgow
No 603 City of Edinburgh
No 604 County of Middlesex
No 605 County of Warwick
No 607 County of Durham
No 608 North Riding
No 609 West Riding
No 610 County of Chester
No 611 West Lancashire
No 612 County of Aberdeen
No 613 City of Manchester
No 614 County of Glamorgan
No 615 County of Surrey
No 616 South Yorkshire
No 692 Fellowship of the Bellows

Hyderabad, J8807, of No 503 (County of Lincoln) Sqn at Waddington. (Museum of Army Flying)

Tempest V, EJ608/SD·P, of No 501 (County of Gloucester) Sqn. (Air Britain M5598)

Airacobra, AH601, of No 601 (County of London) Sqn. This particular aircraft, the serial number of which matched the squadron number, was flown by the CO, Sqn Ldr E J Gracie. Although it carried the unit identity code, UF, it had no individual letter; in its place it had the squadron's winged sword emblem painted on the fuselage, just ahead of the Sqn Ldr's pennant on the cockpit door. (RAF Museum P9502)

Vampire FB 5, VV617, wearing the interlocking mauve and stone triangle markings of No 607 (County of Durham) Sqn. (R C Sturtivant)

Spitfire VB, BM594/FY·X, of No 611 (West Lancashire) Sqn at Coltishall in 1944. (RAF Museum P10576)

Appendix 7

Aircraft used by Squadrons

This Appendix cross-refers aircraft types to those squadrons which used them. All types mentioned in the main squadron histories Section are included, sub-divided into variants where these are significant.

Squadrons using each type are listed numerically using the following conventions: '3' indicates No 3 Sqn, RFC or RAF; '4N' indicates No 4 (Naval) Sqn, RNAS; and '9N/209' indicates that the type concerned was being flown by the unit on 1 Apr 18, i.e. when the squadron was remustered from the RNAS into the RAF.

No 210 Sqn is recorded in the main text as having operated Singapore IIIs three times, thus possibly creating an impression that these aeroplanes were more numerous than they really were. The explanation lies in the fact that No 210 was twice used to ferry aircraft to their overseas operators. This one, K3593, was the second Singapore III to be built and was delivered to Seletar, by No 210 Sqn, on 2 Apr 35. The first four aircraft received by No 205 Sqn in Singapore were marked with playing card insignia, in this case the ace of spades. (RAF Museum P18120)

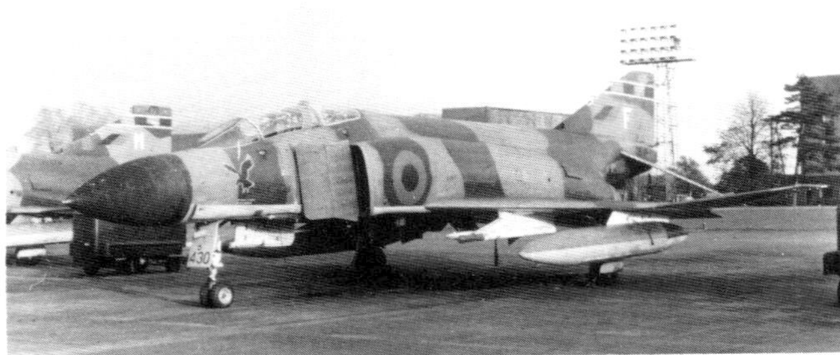

The Phantom FGR 2 served with two separate sets of squadrons during its two-stage career. This is XV430 seen during its service with No 23 Sqn in the air defence role. (RAF Museum P14939)

It should be appreciated that some aeroplanes were used by several squadrons in turn. A casual glance at the units listed as having used a particular type of aircraft may therefore give a false impression. For instance thirteen squadrons are shown as having flown the Spitfire VI in the UK. However, only 100 of these aircraft were built, and five of them went to Egypt. The explanation lies in the way in which the aircraft were deployed. A significant number of Spitfire VIs spent their operational careers in the Orkneys, where they were flown by a succession of squadrons in rotation as each spent a rest period in the extreme North of Scotland before returning to the more intensive operational arena of the South. Another example is provided by the Phantom FGR 2. This aircraft is listed as having been used by thirteen units; however, the Phantom's career was in two distinct phases. Initially seven squadrons flew it in the tactical reconnaissance and attack roles. These squadrons were re-equipped with the Jaguar and the Phantoms began a new lease of life as air defence fighters with six different squadrons.

Aircraft	Squadrons
Airacobra I	601
Albacore	36, 119, 415
Albatross	271
Albemarle I	161, 295, 296, 297, 511, 570
Albemarle II	295, 296, 297, 570
Albemarle V	295, 296, 297, 570
Albemarle VI	296, 297
Aldershot III	99
Andover C.1	32, 46, 52, 60, 84
Andover CC 2	21, 32, 60
Andover E.3	115
Anson I	7, 24, 35, 44, 48, 51, 52, 58, 61, 63, 75, 76, 97, 104, 106, 108, 109, 116, 144, 148, 173, 185, 192, 206, 207, 215, 217, 220, 224, 233, 251, 267, 269, 275, 276, 278, 280, 281, 282, 320, 321, 500, 502, 510, 516, 544, 608, 612
Anson X	24, 353
Anson C.11	58
Anson XII	31, 116, 147, 167, 187
Anson C.19	8, 31, 58, 81, 116, 147, 173, 187, 527
Anson T.21	228, 275
Argosy C.1	70, 105, 114, 215, 267
Argosy E.1	115
Argus	173, 680
Atlas	2, 4, 13, 16, 26, 208
Audax	2, 4, 5, 13, 16, 20, 24, 26, 28, 52, 61, 63, 77, 105, 114, 144, 146, 148, 173, 208, 211, 226, 237, 267, 615
Auster I	651, 652, 653, 654, 655, 656, 657
Auster III	651, 652, 653, 654, 655, 656, 657, 658, 659, 660, 661, 662
Auster IV	651, 652, 653, 654, 655, 656, 657, 658, 659, 660, 661, 662, 663, 664
Auster V	275, 651, 652, 653, 654, 655, 656, 657, 658, 659, 660, 661, 662, 663, 664, 665, 666
Auster AOP 6	8, 209, 267, 651, 652, 656, 657, 659, 661, 662, 663, 664, 666
Auster AOP 9	652, 656
Avro Type E/Es	3, 5, 7
Avro 504	1, 5, 9, 12, 15, 19, 22, 23, 24, 25, 28, 29, 40, 43, 45, 49, 53, 54, 55, 57, 63, 64, 66, 67, 72, 84, 100
Avro 504K(NF)	33, 75, 76, 77, 90
Avro 504N	24
AW FK 3	43, 47, 53, 55, 63
AW FK 8	2, 8, 10, 17, 35, 39, 47, 50, 82, 142, 143, 150
Balliol T.2	288
Baltimore I	69, 162, 203, 223
Baltimore II	14, 55, 69, 162, 203, 223
Baltimore III	52, 55, 69, 162, 203, 223, 454
Baltimore IV	13, 52, 55, 69, 203, 223, 454, 459, 500
Baltimore V	13, 52, 55, 69, 223, 249, 454, 459, 500, 680
Barracuda II	567, 667, 679, 691
Basset CC 1	26, 32, 207
Battle I	12, 15, 35, 40, 52, 63, 88, 98, 103, 105, 106, 142, 150, 185, 207, 218, 226, 234, 235, 242, 245, 253, 266, 300, 301, 304, 305, 616
BE 1	2, 4, 5
BE 2	2, 4, 6
BE 2A	2, 3, 4, 6, 8, 9, 16, 28
BE 2B	2, 4, 8, 9, 12, 16, 29, 66
BE 2C	2, 3, 4, 5, 6, 7, 8, 9, 10, 12, 13, 14, 15, 16, 17, 19, 20, 21, 22, 23, 24, 25, 26, 28, 29, 30, 31, 33, 34, 35, 36, 39, 40, 43, 45, 46, 47, 49, 50, 51, 52, 54, 55, 57, 64, 66, 67, 75, 76, 77, 78, 84, 100, 114
BE 2D	2, 4, 5, 6, 7, 8, 9, 10, 12, 13, 15, 16, 37, 42, 66, 77
BE 2E	2, 4, 5, 6, 7, 8, 9, 10, 12, 13, 14, 15, 16, 21, 30, 31, 33, 34, 36, 37, 38, 39, 42, 46, 47, 50, 51, 53, 63, 67, 75, 76, 77, 78, 100, 113, 114, 141, 142, 144, 150, 269

Aircraft	Squadrons
BE 2F	5, 6, 7, 10, 15, 16, 34, 52
BE 2G	4, 5, 6, 7, 10, 15, 16, 34, 52, 53
BE 3	3
BE 4	3, 4
BE 8/8A	1, 3, 5, 6, 7, 8, 9, 22
BE 12	10, 19, 21, 33, 36, 37, 38, 39, 47, 50, 51, 52, 54, 63, 66, 75, 76, 77, 78, 84, 101, 141
BE 12A	17, 33, 37, 39, 47, 50, 67, 76, 78, 84, 101, 142, 144, 150
BE 12B	37, 50, 51, 75, 76, 77, 78
Beaufighter I	25, 29, 46, 68, 69, 89, 141, 143, 153, 173, 176, 219, 227, 235, 236, 239, 248, 252, 256, 272, 285, 577, 598, 600, 603, 604, 680
Beaufighter II	48, 96, 125, 143, 255, 307, 404, 406, 409, 410, 456, 488, 515, 600, 618
Beaufighter VI	27, 29, 46, 68, 89, 96, 108, 125, 141, 144, 153, 176, 177, 219, 227, 235, 236, 248, 252, 254, 255, 256, 272, 287, 288, 307, 406, 409, 456, 488, 600, 603, 604, 684
Beaufighter X	5, 17, 20, 22, 27, 34, 39, 42, 45, 46, 47, 84, 143, 144, 177, 211, 217, 227, 235, 236, 248, 252, 254, 272, 404, 455, 489, 603, 684, 695
Beaufighter XI	46, 143, 177, 227, 235, 252, 272, 404, 603
Beaufort I	22, 39, 42, 47, 48, 69, 86, 100, 217, 415, 489
Beaufort II	39, 42, 86, 217
Beech 17 Traveller	24
Belfast C.1	53
Belvedere HC 1	26, 66, 72
Beverley	30, 34, 47, 48, 53, 84
Blenheim I	8, 11, 18, 21, 23, 25, 27, 29, 30, 34, 39, 44, 45, 55, 57, 60, 61, 62, 64, 68, 82, 84, 88, 90, 92, 101, 104, 107, 108, 110, 113, 114, 139, 141, 144, 145, 203, 211, 219, 222, 223, 229, 234, 235, 236, 242, 245, 248, 252, 254, 267, 285, 406, 600, 601, 604, 608
Blenheim IV	6, 8, 11, 13, 14, 15, 18, 21, 34, 35, 39, 40, 45, 52, 53, 55, 57, 59, 60, 82, 84, 86, 88, 90, 101, 104, 105, 107, 108, 110, 113, 114, 139, 140, 143, 162, 173, 203, 211, 212, 218, 226, 233, 235, 236, 244, 248, 252, 254, 272, 287, 288, 289, 404, 406, 407, 459, 489, 500, 516, 521, 526, 527, 528, 600, 608, 614
Blenheim V	8, 13, 18, 34, 42, 113, 114, 139, 162, 203, 244, 454, 614
Bleriot XI	3, 6, 7, 9, 10, 15, 16, 22, 23, 24
Bleriot XXI	3
Bleriot Parasol	3, 5, 9
Bloodhound I	62, 94, 112, 141, 222, 242, 247, 257, 263, 264, 266
Bloodhound II	25, 33, 41, 65, 85, 112
Bombay	117, 216, 271
Boston I	88, 93, 534, 539
Boston II	88
Boston III	18, 23, 88, 107, 114, 173, 223, 226, 267, 342, 418, 532, 605
Boston III (Turbinlite)	530, 531, 532, 533, 534, 535, 537, 538, 539
Boston IV	13, 18, 55, 88, 114, 342
Boston V	13, 18, 55, 114
Botha I	24, 502, 608
Breguet Biplane	2, 4
Brigand B.1	8, 45, 84
Brigand Met 3	45
Bristol Boxkite	1, 2, 3
Bristol Coanda Monoplane	3
Bristol F2b Fighter	2, 4, 5, 6, 8, 9, 10, 11, 12, 13, 14, 16, 20, 22, 24, 28, 31, 33, 34, 35, 36, 39, 48, 59, 62, 67, 76, 88, 100, 105, 106, 111, 114, 138, 139, 141, 208
Bristol M.1B	50, 111
Bristol M.1C	47, 63, 72, 150
Bristol Prier Monoplane	3
Bristol Scout	1, 2, 3, 4, 5, 6, 7, 8, 9, 11, 12, 13, 16, 17, 18, 19, 21, 22, 24, 28, 30, 33, 36, 39, 43, 45, 47, 63, 67, 111, 3N
Britannia C.1	99, 511
Britannia C.2	99, 511
Buccaneer S.2	12, 15, 16, 208, 216
Buffalo I	60, 67, 71, 146, 243, 453, 488
Bulldog II	3, 17, 19, 23, 29, 32, 41, 54, 56, 111
Camel	3, 17, 28, 37, 39, 43, 44, 45, 46, 47, 50, 51, 54, 61, 63, 65, 66, 70, 71, 73, 78, 80, 112, 143, 150, 151, 152, 153, 1N/201, 3N/203, 4N/204, 8N/208, 9N/209, 10N/210, 212, 13N/213, 219, 220, 221, 222, 223, 225, 226, 230, 233, 273
Campania	240, 241, 242, 253
Canberra B.2	6, 7, 9, 10, 12, 15, 18, 21, 27, 32, 35, 40, 44, 45, 50, 51, 57, 59, 61, 73, 76, 85, 90, 97, 98, 100, 101, 102, 103, 104, 109, 115, 139, 149, 151, 192, 199, 207, 245, 249, 360, 527, 540, 542, 617
Canberra PR 3	39, 58, 69, 82, 85, 540
Canberra B.6	6, 9, 12, 21, 51, 76, 100, 101, 109, 139, 192, 213, 249, 360, 542, 617
Canberra PR 7	13, 17, 31, 39, 58, 80, 81, 82, 100, 214, 527, 540, 542
Canberra B(I) 8	3, 14, 16, 59, 88, 100
Canberra PR 9	13, 39, 58
Canberra T.11	85
Canberra B.15/E.15	32, 45, 73, 98, 100
Canberra B.16	6, 249
Canberra T.17	360, 361
Canberra TT 18	7, 100
Canberra T.19	85, 100
Caproni Ca 42	227
Catalina I	119, 190, 191, 202, 205, 209, 210, 212, 240, 259, 262, 265, 270, 333, 413, 422, 490, 628
Catalina II	209, 210, 240, 321
Catalina III	119, 321, 330
Catalina IV	190, 191, 202, 205, 210, 212, 240, 262, 321, 333, 357, 413, 628
Caudron G II	4
Caudron G III	1, 4, 5, 14, 19, 22, 23, 24, 25, 29, 30, 34
Caudron G IV	7N
Chinook HC 1	7, 18, 78
Chipmunk T.10	31, 114, 275
Cierva C.40	81
Cloud	48
Cody V	2, 4
Comet C.2	216
Comet C.2(R)	51, 192
Comet C.4	216
Coronado I	231
Cuckoo	185, 186, 210
Curtiss JN 3 & 4	20, 22, 24, 25, 84
Curtiss H.12	228, 234, 240
Curtiss H.16	228, 230, 238, 257
Cygnet	24, 510
Dakota	10, 18, 21, 24, 27, 30, 31, 46, 48, 52, 53, 62, 70, 76, 77, 78, 96, 110, 113, 114, 117, 147, 167, 187, 194, 204, 206, 209, 215, 216, 231, 233, 238, 243, 267, 271, 353, 357, 435, 436, 437, 511, 512, 525, 575, 620
DC 2	31, 117, 267
DC 3	24, 31, 117, 267
Defiant I	85, 96, 125, 141, 151, 153, 255, 256, 264, 275, 276, 277, 281, 285, 286, 287, 288, 289, 307, 409, 410, 456, 667, 691
Defiant II	96, 125, 151, 256, 264, 515
Defiant III	285, 286, 287, 289, 667, 691
Demon	6, 8, 23, 25, 29, 41, 64, 65, 74, 208, 600, 601, 604, 607, 608

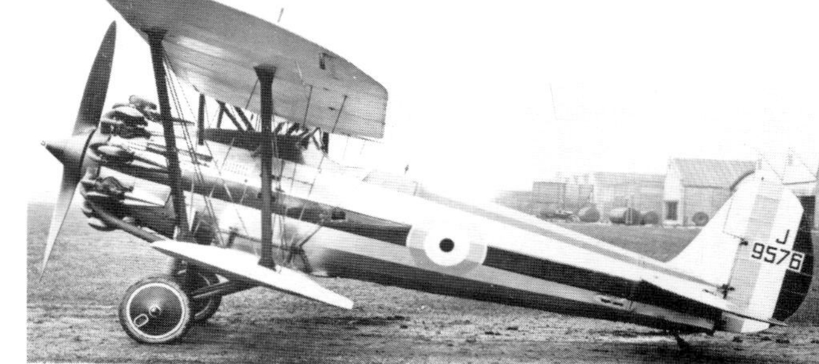

A Bulldog II, J9576, of No 3 Sqn. (RAF Museum P2422)

A Fury I, K2071, of No 25 Sqn. Note that the Moth, G-EBDT, in the background wears the black zig-zag markings of No 17 Sqn. (RAF Museum P8789)

Aircraft	Squadrons
Deperdussin Monoplane	3
Devon C.1 & C.2	21, 26, 31, 207
DH 1A	14
DH 2	5, 11, 17, 18, 24, 28, 29, 32, 35, 41, 47, 111
DH 4	18, 25, 27, 30, 49, 55, 57, 63, 72, 2N/202, 5N/205, 6N, 11N/211, 212, 17N/217, 220, 221, 222, 223, 224, 226, 227, 233, 273
DH 5	24, 28, 32, 41, 64, 68
DH 6	76, 77, 236, 241, 242, 244, 250, 251, 252, 253, 254, 255, 256, 258, 260, 272
DH 9	17, 27, 47, 49, 55, 98, 99, 103, 104, 107, 108, 109, 117, 119, 120, 142, 144, 202, 6N/206, 11N/211, 212, 218, 219, 220, 221, 222, 223, 224, 226, 227, 233, 236, 250, 254, 260, 269, 270, 273
DH 9A	3, 8, 11, 12, 14, 15, 18, 22, 24, 25, 27, 30, 35, 39, 45, 47, 55, 57, 60, 84, 99, 100, 110, 123, 155, 156, 205, 207, 212, 221, 501, 600, 601, 602, 603, 604, 605
DH 10/10A	60, 97, 104, 216
Dolphin	19, 23, 79, 81, 87, 90, 91, 93, 141
Dominie (DH 89)	24, 271, 526, 527
Dornier Do 22	230
Dragon (DH 84)	24
Dragonfly HC 2	194
Dragon Rapide (DH 89)	24, 173
Electra	24, 173, 267, 680
Ensign	24
Envoy	24
Executive	231
Expediter I	353
Express (DH 86)	24, 117, 216
Fairey IIIA	258, 272
Fairey IIIB	219, 230
Fairey IIIC	229, 230
Fairey IIID	202, 267
Fairey IIIF	8, 14, 24, 35, 45, 47, 202, 203, 207
Farman F.40	2N
Farman	see Henry Farman and Maurice Farman
Fawn	11, 12, 100, 503, 602
FE 2A	6, 16, 20
FE 2B	6, 11, 12, 16, 18, 19, 20, 22, 23, 25, 28, 33, 35, 36, 38, 45, 51, 58, 64, 75, 83, 90, 100, 101, 102, 148, 149, 166, 246
FE 2C	25, 100
FE 2D	20, 25, 33, 36, 38, 57, 77
FE 8	5, 29, 40, 41
Felixstowe F.2A	228, 230, 231, 232, 238, 240, 247, 257, 267
Felixstowe F.3	230, 231, 232, 234, 238, 247, 263, 267, 270, 271
Felixstowe F.5	230, 231
Flamingo (DH 95)	24
Fokker F.XXII	24
Fokker T.VIIIw/G	320
Ford 5AT-D	271
Fortress I	90, 220
Fortress II	59, 206, 214, 220, 223, 251, 517 (B-17F), 519, 521
Fortress III	214, 220, 223, 251
Fox	12
Fox Moth (DH 83)	24
Fulmar II	273
Fury I	1, 25, 43
Fury II	25, 41, 73, 87
Gamecock I	3, 17, 23, 32, 43
Gazelle HCC 4	32
Gauntlet I	6, 19, 111
Gauntlet II	6, 17, 19, 32, 33, 46, 54, 56, 65, 66, 74, 79, 80, 111, 112, 151, 213, 234, 504, 601, 602, 615, 616
Gipsy Moth (DH 60)	510
Gladiator I	1, 3, 6, 14, 25, 33, 54, 56, 65, 72, 73, 80, 85, 87, 94, 112, 117, 127, 141, 152, 261, 263, 267, 604, 605, 607, 615
Gladiator II	6, 33, 72, 80, 94, 112, 123, 127, 152, 237, 247, 263, 267, 274, 520, 521, 603, 615
Goose	24
Gordon I & II	6, 14, 29, 35, 40, 45, 47, 207, 223
Grebe II	19, 25, 29, 32, 56, 111
Gull Six	173
Hadrian	668, 669, 670, 671, 672, 673
Halifax I	10, 35, 76
Halifax II	10, 35, 51, 58, 76, 77, 78, 102, 103, 138, 148, 158, 161, 178, 192, 301, 405, 408, 419, 428, 429, 460, 462, 466, 502, 511, 614, 624
Halifax III	10, 35, 51, 58, 76, 77, 78, 96, 102, 158, 171, 187, 190, 192, 199, 246, 296, 297, 298, 346, 347, 408, 415, 420, 424, 425, 426, 427, 429, 431, 432, 433, 434, 462, 466, 502, 517, 518, 519, 520, 521, 578, 640, 644

A Hind, K6820, of No 50 Sqn at Waddington in Nov 38 fitted with smoke dispensers beneath the wings. (D J French)

Halifax V	76, 77, 138, 148, 161, 192, 295, 296, 297, 298, 301, 346, 347, 408, 427, 428, 429, 431, 434, 517, 518, 520, 624, 644
Halifax VI	76, 77, 78, 102, 158, 202, 224, 346, 347, 466, 518, 640
Halifax VII/A.7	47, 113, 190, 295, 296, 297, 298, 408, 415, 426, 432, 620, 644
Halifax VIII	301, 304
Halifax A.9	47, 113, 202, 295, 297, 620, 644
Hamble Baby	219, 229, 249, 253, 263
Hamble Baby Convert	225
Hampden	7, 44, 49, 50, 61, 76, 83, 97, 106, 144, 185, 207, 408, 415, 420, 455, 489, 517, 519, 521
Hardy	6, 30, 173, 237
Harrier GR 1	1, 3, 4, 20
Harrier GR 3	1, 3, 4, 20
Harrow I & II	37, 75, 93, 115, 214, 215, 271
Hart	5, 6, 11, 12, 15, 18, 23, 24, 27, 33, 39, 40, 45, 57, 142, 173, 218, 237, 296, 500, 501, 503, 510, 600, 601, 602, 603, 604, 605, 609, 610, 611
Harvard T.2	1, 5, 17, 20, 34, 41, 267, 691, 695
Hastings C.1	24, 36, 47, 48, 51, 53, 70, 99, 114, 116, 151, 242, 297, 511
Hastings C.2	24, 36, 47, 48, 53, 70, 97, 99, 114, 115, 151, 511
Hastings C.4	24
Hastings Met 1	202
Havoc I	23, 25, 85, 93, 161, 531, 533, 537, 605
Havoc I (Turbinlite)	93, 531, 532, 533, 534, 535, 537, 538, 539
Havoc II	85, 605
Havoc II (Turbinlite)	530, 533, 534, 535, 536, 538, 539
Heck III	24
Hector	2, 4, 13, 26, 53, 59, 296, 602, 612, 613, 614, 615
Hendon II	38, 115
Henley III	291, 587, 595, 631, 639, 679, 695
Henry Farman III	3
Henry Farman Biplane	2
Henry Farman F.20	3, 5, 6, 7, 11, 15, 28, 32, 35, 45, 64
Henry Farman F.27	5, 26, 30, 31, 114
Hercules C.1	24, 30, 36, 47, 48, 70
Hercules C.3	24, 30, 47, 70
Hereford	185
Heron C.4	60
Hertfordshire	See Flamingo
Heyford I, II, III	7, 9, 10, 38, 58, 78, 97, 99, 102, 148, 149, 166
Hiller HTE-2	275
Hinaidi	10, 99, 503
Hind	12, 15, 18, 21, 34, 40, 44, 49, 50, 52, 57, 62, 63, 82, 83, 88, 90, 98, 103, 104, 106, 107, 108, 110, 113, 114, 139, 142, 185, 211, 267, 500, 501, 502, 503, 504, 602, 603, 605, 609, 610, 611, 613, 614, 616
Hornet F.1	19, 41, 64, 65
Hornet F.3	19, 33, 41, 45, 64, 65, 80
Hornet Moth (DH 87)	24, 116, 510, 526, 527, 528, 529
Horsley	11, 15, 22, 33, 36, 100, 504

Hoverfly I	529
Hoverfly II	657
HP 42	271
HS 125 CC 1, 2, 3	32
Hudson I	24, 161, 206, 212, 220, 224, 233, 267, 269, 320
Hudson II	24, 206, 320
Hudson III	24, 48, 59, 62, 139, 161, 163, 200, 203, 206, 217, 220, 224, 231, 233, 251, 267, 269, 279, 285, 287, 288, 289, 320, 353, 357, 407, 459, 517, 519, 520, 521, 608
Hudson IV	24, 117, 200, 206, 267
Hudson V	24, 48, 53, 59, 161, 206, 224, 233, 271, 279, 320, 407, 500, 608
Hudson VI	8, 24, 48, 59, 62, 117, 163, 194, 200, 216, 217, 220, 231, 267, 279, 320, 353, 459, 500, 520, 521, 608
Hunter F.1	43, 54, 222
Hunter F.2	257, 263
Hunter F.4	3, 4, 14, 20, 26, 43, 54, 66, 67, 71, 74, 92, 93, 98, 111, 112, 118, 130, 222, 234, 245, 247
Hunter F.5	1, 34, 41, 56, 263
Hunter F.6	1, 4, 14, 19, 20, 26, 43, 54, 56, 63, 65, 66, 74, 92, 93, 111, 208, 247, 263
Hunter FGA 9	1, 4, 8, 20, 28, 43, 45, 54, 58, 208
Hunter FR 10	2, 4, 8, 79
Hurricane I	1, 3, 6, 17, 30, 32, 33, 43, 46, 56, 69, 71, 73, 74, 79, 80, 85, 87, 94, 95, 96, 98, 111, 112, 116, 121, 127, 128, 145, 151, 173, 181, 182, 183, 185, 208, 213, 225, 229, 232, 237, 238, 239, 242, 245, 247, 249, 250, 253, 255, 256, 257, 258, 260, 261, 263, 267, 273, 274, 276, 286, 287, 288, 289, 302, 303, 306, 308, 310, 312, 315, 316, 317, 318, 331, 335, 401, 402, 450, 451, 501, 504, 527, 538, 601, 605, 607, 610, 615, 680, 691
Hurricane II	1, 3, 5, 6, 11, 17, 20, 26, 28, 30, 32, 33, 34, 42, 43, 56, 60, 67, 69, 71, 73, 74, 79, 80, 81, 87, 94, 96, 113, 121, 123, 126, 127, 128, 133, 134, 135, 136, 146, 151, 153, 164, 174, 175, 176, 184, 185, 193, 208, 213, 225, 229, 232, 237, 238, 239, 241, 242, 245, 247, 249, 250, 253, 256, 257, 258, 261, 273, 274, 279, 284, 285, 286, 287, 289, 290, 291, 302, 306, 309, 310, 312, 316, 317, 318, 331, 335, 336, 351, 352, 401, 402, 417, 451, 486, 488, 504, 516, 518, 520, 521, 527, 530, 531, 532, 533, 534, 535, 536, 537, 538, 539, 577, 587, 595, 598, 601, 605, 607, 615, 631, 667, 679, 680, 681, 691, 695
Hurricane IV	6, 20, 28, 42, 63, 137, 164, 184, 186, 285, 287, 289, 291, 309, 351, 438, 439, 440, 567, 577, 587, 595, 598, 639, 650, 679
Hyderabad	10, 99, 502, 503
Iris III & V	209
Jaguar GR 1	2, 6, 14, 17, 20, 31, 41, 54
Javelin FAW 1	46, 87
Javelin FAW 2	46, 85, 89
Javelin FAW 4	3, 11, 23, 41, 72, 87, 96, 141

A Heyford III, K5190, of No 9 Sqn in front of the partly complete hangars at Scampton which became the unit's home on 1 Oct 36, well before it was really ready for occupation. (Lincolnshire Echo)

A Lysander IIIA, V9547, of No 277 Sqn. (*RAF Museum P7335*)

Javelin FAW 5	5, 11, 41, 72, 87, 151
Javelin FAW 6	29, 46, 85, 89
Javelin FAW 7	23, 25, 33, 64
Javelin FAW 8	41, 85
Javelin FAW 9	5, 11, 23, 25, 29, 33, 60, 64
Junkers Ju 52/3m	173
Kangaroo	246, 252, 256
Kittyhawk I	94, 112, 250, 260, 450
Kittyhawk II	260
Kittyhawk III	112, 250, 260, 450
Kittyhawk IV	112, 250, 450
Koolhoven FK 43	510
Lancaster I/III	7, 9, 12, 15, 35, 37, 44, 49, 50, 57, 61, 70, 75, 83, 90, 97, 100, 101, 103, 106, 109, 115, 138, 148, 149, 150, 153, 156, 166, 170, 178, 186, 189, 195, 207, 214, 218, 227, 300, 405, 424, 427, 429, 433, 434, 460, 463, 467, 514, 550, 576, 582, 617, 619, 622, 625, 626, 630, 635
Lancaster PR 1	82, 541, 683
Lancaster II	61, 115, 408, 426, 432, 514
Lancaster GR/ASR 3	18, 37, 38, 120, 160, 179, 203, 210, 224, 279, 621
Lancaster VI	635
Lancaster VII/B.7	9, 37, 40, 104, 617
Lancaster X	405, 408, 419, 420, 425, 428, 431, 434
Lancastrian C.2	24, 231, 232, 511
Lerwick I	209, 240, 422
Leopard Moth (DH 85)	24
Liberator I	120, 231, 511
Liberator II	108, 120, 148, 159, 160, 178, 224, 231, 511
Liberator III	59, 86, 120, 159, 160, 178, 224, 231, 232, 246, 311, 354, 355, 357
Liberator IV	223
Liberator V	53, 59, 86, 120, 159, 160, 200, 224, 311, 354, 547
Liberator VI	8, 37, 40, 52, 53, 59, 70, 86, 99, 102, 104, 148, 159, 160, 178, 200, 203, 206, 215, 220, 224, 232, 246, 292, 301, 311, 321, 354, 355, 356, 357, 358, 422, 423, 426, 547
Liberator VII	232, 246, 511
Liberator VIII	53, 59, 86, 102, 120, 159, 160, 203, 206, 214, 220, 224, 228, 232, 355, 422, 423, 426, 466, 547, 614
Liberator IX	231
Lightning F.1/1A	5, 56, 74, 111
Lightning F.2/2A	19, 92
Lightning F.3	5, 11, 23, 29, 56, 74, 111
Lightning F.6	5, 11, 23, 56, 74, 111
Lincoln B.2	7, 9, 12, 15, 35, 44, 49, 50, 57, 58, 61, 75, 83, 90, 97, 100, 101, 115, 116, 138, 148, 149, 151, 192, 199, 207, 214, 527, 617
Lockheed 10a	see Electra
Lockheed 12	24
Lockheed 14	267
Lodestar	117, 173, 267
London I & II	201, 202, 204, 209, 210, 228, 240
Longhorn	1, 2, 3, 4, 5, 6, 7, 9, 10, 14, 15, 22, 24, 29, 30
Lysander I	2, 6, 16, 208, 237, 267, 510, 695
Lysander II	2, 4, 6, 13, 16, 20, 26, 28, 173, 208, 225, 231, 237, 239, 241, 267, 268, 288, 516, 613, 614, 695
Lysander III	2, 4, 13, 16, 26, 116, 138, 148, 161, 225, 231, 239, 241, 268, 275, 276, 277, 278, 285, 287, 288, 289, 309, 357, 400, 414, 598, 613, 614
Magister I	24, 173, 267, 271
Manchester I	49, 50, 61, 83, 97, 106, 207
Marauder I	14, 231, (B-26A)
Marauder II	14
Marauder III	14, 39
Mariner I	524
Martinet I	5, 17, 20, 34, 269, 285, 286, 287, 288, 289, 290, 291, 520, 567, 587, 595, 598, 631, 650, 679, 691, 695
Martinsyde S.1	1, 4, 5, 6, 9, 10, 12, 14, 16, 18, 19, 20, 22, 23, 25, 30, 45, 144
Martinsyde G.100/102	6, 14, 18, 20, 21, 23, 27, 30, 49, 51, 63, 67, 72, 142
Maryland	8, 39, 69, 203, 223, 544
Master III	286, 287
Maurice Farman	see Longhorn and Shorthorn
Mentor	24
Messerschmitt Bf 108	24
Messerschmitt Bf 109F	267
Messerschmitt Bf 110C	267
Meteor I	616
Meteor III/F.3	1, 56, 63, 66, 74, 91, 92, 124, 222, 234, 245, 257, 263, 266, 500, 504, 541, 616
Meteor F.4	1, 19, 41, 43, 56, 63, 64, 65, 66, 74, 92, 222, 245, 257, 263, 266, 500, 504, 600, 609, 610, 611, 615, 616
Meteor F.8	1, 19, 34, 41, 43, 54, 56, 63, 64, 65, 66, 72, 74, 85, 92, 111, 222, 245, 247, 257, 263, 500, 504, 600, 601, 604, 609, 610, 611, 615, 616
Meteor FR 9	2, 8, 79, 208
Meteor PR 10	2, 13, 81, 541
Meteor NF 11	5, 11, 29, 68, 85, 87, 96, 125, 141, 151, 256, 264, 527
Meteor NF 12	25, 29, 46, 64, 72, 85, 152, 153
Meteor NF 13	39, 219
Meteor NF 14	25, 33, 46, 60, 64, 72, 85, 152, 153, 264, 527
Mitchell II	98, 180, 226, 305, 320, 342, 681, 684
Mitchell III	98, 180, 226, 320, 342
Mohawk III	510
Mohawk IV	5, 146, 155
Morane BB	1, 3, 12, 60
Morane H	4, 7, 12, 15, 60
Morane I	60
Morane L	1, 3, 15, 25
Morane LA	1, 3, 7, 12, 60
Morane N	1, 3, 60
Morane P	1, 3
Morane V	60
Mosquito I	69, 540

A Mitchell II, FV914/VO·A, of No 98 Sqn. No 98 Sqn was affiliated to Derby during World War II and this aircraft wears that city's coat of arms painted beneath the cockpit sill. (*RAF Museum P7449*)

Aircraft	Squadrons
Mosquito II	23, 25, 27, 85, 141, 143, 151, 157, 169, 239, 264, 307, 333, 410, 418, 456, 515, 605, 681, 684
Mosquito IV	105, 109, 139, 192, 521, 540, 544, 618, 627, 683, 692
Mosquito VI	4, 8, 11, 14, 18, 21, 22, 23, 25, 27, 29, 36, 39, 45, 47, 69, 82, 84, 89, 107, 110, 114, 141, 143, 151, 157, 162, 169, 211, 235, 239, 248, 256, 264, 268, 305, 307, 333, 334, 404, 410, 418, 456, 464, 487, 489, 515, 540, 605, 613, 617, 618, 681, 684
Mosquito VIII	540
Mosquito IX	105, 109, 139, 140, 540, 544, 680, 681, 684
Mosquito XII	29, 46, 85, 108, 151, 256, 307, 406, 488, 604
Mosquito XIII	29, 85, 96, 108, 151, 256, 264, 409, 410, 488, 604
Mosquito XV	85
Mosquito XVI	4, 14, 69, 98, 105, 109, 128, 139, 140, 163, 176, 180, 192, 256, 400, 540, 544, 571, 608, 618, 627, 680, 684, 692
Mosquito XVII	25, 68, 85, 125, 219, 456
Mosquito XVIII	248, 254, 618
Mosquito XIX	68, 89, 157, 169, 176, 255, 256, 500, 600
Mosquito XX/B.20	128, 139, 162, 608, 627
Mosquito XXV/B.25	128, 139, 142, 162, 163, 502, 608, 627
Mosquito FB 26	39, 55, 249
Mosquito XXX/NF 30	23, 25, 29, 68, 85, 125, 141, 151, 157, 219, 239, 255, 264, 307, 406, 410, 456, 488, 500, 502, 504, 605, 608, 609, 616
Mosquito XXXII	540, 544
Mosquito XXXIV/PR34	13, 58, 81, 192, 540, 544, 680, 684
Mosquito XXXV/B.35	14, 98, 109, 139, 527
Mosquito PR 35	58
Mosquito XXXVI/NF 36	23, 25, 29, 39, 85, 141, 199, 219, 264
Moth (DH 60)	24, 267
Moth Major (DH 60)	173
Mustang I	2, 4, 14, 16, 26, 63, 168, 169, 170, 171, 225, 231, 239, 241, 268, 285, 303, 309, 400, 414, 430, 516, 587, 613
Mustang II	2, 225, 268
Mustang III	19, 64, 65, 112, 118, 122, 126, 129, 165, 213, 234, 249, 250, 260, 306, 309, 315, 316, 441, 442, 450, 541
Mustang IV	19, 64, 65, 93, 112, 122, 126, 154, 213, 234, 249, 250, 260, 303, 611
Neptune MR 1	36, 203, 210, 217
Nieuport Monoplane	3
Nieuport 11	3N
Nieuport 12	45, 46, 84, 10N
Nieuport 16	1, 3, 11, 29, 60
Nieuport 17	1, 11, 14, 17, 29, 40, 60, 111, 113, 1N, 8N, 9N, 10N
Nieuport 20	1, 39, 45, 46
Nieuport 23	1, 14, 29, 40, 60, 111, 113
Nieuport 24	1, 29, 40, 111, 113
Nieuport 27	1, 29
Nighthawk (Nieuport)	1
Nighthawk (Miles)	24
Nightjar	203
Nimrod MR 1	42, 120, 201, 203, 206
Nimrod MR 2	42, 120, 201, 206
Nimrod R.1	51
Northrop N3P-B	330
0/100	7N/207, 14N/214, 15N/215, 16N
0/400	58, 70, 97, 100, 115, 116, 207, 214, 215, 16N/216
Overstrand	101, 144
Oxford	1, 5, 17, 20, 24, 34, 41, 116, 173, 192, 285, 286, 287, 288, 289, 290, 510, 526, 527, 529, 567, 577, 587, 595, 598, 631, 667, 691, 695
Panther	205
Pembroke C.1	21, 32, 60, 78, 84, 152, 207, 209, 267
Pembroke C(PR) 1	81
Percival Q.6	24, 267, 510
Perth	209
Phantom FG 1	43, 111
Phantom FGR 2	2, 6, 14, 17, 19, 23, 29, 31, 41, 54, 56, 92, 111
Phantom (F-4J[UK])	74
Phoenix	24
Pioneer CC 1	20, 78, 209, 215, 230, 267
Prentice T.1	31
Proctor I-IV	24, 31, 117, 173, 267, 510
Puma HC 1	33, 230
Pup	28, 36, 37, 46, 50, 54, 61, 64, 66, 72, 92, 112, 141, 2N, 3N, 4N, 8N, 9N
Puss Moth (DH 80)	24, 510

One of the unusual Mosquito XVIIIs which were armed with a 75mm Molins gun. This one, PX468, served with No 254 Sqn as QM·D.
(RAF Museum P6640)

A Siskin IIIA, J9901, wearing the pale blue and white checks of No 19 Sqn. (RAF Museum P9791)

Rangoon	203, 210
RE 1	2, 6
RE 5	2, 6, 7, 12, 16, 19
RE 7	9, 12, 19, 20, 21, 37, 49
RE 8	4, 5, 6, 7, 9, 12, 13, 14, 15, 16, 21, 30, 34, 42, 50, 52, 53, 59, 63, 67, 69, 76, 77, 105, 106, 113, 142, 144, 208
Reliant	24, 173, 510
Roc	241
Rota	529
Sabre F.4	3, 4, 20, 26, 66, 67, 71, 92, 93, 112, 130, 234
Salamander	96, 157
Saro A.7	209
Scapa	202, 204, 228, 240
Scion Senior	173
SE 2/2A	3, 5
SE 5	39, 40, 56, 60, 78
SE 5A	1, 17, 24, 29, 30, 32, 37, 40, 41, 47, 50, 56, 60, 61, 63, 64, 68, 72, 74, 81, 84, 85, 89, 92, 94, 111, 143, 145, 150
Seaford	201
Sea Gladiator I	261
Sea King HAR 3	78, 202
Seal	273
Sea Otter	276, 277, 278, 279, 281, 282, 292
Sentinel	27, 117, 194, 357
Shackleton MR 1	42, 120, 203, 204, 205, 206, 220, 224, 240, 269
Shackleton MR 2	37, 38, 42, 120, 203, 204, 205, 206, 210, 220, 224, 228, 240, 269
Shackleton AEW 2	8
Shackleton MR 3	42, 120, 201, 203, 206, 220
Short 184	202, 219, 229, 230, 233, 234, 235, 237, 238, 239, 240, 241, 242, 243, 245, 246, 248, 249, 253, 263, 264, 266, 267, 268, 269, 270, 271
Short 320	229, 240, 248, 263, 266, 268
Short Bomber	7N
Short R.24/31	209
Short S.23M 'C' Class	119
Short S.26M 'G' Class	119
Shorthorn	2, 4, 6, 9, 10, 14, 15, 16, 18, 19, 23, 24, 25, 30
Sidestrand	101
Simoun	267
Singapore II	209
Singapore III	203, 205, 209, 210, 228, 230, 240
Siskin III	41, 111
Siskin IIIA	1, 17, 19, 25, 29, 32, 41, 43, 54, 56, 111
Skymaster I	24, 232, 246
SM 73P	24, 271
SM 79K	117, 173
Snipe	1, 3, 17, 19, 23, 25, 29, 32, 37, 39, 41, 43, 45, 56, 70, 78, 80, 111, 112, 143, 201, 208
Sopwith 1½ Strutter	37, 43, 44, 45, 70, 78, 84, 2N, 4N, 5N, 7N, 8N, 225
Sopwith 3-Seater	5
Sopwith Baby	219, 229, 246, 248, 249, 263, 270
Sopwith Triplane	1N, 8N, 9N, 10N
Southampton	201, 203, 204, 205, 209, 210
SPAD S.VII	17, 19, 23, 30, 63, 72
SPAD S.XIII	23
Spitfire C/D	140, 212, 541
Spitfire I	19, 41, 54, 64, 65, 66, 72, 74, 92, 111, 118, 122, 123, 124, 129, 131, 132, 140, 145, 152, 222, 234, 238, 249, 257, 266, 303, 308, 313, 403, 411, 452, 457, 485, 501, 510, 602, 603, 609, 610, 611, 616
Spitfire II	19, 41, 54, 64, 65, 66, 71, 72, 74, 91, 111, 118, 121, 122, 123, 124, 129, 130, 131, 132, 133, 134, 145, 152, 154, 222, 234, 266, 276, 277, 278, 302, 303, 306, 308, 310, 312, 313, 315, 316, 331, 340, 350, 401, 403, 411, 412, 416, 417, 452, 457, 485, 501, 504, 602, 603, 609, 610, 611, 616

Spitfire IV	69, 140, 540, 541, 542, 543, 544, 680, 681, 683
Spitfire V	16, 19, 26, 32, 33, 41, 43, 54, 63, 64, 65, 66, 71, 72, 73, 74, 80, 81, 87, 91, 92, 93, 94, 111, 118, 121, 122, 123, 124, 126, 127, 129, 130, 131, 132, 133, 134, 136, 145, 152, 154, 164, 165, 167, 184, 185, 186, 208, 213, 222, 225, 229, 232, 234, 237, 238, 241, 242, 243, 249, 253, 257, 266, 269, 274, 275, 276, 277, 278, 287, 288, 290, 302, 303, 306, 308, 310, 312, 313, 315, 316, 317, 318, 322, 326, 327, 328, 329, 331, 332, 335, 336, 340, 341, 345, 349, 350, 352, 401, 402, 403, 411, 412, 416, 417, 421, 441, 442, 443, 451, 452, 453, 457, 485, 501, 504, 520, 521, 527, 567, 577, 595, 601, 602, 603, 607, 609, 610, 611, 615, 616, 631, 691, 695, 1435
Spitfire VI	66, 118, 124, 129, 132, 234, 310, 313, 504, 519, 602, 616, 680
Spitfire PR VII	140
Spitfire VII	118, 124, 131, 154, 313, 518, 519, 611, 616
Spitfire VIII	17, 20, 28, 32, 43, 54, 67, 73, 81, 87, 92, 94, 131, 132, 136, 145, 152, 153, 154, 155, 185, 208, 238, 241, 253, 256, 273, 326, 327, 328, 417, 451, 452, 457, 548, 549, 601, 607, 615
Spitfire IX	1, 6, 16, 19, 32, 33, 43, 56, 64, 65, 66, 72, 73, 74, 80, 81, 87, 91, 92, 93, 94, 111, 118, 122, 123, 124, 126, 127, 129, 130, 131, 132, 133, 145, 152, 153, 154, 164, 165, 183, 185, 208, 213, 222, 225, 229, 232, 234, 237, 238, 241, 242, 243, 249, 253, 256, 274, 287, 288, 302, 303, 306, 308, 310, 312, 313, 315, 316, 317, 318, 322, 326, 327, 328, 329, 331, 332, 336, 340, 341, 345, 349, 350, 401, 402, 403, 411, 412, 414, 416, 417, 421, 441, 442, 443, 451, 453, 485, 501, 504, 521, 541, 595, 601, 602, 611, 680, 683, 1435
Spitfire X	541, 542
Spitfire XI	2, 4, 13, 16, 26, 28, 140, 253, 400, 541, 542, 543, 544, 680, 681, 682, 683
Spitfire XII	41, 91, 595
Spitfire XIV/14	2, 11, 16, 17, 20, 26, 28, 41, 91, 130, 132, 136, 152, 155, 268, 273, 322, 350, 401, 402, 411, 412, 414, 416, 430, 443, 451, 453, 600, 602, 607, 610, 611, 612, 613, 615
Spitfire XVI/16	5, 16, 17, 19, 20, 31, 34, 63, 65, 66, 74, 126, 127, 164, 229, 287, 288, 302, 303, 308, 317, 322, 329, 340, 341, 345, 349, 350, 401, 402, 403, 411, 412, 416, 421, 443, 451, 453, 501, 567, 577, 587, 595, 601, 602, 603, 604, 609, 612, 614, 631, 667, 691, 695
Spitfire XVIII/18	28, 32, 60, 81, 208
Spitfire XIX/PR 19	2, 16, 31, 34, 81, 82, 268, 541, 542, 681, 682, 683
Spitfire F.21	1, 41, 91, 122, 595, 600, 602, 615
Spitfire F.22	73, 500, 502, 504, 600, 602, 603, 607, 608, 610, 611, 613, 614, 615
Spitfire F.24	80
Stampe SV 4B	510

A Spitfire IIA, P7753/QJ·X, of No 616 Sqn at Tangmere in 1941; this aircraft was lost on a sortie on 5 May 41. Squadron identification codes were changed on 4 Sep 39 with the declaration of war, but a few units continued to use their pre-war allocations. No 616 Sqn failed to take up its YQ combination when it should have done and until 1941 it shared the use of the QJ combination with No 92 Sqn to whom it rightly belonged. Perhaps it confused the enemy . . . (RAF Museum P8128)

A Spitfire PR 19, PM628, of No 541 Sqn. (RAF Museum P19007)

Stirling I	7, 15, 75, 90, 149, 214, 218, 620
Stirling III	7, 15, 75, 90, 149, 171, 196, 199, 214, 218, 513, 525, 620, 622, 623
Stirling IV	46, 51, 138, 148, 158, 161, 190, 196, 242, 295, 299, 570, 620, 624
Stirling V	46, 51, 158, 196, 242, 299
Stranraer	209, 210, 228, 240
Sunderland I	95, 201, 202, 204, 210, 228, 230
Sunderland II	201, 202, 204, 228, 230, 330, 423, 461
Sunderland III	95, 119, 201, 202, 204, 228, 230, 246, 270, 330, 343, 422, 423, 461, 490
Sunderland V/GR 5	88, 201, 204, 205, 209, 228, 230, 240, 259, 330, 461
Swift F.1	56
Swift F.2	56
Swift FR 5	2, 4, 79
Swordfish I	8, 202
Swordfish III	119
Sycamore HC 11	651, 657
Sycamore HC 12	22
Sycamore HR 13	275
Sycamore HR 14	22, 32, 84, 103, 110, 118, 194, 225, 228, 275, 284
Tabloid	3, 4, 5, 7
Taylorcraft Plus C	651
Taylorcraft Plus C.2	651, 652, 653, 654
Taylorcraft Plus D	651
Tempest II/F.2	5, 16, 20, 26, 30, 33, 54, 152, 183, 247
Tempest V	3, 16, 26, 33, 41, 56, 80, 174, 222, 274, 287, 349, 485, 486, 501
Tempest VI/F.6	6, 8, 39, 213, 249
Thor	77, 82, 97, 98, 102, 104, 106, 107, 113, 130, 142, 144, 150, 218, 220, 223, 226, 240, 254, 269
Thunderbolt I	5, 30, 79, 113, 123, 134, 135, 146, 258, 261
Thunderbolt II	5, 30, 34, 42, 60, 79, 81, 113, 123, 131, 134, 146, 258, 261, 615
Tiger Moth	24, 27, 31, 81, 116, 510, 652, 653, 654, 656, 668, 669, 670, 671, 672, 673
Tomahawk I & II	2, 4, 16, 26, 73, 112, 168, 171, 208, 231, 239, 241, 250, 260, 268, 349, 400, 403, 414, 430, 613
Tomtit	24
Tornado F3	5, 29
Tornado GR 1	9, 14, 15, 16, 17, 20, 27, 31, 617
Tristar C.1/K.1	216
Tutor	24
Twin Pioneer CC 1	21, 78, 152, 209, 230
Twin Pioneer CC 2	152, 209, 230
Typhoon I	1, 3, 4, 56, 137, 164, 168, 174, 175, 181, 182, 183, 184, 186, 193, 195, 197, 198, 245, 247, 257, 263, 266, 268, 438, 439, 440, 485, 486, 609
V/1500	166, 167, 274
Valentia	31, 70, 216
Valetta C.1	24, 30, 48, 52, 70, 78, 84, 110, 114, 115, 204, 216, 233, 622, 683
Valiant B.1	7, 18, 49, 138, 148, 199, 207, 214
Valiant B(K) 1	7, 49, 90, 138, 148, 207, 214
Valiant B(PR) 1	7, 49, 90, 138, 148, 207, 214, 543

A VC 10 C.1, XV104, of No 10 Sqn at Brize Norton in 1987. All the RAF's transport VC 10s were allocated individual names commemorating air VCs; XV104 bears the name James McCudden on a scroll alongside the entrance door. (J M Webber)

Aircraft	Squadrons
Valiant B(PR)K 1	7, 90, 138, 148, 214, 543
Vampire F.1	3, 20, 54, 72, 130, 247, 501, 595, 605, 608, 613, 631
Vampire F.3	5, 20, 32, 54, 72, 73, 247, 502, 601, 604, 605, 608, 614
Vampire FB 5	3, 4, 5, 6, 11, 14, 16, 20, 26, 28, 32, 54, 60, 67, 71, 72, 73, 93, 94, 98, 112, 118, 145, 185, 213, 234, 247, 249, 266, 501, 502, 602, 603, 605, 607, 608, 609, 612, 613, 614
Vampire FB 9	4, 6, 8, 20, 26, 28, 32, 45, 60, 73, 213, 234, 249, 501, 502, 608, 613, 614
Vampire NF 10	23, 25, 151
Varsity T.1	97, 115, 116, 151, 173, 187, 192, 527
VC 10 C.1	10
VC 10 K.2	101
VC 10 K.3	101
Vega Gull	24, 267, 510
Vengeance I & II	45, 82, 84, 110
Vengeance III	82, 84, 110
Vengeance IV	110, 288, 289, 291, 567, 577, 587, 595, 631, 667, 679, 691, 695
Venom FB 1	5, 6, 8, 11, 14, 16, 28, 32, 45, 60, 73, 94, 98, 118, 145, 249, 266
Venom NF 2	23, 33, 219, 253
Venom NF 3	23, 89, 125, 141, 151
Venom FB 4	5, 6, 8, 11, 28, 60, 73, 142, 208, 249, 266
Ventura I	21, 140, 251, 299, 464
Ventura II	21, 299, 464, 487, 624
Ventura V	13, 459, 500, 519, 521
Vernon	45, 70
Vickers Boxkite	1
Vickers FB 'Gun Carrier'	6, 7, 11
Vickers FB 5	2, 5, 6, 11, 16, 18, 24, 25, 32, 35, 41
Vickers FB 9	11
Vickers ES 1	11, 32, 50
Vickers FB 19 Mk II	14, 30, 47, 111
Victor B.1	10, 15, 55, 57
Victor K.1	55, 57, 214
Victor B.2	100, 139
Victor B.2(SR)	543
Victor K.2	55, 57
Victoria	70, 216
Vildebeeste I	22, 42, 100
Vildebeeste II	100
Vildebeeste III	22, 36, 42, 100, 273
Vildebeeste IV	22, 42
Vimy	7, 9, 45, 58, 70, 99, 100, 216, 502
Vincent	8, 45, 47, 55, 84, 207, 223, 244
Virginia II	7
Virginia III	7, 58
Virginia IV	7, 9
Virginia V	7, 9, 58
Virginia VI	7, 9, 58
Virginia VII	7, 9, 58
Virginia VIII	9
Virginia IX	7, 9, 58
Virginia X	7, 9, 10, 51, 58, 75, 214, 215, 500, 502
Voisin LA	4, 5, 7, 12, 16
Voisin LA.S	30
Vulcan B.1	44, 50, 83, 101, 617
Vulcan B.2	9, 12, 27, 35, 44, 50, 83, 101, 617
Vulcan B.2(MRR)	27
Vulcan B.2(K)	50
Wallace	501, 502, 503, 504
Walrus (Westland)	3
Walrus (Supermarine)	89, 269, 275, 276, 277, 278, 281, 282, 283, 284, 292, 293, 294, 624
Wapiti	5, 11, 20, 24, 27, 28, 30, 31, 39, 55, 60, 84, 501, 600, 601, 602, 603, 604, 605, 607, 608
Warwick I	38, 167, 251, 269, 276, 277, 278, 279, 280, 281, 282, 283, 284, 292, 293, 294, 301, 304, 520, 525
Warwick III	167, 301, 304, 353, 525
Warwick V	179, 621
Warwick VI	281
Washington B.1	15, 35, 44, 57, 90, 115, 149, 192, 207
Wellesley	7, 14, 35, 45, 47, 76, 77, 117, 148, 207, 223, 267
Wellington I	9, 15, 36, 37, 38, 40, 57, 70, 75, 93, 99, 101, 103, 108, 109, 115, 148, 149, 150, 156, 162, 192, 214, 215, 218, 221, 294, 300, 301, 304, 305, 311, 419, 458
Wellington II	9, 12, 38, 57, 99, 104, 142, 148, 158, 214, 218, 305, 405, 466
Wellington III	9, 12, 37, 40, 57, 70, 75, 99, 101, 115, 142, 150, 156, 162, 166, 192, 196, 199, 300, 419, 420, 424, 425, 426, 427, 428, 429
Wellington IV	142, 300, 301, 305, 458, 460, 544
Wellington VI	109
Wellington VIII	36, 38, 69, 172, 179, 221, 458, 547, 612
Wellington X	36, 37, 40, 70, 99, 104, 142, 150, 162, 166, 192, 196, 199, 215, 300, 304, 305, 420, 424, 425, 426, 427, 428, 429, 431, 432, 466, 527
Wellington XI	36, 38, 221, 294, 344, 407, 547
Wellington XII	36, 38, 172, 221, 407
Wellington XIII	8, 36, 38, 69, 203, 221, 244, 281, 294, 304, 344, 415, 458, 524, 547, 612, 621
Wellington XIV	14, 36, 38, 172, 179, 304, 407, 458, 524, 612, 621
Wellington XVI	24, 232, 242
Wessex HC 2	18, 28, 72, 78, 84, 103
Wessex HAR 2	22, 202
Whirlwind I	137, 263
Whirlwind HAR/HC 2	22, 225, 228, 275
Whirlwind HAR 4	110, 155, 217, 228, 275
Whirlwind HAR/HC 10	22, 28, 84, 103, 110, 202, 225, 228, 230
Whirlwind HCC 12	32
Whitley I	10, 58, 78, 166
Whitley II	7, 51, 58, 97
Whitley III	7, 51, 58, 77, 97, 102, 166
Whitley IV	10, 51, 78
Whitley V	10, 51, 58, 77, 78, 102, 109, 138, 161, 295, 296, 297, 298, 502, 612
Whitley VII	53, 58, 502, 612
Whitney Straight	24, 271
Wicko	24
Wight Converted	241, 243
Woodcock II	3, 17
York C.1	24, 40, 51, 59, 99, 206, 242, 246, 511

Appendix 8

Aircraft Manufacturers

Apart from where the name of the designer or builder forms an integral part of the conventional/familiar designation of a particular type of aeroplane, as in 'Deperdussin Monoplane', or 'Nieuport 17', no reference to manufacturers has been made in the main text of this book. This approach has been adopted partly for brevity, and partly to avoid the duplication which would be necessary to reflect the various changes of manufacturer as the aircraft industry evolved through its succession of mergers. Inherent in these re-organisations were retrospective redesignations of aircraft types, thus the Avro Vulcan became, first, the Hawker Siddeley Vulcan and, ultimately, the British Aerospace Vulcan. Such changes have not been confined to the British aircraft industry, and in the United States for instance the Phantom's original manufacturer, McDonnell, is now McDonnell Douglas. Another potential source of confusion arises from an aeroplane design being taken over by a second manufacturer for development and/or production, resulting in the foster-company becoming more familiarly associated with the type than the parent organisation. The Sopwith Baby floatplane, for instance, evolved into the Fairey Hamble Baby, and the Meteor may be accredited to either Gloster (the originators) or to Armstrong Whitworth, depending on the variant concerned.

In this Appendix are listed the manufacturers conventionally associated with a design. Where necessary both the original company and its successor(s) have been included, although this has been restricted to nomenclature which achieved common contemporary use. Thus the Tiger Moth is listed only against DeHavilland. The technically correct, but little used, designation 'British Aerospace Tiger Moth' has not been acknowledged.

The Belvedere was originally conceived and developed by Bristols but that company's helicopter division was absorbed by Westlands in Mar 60. Production aircraft, delivery of which began in Oct 60, are therefore more properly associated with the latter organisation. This is Belvedere HC 1, XG453, of No 66 Sqn in the Far East. (RAF Museum P14444)

Airacobra	Bell
Albacore	Fairey
Albatross	DeHavilland
Albemarle	Armstrong Whitworth
Aldershot	Avro
Andover	Avro, Hawker Siddeley, British Aerospace
Anson	Avro
Argosy	Armstrong Whitworth, Hawker Siddeley
Argus	Fairchild
Atlas	Armstrong Whitworth
Audax	Hawker
Auster variants	Auster
Avro Type E	Avro
Avro 504	Avro
AW FK 3	Armstrong Whitworth
AW FK 8	Armstrong Whitworth
Balliol	Boulton Paul
Baltimore	Martin
Barracuda	Fairey
Basset	Beagle
Battle	Fairey
BE types	Royal Aircraft Factory
Beaufighter	Bristol
Beaufort	Bristol
Beech 17 Traveller	Beech
Belfast	Short
Belvedere	Bristol, Westland
Beverley	Blackburn
Blenheim	Bristol
Bleriot types	Bleriot
Bloodhound	Bristol-Ferranti
Bombay	Bristol
Boston	Douglas

Originally a Gloster design, responsibility for the two-seat night-fighter variants of the Meteor was delegated to a sister company within the Hawker Siddeley Group. This is an Armstrong Whitworth Meteor NF 14, WS724, of No 46 Sqn. (R C Sturtivant)

Currently (1987) the Canberra is accredited to British Aerospace, however, the type is still most commonly associated with the English Electric Company. These Canberra B.15s, WH956 and WH974, of No 45 Sqn are seen at Labuan in 1965 armed with Nord AS 30 missiles. (Author's collection)

Botha	Blackburn
Breguet Biplane	Breguet
Brigand	Bristol
Bristol Boxkite	Bristol
Bristol Coanda	Bristol
Bristol F2b Fighter	Bristol
Bristol M.1	Bristol
Bristol Prier	Bristol
Bristol Scout	Bristol
Britannia	Bristol
Buccaneer	Blackburn, Hawker Siddeley, British Aerospace
Buffalo	Brewster
Bulldog	Bristol
Camel	Sopwith
Campania	Fairey
Canberra	English Electric, British Aircraft Corporation, British Aerospace
Caproni Ca 42	Caproni
Catalina	Consolidated
Caudron GII-GIV	Caudron
Chinook	Boeing-Vertol
Chipmunk	DeHavilland (Canada)
Cierva C.40	Cierva
Cloud	Saunders Roe (Saro)
Cody V	Cody
Comet	DeHavilland
Coronado	Consolidated
Cuckoo	Sopwith
Curtiss JN	Curtiss
Curtiss H Boats	Curtiss
Cygnet	General Aircraft
Dakota	Douglas
DC 2	Douglas
DC 3	Douglas
Defiant	Boulton Paul
Demon	Hawker
Deperdussin Monoplane	Deperdussin
Devon	DeHavilland
DH 1	Airco, DeHavilland
DH 2	Airco, DeHavilland
DH 4	Airco, DeHavilland
DH 5	Airco, DeHavilland
DH 6	Airco, DeHavilland
DH 9	Airco, DeHavilland
DH 10	Airco, DeHavilland
Dolphin	Sopwith
Dominie (DH89)	DeHavilland
Dornier Do 22	Dornier
Dragon (DH 84)	DeHavilland
Dragonfly	Westland
Dragon Rapide (DH 89)	DeHavilland
Electra	Lockheed
Ensign	Armstrong Whitworth
Envoy	Airspeed
Executive	Spartan
Expediter	Beech
Express (DH 86)	DeHavilland
Fairey III	Fairey
Farman F.40	Farman
Fawn	Fairey
FE types	Royal Aircraft Factory
Felixstowe Boats	Felixstowe
Flamingo (DH 95)	DeHavilland
Fokker F.XXII	Fokker
Fokker T. VIIIw/G	Fokker
Ford 5AT-D	Ford
Fortress	Boeing
Fox	Fairey
Fox Moth (DH 83)	DeHavilland
Fulmar	Fairey
Fury	Hawker
Gamecock	Gloster
Gazelle	Westland
Gauntlet	Gloster
Gipsy Moth (DH 60)	DeHavilland
Gladiator	Gloster
Goose	Grumman
Gordon	Fairey
Grebe	Gloster
Gull Six	Percival
Hadrian	Waco
Halifax	Handley Page
Hamble Baby	Fairey
Hamble Baby Convert	Parnall
Hampden	Handley Page
Hardy	Hawker
Harrier	Hawker Siddeley, British Aerospace
Harrow	Handley Page
Hart	Hawker
Harvard	North American
Hastings	Handley Page
Havoc	Douglas
Heck	Parnall Hendy
Hector	Hawker
Hendon	Fairey
Henley	Hawker
Henry Farman types	Henry Farman
Hercules	Lockheed
Hereford	Handley Page
Heron	DeHavilland
Hertfordshire	DeHavilland
Heyford	Handley Page
Hiller HTE	Hiller
Hinaidi	Handley Page
Hind	Hawker
Hornet	DeHavilland
Hornet Moth (DH 87)	DeHavilland
Horsley	Hawker
Hoverfly	Sikorsky
HP 42	Handley Page
HS 125	Hawker Siddeley, British Aerospace
Hudson	Lockheed
Hunter	Hawker
Hurricane	Hawker
Hyderabad	Handley Page
Iris	Blackburn
Jaguar	SEPECAT
Javelin	Gloster
Junkers Ju 52	Junkers

A Canberra PR 7, WH795, of No 81 Sqn over the South China Sea in 1961 displaying the squadron's Ace of Spaces insignia below the cockpit rim and sun-bleached upper wing roundels. (Sqn Ldr J West)

Kangaroo	Blackburn
Kittyhawk	Curtiss
Koolhoven FK 43	Koolhoven
Lancaster	Avro
Lancastrian	Avro
Lerwick	Saunders Roe (Saro)
Leopard Moth (DH 85)	DeHavilland
Liberator	Consolidated
Lightning	English Electric, British Aircraft Corporation, British Aerospace
Lincoln	Avro
Lockheed 10, 12, 14	Lockheed
Lodestar	Lockheed
London	Saunders Roe (Saro)
Longhorn	Maurice Farman
Lysander	Westland
Magister	Miles
Manchester	Avro
Marauder	Martin
Mariner	Martin
Martinet	Miles
Martinsyde S.1	Martinsyde
Martinsyde G.100/102	Martinsyde
Maryland	Martin
Master	Miles
Mentor	Miles
Messerschmitt Bf 108	Messerschmitt
Messerschmitt Bf 109	Messerschmitt
Messerschmitt Bf 110	Messerschmitt
Meteor	Gloster
Meteor NF	Armstrong Whitworth
Mitchell	North American
Mohawk	Curtiss
Morane types	Morane
Mosquito	DeHavilland
Moth (DH 60)	DeHavilland
Moth Major (DH 60)	DeHavilland
Mustang	North American
Neptune	Lockheed
Nieuport Monoplane	Nieuport
Nieuport types	Nieuport
Nighthawk	Miles
Nighthawk	Nieuport & General, Gloster
Nightjar	Nieuport & General, Gloster
Nimrod	Hawker Siddeley, British Aerospace
Northrop N3P-B	Northrop
0/100	Handley Page
0/400	Handley Page
Overstrand	Boulton Paul
Oxford	Airspeed
Panther	Parnall
Pembroke	Percival, Hunting Percival
Percival Q.6	Percival
Perth	Blackburn
Phantom	McDonnell, McDonnell Douglas
Phoenix	Heston
Pioneer	Scottish Aviation
Prentice	Percival
Proctor	Percival
Puma	Westland
Pup	Sopwith
Puss Moth (DH 80)	DeHavilland
Rangoon	Short
RE types	Royal Aircraft Factory
Reliant	Stinson
Roc	Blackburn
Rota	Cierva, Avro
Sabre	North American
Salamander	Sopwith
Saro A.7	Saunders Roe (Saro)
Scapa	Supermarine
Scion Senior	Short
SE types	Royal Aircraft Factory
Seaford	Short
Sea Gladiator	Gloster
Sea King	Westland
Seal	Fairey
Sea Otter	Supermarine
Sentinel	Stinson
Shackleton	Avro, Hawker Siddeley, British Aerospace
Short 184	Short
Short 320	Short
Short Bomber	Short
Short R.24/31	Short
Short S.23M 'C' Class	Short
Short S.26M 'G' Class	Short
Shorthorn	Maurice Farman
Sidestrand	Boulton Paul
Simoun	Caudron
Singapore	Short
Siskin	Armstrong Whitworth
Skymaster	Douglas
SM 73P	Savoia Marchetti
SM 79K	Savoia Marchetti
Snipe	Sopwith
Sopwith 1½ Strutter	Sopwith
Sopwith 3-Seater	Sopwith
Sopwith Baby	Sopwith
Sopwith Triplane	Sopwith
Southampton	Supermarine
SPAD types	SPAD
Spitfire	Supermarine
Stampe SV 4	Stampe et Vertongen
Stirling	Short
Stranraer	Supermarine
Sunderland	Short
Swift	Supermarine
Swordfish	Fairey
Sycamore	Bristol
Tabloid	Sopwith
Taylorcraft types	British Taylorcraft
Tempest	Hawker
Thor	Douglas
Thunderbolt	Republic
Tiger Moth	DeHavilland
Tomahawk	Curtiss
Tomtit	Hawker
Tornado	Panavia
Tristar	Lockheed
Tutor	Avro
Twin Pioneer	Scottish Aviation
Typhoon	Hawker
V/1500	Handley Page
Valentia	Vickers
Valetta	Vickers
Valiant	Vickers
Vampire	DeHavilland
Varsity	Vickers
VC 10	Vickers, British Aircraft Corporation, British Aerospace
Vega Gull	Percival
Vegeance	Vultee
Venom	DeHavilland
Ventura	Lockheed
Vernon	Vickers
Vickers Boxkite	Vickers
Vickers FB types	Vickers
Victor	Handley Page
Victoria	Vickers
Vildebeest	Vickers
Vimy	Vickers
Vincent	Vickers
Virginia	Vickers
Voisin types	Voisin
Vulcan	Avro, Hawker Siddeley, British Aerospace
Wallace	Westland
Walrus	Westland
Walrus	Supermarine
Wapiti	Westland
Warwick	Vickers
Washington	Boeing
Wellesley	Vickers
Wellington	Vickers
Wessex	Westland
Whirlwind (fighter)	Westland
Whirlwind (helicopter)	Westland
Whitley	Armstrong Whitworth
Whitney Straight	Miles
Wicko	Foster Wikner
Wight Converted	Wight
Woodcock	Hawker
York	Avro

Appendix 9

Locations used by Squadrons

This Appendix cross-refers squadron locations to those units which used them, and to the appropriate map at Appendix 11. The vast majority, but not all, of these locations were airfields of some description. A brief summary of what is embraced by the term 'airfield' is at Appendix 10. Those locations which were not airfields included such establishments as:-

a. **Administrative Units.** In the period 1918-1920 several squadrons were nominally located at non-flying stations. For instance Nos 26 and 139 Sqns were officially disbanded at the Records Office at Blandford after their return from overseas service in 1918 and 1919 respectively, and Nos 1, 3, 4, 24, 39 and 207 Sqns all languished at the RAF Depot, Uxbridge, in 1920 while they existed only as cadres.

b. **Transit Camps.** During World War Two there was a variety of transit camps where personnel assembled prior to, or were temporarily accommodated during, transfers to other theatres. These were not always located at airfields. Examples are: No 56 Personnel Transit Camp at Gragnano, near Naples; No 1 Personnel Depot at Melbourne, Australia; No 1 Base Personnel Depot at Hussein Dey, Algiers; No 10 Personnel Transit Camp which was based on the Bellgrove Hotel, at 609 Gallowgate, Glasgow; No 1 Personnel Despatch Centre at RAF West Kirby, Cheshire; and No 104 Personnel Receipt and Despatch Centre at RAF Hednesford, near Birmingham.

c. **Training and/or Recreational Centres.** In overseas theatres, particularly in India, where the practice was well-established in peacetime, camps were set up through which personnel could be rotated, mainly to experience a beneficial change of climate but sometimes to receive some useful field training at the same time. Examples of these were Nos 1 and 2 Hill Depots at Lower Topa and Solan.

d. **Squadron Headquarters.** In the early days of the UK's air defence organisation, the squadrons of the Home Defence Brigade were established with a Headquarters, which was not necessarily at an airfield, supporting detached Flights. Examples of these remote Headquarters were: 'The Grange' at Woodham Mortimer, which was the HQ for No 37 Sqn; 'Old Dick's Veterinary College' in Clyde Street, Edinburgh, which housed No 77 Sqn's HQ; No 36 Sqn's HQ, which was at 'Monaise' in Fernwood Road, Jesmond, Newcastle; No 39 Sqn's HQ which was at 'Selway Lodge', Woodford Green, in North London; and 'The Old Grammar School' at Hingham, Norfolk, which accommodated No 51 Sqn's HQ.

No 51 Sqn's HQ spent some months at 'the Old Grammar School', Hingham; there was no airfield at Hingham. For its Home Defence role No 51 Sqn converted some of its FE 2Bs into single-seaters by fairing over the front cockpits. This is one of these modified aeroplanes, A5549, pictured on 12 Nov 18. On the original print the inscription on the nose can be deciphered as 'Per Ardua Ad Astra' with 'Royal Aircraft Factory, Farnborough' beneath it. (RAF Museum P22085)

When No 45 Sqn posed its Fairey IIIFs for this picture in 1930 its home base was referred to as Helwan; the spelling had previously often been rendered as Helouan. (No 45 Sqn archives)

Within this Appendix, squadrons (third column) associated with each location (first column) have been listed numerically using the following conventions: '3' indicates No 3 Sqn, RFC or RAF; '4N' indicates No 4 (Naval) Sqn, RNAS; and '6N/206' indicates that the unit concerned was at that particular location on 1 Apr 18, i.e. when the squadron was remustered from the RNAS into the RAF. The figures in the second column provide a cross-reference to the maps at Appendix 11. The first figure indentifies the particular map, and the second, the specific location symbol.

The spelling of place names can be problematical for a variety of reasons and the subject warrants a brief examination. The translation of an Arabic name, for example, can easily result in several alternative renderings in English. A literal transcription of the Arabic characters into English ones will produce one spelling while a phonetic translation of the Arabic sounds will frequently result in one or more additional variations. Thus Qantara and Kantara, Aboukir and Abu Qir, Helwan and Helouan, Minnigh and Minnick, and so on, are all valid alternatives. This syndrome is not confined to Arabic and in Greece, for example, Yanina, Ioanina and Janina may all be found in various references to indicate the same place. Similarly, in Malta, Ta Qali and Ta Kali are synonymous, as are Qrendi and Krendi (although none really convey the distinctly glottal pronunciation adequately). Within this book spellings have been standardised but cross-references have been provided where it has been considered necessary.

A particular case where alternative spellings has given rise to permanent confusion manifested itself in Egypt. Idku, also later designated as LG 229, was a much used airfield, well situated, just east of Alexandria (at 3117N 3015E), for the defence of the Nile Delta. However, its name was also frequently rendered as Edcu and Edku. In general a particular

Idku (or Edku or Edcu) in Egypt was an extensively used airfield during WW II. This is a Beaufighter I, X7760, of the Idku-based No 46 Sqn. (F F Smith)

unit would tend to standardise on one spelling and the resultant situation, where one squadron consistantly recorded 'Idku' while another recorded 'Edku', has led to a widespread, but erroneous, impression that there were two, or even three, different locations involved. It is interesting to observe that some units evidently regarded the different spellings as quite interchangeable and used them at random, depending upon who was writing the account. In its Operations Record Book No 74 Sqn, for instance, refers to 'Edku' on 1 Sep 43, 'Edcu' on 13 Sep 43 and 'Idku' on 22 Sep 43. No 145 Sqn managed all three variations on a single day! Their narrative account for 15 Aug 42 uses 'Edku', while the Record of Flights for that date begins with 'Idku' but ends with 'Edcu'.

Other examples can be found where similar spellings have led to misconceptions in the opposite sense. For instance, in France, Acq and Ascq were different places although they are sometimes treated as the same place with interchangeable spellings. The same is true of Aulnoy and Aulnoye. Similarly Kalyan and Kalyanpur in India have in the past sometimes been confused.

A further cause of differing spellings is that they may actually change with contemporary useage and the passage of time. Thus Miram Shah and Miranshah in North West India, Vert Galant and Vert Galand in France, and Rendcombe and Rendcomb in the UK, might all be correct at different times. Allied to this is the use of different spellings in alternative languages. Belgium provides numerous examples of this, where Bruges may be Brugge, and Courtrai may be Kortrijk, to quote just two examples.

The location at which this incident occurred was known at the time (Jul 28) as Miranshah; today it is usually referred to as Miram Shah. E8584 was a DH 9A of No 60 Sqn which suffered an undercarriage collapse; the damage was repaired and the aircraft was restored to use. (RAF Museum P22346)

Another explanation for incorrect spellings is that they may have been perpetrated in original documents and perpetuated ever since. Related to this are errors arising from the misinterpretation of correctly rendered spellings, written perhaps in an ornate copperplate script, which have subsequently been accepted as correct. Some examples of this are given below.

a. A summary of No 66 Sqn's service in Italy during the First World War was included in the squadron's new Operations Record Book when it was opened in 1936. This incorrectly records Treviso as 'Treorso', presumably a typing error arising from interpretation of a poorly written original. Unfortunately this incorrect spelling has been reproduced in several subsequent accounts of the unit's movements. Incidentally, the official contemporary account of the squadron's early history does spell Treviso correctly.

b. In various accounts of No 55 Sqn's service in France in 1918 can be found 'Le Planey', 'Le Planly' and 'Le Planty', all referring to the same place. The latter was the accepted contemporary spelling, but it is interesting to note that on current maps the spelling now appears as 'Le Plantis'.

c. During the retreat across France in the face of the German offensive of Mar 18, several new airfields being prepared for the RNAS were taken over by the RFC. One of these was at Nielles-lès-Calais, near Fréthun. However, on the site drawings, the town name was rendered in a rather stylised fashion, thus:

   This was misinterpreted at the time as 'Fretnum' and this spelling is prevalent in various contemporary documents. Consequently all accounts of the history of No 218 Sqn, the only squadron to use the aerodrome, have sustained this error.

d. There have been some near misses in this context, where mis-spellings have occurred in documents but have escaped being carried forward. One published account of No 38 Sqn's history, for example, notes the unit as having been at 'South Cerney' (i.e. in Gloucestershire) in 1918, when it should have indicated 'Serny', in France. Another example is provided by No 46 Sqn's Operations Record Book, which was opened in 1936 with an account of the squadron's previous service. This includes 'Lippets' (for Liettres), 'Sermy' (for Serny), 'Catty' (for Cappy), 'Beusigny' (for Busigny), and 'Poulainfville' (for Poulainville). All were, presumably, a result of inadequate proofreading of a typescript prepared from a handwritten draft.

No 423 Sqn was resident at Lough Erne when it was renamed as Castle Archdale. This picture, dated 28 Sep 44, shows one of No 423 Sqn's Sunderland IIIs, NJ184/3-C, at its moorings in Northern Ireland. (PAC PL-33246)

Fortunately none of these errors gained any currency but the examples serve to show how such errors could, and did, occur.

A further factor which must be considered in the context of airfield names is that, for various administrative reasons, these may be formally changed. For instance Church Stanton was renamed Culmhead to avoid confusion with Church Fenton. Other aerodromes operated under different names during two separate periods of service. Where they are significant within this book alternative names have been cross-referenced in this Appendix. A list of formal name changes is on the adjacent page.

One further aspect of airfield naming needs to be addressed. There have been several systems under which airfields have had one or more names or designations at the same time. These are discussed briefly below.

North African Landing Grounds. In the Western Desert of Egypt and Cyrenaica a series of rudimentary airstrips were surveyed and designated as numbered Landing Grounds, eg LG 81. Where a significant feature or settlement was close at hand a name was also used, eg LG 10 was also known as Gerawala, and LG 219 was known variously as Matariyah, Kilo 8 and Payne Field. In contemporary records, names and LG numbers were used at random and both may appear in squadron Operations Record Books. The use of LG numbers has, incidentally, led to a permanent misconception in one instance. In early 1942, three airfields were laid out around the well-established pre-war aerodrome at Abu Sueir near Ismailia on the Suez Canal. These were initially referred to as LG 'X', LG 'Y' and LG 'Z', later becoming LG 206/Abu Sueir North, LG 207/Mahsma and LG 208/Qassassin respectively. However, in 1940/41 there had previously been an 'X' LG, a 'Y' LG and a 'Z' LG on the coast road between Sidi Barrani and Mersah Matruh; these later became LGs 05, 06 and 07 respectively. Most subsequent accounts of squadron movements have not acknowledged the significance of placing the letter designation in front of or behind the 'LG' and they are all usually presented in the latter form. This, unfortunately, indicates that some units were in the comparative safety of the Canal Zone when they were in fact at forward locations 250 or more miles to the west.

North West Europe 1944/45. After the invasion of Europe in 1944, all continental airfields were allocated a coded letter/number designation as well as a name. This applied both to established aerodromes and to temporary airstrips constructed of Pierced Steel Planking. Airfields under British jurisdiction were designated with a 'B' while those controlled by the Americans had an 'A'. Airfields taken over by the Allies advancing from the South of France were designated with a 'Y', while those occupied by the Americans in Germany had an 'R'. There were several instances of duplicated designations. Epinoy airfield at Cambrai, for instance, was both A 75 and B 72, and Beauvais/Tillé was both A 61 and B 42. In contemporary records, both names and coded designators appear indiscriminately. It should also be noted that, although the

Some of the designations which were applied to North African Landing Grounds are potentially confusing. For instance, there was an LG'Y' and a 'Y'LG, but they were different places. No 55 Sqn was a sometime resident of LG'Y', which was east of the Nile Delta, close to the Suez Canal, during the time that it flew Baltimores; this is a Baltimore II, AG781, of No 55 Sqn. (RAF Museum P14682)

Typical of the temporary airfields laid down in Europe after D-Day, B 3/ Ste-Croix-sur-Mer was built by No 24 Airfield Construction Group and was basically a 4,200' x 540' graded earth flight strip with a 3,600' x 120' overlay of Square Meshed Track. In use on a daily basis from 10 Jul 44, the first permanent residents were the three Canadian Spitfire squadrons of No 144 Wg which moved in on 15 Jun 44. A month later these were replaced by the Typhoons of No 146 Wg which remained until early Sep. The airfield was decommissioned on 10 Sep 44. This photograph was taken on 19 Aug and 78 aeroplanes can be seen on it, most, if not all, of them being Typhoons. (Author's collection)

temporary airstrips had official names, alternatives were also current; thus Godelmesnil was also frequently referred to as Baromesnil, Coulombs was also Cully, and Fresnoy-Folny was also Londinière. This probably arose from the proximity of another village, in or near which a unit was billeted, seeming at the time to offer a more logical choice of name.

Airfield Complexes. During the Second World War, groups of airfields were occasionally laid down, all using the same generic title, but each distinguished by a suffix. Examples are the four airstrips at Gardabia in Libya, the fifteen airfields which constituted the Sicilian Gerbini complex, and the twelve aerodromes in the vicinity of Foggia. Not all of the component airfields were necessarily used by operational RAF units. Some were used by the USAAF, some were occupied by the Repair and Salvage organisation, while others functioned as supply dumps and airlift terminals to support the logistic system. Where known, the specific airfield within a complex which a squadron used has been identified in that unit's record of movements. However, where the surviving records are not that precise this has not always been possible; thus a unit noted only as having been at, say, La Sebala may have been at either La Sebala I or La Sebala II, while other squadrons will have the particular airstrip identified.

Airfield/Town Names. Some aerodromes are sometimes referred to by the name of an adjacent town rather than by their own specific name. Peretola, for example, was often recorded as Florence; Alexandria was sometimes used to mean Maryut; Cardiff was, more precisely, Pengam Moors; and Inverness could mean either Dalcross or Longman. Within this book the airfield name has generally been used, but significant cross-references are provided in this Appendix.

The remaining method of naming airfields which should be acknowledged was the practice of allocating random designations. This was sometimes done for want of any more suitable means of identification, as in North West Africa where the complex of airfields laid down around Souk el Khemis, for example, were named after major London railway stations, or to provide a measure of security through the use of code-

Hatfield Woodhouse was renamed Lindholme on 1 Aug 40. This is Hampden, AE184/VN·Z, of No 50 Sqn, the resident bomber squadron at the time. (No 50 Sqn archives)

Original Name	Revised Name	Date of Change
Bathurst	Half Die	3 Jun 43
Bawtry	Bircotes	5 Jun 42
Bowldown Farm	Leighterton	17 Oct 17
Brackley	Croughton	19 Jul 41
Bramham Moor	Tadcaster	6 Oct 17
Brattleby	Scampton	29 Dec 16
Butley	Bentwaters	15 Jan 44
Castel Benito	Idris	1 Aug 52
Cattewater	Mount Batten	1 Oct 29
Chiddingstone Causeway	Penshurst	20 Jul 17
Church Stanton	Culmhead	15 Dec 43
Dhibban	Habbaniyah	1 May 38
Dimapur	Manipur Road	29 Nov 44
Elford	Seahouses	3 Oct 18
Erkowit	Carthago	7 Jul 40
Folkestone	Hawkinge	29 Dec 16
Ford Farm	Old Sarum	17 Oct 17
Grantham	Spitalgate*	29 Mar 44
Gullane	Drem	WW I/WW II
Harpswell	Hemswell	WW I/WW II
Hartford Bridge	Blackbushe	18 Nov 44
Hatfield Woodhouse	Lindholme	1 Aug 40
Hollom Down	Lopcombe Corner	17 Oct 17
Hylton	Usworth	15 Jul 18
Invergordon	Alness	10 Feb 43
Ingham	Cammeringham	28 Nov 44
Islay	Port Ellen	22 Oct 42
Kalamaki	Hassani	1 Dec 44
Katunayake	Negombo	14 Mar 44
Lough Erne	Castle Archdale	1 Feb 43
Luce Bay	West Freugh	WW I/WW II
Newcastle-on-Tyne	Woolsington	5 Jun 42
Old Weston	Molesworth	WW I/WW II
Pembroke	Carew Cheriton	WW I/WW II
Penston	Macmerry	WW I/WW II
'Racecourse'	Colombo	20 Mar 42
Red House Farm	Boscombe Down	17 Oct 17
Rochford	Southend	20 Oct 40
Rosneigr	Valley	4 Apr 41
Scopwick	Digby	22 Jul 20
Shotwick	Sealand	25 Jun 24
Spitalgate*	Spittlegate	15 Oct 52
Spittlegate	Grantham	2 Apr 28
Stamford	Wittering	10 Apr 18
Suttons Farm	Hornchurch	1 Jun 28
Tatoi	Menidi	28 Nov 40
Treblezue	St Mawgan	24 Feb 43
West Wickham	Wratting Common	21 Aug 43
Weyhill	Andover	17 Oct 17

* 'Spitalgate' was a mis-spelling of 'Spittlegate' nevertheless it was the official rendering of the station name from 1944 until 1952, when the error was rectified.

The aerodrome known as Luce Bay during WW I became West Freugh when it was re-established in 1936. This picture of Hind, K6692, was taken at West Freugh on 29 Apr 37 following a landing accident during No 107 Sqn's Armament Practice Camp. The photograph shows some of the more intimate details of the Hind's undersides, bomb racks, aerial fairlead, downward identification light, bomb-aimer's hatch, retractable radiator, leading edge slats, etc. (Sqn Ldr C W Jefford)

Originally, and currently, called Spittlegate, this airfield has also been known as Grantham and Spitalgate at various times. This photograph was taken on 18 Nov 17 and shows a typical well-developed UK aerodrome of the period. Although relatively substantial most of the buildings were of timber construction and were essentially temporary. Much of the RAF's budget in the early 1920s had to be spent on erecting brick structures on its permanent peacetime airfields – of which Spittlegate was one. At the time that the photograph was taken the resident units were Nos 15 and 37 TSs; these were merged into No 39 TDS on 15 Jul 18. (Museum of Army Flying)

No 107 Sqn's Hinds lined up at West Freugh during an Armament Practice Camp in the spring of 1937. (Sqn Ldr C W Jefford)

names. An example of the latter practice occurred in 1942, when a network of airstrips around Rangoon was created, each being named for an alcoholic beverage. Another notable instance of the use of a non-geographical name was the Pierced Steel Planking airstrip built in early 1943 near Bone in Algeria. This came to be known as Tingley after the major commanding the construction engineers who built it.

Detachments

All place names mentioned in the main text are cross-referred in this Appendix and their whereabouts are indicated on the maps at Appendix 11. However, within the confines of this book it has not been possible to list every airfield from which every squadron has ever operated. All main bases have been listed, with dates of occupation. Major wartime detachments, and operational deployments between the wars, from those bases have been noted, but without dates. A degree of personal judgement has been exercised in deciding whether to regard some movements as having been of sufficient significance to warrant recording, with dates, as 'temporary changes of base' or without dates as 'detachments'. The aim has been to try to indicate where the 'core' of the squadron was. This procedure has been followed in general up to 1948. Thereafter, recording of movements has been largely confined to changes of main base.

It should be appreciated that, even in peacetime, the RAF is a dynamic organisation and its squadrons are continually involved in movements associated with their training task. Such movements have not been included in this book after about 1948. Between the Wars such activities included: the deployment of Army Co-operation squadrons to Salisbury Plain and Dartmoor to join the Army for annual manoeuvres; flying-boat cruises around the UK, Europe, the Mediterranean and, sometimes, even further afield; and the detachment of bomber squadrons to Armament Training Stations like North Coates for intensive weapons training. After the War the pattern was resumed: Lincoln squadrons visited Shallufa in the

RAF flying boats undertook a series of long-range flights in the 1920s and 1930s. Representative of these is S1263, named 'Leda', which was originally delivered to No 209 Sqn as an Iris III on the date of its first flight, 5 Feb 30. This aeroplane subsequently undertook a cruise of the west coast of the UK, took part in the RAF's first flight to Iceland, and a flight to Egypt. S1263 is seen here after having its Condor engines replaced by Buzzards, making it an Iris V. It did not survive for long in this guise, however, since it was lost in Plymouth Sound on 12 Jan 33 following a collision with a naval steam pinnace. (MOD H1792)

'V-bombers routinely deployed to Goose Bay, Canada, for low-level training'. This Vulcan B.2, XM650, of No 50 Sqn is seen at Goose Bay on just such a detachment in Oct 80. (Author)

Canal Zone in the 1940s and 1950s for bombing practice; fighter-bomber squadrons based around the Mediterranean attended courses at No 26 APC, Nicosia during the same period; Shackleton squadrons maintained various detachments for prolonged periods, for example No 205 Sqn maintained an Air-Sea Rescue aircraft on standby at Gan for many years, and UK-based maritime squadrons supported the blockade of East African ports during the Rhodesian UDI crisis of the late 1960s with detachments at Majunga; and V-bombers routinely deployed to Goose Bay, Canada, and Offut AFB, Nebraska for low-level flying training for 20 years starting in 1962. Such activities continue today, for instance: fighter squadrons detach to Akrotiri for live gun-firing, to Valley for missile firing, and to Decimommanu to use the instrumented NATO range for Air Combat Manoeuvre Training; Tornados visit Goose Bay, in Labrador, and Nellis AFB, Nevada for realistic low flying practice; and Jaguar and Harrier squadrons from the UK regularly exercise their forward deployment commitments to airfields in Denmark, Norway and West Germany.

Although peacetime detachments have not generally been

Apart from routine training detachments squadrons of the RAF are frequently involved in exercise deployments across the length and breadth of Europe in pursuit of their NATO commitments. Two extreme examples are represented here by (left) Vulcan B.2s of No 50 Sqn at Bödo, inside the Norwegian Arctic Circle in 1978 for Exercise Northern Wedding (Author)*; and (above) Buccaneer S.2s of No 12 Sqn at Gibraltar for Exercise Spring Train in 1981.* (Andrew Thomas)

Ever since the early-1960s elements of the RAF's offensive arm, ranging in size from single aircraft to whole squadrons, have frequently visited North America to hone their skills in a variety of exercises and competitions with the USAF and RCAF. This Tornado GR 1, of No 27 Sqn, is seen approaching the dramatic shape of the Devil's Tower in Wyoming during such a detachment in 1986. (British Aerospace, Warton — photographer Sqn Ldr Terry Cook)

included in the main movement listings those associated with the major post-war operations have been listed below because of their particular significance. These lists are only concerned with those units which were detached to the region in question. It can generally be assumed that any locally based units would automatically have been involved.

The Berlin Airlift

Begun on 25 Jun 48 under the codename Operation 'Knicker', the aim of the initial Berlin Airlift was to supply the military garrison. The first sorties were flown by Dakotas of No 77 Sqn on 28 Jun. The following day Operation 'Carter-Paterson' was begun with the objective of sustaining the civilian population of the city. On 3 Jul 48 the two operations were combined under the codename 'Plainfare'. Control over the RAF contribution to the undertaking was provided initially by a Cell of HQ BAFO operating from Wunstorf. This moved to Bückeburg in Jul 48 where, on 22 Sep 48, it handed over to HQ No 46 Gp whose staff continued to direct operations until 15 Oct 49, by which time all detached squadrons had returned to the UK. Squadrons involved were deployed forward to Germany for intensive airlift flying, virtually losing their individual identities in the process. Their maintenance facilities remained in the UK and aircraft were rotated to their parent bases as necessary for rectification or routine overhaul. Units and bases concerned were:

a. Dakotas of Nos 10, 18, 27, 30, 46, 53, 62 and 77 Sqns operating from Wunstorf (25 Jun 48 - 19 Jul 48), Fassberg (19 Jul 48 - 20 Aug 48) and Lübeck (20 Aug 48 - 23 Sep 49). Some schedules were flown from Bückeburg by, for example, Nos 10, 30 and 46 Sqns, but this was not a major lift airhead.

Mainstay of the RAF's contribution to the Berlin Airlift was the York. This one is MW232 of No 511 Sqn seen at Lübeck in 1948. (R C Sturtivant)

The first flying boat into Berlin for the Airlift was this Sunderland GR 5, VB887/4X·X, of No 230 Sqn seen here moored on Lake Havel. (RAF Musem P21269)

b. Yorks of Nos 40, 51, 59, 99, 206, 242 and 511 Sqns operating from Wunstorf (1 Jul 48 - 29 Aug 49).

c. Hastings of Nos 47 and 297 Sqns operating from Schleswig (11 Nov 48 - 6 Oct 49).

d. Sunderlands of Nos 201 and 230 Sqns flying from Finkenwerder (5 Jul 48 - 15 Dec 48).

Kenya — Anti-Mau Mau Operations

Lincolns of No 49 Sqn, detached to Shallufa in 1953 on a routine Exercise 'Sunray' (bombing practice), were redeployed to Eastleigh (Nairobi) to assist in the campaign against the Mau Mau on an experimental basis. The deployment was considered to have been a success and a Lincoln presence was maintained in East Africa for some time afterwards. Units detached to Eastleigh were:

No 49 Sqn	Nov 53 - Jan 54
No 100 Sqn	Jan 54 - Mar 54
No 61 Sqn	Mar 54 - Jun 54
No 214 Sqn	Jun 54 - Dec 54
No 49 Sqn	Nov 54 - Jul 55

Lincoln B.2s of No 49 Sqn, including RF349 and SX979, line up at Eastleigh during their initial deployment to East Africa in connection with the anti-Mau Mau campaign in 1953. (Flt Lt A Clarke)

Malaya

Operation 'Firedog', the campaign against Communist terrorists in Malaya, began with the declaration of a State of Emergency on 17 Jul 48, and continued until 31 Jul 60. The air campaign was largely conducted with the available resources stationed in the Far East, but UK-based bomber squadrons were detached to the theatre from time to time to provide reinforcements. These units were:

Unit	Type	Period	Deployment Base(s)
No 97 Sqn	Lincoln	Apr 48 - Jun 48	Tengah
No 57 Sqn	Lincoln	Mar 50 - Jun 50	Tengah
No 100 Sqn	Lincoln	May 50 - Dec 50	Tengah
No 61 Sqn	Lincoln	Dec 50 - Apr 51	Tengah
No 83 Sqn	Lincoln	Sep 53 - Jan 54	Tengah
No 7 Sqn	Lincoln	Jan 54 - Apr 54	Tengah
No 7 Sqn	Lincoln	Jul 54 - Oct 54	Tengah
No 148 Sqn	Lincoln	Oct 54 - Feb 55	Tengah
No 101 Sqn	Canberra	Feb 55 - Jun 55	Butterworth, Changi
No 617 Sqn	Canberra	Jul 55 - Nov 55	Butterworth
No 12 Sqn	Canberra	Oct 55 - Mar 56	Butterworth
No 9 Sqn	Canberra	Mar 56 - Jun 56	Butterworth

Brigand B.1s of No 45 Sqn about to take-off from Tengah on a 'Firedog' sortie. (No 45 Sqn archives)

No 45 Sqn was involved in the anti-terrorist campaign in Malaya from start to finish; during these twelve years the squadron flew six types of aircraft. Here the squadron poses its Venoms 'for the album'. (No 45 Sqn archives)

Suez

Operation 'Musketeer' involved some redeployment of units already stationed in and around the Mediterranean theatre and the despatch of large-scale reinforcements from the UK to Malta and Cyprus. The campaign itself was relatively brief, fighting lasting from 31 Oct 56 to 7 Nov 56; however, the overall period during which UK reinforcements were present occupied some six months. Squadrons deployed from the UK were:

Unit	Type	Period	Deployment Base(s)
No 1 Sqn	Hunter	Aug 56 - Dec 56	Akrotiri, Nicosia
No 9 Sqn	Canberra	Oct 56 - Dec 56	Hal Far, Luqa
No 10 Sqn	Canberra	Oct 56 - Nov 56	Nicosia
No 12 Sqn	Canberra	Sep 56 - Dec 56	Luqa, Hal Far
No 15 Sqn	Canberra	Oct 56 - Nov 56	Nicosia
No 18 Sqn	Canberra	Oct 56 - Dec 56	Nicosia
No 27 Sqn	Canberra	Oct 56 - Dec 56	Nicosia
No 30 Sqn	Valetta	Oct 56 - Nov 56	Nicosia
No 34 Sqn	Hunter	Aug 56 - Dec 56	Akrotiri, Nicosia
No 44 Sqn	Canberra	Oct 56 - Nov 56	Nicosia
No 61 Sqn	Canberra	Oct 56 - Jan 57	Nicosia
No 99 Sqn	Hastings	Oct 56 - Nov 56	Nicosia
No 101 Sqn	Canberra	Sep 56 - Nov 56	Luqa, Hal Far
No 109 Sqn	Canberra	Sep 56 - Dec 56	Luqa
No 138 Sqn	Valiant	Oct 56 - Dec 56	Luqa
No 139 Sqn	Canberra	Sep 56 - Dec 56	Luqa, Nicosia
No 148 Sqn	Valiant	Oct 56 - Nov 56	Luqa
No 207 Sqn	Valiant	Oct 56 - Nov 56	Luqa
No 214 Sqn	Valiant	Oct 56 - Dec 56	Luqa
No 511 Sqn	Hastings	Oct 56 - Nov 56	Nicosia

Venom FB 4, WR444, of No 249 Sqn at Akrotiri in Nov 56 wearing its black and yellow Suez campaign markings. (Sqn Ldr E B Goldsmith via Bruce Robertson)

In addition to the above an element of No 58 Sqn (Canberra) was deployed to Akrotiri to reinforce the resident No 13 Sqn; and aircraft and crews of Nos 35 and 115 Sqns were used to bolster the deployed Canberra bomber squadrons. Nos 6, 13, 37, 70, 84 and 114 Sqns also took part in the operation, flying from their home bases; while Nos 8, 39, 208 and 249 Sqns flew from temporary locations (although in the cases of Nos 208 and 249 Sqns these subsequently became their 'home' stations).

A Meteor NF 13, WM315, of No 39 Sqn wearing the unit's black and yellow triangle markings. These were later obscured by the black and yellow bands worn by all aircraft involved in Operation Musketeer in which No 39 Sqn participated as an in-theatre unit. (Air Britain X74)

Falklands

The nature of the South Atlantic campaign of 1982, Operation 'Corporate', gave rise to unit deployments which varied in strength from single aircraft to whole squadrons. In the majority of cases this involved flying into, or from, Wideawake airfield on Ascension Island. During the actual fighting, the only RAF aircraft which came to be based in the combat area, as distinct from operating over it, were: the Harriers of No 1 Sqn, initially on board HMS *Hermes*, and later shore-based in the Falkland Islands; and a Chinook of No 18 Sqn (sole survivor of an attack on the merchant ship *Atlantic Conveyor* while in transit) which also flew from Falklands territory. Other units which were officially gazetted as having taken part in the operation were: No 10 Sqn (VC 10); Nos 24, 30, 47 and 70 Sqns (Hercules); No 29 Sqn (Phantom); Nos 42, 120, 201 and 206 Sqns (Nimrod); Nos 44, 50 and 101 Sqns (Vulcan); Nos 55 and 57 Sqns (Victor); and No 202 Sqn (Sea King).

A Harrier GR 3 of No 1 Sqn prepares to launch from HMS Hermes' ski-jump during Operation Corporate in 1982. (RAF Museum P21365)

The operations dealt with above are those which involved both the deployment of reinforcements and their subsequent employment. There have been many other incidents since 1945 which have been largely contained by units already based within the theatre. The 1960s, a particularly troubled decade, provided several examples of such campaigns. The Brunei Revolution of 1962-63, for instance, was dealt with by the resident squadrons of the Far East Air Force, while the operations in the Radfan in 1964 were handled by local units based at Khormaksar. The same period also provides examples of deployments which, in themselves, were sufficient to avert the need for more than a token use of force. One such operation was the reinforcement of Kuwait, in 1961, where a potential crisis was contained by the squadrons of Air Forces Middle East from Aden, Kenya and Bahrain, supported by detachments of Canberras from Nos 13, 88 and 213 Sqns. Another relatively bloodless, but large-scale, campaign was the Indonesian 'Confrontation' of 1963-66, which involved the deployment, at various times, of all, or elements of, Nos 3, 6, 14, 16, 32, 73 and 249 Sqns (Canberra), and Nos 23 and 64 Sqns (Javelin). In addition there were usually detachments of Victors and/or Vulcans and Shackletons in the theatre throughout the period of tension.

In all of the operations mentioned above, and in many more, all over the world, the squadrons of the transport force have invariably been engaged. Their activities have involved: the provision of logistic support to the military; the flying-in of aid to civilian authorities in disaster areas; the delivery of troops to trouble spots; and the evacuation of British citizens from crisis situations.

If the Indonesian Confrontation had developed into a shooting war the Far East Air Force's resident bomber unit, No 45 Sqn, would have been the spearhead of the offensive campaign. This picture shows five of the squadron's Canberra B.15s and a single T.4 in the unit's traditional pose. (No 45 Sqn archives)

Representing the world-ranging transport force of the post-war RAF are: a Dishforth-based Valetta C.1, VW204, of No 30 Sqn in the mid-1950s. (Air Britain X202);

a Beverly C.1, XB269, of No 47 Sqn seen at Akrotiri in 1956 dwarfing the Venom in the foreground. (RAF Museum P8766);

a Britannia C.1, XL636 'Argo', long-range strategic transport of the Lyneham-based Nos 99 and 511 Sqns, which operated their fleet on a pooled basis. (Air Britain M756)

Location	Map & Symbol (see Appx 11)	Squadron/Remarks
A 8		see Picauville
A 12		see Balleroy
A 15		see Maupertus
A 23		see Querqueville
A 41		see Dreux
A 58		see Coulommiers
A 61		see Beavais/Tillé (B 42)
A 75		see Cambrai/Epinoy (B 72)
A 84		see Chièvres
A 92		see Brustem (St Trond)
Aalborg	16/5	69
Aalten	14/54	662
Aandalsnes	16/11	263
Abadan	42/20	74, 123, 237
Abbeville	11/109	2, 3, 4, 5, 35, 52
Abbeville (Drucat)	12/18	13, 26, 151, 607, 615
Abbotsinch	4/96	21, 34, 88, 225, 232, 239, 254, 269, 309, 602, 666
Abeele	11/41	4, 5, 6, 8, 10, 29, 32, 41, 42, 53, 149
Aberporth	5/9	595
Abidjan	40/18	204, 270, 490
Abingdon	8/23	15, 24, 27, 30, 40, 46, 47, 51, 52, 53, 59, 62, 63, 97, 98, 103, 104, 106, 147, 166, 167, 185, 238, 242, 525
Ablainzevelle	11/166	12
Aboukir (LG 34)	18/9	29, 56, 64, 80, 94, 112, 123, 142, 145, 208, 237, 252, 294, 451, 603, 651
Aboukir (Seaplanes)	18/10	204, 228, 230
Abscon	11/206	19, 42, 98
Abu Gandir	37/2	14
Abu Kamal	42/3	6
Abu Sueir	18/55	6, 13, 37, 40, 46, 70, 80, 84, 89, 104, 114, 145, 208, 213, 214, 216, 223, 252, 272, 450, 458
Abu Zenima	37/6	213
Acaster Malbis	4/69	601
Accra	40/20	82, 200, 541
Achmer (B 110)	15/9	98, 175, 180, 184, 245, 320, 438, 440, 658
Acklington	4/19	1, 18, 19, 23, 25, 29, 32, 41, 43, 46, 54, 56, 63, 64, 65, 66, 72, 74, 79, 85, 91, 92, 111, 130, 140, 141, 152, 164, 167, 198, 202, 219, 222, 228, 245, 247, 257, 258, 263, 264, 266, 275, 278, 288, 289, 291, 309, 315, 316, 317, 322, 349, 350, 406, 409, 410, 504, 539, 600, 607, 609, 610
'Acorn'		see Kalyanpur
Acq	11/161	5,6
Acroma	20/46	208
Addu Atoll	53/4	160, 205, 217, 230, 240, 321, 413
Adelaide	50/46	453
Aden		see Khormaksar, Isthmus, Sheikh Othman, Robat
Afisse	36/44	242
Afrikanda	16/18	144
Agadir	40/3	48, 179, 544
Agartala	46/12	5, 17, 27, 28, 31, 60, 62, 99, 113, 117, 155, 194, 216, 292, 681
Agedabia	20/5-6	6, 145, 208
Agenvillers	11/107	9, 82
Agnone	25/16	112, 250, 260, 450
Agordat	37/33	47, 237
Agra	44/46	20, 30, 114
Agrinion	35/3	112, 211
Ahaus	14/52	653
Ahlhorn (B 111)	15/19	14, 16, 20, 26, 33, 96, 149, 193, 197, 213, 256, 263, 266, 302, 308, 317
Ailly	13/71	660
Aire	11/90	10, 16 — see Treizennes
Aischa	38/16	8
Ajaccio	29/8	154, 232, 242, 243, 283, 326, 327, 328 — see Campo d'il Oro
Akab	42/43	63
Akrotiri	26/4	6, 8, 9, 13, 29, 32, 35, 56, 70, 73, 84, 208, 249
Akureyri	17/4	330
Akyab	46/45	17, 27, 30, 31, 45, 60, 62, 67, 89, 135, 136, 139, 159, 176, 194, 203, 211, 212, 230, 267, 298, 357, 436, 615
Alatri	31/66	654
Alconbury	7/96	15, 40, 52, 156
Aldergrove	3/5	2, 4, 9, 48, 59, 72, 85, 86, 102, 118, 120, 143, 202, 206, 214, 220, 224, 231, 233, 235, 240, 245, 252, 254, 272, 275, 280, 311, 502, 518, 547, 651
Alem el Chel	21/30	73, 92, 250, 450, 601
Aleppo	36/46	14, 111, 243
Alexandria	18/8	14, 17, 113, 202, 204, 228, 230, 267, 269, 270 — see Maryut
Algiers	24/6	651 — see Hussein Dey & Fort de l'Eau
Alghero	28/1	14, 23, 36, 39, 108, 153, 256, 272, 284, 458, 682
Ali Gharbi	42/21	30
Alimini	30/27	224, 225 — see Otranto
Alipore	46/3	17, 28, 34, 67, 79, 81, 136, 146, 155, 215, 261, 298, 607, 615, 681, 684
Allahabad	44/53	34, 97, 110, 177
Allonville	11/143	4, 9, 34, 53, 80, 82, 203
Almaza	18/40	45, 78, 94, 154, 216, 232, 242, 243, 318, 451, 459, 500
Almondbank		see Methven
Almyros	35/14	11
Alness		see Invergordon
Alor Star	48/1	62
Alquines	11/26	41, 58, 98, 149, 14N, 206, 215
Altamura	30/19	651
Alto	29/6	154, 232, 242, 243
Altona	15/55	653
Amarda Road	45/55	5, 20, 27, 45, 67, 81, 110, 131, 135, 136, 177, 215, 607
Ambala	44/43	3, 5, 20, 28, 31, 60, 99, 114, 659
Amberkoj	35/24	17, 47, 144, 150, 222
Amberley	50/34	548, 549
Amblie (B 14)	13/9	661
Amendola	30/11	142, 150, 178, 214, 614
Amiens	11/136	2, 3, 4, 5, 9
Amiens/Glisy (B 48)	12/21 & 13/19	16, 69, 87, 137, 140, 181, 182, 219, 247, 276, 409, 410, 438, 439, 440, 488
Amifontaine	12/29	12
Amiriya (LG 29)	18/13	29, 30, 33, 47, 80, 84, 94, 112, 117, 208, 216, 250, 267, 274 — note that LGs 85-99, 154 and 171-175 (qv) were also loosely referred to as 'Amiriya'
Amman	36/26	6, 14, 32, 33, 45, 73, 208, 249, 450, 651
Amphiklia	35/6	208
Amseat	19/15-16	55, 73
Amy		see Roye
Anagni	31/67	657
Ancenis	12/72	242
Ancona		see Falconara
Andaman Islands		see Port Blair
Andir	49/10	36, 242 — see Bandoeng
Andover	8/43	2, 9, 11, 12, 13, 16, 21, 44, 51, 53, 59, 63, 82, 101, 103, 104, 105, 106, 107, 116, 119, 142, 148, 169, 170, 207, 214, 215, 225, 285, 289, 296, 613, 651, 657, 660, 661, 664, 665, 666
Andrano	30/29	224, 225, 226
Andreas	4/79	93, 275, 452, 457
Andrews Field	9/7	19, 65, 122, 129, 276, 303, 306, 309, 315, 316, 504, 616
Angel		see Red Road

Angers	12/71	1
Angerville-l'Orchier	13/67	652
Angle	5/16	32, 152, 263, 312, 412, 421, 615
Anglure	12/46	1, 501
Aniche	11/207	22, 40, 64
Annah	42/5	6
Annan	4/84	107
Anstedt	15/26	662
Antelat	20/7-8	6, 33, 94, 112, 208, 229 238, 250, 260, 450
Antwerp		see Deurne (B 70)
Anzio	31/71	655
Apapa	40/21	95, 200, 270, 490
Apeldoorn	14/43	661, 664, 665, 666
Appeldorn	14/61	662
Apollonia	20/32	94
Appledram	8/85	175, 181, 182, 302, 308, 310, 312, 313, 317
Aqaba	37/5	14
Aqir	36/15	6, 10, 11, 32, 37, 45, 55, 70, 76, 80, 84, 113, 147, 159, 160, 162, 208, 211, 215, 221, 227, 250, 294, 335, 450, 454, 458, 620, 621, 680
Aqsu	42/52	208
Aquino	31/64	208, 683
Arab Village	42/27	30
Arawali	44/19	5, 11, 20, 27, 28, 60
Araxos	35/4	6, 32, 108, 252, 336
Arcade	32/23	66, 139
Ardres	13/115	660
Arezzo	31/93	654
Argos	35/5	11, 33, 80, 208
Ariana	23/18	225, 241
Arkonam	45/37	30, 79, 134, 146, 258, 261
Arnhem	14/46	661
Arras	12/8	26
Artins	12/67	226
Arzeu	24/3	209, 210
Asa	30/42	152, 225, 232, 242
Asansol	44/59	28, 45, 60, 62, 82, 113, 136, 215
Ascension Island		see Wideawake
Ascq/Asq	11/70	4, 42, 85, 88
Ashford	9/77	65, 122, 414, 430
Ashington	4/21	36, 256
Asmara	37/34	8, 39, 47, 163, 237
Aspelaere	12/1	4
Assab	38/18	8
Assevillers	11/174	80, 84
Assiyut	37/8	17
Aston Down	8/5	4, 180, 187
Atcham	5/60	74, 131, 232, 350, 577
Athies	11/185	9, 24, 46
Attlebridge	7/32	88, 247, 320
Atwick	4/51	251
Auberchicourt	11/208	203
Auberives-sur-Suippes	12/38	88, 218
Auchel/Lozinghem	11/85	3, 18, 22, 23, 25, 32, 40, 43, 58, 70, 83, 101, 148, 8N
Auchy	11/67	16
Augusta	25/17	608
Aulnoy	10/39	5, 42, 52, 88, 99
Aulnoye	10/36	11, 22, 62
Autouillet	13/72	658
Autreville	10/63	216
Auxi-le-Chateau	11/115	6, 8, 52, 99, 110
Avesnes-le-Comte	11/155	8, 12, 43, 54
Avesnes-le-Sec	11/210	52
Aviano	32/24	13, 18, 55, 114, 256, 600
Avret Hisar	35/26	17
Avrilly (B 34)	13/75	168, 400, 430
Ayr	4/91	1, 3, 18, 26, 56, 64, 72, 81, 105, 106, 130, 141, 165, 169, 186, 219, 222, 232, 239, 241, 278, 281, 282, 289, 312, 313, 322, 329, 340, 345, 402, 406, 410, 438, 439, 440, 486, 488, 516, 602, 611, 652
Azelot	10/65	55, 99, 104
Aziziya	42/31	30
B 2		see Bazenville

B 3	see Ste-Croix-sur-Mer
B 4	see Bény-sur-Mer
B 5	see Camilly
B 6	see Coulombs
B 7	see Martragny
B 8	see Sommervieu
B 9	see Lantheuil
B 10	see Plumetot
B 11	see Longues
B 12	see Ellon
B 14	see Amblie
B 15	see Ryes
B 16	see Villons-les-Buissons
B 17	see Carpiquet
B 18	see Cristot
B 19	see Lingèvres
B 21	see Ste-Honorine-de-Ducy
B 23	see Morainville
B 24	see St-André-de-l'Eure
B 26	see Illiers-l'Évêque
B 27	see Boisney
B 28	see Evreux
B 29	see Bernay
B 30	see Créton
B 31	see Fresnoy-Folny
B 33	see Campneuseville
B 34	see Avrilly
B 35	see Godelmesnil
B 37	see Corroy
B 40	see Beauvais/Nivillers
B 42	see Tillé
B 43	see Fort Rouge
B 44	see Poix
B 48	see Amiens/Glisy
B 50	see Vitry-en-Artois
B 51	see Lille/Vendeville
B 52	see Douai
B 53	see Merville
B 55	see Wevelghem
B 56	see Evere
B 57	see Lille/Nord
B 58	see Melsbroek
B 60	see Grimbergen
B 61	see St Denis-Westrem
B 63	see St Croix
B 64	see Diest
B 65	see Maldeghem
B 66	see Blankenberg
B 67	see Ursel
B 68	see Le Culot
B 70	see Deurne
B 71	see Coxyde
B 72	see Cambrai/Epinoy
B 75	see Nivelles
B 76	see Peer
B 77	see Gilze-Rijen
B 78	see Eindhoven
B 79	see Woensdrecht
B 80	see Volkel
B 82	see Grave
B 83	see Knocke le Zout
B 84	see Rips
B 85	see Schjindel
B 86	see Helmond
B 87	see Rosières-en-Santerre
B 88	see Heesch
B 89	see Mill
B 90	see Petit Brogel
B 91	see Kluis
B 92	see Abbeville/Drucat
B 100	see Goch
B 101	see Nordhorn
B 103	see Plantlunne
B 105	see Drope
B 106	see Twente
B 108	see Rheine
B 109	see Quackenbrück
B 110	see Achmer
B 111	see Ahlhorn
B 112	see Hopsten

Biggin Hill	9/55	1, 3, 19, 23, 32, 37, 39, 41, 56, 64, 66, 72, 74, 78, 79, 91, 92, 124, 133, 141, 154, 213, 222, 229, 242, 264, 287, 322, 340, 341, 345, 401, 411, 412, 436, 485, 600, 601, 602, 609, 610, 611, 615
Bikram	44/55	117, 669, 671, 672, 673
Bilaspur	45/52	10, 96, 267, 673
Bilbeis	18/43	31, 117, 162, 267
Binbrook	7/6	5, 9, 11, 12, 50, 64, 85, 101, 109, 139, 142, 460, 617
Birch	9/14	48
Bircham Newton	7/22	7, 11, 18, 21, 34, 35, 39, 42, 48, 49, 53, 56, 59, 60, 90, 99, 101, 119, 166, 167, 200, 206, 207, 220, 221, 229, 233, 235, 248, 252, 254, 269, 274, 279, 280, 320, 407, 415, 500, 502, 521, 524, 598, 695
Bir Dufan	21/14-19	73, 112, 250, 260
Bir el Baheira	19/8-9	14, 260 — see LG 140, LG 167 and Baheria
Bir el Gubi/Gobi (LG 170)	20/55	208
Bir El Regal	20/9	208 — see LG 165
Bir Kenayis (LG 43)	19/46	80, 208
Bir Korayim		see LG 09
Bir Mella	19/37	208
Birr	3/19	106, 141
Bishnapur	44/57	358
Bisseghem	11/56	7, 24, 43, 65, 82, 108
Bissendorf	15/36	659
Bizerta	23/9	230 — see Sidi Ahmed
Blackbushe	8/33	128, 162, 167, 301, 418, 605, 622 — see Hartford Bridge
Blackdown	37/29	47, 237
Blainville	13/16	652
Blairville	13/102	658
Blakehill Farm	8/12	233, 271, 437, 575
Blandford	8/62	26, 139
Blangermont	11/122	98
Blankenberg (B 66)	14/14	168, 400, 414, 430
Blida	24/5	13, 14, 18, 23, 36, 114, 142, 144, 150, 179, 283, 293, 458, 500, 600, 608, 614, 624
Blyton	6/7	199
Bobbili	45/49	5, 81, 131, 258
Bodney	7/57	21
Bodö	16/13	263
Bodorgan	5/3	577, 650
Boffles	11/118	60
Bognor	8/83	19, 66, 122, 331, 332, 602
Bogs O'Mayne	2/15	57 — see Elgin
Boiry-St-Martin	11/164	8, 12
Boischot	14/17	653
Bois-de-Roche	11/114	5N/205
Boisdinghem	11/27	20, 21, 22, 25, 45, 46, 48, 49, 53, 54, 55, 57, 60, 70, 80, 203, 206
Boisney (B 27)	13/63	2, 4, 268
Bologna	31/6	87, 185, 208, 225
Bolt Head	5/47	16, 41, 234, 257, 263, 266, 275, 276, 310, 421, 610, 611
Bombay		see Juhu, Santa Cruz and Worli
Bone	24/22	14, 36, 72, 81, 111, 152, 153, 154, 219, 225, 232, 242, 243, 255, 284, 293, 458, 500, 600, 608, 624, 651, 655, 657
Bonneuil		see Golancourt
Boos	12/56 & 13/85	1, 59, 85, 87, 660
Bordeaux-Merignac (Y 37)	33/4	346, 347
Borghetto	31/39	87, 185
Borgo	29/3	6, 253, 272, 283, 327, 328, 682
Borgo Lucrezia	31/35	654
Borgo San Lorenzo	31/102	655
Bo Rizzo	25/1	13, 36, 52, 87, 219, 255, 272, 458, 500, 603, 608, 614
Borne	14/50	661, 665
Boscombe Down	8/49	9, 10, 35, 51, 56, 58, 78, 88, 97, 109, 150, 166, 214, 217, 218, 224, 249
Boshoven	14/80	653
Bottesford	6/36	90, 207, 467
Bottisham	7/79	2, 4, 168, 169, 241, 268, 288, 400, 613, 652, 654
Bou Ficha	23/25-26	225, 241
Bouge	10/17	62
Boulmer	4/18	202
Boulogne	11/25 & 12/15	2, 6, 7, 56, 85
Bourg Leopold	14/91	658, 662
Bourlon	11/200	52
Bourn	7/89	15, 97, 101, 105, 162, 609
Bournemouth	8/66	413
Boussières	11/213	87, 210
Bouvincourt	11/188	1, 43, 80, 84
Bovelles	11/137	5, 6, 205
Bowmore	4/100	119, 246, 422
Boxted	9/11	25, 56, 222, 234, 263, 266
Bracebridge Heath	6/25	120
Brackley	8/17	78 — see Croughton
Brading	8/88	253
Bradwell Bay	9/15	3, 19, 23, 25, 29, 56, 64, 85, 124, 125, 126, 151, 157, 198, 219, 247, 264, 278, 287, 309, 310, 312, 313, 418, 456, 488, 501, 605, 611
Bramcote	6/61	151, 215, 300, 301, 304, 305
Bramham Moor	4/73	33 — see Tadcaster
Brasschaat	14/27	652
Brattleby		see Scampton
Brawdy	5/12	22, 202, 517, 521, 595
Bray Dunes	11/8	34, 48, 54, 65, 92, 3N, 4N/204, 8N, 9N
Breda	14/34	661, 664
Breighton	4/60	78, 112, 240, 460
Brenzett	9/74	122, 129, 306, 315
Bremerhaven	15/47	662
Bretteville	13/22	653
Bretteville-sur-Laize	13/50	660
Bricy		see Orléans/Bricy
Brindisi	30/24	6, 18, 32, 55, 73, 112, 114, 148, 185, 213, 223, 249, 253, 284, 301, 600, 624, 1435
Brize Norton	8/15	10, 53, 99, 101, 110, 115, 296, 297, 511
'Broadway'	46/82	81
Broadwell	8/14	10, 76, 77, 271, 512, 575
Brockworth	8/6	90
Bron		see Lyons/Bron
Brooklands	9/37	1, 8, 9, 10, 46
Brough	4/54A	228
Bruay	11/84	3, 8, 16, 18, 23, 35, 40, 46, 54, 71
Bruges	11/1	6 — see St Croix (B 63)
Brüggen	14/98	2, 9, 14, 17, 20, 25, 31, 67, 71, 80, 87, 112, 130, 213
Bruille	11/204	203, 209
Brunei	47/20	66, 110
Brussels		see Evere (B 56) & Melsbroek (B 58)
Brustem	14/93	349, 350
Bryas	11/124	40
Bu Amud (LG 147)	20/53	6, 11, 14, 39, 45, 46, 55, 73, 80, 89, 94, 108, 123, 134, 203, 229, 237, 336
Buchheim	10/2	7
Bückeburg	15/29	2, 541
Buckminster	6/42	38, 90
Budareyri	17/5	330
Budrio	31/7	655
Bueken	14/18	652
Bu Grara	22/5	92, 145, 601
Buna	38/4	237
Burao	38/13	8
Burgh Castle	7/42	219, 273
Burgh el Arab	18/4-5	39, 47, 73, 203, 450 — see LG 28 & LG 39
Burn	4/70	431, 578, 658, 659

Burrumbul	18/37	208
Bury St Edmunds	7/72	241, 268 — see Westley
Bushire	43/3	6, 30, 55, 63, 84
Busigny	11/230	24, 46
Bustan	42/34	30
Butley	7/47	230
Butterworth	48/3	18, 27, 33, 34, 45, 47, 52, 60, 62, 66, 81, 110
Cachy	11/40	62, 73, 79, 80
Caen		see Carpiquet (B 17)
Caffiers	10/23	54
Cailly	13/86	661
Cairncross	4/10	256
Cairo West	18/35	14, 74, 89, 96, 216, 220 — see Kilo 26 and LG 224
Caistor	6/4	85, 269
Calafrana		see Kalafrana
Calais/Marcke	11/19	9, 29, 66, 74
Calcutta	46/2	658, 668
Caldiero	32/7	34, 139
Calenzana	29/2	154, 232, 242, 243
Calshot	8/73	201, 228, 230, 240
Calvi	29/1	43, 72, 93, 111, 148, 225, 237, 238, 284, 326, 327, 328, 451 — see St Catherine
Camblain l'Abbé	11/159	16, 148
Cambrai		see Epinoy (B 72)
Cambridge	7/80	2, 16, 26, 239, 268
Camden	50/38	243, 457
Camilly (B 5)	13/15	174, 175, 184, 198, 245, 609
Campneuseville (B 33)	13/92	66, 127, 331, 332
Campo d'il Oro		see Ajaccio
Campoformido	32/29	72, 87, 93, 185, 225, 600, 654 — see Udine
Campomarino	30/2	6, 249 — see Biferno
Campozillone	30/56	657
Camp Wadi	42/24	30
Canda	32/8	655
Candas	11/130	28, 34, 42, 45, 66
Canne	30/3	6, 32, 73, 80, 92, 145, 241, 249, 253, 274, 336, 351, 352, 417, 601
Canosa	30/16	651
Canrobert	24/23	13, 18, 114, 614
Canteloup	13/51	662
Capetown	41/4	26
Capodichino	30/47	43, 72, 93, 111, 225, 243, 253, 654
Cappelle	11/16	19, 38, 65, 88, 108, 204, 9N, 11N, 12N
Cappy	11/172	23, 24, 46
Cardiff		see Pengam Moors
Carew Cheriton	5/18	32, 48, 75, 217, 236, 238, 254, 286, 320, 321, 500, 587 — see Pembroke
Cark	4/77	650
Carnaby	4/49	150, 247
Carnières	11/212	13
Carpiquet (B 17)	13/20	33, 222, 264, 349, 409, 485, 604
Carraia	31/88	657
Carthago	37/20	45, 47 — see Erkowit
Carvin	11/78	152, 207
Cassala	25/8	43, 72, 93, 111, 243
Cassandro	31/32	241, 318, 654, 683
Cassel	13/111	660
Cassibile	25/19	92, 145, 284, 296, 417, 600, 601
Castel Benito	21/3	6, 73, 89, 92, 108, 112, 117, 145, 208, 250, 260, 283, 294, 318, 417, 450, 601, 651, 680 — see Idris
Castellamare	30/35	654
Castiglione (del Lago)	31/90	208, 318, 683
Castle Archdale	3/24	201, 202, 228, 230, 422, 423 — see Lough Erne
Castlebar	3/21	2, 100, 105
Castle Bromwich	6/76	9, 19, 34, 38, 54, 55, 71, 115, 132, 577, 605, 663
Castle Camps	9/3	25, 68, 73, 85, 91, 151, 157, 307, 410, 456, 486, 527, 605

Castletown	2/5	3, 17, 54, 66, 118, 123, 124, 131, 132, 167, 213, 232, 260, 278, 282, 310, 331, 404, 504, 607, 610
Castrocaro	31/18	663
Catania	25/10	43, 87, 108, 117, 185, 229, 243, 255, 267, 272, 1435
Catfoss	4/52	97, 226, 616
Catigny	11/178	52, 82, 101
Catillon	10/41	101
Catterick	4/36	17, 26, 41, 44, 53, 54, 63, 64, 68, 76, 89, 107, 115, 118, 122, 127, 130, 131, 134, 145, 219, 222, 256, 289, 306, 313, 331, 332, 401, 403, 504, 600, 609
Cattewater	5/46	237, 238 — see Mount Batten
Caudry	11/219	59
Cawnpore	44/51	31, 60, 114
Cecina	31/109	13, 18, 55, 114, 682
Celle (B 118)	15/37	2, 4, 11, 14, 16, 41, 93, 94, 98, 130, 137, 145, 268, 350, 414, 486, 652, 659
Celone	30/13A	18, 55, 114, 178, 223, 225, 462, 614
Cercola	30/45	654
Cerignola	30/15	37, 40, 70, 104, 142, 150
Cervia	31/21	112, 250, 260, 450, 657
Cesena	31/22	651, 657
Cesenatico	31/23	293, 454, 500, 600
Chailey	9/43	302, 308, 317
Chailly	10/56	27, 98, 107
Chaklala	44/33	5, 10, 62, 99, 194, 215, 298, 670, 672
Chakrata	44/42	34, 159
Chakulia	45/58	20, 30, 42, 135, 615
Challerange	12/33	103, 150
Champien	11/177	48, 54, 73, 79, 80, 84, 5N
Chandina	46/13	62, 113, 681
Changi	48/24	33, 48, 52, 81, 84, 103, 110, 205, 215, 656
Charmy Down	8/60	87, 88, 107, 125, 137, 234, 245, 247, 263, 286, 417, 421, 533
Charra	44/58	20, 82, 84, 615
Chart Court	9/80	653
Charterhall	4/12	130, 165, 263, 303
Château Bernard		see Cognac
Château Bougon		see Nantes
Châteaubriant	12/74	13
Châteaudun (France)	12/62	1, 242
Châteaudun (Algeria)	24/15	655, 657
Chattis Hill	8/40	91, 92, 93
Chechen	52/9	221, 266
Chedburgh	7/73	214, 218, 301, 304, 620
Chemy	11/77	214
Cherbourg (Harbour)	13/36	243
Cheria	23/30	104 — see Kairouan/El Alem
Chettinad	45/16	11, 20
Cheux	13/23	653
Chiaravalle	31/43	241, 318, 683
Chickerall	5/54	241, 253
Chiddingstone Causeway	9/56	78 — see Penshurst
Chieng Mai	47/6	20
Chièvres (A 84)	14/8	164, 183, 198, 609
Chilbolton	8/39	26, 54, 174, 183, 184, 222, 238, 245, 247, 308, 501, 504
China Bay	45/19	17, 159, 205, 240, 258, 261, 273, 321, 357, 684
Chingford	9/23	138, 154, 155
Chipilly	11/171	8, 9, 22, 24, 35, 52, 54, 1N
Chiringa	46/24	20, 22, 27, 45, 89, 177, 211, 261
Chittagong/Patenga	46/22	5, 20, 30, 45, 48, 67, 79, 82, 89, 110, 117, 135, 136, 146, 152, 176, 177, 215, 258, 261, 273, 292, 607, 615
Chivenor	5/26	5, 14, 17, 22, 26, 36, 51, 59, 77, 172, 179, 235, 248, 252, 254, 272, 275, 304, 404, 407, 459, 517, 521, 547, 612, 691

Chocques	11/82	3, 4, 9, 10, 16, 42
Cholavaram	45/43	5, 11, 27, 34, 45, 47, 60, 82, 84, 113, 123
Christmas Island	53/9	49, 76, 100, 217
Church Fenton	4/72	19, 23, 25, 26, 41, 46, 64, 68, 71, 72, 73, 85, 87, 96, 112, 124, 125, 129, 141, 183, 213, 234, 242, 245, 249, 257, 263, 264, 288, 306, 307, 308, 409, 456, 488, 600, 604, 609
Church Stanton	5/51	66, 131, 154, 165, 234, 302, 306, 312, 313, 316, 504 — see Culmhead
Citadel		see Méaulte
Citta della Pieve	31/87	657
Civita Castellana	31/77	657
Clairfaye Farm		see Léalvillers
Clairmarais	11/32 & 12/12	1, 4, 13, 15, 20, 27, 53, 54, 58, 65, 74, 98, 101, 149, 9N/209
Clary		see Iris Farm
Clavier	10/14	9, 12
Cleave	5/30	639
Clermont	10/23	23, 80
Clifton	4/65	4, 169, 231, 430, 613, 614, 657, 658, 659
Coal Aston	6/66	33
Cobham	9/38	652
Cochin	45/14	191, 203, 212, 217, 240, 321
Coconada	45/47	191, 205, 240
Cocos Islands	53/7	99, 136, 203, 205, 321, 356, 684
Cognac (Y 36)	33/3	26
Cognelée		see Fort Cognelée
Coimbatore	45/13	656
Coleby Grange	6/27	68, 142, 253, 264, 288, 307, 409, 410
Colerne	8/59	19, 24, 29, 36, 74, 87, 89, 114, 118, 124, 125, 131, 137, 151, 165, 175, 183, 184, 219, 245, 256, 263, 264, 285, 286, 307, 316, 317, 402, 406, 410, 417, 456, 488, 501, 504, 511, 587, 600, 604, 616, 662
Collyweston	6/47	23, 133, 152, 266, 288, 349, 658
Colmar (Y 53)	33/22	326, 327, 328
Colombo	45/29	11, 30, 230, 258
Coltishall	7/37	1, 6, 22, 23, 25, 26, 29, 41, 42, 54, 64, 66, 68, 72, 74, 80, 93, 118, 124, 125, 133, 137, 141, 151, 152, 154, 195, 202, 222, 229, 234, 242, 255, 257, 264, 266, 274, 278, 288, 303, 306, 307, 309, 312, 315, 316, 318, 409, 453, 488, 602, 603, 604, 611, 616
Comilla	46/14	30, 31, 62, 67, 79, 96, 113, 134, 146, 152, 194, 238, 258, 681, 684,
Comiso	25/21	18, 43, 72, 93, 111, 114, 243, 654
Compiègne	10/46	2, 3, 4, 5
Condé/Vraux	12/41	1, 15, 114
Congella	41/5	209, 259, 262, 265, 321
Coningsby	7/13	5, 6, 9, 12, 15, 23, 29, 35, 40, 41, 44, 45, 54, 56, 57, 61, 83, 97, 106, 109, 111, 139, 149, 249, 617, 619
Constantine	24/18	72, 81, 152, 225, 232, 241, 242, 243 — see Le Kroube
Conteville	11/113	24, 41, 48, 49, 54, 65, 84
Coolham	9/39	129, 222, 306, 315, 349, 485
Copenhagen		see Kastrup (B 160)
Copmanthorpe	4/68	33, 57, 76
Coronella	31/1	655
Corroy (B 37)	13/90	74, 329, 340, 341
Cos	35/51	74
Cottesmore	6/44	9, 10, 12, 15, 35, 44, 57, 98, 106, 115, 149, 185, 207, 360
Coucou	11/52	21, 53
Coudekerque	11/11	98, 4N, 5N, 7N/207, 7(A)N, 14N/214, 15N/215
Coudray-en-Vexin	13/84	653
Coulombs (B 6)	13/25	137, 181, 182, 247, 264 — see Cully
Coulommiers (A 58)	10/57, 12/52 & 13/80	2, 3, 4, 5, 540, 541
Courcelles-le-Comte	11/165	12, 15, 59
Covehithe	7/44	273
Cox's Bazaar	46/27	5, 28, 30, 67, 89, 123, 134, 135, 146, 176, 258, 261, 273, 357
Coxyde (B 71)	13/110	418, 605
Crail	2/30	43, 104
Cramaille	10/44	52, 216
Cramlington	4/23	36, 58, 63, 76, 120, 252
Cranage	6/73	96, 307
Cranfield	6/57	2, 4, 35, 62, 82, 108, 181, 183, 207, 239
Crazies Hill		see Henley
Crécy	12/17	18, 53, 57, 59, 114
Creti	31/92	112, 250, 260, 450, 657 — see Foiano
Créton (B 30)	13/77	137, 181, 182, 247
Cristot (B 18)	13/24	401, 411 412, 442
Crochte	11/14	217
Croft	4/34	78, 419, 427, 431, 434
Croisette	11/125	62
Crotone	30/32	225
Croughton	8/17	124, 421 — see Brackley
Croydon	9/53	1, 3, 10, 17, 22, 32, 41, 72, 83, 84, 85, 92, 93, 111, 116, 145, 147, 167, 207, 271, 285, 287, 302, 317, 414, 435, 437, 501, 605, 607, 615
Cuerne	11/58	74
Cuers (Y 13)	33/11	237, 238, 451
Cully	13/25	659 — see Coulombs
Culmhead	5/51	126, 131, 165, 286, 587, 610, 616 — see Church Stanton
the Curragh	3/16	105, 141
Cutella	30/1	112, 250, 260, 450
Cuttack	45/54	20, 60, 62, 134, 135, 160, 200, 215, 353, 354, 615
Cyrene	20/30	94
Dabaing	46/42	67
Dakar (Seaplanes)	40/5	95, 344
Dakar	40/6	343
Dakawa	39/10	26
Dalbumgarh	45/57	28, 42, 45, 131
Dalcross	2/12	41, 63, 88, 122
Dale	5/15	304
Dallachy	2/17	144, 281, 404, 455, 489, 618
Dalton	4/41	102, 420, 424, 428
Damascus	36/40	14, 111, 142, 450
Dambulla	45/23	30, 258
Dardoni	44/17	5, 27, 28, 31, 60
Dar-es-Salaam	39/13 & 41/17	26, 82, 230, 259, 683
Darragh	20/20-22	601 — see Wadi Surri
Dartmouth, NS	51/4	431, 434
Davidstow Moor	5/31	53, 144, 206, 269, 281, 282, 304, 404, 524, 547, 612
Darwin/Civil	50/13	54, 542, 548, 549
Darwin/Nightcliffe	50/14	54
Deanland	9/46	64, 91, 234, 302, 308, 317, 322, 345, 611
Debden	9/4	17, 25, 29, 41, 54, 65, 71, 73, 80, 85, 87, 111, 121, 124, 129, 157, 219, 232, 257, 258, 264, 287, 303, 350, 403, 418, 504, 531, 601, 616
Debert, NS	51/3	420, 425
Dedeagatch	35/41	47, 150, 222
Dedelsdorf (B 155)	15/40	3, 33, 56, 80, 174, 222, 274
Deilinghofen	15/1	652, 658, 662
Deir el Ballah	36/9	14, 67, 111
Deir es Zor	42/1	208, 261
Dekheila (LG 32)	18/7	73, 74, 80, 89, 145, 213, 335
Delden	14/48	661
Delhi	44/45	11, 20, 28, 39, 60 — see Palam
Denham	8/31	652
Deolali	45/4	20, 28, 159, 656, 659
Dera Ghazi Khan	44/6	31
Dera Ismail Khan	44/11	31
Dergaon	46/111	5, 34, 60, 615
Derna	20/34	6, 45, 55, 80, 148, 223, 227, 274, 294, 680
Desford	6/63	664

Detling	9/59	1, 4, 13, 26, 48, 50, 53, 59, 80, 112, 118, 124, 132, 143, 165, 184, 229, 235, 239, 274, 280, 318, 453, 500, 504, 567, 602, 651, 655, 657
Detmold	15/30	652
Deurne (B 70)	14/24	2, 4, 74, 80, 130, 132, 174, 175, 184, 193, 197, 245, 257, 263, 266, 268, 274, 302, 308, 317, 329, 341, 345, 402, 441, 453, 602
Deversoir	18/53	6, 8, 32, 73, 213, 249, 256, 417, 680
Dhamial	44/34	117, 670
Dhibban	42/11	30, 55, 70 — see Habbaniyah
Dhubalia	46/9	31, 36, 62, 99, 159, 215, 353, 355, 658, 659
Diego Garcia	53/3	205, 230, 240
Diego Suarez	41/19	209, 259, 265
Diepholz (B 114)	15/18	416, 421, 443
Dieppe	12/57	26
Diersfordt	14/60	658
Diest (B 64)	14/15	41, 130, 402, 653, 658, 659, 662
Digby	6/29	2, 19, 29, 46, 56, 73, 79, 92, 111, 121, 151, 167, 198, 222, 229, 242, 288, 302, 310, 349, 350, 401, 402, 409, 411, 412, 416, 421, 438, 441, 442, 443, 504, 527, 528, 601, 609, 611 — see Scopwick
Digri	45/62	45, 99, 110, 159, 215, 298, 355, 357, 358, 617
Dijon		see Longevic
Dimapur	46/110	11, 113, 656 — see Manipur Road
Dinant	14/10	662
Dinard	12/76	17, 501
Dinjan	46/113	5, 20, 31, 60, 146
Dinther	14/72	653
Dishforth	4/43	10, 30, 47, 51, 78, 215, 230, 297, 425, 426
Djedeida	23/19-20	37, 70
Djedjelli	24/13	87, 154, 242
Docking	7/24	53, 143, 221, 235, 241, 254, 268, 288, 304, 407, 415, 502, 521, 524
Dodoma	39/29	26
Doetinchem	14/47	657, 661
Dohazari	46/23	27, 60, 79, 82, 110, 135, 258, 615
Doncaster	6/70	7, 82, 169, 271, 613, 616, 658
Donibristle	4/2	22, 36, 42, 100, 271
Don Muang	47/8	20, 62, 211, 273, 357, 681, 684
Dorfmark	15/43	658
Dorval	51/7	231, 243
Doshen Tapeh	42/62	74, 123
Douai (B 52)	12/6 & 13/104	13, 132, 441, 453, 602
Douains	13/73	662
Double Moorings	46/21	67, 152
Dour	10/33	88
Dover		see Swingate Down and Guston Road
Dover, St Margarets		see Swingate Down
Dover Harbour	9/66	233
Down Ampney	8/11	48, 271, 435, 436
Downham Market	7/16	214, 218, 571, 608, 623, 635
Drem	4/7	29, 43, 64, 65, 72, 81, 91, 96, 111, 123, 124, 130, 137, 141, 145, 165, 186, 197, 219, 222, 226, 232, 242, 245, 258, 260, 263, 278, 281, 282, 289, 307, 309, 340, 409, 410, 453, 485, 486, 488, 600, 602, 603, 605, 607, 609, 611 — see Gullane
Dreux (A 41)	12/60 & 13/79	59, 329, 340, 341, 345
Driffield	4/57	33, 51, 58, 75, 77, 88, 97, 98, 102, 104, 158, 196, 202, 213, 215, 217, 219, 405, 426, 462, 466, 485
Drigh Road	44/3	5, 28, 31, 60, 84, 159, 160, 354
Drionville	11/93	88, 92, 98, 107
Droglandt	11/39	5, 6, 7, 10, 15, 21, 28, 32, 41, 46, 57, 65, 70, 82, 10N
Drope (B 105)	15/15	74, 193, 197, 263, 266, 340, 341, 345, 485
Drucat		see Abbeville/Drucat
Drysdale Mission	50/11	54, 457
Dudhkundi	45/59	113, 159
Dumfries	4/85	225, 614, 651, 652
Dum Dum	46/5	5, 28, 31, 45, 52, 60, 62, 113, 135, 136, 139, 146, 176, 194, 215, 258, 353, 357, 681, 684
Dundee	2/25	249, 257
Dundonald	4/93	2, 18, 26, 63, 268, 414, 516
Dunholme Lodge	6/18	44, 141, 170, 619
Dunino	2/29	309
Dunkirk	12/13	4 — see Cappelle, St Pol & Bierne
Dunsfold	8/35	21, 98, 180, 231, 276, 320, 400, 414, 430
Düren	10/9	12, 59
Duxford	7/81	2, 3, 4, 8, 19, 29, 56, 64, 65, 66, 80, 91, 92, 111, 119, 123, 124, 129, 133, 169, 181, 195, 222, 242, 258, 264, 266, 268, 288, 302, 310, 312, 601, 609, 611
Dwelha	46/78	89, 155, 607
Dyce	2/21	3, 17, 91, 111, 122, 129, 130, 141, 143, 145, 165, 234, 235, 248, 254, 289, 310, 331, 332, 404, 410, 416, 540, 602, 603, 612, 618
Earles Colne	9/12	296, 297
Eastchurch	9/60	4, 19, 21, 33, 48, 53, 59, 65, 100, 122, 124, 132, 142, 165, 174, 175, 181, 182, 183, 184, 207, 245, 247, 263, 266, 291, 401, 567
East Fortune	4/8	185
East Grinstead	9/48	659, 660
East Kirkby	7/11	57, 460, 630
Eastleigh (UK)	8/75	7, 28, 42, 45, 101, 201, 224, 269
Eastleigh (Nairobi)	41/14	8, 13, 21, 30, 39, 45, 78, 82, 142, 208, 216, 223, 237, 249, 500, 683
Eastmanton Down	8/46	26, 239
East Moor	4/47	158, 288, 415, 429, 432
East Wretham	7/58	115, 311
Ebblinghem	11/33	5
Eboli	30/38	663
Echemines	12/50	12, 24, 73, 88, 103, 105
Ecoivres	11/126	107
Écury-sur-Coole	12/42	150
Ed Damer	37/21	35, 207
Edinburgh	4/5	77
Edinburgh Field	50/48	49, 76, 542
Edinburgh Field (BWI)	51/12	53
Edku		see Idku (LG 229)
Edzell	2/22	612
Eglinton	3/1	41, 133, 134, 152, 153, 275, 485, 501, 504
Eil	10/5	43, 84, 92, 208
Eindhoven (B 78)	14/79	16, 41, 69, 130, 137, 140, 168, 181, 182, 247, 350, 400, 403, 414, 416, 421, 430, 438, 439, 440, 443, 610, 653, 658
Ein Shemar	36/30	6, 13, 18, 32, 37, 38, 178, 208, 214, 621, 651, 680
Ekaterinodar	52/3	47
El Adem (LG 144)	20/51	33, 38, 46, 47, 70, 73, 80, 94, 103, 112, 117, 178, 208, 213, 216, 221, 238, 249, 267, 274, 294, 336, 450, 459, 462, 603, 614
El Affule	36/33	113, 142
El Alem	23/30	40, 73 — see Kairouan/Cheria
El Aouina	23/17	241, 284, 683
El Assa	22/13	73, 112, 250, 260, 450
El Ballah	18/61	73, 94, 256
El Bassa	36/37	6, 73, 80, 208, 260, 450, 451
El Chel		see Alem el Chel
El Daba	19/70	30, 33, 45, 73, 113, 211 — see LG 105
El Djem	34/40	112, 117, 250, 450, 680
El Dwabis	19/40	274
Elevsis	35/7	30, 33, 38, 80, 112, 208
El Firdan	18/60	14, 229, 237, 238
El Gamil/Port Said	18/62	33, 73, 80, 89, 94, 213, 238, 250, 451
Elgin	2/15	17, 232, 614 — see Bogs O'Mayne
El Gubbi/El Gubsi	20/43-49	6, 39, 45, 46, 55, 73, 80, 203, 208,

(LGs 145 & 146)		223, 238, 250, 252, 451 — see Tobruk
El Hamma	22/3	112, 250, 260, 450, 601
El Hammam	18/2	14, 17 — see LG 37
El Hassiet	20/1	92, 145, 601
Elincourt	11/227	35
El Khanka	18/42	213, 216, 272, 274
Ellon (B 12)	13/26	19, 65, 122, 658
El Magrun	20/13-14	37, 40, 70, 73, 227, 252, 603
Elmas	28/2	38, 284
El Merduma	21/33-36	73, 92, 145, 601
Elm	15/48	662
Elmswell	7/61	75
El Nogra	20/4	92, 601
Elsenborn	10/10	5, 7, 70
Elsham	6/1	33
Elsham Wolds	6/1	57, 100, 103, 576
El Sirtan		see Sirtan
Elvington	4/64	77, 346, 347
El Weigh	37/12	14
Emerchicourt	11/209	5
Enfindaville	23/28	55, 223
Ennetières	11/73	24
Enschede		see Twente (B 106)
Entzheim	33/24	326, 327, 328, 341
Epinoy (B 72)	13/103	14, 69, 107, 180, 268, 305, 487, 613
Eringhem	11/15	210
Episkopi	26/3	112
Erkowit	37/20	47, 112
Erle	14/56	659
Ernes	13/53	661
Erquinghem	11/48	23
Erre	11/205	148
Escaudoeuvres	11/211	52
Escaufourt	11/229	85
Escharen	14/68	658
Eshott	4/20	289, 291
Esnes	11/221	56
Esquerdes	11/29	70
Essey		see Nancy
Estabel	36/41	451
Estourmel	11/216	12
Estrée-Blanche	11/91	22, 41, 43, 66, 79 — see Liettres
Estrées-en-Chaussée	11/187	8, 9, 34, 35, 59, 73, 83, 85, 92, 207, 208
Estrées-lès-Crécy	11/105	87
Etrun	11/162	13
Eu		see Godelmesnil (B 35)
'Euston'		see Souk el Khemis
Evanton	2/10	64, 106, 614
Evere (B 56)	14/20	349, 350, 401, 403, 411, 412, 414, 416, 421, 437, 442, 443, 512, 575, 610, 660
Evreux (B 28)	13/74	401, 412
Exeter	5/50	16, 19, 21, 26, 66, 87, 93, 124, 125, 131, 151, 165, 213, 222, 225, 247, 257, 263, 266, 275, 278, 282, 286, 307, 308, 310, 317, 329, 406, 421, 504, 536, 601, 610, 616, 691
Exmouth Gulf		see Learmonth
Fabriano	31/41	651
Fabrica	31/79	92, 145, 417, 601
Fairchildes	9/54	661
Fairford	8/10	10, 30, 47, 53, 113, 190, 295, 297, 620
Fairlop	9/21A	19, 64, 65, 81, 122, 154, 164, 182, 193, 195, 239, 245, 247, 287, 302, 313, 317, 350, 602, 603
Fairwood Common	5/21	19, 33, 41, 65, 66, 68, 74, 79, 91, 118, 124, 125, 127, 131, 132, 164, 165, 183, 193, 197, 198, 222, 245, 247, 257, 263, 264, 266, 268, 276, 285, 286, 288, 302, 306, 307, 308, 312, 315, 316, 317, 322, 329, 331, 332, 345, 401, 402, 403, 411, 412, 421, 456, 485, 504, 536, 577, 595, 600, 609, 610, 615, 616, 691
Falconara	31/45	6, 13, 18, 38, 55, 114, 237, 241, 255, 256, 272, 318, 454, 458, 600, 624, 1435
Falcone	25/3	43, 72, 93, 111, 243
Faldingworth	6/14	300, 305
Falerium	31/78	112, 208, 250, 260, 450, 683
Falluja	42/12	30
Falmouth	5/43	209, 240
Famagusta	26/10	80, 213, 651
Famechon	11/110	101, 102, 151
Fanara	18/51	230
Fano	31/36	87, 92, 112, 145, 185, 241, 250, 260, 417, 450, 601
Farnborough	8/34	1, 2, 4, 5, 6, 7, 10, 15, 16, 31, 53, 70, 100, 101, 108, 285, 287, 290, 653
Farwania	43/5	8, 208
Fassberg (B 152)	15/42	3, 5, 11, 14, 16, 18, 26, 27, 30, 33, 46, 53, 56, 62, 77, 80, 98, 112, 118, 130, 174, 266, 340, 341, 345, 349, 350, 401, 402, 411, 412, 416, 421, 443, 451, 453, 616
Fatehjang	44/27	668, 669, 670, 672
Fauquembergues	11/94 & 13/114	58, 661
Faux-Villecerf	12/51	88, 103, 142, 226
Fayid	18/52	6, 13, 14, 37, 38, 39, 70, 76, 78, 84, 92, 108, 112, 114, 147, 159, 160, 178, 204, 208, 214, 216, 454, 458, 462, 651, 683
Fayoum	37/3	14, 17
Fayoum Road		see LG 222 and Kilo 17
Fazilpur	46/19	30, 134
Felixstowe	9/10	22, 203, 209, 210, 230, 231, 232, 247, 259, 261
Feltham	9/35	116
Feltwell	7/68	37, 57, 75, 77, 192, 214, 464, 487, 651
Feni	46/18	11, 20, 30, 60, 82, 113, 123, 146, 176, 177, 211, 607, 615
Fenny		see Feni
Fère-en Tardenois	10/43	2, 3, 4, 5
Ferme Guillemin		see Selvigny
Fermo	31/51	241, 318, 651 — see Porto San Giorgio
Fermoy	3/17	2, 105, 106
Ferrara		see La Russia
Fersfield	7/52	98, 107, 140, 180, 226, 605, 613
Fienvillers	11/129	1, 6, 11, 15, 19, 21, 23, 27, 41, 42, 43, 45, 53, 54, 55, 57, 59, 60, 70, 101, 1N/201
Figline	31/98	655
Filescamp Farm	11/157	46, 60, 203
Filton	5/57	19, 20, 25, 33, 42, 62, 66, 101, 118, 121, 145, 236, 263, 286, 501, 504, 528
Findo Gask	2/33	309
Finkenwerder	15/49	201, 230
Finningley	6/9	7, 12, 18, 22, 76, 77, 98, 101, 102, 106, 202, 616
Firbeck	6/69	2, 613, 654, 659
Firmo	30/34	651
Fishermans Lake	40/16	95, 204, 270, 490
Fishguard	5/10	245
Fiskerton	6/21	49, 141, 150, 576
Fismes	10/42	52
Flamicourt	12/22	13
Flaumont	10/30	35, 80
Flensburg (B 166)	15/60	181, 182, 438, 439, 440
Flers	13/44	659
Flesselles	11/133	35
Flez	11/184	22, 24, 48, 54, 84, 9N — see Monchy Lagache
Florence		see Peretola
Florina	35/21	17, 47
Floringhem	11/86	2, 21, 88, 103
Foggia	30/13	6, 14, 32, 38, 40, 73, 87, 104, 112, 148, 154, 221, 250, 253, 255, 256, 260, 272, 293, 450, 458, 624, 682, 1435 — see Celone, Mileni, Tortorella, Triolo
Foiano	31/92	450 — see Creti
Folkestone	9/68	25 — see Hawkinge

Folkingham	6/41	223
Follonica	31/95	225, 600, 682
Fontaine Chaude	24/17	142, 150
Fontaine-sur-Maye	11/106	151
Ford	8/82	16, 19, 23, 29, 43, 65, 66, 88, 96, 107, 122, 127, 129, 132, 141, 170, 174, 256, 287, 288, 302, 306, 308, 315, 317, 331, 332, 418, 441, 442, 443, 453, 456, 602, 604, 605, 611 — see Ford Junction
Ford Farm	8/50	99 — see Old Sarum
Ford Junction	8/82	10, 22, 97, 115, 144, 148, 149, 215 — see Ford
Forêt de Cinglais	13/49	653
Forli	31/19	13, 18, 55, 114, 256, 318, 454, 651, 654, 663, 683
Fornebu	16/7	333
Fort Cognelée	10/16	5, 7, 9, 43, 70, 149
Fort de l'Eau	24/9	655, 657
Fort Grange		see Gosport
Fort Johnson	39/19	26
Fort Kermea	42/40	30
Fort Maddelena		see LG 123 and LG 124
Fort Rouge (B 43)	13/113	2, 4, 268
Fort Rowner		see Gosport
Fort Sandeman	44/10	5, 28, 31
Fossalunga		see Istrana
Fossombrone	31/34	651
Foucart	13/68	652
Foucaucourt	11/175	8, 73, 85, 208
Foulsham	7/29	98, 180, 192, 463, 514
Fouquerolles	10/47	32, 43, 73, 80
Fourneuil	10/48	27, 49, 103
Fowlmere	7/82	2, 15, 16, 19, 21, 111, 124, 125, 126, 133, 154, 167, 174, 264, 411, 421, 655
Franc Waret	10/15	57, 88, 107
Franqueville	11/112	83
Fraserburgh	2/19	279
Fremantle	50/1	205, 488
Freetown		see Hastings, Waterloo, Jui and Lungi
Frejus (Y 12)	33/14	154, 232, 242, 243
Freren	15/14	662
Fresney-le-Vieux	13/47	658
Fresnoy-Folny (B 31)	13/88	2, 4, 268, 308, 317
Fréthun	11/20	218
Friedrichshaven (R 58)	33/26	340, 341, 345
Friston	9/45	32, 41, 64, 131, 253, 306, 308, 316, 349, 350, 412, 501, 610, 666
Froha	24/4	296
Froidmont	11/66	21, 64, 74, 209
Frontier Aerodrome	11/8	9N
Fuka	19/62-65	11, 18, 30, 33, 38, 45, 55, 84, 89, 203, 223, 252 — see LGs 16, 17 & 18
Fulbeck	6/32	49, 189
Full Sutton	4/63	77, 102, 231
Funtington	8/79	4, 19, 33, 65, 66, 122, 127, 164, 183, 198, 222, 268, 329, 331, 332, 340, 341, 349, 438, 439, 440, 441, 442, 443, 485, 609
Furnes	11/5	1N, 3N, 8N, 9N, 10N
Furth		see Nuremburg/Furth
Fyzabad	44/52	45, 113
Gabes	22/4	6, 73, 117, 601
Gabr Saleh (LG 163)	19/2	208
Gacé	13/57	658
Gainsborough	6/11	33
Galeria	31/75	225
Gambut Nos 1-4 LGs 139, 142, 143 & 156)	19/3-6	6, 11, 14, 33, 38, 45, 46, 47, 55, 73, 80, 84, 92, 108, 112, 113, 145, 148, 162, 203, 208, 213, 227, 229, 237, 238, 250, 252, 260, 274, 294, 450, 454, 458, 459, 601, 603 — see LG 143
Gan		see Addu Atoll
Gannavaram	45/46	22, 217
Gardabia	21/10-13	37, 40, 70, 104, 227, 272, 462
Gardermoen	16/6	129, 130, 276, 331, 332, 334, 437
Garissa	38/2	237
Gasr el Arid (LG 141)	19/7	73, 94, 208, 260, 274
Gasr Garabulli	21/5	73
Gatow	16/2	3, 14, 16, 26, 33, 56, 69, 80, 98, 107, 174, 451, 453
Gatwick	9/50	2, 4, 14, 18, 19, 26, 53, 57, 63, 65, 80, 92, 98, 116, 141, 168, 171, 175, 183, 229, 239, 268, 274, 287, 309, 400, 414, 430, 613, 655
Gaudo	30/36	600, 608
Gaydon	6/58	138, 543
Gaye	12/45	73
Gaza	36/12	33, 45, 127, 208, 318, 451
Gazala (LGs 149, 150 & 152)	20/43-45	33, 45, 55, 73, 80, 94, 112, 216, 229, 238, 250, 260, 274, 450
Gebeit	37/17	35, 207
Gedaref	37/28	47
Geilenkirchen	14/97	2, 3, 5, 11, 59, 92, 96, 234, 256
Gela		see Ponte Olivo and Monte Lungo
Geldrop	14/81	659
Geleen	14/95	653
Gemert	14/78	658
Genech	11/69	2, 19

Geographic Co-ordinates — While operating in the field some AOP squadrons recorded their locations as contemporary grid references rather than by place name. Where this was the case the co-ordinates have been converted into latitude and longitude:

3727N 1500E	25/9	651
4105N 1413E	30/49	654
4113N 1404E	30/53	654
4201N 1235E	31/76	654
4402N 1230E	31/28	651
4423N 1201E	31/13	651
4428N 1212E	31/14	651
4431N 1203E	31/12	651
4913N 0029E	13/66	652
5117N 0439E	14/26	652
5123N 0445E	14/31	653
5140N 0505E	14/37	653
5145N 0509E	14/39	653
5150N 0515E	14/40	653
5158N 0559E	14/47	661
'George'	46/34	135 — see Nidania
Gerawala	19/48	30, 33, 112, 127, 208, 238, 274 — see LG 10
Gerbini	25/6	18, 23, 126
Gerpinnes	10/20	6, 12, 59
Gescher	14/53	659
Ghedi	32/4	28, 34
Ghemines		see Hosc Raui
Ghent	14/5	660, 661 — see St Denis-Westrem
Ghisonaccia	29/7	14, 36, 284, 458, 500
Gianaclis	18/29	38, 39, 47, 148, 221, 252, 255, 272, 459, 512
Giarabub	19/28-29	33, 113 — see LGs 107 & 108
Gibraltar	40/1	36, 48, 52, 87, 95, 172, 179, 202, 204, 210, 220, 224, 233, 248, 256, 265, 269, 458, 500, 511, 520, 540, 541, 544, 608
Gilgit	44/31	11, 27, 39, 60
Gilze-Rijen (B 77)	14/35	2, 4, 33, 164, 183, 198, 219, 222, 226, 264, 268, 274, 302, 305, 308, 317, 342, 345, 349, 409, 410, 485, 488, 609, 616, 657, 665, 666
Gioia (del Colle)	30/20	81, 92, 145, 152, 154, 225, 232, 242, 243, 284, 417, 651
Giovanni	31/65	655
Glasgow	4/94	69
Glisy		see Amiens/Glisy (B 48)
Gniloaksaiskaya	52/7	47
Goch (B 100)	14/76	174, 175, 184, 245, 403, 416, 421, 438, 439, 440, 443, 662 — see Laarbruch
Godelmesnil (B 35)	13/89	33, 164, 183, 198, 222, 349, 485, 609
Golancourt	11/181	52, 82
Goldhanger	9/16	37, 74

Goldington	6/56	75
Gondecourt	11/76	6, 88, 108
Gong Kedak	48/28	36
Gonneham		see Chocques
Gordon's Tree	37/23	47, 223, 237 — see Khartoum
Gorizia	32/33	651
Gormanston	3/13	117, 141
Goslar	15/31	657, 662
Gosport	8/77	3, 5, 8, 13, 14, 17, 22, 23, 28, 29, 31, 39, 40, 41, 42, 45, 48, 56, 60, 78, 79, 81, 86, 88, 186, 210, 224, 248, 608, 667
Goubrine	23/34 & 38	6, 92, 145, 295, 296, 417, 601
Gourock	4/97	651, 654
Gouy-l'Hôpital	13/93	653
Gouy-Servins	13/106	653
Gragnano	30/43	14, 154, 232, 238, 242, 243, 272, 451, 1435
Grand Fayt	10/37	35, 80
Grangemouth	4/1	141, 263, 602, 614
Gransden Lodge	7/86	53, 97, 142, 169, 192, 405, 421, 692
Grantham	6/39	106, 113, 185, 211 — see Spittlegate
Grasnaya	16/16	210
Grave (B 82)	14/67	80, 130, 274, 317, 402, 403, 416, 421, 443, 661
Graveley	7/88	35, 97, 115, 161, 227, 571, 692
Gravesend	9/57	2, 4, 19, 21, 32, 64, 65, 66, 71, 72, 74, 85, 92, 111, 122, 124, 132, 133, 141, 165, 174, 181, 193, 232, 245, 247, 257, 264, 266, 277, 284, 306, 350, 401, 464, 487, 501, 604, 609, 610
Great Dunmow	9/6	190, 620
Greatham	4/29	243 — see West Hartlepool
Great Massingham	7/20	18, 90, 107, 169, 342
Great Orton	4/81	281, 282
Great Sampford	9/5	65, 133, 616
Great Yarmouth	7/41	212, 228, 229, 273
Greenland Top	7/3	251
Greenwood, NS	51/5	405, 408
Grentheville	13/18	652
Greven	15/5	659
Grimbergen (B 60)	14/22	3, 19, 56, 65, 66, 122, 127, 302, 308, 317, 331, 332, 486
Grimsetter	1/5	129, 132, 234
Grombalia	23/23	18, 114
Grossa	32/11	28, 34, 42, 45, 66, 139
Grossachsenheim		see Sachsenheim
Grosseto	31/94	43, 72, 93, 111
Grottaglie	30/22	6, 14, 36, 38, 39, 92, 112, 126, 185, 221, 249, 250, 255, 336, 417, 450, 458, 500, 608, 624, 1435
Grove	8/24	174, 184
Guernsey	12/78	17, 48
Guidonia	31/74	112, 250, 260, 450
Guildford	50/3	452, 457
Guindy	45/41	84
Gujrat	44/36	435, 436
Gullane	4/7	151, 152 — see Drem
Gumuljina	35/40	47, 150
Guston Road (Dover)	9/65A	1N, 6N, 9N, 218, 233
Gütersloh (Y 99)	15/3	2, 3, 4, 14, 16, 18, 19, 20, 21, 26, 33, 59, 67, 69, 71, 79, 80, 92, 102, 103, 104, 107, 149, 230, 541
Guyencourt	12/54	18
Gzina	21/29	260 — see Sidi Azzab
H4	36/27	84, 203, 208
Habbaniyah	42/11	6, 8, 11, 14, 45, 52, 55, 70, 73, 74, 82, 84, 94, 123, 127, 162, 185, 203, 208, 216, 223, 249, 261, 651, 680, 683 — see Dhibban
Habighorst	15/39	659
Hadera	36/31	74, 123
Haditha (K3)	42/6	127
Hadleigh	7/63	75
Hadzi Junas	35/29	47
Haifa	36/35	6, 30, 80, 112, 113, 142, 144, 208, 213, 260, 261, 450, 651
Hainault Farm	9/21B	39, 44, 151, 153
Hajdarli	35/28	47
Hakimpet	45/45	5, 31, 658
Hal Far	27/6	22, 38, 43, 72, 73, 74, 93, 108, 185, 208, 229, 242, 243, 249, 250, 255, 283, 284, 605, 624, 1435
Halfaya	19/17	208
Half Die	40/8	95, 204, 490 — see Bathurst
Halluin	11/54	41, 74
Halton	8/30	529
Hamadan	42/58	30, 72
Hamburg		see Altona and Finkenwerder
Hamman		see LG 37
Hamraiet	20/25-27	92, 112, 145, 250, 260, 450, 601
Hamworthy	8/65	210, 461
Hancourt	11/189	23, 101
Handorf (Y 94)	15/4	4, 21, 107, 305
Hangelar	10/7	5, 207
Hani	23/33	40, 104, 420, 424, 425
Harburg	15/50	653
Harlaxton	6/40	68, 98
Harlebeke	11/60	38
Harling Road	7/59	51, 75, 88, 89, 94
Harpswell	6/13	33 — see Hemswell
Harrietsham	9/81	50
Harrington	6/51	218
Harrowbeer	5/44	1, 19, 26, 64, 126, 130, 131, 165, 175, 183, 193, 263, 266, 275, 276, 286, 302, 312, 329, 414, 610, 611, 616, 691
Hartfield	9/47	658
Hartford Bridge	8/33	16, 21, 88, 107, 140, 171, 226, 264, 305, 322, 342, 430, 613 — see Blackbushe
Harwell	8/25	75, 105, 107, 148, 215, 226, 295, 570
Hassani	35/9	13, 18, 38, 39, 55, 221, 252, 283, 294, 335, 336, 624, 680, 683 — see Kalamaki
Hassani Abdel	44/28	5, 20, 28, 60
Hastings	40/14	95, 128, 200
Hatfield	9/28	2, 116, 239
Hatfield Woodhouse		see Lindholme
Hathazari	46/20	31, 62, 117, 177
Hatston	1/4	254
Haussimont	10/62	82
Haute Vissée	11/128	101
Haverfordwest	5/13	516
Hawarden	5/67	173, 577
Hawkinge	9/68	1, 2, 3, 16, 17, 25, 26, 38, 41, 56, 65, 66, 79, 83, 91, 120, 122, 124, 132, 234, 245, 277, 278, 313, 322, 350, 402, 416, 441, 451, 453, 501, 504, 567, 605, 611, 613, 616, 658 — see Folkestone
'Hay'	46/29	79, 134, 136, 258 — see Ramu 3
Hazbub	22/7	92, 601
Headcorn	9/82	403, 421
Heathfield		see Ayr
Heathrow	9/34	1
Hébécourt	13/98	662
Hednesford	6/74	262
Heesch (B 88)	14/70	401, 402, 411, 412, 442
Heliopolis	18/39	6, 11, 14, 17, 30, 33, 39, 40, 45, 55, 58, 64, 67, 70, 73, 80, 84, 92, 113, 173, 206, 208, 211, 216, 267, 272, 417, 451, 603
Helmond (B 86)	14/83	137, 181, 182, 247
Helperby	4/44	76
Helvoirt	14/38	653
Helwan	18/38	6, 8, 11, 18, 29, 30, 33, 39, 45, 47, 55, 70, 74, 80, 112, 113, 134, 142, 145, 206, 208, 211, 318, 601
Hemswell	6/13	12, 61, 76, 83, 97, 100, 109, 139, 144, 150, 170, 199, 300, 301, 305, 542 — see Harpswell

Jullundur	44/40	28, 659
Jumchar	46/26	30, 82, 135
Junction Station	36/16	14, 144, 145
Jurby	4/80	166, 215, 258, 302, 307, 312, 457
K1		see Kirkuk
K3		see Haditha
Kabrit	18/49	13, 14, 32, 37, 39, 40, 55, 70, 73, 78, 80, 104, 108, 113, 114, 148, 162, 203, 204, 208, 215, 216, 219, 458, 683
Kahe	39/4	26
Kairouan	23/30-32	37, 112, 142, 150, 250, 260, 420, 424, 425, 450, 654 — see Cheria, Temmar and El Alem
Kai Tak	47/5	28, 45, 60, 80, 81, 88, 96, 103, 110, 132, 205, 209, 215, 656, 681
Kajamalai	45/31	123 — see Trichinopoly
Kalabac	35/20	47
Kalafrana	27/5	202, 209, 228, 230, 267, 268
Kalamaki	35/9	32, 38, 73, 94, 108, 112, 208, 221, 283, 335, 336 — see Hassani
Kalaywa	46/65	60, 607
Kaldadarnes	17/3	48, 98, 269
Kalametiya	45/25	30, 258
Kalemyo	46/93	28, 656
Kalidjati	49/9	36, 84, 211
Kallang	48/23	11, 27, 31, 34, 39, 48, 62, 67, 84, 110, 152, 155, 215, 232, 242, 243, 488
Kalyan	45/5	20, 110
Kalyanpur	46/1	17, 155
Kan	46/91	11, 152
Kanchrapara	46/8	27, 45, 79
Kandy	45/24	160
Kangla	46/101	11, 42, 60, 62, 81, 113, 176, 194, 436
Kankesanterai	45/17	160, 203, 292, 354
Kano	40/23	82, 541
Kanpur		see Cawnpore
Kantara		see Qantara
Kapoeta	40/32	47
Karachi	44/1	11, 34, 60, 82, 97, 110, 216 — see Drigh Road and Mauripur
Kargi Road	45/53	77, 671, 672, 673
Kars	52/14	17
Kasfareet	18/50	14, 47, 127, 237, 417, 603, 651
Kasirin	42/38	30
Kassala	37/30	47
Kastrup (B 160)	16/4	3, 41, 56, 80, 137, 175, 181, 182, 184, 400, 486
Katukurunda	45/27	273
Kazaklar	35/18	208
Kazvin	42/60	30, 63, 72
Keevil	8/58	196, 299
Kelai	53/5	205, 230, 240
Kelanang	48/13	11, 17, 656
Kelstern	7/7	170, 625
Kemajoran	49/4	27, 31, 47, 48, 60, 81, 84, 100, 110, 321, 453, 656, 681
Kemble	8/4	286
Kenley	9/52	1, 3, 13, 17, 23, 24, 32, 39, 46, 64, 66, 80, 84, 88, 91, 95, 108, 110, 111, 116, 165, 207, 229, 253, 258, 302, 312, 350, 400, 401, 402, 403, 411, 412, 416, 421, 452, 485, 501, 600, 602, 611, 615, 616, 661
Kermanshah	42/57	63, 237
Khanka		see El Khanka
Khanpur	44/5	31
Kharga	37/9	17 — see Sherika
Kharagpur	45/60	5, 31
Khartoum	37/22	3, 6, 8, 39, 47, 117, 208, 213, 216 — see Gordon's Tree
Khirbet Deiran	36/17	113
Khormaksar	38/8	8, 12, 21, 26, 37, 41, 43, 73, 78, 84, 94, 105, 114, 203, 208, 209, 216, 233, 244, 259, 265, 413, 459, 621, 683
Kidlington	8/21	52, 167, 239, 411
Kidsdale	4/87	651
Kiel/Holtenau	15/57	659, 660
Kifri	42/53	30
Killadeas	3/23	240
Kilid el Bahr	35/46	4
Killingholme	7/2	228, 229, 238, 249, 251, 252, 256
Kilo 8	18/41	73, 127, 213 — see LG 219
Kilo 17	18/36	46 — see LG 222
Kilo 26	18/35	6 — see LG 224 and Cairo West
Kilo 40	18/34	148 — see LG 237
Kilo 61	18/44	55 — see LG 209
Kilo 143		see Ujret el Zol
Kilwa	39/14	26
Kilya Bay	35/45	4, 203, 267
Kingscliffe	6/49	91, 93, 266, 349, 485, 616
'Kings Cross'		see Souk el Khemis
Kingsnorth	9/75	19, 65, 122, 184, 602
Kinloss	2/13	8, 10, 49, 50, 51, 77, 90, 102, 115, 120, 161, 201, 206, 217, 220, 609
Kinmagon	46/77	34, 47, 110, 113, 436
Kipevu	41/16	209, 259, 265, 413
Kirchdorf	15/27	653
Kirec	35/27	47, 150
Kirkistown	3/12	485, 504
Kirknewtown	4/4	289, 309
Kirkuk (K1)	42/49	6, 30, 63, 208, 237
Kirmington	6/3	142, 150, 153, 166
Kirton-in-Lindsey	6/6A	33
Kirton-in-Lindsey	6/6B	43, 65, 71, 74, 85, 121, 133, 136, 169, 222, 253, 255, 264, 302, 303, 306, 307, 317, 409, 452, 457, 486, 616
Kisumu	41/13	209
Kjevik	16/8	130, 276
Klagenfurt	32/34	43, 72, 93, 111, 225, 651
Kleine Brogel		see Petit Brogel
Kleve	14/62	652, 660
Kluang	48/18	155, 488, 656
Kluis (B 91)	14/64	33, 164, 183, 198, 222, 274, 609, 616 — see Nijmegen
the Knavesmire		see York
Knocke le Zout (B 83)	14/1	119, 276, 290
Koggala	45/26	191, 205, 209, 212, 230, 240, 413
Kohat	44/21	5, 20, 27, 28, 31, 34, 60, 114
Kolar	45/36	82, 110, 215, 258, 358
Korangi Creek	44/4	191, 212
Korba	23/24	225
Kota Bahru	48/29	36, 243
Kotelnikovo	52/6	47
Krendi	27/3	185, 229, 249
Kristiansand		see Kjevik
Kuala Lumpur	48/11	11, 17, 28, 33, 45, 48, 52, 60, 81, 84, 89, 110, 131, 136, 155, 194, 209, 258, 267, 453, 656, 681 — see Noble Field
Kuala Trengganu	48/27	656
Kuantan	48/26	32, 36, 45, 60, 62, 100
Kuching	47/12	20, 45, 60, 62, 64, 66, 103, 110, 209, 225, 230
Kufra	37/1	6, 237, 417
Kukush	35/24	47
Kut al Imara	42/28	30
Kuwait		see Farwania
Kuwar Reach		see Sindiya
Kwa-Lokua	39/7	26
Kwetnge	46/72	34, 89, 113, 155, 607
Kumbhirgram	46/103	22, 34, 42, 45, 47, 60, 81, 82, 84, 99, 110, 146, 261
Kyaukpyu	46/46	5, 31, 117, 123, 134, 258, 273, 357, 436, 615
Laarbruch	14/76	2, 3, 5, 15, 16, 20, 25, 31, 68, 69, 79, 80, 214, 541 — see Goch
La Banca	31/68	18, 114, 600
La Barre-en-Ouche	13/61	653
La Bellevue	11/153	8, 11, 18, 32, 35, 48, 49, 59, 60, 62, 73, 80, 1N
La Boiserotte	10/55	5
La Brayelle	11/203	16, 18, 25, 32

Labuan	47/21	20, 45, 60, 64, 66, 81, 103, 110, 209, 230
La Buissière	12/9	2, 607
La Fauconnerie	23/41	55, 92, 145, 223, 417, 601
La Fère	11/179	2, 3, 4, 5
La Ferté	10/58	52
Laferug	38/14	94
La Fouquerie	13/39	659
Lagan	52/10	221
Lagens	51/11	172, 179, 206, 220, 233, 269, 280
Lago	30/51	43, 72, 93, 111, 145, 225, 600
La Gorgue	11/46	5, 15, 16, 35, 42, 43, 46, 208
Lagos		see Apapa and Ikeja
Lahana	35/34	17
Lahat	47/11	34
Lahore	44/39	5, 11, 28, 31, 39, 60, 97, 114, 194, 659
Lahoussoye	11/144	3, 15, 52, 54, 83, 101
La Jasse (Y 19)	33/8	43, 72, 93, 111, 225
Lajes		see Lagens
Lajj	42/33	30
Lakatamia	26/8	46, 127, 154, 162, 203, 213, 227, 232, 252, 294, 451, 454, 603, 680
Lake Down	8/51	107, 108, 109, 136, 201
Lake Indawgyi	46/83	230
Lake Lesjeskog	16/10	263
Lake Timsah	18/54	230
Lakenheath	7/69	149, 199
Lalaghat	46/105	668 — see Rajyeswarpur
Lalmai	46/15	11, 117
La Louveterie	10/11	57, 205
La Lovie	11/42	21, 23, 29, 35, 65, 74
La Marsa	23/16	651, 682
Lampedusa	23/39	253
Landes	13/42	653
Laneffe	10/22	53, 101
Lanenburg		see Langenhagen
Langar	6/37	207
Langebaan	41/3	259, 262, 321, 413
Langenhagen (B 120)	15/34	137, 181, 182, 247
Langham	7/27	254, 280, 455, 489, 521, 524, 621
Lanka	46/109	5, 11, 20
Lantheuil (B 9)	13/8	438, 439, 440, 659
Laon/Athies	12/28	26
La Queue-d'Haye	13/81	662
Larissa	35/17	11, 33, 80, 113, 208
Larkhill	8/54	3, 657
La Rochelle	33/2	212
La Rue Huguenot		see Morainville (B 23)
La Russia	31/2	318, 651, 654, 683
La Salanque		see Perpignan/La Salanque
La Sebala	23/13-14	13, 32, 72, 73, 81, 87, 93, 153, 219, 243, 253, 255, 283
La Senia	24/1	32, 36, 153, 256, 500
Lasham	8/37	33, 107, 175, 181, 182, 183, 239, 305, 320, 412, 451, 453, 602, 609, 613
Lashenden	9/84	403, 421
Lashio	46/79	17, 28, 45, 60, 113
Lassiti	39/6	26
Lasson	13/19	660
La Targette	11/217	56, 102, 201
La Terrière	13/40	659
Lavariano	32/30	93, 112, 225, 237, 250, 260, 318, 450
Laverton	50/44	21, 54, 542
Laviéville	11/146	3, 15, 18, 56
Lawntown	50/31	548, 549
Leadenham	6/31	38, 90
Léalvillers	11/149	15, 32, 41, 59
Learmonth	50/5	54, 457
Le Casteau	10/32	57
Le Cateau	10/40	2, 3, 4, 5
Lecce	30/26	108, 256, 500
Léchelle	11/195	3, 15, 56
Leconfield	4/55	19, 22, 26, 51, 64, 72, 74, 81, 92, 96, 97, 129, 134, 152, 166, 196, 202, 213, 228, 234, 245, 249, 253, 258, 275, 302, 303, 313, 466, 485, 610, 616, 640
Le Crotoy	11/104	6
Le Culot (B 68)	14/13	401. 403, 409, 411, 412, 416, 421, 442, 443 — see Beauvechain
Leeming	4/37	7, 10, 33, 35, 60, 77, 102, 219, 264, 405, 408, 419, 424, 427, 429
Le Fresne-Camilly		see Camilly (B 5)
Lee-on-Solent	8/76	16, 26, 42, 63
Le Favril	13/64	661
Leffrinckhoucke	11/9	48, 54, 9N, 10N
Leghorn	31/107	657
Le Hameau	11/156	1, 5, 11, 13, 18, 22, 23, 29, 32, 45, 52, 58, 59, 60, 64, 84, 94, 100, 101, 102, 203, 9N, 209
Le Hamel	13/5	662
Le Havre		see Octeville
Leicester East	6/62	190, 196, 620
Leighterton	8/1	28, 66
Le Kroube		654 — see Constantine
Le Luc	33/12	682
Le Mans	12/69	17, 501
Le Mesnil-Jourdain	13/70	653
Lentini	25/13 & 15	81, 92, 145, 152, 154, 232, 242, 284, 417, 601, 651
Le Planquay	13/60	660
Le Planty	11/117	55
Le Quesnoy	11/102	11, 57, 107
Les Eauvis	11/121	49
Les Grandes-Chappelles	12/49	88
Lesjeskog		see Lake Lesjeskog
Les Moëres	11/7	5
Les Thilliers-en-Vexin	13/82	658
Lete	20/21	352
Le Touquet	12/16	85, 87, 615
Leuchars	2/28	3, 11, 22, 23, 25, 29, 36, 42, 43, 72, 74, 82, 86, 105, 107, 111, 114, 120, 144, 151, 160, 202, 203, 205, 206, 217, 222, 224, 228, 233, 235, 264, 275, 281, 320, 333, 415, 455, 489, 519, 540, 544, 547, 602, 603, 605, 612
Le Vallon (Y 18)	33/7	154, 238, 242, 243, 255, 256, 326, 327, 458
Leverano	30/25	32, 213, 249, 253
LG 02		see Sidi Barrani
LG 05	19/42	18, 30, 39, 203, 213, 221, 252, 272, 459 — see 'X' LG
LG 06		see 'Y' LG
LG 07 (Matruh West)	19/45	47, 213, 238, 250, 272, 274, 294, 459 — see 'Z' LG
LG 08 (Matruh)	19/47	47, 74, 127, 335, 336, 451
LG 09 (Bir Koraiyim)	19/66	11, 37, 38, 108, 148, 162, 462
LG 10 (Gerawala)	19/48	208, 237, 272, 335
LG 11		see Qasaba
LG 12 (Sidi Haneish N)	19/50	33, 213, 229, 238, 250, 450
LG 13 (Sidi Haneish S)	19/51 601	73, 80, 92, 145, 238, 250, 274, 335,
LG 14		see Maaten Bagush
LG 15 (Maaten Bagush Satellite)	19/57	14, 39, 55, 127, 145, 238
LG 16 (Fuka Satellite)	19/62	39, 45
LG 17 (Fuka Main)	19/64	39, 55
LG 18 (Fuka South)	19/63	80
LG 20 (Qotafiya I)	19/69	73, 127, 213, 238, 335
LG 21 (Qotafiya III)	19/67	14, 55, 73, 92, 145, 601
LG 28 (Burgh el Arab)	18/5	208
LG 29		see Amiriya
LG 32		see Dekheila
LG 34		see Aboukir
LG 37 (Hamman S)	18/2	6, 80, 127, 274, 335

LG 39 (Burgh el Arab S)	18/4	73, 145, 203, 208, 221, 459
LG 40 (Bahig S)	18/6	459
LG 43		see Bir Kenayis
LG 60	19/58	38, 148
LG 66		see Siwa N
LG 67		see Siwa S
LG 68		see 'Waterloo'
LG 75	19/38	6, 14, 33, 45, 70, 84, 112, 113, 208, 213, 237, 250, 260, 450, 451
LG 76	19/39	11, 14, 33, 37, 73, 112, 145, 213, 238, 250, 260, 450
LG 79	19/30	55, 112, 208
LG 81	19/19	45
LG 85	18/21	33, 73, 80, 213, 260, 335, 601
LG 86	18/18	22, 39, 55, 162, 223
LG 87	18/19	47, 221
LG 88	18/14	14, 127, 274
LG 89	18/20	6, 47, 73, 127, 221, 274
LG 90	18/26	213, 451
LG 91	18/27	6, 38, 52, 112, 162, 203, 250, 252, 294, 450, 454, 458, 459, 603
LG 92	18/16	80, 127, 145, 238, 274, 601
LG 93	18/11	229
LG 95 (Ikingi)	18/12	55
LG 97	18/25	14, 260
LG 98	18/24	14, 55, 223
LG 99	18/23	55, 221, 223
LG 100 (Wadi Natrun)	18/31	55, 208
LG 101	19/52	33, 74, 203, 213, 238, 250, 260, 450
LG 102	19/53	6, 30, 80, 112, 229, 250, 450
LG 103	19/60	80, 94, 208, 274
LG 104 (Qotafiyah II)	19/68	11, 40, 70, 104, 148, 162, 208, 272, 335
LG 105 (El Daba)	19/70	74, 108, 238, 274
LG 106	18/1	6, 37, 70, 74, 104, 108, 112, 148, 237, 238, 250, 450, 451
LG 107		see Giarabub
LG 108 (Giarabub No 2)	19/28	6
LG 109	19/33	80, 94, 250, 260
LG 110	19/34	94, 112, 250, 274
LG 111	19/35	80, 229, 274
LG 112	19/31	208, 237
LG 115	19/55	73, 94, 112, 260
LG 116	19/56	11, 14, 84, 113, 223
LG 117	19/59	38
LG 121	19/43	30, 80, 134, 223, 238, 335, 336
LG 122	19/24	112, 250
LG 123 (Fort Maddelena)	19/27	80, 208, 229, 238, 250
LG 124 (Fort Maddelena)	19/25	94, 260, 274
LG 125	20/56	33, 113, 213, 238
LG 128	19/23	80, 208, 237, 451
LG 130	19/32	274
LG 131	19/21	208, 451
LG 132	19/20	237, 451
LG 133	19/22	80
LG 134	19/1	208
LG 139 (Gambut No 1)		see Gambut
LG 140 (Bir el Baheira No 1)	19/8	37, 70
LG 141		see Gasr el Arid
LG 142 (Gambut No 2)		see Gambut
LG 143 (Gambut No 3)	19/6	221, 272, 459
LG 144		see El Adem
LG 145		see Tobruk No 2/El Gubsi East
LG 146		see Tobruk No 3/El Gubsi West
LG 147		see Bu Amud
LG 148		see Sidi Azeiz
LG 149		see Gazala No 1
LG 150		see Gazala No 2
LG 152		see Gazala No 3
LG 153		see Sidi Rezegh
LG 154	18/22	33, 145, 213, 238, 601
LG 155	19/36	73, 145, 213, 238, 601
LG 156 (Gambut No 4)		see Gambut
LG 157 (El Adem South)		see El Adem
LG 163		see Gabr Selah
LG 165 (Bir el Regal)	20/9	274
LG 167 (Bir el Baheira No 2)	19/9	148, 462
LG 170		see El Gubbi
LG 172	18/3	6, 33, 127, 145, 213, 238
LG 173	18/17	92, 145, 264, 335, 601
LG 175	18/15	112, 417, 450
LG 202	18/30	208
LG 206 (Abu Sueir North)		see LG 'X'
LG 207 (Qassassin)	18/56	55, 318 — see LG 'Y'
LG 208 (Mahsma)	18/57	459 — see LG 'Z'
LG 209 (Suez Road No 2)	18/44	223 — see Kilo 61
LG 219 (Matariyah)	18/41	134, 336, 601, 680 — see Payne Field and Kilo 8
LG 222 (Fayoum Road)	18/36	40, 134 — see Kilo 17
LG 224 (Cairo West)	18/35	14, 37, 39, 46, 70, 76, 104, 267, 450, 454 — see Kilo 26
LG 226	18/32	38, 203, 459
LG 227	18/28	47, 203, 454, 459
LG 229 (Idku)	18/33	274
LG 237 (Jebel Hamzi)	18/34	40, 104, 108, 148, 462 — see Kilo 40
LG 251		see Shallufa Satellite
LG 'X'	18/58	203 — see LG 206
LG 'Y'	18/56	55, 203, 223, 450 — see LG 207
LG 'Z'	18/57	459 — see LG 208
Libreville	41/1	95, 270
Liettres	11/91	19, 45, 46, 54, 56, 66, 70, 73, 80, 84, 151, 152, 203, 210 — see Estrée-Blanche
Ligescourt	11/103	100, 207
Likuju	39/24	26
Lilbourne	6/60	34, 55, 73, 84
Lille/Marcq	12/3	504 — see Lille/Nord
Lille/Nord (B 57)	13/108	66, 127, 331, 332 — see Lille/Marcq
Lille/Ronchin	11/71 & 12/4	4, 26, 103
Lille/Seclin	11/74 & 12/5	21, 53, 85, 87, 212
Lille/Vendeville (B 51)	13/107	74, 193, 197, 219, 257, 263, 264, 266, 302, 308, 317, 329, 340, 341, 409, 410, 604
Limassol	26/5	227, 252, 294
Limavady	3/3	48, 53, 143, 153, 172, 221, 224, 245, 281, 304, 407, 500, 502, 612
Limbraga	32/22	42
Limerick	3/18	2
Linde	14/90	659
Lindholme	6/8	50, 57, 100, 110, 304, 305, 408
Lingèvres (B 19)	13/27	132, 441, 453, 602
Linselles	11/51	4, 52, 206
Linton-on-Ouse	4/46	4, 35, 51, 58, 64, 65, 66, 76, 77, 78, 92, 102, 264, 275, 405, 408, 426
Lisieux	13/59	652
Lisset	4/50	158
Little Aden	38/10	94
Little Snoring	7/28	23, 115, 141, 169, 515
Little Staughton	6/53	109, 582
Littorio	31/72	92, 145, 417, 601, 624
Livingstone	41/9	82, 683
Livingstone	50/18	54, 457, 548
Llanbedr	5/7	20, 41, 66, 74, 129, 131, 164, 168, 183, 193, 198, 232, 268, 302, 306, 308, 310, 312, 315, 322, 329, 331, 332, 340, 341, 349, 350, 485, 504, 602, 609, 631
Llandow	5/22	5, 614, 663
Llangefni	5/4	244, 255
Loiwing	46/80	17, 45, 113

Lonato	32/5	663
Londinière		see Fresnoy Folny (B 31)
London Colney	9/29	1, 24, 54, 56, 74, 92
Longavesnes	11/192	3, 6, 8, 15, 35, 52, 59
Longevic (Y 9)	33/20	326, 327, 328, 682
Long Kesh	3/8	74, 88, 226, 231, 290, 422
Longman	2/11	241, 289, 309, 526, 527, 598, 614
Longtown	4/83	41
Longues (B 11)	13/2	132, 441, 453, 602
Lopcombe Corner	8/41	52, 74, 85, 91
Loralai	44/7	5, 20, 31, 48, 114
Loreto	31/48	87, 92, 145, 185, 417, 601
Lossiemouth	2/14	6, 8, 9, 10, 12, 15, 21, 44, 50, 54, 57, 63, 76, 82, 83, 88, 99, 105, 107, 110, 114, 202, 208, 216, 254, 280, 617
Lough Erne	3/24	119, 201, 228, 240, 422 — see Castle Archdale
Lower Topa	44/29	155
Lozinghem		see Auchel/Lozinghem
Lübeck (B 158)	15/53	1, 2, 3, 4, 10, 16, 18, 19, 23, 25, 26, 29, 30, 33, 41, 46, 53, 56, 62, 63, 66, 74, 77, 80, 85, 91, 92, 107, 129, 137, 141, 151, 174, 181, 182, 219, 222, 245, 247, 257, 263, 264, 266, 307, 486, 504, 616, 659
Luce Bay	4/88	244, 255, 258 — see West Freugh
Ludendorf	10/8	9
Ludford Magna	7/8	101, 104
Ludham	7/40	1, 19, 91, 167, 195, 245, 602, 603, 610, 611
Lugo	31/11	655
Lulsgate Bottom	5/56	286
Luneburg (B 156)	15/51	3, 137, 181, 182, 247, 400, 414, 430, 616, 652, 659
Lungi	40/11	82
Luqa	27/2	13, 18, 21, 22, 23, 37, 38, 39, 40, 42, 46, 55, 69, 73, 78, 82, 86, 89, 92, 104, 105, 107, 108, 110, 113, 126, 138, 139, 145, 148, 162, 185, 203, 217, 219, 221, 223, 227, 242, 250, 252, 256, 260, 261, 272, 417, 450, 458, 600, 601, 605, 683, 1435
Lusaka	41/10	29, 82
Luton	9/2	264
Luxeuil (Y 8)	33/21	326, 327, 328
Luxor	37/11	55, 294
Lydd	9/73	174, 175, 245
Lydda	36/21	14, 33, 55, 134, 162, 203, 211, 213, 294, 458, 459
Lympne	9/70	1, 2, 16, 18, 21, 26, 33, 34, 41, 53, 59, 65, 69, 72, 74, 83, 91, 98, 102, 108, 120, 127, 130, 133, 137, 165, 186, 245, 310, 312, 313, 350, 401, 451, 453, 504, 567, 598, 609, 610, 659
Lyneham	8/3	24, 30, 36, 47, 48, 53, 70, 99, 159, 160, 206, 216, 242, 246, 511, 525
Lyons/Bron (Y 6)	33/19	43, 72, 93, 111, 326, 327, 328, 682
Lyons/Satolas (Y 24)	33/18	225
'Lyons'	46/31	11, 79, 136 — see Ramu 2
Maaten Bagush (LG 14)	19/54	6, 30, 31, 113, 162, 208, 213, 216 — see LG 15
Macaaca		see Assab
Macmerry	4/6	13, 63, 225, 241, 263, 607, 614 — see Penston
Machrihanish	4/98	65, 272
Madhaiganj	44/61	82, 110, 159
Madhij	42/10	30
Madna	30/4	80, 241, 274, 318, 601
Madioen	49/14	36
Madley	5/58	26
Madras	45/38	656 — see St Thomas Mount, Red Hills Lake and Guindy
Madura	45/15	11, 17, 132, 203
Mafraq	36/28	6, 14, 32, 249
Maghaberry	3/27	231
Magwe	46/70-71	11, 17, 28, 45, 60, 67, 113, 135
Maharajpur	44/47	84
Mahsma		see LG 'Z' and LG 208
Maidan	46/4	136 — see Red Road
'Maida Vale'	46/71	42, 152 — see Magwe
Maison Blanche	24/10	32, 43, 72, 81, 89, 93, 111, 152, 153, 219, 225, 241, 242, 253, 255, 283, 600, 682
Maison Carrée	24/8	500
Maisoncelle	11/98	18, 22, 57, 103, 104, 110
Majunga	41/20	204
Maldeghem (B 65)	14/3	33, 119, 222, 349, 485, 504
Maleme	35/52	30, 33, 80, 113, 208
Malignano	31/97	208, 225, 682, 683
Malincourt	11/226	8, 73
Malindini	38/1	237
Maltepe	35/44	55
Mamfe	40/24	230
Manipur Road	46/110	79, 113 — see Dimapur
Manorbier	5/19	595
Manston	9/62	1, 2, 3, 4, 9, 16, 18, 21, 22, 23, 26, 29, 32, 33, 39, 46, 48, 56, 59, 62, 63, 69, 72, 74, 77, 79, 80, 88, 91, 92, 101, 107, 110, 118, 119, 124, 130, 137, 139, 143, 151, 158, 164, 174, 175, 183, 184, 193, 197, 198, 206, 7N, 213, 217, 219, 222, 224, 226, 229, 235, 242, 253, 257, 263, 266, 273, 274, 305, 310, 311, 312, 313, 331, 332, 403, 406, 415, 421, 451, 455, 500, 501, 504, 567, 600, 601, 604, 605, 607, 609, 611, 615, 616, 618
Manzai	44/13	20, 27, 28, 60
Marago-Opuni	39/5	26
Maranda	39/26	26
Marawa	20/27	6, 55, 208, 274
Marble Arch	21/37	117, 250, 260, 267, 318, 450
Marcianese	30/48	13, 18, 55, 92, 114, 145, 417, 600, 601
Marcon	32/18	34
Marcke		see Calais/Marcke
Marcq		see Lille/Marcq
Mardhaibunia	46/36	20 — see 'Hove'
Maretz	11/228	6, 208
Marham	7/18	15, 27, 35, 38, 44, 49, 51, 55, 57, 90, 100, 105, 109, 115, 139, 148, 149, 207, 214, 218, 242, 617
Maria ter Heide	14/28	652
Marian	35/36	17, 150, 222
Marieux	11/150	4, 5, 8, 15, 24, 41, 70, 3N
Maryut	18/8	39, 74, 94, 112, 250, 274, 601 — see Alexandria
Marquain	11/65	42, 98
Marquise	11/24	57, 85, 110, 149, 151, 216
Marseilles	33/10	6, 58, 80, 99, 657
Martlesham Heath	7/49	1, 2, 3, 15, 17, 22, 25, 26, 29, 41, 54, 56, 64, 65, 71, 85, 110, 111, 122, 124, 132, 133, 151, 165, 182, 198, 222, 236, 239, 242, 257, 258, 264, 266, 277, 278, 284, 287, 303, 310, 312, 317, 332, 350, 401, 402, 403, 412, 416, 421, 453, 501, 504, 604, 605, 607, 611, 613
Martagny (B 7)	13/32	19, 65, 122, 164, 183, 198, 609
Martuba	20/35-39	94, 112, 208, 213, 238, 250, 260, 274, 450
'Marylebone'		see Souk el Khemis
Mascot	50/40	452
Masirah	43/14	8, 204, 209, 212, 244, 259, 265, 294, 321
Massawa	37/35	47
Matariyah		see LG 219
Mateur	23/6-7	43, 72, 93, 111, 243
Matigny	11/182	7, 23, 24, 52
Matlask	7/35	3, 19, 56, 65, 72, 122, 137, 195, 222, 229, 245, 266, 278, 451, 453, 486, 601, 602, 609, 611, 658, 659
Matruh		see Mersah Matruh
Mattishall	7/31	51
Maubeuge	10/31	2, 3, 4, 5, 18, 25, 107, 205, 206
Maulde	14/7	658
Maungdaw	46/39-41	20, 28

Maunghnama	46/38	67, 273, 656
Maunubyin		see Akyab
Maupertus (A 15)	13/37	604
Mauripur	44/2	5, 10, 20, 31, 62, 77, 117, 267, 298
Mauritius	53/2	259, 265
Mazingarbe	11/80	2
Mbagui	39/9	26
Mbarangandu	39/25	26
Mbuyuni	39/2	26
Méaulte	11/168	52
Meaux	12/53	212
Mechili	20/28-29	33, 94, 112, 208, 229, 238, 250, 274
Medan	47/9	60, 155, 656
Medanine	22/6	55, 112, 145, 223, 250, 260, 450
Medicina	31/8	655
Medjez el Bab	23/4	651
Megiddo	36/32	6, 208
Meherabad	42/61	74, 123, 127, 680
Meiktila	46/73	10, 17, 27, 28, 34, 42, 47, 62, 79, 89, 113, 146, 194, 298, 357, 656, 681
Melbourne	50/43	54, 452, 457, 548, 549, 618
Melbourne (UK)	4/61	10, 575
Meldola	31/20	663
Mellaha	21/4	162, 274, 294, 417
Melbroek (B 58)	14/19	16, 21, 69, 98, 107, 128, 137, 140, 180, 181, 182, 247, 268, 305, 320, 340, 403, 416, 421, 437, 438, 439, 440, 443, 464, 487, 616, 662
Melton Mowbray	6/43A	38
Melton Mowbray	6/43B	254
Melun	10/52	2, 3, 4, 5
Membury	8/45	19, 187, 525
Menastir	19/10	45
Mendlesham	7/51	310, 312, 313
Menidi	35/12	11, 37, 84, 113, 211 — see Tatoi
Menin	11/53	7, 10, 70, 82
Mepal	7/93	7, 44, 49, 75, 113
Meppen	15/16	660, 664
Merchin	11/72	54
Merduma		see El Merduma
Mergui	47/9	60, 67
Merheim	10/3	18, 25, 207
Merrekesh	40/2	32, 39, 544
Merryfield	5/52	53, 187, 238, 242, 243
Mersah Matruh	19/47	14, 33, 113, 142, 162, 208, 252, 451, 621 — see LG 07 and LG 08
Merston	8/84	41, 80, 118, 130, 131, 145, 174, 181, 182, 184, 229, 232, 247, 274, 287, 303, 329, 340, 341, 402, 412, 416, 485
Merville (B 53)	13/112	33, 164, 183, 198, 222, 349, 485, 609
Merville	11/45 & 12/10	2, 3, 16, 79, 85, 87, 213, 601, 607, 615
Mestre	32/16	655
Mesum		see Westerkappelen
Meteren	11/44	5
Metheringham	6/28	106, 189, 467
Methven	2/32	652
Methwold	7/67	21, 57, 149, 207, 214, 218, 320, 464, 487
Metokhi	35/10	32
Mezze		see Damascus
Mhow	45/3	28, 31
Mianwali	44/25	27, 60, 97, 99
Middle Aerodrome		see Bray-Dunes
Middleton St George	4/33	33, 76, 78, 92, 264, 419, 420, 428
Middle Wallop	8/42	16, 19, 23, 32, 56, 63, 80, 93, 125, 151, 164, 165, 169, 182, 234, 236, 238, 245, 247, 256, 285, 286, 288, 400, 406, 414, 418, 456, 501, 504, 537, 587, 601, 604, 609, 651, 657, 662
Mierlo	14/82	659
Miho	47/1	11, 17
Mikra Bay	35/23	14, 17, 47, 144, 150
Milan	32/3	28, 34, 66
Milazzo	25/4-5	81, 152, 154, 225, 232, 242, 284, 654
Mildenhall	7/70	15, 35, 38, 44, 73, 75, 99, 115, 149, 207, 211, 218, 419, 622
Mileni	30/10	112, 250, 260, 450
Mill (B 98)	14/75	2, 4, 193, 197, 257, 263, 266, 268, 659
Milfield	4/13	164, 183, 184
Millingimbi	50/19	54, 452, 457
Milltown	2/16	224
Mingaladon	46/50	17, 18, 20, 27, 28, 31, 45, 52, 60, 62, 67, 81, 89, 113, 135, 136, 176, 194, 267, 273, 357, 607, 656, 681
Minneriya	45/21	8, 17, 22, 30, 81, 89, 135, 136, 160, 176, 217, 354, 357
Minnigh	36/47	154
Minya	37/7	17
Miranshah	44/16	5, 11, 20, 27, 28, 39, 60, 659
Miri	47/19	62
Mirjana	42/54	72
Missindyi	39/16	26
Misson	6/10	94
Misurata	21/9	33, 38, 47, 89, 162, 213, 252, 274, 603
Mitylene	35/50	223
Moascar	18/59	30, 208 — see Ismailia
Mogadishu	38/5	6, 8, 78, 84, 213, 244, 621
Moislains	11/193	6, 20, 35, 107, 205
Moisy	12/63	88 — see Ozouer-le-Doyen
Molesworth	6/52	19, 54, 124, 129, 159, 222, 234, 441, 442, 460 — see Old Weston
Mombasa	39/1	26 — see Kipevu and Port Reitz
Mona	5/2	577
Monastir	23/36	13, 73, 87, 219, 255, 600, 680
Monchy-Lagache	12/24	4 — see Flez
Mondeville	13/17	660
Mons-en-Chaussée	11/86 & 12/23	4, 8, 9, 13, 35, 59, 85, 5N
Mont-de-Soissons	10/45	52
Montechiari		see Ghedi
Montecorvino	30/41	32, 36, 69, 73, 111, 253, 500, 600, 608, 663
Montelimar (Y 21)	33/16	154, 242, 243
Monte Lungo	25/25	18, 55, 114, 223
Monte Marciano	31/44	651
Montesanto	31/5	651
Montford Bridge	5/61	577
Montigny Farm	11/190	9
Mont Jois	12/20	81
Montrose	2/23	2, 3, 17, 25 43, 80, 83, 108, 111, 132, 141, 145, 224, 232, 233, 248, 263, 269, 310, 416, 598, 602, 603, 614
Monywa	46/90	20, 27, 60, 194, 656
Monza	32/2	663
Morainville (B 23)	13/65	164, 183, 193, 198, 257, 266, 609
Morbecque	11/35	5
Morciano	31/31	651
Morecombe	4/76	243
Moreuil	11/139	7, 23, 24
Morib		see Kelanang
Morlancourt	11/170	9
Morogoro	39/11	26
Morpeth	4/22	72
Morville	10/19	57, 101
Mory	11/198	11, 12, 13, 57
Mosul	42/48	6, 30, 45, 52, 55, 63, 84, 237, 244, 261
Moulmein	46/58	60
Mount Batten	5/46	203, 204, 209, 461 — see Cattewater
Mount Farm	8/26	140, 540, 543
Mount Pleasant	51/15	23, 78
Mourmelon-le-Grande	12/40	88
Mousehould Heath	7/39	18, 37, 85, 117
Moyenneville	11/108 & 13/91	3, 4, 5, 600
Msaken	23/37	654

Msus	20/10-12	6, 33, 92, 94, 112, 145, 208, 229, 238, 250, 260, 274, 601
Mtonia	39/20	26
Mtua	39/18	26
Muar	48/17	656
Mudros	35/49	17, 47, 144, 220, 221, 222, 223, 226, 266
Muharraq	43/6	8, 30, 73, 84, 105, 152, 208, 294 — see Bahrain
Mullaghmore	3/4	281
Mullion	5/41	236, 254
Munster		see Handorf (Y 94)
Muqueibila	36/29	45, 123, 154, 208, 232, 242, 318
Murree	44/32	31
Musandeg	42/22	30
Mustabig	36/5	14, 67
Mustapha Pasha	35/42	17
Mwembe	39/21	26
Myingyan	46/76	34, 79, 113, 146, 261
Nahud	40/33	17
Nahunga	39/17	26
Nairobi		see Eastleigh
Nancy	12/36	212
Nancy/Essey (Y 24)	33/23	327, 328, 682
Nantes/Château Bougon	12/73	1, 73, 98, 105, 114, 218, 242
Naples		see Portici and Gragnano
Narborough	6/19	35, 56, 59, 60, 64, 83, 121
Narni	31/81	654
Narromine	50/41	618
Narungombe	39/15	26
Nasiriyah	42/15	30, 84
Nazir	46/35	5, 123, 211, 615
Ndola	41/11	29
Needs Oar Point	8/72	193, 197, 257, 266
Nefatia	22/9-10	73, 112, 250, 260, 450
Nefza	23/5	43
Negenborn	15/35	659
Negombo	45/30	45, 232, 249
Neheim	15/2	662
Nesle	11/176	7
Netheravon	8/48	1, 2, 3, 4, 5, 6, 7, 10, 11, 12, 13, 18, 19, 20, 21, 26, 27, 32, 33, 35, 42, 43, 48, 52, 53, 57, 62, 66, 72, 97, 99, 115, 116, 118, 142, 187, 207, 208, 215, 239, 295, 296, 297
Netherthorpe	6/67	613
Nettuno	31/69	43, 93, 417, 682
Neufcampville		see Campneuseville (B 33)
Newcastle	4/26	36
Newchurch	9/71	3, 19, 56, 132, 184, 486, 602
New Haggerston	4/14	77, 256
Newhaven	9/44	78, 242
Newlyn	5/37	235
Newmarket	7/78	2, 75, 99, 107, 138, 161, 215, 453
New Romney	9/72	181, 182, 247
Newton	6/35	103, 150
Newtownards	3/10	231, 290
Niamata	35/16	113
Nicosia	26/7	6, 8, 29, 32, 39, 43, 46, 70, 73, 74, 80, 84, 103, 114, 127, 162, 185, 203, 208, 213, 230, 243, 249, 250, 256, 261, 272, 284, 294, 451, 459, 603, 680
Nidania	46/34	20, 607, 615 — see 'George'
Nidiani		see Nidania
Nightcliffe		see Darwin/Nightcliffe
Nijmegen	14/66	653, 660, 662 — see Kluis (B 91)
Niksic	34/6	6
Nivelles (B 75)	10/27 & 14/9	11, 22, 29, 48, 57, 62, 79, 88, 107, 206, 437
Nivillers		see Beauvais/Nivillers (B 40)
Noble Field	48/10	656
Nordhorn (B 101)	15/12	302, 308, 317, 662
Norfolk, Va	51/9	53
Noron-la-Poterie	13/31	659
Norrent-Fontes	11/89 & 12/11	1, 56, 73, 79, 504
North Coates	7/5	22, 25, 42, 53, 59, 85, 86, 143, 217, 235, 236, 248, 254, 264, 275, 278, 407, 415, 611
North Creake	7/26	171, 199
North Front		see Gibraltar
North Killingholme	6/2	550
North Luffenham	6/46	61, 111, 144, 408
Northolt	9/31	1, 4, 12, 16, 18, 23, 24, 25, 32, 41, 43, 65, 69, 74, 86, 92, 111, 124, 140, 207, 213, 229, 246, 253, 257, 264, 271, 287, 302, 303, 306, 308, 315, 316, 317, 515, 600, 601, 604, 609, 615
North Pickenham	7/56	220
North Weald	9/25	1, 2, 4, 17, 25, 26, 29, 33, 39, 46, 56, 63, 66, 71, 72, 74, 111, 116, 121, 124, 127, 130, 151, 168, 222, 234, 242, 249, 257, 268 275, 285, 287, 288, 301, 304, 310, 312, 313, 331, 332, 403, 412, 486, 601, 604
North Weald Basset	9/25	39, 44, 75
Norwich		see Mousehold Heath
Nouex-les-Auxi	11/116	201
Novorossisk	52/2	47
Nowshera	44/24	31
Nuova	30/5	335, 336
Nuremburg/Furth (R 28)	34/1	21
Nurlu	11/194	8, 9, 34
Nutts Corner	3/6	44, 120, 160, 220, 231
Oakington	7/90	7, 10, 18, 24, 27, 30, 46, 75, 86, 97, 101, 206, 218, 238, 242, 571, 627
Oatland Hill	8/52	658, 665
Oban	2/1	209, 210, 228, 330, 422, 423, 524
Ochey	10/64	55, 100, 16N, 216
Octeville	12/59	1, 73
Odiham	8/36	2, 4, 7, 13, 18, 26, 33, 46, 53, 54, 59, 63, 66, 72, 82, 96, 114, 130, 168, 170, 171, 174, 175, 181, 182, 184, 225, 230, 233, 239, 247, 264, 268, 271, 400, 412, 414, 430, 436, 437, 604, 613, 614
Oesthaven	49/3	205
Okehampton	5/29	16, 225
Oldenburg	15/23	14, 20, 26, 234
Old Sarum	8/50	7, 13, 16, 34, 53, 59, 98, 103, 107, 124, 125, 126, 225, 651, 652, 653, 654, 655, 658, 660, 661, 662, — see Ford Farm
Old Weston	6/52	75 — see Molesworth
Omagh	3/25	105
Onbauk	46/86	36, 42, 113
Ondal	44/60	34, 110
Ondaw	46/88	34, 42, 113
Ondefontaine	13/41	662
Ophoven (Y 32)	14/92	41, 130, 350, 430, 610
Ora	42/25	30
Oranmore	3/20	2, 100, 105, 106
Orcq	11/64	40, 203
Orfordness	7/45	37
Orléans/Bricy	12/61	212
Orlyak	35/35	17
Orvieto	31/85	208, 683
Osa	31/73	208, 683
Osnabrück	15/7	658
Ossenpass	14/58	662
Ossogne	10/24	20
Ostende	11/4	6
Otranto	30/28	263, 271 — see Alimini
Otricole	31/80	654
Otterloo	14/42	657
Oudna	23/21-22	40, 104, 142, 150
Oulmene	24/24	13, 18, 614
Oulton	7/34	18, 21, 65, 88, 114, 139, 214, 223, 236
Ouston	4/24	72, 81, 122, 131, 198, 202, 226, 232, 242, 243, 281, 288, 289, 291, 317, 350, 410, 607, 613, 657, 664
Owthorne	7/1	251
Oxelaere	11/36	8

Oxford		see Port Meadow
Ozouer-le-Doyen	12/63	103 — see Moisy
P I (Palembang)	49/1	34, 84, 232, 242, 258, 605
P II (Parabumilih)	49/2	27, 34, 62, 84, 211, 232, 242, 258, 453, 605
Pachino	25/20	43, 72, 92, 93, 111, 112, 145, 243, 250, 260, 450, 601
Padang	47/10	656
'Paddington'		see Souk el Khemis
Padstow	5/32	250
Padua	32/10	42, 45, 651
Paglieta	31/58	651, 655
Palam	44/44	31, 34, 62, 76, 194, 232, 353, 681
Palata	30/12	241
Palazzo	30/17	225
Palel	46/97	17, 34, 42, 79, 81, 113, 146, 152, 155, 261, 615, 656
Palembang		see P I
Palermo	25/2	87, 283
Palese		see Bari
Palms	39/8	26
Pamanzi	41/18	209, 230, 265
Pandeveswar	44/62	99, 110, 215
Panebianco	25/11	43, 72, 93, 111, 243
Pankham Fort	46/67	17
Paphos	26/1	127, 213, 237, 252,272, 274, 603
Parabumilih		see P II
Parachinar	44/20	20, 28
Parafield	50/47	238
Paramali	26/2	112
Paramythia	35/2	11, 30, 33, 37, 80, 84, 112, 211
Parashuram	46/17	27, 134
Parfondeval	13/87	652
'Park Lane'	46/62	17, 135
Patenga		see Chittagong
Patharkandi	46/106	5, 113, 123
Payne Field		see LG 219
Pearce	50/2	76
Pecq	11/63	5, 6
Peer (B 76)	14/89	653
Pegu	46/60	159, 279, 335
Pembrey	5/20	5, 32, 79, 92, 118, 225, 238, 248, 256, 307, 316, 595
Pembroke	5/18	255 — see Carew Cheriton
Pembroke Dock	5/17	95, 119, 201, 203, 204, 209, 210, 228, 230, 240, 320, 321, 422, 461
Penang	48/4	230, 240 — see Bayan Lepas
Pengam Moors	5/24	286, 587, 614, 663
Penhros	5/6	63, 90, 258, 312
Penshurst	9/56	268, 653, 661, 664
Penston	4/6	77 — see Macmerry
Perk	14/21	658
Peretola	31/103	43, 72, 87, 93, 111, 185, 208, 225, 682
Pergola	31/37	651
Perim Island	38/17	8, 223
Peristerona	26/6	74
Peronnes	10/28	7
Perpignan/ La Salanque	33/5	12, 88, 105, 114, 142, 150, 218, 226
Perranporth	5/35	19, 65, 66, 118, 130, 132, 183, 234, 276, 286, 302, 310, 317, 329, 340, 341, 412, 453, 602, 610, 639
Perrières	13/54	660
Perth		see (UK) Methven and Scone and (Australia) Pearce
Perugia	31/86	13, 55, 87, 92, 114, 145, 185, 417, 500, 601, 654
Pescara	31/55	6, 223, 454, 500
Peshawar	44/22	5, 20, 27, 28, 31, 34, 39, 60, 155, 659
Petah Tiqva	36/23	6, 14, 32, 208, 651
Peterhead	2/20	19, 26, 63, 65, 68, 118, 122, 125, 129, 132, 164, 165, 167, 234, 245, 278, 282, 309, 312, 313, 315, 350, 402, 409, 411, 414, 416, 430, 453, 504, 598, 602, 603, 611
Petit Brogel (B 90)	14/88	400, 403, 414, 416, 421, 430, 443
Petite Synthe	11/17	49, 65, 85, 87, 5N, 6N, 7N, 11N/211, 218
Petrovsk Kaskar	52/11	221
Petrovsk Port	52/12	266
Pezarche		see Touquin
Phalempin	11/75	85
Phaphamau	44/54	177, 211
Pharsala	35/15	208
Phillipeville	24/19	32, 87, 232, 241, 243, 253, 657
Phillipopolis	35/39	17
Piagiolino	31/38	241, 318, 683
Picauville (A 8)	13/38	264, 604
Pierrepont	13/21	660
'Pilsener'		see Pegu
Piombino	31/96	43, 72, 93, 111
Pisa	31/106	237, 293
Pizzone	30/23	224, 225, 226, 227 — see Taranto
Planques	11/99	62
Plantlunne (B 103)	15/13	164, 183, 198, 609
Plivot	12/43	53, 103, 139, 142
Plumetot (B 10)	13/13	2, 4, 33, 184, 198, 268, 302, 308, 310, 312, 313, 317, 609, 652
Pocklington	4/62	102, 405
Poggio Renatico	31/3	42
Pointe Noire	41/2	95, 200
Poitiers	33/1	212
Poix (B 44)	12/55 & 13/94	53, 57, 59, 253, 401, 411, 412, 414, 442, 615
Polebrook	6/50	90, 130, 159, 160, 220
Pomigliano	30/46	23, 114, 241, 255, 256, 284, 293, 600, 608, 682
Pont-de-Fresney	13/48	661
Pontecorvo	31/63	654
Pontedera	31/105	87, 185
Ponte Olivo	25/22	18, 114
Poole Harbour		see Hamworthy
Poona	45/10	5, 10, 20, 28, 31, 76, 232
Poperinghe	11/43	4, 5, 6, 19, 29, 65, 70
Poretta	29/4	154, 232, 237, 238, 242, 243, 451
Port Blair	53/6	28, 139
Port Dickson	48/15	656
Port Ellen	4/99	48
Port Etienne	40/4	95, 200, 204, 343, 344
Portici	30/44	80, 229, 274, 500
Portland	5/55	241
Port Loko	40/12	128
Port Meadow	8/22	93
Portogruaro	32/25	655
Porto Potenza	31/49	55
Porto San Elpidio	31/50	651
Porto San Giorgio	31/51	663 — see Fermo
Portreath	5/36	66, 130, 143, 152, 153, 234, 235, 247, 248, 263, 264, 275, 276, 277, 286, 313, 400, 414, 613, 639
Port Reitz	41/15	621
Port Said	18/62 & 31/1	14, 144, 269 — see El Gamil
Port Stanley	51/16	1, 7, 18, 23, 29, 202
Port Sudan	37/16	3, 14, 17, 112
Port Swettenham	48/12	60, 81, 656
Port Victoria	53/1	205, 209, 259, 265, 413
Pouan	12/48	150
Poulainville	11/142	8, 35, 46, 52, 201
Poulton	5/66	595
Prague	34/2	310, 311, 312, 313
Prawle Point	5/48	254
Predannack	5/42	1, 25, 33, 64, 66, 85, 118, 120, 141 151, 157, 165, 179, 183, 222, 234, 236, 247, 248, 263, 264, 266, 304, 307, 310, 311, 349, 406, 410, 414, 456, 485, 536, 600, 604, 611, 618
Prémont Farm	11/231	9
Presenzano	30/55	654, 657
Prestwick	4/92	102, 114, 141, 253, 263, 600, 602, 603, 610, 615
Prkos	34/4	6, 73, 213, 249, 253, 351, 352
Pronville	11/199	5, 32
Protville	23/10-12	13, 14, 39, 47, 52, 111, 144, 152, 154, 232, 458, 608, 624 — see Utique and Sidi Athman

Proven	11/40	7, 9, 82
Provin	11/79	58
Proyart	11/173	9, 20, 92, 101, 205
Qaiyarh	42/47	14, 237, 454
Qalat Mufti	42/56	30
Qantara	36/2	14, 67, 111, 113, 142, 145, 216
Qasaba (LG 11)	19/49	6, 14, 30, 33, 45, 73, 208, 451
Qassassin	18/56	14, 123, 134 — see LG 207 and LG 'Y'
Qastina	36/14	47, 512, 644, 651
Qotafiyah	19/67-69	39, 45, 84, 211 — see LGs 20, 21 and 104
Quackenbrück (B 109)	15/17	33, 222, 274, 616
Quatre Vents Farm		see Lechelle
Qubba	42/8	30
Quelmes	11/28	82, 209
Querqueville (A 23)	13/35	276
Quesnoy	11/102	11, 57, 107
Quetta	44/9	5, 20, 28, 31, 48, 60, 82, 84, 110, 114, 160 — see Samungli
Quevauvillers	11/138	9, 82
Quiévy	11/215	60
Quilen	11/95	100, 149, 214, 216
Quonset Point, RI	51/8	53
R 16		see Hildesheim
R 27		see Grossachsenheim
R 28		see Nuremburg/Furth
R 58		see Friedrichshaven
Rabigh	37/15	14
Racecourse		see Colombo
Radovo	35/32	17
Rafah	36/8	14, 67
Rahad	40/31	17
Raipur	45/50	238, 298
Rajkot	45/1	60, 97
Rajyeswarpur	46/105	42, 155 — see Lalaghat
Ramadi	42/9	30, 63
Ramat David	36/34	6, 32, 37, 46, 74, 127, 154, 208, 213, 216, 232, 242, 243, 249, 294, 459, 651
Ramatuelle	33/13	43, 72, 93, 111, 225, 284
Ramleh	36/18	6, 11, 14, 33, 45, 55, 80, 111, 113, 142, 145, 208, 211, 651
Ramree Island		see Kyaukpyu
Ramu 1-4	46/28-31	20, 28, 79, 81, 152, 211, 607 — see 'Hay', 'Lyons' and 'Reindeer'
Ranchi	44/56	11, 20, 27, 28, 45, 47, 79, 82, 84, 110, 177, 211, 656
Rangoon	46/49	136, 230, 240 — see Mingaladon
Ras al Hadd	43/13	244
Ratmalana	45/28	22, 30, 42, 81, 84, 89, 136, 160, 176, 203, 217, 232, 258, 261, 273, 292
Ratnap	46/33	28, 134, 258
Rattlesden	7/64	266
Ravenna	31/17	43, 72, 93, 111, 657
Ravigliano	31/89	657
Rawcliffe		see Clifton
Rayak	36/42	80, 162, 208, 450, 451
Razmak	44/15	659
Rebais	10/59	5
Recanati	31/47	651
Reckem	11/55	10, 48, 79
Red Barn	8/13	26
Redcar	4/31	7N, 251, 252
Redhill	9/51	1, 16, 66, 116, 131, 219, 231, 258, 287, 303, 308, 310, 312, 340, 350, 400, 401, 402, 411, 412, 414, 416, 421, 452, 457, 485, 504, 600, 602, 611
Red Hills Lake	45/42	191, 205, 212, 230, 240, 321, 357, 628
Red Road	46/4	17, 136
Reghaia	24/11	32, 36, 39, 153, 227, 256, 272, 328, 458
Regina	30/9	13, 55, 114, 142, 150 — see San Severo
Reichswalde	14/63	660, 662
Reims/Champagne	12/31	24, 58, 73, 105, 226
'Reindeer'	46/28 & 30	5, 81, 135, 146, 258, 261 — see Ramu 1 and 4
Reinsehlen (B 154)	15/44	400, 403, 414, 416, 421, 430, 443
Rely	11/88	6, 42, 54
Remaisnil	11/127	11, 62, 70, 73, 80
Renaix	14/6	653
Rendcomb	8/8	45, 46, 48, 62, 110
Renfrew	4/95	33, 55, 80, 309, 602, 666
Rennes	12/75	57, 59
Rennington	4/17	256
Reumont	11/225	53, 218
Reviers	13/10	652
Reykjavik	17/2	53, 86, 120, 190, 204, 209, 210, 220, 221, 251, 269, 279, 280, 330, 612
Reyville	23/27	55, 223
Rhede	14/55	652
Rheine (B 108)	15/11	264, 400, 401, 402, 409, 411, 412, 414, 430
Riccione	31/30	654
Richmond	50/37	54, 452, 457
Ridgewell	7/75	90
Rillaar	14/16	662
Rimini	31/29	43, 72, 87, 93, 111, 241, 318, 654, 657, 683
Ringway	6/72	4, 64, 78, 253, 264, 296, 613, 663
Ripon	4/42	76
Rips (B 84)	14/77	401, 411, 412, 442
Risalpur	44/23	1, 5, 11, 20, 27, 31, 39, 60, 97, 117, 146, 152, 298
'Ritz'		see Maungdaw
Rivenhall	9/13	295, 570
River Foglia	31/33	657
River Sangro	31/57	655
Rivolto	32/26	39, 43, 72, 111, 293
Riyan	43/16	8, 621
Robat	38/12	12
Robertsfield	40/17	200
Roborough	5/45	16, 247, 276, 691
Rochford	9/17	37, 54, 61, 74, 141, 151, 152, 600, 616 — see Southend
Rollestone Camp	8/55	657
Ronchi	32/32	654, 655
Ronchin		see Lille/Ronchin
Rongotai	53/8	488
Roosendaal	14/30	652
Roseto degli Abruzzi	31/54	651
Rosh Pinna	36/39	208
Rosières-en-Santerre (B 87)	12/25 & 13/100	18, 21, 57, 464, 487
Rosignano	31/108	38, 92, 112, 145, 225, 237, 255, 293, 458, 600, 624
Rostrup	15/21	661, 664
Rouen/Boos		see Boos
Rougefay	11/119	87
Rouvres	12/35	1, 73
Rovigo	32/9	654
Rovilles-aux-Chênes	10/68	115, 216
Roye/Amy	12/26	18, 57
Rozay-en-Brie	10/53	49
Ruaudin	12/68	73
Rucqueville	13/33	653
Rufforth	4/66	158, 664
Rufisque	40/7	200
Ruisseauville	11/96	25, 27, 32, 98
Rumkha	46/32	136, 152, 607
Ryes (B 15)	13/4	193, 257
St-André	13/30	662
St-André-aux Bois	11/101	6, 21, 27, 35, 55, 57, 60, 99, 100, 101, 102
St-André-d'Echauffour	13/56	662
St-André-de-l'Eure (B 24)	13/76	19, 65, 122, 174, 175, 184, 245, 401, 409, 411, 412, 438, 439, 440, 442
St Angelo	3/22	153, 235, 422
St Catherine	29/1	451 — see Calvi

St Croix (B 63)	14/2	119, 276 — see Bruges
St Davids	5/11	53, 58, 220, 502, 517
St Denis-Westrem (B 61)	14/5	2, 4, 268, 276, 302, 308, 317 — see Ghent
Ste-Croix-sur-Mer (B 3)	13/7	175, 193, 197, 257, 263, 266, 441, 442, 443
Ste-Foy-de-Montgommery	13/58	660
Ste-Honorine-de-Ducy (B 21)	13/28	168, 400, 414, 430
St-Eloi	11/160	3N, 8N
Ste-Marguerite	11/50	149
Ste-Marie-Cappel	11/37	1, 4, 19, 20, 35, 45, 46, 48, 53, 57, 60, 79, 1N, 6N/206, 210
St Eval	5/33	22, 42, 48, 53, 58, 59, 61, 86, 140, 143, 161, 179, 203, 206, 210, 217, 220, 221, 224, 228, 233, 234, 235, 236, 238, 240, 247, 248, 254, 263, 280, 282, 304, 407, 415, 489, 500, 502, 517, 541, 543, 547, 612
St-Germain	14/12	659
St-Germain-Langot	13/46	653
St Helier	12/77	17, 501
St Hubert	14/86	658
St-Inglevert	11/21 & 12/14	21, 85, 97, 100, 115, 214, 607, 615
St Jean	36/36	38, 46, 47, 74, 80, 89, 127, 147, 159, 162, 213, 221, 252, 261, 272, 294, 335, 451, 454, 458, 459
St Just	5/38	16
St-Léger-les-Authie	11/151	18
St Lucia	41/6	262, 265
St-Lucien Ferme	12/47	103, 218
St Mary's	5/40	87
St Mawgan	5/34	7, 22, 42, 201, 206, 217, 220, 228, 282 — see Treblezue
St-Omer	11/30	1, 2, 3, 4, 5, 6, 7, 8, 9, 10, 11, 12, 13, 15, 16, 18, 19, 20, 22, 23, 24, 25, 27, 28, 29, 32, 40, 41, 42, 43, 45, 46, 52, 53, 54, 56, 58, 59, 60, 62, 64, 66, 69, 71, 73, 74, 79, 82, 83, 85, 87, 98, 99, 104, 210
St-Paul	13/43	659
St-Pierre-sur-Dives	13/52	652
St-Pol	11/20	6, 38, 2N, 3N, 8N, 9N, 10N, 13N
St-Quentin	11/183	2, 3, 4, 5
St Thomas Mount	45/50	5, 11, 20, 27, 30, 34, 42, 45, 60, 82, 84, 89, 113, 123, 135, 146, 155, 176, 200, 203, 211, 215, 261, 354
St-Valéry	12/58	601
Sachsenheim (R 27)	33/25	326, 328 — see Sersheim
Sadaung	46/87	5, 28, 89, 155, 258
Safi	27/4	111, 112, 126
Saigon		see Tan Son Nhut
Sains-lès-Pernes	11/87	148
Saki	52/1	283
Salalah	43/15	8
Salbani	45/61	9, 82, 134, 159, 160, 355, 356
Salmana	36/4	14
Salon	33/9	37, 75, 99, 149
Salonika		see Mikra Bay
Samarra	42/45	63, 72
Samawah	42/14	6, 30
Sambre	45/12	20
Samungli	44/8	84
San Angelo	30/54	112, 208, 241, 250, 260, 450
San Basilio	30/21	663
San Bernardino	31/46	651
San Francesco	25/14	225
San Giorgio	31/62	654
San Luca	32/15	34, 42
San Marco	31/4	655
San Pancrazio	31/16	657
San Pelagio	32/21	42, 45
San Piero in Bagno	31/100	654
San Pietro in Gu	32/14	66
San Severo	30/8	651, 680, 682, 683 — see Regina
San Stephano	35/43	17, 25, 55, 56, 150, 207, 208, 220, 222
Santa Arcangelo	31/25	651
Santa Cruz	45/7	159, 203, 217, 244
Santa Maria di Leucca	30/30	263
Santa Maria la Fossa	30/50	654, 655
San Vito	31/56	241, 318, 651
Sapam	46/98	5, 11, 17, 20, 136, 155, 607
Sarafand	36/19	651
Sarcedo	32/13	28
Sarona	36/20	111, 113, 142
Sart	10/12	6, 8, 57
Satolas		see Lyons/Satolas
Sattler	50/16	452
Saugor	44/49	5, 20, 28
Saultain	10/38	42, 64, 209
Saumur	12/70	73
Saussay-la-Campagne	13/83	653
Savignano	31/24	657
Savoia	20/31	80, 94, 237
Savy	11/158	5, 11, 13, 15, 19, 35, 41, 52, 60, 69, 82, 85
Sawbridgeworth	9/26	2, 4, 63, 80, 126, 168, 170, 182, 239, 268, 652
Sbiba	23/42	654
Scampton	6/16	9, 10, 18, 21, 27, 33, 35, 49, 57, 81, 83, 98, 100, 148, 153, 214, 467, 617, 625
Scandicci	31/104	655
Scanzano	30/31	225, 284
Scapa Flow	1/6	46, 263
Scaramanga	35/8	230
Schaft		see Eindhoven
Schaijk	14/69	661, 662
Schjindel (B 85)	14/73	66, 74, 127, 322, 329, 331, 332, 340, 341, 345
Schleswig (B 164)	15/58	26, 47, 56, 175, 181, 182, 184, 245, 297
Schwecat	34/3	187, 238, 525
Scone	2/31	309, 666
Scopwick	6/29	11, 25, 203, 205, 209, 210, 213 — see Digby
Scordia	25/12	651
Scorton	4/35	26, 56, 122, 130, 167, 219, 406, 410, 604
Sculthorpe	7/25	21, 214, 342, 464, 487
Scuscuiban	38/6	8, 621
Sealand	5/68	79, 577 — see Shotwick
Seahouses	4/16	256
Seaton Carew	4/30	36, 246, 251, 252
Sebala		see La Sebala
Seclin		see Lille/Seclin
Secqueville-en-Bessin	13/34	658
Secunderabad	45/44	5, 28, 31 — see Begumpet
Sedadah	20/23	250, 260, 450
Sedes	35/22	32, 94, 335, 336, 624
Sedgeford	7/23	13, 45, 64, 72, 87, 110, 122
Sek Kong	47/4	28, 80
Seletar	48/25	11, 17, 22, 34, 36, 52, 60, 65, 66, 81, 84, 88, 89, 100, 103, 110, 155, 205, 209, 225, 230, 232, 258, 605, 681, 684
Selsey	8/86	33, 65, 74, 222, 245, 329, 340, 341, 349, 485
Selvigny	11/222	15
Semakh	36/38	6, 211
Sembawang	48/21	28, 60, 62, 194, 453, 656
Semerang	49/13	656
Semplak	49/6	62
Senem	22/8	6, 680
Senigallia	31/40	654
Senlis	10/49	2, 3, 4, 5
Senlis-le-Sec	11/148	1, 15, 43, 94
Sennar	37/25	47
Senon	12/34	2, 87
Sepulot	47/22	230
Serches		see Mont-de-Soissons
Seremban	48/14	656

Serny	11/92	18, 22, 25, 27, 32, 38, 41, 46, 62, 80, 83, 88, 92, 102, 103, 148, 208
Serracapriola	30/6	651
Serragia	29/5	237, 238, 451
Serravalle	31/27	651
Serretelle	30/39	81, 152, 154, 225, 232, 242
Serris	10/51	2, 3, 4, 5
Sersheim	33/25	327 — see Sachsenheim (R 27)
Setif	24/12	13, 18, 87, 114, 152, 242, 253, 255, 600
Seychelles		see Port Victoria
Sfax	22/2	6, 43, 73, 651 — see Sidi Mansour
Shahraban	42/55	30
Shaibah	42/16	6, 8, 31, 32, 37, 45, 70, 73, 74, 84, 162, 244, 249, 261, 680, 683
Shallufa	18/46	6, 14, 32, 37, 38, 39, 40, 46, 70, 76, 82, 90, 104, 162, 213, 220, 221, 252, 351, 454, 458, 620
Shallufa Satellite (LG 251)	18/47	221
Shandur	18/48	6, 39, 42, 47, 73, 89, 108, 127, 134, 147, 160, 178, 213, 221, 223, 237, 417
Shanghai	47/3	2
Sharjah	43/11	6, 8, 60, 73, 78, 84, 152, 208, 210, 244, 249, 294, 680, 683
Shawbury	5/63	90, 131, 137, 411
Sheikh Jaad	42/30	30
Sheikh Nuran	36/10	113 — see Weli Sheikh Nuran
Sheikh Othman	38/11	8, 11, 39, 41, 94, 203
Sheikh Saad	42/23	30
Shepherds Grove	7/60	82, 196, 299
Sherburn-in-Elmet	4/71	46, 73
Sherika	37/9	67
Shinyanga	39/32	26

Ships — Reference to named ships in the main body of the text has generally been confined to those vessels whose role normally involved them in the carriage or operation of aircraft. Troopships, which were frequently employed in the redeployment of squadrons, have not been named except for HMT *Neuralia* which was particularly significant since No 74 Sqn was reformed aboard her in 1936. Ships named in the text are:

HMS *Argus*		4, 65, 81, 112, 134, 186, 203, 242, 605
HMS *Ark Royal*		4, 55, 242, 249, 267, 605
HMS *Empress*		221
HMS *Fencer*		618
HMS *Furious*		73, 213, 229, 249, 263
HMS *Glorious*		46, 263
HMS *Hermes*		2
HMS *Indomitable*		30, 258, 261
HMS *Ocean*		33, 80
HMS *Riviera*		221
HMS *Smiter*		132, 136
HMS *Striker*		618
HMS *Trumpeter*		11, 17, 656
HMS *Vengeance*		11, 17
HMS *Victorious*		238
HMT *Neuralia*		74
SS *Manela*		230
USS *Wasp*		601, 603
Shobdon	5/59	88, 577
Shoreham	9/40	3, 14, 81, 82, 86, 94, 123, 225, 245, 253, 277, 345, 667
Shotwick	5/68	27, 55, 90, 95, 96, 98, 103 — see Sealand
Shumran	42/29	30
Sialkot	44/38	5, 28
Sibu	47/18	110
Sidi Ahmed	23/9	13, 219, 655
Sidi Amor	23/15	13, 14, 39, 47, 219, 624
Sidi Athman	23/10	242 — see Protville
Sidi Azeiz (LG 148)	19/13	33, 38, 112, 208, 223, 260, 274, 450, 451
Sidi Azzab	21/29	145 — see Gzina
Sidi Barrani (LG 02)	19/41	14, 22, 33, 39, 55, 80, 112, 113, 127, 203, 208, 237, 274
Sidi Haneish	19/50-51	33, 73, 80, 112, 238, 274 — see LG 12 and LG 13
Sidi Mansour	22/1	654 — see Sfax
Sidi Rezegh (LG 153)	20/54	94, 208, 260
Sigiriya	45/22	8, 160, 200, 203, 354
Sigonela	25/6C	23, 55, 114, 203, 223
Silchar West	46/104	34, 60, 113, 211, 615
Silloth	4/82	215, 320
Sindiya	42/21	30
Singerbil	46/11	60
Sinello	31/59	241
Sinn Abtar	42/26	30
Sinthe	46/75	5, 11, 42, 146, 152, 261
Siros	35/11	264
Sirtan	21/6-8	55, 223
Sissinghurst	9/85	653
Sisteron (Y 20)	33/15	43, 72, 93, 111, 225
Siwa (LG 66/67)	40/35-36	6, 208
Skaanland	16/14	46
Skaebrae	1/3	3, 66, 118, 129, 132, 164, 234, 253, 312, 313, 329, 331, 441, 451, 453, 598, 602, 603, 611
Skellingthorpe	6/22	50, 61, 463, 619
Skipton-on-Swale	4/38	420, 424, 432, 433
Skitten	2/6	48, 86, 144, 172, 179, 217, 232, 260, 404, 407, 489, 519, 607, 608, 612, 618
Skyros	35/13	266
'Sloane Square'		see Souk el Arba
Snailwell	7/77	26, 56, 137, 152, 168, 170, 181, 182, 183, 184, 239, 241, 247, 268, 309, 527, 613, 614
Snaith	6/71	51, 150, 266, 578
Snevche	35/33	47
Socotra	43/17	321, 621
Soerabaya	49/15	60, 84, 321, 656
Sola		see Stavanger
Solan	44/41	99
Sollum	19/14	14
Soltau		see Reinsehlen
Soluch	20/15	104, 462
Sommervieu (B 8)	13/3	74, 164, 168, 266, 329, 340, 341, 400, 430
Soncamp	11/154	8, 12, 87
Songea	39/23	26
Sookerating	46/114	159
Sorarogha	44/14	20
Sorman	21/2	6, 260
Sougé	12/66	12, 103
Souk el Arba	23/1	72, 93, 111, 152, 225, 241, 255, 651
Souk el Khemis		
,, 'Euston'	23/2E	72, 93, 241, 243
,, 'Kings Cross'	23/2F	18, 114
,, 'Marylebone'	23/2C	242
,, 'Paddington'	23/2A	32, 81, 152, 242, 255, 600
,, 'Victoria'	23/2B	154, 232
,, 'Waterloo'	23/2D	111, 225
Sousse	23/35	134, 152, 154, 232, 242, 253, 651
South Carlton	6/17	25, 57, 69, 96, 109
Southend	9/17	19, 41, 54, 64, 65, 66, 74, 121, 122, 124, 127, 137, 222, 234, 264, 287, 291, 302, 310, 312, 313, 317, 331, 332, 349, 350, 402, 403, 411, 453, 501, 603, 611 — see Rochford
South Farnborough		see Farnborough
Spa	10/13	57
Sparinese	30/52	654
Speke	5/71	13, 229, 236, 303, 306, 308, 312, 315, 611
Spich	10/6	7, 11, 22, 62
Spilsby	7/10	29, 44, 65, 75, 129, 207, 219, 222, 264
Spitalgate		see Spittlegate
Spittlegate	6/39	29, 39, 43, 70, 83, 91, 100, 106, 202 — see Grantham
Spy	10/18	57
Squires Gate	4/75	63, 75, 96, 215, 256, 307, 308
Staceghem	11/61	7, 10
Stalhille	11/3	213

Stamford	6/48	38, 90 — see Wittering
Stapleford (Tawney)	9/24	3, 46, 151, 242, 277, 656, 658
Staplehurst	9/83	401, 411, 412
Stavanger/Sola	16/9	130, 276, 330
Staverton	8/7	225
Stavros	35/37	221, 222, 223
Stein	14/96	653
Stirling	2/34	43, 63
Stojakovo	35/31	17
Stonehenge	8/53	4, 97, 107, 108, 109
Stoney Cross	8/70	26, 46, 175, 232, 239, 242, 243, 296, 297, 299
Stornara	30/14	614
Stornoway	2/4	48, 58, 224, 500, 502, 518, 612
Stow Maries	9/18	37
Stradishall	7/74	1, 9, 35, 51, 54, 75, 85, 89, 101, 109, 115, 125, 138, 148, 149, 150, 152, 158, 186, 207, 208, 214, 215, 236, 245, 254, 263, 311
Stranraer	4/89	209, 210, 228, 240, 413, 490
Strasbourg		see Entzheim
Strathpine	50/32	548, 549
Strauss	50/17	452, 549
Strée	10/25	80, 101, 208
Strubby	7/9	144, 227, 280, 404, 619
Sturgate	6/12	50, 61
Suda Bay	35/53	113, 264
Suez	18/45 & 37/4	8, 14, 17, 55, 67, 142, 145, 163
Suez Road No 2		see Kilo 61 and LG 209
Sulaimania	42/50	1, 6, 30
Sullom Voe	1/1	190, 201, 204, 210, 240, 330, 333, 413
Sumburgh	1/2	3, 17, 42, 48, 66, 86, 118, 125, 129, 132, 143, 144, 152, 164, 217, 232, 234, 235, 236, 248, 254, 272, 278, 307, 310, 313, 331, 404, 453, 455, 504, 598, 602, 608, 611
Summit	37/18	45, 112, 223
Sungei Patani	48/2	27
Surabaya		see Soerabaya
Surcamps	11/111	102
Sutton Bridge	7/14	64, 254, 264, 266, 613
Suttons Farm	9/20	23, 39, 46, 51, 78 — see Hornchurch
Suzanne	11/169	20, 35
Swannington	7/33	85, 157, 229, 451, 453, 602
Swanton Morley	7/30	3, 88, 98, 105, 107, 110, 152, 180, 226, 305, 320, 464, 487, 613
Sweveghem	11/62	21, 53
Swinderby	6/24	50, 300, 301, 455
Swingate Down	9/65B	2, 3, 4, 5, 7, 9, 15, 27, 49, 50, 58, 110, 212
Swingfield	9/67	119
Sydenham	3/9	88, 226
Syerston	6/34	49, 61, 106, 304, 305, 408, 504
Sylhet	46/107	117
Sylt (B 170)	15/61	2, 3, 4, 14, 16, 21, 26, 33, 41, 56, 69, 80, 107, 302, 305, 308, 317, 349, 350, 411, 412
Syracuse	25/18	651, 654
Tl	42/4	127
Tabingaung	46/85	17, 89, 155, 607
Tabora	39/31 & 41/12	26, 82
Tadcaster	4/73	33, 57, 75, 76, 94 — see Bramham Moor
Tafaraoui	24/2	32, 36, 500, 614
Taher	24/14	87, 153, 219, 328
Tahoune Guemac	42/2	127
Taillebois	13/45	662
Tain	2/8	17, 76, 86, 123, 132, 144, 186, 235, 279, 280, 281, 311, 404, 415, 417, 455, 518, 519, 547
Taiping	48/6	62, 656
Ta Kali	27/1	32, 69, 73, 81, 89, 126, 152, 154, 185, 208, 227, 229, 232, 238, 242, 248, 249, 261, 272, 603, 605
Takoradi	40/19	82, 110, 200, 541
Talbenny	5/14	248, 304, 311
Tallaght	3/14	105, 117, 141, 149, 244
Tamet	21/24	73, 92
Tamu	46/96	11, 28, 152, 155
Tangmere	8/81	1, 14, 17, 22, 23, 25, 26, 29, 32, 33, 34, 40, 41, 42, 43, 56, 65, 66, 69, 72, 74, 82, 84, 85, 87, 91, 92, 93, 96, 98, 115, 118, 124, 127, 129, 130, 131, 141, 145, 148, 161, 164, 165, 168, 170, 183, 197, 198, 207, 208, 213, 217, 219, 222, 229, 238, 245, 257, 266, 268, 302, 310, 312, 313, 329, 331, 332, 340, 341, 349, 401, 403, 411, 412, 416, 421, 485, 486, 501, 534, 587, 601, 605, 607, 609, 614, 616
Tanjore	45/32	11, 36, 60, 261, 353
Tank	44/12	5, 20, 27, 28, 31, 60
Tan Son Nhut	47/11	81, 273, 681, 684
Tantonville	10/66	55, 99
Taranto	30/23	226, 263, 271 — see Pizzone
Tarcienne	10/21	9
Tarquinia	31/82	13, 18, 26, 43, 55, 72, 93, 111, 114
Tarrant Rushton	8/63	196, 295, 297, 298, 644
Tasikmalaja	49/11	36, 242
Tatoi	35/12	70, 84, 211 — see Menidi
Taukkyan	46/92	17, 60
Taveta	39/3	26
Tawau	47/23	230
Tayport	2/27	210
Tealing	2/24	63, 257
Tecklenburg	15/6	659
Tel Aviv	36/22	6
Telergma	24/16	14
Telscombe Cliffs	9/42	78, 242
Temerloh	48/9	656
Temmar	23/31	70 — see Kairouan
Templeux-la-Fosse		see Nurlu
Temploux	14/11	662
Tempsford	7/85	53, 109, 138, 149, 161, 426, 617
Tengah	48/22	11, 17, 20, 28, 32, 33, 34, 39, 45, 60, 62, 64, 74, 81, 84, 103, 136, 152, 155, 204, 242, 258
'Tennant'	46/64	17, 20, 60, 79, 146, 155, 261, 607
Ternhill	5/64	19, 46, 78, 87, 95, 131, 132, 133, 134, 306, 403, 605, 611
Terria	20/16	178, 462
Teteghem	11/10	24, 29, 54, 74, 1N, 204, 8N/208, 9N, 10N/210
Teuge	14/44	657
Teversham		see Cambridge
Tezpur	46/108	5, 20, 31, 113, 194
Thasos	35/38	47, 222
Thazi	46/94	20, 47
Thedaw	46/74	17, 20, 60, 152, 155, 607
Thelepte	23/43	241
Therfield	7/83	75
Thetford	7/66	25, 35, 38, 45, 51, 77, 80, 119, 128
Thirsk	4/39	226
Tholthorpe	4/45	420, 425, 431, 434
Thornaby	4/32	42, 92, 106, 114, 143, 185, 220, 224, 233, 269, 275, 279, 280, 281, 306, 332, 401, 608
Thorney Island	8/78	21, 22, 36, 42, 46, 48, 53, 56, 59, 63, 80, 86, 129, 130, 131, 143, 164, 183, 193, 198, 217, 220, 222, 233, 235, 236, 248, 254, 278, 280, 404, 407, 415, 455, 464, 487, 489, 547, 609, 612
Throwley	9/79	50, 112, 143
Thruxton	8/44	12, 13, 16, 63, 168, 170, 225, 226, 268, 297, 298, 614
Thuilles	10/26	84, 92, 211
Thurleigh	6/54	160
Tienraij	14/85	658
Tiflis	52/15	17
Tikrit	42/46	63, 72
Tilburg	14/36	652, 661, 664
Tilda	45/51	31, 76, 673
Tillé (B 42)	13/95	175, 184, 245

Tilshead	8/56	16, 225
Tingley	24/21	32, 43, 81, 87, 154, 232, 242, 243, 255, 283, 600
Tiree	2/2	224, 281, 304, 518
Tissano	32/31	43, 72, 87, 93, 111, 112, 208, 225, 250, 318
Tjikampek	49/8	36
Tjikembar	49/7	36
Tjilitjan	49/5	232, 242, 258, 488, 605
Tjilitjap	49/12	205
Tmimi	20/41-42	208, 223, 237
Tobruk	20/47-50	6 — see also El Gubbi/El Gubsi
Tocra	20/25	46, 148, 335, 624, 680
Topcliffe	4/40	24, 36, 47, 53, 77, 102, 203, 210, 297, 405, 419, 424
Torre di Palme	31/52	651
Torremaggiore	30/7	651
Torquay	5/49	239
Tortorella	30/13B	37, 70, 92, 145, 417, 600, 601
Tortoreto	31/53	241, 318
Toungoo	46/63	31, 60, 67, 113, 152, 155, 233, 357
Touquin	10/54	2, 3, 4, 5, 32, 43, 54, 73, 80
Towyn	5/8	631
Tramecourt	11/97	208
Tranent		see Macmerry
Treblezue	5/34	264, 400 — see St Mawgan
Tre Cancelli	31/70	43, 72, 93, 111, 225
Trécon	10/60	52
Treizennes	11/90	4, 6, 18, 22, 27, 32, 40, 42, 43, 58, 100, 102, 3N/203, 210 — see Aire
Trescoe	5/39	234
Treviso	32/19	28, 43, 66, 87, 92, 93, 111, 112, 145, 241, 250, 253, 318, 417, 601, 624, 683
Tricesimo	32/28	654
Trichinopoly	45/31	5, 20 — see Kajamalai
Trigno	31/61	80, 208, 241, 318, 682
Trikkala	35/19	80
Trincomalee	45/20	230
Triolo	30/13G	92, 145, 417, 601
Trombay	45/9	191, 212
Trondheim		see Vaernes
Trun	13/55	653
Truscott	50/10	548, 549
Tuddenham	7/71	90, 107, 138, 149, 186, 207
Tulear	41/21	209, 230, 259, 262, 265
Tulihal	46/100	11, 42, 62, 81, 89, 113, 117, 152, 155, 176, 177, 215, 233, 267, 435, 607
Tulo	39/12	26
Tunduru	39/22	26
Turnberry	4/90	618
Turnhouse	4/3	3, 44, 63, 64, 65, 77, 81, 83, 104, 122, 123, 141, 151, 164, 165, 197, 207, 232, 241, 242, 243, 245, 253, 263, 268, 289, 290, 303, 312, 329, 340, 341, 598, 603, 607, 666
Turnhout	14/32	652
Tusciano	30/40	43, 72, 243, 654
Tuz Khurmatli	42/51	30, 63
Twente (B 106)	14/51	2, 3, 4, 33, 41, 56, 66, 127, 130, 137, 181, 182, 219, 247, 264, 268, 322, 331, 332, 349, 350, 409, 485
Twinwood Farm	6/55	26, 164, 169, 239, 268, 613
Tydd St Mary	7/15	51
Tynemouth	4/27	252
Ubena	39/27	26
Udine	32/29	293, 651, 655, 683 — see Campoformido
Ujret el Zol	36/6	14, 67
Ulunderpet	45/33	131, 134, 258
Umbertide	31/91	654
Umritsar	37/32	237
Umtali	41/8	237
Upavon	8/47	3, 9, 17, 72, 73, 85, 87, 230
Upper Heyford	8/18	7, 10, 18, 33, 34, 40, 57, 58, 76, 81, 89, 94, 99, 105, 108, 109, 113, 122, 123, 157, 158, 215, 218, 226, 233
Upper Topa	44/30	668, 669, 670
Upwood	7/97	7, 18, 21, 26, 35, 40, 49, 50, 52, 53, 61, 63, 76, 90, 98, 102, 105, 139, 148, 156, 214, 542
Ursel (B 67)	14/4	164, 183, 198, 276, 609
Usworth	4/28	36, 43, 64, 103, 607, 664 — see Hylton
Utersen (B 174)	15/56	411, 412, 416, 421, 443
Utique	23/10	72, 81 — see Protville
Uxbridge	9/32	1, 3, 4, 24, 39, 207
Vaenga	16/17	81, 134, 144, 455, 543
Vaernes	16/12	129, 165, 276, 332, 540
Valence (Y 23)	33/17	682
Valheureux	11/131	3, 56
Valley	5/1	20, 22, 125, 131, 157, 219, 242, 247, 258, 275, 281, 285, 312, 315, 350, 406, 456, 615, 650
Varrelbusch (B 113)	15/20	302, 308, 317, 322, 349
Varssenaere	11/2	202, 217
Vassincourt	12/37	1
Vasto	31/60	651. 657, 683
Vavuniya	45/18	17, 22, 60, 89, 132, 176, 217
Velikoknyajaskaya	52/4	47
Venafro	30/57	92, 145, 208, 417, 601
Vendeville		see Lille/Vendeville
Venice	32/17	655
Vermeppen		see Meppen
Verona	32/6	28, 34, 66 — see Villafranca
Vert Galand	11/132	3, 4, 8, 11, 12, 13, 15, 19, 22, 23, 32, 56, 57, 59, 60, 66, 70, 84, 3N, 8N, 218
Vibo Valentia	30/33	651
Vicchio	31/101	655
'Victoria'		see Souk el Khemis
Victoria Point	47/12	60
Vignacourt	11/134	8, 15, 20, 29, 54, 80, 151
Villa Arzana	31/10	663
Villa Brocchi	31/15	651
Villa Carpena		see Forli
Villafranca	32/6	87, 185, 208, 225 — see Verona
Villa Orba	32/27	454, 500
Villaverla	32/12	34, 139
Villeneuve (Vertus)	12/44	10, 73, 77, 102, 105
Villers-Bocage		see Fleselles
Villers-Bretonneux	11/141	11, 24, 25, 27, 34, 35, 5N
Villers-lès-Cagicourt	11/202	27, 49, 62
Villeselve	11/180	53
Villesneux	10/61	100, 16N/216
Villiersfaux	12/64	142
Villons-les-Buissons (B 16)	13/14	66, 127, 331, 332
Vis	34/5	6, 73, 249, 253, 351, 352, 1435
Vitry-en-Artois (B 50)	12/7 & 13/105	53, 56, 59, 88, 151, 174, 175, 184, 226, 245, 342, 607, 615
Vizagapatam	45/48	5, 30, 42, 62, 81, 84, 89, 135, 136, 155, 203, 215, 615
Volkel (B 80)	14/74	3, 4, 41, 56, 80, 174, 175, 184, 245, 274, 305, 401, 411, 412, 418, 442, 486, 605
Voltone	31/83	225, 600, 682
Waddington	6/26	9, 12, 21, 23, 27, 44, 49, 50, 57, 61, 82, 83, 88, 97, 100, 101, 105, 110, 117, 123, 142, 203, 204, 207, 420, 463, 467, 503, 617
Wadi Gazouza	37/19	45, 211, 223
Wadi Halfa	37/13	6, 237
Wadi Natrun	18/31	39, 45 — see LG 100
Wadi Surri	20/20	92, 145 — see Darragh North
Wagnonlieu	11/163	12
Wahn (B 119)	14/100	2, 4, 11, 14, 17, 21, 68, 69, 87, 98, 107, 128, 180, 305
Wailly	13/97	658
Wajir	38/3	237
Waller Field (BWI)	51/13	53
Wallon-Cappel	11/34	5
Walmer	9/64	3N, 4N, 8N, 233
Waltham	7/4	100, 142, 550
Wamin	11/100	80
Wangelau	15/52	659

Appendix 10

Airfield Development

As aeroplanes have grown larger and more complex with the passage of time, so the aerodrome facilities needed to support them have had to keep pace. This Appendix, by examining a few typical examples from different theatres and eras, is intended to provide an impression of the way in which airfields have evolved over the years.

The earliest aeroplanes required only a few hundred yards of level ground, reasonably short grass, and an absence of significant vertical obstructions. For aircraft, shelter from the elements was afforded either by canvas hangars or by sheds of wooden construction (clad in either timber or galvanised iron) drawn from Army stocks. Similar structures provided technical, office and domestic accommodation for personnel. Although a variety of canvas hangar designs was available in the early days, the French Bessoneau pattern was the most prevalent and its use was to become widespread, both at home and abroad. By 1917, a purpose built aeroplane hangar of substantial construction, often referred to as the 'Belfast Type' after the Belfast truss which supported the arched roof, began to appear on major UK aerodromes. Both the canvas Bessoneaux and the permanent 1917 pattern hangars remained in general use until well after the Second World War. The latter dominated the skyline at most RAF aerodromes at home until they began to be eclipsed by newer and larger structures in the mid-1930s.

As military aviation evolved during the First World War the aerodromes in the UK became broadly classifiable according to their function. Most combat flying took place overseas, so few of the airfields at home housed operational units. One group which did was that from which the air defence of the UK was mounted. Initially Home Defence Squadrons* tended to be organised with a Headquarters, often not located at an airfield, controlling operational flights at dispersed sites. As the incidence of attacks on the UK declined the detached flights were withdrawn and the squadrons became concentrated on main bases. Bekesbourne and Leadenham are illustrated, at Figs 8 and 9, as typical examples of a Home Defence station and a subordinate flight station. A second category of operational flying station in the UK supported the operations of the landplanes and seaplanes of the coastal defence squadrons. An example of a seaplane facility, Cattewater, is illustrated at Fig 10.

The majority of aerodromes in the UK during the First World War were concerned with flying training or the preparation of newly formed squadrons for service abroad. By late 1918, many of these airfields had become quite well established and a large proportion of them featured permanent hangars and orderly rows of ancilliary buildings and

*Home Defence (HD) Squadrons were initially distinguished by having their role incorporated into their designations, e.g. No 39 (HD) Sqn. This practice was terminated from 17 Oct 17 on the authority of A0 639.

Typical of early aircraft sheds are these, of timber construction with canvas 'doors', at Abeele housing the DH 2s of No 29 Sqn in 1916. (RAF Museum P11965)

An interior view of the 1917 pattern 'Belfast type' hangar housing DH 4s of No 40 TDS at Harlaxton in 1918. (MOD H2385)

Underlining their portability, these Bessoneaux hangars were erected at San Stephano to house the Bristol Fighters of No 208 Sqn. The occasion which is the subject of the picture was an 'At Home Day' held on 11 Aug 23 following the resolution of the Chanak crisis. (RAF Museum P693)

The Belfast type hangar "dominated the skyline at most RAF aerodromes". This is Hendon in 1931. The aeroplanes are: thirteen Wapitis, three Avro 504Ns and two Moths of Nos 600 and 601 Sqns. (RAF Museum P10422)

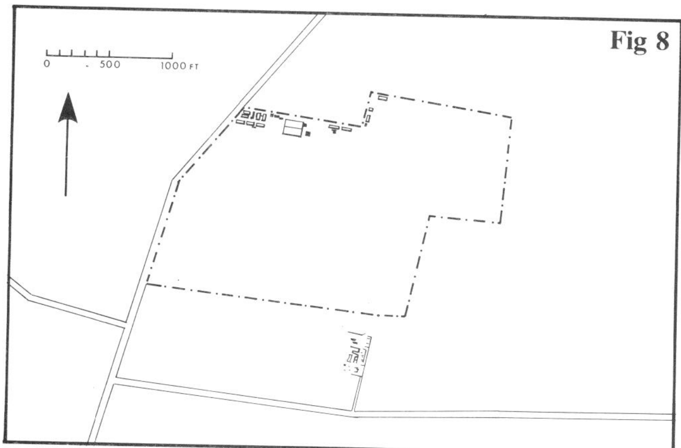

Opened in 1916 to house 'C' Flight of No 38 Sqn on Home Defence duties, Leadenham is illustrated as it appeared in late 1918, by which time the residents were 'A' Flight of No 90 Sqn. Located 2 miles west of Cranwell aerodrome, Leadenham was one of the many airfields, several of which still remain, which were established along the line of the Lincolnshire Edge, a ridge running north/south down the county. The landing ground measured 800 yds by 600 yds. Shelter for the eight authorised Avro 504s was provided by a pair of adjacent 130′ by 80′ sheds. Hutted accommodation for a total of 51 personnel was also available. The RAF left the site in 1919 and it was never used for flying again. Few traces of its brief association with military aviation now remain.

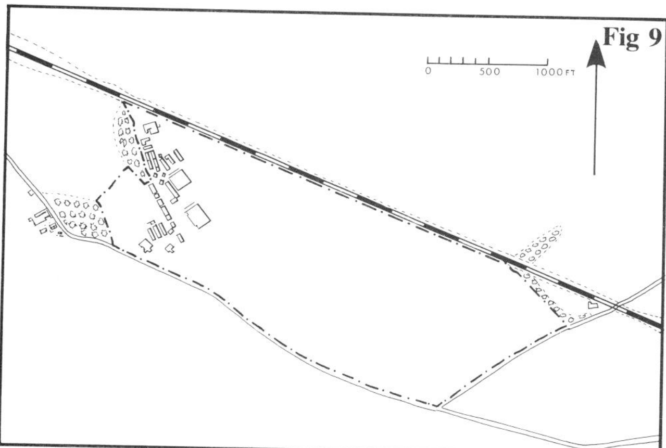

Bekesbourne aerodrome was located to the south east of Canterbury alongside the then South Eastern and Chatham Railway. The airfield was some 1,160 yds by 450 yds and was occupied by 'B' Flt of No 50 Sqn initially, although later the whole squadron concentrated there. By late 1918, development of the facilities was almost complete and there was accommodation available for the establishment of 261 personnel required to operate the squadron's 24 Camels. These were housed in two 1917 pattern Belfast-type hangars. The site was abandoned by the RAF in 1919 but continued to function as a civil aerodrome. In 1939 the RAF returned briefly but the following year the airfield was closed for good. Nevertheless, several of the 1918 era buildings remained standing until well after the Second World War.

Waddington was a typical UK training aerodrome. It is seen here on 5 Apr 18 (see Fig 12) at which time its resident units were Nos 47 and 48 TSs. (RAF Waddington archives)

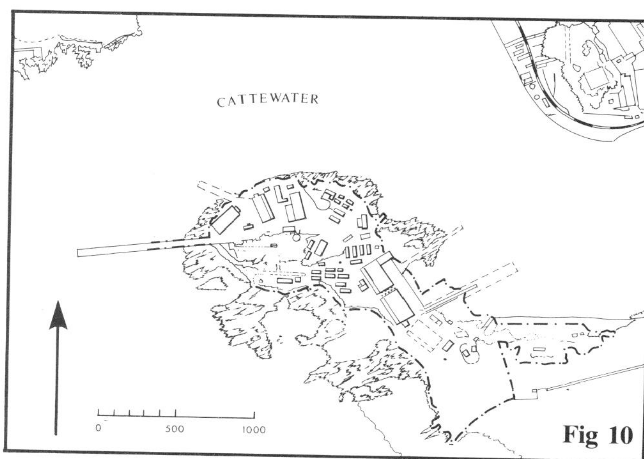

First opened in 1917 as an RNAS seaplane station, Cattewater shared an historic site on Mount Batten Point with an old castle, which still stands. The facilities continued to be developed after they were taken over by the RAF in Apr 18 and by the end of the war there were three slipways and three substantial seaplane sheds (a planned fourth shed, the site of which is indicated in the sketch, was never completed). These supported the operations of the Short seaplanes and Felixstowe flying boats of Nos 237 and 238 Sqns. After some initial post-war uncertainty, Cattewater became a permanent RAF Station in 1925 and thereafter continued to undergo progressive development. The WW I era huts on the south side of the Point were eventually replaced by brick barracks and additional land to the east of that shown on the plan was taken over to permit the erection of permanent messes and married accommodation. Mount Batten, as Cattewater became in 1929, remains in use today.

Cattewater mole in 1918 with a bomb-laden Short 184 of No 237 Sqn suspended from the mobile steam crane – see Fig 10. (J M Bruce/G S Leslie collection)

This picture shows a typical French airfield, part of the eastern aerodrome at Bertangles, on 16 Jun 18. In the foreground are Dolphins of No 23 Sqn and Bristol Fighters of No 48 Sqn can just be discerned at top right. The ragged white lines are entrenchments. The domestic and technical facilities are relatively substantial huts and aeroplane sheds rather than the tentage which was prevalent at many other aerodromes. (Museum of Army Flying)

hutted accommodation. The number still exhibiting the gipsy-encampment-like air conferred by the use of tents was rapidly decreasing. By the time that the War ended, the majority of these fairly sophisticated facilities had become TDSs although some, like Bicester, Chingford and Castle Bromwich were designated as Mobilisation Stations. The difference in role, however, led to no noticeable difference in appearance. Two examples of TDSs are illustrated: No 14 TDS, Lake Down, at Fig 11; and No 48 TDS, Waddington, at Fig 12.

During 1914-19 the majority of the operational squadrons of the RFC, RNAS and RAF were in France. The earliest squadrons to deploy protected their aeroplanes from the weather during the winter of 1914-15 as best they could with makeshift shelters of wattle or canvas stretched over hop poles. No 5 Sqn was probably the first unit to have proper facilities when the Royal Engineers erected some sheds for them at Bailleul in Mar 15. Aerodromes in France were not very different from the earlier airfields in the UK although, being essentially temporary by nature, they never acquired the full trappings of permanence which began to transform the home bases from 1917. Two examples of typical RFC airfields in France are illustrated as they were in 1917: Léalvillers at Fig 13; and Le Hameau/Filescamp Farm at Fig 14.

After the run-down of the RAF in 1919 a selection of permanent aerodromes was retained for the peacetime air force and these continued to be developed. Temporary wartime huts were gradually replaced by brick guardrooms, offices, workshops, messes and barracks, and a few married quarters began to appear. The next major change came with the Expansion Programmes of the mid-1930s which led to the construction of many additional aerodromes and brought a new generation of buildings. The new structures were both attractive in appearance and practical in design. The large 'C-type' hangars in particular were most successful and continue to house most of the RAF's aeroplanes more than

'C' Type hangars first appeared in 1927. The basic design underwent progressive amendment thereafter. This one, providing a backdrop to Overstrand, K4560, of No 101 Sqn, is of the mid-1930s pattern. (Author's collection)

Waddington in 1939 with the classic 'Expansion Pattern' development in the distance; see Fig 15. This picture makes an interesting comparison with that on the previous page and shows that the south eastern technical site had changed little in over 20 years. These buildings were not demolished until 1943 (some survived until even later) when the airfield was remodelled and paved runways were laid. (D French)

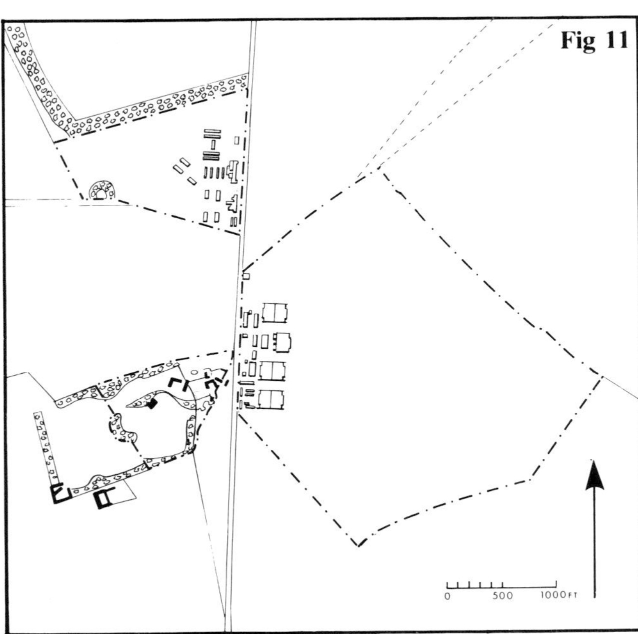

Initially opened in 1917 to house the nuclei of several bombing squadrons, Lake Down was located on the southern edge of Salisbury Plain, 5 miles to the west of Amesbury. It evolved into No 14 TDS, which opened on 6 Jun 18 with the task of training day bomber crews. The aerodrome itself was a somewhat undulating area which had maximum dimensions of 880 yds and 950 yds. The six hangars and one Aeroplane Repair Shed supported the establishment of 36 DH 4s and/or DH 9s and 36 Avro 504s. Just to the north west of the aerodrome, domestic accommodation was available for up to 858 personnel of whom 180 could be students. A further site, due west of the hangars, housed the 42 personnel comprising the staff of Headquarters 33rd Training Wing in the existing buildings of "Druid's Lodge". The Station closed in 1919 and was not redeveloped as an airfield. "Druid's Lodge" itself remains and some traces of the technical site can still be discerned.

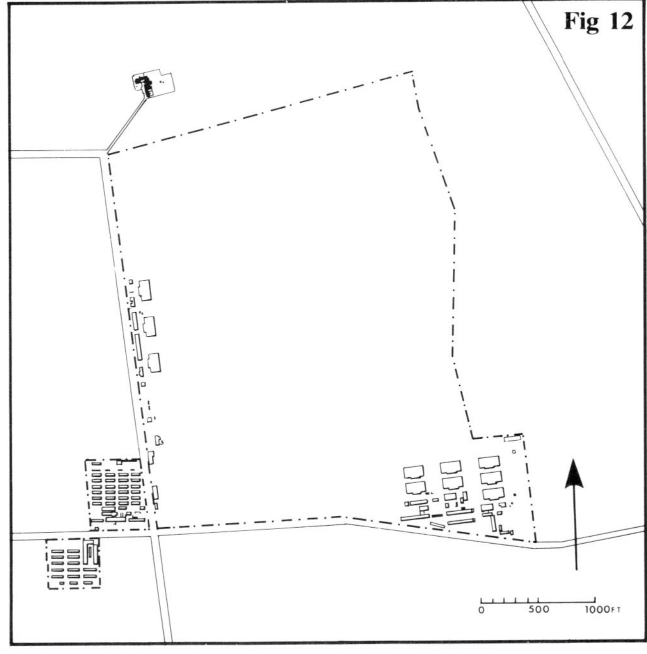

Opened in 1916, Waddington, like Leadenham, was one of the airfields built along the Lincolnshire Edge. It became No 48 TDS and was concerned with training for day bombing. Waddington also housed the HQ of 27th Training Wing, could house an operational bomber squadron and was available, if necessary, as a Landing Ground for Home Defence operations. There was by late 1918 an establishment of 36 Avro 504s and 36 DH 4/9s and 858 personnel, of whom 180 were under instruction. The aircraft sheds, which were of the permanent Belfast-type, were erected in two groups. Waddington became a permanent RAF aerodrome after the war and was subsequently extensively enlarged and developed – see Figs 15, 16 and 27.

half a century later. Waddington, apart from a brief period in the early 1920s, remained in use between the wars and was not substantially changed from the way it had appeared in 1918 (see Fig 12) until it was expanded and redeveloped to take on the characteristics of a typical 'Expansion Aerodrome'. It is illustrated in this later form as an example of such an airfield, circa 1939, at Fig 15.

When the Expansion took place, runways were still not regarded as essential facilities. However, the effects of

Runways were not considered necessary during the Expansion period and did not become common until 1942. One class of aeroplane which avoided the enormous expense associated with airfield pavements was the flying boat; a class which the RAF operated from its inception until 1957. This is Stranraer, K7297, of No 209 Sqn taking-off from Felixstowe in 1938. (RAF Museum P4518)

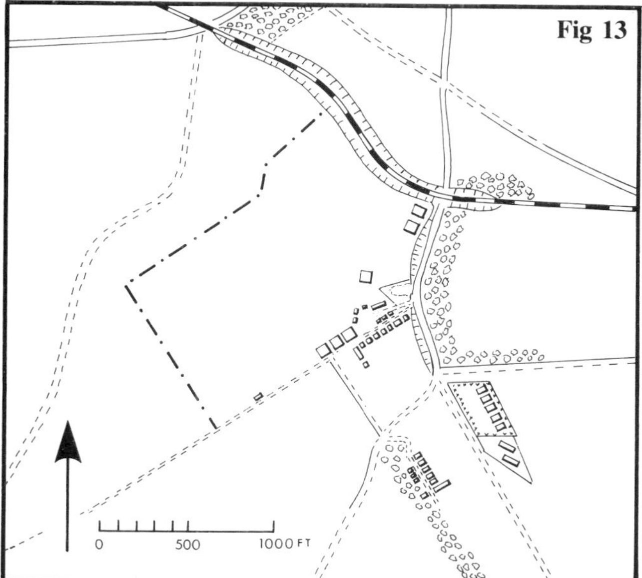

Representative of many of the small operational airfields used by the RFC/RAF in France, Léalvillers is illustrated as it was in Jul 17. The landing ground had maximum dimensions of 475 yds by 350 yds. There were three unoccupied corrugated iron clad aircraft sheds of steel construction (the isolated large structure and the most north-easterly pair on the plan). The other three hangars, in a line on the southern boundary of the flying area, were Bessoneau type and were occupied by No 41 Sqn, which had just converted to DH 5s from FE 8s. To the north east of these was a scattering of huts providing: an Engineer Officer's office, a transport shed, a guardroom, a Flight Office, and other ancilliary facilities. To the south east of the Bessoneaux were a workshop and a smith's, and a line of huts running north east from these constituted the men's camp. Four hundred yards or so to the south, and at right angles to the men's camp, was another line of huts which were the officers' quarters. To the east of the officers' quarters, and within a wire compound, was a prisoner-of-war camp.

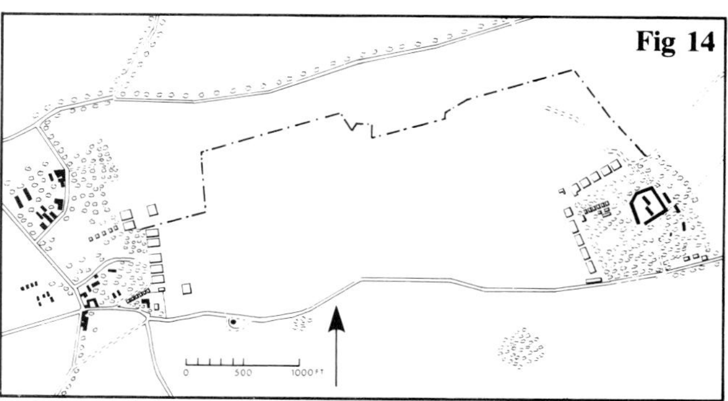

Filescamp Farm and Le Hameau were really two camps which shared the same large landing ground, this being some 1,300 yds by 500 yds in extent. Filescamp Farm itself is set in orchards at the eastern end of the aerodrome. The village shown at the extreme left of the sketch (to the west) is Le Hameau. A mile further west is a larger village called Izel-les-Hameaux (contemporary WW I renderings usually omitted the final 'x'). All three names were used to identify the aerodrome, although when Filescamp Farm was specified it always meant the eastern camp in particular. A survey of available hangarage within 3rd Brigade dated 9 May 17, for instance, recorded that: Nos 11 and 100 Sqns at Izel-les-Hameau (sic) had 6 and 3 Bessoneaux respectively; No 60 Sqn at Filescamp Farm had 5 permanent sheds; and No 29 Sqn at Le Hameau had a further 4½ sheds. The sketch is based on an original dated Jul 17. It shows Le Hameau, to the west, which could accommodate two 2-seater squadrons. Nine aeroplane sheds were available with officers' accommodation in the trees behind the hangars. A CO's office was available at the southern end of the main line of five sheds. At Filescamp Farm there were nine aeroplane sheds erected along the aerodrome sides of the orchard; these could accommodate two single-seat scout squadrons. One additional shed was available to house the men, while officers lived either in the farm itself or in huts erected among the trees. A CO's office was in the angle made by the two lines of hangars. The aerodrome was extensively used throughout the war by a variety of squadrons and remained in use by the RAF until mid-1919.

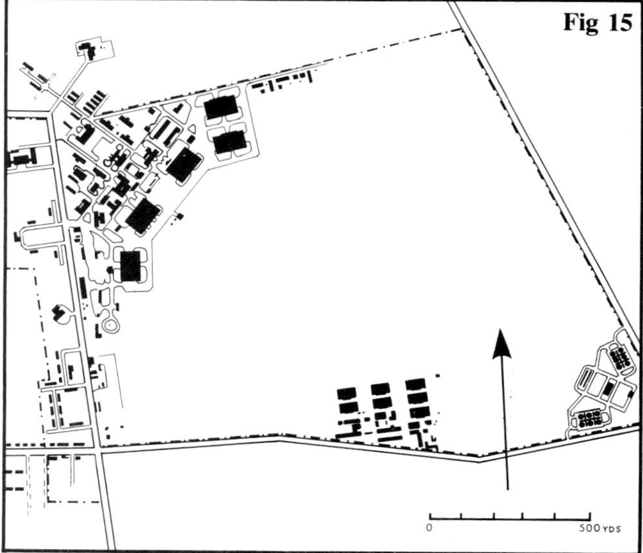

By 1939 Waddington (see Fig 12) had taken on much of the appearance of an Expansion Pattern aerodrome. Five of the large C Type hangars and a full complement of modern workshop, administrative and barrack facilities had been built in the north western corner of the airfield, replacing three of the original WW I hangars. At this stage the southern complex of buildings, including seven hangars dating from 1917, still stood. Additional land had been acquired to the west of the aerodrome, on which had been erected some married quarters and a new Officers' Mess. The airfield area had also been increased to the east and it now extended to the Lincoln-Sleaford (A15) road. In the south eastern corner of the aerodrome a new fuel storage complex had been built.

operating increasingly heavy aircraft, and the inherent tendency of grass surfaces to become waterlogged, and thus inhibit flying, brought an acceptance of the need, first for paved taxitracks, and ultimately for runways. It is, perhaps, not generally appreciated that the 'Dambusters' raid was launched from a grass airfield. Most major aerodromes constructed from 1942 onwards were laid out with paved runways from the outset and most of the older aerodromes were progressively closed, provided with paved surfaces and restored to use. In general three runways were built, a major one aligned with the prevailing wind, and two subsidiary strips, arranged at 60° to the main axis, to cater for cross-wind conditions. This ideal arrangement frequently had to be adapted, however, to conform with constraints imposed by local geography. Fig 16 shows Waddington again, this time as it was in 1945 after its runways had been laid some two years before.

In addition to the UK's major wartime operational airfields there were several hundred minor aerodromes of varying degrees of sophistication, few of which had many permanent buildings and which were never provided with paved runways. A typical example of such a minor facility was Coleby Grange (Fig 17).

Another category of minor airfield which accomodated operational units was the Advanced Landing Ground (ALG). The ALGs were laid out along the south coast of England and initially provided opportunities for tactical fighter squadrons to familiarise themselves with the techniques involved in mounting operations from the somewhat spartan facilities which they provided, and which could be expected to be available to them on the Continent after the invasion of Europe. They also served as the air bases from which most of the direct air support and fighter cover missions for the

Portable runway surfaces were not confined to north west Europe. This bomb-laden Kittyhawk IV, FX561/GA-?, of No 112 Sqn is seen taking-off from the PSP strip at Cutella in the spring of 1944. (RAF Museum P10932)

PSP even reached the Far East. This well-used but unidentified Mosquito PR 16 of No 684 Sqn is parked on a PSP dispersal at Kallang in 1946. (Sqn Ldr N J Haine)

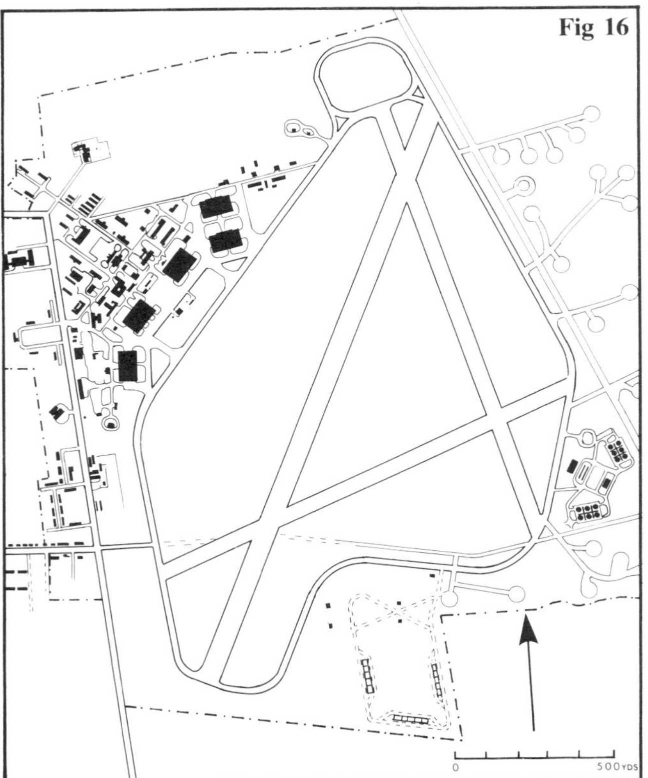

Waddington was closed in 1943 to permit the construction of paved runways and the demolition of the remaining buildings in the southern complex dating from 1917. The illustration shows the airfield as it appeared circa 1945. Further land had been acquired both to the north and south to cater for the runways, the largest of which measured some 2,000 yds while the other two were 1,500 yds long. A weapons storage and preparation facility had been built to the south of the public road (the B1178) which had formed the southern boundary of the airfield but which had now been permanently closed. Yet more land had been taken over to the east of the A15, where extensive aircraft dispersal facilities had been provided.

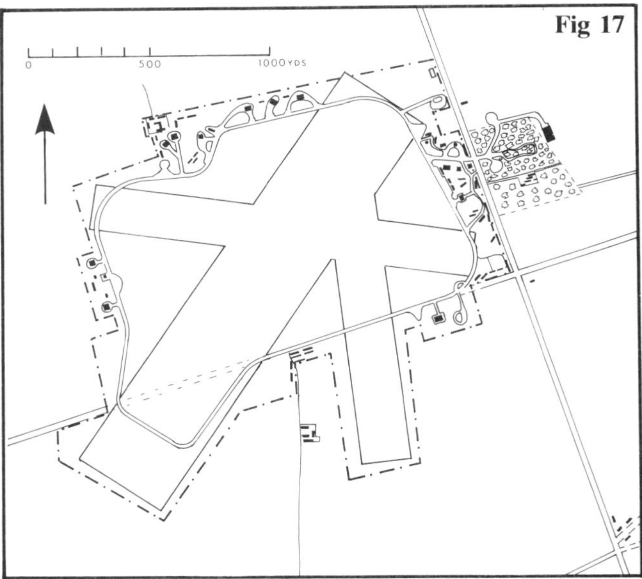

Coleby Grange, some 8 miles south of Lincoln, is shown as it was in 1945. Opened in 1940, the aerodrome had a 2,000 yd main runway and two others each providing 1,400 yd runs. All three were grass surfaced. The airfield layout necessitated the closure of the public road which crossed the southern part of the main runway and provided a section of the tarmac perimeter track. A few hardstandings were available with eight blister hangars. One larger hangar, a T1 type, was erected behind the wooded area to the east of the aerodrome, on the far side of the Lincoln to Sleaford (A15) road. A permanent control tower, or Watch Office, was built near the eastern perimeter track. Accommodation could be provided for nearly 1,400 personnel in either temporary huts or locally requisitioned billets. Coleby Grange was initially a fighter airfield serving as a satellite, first for Kirton-in-Lindsey, and then for Digby, and operated squadrons of Hurricanes, Defiants, Beaufighters and Mosquitos. Later it became a training airfield and supported a series of units until flying, apart from some elementary gliding, ceased in 1947. The Air Ministry retained title to the land, however, and it was brought back into use in 1958-63, being provided with launch pads for the three Thor IRBMs of No 142 Sqn as part of the Hemswell missile wing. The land was finally disposed of in 1965.

actual invasion were flown. Temporary runways were laid out in a variety of materials including Square Meshed Track (SMT), Somerfeld Track and Pierced Steel Planking (PSP), with the latter becoming predominant. After the invasion the ALGs rapidly became redundant and, with a few exceptions, their effective lives only spanned the period 1942-44. Deanland is illustrated at Fig 18 as an example of an ALG.

Once on the Continent the experience gained in building the temporary airfields* in the UK was put to good use and the engineers of the RAF's Airfield Construction Branch built a succession of ALGs, keeping pace with the Army's advance across North West Europe. Two examples are illustrated: Camilly (B 5) at Fig 19, an airfield built within the initial Normandy beachead, and Goch (B 100) at Fig 20, a similar airstrip constructed just inside Germany in the early spring of 1945. Not all airfields on the Continent had to be built from scratch, of course, and Brussels/Evere (B 56) is illustrated at Fig 21 as an example of an existing airfield in Belgium which was taken over by the liberating forces, repaired, developed and brought into use.

*AMO A1089 of 28 Oct 43 ruled that the term 'aerodrome' was thenceforth to be superseded by 'airfield', or 'airport' as appropriate. The same Order also ruled that 'aircraft' was to be used in place of 'aeroplane' (except for specific legal applications). The older terminology was well-established, however, and even today has not completely disappeared from use.

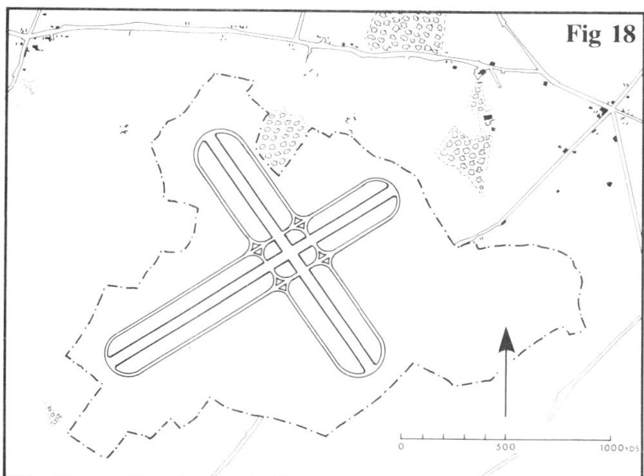

Deanland was built in the summer of 1943 by No 16 Airfield Construction Group of the Royal Engineers. The layout was that of a classic Advanced Landing Ground, with 1,600 yd and 1,400 yd Sommerfeld Track runways at 90° to each other, each flanked by parallel taxiways. Four small concrete hardstandings were also provided and four blister hangars were erected. Accommodation for personnel was tented, although a few huts were built in the woods to the east of the airfield later. Opened in Apr 44, Deanland operated various Spitfire squadrons up to and during the invasion of Europe, but by Nov 44 the airfield had closed again and before the end of the year the tracking had been lifted and the land had been derequisitioned.

PSP remained in widespread use after the war, indeed it is still used today. This Meteor PR 10, WB165, of No 81 Sqn is parked on PSP at Kuala Lumpur in 1956. (Sqn Ldr P J Mason)

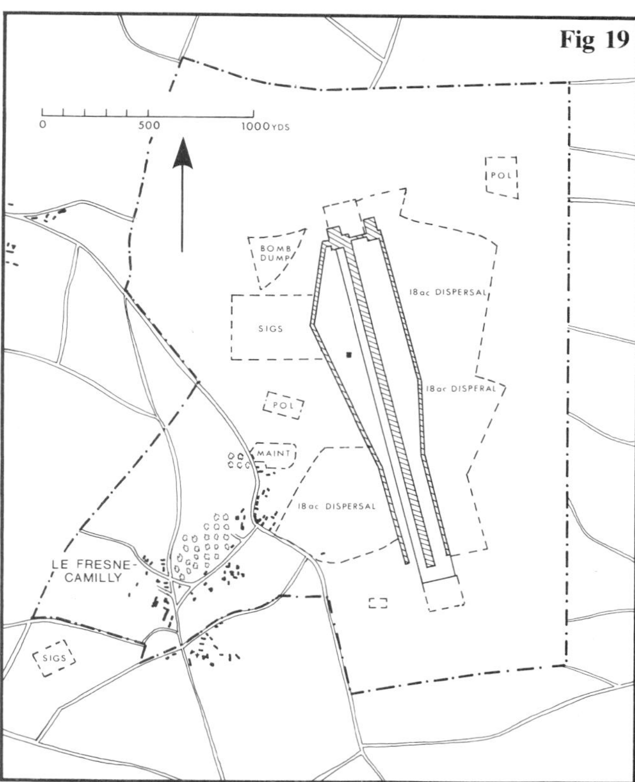

Typical of the temporary landing grounds created within the Normandy beachhead, B 5 was built by No 23 Airfield Construction Group and located 10 miles east of Bayeux and 8 miles north-west of Caen. Completed on 16 Jun 44 (just 10 days after the initial landings) the flying strip, which was of graded earth, measured 5,000 ft by 360 ft. A 120 ft wide runway of Square Meshed Track was provided, as were marshalling areas and 30 ft taxiways. All facilities were temporary; refuelling was by bowser and/or jerry cans, and accommodation was under canvas. The first Typhoons, No 174 Sqn, arrived on 17 Jun 44 and were joined subsequently by those of Nos 175, 184 and 245 Sqns to complete No 121 Wing. The Wing moved out on 28 Aug 44 and the strip was abandoned on 4 Sep 44. No trace now remains.

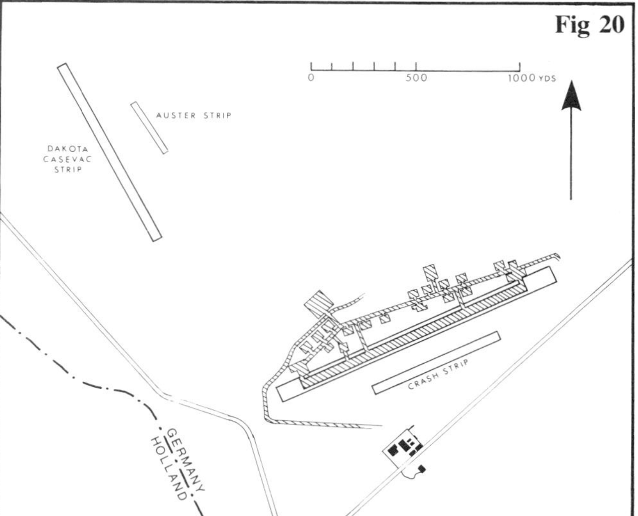

The first landing ground at Goch was a small strip used by the Austers of No 662 Sqn between 4 and 26 Mar 45. Not dissimilar to B 5 (see Fig 19), the main B 100 landing ground was located just across the German border from Holland, 8 miles south-east of the village of the same name and 3 miles south-west of Weeze. Laid out in Pierced Steel Planking on grass, the runway was 3,600 ft long with a grass-surfaced parallel crash strip. A mile to the north-west, near the Auster strip, was a 3,000 ft grass runway provided for casualty evacuation. As at B 5, supporting facilities were adequate but unsophisticated: accommodation was in tents; refuelling was by jerry can; and a mobile lighting array was available to permit night-flying. Capable of operating two Wings, the first aircraft of No 121 (Typhoon) Wing arrived at Goch on 20 Mar 45, being joined 10 days later by those of No 143 Canadian Wing. The Typhoons were replaced in mid-Apr by the Spitfires of No 127 Canadian Wing but they too had moved on by the end of the month. B 100 as such then fell into disuse but the site was later selected for development as one of the new permanent airfields to be constructed for the RAF in Germany. Opened, as Laarbruch, in 1954 it was initially used by reconnaissance aircraft and housed the Meteors and Canberras of Nos 69, 79 and 541 Sqns before the end of the year. Laarbruch remains one of the RAF's major facilities in Germany today (1987).

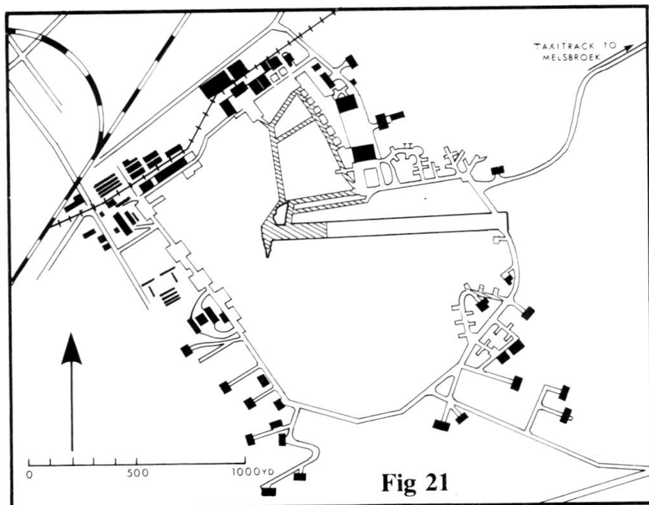

An example of an existing facility which was restored to use after its occupation, Evere was a pre-war commercial airport 4 miles north-east of Brussels. The original facilities had included a 2,700 ft concrete runway, extensive hangarage, a terminal building on the south-western perimeter track, a freight handling area to the north which was connected to the railway system via its own branch line, and a concrete perimeter track encircling the whole aerodrome. To improve the utility of the airfield after its capture in Sep 44, the runway was extended by 600 ft with Square Meshed Track and a network of taxiways and hardstandings was provided in the same material (shown hatched in the sketch). Used initially by Canadian Spitfire squadrons from 6 Sep, the airfield later became an Army resupply airhead and was used extensively by Dakotas plying back and forth between Belgium and the UK. The aerodrome continued to function as an airport after the war but was superseded by Brussels International at Zaventem. The old Evere site has now been redeveloped and accommodates, among other facilities, the NATO Headquarters complex.

In the Middle East a handful of permanent aerodromes, like Shaibah, Abu Sueir and Heliopolis (Fig 22) had been developed between the wars. The majority of combat missions flown in this theatre during the Second World War did not involve these sophisticated facilities, however. Most operations were conducted from temporary Landing Grounds (LG). These had natural surfaces, few, if any, buildings and usually lacked even a name, being identified only by a number. Some locations had been selected and surveyed before the war but as the campaigns in the Western Desert and Cyrenaica developed so LGs proliferated until there were well over 200 designated sites. Most of these were temporary but later on the original permanent aerodromes in Egypt also acquired numerical identities. There was little to distinguish most LGs and descriptive information was often sparse. An airfield directory dated 1942 provides, as an example, the following information on LG 75:

> Location: 3112N 2604E, approximately 4 mls north of the escarpment, 30 mls south south east of Sidi Barrani. Hard sand surface with some stone. Maximum runs 1,900 yds north/south and 1,200 yds east/west.

Burgh el Arab, later LG 39, was an early example of such a desert strip and is illustrated at Fig 23 as it was in late 1939.

View of a typical desert airstrip. This was part of No 260 Sqn's site at LG 109 in Nov 41. (M Gidman)

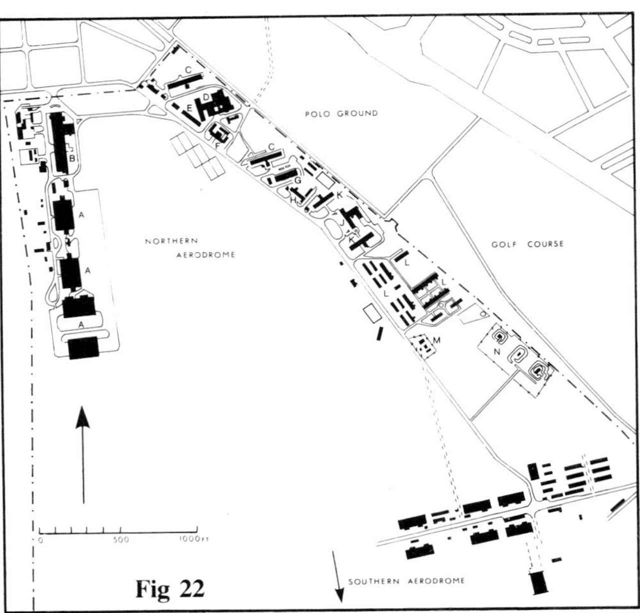

Heliopolis, located on the north eastern outskirts of Cairo, was first used by Nos 14 and 17 Sqns when an RFC presence was established in the Middle East in 1915. For most of the war it housed training units but it was then selected to be a permanent peacetime aerodrome. It is shown in the sketch as it was in the early 1930s after the construction of permanent buildings had begun. There were actually two adjacent aerodromes. At this time the southern site had seven aeroplane sheds, and associated technical and barrack accommodation, mostly temporary structures, housing No 208 Sqn. The northern aerodrome was undergoing extensive modernisation. The western side was flanked by four hangars (A), accommodating No 216 Sqn, and the MT Section (B). On the eastern side were: barrack blocks (C); the Airmen's Mess and Institute (D); a church (E); the Sergeants' Mess (F); Station Sick Quarters (G); Station Headquarters (H); the Officers' Mess (J) flanked by single officers' quarters (K); and quarters for married airmen (L). Further south were a petrol pumping installation (M) and a storage compound for bombs and pyrotechnics (N). The building programme continued throughout the 1930s and into the war years. The southern site was also redeveloped and extended. Additional hangars were erected, some to the south east of the area shown on the plan, and others replacing some of the original aeroplane sheds. During the Second World War, although Heliopolis accommodated a variety of units including No 168 MU and a number of combat squadrons, mostly on a transitory basis, its main function was to provide air communications facilities for the staffs of the various HQs located in Cairo. It was thus the base for the Heliopolis Communications Flight (later No 267 Sqn) and No 173 Sqn (later the Middle East Communications Squadron). After the war the airfield eventually passed to the control of the Royal Egyptian Air Force but, since it was steadily being engulfed by the expansion of the city, it saw little further use and is no longer an active aerodrome.

This picture, dated 8 Mar 29, is of Heliopolis; it shows the area in the south eastern corner of the sketch at Fig 22. The large aeroplane to the right of the picture is a DH 66 airliner of Imperial Airways, the smaller types include Fairey IIIFs and Bristol Fighters. (MOD H480)

One of the RAF's most important overseas bases between the wars was Hinaidi in Iraq. This picture was taken on 20 Mar 24 and shows the extensive technical and domestic accommodation flanking the aerodrome. Resident units at this time were: No 6 Sqn (Bristol Fighter); Nos 8 and 30 Sqns (DH 9A); and Nos 45 and 70 Sqns (Vernon). (RAF Museum P490)

Once the Axis forces had been defeated in North Africa, few of the temporary LGs had any further value and they were quickly reclaimed by the desert. The RAF concentrated on a chain of selected sites along the coast, often those which had originally been developed by the Italian colonists in the 1930s. These were progressively improved by the erection of permanent buildings and, eventually, the laying of paved runways. Fig 24 shows El Adem as it was in early 1944.

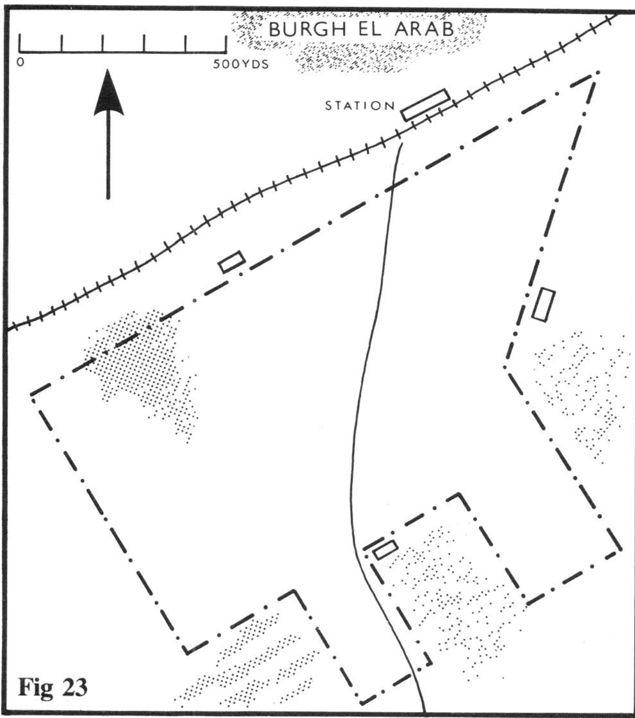

Burgh el Arab, located one mile south of the town of that name, alongside the coastal railway between Alexandria and Mersah Matruh, is illustrated as it was on 3 Oct 39, when it was the subject of a report submitted by No 80 Sqn. The overall dimensions of the aerodrome, which was bisected by a rough track, were approximately 1,000 yds by 800 yds. The surface was of natural clay which became unusable in wet weather. There was a depression in the ground in the north-western corner, some low sandhills in the south west and broken ground to the south and east. No night flying or technical facilities were available, apart from three water tanks on the boundaries of the airfield. The recommended approach was from the south to touch down on the eastern side of the landing ground. During the war Burgh el Arab acquired the designation LG 39 and underwent some development, being used quite extensively, particularly by maritime strike and reconnaissance units.

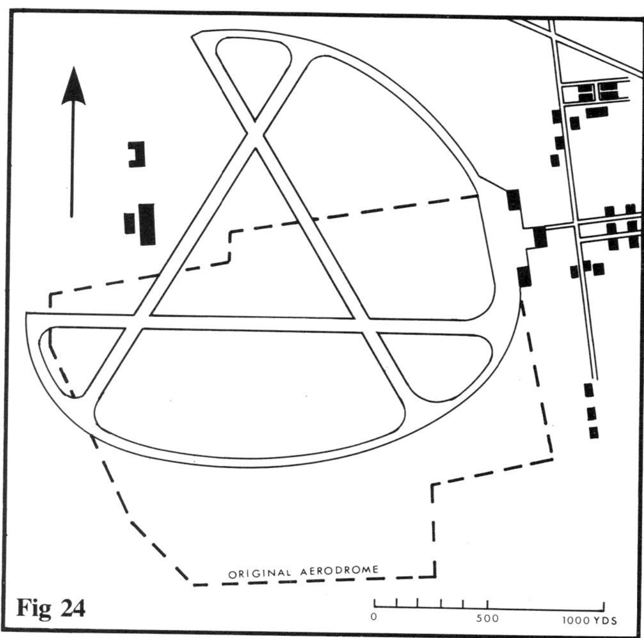

El Adem was initially selected as an airfield site by the Italian colonists in the late 1930s. During the Western Desert campaigns of 1940-42, its location just south of Tobruk on the Trigh Capuzzo, the ancient desert highway, endowed it with considerable tactical significance. It changed hands several times and was regarded as either an asset or a target by each side in turn, depending upon who was in possession. The site, which was well chosen, was a level area of rock with a shallow sand covering which provided, apart from sandstorms, an all-weather surface. After the fighting had receded to the west, El Adem was selected for further development and it is shown here as it was in late 1943. By this time the NNW/SSE and E/W runways were each 2,000 yds long and 50 yds wide and tracked. The third runway was a graded but unsurfaced strip. All three were interconnected by an all-weather taxi track and a tarmac apron was available in front of the three hangars. Extensive aircraft parking areas were also available on the natural surfaces to the south and west of the aerodrome. Facilities included a comprehensive range of workshops, a flarepath, a bulk fuel installation, barrack and transit accommodation and there was a tarmac road connecting the airfield to Tobruk. El Adem continued to undergo development after the war and it remained in use mainly as a staging post and as the host airfield for detachments using the adjacent desert air weapons ranges. The RAF finally withdrew in 1970, the last flight, an Argosy of No 70 Sqn, departing on 23 Mar 70.

The handful of rudimentary pre-war landing grounds in the Western Desert were used on an occasional basis by the squadrons based in Egypt for practice deployments. One such unit was No 33 Sqn. This picture of a 33 Sqn Gladiator I, L7619, was taken at Ismailia in 1939 and shows a locally devised camouflage scheme. (RAF Museum P8548)

In India and the Far East the situation was similar to that in North Africa, with the combat zone becoming concentrated in the North Eastern provinces of India, and airfields proliferated in Bengal, Assam and the Arakan. The regional climate and the terrain were even less hospitable than those of the North African desert and the monsoon season often turned airfields into inoperable quagmires for prolonged periods. To counter this, the laying of paved runways to provide all-weather strips was more prevalent than in most other war zones. An example of such a relatively sophisticated airfield, Baigachi, is illustrated at Fig 25. Not all airfields could offer these facilities, however, and descriptive information on the more primitive strips was confined to a brief specification similar to that provided for the desert LGs.

After 1945 the number of RAF airfields overseas dwindled rapidly and the RAF concentrated on a selection of permanent strategic bases which became steadily larger and more complex. Tengah, in Singapore, is illustrated at Fig 26 as an example of such a base, shortly before the British withdrew from most of their overseas commitments.

At home the number of airfields in use decreased slowly as the RAF contracted and, although many aerodromes were restored to agricultural use, title to the land was often retained by the Air Ministry (later Ministry of Defence) for many years. Some disused sites, Bardney, Caistor and Mepal for example, were reoccupied briefly in 1957-63 during the RAF's initial deployment of SAMs and IRBMs. Overall, however, the number of active airfield sites has continued to decrease and in recent years much real estate has been permanently disposed of. Some ex-RAF airfields have been taken over by the Army (Oakington, Waterbeach, Little Rissington, Bassingbourn and Kirton-in-Lindsey are examples) since their Expansion Pattern buildings and the

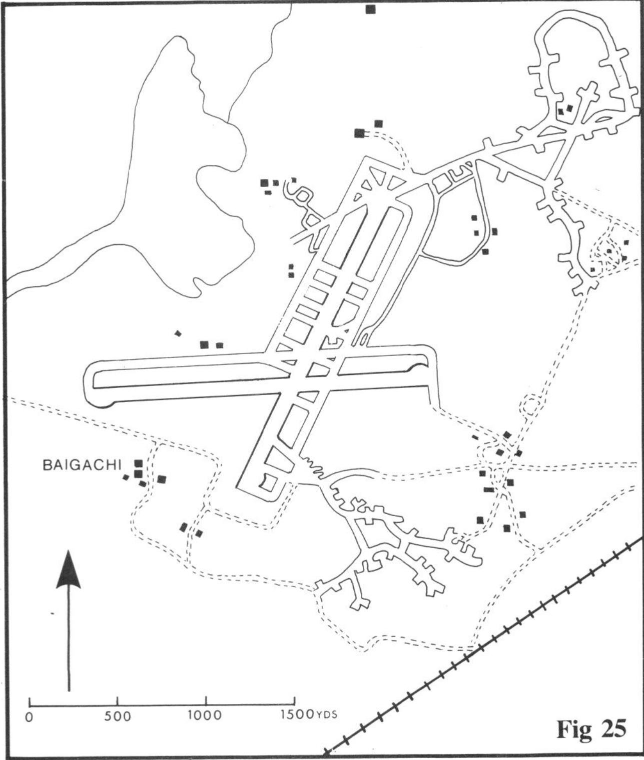

Baigachi, one of the all-weather airfields in the vicinity of Calcutta, was located alongside the Bengal-Assam Railway midway between that city and Jessore. The sketch shows the aerodrome as it was in late 1944. The E/W runway was 2,000 yds long by 50 yds wide and made of concrete, while the other was of the same size but tarmac surfaced. Full night flying facilities were available. Both runways were flanked on either side by 75 yd wide natural surfaced strips but these were prone to cracking in dry weather and became waterlogged during the rainy season. The taxi tracks were 50′ wide and led to well dispersed blast pens and hardstandings intended to accommodate a nominal 36 fighters and 64 heavy bombers. There were also eight hangarettes and sufficient storage for bombs and fuel to support two heavy bomber squadrons. Accommodation for over 1,800 men was available in three camp areas, each about 2 miles from the airfield, two to the east and the other to the west. Baigachi was used intensively throughout the war as a fighter aerodrome for the defence of Calcutta. After the war it passed to the jurisdiction of the Indian Air Force.

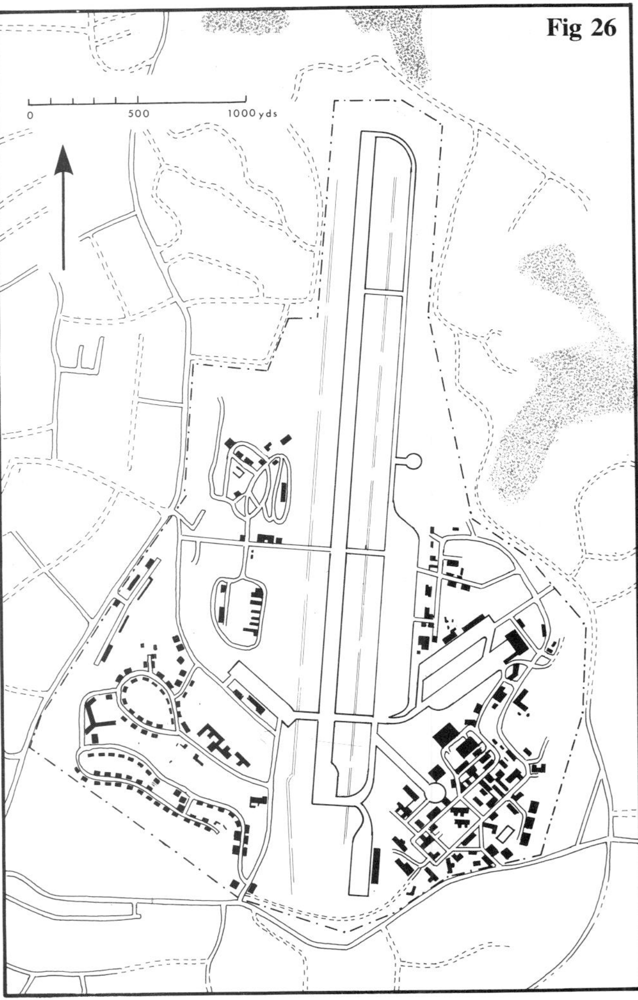

Construction of an aerodrome at Tengah was begun in 1937. The selected site was among a network of laterite roads and small villages on the western side of Singapore island with mangrove swamp to the north and east. By Sep 39, when Nos 34 and 62 Sqns (Blenheims) arrived from the UK to become the resident units, two hangars were available along with a grass airfield and some domestic and technical accommodation. In 1941 a 2,500 ft metalled runway running NW/SE was laid. In Feb 42 Tengah was occupied by the Japanese. While under Japanese jurisdiction prisoners were used, first to extend the existing runway by 300 yds, and then to construct a second strip which was 800 yds long and ran NE/SW. After intermittent use by fighters of the Japanese Army Air Force the RAF returned to Tengah in Sep 45. Japanese personnel were used to restore the now somewhat neglected airfield to use and in 1946-47 a third runway was constructed. This was 2,000 yds long and ran N/S. It was completed in time to support the station's twelve-year involvement in the Malayan Emergency, 'Operation Firedog'. Recurrent problems with the poor quality of the runways and flooding led to a major reconstruction of the airfield in 1959-61. A completely new, 9,100 ft long, N/S runway was laid. This was heavily cambered and flanked, 100 yds to each side, by parallel ditches to drain off the monsoon rains. At the same time large concrete dispersal areas (utilising parts of the old three runway layout), a new Operations Block and a modern Control Tower were built. The plan shows Tengah as it was in about 1962 after completion of the rebuilding programme. For a period during the Indonesian Confrontation of 1963-66 the airfield was the busiest in the RAF but thereafter a gradual withdrawal began. By 1972 the airfield had been transferred to the Singapore Air Defence Command and the only remaining RAF unit was No 103 Sqn (Wessex). In 1975 the last RAF element left and Tengah became, and remains, the main base for the combat aircraft of the newly constituted Republic of Singapore Air Force.

adjacent areas of open space for training represented a significant improvement over the Nissen-hutted camps or Victorian barracks in which some units had previously been accommodated.

Those operational airfields which the RAF continued to occupy underwent further development. New purpose-built buildings were erected, where necessary, to house specialist facilities associated with the storage or maintenance of various types of advanced avionic equipment or weapons as these were introduced into service. Radar became an essential tool, for all-weather operation and for air traffic control, and most airfields soon sprouted a prominent rotating aerial array. The most obvious changes occurred in the 1950s. These were: the large-scale construction of on-base married accommodation, so that each station acquired an estate of red brick 'council houses'; and the superimposing onto the old three-runway pattern of a single major pavement whose length, of about 3,000 yds, was basically tailored to the requirements of the new V-bombers. Waddington is illustrated once again, at Fig 27, this time as it appeared in about 1960 as a fully-developed main operating base for a three squadron Wing of Vulcans.

Recognition of the inherent vulnerability of airfields has led to the latest developments in the external appearance of RAF airfields. This phase began in the late 1970s with a 'tone down' programme aimed at reducing the 'visual signature' of airfields, especially as seen from the air. This was most apparent in the liberal application of green paint to buildings in a successful attempt to make them blend with their surroundings. This was followed by the 'hardening' of essential facilities leading to another spate of construction work as Hardened Aircraft Shelters (HAS) were built on many of the major airfields operating combat aircraft.

The ultimate solution to the problem of airfield vulnerability is, of course, not to use airfields at all. The development of practical V/STOL technology made this a possibility which was realised with the introduction into service of the Harrier. In a sense this completed the cycle of airfield evolution, since the earliest type of aerodrome described in this Appendix would also provide perfectly adequate facilities from which to fly a modern V/STOL combat aircraft.

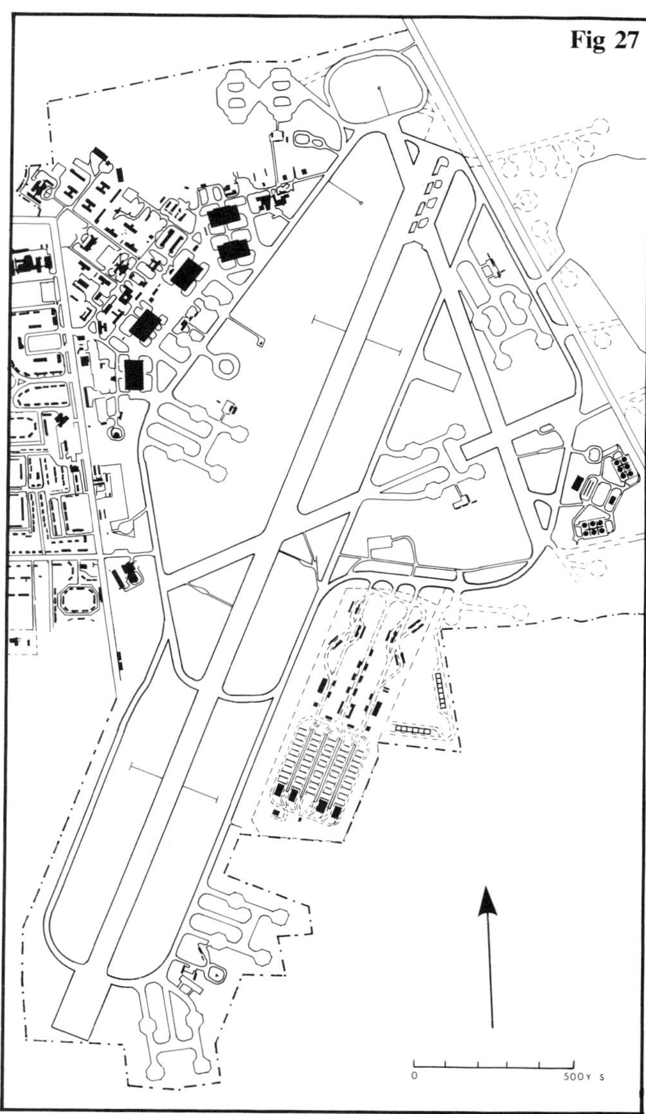

Waddington was closed again in 1953 and the aerodrome underwent a further major redevelopment, this time to transform it into a main base for the operation of V-Bombers. Yet more land was acquired to the south to permit the extension of the main runway to 9,000′. The conventional weapons storage area was redeveloped and extensive aircraft parking facilities were provided within the camp perimeter, those to the east of the A15 becoming redundant. Further support facilities were built, including an electronics servicing building, an Operations Block and a new control tower. A major building programme was also undertaken on the further enlarged domestic area to the west of the technical site to provide several hundred married quarters. The sketch shows the aerodrome as it appeared with all this work complete, circa 1960.

A Harrier GR 3, XV792, of No 3 Sqn approaching to land at a field strip in Germany. Note the transportable 'runway' and the aircraft hidden under camouflage netting in the background. The unique V/STOL capabilities of the Harrier makes any piece of reasonably level firm ground a potential airfield and restores a degree of operational flexibility which had been lost through the evolution of successive generations of ever faster and heavier conventional aircraft. (British Aerospace, Kingston)

A Tornado GR 1 of No 27 Sqn parked in front of a Hardened Aircraft Shelter at RAF Marham in 1986. (British Aerospace, Warton)

Appendix 11

Location Maps

The maps in this Appendix indicate the whereabouts of all the locations which appear in the main text, and which are cross-referred in Appendix 8.

The maps are of various scales and projections and have been selected as the best compromises between accuracy and the extent of the geographical areas represented. Thus, where airfields are/were relatively numerous, as in the UK and North Western Europe, larger scales have been used to permit the accurate representation of a location relative to other airfields, towns and lines of communication. Conversely, where the distribution of significant locations was less dense, as for instance in Southern Africa, a small scale has been considered adequate. However, where necessary, expanded insets have been used in such cases to illustrate areas where concentrations of facilities occurred in an otherwise sparsely used region.

The maps are generally orientated with North at the top. Where this is not the case an arrow symbol has been provided to indicate the direction of True North as an aid to orientation. The numbers running around the edges of the maps are degrees of latitude and longitude. The location symbols are the same in every case and are intended only to indicate the whereabouts of a facility, whether it is an aerodrome or a transit camp. They should not be interpreted as indicating the physical extent of the airfield concerned.

No attempt has been made to illustrate the location of every airfield, only, with a very few additions, those named in the main text, that is, those which have accommodated a significant element of a squadron at some time. As a result many aerodromes are not represented at all. In the UK for instance, neither Cranwell nor Little Rissington appear, and in North Africa fewer than half of the numbered Landing Grounds are indicated. An exception to this occurs where there were concentrations of airfields, all having the same generic name, for instance those at Gerbini in Sicily, the Foggia airfields in Italy, and various complexes in North Africa like those at Bir Dufan, Martuba and Gardabia.

Although basic lines of communication have been shown on the larger scale maps, these should be treated with some circumspection since many of the maps cover a lengthy period of social evolution. This is particularly significant in the UK where single maps serve to represent some 80 years of historical development. The actual period illustrated is approximately 1950, thus the modern motorway network is not shown and the railways are 'pre-Beeching'.

The areas covered by the maps are as follows:

1 The Orkney and Shetland Islands
2 Northern Scotland
3 Ireland
4 Southern Scotland and Northern England
5 Wales and South Western England
6 The Midlands
7 East Anglia, the Wash and the Lincolnshire Wolds
8 Central Southern England
9 London and South Eastern England
10 France, Belgium and Germany, 1914-20
11 The Western Front — France and Belgium, 1914-19
12 France, 1940
13 Normandy and Northern France, 1944-45
14 Belgium, Holland and (West) Germany, 1944 to date
15 Germany, 1945 and after
16 Scandinavia
17 Iceland
18 The Nile Delta and the Suez Canal
19 The Western Desert
20 Cyrenaica
21 Libya (Sirte and Tripolitania)
22 Tunisia (Gabes)
23 Tunisia
24 Algeria
25 Sicily
26 Cyprus
27 Malta
28 Sardinia
29 Corsica
30 Southern Italy
31 Central Italy
32 Northern Italy
33 South Eastern France, 1944-45
34 Eastern Europe, Jugoslavia and the Adriatic Sea
35 Greece, Macedonia and Turkey
36 The Levant — Syria and Palestine
37 The Nile and the Red Sea
38 The Horn of Africa
39 Tanganikya
40 Northern Africa
41 Southern Africa
42 Iran (Persia) and Iraq (Mesopotamia)
43 The Persian Gulf
44 Northern India
45 Southern India and Ceylon
46 North Eastern India (Assam, Bengal, the Arakan) and Burma
47 South East Asia, Borneo, Sumatra
48 Malaya
49 Java
50 Australia
51 The Atlantic Ocean
52 South Russia
53 The Indian and Pacific Oceans

This appendix only shows the locations of sites recognised to be airfields or landing grounds of some sort. To cover every site ever used by aeroplanes would be a task of almost infinite length. This Auster III of No 656 Sqn, for instance was quite happy to use the beach at Akyab as an impromptu aerodrome. (Museum of Army Flying)

SHETLANDS

ORKNEYS

Naut Mls

0 5 10 20 30

Map 1

Map 1 – Orkney and Shetland Islands

1 Sullom Voe
2 Sumburgh
3 Skaebrae
4 Hatston
5 Grimsetter
6 Scapa Flow

Sumburgh was a familiar haunt of Coastal Command's maritime strike squadrons, of which No 248 Sqn was one. This is a Beaufighter VIC, JL447, which flew with No 248 Sqn between 23 Nov 42 and 30 Jan 43. (RAF Museum P7179)

When No 46 Sqn was deployed to Norway its Hurricanes were ferried there by HMS Glorious, *which was obliged to return to Scapa Flow before heading north again and successfully flying-off the aircraft on 26 May 40. When they withdrew, on 7/8 Jun 40, No 46 Sqn flew its thirteen Hurricanes back to the ship and all successfully landed-on. Intercepted en route Scapa Flow, and unable to operate its own aircraft because of the RAF machines on the deck, HMS* Glorious *and her two escorts were sunk by the* Scharnhorst *and* Gneisenau; *only forty men, two of them from No 46 Sqn, survived. The photograph shows one of No 46 Sqn's Hurricanes being loaded aboard in the UK.* (RAF Museum P9372)

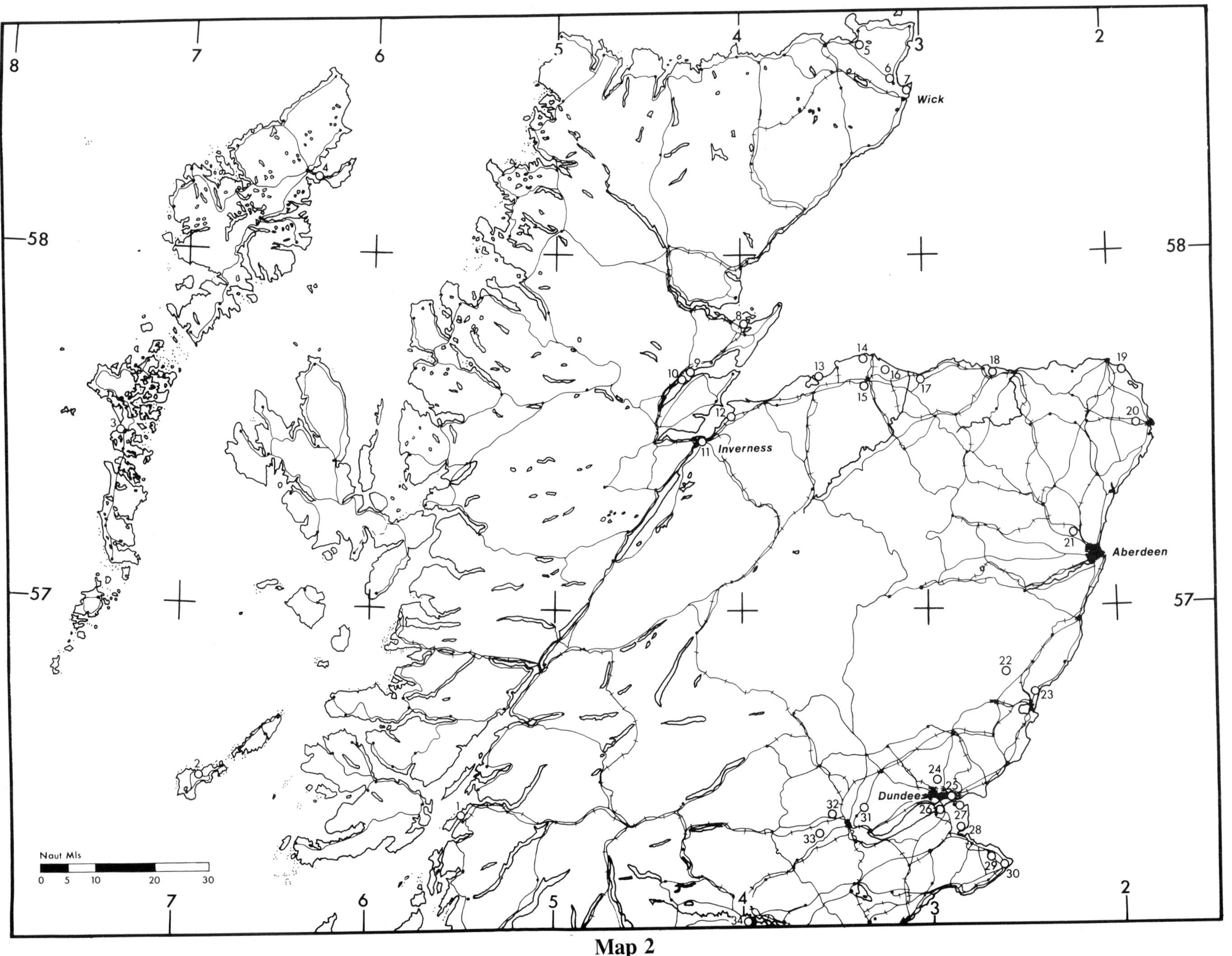

Map 2

Map 2 – Northern Scotland

1 Oban
2 Tiree
3 Benbecula
4 Stornoway
5 Castletown
6 Skitten
7 Wick
8 Tain
9 Invergordon/Alness
10 Evanton
11 Longman
12 Dalcross
13 Kinloss
14 Lossiemouth
15 Elgin/Bogs O'Mayne
16 Milltown
17 Dallachy
18 Banff
19 Fraserburgh
20 Peterhead
21 Dyce
22 Edzell
23 Montrose
24 Tealing
25 Dundee
26 Woodhaven
27 Tayport
28 Leuchars
29 Dunino
30 Crail
31 Perth/Scone
32 Methven
33 Findo Gask
34 Stirling/Raploch

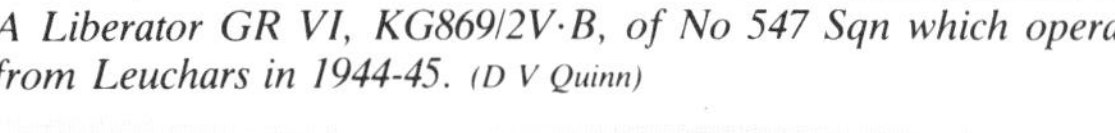
A Liberator GR VI, KG869/2V·B, of No 547 Sqn which operated from Leuchars in 1944-45. (D V Quinn)

No 151 Sqn has strong Scottish affiliations and uses the Cross of St Andrew as its insignia: it can be seen here on a Meteor NF 11, WM 245, which the squadron flew from Leuchars in 1953-55. (J D R Rawlings)

Following World War II No 120 Sqn's numberplate was selected for preservation in recognition of the unit's outstanding operational record – sixteen U-Boats destroyed. This is one of the squadron's Kinloss-based Shackleton MR 3s, WR981. (Air Britain M5329)

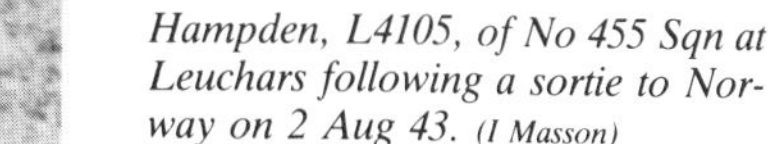
Hampden, L4105, of No 455 Sqn at Leuchars following a sortie to Norway on 2 Aug 43. (I Masson)

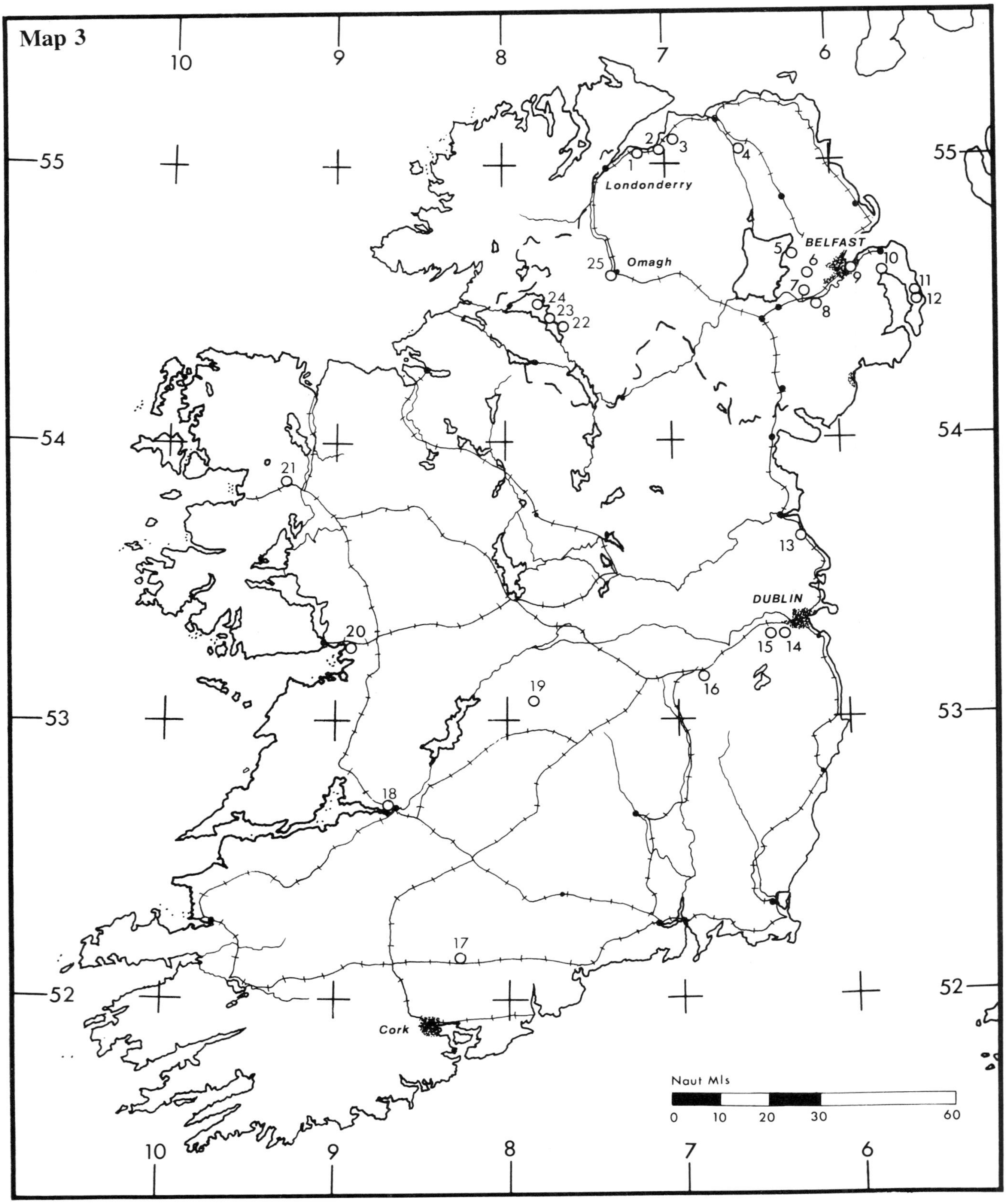

Map 3

Map 3 – Ireland

1 Eglinton
2 Ballykelly
3 Limavady
4 Mullaghmore
5 Aldergrove
6 Nutts Corner
7 Maghaberry
8 Long Kesh
9 Sydenham
10 Newtownards
11 Ballyhalbert
12 Kirkistown
13 Gormanston
14 Tallaght
15 Baldonnel
16 The Curragh
17 Fermoy
18 Limerick
19 Birr
20 Oranmore
21 Castlebar
22 St Angelo
23 Killadeas
24 Castle Archdale/Lough Erne
25 Omagh

A Sunderland III, EK591/2·U, of No 422 Sqn alighting at Castle Archdale on 15 Jul 44. (RCAF)

Shackleton MR 1, VP287, of No 269 Sqn making a low run at Ballykelly in the 1950s. (Author's collection)

No 118 Sqn retained its fighter-style markings when it reformed as a utility helicopter squadron at Aldergrove in 1959. These can be seen on this Sycamore HC 14, XG506. (via R C Sturtivant)

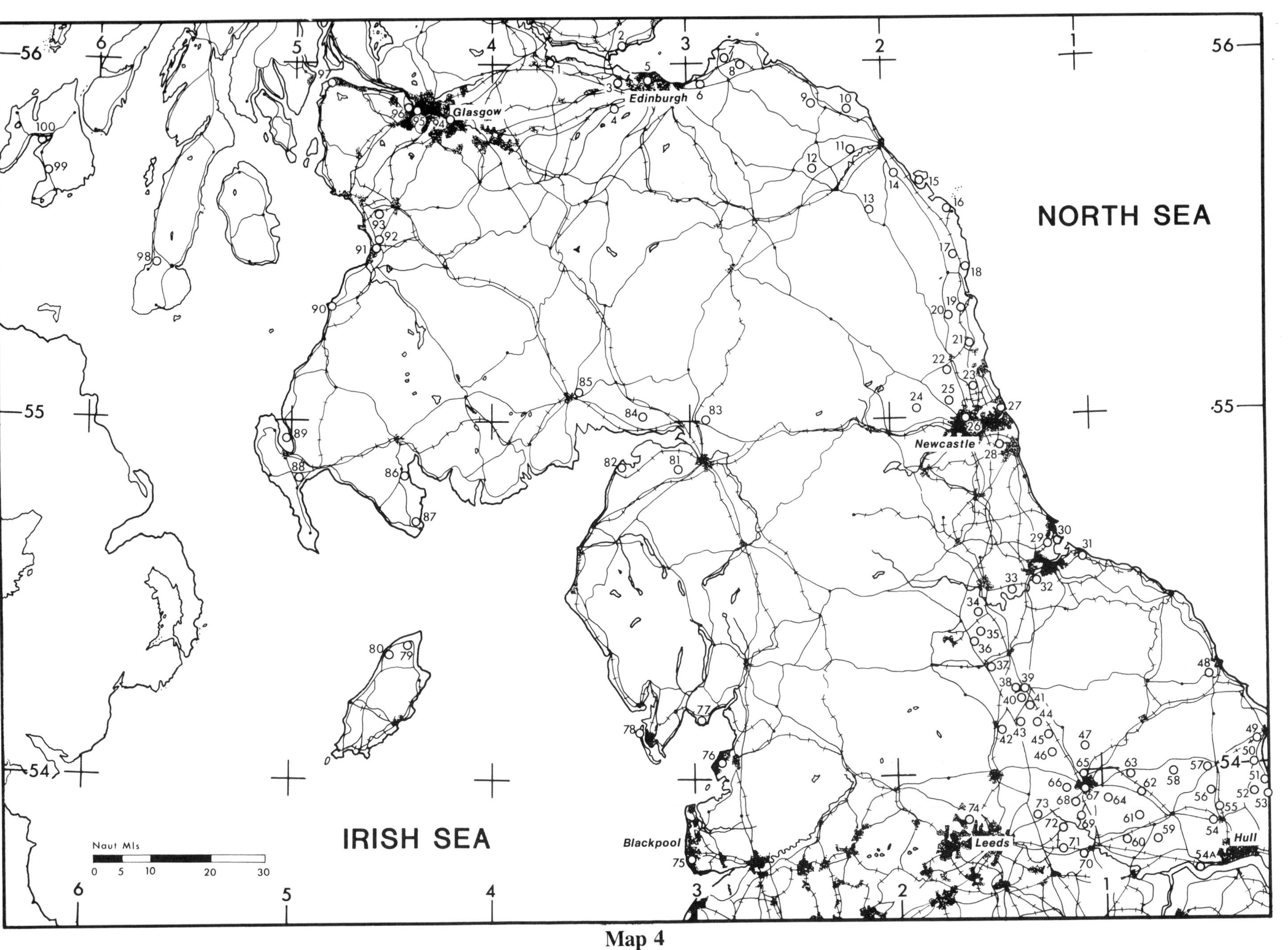
NORTH SEA
IRISH SEA
Edinburgh
Glasgow
Newcastle
Leeds
Hull
Blackpool
Naut Mls

Map 4

Map 4 – Northern England and Southern Scotland

1 Grangemouth
2 Donibristle
3 Turnhouse
4 Kirknewton
5 Edinburgh
6 Macmerry/Tranent/Penston
7 Drem/Gullane
8 East Fortune
9 Whiteburn
10 Cairncross
11 Winfield
12 Charterhall
13 Milfield
14 New Haggerston
15 Holy Island
16 Seahouses/Elford
17 Rennington
18 Boulmer
19 Acklington
20 Eshott
21 Ashington
22 Morpeth
23 Cramlington
24 Ouston
25 Woolsington
26 Newcastle
27 Tynemouth
28 Usworth/Hylton
29 West Hartlepool/Greatham
30 Seaton Carew
31 Redcar
32 Thornaby
33 Middleton St George
34 Croft
35 Scorton
36 Catterick
37 Leeming
38 Skipton-on-Swale
39 Thirsk
40 Topcliffe
41 Dalton
42 Ripon
43 Dishforth
44 Helperby
45 Tholthorpe
46 Linton-on-Ouse
47 East Moor
48 West Ayton
49 Carnaby
50 Lisset
51 Atwick
52 Catfoss
53 Hornsea
54 Beverley
54A Brough
55 Leconfield
56 Hutton Cranswick
57 Driffield
58 Huggate
59 Holme-on-Spalding Moor
60 Breighton
61 Melbourne
62 Pocklington
63 Full Sutton
64 Elvington
65 York/Clifton/ Rawcliffe
66 Rufforth
67 The Knavesmire
68 Copmanthorpe
69 Acaster Malbis
70 Burn
71 Sherburn-in-Elmet
72 Church Fenton
73 Tadcaster/Bramham Moor
74 Yeadon
75 Squires Gate
76 Morecombe
77 Cark
78 Barrow-in-Furness
79 Andreas
80 Jurby
81 Great Orton
82 Silloth
83 Longtown
84 Annan
85 Dumfries
86 Wigtown
87 Kidsdale
88 Luce Bay/West Freugh
89 Stranraer/Wig Bay
90 Turnberry
91 Ayr
92 Prestwick
93 Dundonald
94 Glasgow
95 Renfrew
96 Abbotsinch
97 Gourock
98 Machrihanish
99 Port Ellen/Islay
100 Bowmore

This BE 12, 6478, served with No 76 Sqn on Home Defence duties in 1917. The squadron flew from a variety of landing grounds in Yorkshire. (J M Bruce/G S Leslie collection)

The first Auxiliary Squadron to form, in Sep 25, was No 602 Sqn. This is one of the squadron's Abbotsinch-based Harts, K3858, in about 1935. (RAF Museum P9430)

Catfoss was used for Armament Practice Camps between the wars. This Sidestrand III, J9178, of No 101 Sqn is seen at Catfoss in the early 1930s. (Museum of Army Flying)

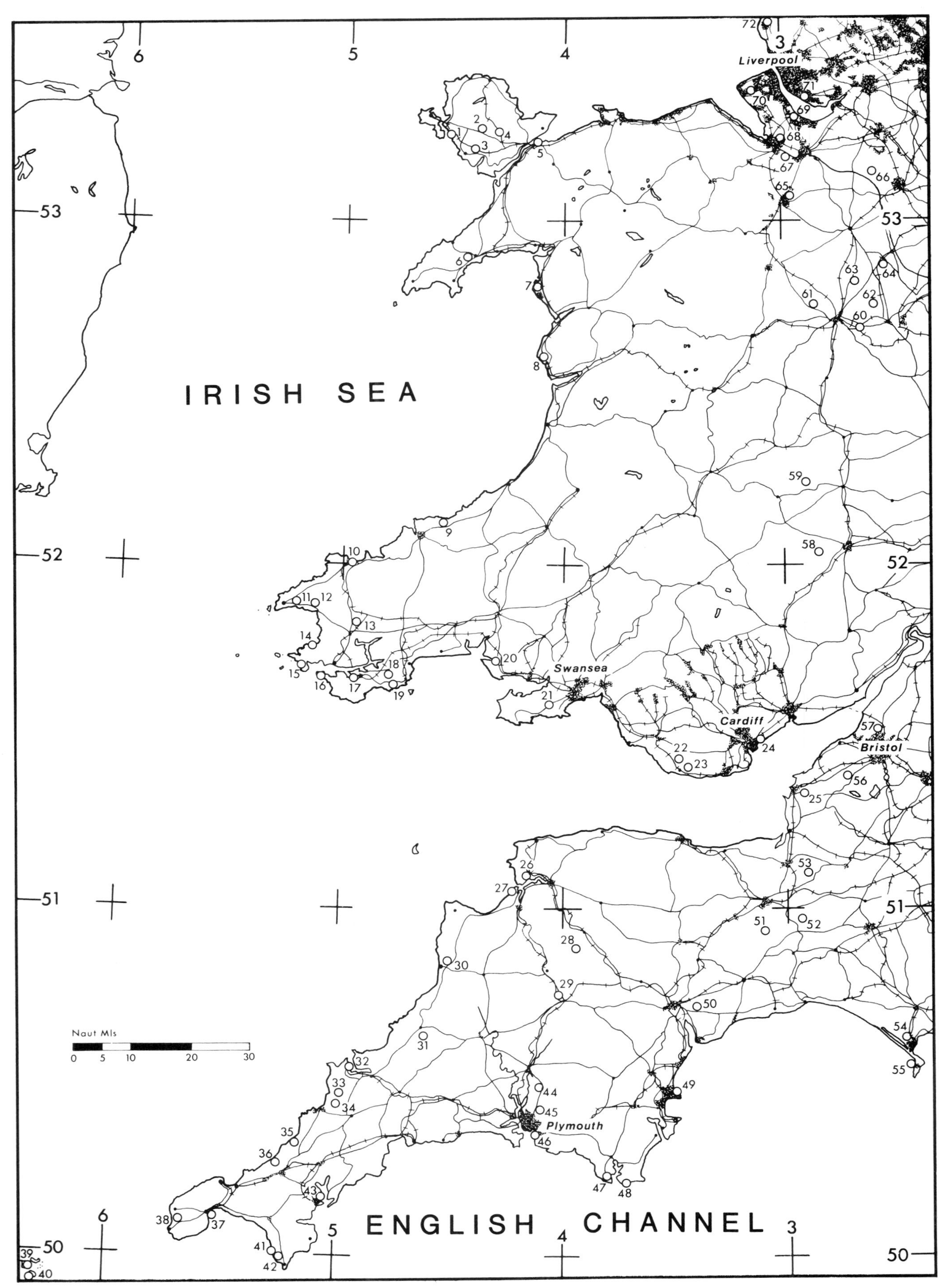
Liverpool
IRISH SEA
Swansea
Cardiff
Bristol
Plymouth
ENGLISH CHANNEL
Naut Mls
0 5 10 20 30

Map 5

Map 5 – Wales and South West England

1 Valley
2 Mona
3 Bodorgan
4 Llangefni
5 Bangor
6 Penrhos
7 Llanbedr
8 Towyn
9 Aberporth
10 Fishguard
11 St Davids
12 Brawdy
13 Haverfordwest
14 Talbenny
15 Dale
16 Angle
17 Pembroke Dock
18 Carew Cheriton/Pembroke
19 Manorbier
20 Pembrey
21 Fairwood Common
22 Llandow
23 St Athan
24 Pengam Moors
25 Weston-super-Mare
26 Chivenor
27 Westward Ho!
28 Winkleigh
29 Okehampton
30 Cleave
31 Davidstow Moor
32 Padstow
33 St Eval
34 St Mawgan/Treblezue
35 Perranporth
36 Portreath
37 Newlyn
38 St Just
39 Trescoe
40 St Marys
41 Mullion
42 Predannack
43 Falmouth
44 Harrowbeer
45 Roborough
46 Cattewater/Mount Batten
47 Bolt Head
48 Prawle Point
49 Torquay
50 Exeter
51 Culmhead/Church Stanton
52 Merryfield
53 Weston Zoyland
54 Chickerall
55 Portland
56 Lulsgate
57 Filton
58 Madley
59 Shobdon
60 Atcham
61 Montford Bridge
62 High Ercall
63 Shawbury
64 Ternhill
65 Wrexham
66 Poulton
67 Hawarden
68 Sealand/Shotwick
69 Hooton Park
70 West Kirby
71 Speke
72 Woodvale

A Felixstowe F.3, N4415, of No 234 Sqn at Trescoe in 1918. (RAF Museum P10174)

A Beaufighter IF, X7583/WM·E, of No 68 Sqn which was based at High Ercall in 1941 for the defence of the West Midlands. (RAF Museum P12519)

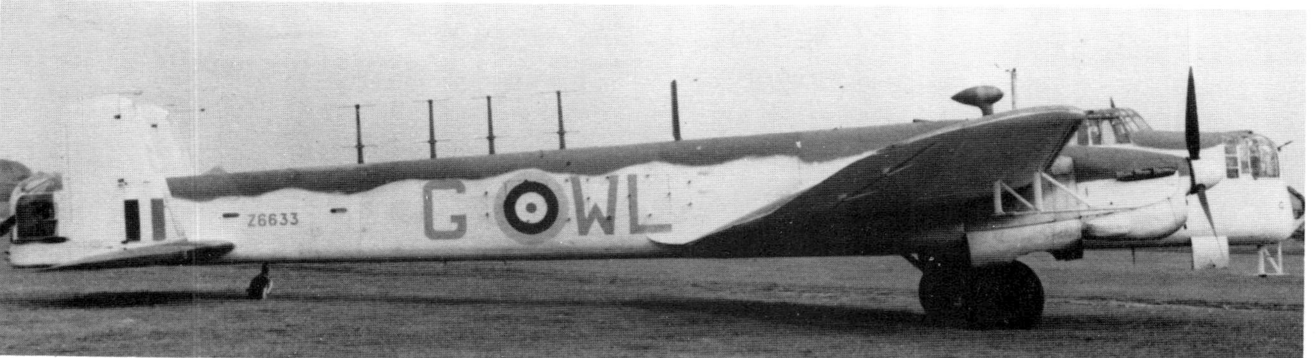

A Whitley VII, Z6633/WL·G, of No 612 Sqn who were based at Davidstow Moor, Chivenor and St Eval (among other places) while operating this type. (RAF Museum P9561)

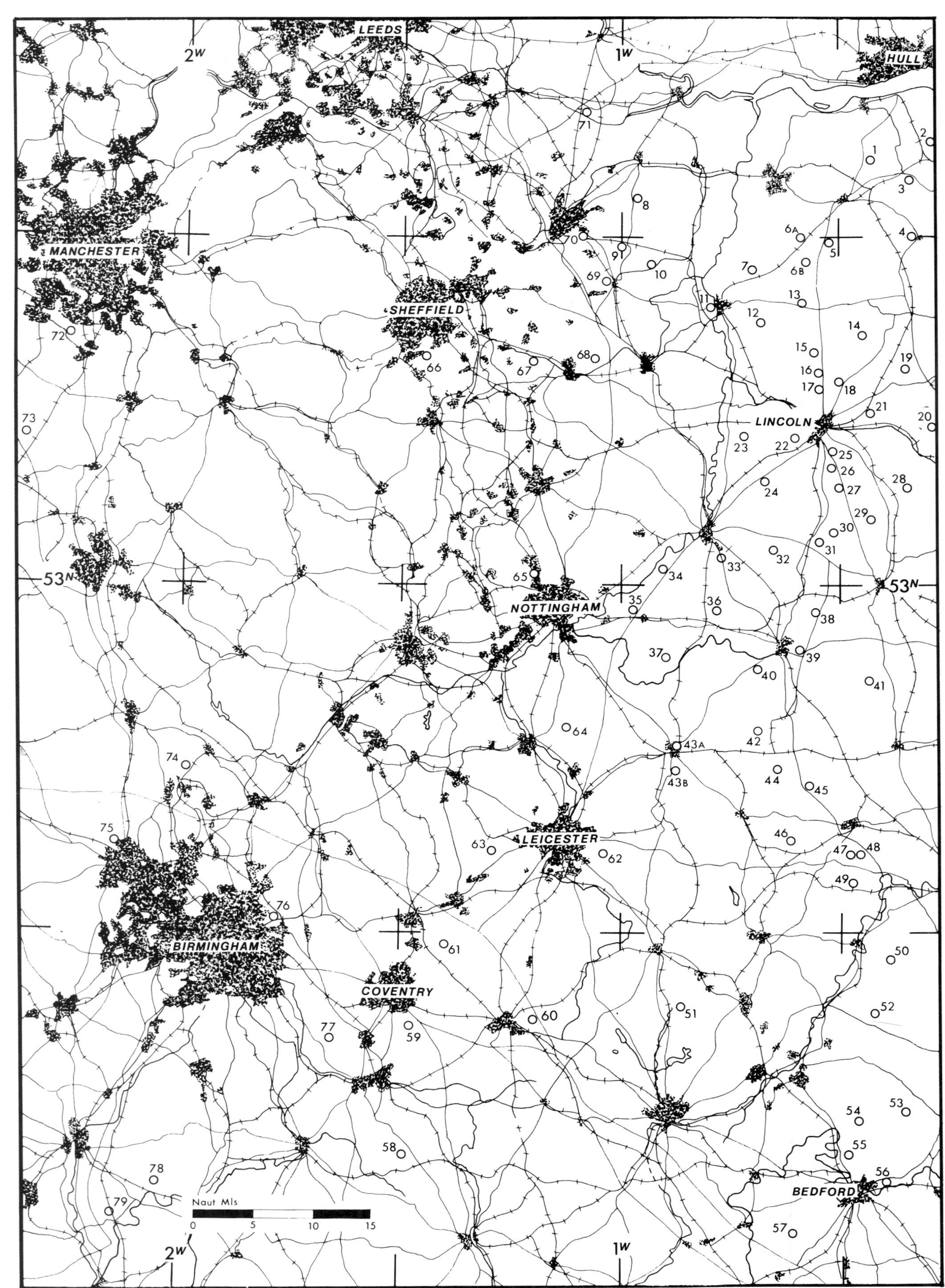
LEEDS
HULL
MANCHESTER
SHEFFIELD
LINCOLN
NOTTINGHAM
LEICESTER
BIRMINGHAM
COVENTRY
BEDFORD
2W
1W
53N
Naut Mls
0
5
10
15
1
2
3
4
5
6A
6B
7
8
9
10
11
12
13
14
15
16
17
18
19
20
21
22
23
24
25
26
27
28
29
30
31
32
33
34
35
36
37
38
39
40
41
42
43A
43B
44
45
46
47
48
49
50
51
52
53
54
55
56
57
58
59
60
61
62
63
64
65
66
67
68
69
70
71
72
73
74
75
76
77
78
79

Map 6

Map 6 – The Midlands

1 Elsham/Elsham Wolds
2 North Killingholme
3 Kirmington
4 Caistor
5 Hibaldstow
6A Kirton-in-Lindsey (WW I)
6B Kirton-in-Lindsey (WW II)
7 Blyton
8 Lindholme/Hatfield Woodhouse
9 Finningley
10 Misson
11 Gainsborough
12 Sturgate
13 Hemswell/Harpswell
14 Faldingworth
15 Ingham
16 Scampton
17 South Carlton
18 Dunholme Lodge
19 Wickenby
20 Bardney
21 Fiskerton
22 Skellingthorpe
23 Wigsley
24 Swinderby
25 Bracebridge Heath
26 Waddington
27 Coleby Grange
28 Metheringham
29 Digby/Scopwick
30 Wellingore
31 Leadenham
32 Fulbeck
33 Balderton
34 Syerston
35 Newton
36 Bottesford
37 Langar
38 Barkston Heath
39 Spittlegate/Grantham
40 Harlaxton
41 Folkingham
42 Buckminster
43A Melton Mowbray (WW I)
43B Melton Mowbray (WW II)
44 Cottesmore
45 Woolfox Lodge
46 North Luffenham
47 Collyweston
48 Wittering/Stamford
49 Kingscliffe
50 Polebrook
51 Harrington
52 Old Weston/ Molesworth
53 Little Staughton
54 Thurleigh
55 Twinwood Farm
56 Goldington
57 Cranfield
58 Gaydon
59 Baginton
60 Lilbourne
61 Bramcote
62 Leicester East
63 Desford
64 Wymeswold
65 Hucknall
66 Coal Aston
67 Netherthorpe
68 Worksop
69 Firbeck
70 Doncaster
71 Snaith
72 Ringway
73 Cranage
74 Hednesford
75 Wolverhampton
76 Castle Bromwich
77 Honiley
78 Pershore
79 Defford

Among the rather motley collection of aircraft flown by No 271 Sqn when it reformed at Doncaster in 1940 were three HP 42 airliners. This one, G-AAUC 'Horsa', is seen in full warpaint after it had been impressed as AS981. Its military career was relatively brief, since it was written-off in a forced landing on 7 Aug 40. (RAF Museum P7384)

Hampden, L4099/JW·J, of No 44 Sqn at Waddington in 1939 prior to adoption of the unit's wartime code, KM. L4099 was finally lost to a Bf 109 on a sortie to Norway on 12 Apr 40. (H Moyle)

Apart from a short period while it was closed for the laying of runways Waddington was a Main Force bomber base within No 5 Gp throughout the war. In 1943-45 it was home to Australian units; this Lancaster belonged to No 467 Sqn. (RAF Waddington archives)

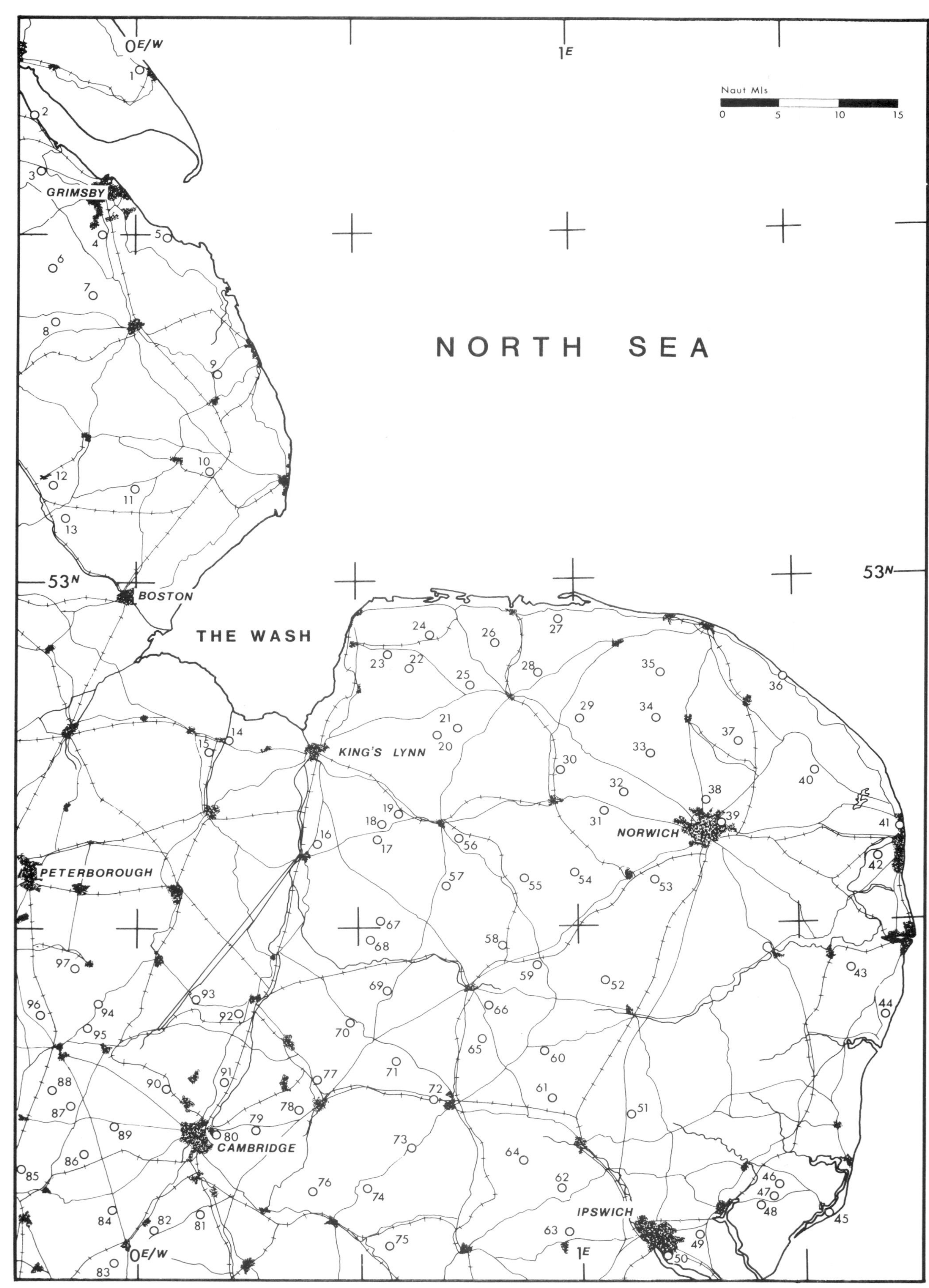
NORTH SEA
THE WASH
GRIMSBY
BOSTON
KING'S LYNN
NORWICH
PETERBOROUGH
CAMBRIDGE
IPSWICH
53N
0E/W
1E
Naut Mls
0
5
10
15

Map 7

Map 7 – East Anglia, the Wash & the Lincolnshire Wolds

1 Owthorne
2 Killingholme
3 Greenland Top
4 Waltham
5 North Coates
6 Binbrook
7 Kelstern
8 Ludford Magna
9 Strubby
10 Spilsby
11 East Kirkby
12 Woodhall Spa
13 Coningsby
14 Sutton Bridge
15 Tydd St Mary
16 Downham Market
17 Barton Bendish
18 Marham
19 Narborough
20 Great Massingham
21 West Raynham
22 Bircham Newton
23 Sedgeford
24 Docking
25 Sculthorpe
26 North Creake
27 Langham
28 Little Snoring
29 Foulsham
30 Swanton Morley
31 Mattishall
32 Attlebridge
33 Swannington
34 Oulton
35 Matlask
36 Bacton
37 Coltishall
38 Horsham St Faith
39 Norwich/Mousehold Heath
40 Ludham
41 Great Yarmouth
42 Burgh Castle
43 Beccles
44 Covehithe
45 Orfordness
46 Bentwaters
47 Butley
48 Woodbridge
49 Martlesham Heath
50 Ipswich
51 Mendlesham
52 Fersfield
53 Hethel
54 Hingham
55 Watton
56 North Pickenham
57 Bodney
58 East Wretham
59 Harling Road
60 Shepherds Grove
61 Elmswell
62 Wattisham
63 Hadleigh
64 Rattlesden
65 Honington
66 Thetford
67 Methwold
68 Feltwell
69 Lakenheath
70 Mildenhall
71 Tuddenham
72 Westley/Bury St Edmunds
73 Chedburgh
74 Stradishall
75 Ridgewell
76 West Wickham/ Wratting Common
77 Snailwell
78 Newmarket
79 Bottisham
80 Cambridge/Teversham
81 Duxford
82 Fowlmere
83 Therfield
84 Bassingbourn
85 Tempsford
86 Gransden Lodge
87 Yelling
88 Graveley
89 Bourn
90 Oakington
91 Waterbeach
92 Witchford
93 Mepal
94 Warboys
95 Wyton
96 Alconbury
97 Upwood

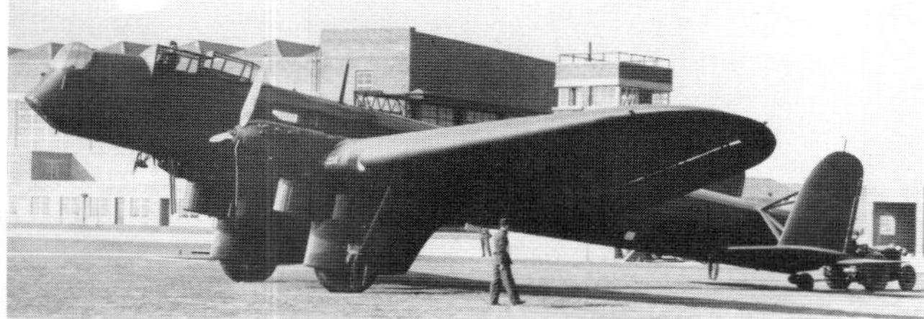

The Hendon, the first of the monoplane heavy bombers entered service with No 38 Sqn at Marham in 1936. This one was serialled K5088. (RAF Museum P15333)

Following the 'Munich Crisis' of 1938 two-letter squadron identification codes were introduced. The Upwood-based No 63 Sqn was unusual in that it had two allocations, NE and ON. These Battles, the nearest is K7613, wear the latter. On the outbreak of war codes were re-allocated; NE went to No 143 Sqn and ON to No 124 Sqn. (RAF Museum P10484)

Out of their usual No 4 Gp (Yorkshire) environment, these Halifax V, Srs IAs LK735/ZL·Z and EB248/ZL·U, of No 427 Sqn, based at Leeming, were photographed at Coltishall in Feb 44. (RAF Museum P10578)

No 216 Sqn was to have been the third UK-based Buccaneer squadron and was to have operated alongside No 12 Sqn in the maritime role. These plans did not come to fruition and the squadron was short-lived. This is one of No 216 Sqn's Buccaneer S.2s, XW533, at Honington in 1979 with the unit badge painted on the intake flank. (Andrew Thomas)

A Lancaster III, PB509/OJ·C, of No 149 Sqn at Mildenhall. Note the two yellow bars painted on the fins; these are believed to have been associated with daylight operations and indicated that the aircraft was fitted with the Gee-H bombing aid. (RAF Museum P14542)

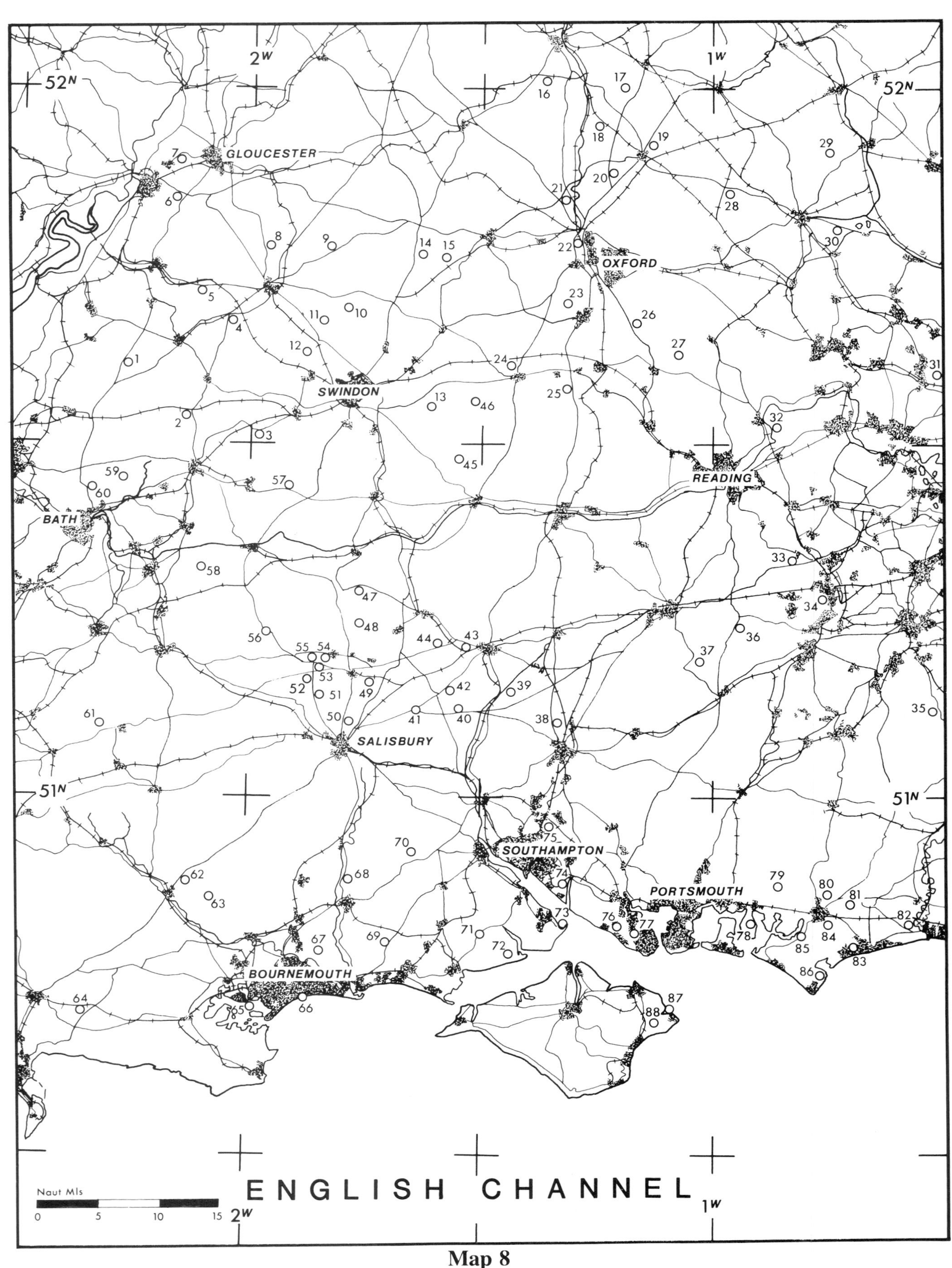

52N
2W
1W
GLOUCESTER
OXFORD
SWINDON
READING
BATH
SALISBURY
SOUTHAMPTON
PORTSMOUTH
BOURNEMOUTH
51N
ENGLISH CHANNEL
Naut Mls
0 5 10 15
1 2 3 4 5 6 7 8 9 10 11 12 13 14 15 16 17 18 19 20 21 22 23 24 25 26 27 28 29 30 31 32 33 34 35 36 37 38 39 40 41 42 43 44 45 46 47 48 49 50 51 52 53 54 55 56 57 58 59 60 61 62 63 64 65 66 67 68 69 70 71 72 73 74 75 76 77 78 79 80 81 82 83 84 85 86 87 88

Map 8

Map 8 – Central Southern England

1 Leighterton
2 Hullavington
3 Lyneham
4 Kemble
5 Aston Down
6 Brockworth
7 Staverton
8 Rendcomb
9 Bibury
10 Fairford
11 Down Ampney
12 Blakehill Farm
13 Red Barn
14 Broadwell
15 Brize Norton
16 Barford St John
17 Brackley/Croughton
18 Upper Heyford
19 Bicester
20 Weston-on-the-Green
21 Kidlington
22 Port Meadow
23 Abingdon
24 Grove
25 Harwell
26 Mount Farm
27 Benson
28 Westcott
29 Wing
30 Halton
31 Denham
32 Henley/Crazies Hill Farm
33 Hartford Bridge/ Blackbushe
34 Farnborough
35 Dunsfold
36 Odiham
37 Lasham
38 Worthy Down
39 Chilbolton
40 Chattis Hill
41 Lopcombe Corner
42 Middle Wallop
43 Andover
44 Thruxton
45 Membury
46 Eastmanton Down
47 Upavon
48 Netheravon
49 Boscombe Down
50 Ford Farm/Old Sarum
51 Lake Down
52 Oatland Hill
53 Stonehenge
54 Larkhill
55 Rollestone Camp
56 Tilshead
57 Yatesbury
58 Keevil
59 Colerne
60 Charmy Down
61 Zeals
62 Blandford
63 Tarrant Rushton
64 Warmwell
65 Hamworthy
66 Bournemouth
67 Hurn
68 Ibsley
69 Holmsley South
70 Stoney Cross
71 Beaulieu
72 Needs Oar Point
73 Calshot
74 Hamble
75 Eastleigh
76 Lee-on-Solent
77 Gosport/Forts Grange & Rowner
78 Thorney Island
79 Funtington
80 Westhampnett
81 Tangmere
82 Ford (Junction)/Yapton
83 Bognor
84 Merston
85 Appledram
86 Selsey
87 Bembridge
88 Brading

A Virginia X, J8907, of No 10 Sqn at Boscombe Down in Jul 33. (Museum of Army Flying)

A Boston III, W8346, of No 537 Sqn from Middle Wallop. The aeroplane has one of Walt Disney's Seven Dwarfs painted on the nose between the Turbinlite and the AI radar dipole aerial mounted on the fuselage side beneath the cockpit. (W Huntley via Andrew Thomas)

A Halifax V glider tug, LL312/9U·T, of No 644 Sqn from Tarrant Rushton in the summer of 1944. The aeroplane has ten mission symbols painted beneath the cockpit sill. (RAF Museum 6030-7)

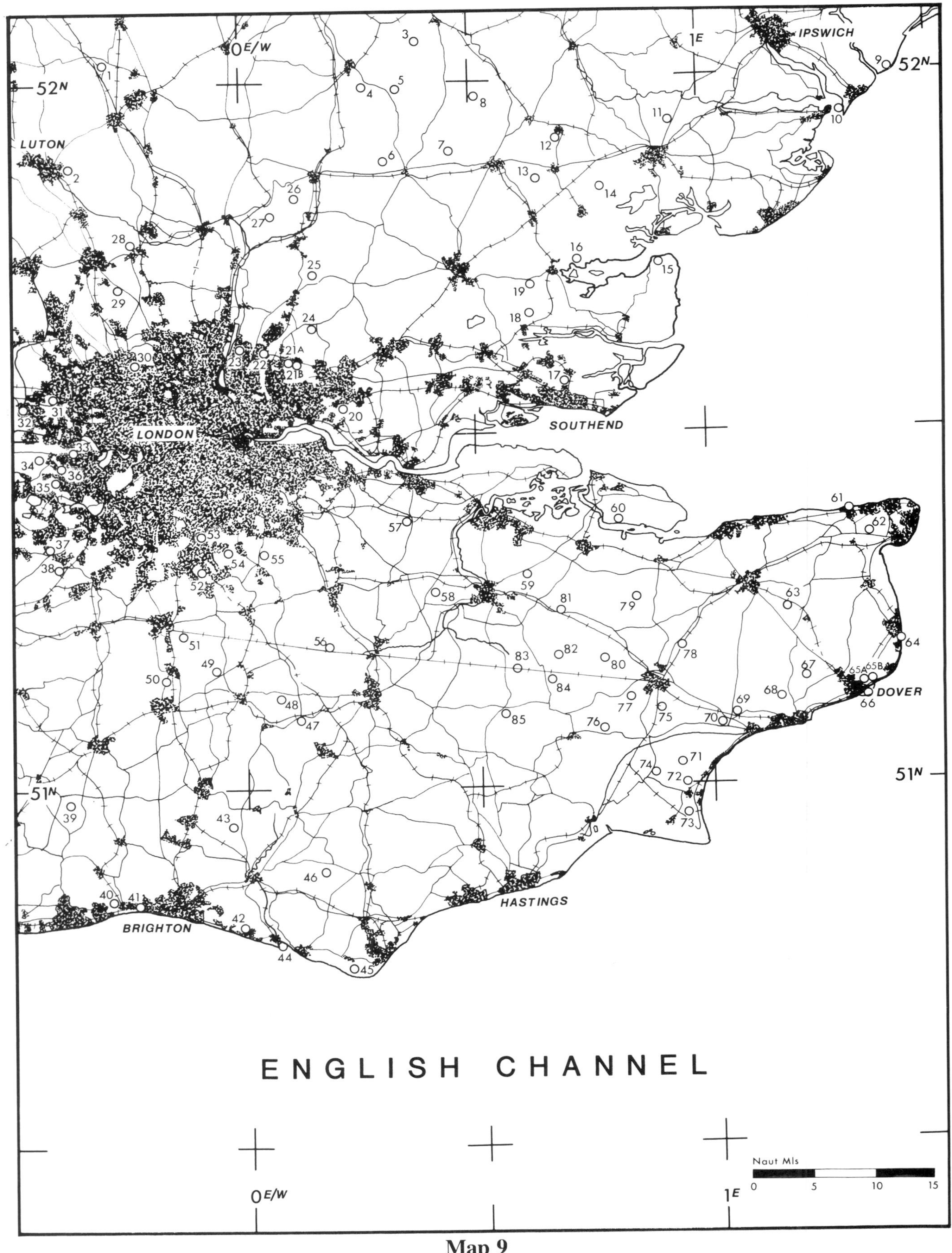
IPSWICH
LUTON
LONDON
SOUTHEND
DOVER
HASTINGS
BRIGHTON
ENGLISH CHANNEL
52N
51N
0E/W
1E
Naut Mls
0
5
10
15

Map 9

Map 9 – London and South East England

1 Henlow
2 Luton
3 Castle Camps
4 Debden
5 Great Sampford
6 Great Dunmow
7 Andrews Field
8 Wethersfield
9 Bawdsey
10 Felixstowe
11 Boxted
12 Earles Colne
13 Rivenhall
14 Birch
15 Bradwell Bay
16 Goldhangar
17 Rochford/Southend
18 Stow Maries
19 Woodham Mortimer
20 Suttons Farm/ Hornchurch
21A Fairlop
21B Hainault Farm
22 Woodford Green
23 Chingford
24 Stapleford (Tawney)
25 North Weald (Bassett)
26 Sawbridgeworth
27 Hunsdon
28 Hatfield
29 London Colney
30 Hendon
31 Northolt
32 Uxbridge
33 Heston
34 Heathrow
35 Feltham/Hanworth
36 Hounslow
37 Brooklands
38 Cobham
39 Coolham
40 Shoreham
41 Hove
42 Telscombe Cliffs
43 Chailey
44 Newhaven
45 Friston
46 Deanland
47 Hartfield
48 East Grinstead
49 Horne
50 Gatwick
51 Redhill
52 Kenley
53 Croydon
54 Fairchildes
55 Biggin Hill
56 Penshurst/ Chiddingstone Causeway
57 Gravesend
58 West Malling
59 Detling
60 Eastchurch
61 Westgate
62 Manston
63 Bekesbourne
64 Walmer
65A Dover/Guston Road
65B Dover/Swingate Down
66 Dover Harbour
67 Swingfield
68 Hawkinge/Folkestone
69 Westenhanger
70 Lympne
71 Newchurch
72 New Romney
73 Lydd
74 Brenzett
75 Kingsnorth
76 Woodchurch
77 Ashford
78 Wye
79 Throwley
80 Chart Court
81 Harrietsham
82 Headcorn
83 Staplehurst
84 Lashenden
85 Sissinghurst

A night-fighter Camel, C8372, of No 50 Sqn at Bekesbourne in 1918. In the course of early efforts to establish an air defence network using radio control all the Home Defence squadrons based around London were given call signs. No 50 Sqn's radio identification was 'Dingo', hence the running dogs device painted beneath the cockpit. This emblem reappeared on the fins of the squadron's Vulcans over half a century later. (No 50 Sqn archives)

An SE 5A, D5995, of No 143 Sqn from Detling exhibits flame-damped exhaust pipes and toned down night-flying markings. (RAF Museum P10957)

Virginia X, J7438, "Isle of Sheppey" (painted beneath the rim of the front-gunner's cockpit), of No 500 Sqn at Manston. (D R Neate)

A Cloud, K3729, while serving with No 48 Sqn at Manston in 1936-38 where the unit functioned as an air navigation school. (Author's collection)

An immaculate Bulldog IIA, K2184, of No 41 Sqn from Northolt. Note the camera gun fitted above the centre section. (RAF Museum P19253)

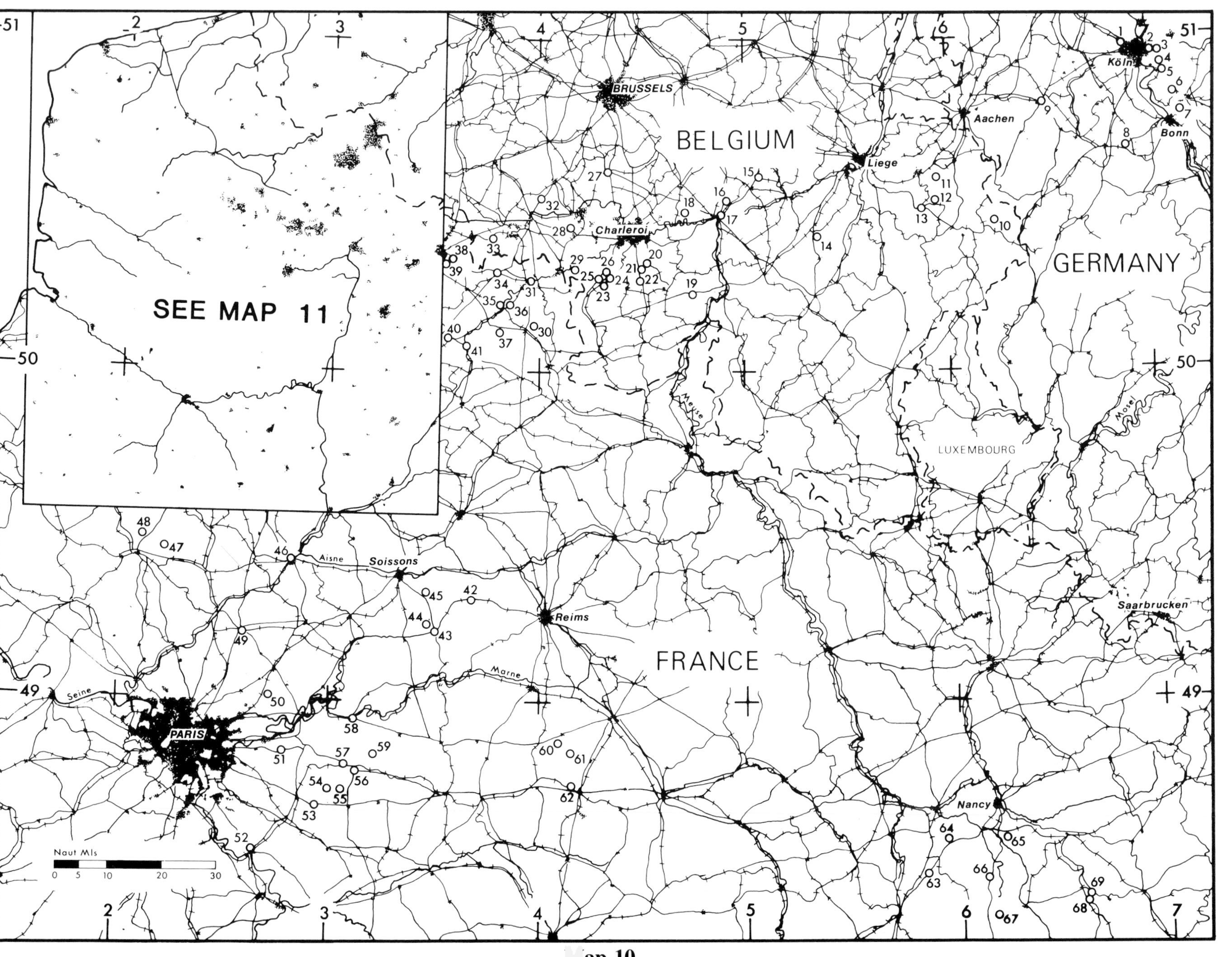
SEE MAP 11
BELGIUM
GERMANY
FRANCE
LUXEMBOURG
BRUSSELS
Charleroi
Liege
Aachen
Köln
Bonn
Meuse
Mosel
Saarbrucken
Aisne
Soissons
Reims
Marne
Seine
PARIS
Nancy
Naut Mls
0 5 10 20 30

Map 10 – France, Belgium, Germany, 1914-1920

1 Bickendorf
2 Buchheim
3 Merheim
4 Heumar
5 Eil
6 Spich
7 Hangelar
8 Ludendorf
9 Düren
10 Elsenborn
11 La Louveterie
12 Sart
13 Spa
14 Clavier
15 Franc Waret/Burdinne
16 Fort Cognelée
17 Bouge
18 Spy
19 Morville
20 Gerpinnes
21 Tarcienne
22 Laneffe
23 Clermont
24 Ossogne
25 Strée
26 Thuilles
27 Nivelles
28 Peronnes
29 Wiheries
30 Flaumont
31 Maubeuge
32 Le Casteau/Les Bruyères
33 Dour
34 Bavai
35 Berlaimont
36 Aulnoye
37 Grand Fayt
38 Saultain
39 Aulnoy
40 Le Cateau
41 Catillon
42 Fismes
43 Fère-en-Tardenois/ Saponay
44 Cramaille
45 Mont-de-Soissons/ Serches
46 Compiègne
47 Fouquerolles
48 Fourneuil
49 Senlis
50 Juilly
51 Serris
52 Melun
53 Rozay-en-Brie
54 Touquin/Pezarches
55 La Boiserotte
56 Chailly
57 Coulommiers
58 La Ferté
59 Rebais
60 Trécon
61 Villesneux
62 Haussimont
63 Autreville
64 Ochey
65 Azelot
66 Tantonville
67 Bettoncourt
68 Roville-aux-Chênes
69 Xaffévillers

No 49 Sqn remained on the Continent for a time after the Armistice as part of the Occupation Force. This DH 4, D8364, was still on charge to No 49 Sqn in 1919 and is seen here at Bickendorf. (RAF Museum P9971)

No 104 Sqn was an element of the Independent Air Force and operated its DH 9s, including this one, D559, from Azelot in 1918. (RAF Museum P8295)

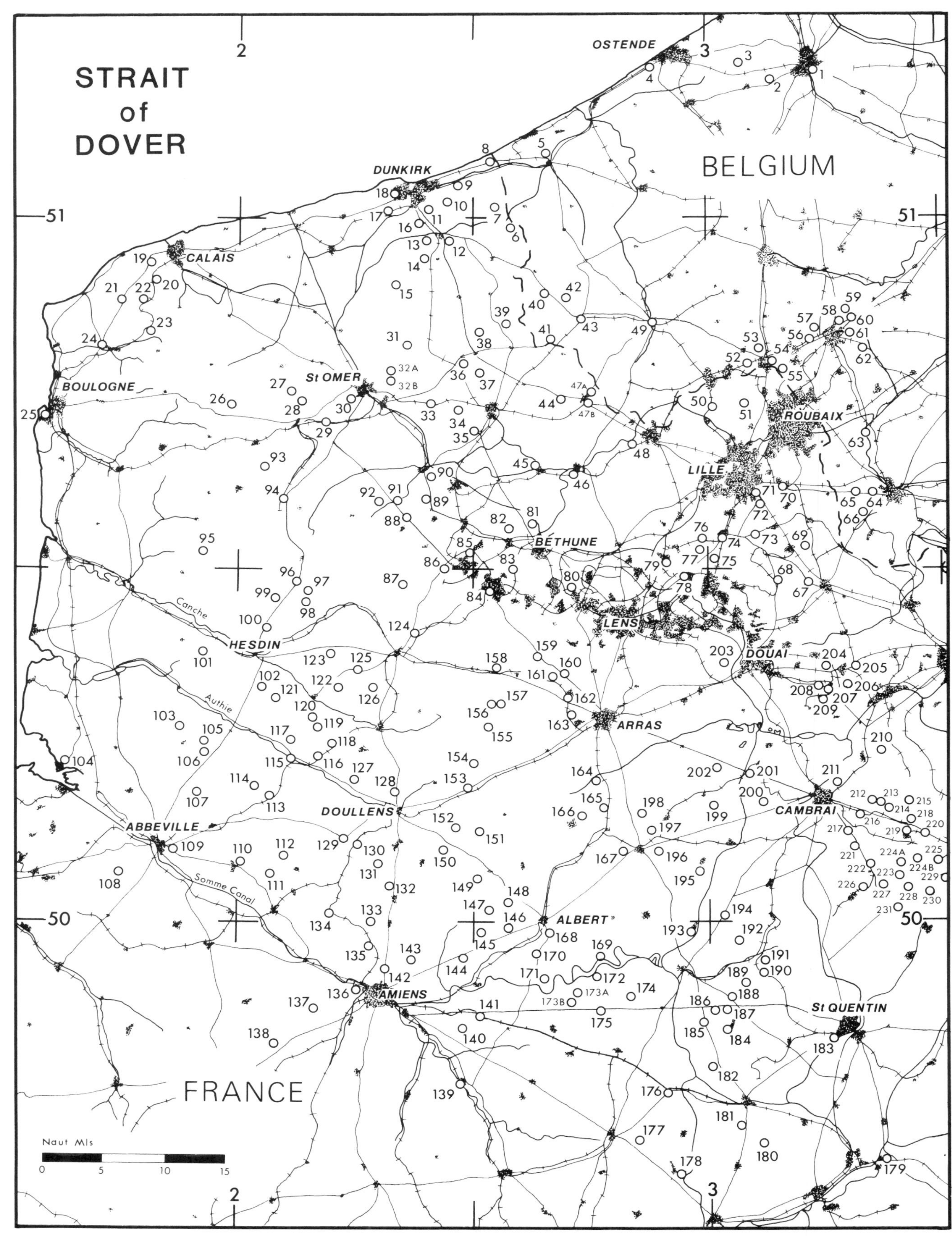
STRAIT of DOVER
BELGIUM
FRANCE
OSTENDE
DUNKIRK
CALAIS
BOULOGNE
St OMER
ROUBAIX
LILLE
BÉTHUNE
LENS
HESDIN
DOUAI
ARRAS
DOULLENS
ABBEVILLE
CAMBRAI
ALBERT
AMIENS
St QUENTIN
Canche
Authie
Somme Canal
2
3
51
50
Naut Mls
0 5 10 15

Map 11

Map 11 – The Western Front – France and Belgium, 1914-19

1 Bruges
2 Varssenaere
3 Stalhille
4 Ostende
5 Furnes
6 Hondschoote
7 Les Moëres
8 Bray Dunes (Frontier Aerodrome)
9 Leffrinckhoucke
10 Teteghem
11 Coudekerque
12 Bergues
13 Bierne
14 Crochte
15 Eringhem
16 Capelle
17 Petite Synthe
18 St-Pol
19 Calais/Marcke
20 Fréthun/Nielles-lès-Calais
21 St-Inglevert
22 Beauregard
23 Caffiers
24 Marquise
25 Boulogne
26 Alquines
27 Boisdinghem
28 Quelmes
29 Esquerdes
30 St-Omer
31 Hoog Huis/Huys
32A Clairmarais North
32B Clairmarais South
33 Ebblinghem
34 Wallon-Cappel
35 Morbecque
36 Oxelaere
37 Ste-Marie-Cappel
38 Oudezeele
39 Droglandt
40 Proven
41 Abeele
42 La Lovie
43 Poperinghe
44 Meteren
45 Merville
46 La Gorgue
47A Bailleul (Asylum Ground)
47B Bailleul (Town Ground)
48 Erquinghem
49 Ypres
50 Ste-Marguerite
51 Linselles
52 Coucou
53 Menin
54 Halluin
55 Reckem
56 Bisseghem
57 Heule
58 Cuerne
59 Bavichove
60 Harlebeke
61 Staceghem
62 Sweveghem
63 Pecq
64 Orcq
65 Marquain
66 Froidmont
67 Auchy
68 Bersée
69 Genech
70 Asq/Ascq
71 Lille/Ronchin
72 Merchin
73 Ennetières
74 Lille/Seclin
75 Phalempin
76 Gondecourt
77 Chemy
78 Carvin
79 Provin
80 Mazingarbe
81 Hinges
82 Chocques/Gonneham
83 Hesdigneul
84 Bruay
85 Auchel/Lozinghem
86 Floringhem
87 Sains-lès-Pernes
88 Rely
89 Norrent-Fontes
90 Aire/Treizennes
91 Estrée-Blanche/Liettres
92 Serny
93 Drionville
94 Fauquembergues
95 Quilen
96 Ruisseauville
97 Tramecourt
98 Maisoncelle
99 Planques
100 Wamin
101 St-André-aux Bois
102 Le Quesnoy
103 Ligescourt/Crécy-en-Ponthieu
104 Le Crotoy
105 Estrées-lès-Crécy
106 Fontaine-sur-Maye
107 Agenvillers
108 Moyenneville
109 Abbeville
110 Famechon
111 Surcamps
112 Franqueville
113 Conteville
114 Bois-de-Roche
115 Auxi-le-Château
116 Nouex-les-Auxi
117 Le Planty
118 Boffles
119 Rougefay
120 Belleville Farm
121 Les Eauvis
122 Blangermont
123 Beauvois/Humières
124 Bryas
125 Croisette
126 Ecoivres
127 Remaisnil
128 Haute Visée
129 Fienvillers
130 Candas
131 Valheureux
132 Vert Galand
133 Fleselles/Villers-Bocage
134 Vignacourt
135 Bertangles
136 Amiens
137 Bovelles
138 Quevauvillers
139 Moreuil
140 Cachy
141 Villers-Bretonneux
142 Poulainville
143 Allonville
144 Lahoussoye
145 Baizieux
146 Laviéville
147 Warloy-Baillon
148 Senlis-le-Sec
149 Léalvillers/Clairfaye Farm
150 Marieux
151 St-Léger-les-Authie
152 Hurtebise Farm
153 La Bellevue
154 Soncamp
155 Avesnes-le-Comte
156 Le Hameau/Izel le Hameau
157 Filescamp Farm
158 Savy
159 Camblain-l'Abbé
160 St-Eloi
161 Acq
162 Etrun
163 Wagnonlieu
164 Boiry-St-Martin
165 Courcelles-le-Comte
166 Ablainzevelle
167 Bapaume
168 Méaulte/Citadel
169 Suzanne
170 Morlancourt
171 Chipilly
172 Cappy
173A Proyart East
173B Proyart South
174 Assevillers
175 Foucaucourt
176 Nesle
177 Champien
178 Catigny
179 La Fère
180 Villeselve
181 Golancourt (Bonneuil)
182 Matigny
183 St-Quentin
184 Flez
185 Athies
186 Mons-en-Chaussée
187 Estrées-en-Chaussée
188 Bouvincourt
189 Hancourt
190 Montigny Farm
191 Hervilly
192 Longavesnes
193 Moislains
194 Nurlu
195 Léchelle
196 Bancourt
197 Beugnâtre
198 Mory
199 Pronville
200 Bourlon
201 Marquion
202 Villers-lès-Cagnicourt
203 La Brayelle
204 Bruille
205 Erre
206 Abscon
207 Aniche
208 Auberchicourt
209 Emerchicourt
210 Avesnes-le-Sec
211 Escaudoeuvres
212 Carnières
213 Boussières
214 Bévillers
215 Quiévy
216 Estourmel
217 La Targette
218 Béthencourt
219 Caudry
220 Inchy
221 Esnes
222 Selvigny/Ferme Guillemin
223 Iris Farm (Clary)
224A Bertry West
224B Bertry East
225 Reumont
226 Malincourt
227 Elincourt
228 Maretz
229 Escaufourt
230 Busigny
231 Prémont Farm

A DH 4, A7624, wearing No 55 Sqn's white triangle 'somewhere in France' in 1918. (RAF Museum P2502)

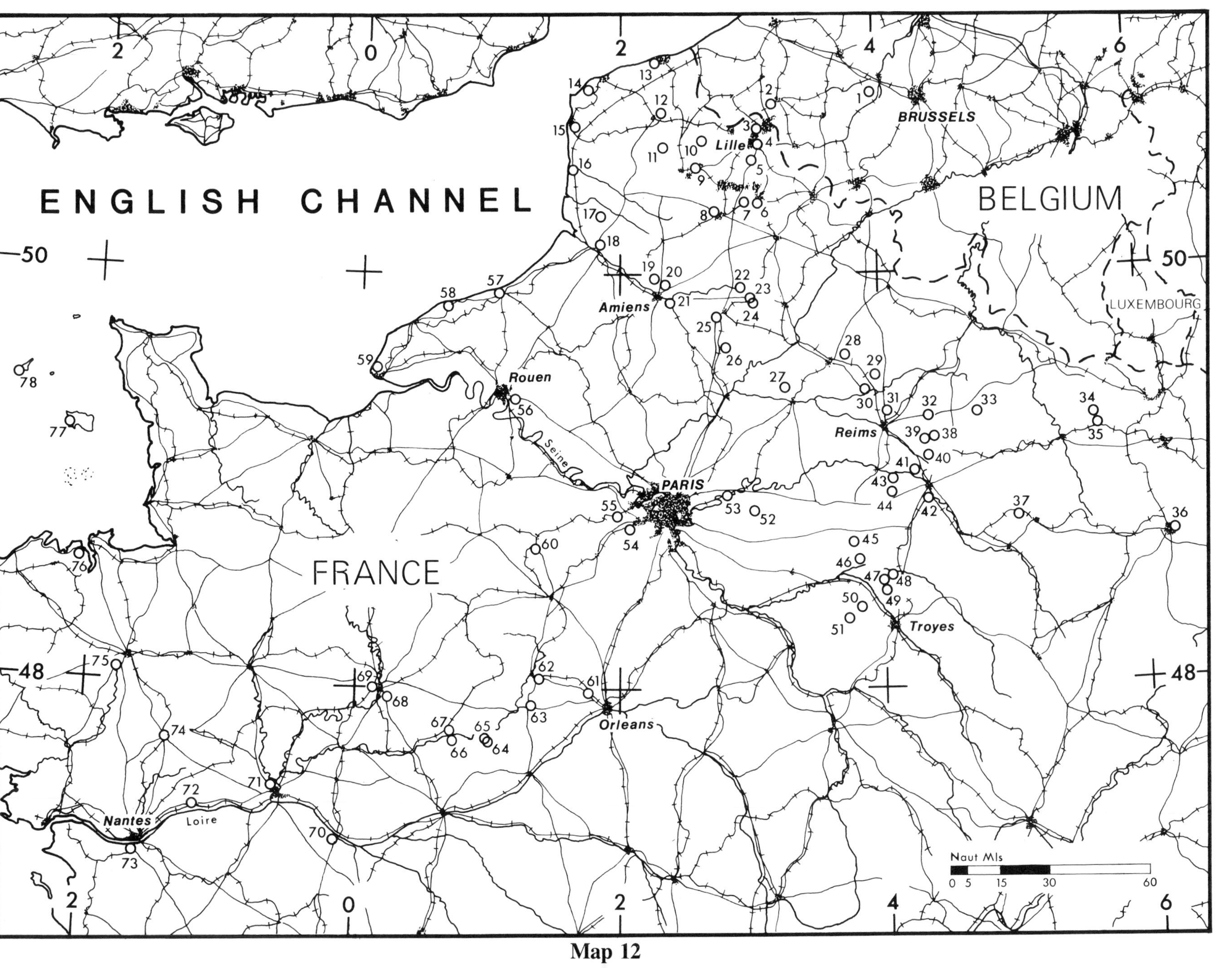
ENGLISH CHANNEL
BELGIUM
LUXEMBOURG
FRANCE
BRUSSELS
Lille
Amiens
Reims
PARIS
Rouen
Seine
Troyes
Orleans
Nantes
Loire
Naut Mls
0 5 15 30 60

Map 12

Map 12 – France, 1939-40

1 Aspelaere
2 Wevelghem
3 Lille/Nord/Marcq
4 Lille/Ronchin
5 Lille/Seclin
6 Douai
7 Vitry-en-Artois
8 Arras
9 Béthune/Labuissière
10 Merville
11 Norrent-Fontes
12 Clairmarais
13 Dunkirk
14 St-Inglevert
15 Boulogne
16 Le Touquet
17 Crécy
18 Abbeville
19 Bertangles
20 Mont Jois
21 Amiens
22 Flamicourt
23 Mons-en-Chaussée
24 Monchy-Lagache
25 Rosières-en-Santerre
26 Roye/Amy
27 Bagneux
28 Laon/Athies
29 Amifontaine
30 Berry-au-Bac
31 Reims/Champagne
32 Bétheniville
33 Challerange
34 Senon
35 Rouvres
36 Nancy
37 Vassincourt
38 Auberives-sur-Suippes
39 Moscou Ferme
40 Mourmelon-le-Grande
41 Condé/Vraux
42 Écury-sur-Coole
43 Plivot
44 Villeneuve (Vertus)
45 Gaye
46 Anglure/Allemanche
47 Rhèges/St-Lucien Ferme
48 Pouan
49 Les Grandes-Chappelles
50 Echemines
51 Faux-Villecerf
52 Coulommiers
53 Meaux
54 Guyencourt
55 Poix
56 Rouen/Boos
57 Dieppe
58 St-Valéry
59 Le Havre/Octeville
60 Dreux
61 Orléans/Bricy
62 Châteaudun
63 Moisy/Ozouer-le-Doyen
64 Villiersfaux
65 Houssay
66 Sougé
67 Artins
68 Ruaudin
69 Le Mans
70 Saumur
71 Angers
72 Ancenis
73 Nantes/Château Bougon
74 Châteaubriant
75 Rennes
76 Dinard
77 St Helier
78 Guernsey

A Battle, K9264/PM·L, of No 103 Sqn over France in 1940. Note the blanking-off of much of the cockpit glazing, apparently by doping fabric over the framework. This aeroplane was lost on 10 May 40, the first day of the German offensive. (RAF Museum P10623)

A number of fighter squadrons were despatched to France in Jun 40 in a vain attempt to blunt the German assault and to provide cover for the retreating British Forces. No 17 Sqn was among these, operating briefly from Le Mans and Dinard and falling back to the UK via the Channel Islands. This photograph of one of the squadron's Hurricane Is, P3878/YB·W, was taken in England a little later in the year. The aeroplane crashed at Debden on 24 Sep 40. (RAF Museum P10064)

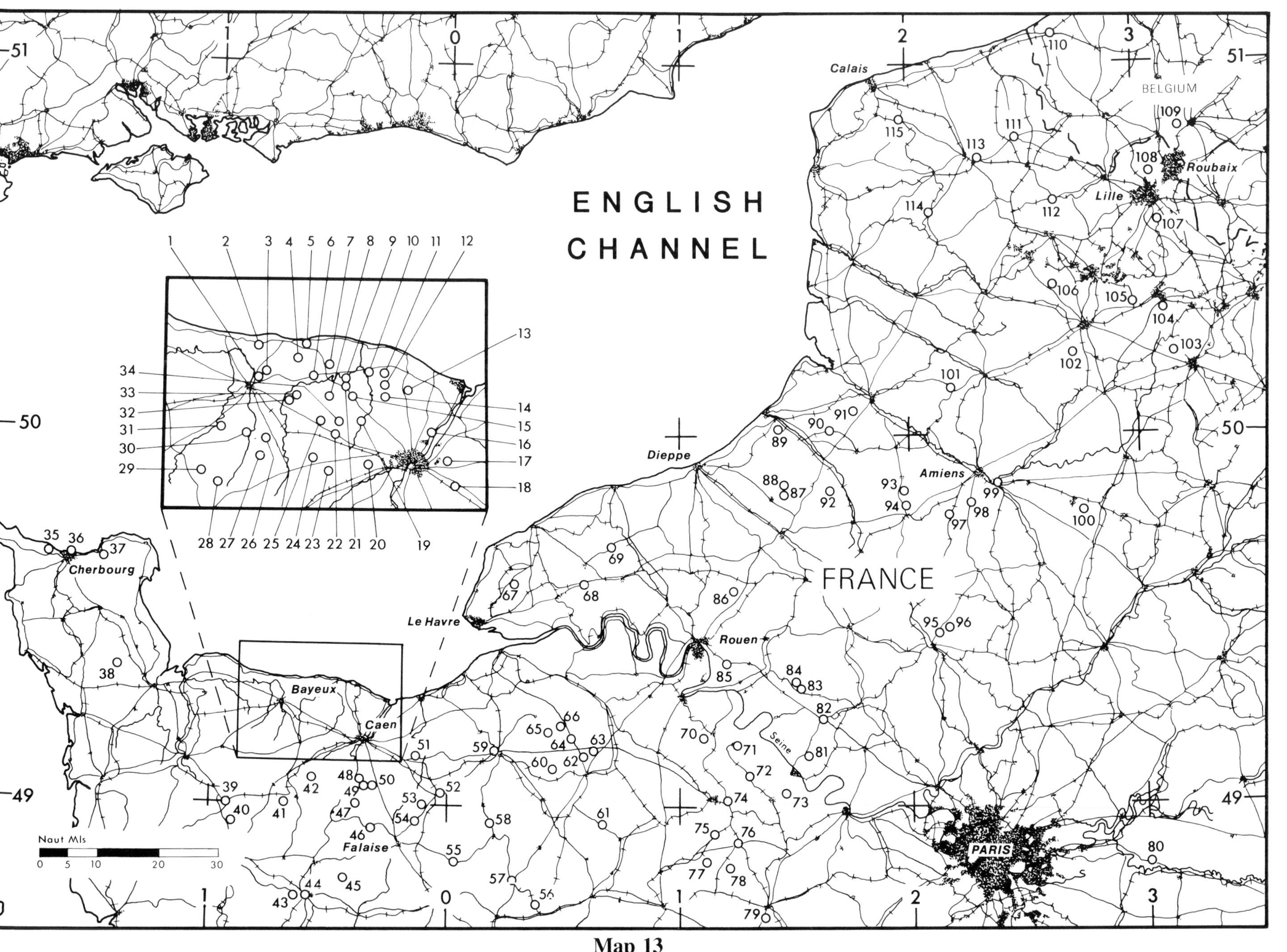
ENGLISH
CHANNEL
FRANCE
BELGIUM
Calais
Lille
Roubaix
Amiens
Dieppe
Rouen
Seine
Le Havre
PARIS
Bayeux
Caen
Falaise
Cherbourg
Naut Mls
0 5 10 20 30
51
50
49
1
0
1
2
3
1 2 3 4 5 6 7 8 9 10 11 12 13 14 15 16 17 18 19 20 21 22 23 24 25 26 27 28 29 30 31 32 33 34
35 36 37 38 39 40 41 42 43 44 45 46 47 48 49 50 51 52 53 54 55 56 57 58 59 60 61 62 63 64 65 66 67 68 69 70 71 72 73 74 75 76 77 78 79 80 81 82 83 84 85 86 87 88 89 90 91 92 93 94 95 96 97 98 99 100 101 102 103 104 105 106 107 108 109 110 111 112 113 114 115
Map 13

Map 13 – Northern France, 1944-45

1 Bayeux
2 B 11/Longues
3 B 8/Sommervieu
4 B 15/Ryes
5 Le Hamel
6 B 2/Bazenville
7 B 3/Ste-Croix-sur-Mer
8 B 9/Lantheuil
9 B 14/Amblie
10 Reviers
11 B 4/Bény-sur-Mer
12 Basly
13 B 10/Plumetot
14 B 16/Villons-les-Buissons
15 B 5/(Le Fresne-) Camilly
16 Blainville
17 Mondeville
18 Grentheville
19 Lasson
20 B 17/Carpiquet
21 Pierrepont
22 Bretteville
23 Cheux
24 B 18/Cristot
25 B 6/Coulombs/Cully
26 B 12/Ellon
27 B 19/Lingèvres
28 B 21/Ste-Honorine-de-Ducy
29 A 12/Balleroy
30 St-André
31 Noron-le-Poterie
32 B 7/Martragny
33 Rucqueville
34 Secqueville-en-Bessin
35 A 23/Querqueville
36 Cherbourg Harbour
37 A 15/Maupertus
38 A 8/Picauville
39 La Fouquerie
40 La Terrière
41 Ondefontaine
42 Landes
43 St-Paul
44 Flers
45 Taillebois
46 St-Germain-Langot
47 Fresney-le-Vieux
48 Pont-de-Fresney
49 Forêt de Cinglais
50 Bretteville-sur-Laize
51 Canteloup
52 St-Pierre-sur-Dives
53 Ernes
54 Perrières
55 Trun
56 St-André-d'Echauffour
57 Gacé
58 Ste-Foy-de-Montgomery
59 Lisieux
60 Le Planquay
61 La Barre-en-Ouche
62 B 28/Bernay
63 B 27/Boisney
64 Le Favril
65 B 23/Morainville/La Rue Huguenot
66 4913N 0029E
67 Angerville-l'Orchier
68 Foucart
69 Héricourt-en-Caux
70 Le Mesnil-Jourdain
71 Ailly
72 Autouillet
73 Douains
74 B 28/Evreux
75 B 34/Avrilly
76 B 24/St-André-de-l'Eure
77 B 30/Créton
78 B 26/Illiers-l'Évêque
79 A 41/Dreux
80 A 58/Coulommiers
81 La Queue-d'Haye
82 Les Thilliers-en-Vexin
83 Saussay-la-Campagne
84 Coudray-en-Vexin
85 Boos (Rouen)
86 Cailly
87 Parfondeval
88 B 31/Fresnoy-Folny/Londinière
89 B 35/Godelmesnil
90 B 37/Corroy
91 Moyenneville
92 B 33/Campneuseville
93 Gouy-l'Hôpital
94 B 44/Poix
95 B 42/Beauvais/Tillé
96 B 40/Beauvais/Nivillers
97 Wailly
98 Hébécourt
99 B 48/Amiens/Glisy
100 B 87/Rosières-en-Santerre
101 Bernaville
102 Blairville
103 B 72/Cambria/Epinoy
104 B 52/Douai
105 B 50/Vitry-en-Artois
106 Gouy-Servins
107 B 51/Lille/Vendeville
108 B 57/Lille/Nord/Wambrechies
109 B 55/Wevelghem
110 B 71/Coxyde
111 Cassel
112 B 53/Merville
113 B 43/Fort Rouge
114 Fauquembergues
115 Ardres

One of the many RAF aeroplanes to fall over France in 1941-42 this Spitfire V, AA837/SD·E, of No 501 Sqn force-landed on 4 Nov 41 after being damaged by a Bf 109. (RAF Museum P9885)

Downed over Glisy on 16 Aug 43 this Typhoon IB, JP577/HH·T, of No 175 Sqn is being examined by Luftwaffe personnel. (RAF Museum P15783)

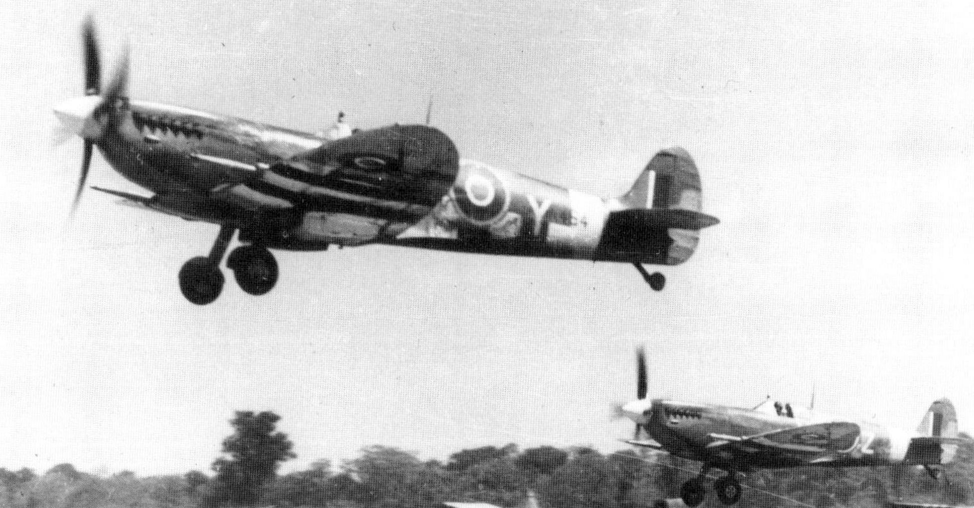

A pair of Spitfire IXs, MK464/Y2·Y and MK777/Y2·Z, of No 442 Sqn taking off, probably from Ford, for a sortie over the Normandy beaches. (RAF Museum P21632)

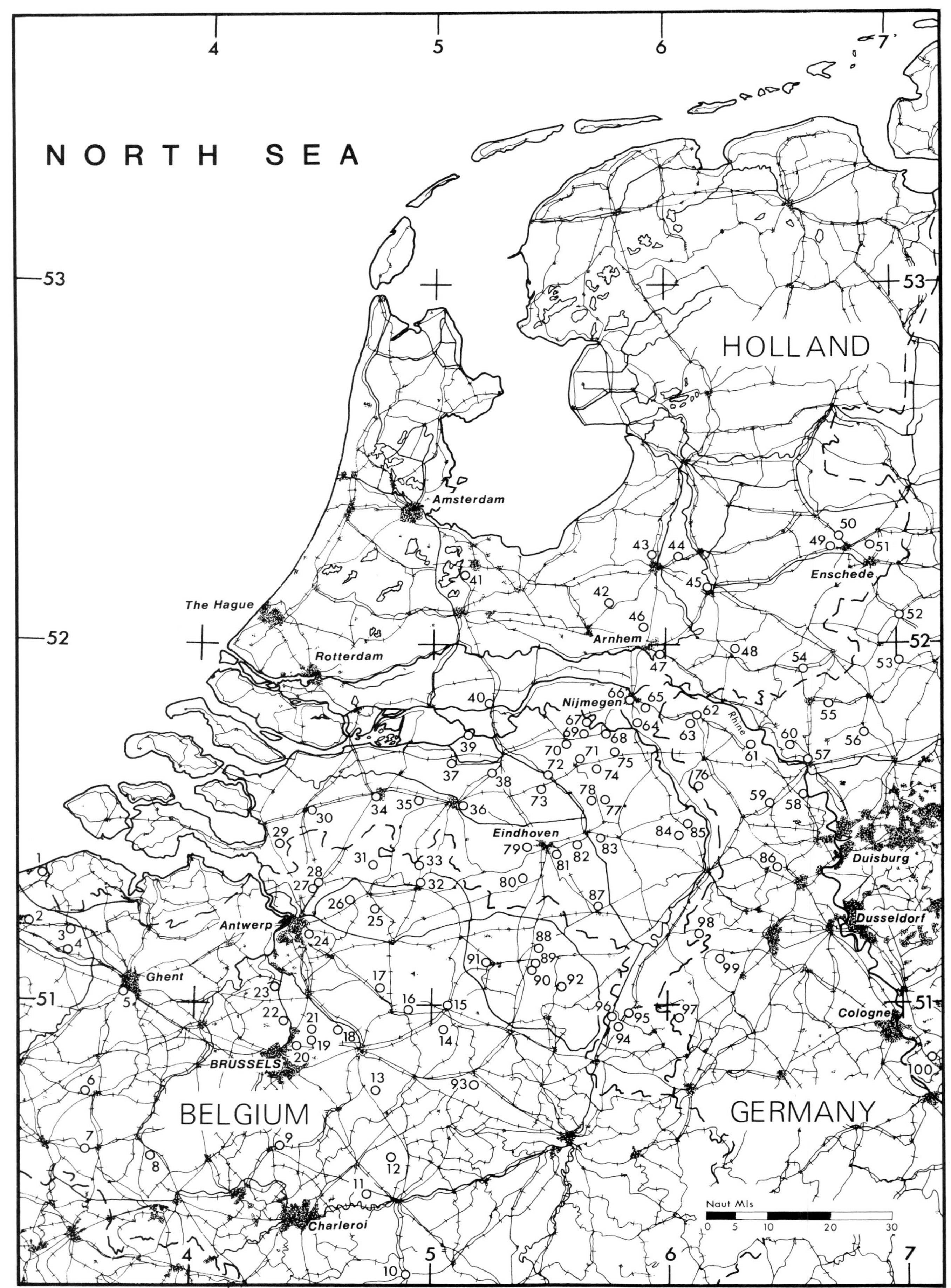
NORTH SEA
HOLLAND
BELGIUM
GERMANY
Amsterdam
The Hague
Rotterdam
Arnhem
Nijmegen
Enschede
Eindhoven
Antwerp
Ghent
BRUSSELS
Charleroi
Duisburg
Dusseldorf
Cologne
Rhine
Naut Mls
0 5 10 20 30
4
5
6
7
53
52
51

Map 14

Map 14 – Belgium, Holland & West Germany, 1944 to date

1 B 83/Knocke le Zout
2 B 63/Bruges/St Croix
3 B 65/Maldeghem
4 B 67/Ursel
5 B 61/St Denis-Westrem
6 Renaix
7 Maulde
8 A 84/Chièvres
9 B 75/Nivelles
10 Dinant
11 Temploux
12 St-Germain
13 B 68/Le Culot/Beauvechain
14 B 66/Blankenberg
15 B 64/Diest
16 Rillaar
17 Boischot
18 Bueken
19 B 58/Melsbroek
20 B 56/Evere
21 Perk
22 B 60/Grimbergen
23 Willebroek
24 B 70/Deurne
25 Zoersal
26 5117½N 0439E
27 Brasschaat
28 Maria ter Heide
29 B 79/Woensdrecht
30 Roosendaal
31 5123N 0445E
32 Turnhout
33 Het Gehaul
34 Breda
35 B 77/Gilze-Rijen
36 Tilburg
37 5140N 0505E
38 Helvoirt
39 5140N 0509E
40 5150N 0515E
41 Hilversum
42 Otterloo
43 Apeldoorn
44 Teuge
45 Zutphen
46 Arnhem
47 5158N 0559E
48 Doetinchem
49 Delden
50 Borne
51 B 106/Twente
52 Ahaus
53 Gescher
54 Aalten
55 Rhede
56 Erle
57 Wesel
58 Ossenpass
59 Issum
60 Diersfordt
61 Appeldorn
62 Kleve
63 Reichswalde
64 B 91/Kluis
65 Berg en Dal
66 Nijmegen
67 B 82/Grave
68 Escharen
69 Schaijk
70 B 88/Heesch
71 Hoeven
72 Dinther
73 B 85/Schjindel
74 B 80/Volkel
75 B 89/Mill
76 B 100/Goch/Laarbruch
77 B 84/Rips
78 Gemert
79 B 78/Eindhoven
80 Boshoven
81 Geldrop
82 Mierlo
83 B 86/Helmond
84 Horst
85 Tienraij
86 St Hubert
87 Weert
88 B 90/Petit Brogel
89 B 76/Peer
90 Linde
91 Bourg Leopold
92 Y 32/Ophoven
93 A 92/St Trond/Brustem
94 Beek
95 Geleen
96 Stein
97 Geilenkirchen
98 Bruggen
99 Wildenwrath
100 B 119/Wahn

An ASV-equipped Swordfish III, NF374/NH·M, of No 119 Sqn which flew these venerable naval biplanes in pursuit of German midget submarines operating off the Belgian coast. (RAF Museum P1620)

One of No 140 Sqn's photo-reconnaissance Mosquito XVIs, NS777, at Melsbroek in 1944. (RAF Museum P1000157)

A Typhoon IB, MN424/F3·G, of No 438 Sqn at Eindhoven in Dec 44. (RAF Museum 302-22)

A Sabre F.4, XB671, of No 67 Sqn taking-off from Brüggen in 1953. The practice of displaying the unit badge on the white stripe of the fin tricolour is not officially sanctioned and, while not unique, it is unusual. (Wg Cdr P Cornell)

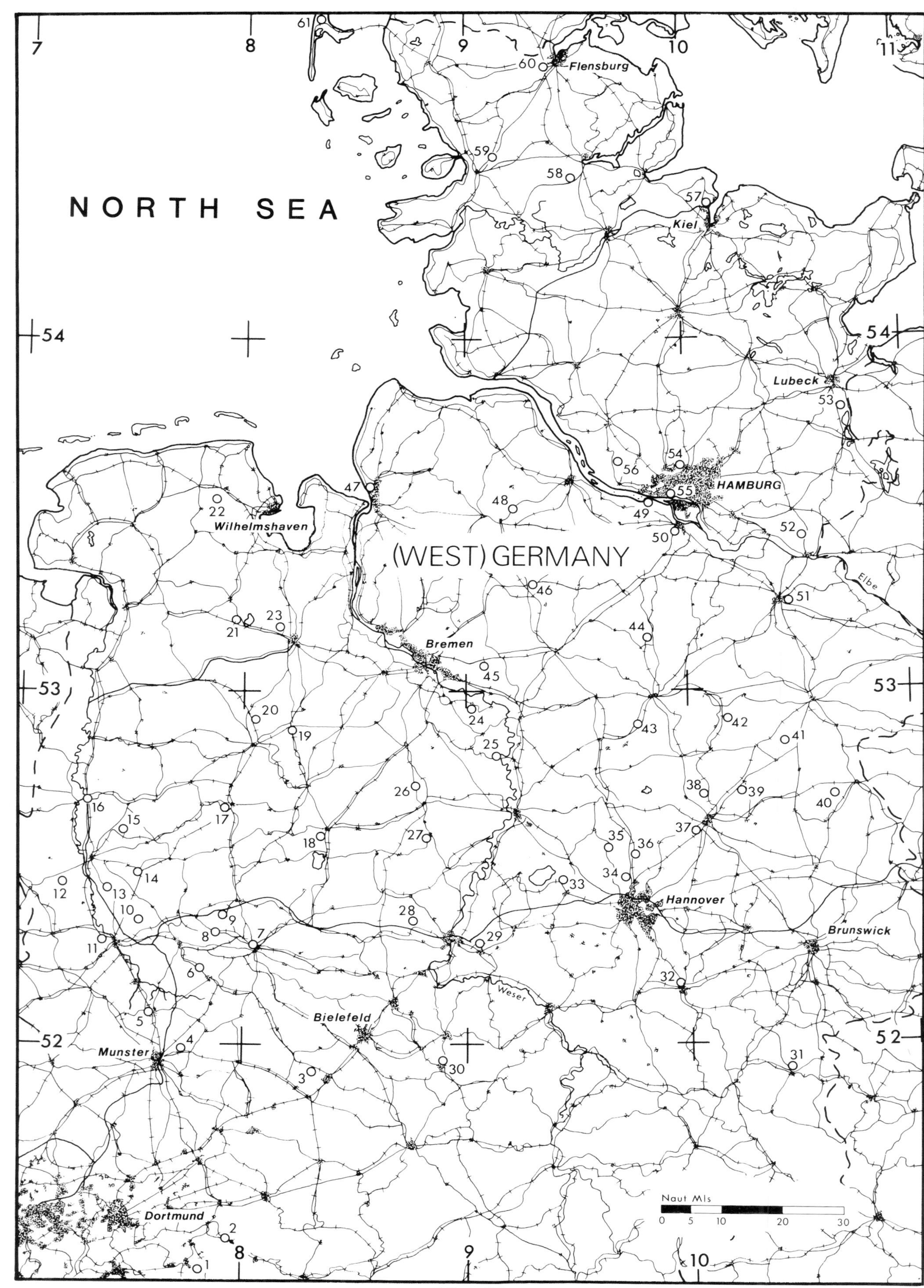
NORTH SEA
(WEST) GERMANY
Flensburg
Kiel
Lubeck
HAMBURG
Elbe
Wilhelmshaven
Bremen
Hannover
Brunswick
Weser
Bielefeld
Munster
Dortmund
Naut Mls
0 5 10 20 30
7
8
9
10
11
54
53
52
1
2
3
4
5
6
7
8
9
10
11
12
13
14
15
16
17
18
19
20
21
22
23
24
25
26
27
28
29
30
31
32
33
34
35
36
37
38
39
40
41
42
43
44
45
46
47
48
49
50
51
52
53
54
55
56
57
58
59
60
61

Map 15

Map 15 – Germany, 1945 and after

1 Deilingenhofen
2 Neheim
3 Y 99/Gütersloh
4 Y 94/Handorf
5 Greven
6 Tecklenburg
7 Osnabrück
8 Westerkappelen
9 B 110/Achmer
10 B 112/Hopsten
11 B 108/Rheine
12 B 101/Nordhorn
13 B 103/Plantlunne
14 Freren
15 B 105/Drope
16 Meppen/Vermeppen
17 B 109/Quackenbrück
18 B 114/Diepholz
19 B 111/Ahlhorn
20 B 113/Varrelbusch
21 Rostrup
22 B 117/Jever
23 Oldenburg
24 Wester-Wisch
25 Hoya
26 Anstedt
27 Kirchdorf
28 Hille
29 B 151/Bückeburg
30 Detmold
31 Goslar
32 R 16/Hildesheim
33 B 116/Wunstorf
34 B 120/Langenhagen
35 Negenborn
36 Bissendorf
37 B 118/Celle
38 B 150/Hustedt
39 Habighorst
40 B 155/Dedelsdorf
41 Hösseringen
42 B 152/Fassberg
43 Dorfmark
44 B 154/Reinsehlen
45 Bassen
46 Zeven
47 Bremerhaven
48 Elm
49 Finkenwerder
50 Harburg
51 B 156/Lüneburg
52 Wangelau
53 B 158/Lübeck
54 B 168/Fuhlsbüttel
55 Altona
56 B 174/Utersen
57 Kiel/Holtenau
58 B 164/Schleswig
59 B 172/Husum
60 B 166/Flensburg
61 B 170/Sylt

Symbolising the defeat of the Luftwaffe, a pristine Typhoon IB, RB458/ZY·B, of No 247 Sqn stands amid the wreckage at Lübeck shortly after VE-day. (RAF Museum 6051-7)

A Meteor F.3, EE253/A6·E, of No 257 Sqn photographed at Wunstorf in 1947 during one of the routine deployments of UK fighter squadrons to Germany. (P H Dobbs)

The Hastings entered service shortly after the Berlin Airlift began. This one, TG535, took part in the operation, flying from Schleswig with No 47 Sqn. (via R C Sturtivant)

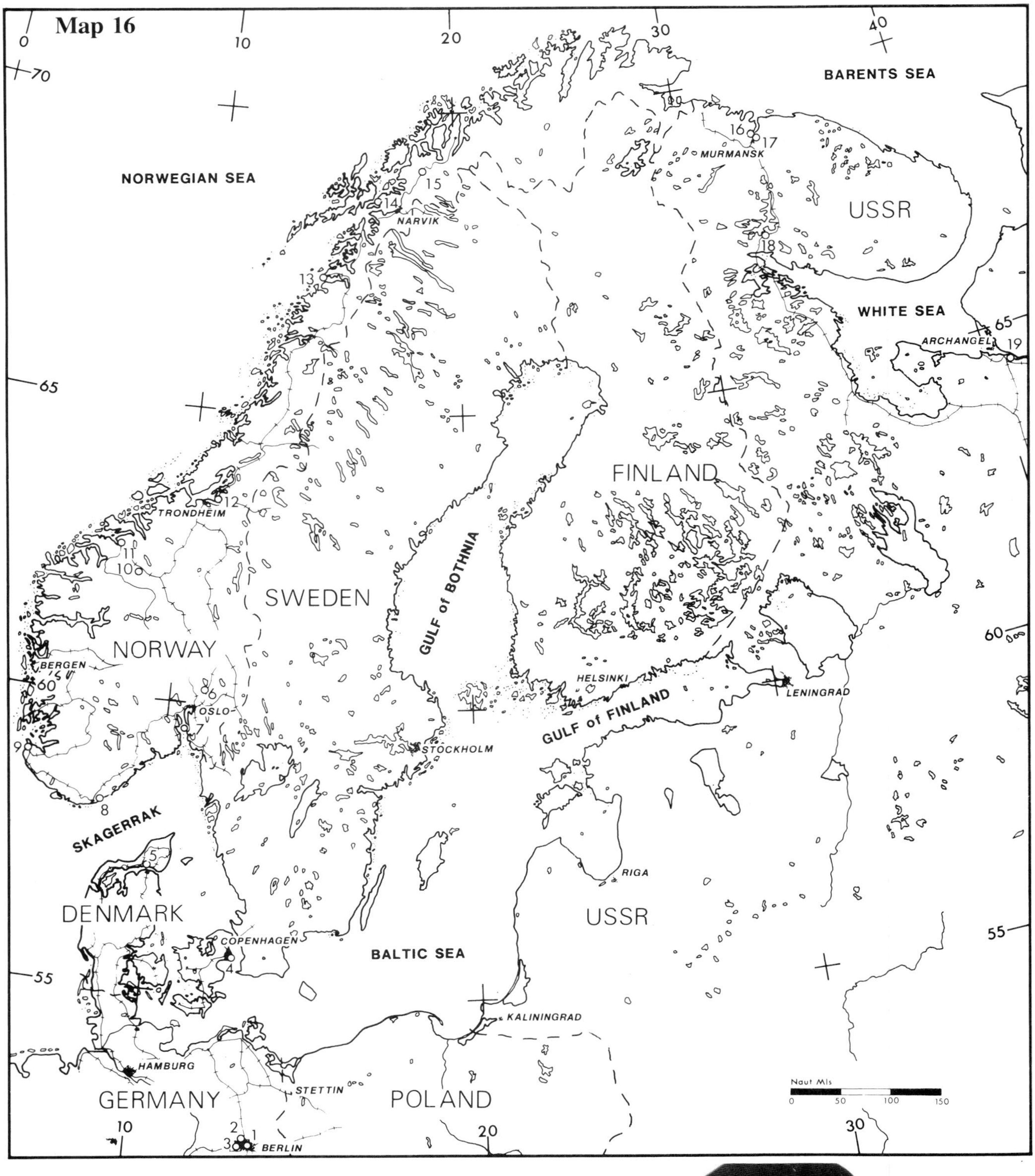

Map 16

NORWEGIAN SEA
BARENTS SEA
WHITE SEA
USSR
FINLAND
SWEDEN
NORWAY
GULF of BOTHNIA
GULF of FINLAND
SKAGERRAK
DENMARK
BALTIC SEA
GERMANY
POLAND
MURMANSK
NARVIK
ARCHANGEL
TRONDHEIM
BERGEN
OSLO
STOCKHOLM
HELSINKI
LENINGRAD
RIGA
COPENHAGEN
KALININGRAD
HAMBURG
STETTIN
BERLIN
Naut Mls
0 50 100 150

Map 16 – Scandinavia

1 Tempelhof
2 Gatow
3 Tegel
4 B 160/Kastrup
5 Aalborg
6 Gardermoen
7 Oslo/Fornebu
8 Kristiansand/Kjevik
9 Stavangar/Sola
10 Lake Lesjeskog
11 Aandalsnes
12 Trondheim/Vaernes
13 Bodö
14 Skaanland
15 Bardufoss
16 Grasnaya
17 Vaenga
18 Afrikanda
19 Yagodnik

No 263 Sqn fought a brief but gallant campaign in the defence of Norway. This Gladiator II, N5626, is seen on the shores of Lake Lesjeskog in Jun 40. Note the bizarre black and white underwing camouflage scheme which was then in vogue for British fighters. (RAF Museum P1636)

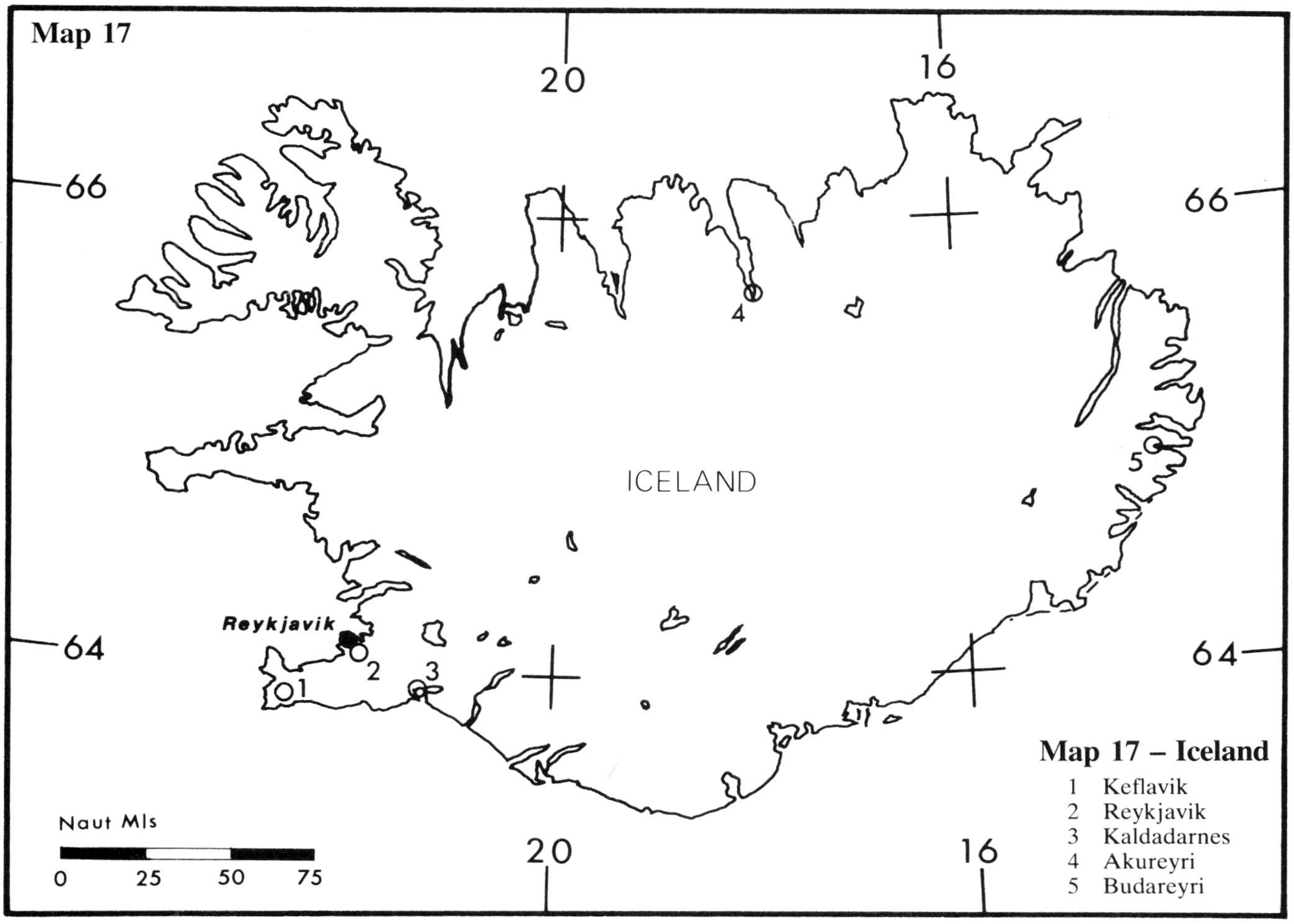

Map 17

20 16
66 66
64 64
Reykjavik
ICELAND
Naut Mls
0 25 50 75
20 16

Map 17 – Iceland

1 Keflavik
2 Reykjavik
3 Kaldadarnes
4 Akureyri
5 Budareyri

Hudson III, T9465/UA·N, was a much photographed aeroplane having been presented to the RAF by its manufacturers; it bore the legend "Spirit of Lockheed-Vega Employees" on the side of the fuselage. T9465 spent the early part of its career with No 269 Sqn in Iceland and is seen here at Kaldadarnes. (RAF Museum P11813)

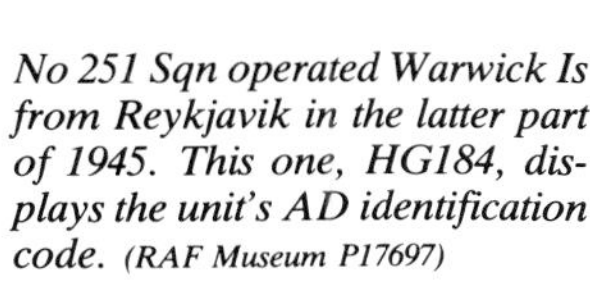

No 251 Sqn operated Warwick Is from Reykjavik in the latter part of 1945. This one, HG184, displays the unit's AD identification code. (RAF Museum P17697)

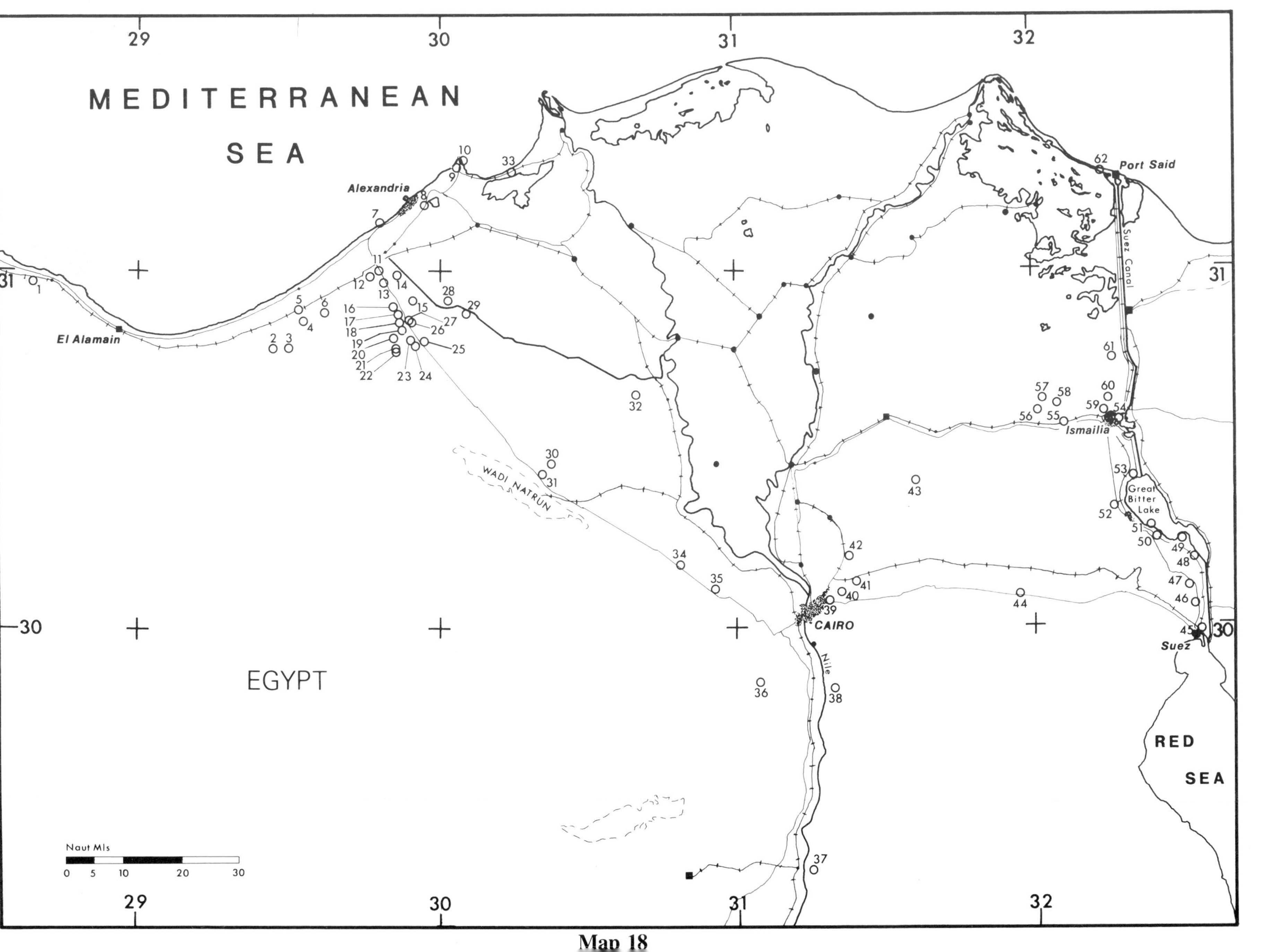
MEDITERRANEAN
SEA
RED
SEA
EGYPT
Port Said
Suez Canal
Ismailia
Great Bitter Lake
Suez
CAIRO
Nile
Alexandria
El Alamain
WADI NATRUN
Naut Mls
0 5 10 20 30

Map 18

Map 18 – Nile Delta and Suez Canal

1 LG 106
2 LG 37 Hamman S
3 LG 172
4 LG 39 Burgh el Arab S
5 LG 28 Burgh el Arab
6 LG 40 Bahig S
7 LG 32 Dekheila
8 Alexandria/Maryut
9 LG 34 Aboukir
10 Aboukir Bay
11 LG 93
12 LG 95 Ikingi
13 LG 29 Amiriya
14 LG 88
15 LG 175
16 LG 92
17 LG 173
18 LG 86
19 LG 87
20 LG 89
21 LG 85
22 LG 154
23 LG 99
24 LG 98
25 LG 97
26 LG 90
27 LG 91
28 LG 227
29 Gianaclis
30 LG 202
31 LG 100 Wadi Natrun
32 LG 226
33 LG 229 Idku
34 LG 237 Kilo 40/Gebel Hamzi
35 LG 224 Kilo 26/Cairo West/Mena Road
36 LG 222 Kilo 17/Fayoum Road
37 Burrumbul
38 Helwan
39 Heliopolis
40 Almaza
41 LG 219 Kilo 8/Matariyah/Payne Field
42 El Khanka
43 Bilbeis
44 LG 209 Kilo 61/Suez Road No 2
45 Suez
46 Shallufa
47 LG 251 Shallufa Satellite
48 Shandur
49 Kabrit
50 Kasfareet
51 Fanara
52 Fayid
53 Deversoir
54 Lake Timsah
55 Abu Sueir
56 LG 207/LG 'Y' Qassassin
57 LG 208/LG 'Z' Mahsma
58 LG 206/LG 'X' Abu Sueir North
59 Ismailia/Moascar
60 El Firdan
61 El Ballah
62 El Gamil/Port Said

A Vincent, K4671, of No 45 Sqn flown by F S Hyett, which stalled during a formation take-off from Aboukir on 24 Mar 36. (Andrew Thomas)

No 113 Sqn began trials of a new style of camouflage in Mar 40. This may account for the unusual colour scheme on this Blenheim I, L4823, seen at Heliopolis after a minor mishap. (S W Lee)

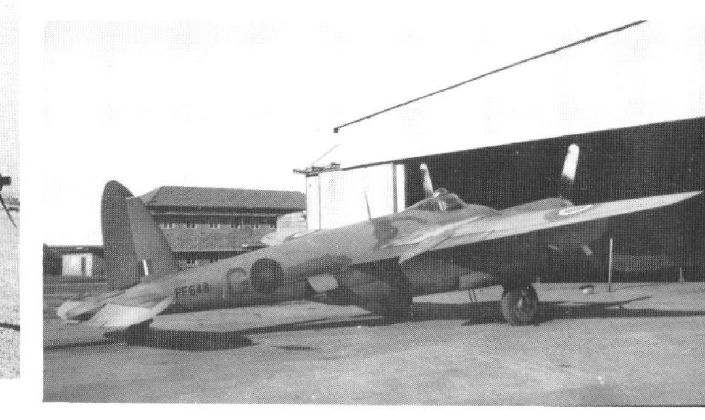

A Mosquito PR 34, PF648, of No 13 Sqn at Kabrit not long after the war. (H Holmes via R C Sturtivant)

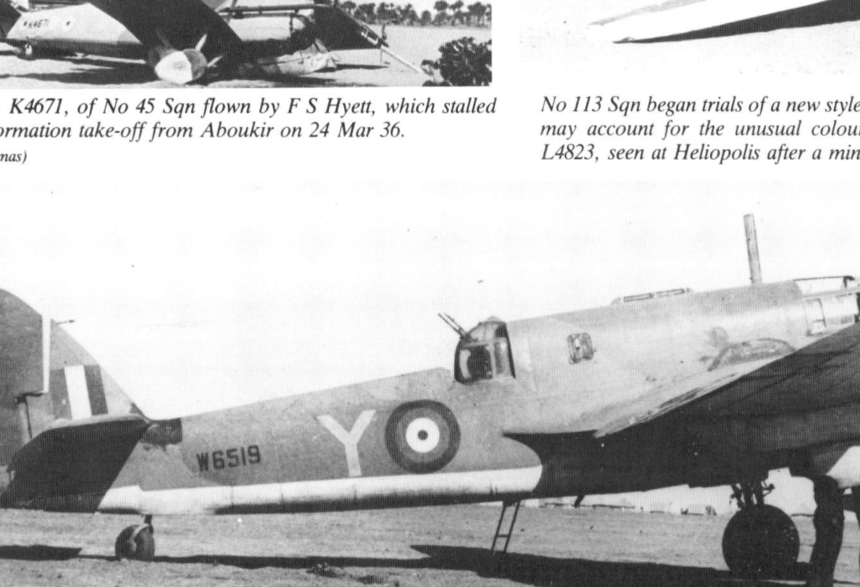

No 39 Sqn was very active in the anti-shipping role from Egyptian airfields throughout 1941-43. This is one of the squadron's Beaufort Is, W6519, which was lost on such a mission on 23 Jun 42. (RAF Museum P13015)

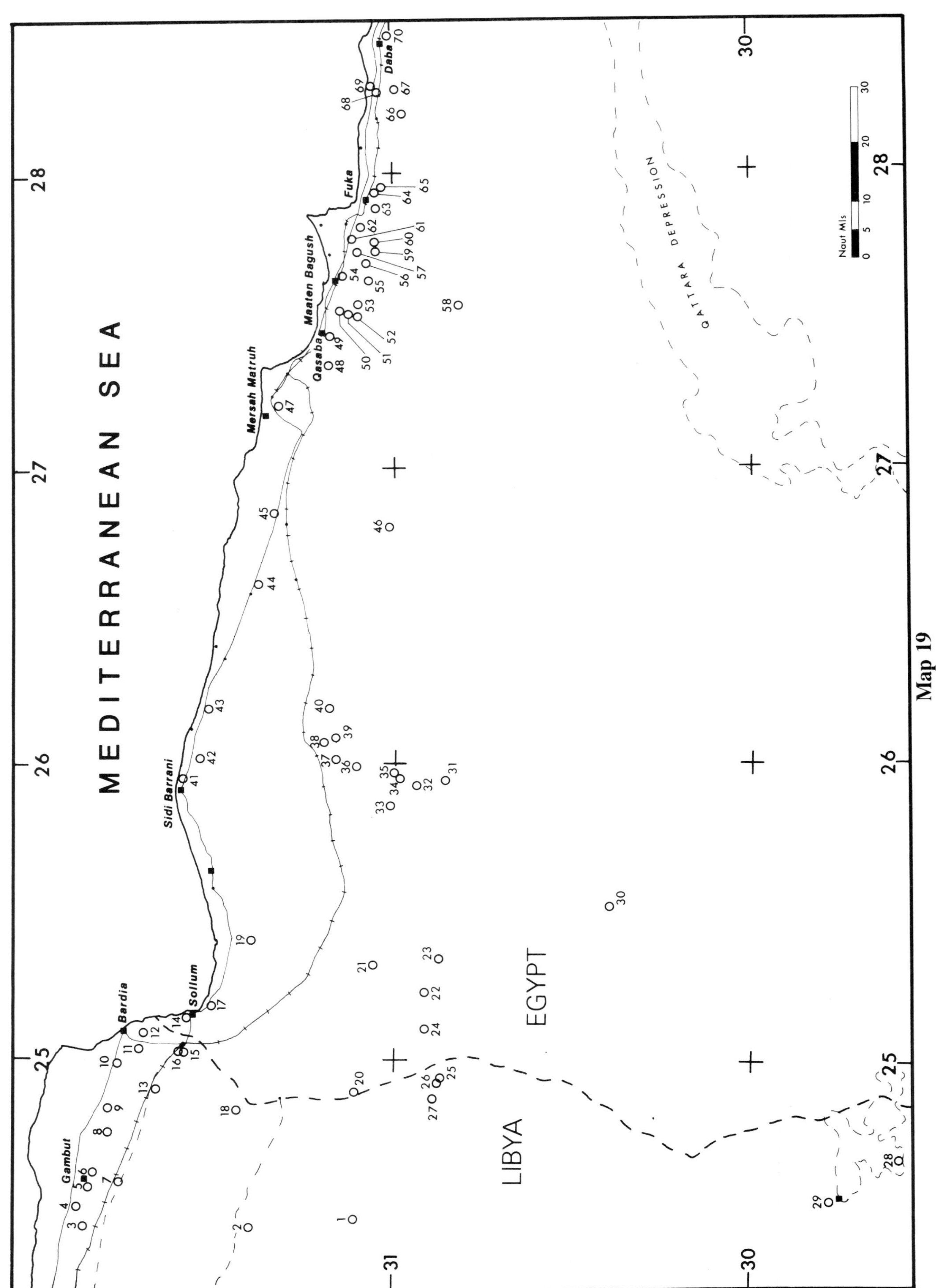
MEDITERRANEAN SEA
LIBYA
EGYPT
QATTARA DEPRESSION
Gambut
Bardia
Sollum
Sidi Barrani
Mersah Matruh
Qasaba
Maaten Bagush
Fuka
Daba
Naut Mls

Map 19

Map 19 – Western Desert

1 LG 134
2 LG 163 Gabr Selah
3 LG 156 Gambut No 4
4 LG 139 Gambut No 1/Main
5 LG 142 Gambut No 2
6 LG 143 Gambut No 3
7 LG 141 Gasr el Arid
8 LG 140 Bir el Beheira No 1
9 LG 167 Bir el Beheira No 2
10 Menastir
11 Bardia
12 Bardia South
13 LG 148 Sidi Azeiz
14 Sollum
15 Capuzzo/Amseat No 1
16 Capuzzo North/Amseat No 2
17 Halfaya
18 Sidi Omar
19 LG 81
20 LG 132
21 LG 131
22 LG 133
23 LG 128
24 LG 122
25 LG 124 Fort Maddelena/Esc Scegga
26 Fort Maddelena No 2
27 LG 123 Fort Maddelena No 3
28 LG 108 Giarabub No 2
29 LG 107 Giarabub
30 LG 79
31 LG 112
32 LG 130
33 LG 109
34 LG 110
35 LG 111
36 LG 155
37 Bir Mella
38 LG 75
39 LG 76
40 El Dwabis
41 LG 02 Sidi Barrani
42 LG 05/'X' LG
43 LG 121
44 LG 06/'Y' LG
45 LG 07/'Z' LG/Matruh West
46 LG 43 Bir Kenayis
47 LG 08 Mersah Matruh
48 LG 10 Gerawala
49 LG 11 Qasaba
50 LG 12 Sidi Haneish North
51 LG 13 Sidi Haneish South
52 LG 101
53 LG 102
54 LG 14 Maaten Bagush
55 LG 115
56 LG 116
57 LG 15 Maaten Bagush Satellite
58 LG 60
59 LG 117
60 LG 103
61 LG 68 'Waterloo'
62 LG 16 Fuka Satellite
63 LG 18 Fuka South
64 LG 17 Fuka Main
65 LG 19 Fuka East
66 LG 09 Bir Koraiyim
67 LG 21 Qotafiyah III
68 LG 104 Qotafiyah II
69 LG 20 Qotafiyah I
70 LG 105 El Daba

A Beaufighter X, NE400, of No 603 Sqn being serviced at Gambut in 1944. The photograph exudes atmosphere and the aeroplane exhibits several interesting details including a nose blister housing for the F.24 strike camera, underwing racks for rocket projectiles and a Yagi aerial array for the ASV Mk III radar projecting forwards from beneath the nose. (Sqn Ldr J B Blanche)

A Hurricane IIB, BP166/KC·J, of No 238 Sqn which operated on a very mobile basis in Egypt and Cyrenaica. (RAF Museum P8450)

One of No 39 Sqn's Beaufort Is, N1170, after a crash landing at Sidi Barrani on 27 Mar 42. (RAF Museum P8136)

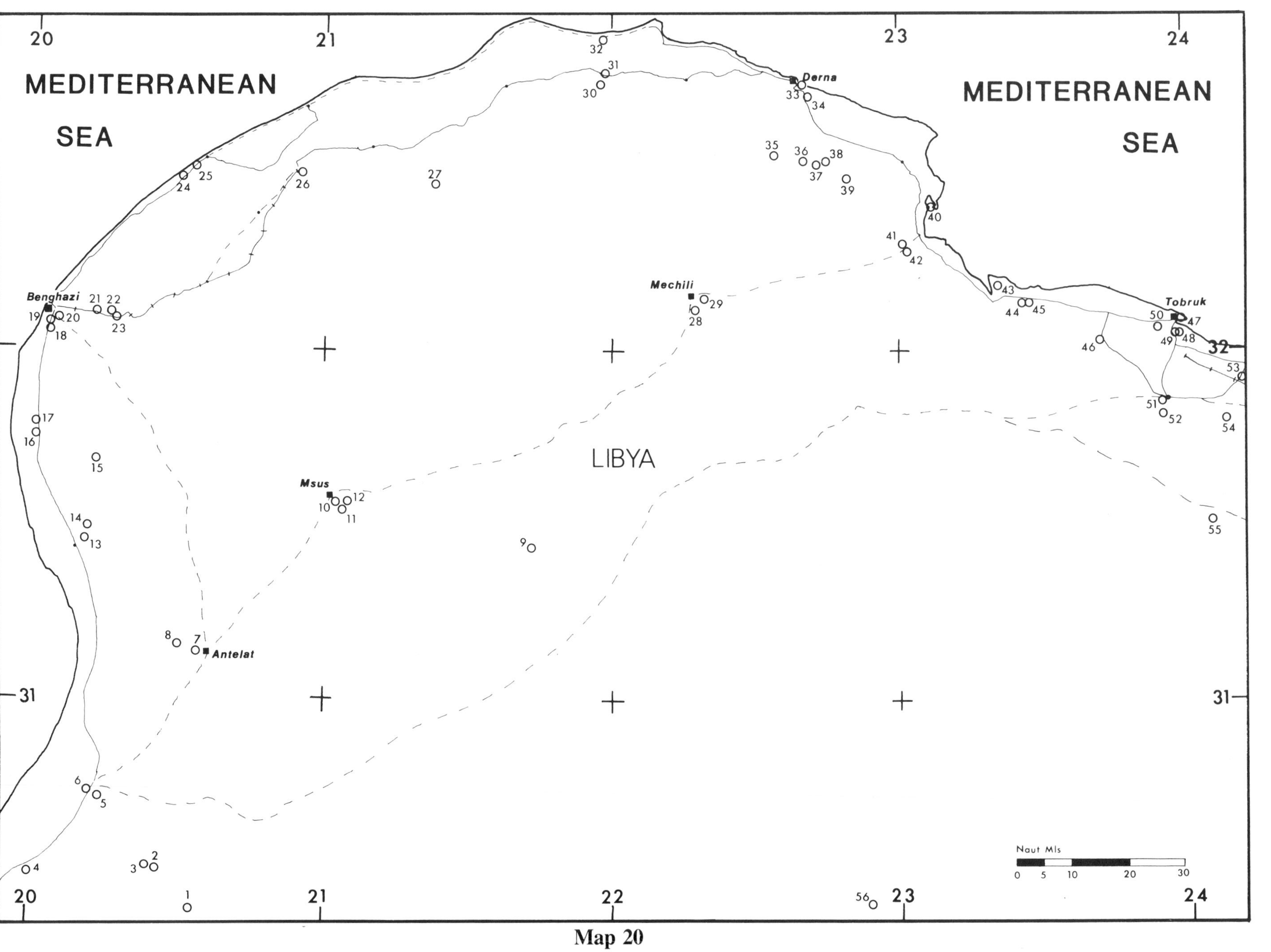
MEDITERRANEAN SEA
MEDITERRANEAN SEA
LIBYA
Benghazi
Derna
Mechili
Msus
Antelat
Tobruk
Naut Mls

Map 20

Map 20 – Cyrenaica

1 El Hassiet
2 Belandah No 1
3 Belandah No 2
4 El Nogra
5 Agedabia East
6 Agedabia West
7 Antelat No 1
8 Antelat No 2
9 LG 165 Bir el Regal
10 Msus No 1
11 Msus No 2
12 Msus No 3
13 El Magrun
14 Magrun North
15 Soluch
16 Terria
17 Hosc Raui
18 Berka III
19 Berka II
20 Berka I
21 Lete
22 Benina North
23 Benina
24 Bersis
25 Tocra
26 Barce
27 Marawa/Maraua
28 Mechili No 1
29 Mechili No 2
30 Cyrene
31 Savoia
32 Apollonia
33 Derna Harbour
34 Derna
35 Martuba No 5
36 Martuba No 3
37 Martuba No 1
38 Martuba No 4
39 Martuba No 2
40 Mendalao Bay
41 Tmimi 2
42 Tmimi 1
43 LG 149 Gazala No 1
44 LG 150 Gazala No 2
45 LG 152 Gazala No 3
46 Acroma
47 Tobruk No 1
48 LG 145 Tobruk No 2/El Gubbi (or Gubsi) West
49 LG 146 Tobruk No 3/El Gubbi (or Gubsi) East
50 Tobruk No 4/Crum el Chel
51 LG 144 El Adem
52 LG 157 El Adem South
53 LG 147 Bu Amud
54 LG 153 Sidi Rezegh
55 LG 170/Bir el Gubi (or Gobi)
56 LG 125

Mainly based in Egypt, No 108 Sqn sometimes operated from as far west as LG 237 in Cyrenaica. This picture shows a Wellington IC, HX425, of No 108 Sqn with 15 mission symbols, a Red Indian's head and the name 'Hiawatha' painted on its forward fuselage. (Chaz Bowyer)

No 73 Sqn was one of those involved in the highly mobile campaign which ebbed and flowed across the North African desert. This is one of No 73 Sqn's Hurricane Is, V7544, which came to grief at El Adem on 12 Feb 41. (RAF Museum P5095)

A Halifax II, Srs IA, with the early triangular style of fin, in North African service with No 462 Sqn. (Chris Shores)

A Spitfire IX, MH599/GO·C, of No 94 Sqn from Bu Amud in May 44. (RAF Museum P20401)

Map 21

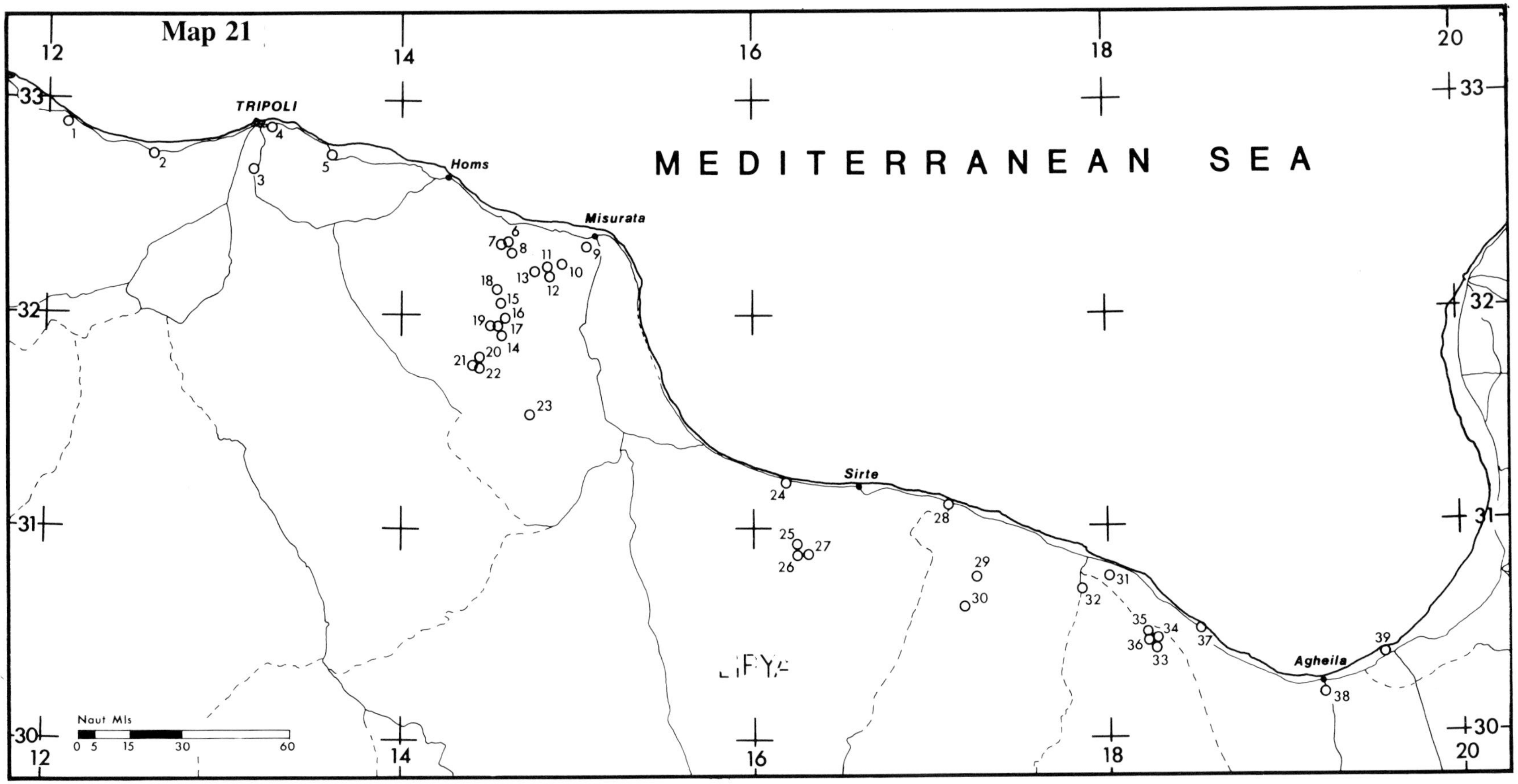

Map 21 – Libya (Sirte and Tripolitania)

1	Zuara	15	Bir Dufan 2	28	Sultan
2	Sorman	16	Bir Dufan 3	29	Gzina/Sidi Azzab
3	Castel Benito/Idris	17	Bir Dufan 4	30	Alem el Chel
4	Mellaha	18	Bir Dufan 5	31	Nofilia 1
5	Gasr Garabulli	19	Bir Dufan 6	32	Nofilia 2
6	Sirtan North	20	Darragh North/Wadi Surri	33	El Merduma 1
7	Sirtan West	21	Darragh West	34	El Merduma 2
8	Sirtan Main	22	Darragh Main	35	El Merduma 3
9	Misurata	23	Sedadah	36	El Merduma 4
10	Gardabia East	24	Tamet	37	Marble Arch
11	Gardabia Main	25	Hamraiet North	38	El Agheila
12	Gardabia South	26	Hamraiet Main	39	Mersa el Brega
13	Gardabia West	27	Hamraiet East		
14	Bir Dufan 1				

Kittyhawk IIIs of No 260 Sqn lined up at Castel Benito in early 1943. Delivered in a temperate camouflage scheme, desert colours were applied in-theatre. An attempt has been made to avoid overpainting the serial number on some aircraft but even these have been obscured by the subsequent application of individual code letters. (Edwards)

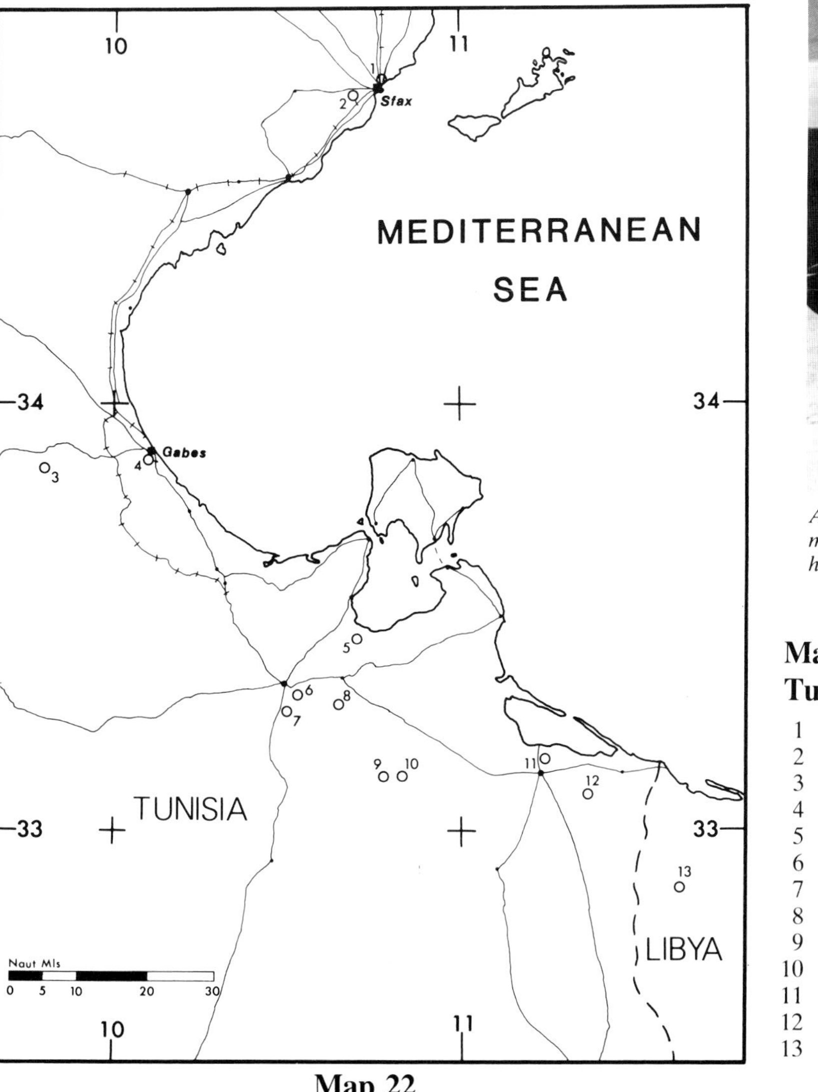

Map 22

As the 8th Army pursued the Afrika Korps into Tunisia the transport squadrons in the Middle East were fully occupied moving urgent supplies forward and evacuating casualties. One such unit was No 216 Sqn one of whose Hudsons is seen here coded LO·K. (G J Thomas)

Map 22 – Tunisia (Gabes)

1 Sidi Mansour/Sfax
2 Sfax
3 El Hamma
4 Gabes
5 Bu Grara
6 Medanine
7 Hazbub
8 Senem
9 Nefatia West
10 Nefatia Main
11 Ben Gardane North
12 Ben Gardane South
13 El Assa

One of the units that was based briefly in the Gabes sector was No 223 Sqn. This is one of No 223 Sqn's Baltimore IIIs, AG950. (RAF Museum P22508)

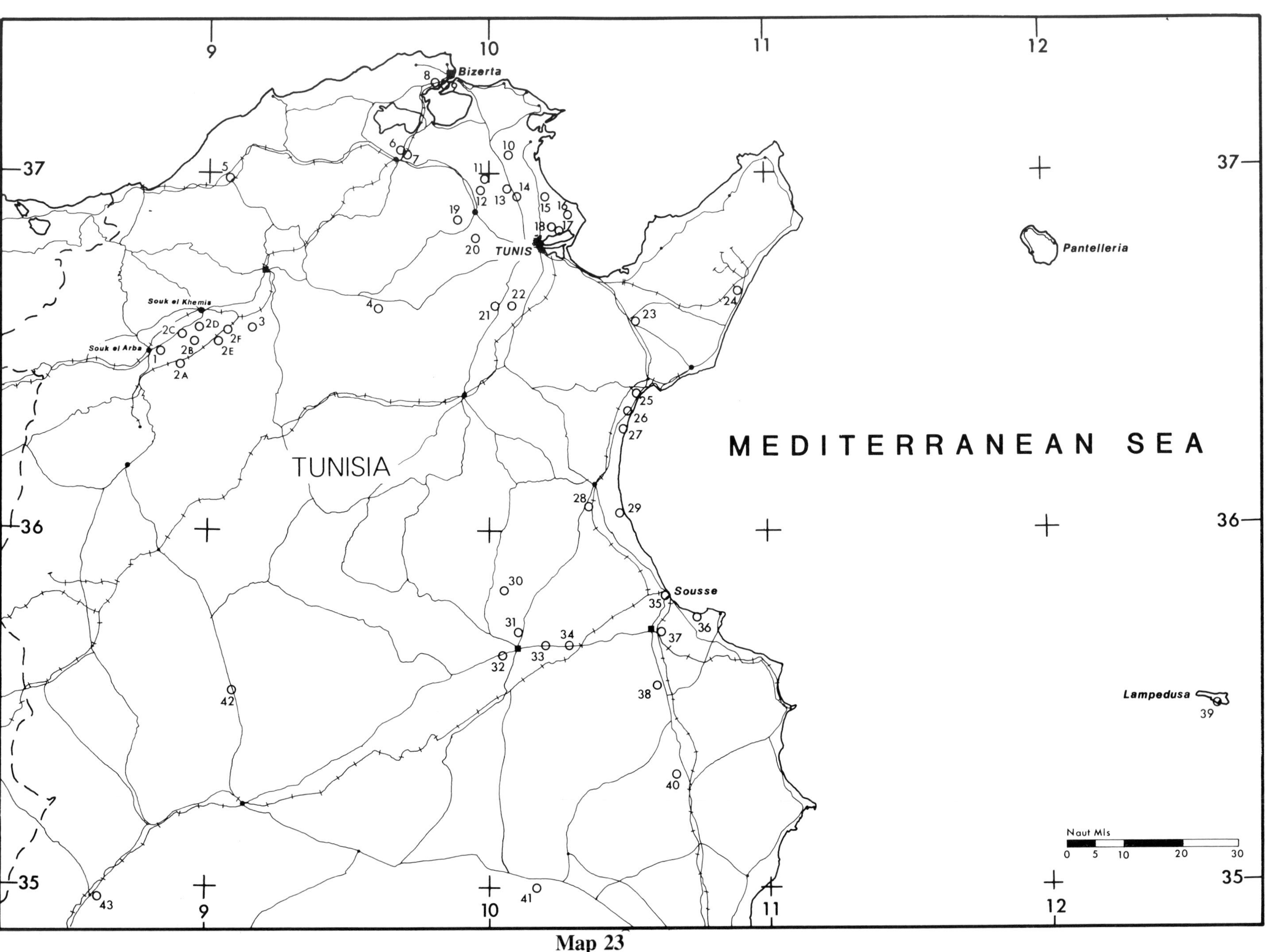
MEDITERRANEAN SEA
TUNISIA
Bizerta
TUNIS
Sousse
Souk el Khemis
Souk el Arba
Pantelleria
Lampedusa
Naut Mls
0 5 10 20 30
9
10
11
12
37
36
35

Map 23

Map 23 – Tunisia

1 Souk el Arba 'Sloane Square'
2A Souk el Khemis 'Paddington'
2B Souk el Khemis 'Victoria'
2C Souk el Khemis 'Marylebone'
2D Souk el Khemis 'Waterloo'
2E Souk el Khemis 'Euston'
2F Souk el Khemis 'Kings Cross'
3 Beja/Sidi Small
4 Medjez el Bab
5 Nefza
6 Mateur II
7 Mateur I/Bel Aid
8 Sidi Ahmed
9 Bizerta
10 Protville III/Utique/Sidi Athman
11 Protville I
12 Protville II
13 Le Sebala II
14 Le Sebala I
15 Sidi Amor
16 La Marsa
17 El Aouina
18 Ariana
19 Djedeida 1
20 Djedeida 2
21 Oudna No 2
22 Oudna No 1
23 Grombalia
24 Korba
25 Bou Ficha North
26 Bou Ficha South
27 Reyville
28 Enfidaville
29 Hergla
30 Kairouan/El Alem/Cheria
31 Kairouan/Temmar
32 Kairouan/Allami
33 Hani
34 Goubrine II
35 Sousse
36 Monastir
37 Msaken
38 Goubrine Main
39 Lampedusa
40 El Djam
41 La Fauconnerie
42 Sbiba
43 Thelepte

Hurricane IIC, HW421, of No 241 Sqn at Souk el Khemis.
(RAF Museum P7913)

Map 24

MEDITERRANEAN SEA

ALGERIA

ALGIERS

Oran

Constantine

Bone

Naut Mls 0 5 15 30 60

Map 24 – Algeria

1 La Senia
2 Tafaraoui
3 Arzeu
4 Froha
5 Blida
6 Algiers
7 Hussein Dey
8 Maison Carrée
9 Fort de l'Eau
10 Maison Blanche
11 Reghaia
12 Setif
13 Djedjelli
14 Taher
15 Châteaudun
16 Telergma
17 Fontaine Chaude
18 Constantine/Le Kroube
19 Phillipeville
20 Jemappes
21 Tingley
22 Bone
23 Canrobert
24 Oulmene
25 Youks les Bains

Hurricane IIC, HV817/FT·C, of No 43 Sqn at Maison Blanche in Nov 42. (RAF Museum P8020)

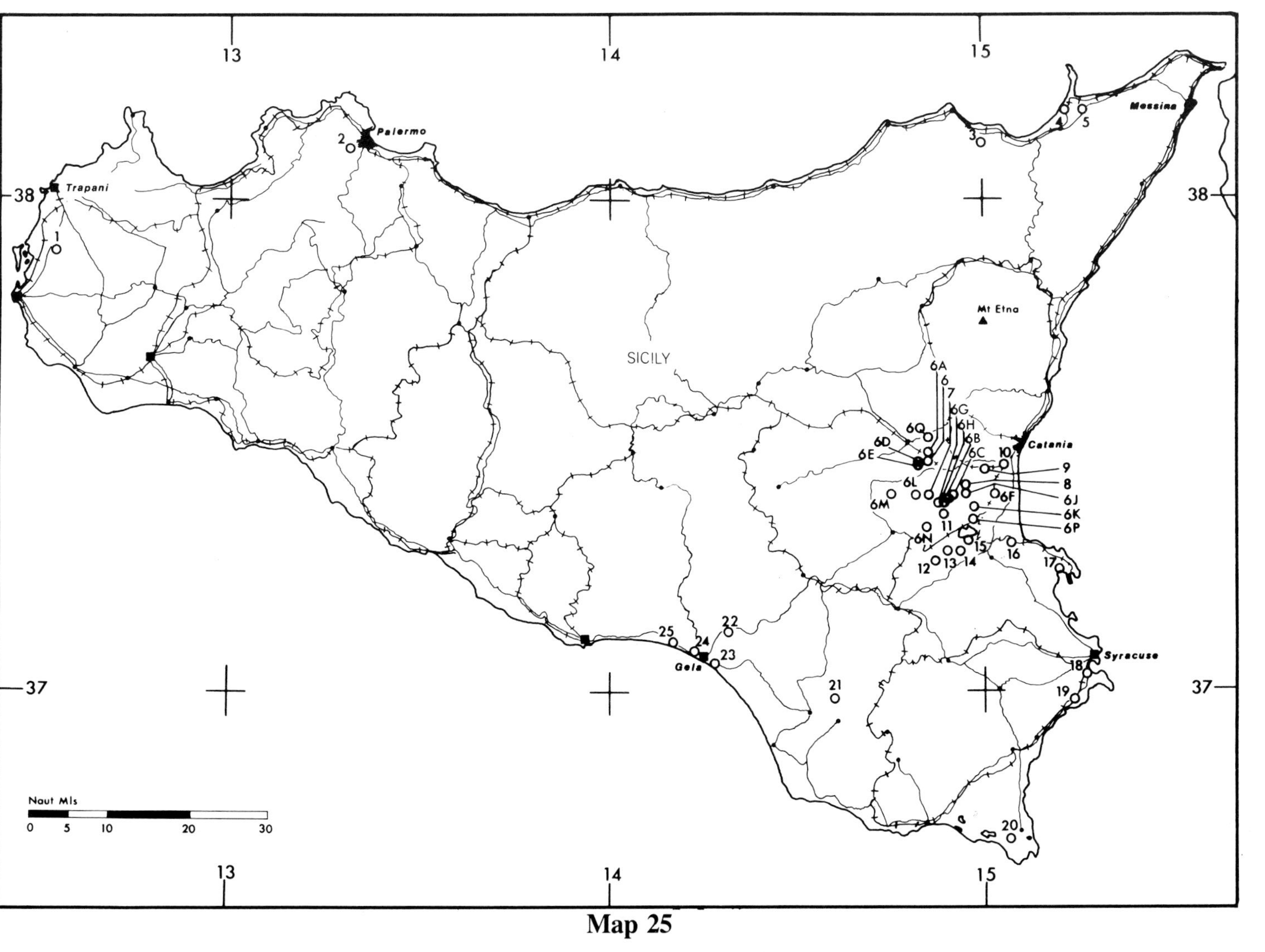

Map 25

Map 25 – Sicily

1 Bo Rizzo
2 Palermo
3 Falcone
4 Milazzo West
5 Milazzo East
6 Gerbini
6A Gerbini Satellite No 1
6B Gerbini Satellite No 2
6C Gerbini Satellite No 3/ Sigonella
6D Gerbini Satellite No 4
6E Gerbini Satellite No 5
6F Gerbini Satellite No 6
6G Gerbini Satellite No 7
6H Gerbini Satellite No 8
6J Gerbini Satellite No 9
6K Gerbini Satellite No 10
6L Gerbini Satellite No 11
6M Gerbini Satellite No 12
6N Gerbini Satellite No 13
6P Gerbini Satellite No 14
6Q Gerbini Satellite No 15
7 Fano
8 Cassala
9 3727N 1500E
10 Catania
11 Panebianco
12 Scordia
13 Lentini West
14 San Francesco
15 Lentini East
16 Agnone
17 Augusta
18 Syracuse
19 Cassibile
20 Pachino
21 Comiso
22 Gela/Ponte Olivo
23 Gela East
24 Gela West
25 Monte Lungo

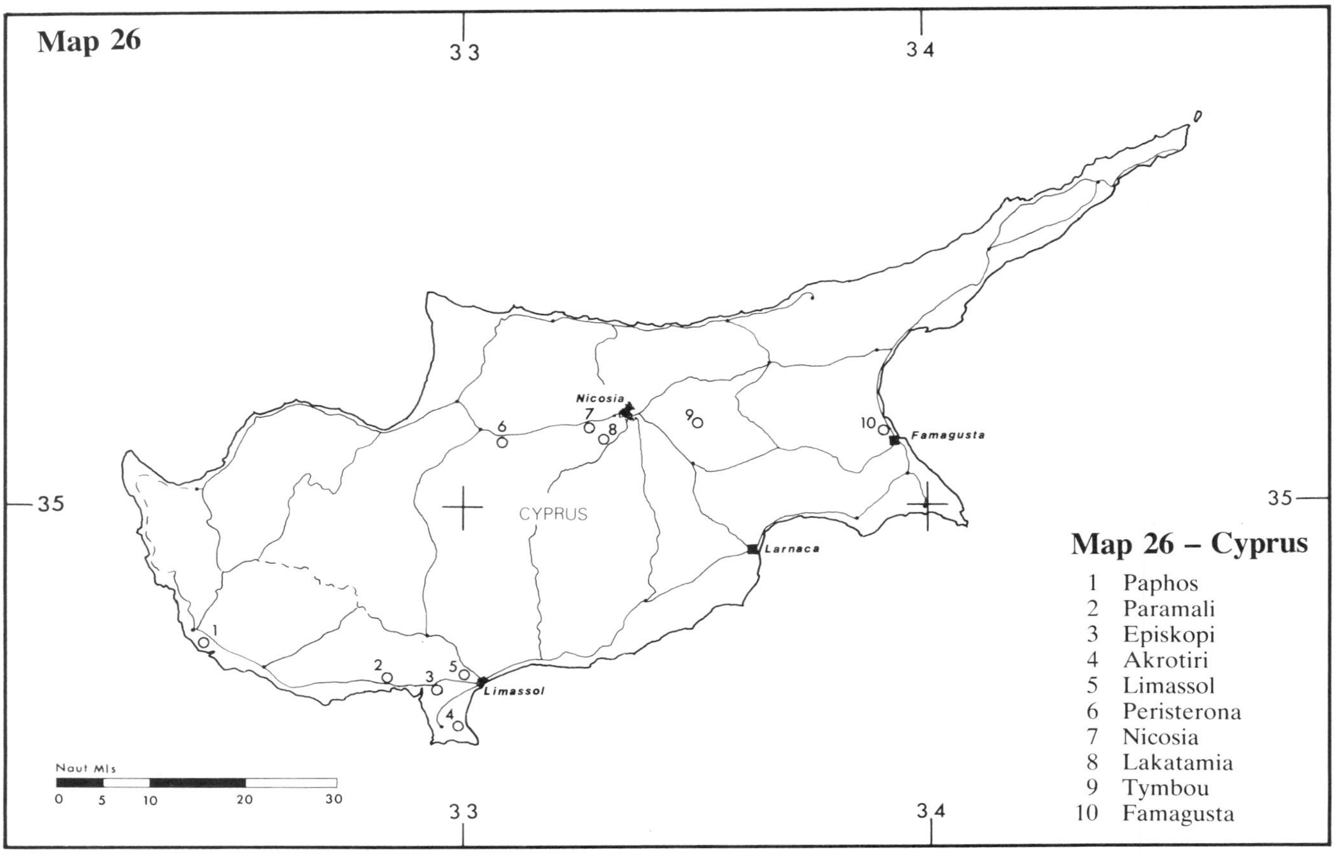

Map 26

Map 26 – Cyprus

1 Paphos
2 Paramali
3 Episkopi
4 Akrotiri
5 Limassol
6 Peristerona
7 Nicosia
8 Lakatamia
9 Tymbou
10 Famagusta

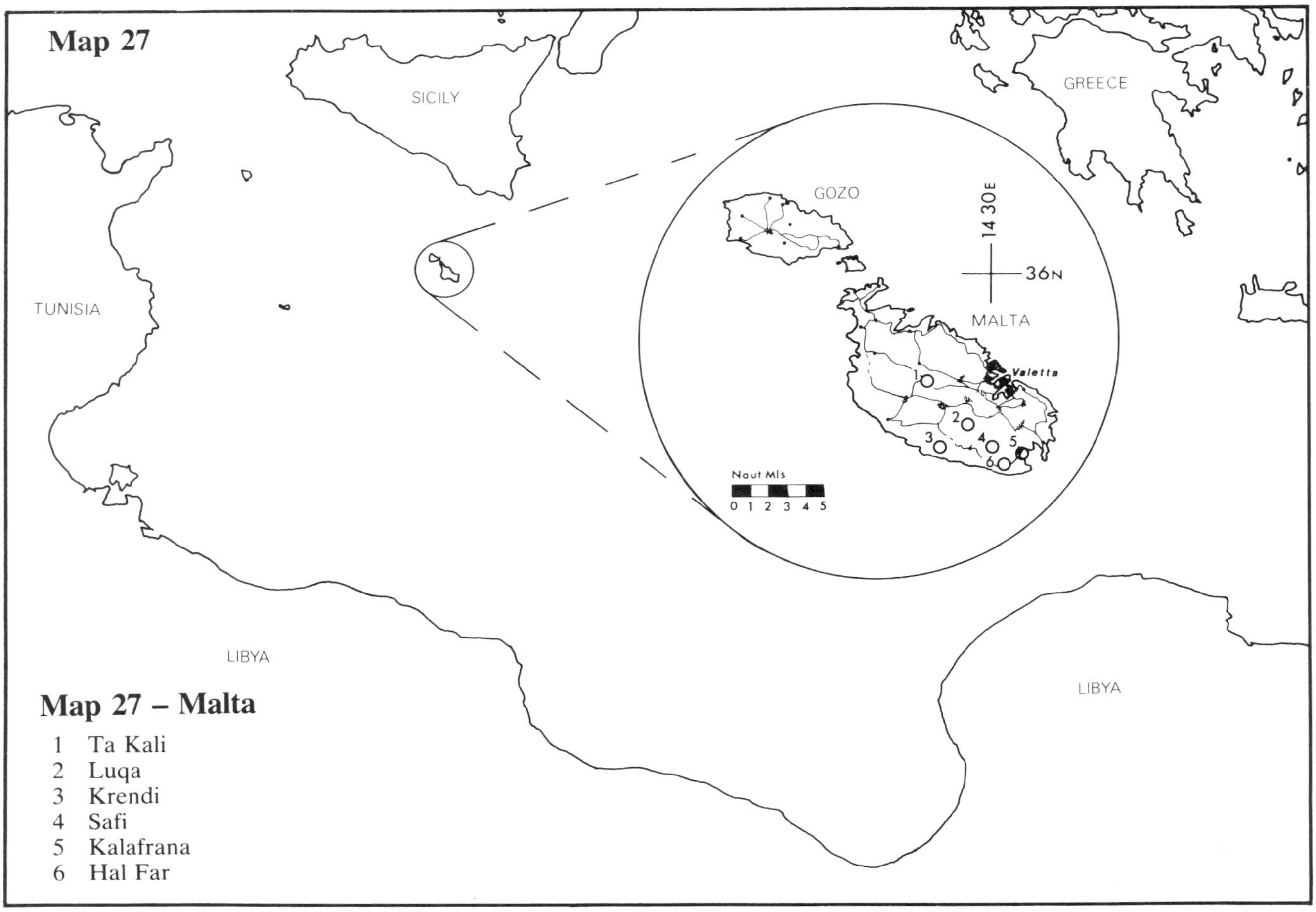

Map 27

Map 27 – Malta

1 Ta Kali
2 Luqa
3 Krendi
4 Safi
5 Kalafrana
6 Hal Far

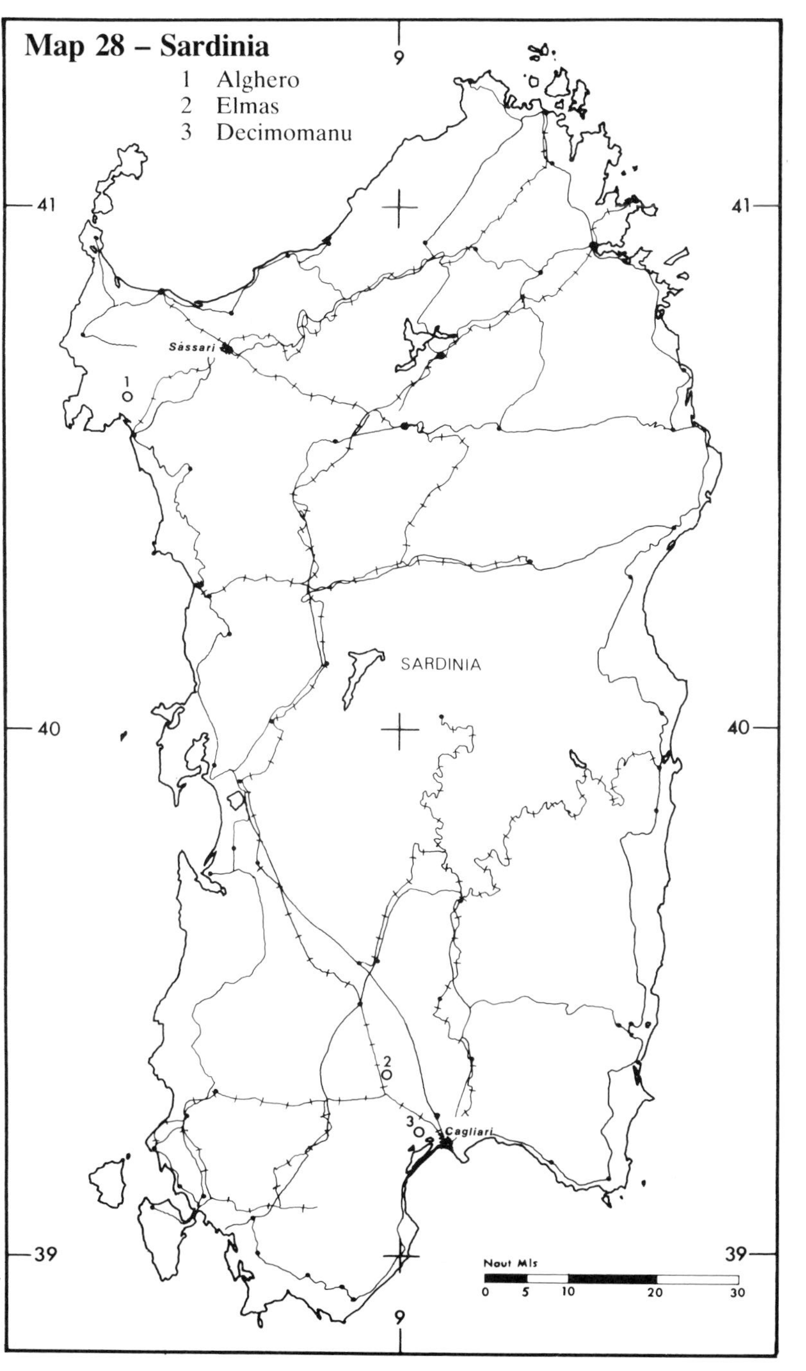

Map 29

Bastia

Calvi

CORSICA

AJACCIO

Naut Mls

0 5 10 20 30

9 10 43 42

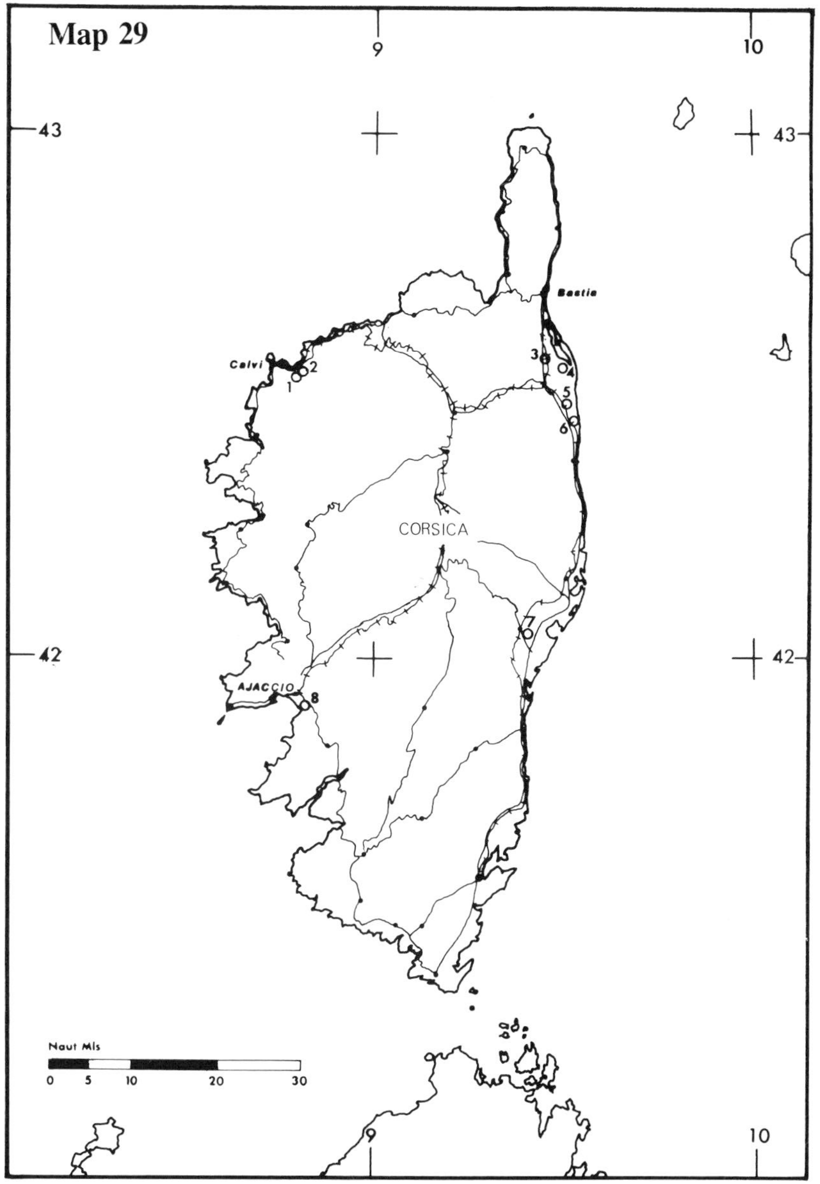

Map 29 – Corsica

1 Calvi/St Catherine
2 Calenzana
3 Borgo
4 Poretta
5 Serragia
6 Alto
7 Ghisonnacia
8 Ajaccio/Campo d'il Oro

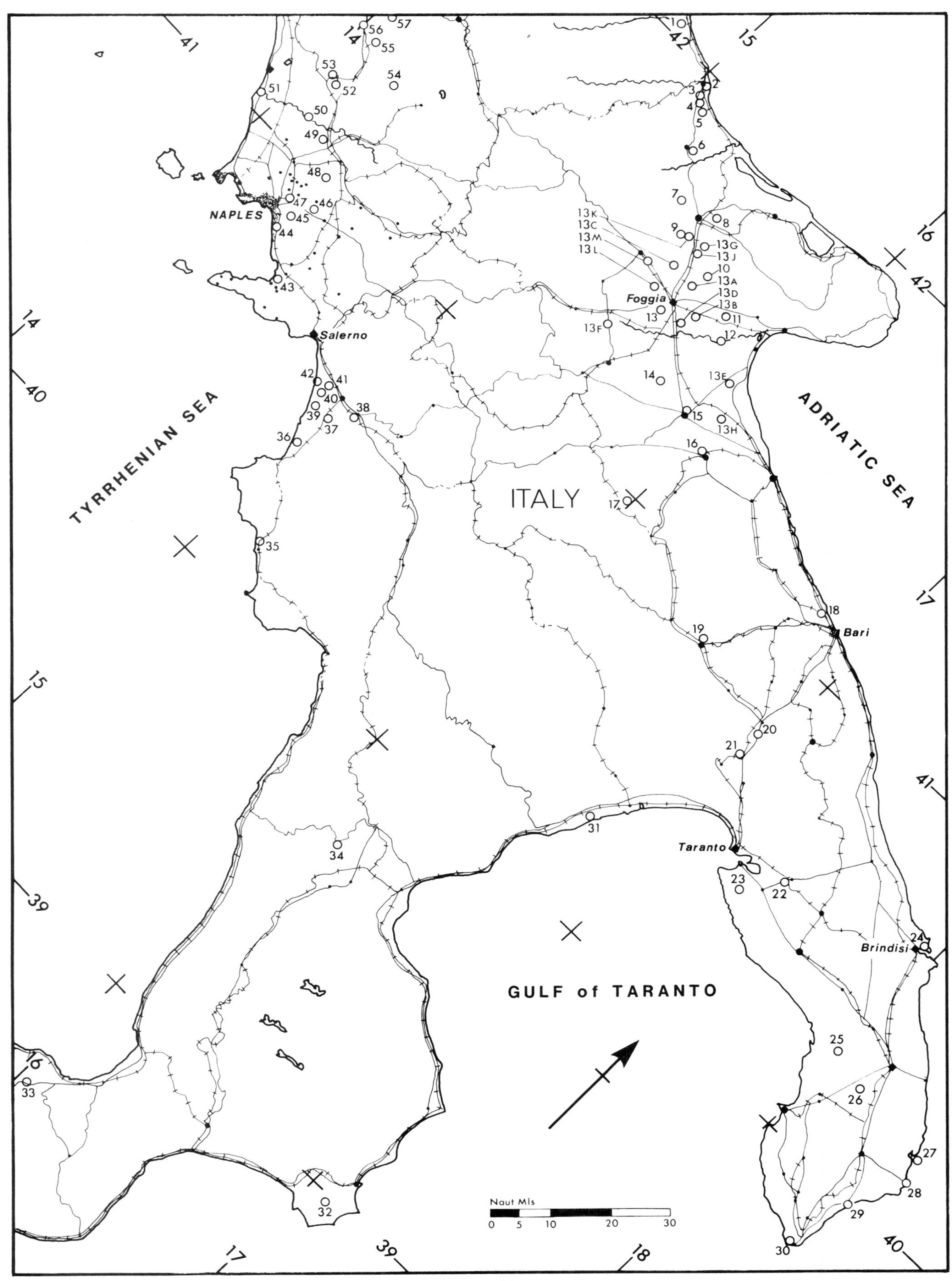

NAPLES
Salerno
Foggia
Bari
Taranto
Brindisi
TYRRHENIAN SEA
ADRIATIC SEA
ITALY
GULF of TARANTO
Naut Mls
0 5 10 20 30

Map 30

Map 30 – Southern Italy

1 Cutella
2 Biferno/Campomarino
3 Canne
4 Madna
5 Nuova
6 Serracapriola
7 Torremaggiore
8 San Severo
9 Regina
10 Mileni
11 Amendola
12 Palata
13 Foggia Main
13A Foggia No 1/San Nicola/Capelli/Celone
13B Foggia No 2/Tortorella
13C Foggia No 3/Schifara/Salsola
13D Foggia No 4/Fandetta
13E Foggia No 5/Morin
13F Foggia No 6/Radogno
13G Foggia No 7/Zanotti/Triolo
13H Foggia No 8/Posta Augello
13J Foggia No 9/Amendola/Triolo LG
13K Foggia No 10/San Andrea
13L Foggia No 11/Nocelli
13M Foggia No 12/Lucera
14 Stornara
15 Cerignola
16 Canosa
17 Palazzo
18 Bari/Palese
19 Altamura
20 Gioia del Colle
21 San Basilio
22 Grottaglie
23 Taranto/Pizzone
24 Brindisi
25 Leverano
26 Lecce
27 Alimini
28 Otranto
29 Andrano
30 Santa Maria de Leucca
31 Scanzano
32 Crotone
33 Vibo Valentia
34 Firmo
35 Castellamare
36 Gaudo
37 Battipaglia
38 Eboli
39 Serretelle
40 Tusciano
41 Montecorvino
42 Asa
43 Gragnano
44 Portici
45 Cercola
46 Pomigliano
47 Capodichino
48 Marcianese
49 4105N 1413E
50 Santa Maria la Fosse
51 Lago
52 Sparinese
53 4113½N 1404½E
54 San Angelo
55 Presenzano
56 Campozillone
57 Venafro

Dakotas, including KG496 and FL589, of No 267 Sqn lined up at Bari. Apart from some Wellingtons the rest of the aircraft in the background are all American and include examples of the B-17, B-24, B-26, C-47, P-38, P-47 and P-51.
(RAF Museum P1691)

A Spitfire VC of No 43 Sqn kicks up the dust of Tusciano in Sep 43.
(RAF Museum P8054)

A Liberator VI carrying the 'SNAKE' annotation ahead of the serial number on the fuselage. This was intended to ensure that the aircraft arrived at its destination (the Far East) and was not diverted en route. The system appears not to have been 100 per cent effective, since KL732 is seen here as EP·C of No 104 Sqn in Italy.
(RAF Museum P7565)

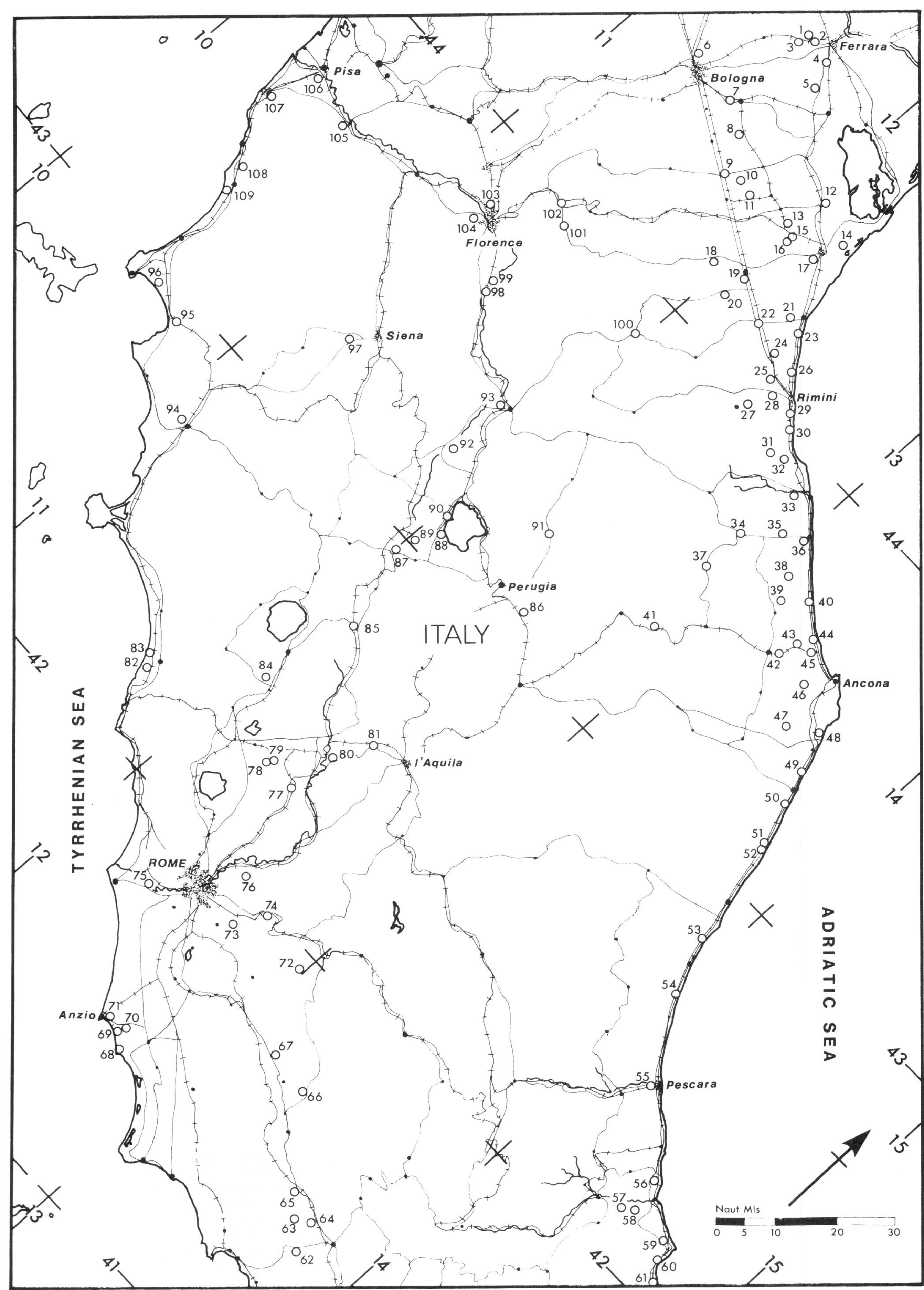
Ferrara
Bologna
Pisa
Florence
Siena
Rimini
Perugia
ITALY
Ancona
l'Aquila
ROME
Anzio
Pescara
TYRRHENIAN SEA
ADRIATIC SEA
Naut Mls
0 5 10 20 30

Map 31

Map 31 – Central Italy

1 Coronella
2 Ferrara/La Russia
3 Poggio Renatico
4 San Marco
5 Montesanto
6 Bologna
7 Budrio
8 Medicina
9 Imola
10 Villa Arzana
11 Lugo
12 4431N 1203E
13 4423N 1201E
14 4428N 1212E
15 Villa Brocchi
16 San Pancrazio
17 Ravenna
18 Castrocaro
19 Forli
20 Meldola
21 Cervia
22 Cesena
23 Cesenatico
24 Savignano
25 Santa Arcengelo
26 Bellaria
27 Serravalle
28 4402N 1230E
29 Rimini
30 Riccione
31 Morciano
32 Cassandro
33 'River Foglia'
34 Fossombrone
35 Borgo Lucrezia
36 Fano
37 Pergola
38 Piagiolino
39 Borghetto
40 Senigallia
41 Fabriano
42 Iesi
43 Chiaravalle
44 Monte Marciano
45 Falconara
46 San Bernadino
47 Recanati
48 Loreto
49 Porto Potenza
50 Porto San Elpidio
51 Fermo/Porto San Giorgio
52 Torre di Palme
53 Tortoreto
54 Roseto degli Abruzzi
55 Pescara
56 San Vito
57 'River Sangro'
58 Paglieta
59 Sinello
60 Vasto
61 Trigno
62 San Giorgio
63 Pontecorvo
64 Aquino
65 Giovanni
66 Alatri
67 Anagni
68 La Banca
69 Nettuno
70 Tre Cancelli
71 Anzio
72 Littorio
73 Osa
74 Guidonia
75 Galeria
76 4201N 1235E
77 Civita Castellana
78 Falerium
79 Fabrica
80 Otricole
81 Narni
82 Tarquinia
83 Voltone
84 Viterbo
85 Orvieto
86 Perugia
87 Citta della Pieve
88 Carraia
89 Ravigliano
90 Castiglione del Lago
91 Umbertide
92 Creti/Foiano
93 Arezzo
94 Grosseto
95 Follonica
96 Piombino
97 Malignano
98 Figline
99 Incisa
100 San Piero in Bagno
101 Vicchio
102 Borgo San Lorenzo
103 Peretola
104 Scandicci
105 Pontedera
106 Pisa
107 Leghorn
108 Rosignano
109 Cecina

A Kittyhawk IV of No 450 Sqn. (F F Smith via Chris Shores)

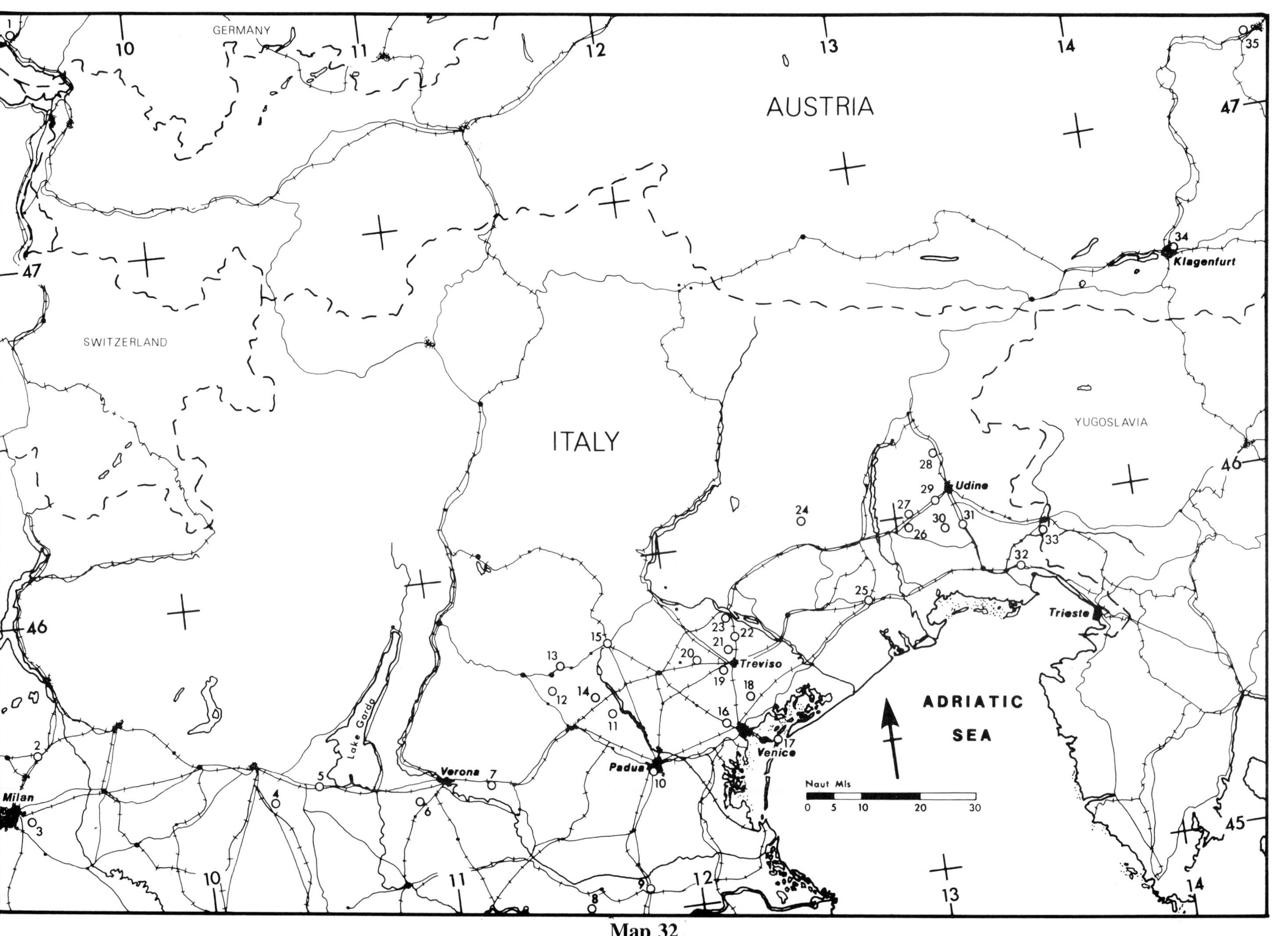
GERMANY
AUSTRIA
SWITZERLAND
ITALY
YUGOSLAVIA
Klagenfurt
Udine
Trieste
Treviso
Venice
Padua
Verona
Milan
Lake Garda
ADRIATIC
SEA
Naut Mls
0 5 10 20 30

Map 32

Map 32 – Northern Italy

1 Friedrichshaven
2 Monza
3 Milan
4 Ghedi
5 Lonato
6 Verona/Villafranca
7 Caldiero
8 Canda
9 Rovigo
10 Padua
11 Grossa
12 Villaverla
13 Sarcedo
14 San Pietro in Gu
15 San Luca
16 Mestre
17 Venice/San Nicola
18 Marcon
19 Treviso
20 Istrana/Fossalunga
21 San Pelagio
22 Limbraga
23 Arcade
24 Aviano
25 Portogruaro
26 Rivolto
27 Villa Orba
28 Tricisimo
29 Udine/Campoformido
30 Lavariano
31 Tissano
32 Ronchi
33 Gorizia
34 Klagenfurt
35 Zeltweg

A Mustang IV wearing No 112 Sqn's well known sharkmouth marking flying over northern Italy in 1946. (Andrew Thomas)

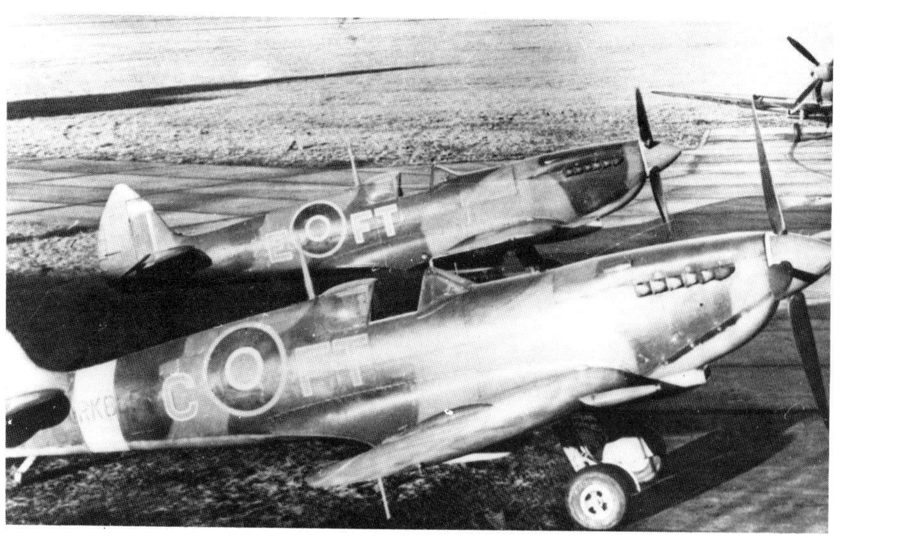

Spitfire IXs, RK885/FT·C and TB546/FT·E, of No 43 Sqn at Zeltweg in Sep 45. (RAF Museum P8030)

No 250 Sqn traded-in its Kittyhawks for Mustang IIIs and IVs at Lavariano in Aug 45. This one appears to have the eye of one of No 112 Sqn's sharks painted on its cowling. (RAF Museum P10497)

A Tempest F.2 of No 26 Sqn at Zeltweg in 1947. (Sqn Ldr D L Rowell)

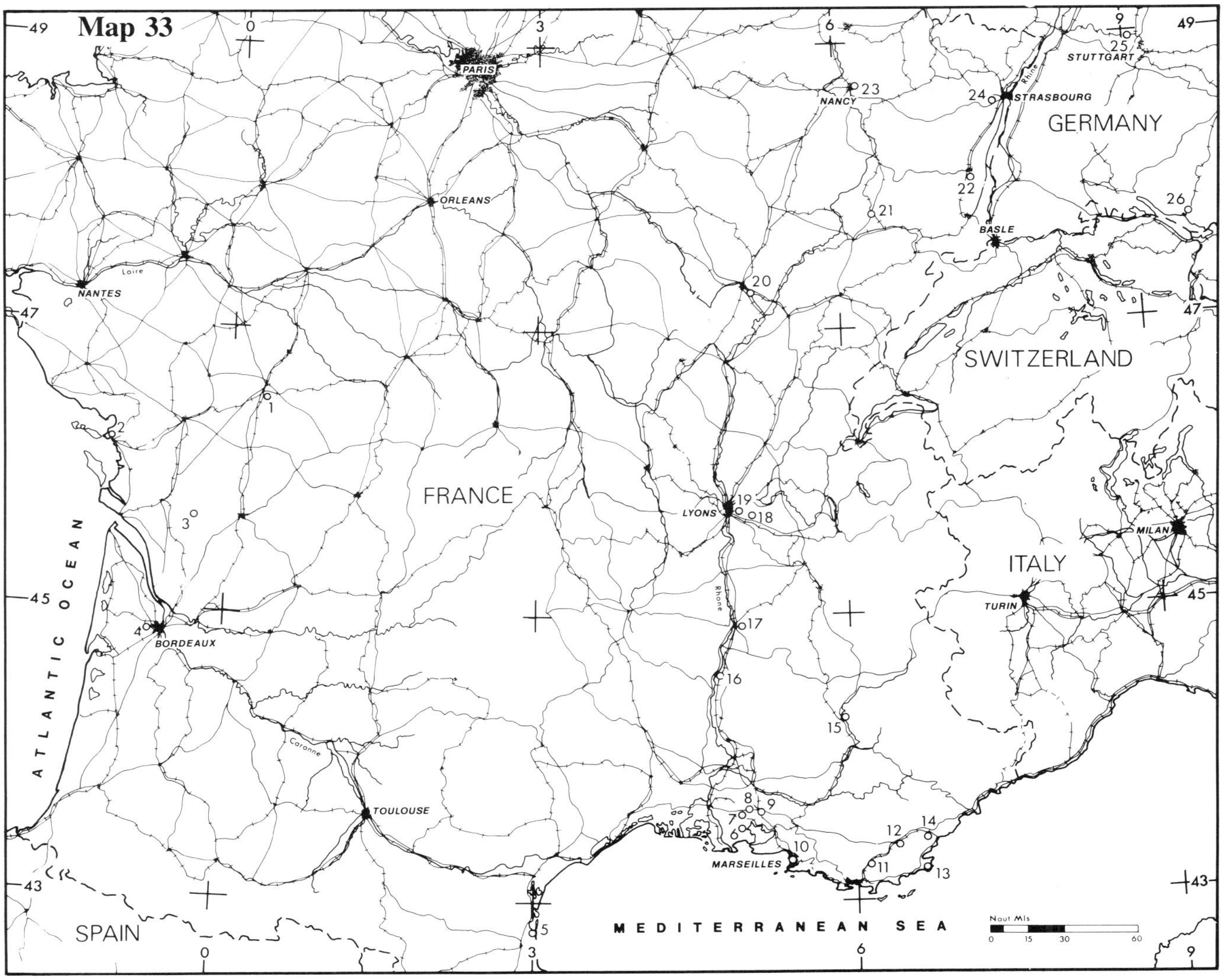

Map 33 – South Eastern France, 1940-45

1	Poitiers	8	Y 19/Le Jasse	16	Y 21/Montelimar	24	Y 40/Strasbourg/ Entzheim
2	La Rochelle	9	Y 16/Salon	17	Y 23/Valence	25	R 27/Sersheim/ Sachsenheim
3	Y 36/Cognac/Château Bernard	10	Marseilles	18	Y 24/Lyons/Satolas	26	R 58/Friedrichshaven
4	Y 37/Bordeaux/Merignac	11	Y 13/Cuers	19	Y 6/Lyons/Bron		
5	Perpignan/La Salanque	12	Le Luc	20	Y 9/Dijon/Longevic		
6	Y 17/Istres	13	Ramatuelle	21	Y 8/Luxeuil		
7	Y 18/Le Vallon	14	Y 12/Frejus	22	Y 53/Colmar		
		15	Y 20/Sisteron	23	Y 42/Nancy/Essey		

No 93 Sqn was one of the units which took part in Operation Dragoon, the invasion of southern France. This is one of the squadron's Spitfire IXs, RR239/HN·Y. (RAF Museum P17681)

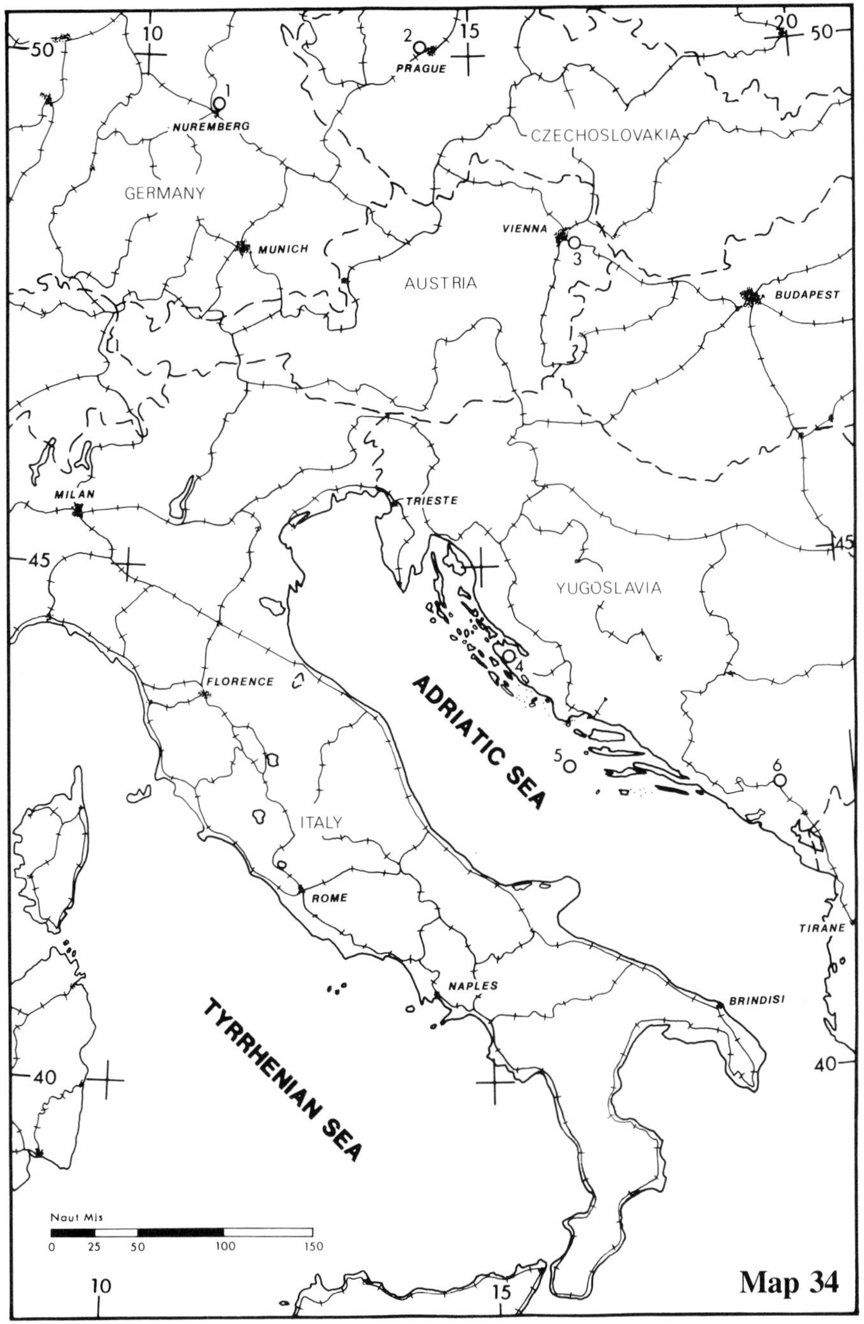

Map 34

Map 34 – Eastern Europe and the Adriatic/Jugoslavia

1	R 28/Nuremburg/Furth	4	Prkos
2	Prague	5	Vis
3	Vienna/Schwecat	6	Niksic

A Dakota, KN478, of No 78 Sqn seen at Schwecat in 1946. (RAF Museum P7758)

These Walruses of No 624 Sqn, including L2201 'B', W2741 'E' and Z1769 'A', were transferred to the RAF from RN stocks and used on mine-spotting duties in the Adriatic, Aegean and Mediterranean from bases in Italy, Greece and Malta. (via Chaz Bowyer)

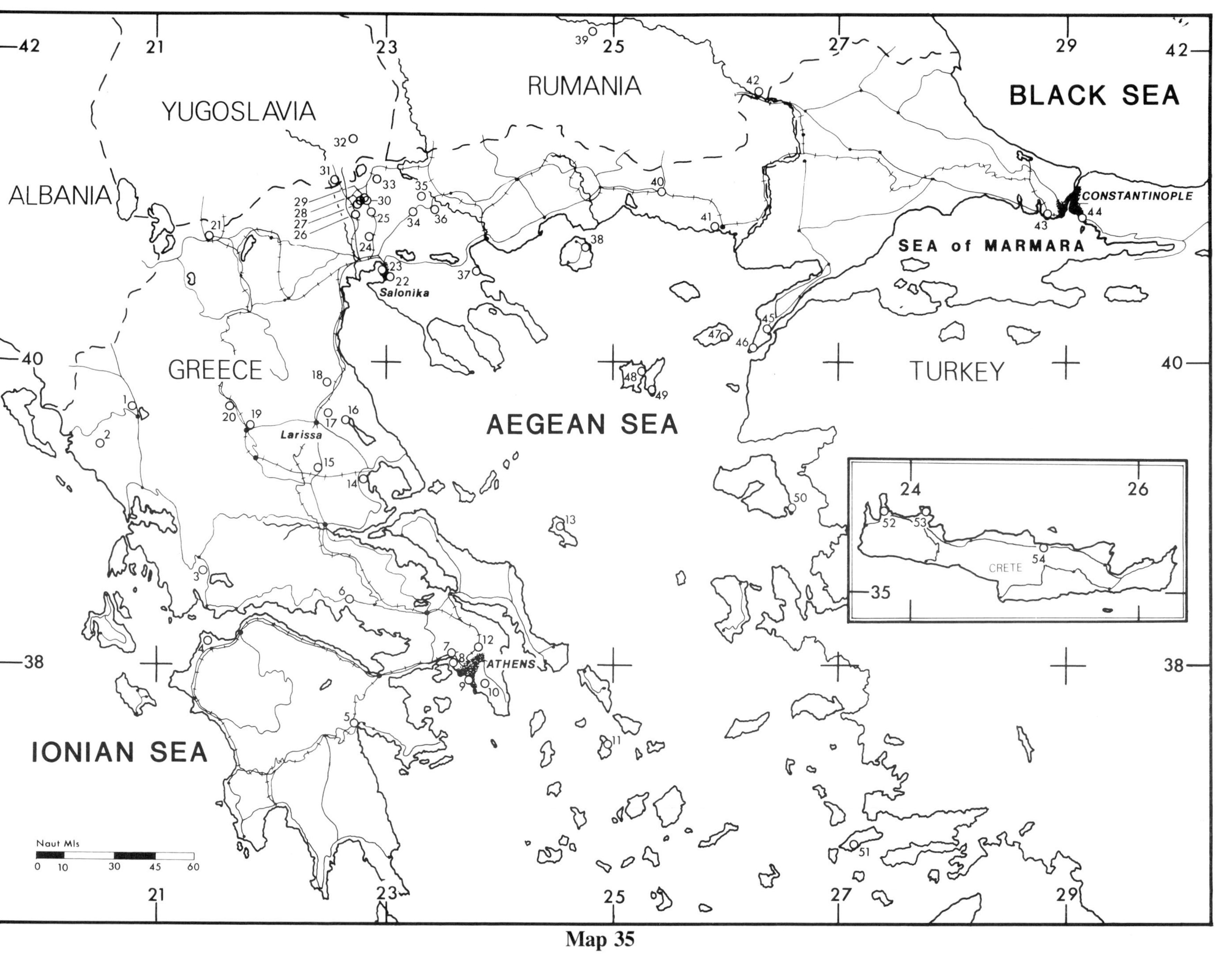
ALBANIA
YUGOSLAVIA
RUMANIA
BLACK SEA
CONSTANTINOPLE
SEA of MARMARA
TURKEY
GREECE
Salonika
Larissa
AEGEAN SEA
ATHENS
IONIAN SEA
CRETE
Naut Mls
0 10 30 45 60

Map 35

Map 35 – Greece/Macedonia and Turkey

1 Yanina
2 Paramythia
3 Agrinion
4 Araxos
5 Argos
6 Amphiklia
7 Elevsis
8 Scaramanga
9 Hassani/Kalamaki
10 Metokhi
11 Siros/Syra (Phoenika)
12 Menidi/Tatoi
13 Skyros
14 Almyros
15 Pharsala
16 Niamata
17 Larissa
18 Kazaklar
19 Trikkala
20 Kalabac
21 Florina
22 Sedes
23 Mikra Bay
24 Amberkoj
25 Kukush
26 Avret Hisar
27 Kirec
28 Hajdarli
29 Hadzi Junas
30 Yanesh
31 Stojakovo
32 Radovo
33 Snevche
34 Lahana
35 Orlyak
36 Marian
37 Stavros
38 Thasos
39 Phillipopolis
40 Gumuldjina
41 Dedeagatch
42 Mustapha Pasha
43 San Stephano
44 Maltepe
45 Kilya Bay
46 Kilid el Bahr
47 Imbros
48 Lemnos (Gliki)
49 Mudros (Marsh — Romanos/Landplanes, Talikna/Seaplanes)
50 Mitylene (Kalloni)
51 Cos
52 Maleme
53 Suda Bay
54 Heraklion

RNAS floatplanes operated in the Aegean, from ships and from shore bases, before being absorbed into the RAF and evolving into Nos 264 and 266 Sqns. This is an RNAS Short 184, 8095, from HMS Springbok, *on the beach at Mudros.* (RAF Museum P15604)

The Nightjar served only with No 203 Sqn. The highlight of its career was participation in the British intervention in Turkey during the Chanak Crisis of 1922-23. This picture was taken at Kilya Bay. (RAF Museum P14803)

The rather nondescript appearance of this Spitfire IV is misleading. It resulted from the rubbing down of filler which had been applied to produce as smooth a finish as possible in pursuit of maximum performance. The aeroplane was operated by No 680 Sqn and flew photo-reconnaissance sorties over the Aegean from Egypt. (Chaz Bowyer)

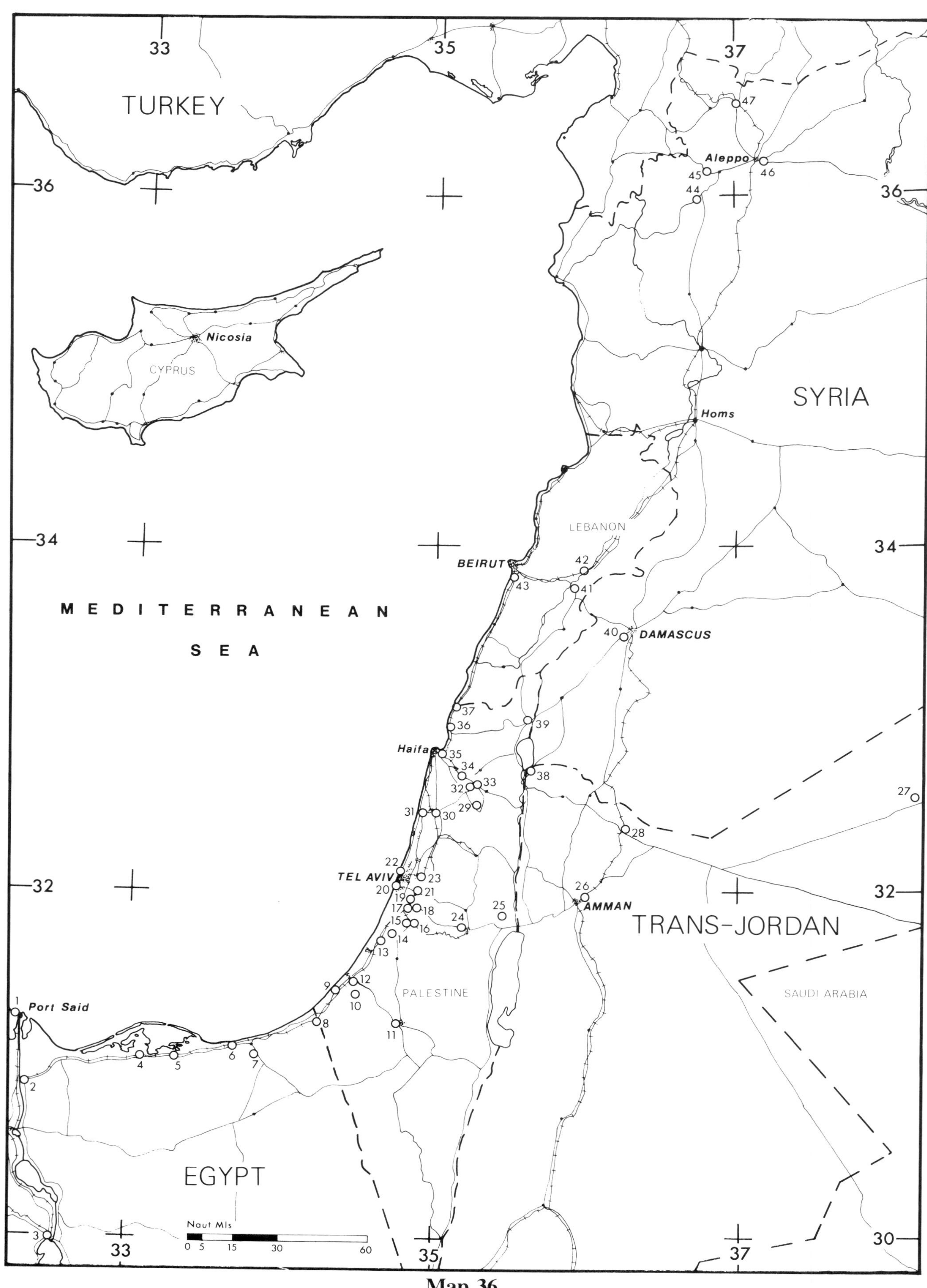

TURKEY
SYRIA
CYPRUS
Nicosia
LEBANON
MEDITERRANEAN
SEA
PALESTINE
TRANS-JORDAN
SAUDI ARABIA
EGYPT
Aleppo
Homs
BEIRUT
DAMASCUS
Haifa
TEL AVIV
AMMAN
Port Said
Naut Mls
0 5 15 30 60
33
35
37
36
34
32
30

Map 36

Map 36 – The Levant – Syria, Palestine

1 Port Said
2 Qantara
3 Suez
4 Salmana
5 Mustabig
6 Ujret el Zol
7 El Arish
8 Rafah
9 Deir el Ballah
10 (Weli) Sheikh Nuran
11 Beersheba
12 Gaza
13 Julis
14 Qastina
15 Aqir
16 Junction Station
17 Khirbet Deiran
18 Ramleh
19 Sarafand
20 Sarona
21 Lydda
22 Tel Aviv
23 Petah Tiqva
24 Jersusalem
25 Jericho
26 Amman
27 H4
28 Mafraq
29 Muqueibila
30 Ein Shemar
31 Hadera
32 Megiddo
33 El Affule
34 Ramat David
35 Haifa
36 St Jean
37 El Bassa
38 Semakh
39 Rosh Pinna
40 Damascus/Mezze
41 Estabel
42 Rayak
43 Beirut
44 Afisse
45 Bab el Haoua
46 Aleppo
47 Minnigh

No 14 Sqn arrived in Egypt in Nov 15 and spent most of the next thirty years in the region. This BE 2C, 4395, belonged to the squadron. The picture clearly illustrates the common practice in early two-seaters of having the pilot in the rear cockpit with the observer/gunner in the front seat. (Chaz Bowyer)

A Bristol Fighter, B1148, of No 67 Sqn at Julis. No 67 Sqn was formed from, and subsequently reverted to being, No 1 Sqn, AFC. Its Australian character can be deduced from the distinctive slouch hats worn by many of the personnel in this picture. (RAF Museum P11635)

An RE 8, B6557, of No 142 Sqn in Palestine. (RAF Museum P8277)

SE 5As of No 111 Sqn in Palestine in 1918. The nearest, B139, has four 20lb Cooper bombs on a rack beneath its fuselage. (RAF Museum P1102)

An Auster AOP 6, VF494, of No 651 Sqn landing on HMS Ocean *in the Mediterranean in 1947.* (Museum of Army Flying)

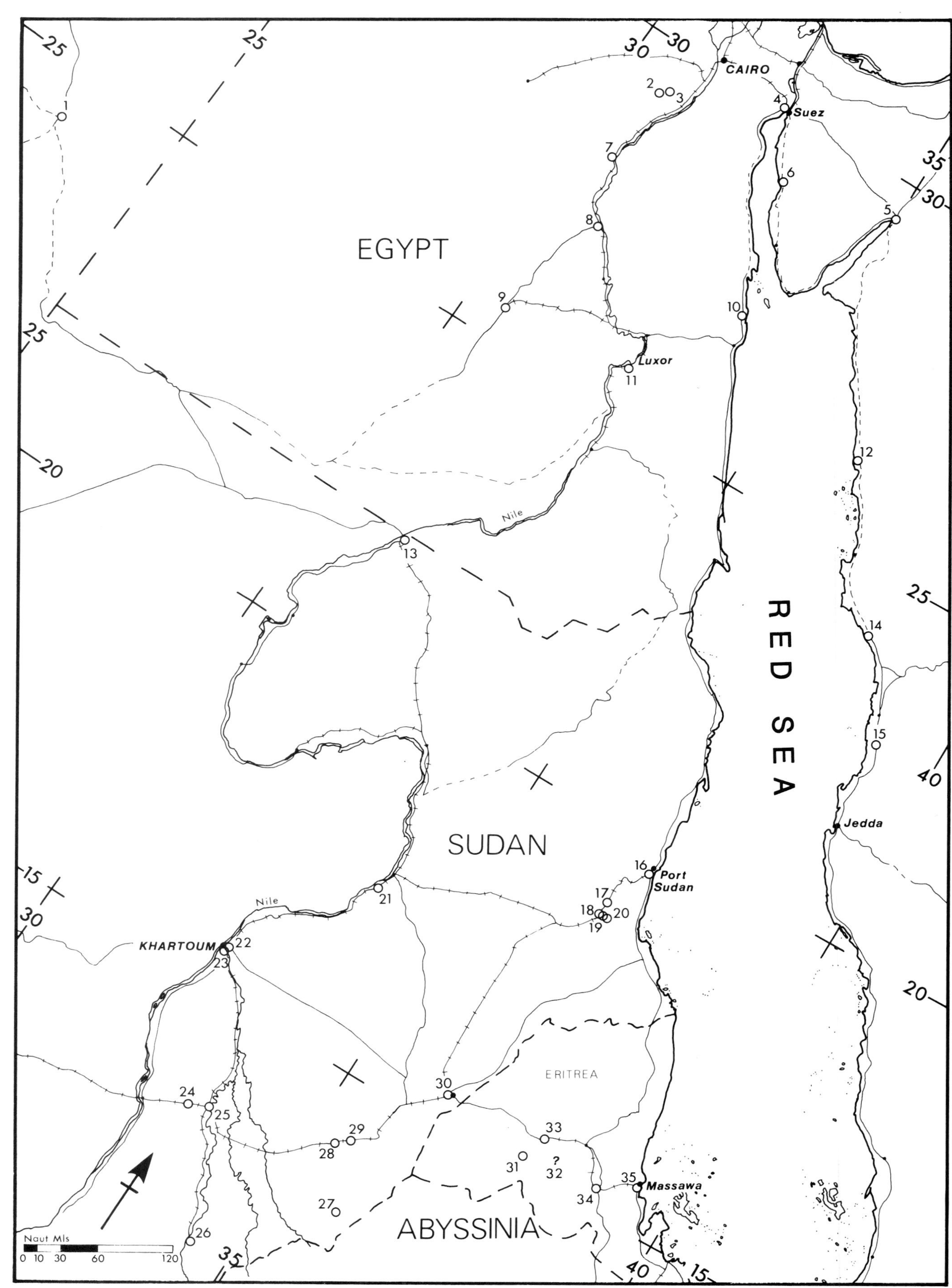
EGYPT
CAIRO
Suez
Luxor
Nile
SUDAN
RED SEA
Jedda
Port Sudan
KHARTOUM
ERITREA
Massawa
ABYSSINIA
Naut Mls
0 10 30 60 120

Map 37

Map 37 – The Nile and the Red Sea

1 Kufra
2 Abu Gandir
3 Fayoum
4 Suez
5 Aqaba
6 Abu Zenima
7 Minya
8 Assiyut
9 Kharga/Sherika
10 Hurghada
11 Luxor
12 El Weigh
13 Wadi Halfa
14 Yenbo
15 Rabigh
16 Port Sudan
17 Gebeit
18 Summit
19 Wadi Gazouza
20 Erkowit/Carthago
21 Ed Damer
22 Khartoum
23 Gordon's Tree
24 'Hamble'
25 Sennar
26 Roseires
27 'Heston'
28 Gedaref
29 'Blackdown'
30 Kassala
31 Barentu
32* Um Ritsar
33 Agordat
34 Asmara
35 Massawa

*The exact location of Um Ritsar (No 237 Sqn Mar/Apr 41) has remained obscure, but it must, logically, have been somewhere between Barentu and Asmara.

Gordons, including K2622 and K2624, of the Khartoum-based No 47 Sqn. Judging from the fact that some of these aeroplanes have rudder stripes while others do not the photograph was probably taken shortly after 1 Aug 34 when such markings were discontinued. (RAF Museum P10734)

When No 14 Sqn re-equipped with Blenheims in Dec 40 it passed its Wellesleys on to Nos 47 and 223 Sqns. This one, L2665, was lost in an Italian Air Force attack on Agordat on 9 Feb 41. It is not certain that this photograph depicts this incident – the damage looks more like a landing accident and the retention of No 14 Sqn's badge on the fin, in place of fin stripes, suggests an earlier date. (RAF Museum P7019)

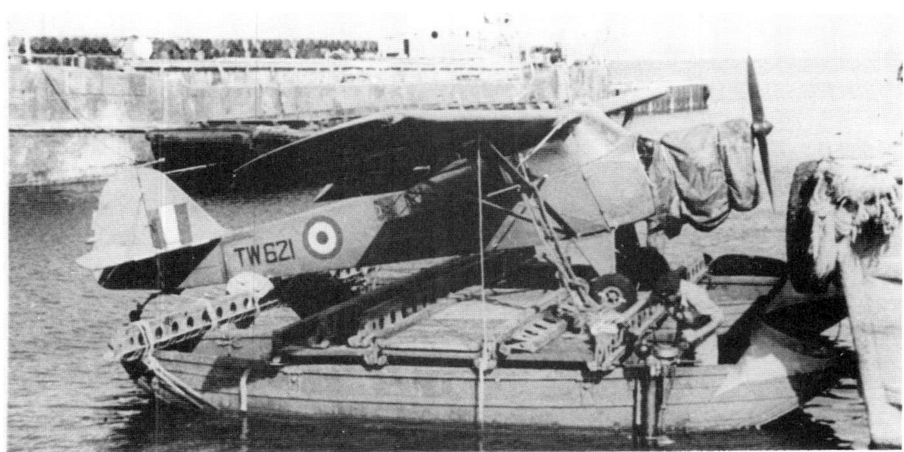

On 24 Aug 54 Capt Sargent, RA, forced-landed on a narrow beach while en route Ismailia-Amman in this Auster AOP 6, TW621, of No 651 Sqn. The aircraft was floated off on pontoons, towed eleven miles up the Gulf of Aqaba, fitted with a new engine and flown back to Ismailia. It did not survive for long; it crashed in Egypt on 27 Aug 55. (Museum of Army Flying)

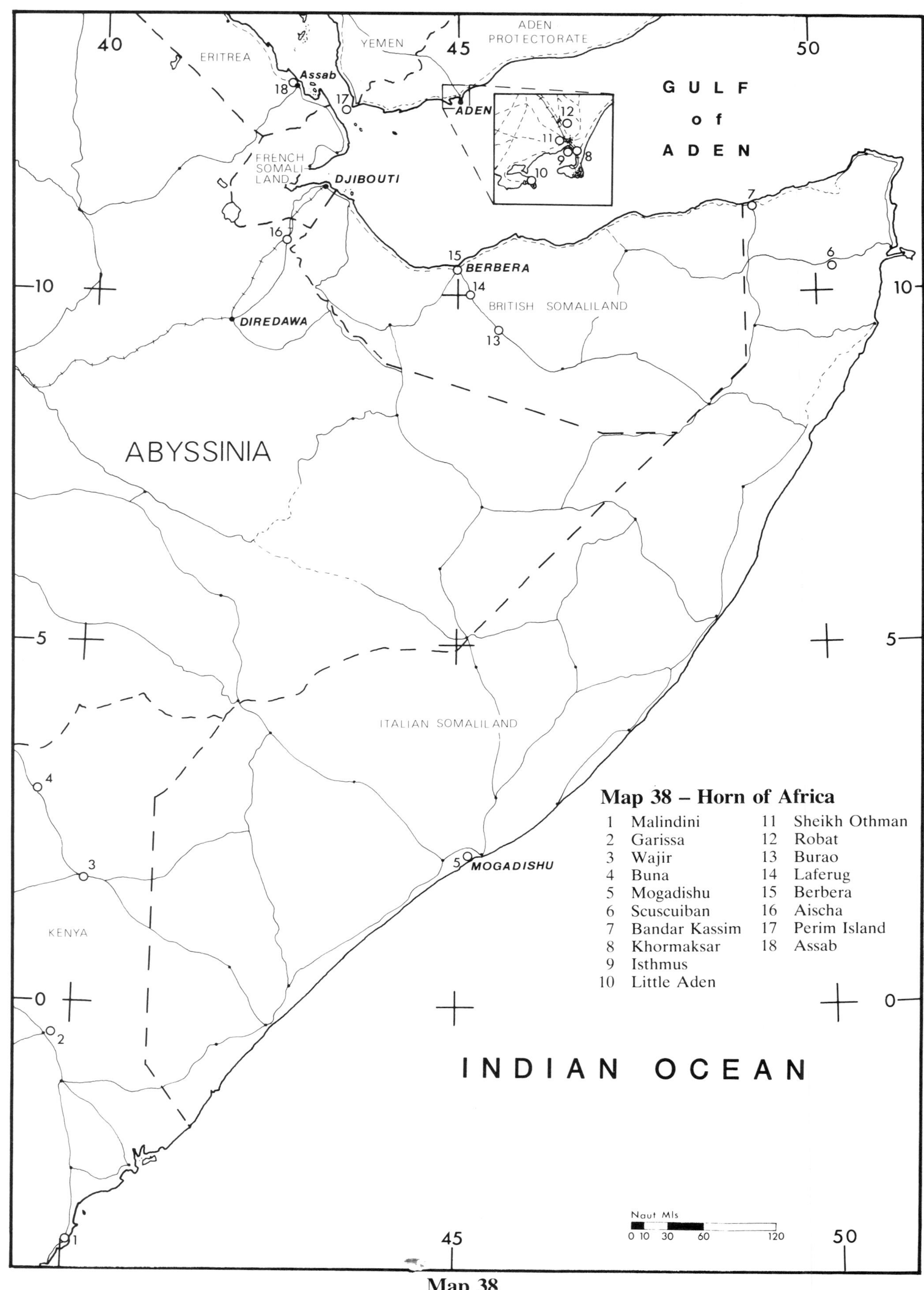
ERITREA
YEMEN
ADEN PROTECTORATE
GULF of ADEN
Assab
ADEN
FRENCH SOMALI-LAND
DJIBOUTI
BERBERA
BRITISH SOMALILAND
DIREDAWA
ABYSSINIA
ITALIAN SOMALILAND
MOGADISHU
KENYA
INDIAN OCEAN
Map 38 – Horn of Africa
1 Malindini
2 Garissa
3 Wajir
4 Buna
5 Mogadishu
6 Scuscuiban
7 Bandar Kassim
8 Khormaksar
9 Isthmus
10 Little Aden
11 Sheikh Othman
12 Robat
13 Burao
14 Laferug
15 Berbera
16 Aischa
17 Perim Island
18 Assab
Naut Mls
0 10 30 60 120

Map 38

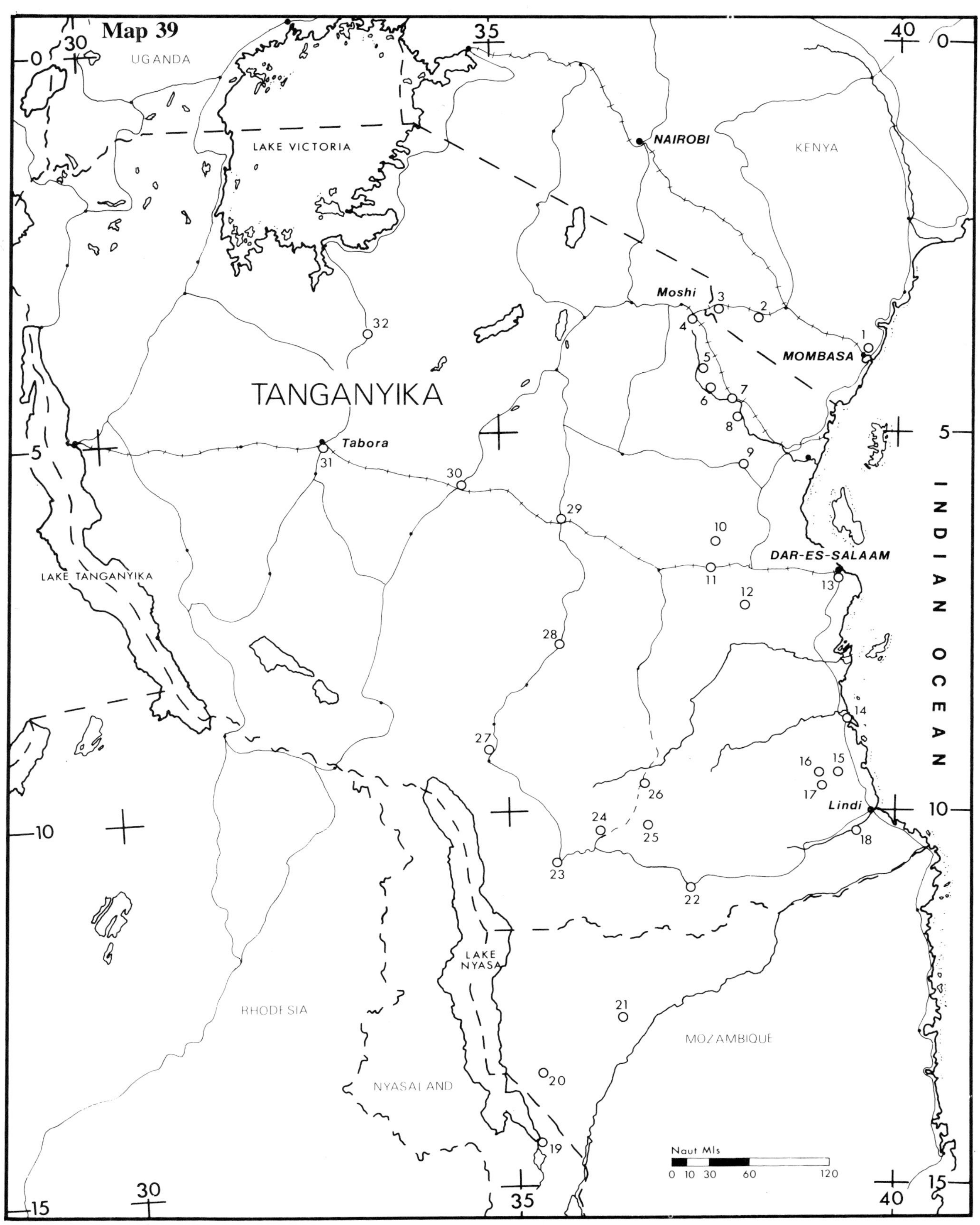

Map 39 – Tanganyika

1	Mombasa	9	Mbagui	17	Nahunga	25	Mbarangandu
2	Mbuyuni	10	Dakawa	18	Mtua	26	Maranda
3	Taveta	11	Morogoro	19	Fort Johnson	27	Ubena
4	Kahe	12	Tulo	20	Mtonia	28	Iringa
5	Marago Opuni	13	Dar-es-Salaam	21	Mwembe	29	Dodoma
6	Lassiti	14	Kilwa	22	Tunduru	30	Itigi
7	Kwa-Lokua	15	Narungombe	23	Songea	31	Tabora
8	Palmas	16	Missindyi	24	Likuju	32	Shinyanga

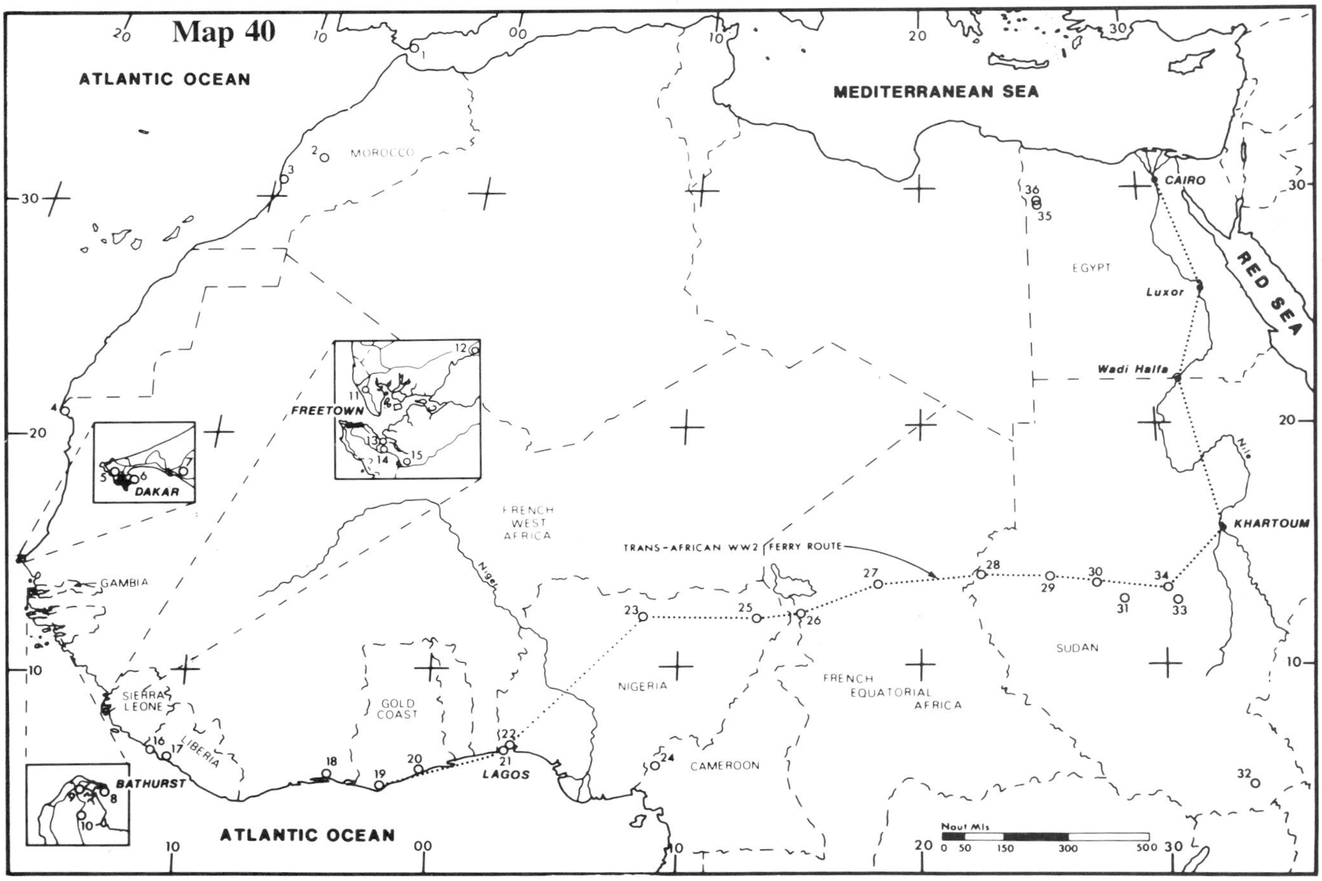

Map 40 – Northern Africa

1 Gibraltar/North Front
2 Merrakesh
3 Agadir
4 Port Etienne
5 Dakar
6 Dakar (seaplanes)
7 Rufisque
8 Bathurst/Half Die
9 Jeswang
10 Bathurst/Yundum
11 Lungi
12 Port Loko
13 Jui
14 Hastings
15 Waterloo
16 Fishermans Lake
17 Robertsfield
18 Abidjan
19 Takoradi
20 Accra
21 Apapa
22 Ikeja
23 Kano
24 Mamfe
25 Maidugri
26 Fort Lamy
27 Ati
28 El Geneina
29 El Fasher
30 Jebel el Hillah
31 Rahad
32 Kapoeta
33 Nahud
34 El Obeid
35 LG 67 Siwa South
36 LG 66 Siwa North

A London II, K6932/TQ·B, of No 202 Sqn rides at her moorings off Gibraltar in 1939. (RAF Museum P13666)

No 26 Sqn landed at Mombasa in Dec 15 and spent the next two years operating all over Tanganyika (see Map 39). This is one of the squadron's BE 2Cs, 4309. (RAF Museum P12529)

No 82 Sqn spent the period from 1946 to 1952 carrying out a photographic survey of East and West Africa. This picture shows one of the squadron's Lancaster PR 1s, TW901, undergoing engine maintenance under field conditions. (Andrew Thomas)

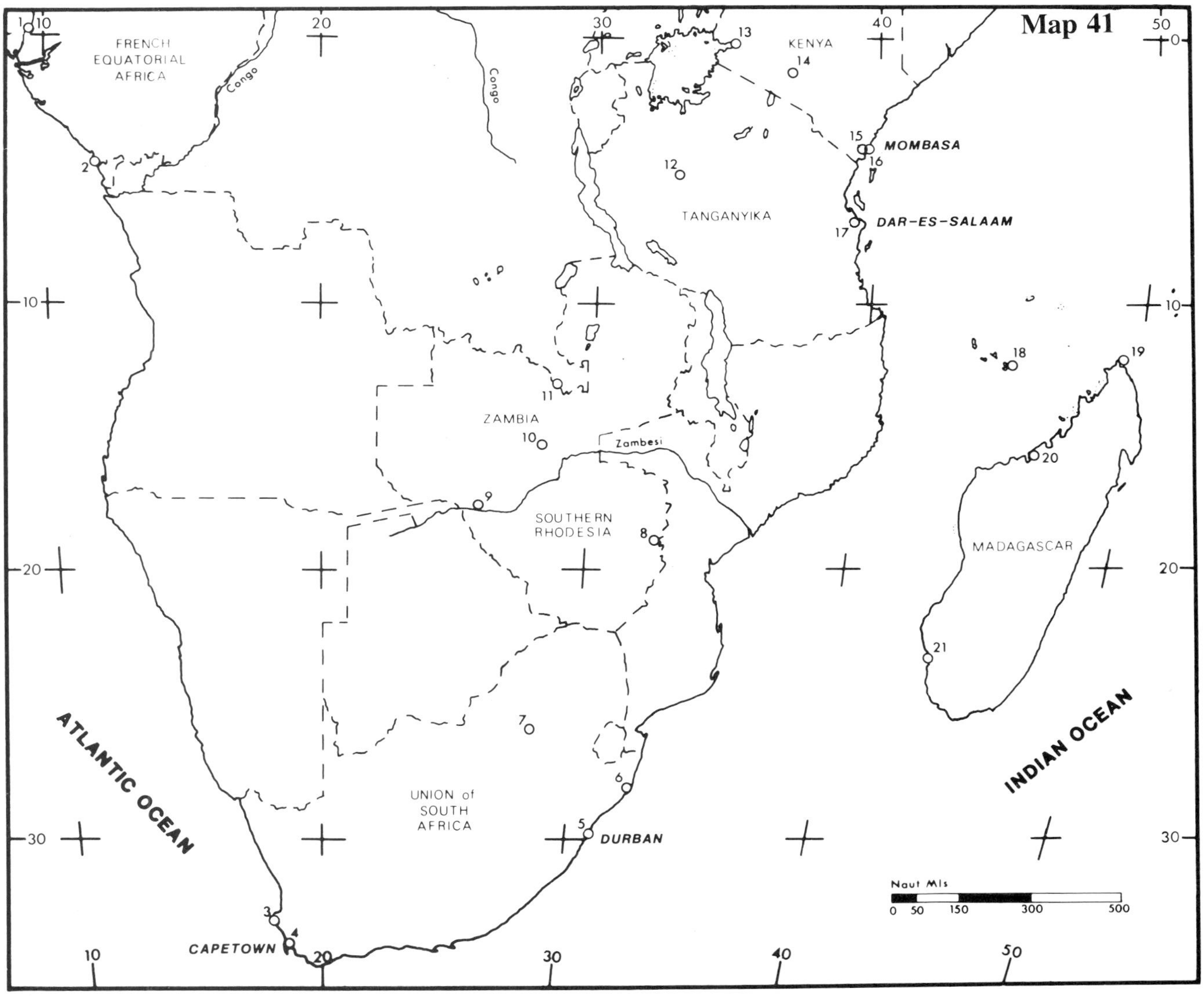

Map 41 – Southern Africa

1 Libreville
2 Pointe Noire
3 Langebaan
4 Capetown
5 Congella
6 St Lucia
7 Zwartkop
8 Umtali
9 Livingstone
10 Lusaka
11 Ndola
12 Tabora
13 Kisumu
14 Eastleigh
15 Port Reitz
16 Kipevu
17 Dar-es-Salaam
18 Pamanzi
19 Diego Suarez
20 Majunga
21 Tulear

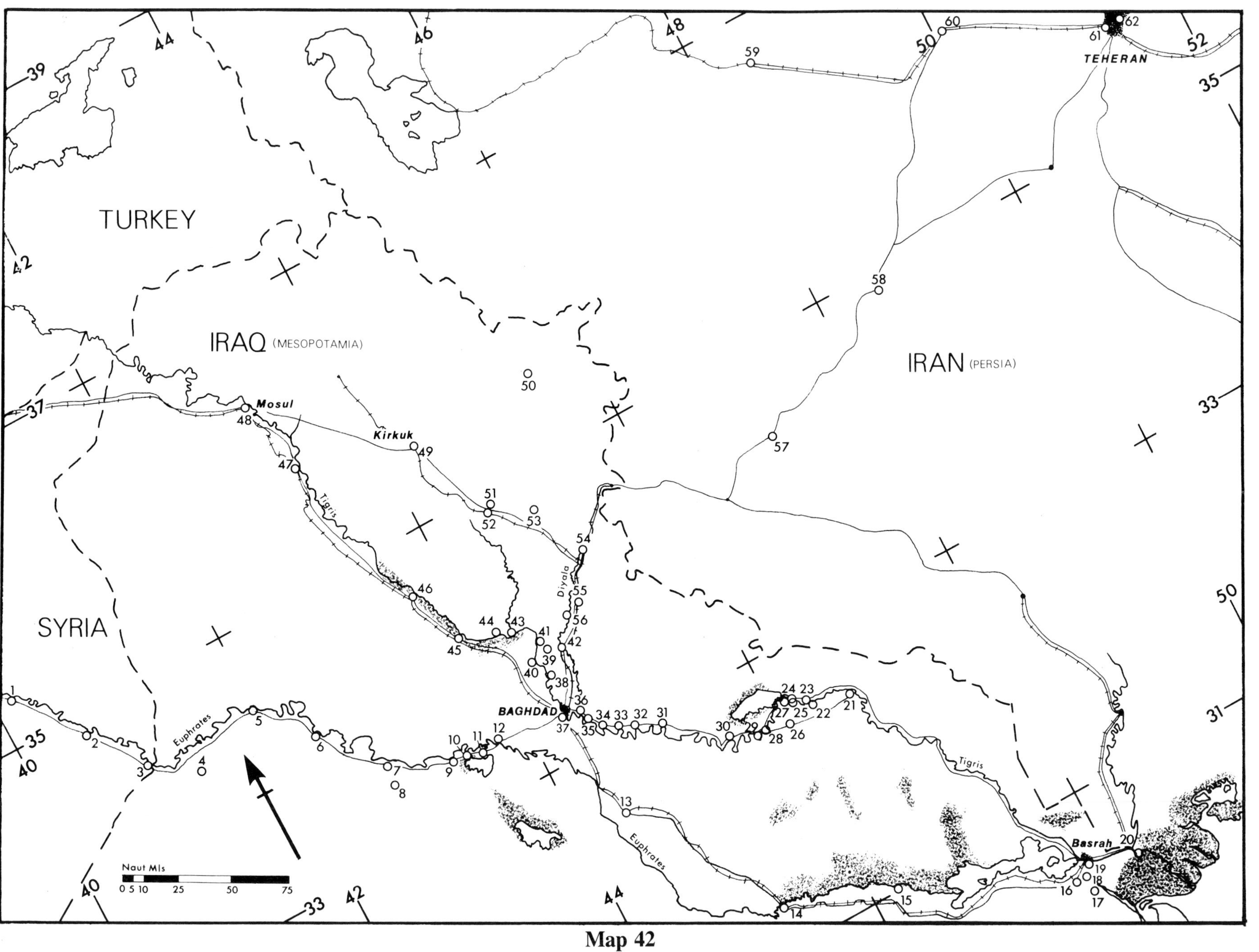
TURKEY
IRAQ (MESOPOTAMIA)
IRAN (PERSIA)
SYRIA
TEHERAN
Mosul
Kirkuk
BAGHDAD
Basrah
Tigris
Euphrates
Diyala
Naut Mls
0 5 10 25 50 75

Map 42

Map 42 – Iran (Persia) and Iraq (Mesopotamia)

1 Deir es Zor
2 Tahoune Guemac
3 Abu Kamal
4 T.1
5 Annah
6 K.3/Haditha
7 Hit
8 Qubba
9 Ramadi
10 Madhij
11 Habbaniyah/Dhibban
12 Falluja
13 Hillah
14 Samawah
15 Nasiriyah
16 Shaibah
17 Barjisayah
18 Zobeir
19 Basrah/Tanouma
20 Abadan
21 Ali Gharbi
22 Musandeg
23 Sheikh Saad
24 Camp Wadi
25 Ora
26 Sinn Abtar
27 Arab Village
28 Kut al Imara
29 Shumran
30 Sheikh Jaad
31 Aziziya
32 Zeur
33 Lajj
34 Bustan
35 Bawi
36 Hinaidi
37 Baghdad (West)
38 Kasirin
39 Jadida
40 Fort Kermea
41 Sindiya/Kuwar Reach
42 Baquba
43 Akab
44 Barura
45 Samarra
46 Tikrit
47 Qaiyarh
48 Mosul
49 K.1/Kirkuk
50 Sulaimania
51 Tuz Khurmatli
52 Aqsu
53 Kifri
54 Mirjana
55 Shahraban
56 Qalat Mufti
57 Kermanshah
58 Hamadan
59 Zinjan
60 Kazvin
61 Meherabad
62 Doshen Tapeh

A SPAD S.VII, A8807, of No 30 Sqn at Baquba in 1918. (RAF Museum P1247)

One of only a handful of Nighthawks which saw service in Iraq in the early 1920s. JR6925 was on the strength of No 8 Sqn at Hinaidi when this picture was taken. (RAF Museum)

A Wapiti IIA, K1125, of No 55 Sqn's B Flt, at Hinaidi. (RAF Museum P3275)

Basrah
50
55
60
30
30
Shiraz
KUWAIT
IRAN
PERSIAN GULF
Bahrain
QATAR
Sharjah
GULF of OMAN
25
25
TRUCIAL STATES
MUSCAT and OMAN
SAUDI ARABIA
Masirah
20
20
MUSCAT and OMAN
Salalah
ARABIAN SEA
ADEN and SOUTH ARABIA
15
15
Riyan
Socotra
50
55
60
Naut Mls
0 10 30 60 120
1
2
3
4
5
6
7
8
9
10
11
12
13
14
15
15
16
17

Map 43

Map 43 – Persian Gulf

1 Jiwani
2 Jask
3 Bushire
4 Kuwait
5 Farwania (Kuwait New)
6 Muharraq
7 Bahrain
8 Doha
9 Abu Dhabi
10 Dubai
11 Sharjah
12 Muscat
13 Ras al Hadd
14 Masirah
15 Salalah
16 Riyan
17 Socotra

A Wellington XIV, NC828, of No 621 Sqn parked at Khormaksar. This unit spent many hours on largely uneventful patrols of the Arabian Sea and Persian Gulf. (E Woodhouse)

The staging posts along the coast of the Arabian Sea and Persian Gulf were at 200-300 mile intervals permitting short-range types like this Twin Pioneer CC 1, XL992, of No 21 Sqn, to move about the theatre from the main base in Aden. (Andrew Thomas)

Based at Khormaksar, No 37 Sqn was the resident anti-submarine unit at the disposal of HQ Air Forces Middle East for the last ten years of the British presence in the area. The squadron was often required to operate in the bomber role flying over terrain as rugged as that in the background to this picture of Shackleton MR 2, WL752; the open hatch under the tail houses a camera. Detachments were frequent, prolonged and often involved active operations. For example in the course of an 18 month detachment to Muscat in 1957-59 No 37 Sqn dropped 3,457,670lbs of bombs and fired 7,000 rounds of 20mm ammunition. (RAF Museum P1502)

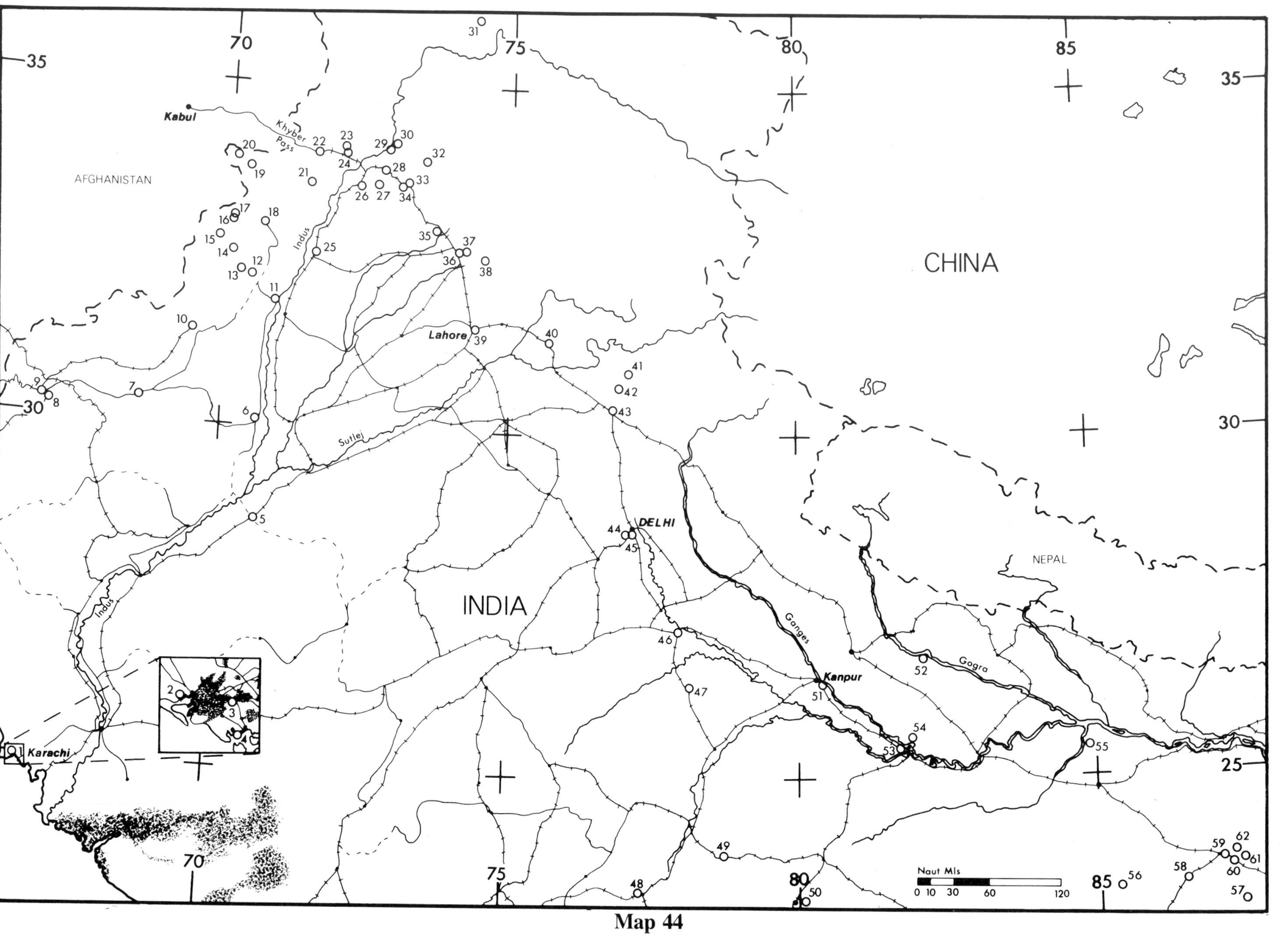
CHINA
NEPAL
INDIA
AFGHANISTAN
Kabul
Khyber Pass
Indus
Lahore
Sutlej
DELHI
Kanpur
Ganges
Gogra
Karachi
Naut Mls
0 10 30 60 120

Map 44

Map 44 – Northern India

1 Karachi
2 Mauripur
3 Drigh Road
4 Korangi Creek
5 Khanpur
6 Dera Ghazi Khan
7 Loralai
8 Samungli
9 Quetta
10 Fort Sandeman
11 Dera Ismail Khan
12 Tank
13 Manzai
14 Sorarogha
15 Razmak
16 Miranshah
17 Dardoni
18 Bannu
19 Arawali
20 Parachinar
21 Kohat
22 Peshawar
23 Risalpur
24 Nowshera
25 Mianwali
26 Basal
27 Fatehjang
28 Hassani Abdel/Wah
29 Lower Topa
30 Upper Topa
31 Gilgit
32 Murree
33 Chaklala
34 Dhamial
35 Jhelum
36 Gujrat
37 Julalpur
38 Sialkot
39 Lahore
40 Jullundur
41 Solan
42 Chakrata
43 Ambala
44 Palam
45 Delhi
46 Agra
47 Maharajpur
48 Bhopal
49 Saugor
50 Jubbulpore
51 Cawnpore/Kanpur
52 Fyzabad
53 Allahabad
54 Phaphamau
55 Bikram
56 Ranchi
57 Bishnapur
58 Charra
59 Asansol
60 Ondal
61 Madhaiganj
62 Pandeveswar

A DH 9A, E8673, of No 27 Sqn. (RAF Museum P7557)

An Audax, K4854, of No 20 Sqn wearing the squadron's red fuselage band. The star-shaped badge frame on the fin is appropriate for an Army Co-operation squadron; the wheel hubs and individual letter N are in yellow, officially the colour of B Flt, although this aeroplane is reported as having been with C Flt.
(Gp Capt R C F Lister)

This Auster V, TJ643, of No 659 Sqn suffered an engine failure on 19 Mar 46 while being flown from Miranshah to Quetta by Capt D A Scott. It lost its undercarriage in the ensuing forced-landing in Baluchistan and, despite the apparently relatively minor damage, the aircraft was struck off charge on 25 Apr 46.
(Museum of Army Flying)

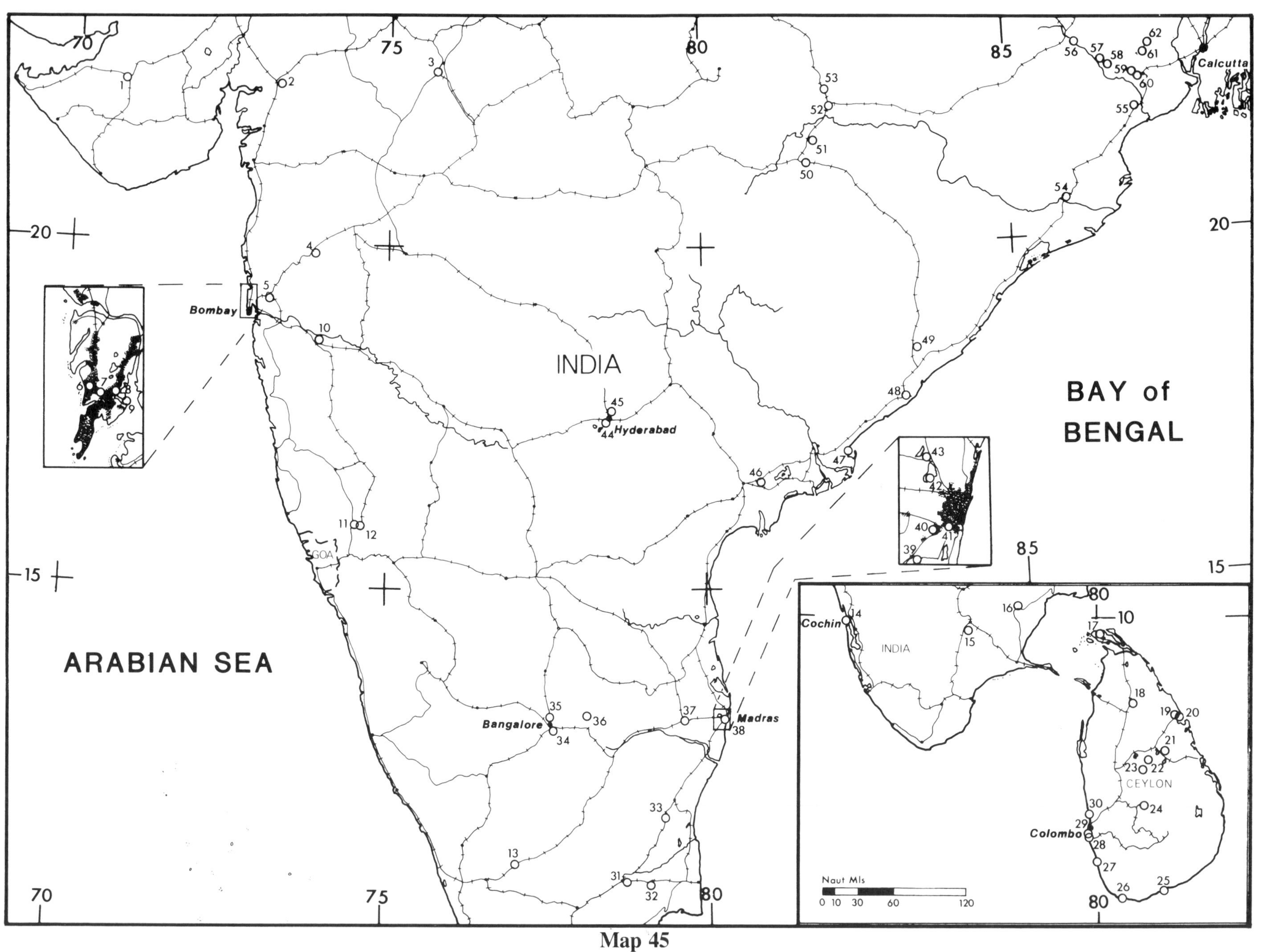
BAY of BENGAL
ARABIAN SEA
INDIA
CEYLON
Calcutta
Madras
Hyderabad
Bangalore
Bombay
Cochin
Colombo
GOA
Naut Mls
0 10 30 60 120

Map 45

Map 45 – Southern India and Ceylon

1 Rajkot
2 Baroda
3 Mhow
4 Deolali
5 Kalyan
6 Juhu
7 Santa Cruz
8 Worli
9 Trombay
10 Poona
11 Belgaum
12 Sambre
13 Coimbatore
14 Cochin
15 Madura
16 Chettinad
17 Kankesanterai
18 Vavuniya
19 China Bay
20 Trincomalee
21 Minneriya
22 Sigiriya
23 Dambulla
24 Kandy
25 Kalametiya
26 Koggala
27 Katukurunda
28 Ratmalana
29 Colombo (Racecourse)
30 Negombo
31 Trichinopoly/Kajamalai
32 Tanjore
33 Ulunderpet
34 Bangalore
35 Yelahanka
36 Kolar
37 Arkonam
38 Madras
39 Tambaram
40 St Thomas Mount
41 Guindy
42 Red Hills Lake
43 Cholavaram
44 Secunderabad/ Begumpet
45 Hakimpet
46 Gannavaram
47 Coconada
48 Vizagapatam
49 Bobbili
50 Raipur
51 Tilda
52 Bilaspur
53 Kargi Road
54 Cuttack
55 Amarda Road
56 Jamshedpur
57 Dalbumgarh
58 Chakulia
59 Dudhkundi
60 Kharagpur
61 Salbani
62 Digri

A Catalina IVB, JX431, of No 205 Sqn from Ceylon. (RAF Museum P2001)

A Mosquito VI, TE640/OB·F, of No 45 Sqn at Santa Cruz in 1946. (Author's collection)

Liberator VI, KH331/G, "the Winniemae", of No 200 Sqn at Jessore in 1945. The codeword SNAKE in front of the serial number indicated that the aeroplane was destined for service in the Far East and was not to be diverted en route (but see the photograph of Liberator VI, KL732, of No 104 Sqn illustrating Map 30). The suffix G after the serial number indicated that the aircraft was fitted with devices of sufficient sensitivity to require the provision of guards at all times.
(F F H Charlton via Andrew Thomas)

A Lancaster VII, NX678/WS·S, of No 9 Sqn photographed at Salbani in the black and white tropical bomber scheme specified for use by Tiger Force in the final assault on Japan. The early end of the war stopped further development of Tiger Force, which had just begun to assemble, but two of its designated units, Nos 9 and 617 Sqns were deployed to India for a short period in 1946.
(RAF Museum P2768)

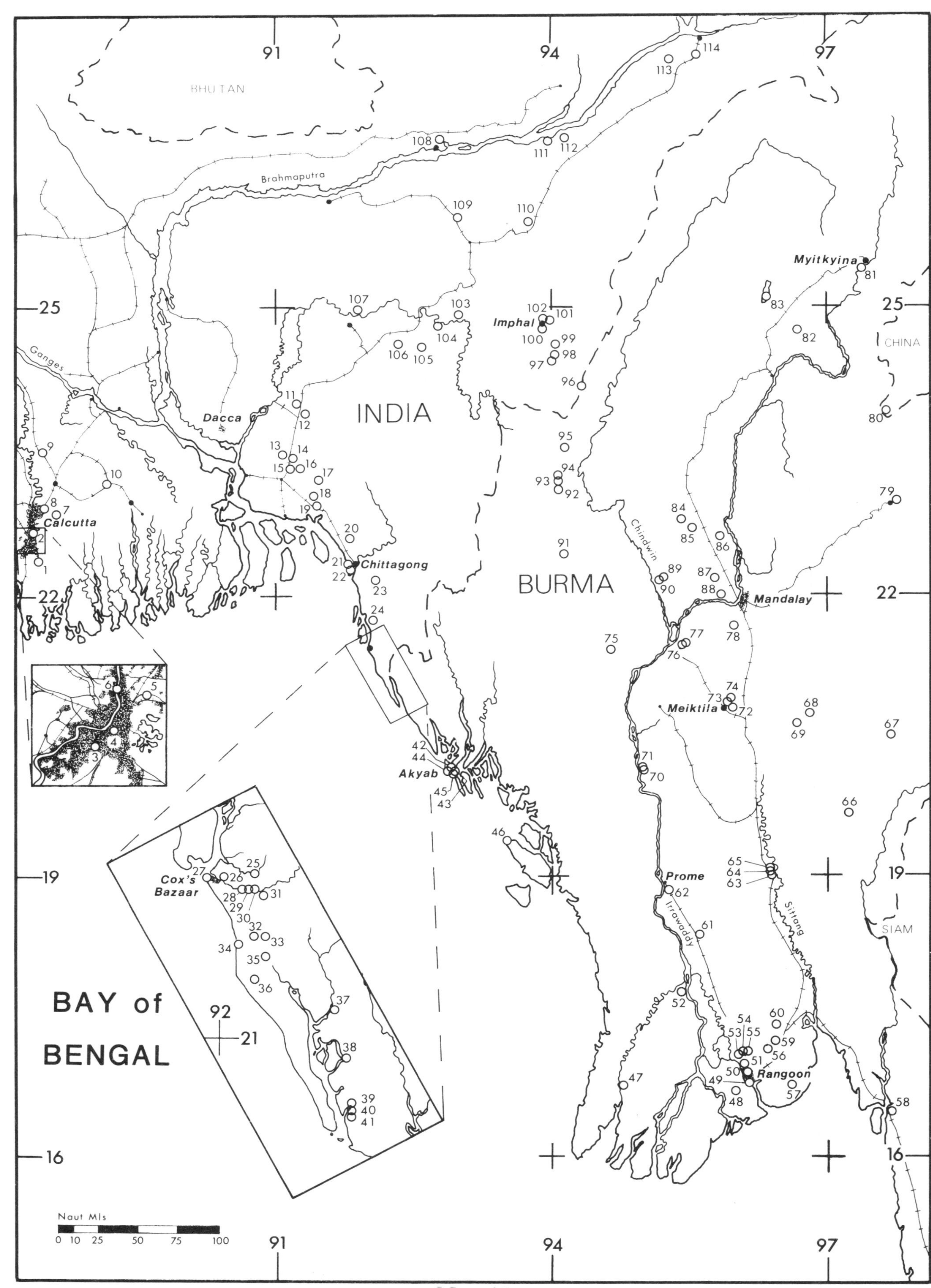
BHUTAN
Brahmaputra
Ganges
INDIA
BURMA
CHINA
SIAM
Dacca
Calcutta
Chittagong
Imphal
Myitkyina
Mandalay
Meiktila
Akyab
Prome
Rangoon
Cox's Bazaar
Chindwin
Irrawaddy
Sittang
BAY of BENGAL
Naut Mls
0 10 25 50 75 100

Map 46

Map 46 – North East India (Assam, Bengal, the Arakan) and Burma

1 Kalyanpur/'Acorn'
2 Calcutta
3 Alipore
4 Red Road/Maidan/ 'Angel'
5 Dum Dum
6 Bally/Willingdon Reach
7 Baigachi
8 Kanchrapara
9 Dhubalia
10 Jessore
11 Singerbil
12 Agartala
13 Chandina
14 Comilla
15 Lalmai
16 Bhatpara
17 Parashuram
18 Feni/Fenny
19 Fazilpur
20 Hathazari
21 Double Moorings
22 Chittagong/Patenga
23 Dohazari
24 Chiringa
25 Joari
26 Jumchar
27 Cox's Bazaar
28 Ramu 3/'Hay'
29 Ramu 1/'Reindeer I'
30 Ramu 4/'Reindeer II'
31 Ramu 2/'Lyons'
32 Rumkha
33 Ratnap
34 Nidania/'George'/ Nidiani
35 Nazir/Ukhia
36 Mardhaibunia/'Hove'
37 Bawli
38 Maunghnama
39 Maungdaw 1/'Ritz'
40 Maungdaw 2
41 Maungdaw 3
42 Dabaing 1
43 Dabaing 2
44 Dabaing 3
45 Akyab Main
46 Kyaukpyu/Ramree Island
47 'Dewar'
48 Twante
49 Rangoon
50 Mingaladon
51 'John Haig'
52 'Black & White'
53 'Highland Queen'
54 Hmawbi
55 'Johnny Walker'
56 Zayatkwin
57 'Scotts Club'
58 Moulmein
59 'Canadian Club'
60 Pegu/'Pilsener'
61 Zigon
62 Prome/'Park Lane'
63 Toungoo
64 'Tennant'
65 Kalaywa
66 Loikaw
67 Pankham Fort
68 Heho
69 'Huntsman'
70 Magwe Satellite
71 Magwe/'Maida Vale'
72 Kwetnge
73 Meiktila
74 Thedaw
75 Sinthe
76 Myingyan
77 Kinmagon
78 Dwelha
79 Lashio
80 Loiwing
81 Myitkyina
82 'Broadway'
83 Lake Indawgyi
84 Ye-U
85 Tabingaung
86 Onbauk
87 Sadaung
88 Ondaw
89 Ywadon
90 Monywa
91 Kan
92 Taukkyan
93 Kalemyo
94 Thazi
95 Yazagyo
96 Tamu
97 Palel
98 Sapam
99 Wangjing
100 Tulihal
101 Kangla
102 Imphal
103 Kumbhirgram
104 Silchar West
105 Lalaghat/Rajyeswarpur
106 Patharkandi
107 Sylhet
108 Tezpur
109 Lanka
110 Dimapur/Manipur Road
111 Dergaon
112 Jorhat
113 Dinjan
114 Sookerating

A Liberator VIII, KP136, of No 355 Sqn. (RAF Museum P2756)

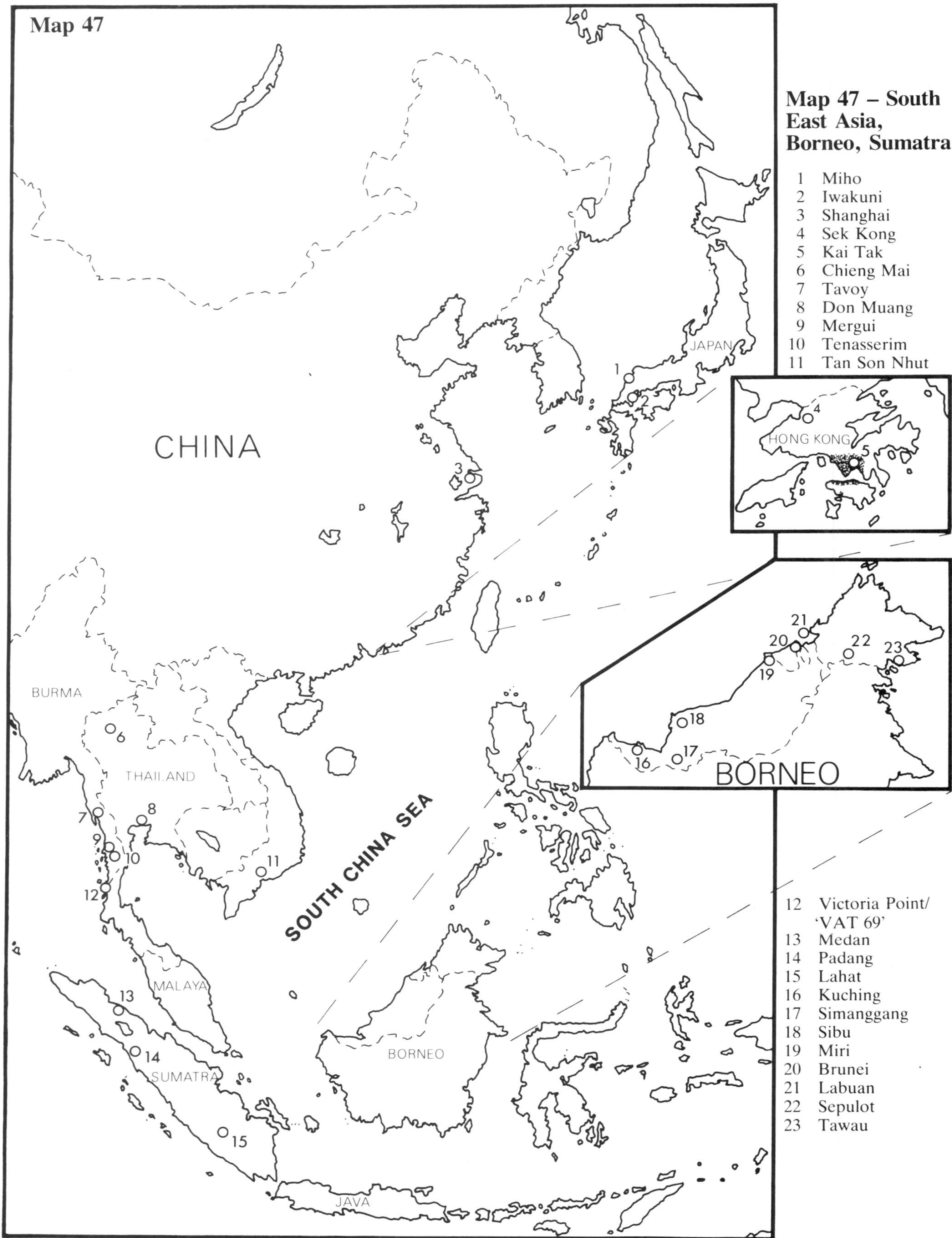
Map 47
CHINA
JAPAN
HONG KONG
BURMA
THAILAND
SOUTH CHINA SEA
MALAYA
SUMATRA
BORNEO
JAVA
BORNEO
Map 47 – South East Asia, Borneo, Sumatra
1 Miho
2 Iwakuni
3 Shanghai
4 Sek Kong
5 Kai Tak
6 Chieng Mai
7 Tavoy
8 Don Muang
9 Mergui
10 Tenasserim
11 Tan Son Nhut
12 Victoria Point/ 'VAT 69'
13 Medan
14 Padang
15 Lahat
16 Kuching
17 Simanggang
18 Sibu
19 Miri
20 Brunei
21 Labuan
22 Sepulot
23 Tawau

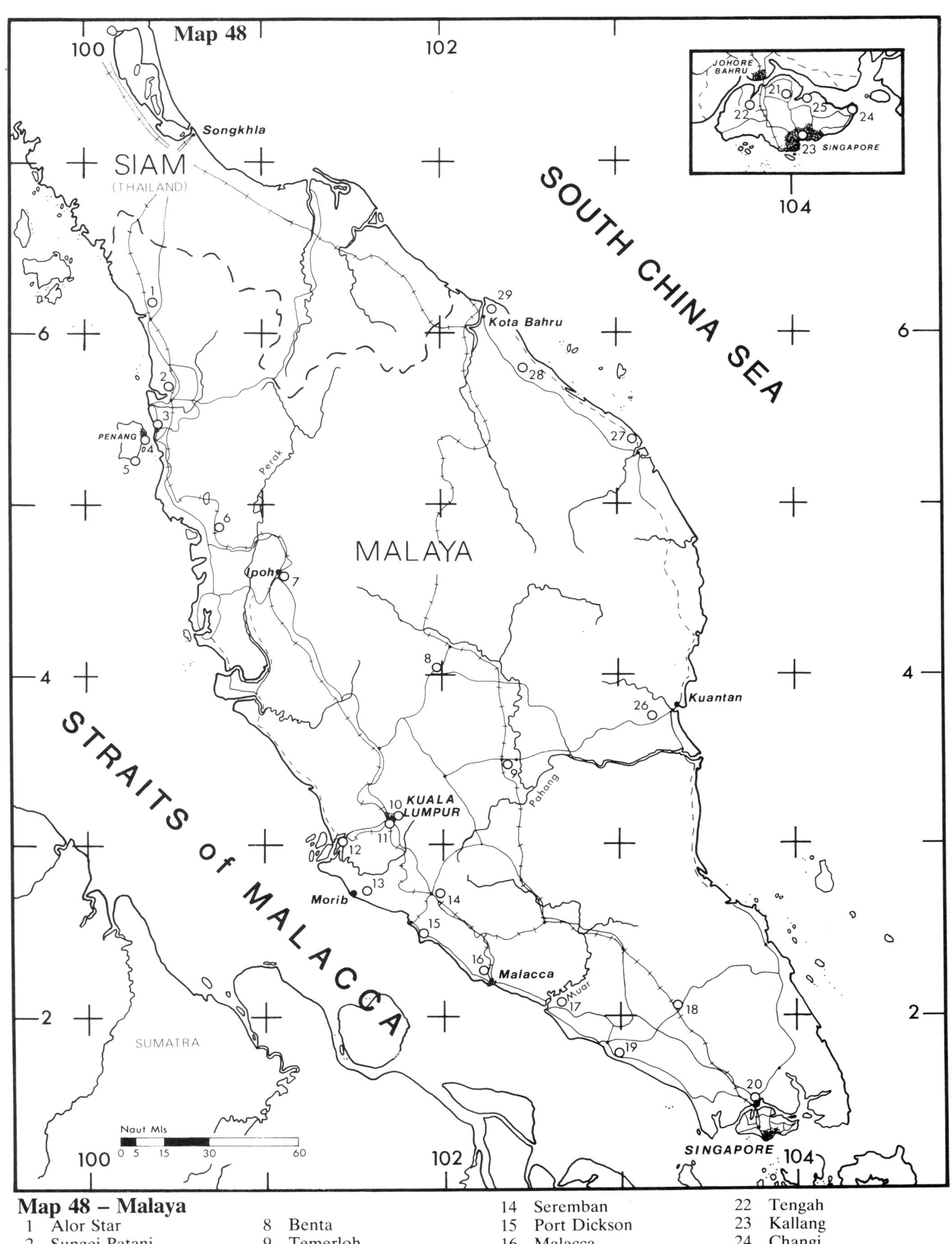

Map 48 – Malaya

1 Alor Star
2 Sungei Patani
3 Butterworth
4 Penang
5 Bayan Lepas
6 Taiping
7 Ipoh
8 Benta
9 Temerloh
10 Noble Field (Kuala Lumpur)
11 Kuala Lumpur
12 Port Swettenham
13 Kelanang/Morib
14 Seremban
15 Port Dickson
16 Malacca
17 Muar
18 Kluang
19 Batu Pahat
20 Johore Bahru
21 Sembawang
22 Tengah
23 Kallang
24 Changi
25 Seletar
26 Kuantan
27 Kuala Trengganu
28 Gong Kedak
29 Kota Bahru

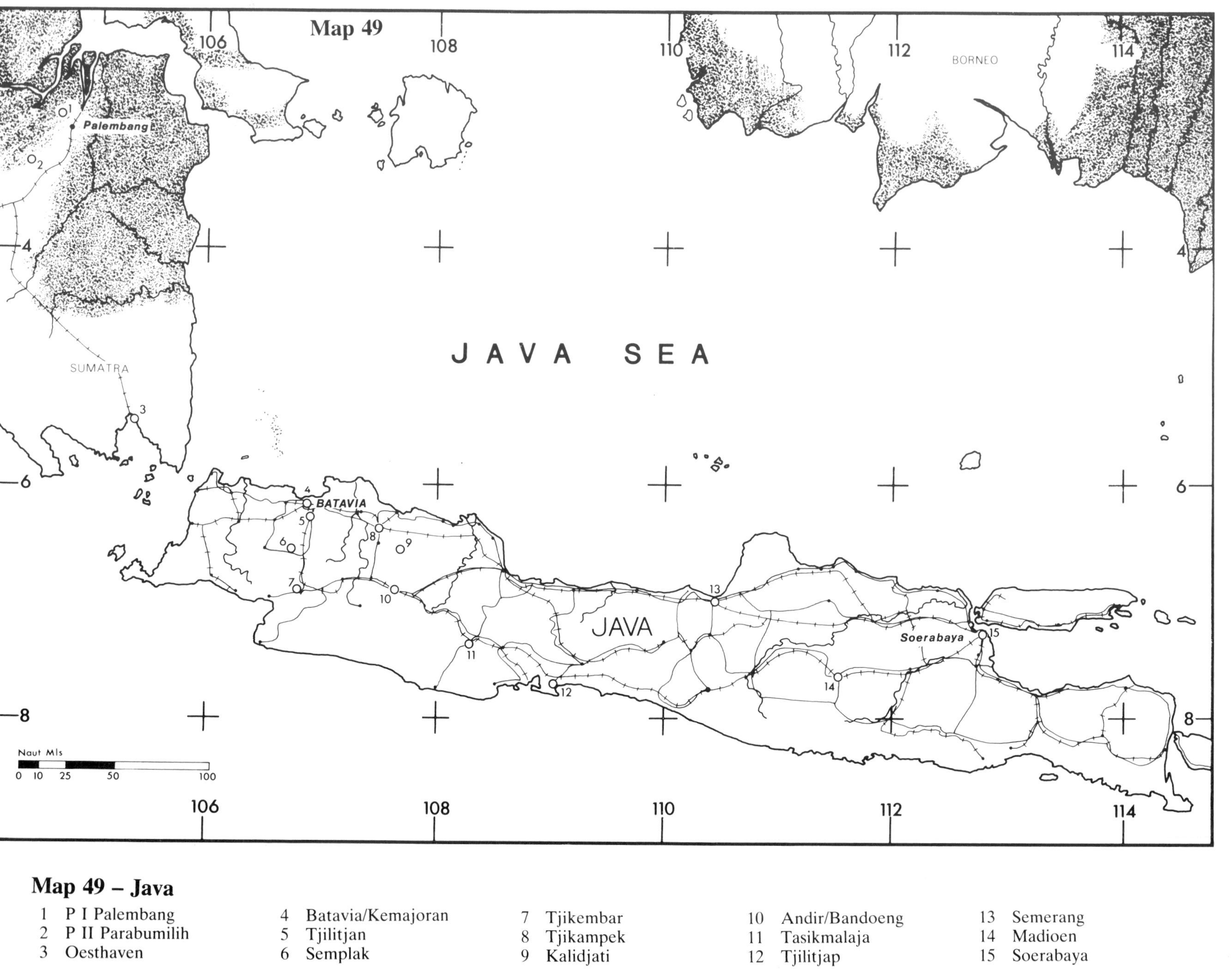

Map 49 – Java

1 P I Palembang
2 P II Parabumilih
3 Oesthaven
4 Batavia/Kemajoran
5 Tjilitjan
6 Semplak
7 Tjikembar
8 Tjikampek
9 Kalidjati
10 Andir/Bandoeng
11 Tasikmalaja
12 Tjilitjap
13 Semerang
14 Madioen
15 Soerabaya

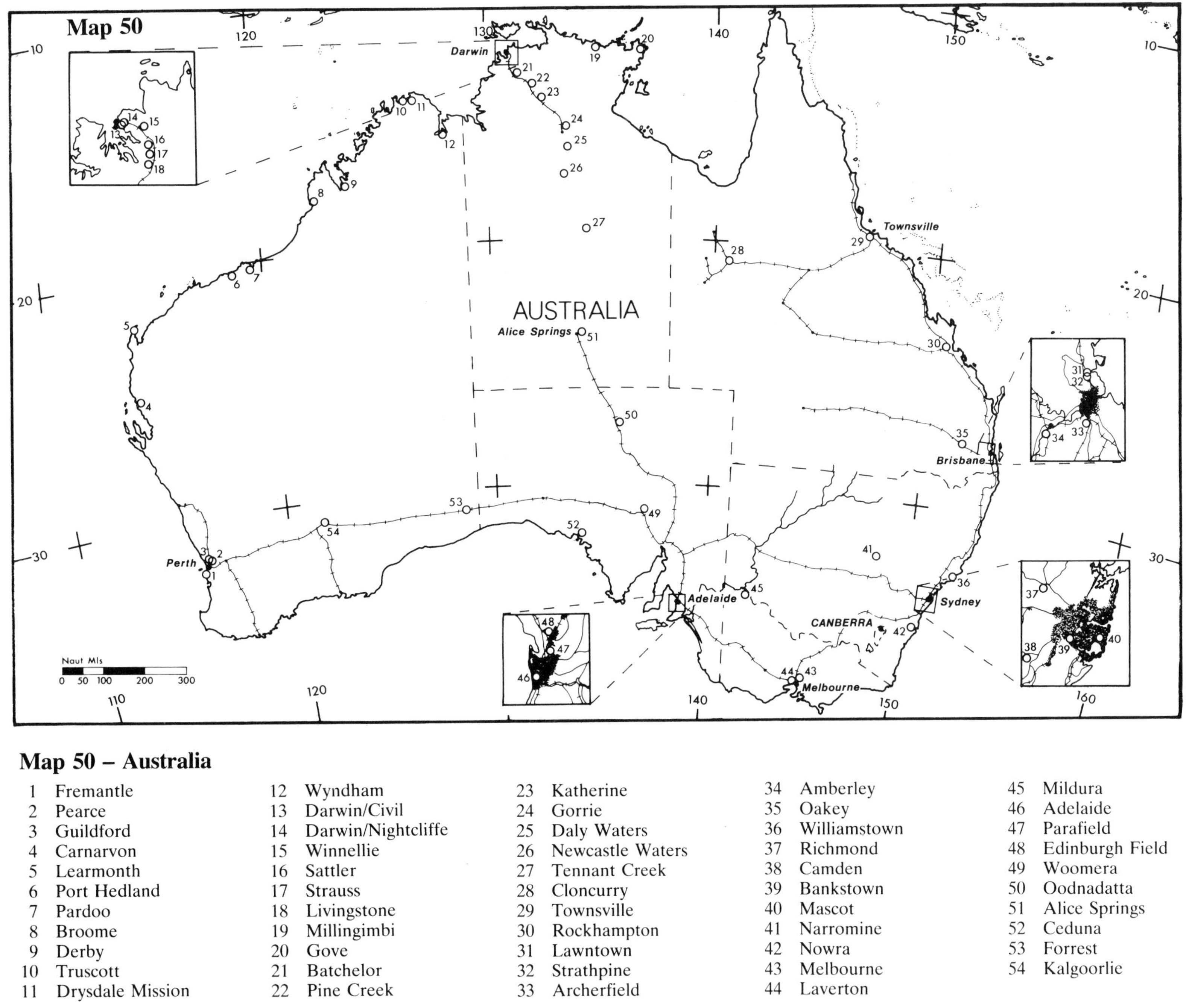

Map 50 – Australia

1 Fremantle
2 Pearce
3 Guildford
4 Carnarvon
5 Learmonth
6 Port Hedland
7 Pardoo
8 Broome
9 Derby
10 Truscott
11 Drysdale Mission
12 Wyndham
13 Darwin/Civil
14 Darwin/Nightcliffe
15 Winnellie
16 Sattler
17 Strauss
18 Livingstone
19 Millingimbi
20 Gove
21 Batchelor
22 Pine Creek
23 Katherine
24 Gorrie
25 Daly Waters
26 Newcastle Waters
27 Tennant Creek
28 Cloncurry
29 Townsville
30 Rockhampton
31 Lawntown
32 Strathpine
33 Archerfield
34 Amberley
35 Oakey
36 Williamstown
37 Richmond
38 Camden
39 Bankstown
40 Mascot
41 Narromine
42 Nowra
43 Melbourne
44 Laverton
45 Mildura
46 Adelaide
47 Parafield
48 Edinburgh Field
49 Woomera
50 Oodnadatta
51 Alice Springs
52 Ceduna
53 Forrest
54 Kalgoorlie

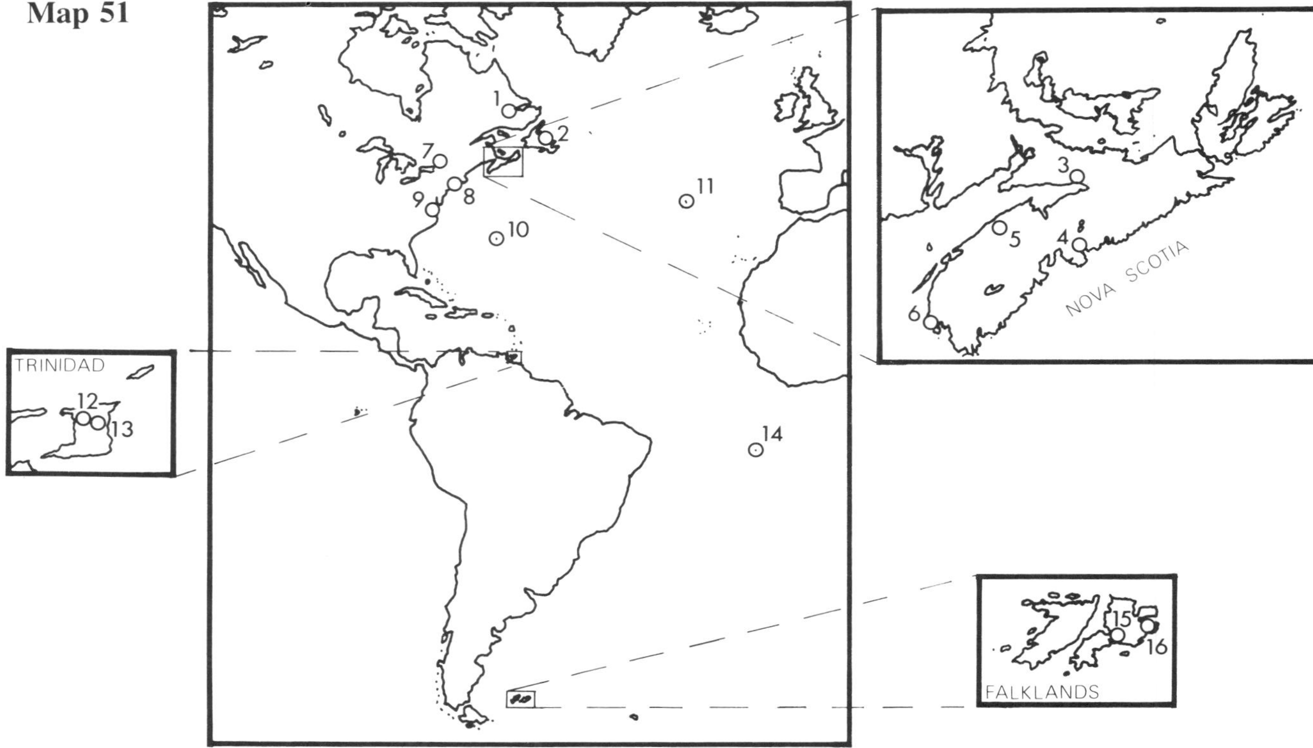

Map 51 – Atlantic Ocean

1 Goose Bay
2 Gander
3 Debert
4 Dartmouth
5 Greenwood
6 Yarmouth
7 Dorval
8 Quonset Point, RI
9 Norfolk, Va
10 Bermuda
11 Lagens (Azores)
12 Edinburgh Field
13 Waller Field
14 Wideawake (Ascension Island)
15 Mount Pleasant
16 Port Stanley

A Lancaster B.1(FE), TW659/TL·M, of No 35 Sqn photographed taking off from Mitchell Field, New York during the squadron's highly successful 16 aircraft tour of the USA in Jul-Aug 46. (Chaz Bowyer)

A Lincoln B.2, RF507/KC·0, of No 617 Sqn photographed during that unit's tour of the USA in 1947. (R C Sturtivant)

A Vulcan B.2 of No 50 Sqn shows off its camouflage scheme during a low-level training sortie from Goose Bay in 1977. (Author's collection)

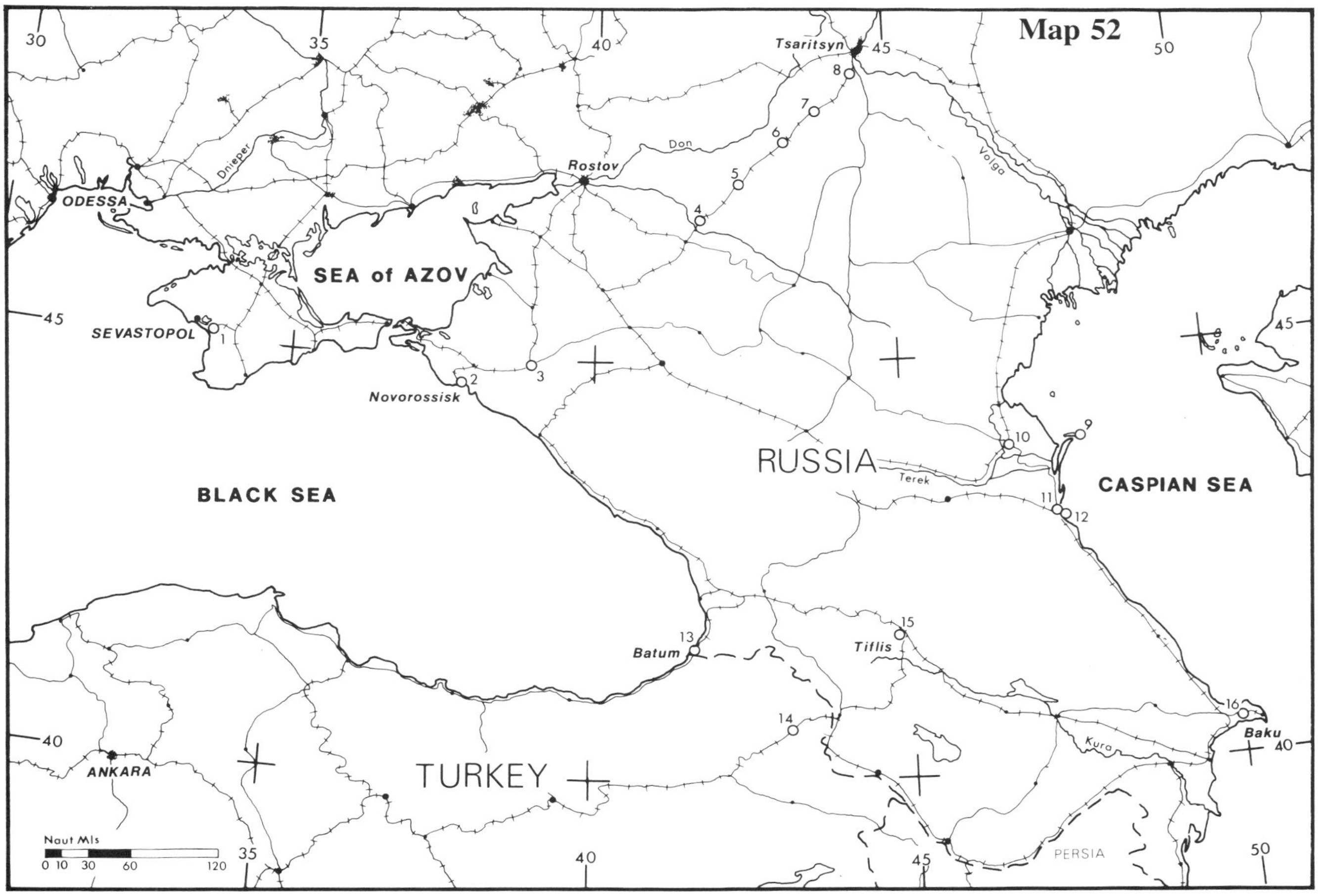

Map 52 – South Russia

1	Saki	5	Zimovniki	9	Chechen	13	Batum
2	Novorossisk	6	Kotelnikovo	10	Lagan	14	Kars
3	Ekaterinodar	7	Gniloaksaiskaya	11	Petrovsk Kaskar	15	Tiflis
4	Velikoknyajaskaya	8	Beketovka	12	Petrovsk Port	16	Baku

While No 266 Sqn was based at Petrovsk in 1919 it sometimes operated its seaplanes from this commandeered merchant vessel, the Aleydar Useynoff. *Two Short 184s, N9079 and N9082, with their wings folded can be discerned on deck between the bridge and the forward mast.* (RAF Museum P1341)

When plans to deploy No 186 Sqn to the Caucusus were abandoned its assigned aircraft were changed to DH 9As and ferried to the theatre by HMS Argus. *This one, E764, is seen in service with No 221 Sqn.* (RAF Museum P12305)

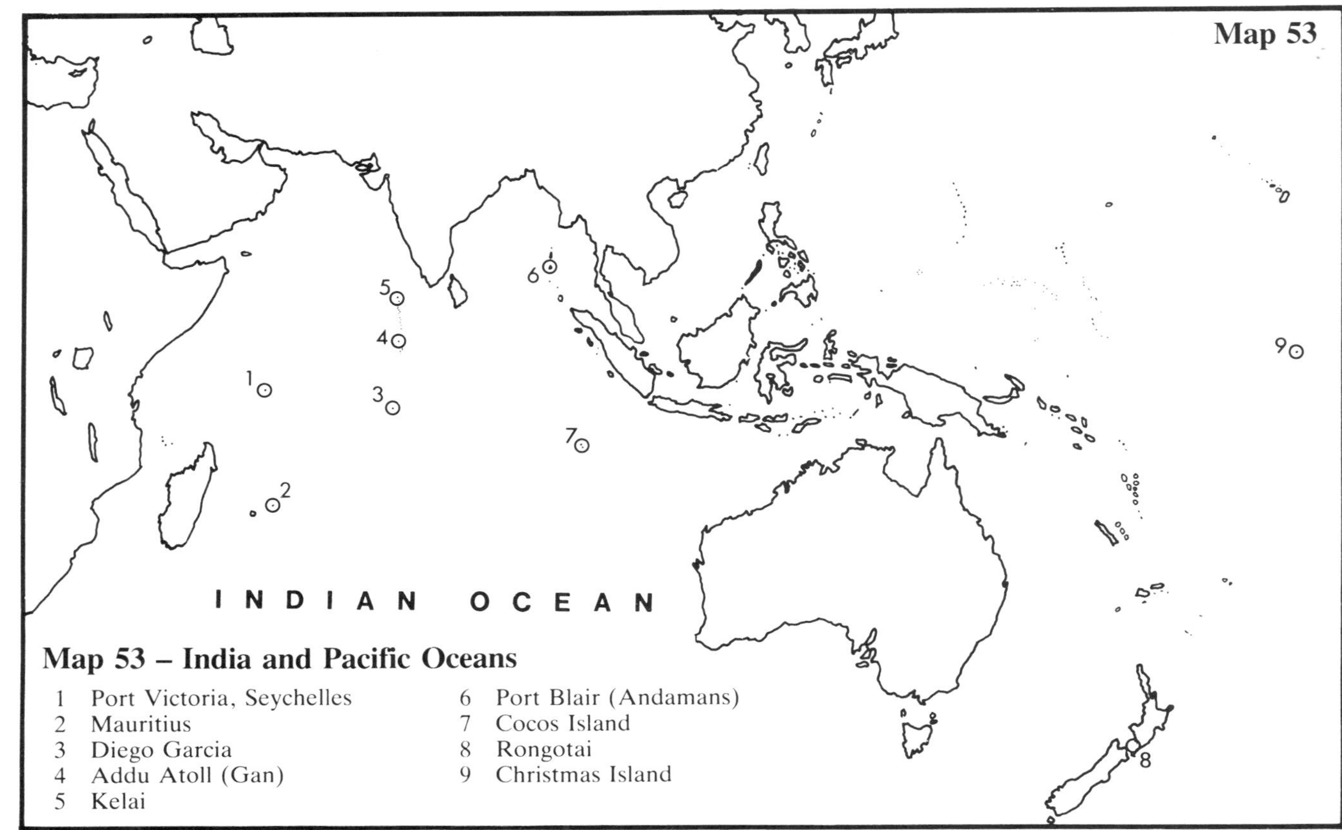

Map 53 – India and Pacific Oceans

1 Port Victoria, Seychelles
2 Mauritius
3 Diego Garcia
4 Addu Atoll (Gan)
5 Kelai
6 Port Blair (Andamans)
7 Cocos Island
8 Rongotai
9 Christmas Island

Among the maritime units which patrolled the western side of the Indian Ocean was No 209 Sqn based at Kipevu. Seen here at take-off is one of the squadron's Catalina IBs, FP285. (RAF Museum P1514)

This Liberator VI, EW157, of No 356 Sqn, with a Wg Cdr's pennant painted on its nose, was photographed over north east India. In Jul 45 No 356 Sqn moved to the Cocos Islands in preparation for Operation Zipper, the invasion of Malaya. With the premature end of the war this operation never took place and No 356 Sqn disbanded in Nov 45. (RAF Museum P14745)

Appendix 12

The Origins of the Squadrons of the Aegean Group, 1918

The early histories of the units which operated in the Aegean theatre during the First World War are difficult to unravel with any certainty. A0 800, which was published on 9 Mar 18, announced the designations which were to be applied to existing Naval units of squadron status on their absorption into the RAF on 1 Apr 18. In the case of squadrons serving in France this merely involved the addition of 200 to the current unit number, however, A0 800 also provided numbers for more remote units. These were expressed as follows.

No 220 Sqn	Reconnaissance Squadron (Aegean)
No 221 Sqn	Anti-submarine Squadron (Aegean)
No 222 Sqn	No 1 Fighter Squadron (Aegean)
No 223 Sqn	No 2 Fighter Squadron (Aegean)
No 224 Sqn	Anti-submarine Squadron (Otranto)
No 225 Sqn	Fighter Squadron (Otranto)
No 226 Sqn	Bombing Squadron (Taranto)
No 227 Sqn	Caproni Squadron (Taranto)

The squadrons operating from Southern Italy are relatively well recorded but this is not the case for the four units within the Aegean Group (these were eventually reorganised into Nos 62 and 63 Wings of No 15 [Aegean] Group). From surviving records in the Public Record Office it can be established that on 31 Mar 18, the day before the RAF was created, the units in the Aegean Theatre were:

A Sqn at Thasos.
B Sqn at Mitylene.
C Sqn at Imbros.
D Sqn at Stavros.
Seaplane units at Suda Bay and Siros

A further unit listed, Z Sqn, was a Greek unit operating with the British air forces.

It is also apparent from contemporary documents that the new designations were not brought into use in the Aegean until Sep 18. Nevertheless, despite an absence of routine reporting from units which had not yet acknowledged their new identities, the Location Lists of Units of the Royal Air Force began to include these squadrons. Surviving Lists include the following:

Camel, B3769, served in the Aegean theatre from Dec 17 when it was on the strength of D Sqn at Stavros. It remained in the area until the end of the war when, in Nov 18, it was transferred to Greece.

A Short 320 of No 6 Wg, RNAS at Otranto in 1918. When the RAF was formed the seaplanes of No 6 (later No 66) Wg should have been reorganised into No 224 Sqn. In the event it was not until Aug 18 that this regrouping occurred and when it did the designation adopted was No 263 Sqn. (RAF Museum P12593)

One of the Camels identifiable in this picture, C133, is known to have served with No 227 Sqn, while another, C53, is recorded as having been with No 226 Sqn. Both of these units were stationed in southern Italy; however, that region lacks mountains like those in the background to this photograph. It is concluded that this picture was taken at Mudros during No 266 Sqn's detachment to the Aegean in late 1918. (J M Bruce/G S Leslie collection)

The seaplane unit which, to conform with A0 800, should logically have been No 221 Sqn eventually became No 264 Sqn in about Aug 18. A similar discontinuity between London's intentions and their interpretation in the field appears to have resulted in the anti-submarine squadron in Italy becoming No 263 Sqn, rather than No 224 Sqn as A0 800 indicated.

	1 May 18	18 Jun 18	1 Aug 18	17 Sep 18	1 Nov & 1 Dec 18
No 220 Sqn	Imbros	Imbros	Imbros	Imbros	
No 221 Sqn	Suda Bay	Suda Bay	Mudros	Mudros	15 (Aegean)
No 222 Sqn	Thasos	Thasos	Thasos	Thasos	Group
	& Stavros	& Stavros	& Stavros	& Stavros	Mudros
No 223 Sqn	Mitylene	Mitylene	Mitylene	Mitylene	

It would appear from the above that, theoretically at least, the lineal descent of the Agean squadrons was:

A Sqn became No 222 Sqn at Thasos
B Sqn became No 223 Sqn at Mitylene
C Sqn became No 220 Sqn at Imbros
D Sqn became No 221 Sqn at Stavros

The records of the Aegean Group are incomplete but they do permit certain facts to be established. Significant among these are the following:

a. B Sqn left Mitylene in Apr 18 and the base was

largely evacuated by the end of Jun 18. The Air Ministry's location listing for 'No 223 Sqn' must therefore have been consistantly incorrect.
b. The last Camel of A Sqn was withdrawn from Thasos on 6 May 18. The Air Ministry's inclusion of Thasos as a location for 'No 222 Sqn' after this date was therefore wrong.
c. After their withdrawal to Stavros, in Apr and May 18 respectively, A and B Sqns cease to feature in contemporary records.
d. An F Sqn formed at Mudros in Apr/May 18 and operated on a mobile basis until it took up permanent residence on Mudros from 7 Jul 18.
e. Numerical designations were adopted from 14 Sep 18, as follows:

C Sqn at Imbros became No 220 Sqn
D Sqn at Stavros became No 221 Sqn
F Sqn at Mudros became No 222 Sqn.

f. The author has found no reference to No 223 Sqn in any contemporary records, apart from the suspect Air Ministry listings and a formal announcement of its final disbandment.
g. In Oct 18 No 221 left Stavros for Mudros and its assets were used to reinforce Nos 220 and 222 Sqns. Thereafter No 221 Sqn does not appear in any records until it begins preparations for its post-war deployment to the Caucasus.

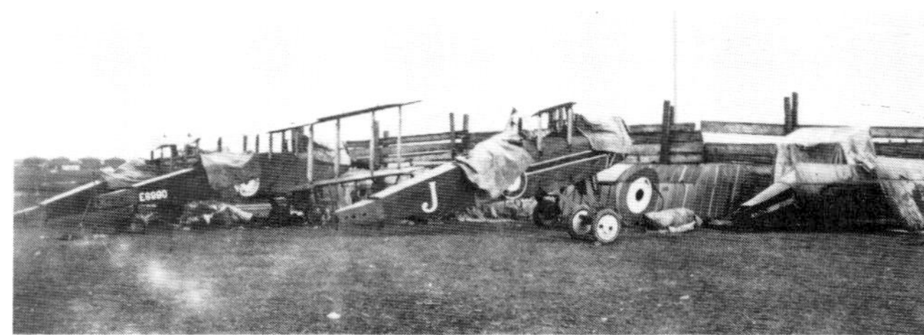

No 221 Sqn seems to have had a very low-key existence from Oct 18 until Dec 18, when it began to mobilise for deployment to the Caucasus where it was to assist General Denikin's White Russians in their struggle with the Bolsheviks. This photograph was taken on 20 Jan 19 and shows DH 9s, including E8990, of No 221 Sqn being erected after their arrival at Petrovsk. (RAF Museum P12291)

It is acknowledged that several versions of the early days of Nos 220-223 Sqns have appeared before but the author has not been able to substantiate these. The specific movement dates contained in the main text have all been drawn from surviving documents. The problem, with the earlier dates, has been to decide to which 'squadron' they should be related. While admitting that the information presented on these units in the main text is, to a degree, conjectural it is believed that it represents a more accurate reconstruction of events than any of those which have been published previously.

One of the first DH 9s to be erected at Petrovsk by No 221 Sqn after its deployment from the Aegean was D2803. It did not survive for long; this picture was taken on 3 Feb 19. (RAF Museum P12286)

A Short 184, N9085, of No 266 Sqn at Petrovsk in 1919. (RAF Museum P1337)

Abbreviations

AAC(U)	Anti-Aircraft Co-operation (Unit)
A&AEE	Aeroplane and Armament Experimental Establishment
AAF	Auxiliary Air Force
ACSEA	Air Command, South East Asia
AFB	(US) Air Force Base
AFC	Australian Flying Corps
ALG	Advanced Landing Ground
AMO	Air Ministry Order
AMWO	Air Ministry Weekly Order
AO	Air Organisation (Memorandum)
AOP	Air Observation Post
APC	Armament Practice Camp
ASR	Air/Sea Rescue
AWF	All-Weather Fighter
BAFO	British Air Forces of Occupation
BAL	Berlin Air Lift
BCATP	British Commonwealth Air Training Plan
Bde	Brigade
BPD	Base Personnel Depot
Btn	Battalion
BWI	British West Indies
CAF	Canadian Air Force
CasEvac	Casualty Evacuation
CD Flt	(Indian) Coastal Defence Flight
CFS	Central Flying School
CO	Commanding Officer
Comm(s)	Communication(s), as in 'Comm Flt'
Coy	Company
DB	Disbanded. Used freely to indicate when a unit ceased to have a tangible existence within the RAF, eg when it was: formally disbanded; renumbered; passed to the control of another service or nation; reduced to a 'numberplate only' basis; nominated as the dormant half of a Linked Squadron.
det	Detachment or detached
F	Formed. Used freely to indicate the original formation of a squadron - possibly by the renumbering of a previously existing unit.
FAA	Fleet Air Arm
FE	Far East
Flt	Flight
FTS	Flying Trainig School
Gp	Group
HAS	Hardened Aircraft Shelter
HCU	Heavy Conversion Unit
HD	Home Defence
HMS	His/Her Majesty's Ship
HMT	His Majesty's Troopship
HQ	Headquarters
IRBM	Intermediate Range Ballistic Missle
LG	Landing Ground
ME	Middle East
MOD	Ministry of Defence
MU	Maintenance Unit
NATO	North Atlantic Treaty Organisation
NCS	Northern Communications Squadron
NS	Nova Scotia
OCU	Operational Conversion Unit
OTU	Operational Training Unit
PAC	Public Archives of Canada
PD	(RAAF) Personnel Depot
PDC	Personnel Despatch Centre
PDU	Photographic Development Unit
PR	Photographic Reconnaissance
PRC	Personnel Reception Centre
PRU	Photographic Reconnaissance Unit
PSP	Pierced Steel Planking
PTC	Personnel Transit Centre
RAAF	Royal Australian Air Force
RAF	Royal Air Force
RAFVR	Royal Air Force Volunteer Reserve
RAS	Reserve Aeroplane Squadron
RAuxAF	Royal Auxiliary Air Force
RCAF	Royal Canadian Air Force
RDU	(Aircraft) Receipt and Despatch Unit
RE	Royal Engineers
RF	Reformed. Used freely to indicate the second, or subsequent, existence of a unit, whether by actual reformation or by the redesignation of a previously existing unit.
RFC	Royal Flying Corps
RN	Royal Navy
RNAS	Royal Naval Air Service
RNZAF	Royal New Zealand Air Force
RS	Reserve Squadron
SAAF	South African Air Force
SAM	Surface-to-Air Missile
SEAC	South East Asia Command
SFTS	Service Flying Training School
SMT	Square Meshed Track
Sqn	Squadron
SRAF	Southern Rhodesian Air Force
SS	Steamship
TDS	Training Depot Station
TS	Training Squadron
TWCU	Tornado Weapons Conversion Unit
TWU	Tactical Weapons Unit
UDI	Unilateral Declaration of Independence (by Rhodesia)
USAAF	United States Army Air Force
V/STOL	Vertical/Short Take Off
wef	with effect from
Wg	Wing
WWI	World War One (1914-1918)
WWII	World War Two (1939-1945)

The most recent Operational Conversion Unit to form, No 229 OCU, is responsible for training fighter crews. The three aeroplanes seen here are: Tornado F.2T, ZD934 (left), and Tornado F.3s, ZE166 (rear) and ZE168 (right). The latter wears the red chevron marking of No 65 Sqn, No 229 OCU's operational identity. (J M Webber)